Emilia-Romagna
Pages 258–273

Trentino–Alto Adige
Pages 170–179

The Veneto and Friuli
Pages 142–169

Venice
Pages 88–141

Umbria
Pages 352–367

Le Marche
Pages 368–377

Abruzzo, Molise, and Puglia
Pages 504–517

Basilicata and Calabria
Pages 518–525

Sicily
Pages 526–547

Trieste

nice

Ancona

Pescara

L'Aquila

ME
LAZIO

Foggia

Bari

SOUTHERN ITALY

Napoli

Salerno

Potenza

Taranto

Catanzaro

Palermo

Messina

Reggio di Calabria

SICILY

Catania

Agrigento

EYEWITNESS TRAVEL

ITALY

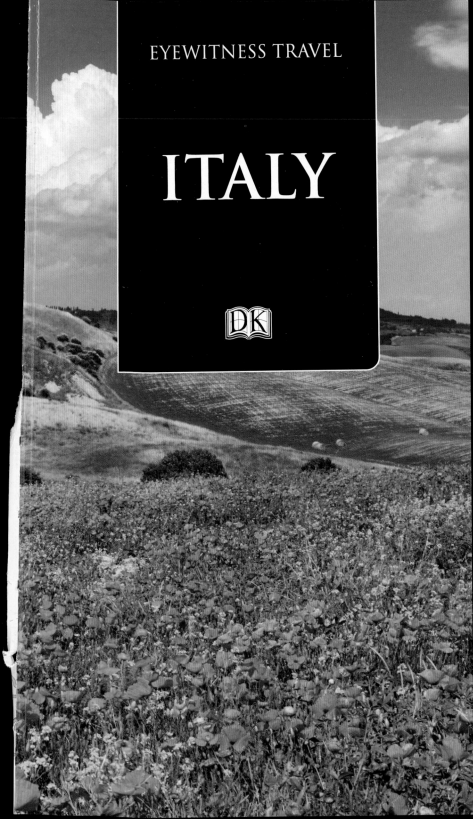

EYEWITNESS TRAVEL

ITALY

LONDON, NEW YORK,
MELBOURNE, MUNICH AND DELHI
www.dk.com

Project Editor Fiona Wild
Art Editors Vanessa Courtier, Annette Jacobs
Editors Francesca Machiavelli, Sophie Martin, Helen Townsend, Nicky Tyrrell
Designers Jo Doran, Anthea Forlee, Paul Jackson, Marisa Renzullo
Main Contributors Ros Belford, Susie Boulton, Christopher Catling, Sam Cole, Paul Duncan,
Olivia Ercoli, Andrew Gumbel, Tim Jepson, Ferdie McDonald, Jane Shaw

Maps
Lovell Johns Ltd., Dorling Kindersley Cartography

Photographer
John Heseltine

Illustrators
Stephen Conlin, Donati Giudici Associati srl, Stephen Gyapay, Roger Hutchins, Maltings
Partnership, Simon Roulstone, Paul Weston, John Woodcock

Printed and bound by South China Printing Co. Ltd., China

First published in the UK in 1996 by Dorling Kindersley Limited
80 Strand, London WC2R 0RL

13 14 15 16 10 9 8 7 6 5 4 3 2 1

Reprinted with revisions 1997, 1999, 2000, 2001, 2002, 2003, 2004, 2005,
2006, 2007, 2008, 2009, 2010, 2011, 2012, 2013

Copyright 1996, 2013 © Dorling Kindersley Limited,
London A Penguin Company

A catalog record for this book is available from the Library of Congress.

ISSN 1542-1554

ISBN 978-1-46540-057-4

Floors are referred to throughout in accordance with European usage;
i.e., the "first floor" is the floor above ground level.

MIX
Paper from
responsible sources
FSC
www.fsc.org FSC™ C018179

The information in this DK Eyewitness Travel Guide is checked annually.
Every effort has been made to ensure that this book is as up-to-date as possible at
the time of going to press. Some details, however, such as telephone numbers,
opening hours, prices, gallery hanging arrangements, and travel information are
liable to change. The publishers cannot accept responsibility for any consequences
arising from the use of this book, nor for any material on third party websites, and
cannot guarantee that any website address in this book will be a suitable source of
travel information. We value the views and suggestions of our readers very highly.
Please write to: Publisher, DK Eyewitness Travel Guides, Dorling Kindersley,
80 Strand, London WC2R 0RL, UK, or email: travelguides@uk.dk.com.

Front cover main image: Basilica di San Francesco, Assisi, Umbria

◀ Rolling landscape of poppies and cypresses in San Quirico d'Orcia, Tuscany

Contents

How to Use This Guide **6**

David by Bernini, Rome

Introducing Italy

Discovering Italy **10**

Putting Italy on
the Map **18**

A Portrait of Italy **24**

The History of Italy **46**

Italy Through the Year **70**

Northeast Italy

Introducing Northeast
Italy **78**

Venice **88**

Venice Street Finder **130**

The Veneto and Friuli **142**

Trentino–Alto Adige **170**

Northwest Italy

Introducing Northwest
Italy **180**

Lombardy **190**

Valle D'Aosta and
Piedmont **214**

Liguria **234**

Central Italy

Introducing Central Italy **248**

Emilia-Romagna **258**

Florence **274**

Florence Street Finder **311**

Tuscany **318**

Umbria **352**

Le Marche **368**

Gondolas weaving through the maze of canals in Venice

Rome Street Finder **451**

Lazio **464**

Southern Italy

Introducing Southern Italy **476**

Naples and Campania **486**

Abruzzo, Molise, and Puglia **504**

Basilicata and Calabria **518**

Sicily **526**

Sardinia **548**

Travelers' Needs

Where to Stay **558**

Where to Eat **578**

Shopping in Italy **606**

Entertainment in Italy **608**

Survival Guide

Practical Information **614**

Travel Information **624**

General Index **636**

Acknowledgments **667**

Phrase Book **671**

A traditional small shop in Volterra, Tuscany

Rome and Lazio

Introducing Rome and Lazio **378**

The Ancient Center **386**

Around Piazza Navona **400**

Northeast Rome **410**

The Vatican and Trastevere **418**

Aventine and Lateran **434**

Farther Afield **442**

Shopping in Rome **447**

Entertainment in Rome **449**

Basilica of San Francesco in Assisi, started in 1228

HOW TO USE THIS GUIDE

This guide helps you get the most from your visit to Italy, providing expert recommendations as well as detailed practical information. *Introducing Italy* maps the whole country and sets it in its historical and cultural context. The 15 regional chapters, plus *Rome, Florence,* and *Venice,* describe important sights with the help of maps and images. Each section is introduced with features on regional architecture and food specialties. *Travelers' Needs* gives details of hotels and restaurants, and the *Survival Guide* contains practical information on everything from transportation to personal safety.

Rome

The center of Rome has been divided into five sightseeing areas. Each area has its own chapter, which opens with a list of the sights described. All the sights are numbered and plotted on an Area Map. The detailed information for each sight is presented in numerical order, making it easy to locate within the chapter.

All pages relating to Rome have red thumb tabs.

1 Area Map For easy reference, the sights are numbered and located on a map. The sights are also shown on the Street Finder on pages 447–57.

A locator map shows where you are in relation to other areas of the city center.

Sights at a Glance lists the chapter's sights by category: Churches, Museums and Galleries, Historic Buildings, Streets and Piazzas.

Stars indicate the sights that no visitor should miss.

2 Street-by-Street Map This gives a bird's-eye view of the heart of each sightseeing area.

A suggested route for a walk is shown in red.

3 Detailed information All the sights in Rome are described individually. Addresses and practical information are provided. The key to the symbols used in the information block is shown on the back flap.

1 Introduction
The landscape, history, and character of each region is described here, showing how the area has developed over the centuries and what it offers to the visitor today.

Italy Area by Area

Apart from Rome, Florence, and Venice, Italy has been divided into 15 areas, each of which has a separate chapter. The most interesting towns and places to visit have been numbered on a Regional Map.

Each area of Italy can be identified quickly by its color coding, shown on the inside front cover.

2 Regional Map This shows the main road network and gives an illustrated overview of the whole region. All entries are numbered and there are also useful tips on getting around the region by car and train.

3 Detailed information
All the important towns and other places to visit are described individually. They are listed in order, following the numbering given on the Regional Map. Within each entry, information is given on the most important sights. The name of the provincial capital is given for smaller towns at the top of each entry.

Story boxes explore specific subjects further.

For all the top sights, a Visitors' Checklist provides the practical information you need to plan your visit.

4 Italy's top sights
These are given two or more full pages. Historic buildings are dissected to reveal their interiors; museums and galleries have color-coded floorplans to help you locate the most interesting exhibits.

INTRODUCING ITALY

Discovering Italy 10–17

Putting Italy on the Map 18–23

A Portrait of Italy 24–45

The History of Italy 46–69

Italy Through the Year 70–77

DISCOVERING ITALY

The following tours have been designed to take in as many of the country's highlights as possible, while keeping long-distance travel to a minimum. First come three 2-day tours of Italy's most glamorous cities: Rome, Florence and Venice. These itineraries can be followed individually or combined to form a weeklong tour. Extra suggestions are provided for those who want to extend their stay to 10 days.

Next come two seven-day tours, covering the north and the south of Italy. These can be combined to make a superb two-week tour of the whole country. Finally, two themed itineraries have been designed for anyone looking to tailor their trip according to a specific interest. Pick, combine, and follow your favourite tours, or simply dip in and out and be inspired.

Golden fields of Tuscany
The Tuscan countryside, with its rolling hills and pencil-thin cypress trees, is a dream for artists and visitors alike.

A Week in Northern Italy

- See the artworks of the Pinoteca di Brera and shop in fashionable **Milan**.

- Take a relaxing cruise on **Lake Como** and walk in the surrounding countryside.

- Look up at Juliet's balcony in **Verona**; marvel at the architecture of **Vicenza**; admire frescoes in **Padua**.

- Enjoy a *vaporetto* ride along **Venice's** magnificent waterway, the Grand Canal.

- Take in the views of **Florence** from the Duomo and visit the city's world-famous galleries.

- Walk the dizzying pathways and hillsides of the **Cinque Terre** coastline.

- Explore the three enchanting Tuscan towns of **Lucca**, **Pisa** and **Siena**.

A Week in Southern Italy

- See treasures of the Classical World in **Rome's** museums and people-watch from the Spanish Steps.

- Marvel at sculptures and mosaics in Museo Archeologico in **Naples**; sample fantastic pizza in the city of its origin.

- Visit the evocative ruins of **Pompeii**; take a ferry to the island of **Capri**.

- Marvel at the beautiful views from the towns along the **Amalfi Coast**; enjoy the sea air at **Ravello**.

- Take a night ferry to Palermo in **Sicily** and visit the glittering Palazzo dei Normanni.

- Discover the Valley of the Temples near **Agrigento**; explore the magnificent Baroque town of **Noto**.

Key

— Northern Italy tour

— Southern Italy tour

A Gourmet Tour of Central Italy

- Try fine cheeses and ham in the delightful town of **Parma**; sample vintage balsamic vinegar in **Moderna**.

- Dine in style in **Bologna** and soak up the atmosphere in the city's *entoce* (wine bars).

- Try the Tuscan speciality *Bistecca Fiorentina* in **Pisa**; enjoy *panforte* in **Siena**.

- Visit **Perugia** and stock up on the town's famous Baci chocolates; travel to **Norcia** to enjoy truffles, and pork from the region's black pigs.

- Spend a day in **Orvieto**, seeking out pecorino cheese, delicious salami and Orvieto Classico wine.

A Tour of Etruscan Italy

- Explore fabulous museums dedicated to the Etruscan civilization in **Rome**.

- Visit the vast "city of the dead" at **Cerveteri**; marvel at the frescoed tombs in **Tarquinia**.

- See remnants of Etruscan life at the Necropoli Etrusca in **Orvieto**; spend an afternoon in the hilltop town of **Todi**.

- Travel to **Chiusi** for the fine Museo Nazionale Etrusco; visit medieval **Gubbio** to see the Eugubine Tablets.

- Spend a day in **Volterra** and see Etruscan funerary urns at the Museo Guarnacci; travel to **Florence** for the fabulous Medici Etruscan collection.

0 kilometers   150

0 miles   150

Key

— Gourmet Italy tour

··· Etruscan Italy tour

Colosseum, Rome
Once the site of deadly gladiatorial combat, the Colosseum is the highlight of a trip to Rome. Tickets include access to the Forum and Palatine Museum.

Beautiful spiral staircase leading down from the Vatican Museums, Rome

2 days in Rome

The nation's capital has an overwhelming array of memorable sights, including the wonderful Vatican Museums and the Colosseum.

- **Arriving** Fiumicino (Leonardo da Vinci) is Rome's main airport, located about 18 miles (30 km) southwest of the city. The "Leonardo Express" train runs nonstop to Termini station, the city's main train station.

- **Moving on** Rome to Florence takes 1 hour 37 minutes by Eurostar.

Day 1
Morning A couple of days in **Rome** *(pp387–463)* will only scrape its surface, but do devote one day to the Vatican and St Peter's. The fast route through the **Vatican Museums** *(pp424–31)* takes in the **Sistine Chapel** *(pp428–30)*. Don't miss Michelangelo's *Creation of Adam* on the ceiling and his dynamic altarpiece, *The Last Judgment*. The four **Raphael Rooms** *(p431)* show another Renaissance master, Raphael, at the peak of his artistic powers.
Afternoon Inside the awe-inspiring **St Peter's** *(pp422–25)*, be sure to see Michelangelo's moving *Pietà*. Climb the dome for views, then descend to the grottoes for the papal tombs. Afterward, cross the Tiber to the *centro storico*. Look in at the **Pantheon** *(p408)*, the only ancient Roman temple to survive intact, then spend the

evening among the exuberant Baroque fountains and cafés of **Piazza Navona** *(pp402–3)*.

Day 2
Morning Wander through the evocative ruins of the **Roman Forum** *(pp394–6)*, and on to the monumental **Colosseum** *(p397)*. Nearby, the church of **San Clemente** *(p439)* reveals its layers of history from pagan temple to 15th-century church.
Afternoon For great city views, head up to the **Capitoline Museums** *(pp390–91)*. The Palazzo Nuovo has a fine selection of Greek and Roman statues. For some respite, visit the pretty 17th-century pleasure gardens of **Villa Borghese** *(pp442–3)*. Visit **Piazza di Spagna** and the **Spanish Steps** *(p413)* and cast a coin in the Baroque **Trevi Fountain** *(pp414–5)*.

> **To extend your trip…**
> Take a day trip to the lovely hill-town of **Tivoli** and **Hadrian's Villa** *(p472)*, about 5 km (3 miles) west of Tivoli.

2 days in Florence

Florence is the city for art lovers, with a wealth of breathtaking museums and galleries.

- **Arriving** Florence is served by two airports – Amerigo Vespucci airport, 2 miles (4 km) from the center, and Pisa airport. From Amerigo Vespucci, buses run to Florence's Santa Maria Novella train station; from Pisa, catch a direct train to Santa Maria Novella.

- **Moving on** The journey from Florence to Venice is just 2 hours by train.

Day 1
Morning Florence *(pp274–317)*, the embodiment of the Renaissance, is much more compact than Rome. Feel the pull of Brunelleschi's immense orange-tiled dome, which crowns the **Duomo** *(pp284–6)*. Climb the dome for stunning views, then admire Ghiberti's

View of the Vatican, with St Peter's Basilica and Sant'Angelo bridge, Rome

Looking south from the upper terrace of the Boboli Gardens, Florence

famous bronze doors on the **Baptistry** *(pp284–6)*. A few streets away, the **Bargello** *(p287)* holds a fantastic collection of Renaissance sculpture.

Afternoon Take a stroll around **Piazza della Signoria** *(pp294–5)*, dominated by its towering city hall, the Palazzo Vecchio, and a copy of Michelangelo's *David*. Stop off at the famous Bar Vivioli Gelateria for an ice cream before tackling the **Uffizi** *(pp290–93)*. Caravaggio, Titian, Raphael – works by all the major artists of the Renaissance and beyond are on display here.

Day 2
Morning See the real statue of *David* by Michelangelo in the **Galleria dell' Accademia** *(p279)*, then visit the church of **Santa Maria Novella** *(pp300–301)* for Masaccio's *Trinity*, with its novel use of perspective.
Afternoon Visit the Gothic church of **Santa Croce** *(pp288–9)*, the final resting place of Michelangelo, Galileo and Machiavelli. Next, cross **Ponte Vecchio** *(p289)* for the **Cappella Brancacci** *(pp302–3)* to see more frescoes by Masaccio. The fountains, grottoes and woods of the **Boboli Gardens** *(p307)* are perfect for a picnic, and there is plenty more art in the **Palazzo Pitti** *(pp306–7)*.

> **To extend your trip…**
> Spend a day in the **Cinque Terre** *(p245)* and another exploring **Pisa** *(pp328–30)* and **Lucca** *(pp324–7)*.

2 days in Venice

This unique city on the water has romantic gondolas, magnificent churches and wonderful art.

- **Arriving** Marco Polo airport is located at Tessera, 5 miles (8 km) north of the city. Alilaguna ferries, which stop at various points in the city, can be picked up a short walk from the airport. The travel time is around an hour. Water taxis are also available, but are expensive. Venice's main train station is Venezia Santa Lucia station.

Day 1
Morning Merely getting lost in **Venice** *(pp88–141)* will exceed expectations, as will the reality of the familiar images. To make the most of a visit to this watery city, travel by *vaporetto* or gondola along the **Grand Canal** *(pp92–5)* to **Piazza San Marco** *(pp112–13)* and the **Basilica di San Marco** *(pp114–17)*. The mosaics inside and out are ravishing, but so too are the Pala d'Oro (golden altarpiece), the jewels of the Treasury and the four Horses of St Mark on the balcony. Take the elevator to the top of the adjacent Campanile to be rewarded with a view stretching all the way to the Alps.

Afternoon Join a pre-booked Secret Itineraries tour to get the most out of the **Palazzo Ducale** *(pp118–20)*, where the vast Sala del Maggior Consiglio, with its magnificent Tintoretto, is the highlight. Have coffee at Caffè Florian or Grancaffè Quadri on **Piazza San Marco** *(pp112–13)*, then cross the Grand Canal to the **Accademia** *(pp110–11)* for the best of the Venetian painters. If you prefer modern art, visit the **Peggy Guggenheim Collection** *(pp108–9)*, housed in the 18th-century Palazzo Venier dei Leoni.

Day 2
Morning Make for the **Rialto** *(p101)* to watch boats go by from the bridge, and stock up at the city's busiest market. Nearby is the church of **Santa Maria Gloriosa dei Frari** *(pp102–3)* with its exquisite altarpiece, a *Madonna and Child* by Bellini.
Afternoon Tour the islands of **Torcello** *(pp126–7)* for 12th- and 13th-century mosaics, **Murano** *(p125)* for the glass museum and colorful **Burano** *(p125)* for lace. Be sure to sample some local snacks and drink an *aperitivo* in one of the many enticing bars back in Venice.

> **To extend your trip…**
> Take a day-trip to **Verona** *(pp146–51)*, which has a fine Roman arena.

Stylish waiters serve drinks in refined Caffè Florian, Venice

A Week in Northern Italy

- **Airports** Arrive at Milano Malpensa airport and depart from Pisa Galileo Galilei.

- **Transportation** Trains connect the cities in 2 hours or less. Use the bus to reach Siena from Florence, and rent a car for the Cinque Terre, leaving it at La Spezia for the local train. It is easy to make day trips to Lake Como from Milan, the Veneto from Venice and the Cinque Terre from Florence.

- **Booking ahead** *Milan:* Viewing of *Last Supper; Venice:* Basilica di San Marco; *Florence:* Accademia, Uffizi; *Pisa:* ascent of the Leaning Tower.

Day 1: Milan

If you're looking for Italian style, high fashion, art and architecture, **Milan** *(pp196–205)*, the largest city of the north, has it all. Heading up the list of sights is Leonardo da Vinci's world-famous *Last Supper* *(p204)*. Visit the enormous Gothic Duomo *(p197)*, which invites a climb to its roof for the best city view. For glorious paintings from the Renaissance to the present day, don't miss the Pinacoteca di Brera *(pp202–203)*, and for those who enjoy shopping, Galleria Vittorio Emanuele II *(p198)*, with its magnificent glass dome and floor mosaics, is a must.

Day 2: Lake Como

Lake Como *(pp194–5)*, its long arms nestling between steep hillsides, is a prime example of Italy's exquisite landscapes. Cruise the lake or take short ferry hops across the water, admiring the resplendent villas along the way. Explore Bellagio, or take a funicular up into the hills.

Day 3: Venice

Pick a day from the city itinerary on p13.

Day 4: The Veneto – Verona, Vicenza and Padua

Pick from a trio of towns, all within striking distance of Venice. Lively **Verona** *(pp142–7)* conjures up Shakespeare's *Romeo and Juliet*, and crowds still flock to see Juliet's balcony. Famous for concerts is the well-preserved Roman Arena *(p147)*, while the Romanesque church of San Zeno Maggiore *(pp150–51)* has a lovely cloister. Admirers of Palladio will appreciate **Vicenza** *(pp154–7)*, where his elegant Classical buildings surround the Piazza dei Signori. **Padua** *(pp158–63)* is known for its Cappella dei Scrovegni *(pp160–61)*, containing some wonderful frescoes by Giotto.

Day 5: Florence

Pick a day from the city itinerary on p12.

Day 6 : Cinque Terre

The five tiny villages of the **Cinque Terre** *(p245)* – Monterosso, Vernazza, Corniglia,

Rolling fields in Tuscany

Manarola and Riomaggiore – are the jewels of Italy's northwest coast. Colorful houses cling to the rocky cliffs, making a hike along the connecting path a delight to the eye. You can do the whole trail (north to south is less steep) in five or six hours.

Day 7: Tuscany – Lucca, Pisa, Siena

These three Tuscan towns are less busy than Florence, yet they offer a cultural feast with the bonus of an enchanting landscape. If time is tight, visit two. In **Lucca** *(pp324–7)*, promenade the encircling 17th-century grassy ramparts and visit the church of San Michele in Foro, its exquisite Pisan-Romanesque façade bursting with decoration. **Pisa** *(pp328–30)* is the home of the iconic 13th-century Leaning Tower, which, together with the Duomo and Baptistry, forms the Campo dei Miracoli. **Siena** *(pp342–7)* is one of Italy's most appealing medieval towns and home to the twice-yearly Palio *(p345)*, when Piazza del Campo comes alive with spirited bareback horse racing. Within striking distance of the piazza are the Gothic Palazzo Pubblico, which contains a treasure trove of frescoes from the Middle Ages, and the magnificent Duomo *(pp346–7)*. En route from Pisa to Siena, try to catch a glimpse of the 13 medieval towers that pierce the skyline in **San Gimignano** *(pp348–9)*. The view is magical in the evening.

Pretty Bellagio, which sits on a peninsula at the top of Lake Como's two "arms"

A Week in Southern Italy

- **Airports** Arrive at Rome Fiumicino and depart from Catania airport, Sicily.

- **Transportation** Train travel from Rome to Naples is fast and easy (1 hour 10 minutes is the fastest). Take the ferry for Capri and Sicily, the bus for the coastal towns of Sorrento, Positano, Amalfi and Ravenna, and for Agrigento from Palermo (2 hours). You will need a car to see inland Sicily: Piazza Armerina and Noto. Pompeii and Capri are easy to visit as day trips from Naples.

- **Booking ahead** *Rome*: Vatican Museums, Colosseum, Forum and Palatine; *Naples*: Museo Archeologico Nazionale, Secret Cabinet Tour.

Days 1 and 2: Rome
See the city itinerary on p12.

Day 3: Naples
Naples *(pp490–97)* is chaotic, but the rewards of visiting are manifold. The main attraction is the world-renowned Museo Archeologico Nazionale *(pp494–5)* and its vast collection of Roman and Pompeiian treasures; allow at least half a day here. Book ahead for the Secret Cabinet tour to view the erotic works from Pompeii. Tiny Cappella Sansevero *(p491)* holds intriguing works from the 18th century, notably the virtuoso alabaster and marble *Veiled Christ* by Sammartino. Santa Chiara *(p493)* is worth seeing for its charming majolica-tiled cloisters. Don't leave without eating pizza in the city of its invention.

Day 4: Pompeii and Capri
The Circumvesuviana train skirts the base of Vesuvius from Naples to Pompeii and on to Sorrento. **Pompeii** *(pp498–9)* gives you an insight into a Roman town as it was in AD 79 before it was destroyed,

The evocative ancient temple ruins at Selinunte, Sicily

most poignantly through the body casts of the people who perished here. Arrange a trip up the infamous volcano, or take a ferry from Naples or Sorrento to the idyllic island of **Capri** *(pp502–503)*, best enjoyed in the quiet of evening. Blue Grotto sea cave and Villa Jovis of Emperor Tiberius are secondary attractions to the captivating vistas you will find here.

Marina Grande on the pretty island of Capri

Day 5: Amalfi Coast
Take the hair-raising bus ride along the coast for views of a lifetime and stop off at your leisure at some of Italy's most beautiful towns. **Sorrento** *(p501)* is the most prosaic and popular, while chic **Positano** *(p501)* favors the jet set and comes with a good beach. **Amalfi** *(p501)* has a stunning 9th-century cathedral, while **Ravello** *(p501)*, set high above terraces of lemon groves, has the best of the views. Lose yourself among the bougainvillea in the lush gardens of the Villa Cimbrone or Villa Rufolo.

Days 6 and 7: Sicily
Sicily is a melting pot of Norman, Byzantine, Greek and Arab influences and deserves at least two days' exploration. Taking the night ferry from Naples to Palermo, the island's largest town, will save you time. **Palermo** *(pp530–33)* exemplifies all these influences, notably in the Palazzo dei Normanni, whose Cappella Palatina is a glittering mix of mosaics, marble and gold. The most famous Norman mosaics, however, are outside Palermo, at the highly ornamented Duomo of Monreale *(pp534–5)*. Seek out the intricate Norman cloisters here. To the south you can discover the ancient Greek legacy in the Valley of the Temples *(p540)*, near Agrigento, or at Selinunte *(p538)*, which has the benefit of a long and sandy beach. In the interior, the Villa Romana del Casale at **Piazza Armerina** *(p541)* sports some of Italy's liveliest mosaics, and beautiful **Noto** *(p547)*, aglow with golden stone, is a unique Baroque town rebuilt after the earthquake of 1693.

A Gourmet Tour of Central Italy

- **Duration** 7 days – but extends to a 10-day tour with the extra suggestions.
- **Airports** Arrive at Milan Linate airport and depart from Rome Fiumicino airport. From Milan, travel by train or car to Parma for the first stop on the tour.
- **Transportation** This tour can be made using Italy's railroad network, but renting a car allows more flexibility.

This itinerary takes you to Italy's central regions – Emilia-Romagna, Tuscany and Umbria – focusing on the regional food specialities along the way. If you are traveling in summer or fall, look out for the copious food festivals held across the region.

Day 1: Parma

Affluent **Parma** (p263) is synonymous with cheese and ham – *Parmigiano Reggiano* (parmesan) and *prosciutto crudo* (Parma ham). The delicatessens here are a feast for the eyes, as are the city's main sights, which include an exquisite 12th-century Baptistry and paintings by Correggio in the lovely Duomo.

Day 2: Modena

The handsome city of **Modena** (p264) has two main claims to fame: it is the producer of fast cars (Ferrari and Maserati) and balsamic vinegar – try the city's market for the best vintage variety. In between sampling some of the region's other specialities, such as mortadella, spicy sausage and pig's feet, be sure to visit the very fine Romanesque Duomo and the Este collection of paintings in the Palazzo dei Musei.

Day: 3 Bologna

Dress up for dinner here – **Bologna** (pp266–9) has some of the country's finest restaurants and atmospheric *enotece* (wine bars). Home-made pasta comes with the famous Bolognese (*ragù*) or cream sauce, or stuffed with ricotta, pork or pumpkin. During the day, check out the medieval skyscrapers of the Due Torri and the Gothic church of San Petronio.

> **To extend your trip...**
> Cycle around the lagoons of the **Po Delta** (p271), 60 miles (97 km) from Bologna.

Day 4: Pisa

Spend a day in **Pisa** (pp328–30). The city's main draw is the Campo dei Miracoli, which contains the Duomo, Baptistry and the Leaning Tower. Pisa's culinary attractions include fish dishes, such as *cacciucco*, a hearty fish soup, and *baccala alla Pisana*, salt cod with tomato sauce. Meat-eaters will love *Bistecca Fiorentina* (thick charcoal-grilled steak).

The iconic Leaning Tower of Pisa

Day 5: Siena

Life in **Siena** (pp342–7) centers on the beautiful fan-shaped piazza of Il Campo, around which *pasticcerie* sell the city's famous *panforte* cake and *ricciarelli* (almond biscuits). Admire the frescoes in the medieval Palazzo Pubblico and the treasures of the spectacular Duomo and its Museo.

> **To extend your trip...**
> Head for the coast at **Maremma Park** (pp350–51), 50 miles (81 km) from Siena.

Day 6: Perugia and Norcia

Stop at **Perugia** (pp356–7) to stock up on Baci chocolate and see the frescoes in the Palazzo dei Priori, before traveling to the gastromic hotspot of **Norcia** (pp366–7), where black truffles, salami, and pork from the local black pigs are the specialities.

> **To extend your trip...**
> Explore the mountains of the **Valnerina** (p367), 30 miles (48 km) from Norcia.

Day 7: Orvieto

You can be assured of good-quality food here as **Orvieto** (pp362–3) is headquarters of the Città Slow movement and an advocate of slow food. Look out for pecorino cheese and salami, and of course, Orvieto Classico wine. Take time to visit the Romanesque-Gothic Duomo and the 16th-century Pozzo di San Patrizio.

Atmospheric outdoor dining in Piazza della Mercanzia, Bologna

For practical information on traveling around Italy, see pp628–35

A Tour of Etruscan Italy

- **Duration** 7 days – but extends to a 10-day tour with the extra suggestions.
- **Airports** Arrive at Rome Fiumicino airport and depart from Pisa Galileo Galilei (trains from Florence to Pisa take 1 hour).
- **Transportation** This tour is most easily done by car, though Cerveteri is accessible by bus from Rome and Tarquinia and Orvieto by train.

This tour focuses on the ancient Etruscan sights and museums of Lazio, Umbria and Tuscany, as well as other interesting sights along the way. For more on Italy's first major civilization, see pp48–9.

Day 1: Rome
Be inspired by the world's best collections of Etruscan treasures in the **Etruscan Museum of the Vatican** *(p424)* and the **Museo Nazionale Etrusco** in the **Villa Giulia** *(p444)*. The tender portrayals of people on the sarcophagi, the delicate and intricate gold jewelry, and lifelike bronze sculptures display amazing craftsmanship. Leave time for the lovely gardens of the **Villa Borghese** *(pp442–3)*.

Day 2: Cerveteri
Feel the mystery of the vast necropolis at **Cerveteri** *(p470)* as you stroll its silent streets. Here, see the tombs that were built as replicas of homes, decorated with frescoes and filled with domestic furnishings. Fifty thousand Etruscans were entombed here from the 7th to the 1st century BC in what was one of the most powerful of the 12 Etruscan cities. Visit the Museo Nazionale Cerite to see displays of objects that were buried with the bodies.

To extend your trip…
Head 40 miles (64 km) from Rome to the Etruscan amphitheatre at **Sutri** *(p470)*.

Well-preserved "Street" of Etruscan tombs, Cerveteri

Day 3: Tarquinia
Spend some time in **Tarquinia** *(p470)*, the medieval center of which was the capital of Etruria 2,500 years ago. Head uphill to the necropolis, a warren of tombs that hold lively and colorful frescoes depicting the lives of their inhabitants. For more revelations of everyday life and artistry, head for the Museo Archeologico, where, alongside the famous terracotta winged horses, are fine displays of jewelry, bronzes and ceramics.

To extend your trip…
Visit the Renaissance gardens of Villa Lante at **Viterbo** *(pp468–9)*, 40 miles (64 km) from Tarquinia.

Day 4: Orvieto and Todi
You can see more Etruscan remains in **Orvieto** *(pp362–3)*, at the Museo Archeologico Faina and Museo Civico, at the Necropoli Etrusca, and even during a tour of Orvieto Underground *(www.orvieto underground.it)*. The fine beautiful Duomo and the 16th-century Pozzo di San Patrizio add to the attractions. From here travel to nearby **Todi** *(p363)*. This dramatic hilltop town is home to the Museo Etrusco-Romano.

Day 5: Chiusi and Gubbio
Make your way northwards for **Chiusi** *(p336)* and the Museo Nazionale Etrusco for its fine display of urns and vases taken from the surrounding tombs.

Then head towards the forest-clad Appenines for charming **Gubbio** *(p356)*, where the Palazzo dei Consoli houses the famous seven bronze Eugubine Tablets inscribed with Etruscan letters, and where the strange Porte della Morte, walled up doors, were once supposedly used for the transport of coffins.

Volterra, once an important Etruscan city

Day 6: Volterra
The city of **Volterra** *(p338)* is home to the excellent Museo Guarnacci and beautiful Etruscan funerary urns, made out of alabaster, for which the region is famous. For more alabaster visit the Pinacoteca e Museo Civico and browse the craft shops.

To extend your trip…
A 20 mile (32 km) drive from Volterra takes you to **San Gimignano** *(pp348–9)* and its 13th-century towers.

Day 7: Florence
Finish your tour in Florence and visit the Medici Etruscan collection in the **Museo Archeologico** *(p281)*, which includes two outstanding sculptures – the Chimera and the Arringatore (Orator) bronze.

Putting Italy on the Map

Italy sits at the heart of the Mediterranean, shielded from the rest of Europe by the vast sweep of the Alps. The Po, its longest river, arcs across the industrial north, while the Apennine mountains split the boot-shaped peninsula down its length. Italy, with a population of 58 million governed from Rome, covers 116,320 sq miles (301,268 sq km) and includes Sicily and Sardinia.

SWITZERLAND

Lago Maggiore
Lago di Como
Trente

Aosta
Lecco
Lago di Garda

Arona
Bergamo
Verona

Ivrea
Milan
Brescia

Po
Mantova

Turin
Po

Tanaro

Parma
Modena

Cuneo
Genoa

Avignon
La Spezia
Lucca

FRANCE
Nice
San Remo
Pisa

Monaco
Livorno

Ligurian Sea
Piombino

Marseille
Elba

Bastia
Orbetello

Corsica

Tyrrhenian Sea

Ajaccio

Porto Torres
Olbia

Alghero

Sardinia
Arbatax

Key

— Highway
— Major road
-- Ferry service
— International boundary

Cagliari

Europe

NORWAY
North Sea
SWEDEN
ESTONIA
LATVIA
REP. OF IRELAND
UNITED KINGDOM
DENMARK
LITHUANIA
BELARUS
NETH.
GERMANY
POLAND
BELGIUM
CZECH REPUBLIC
UKRAINE
FRANCE
AUSTRIA
SLOVAKIA
HUNGARY
Atlantic Ocean
ITALY
CROATIA
ROMANIA
SERBIA
BULGARIA
MONTEN.
KOS.
MAC.
SPAIN
ALBANIA
GREECE
PORTUGAL
MOROCCO
ALGERIA
TUNISIA

Mediterranean Sea

Bizerte

Annaba
TUNISIA
Tunis

Northern Italy

Airline connections link the rest of Europe with Milan, Turin, Bologna, Pisa, Florence, Verona, and Venice. Major roads and railroads also provide excellent links to cities all over Europe. Transportation services are very efficient, with highways and railroads along both coasts, and across the area's main east-to-west axis at the foot of the Alps. Milan, Verona, and Bologna are the key transportation hubs, while Florence forms the focus of links to the south.

Florence by Road

Good fast roads link Florence to Pisa to the west, Rome and Siena to the south, and Bologna to the north.

Florence and Environs

Key

- – – International boundary
- – – Regional boundary
- ▨▨ Highway
- ▨▨ Main road
- — Railroad line

| 0 kilometers | 4 |
| 0 miles | 2 |

For additional map symbols *see back flap*

Venice by Road
Venice is joined to the mainland by a causeway. This provides easy access to highway links with Verona and Padua.

Venice

Mestre
FS
Marco Polo
Canale Oselino
S14b
S14
S11
Laguna veneta

FS Santa Lucia
San Marco

0 kilometers 4
0 miles 2

AUSTRIA

rtina d'Ampezzo
Tolmezzo
S52
Belluno
A23
Cividale del Friuli
Udine
SLOVENIA
Pordenone
S13
Gorizia
Aquileia
Treviso
Trieste

VENICE
see inset above

Po Delta
Greece, Turkey, Egypt

Ravenna

Rimini
Pèsaro
SAN MARINO
Fano

Urbino
S3
ansepolcro
Sibillini
Ancona
Conero Peninsula
Jesi
Grotte di Frasassi
Loreto
Greece, Turkey, Cyprus

rtona
Gubbio
S316
Perugia
Assisi
Lago asimeno
usi
Spello
Montefalco
Todi
eto
Norcia
Spoleto

Ascoli Piceno

Viterbo
S2
L'Aquila
A24
Pescara
A25
Lanciano
Sulmona
ROME
Scanno
A1
S17
Sermoneta
Sperlonga
Terracina
Formia
Benevento
Caserta

Isole Tremiti

San Severo
A14
Lucera
S89
Troia
Foggia
Trani
Bari

Key to Color-Coding

Northeast Italy

Venice
The Veneto and Friuli
Trentino–Alto Adige

Northwest Italy

Lombardy
Valle d'Aosta and Piedmont
Liguria

Central Italy

Emilia-Romagna
Florence
Tuscany
Umbria
Le Marche

0 kilometers 100
0 miles 50

Southern Italy

International airline services operate to Rome, Naples, and Palermo in southern Italy. Transportation links within the region are generally slower than in the north, particularly inland and on the islands of Sicily and Sardinia, where buses are often a faster option than trains. Mainland coastal road and railroad links are good, however, especially those linking Rome and Naples, the region's main transportation hubs, which are connected by a high-speed train service. Two trans-Apennine highways offer the quickest cross-country routes.

Sicily and Sardinia

Ferries operate to Sicily from Naples, Villa San Giovanni, and Reggio di Calabria. Onward connections include boats to Malta and Tunisia. Ferries run to Sardinia from several mainland ports, notably Civitavecchia, Genoa, and Livorno.

Key

- ▬ ▬ International boundary
- ‑ ‑ Regional boundary
- ▭ Highway
- ▭ Main road
- ── Railroad line

For additional map symbols see back flap

Rome by Road
Highway links approach Rome from Naples, Pescara, and Florence. All feed into the city's ring road, the Grande Raccordo Anulare.

Rome and Environs

0 kilometers   10
0 miles   5

GRANDE RACCORDO ANULARE (GRA)
VIA CASSIA
VIA NOMENTANA
VIA AURELIA
VATICAN CITY
VIA TIBURTINA
A24
VIA CASILINA
VIA APPIA NUOVA
VIA CRISTOFORO COLOMBO
FS
S2
S3
A1
A1
S5
S1
A12
A91
S7
Leonardo da Vinci di Fiumicino
Tevere (Tiber)
Ciampino

Vasto
Isole Tremiti
Termoli
Rodi Garganico
Vieste
Gargano Peninsula
San Severo
Manfredonia
Lucera
Foggia
Troia
Trani
Bari
Croatia, Greece, Egypt
enevento
Castel del Monte
Ruvo di Puglia
aserta
Melfi
Alberobello
Brindisi
Greece
Pompei
Matera
Lecce
Salerno
Potenza
Taranto
Amalfi
Metaponto
Galatina
Otranto
Paestum
Sala Consilina
Policoro
Greece
Cilento
Maratea
Castrovillari
Rossano
Cosenza
Crotone
Catanzaro
Lamezia
Isole Eolie
Tropea
Vibo Valentia
↑ *Naples*
Stilo
Gerace
Milazzo
Messina
Tindari
Reggio di Calabria
↑ *Naples*
Taormina
enna
Catania
iazza erina
Malta
Pantalica
Siracusa
ela
Noto
Modica

A14
S47
S17
A16
S96
A3
A16
S407
S106
S18
S18
S107
S106
S280
43
S106
A20
A18
A19
S417
A18
S115

0 kilometers   100
0 miles   50

Key to Color-Coding

Rome and Lazio

Rome
Lazio

Southern Italy

Naples and Campania
Abruzzo, Molise, and Puglia
Basilicata and Calabria
Sicily
Sardinia

A PORTRAIT OF ITALY

Italy has drawn people in search of culture and romance for many centuries Few countries can compete with its Classical origins, its art, architecture, musical and literary traditions, its scenery or food and wine. The ambiguity of its modern image is also fascinating: since World War II Italy has climbed into the top ten world economies, yet at its heart it retains many of the customs, traditions, and regional allegiances of its agricultural heritage.

Italy has no single cultural identity. From the northern snowcapped peaks of the Alps, to the rugged southern shores of Sicily, lies a plethora of distinctive regions and peoples. Politically, Italy is a young country: it did not exist as a unified nation state until 1870, and its 20 regions have maintained their cultural individuality. Visitors to Italy are often pleasantly surprised by the diversity of its dialects, cuisines, and architecture. There is also a larger regional division. People speak of two distinct Italies: the rich industrial north and the poorer agricultural south, known as *Il Mezzogiorno* or Land of the Midday Sun. The frontier separating the two is indeterminate, lying somewhere between Rome and Naples.

The north is directly responsible for Italy's place among the world's top industrial nations. It has been the powerhouse behind the Italian economic miracle, its success achieved by internationally renowned names such as FIAT, Prada, Ferragamo, Pirelli, Olivetti, Zanussi, Alessi, and Armani. In contrast, the south, once a cradle of high culture and civilization, has been dogged by

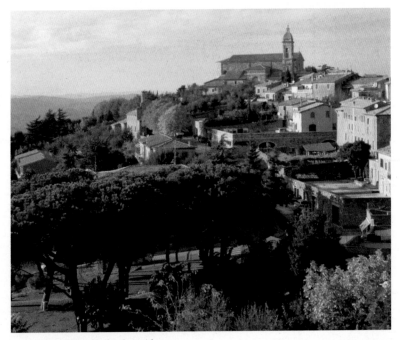

View of the rooftops of Montalcino from the town's fortress

◀ Cobbled lane in the coastal fishing resort town of Cefalu, Sicily unemployment and organized crime. Some of its areas rank among the most depressed in Europe, although many southern towns did benefit from an injection of Millennium funds.

The historic divide between north and south is a powerful factor in contemporary politics. The federalist party, the Northern League, owes its popularity to this split. Those in favor of separation complain that the south is a drain on resources: Milan is seen as efficient and rich, while Naples is viewed as chaotic, dirty, and corrupt.

History and geography have both contributed to the division. The north is closer in both location and spirit to Germany and France, while the south has suffered a succession of invasions from foreign powers: Carthaginians and Greeks in ancient times, Saracens and Normans in the Middle Ages, and until the middle of the 19th century, the Bourbons from Spain held sway.

Tradition

Distinctive variations in Italy's regions have much to do with the mountainous landscape and inaccessible valleys. Tuscan and Ligurian hill towns, for instance, have quite different silhouettes, and the farmhouses in Puglia, the famous *trulli*, are unlike those found in the landscape of Emilia-Romagna.

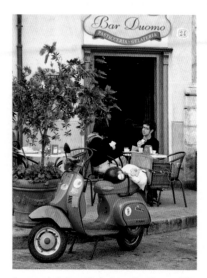

A scooter parked in front of The Bar Duomo, Piazza Duomo in Cefalù

In southern Italy the landscape, architecture, dialects, food, and even the appearance of the people have closer affinities with the Eastern Mediterranean and North Africa than with Europe. In the far south, study of the local dialects has revealed traces of ancient Greek and old Albanian, preserved in tightly knit communities isolated by the rugged geography. Christianity and pagan ritual are closely linked; sometimes the Virgin is portrayed as a thinly disguised Demeter, the Earth goddess.

Café-goers relaxing in Marina di Pisa, Tuscany

Medieval skyscrapers emerging from the Tuscan landscape of San Gimignano

Throughout Italy, ancient techniques of husbandry endure, and many livelihoods are closely connected to the land and the seasons. Main crops include sugar beet, corn, wheat, olives, and grapes; colorful Easter celebrations *(see p70)* pay tribute to the bounty of the soil. Although some of the north's postwar economic prosperity can be attributed to industry (especially car production in and around Turin), much of it has grown from the expansion of family-owned artisan businesses and the export of handmade goods abroad. This is recognized as a distinct sector of the economy. The internationally successful retail clothes chain Prada is a good example. The "Made in Italy" label, found on goods such as clothes, shoes, and leather bags, guarantees a high standard.

Culture and Arts

The arts in Italy have had a long and glorious history and Italians are very proud of this. Given the fact that Italy has more than 100,000 monuments (archeological sites, cathedrals, churches, houses, and statues), all of which have major historical significance, it is not surprising that there is a shortage of funds to keep

them in good repair. Many museums in Italy, particularly those in the south, are closed, or partially closed. You may find churches in Venice hidden behind permanent scaffolding, or those in Abruzzo shut due to earthquake damage. However, with tourism accounting for around 12 percent of Italy's Gross Domestic Product,

Bernini's 17th-century Fontana del Tritone, Rome

Roadside stall near Positano, Campania

efforts are being made to put as many buildings and collections on show as possible. The Jubilee 2000 helped matters by allocating large amounts of money for the restoration of buildings and sites belonging to the Catholic Church.

The performing arts are also underfunded, yet there are some spectacular cultural festivals. Almost every town of any size has its own opera house, and La Scala opera house in Milan stages world-class productions.

Cinema is another flourishing art form in Italy and has been so since its invention. The sets at Cinecittà, on the outskirts of Rome, have been used by many famous directors, including Fellini, Pasolini, de Sica, Visconti, and many others. Italian films such as *La Vita è Bella* and *The Son's Room* have found critical acclaim and box-office success both in Italy and abroad. In Italy the arts belong to everyone: opera is attended by people from all backgrounds, regardless of social status, as are movie theaters and galleries.

Social Customs and Politics

Italian society is still highly traditional, and Italians can be very formal. Between the generations degrees of familiarity exist:

reserve *ciao* (hello or goodbye) for friends your age or younger, and greet older people with *piacere* (pleased to meet you), *buon giorno* (good day) or *buona sera* (good evening), and on parting, say *arrivederci* (goodbye). Strangers are met with a handshake, but family and friends receive a kiss.

Italian chic decrees that the clothes you wear should give the impression of wealth. If Italians wear similar outfits, it is because they are conformists in fashion as in other aspects of daily life.

Italian politics, in contrast, are not so well regulated. Governments in the postwar era were characterized by short-lived coalitions, dominated by the Christian Democrats. In 1993 Italy experienced a political crisis when an organized network of corruption was exposed, disgracing a huge number of politicians and businessmen. Although the investigations failed to eradicate corruption, they led to the formation of two large coalitions, centre-left and centre-right. Silvio Berlusconi, leader of Forza Italia, became prime minister in 1994 but lasted a short while as he, too, was accused of corruption. In 1998 Massimo D'Alema became Italy's first left-wing Prime Minister. Recent years have seen an alternation of centre-right and centre-left

Diners relaxing at a restaurant in Orta San Giulio, Piedmont

The solution to heavy traffic in Rome: motorbikes and scooters

governments, with Berlusconi dominating. Economist and academic Mario Monti became prime minister in November 2011. In April 2013 a coalition was sworn in made up of the Democratic Party and Berlusconi's People of Freedom Party.

Modern Life

Food and soccer are the great constants; Italians live for both. Much time is spent on preparing food and eating. The Italian diet, particularly in the south, is among the healthiest in the world. Soccer is a national passion and inspires massive public interest and media attention, not least as a way of expressing regional loyalties.

As far as religion is concerned, the number of practicing Catholics has been in decline for some years. Although Rome lies at the center of world Catholicism, today many Italians are uninterested in religion, but still attend mass in number on saints' days or feast days. As a result of immigration, other religions are now on the increase.

The emphasis on conformity and a commitment to the institution of the family remain key factors in Italian society despite the country's low birth rate. Grandparents, children, and grandchildren often still live in family units, although this is becoming less common. All children are pampered, but the most cherished ones are, usually, male. Women's Liberation fought a powerful campaign in the 1970s and did much to change attitudes toward women in the workplace, particularly in metropolitan areas. However, the idea that men should help with housework and the care of the children is still a fairly foreign notion among the older generation.

With the miracle of its postwar economic recovery, where industry and technology were united with design, Italy became a success story. Although the economy was dented by the worldwide recessions of recent years, the exposure of corruption in many walks of public life, and political upheaval, Italy appears unchanged to foreign visitors. Its ability to keep its regional identities and traditional values seems to allow it to ride out any changes relatively unscathed.

Medieval and Early Renaissance Art

The story of early Italian art, from the 13th century until the late 15th century, illuminates one of the richest periods in European art history. For the first time since Classical antiquity, painters and sculptors created a convincing pictorial space in which figures, modeled "in the round," were given life. Ethereal buildings were replaced by those firmly rooted in the real world, reproducing what artists actually saw. This revolution in art included the reintroduction of the fresco technique, giving artists huge surfaces for telling pictorial stories.

c.1305 Giotto di Bondone, *The Meeting at the Golden Gate* (Cappella degli Scrovegni, Padua) Giotto broke away from the ornate Byzantine style to visualize naturalness and human emotions. His way of working would later be dubbed the Florentine style.

1235 Bonaventura Berlinghieri, *St. Francis Altarpiece* (San Francesco, Pescia)

1285 Duccio di Buoninsegna, *Rucellai Madonna*, panel (Uffizi, Florence). Duccio dominated the Sienese painting style, which combined bold linear movements with a new human intimacy.

1339 Ambrogio Lorenzetti, *Good Government Enthroned* (Sala dei Nove, Palazzo Pubblico, Siena)

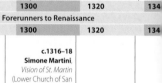

1220	1240	1260	1280	1300	1320	134
Middle Ages				Forerunners to Renaissance		
1220	1240	1260	1280	1300	1320	134

c.1259 Nicola Pisano, Pulpit (Baptistry, Pisa cathedral)

c.1265 Coppo di Marcovaldo, *Madonna and Child* (Santa Monica dei Servi, Orvieto)

c.1280 Cimabue, *Madonna Enthroned with Angels and Prophets*, also known as *Santa Trinità Madonna* (Uffizi, Florence)

c.1291 Pietro Cavallini, *Last Judgment*, detail (Santa Cecilia, Trastevere, Rome)

c.1316–18 Simone Martini, *Vision of St. Martin* (Lower Church of San Francesco, Assisi)

c.1297 Giovanni Pisano, Pulpit (Sant'Andrea, Pistoia)

c.1336 Andrea Pisano, *Baptism of St. John the Baptist*, panel on the South Doors (Baptistry, Florence cathedral)

c.1425–52 Lorenzo Ghiberti, *Gates of Paradise*, panel on the East Doors. (Baptistry, Florence cathedral). These elaborate doors mark a transition from the Gothic style to the Early Renaissance style, in Florence.

c.1435 Donatello, *David* (Museo del Bargello, Florence)

1357 Andrea Orcagna, *Enthroned Christ with Madonna and Saints* (Strozzi Altarpiece, Santa Maria Novella, Florence)

c.1452–65 Piero della Francesca, detail of *The Dream of Constantine* (San Francesco, Arezzo)

c.1456 Paolo Uccello, *Battle of San Romano* (Uffizi, Florence)

c.1410 Nanni di Banco, *Four Crowned Martyrs* (Orsanmichele, Florence)

1360	1380	1400	1420	1440	1460

Early Renaissance

1360	1380	1400	1420	1440	1460

1423 Gentile da Fabriano, *Adoration of the Magi* (Uffizi, Florence)

c.1440 Fra Angelico, *Annunciation* (San Marco, Florence)

c.1350 Francesco Traini, *Triumph of Death* (Campo Santo, Pisa)

c.1463 Piero della Francesca, *Resurrection* (Pinacoteca, Sansepolcro)

c.1465 Fra Filippo Lippi, *Madonna with Child and Angels* (Uffizi, Florence)

c.1425–8 Masaccio, *The Tribute Money* (Cappella Brancacci, Florence)

c.1465–74 Andrea Mantegna, *Arrival of Cardinal Francesco Gonzaga* (Palazzo Ducale, Mantova)

c.1470 Andrea del Verrocchio, *David* (Bargello, Florence)

Fresco Technique

Fresco, meaning "fresh," refers to the technique of painting onto a thin layer of damp, freshly laid plaster. Pigments are drawn into the plaster by surface tension, and the color becomes fixed as the plaster dries. The pigments react with the lime in the plaster to produce strong, rich colors, such as those in Masaccio's *The Tribute Money*.

The Tribute Money by Masaccio (Cappella Brancacci, Florence)

High Renaissance Art

The High Renaissance in the late 15th century was marked by an increasing sense of realism in many religious works and by the technical mastery of such renowned artists as Michelangelo, Leonardo da Vinci, and Raphael. The different schools of Renaissance painting, while drawing on Classical models, produced varying styles: Florentine painting was noted for its cool clarity, while sensuous color and warm light characterized many Venetian works. By the mid-16th century, however, these styles shifted to the fanciful, contorted imagery of Mannerism.

c.1480 Andrea Mantegna, *Dead Christ* (Brera, Milan)

1481–2 Sistine Chapel wall frescoes painted by various artists.

c.1481–2 Pietro Perugino, *Christ Delivering the Keys of the Kingdom to St. Peter*, wall fresco (Sistine Chapel, Rome)

c.1483–88 Andrea del Verrocchio, completed by Alessandro Leopardi, *Equestrian Monument of Bartolomeo Colleoni* (Campo dei Santi Giovanni e Paolo, Venice)

c.1487 Giovanni Bellini, *San Giobbe Altarpiece* (Accademia, Venice)

c.1503–1505 Leonardo da Vinci, *Mona Lisa* (Louvre, Paris)

c.1495 Leonardo da Vinci, *Last Supper* (Santa Maria delle Grazie, Milan)

1519–26 Titian, *Madonna of the Pesaro Family* (Santa Maria Gloriosa dei Frari, Venice)

1505 Raphael, *Madonna of the Goldfinch* (Uffizi, Florence)

1508–12 Michelangelo, *Sistine Chapel ceiling* (The Vatican, Rome). Over 200 preliminary drawings were made for this incredible vision of God's power and humanity's spiritual awakening.

1480	1500	1520
	High Renaissance	**Manneris**
1480	1500	1520

1485 Leonardo da Vinci, *Virgin of the Rocks* (Louvre, Paris)

c.1485 Sandro Botticelli, *Birth of Venus* (Uffizi, Florence)

c.1486 Leonardo da Vinci, *Uomo Vitruviano* (Accademia, Venice)

1499–1504 Luca Signorelli, *Damned Consigned to Hell* (Cappella Nuova, Orvieto cathedral)

1501–1504 Michelangelo, *David* (Galleria dell'Accademia, Florence)

1505 Giovanni Bellini, *Madonna and Child with Four Saints* (San Zaccaria altarpiece, Accademia, Venice)

c.1508 Giorgione, *Tempesta* (Accademia, Venice)

1509 Raphael, *School of Athens* (Stanza della Segnatura, The Vatican, Rome). The scale, magnificence, and harmony of this fresco represent the ideals of the High Renaissance. These ideals sought to express superhuman rather than human values.

1517 Sodoma, *Marriage of Alexander and Roxana* (Villa Farnesina, Rome)

1516 Michelangelo, *Dying Slave* (Louvre, Paris)

1512–14 Raphael, *Angel Delivering St. Peter from Prison*, detail from the *Liberation of St. Peter from Prison* (Stanza di Eliodoro, The Vatican, Rome)

1523 Rosso Fiorentino, *Moses Defends the Daughters of Jethro* (Uffizi, Florence)

1530–32 Giulio Romano, *Ceiling and wall frescoes* (Sala dei Giganti, Palazzo del Tè, Mantova)

c.1532 Michelangelo, *"Blockhead" Captive* (Galleria dell' Accademia, Florence)

1534–5 Paris Bordone, *Fisherman Delivering the Ring* (Accademia, Venice)

1534–41 Michelangelo, *Last Judgment*, wall fresco (Sistine Chapel, Rome)

c.1540–42 Titian, *David and Goliath* (Santa Maria della Salute, Venice)

c.1562–6 Jacopo Tintoretto, *Finding of the Body of St. Mark* (Brera, Milan)

c.1550 Moretto, *Ecce Homo with Angel* (Pinacoteca Tosio Martinengo, Brescia)

| 1540 | 1560 |
| 1540 | 1560 |

1538 Titian, *Venus of Urbino* (Uffizi, Florence)

c.1546 Titian, *Portrait of Pope Paul III Farnese with his Nephews*, (Museo di Capodimonte, Naples)

c.1534–40 Parmigianino, *Madonna and Angels or Madonna with the Long Neck* (Uffizi, Florence). Attenuated proportions and contrasting colors make this a fine example of the Mannerist style.

c.1540 Agnolo Bronzino, *Portrait of Lucrezia Panciatichi* (Uffizi, Florence). Elongated features, such as Lucrezia's fingers, are typical of the exaggerated Mannerist style.

1556 Veronese, *Triumph of Mordecai* (San Sebastiano, Venice)

c.1526–30 Correggio, *Assumption of the Virgin* (Dome of Parma cathedral). Neither a Mannerist nor a High Renaissance painter, Correggio was a master of illusion, skilled at making ascending figures float convincingly, as seen in the fresco above.

Italian Architecture

The buildings of Italy span almost 3,000 years, drawing influences from a wide variety of sources. Etruscan and Roman buildings borrowed heavily from ancient Greece, while in later centuries Norman, Arabic, and Byzantine styles colored Italy's Romanesque and Gothic architecture. Classical ideals infused the country's Renaissance buildings, later giving way to the inspired innovations of the Baroque period.

Orvieto's Duomo displays the ornate and intricate decoration, notably sculpture, common to many Gothic cathedrals. Building stretched from the 13th to the early 17th centuries.

The Basilica di San Marco

The Basilica di San Marco (AD 832–1094) in Venice combines Classical, Romanesque, and Gothic architecture, but its key inspiration was Byzantine *(see pp114–15)*.

200	400	600	800	1000
Classical		Byzantine		Romanesque
200	400	600	800	1000

Triumphal arches such as Rome's Arch of Constantine (AD 313) were a uniquely Roman invention. Built to celebrate military victories, they were adorned with reliefs depicting episodes from successful campaigns *(see p384)*.

The round-arched Romanesque style emerged from the Dark Ages in structures such as the Duomo in Modena. The churches usually had simple interiors that derived from Roman basilicas.

The building of domes over square or rectangular spaces was a major development of the Byzantine era.

Etruscan Architecture

Virtually the only architectural memorials to the Etruscans are their necropolises (circa 6th century BC), found primarily in Tuscany, Lazio, and Umbria. Little else survives, probably because most day-to-day buildings were made from wood. The Etruscans' close cultural and trading ties with Greece, however, suggest their architecture would have borrowed heavily from Greek models. Rome, in turn, looked to Etruscan architecture for inspiration, and most early Roman public buildings were probably Etruscan in style.

Model of Etruscan temple with Classical Greek portico

The cathedral of Monreale in Sicily, built in the 12th century, contains Norman elements blended with exotic Arabic and Byzantine decoration *(see pp534–5)*.

Bramante's Tempietto at San Pietro in Montorio, Rome (buwto the precise, Classical temples of ancient Rome *(see p384).*

Baroque façades, such as this one added to Syracuse's Duomo between 1728 and 1754, were often grafted onto older churches.

Industrial innovations in glass and metal were applied in new buildings, like Mengoni's imposing Galleria Vittorio Emanuele II (1865) in Milan *(see p198).*

The Classical ideals of Rome and ancient Greece were reintroduced into Italian architecture during the Renaissance.

Papal patronage and the vigor of the Counter-Reformation fueled the Baroque, a period of architectural splendor, invention, and exuberance.

The Mole Antonelliana (1863–89), in Turin, topped by a soaring granite spire, was for a time the tallest building in the world *(p228).*

Torre Velasca's 26-floor tower in Milan (1950s) pioneered the use of reinforced concrete.

00	1400	1600	1800	2000
	Renaissance	Baroque	19th Century	20th Century
00	1400	1600	1800	2000

Siena's Duomo (1136–1382), an imposing Romanesque-Gothic cathedral, went through 200 years of architectural transformation *(see pp346–7).*

Santa Maria Novella in Florence has a Renaissance façade (1456–70) by Alberti and a Gothic interior.

Gian Lorenzo Bernini (1598–1680), architect of St. Peter's Square, was a dominant figure in the Roman Baroque.

Andrea Palladio (1508–80) built Neo-Classical villas and palazzi. His style was imitated in Europe for over two centuries *(see p84).*

Outer skin of dome, supported by 24 ribs

Lantern

Inner shell

Brunelleschi's dome for the Duomo in Florence, completed in 1436, was a masterpiece of Renaissance design and ingenious engineering *(see p257).*

The Gesù in Rome was designed for the Jesuits by Vignola in 1568. With its powerful façade and lavish decoration, it was the prototype for countless other Baroque churches *(see p385).*

The Pirelli building in Milan, designed by Ponti and Nervi (late 1950s), is a great example of modern Italian architecture *(see p189).*

Saints and Symbols in Italian Art

Saints and symbols are especially important in Italian art. They form part of an established visual language used by artists to narrate stories of the Bible and the Catholic church to church-goers. Paintings of the saints were the focus for prayer and each offered assistance in a particular aspect of daily life. Patron saints protected specific cities, or trades, and individuals who bore their name. Saints' days and religious festivals still play an important part in Italian life.

The Evangelists

The four evangelists, Matthew, Mark, Luke, and John, are each represented by a winged creature, standing for a divine mission

Eagle
(St. John)

St. Dominic is usually portrayed wearing the habit of his order. The lily is another of his attributes.

St. Cosmas and St. Damian are always shown together, dressed in physicians' clothing.

St. Mark the Evangelist often holds his book of the Gospels.

St. John carries a book of the Gospel bearing his name.

St. Thomas Aquinas is usually shown with a star, barely visible in this painting, on his Dominican habit.

St. Lawrence carries a palm leaf as well as the gridiron on which he was roasted.

Virgin Enthroned with the Child and Saints (c.1450) was painted on dry plaster by the Dominican friar Fra Angelico. It is on display at the Museo di San Marco, Florence *(see p280).*

The Virgin, usually shown in blue robes, is depicted as Mater Amabilis – the "Mother Worthy of Love."

St. Peter Martyr, here with a palm leaf, is sometimes depicted with a head wound, carrying a sword.

Symbols

Different saints or martyrs were made more identifiable by being given "attributes" or symbols – particular objects to carry or clothing to wear. These were items that played a particular role in their life story. Martyrs were known by their instruments of torture or death. Symbolism also appears in the sky, animals, flowers, colors, and numbers.

The lamb symbolizes Christ, the Lamb of God, or in early Christian art, the sinner.

The skull is a "memento mori" to remind us of death and impermanence.

Winged man
(St. Matthew)

Winged lion
(St. Mark)

Winged ox
(St. Luke)

Giovanni Bellini's painting of
Madonna and Child with Four Saints
(see p123)

St. Peter the Apostle, the "rock" on which the Christian church was founded, carries the keys to heaven.

The Madonna, with the Christ Child, is an emblem of perfect motherly love.

St. Catherine of Alexandria is shown here with a piece of the wheel on which she was martyred.

St. Jerome is always portrayed as an old man, often a hermit, whose life was devoted to scholarship.

Detail from Madonna and Child with Four Saints, by Giovanni Bellini. The painting was produced for an altarpiece at San Zaccaria, Venice, in 1505, where it is still on display.

The angel, a messenger of God to man, is portrayed in this scene as a musician of Heaven.

St. Lucy is depicted here holding her own eyes in a dish. She became the patron saint of the blind and symbolizes light.

The lily, flower of the Virgin, is the symbol of purity, resurrection, peace, and chastity.

The cockle shell most often represents pilgrimage. It is a particular attribute of St. Roch.

The palm represents, in Christian art, a martyr's triumph over death.

Writers, Poets, and Dramatists

Italy has produced many writers (in Latin and Italian) who have won worldwide acclaim. Each of them provides an illuminating insight into the country's turbulent past: the Classical poets Virgil, Horace, and Ovid give vivid accounts of the concerns and values of ancient Rome; medieval Florence and Tuscany are brought to life in the poetry of Dante and Petrarch and the salacious tales of Boccaccio. In less than a century these three great writers created a new literary language to rank with any in Europe. Italy's modern literature still commands international attention – Umberto Eco has to his credit one of the most widely read books of the 20th century.

Primo Levi (1919–87) gave an astonishing account of his survival of the Jewish Holocaust and World War II's aftermath in *The Truce* and *If This Is a Man.*

Trentino
Alto Ad

Lombardy

Valle d'Aosta
and Piedmont

Liguria

Emilia-
Romagna

Dario Fo (born 1926) won the Nobel prize for Literature in 1997.

Tuscany

Umberto Eco (born 1932), a professor at the University of Bologna, wrote the novel *The Name of the Rose*, which explored his passion for the Middle Ages. The book was made into a film (above) in 1986.

Giovanni Boccaccio (1313–75) is notable for providing a fascinating social record of his era. *The Decameron*, his captivating collection of 100 short stories, is set in the plague-stricken Florence of 1348.

Pinocchio, written by Carlo Collodi (1826–90) in 1883, is one of the world's best known children's stories. "Collodi" was Carlo Lorenzini's pseudonym, taken after his mother's birthplace in Tuscany.

Dante's (1265–1321) *Divine Comedy* (c.1308–21), is a journey through Hell, Purgatory, and Paradise. It includes horrific accounts of the torments suffered by the damned.

Venetian author
Carlo Goldoni (1707–93) reacted against the satirical tradition of *La Commedia dell'Arte*, preferring to write more forgiving plays on contemporary Venice society.

The Veneto and Friuli

Classical Roman Writers

Texts in Latin by Classical Roman philosophers, poets, dramatists, and politicians are part of the bedrock of Western culture. Today the names Virgil *(The Aeneid)*, Ovid *(Metamorphoses)*, and Pliny *(Historia Naturalis)* are literary legends. Fascinating histories such as Livy's *Early History of Rome*, Caesar's *Gallic Wars*, Tacitus's *Annals*, and Suetonius's *The Twelve Caesars* give us an invaluable window on the distant Roman past, as do the caustic *Satires* of Juvenal. Many Latin works owe their survival to the teams of medieval monks who diligently copied and illustrated them. In the Renaissance the stories of Ovid's *Metamorphoses* were plundered by many writers and the works of Cicero had a profound influence on prose style; Seneca was seen as a master of tragedy and Plautus's *Pot of Gold* served as a model for comedies.

Detail from medieval copy of Pliny's *Historia Naturalis*

Petrarch (1304–74), one of the earliest and greatest lyric poets, produced works which showed the first indications of Humanism.

Le Marche

Umbria

Lazio

St. Francis of Assisi (1182–1226) was the first author to write in Italian instead of formal Latin. As well as letters and sermons, he wrote poems and songs, including the popular *Canticle of the Sun*.

Abruzzo, Molise, and Puglia

Campania

Basilicata and Calabria

Roman writer Alberto Moravia (1907–90) is usually labeled a "Neo-Realist." His novels and short stories focus on the corrupt values of contemporary society. Among his best known works are *Gli Indifferenti* and *Agostino*.

Sicily

The Sicilian Nobel Prize-winner Luigi Pirandello (1867–1936) was preoccupied with themes of illusion and reality. *Six Characters in Search of an Author* is his most famous work.

| 0 kilometers | | 200 |
| 0 miles | 100 | |

Music and Opera in Italy

Before Italy's unification, particularly during the 17th and 18th centuries, each major city had its own traditions of music-making. Rome, as the papal city, had musical traditions less hedonistic than elsewhere, and avoided opera. Florence had its day at the turn of the 16th century, with its celebrated *camerata* (groups set on reviving the traditions of Ancient Greek spectacle). Venice fostered church music on a grand scale, and Naples, during the 18th century, was renowned for comic opera. In the 19th century, Milan became the undisputed center of Italian opera, centered on La Scala.

The Medieval and Renaissance Periods

Through Boccaccio (see p38), among others, it is known that singing, dancing, and poetry often went hand in hand in medieval and Renaissance Italy. Italy concentrated on music as part of a spectacle rather than as a pure art form.

Important contributors to the music of these periods include Guido d'Arezzo (c.995–1050), a monk who perfected musical notation, and Francesco Landini (1325–97), one of the first known composers whose songs displayed a distinct concern for lyricism. The next 150 years were to be characterized by the *Ars Perfecta* style, culminating with composer Giovanni Palestrina (1525–94). His vocal style subjected dissonance to strict control, and it was employed for most church music during his lifetime. Madrigals (vocal settings of poems by Petrarch and other poets) were also popular.

The early 17th century saw Italian composers such as Carlo Gesualdo (c.1561–1613) and Claudio Monteverdi challenge these traditions by introducing more declamation and more of the unexpected.

La Pietà, Venice, where Vivaldi performed

The Baroque Era

Claudio Monteverdi's music straddled the transition from the Renaissance period to 17th-century Baroque. The word "baroque" means highly ornamented, even bizarre, and embellishment was rife. Monteverdi's madrigals began as standard pieces for four voices but ended up as mini-operas. This was due to the popularity of an individual instrumental style and the development of the *basso continuo* (a supporting organ, harpsichord, or lute that unleashed the possibility for solos and duets). At this point, the beginnings of the string orchestra were in place.

A new fashion for declamation meant that various emotional states were being represented with sighs and sobs rather than just description. Monteverdi's *Vespers* followed others' in exploiting the stereophonic possibilities of San Marco in Venice by contrasting different

Major Italian Composers through the Ages

Claudio Monteverdi (1567–1643) was best known for his *Vespers* of 1610. Both his madrigals and operas are considered major landmarks in the development of music.

Antonio Vivaldi (1678–1741) wrote over 600 concertos, many of which are for the violin. *The Four Seasons*, a set of concertos, is among the best-selling classical music of all time.

Gioacchino Rossini (1792–1868) was most famous for his comic operas, like *The Barber of Seville* and *La Cenerentola*. The romantic, expressive side of his more serious works, such as *Otello*, was often overlooked.

Luciano Pavarotti performed in the most modern surroundings

forces in different parts of the building. In the 1680s, Arcangelo Corelli (1653–1713) turned to classicism. Corelli was famous for the *concerto grosso*, a style that contrasted the solo string group with the full ensemble. He was followed by Antonio Vivaldi (1678–1741), who concentrated his efforts on developing the solo form of the *concerto grosso*. He used wind and plucked instruments as well as violins.

The Emergence of Opera

Opera first emerged during the wedding celebrations of Italy's wealthy 16th-century families. Monteverdi was the first composer to establish his work

Puccini's *Tosca*, first staged in 1900

firmly in the opera repertoire. During the 17th century, Alessandro Scarlatti (1660–1725) formulated a model which consisted of an orchestral overture followed by a sequence of narrative, set as *recitative*, and interrupted by *da capo* (three-part) arias. Themes for the weightier *opera seria* were largely drawn from mythology, while the lighter *opera buffa* had stock scenes that sometimes owed a large debt to the traditions of *Commedia dell'Arte*. Famous for his comic operas, such as *The Barber of Seville*, was the composer Gioacchino Rossini. Among other contributors, Vincenzo Bellini (1801–35) and Gaetano Donizetti (1797–1848) developed *bel canto* singing, a style stressing fine tone and ornamentation.

The two most prominent opera composers of the latter half of the 19th century were Giuseppe Verdi and Giacomo Puccini (1858–1924). Verdi often turned to the works of Shakespeare as well as to contemporary subjects in order to form a basis for his work, while many composers, like Puccini, turned to the new trend of *verismo* (slices of realism) – *La Bohème* is one of the most refined examples of this style.

The 20th Century

In the early 20th century, Puccini's *La Fanciulla del West* (The Girl of the West) brought cowboys into opera, *Turandot* looked towards the Orient, and *Tosca* brought torture and murder. Some composers have attempted to emulate French and German music, and only a few Italian pieces, such as those by Ottorino Respighi (1879–1936), have been regularly performed. The most important name in post-war Italian music was Luciano Berio (1925–2003), who developed Music Theater, an art form lying somewhere between drama and opera. In later years, however, Berio continued the tradition of Grand Opera with his elaborate production of *Un Re in Ascolto*. But it is Luciano Pavarotti (1935–2007) who must be credited with renewing an international interest in opera. In the 1990s, his televised performances with "Three Tenors" co-stars José Carreras and Placido Domingo secured a massive world audience for opera. Another star of opera and classical music is internationally renowned conductor Riccardo Muti, former director of La Scala.

The illuminated interior of Rome's Teatro dell'Opera

Giuseppe Verdi (1813–1901), whose first works were for the opera house La Scala *(see p197)*, was the most important opera composer of the 19th century. His most celebrated works include *Rigoletto* and *Aida*.

Italian Design

Italy has had phenomenal success evolving stylish, desirable forms for everyday objects. Its 20th-century achievements can be credited to a handful of forward-thinking industrial giants, such as Olivetti, willing to entrust important product decisions to a group of inspired designers, like Ettore Sottsass. The design genius was to rethink the function of consumer objects, apply new technology, and then make the result look seductive.

The streamlined aesthetic of Italian design extends even to pasta; this Marille version was created by car designer Giorgio Giugiaro for Voiello in 1983.

Sleek, sculptural Alessi cutlery (1988), designed by Ettore Sottsass, combines maximum utility with elegance and aesthetic integrity.

The Alessi kettle (1985), designed by Michael Graves, achieved such popularity in its first year of production that over 100,000 were sold.

One of the best known coffeemakers is Bialetti's Moka Express. Although designed in 1930, it is still enormously popular today.

Christophe Pilet's chair, designed for Giulio Cappellini's collection of contemporary furniture, expresses the idea of the living style of the 1990s.

The folding Cumano table, designed by Achille Castiglione for Zanotta in 1979, is still revered as a "designer object."

The Patty Difusa chair, with unusual wooden arms that curve into legs, was designed by William Sawaya for Sawaya & Moroni in Milan.

Pininfarina's streamlined form for the Ferrari Testarossa (1986) pushes car design almost into the realms of sculpture.

Light in weight, and compact in shape, Olivetti's Valentine typewriter revolutionized the role of the desk typewriter. Designed by Ettore Sottsass in 1969, its portability allowed the user to work anywhere.

Babc

Italian printer Giambattista Bodoni (1740–1813) designed the sophisticated typeface that bears his name and is still popular 200 years after its creation.

Milan's Giorgio Armani is best known for his updating of classic items such as the jacket, creating a flattering, smart, and comfortable, "deconstructed" look.

Prada, the Milan-based fashion house headed by Miuccia Prada, features minimalist, cutting-edge designs and the use of innovative fabrics.

Florence has a long reputation as a producer of high-quality crafts, particularly fashion accessories such as handbags, shoes, belts, jewelry, and briefcases.

Gucci's classic items, including bags and shoes, are a revered totem for the fashion-conscious.

The Artemide company is renowned for combining metal and glass in many of their designs, especially lamps and lighting fixtures.

Piaggio's innovative Vespa scooter (1946), by Corradino d'Ascanio, provided cheap, fast, and reliable transportation at a time when few could afford the expense of a car. Hugely successful, the Vespa is still a common sight on Italy's streets.

The FIAT 500 (1957), like the Vespa, became a symbol of mobility and democratization, an expression of Italy's rapid postwar recovery.

Scientists, Inventors, and Explorers

Italy has fostered a long tradition of important scientific thought and discovery, fueled in the Renaissance by such men as Galileo, who searched for a new understanding of the universe. Meanwhile, explorers such as Columbus had set off to find new worlds, a move heralded in the 13th century by Marco Polo. The spirit of scientific inquiry continued up to the 20th century, with the invention of radio and pioneering work in the field of nuclear physics.

Trentino Alto Adige

Lombardy

Valle d'Aosta and Piedmont

Liguria

Emilia-Romagna

Tuscany

Genoese-born Christopher Columbus sailed west from Spain in 1492. He reached the Indies in three months, navigating with such aids as an astrolabe.

The explorer Amerigo Vespucci established that the New World was a separate land mass. A pamphlet wrongly described him as its discoverer, and so, in 1507, America acquired its name.

Guglielmo Marconi invented the first practical system for sending radio signals. In 1901, he succeeded in picking up a signal that had been sent to England from Newfoundland.

Leonardo da Vinci was the ultimate Renaissance man, accomplished in both arts and sciences. He conceived his first design for a flying machine in c.1488, more than 400 years before the first airplane took off. This model is based on one of his technical drawings.

The telescope enabled astronomers to produce accurate lunar maps. Domenico Cassini, astronomy professor at Bologna University, refined the instrument. In 1665 he traced the meridian line in the church of San Petronio.

| 0 kilometers | | 200 |
| 0 miles | 100 | |

Padua University, founded in 1222, was a center of scientific learning in the Renaissance. Galileo, inventor of the telescope, taught physics here, and the lectern he used is still on view.

The Veneto and Friuli

The Venetian Marco Polo set off for the east as a youth in 1271. He stayed at the court of the Mongol emperor, Kublai Khan, for nearly two decades before returning home. He is seen here arriving at Hormuz in the Persian Gulf from India.

Galileo Galilei proved that the earth revolved around the sun, overturning Church doctrine. He was convicted of heresy in 1633. Here he shows the rings of Saturn to Venetian senators.

Le Marche

Umbria

Winner of the Nobel Prize for Physics in 1938, Enrico Fermi directed the first controlled nuclear chain reaction. He built the world's first nuclear reactor for producing power at the University of Chicago.

Lazio

Abruzzo, Molise, and Puglia

Campania

Pliny the Elder wrote his catalog of human knowledge, *Natural History*, in AD 77. He died when Vesuvius erupted two years later, but his book retained its authority for 1,500 years.

Basilicata and Calabria

Spectacles were invented in Italy in the 13th century. They are first recorded in Venice, still an important center for glasswork today.

Sicily

The mathematician Archimedes was born in c.287 BC in Syracuse, Sicily, then a Greek colony. Legend has it that he discovered the principle of specific gravity while in the bath.

THE HISTORY OF ITALY

The concept of Italy as a geographic entity goes back to the time of the Etruscans, but Italy's history is one of discord and division. Prior to the 19th century, the only time the peninsula was united was under the Romans, who by the 2nd century BC had subdued the other Italian tribes. Rome became the capital of a huge empire, introducing its language, laws, and calendar to most of Europe before succumbing to Germanic invaders in the 5th century AD. Another important legacy of the Roman empire was Christianity and the position of the pope as head of the Catholic church. The medieval papacy summoned the Franks to drive out the Lombards and, in AD 800, crowned the Frankish king Charlemagne Holy Roman Emperor. Unfortunately, what seemed to be the dawn of a new age turned out to be anything but. For five centuries popes and emperors fought to decide which of them should be in charge of their nebulous empire.

Meanwhile, a succession of foreign invaders – Normans, Angevins, and Aragonese – took advantage of the situation to conquer Sicily and the south. The north,

in contrast, saw a growth of independent city-states, the most powerful being Venice, fabulously wealthy through trade with the East. Other cities, such as Genoa, Florence, Milan, Pisa, and Siena, also had their days of glory. Northern Italy became the most prosperous and cultured region in western Europe, and it was the artists and scholars of 15th-century Florence who inspired the Renaissance. Small, fragmented states, however, could not compete with great powers. In the 16th century Italy's petty kingdoms fell prey to a foreign invader, this time to Spain, and the north subsequently came under the control of Austria.

One small kingdom that remained independent was Piedmont, but during a war between Austria and France it fell to Napoleon in 1796. In the 19th century, however, it was Piedmont that became the focus for a movement toward a united Italy, a goal that was achieved in 1870, thanks largely to the heroic military exploits of Garibaldi. In the 1920s, the Fascists seized power, and in 1946, the monarchy was abandoned for today's republic.

16th-century map of Italy, of the kind used by Venetian and Genoese sailors

◄ *Fall of the Rebel Angels* fresco by Giacinto Brandi on the ceiling of Sant'Ambrogio e Carlo al Corso

The Age of the Etruscans

The Etruscans were Italy's first major civilization. The frescoes, jewelry, and pottery found in their tombs are evidence of a highly artistic, cultured people. Their origin is a mystery, as is their language, but from the 9th century BC they spread through central Italy, their chief rivals being the Greeks in the south. Etruria was never a unified state, just a loose confederation of cities. In the 6th century Etruscan kings ruled Rome, the city that would ultimately eclipse them.

Italy in 650 BC

- Etruscan kingdoms
- Greek colonies

The double flute was a specialty of the Etruscans. The instrument was played at festivals and funerals alike.

Terracotta Winged Horses
This beautiful relief of yoked horses (4th century BC) decorated the façade of the Ara della Regina temple at Tarquinia.

Bronze Sheep's Liver
The inscriptions served as a guide for telling the future from animals' entrails.

Terracotta Cremation Urn
The lid of the urn shows the deceased holding a writing tablet. The Etruscans introduced the alphabet to Italy.

Tomb of the Leopards

Feasts and revelry are common themes in the frescoes that decorate Etruscan tombs. These musicians are from a tomb fresco (c.500 BC) at Tarquinia (see p470).

900 BC	800 BC	700 BC
9th century BC Pre-urban communities established along river valleys in Etruria	**753 BC** Legendary date of foundation of Rome by Romulus	**c.700 BC** Growth of cities in Etruria; earliest Etruscan inscriptions
		616 BC Etruscans become rulers of Rome under Tarquino the Older
c.900 BC First traces of Iron Age in Italy; Villanovan period	**715–673 BC** Reign of the wise Numa Pompilius, second king of Rome	
c.800 BC Greeks settle in Sicily and south of Italy		*Etruscan gold earrings*

A Boxing Match
Athletic competitions were held at funerals. This vase, which dates from about 500 BC, was made in Etruria, but imitates the Greek black-figure style of pottery.

The musicians and the dancer in the tomb painting are painted with a realism that indicates the influence of Greek art.

The lyre was made from a tortoise shell and played with a plectrum.

Apollo of Veii
This magnificent statue of Apollo (c.500 BC) shows the stylized facial features characteristic of Etruscan art.

Bronze Mirror
Wealthy Etruscans lived in great luxury. The women used polished bronze mirrors with engraved backs. This one shows Helen of Troy and the goddess Aphrodite.

Where to See Etruscan Italy

Rock tombs like these at Sovana (p336) are common in the volcanic tufa of central Italy.

Tuscany, Lazio, and Umbria are rich in Etruscan remains, especially tombs. There are huge necropolises in Lazio at Cerveteri and Tarquinia (p470). The latter also has an important museum. Other museums with major collections of Etruscan art and artifacts include Villa Giulia (p444) and the Vatican's Museo Gregoriano (p426) in Rome, the Museo Archeologico in Florence (p281), the Museo Nazionale in Chiusi (p336), and the Museo Guarnacci in Volterra (p338).

Temple of Neptune
This fine temple at Paestum (5th century BC) is a legacy of Greek colonization of the south.

---

509 BC Last Etruscan king, Tarquinius Superbus, expelled from Rome; establishment of Roman Republic

Mixing bowl, imported from Greece

450 BC Roman law codified in the Twelve Tables

390 BC Gauls sack Rome; Capitol saved thanks to alarm sounded by cackling geese

600 BC	500 BC	400 BC

499 BC Battle of Lake Regillus; Romans defeat alliance of Latins and Etruscans

474 BC Etruscan fleet defeated by Greeks off Cumae; blow to Etruscan naval power

c.400 BC Gauls start to settle along valley of the Po

396 BC Veii, a major Etruscan city in present-day Lazio, falls to Rome

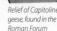

Relief of Capitoline geese, found in the Roman Forum

From Republic to Empire

From the scores of tribes inhabiting ancient Italy, one people, the Romans, emerged to conquer the peninsula and impose their language, customs, and laws on the rest. Rome's success was due to superb skill in military and civil organization. The state was a republic ruled by two consuls, elected each year, but as the extent of Rome's conquests grew, power passed to generals such as Julius Caesar. The Republic became unworkable and Caesar's heirs became the first Roman emperors.

Aquileia
Via Postumia
VERONA
Padus
PLACENTIA
Piacenza
Via Aemilia
BONONIA
Bologna
GENUA
Genoa

Cisalpine Gaul was annexed in 202–191 BC.

FLORENTIA
Florence
Via Cassia
ARIMINUM
Rimini
FAN
FOR
Fanc
PISAE
Pisa
Anus
ARRETIUM
Arezzo

POPULONIA

Via Aurelia
CLUSIUM
Chiusi
Tiberis
Via Flaminia

Etruria was in Roman hands by 265 BC.

ALBA FUCENS

ROMA
TIBUF
Tivoli

Julius Caesar
The great general, conqueror of Gaul, returned to Italy in 49 BC to defeat Pompey. His rise to absolute power marked the end of the Republic.

Oscan Inscription
The languages of the peoples conquered by Rome lived on for centuries before being replaced by Latin. The Oscans lived in what is now Campania.

War Elephant
In 218 BC, the great Carthaginian general Hannibal brought 37 elephants across the Alps – to spread alarm in the Roman ranks.

Roman Aqueduct
The Romans' talent for engineering found its most spectacular expression in huge aqueducts. These could be up to 50 miles (80 km) long, though for most of that distance the water ran underground.

High ground

Cleaning vent

Underground water channel

Arches carrying water across low ground

Reservoir

PANORMUS
Palermo

312 BC Building of Via Appia and Aqua Appia aqueduct

308 BC Etruscan city of Tarquinii falls to Rome

275 BC Greek King Pyrrhus defeated by Romans at Beneventum

264–241 BC First Punic War (between Rome and Carthage)

218 BC Second Punic War; Hannibal crosses the Alps

216 BC Roman defeat at Battle of Cannae

300 BC

250 BC

200 BC

Via Appia

287–212 BC Life of Archimedes, the great Greek mathematician of Syracuse

265 BC Romans capture last Etruscan city

237 BC Romans occupy Corsica and Sardinia

Hannibal, Carthaginian leader in the Second Punic War

191 BC Gaulish territory south of the Alps falls to Rome

Cicero Addresses the Senate
State business was debated in the Senate. The great orator Cicero (106–143 BC) argued for the Republic and against tyranny.

Roman Legionary
This bronze shows a legionary in standard kit of helmet, breastplate, leather kilt with iron plates, greaves on his shins, and sandals.

The Via Appia was extended from Capua to Brindisi in 190 BC.

Sicily became the first Roman province in 241 BC.

Where to See
Italy from the Republican Era

Republican structures are very rare, most having been rebuilt under the Empire. In Rome itself, two notable exceptions are the 2nd-century BC Temples of the Forum Boarium (p437). However, the legacy of the age to modern Italy is not hard to appreciate. Countless roads, such as the Via Appia Antica (p445), and towns were planned originally by Roman engineers. Two striking examples of towns with original Roman street plans are Lucca (pp324–5) and Como (p195).

These huge basalt blocks at Tharros in Sardinia (p555) were part of a Roman road.

Roman Roads

After conquering other tribes, the Romans imposed their authority by building roads along which legions could march rapidly to deal with any trouble. They also built towns. Many, such as Ariminum (Rimini), were "colonies," settlements for Roman citizens – often veteran legionaries.

Aerial View of Bologna
Roman street plans are still visible in city centers today. The route of the old Via Aemilia cuts straight through the center of Bologna.

Milestone from the Via Aemilia

168 BC End of Third Macedonian War; Romans now masters of Greece

150 BC

146 BC End of Third Punic War; Carthage destroyed

104 BC Slave revolt in Sicily

100 BC

89 BC Social War: Rome's Italian allies granted citizenship

80 BC Building starts on the first Roman amphitheater, at Pompeii

73–71 BC Slave revolt led by Spartacus

49 BC Caesar crosses the Rubicon and drives Pompey from Rome

50 BC

45 BC Introduction of 12-month Julian calendar

44 BC Murder of Julius Caesar; end of Roman Republic

31 BC Octavian defeats Mark Antony at Battle of Actium

30 BC Suicide of Mark Antony and Cleopatra in Egypt

The Golden Age of Rome

From the age of Augustus to the reign of Trajan, Rome's power grew until her empire stretched from Britain to the Red Sea. Despite the extravagance of emperors such as Nero, taxes and booty from military campaigns continually refilled the Imperial coffers. Under the wiser rule of Trajan, Hadrian, and Marcus Aurelius in the 2nd century AD, Roman citizens enjoyed wealth and comfort, with most of the work performed by slaves. Entertainment included visits to the baths, the theater, and the games. The town of Pompeii, buried when Vesuvius erupted in AD 79, preserves many fascinating details of everyday life.

Roman Empire in AD 117

Maximum extent of the Empire

Mosaic of Gladiators
Bloodthirsty gladiatorial combats were very popular. The gladiators were mostly slaves captured in war.

Frescoes of festoons and medallions

Trajan's Column
The carvings record Trajan's successful campaigns in Dacia (present-day Romania) in the first decade of the 2nd century AD.

The triclinium
(main dining room) had a beautiful frieze of cupids.

House of the Vettii
This reconstruction shows one of Pompeii's finest houses (see pp498–9). The Vettii were not aristocrats, but freedmen, former slaves, who had made a fortune through trade. The rooms were richly decorated with frescoes and sculptures.

Roman Shops
Buildings in towns were lined with small shops open to the street, like this pharmacy. The front was closed with wooden panels and locked at night.

9 BC Dedication of Ara Pacis *(see p414)* in Rome to celebrate peace after wars in Gaul and Spain

AD 17 Tiberius fixes boundary of Empire along the Rhine and Danube

Bronze cooking pots from kitchen at Pompeii

AD 79 Eruption of Vesuvius destroys Pompeii and Herculaneum

50 BC | **AD 1** | **AD 50**

27 BC Augustus takes title Princeps, in effect becoming the first Roman emperor

AD 37–41 Reign of Caligula

AD 43 Roman conquest of Britain in reign of Claudius

AD 67 Traditional date for martyrdom of St. Peter and St. Paul in Rome

AD 68 Deposition and suicide of Nero

AD 80 Inaugural games in Colosseum

Augustus
The adopted son of Julius Caesar became the first emperor, reducing the Roman Senate to impotence and ruling by decree.

The atrium had a skylight in the roof with a pool that collected rainwater below.

Front entrance

Where to See Imperial Rome

The best places to discover how people lived are Pompeii (pp498–9) and Herculaneum. Artifacts and works of art from these sites are held at the Museo Archeologico in Naples (pp494–5), while local museums all over Italy contain statues and other remains. Famous sights in Rome include the Pantheon (p408) and the Colosseum (p397). Hadrian's Villa, at Tivoli (p472) and Ostia (p471) are also fascinating to visit, but the whole country preserves traces of Rome's glory – from the Arch of Augustus in Aosta (p219) to Villa del Casale (p541) in Sicily.

The Forum (pp394–5), with its temples and law courts, was the center of daily life in ancient Rome.

Reception room

Mosaic of a Banquet
The Romans ate reclining on low couches. A popular accompaniment for many dishes was *garum*, a salty sauce made of dried fish.

Peristyle or colonnade

The internal garden was a feature borrowed by the Romans from the Greeks.

Household Shrine
Religious rites were practiced both in public and in private. This shrine from the House of the Vettii was dedicated to the *lares*, the household gods.

AD 97 Roman Empire reaches largest extent in reign of Trajan

AD 161–180 Reign of Marcus Aurelius

AD 193–211 Reign of Septimius Severus

AD 212 Roman citizenship extended to include people from all parts of the Empire

AD 100

AD 150

AD 200

Late 1st century AD Amphitheater of Verona built

AD 134 Hadrian's Villa at Tivoli completed

Emperor Septimius Severus

AD 125 Pantheon rebuilt by Hadrian

AD 216 Baths of Caracalla completed in Rome

The Splitting of the Empire

A decisive turning point in the history of the Roman Empire came with Emperor Constantine's conversion to Christianity in AD 312 and his decision to build a new capital at Constantinople (Byzantium). By the 5th century the Empire was split into two. Rome and the Western Empire could not stem the tide of Germanic invaders migrating southward, and Italy fell first to the Goths and later to the Lombards. The Eastern Empire retained nominal control over parts of Italy from its stronghold at Ravenna, which became the richest, most powerful city of the age, while the great palaces and arenas of Rome were reduced to ruins.

Italy in AD 600

Byzantine territories

Lombard territories

The Donation of Constantine
A medieval legend, encouraged by the papacy, tells how Constantine granted Pope Sylvester temporal power over Rome.

Belisarius
(500–565) was a general who won much of Italy back from the Goths.

Theodolinda of the Lombards
The 6th-century queen converted her people to orthodox Catholicism. Here, gold is melted for the church she built at Monza (see p205).

Justinian reigned from 527 to 565. He was a great lawgiver and one of the most powerful Byzantine emperors.

303–5 Persecution of Christians throughout the Empire in the reign of Diocletian

312 Constantine defeats rival Maxentius at Battle of the Milvian Bridge

404 Ravenna becomes seat of western emperor

Gold coin of Theodoric

488 Italy invaded by Theodoric the Ostrogoth

547 Church of San Vitale in Ravenna

200	300	400	500

270 Aurelian Wall built to protect Rome from Germanic invaders

313 Edict of Milan grants freedom of worship to Christians

324 Christianity becomes state religion

c.320 Building of first St. Peter's in Rome

476 End of Western Empire

410 Sack of Rome by Alaric the Visigoth

535 Belisarius lands in Sicily; reconquest of most of Italy by Byzantine Empire

564 Lombards invade Italy establishing their capital at Pav

Charlemagne
The King of the Franks was invited by the pope to crush the Lombards. In return, he was crowned Holy Roman Emperor in AD 800.

Saracens Besieging Messina (843)
In the 9th century, Sicily was conquered by Muslims from Africa. Saracen raiders even reached Rome, where Pope Leo IV built a new wall to defend the Vatican.

The emperor holds a large gold paten, the dish in which the bread is placed for Mass.

Maximian, Archbishop of Ravenna

Where to See Early Christian and Byzantine Italy

Though the fall of the Roman Empire led to war, famine, and depopulation, the continuity of the Christian religion has preserved many monuments of the late Empire and Byzantine period. Rome has the catacombs (p446) and great basilicas, such as Santa Maria Maggiore (p417). In Ravenna, the

administrative capital of the Byzantine Empire, are the churches of San Vitale and Sant'Apollinare (pp272–3) with their magnificent mosaics. Sicily and the south also preserve many Byzantine churches, while the finest example of late Byzantine architecture is San Marco in Venice (pp114–15).

Stilo in Calabria has a beautiful Byzantine church, the Cattolica (p524), dating from the 10th century.

Santa Costanza in Rome (p445) was built in the 4th century as the mausoleum of Constantine's daughter. Late Roman mosaics decorate the vaults.

Priests

The Court of Justinian
Byzantine churches were decorated with glorious mosaics of colored glass and gold leaf. This one from the apse of the church of San Vitale in Ravenna (see p272), completed in 547, depicts members of the Imperial court.

595 Lombards control two thirds of Italy

752 Lombard King Aistulf takes Byzantine stronghold of Ravenna

774 Charlemagne conquers Italy and takes Lombard crown

800 Charlemagne crowned Holy Roman Emperor in St. Peter's

878 Saracens capture city of Syracuse from Byzantine Empire and gain control of Sicily

600 | **700** | **800** | **900**

Gregory the Great (reigned 590–604)

599 Pope Gregory negotiates peace between the Lombards and the Byzantine Empire

754 Pope appeals to Franks for help; King Pepin invades Italy and defeats Lombards

6th-century Lombard gold helmet in the Bargello museum, Florence (see p287)

The Rise of Venice

Medieval Italy saw waves of foreign invaders joining in the struggle for power between popes and emperors. In the confusion, many northern cities asserted their independence from feudal overlords. The most powerful was Venice, governed by its doge and Great Council, which grew rich through trade with the East and by shipping Crusaders to fight the Saracens in the Holy Land. Its maritime rivals on the west coast were Genoa and Pisa.

The Mediterranean (1250)
— Genoese trade routes
— Venetian trade routes

Matilda of Tuscany
Matilda, Countess of Tuscany (1046–1115) supported the radical Pope Gregory VII against the Emperor Henry IV. When she died, she left her lands to the church.

Sails – for added speed

Canopy over the half-deck

The oars, pulled by slaves, were the principal means of propulsion.

Venetian Galley
The galleys used by Venice, both as warships and for carrying cargo, were similar to ancient Greek vessels.

Basilica San Marco

Doge's Palace

The columns of San Marco and San Teodoro had been erected in the 12th century.

Marco Polo's Departure for China

Venice traded in Chinese silks and spices imported via the Middle East, but no Venetian had been to China before Marco Polo's father Nicolò. Marco Polo set off with his father in 1271, returning 25 years later with fantastic tales of his time at the court of Kublai Khan.

1000 Doge of Venice, Pietro Orseolo II, defeats Dalmatian pirates in Adriatic

11th century School of Law at Bologna develops into Europe's first university

Medieval students

1139 Naples incorporated into Kingdom of Sicily

1000

1050

1100

1030 Norman knight Rainulf granted county of Aversa by Duke of Naples

1061 Normans Robert Guiscard and Roger de Hauteville capture Messina from the Arabs

1063 San Marco in Venice rebuilt

1084 Normans sack Rome

1076 Salerno, last Lombard city, falls to Normans

1073–85 Pope Gregory VII reforms church and papacy

1130 Roger II crowned king of Sicily

1115 Death of Countess Matilda

St. Francis of Assisi

(1181–1226)
In *The Dream of Pope Innocent III* by Giotto, painted around 1290–1295, St. Francis holds up the tottering edifice of the Roman church. The Franciscans' rule of poverty brought about a religious revival in reaction to the wealth of the church.

Where to See Early Medieval Italy

Of the many churches built in this period, especially fine examples are Venice's San Marco *(p114)*, Sant'Antonio *(p162)* in Padua, and the Duomo in Pisa *(p328)*.

Castello dell' Imperatore, Prato, was built about 1240.

The Leaning Tower *(p330)* also dates back to the 12th century. Medieval castles include Frederick II's Castel del Monte in Puglia *(p513)* and Castello dell'Imperatore in Prato.

Monastery of Sant'Apollonia

Today's Riva degli Schiavoni

Nicolò Polo, his brother Maffeo, and son Marco prepare to embark. They sailed first to Acre in the Levant.

Fourth Crusade

Discord between the leaders of the crusade and Pope Innocent III culminated in the sacking of Constantinople in 1204.

Frederick II

(1194–1250) The emperor kept a court of poets and scholars in Sicily. He won Jerusalem from the Arabs by diplomacy, but was constantly at war with the pope and the cities of Lombardy.

1155 Frederick Barbarossa crowned Holy Roman Emperor

1198 Frederick II becomes king of Sicily

1204 Sacking of Constantinople

1209 Franciscan Order founded

1216 Dominican Order founded

1250 Death of Frederick II

1260 Urban IV invites Charles of Anjou to rule Naples and Sicily

1265 Birth of Dante

150 **1200** **1250**

Frederick Barbarossa dressed as a Crusader

1220 Frederick II crowned Holy Roman Emperor

1237 Lombard League defeats Frederick at Battle of Cortenuova

1228 Gregory IX excommunicates Frederick II; struggle between Guelphs (the papal party) and Ghibellines (supporters of the emperor)

1271 Marco Polo sets off on journey to China

The Late Middle Ages

Old feuds between pope and emperor thrived throughout the 14th century, kept alive by two warring factions – the Guelphs, who backed the papacy, and the Ghibellines, who favored Imperial power. The cities of Lombardy and Tuscany used the political confusion to grow in strength. It was against this turbulent backdrop that a great new age in painting was inspired by artists such as Duccio and Giotto. Also at this time the Florentine poets Dante and Petrarch laid the foundations of Italian literature.

Italy in 1350
- Papal States
- Holy Roman Empire
- Angevin Kingdom of Naples

The campanile or bell tower

Medieval Town Square

Throughout central Italy, the town square was an expression of civic pride and independence. Towns, such as Perugia (see pp356–7), tried to overshadow their rivals in the splendor of their town halls. The center of Perugia has changed little since the 14th century when the town's main rival was Siena.

A griffin, symbol of Perugia

Condottieri

Cities paid *condottieri*, leaders of bands of mercenaries, to fight their wars. Siena hired Guidoriccio da Fogliano, seen here in a fresco by Simone Martini (1330).

The main chamber of the town hall, the Sala dei Notari, is decorated with the coats of arms of Perugia's mayors.

The Fontana Maggiore was begun in 1275 and includes panels by Nicola Pisano. Prominently placed, it is an emblem of the town's wealth.

Dante's Inferno

One of the harshest punishments in Dante's vision of hell is reserved for corrupt popes, such as Boniface VIII (reigned 1294–1303), who are placed upside down in fiery pits.

1282 Sicilian Vespers; uprising against French rule in Palermo; 2,000 French soldiers killed

1296 Work begins on the Duomo in Florence

1298 Marco Polo returns from China to Venice

1309–43 Reign of Robert the Wise of Naples

1310 Work begins on Palazzo Ducale in Venice

1313 Birth of Boccaccio

1339 Simon Boccanegra becomes first doge of Genoa; Giovanna I Queen of Naples

1275

1300

1325

1282 Peter of Aragon lands at Trapani, conquers Sicily, and is crowned king in Palermo

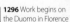

The poet and scholar Petrarch

1304 Birth of Petrarch

1309 Clement V moves papacy to Avignon

1321 Dante completes *La Divina Commedia* and dies the same year

1337 Death of Giotto

The Black Death
Bubonic plague reached Italy in 1347, carried on Genoese ships from the Black Sea. It killed over a third of the population, reducing the remainder to a state of superstitious terror.

Where to See Late Medieval Italy

Many central Italian cities and towns have public buildings from the 13th and 14th centuries; among the most impressive are Palazzo Vecchio (p295) in Florence and Siena's Palazzo Pubblico (p344). Smaller towns that preserve much of their medieval character include Volterra (p338) and the walled Monteriggioni (p338) in Tuscany, Gubbio (p356) and Todi (p363) in Umbria, and Viterbo (pp468–9) in Lazio. The Duomo in Orvieto (pp362–3) is a fine example of a late 13th-century Gothic cathedral.

Piazza dei Priori in Volterra (p328) is one of the most beautiful medieval squares in Italy.

The cathedral was started in 1350 and used to include an outside pulpit in the square.

Construction of Alessandria
Almost all towns were ringed with strong walls. This fresco (1407) by Spinello Aretino is a valuable record of medieval building techniques.

Return of Pope Gregory XI to Rome (1378)
For 70 years the popes had lived in Avignon, protected by the French kings, while nobles and republicans fought for control of Rome.

1347–9 Black Death

Medieval doctor

1378–1415 Period of Schism, with rival popes and antipopes in Rome and Avignon

1380 Genoese fleet surrenders to Venetians at Chioggia

1350

1375

1400

1354 Cola di Rienzo killed in Rome

1347 Cola di Rienzo tries to re-establish Roman Republic

1385 Gian Galeazzo Visconti becomes ruler of Milan

1378 Gregory XI returns from Avignon to Rome

1406 Pisa annexed by Florence

The Renaissance

Fifteenth-century Italy saw a flowering of the arts and scholarship unmatched in Europe since the days of Greece and Rome. Architects turned from the Gothic to Classical models for inspiration, while painting, with its new understanding of perspective and anatomy, produced a generation of artists that included such giants as Leonardo da Vinci, Raphael, and Michelangelo. The patronage for this cultural "rebirth" came from the wealthy families that ruled the city states of the north, led by the Medici of Florence. In spite of intense rivalry, they oversaw a period of uneasy stability out of which the Renaissance grew.

Italy in 1492

Republic of Florence

Papal States

Aragonese possessions

Handing over the Keys of St. Peter
Perugino's fresco in the Sistine Chapel *(see p430)* links the authority of the pope to the New Testament and, through the Classical buildings in the background, to ancient Rome.

Galeazzo Maria Sforza was the son of Milan's ruler.

Piero de' Medici, Lorenzo's father, was given the nickname "the Gouty."

Self-portrait of the artist

Execution of Savonarola *(1498)*
Having assumed the leadership of Florence in 1494, the fanatical monk was hanged, then burned for heresy in Piazza della Signoria.

1420 Martin V re-establishes papacy in Rome

1435 Publication of *On Painting* by Alberti, which contains the first system for the use of linear perspective

1436 Brunelleschi completes dome of Florence cathedral

1458–64 War between Houses of Aragon and Anjou over Kingdom of Naples

1469 Lorenzo the Magnificent becomes ruler of Florence

1400

1425

1450

1434 Cosimo de' Medici comes to power in Florence

1442 Naples captured by Alfonso of Aragon

1452 Birth of Leonardo da Vinci

1444 Federico da Montefeltro becomes Duke of Urbino

1453 Fall of Constantinople

Cosimo de' Medici

Filippo Brunelleschi

The Battle of Pavia *(1525)*
The French King Francis I was captured at this battle against the army of the Habsburg Emperor Charles V, who won control of Italy.

The Procession of the Magi

Benozzo Gozzoli's fresco (1459) in the Palazzo Medici-Riccardi, Florence, depicts members of the Medici family and other contemporary notables. It contains many references to a great church council held in Florence in 1439.

Where to See Renaissance Italy

Many cities were flourishing centers of the arts in the 15th century. None can rival Florence *(pp274–317)* with its great palazzi and the Uffizi gallery *(pp290–93)*, but Venice *(pp88–141)*, Urbino *(pp374–5)*, and Mantova *(p211)* all preserve great treasures. In Rome, do not miss the Vatican's Sistine Chapel and Raphael Rooms *(pp428–31)*.

The Spedale degli Innocenti by Brunelleschi in Florence *(p281)* shows the Classical symmetry and restraint of Renaissance architecture.

Humanism
Carpaccio's painting of St. Augustine is thought to show Cardinal Bessarion (c.1395–1472), one of the scholars who revived interest in Classical philosophy, especially Plato.

Lorenzo de' Medici (the Magnificent) was depicted as one of the three kings traveling to Bethlehem.

Pope Julius II
During his reign (1503–13), the worldly Julius made the papacy a major power in European politics. Raphael's portrait shows him as a shrewd old statesman.

1487 Birth of Titian

1483 Sixtus IV consecrates Sistine Chapel

1494 Italy invaded by Charles VIII of France

1503 Giuliano della Rovere elected Pope Julius II; he proves the most powerful of the Renaissance popes

1527 Rome sacked by Imperial troops

Niccolò Machiavelli

1475

1500

1525

1475 Birth of Michelangelo

Raphael

1483 Birth of Raphael

1498 Savonarola executed; Machiavelli secretary to ruling Council in Florence

1512 Michelangelo completes Sistine Chapel ceiling

1513 Giovanni de' Medici crowned Pope Leo X

1525 Francis I of France captured at Battle of Pavia

1532 Machiavelli's book *The Prince* is published, five years after his death

The Counter-Reformation

After the Sack of Rome in 1527, Italy was at the mercy of Charles V, Holy Roman Emperor and King of Spain. Pope Clement VII, who had opposed Charles, crowned him emperor in Bologna. In response to the growing threat from Protestantism, a series of reforms, known as the Counter-Reformation and backed by the Inquisition, imposed rigid orthodoxy. New religious orders, such as the Jesuits, were set up to take the battle for men's souls far overseas. The missionary spirit of the age inspired the dramatic forms of the Baroque.

Italy in 1550
- Spanish possessions
- States allied with Spain

Emperor Charles V and Pope Clement VII
The two former enemies settled their differences and the future destiny of Italy in the Treaty of Barcelona (1529).

The Virgin Mary intervenes on the side of the Christians.

Baroque Stucco Decoration

This stucco relief by Giacomo Serpotta (c.1690) in the Oratory of Santa Zita in Palermo is a magnificent example of Late Baroque exuberance. The subject is a favorite of the period, the Battle of Lepanto, a great naval triumph for the combined forces of Christendom against the Turks (1571).

The center of the ingenious creation is, in effect, a framed painting in perspective.

Baroque Architecture
Guarino Guarini's decoration of the dome of the Chapel of the Holy Shroud in Turin (*see p225*) was completed in 1694.

The young boy rests his hand on a helmet, symbol of the victorious Christians.

1530–37 Alessandro de' Medici ruler of Florence

1542 Inquisition established in Rome

1545–63 Council of Trent sets out agenda of Counter-Reformation

Andrea Palladio

1580 Death of architect Palladio

1600 Philosopher Giordano Bruno burned for heresy in Rome

1589 Palestrina publishes setting of the Latin Hymnal

1525	1550	1575	160

1540 Founding of Jesuit Order

1541 Michelangelo completes *Last Judgment* in Sistine Chapel

1529 Charles V crowned Holy Roman Emperor in San Petronio, Bologna

1564 Birth of Galileo

1560 San Carlo Borromeo appointed Bishop of Milan

1571 Victory over Turkish fleet at Battle of Lepanto

Giovanni Pierluigi da Palestrina

Trial of Galileo
The great astronomer was often in trouble with the Inquisition. He was summoned to Rome in 1633 and forced to deny that the Earth and planets moved round the sun.

Lepanto was the last major sea battle in which Venetian galleys played an important role.

St. Ignatius Loyola
The Spanish saint was the founder of the Jesuits – sanctioned by the pope in Rome in 1540.

Cherubs, a favorite motif in Baroque decoration

The turban, symbol of the defeated Turks

Where to See Baroque Italy

The Ecstasy of St. Teresa
by Bernini (p416) has the dynamic theatricality characteristic of the best Baroque sculpture.

The Baroque is strongly associated with Rome and in particular with its great public spaces such as Piazza Navona (pp402–3) and the many churches by Borromini and Bernini. Other cities and towns with striking Baroque architecture include Lecce (pp516–17) in Puglia, Palermo (pp530–33), Noto (p547), and Syracuse (pp546–7) in Sicily, and Turin (pp224–5).

Revolt of Masaniello (1647)
High taxes made Spanish rule in Naples unpopular. A proposed tax on fruit sparked off this failed revolt.

1626 New St. Peter's consecrated in Rome

1631 Duchy of Urbino absorbed by Papal States

1669 Venice loses island of Crete to the Turks

1694 Andrea Pozzo completes ceiling fresco for the church of Sant'Ignazio in Rome

1678 Birth of Vivaldi

1625   **1650**   **1675**

1633 Galileo condemned by papal authorities

1642 L'Incoronazione di Poppea by Monteverdi

1647 Revolt in Naples in response to tax on fruit

1669 Major eruption of Mount Etna

1674 Revolt against Spanish rule in Messina

1693 Eastern Sicily ruined by earthquake that kills 5 percent of the island's population

The Grand Tour

The treaty of Aix-la-Chapelle in 1748 marked the start of 50 years of peace. It was about this time that Italy, with its great art treasures and Classical ruins, including the newly excavated Pompeii, became Europe's first great tourist destination. Young English "milords" visited Rome, Florence, and Venice as part of a new type of pilgrimage, the Grand Tour, while artists and poets sought inspiration in Rome's glorious past. In 1800, Napoleon, who conquered and briefly united Italy, threatened to destroy the old order, but in 1815 the status quo was restored.

Charles III's Fleet at Naples *(1753)* Ruler of Naples from 1734 to 1759, when he became King of Spain, Charles attempted genuine political reforms.

Goethe in the Roman Campagna
Goethe toured Italy in the 1780s. Great poets who followed his example included the Romantics Keats, Shelley, and Byron.

Farnese Hercules
(see p495)

The Dying Galatian
(see p390)

Venetian Carnival
The colorful folklore of Carnival attracted many tourists, but Venice's days of greatness were over. In 1797, the proud maritime republic was ceded to Austria by Napoleon.

Gallery of Views of Ancient Rome by Pannini
Giovanni Pannini (1691–1765) painted views of Roman ruins for foreigners. This painting is a capriccio, an imaginary scene incorporating many well-known views and Classical statues.

1713 Treaty of Utrecht gives Naples and Sardinia to Austria and Sicily to Piedmont

Medici coat of arms

1725 *The Four Seasons* by Vivaldi

1735 Peace of Vienna confirms Charles III as King of the Two Sicilies (Naples and Sicily)

1748 First excavations at Pompeii

1700

1720

1740

1707 Birth of playwright Carlo Goldoni

1737 End of Medici dynasty in Florence; Grand Duchy of Tuscany passes to Austrian House of Lorraine

Antonio Vivaldi, great Venetian composer

1718 Piedmont and Sardinia united under House of Savoy; Sicily passes to Austria

THE HISTORY OF ITALY | 65

View of the Roman Forum by Piranesi
The popular series of etchings *Vedute di Roma* (Views of Rome) by Giovanni Battista Piranesi (1720–78) inspired a new interest in excavating the ruins of ancient Rome.

Where to See 18th-Century Italy

The 18th century produced two of Rome's best-loved tourist attractions: the Spanish Steps (p413) and the Trevi Fountain (p414). It was also the age of the first purpose-built museums, including the Vatican's Museo Pio-Clementino (p425). The Neo-Classical sculpture of Antonio Canova (1757–1822) was immensely popular during this period. His tomb is in Santa Maria Gloriosa dei Frari in Venice (pp102–3). Of Neo-Classical buildings, the most imposing is a vast monument to enlightened despotism: the Palazzo Reale at Caserta (p500).

Pauline Borghese, Napoleon's sister, was the model for Antonio Canova's *Venus (1805)* in the Villa Borghese collection in Rome (p443).

The Colosseum was as popular a subject in the 18th century as it is on today's picture postcards.

The Laocoön
(see p421)

View of the Pantheon
(see p408)

Napoleon
When Napoleon conquered Italy in 1800, he was seen by many as a liberator. The enchantment wore off as he took priceless works of art back to Paris.

Congress of Vienna (1815) The conference decided that Austria should keep Lombardy and Venice, thereby sowing the seeds of the Italian unification movement.

La Scala Opera House, Milan (see p191)

1778 La Scala opened in Milan

1797 Venice given to Austria by Treaty of Campo Formio; France controls rest of northern Italy

1800–1801 Napoleon conquers Italy

1808 Murat becomes King of Naples

1809 Pope Pius VII exiled from Rome

1760   **1780**   **1800**

1773 Pope dissolves Jesuit Order

1780 Joseph II succeeds to Austrian throne; minor reforms in Lombardy

1806 Joseph Bonaparte becomes King of Naples

1768 Corsica sold by Genoa to France

1796–7 Napoleon's first campaign in northern Italy

1765–90 Reign of Leopold Grand Duke of Tuscany, who introduces enlightened reforms

1815 Congress of Vienna restores status quo in Italy, though Austria keeps Venice

The Risorgimento

The word "Risorgimento" (resurgence) describes the five decades of struggle for liberation from foreign rule, culminating in the unification of Italy in 1870. In 1848, patriots rose up against the Austrians in Milan and Venice, the Bourbons in Sicily, and the pope in Rome, where a republic was declared. Garibaldi valiantly defended the republic, but all the uprisings were too localized. By 1859, the movement was better organized with Vittorio Emanuele II at its head. Two years saw the conquest of all but Venice and Rome, both of which fell within a decade.

Italy in 1861

Kingdom of Italy

Giuseppe Mazzini
(1805–72)
An exile for much of his life, Mazzini fought alongside Garibaldi to unite Italy as a republic, rather than a kingdom.

The guns were rusty, old converted flintlocks.

The red shirt was the badge of the Garibaldini.

Italian Railroads
The short railroad line from Naples to Portici was opened in 1839. Politically fragmented, Italy was slow to create an effective rail network.

Revolt of Messina
When, in 1848, Messina revolted, Ferdinand II subjected the town to a savage bombardment, earning himself the nickname King Bomba.

1831 Insurrection in Romagna and Le Marche against papal rule

1840 First major railroad lines established

1849 Accession of Vittorio Emanuele II as ruler of Piedmont

1852 Cavour becomes prime minister of Piedmont

1820 **1830** **1840** **1850**

1820s Carbonari secret society active in Papal States

1831 Mazzini founds *Giovine Italia* (Young Italy) movement

Daniele Manin, hero of the Venetian uprising of 1848

1847 Economic crisis

1848 Revolutions throughout Italy

1849 Republic of Rome crushed by French troops

Battle of Solferino (1859)
With the help of a French army led by
Napoleon III, the Piedmontese won Milan
and Lombardy from the Austrians.

Where to See Risorgimento Italy

Almost every town in Italy honors the heroes of
the Risorgimento with a Via Garibaldi, a Via Cavour, a
Piazza Vittorio, a Via Mazzini, and a Via XX Settembre
(the date of the fall of Rome in 1870). Many cities
also have Risorgimento museums. One of the best
is in Turin (p227).

The Victor Emmanuel Monument (p388) is a
prominent, but largely unloved, Roman landmark.

Two old paddle steamers
brought the Thousand from
Quarto near Genoa.

**Count Camillo di
Cavour** (1810–61)
Cavour's diplomacy
as prime minister of
Piedmont ensured that
the House of Savoy
became rulers of the
new Italy. He also
coined the word
"Risorgimento."

The skiffs were lent
by other ships moored
in Marsala harbor.

Garibaldi and the Thousand

*Giuseppe Garibaldi (1807–82) was a leader
of courage and genius. In 1860, he landed at
Marsala with 1,000 volunteers. The garrison
at Palermo surrendered, Sicily fell, and he
went on to conquer Naples, thus presenting
Vittorio Emanuele with half a kingdom.*

Giuseppe Verdi
(1813–1901)
Composers such as
Verdi, Donizetti, and
Rossini made the 19th
century the great era of
Italian opera. Verdi's
early operas inspired
the Risorgimento.

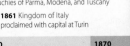

59 Battles of Magenta and Solferino;
edmont acquires Lombardy from Austria
d duchies of Parma, Modena, and Tuscany

1861 Kingdom of Italy
proclaimed with capital at Turin

860

1866 Italy wins
Venice from Austria

860 Garibaldi and the Thousand
apture Kingdom of the Two Sicilies

1870

1870 Rome falls to royalist
troops and is made capital
of new kingdom; Vatican
announces doctrine of
papal infallibility

*Pope Pius IX, who remained a virtual
prisoner in the Vatican when Rome
became capital of Italy*

1882 Deaths of Garibaldi
and Pope Pius IX

1880

1878 Death of Vittorio Emanuele;
accession of King Umberto I

1893 Troops
sent to suppress
insurrection
in Sicily

1890

1890 Italian colony
of Eritrea established
by royal decree

Modern Italy

Fascism under Mussolini (1922–43) promised the Italians greatness, but delivered only humiliation. In spite of this, Italy has become one of Europe's leading economies with a standard of living undreamed of at the turn of the 20th century. This has been achieved in the face of great obstacles. Since 1946, the Republic has passed through many crises: a series of unstable coalitions, the terrorist outrages in the 1970s, and in the 1990s, corruption scandals involving numerous government ministers and officials.

1936 FIAT produces first "Topolino" car

1960 *La Dolce Vita,* Federico Fellini's film satire on Rome's decadent café society, is released

1922 Fascists march on Rome; Mussolini invited to form government

1940 Italy enters World War II

1918 Austrian advance halted at the river Piave, just north of Venice

1900 Assassination of King Umberto I

1911–12 Italy conquers Libya

1943 Allies land in Sicily; Italy signs armistice and new Badoglio government declares war on Germany

1900	1910	1920	1930	1940	1950

1900	1910	1920	1930	1940	1950

1908 Earthquake destroys many towns and villages in Calabria and eastern Sicily; Messina almost completely razed to the ground; over 150,000 die

1915 Italy enters World War I

1936 Italy conquers Abyssinia; pact with Germany, forming anti-Communist "Axis"

1943 Mussolini imprisoned, then freed by Germans

1946 Referendum in which Italy votes to become a republic; Christian Democrat party forms first of a long series of coalition governments

1920s Postwar years see continued emigration to the United States. Here, emigrants cheer as they reach New York aboard the *Giulio Cesare*

1957 Treaty of Rome; Italy one of the six founder members of the European Economic Community

1960 Olympic Games held in Rome

1917 Defeat at Caporetto on Italy's northeastern border; Italian troops, such as these Alpini, retreat to defensive positions

1909 In his *Futurist Manifesto,* Filippo Marinetti condemns all traditional art as too static. His idea of a new dynamic art is expressed in works such as Umberto Boccioni's bronze *Unique Forms of Continuity in Space*

1978 Ex-prime minister Aldo Moro kidnapped and assassinated by the Red Brigades

1996 Fire destroys La Fenice theater in Venice

1994 TV magnate Silvio Berlusconi becomes prime minister after forming political party "Forza Italia." Alleged financial irregularities force him to resign later that year

1997 Earthquake in Assisi seriously damages the Basilica di San Francesco, destroying Giotto's frescoes

2000 Rome celebrates the Holy Year known as the Jubilee

1992 Judge Giovanni Falcone killed by Mafia in Sicily

2002 Euro is adopted

2006 Italy wins World Cup in Germany

1992 Scandals expose widespread corruption in the postwar political system

2008 Silvio Berlusconi wins third term as prime minister but resigns in 2011 as the country is gripped by financial crisis

66 River Arno rsts its banks, oding Florence d damaging ny priceless rks of art

1983 Bettino Craxi, Italy's first Socialist prime minister, forms government

2011 Mario Monti sworn in as prime minister

2013 Pope Benedict XVI resigns and Pope Francis is elected

1970	1980	1990	2000	2010	2020

1970	1980	1990	2000	2010	2020

1990 World Cup staged in Italy

2015 Milan hosts the Universal Exposition

1978 Election of Pope John Paul II

2013 Election results in coalition government.

2011 Italy celebrates 150 years of unification

1982 Italian football team wins World Cup in Spain

2006 Romano Prodi sworn in as prime minister

2005 Election of Pope Benedict XVI

1999 Roberto Benigni wins 3 Oscars for his film *La Vita è Bella*, including best actor and best foreign language film

1969 Bomb outrage in Milan at Piazza Fontana; 13 killed and many injured

1997 Dario Fo wins the Nobel prize for literature

Italian Cinema Since World War II

The social problems of late 1940s Italy inspired a wave of cinema known as Neo-Realism. Leading exponents included Roberto Rossellini, who made *Roma Città Aperta* (1945), Vittorio de Sica, the director of *Bicycle Thieves* (1948), Pier Paolo Pasolini, and Luchino Visconti. Since that time, the major Italian directors have cultivated their own personal styles. Visconti's later movies,

Vittorio de Sica (1901–74)

such as *Death in Venice* (1971), show formal beauty and decadence, while Federico Fellini's *La Dolce Vita* (1960) and *Roma* (1972) depict life as a grotesque carnival. Italy has also produced some commercially successful movies, such as Sergio Leone's late 1960s westerns and the Oscar-winning *Cinema Paradiso* and *La Vita è Bella*.

ITALY THROUGH THE YEAR

Throughout Italy, the variety of local character and color is astonishing. This is mainly due to the survival of regionalism, particularly in the southern parts of the country. Old traditions, customs, and lifestyles are still greatly respected and there is a deep attachment to the land, which is reflected in a healthy interest in the food and produce, as well as a perseverance of seasonal religious and secular events. Annual festivals, whether in rural or urban areas, range from wine-tasting and gastronomic celebrations to elaborate commemorations of every patron saint imaginable.

Spring

The Italian spring begins early, particularly in the south. City streets and main sights are rarely overcrowded (except at Easter in Rome). The weather, however, can be unpredictable and wet in the central and northern parts of the country. Spring specialties, such as asparagus, spinach, and arugula, begin to feature on restaurant menus. This is a season of great celebration; festivals and fairs abound, especially in Sicily, and the Easter papal address always draws massive crowds to St. Peter's.

Tuscan asparagus

March

Dolomiti Ski Jazz Festival, *(mid-Mar)*, Val di Fiemme, Trentino–Alto Adige. Live jazz on the ski slopes.
Sa Sartiglia, Oristano, Sardinia. Three-day carnival ending on Shrove Tuesday.
Su e zo per i ponti *(Sun, varies)*, Venice. A lively race through the city's streets, up and down the bridges.

April

Procession of the Grieving Madonna *(Good Friday)*, Procida, Campania. A colorful religious procession throughout the island.
Holy Week *(Easter Week)*. Numerous Easter celebrations from Palm Sunday to Easter Sunday, throughout the country.
Papal Address *(Easter Sunday)*, Rome. The pope makes his Easter address from the Vatican.
Dance of the Devils *(Easter Sunday)*, Prizzi, Sicily. Dance recital symbolizing the attempts of evil to vanquish the forces of good.
Scoppio del Carro *(Easter Sunday)*, Florence. Firework display is lit by a mechanical dove in front of the Duomo.
Festa della Madonna che Scappa in Piazza *(Easter Sunday)*, Sulmona, Abruzzo. Re-enactment of a meeting between the Virgin and the Risen Christ.
Festa degli Aquiloni *(first Sun after Easter)*, San Miniato, Tuscany. Kite lovers perform aerial acrobatics at this festival.
Festa di San Marco *(Apr 25)*, Venice. St. Mark, the patron saint of Venice, is commemorated by a gondola race across St. Mark's Basin.
Mostra Mercato Internazionale dell'Artigianato *(last week)*, Florence. An important European exhibition of arts and crafts.

Spring strawberries

Scoppio del Carro (Explosion of the Carriage) festival in Florence

Sagra Musicale Lucchese *(dates vary)*, Lucca, Tuscany. Festival of sacred music held in Romanesque churches.

May

Festa di Sant'Efisio *(May 1)*, Cagliari, Sardinia. Paraders in traditional Sardinian costume.
Festa di San Nicola *(May 7–9)*, Bari, Puglia. A statue of St. Nicholas is taken to the sea.
Festa dei Ceri *(May 15)*, Gubbio, Umbria. Festival, including a race with four teams carrying large candles.
Festa di San Domenico Abate *(first Thu)*, Cocullo, Abruzzo. Includes a procession with a statue of St. Dominic covered with live snakes.
Festa dello Speck *(late May)*, Bolzano, Trentino–Alto Adige. A celebration of the famed ham.
Greek Drama in Theater *(May–Jun)*, Syracuse, Sicily. Festival of Greek drama.
Maggio Musicale *(May–Jun)*, Florence. This is the city's biggest arts festival, including music, drama, and dance.

Procession of the Grieving Madonna on the isle of Procida

Street carpeted with flowers for the Infiorata in Genzano

Summer

Summer brings the crowds to Italy, particularly the cities. Italians, however, flee and head for the coast, usually in August. The lines for tourist attractions can be long and hotels are often fully booked. Festivals vary; religious events are interspersed with those of the arts and local folklore.

June

Festa della Fragola
(Jun 1), Borgo San Martino, Piedmont. Musical and folkloric performances in celebration of the strawberry.
Biennale *(Jun–Sep)*, Venice. The world's biggest exhibition of contemporary art takes place during odd-numbered years only.
Infiorata *(Corpus Christi day)*, Genzano, Lazio. A procession through streets carpeted with flowers.
International Film Festival *(mid-Jun)*, Taormina, Sicily.
Festa di San Giovanni *(mid-Jun–mid-Jul)*, Turin, Piedmont. Festival in honor of the city's patron saint, John.
Calcio Storico *(Jun 24 and two other days in Jun)*, Florence. Soccer in 16th-century costumes; fireworks.
Festa di Sant'Andrea *(Jun 27)*,

Amalfi, Campania. Fireworks and processions.
Festival dei Due Mondi *(late Jun–early Jul)*, Spoleto, Umbria. International festival of drama, music, and dance.
Gioco del Ponte *(last Sun)*, Pisa. "The Bridge Parade" of marchers in antique armor.
Estate Romana *(late Jun–mid-Sep)*, Rome. Outdoor movies, performances, ballet, and concerts.

July

Corsa del Palio *(Jul 2)*, Siena. Tuscany's most famous event *(see p345)* presents a medieval flag-waving exhibition and horse race.
Festa della Madonna della Bruna *(first Sun)*, Matera, Basilicata. A lively procession of clergymen and knights in costume.
Festa dei Noiantri *(last two weeks Jul)*, Rome. A colorful festival in Trastevere.
Festa della Santa Maria del Carmine *(Jul 16)*, Naples. Featuring the illumination of the city's bell tower.
Umbria Jazz *(Jul)*, Perugia. World-famous jazz artists perform in various settings.
Opera Festival *(Jul–Aug)*, Verona, Veneto. Renowned

Musician from Florence's Calcio

The Sienese Palio in action

opera festival *(see p141)* overlapping with the **Shakespeare Festival**, providing music, drama, opera, and dance.

August

Medieval Palio *(first weekend Aug)* Feltre, Veneto. Parades and archery competitions, medieval-style.
Festa dei Candelieri *(Aug 14)*, Sassari, Sardinia. "Festival of the Candle," dating from the 16th century.
Festa del Mare *(Aug 15)*, Diano Marina, Liguria. This "Festival of the Sea" boasts a spectacular firework display.
Corsa del Palio *(Aug 16)*, Siena, Tuscany. See July entry.
Rossini Festival *(mid-Aug)*, Pesaro, Le Marche. A celebration of the composer's work, in his birthplace.
Venice Film Festival *(late Aug–early Sep)*. International festival on the Lido.
Settimane Musicali di Stresa *(late Aug–end Sep)*, Stresa, Lombardy. Four weeks of concerts and recitals.

Sun, sand, and sea – essential ingredients of a Tuscan beach holiday

Fall

Fall is a slow, gentle season in Italy, but that doesn't mean there are fewer festivals and fairs. In addition to the various religious events at this time of year, gastronomic festivals are especially popular, commemorating such delectables as chestnuts, local cheeses, sausages, and mushrooms. Fall is the season of the *vendemmia*, the grape harvest, which is often used as an excuse for village festivities at which the latest local wines flow freely.

The climate (*see pp76–7*) in late fall is often cold and wet in the north. The south, however, can be quite warm right through October.

The widely cultivated olive tree

held in the main square every even year.
Rassegna del Chianti Classico *(second week)*, Chianti, Tuscany. Celebration of the local wines.
La Notte Bianca *(mid-Sep)*, Rome. Concerts, events, and free admission to some museums during the night.
The Miracle of San Gennaro *(Sep 19)*, Naples. Re-enactment of the liquefaction of the saint's blood, in a lively mass at the Duomo.
Palio *(third Sun)*, Asti, Piedmont. Includes a costumed medieval procession and bareback horse racing.

October
Amici della Musica *(Oct–Apr)*, Florence, Tuscany. The popular "Friends of Music" concert season begins.
Fiera del Tartufo *(Oct–Nov)*, Alba, Piedmont. A variety of events centered around the locally grown white truffle.
Festa di San Francesco *(Oct 4)*, Assisi, Umbria. Feast in honor of one of Italy's patron saints.

Advertisement for the September Palio in Asti, Piedmont

September
Festa di Santa Lucia *(first Sun)*, Lodè, Sardinia. Includes a contest where competitors improvise short poems.
Procession of the Macchina di Santa Rosa *(Sep 3)*, Viterbo, Lazio. Commemoration of the saint's body being transported to the Church of Santa Rosa in 1258.
Giostra del Saracino *(first Sun)*, Arezzo, Umbria. Joust of the Saracen and knights, dating from the 13th century.
Regata Storica *(first Sun)*, Venice. A procession of historic boats followed by a colorful gondola race.
Human chess game *(second week)*, Marostica, near Vicenza. A popular costumed game

Wine festivals *(first week)*, Castelli Romani, Lazio.
Sagra del Tordo *(last Sun)* Montalcino, Tuscany. Celebration of the thrush; costumed archery contests.
Festa dell'Uva *(dates vary)*, Bolzano, Trentino–Alto Adige. Grape festival with live music and a costumed procession featuring allegoric carts.
International Festival of Cinema *(dates vary)*, Rome. A week of screenings, high-profile events, and celebrity spotting in the capital.

A roasted chestnut stall in autumn

November
Festa dei Popoli *(Nov)*, Florence, Tuscany. Film festival showing documentary films in their original languages with Italian subtitles.
Festa della Salute *(Nov 21)*, Venice. Cherished by Venetian locals, this feast gives thanks to the Virgin Mary in memory of a 1630 plague.

The human chess game in the town square of Marostica

Winter

There are fairs, markets, and religious events up and down the country at this time of year. Neapolitan Christmas cribs are famous and nearly every church has one. The Christmas holiday itself is low-key; more is made of other religious events such as the liquefaction of San Gennaro's blood in Naples and the Carnevale in Venice.

December

Festa di Sant'Ambrogio
(early Dec), Milan. The official opening of La Scala Opera season *(see p197)*.
Festa della Madonnadi Loreto
(Dec 10), Loreto, Le Marche. Celebration of the Virgin's Holy House.
Mercato della Befana
(mid-Dec–Jan 6), Rome. Well-known Christmas fair held in Piazza Navona.
The Miracle of San Gennaro
(Dec 16), Naples. See September. **Christmas fair** *(mid-Dec)*, Naples. Fair selling crib figures and decorations.
Fiaccole di Natale
(Christmas Eve), Abbadia di San Salvatore, Tuscany. Features carols and processions in memory of the first shepherds.
Midnight Mass *(Dec 24)*, at churches all over the country.
Christmas Day *(Dec 25)*, St. Peter's Square, Rome. Public blessing by the pope.

Rome during one of its rare snowfalls

La Befana at Piazza Navona, Rome

January

Capodanno *(Jan 1)*, all over the country. New Year's Day is celebrated with fireworks and volleys from hunters firing into the air to scare off ghosts and spirits of the old year and welcome in the new.
La Befana *(Jan 6)*, throughout Italy. Children's holiday with presents and sweets.
Pitti Immagine Uomo, Pitti Immagine Donna, Pitti Immagine Bimbo, Fortezza da Basso, Florence. Month of international fashion shows for women, men, and children.
Festa di San Sebastiano *(Sun nearest Jan 20)*, Dolceacqua, Liguria. A laurel tree covered with colorful communion hosts is carried through town.

Carnevale, Viareggio

Festa d'o'Cippo di Sant'Antonio *(Jan 17)*, Naples. A procession for St. Anthony, protector of animals.
Carnevale *(a month-long event finishing Shrove Tue)*, Viareggio, Tuscany. A carnival famous for its lively, topically themed floats.
Fair of St. Orsa *(Jan 30–31)*, Aosta, Valle d'Aosta. Exhibition of traditional arts and crafts.

February

Carnevale *(last 10 days before Lent, finishing Shrove Tuesday)*, Venice. Pre-Lent festival meaning "farewell to meat." Events are organized, but anyone can buy a mask and watch the array of gorgeous costumes on show.

Public Holidays

New Year's Day (Jan 1)
Epiphany (Jan 6)
Easter Sunday & Monday
Liberation Day (Apr 25)
Labor Day (May 1)
Republic Day (Jun 2)
Ferragosto (Aug 15)
All Saints' Day (Nov 1)
Immaculate Conception (Dec 8)
Christmas Day (Dec 25)
Santo Stefano (Dec 26)

Sagra delle Mandorle in Fiore *(first or second week)*, Agrigento, Sicily. Annual almond blossom celebration.
Bacanal del Gnoco *(dates vary)*, Verona. Traditional masked procession with both international and local allegorical floats. Masked balls are held in the town's squares.
Carnevale *(dates vary)*, Mamoiada, Sardinia. Processions include *mamuthones* wearing sinister black masks.

Carnevale revelers in Venice

The Sporting Year

Soccer is by far the most important sport in Italy, uniting the country when the national team *(Azzurri)* plays. Other sports throughout the year also attract a large following, so fans are never at a loss for varied activities. For most big sporting events, tickets can be obtained for cash at club outlets such as the venue itself. Agencies provide hard-to-get tickets at often higher prices. Beware of the inevitable scalpers at popular events, as their expensive tickets may not be valid.

Calcio Fiorentino, one of Italy's few indigenous sports, is said to be the medieval precursor of modern soccer.

The professional water polo season takes place from March through to July. The Canottieri Napoli team play consistently well through the championship.

Coppa Italia soccer final

Memorial d'Aloia rowing competition, held in Umbria

The Giro d'Italia cycling race takes place over many stages. Ivan Basso (Italian) won the race in 2006 and 2010.

January	February	March	April	May	June

Indoor Athletics Championships

Rome Marathon

International Showjumping, Rome

The Rome Masters, previously known as the Italian Open, takes place in Rome during May. The event is one of the most prestigious clay court tennis competitions in the world.

The Italian leg the Circuito Mondia in Mugello. Valentir Rossi has dominate the MotoGP Wor Championship f over a decac

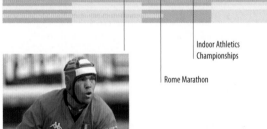

Rugby is becoming increasingly popular. Italy takes part in the Six Nations Championship in February and March, along with England, Scotland, Wales, Ireland, and France.

The Italian Outdoor European Swimming Championships are held every year in July. The Olympic gold medal winner Massimiliano Rosolino, pictured here, celebrates a victory.

Italy has some of the best ski resorts in Europe, and in 2006 Turin hosted the Winter Olympics. Above is Alberto Tomba, once a champion of the slopes.

The Italian Grand Prix, held annually at Monza, is Italy's round of the international Formula One World Championship. Giancarlo Fisichella is one of Italy's most successful drivers.

Trofeo dei Templi rowing competition, Sicily

The Sanremo Car Rally, held each year in October, was made famous by driver Micky Biason and the Lancia Delta Integrale.

August	September	October	November	December

na Palio
e p345),
d on July 2
d August 16

Italy won the World Cup in 2006

The Italian soccer season runs from September through to May. It culminates with the Coppa Italia final, which is equivalent to the British FA Cup. Italy's soccer obsession, however, reaches fever pitch when the World Cup takes place every four years.

The Outdoor Athletics Championship has become very popular. One of Italy's foremost athletes is race walker Alex Schwazer, winner of an Olympic gold medal in 2008.

Key to Sporting Seasons

▬ Soccer
▬ Water polo
▬ Rugby
▬ Basketball
▬ Volleyball
▬ Skiing

The Climate of Italy

The Italian peninsula has a varied climate falling into three distinct geographical regions. Cold Alpine winters and warm, wet summers characterize the northern regions. In the extensive Po Valley, arid summers contrast with freezing, damp winters. The rest of Italy has a pleasant climate with long, hot summers and mild winters. Cooler weather along the backbone of the Apennines can bring snow during the winter months.

TRENTINO–ALTO ADIGE

Average monthly maximum temperature

Average monthly minimum temperature

Average daily hours of sunshine

Average monthly rainfall

°F	Apr	Jul	Oct	Jan
max	61	83	63	41
min	39	63	41	23
hrs	6 hrs	8 hrs	4 hrs	2 hrs
in	2.6 in	3.9 in	3.3 in	0.8 in
month	Apr	Jul	Oct	Jan

LOMBARDY

°F	Apr	Jul	Oct	Jan
max	64	82	63	43
min	46	64	50	30
hrs	5 hrs	9 hrs	5 hrs	3 hrs
in	2.9 in	3.1 in	3.5 in	2.5 in
month	Apr	Jul	Oct	Jan

VALLE D'AOSTA AND PIEDMONT

°F	Apr	Jul	Oct	Jan
max	83	79	63	45
min	43	59	45	28
hrs	5 hrs	9 hrs	4 hrs	3 hrs
in	3.7 in	3.4 in	3.3 in	1.3 in
month	Apr	Jul	Oct	Jan

LIGURIA

°F	Apr	Jul	Oct	Jan
max	64	82	70	54
min	53	68	57	44
hrs	7 hrs	9 hrs	8 hrs	4 hrs
in	2.6 in	1.2 in	2.9 in	2.7 in
month	Apr	Jul	Oct	Jan

SARDINIA

°F	Apr	Jul	Oct	Jan
max	66	84	72	57
min	50	68	57	45
hrs	8 hrs	11 hrs	6 hrs	4 hrs
mm	31 mm	7 mm	48 mm	50 mm
month	Apr	Jul	Oct	Jan

TUSCANY

°F	Apr	Jul	Oct	Jan
max	63	84	68	50
min	46	61	59	36
hrs	8 hrs	11 hrs	6 hrs	5 hrs
mm	72 mm	30 mm	90 mm	65 mm
month	Apr	Jul	Oct	Jan

EMILIA-ROMAGNA

°F	Apr	Jul	Oct	Jan
max	63	86	61	39
min	47	66	50	30
hrs	6 hrs	11 hrs	5 hrs	3 hrs
in	2.3 in	1.5 in	3.2 in	1.8 in
month	Apr	Jul	Oct	Jan

Aosta

Turin

Milan

Verona

Parma

Genoa

Bologna

Florence

Livorno

Olbia

Cagliari

Tre[n]

THE VENETO AND FRIULI

month	Apr	Jul	Oct	Jan
°F	63 / 45	82 / 64	64 / 48	45 / 32
☀	7 hrs	9 hrs	4 hrs	2 hrs
☂	4.4 in	4.3 in	5.3 in	3.5 in

LE MARCHE

month	Apr	Jul	Oct	Jan
°F	61 / 48	81 / 68	66 / 55	47 / 37
☀	6 hrs	10 hrs	5 hrs	3 hrs
☂	2.2 in	2.2 in	3 in	2.6 in

UMBRIA

month	Apr	Jul	Oct	Jan
°F	66 / 43	84 / 61	66 / 48	46 / 34
☀	5 hrs	10 hrs	6 hrs	3 hrs
☂	3.1 in	1.7 in	3.6 in	3 in

ABRUZZO, MOLISE, AND PUGLIA

month	Apr	Jul	Oct	Jan
°F	64 / 50	82 / 68	70 / 57	55 / 43
☀	6 hrs	10 hrs	6 hrs	4 hrs
☂	1.9 in	1.1 in	2.7 in	2.4 in

ROME AND LAZIO

month	Apr	Jul	Oct	Jan
°F	64 / 48	84 / 66	72 / 55	54 / 40
☀	6 hrs	10 hrs	7 hrs	5 hrs
☂	2 in	0.8 in	3.7 in	3.4 in

NAPLES AND CAMPANIA

month	Apr	Jul	Oct	Jan
°F	66 / 54	86 / 70	72 / 64	55 / 45
☀	7 hrs	11 hrs	6 hrs	4 hrs
☂	2.3 in	0.5 in	2.7 in	3.3 in

SICILY

month	Apr	Jul	Oct	Jan
°F	66 / 54	84 / 68	75 / 61	59 / 48
☀	8 hrs	11 hrs	7 hrs	4 hrs
☂	1.1 in	0.3 in	2.3 in	2.3 in

BASILICATA AND CALABRIA

month	Apr	Jul	Oct	Jan
°F	64 / 49	85 / 65	71 / 57	55 / 44
☀	6 hrs	10 hrs	5 hrs	4 hrs
☂	2.8 in	0.5 in	3.4 in	3.5 in

Trieste
Venice
ova
a
Ravenna
Ancona
ugia
Pescara
L'Aquila
Foggia
Bari
Naples
Salerno Potenza
Taranto
Catanzaro
Reggio di Calabria
Messina
Catania
Agrigento

NORTHEAST ITALY

Introducing Northeast Italy   **80–87**

Venice   **89–129**

Venice Street Finder   **130–139**

Venice Vaporetto Routes   **140–141**

The Veneto and Friuli   **142–169**

Trentino–Alto Adige   **170–179**

Northeast Italy at a Glance

The sheer variety to be found in northeast Italy makes it a fascinating area to explore. The majestic Dolomites dominate the north, straddling Trentino–Alto Adige and the Veneto, and are dotted with medieval castles and modern skiing resorts. On the plain, the cities of Verona, Vicenza, and Padua are all noted for outstanding architecture and museums, while the rural hinterland boasts beautiful villas. The incomparable and spectacular city of Venice, with its magnificent monuments, rises from the lagoon. Further east, in Friuli, there are important Roman remains. This map pinpoints some of the highlights.

Alto Adige is a dramatic region of snow-covered mountain valleys scattered with forbidding castles and onion-domed churches in the Tyrolean style *(see pp174–5)*.

TRENTINO-ALTO-ADIGE
(See pp170–79)

THE VENETO AND FRIULI
(See pp142–69)

The Dolomites *(see pp86–7)* form the spectacular backdrop to many towns in northeast Italy, among them Trento, the region's capital *(see pp178–9)*.

Verona is one of the loveliest cities in the Veneto, boasting the Castelvecchio and a Roman arena now used for performances of opera *(see pp146–51)*.

Vicenza, a model Renaissance city, is dominated by the buildings of Palladio, such as the Palazzo della Ragione and La Rotonda *(see pp154–7)*.

◀ Santa Maddalena with the Dolomites in the background

Udine in Friuli is an interesting city that centers on the elegant Piazza della Libertà. The piazza contains imposing statues, such as this colossal Hercules and the Porticato di San Giovanni *(see pp166–7)*.

| 0 kilometers | 40 |
| 0 miles | 20 |

Aquileia, once a splendid Roman city, is filled with ancient remains, such as this Mausoleum. Its Basilica houses early Christian mosaics *(see p168)*.

Brunico

Cortina d'Ampezzo

Tarvisio

Tolmezzo

FRIULI-
VENEZIA
GIULIA

Belluno

Udine

Vittorio Veneto

Pordenone

Gorizia

Piave

Oderzo

Monfalcone

Treviso

VENETO

Caorle

Trieste

Mestre

Padua boasts several major sights, among them the Basilica di Sant'Antonio and the Cappella degli Scrovegni with its frescoes by Giotto *(see pp158–63)*.

Venice
(see inset below)

Chioggia

PO

Basilica di San Marco in Venice is one of Europe's finest Byzantine buildings, with a magnificent gilded interior *(see pp114–17)*.

VENICE
(See pp89–141)

The Palazzo Ducale is a masterpiece of Venetian Gothic architecture *(see pp118–20)*.

| 0 kilometers | 1 |
| 0 miles | 0.5 |

The Flavors of Northeast Italy

This diverse region is the least Italian area of Italy. Bordering on Balkan and Austro-Hungarian territory, its food reflects its rich culture and landscape. Venice's traditional trading links have given a Middle-Eastern flavor to some dishes, such as sweet and sour *saor* sauce, and spices like nutmeg, saffron, and cinnamon feature widely. While pasta is eaten, many dishes are accompanied with the more typical polenta, made from yellow corn flour, and risotto is also a favorite. Butter tends to be used more than olive oil. From hearty, rib-sticking fare to the most delicate and sophisticated of dishes, this is a region full of gastronomic surprises.

Saffron

Delicate, sweet fried pastries in a Trieste bakery

The Veneto & Venice

The Veneto is now one of Italy's main rice-growing regions. Rice was introduced from Spain by the Arabs, and is the staple ingredient for many versatile local dishes. Creamy risottos come in many guises including *di mare* (with seafood), in which cuttlefish ink gives the dish a dramatic, dark appearance. The Veneto's favorite pasta is *bigoli*, a thick spaghetti.

Vegetables are plentiful, including zucchini, asparagus, bitter red radicchio (endive) from Treviso, and variegated radicchio from Castelfranco.

Venetian specialties include *cichetti* and *antipasti* – snacks and appetizers such as marinated sardines, fried artichokes (*articiochi* in the Venetian dialect), and seafood in bite-size portions, especially mussels (*peoci*). Venetian crab (*granceola*) is highly prized, and the local fish soup (*sopa de pesse*) is deliciously hearty. Finely sliced raw beef (*carpaccio*), had its origins here, created by Giuseppe Cipriani at Venice's Harry's Bar.

Delicious, traditional *tiramisù* is also said to originate from Venice, and sorbets are common too. It was the Venetians who introduced cane sugar to Europe and their sweet tooth is still evident in the rich candied fruit, sultana raisins, and pine nuts acquired from the Turks and Byzantines.

Caper berries   Marinated white anchovies   Olives wrapped in anchovies   Seafood cocktail
Selection of Venetian *antipasti*, the perfect appetizer

Regional Dishes and Specialties

Antipasto di frutti di mare (a mixed seafood appetizer) is a special favorite in Venice, where the ingredients come fresh from the Adriatic. From lovely Lake Garda, *anguilla del pescatore* (stewed eel), *lavarelli al vino bianco* (lake fish in white wine), and *carpione* (a type of lake trout) are all fishy delights. Another fish specialty of the region is *baccalà alla veneziana*, made with dried salt cod. Pork and salamis feature throughout the area but in Friuli goose is often used as an alternative to pork, with succulent cured meat offerings such as *salame d'oca* (goose salami). Game is also found on the menu, together with sauerkraut and filling goulash, while desserts often have an Austrian flavor too, such as *apfel strudel*. But the region is also proud of claiming as its own the voluptuous, classic Italian dessert *tiramisù*.

Sarde in Saor Venetian specialty of fried sardines in a sweet and sour onion marinade, with pine nuts.

Asparagus

Delivering fresh vegetables on the waterways of Venice

Friuli–Venezia Giulia

A culinary crossroads, this region marks the meeting point of Slavic, Germanic, and Latin traditions and was once the poorest of the northern Italian regions. Varieties of Hungarian goulash and

Fresh radicchio and peppers piled high in a Treviso market

Austrian strudels often appear on local menus. The area produces fine sweet ham and prosciutto (including the fabled, succulent San Daniele). Goose is a staple dish, as is Istrian lamb, grazed in the open air on local herbs and grasses that impart a delicious flavor.

Trieste is famous for its Viennese pastries and sweet *gnocchi*, prune dumplings sprinkled with sugar and cinnamon. Friuli's dairy speciality is Montasio, a hard cheese made from cow's milk.

Trentino & Alto Adige

Strong Austrian influences from the Alto Adige combine with hearty fare from the mountainous region of Trentino as well as more southern Italian flavors.

Staple dishes include cured meats such as *speck* (smoked ham) and salamis, as well as warming soups including the classic minestrone. Bread dumplings – *canederli* in Italian but *knödel* in Alto Adige – feature more than pasta. Trentino risottos include sweet and savory variations. Especially good are those made with *finferli* mushrooms, highly prized and similar to Tuscan *porcini* in flavor and quality. Alpine trout is flavorsome, and game dishes, especially venison and rabbit, are popular in season, often served with polenta. The Trentino apple is crisp and delicious.

ON THE MENU

Carpaccio *(Venice & the Veneto)* Wafer-thin slices of raw beef in extra virgin olive oil with arugula and slivers of Parmesan cheese.

Fegato alla Veneziana Calf's liver served on a bed of onions.

Jota *(Friuli–Venezia Giulia)* A soup of barley and sauerkraut. This cheap and filling dish is often mixed with *brovada* – turnips that have been steeped in a wooden cask of grape pressings.

Strangolapreti *(Trentino–Alto Adige)* Dumplings *(gnocchi)* made with bread, spinach, or potatoes, coated with butter and cheese. Literally means "priest stranglers."

Risi e bisi Soft and moist risotto mixing rice with fresh peas, sometimes with ham and Parmesan cheese.

Polenta Cornmeal porridge served plain as a side dish, often with rabbit, or *con pancetta* (with bacon).

Tiramisù A rich pudding of mascarpone, sponge fingers, coffee, and marsala. The name means "pick me up."

Understanding Architecture in Venice and the Veneto

Trade contact with the East led medieval Venice to develop its own exotic style – known as Venetian Gothic – blending Byzantine domes and Islamic minarets with European Gothic pointed arches and quatrefoils. In the 16th century, Palladio introduced his interpretations of Classical architecture through a series of churches, public buildings, and rural villas in Venice and the Veneto. The 17th century brought the Baroque style, though its exuberance was tempered by Palladio-influenced restraint.

Andrea Palladio
(1508–80)

The Architecture of Venice: Byzantine to Baroque

Onion-shaped cupolas capping the main domes

Statues added in the 15th century

Upper loggia with copies of the Four Horses of St. Mark

Central portal modeled on the Roman triumphal arch

Byzantine-style façade mosaics

The Basilica di San Marco, western Europe's finest Byzantine church (completed 11th century), was given lavish treatment to make it a dazzling shrine for the relics of St. Mark, the Evangelist, and a fitting symbol of Venetian aspirations *(see pp114–17)*.

The Genius of Palladio

Doric columns supporting the first floor, Ionic above

Shaded loggias for escaping the heat

Palazzo Chiericati is a huge mansion of 1550, its simple style borrowed from the ancient Romans. It was once surrounded by water to reflect the statues of Classical deities along its roof *(see p156)*.

Arcades linking the wings to the central block

Symmetrical façade

Villa Barbaro at Masèr was one of the villas designed by Palladio from the 1550s when it became fashionable for rich Venetians to acquire rural estates. This villa is typical, combining a working farm, housed in the side wings, with the elegant buildings of a country house *(see p153)*.

Where to See the Architecture

A vaporetto trip along the Grand Canal in Venice *(see pp92–5)* is a splendid way of getting an overview of Venetian architecture. Ca' d'Oro, Ca' Rezzonico, and Ca' Pesaro may also be visited for the museums they contain, and a visit

Typical Venetian Gothic window

to the Basilica di San Marco and the Palazzo Ducale is a must. There are numerous examples of Palladio's architecture in the Veneto, but the star is the Villa Barbaro *(see p153)*. Several of his villas line the Brenta Canal *(see p164)*, and the town of Vicenza *(see pp154–7)* is full of his buildings, including La Rotonda, his famous villa.

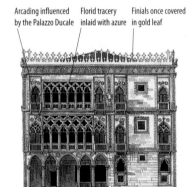

Arcading influenced by the Palazzo Ducale

Florid tracery inlaid with azure

Finials once covered in gold leaf

Ca d'Oro, the 15th-century "House of Gold," reveals Moorish influence in its roof finials and sinuous pointed arches *(see p98)*.

Deep recesses creating play of light and shade

Keystones carved as helmeted heads

Festoons of fruit, ribbons, and flowers

The 17th-century Ca' Pesaro typifies the Venetian Baroque style – Classical columns and rich, but subtle, ornamentation *(see p93)*.

Giant composite columns

Istrian marble, chosen to catch the changing light of the lagoon

Statues and memorials to patrons of the church

San Giorgio Maggiore, built in 1559–80, is marvelously sited at the entrance to the Venetian inner harbor. It broke from the prevailing Gothic style, introducing the clean simplicity and harmonious proportions of Classical architecture to Venice, and more resembles an ancient Roman temple than a Christian church *(see pp124–5)*.

Pediment with coat of arms

Sundials at each end

The Dolomites

The Dolomites are the most distinctive and beautiful mountains in Italy. They were formed of mineralized coral that was laid down beneath the sea during the Triassic era, and uplifted when the European and African continental plates dramatically collided 60 million years ago. Unlike the glacier-eroded saddles and ridges of the main body of the Alps, the pale rocks here have been carved by the corrosive effects of ice, sun, and rain, sculpting the cliffs, spires, and "organ pipes" that we see today. The eastern and western ranges of the Dolomites have slightly different characteristics; the eastern section is the more awe-inspiring, especially the Catinaccio (or Rosengarten) range, which is particularly beautiful, turning rose pink at sunset.

Onion dome, a common local feature

Strada Delle Dolomiti

One of the most spectacular routes through the Dolomites links Bolzano *(see p176)* with Cortina d'Ampezzo *(see p165)*. It follows the lay of the land, passing some of the greatest peaks, and the most majestic landscape.

Distinctive Peaks of the Dolomites

The peaks of the Dolomites include several with distinctive shapes and some of the highest mountains in the range. Many are easily identifiable and have been individually named.

Marmolada 10,968 ft (3,343 m)

Sasso Lungo 10,430 ft (3,179 m)

Cinque Torri 7,762 ft (2,366 m)

13,123 ft (4,000 m)
9,842 ft (3,000 m)
6,562 ft (2,000 m)
3,281 ft (1,000 m)

Approximate heights

The Cinque Torri or Five Towers rise from a single base between Passo Falzarego and Cortina d'Ampezzo.

Sasso Lungo is a tall peak easily recognized by its distinctive scar. It is joined to the Sasso Piatto.

Marmolada is the highest peak in the Dolomite chain. A cable car ascends to 9,842 ft (3,000 m) above the glacier.

Lago di Misurina is a large and beautiful lake lying beside the resort of Misurina. The crystal clear waters reflect the surrounding mountains, mirroring various peaks such as the distinctive and dramatic Sorapiss, in shimmering colors.

Outdoor activities in this area of dramatic landscapes include skiing in winter, and walking and rambling along the footpaths, and to picnic sites, in summer. Chairlifts from the main resorts provide easy access up into the mountains themselves, transporting you into some breathtaking scenery.

Torri del Vaiolet
7,375 ft (2,243 m)

Tre Cime di Lavaredo
9,839 ft (2,999 m)

The Torri del Vaiolet is part of the beautiful Catinaccio range, known for its color.

Tre Cime di Lavaredo or Drei Zinnen dominate the valleys north of the Lago di Misurina.

Nature in the Dolomites

Forests and meadows support a breathtaking richness of wildlife in the region. Alpine plants, which flower between June and September, have evolved their miniature form to survive the harsh winds.

The Flora

Gentian roots are used to make a bitter local liqueur.

The orange mountain lily thrives on sun-baked slopes.

The pretty burser's saxifrage grows in clusters on rocks.

Devil's claw has distinctive pink flower heads.

The Fauna

The ptarmigan changes its plumage from mottled brown in summer to snow white in winter for effective camouflage. It feeds on mountain berries and young plant shoots.

The chamois, a shy mountain antelope prized for its soft skin, is protected in the national parks, where hunting is forbidden.

Roe deer are very common, as their natural predators – wolves and lynx – are decreasing in number. An appetite for tree saplings causes problems for foresters.

VENICE

Lying in the extreme northeast of Italy, Venice, gateway to the Orient, became an independent Byzantine province in the 10th century. Exclusive trading links with the East and victory in the Crusade of 1204 brought wealth and power, which were only gradually eroded by European and Turkish rivals. Today, Venice's ties are with the local Veneto region, which stretches from the flat river plains to the Dolomites.

Venice is one of the few cities in the world that can be truly described as unique. It survives against all the odds, built on a series of low mud banks amid the tidal waters of the Adriatic, and regularly subject to floods. During the Middle Ages, under the leadership of successive doges, Venice expanded its power and influence throughout the Mediterranean to Constantinople (modern Istanbul). The immense wealth of the city was celebrated in art and architecture throughout the city. The riches of St. Mark's alone bear witness to Venice's position as a world power from the 12th to 14th centuries. After slowly losing ground to the new states of Europe, however, it fell to Napoleon in 1797. Finally, Venice joined the Kingdom of Italy in 1866, so bringing unity to the country for the first time in its history. Today, Venice has found a new role. Her palazzi have become museums, shops, hotels, and apartments, and her convents have been turned into centers for art restoration. Yet little of the essential fabric of Venice has altered in 200 years. The city's sounds are still those of footsteps and the cries of boatmen. The only engines are those of barges delivering supplies or waterbuses ferrying passengers between stops. The same well-worn streets are still trodden. More than 14 million visitors a year succumb to the magic of this improbable place whose "streets are full of water" and where the glories of the past are evident at every turn.

Tourists relax at cafés along a canal in Burano, Venice

◀ Dusk settles over the peaceful Venetian Lagoon, Adriatic Coast

Exploring Venice

Venice is divided into six ancient administrative districts or
sestieri: Cannaregio, Castello, San Marco, Dorsoduro, San Polo,
and Santa Croce. You can walk to most places in Venice itself,
and take a ride on a waterbus to any of the islands. The Venice
Card *(see p634)* covers all transportation as well as admission to
most museums, such as Ca' Rezzonico, the Palazzo Ducale,
and Museo Correr.

Sights at a Glance

Churches
① Madonna dell'Orto
③ San Giovanni Grisostomo
④ Santa Maria dei Miracoli
⑥ San Giacomo dell'Orio
⑦ San Polo
⑧ *Santa Maria Gloriosa dei Frari pp102–3*
⑩ San Rocco
⑪ San Pantalon
⑬ San Nicolò dei Mendicoli
⑭ San Sebastiano
⑰ Santa Maria della Salute
⑲ *Basilica di San Marco pp114–15*
㉔ Santo Stefano
㉕ Santi Giovanni e Paolo
㉗ Santa Maria Formosa
㉘ San Zaccaria
㉚ San Giovanni in Bragora

Buildings and Monuments
⑤ Rialto
⑳ *Palazzo Ducale pp118–19*
㉑ Torre dell'Orologio
㉒ Campanile

㉖ Statue of Colleoni
㉙ Scuola di San Giorgio degli Schiavoni
㉛ Arsenale

Museums and Galleries
② Ca' d'Oro
⑨ *Scuola Grande di San Rocco pp104–5*
⑫ *Ca' Rezzonico*
⑮ *Accademia pp110–11*
⑯ *Peggy Guggenheim Collection*
⑱ *Punta della Dogana*
㉓ Museo Correr

Lagoon
㉝ Murano
㉞ Burano
㉟ *Torcello pp126–7*

0 meters — 500
0 yards — 500

Santa Maria della Salute, at the mouth of the Grand Canal

For keys to symbols *see back flap*

A gondola ride along the Grand Canal

The Lagoon

Getting Around

The only road into Venice is the S11 from Mestre, which carries you over the causeway to the Tronchetto and Piazzale Roma where there are parking lots and bus stops. Train travelers arrive at Santa Lucia station on the Grand Canal. In the city, public transportation is by *vaporetto*, or waterbus – the No.1 is best for sightseeing as it travels the length of the Grand Canal *(see pp140–1).*

The Grand Canal: Santa Lucia to the Rialto

The best way to view the Grand Canal as it winds through the heart of the city is from a *vaporetto*, or waterbus. Several lines travel the length of the canal *(see p635)*. The palaces lining the waterway were built over a span of five centuries and present a panoramic survey of the city's history, almost all bearing the name of some once-great Venetian family.

San Geremia houses the relics of St. Lucy, once kept in the church of Santa Lucia where the train station now stands.

San Marcuola
The church was rebuilt in the 18th century, but the planned new façade overlooking the canal was never completed.

Palazzo Labia
Between 1745–50, Giambattista Tiepolo decorated the ballroom with scenes from the life of Cleopatra.

Canale di Cannaregio

Palazzo Corner-Contarini

San Marcuola

Riva di Biasio

Ferrovia

FS

Ponte degli Scalzi

Fondaco dei Turchi
A warehouse for Turkish traders in the 17th–19th centuries, this is now the Natural History Museum.

The Gondolas of Venice

The gondola has been a part of Venice since the 11th century. With its slim hull and flat underside, the craft is perfectly adapted to negotiating narrow, shallow canals. There is a slight leftward curve to the prow, which counteracts the force of the oar, preventing the gondola from going around in circles.

In 1562 it was decreed that all gondolas should be black to stop people making an ostentatious show of their wealth. For special occasions they are decorated with flowers. Today, gondola rides are expensive and usually taken by tourists *(see p635)*. However, *traghetti* (gondola ferries) are a cheap, convenient way of crossing the Grand Canal.

Gondolas tied up by steps

San Simeone Piccolo
This 18th-century domed church is based on the Pantheon in Rome.

Ca' d'Oro
The delicate Gothic tracery of the façade makes this a striking landmark. Its art collection *(see p98)* includes Bernini's model for a fountain (c.1648).

Locator Map

See Venice Street Finder maps 1, 2, 3

Palazzo Vendramin Calergi
This is one of the finest early Renaissance palaces in Venice. The German composer Richard Wagner *(left)* died here in 1883.

The Pescheria has been the site of a busy fish market for six centuries.

Palazzo Sagredo
Graceful Veneto-Byzantine and Gothic arches are both featured on the waterfront façade.

Palazzo Michiel dalle Colonne takes its name from its distinctive colonnade.

The Rialto Bridge *(see p101)* spans the canal in the commercial heart of the city.

San Stae

Ca' d'Oro

Rialto Mercato

San Stae
The façade of this Baroque church is richly adorned with statues. It is a popular concert venue.

Ca' Pesaro
The huge, stately Baroque palace today houses a gallery of modern art and the Oriental Museum.

Rialto

The Grand Canal: the Rialto to San Marco

After passing the Rialto, the canal doubles back on itself along a stretch known as La Volta (the bend). It then widens out and the views become more spectacular approaching San Marco. Façades may have faded and foundations frayed with the tides, yet the canal remains, in the words of the French ambassador in 1495, "the most beautiful street in the world."

Palazzo Mocenigo
Lord Byron stayed in this huge 18th-century palace in 1818.

Sant' Angelo

San Tomà

Palazzo Garzoni is a renovated Gothic palace, now part of the university.

Ca' Rezzonico
Now a museum of 18th-century Venice (see p107), the palace was the last home of the poet Robert Browning, seen here with his son Pen.

San Samuele

Ca' Rezzonico

Palazzo Grassi
This elegant palazzo dates from the 1730s. Bought by French tycoon François-Henri Pinault in 2005, it is now used for art exhibitions.

Ponte dell'Accademia

Palazzo Capello Malipiero
The palace was rebuilt in 1622. Beside it stands the 12th-century campanile of San Samuele.

Accademia

Accademia
The world's greatest collection of Venetian paintings is housed here in the former Scuola della Carità (see pp110–11), which has a Baroque façade by Giorgio Massari.

Palazzo Barbaro
Novelist Henry James wrote The Aspern Papers here in 1888.

The Riva del Vin is the quay where wine *(vin)* used to be unloaded. It is one of the few spots where you can sit and relax on the banks of the Grand Canal.

Locator Map

 See Venice Street Finder maps 6, 7

Palazzo Barzizza, rebuilt in the 17th century, preserves its early 13th-century façade.

Peggy Guggenheim Collection
A one-story palazzo houses Guggenheim's great modern art collection *(see pp108–9)*.

Santa Maria della Salute
The vast weight of this Baroque church is supported by over one million timber piles *(see p109)*.

Palazzo Gritti-Pisani
The former home of the Gritti family is now the luxury Gritti Palace Hotel *(see p560)*.

San Marco
Vallaresso

Santa Maria del Giglio

Salute

Harry's Bar, founded in 1931 by Giuseppe Cipriani, is famous for its cocktails.

Palazzo Dario
Beautiful colored marbles give the 1487 palace a highly individual façade. Legend has it the building is cursed.

The Punta della Dogana customs house, built in the 17th century, now contains the François Pinault Foundation of contemporary art. It is crowned by a golden globe topped by a weathervane *(see p109)*.

Gondolas moored along the Grand Canal at sunrise ▶

Madonna dell'Orto, with 15th-century façade statues of St. Christopher and the Apostles

❶ Madonna dell'Orto

Campo Madonna dell'Orto. **Map** 2 F2. **Tel** 041 275 04 62. 🚇 Madonna dell'Orto. **Open** 10am–5pm Mon–Sat, noon–6pm Sun. **Closed** Jan 1, Dec 25. 🅿 ♿ 🌐 **madonnadellorto.org**

This lovely Gothic church, founded in the mid-14th century, was dedicated to St. Christopher, patron saint of travelers, to protect the boatmen who ferried passengers to the islands in the northern lagoon. A 15th-century statue of the saint, restored by the Venice in Peril fund, stands above the main portal. The dedication was changed and the church reconstructed in the early 15th century, after the discovery, in a nearby vegetable garden (*orto*), of a statue of the Virgin Mary said to have miraculous powers.

The interior, faced almost entirely in brick, is large and uncluttered. On the right is a magnificent painting by Cima da Conegliano, *St. John the Baptist and Other Saints* (c.1493). The vacant space in the chapel opposite belongs to Giovanni Bellini's *Madonna with Child* (c.1478), stolen in 1993 for the third time.

The church's greatest remaining treasures are the works of art by Tintoretto, who was a parishioner of the church. His tomb lies with that of his children, in the chapel to the right of the chancel. The most dramatic of his works are the towering masterpieces that decorate the chancel (1562–4). On the right wall is the *Last Judgment*, whose turbulent content caused John Ruskin's wife, Effie, to flee the church in horror. In *The Adoration of the Golden Calf* on the left wall, the figure carrying the calf, fourth from the left, is believed to be a portrait of the artist. Inside the chapel of San Mauro, off the end of the right nave, stands a statue of the Madonna by Giovanni de' Santi. It was restored by the Venice in Peril fund, and inspired the rededication of the church.

❷ Ca' d'Oro

Calle Ca' d'Oro. **Map** 3 A4. **Tel** 041 520 03 45. 🚇 Ca' d'Oro. **Open** 8:15am–7:15pm daily (last adm: 6:45pm), to 2pm Mon **Closed** Jan 1, May 1, Dec 25; Galleria: Sun & public hols (Jan). 🅿 🏛 ♿ ♿ 🌐 **cadoro.org**

In 1420 Marino Contarini, a wealthy patrician, commissioned the building of what he hoped would be the city's most magnificent palace (*see p85*). The building's intricate carving was entrusted to a team of Venetian and Lombard craftsmen, while the façade was adorned with the most elaborate and expensive decorative finishes, including

Tullio Lombardo's Double Portrait

gold leaf, vermilion, and ultramarine. Over the years the palace was extensively remodeled, and by the 18th century was in a state of semi-dereliction. In 1846 it was bought by the Russian Prince Troubetzkoy for the famous ballerina Maria Taglioni. Under her direction the palace suffered barbaric restoration, losing, among other things, its staircase and much of its original stonework. It was finally rescued by Baron Giorgio Franchetti, a wealthy patron of the arts, who bequeathed both the building and his private art collection to the state in 1915.

Pride of place on the first of the gallery's two floors goes to Andrea Mantegna's *St. Sebastian* (1506), the artist's last work, which occupies a special alcove of its own. Elsewhere, the floor's main exhibits are ranged around the *portego* (gallery). This is largely dominated by the vivid 15th-century *Double Portrait* (c.1493) by the sculptor Tullio Lombardo; Sansovino's lunette of the *Madonna and Child* (c.1530); and several bronze reliefs by the Paduan Andrea Briosco, "Il Riccio" (1470–1532). Rooms leading off the *portego* to the right contain numerous bronzes and medallions, with some examples by Pisanello and Gentile Bellini.

Paintings here also include the famous *Madonna of the Beautiful Eyes*, attributed to Giovanni Bellini, a *Madonna and Child*, attributed to Alvise Vivarini (both late 15th century), and Carpaccio's *Annunciation* and *Death of the Virgin* (both c.1504). A room to the left of the *portego* contains non-Venetian paintings, notably a *Flagellation* by Luca Signorelli (c.1480). A lovely staircase leads to the second floor, which opens with a room hung with tapestries.

The magnificent Gothic façade of the Ca' d'Oro, or House of Gold

It has bronzes by Alessandro Vittoria and paintings by Titian and Van Dyck. The *portego* displays frescoes (c.1532) by Pordenone from the cloister of Santo Stefano, while an anteroom contains damaged frescoes by Titian taken from the Fondaco dei Tedeschi.

Giovanni Bellini's 1513 altarpiece in San Giovanni Grisostomo

❸ San Giovanni Grisostomo

Campo San Giovanni Grisostomo. **Map** 3 B5. **Tel** 041 523 52 93. 🚤 Rialto. **Open** 8:15am–12:15pm, 3–7pm daily. **Closed** during mass. 📷
Ⓦ sancancianovenezia.it

This terracotta-colored church is located near the Rialto. Built between 1479 and 1504, it is a lovely Renaissance design, the last work of Mauro Coducci.

The interior is built on a Greek-cross plan. The light meter illuminates Giovanni Bellini's *St. Jerome with Saints Christopher and Augustine* (1513) above the first altar on the right. This was most probably Bellini's last painting, executed when he was in his eighties.

Over the high altar hangs Sebastiano del Piombo's *St. John Chrysostom and Six Saints* (1509–11).

❹ Santa Maria dei Miracoli

Campo dei Miracoli. **Map** 3 B5. **Tel** 041 275 04 62. 🚤 Rialto, Fondamenta Nuove. **Open** 9am–5pm Mon–Sat. **Closed** Jan 1, Dec 25. 📷 📷
Ⓦ chorusvenezia.org

An exquisite masterpiece of early Renaissance architecture, the Miracoli is the church where many Venetians like to get married. Tucked away in a maze of alleys and waterways in eastern Cannaregio, it is small and somewhat elusive.

Santa Maria dei Miracoli is decorated in various shades of marble, with some fine bas-reliefs and sculpture. It was built in 1481–9 by the architect Pietro Lombardo and his sons to enshrine *The Virgin and Child* (1408), a painting believed to have miraculous powers. The picture, by Nicoló di Pietro, can still be seen above the altar.

The interior of the church is embellished by pink, white, and gray marble. It is crowned by a barrel-vaulted ceiling (1528) that has 50 portraits of saints

Decorative column from inside Santa Maria dei Miracoli

and prophets. The balustrade, between the nave and the chancel, is decorated by Tullio Lombardo's carved figures of St. Francis, Archangel Gabriel, the Virgin, and St. Clare.

The screen around the high altar and the medallions of the Evangelists in the cupola spandrels are also Lombardo's work. Above the main door, the choir gallery was used by the nuns from the neighboring convent, who entered the church through an overhead gallery. Santa Maria dei Miracoli has undergone a major restoration program, which was funded by the American Save Venice organization.

Santa Maria Dei Miracoli

This beautifully proportioned façade is composed of decorated panels and multicolored polished marble.

Carving of saint

The semicircular crowning lunette emphasizes the church's jewel-box appearance.

A false loggia is formed of Ionic arches, inset with windows. The marble used was reportedly left over from the building of San Marco.

Virgin and Child by Giorgio Lascaris

The marble panels are fixed to the bricks by metal hooks. This method prevents the build-up of damp and saltwater behind the panels, and dates from the Renaissance.

Street by Street: San Polo

The Rialto bridge and markets make this area a magnet for visitors. Traditionally the city's commercial quarter, it was here that bankers, brokers, and merchants conducted their affairs. Streets are no longer lined with stalls selling spices and fine fabrics, but the food markets and pasta shops are unmissable. Away from the bridge, streets quickly become less crowded, leading to tiny squares and quiet churches.

The Rialto Markets have existed for centuries and are renowned for their produce. The Pescheria sells fresh fish and seafood.

The 17th-century church of San Cassiano houses a carved altar (1696) and a *Crucifixion* by Tintoretto (1568).

Key

— Suggested route

| 0 meters | 75 |
| 0 yards | 75 |

The Frari

Sant'Aponal has a façade decorated with worn Gothic reliefs. The church was founded in the 11th century, but is now deconsecrated.

San Silvestro

San Giovanni Elemosinario is an inconspicuous church that was rebuilt in the early 16th century, although its campanile dates from the end of the 14th century. Inside it are interesting frescoes by Pordenone.

Locator Map
*See Venice Street Finder
maps 2, 3, 6, 7*

The lively Erberia, selling fresh fruit and vegetables

San Giacomo di Rialto's clock face (1410), which has sadly been a poor timekeeper over the years, adorns one of Venice's oldest churches.

RUGA DEGLI OREFICI

Market entrance

⑤ ★ Rialto
One of Venice's most famous sights, the bridge offers fine views of the Grand Canal, and marks the heart of the city.

⑤ Rialto

Ponte di Rialto. **Map** 7 A1. 🚤 Rialto.

The Rialto takes its name from *rivo alto* (high bank) and was one of the first areas of Venice to be inhabited. A banking and then market district, it remains one of the city's busiest and most bustling areas. Locals and visitors alike jostle among the colorful stalls of the Erberia (fruit and vegetable market) and Pescheria (fish market).

Stone bridges were built in Venice as early as the 12th century, but it was not until 1588, after the collapse, decay, or sabotage of earlier wooden structures, that a solid stone bridge was designed for the Rialto. Completed in 1591, the new bridge remained the only means of crossing the Grand Canal until 1854, when the Accademia bridge was built.

Few visitors leave Venice without crossing the famous bridge. It is a wonderful place to watch and photograph the constant activity of boats on the Grand Canal below.

⑥ San Giacomo dell'Orio

Campo San Giacomo dell'Orio. **Map** 2 E5. **Tel** 041 275 04 62. 🚤 Riva di Biasio or San Stae. **Open** 10am–5pm Mon–Sat. **Closed** Jan 1, Dec 25. 🎫 ✉ 🌐 **chorusvenezia.org**

This church is a focal point of a quiet quarter of Santa Croce. The name "dell'Orio" may derive from a laurel tree *(alloro)* that once stood near the church. San Giacomo was founded in the 9th century, rebuilt in 1225, and thereafter repeatedly modified, resulting in a mixture of styles. The campanile and basilica ground plan survive from the 13th century. The ship's keel roof and the columns are Gothic, and the apses are Renaissance.

The sacristy contains a beautiful ceiling by Veronese in addition to some interesting altar paintings.

⑦ San Polo

Campo San Polo. **Map** 6 F1. **Tel** 041 275 04 62. 🚤 San Silvestro. **Open** 10am–5pm Mon–Sat. **Closed** Jan 1, Dec 25. 🎫 🏛 ✉ 🌐 **chorusvenezia.org**

Founded in the 9th century, rebuilt in the 15th, and revamped in the early 19th in Neo-Classical style, this church is worth visiting for the lovely Gothic portal and the Romanesque lions at the foot of the 14th-century campanile – one holds a serpent between its paws, the other a human head.

Inside, follow the signs for the *Via Crucis del Tiepolo* – 14 pictures of the Stations of the Cross (1749) by the painter Giandomenico Tiepolo: many include vivid portraits of Venetian life. The church also has paintings by Veronese, Palma il Giovane (the Younger) and a dramatic *Last Supper* by Tintoretto.

A Romanesque lion at the base of San Polo's 14th-century campanile

❽ Santa Maria Gloriosa dei Frari

More commonly known as the Frari (a corruption of Frati, meaning brothers), this vast Gothic church dwarfs the eastern area of San Polo. The first church on the site was built by Franciscan friars in 1250–1338, but was replaced by a larger building completed in the mid-15th century. The airy interior is striking for its sheer size and for the quality of its works of art, including masterpieces by Titian and Giovanni Bellini, a statue by Donatello, and several grandiose tombs.

★ **Monks' Choir**
This consists of three-tiered stalls (1468), carved with bas-reliefs of saints and Venetian city scenes.

★ **Assumption of the Virgin**
Titian's glowing and spectacular work (1518) draws the eye through the monk's choir, to the altar, and heavenward.

Rood Screen (1475)
Pietro Lombardo and Bartolomeo Bon carved the rood screen and its decorative marble figures.

KEY

① **The campanile** is 262 ft (83 m) high, the tallest in the city after that of San Marco.

② **The former monastery**, which houses the State Archives, has two cloisters, one in the style of Sansovino, another designed by Palladio.

③ *The Madonna di Ca' Pesaro* (1526) shows Titian's mastery of light and color.

Floorplan

The Frari's imposing cruciform interior, which is 295 ft (90 m) long, holds 12 sights that should not be missed.

VISITORS' CHECKLIST

Practical Information
Campo dei Frari. **Map** 6 D1.
Tel 041 275 04 62. **Open** 9am–6pm Mon–Sat, 1–6pm Sun & religious hols. **Closed** Jan 1, Dec 25. 🈲 unless attending mass. 🕐 frequent. 📧
🌐 basilicadeifrari.it

Transportation
🚤 San Tomà.

Key to Floorplan

1. Tomb of Canova
2. Monument to Titian
3. *Madonna di Ca' Pesaro* by Titian
4. Choir stalls
5. Corner Chapel
6. Tomb of Monteverdi
7. Tomb of Doge Nicolò Tron
8. High altar with *Assumption of the Virgin* (1518) by Titian
9. Tomb of Doge Francesco Foscari
10. *John the Baptist* (c.1450) by Donatello
11. B. Vivarini's altar painting (1474), Bernardo Chapel
12. *Madonna and Child with Saints* (1488) by Bellini

★ Madonna and Child
The sacristy's altarpiece (1488) by Bellini, with its sublime use of color, is one of Venice's most beautiful Renaissance paintings.

Entrance

Tomb of Canova
Canova designed, but never constructed, a Neo-Classical marble pyramid like this as a monument for Titian. After Canova's death in 1822, the sculptor's pupils used a similar design for their master's tomb.

❾ Scuola Grande di San Rocco

Restored main entrance to the Scuola di San Rocco

Founded in honor of San Rocco (St. Roch), a saint who dedicated his life to helping the sick, the Scuola started out as a charitable confraternity. Construction began in 1515 under Bartolomeo Bon and was continued by Scarpagnino until his death in 1549. The work was financed by donations from Venetians keen to invoke San Rocco's protection and the Scuola quickly became one of the wealthiest in Venice. In 1564 its members decided to commission Tintoretto to decorate its walls and ceilings. His earliest paintings, the first of over 50 works he eventually left in the Scuola, fill the small Sala dell'Albergo off the Upper Hall. His later paintings occupy the Ground Floor Hall, immediately within the entrance.

Tintoretto's magnificent *Crucifixion*, painted in 1565 for the Sala dell'Albergo in the Scuola di San Rocco

Ground Floor Hall

The ground floor cycle was executed in 1583–7, when Tintoretto was in his sixties, and consists of eight large paintings illustrating, among others, the life of Mary. The series starts with an *Annunciation* and ends with an *Assumption*.

The calm and tranquil scenes of *The Flight into Egypt*, *St. Mary Magdalene*, and *St. Mary of Egypt* are remarkable for their serenity. This is portrayed most lucidly by the repentant

Detail from *The Flight into Egypt* (1582–7) by Tintoretto

hermit's isolated spiritual contemplation in *St. Mary of Egypt*. In all three paintings, it is noticeable that the landscapes are rendered with rapid strokes, and are an important part of the final composition.

Upper Hall and Sala dell'Albergo

Scarpagnino's great staircase (1544–6), with its upper flight decorated with two vast paintings commemorating the plague of 1630, leads to the Upper Hall. Here, biblical subjects decorate the ceiling and walls, painted by Tintoretto from 1575–81.

The ceiling paintings portray scenes from the Old Testament. The three large and dynamic square paintings in the center show episodes from the Book of Exodus: *Moses Strikes Water from the Rock*, *The Miracle of the Bronze Serpent*, and *The Fall of Manna in the Desert*. These all allude to the charitable aims of the Scuola

in alleviating thirst, sickness, and hunger respectively. All three paintings are crowded compositions displaying much violent movement.

The vast wall paintings in the hall feature episodes from the New Testament, linking with the ceiling paintings. Two of the most striking paintings are *The Temptation of Christ*, which shows a handsome young Satan offering Christ two loaves of bread, and *The Adoration of the Shepherds*. Like *The Temptation of Christ*, *The Adoration* is composed of two halves, with a female figure, shepherds, and an ox below, and the Holy Family and onlookers above.

The breathtakingly beautiful carvings below the paintings were added in the 17th century by sculptor Francesco Pianta. The figures are allegorical and include (near the altar) a caricature of Tintoretto with his palette and brushes, representing Painting.

For hotels and restaurants in this region see pp562–77 and pp580–605

Detail from *The Temptation of Christ* (1578–81) by Tintoretto

The easel painting *Christ Carrying the Cross* was once attributed to Giorgione, though many believe it to be by Titian.

Near the entrance to the Sala dell'Albergo is the *Annunciation* by Titian. The Sala dell'Albergo itself holds the most breathtaking of Tintoretto's works – the *Crucifixion* (1565). Henry James

remarked of this painting: "No single picture contains more of human life; there is everything in it, including the most exquisite beauty." Tintoretto began the cycle of paintings in this room in 1564, when he won the commission with the ceiling painting *San Rocco in Glory*. On the wall opposite the *Crucifixion* are paintings of episodes from the Passion: *Christ before Pilate*, *The Crowning with Thorns*, and *The Ascent to Calvary*.

🔟 San Rocco

Campo San Rocco. **Map** 6 D1. **Tel** 041
523 48 64. 🚤 San Tomà.
Open 9:30am–5:30pm daily. 🎫

On the same square as the celebrated Scuola Grande di San Rocco is the church of the same name. Designed by the sculptor and architect Bartolomeo Bon in 1489 and largely rebuilt in 1725, the exterior suffers from a mixture of styles. The façade was added in 1765–71. Inside, the chancel is decorated with a series of paintings by Tintoretto depicting scenes from the life of San Rocco.

⓫ San Pantalon

Campo San Pantalon. **Map** 6 D2.
Tel 041 523 58 93. 🚤 San Tomà,
Piazzale Roma. **Open** 10am–noon,
1–3pm Mon–Sat. 🎫
🌐 sanpantalon.it

Fumiani's epic ceiling painting (1680–1740) in San Pantalon

The overwhelming feature of this late 17th-century church is its vast painted ceiling, dark, awe-inspiring, and remarkable for its illusionistic effect of height. The ceiling comprises a total of 40 scenes, and admirers claim that this is the world's largest work of art on canvas.

The scenes show the martyrdom and apotheosis of the physician St. Pantalòn. The artist, Gian Antonio Fumiani, took 24 years (1680–1704) to achieve the masterpiece, before allegedly falling to his death from the scaffolding.

Key to Paintings

🟦 Ground Floor Hall **1** The Annunciation; **2** The Adoration of the Three Kings; **3** The Flight into Egypt; **4** The Massacre of the Innocents; **5** St. Mary Magdalene; **6** St. Mary of Egypt; **7** The Presentation in the Temple; **8** The Assumption.

🟦 Upper Hall Walls **9** San Rocco; **10** St. Sebastian; **11** The Adoration of the Shepherds; **12** The Baptism of Christ; **13** The Resurrection; **14** The Agony in the Garden; **15** The Last Supper; **16** The Vision of San Rocco; **17** The Miracle of the Loaves and Fishes; **18** The Resurrection of Lazarus; **19** The Ascension; **20** Christ Heals the Paralytic; **21** The Temptation of Christ.

🟦 Upper Hall Ceiling **22** Moses Saved from the Waters; **23** The Pillar of Fire; **24** Samuel and Saul; **25** Jacob's Ladder; **26** Elijah on a Chariot of Fire; **27** Elijah Fed by the Angels; **28** Daniel Saved by the Angels; **29** The Passover; **30** The Fall of Manna; **31** The Sacrifice of Isaac; **32** The Miracle of the Bronze Serpent; **33** Jonah Emerges from the Whale; **34** Moses Strikes Water from the Rock; **35** Adam and Eve; **36** Three Children in the Furnace; **37** God Appears to Moses; **38** Samson Brings out Water from the Jawbone of an Ass; **39** The Vision of the Prophet Ezekiel; **40** The Vision of Jeremiah; **41** Elisha Distributes Bread; **42** Abraham and Melchizedek.

Ground Floor Hall

Upper Hall

Street by Street: Dorsoduro

Built up on a strata of solid subsoil is the *sestiere* of Dorsoduro – the name means "hard backbone." It has as its focal point the lively Campo Santa Margherita, the largest open space in this part of Venice. The square bustles with activity, particularly in the morning when the market stalls are open, and in the evening when it is the haunt of students from nearby Ca' Foscari, now part of Venice university. The surrounding streets contain some architectural stunners, notably Ca' Rezzonico and the Scuola Grande dei Carmini, which has decorations by Tiepolo. Of the area's waterways, the delightful Rio San Barnaba is best appreciated from the Ponte dei Pugni, near the barge selling fruit and vegetables – itself a time-honored Venetian sight. Alongside the Rio Terrà Canal there are some lively cafés and a fascinating shop selling masks for Carnevale.

Campo Santa Margherita is an ideal place for relaxing in a café.

Palazzo Zenobio, built at the end of the 17th century, has been an Armenian college since 1850. With permission, visitors can see the fine 18th-century ballroom.

Scuola Grande dei Carmini contains nine ceiling panels (1739–44) in the hall on the upper floor, painted by Tiepolo for the Carmelite confraternity.

Santa Maria dei Carmini has a Gothic side porch carved with Byzantine reliefs.

Key

— Suggested route

0 meters	50
0 yards	50

Fondamenta Gherardini runs beside the Rio San Barnaba, one of the prettiest canals in the *sestiere*.

Locator Map
See Venice Street Finder maps 5, 6

Tiepolo's *New World* fresco, part of a series in Ca' Rezzonico

★ Ca' Rezzonico
The ballroom covers the width of the palazzo once owned by Browning.

Palazzo Giustinian
was home to Wagner in 1858.

Ca' Foscari was completed in 1437 for Doge Francesco Foscari.

RIO DI CA FOSCARI

C D ASEO

C SAONERI

C FOSCARI

AGAZEN

C DELLA VIDA

C D BOTTEGHE

CALLE BERNARDO

CANAL GRANDE

CAMPO SAN BARNABA

CALLE DEL TRAGHETTO

Ponte dei Pugni was a traditional scene of fistfights between rival factions. They were finally banned in 1705 for being too violent.

San Barnaba is a thriving community, with its own floating barge stall crammed with fresh fruit and vegetables. It is a focal point for tourists and locals alike.

⑫ Ca' Rezzonico

Fondamenta Rezzonico 3136. **Map** 6 E3.
Tel 041 241 01 00. 🚤 Ca' Rezzonico.
Open 10am–6pm Wed–Mon (Nov–Mar: to 5pm, last adm: 1 hr before closing). **Closed** Jan 1, May 1, Dec 25.
🖼 📷 ♿ 🛗 ♿ 📹 🖥
w museicivicivenezziani.it

This palazzo houses the museum of 18th-century Venice, its rooms furnished with frescoes, paintings, and period pieces taken from other palaces or museums. Building began with Longhena (architect of La Salute, *see p109*) in 1667, but the funds of the Bon family, who commissioned it, ran dry before the second floor was started. In 1712 the unfinished palace was bought by the Rezzonico family of Genoa, who spent a large portion of their fortune on its completion.

The Rezzonico family sold it on, in 1888, to the famous poet Robert Browning and his son, Pen. The outstanding attraction in the palace today is Giorgio Massari's ballroom, which occupies the entire breadth of the building. It is adorned with gilded chandeliers, carved furniture by Andrea Brustolon, and a ceiling with *trompe l'oeil* frescoes. Other rooms have frescoes by Giambattista Tiepolo, including his lively *Nuptial Allegory* (1758), and one by his son, Giandomenico, originally in his villa at Zianigo. There are paintings by Longhi, Guardi, and – rare in Venice – Canaletto. On the top floor is a reconstructed 18th-century apothecary's shop and the Pinacoteca Martini.

Nave of San Nicolò dei Mendicoli, one of the oldest churches in Venice

⑬ San Nicolò dei Mendicoli

Campo San Nicolò. **Map** 5 A3. **Tel** 041 275 03 82. 🚊 San Basilio. **Open** 10am–noon, 3–5:30pm Mon–Sat, 10am–noon Sun & public hols.

Contrasting with the remote and run-down area that surrounds it, this church still remains one of the most charming in Venice. Founded in the 7th century, it has been rebuilt extensively over the years. The little porch on the north flank is 15th century and once sheltered the beggars, or *mendicanti*, who gave the church its name.

Thanks to the Venice in Peril fund, in the 1970s the church underwent one of the most comprehensive restoration programs since the floods of 1966. Flooding had become such a problem that the priest often ferried himself around the church in a small wicker boat. The floor, which was 1 ft (30 cm)

below the level of the canals, was rebuilt and raised slightly to prevent further flood damage. The roofs and lower walls were reconstructed, and paintings and statues restored.

The interior is delightfully embellished, particularly the nave with its 16th-century gilded wooden statues. These include the figure of San Nicolò himself. On the upper walls is a series of paintings of the life of Christ (c.1553) by Alvise dal Friso and other pupils of Veronese.

Outside, a small column supports a stone lion, in a humbler echo of the Column of San Marco in the Piazzetta.

⑭ San Sebastiano

Campo San Sebastiano. **Map** 5 C3. **Tel** 041 275 04 62. 🚊 San Basilio. **Open** 10am–5pm Mon–Sat. **Closed** Jan 1, Dec 25. 🅿 ✉
W **chorusvenezia.org**

This church has one of the most homogeneous interiors in the whole of Venice. The splendor was created by Veronese, who, from 1555 to 1560 and again in the 1570s, was commissioned to decorate the sacristy ceiling, the nave ceiling, the frieze, the east end of the choir, the high altar, the doors of the organ panels, and the chancel.

The paintings feature radiant colors and rich costumes. Those on the sacristy ceiling depict the *Coronation of the Virgin* and the *Four Evangelists*.

Of the other paintings, the finest are the three that tell the story of Esther, Queen of Xerxes I of Persia, famous for securing the deliverance of the Jewish people.

Veronese is buried here. His tomb is in front of the paved chapel to the left of the chancel.

⑮ Accademia

See pp110–11.

⑯ Peggy Guggenheim Collection

Palazzo Venier dei Leoni. **Map** 6 F4. **Tel** 041 240 54 11. 🚊 Accademia. **Open** 10am–6pm Wed–Mon. **Closed** Jan 9, Feb 20, Dec 25. 🅿 🔊 📷 📁 🖥 ✉ 🚻 W **guggenheim-venice.it**

Intended as a four-story palace, the 18th-century Palazzo Venier dei Leoni in fact never rose beyond the ground floor. In 1949 the building was bought as a home by the American

The truncated palazzo housing the Peggy Guggenheim Collection

millionaire Peggy Guggenheim (1898–1979), a collector, dealer, and patron of the arts who befriended, and then furthered the careers of, many innovative abstract and Surrealist artists. One was Max Ernst, who became her second husband. The collection consists of 200 fine paintings and sculptures, each representing the 20th century's most influential modern art movements. The dining room has notable Cubist works of art, including *The Poet* by Pablo Picasso, and an entire room is devoted to Jackson Pollock, who was "discovered" by Guggenheim.

Other artists represented are Braque, Chagall, de Chirico, Dalí, Duchamp, Léger, Kandinsky, Klee, Mondrian, Miró, Malevich, Rothko, Bacon, and Magritte, whose Surreal *Empire of Light* (1953–4) shows a night scene of a darkened house in a wooded setting with a bright day sky above. The sculpture collection, which includes Constantin Brancusi's elegant *Maiastra* (1912), is laid out in the house and garden. Perhaps the most provocative piece is Marino Marini's *Angelo della Città* (Angel of the Citadel, 1948), located on the terrace overlooking the Grand Canal. This shows a prominently displayed man sitting on a horse, erect in all respects.

Maiastra by Constantin Brancusi

The Guggenheim is the best place in the city to see 20th-century art. Light-filled rooms and the large modern canvases provide a striking contrast to the Renaissance paintings in most Venetian churches and museums.

The garden has been paved and features an array of sculptures. Peggy Guggenheim's ashes are also preserved here. A shop and restaurant are located within the grounds. Check the website for information on temporary exhibits.

The large Baroque church of Santa Maria della Salute

⑰ Santa Maria della Salute

Campo della Salute. **Map** 7 A4. **Tel** 041 274 39 11. 🚤 Salute. **Open** 9am–noon, 3–5:30pm daily. **Closed** the sacristy may be closed in the morning during religious holidays. 🔊 to sacristy. 📷

This great Baroque church standing at the entrance of the Grand Canal is one of the most imposing architectural landmarks of Venice. Henry James likened it to "some great lady on the threshold of her salon."

Santa Maria della Salute was built in thanksgiving for the city's deliverance from the plague epidemic of 1630, hence the name *Salute*, which means health and salvation.

Each November, in celebration, worshippers light candles and approach across a bridge of boats spanning the mouth of the Grand Canal for the occasion. Baldassare Longhena started the church in 1630 at the age of 32, and worked on it for the rest of his life. It was completed in

1687, five years after his death. The interior consists of a large octagonal space below the cupola and six chapels radiating from the ambulatory. The large domed chancel and grandiose high altar dominate the view from the main door.

The altar's sculptural group by Giusto Le Corte represents the Virgin and Child giving protection to Venice from the plague. The best of the paintings are in the sacristy to the left of the altar: Titian's early altarpiece of *St. Mark Enthroned with Saints Cosmas, Damian, Roch, and Sebastian* (1511–12) and his dramatic ceiling paintings of *Cain and Abel*, *The Sacrifice of Abraham and Isaac*, and *David and Goliath* (1540–9). *The Wedding at Cana* (1551) on the wall opposite the entrance is by Jacopo Tintoretto.

⑱ Punta della Dogana

Campo della Salute. **Map** 7 A4. **Tel** 199 139 139; 041 271 90 39 from outside Italy. 🚤 Salute. **Open** 10am–7pm Wed–Mon (ticket counter closes at 6pm). **Closed** Jan 1, Dec 25. 🔊 📷 **W** palazzograssi.it

The magnificent 17th-century Punta della Dogana (formerly a customs house) was restored by Japanese architect Tadao Ando and opened in 2009 as a contemporary art gallery. Together with the Palazzo Grassi, it houses the French billionaire François Pinault's large collection of contemporary art. Many well-known artists are represented here, including Jeff Koons and Takeshi Murakami.

Punta della Dogana, a contemporary art museum

⑮ Accademia

The art collection in the Accademia offers a complete spectrum of the Venetian school, from the Byzantine era through the Renaissance to the Baroque and later. The basis of the collection was the Accademia di Belle Arti founded in 1750 by the painter Giovanni Battista Piazzetta. In 1807 Napoleon moved the collection to these premises, enriching it with artworks removed from churches and monasteries. The Accademia is currently undergoing extensive restoration, which may result in changes to the floor plan.

The Tempest
In this enigmatic landscape (c.1507), Giorgione was probably creating a fantasy rather than portraying any specific subject.

Key to Floor Plan

- ☐ Byzantine and International Gothic
- ☐ Renaissance
- ☐ Baroque, Genre, and Landscape
- ☐ Ceremonial Painting
- ☐ Temporary exhibitions
- ☐ Nonexhibition space

The courtyard (1561) designed by Palladio

The former church of Santa Maria della Carità

Feast in the House of Levi (1573) by Paolo Veronese

Entrance

Madonna and Child between St. John the Baptist and a Saint In this beautiful painting (c.1504), Giovanni Bellini places the figures in a spacious landscape, so marking a new phase in his development.

Coronation of the Virgin
Paolo Veneziano's polyptych (1325) has a central image of the Virgin surrounded by a panoply of religious scenes. This detail shows episodes from the *Life of St. Francis.*

Healing of the Madman (c.1496) by Vittore Carpaccio

The long corridor (12) and
the rooms that lead from it are
largely devoted to light-hearted
landscape and genre paintings
from the 18th century. Among
them are pastoral scenes by
Francesco Zuccarelli, works by
Marco Ricci, scenes of Venetian
society by Pietro Longhi, and
a view of Venice by Canaletto
(1763). This is a fine example
of his sense of perspective.

Byzantine and International Gothic

Room 1 shows the influence
of Byzantine art on the early
Venetian painters. In Paolo
Veneziano's glowing *Coronation
of the Virgin* (1325), the linear
rhythms are unmistakably
Gothic, but the gold background and central panel
are distinctly Byzantine.

In contrast, *The Coronation
of the Virgin* (1448) by Michele
Giambono reveals a delicate
naturalism, typical of the
International Gothic style.

Renaissance

The Renaissance came late
to Venice, but by the second
quarter of the 15th century
it had transformed the city
into a thriving art center
rivaling Florence and
Rome. Central to Venetian
art in the 15th century was
the *Sacra Conversazione*,
in which the Madonna is
portrayed with various
saints in a harmonious
composition. Giovanni
Bellini's altarpiece for
San Giobbe (c.1487) in
room 2 is one of the finest
examples of this subject.

In contrast, the High
Renaissance exuberance
of Paolo Veronese is

exemplified in the monumental
Feast in the House of Levi (1573).
The painting occupies a whole
wall in room 10. Tintoretto's
huge masterpiece *The Miracle of
St. Mark Freeing a Slave* (1548) is
also on display here.

Baroque, Genre, and Landscape

Venice lacked native Baroque
painters, but a few non-
Venetians kept the Venetian
school alive in the 17th century.
The most notable was the
Genoese Bernardo Strozzi
(1581–1644). The artist was
a great admirer of the work of
Veronese, as can be seen in his
Feast at the House of Simon (1629)
in room 11. Also represented
in this room is Giambattista
Tiepolo, the greatest Venetian
painter of the 18th century.

Ceremonial Painting

Rooms 20 and 21 return to
the Renaissance, featuring two
great cycles of paintings from
the late 16th century. The detail
in these large-scale anecdotal
canvases provides a fascinating
glimpse of the life, customs,
and appearance of Venice
at the time.

Room 20 houses *The
Stories of the Cross* by Venice's
leading artists. In room 21,
minutely detailed *Scenes
from the Legend of St. Ursula*
(1490s) by Carpaccio mix
reality and imagination
by linking episodes from
the life of the saint to the
settings and costumes of
15th-century Venice.

Feast in the House of Levi (1573) by Paolo Veronese

Street by Street: Piazza San Marco

Throughout its long history, Piazza San Marco has witnessed pageants, processions, political activities, and countless Carnival festivities. Visitors flock here by the thousands for two of the city's most important historic sights – the Basilica and the Palazzo Ducale. These magnificent buildings complement lesser sights, such as the Campanile, Museo Correr, and Torre dell'Orologio, not to mention the gardens of the Giardinetti Reali, open-air orchestras, elegant cafés – notably Quadri and Florian's – and numerous stylish shops.

㉑ Torre dell'Orologio
The clock tower, with hidden clockwork figures, dates from the Renaissance.

Traditionally gondolas have moored in the Bacino Orseolo, which is named after Doge Orseolo.

The Piazza was described by Napoleon as the "most elegant drawing room in Europe."

㉓ Museo Correr
Giovanni Bellini's *Pietà* (1455–60) is one of many masterpieces hanging in the galleries of the Correr.

MERCERIE

PROCURATIE VECCHIE

PIAZZA SAN MARCO

PROCURATIE NUOVE

Harry's Bar has attracted American visitors since Giuseppe Cipriani and his friend Harry set it up in 1931. Shown here is Ernest Hemingway, one of the bar's many famous patrons.

San Marco Vallaresso

⓳ ★ Basilica di San Marco
This 13th-century façade mosaic shows the body of St. Mark being carried into the basilica.

Locator Map
See Venice Street Finder map 7

The Bridge of Sighs
(1600) was built as a passageway between the Palazzo Ducale and the prison. It reputedly took its name from the sighs of prisoners being led to trial.

CALLE LARGA SAN MARCO

RIO DEL PALAZZO

Ponte della Paglia

PIAZZETTA

⓴ ★ Palazzo Ducale
Once home to Venice's rulers, and to the offices of State, the Doges' Palace is a triumph of Gothic architecture.

㉒ The Campanile
The present Campanile replaced one that collapsed in 1902.

MOLO SAN MARCO

San Marco Giardinetti

| 0 meters | | 75 |
| 0 yards | | 75 |

The vaulting of the stairway in the magnificent Libreria Sansoviniana (1588) is decorated with frescoes and gilded stucco. The national library of St. Mark is housed here.

The Zecca, designed by Sansovino and started in 1537, was the city mint until 1870, and gave its name to the *zecchino* or Venetian ducat.

⑲ Basilica di San Marco

Venice's famous Basilica blends the architectural and decorative styles of East and West to create one of the greatest buildings in Europe. The exterior owes its almost Oriental splendor to countless treasures from the Republic's overseas empire. Among these are copies of the famous bronze horses, brought from Constantinople in 1204, and a wealth of columns, bas-reliefs, and colored marbles studded across the main façade. Mosaics from different epochs adorn the five doorways, while the main portal is framed by some of Italy's loveliest Romanesque carving (1240–65).

St. Mark and Angels
The statues crowning the central arch are additions from the early 15th century.

★ Horses of St. Mark
The four horses are replicas of the gilded bronze originals, now protected inside the Basilica's museum.

KEY

① **The elegant arches** echo those of the lower floor, forming a repeat pattern.

② **The Pentecost Dome**, showing the Descent of the Holy Ghost as a dove, was probably the first dome to be decorated with mosaics.

③ **The Ascension Dome** features a magnificent 13th-century mosaic of Christ surrounded by angels, the 12 Apostles, and the Virgin Mary.

④ **St. Mark's body**, believed lost in the fire of AD 976, supposedly reappeared when the new church was consecrated in 1094. The remains are housed in the altar.

⑤ **The Mosaic Sidewalk** shows beautiful pictures of birds and beasts, some of which are allegorical.

⑥ **St. Mark's Treasury**

⑦ **Romanesque carvings** adorn the arches of the main portal.

Entrance

★ Façade Mosaics
A 17th-century mosaic shows the body of St. Mark being taken from Alexandria, reputedly smuggled past Muslim guards under slices of pork.

Ciborium
The fine alabaster columns of the altar canopy, or baldacchino, are adorned with scenes from the New Testament.

The Tetrarchs
This charming sculptured group in porphyry (4th-century Egyptian) is thought to represent Diocletian, Maximian, Valerian, and Constantine. Collectively they were the Tetrarchs, appointed by Diocletian to help rule the Roman Empire.

The Building of St. Mark's

Built on a Greek-cross plan and crowned with five huge domes, this is the third church to stand on the site. The first, which enshrined the body of St. Mark in the 9th century, was destroyed by fire. The second was pulled down in favor of a church that reflected Venice's growing power. The present design was inspired by the Church of the Apostles in Constantinople and was completed and decorated over the centuries. From 1075, all ships returning from abroad had, by law, to bring back a precious gift to adorn "the House of St. Mark." The mosaics inside are mostly 12th–13th century and cover 45,622 sq ft (4,240 sq m). Some were later replaced by such artists as Titian and Tintoretto. Until 1807 St. Mark's was the doge's private chapel, used for ceremonies of State, after which it succeeded San Pietro di Castello as the cathedral of Venice.

13th-century carving of a grape harvester on the main portal

Exploring the Basilica

St. Mark's magnificent interior is clad with dazzling mosaics, which begin in the *narthex*, or atrium of the Basilica, and culminate in the glittering panels of the Pentecost and Ascension domes. The Genesis Cupola in the atrium has a stunning Creation of the World described in concentric circles. The *pavimento* or floor is also patterned with mosaics in marble and glass. Steps from the atrium lead to the Museo Marciano, home to the Basilica's famous horses. Other treasures include the jewel-encrusted Pala d'Oro, behind the high altar, the Nicopeia icon, and the precious hoards of silver, gold, and glassware in the Treasury.

Madonna di Nicopeia
This Byzantine icon, looted in 1204, is one of Venice's most revered images.

★ Pentecost Dome
Showing the Apostles touched by tongues of flame, the Pentecost Dome was lavishly decorated in the 12th century.

★ Ascension Dome
A mosaic of Christ in Glory decorates the enormous central dome. This masterpiece was created by 13th-century Venetian craftsmen, who were strongly influenced by the art and architecture of Byzantium.

★ Treasury
A repository for precious artifacts from both Italy and Constantinople, the treasury houses objects such as this 11th-century silver-gilt coffer.

Mosaics

Clothing the domes, walls, and floor of the Basilica are over 43,000 sq ft (4,000 sq m) of gleaming golden mosaics. The earliest, dating from the 12th century, were the work of mosaicists from the East. Their delicate techniques were soon adopted by Venetian craftsmen, who gradually took over the Basilica's decoration, combining Byzantine inspiration with Western influences. During the 16th century, many sketches by Tintoretto, Titian, Veronese, and other leading artists were reproduced in mosaic.

Among the most dazzling mosaics – many of which have been heavily restored – are those in the 13th-century central Ascension Dome and the 12th-century Pentecost Dome over the nave.

★ Pala d'Oro
The altarpiece, created in the 10th century by medieval goldsmiths, is made up of 250 panels such as this one.

Pala D'Oro

Beyond the Cappella di San Clemente lies the entrance to the most valuable treasure of San Marco: the Pala d'Oro. This jewel-spangled altarpiece, situated behind the high altar, consists of 250 enamel paintings on gold foil, enclosed within a gilded silver Gothic frame. Originally commissioned in Byzantium in AD 976, the altarpiece was further embellished over the centuries.

Napoleon stole some of the precious stones in 1797, but the screen still gleams with pearls, rubies, sapphires, and amethysts.

Museo Marciano

Steps from the atrium, marked Loggia dei Cavalli, take you up to the church museum, where the gallery offers a splendid view into the basilica. The gilded bronze horses, housed in a room at the far end of the museum, were stolen from the top of the Hippodrome (ancient race-course) in Constantinople (modern Istanbul) in 1204 but their origin, either Roman or Hellenistic, remains a mystery. Also on show are mosaics, medieval manuscripts, and antique tapestries.

Baptistry and Chapels

The baptistry (closed to the public) was added by Doge Andrea Dandolo (1343–54), who is buried here, with Sansovino, who designed the font. The adjoining Cappella Zen (also closed to the public) became a funeral chapel for Cardinal Zen in 1504 in return for a bequest to the State. The left transept of the Cappella dei Mascoli is decorated with scenes from the life of Mary, while the third chapel in the same transept houses the icon of the Madonna di Nicopeia. Looted in 1204, it was once carried into battle at the head of the Byzantine army.

KEY

① **North side aisle**

② **The Porta dei Fiori**, or Gate of Flowers, is decorated with 13th-century reliefs.

③ **Cappella dei Mascoli**

④ **The sacristy door** has fine bronze panels by Sansovino, which include portraits of himself with Titian and Aretino.

⑤ **The Altar of the Sacrament** is decorated with mosaics of the parables and miracles of Christ dating from the late 12th or early 13th century.

⑥ **The columns** of the inner façade are thought to be fragments of the first basilica.

⑦ **South side aisle**

⑧ **Baptistry**

⑨ **Cappella Zen**

⑩ **Steps to Museo Marciano**

⑪ **Atrium**

Noah and the Flood, atrium mosaics from the 13th century

⑳ Palazzo Ducale

The Palazzo Ducale (Doges' Palace) was the official residence of each Venetian ruler (doge) and was founded in the 9th century. The present palace owes its external appearance to the building work of the 14th and early 15th centuries. To create their airy Gothic masterpiece, the Venetians broke with tradition by perching the bulk of the palace (built in pink Veronese marble) on top of an apparent fretwork of loggias and arcades (built from white Istrian stone).

★ Giants' Staircase
This 15th-century staircase is crowned by Sansovino's statues of Mars and Neptune, symbols of Venice's power.

★ Porta della Carta
This 15th-century Gothic gate was once the main entrance to the palace. From it, a vaulted passageway leads to the Arco Foscari and the internal courtyard.

★ Sala del Maggior Consiglio
This vast hall was used as a meeting place for members of Venice's Great Council. Tintoretto's huge *Paradise* (1590) fills the end wall.

Sala dello Scudo
The walls of this room, once part of the doge's private apartments, are covered with maps of the world. In the center of the room are two giant 18th-century globes.

VISITORS' CHECKLIST

Practical Information
Piazzetta. **Map** 7 C2. **Tel** 041 271 59 11. **Open** 8:30am–7pm daily (Nov–Mar: to 5:30pm, last adm: 1 hr before closing). **Closed** Jan 1, Dec 25. ♿ 🔊 ♿ partial. 📷 📱 ✉ 🌐 museiciviciveneziani.it

Transportation
🚤 San Marco

Torture Chamber
Interrogations took place in the Torture Chamber. Suspects were hung by their wrists from a cord in the center of the room.

Drunkenness of Noah
This early 15th-century sculpture, symbolic of the frailty of man, is set on the corner of the palace.

Entrance

The Loggia
Each arch of the ground-level portico supports two arches of the loggia, which commands fine views of the lagoon.

KEY

① **Exit**

② **The Arco Foscari** has copies of Antonio Rizzo's 15th-century Adam and Eve.

③ **Courtyard**

④ **Sala del Collegio**

⑤ **Sala del Senato**

⑥ **Anticollegio**

⑦ **Sala delle Quattro Porte**

⑧ **Sala del Consiglio dei Dieci**

⑨ **Sala della Bussola**

⑩ **The Bridge of Sighs**

⑪ **The Ponte della Paglia,** built of Istrian stone, has a pretty balustrade of columns and sculpted pinecones.

Exploring the Palazzo Ducale

A tour of the Palazzo Ducale takes visitors through a succession of richly decorated chambers and halls, arranged over three floors, culminating with the Bridge of Sighs, which links the palace to the prisons. Casanova was once imprisoned here and made a daring escape from the Palazzo through a hole in the roof.

Jacopo and Domenico Tintoretto's *Paradise*, one of the world's largest paintings, in the Sala del Maggior Consiglio

Scala d'Oro and Courtyard

A passage from the Porta del Frumento opens into the palace courtyard. The ticket office and palace entrance are to the left. At the top of Antonio Rizzo's 15th-century Giants' Staircase, the new doge would be crowned with the *zogia* or dogal cap. The Scala d'Oro (golden staircase), designed by Jacopo Sansovino, leads to the palace's upper floors. It takes its name, however, from the elaborate gilt stucco vault created by Alessandro Vittoria (1554–8).

Sala delle Quattro Porte to the Sala del Senato

The second flight of the Scala d'Oro leads to the Sala delle Quattro Porte, with a ceiling designed by Palladio and frescoed by Tintoretto. The end walls of the next room, the Anticollegio, are decorated with mythological scenes by Tintoretto, while Veronese's masterly *Rape of Europa* (1580), opposite the window, is one of the palace's most dramatic works. The adjoining Sala del Collegio was where the doge and his counselors met to receive ambassadors and discuss matters of State. Embellishing the magnificent ceiling are 11 paintings by Veronese. In the next room, the Sala del Senato, the doge and some 200 senators discussed foreign affairs. The paintings are by Tintoretto and pupils.

Sala del Consiglio dei Dieci to the Armeria

The Sala del Consiglio dei Dieci was the meeting room of the powerful Council of Ten, founded in 1310 to protect State security. Two fine works by Veronese adorn the ceiling: *Age and Youth* and *Juno Offering the Ducal Crown to*

A *bocca di leone* for denunciations

Venice (both 1553–4). In the Sala della Bussola, offenders awaited their fate in front of the Council of Ten. The room's *bocca di leone* (lion's mouth), was used to post secret denunciations and was just one of several in the palace. The wooden door here leads to the State Inquisitors' Room and thence to the torture chamber and prisons. The Armory – one of the finest such collections anywhere in Europe – occupies the following rooms.

Sala del Maggior Consiglio

The Scala dei Censori leads to the second floor and past the Sala del Guariento and Antonio Rizzo's statues of Adam and Eve (1480s) to the magnificent Sala del Maggior Consiglio. A vast chamber, it was used as a meeting place for the Great Council and for grand State banquets. By the mid-16th century the Great Council had around 2,000 members. Any Venetian of high birth over 25 was entitled to a seat unless he married a commoner. Tintoretto's huge *Paradise* (1587–90) occupies the eastern wall. Measuring 25 by 81 ft (7.45 by 24.65 m), it is one of the largest paintings in the world. The itinerary then continues in more somber vein, crossing the Bridge of Sighs to enter the dank world of the prisons.

Dialectic (c.1577) by Veronese in the Palazzo Ducale's Sala del Collegio

㉑ Torre dell'Orologio

Piazza San Marco. **Map** 7 B2. **Tel** 041 4273 0892. 🚤 San Marco. 🕐 10 & 11am Mon–Wed, 2 & 3pm Thu–Sun (must be booked in advance). **Closed** Jan 1, May 1, Dec 25. **W** visitmuve.it

This richly decorated clock tower on the north side of the piazza was built in the late 15th century. Mauro Coducci is thought to have worked on the design. With its display of the phases of the moon and the signs of the zodiac, the clock face was designed with seafarers in mind. According to legend, once the clock was completed, the two inventors had their eyes gouged out to prevent them from ever creating a replica.

The clock face of the Torre dell'Orologio

On the upper level, the winged lion of St. Mark stands against a star-spangled blue backdrop. At the very top the two huge bronze figures, known as the *Mori*, or Moors, strike the bell on the hour.

㉒ Campanile

Piazza San Marco. **Map** 7 B2. **Tel** 041 270 83 11. 🚤 San Marco. **Open** Nov–Easter: 9:30am–3:45pm daily; Easter–Jun & Oct: 9am–7pm daily; Jul–Sep: 9am–9pm daily. 🎫 📷 **W** basilicasanmarco.it

From the top of St. Mark's campanile, high above the piazza, visitors can enjoy views of the city, the lagoon, and, visibility permitting, the peaks of the Alps. It was from here that Galileo demonstrated his telescope to Doge Leonardo Donà in 1609. To do so he would have climbed the internal ramp. Access today is by elevator.

The first tower, completed in 1173, was built as a lighthouse to assist navigators in the lagoon. It took on a less benevolent role in the Middle Ages, when offenders were imprisoned – and in some cases left to die – in a cage hung near its summit. With the exception of several 16th-century renovations, the tower survived unharmed until July 1902, when, with little warning, it collapsed. The only casualties were the Loggetta at the foot of the tower and the custodian's cat. Donations flooded in, and in 1903 the foundation stone was laid for a new campanile *"dov'era e com'era"* ("where it was and as it was"). The new tower was opened on April 25 (the Feast of St. Mark) 1912. Due to small structural shifts, the foundations have been reinforced.

㉓ Museo Correr

Procuratie Nuove. Entrance in Ala Napoleonica. **Map** 7 B2. **Tel** 041 240 52 11. 🚤 San Marco. **Open** Apr–Oct: 10am–7pm; Nov–Mar: 10am–5pm (last adm: 1hr before closing). **Closed** Jan 1, Dec 25. 🎫 (includes adm to Libreria Sansoviniana and Museo Archeologico). 🏛 📷 ♿ **W** museiciviciveneziani.it

Teodoro Correr bequeathed his extensive collection of works of art to Venice in 1830, thus forming the core of the city's fine civic museum.

Its first rooms form a suitably Neo-Classical backdrop for early statues by Antonio Canova (1757–1822). The rest of the floor covers the history of the Venetian Republic, with maps,

Young Man in a Red Hat (c.1490) by Carpaccio in the Museo Correr

coins, armor, and a host of doge-related exhibits. The second floor contains a picture collection second only to that of the Accademia.

The paintings, hung chronologically, trace the evolution of Venetian painting, and show the influence of Ferrarese, Paduan, and Flemish artists.

The gallery's most famous works are by Carpaccio: *Portrait of a Young Man in a Red Hat* (c.1490), and *Two Venetian Ladies* (c.1507). The latter is traditionally, but probably incorrectly, known as *The Courtesans* because of the ladies' low-cut dresses. The Museo del Risorgimento on the same floor looks at the history of Venice until unification with Italy in 1866.

The ceiling of Santo Stefano, built in the form of a ship's keel

㉔ Santo Stefano

Campo Santo Stefano. **Map** 6 F2. **Tel** 041 275 04 62. 🚤 Accademia or Sant'Angelo. **Open** 10am–5pm Mon–Sat. **Closed** Jan 1, Dec 25. 🎫 🏛 ♿ **W** chorusvenezia.org

Deconsecrated six times on account of the blood spilled within its walls, Santo Stefano – one of Venice's most beautiful churches – is now remarkably serene. Built in the 14th century, and altered in the 15th, the church has a carved portal by Bartolomeo Bon, and a campanile with a typical Venetian tilt. The interior has a splendid ship's keel ceiling, carved tie-beams, and a sacristy crammed with valuable paintings.

㉕ Santi Giovanni e Paolo

Known more colloquially as San Zanipolo, Santi Giovanni e Paolo vies with the Frari *(see pp102–3)* as the city's greatest Gothic church. Built by the Dominicans in the 14th century, it is striking for its vast scale and architectural austerity. Known as the Pantheon of Venice, it houses monuments to no fewer than 25 doges. Among these are several fine works of art, executed by the Lombardi family and other leading sculptors.

The Nave
The cross-vaulted interior is tied by wooden beams and supported by stone columns.

★ **Tomb of Nicolò Marcello**
This magnificent Renaissance monument to Doge Nicolò Marcello (died 1474) was sculpted by Pietro Lombardo.

Entrance

★ **Tomb of Pietro Mocenigo**
Pietro Lombardo's superb tomb (1481) commemorates the doge's military pursuits when he was Grand Captain of the Venetian forces.

★ **Polyptych by Bellini**
This painting (c.1465) shows St. Vincent Ferrer, a Spanish cleric, flanked by St. Sebastian and St. Christopher.

KEY

① **The doorway**, which is
decorated with Byzantine reliefs and
carvings by Bartolomeo Bon, is one
of Venice's earliest Renaissance
architectural works.

② **The bronze statue** is a
monument to Doge Sebastiano
Venier, who was Commander of the
Fleet at Lepanto.

③ **Tomb of Andrea Vendramin**,
Lombardo's masterpiece (1476–8),
takes the form of a Roman
triumphal arch.

④ **The Baroque high altar**, begun
in 1619, is attributed to Baldassare
Longhena.

⑤ **16th-century altar statues by
Vittoria**

⑥ **16th-century frescoes
attributed to Palma il Giovane**

㉖ Statue of Colleoni

Campo Santi Giovanni e Paolo.
Map 3 C5. 🚤 Ospedale Civile.

Bartolomeo Colleoni, the
famous *condottiere* or
commander of mercenaries,
left his fortune to the Republic
on condition that his statue
was placed in front of San
Marco. A prominent statue in
the piazza would have broken
with precedent, so the Senate
cunningly had Colleoni raised
before the Scuola di San Marco
instead of the basilica. A
touchstone of early Renaissance
sculpture, the equestrian statue
of the proud warrior (1481–8)
is by the Florentine Andrea
Verrocchio, but was cast in
bronze after his death by
Alessandro Leopardi. The statue
has a strong sense of power
and movement, which arguably
ranks it alongside the works
of Donatello.

㉗ Santa Maria Formosa

Campo Santa Maria Formosa. **Map** 7
C1. **Tel** 041 275 04 62. 🚤 Rialto.
Open 10am–5pm Mon–Sat.
Closed Jan 1, Dec 25. 📷 ✉️
🖥️ **chorusvenezia.org**

Designed by Mauro Coducci
in 1492, this church is most
unusual in having two main
façades – one overlooks the
campo, the other the canal.
The bell tower, or campanile,
added in 1688, is noted for the
grotesque face at its base.
   Two paintings stand out in
the interior: a triptych (1473) by
Bartolomeo Vivarini, and Palma
il Vecchio's *St. Barbara* (c.1510).

㉘ San Zaccaria

Campo San Zaccaria. **Map** 8 D2.
Tel 041 522 12 57. 🚤 San Zaccaria.
Open 10am–noon, 4–6pm Mon–Sat,
4–6pm Sun & public hols. 📷 chapels
and crypt. ✉️

Set in a quiet square just a
stone's throw from the Riva
degli Schiavoni, the church
of San Zaccaria is a successful
blend of Flamboyant Gothic
and Classical Renaissance styles.

Palma il Vecchio's *St. Barbara* (c.1510) in
Santa Maria Formosa

Founded in the 9th century,
its façade was later rebuilt by
Antonio Gambello in Gothic
style. When Gambello died in
1481, Mauro Coducci completed
the upper section, adding many
of its Renaissance panels.
   The interior's artistic highlight
is Giovanni Bellini's serene and
sumptuously colored *Madonna
and Child with Saints* (1505) in
the north aisle. A door off the
right nave leads to the Chapel
of St. Athanasius, which in turn
leads to the Chapel of San
Tarasio. The chapel contains
vault frescoes (1442) by Andrea
del Castagno, and polyptychs
(1443–4) by Antonio Vivarini
and Giovanni d'Alemagna.

A Renaissance panel by Coducci on the
façade of San Zaccaria

㉙ Scuola di San Giorgio degli Schiavoni

Calle Furlani. **Map** 8 E1. **Tel** 041 522 88 28. San Zaccaria. **Open** 9:15am–1pm, 2:45–6pm Tue–Sun (Sun am only). **Closed** Jan 1, May 1, Dec 25, and other religious hols.

Within this small gem are some of the finest paintings of Vittore Carpaccio. They were commissioned by the Schiavoni, or Dalmatian Slav community in Venice.

The Scuola was established in 1451 and rebuilt in 1551. It has changed very little since. The exquisite frieze, executed between 1502 and 1508, shows scenes from the lives of patron saints: St. George, St. Tryphone, and St. Jerome. Each episode of the narrative cycle is remarkable for its vivid coloring, minute detail, and historic record of Venetian life. Outstanding among them are *St. George Slaying the Dragon* and *St. Jerome Leading the Tamed Lion to the Monastery*.

㉚ San Giovanni in Bragora

Campo Bandiera e Moro. **Map** 8 E2. **Tel** 041 520 59 06. Arsenale. **Open** 9–11am, 3:30–5:30pm Mon–Sat.

The existing church is essentially Gothic (1475–9), and the interior contains major works of art that demonstrate the transition from Gothic to early Renaissance. Bartolomeo Vivarini's altarpiece *Madonna and Child with Saints* (1478) is unmistakably Gothic.

Lagoon entrance

Arsenale Novissimo, 15th–16th century

Old sail factory

Arsenale Vecchio, 12th–13th century

Corderia

Arsenale Novo, 14th century

18th-century engraving of the Arsenale

Contrasting with this is Cima da Conegliano's large-scale *Baptism of Christ* (1492–5), which adorns the main altar.

㉛ Arsenale

Map 8 F1. Arsenale. Museo Storico Navale Campo San Biagio. **Map** 8 F3. **Tel** 041 244 13 99. **Open** 8:45am–1:30pm Mon–Fri; 8:45am–1pm Sat. **Closed** public hols.

The Arsenale was founded in the 12th century and by the 16th had become the greatest naval shipyard in the world, capable of constructing a whole galley in 24 hours, using an assembly-line system. Surrounded by crenellated walls, it was like a city within a city. Today the site is largely disused. Its impressive 15th-century gateway, twin towers, and guardian lions can be viewed from the *campo* or bridge outside. The gateway was built by Antonio Gambello and is often cited as Venice's first Renaissance construction.

Around the corner, in Campo San Biagio, the **Museo Storico Navale** charts Venetian naval history from the heyday of the Arsenale to the present. Exhibits include friezes from famous galleys of the past and a replica of the *Bucintoro*, the Doge's ceremonial barge.

㉜ San Giorgio Maggiore

Map 8 D4. **Tel** 041 522 78 27. San Giorgio. **Open** 9:30am–12:30pm, 2:30–5:30pm daily (to 4:30pm in winter). (Campanile). Fondazione Cini: **Tel** 041 271 04 02. **Open** by appt Mon–Fri; 10am–4pm Sat & Sun (to 5pm Apr–Sep).

Appearing like a stage set across the water from the Piazzetta is the little island of San Giorgio Maggiore. The church and

St. George Slaying the Dragon (1502–8) by Carpaccio, in the Scuola di San Giorgio degli Schiavoni

monastery, constructed between 1559–80, are among Andrea Palladio's greatest architectural achievements. The church's temple front and the spacious interior with its perfect proportions and cool beauty are typically Palladian *(see pp84–5)*. These qualities are echoed by the church of Il Redentore on the nearby island of Giudecca, built by Palladio in 1577–92.

On the chancel walls of San Giorgio Maggiore are two fine paintings by Tintoretto: *The Last Supper* and *Gathering of the Manna* (both 1594). In the Chapel of the Dead is his last work, *The Deposition* (1592–4), finished by his son Domenico.

The top of the campanile affords superb views of the city and lagoon. You can see the monastery cloisters below, now part of the **Fondazione Cini**, a cultural center that is used to host international exhibitions.

Palladio's San Giorgio Maggiore

㉝ Murano

🚤 4.1 and 4.2 from Fondamente Nuove; 3 from Ferrovia and Piazzale Roma.

Much like Venice, Murano comprises a cluster of small islands, connected by bridges. It has been the center of the glassmaking industry since 1291, when the furnaces were moved here from the city because of the risk of fire and the disagreeable effects of smoke. Some of the houses on the water date from this period.

The colonnaded exterior of Murano's Basilica dei Santi Maria e Donato

🏛 Museo Vetrario

Palazzo Giustinian, Fondamenta Giustinian. **Tel** 041 73 95 86. **Open** 10am–6pm daily (Nov–Mar: to 5pm, last adm: 30 min before closing). **Closed** Jan 1, May 1, Dec 25. 🅿 📷
🆆 visitmuve.it

In the 15th and 16th centuries Murano was the principal glass-producing center in Europe, and today most tourists visit for glass alone. The Museo Vetrario in the Palazzo Giustinian houses a collection of antique pieces. The prize exhibit is the dark blue Barovier wedding cup (1470–80), with enamel work by Angelo Barovier.

🏛 Basilica dei Santi Maria e Donato

Fondamenta Giustinian. **Tel** 041 73 90 56. **Open** 8am–6pm Mon–Sat, 1–6pm Sun (Nov–Mar: to 6pm daily). 📷

With its lovely colonnaded apse, this basilica is the architectural highlight of the island. Despite major restoration in the 19th century, this 12th-century church still retains much of its original beauty. Note the Gothic ship's keel roof, the mosaic Madonna in the apse, and the mosaic floor, which dates from 1140.

Venetian glass goblet

㉞ Burano

🚤 12 from Fondamenta Nuove; 14 from San Zaccaria via Lido and Punta Sabbioni.

Burano is the most colorful of the lagoon islands and can be distinguished from a distance by the tilting tower of its church. In contrast with the haunting Torcello, the island is densely populated, its waterways fringed with brightly painted houses.

The main thoroughfare is Via Baldassare Galuppi, named after the Burano-born composer. It features traditional lace and linen stalls and open-air trattorias serving fresh fish.

🏛 Museo del Merletto

Piazza Baldassare Galuppi 187. **Tel** 041 73 00 34. **Open** Apr–Oct 10am–6pm Tue–Sun (Nov–Mar: to 5pm, last adm: 30 min before closing). **Closed** Jan 1, May 1, Dec 25. 🅿
🆆 visitmuve.it

The people of Burano are fishermen and lacemakers by tradition. You can still see fishermen scraping their boats or mending nets, but today lacemakers are rare. In the 16th century the local lace was the most sought-after in Europe – it was so delicate it became known as *punto in aria* ("points in the air"). After a slump in the 18th century, the industry revived, and a lace-making school was set up here in 1872. Authentic Burano lace is hard to find, but you can watch it being made at the school, now a museum, which displays fine examples of antique lace.

Brightly painted street in Burano

® Torcello

Established between the 5th and 6th centuries, the island of Torcello boasts the oldest building in the lagoon – the cathedral of Santa Maria Assunta. Founded in AD 639, it contains some splendid ancient mosaics. The adjoining church of Santa Fosca, of pure Byzantine design, is another mark of Torcello's former glory – before being eclipsed by Venice, it had a population of 20,000.

★ **Doomsday Mosaics**
The highly decorative 12th-century mosaic of the *Last Judgment* covers the west wall.

Pulpit
The present basilica dates from 1008, but includes earlier features. The pulpit contains 7th-century fragments.

KEY

① **The exquisite Byzantine marble panels** of the iconostasis, or rood screen, are carved with peacocks, lions, and flowers.

② **The Roman sarcophagus**, below the altar, is said to contain the relics of St. Heliodorus.

③ **The 13th-century apse mosaic** of the Madonna against a gold background, is one of the most beautiful in Venice.

④ **The central dome** and cross sections are supported by columns of Greek marble with Corinthian capitals.

⑤ **The Portico** of Santa Fosca, with its elegant stilted arches, is built on three sides of the church, and probably dates from the 12th century.

⑥ **The altar** was rebuilt in 1939 and stands below a 15th-century wood relief of *Santa Fosca Sleeping*.

Nave Columns
Two rows of slender marble columns, 18 in all, separate the three naves. Their finely carved capitals date from the 11th century.

Torcello's Last Canals
Silted canals and malaria hastened Torcello's decline. One of the remaining waterways runs from the *vaporetto* stop to the basilica.

Santa Fosca
Built in the 11th and 12th centuries on a Greek-cross plan, the church has a serene Byzantine interior with a central pentagonal apse.

Vaporetto boarding point →

The Museo dell'Estuario houses many old church treasures

Attila's Throne
It was said that the 5th-century king of the Huns used this marble seat as his throne.

Shopping in Venice

The attractive shop windows that line the narrow streets of Venice are an irresistible attraction for any visitor. Myriad fashion brands are available in gleaming, ultramodern stores, but the city also has a strong artisan tradition. Expert craftspeople in tiny workshops open to the public create delightful and highly original objects in glass, wood, leather, and papier-mâché. Skilled hands transform colored glass rods into playful miniature animals and exquisite flowers, while plaster molds turn out shapes destined to become ornate masks. Interior-design establishments also abound, and sleek kitchenware and fabrics make unusual purchases. Beautiful boutiques offering antique furniture and accessories are concentrated in the city center.

Where to Shop

The glittering Mercerie, which runs from Piazza San Marco to the Rialto, has been Venice's main shopping street since the Middle Ages and, along with the fashion avenue Calle Larga XXII Marzo, is still a draw for the crowds. The zigzagging Frezzeria is full of unusual shops, while across the Grand Canal, the narrow streets from the Rialto southwest toward Campo San Polo are lined with a variety of less expensive stores. The bustling Lista di Spagna, near the station, and the Strada Nova toward the Rialto cater to the everyday needs of the locals.

The islands of Murano and Burano are the places to buy traditional glass and lace.

Food and Markets

One of the delights of Venice is exploring the city's food markets and shops. Fruit and vegetable stalls sprawl to the west of the Rialto Bridge and along the Grand Canal. The Pescheria, or fish market, occupies the farthest section. The neighboring streets are full of gourmet food shops. Wine, olive oil, vinegar, and grappa in decorative bottles, as well as dried pasta in many shapes, colors, and flavors are all good purchases.

Aliani's cheese shop offers a mouthwatering selection of picnic fare, while **Drogheria Mascari** has a fine range of dried fruit, coffee, and alcohol. **Rizzo**, on the other side of the bridge, is a master pasta-maker.

Glass

The island of Murano is a good place to watch expert glass-blowing. However, for contemporary glass creations head back to Venice, around San Marco – try **Venini**'s showroom for stunning platters and huge vases, and **L'Isola** for Carlo Moretti's tumblers in rich colors.

The art of bead-making is alive and flourishing thanks to sisters **Marina e Susanna Sent**'s simple, irresistible necklaces. At **Perle e Dintorni**, customers can sort through an astonishing range of beautiful glass beads and create their own costume jewelry.

Clothing and Accessories

Promod, near San Marco, has reasonably priced fun gear for the young set. Nearby is **Benetton**'s megastore, with its trademark bright clothes, while, opposite, **Max Mara** has superlative womenswear. Other leading names in fashion – **Armani**, **Roberto Cavalli**, **Missoni**, and **Gucci** – also have stylish shops around Piazza San Marco.

Just off San Lio, **Giovanna Zanella** can be found at her cobbler's bench crafting zany shoes and sandals. Her amazing range even includes gondola decorations.

Masks and Costumes

Mass-produced Carnival masks can be found all over the city, but a genuine one makes for a wonderful souvenir. With its striking designs, **Papier Mâché** has revived traditional mask-making. Near Campo San Polo, **Tragicomica** sells masks and costumes, as well as Commedia dell'Arte figures. You will also find these at **Leon d'Oro**, where they make string puppets too. **Ca' Macana** has a great collection of eye-catching masks. You can even participate in a mask-making workshop. Down a winding street in Cannaregio, the husband-and-wife team at **Il Pirata** make papier-mâché masks in their store. Courses are available in the decoration and history of Venetian masks.

Jewelry

Nardi, located in the arcades of Piazza San Marco, crafts an exquisite brooch with a Moor's head, among other things. A short distance away are the sparkling premises of **Bulgari**, while **Cartier**, with its beautiful collection of watches, can be found along the nearby Mercerie. Shops on the Rialto Bridge sell cheaper designs; this is a good place to find bracelets and chains, the prices of which are determined by the weight of the gold. Over the bridge, under the arcades of the ancient goldsmiths' district, is **Attombri** – two brothers who design unusual jewelry from antique Murano glass beads.

Fabric and Interior Design

Venice is famed for fine silks and velvets and sumptuous brocades, many of which are still sold at **Trois**, close to the Gritti Palace hotel. On the Grand Canal, at Sant'Angelo, **Rubelli** is fabric heaven, with a wide range of designs and rich upholstery. More down-to-earth but good-quality household linen and brilliantly colored bath accessories are sold at **TSL**, which has several stores around town.

For original kitchen items, the choice at **Epicentro** is hard to beat; or head to **Marchiol**, hidden away on a Castello backstreet, for modern light fittings and lamps.

Books and Gifts

At the Giardinetti Reali, on the San Marco waterfront, the **Venice Pavilion Bookshop** annex of the Tourist Board has an exhaustive collection of books dealing with many aspects of the city. The **Libreria Marco Polo** bookstore offers a decent English-language section, while **Mare di Carta** offers nautical books and magazines.

Alberto Valese-Ebru uses a distinctive marbling technique on fabric as well as paper. Nearby, **Paolo Olbi** has a wide range of papers and artistic books for sale. On the opposite side of the Grand Canal, at San Tomà, **Daniela Porto** has lovely old printed maps and frames, perfect as gifts, and **Signor Blum** on Campo San Barnaba has charming hand-made carved and painted wooden objects and toys.

DIRECTORY

Food and Markets

Aliani (Casa del Parmigiano)
Erberia Rialto, San Polo 214/8.
Map 3 A5.
Tel 041 520 6525.

Drogheria Mascari
Calle dei Spezieri,
San Polo 381.
Map 3 A5.
Tel 041 522 9762.

Rizzo
Salizzada S. Giovanni Grisostomo, Cannaregio 5778.
Map 3 B5.
Tel 041 522 2824.

Glass

L'Isola – Carlo Moretti
Campo San Moisè,
San Marco 1468.
Map 7 A3.
Tel 041 523 1973.

Marina e Susanna Sent
Campo S. Vio,
Dorsoduro 669.
Map 6 F4.
Tel 041 520 81 36.

Perle e Dintorni
Calle della Mandorla,
San Marco 3740.
Map 7 A2.
Tel 041 346 588 1618.

Venini
Piazzetta dei Leoncini,
San Marco 314.
Map 7 B2.
Tel 041 522 4045.

Clothing and Accessories

Armani
Calle Goldoni,
San Marco 4412.
Map 7 A2.
Tel 041 523 4758.

Benetton

Marzaria (Merceria) Due Aprile, San Marco 5051.
Map 7 B2.
Tel 041 296 0493.

Giovanna Zanella
Calle Carminati, Castello 5641. **Map** 7 B1.
Tel 041 523 5500.

Gucci
Calle Larga XXII Marzo,
San Marco 2102.
Map 7 A3.
Tel 041 241 3968.

Max Mara
Campo San Salvador,
San Marco 5033.
Map 7 A1.
Tel 041 522 6688.

Missoni
Calle Vallaresso, San Marco 1312. **Map** 7 B3.
Tel 041 520 5733.

Promod
Campo S. Bartolomeo,
San Marco 5377.
Map 7 B1.
Tel 041 241 0668.

Roberto Cavalli
Calle Vallaresso,
San Marco 1314.
Map 7 B3.
Tel 041 520 5733.

Masks and Costumes

Ca' Macana
Calle delle Botteghe,
Dorsoduro 3172.
Map 6 D3.
Tel 041 520 32 29.

Leon d'Oro
Calle Frezzeria, San Marco 1770. **Mwap** 7 A2.
Tel 041 520 3375.

Il Pirata
Salizzada San Canciano,
Cannaregio 5559.
Map 3 B5.
Tel 041 520 6529.

Papier Mâché
Calle Lunga Santa Maria Formosa, Castello 5175.
Map 7 C1.
Tel 041 522 9995.

Tragicomica
Calle dei Nomboli, San Polo 2800. **Map** 6 F1.
Tel 041 721 102.

Jewelry

Attombri
Sottoportego degli Orefici, San Polo 74.
Map 3 A5.
Tel 041 521 2524.

Bulgari
Calle Larga XXII Marzo,
San Marco 2282.
Map 7 A3.
Tel 041 241 0553.

Cartier
Mercerie San Zulian,
San Marco 606.
Map 7 B2.
Tel 041 522 2071.

Nardi
Procuratie Nuove, Piazza San Marco, San Marco 69/71.
Map 7 B2.
Tel 041 522 5733.

Fabric and Interior Design

Epicentro
Calle Frezzeria,
San Marco 1728/A.
Map 7 B2.
Tel 041 523 34 92.

Marchiol
Ruga Giuffa, Castello 4920. **Map** 7 C1.
Tel 041 522 5131.

Rubelli
Campiello del Teatro,
San Marco 3877.
Map 6 F2.
Tel 041 523 6110.

Trois
Campo San Maurizio,
San Marco 2666.
Map 6 F3.
Tel 041 522 2905.

TSL Tessile San Leonardo
Rio Terrà San Leonardo,
Cannaregio 1318.
Map 2 D3.
Tel 041 718 524.

Books and Gifts

Alberto Valese-Ebru
Campiello Santo Stefano,
San Marco 3471.
Map 6 F3.
Tel 041 523 8830.

Daniela Porto
Rio Terrà dei Nomboli,
San Polo 2753.
Map 6 E1.
Tel 041 523 1368.

Libreria Marco Polo
Calle del Teatro Malibran,
Cannaregio 5886/a.
Map 3 B5.
Tel 041 522 63 43.

Mare di Carta
Fondamenta dei Tolentini,
Santa Croce 222.
Map 5 C1.
Tel 041 716 304.

Paolo Olbi
Calle della Mandola,
San Marco 3653.
Map 6 F2.
Tel 041 528 5025.

Signor Blum
Campo San Barnaba,
Dorsoduro 2840.
Map 6 D3.
Tel 041 522 6367.

Venice Pavilion Bookshop
Palazzetto Selva, Giardinetti Reali, San Marco 2.
Map 7 B3.
Tel 041 522 5150.

VENICE STREET FINDER

All the map references given for sights, hotels, and restaurants in Venice refer to this section of the book. The key map below shows which areas of the city are covered by the Street Finder. The first figure of the map reference indicates which map to turn to, and the letter and number that follow are for the grid reference. Standard Italian spelling has been used on all the maps in this book, but when exploring Venice you will find that the names on many street signs are written in Venetian dialect. Mostly this means only a slight variation in spelling (as in the word *Sottoportico/Sotoportego* below), but some names look totally different. For example, the church of Santi Giovanni e Paolo *(see map 3)*, is frequently marked on signs as "San Zanipolo." A further map showing the vaporetto routes follows the street maps.

Recognizing Street Names

The signs for street *(calle)*, canal *(rio)*, and square *(campo)* will soon become familiar, but the Venetians have a colorful vocabulary for the maze of alleys that makes up the city. When exploring, the following may help.

FONDAMENTA S.SEVERO

Fondamenta is a street that runs alongside a canal, often named after the canal it follows.

RIO TERRA GESUATI

Rio Terrà is a filled-in canal. Similar to a *rio terrà* is a *piscina*, which often forms a square.

SOTOPORTEGO E PONTE S.CRISTOFORO

Sottoportico or **Sotoportego** means a covered passageway.

SALIZADA PIO X

Salizzada is a main street (formerly a paved street).

RIVA DEI PARTIGIANI

Riva is a wide *fondamenta*, often facing the lagoon.

RUGAGIUFFA

Ruga is a street lined with shops.

CORTE DEI DO POZZI

Corte means a courtyard.

RIO MENUO O DE LA VERONA

Many streets and canals in Venice often have more than one name: *o* means "or."

0 meters   500

0 yards   500

MURANO
(Inset on maps 3–4)

Key to Street Finder

- Major sight
- Place of interest
- FS Train station
- Vaporetto boarding point
- Traghetto crossing
- Gondola mooring
- Bus terminus
- *i* Tourist information
- Hospital with emergency room
- Police station
- Church
- Synagogue
- Railroad line

Scale of map pages

| 0 meters | 150 |
| 0 yards | 150 |

Scale of Murano inset

| 0 meters | 300 |
| 0 yards | 300 |

Aerop
Marco

Venice Vaporetto Routes

The ACTV network runs regular scheduled routes around the city and out to most of the islands. Some routes are circular; others are extended during the peak season. There are also additional lines during the summer months. More details of the different types of *vaporetti* and how to use them are given on pages 634–5.

Key

✈ Airport	▬▬ City center route 1	▬▬ City center route 5.2 (clockwise)	
FS Train station	▬▬ City center route 2 (part seasonal)	▬▬ City center route 6	
🛳 Car ferry	▬▬ City center route 3	▬▬ City center route 7 (seasonal)	
P Car parking lot	▬▬ City center route 4.1 (counterclockwise)	▬▬ City center route 8 (seasonal)	
🚌 Main bus terminal	▬▬ City center route 4.2 (clockwise)	▬▬ City center route 10 (part seasonal)	
O Waterbus stop	▬▬ City center route 5.1 (counterclockwise)	▬▬▬ Night service N	

enella

Venier

Da Mula

Museo

MURANO

Colonna

Faro

Navagero

ero

Celestia

Bacini

CASTELLO

aria

Arsenale

San Pietro

Certosa

Giardini

Sant' Elena

Torcello

Burano

Mazzorbo

Lazzaretto
Nuovo

Punta Vela

Chiesa

Cappannone

Vignole

Forte Massimiliano

Treporti

Punta
Sabbioni

San Nicolò
Ferry-Boat

San Nicolò

LIDO

Lido Santa
Maria Elizabetta

San Servolo

San Lazzaro

Lido Casinò

Chioggia ↓

Lagoon route 9

Lagoon route 12 (part seasonal)

Lagoon route 13

Lagoon route 14

Lagoon route 15

Lagoon route 18 (seasonal)

Lagoon route 19 (seasonal)

Lagoon route 20 (part seasonal)

Lagoon route 22

Terminal route A

Terminal route B

Terminal route O (seasonal)

Terminal route R (part seasonal)

Terminal route 16

Terminal route 17 (car ferry)

Terminal route 21 (seasonal)

THE VENETO AND FRIULI

The Veneto is a region of tremendous contrasts, encompassing the breathtaking natural beauty of the Dolomites, Lake Garda (Italy's largest lake), and the rolling Euganean Hills, and the man-made delights of magnificent ancient cities such as Verona, Vicenza, and Padua. Neighboring Friuli–Venezia Giulia lines the border with Slovenia to the east, taking in the Carnic Hills in the north, the Roman town of Aquileia, and the bustling Adriatic port of Trieste.

The Romans built frontier posts on this fertile land of silt deposits, and these survive today as the cities of Vicenza, Padua, Verona, and Treviso. Strategically placed at the hub of the empire's road network, the cities prospered under Roman rule, but suffered in the wave of Germanic invasions of the 5th century AD.

The region's fortunes revived under the benign rule of the Venetian empire. The medieval cities of the Veneto lay on important trade routes such as the Serenissima, the road connecting the flourishing port cities of Venice and Genoa, and the Brenner Pass, used by commercial travelers crossing the Alps from northern Europe. Wealth from agriculture, commerce, and the spoils of war paid for the beautification of these cities through the building of Renaissance palaces and public buildings, many designed by the Veneto's great architect, Andrea Palladio. His palazzi and villas are telling symbols of the leisured existence once enjoyed by the area's aristocrats.

Today the Veneto is a thriving wine exporter, textile producer, and agricultural center, and Friuli is a focus for new technology, while remaining largely agricultural. Both regions are popular tourist destinations, despite lying a little in the shadow of Venice, and boast an abundant and enchanting variety of attractions.

A leisurely *passeggiata* in one of Verona's ancient streets

◀ The Renaissance Alpini Bridge by Palladio at Bassano del Grappa in the Veneto

Exploring the Veneto and Friuli

The flat landscape of the Veneto plain is dramatically offset by the spectacular Dolomite mountains, which form the northwestern border of the Veneto. Friuli, Italy's most northeasterly region, lies tucked up against Austria to the north and Slovenia to the east. Both the Veneto and Friuli are bordered to the south by the Adriatic, with its beaches and ports, which provide a contrast with the area's gently rolling countryside, the vast stretch of Lake Garda, and the many attractive resorts and ancient towns.

View of Verona from the Teatro Romano

Key

- ━━━ Highway
- ▪ ▪ Highway under construction
- ━━━ Major road
- ━━━ Secondary road
- ┄┄┄ Minor road
- ━━━ Scenic route
- ┄╴┄ Main railroad
- ──── Minor railroad
- ▬▬▬ International border
- ▬▬▬ Regional border
- △ Summit

0 kilometers 25
0 miles 20

For additional map symbols *see back flap*

Getting Around

An extensive railroad network and good bus services make this region easy to explore by public transportation, though only buses operate around Lake Garda. Highways and main roads provide good links between the main cities. The Venice Simplon-Orient-Express train, which operates from London to Venice, offers a novel approach to the area.

The bridge at Cividale del Friuli

A mountain chalet in Cortina d'Ampezzo

Sights at a Glance

1. *Verona pp146–51*
2. Lago di Garda
3. Bassano del Grappa
4. Asolo
5. Castelfranco Veneto
6. *Vicenza pp154–7*
7. *Padua (Padova) pp158–61*
8. Euganean Hills
9. Brenta Canal
10. Treviso
11. Conegliano
12. Belluno
13. Cortina d'Ampezzo
14. Tolmezzo
15. Pordenone
16. Udine
17. Cividale del Friuli
18. Gorizia
19. Aquileia
20. Trieste

VENICE pp88–141

❶ Verona

Verona is a vibrant trading center, the second biggest city in the Veneto region (after Venice), and one of the most prosperous in northern Italy. Its ancient center boasts many magnificent Roman ruins, second only to those of Rome itself, and fine palazzi built of *rosso di Verona*, the local pink-tinged limestone, by the city's medieval rulers. Verona has two main focal points: the massive 1st-century AD Arena, which is still the setting for major events including a large opera festival, and Piazza Erbe with its colorful market. One of the main attractions, however, is the church of San Zeno Maggiore (*see pp154–5*), which boasts unusual medieval bronze door panels: they are carved with extraordinary scenes, some biblical, others on the life of San Zeno.

View of Verona from the Museo Archeologico

Verona's Rulers

In 1263 the Scaligeri began their 124-year rule of Verona. They used ruthless tactics in their rise to power, but once established, the Scaligeri family brought peace to the city. They proved to be relatively just and cultured rulers – the poet Dante was welcomed to their court in 1301, and he dedicated the final part of his epic *Divine Comedy* to the ruling Cangrande I. Today their legacy remains in their ornate tombs and in Castelvecchio.

In 1387 Verona fell to the Visconti of Milan, and a succession of outsiders – Venice, France, and Austria – then ruled the city until the Veneto was united with Italy in 1866.

🏰 Castelvecchio

Corso Castelvecchio 2. **Tel** 045 806 26 11. **Open** 8:30am–7:30pm daily (from 1:30pm Mon, last adm: 45 mins before closing). **Closed** Jan 1, Dec 25 & 26. 📷 🏛 📷

This impressive castle, built by Cangrande II between 1355 and 1375, houses one of the finest art galleries in the Veneto outside Venice.

The first section contains late Roman and early Christian items. The section on medieval and early Renaissance art demonstrates the influence of northern art on local painters: the emphasis is on brutal

Verona's enormous Roman Arena seen from Piazza Brà

Ponte Scaligero, part of the old defense system of Castelvecchio

VISITORS' CHECKLIST

Practical Information

261,000. Via degli Alpini 9 (045 806 86 80). daily. combined churches ticket. Apr: VinItaly wine fair; Jun–Aug: Estate Teatrale Veronese; Nov: International Horse Fair.

w tourism.verona.it

Transportation

Villafranca 9 miles (14 km) SW. Piazzale 25 Aprile.

realism as opposed to serene idealism. The late Renaissance works include a fine collection of 15th-century Madonnas.

Jewelry, armor, swords, and Veronese's *Deposition* (1565) are also on display.

A walkway offers views of the river Adige, the Ponte Scaligero, and the 14th-century statue of Cangrande I from his tomb *(see p152).*

Ponte Scaligero

This medieval bridge was built by Cangrande II between 1354 and 1376. Such is the Veronese affection for the bridge that it was rebuilt after the retreating Germans blew it up in 1945, an operation that involved dredging the river to salvage the masonry. The bridge leads from Castelvecchio to the Arsenal on the north bank, fronted by public gardens.

San Lorenzo

Corso Cavour. **Tel** 045 59 28 13. **Open** daily.

San Lorenzo is one of Verona's lesser-known churches, but is one of the city's most beautiful. Built in 1117 on the remains of a paleo-Christian basilica, the Romanesque exterior, with alternate strips of stone and bricks, is typical of Veronese churches. The bell tower dates to the 15th century, and inside there are some 13th-century frescoes. The church features two unusual cylindrical towers.

Arena

Piazza Brà. **Tel** 045 800 32 04. **Open** 8:30am–7:30pm daily (from 1:30pm Mon, last adm: 1 hr before closing. **Closed** Jan 1, Dec 25 & 26; Jun–Aug: from mid-afternoon on performance days. partial.

Completed in AD 30, this is the world's third-largest Roman amphitheater, after Rome's

Colosseum and the amphitheater at Santa Maria Capua Vetere, near Naples. It could hold almost the entire population of Roman Verona, and visitors came from across the Veneto to watch gladiatorial combats. Since then, the arena has seen executions, fairs, bullfights, and opera productions.

San Fermo Maggiore

Stradone San Fermo. **Tel** 045 59 28 13. **Open** daily.

San Fermo Maggiore is not one but two churches: this is most clearly seen from the outside, where the apse has pointed Gothic elements rising above a sturdy Romanesque base. The lower church, begun in 1065 by Benedictine monks on the site of an earlier sanctuary, has frescoes on the simple arcades.

The more impressive upper church dates from 1313 and is covered with a splendid ship's keel roof. The interior also boasts much medieval fresco work, including a 14th-century section by Stefano da Zevio. Nearby is the Brenzoni mausoleum (c.1440) by Giovanni da Bartolo, and above it a 1426 fresco of the Annunciation by Pisanello (1377–1455).

The 11th-century apse of the lower church of San Fermo Maggiore

Sights at a Glance

① *San Zeno Maggiore (pp154–5)*
② Castelvecchio
③ Ponte Scaligero
④ San Lorenzo
⑤ Arena
⑥ Tomba di Giulietta
⑦ San Fermo Maggiore
⑧ Casa di Giulietta
⑨ Piazza Erbe
⑩ Piazza dei Signori
⑪ Tombs of the Scaligeri
⑫ Sant'Anastasia
⑬ Duomo
⑭ San Giorgio in Braida
⑮ Teatro Romano
⑯ Museo Archeologico
⑰ Giardino Giusti

For keys to symbols *see back flap*

Exploring Verona

Since the days of the Roman Empire, Piazza Erbe – built on the site of the ancient Roman forum – has been the center of Verona. Many of the city's fine palazzi, churches, and monuments are nearly as ancient, several dating from the medieval period.

The fountain, erected in the 14th century at the center of Piazza Erbe

🏛 Piazza Erbe

Piazza Erbe is named after the city's old herb market. Today's stalls, shaded by umbrellas, sell everything from herb-flavored roast suckling pig in bread rolls to succulent fresh-picked fruit and delicious wild mushrooms.

At the northern end of the square is the Baroque **Palazzo Maffei** (1668), surmounted by statues. In front of it rises a column supporting the **Venetian lion** marking Verona's absorption into the Venetian empire (1405). On the west side is the **Casa dei Mercanti**, a largely 17th-century building that dates originally from 1301. Opposite, wall frescoes are still visible above the cafés.

The **fountain** in the middle of the piazza is often overshadowed by the market stalls, though the statue at its center dates from Roman times. It serves as a reminder that this piazza has been used as a marketplace for 2,000 years.

🏛 Piazza dei Signori

Torre dei Lamberti. **Tel** 045 927 30 27.
Open 8:30am–7:30pm daily
(Mar–Oct: to 8:30pm Sat–Thu,
to 11pm Fri). 🎧

In the center of the square is a 19th-century **statue of Dante**, whose gaze seems fixed on the forbidding **Palazzo del Capitano**, once the home of Verona's military

commanders. Beside it is the equally intimidating **Palazzo della Ragione**, the Palace of Reason, or law court; both were built in the 14th century. The courtyard of the law court has a handsome external stone staircase, added in 1446–50. Stunning views of the Alps can be enjoyed from atop the 275-ft (84-m) **Torre dei Lamberti**, which rises from the western side of the courtyard.

Behind the statue of Dante is the **Loggia del Consiglio** (1493), the council chamber. The building is topped by statues of Roman worthies born in Verona: they include Pliny the Elder, the natural historian, and Vitruvius, the architectural theorist.

The square is linked to Piazza Erbe by the Arco della Costa, or the Arch of the Rib, named after the whale rib long ago hung beneath it.

The frescoed Renaissance façade of the Loggia del Consiglio on Piazza dei Signori

🏛 Tombs of the Scaligeri
Via Arche Scaligeri.

Beside the entrance to the tiny Romanesque church of **Santa Maria Antica**, once the parish church of the powerful Scaligeri family, lies a profusion of bizarre tombs of the onetime rulers of Verona.

Over the entrance to the church is the impressive tomb of Cangrande I (died 1329), surmounted by an equestrian statue of the ruler, a copy of the original which is now in Castelvecchio (see p147).

The other Scaligeri tombs are next to the church, behind a wrought iron fence that incorporates the ladder emblem of the family's original name (della Scala, meaning "of the steps"). Towering above the fence are the tombs of Mastino II (died 1351) and Cansignorio (died 1375), splendidly decorated with a profusion of tiny Gothic spires. Other members of the Scaligeri family lie within a series of plainer tombs that stand nearer the church wall.

14th-century Scaligeri tomb

🏛 Sant'Anastasia
Piazza Sant'Anastasia. **Tel** 045 59 28 13.
Open daily. 🎧 ♿ ✉

The huge and lofty church of Sant'Anastasia was begun in 1290. Faded 15th-century frescoes and carved scenes from the life of St. Peter Martyr adorn its Gothic portal.

Inside, there are two holy-water stoups, supported on figures of beggars, known as i gobbi (the hunchbacks). These figures were carved a century apart: the earlier one (on the left) dates from 1495.

The sacristy, off the north aisle, is home to a fine (but damaged) fresco by Pisanello: St. George and the Princess (1433–8).

Romeo and Juliet

The tragic story of Romeo and Juliet, two young lovers from rival families, was written by Luigi da Porto of Vicenza in the 1520s and has inspired countless dramas, films, and ballets.

At the **Casa di Giulietta** (Juliet's house), No. 23 Via Cappello, Romeo is said to have climbed to Juliet's balcony; in reality this is a restored 13th-century inn. Crowds throng to see the simple façade and stand on the small marble balcony. The run-down **Casa di Romeo** is a few streets away, in Via Arche Scaligeri.

The so-called **Tomba di Giulietta** is displayed in a crypt below the cloister of San Francesco al Corso on Via del Pontiere. The stone sarcophagus lies in an extremely atmospheric setting.

Both the Casa and the Tomba di Giulietta are open daily (on Mondays in the afternoon only). There is an admission charge.

The so-called Casa di Giulietta

🏛 Duomo

Piazza Duomo. **Tel** 045 59 28 13. **Open** daily. **Closed** Nov–Feb: Mon. 🅿 ♿ 🅿

Verona's cathedral was begun in 1139 and is fronted by a magnificent Romanesque portal carved by Nicolò, one of the two master masons responsible for the façade of San Zeno *(see pp150–51)*. Here he sculpted the sword-bearing figures of Oliver and Roland, two of Charlemagne's knights, whose exploits were much celebrated in medieval poetry. Alongside them stand evangelists and saints with wide eyes and flowing beards. To the south there is a second Romanesque portal carved with Jonah and the Whale and with comically grotesque caryatids.

The highlight of the interior is Titian's lovely *Assumption* (1535–40), and outside there is a Romanesque cloister in which the excavated ruins of earlier churches are visible. The 8th-century baptistry, or San Giovanni in Fonte (St. John of the Spring), was built from Roman masonry; the marble font was carved in 1200.

🎭 Teatro Romano
🏛 Museo Archeologico

Regaste Redentore 2. **Tel** 045 800 03 60. **Open** 1:30–7:30pm Mon (all day if public hol); 8:30am–7:30pm Tue–Sun. The theater closes early in the afternoon on performance days. **Closed** Jan 1, Dec 25 & 26. 🅿 ♿

This Roman theater was built in the 1st century BC; little survives of the stage area, but the semicircular seating area is largely intact. It offers great views over Verona: in the foreground is the only one of three Roman bridges to have survived, though it was rebuilt after World War II.

A lift carries visitors from the Teatro Romano up the cliffs to the monastery above, now an interesting archaeological museum. The exhibits around the tiny cloister and in the old monks' cells include mosaics, pottery, and glass. There is also a fine bronze bust of the first Roman emperor, Augustus (63 BC–AD 14), who in 31 BC overcame his opponents, including Mark Antony and Cleopatra, to become the sole ruler of the Roman world.

Statuary and formal hedges in the Renaissance Giardino Giusti

🌳 Giardino Giusti

Via Giardino Giusti 2. **Tel** 045 803 40 29. **Open** 9am–8pm daily (Oct–Mar: to 7pm). **Closed** Dec 25. 🅿 ♿

This fine Renaissance garden was laid out in 1580. As with other gardens of the period, there is a deliberate juxtaposition of nature and artifice: the formal lower garden of clipped box hedges, gravel walks, and potted plants contrasts with wilder, natural woods above.

John Evelyn, the English author and diarist who visited Verona in 1661, thought this the finest garden in Europe.

🏛 San Giorgio in Braida

Lungadige San Giorgio. **Tel** 045 834 02 32. **Open** daily. **Closed** during mass.

This lovely domed Renaissance church was begun in about 1530 by Michele Sanmicheli. The altar includes the famous *Martyrdom of St. George* (1566) by Veronese, and above the west door is the *Baptism of Christ*, usually attributed to Tintoretto (1518–94).

The imposing façade of Verona's Duomo, Santa Maria Matricolare

Verona: San Zeno Maggiore

San Zeno, built in 1120–38 to house the shrine of Verona's patron saint, is the most ornate Romanesque church in northern Italy. The façade is adorned with an impressive rose window, marble reliefs, and a graceful porch canopy. The highlight, however, is the fascinating 11th- and 12th-century bronze door panels. A squat tower just north of San Zeno is said to cover the tomb of King Pepin of Italy (777–810).

Nave Ceiling
The nave has a magnificent example of a ship's keel ceiling, so called because it resembles the inside of an upturned boat. This ceiling was constructed in 1386 when the apse was rebuilt.

Altarpiece by Mantegna
The Madonna's halo in Andrea Mantegna's altarpiece of the Virgin and Child with saints (1457–59) echoes the shape of the church's rose window.

VISITORS' CHECKLIST

Practical Information
Piazza San Zeno. **Tel** 045 59 28 13.
Open 8:30am–6pm Mon–Sat,
1–6pm Sun (Nov–Feb: 10am–
1pm, 1:30–5pm Tue–Sat, 12:30–
5pm Sun). **Closed** for mass.
times vary.
w chieseverona.it

★ Cloister (1293–1313)
The arches are rounded Romanesque on one side, pointed Gothic on another.

Bronze Door Panels

The 48 bronze panels of the west doors are primitive but force-ful in their depiction of biblical stories and scenes from the life of San Zeno. Those on the left date from 1030 and survive from an earlier church on the site; those on the right were made after the earthquake in 1137. The panels are the work of three separate craftsmen and are linked with masks. Huge staring eyes and Ottoman-style hats, armor, and architecture feature prominently. Among the scenes, some of which are unclear, are Adam and Eve, Salome dancing for the head of John the Baptist, and a startling Descent into Limbo.

Descent into Limbo   Christ in Glory   Human head

Nave and Main Altar
The plan of the church is modeled on an ancient Roman basilica, the Hall of Justice. The main altar is situated in the raised sanctuary where the judge's throne would have stood.

KEY

① **Former washroom**

② **The bell tower**, started in 1045, reached its present height of 236 ft (72 m) in 1173.

③ **The rose window**, dating from the early 12th century, symbolizes the Wheel of Fortune: figures on the rim show the rise and fall of human luck.

④ **The Romanesque porch** is one of the finest examples of the style in northern Italy. Since 1138 it has shielded biblical bas-reliefs, above the west doors, from the elements.

⑤ **Marble side panels**, which were carved in 1140, depict events from the Life of Christ (to the left of the doors) and scenes from the Book of Genesis (to the right).

⑥ **Striped brickwork** is typical of Romanesque buildings in Verona. Courses of local pink brick are alternated with ivory-colored tufa.

⑦ **The vaulted crypt** contains the tomb of San Zeno, appointed eighth bishop of Verona in AD 362, who died in AD 380.

★ West Doors
Each of the wooden doors has 24 bronze plates nailed on to make the doors look like solid metal. A multicolored bas-relief above them depicts San Zeno, flanked by the people of Verona, vanquishing the devil.

❷ Lago di Garda

Garda, the largest and easternmost of the Italian lakes, borders three regions: Trentino to the north, Lombardy to the west and south, and the Veneto to the south and east. The low-lying countryside around the southern stretches becomes increasingly dramatic farther north, until impressive rocky cliffs, sometimes swathed in pines, hug the shoreline of the northern tip. The numerous sporting facilities, many sights, and splendid scenery of snowcapped mountains help make the lake a favorite summer playground.

VISITORS' CHECKLIST

Practical Information
Brescia, Verona, & Trento.
🛈 Viale Marconi 8, Sirmione (030 91 61 14). Il Vittoriale, Gardone. **Tel** 0365 29 65 11.
Open daily. 🏰 Rocca Scaligera: Sirmione. **Tel** 030 91 64 68.
Open Tue–Sun. 🏰 🗐

Transportation
🚉 Peschiera del Garda, Desenzano del Garda. 🚢 🚌 to all towns.

Eastern tip of Sirmione Peninsula
Beyond the town is a path that follows the rim of the peninsula, passing boiling sulfur springs.

Riva del Garda

Torbole

Riva's waterfront is dominated by a 12th-century fortress. Windsurfers favor this resort because of the consistent off-shore winds.

Limone sul Garda

Tremosine

Malcesine

Campione del Garda

The streets of Malcesine cluster below an imposing medieval castle. A cable car climbs to the summit of Monte Baldo (5,725 ft/ 1,745 m), offering far-reaching views.

Assenza

Tignale

Gardone is noted for its exotically planted park and for Il Vittoriale, the Art Deco villa of the poet Gabriele d'Annunzio, which is filled with curiosities.

Brenzone

Gargnano

Castelletto

Bogliaco

The Republic of Salò was established here by Mussolini in 1943. The cathedral in this elegant town of pastel-painted houses contains a 14th-century altarpiece by Veneziano.

Toscolano Maderno

Gardone Riviera

Salò

Torri del Benaco

Portese

The lake is named after this long-established town.

San Felice del Benaco

Garda

Bardolino

Bardolino gave its name to the well-known red wine.

Manerba Moniga

Peschiera's attractive enclosed harbor and fortress were built by the Austrians in the 1860s, during the Italian Wars of Independence.

Lazise

Padenghe sul Garda

Sirmione

Desenzano

Peschiera del Garda

0 kilometers 5
0 miles 5

Sirmione
A fascinating medieval castle, the Rocca Scaligera dominates the town of Sirmione. At the tip of the peninsula lie Roman ruins.

The hydrofoils, catamarans, and steamers that ply the lake offer glimpses of villas and gardens, which cannot be seen from the coastal road.

Key
••• Steamer route
••• Car ferry

The 16th-century wooden bridge by Palladio at Bassano del Grappa

❸ Bassano del Grappa

Vicenza. 🚐 39,000. 🚆 🚌 **ℹ** Largo Corona d'Italia 35 (0424 52 43 51). 🗓 Thu & Sat am.

This peaceful town lies at the foot of Monte Grappa. The river Brenta is straddled by the graceful Ponte degli Alpini, which was designed in 1569 by Palladio. It is built of timber to allow it to flex when hit by the spring meltwaters. Bassano is well known for its majolica products (decorated and glazed earthenware), some of which are on display in the **Palazzo Sturm**. The town is also synonymous with the popular Italian after-dinner drink, the clear spirit known as *grappa*. It is produced from the lees *(graspa)* left over from wine production; information about the process is given in the **Museo degli Alpini**.

🏛 **Palazzo Sturm**
Via Schiavonetti. **Tel** 0424 52 49 33. **Open** Tue–Sun. 🗓

🏛 **Museo degli Alpini**
Via Angarano 2. **Tel** 0424 50 36 62. **Open** Tue–Sun.

❹ Asolo

Treviso. 🚐 2,000. 🚌 **ℹ** Piazza Garibaldi 73 (0423 52 90 46). 🗓 Sat. 🌐 **asolo.it**

Asolo is beautifully sited among the cypress-clad foothills of the Dolomites. This tiny walled town was once ruled by Queen Caterina Cornaro (1454–1510), the Venetian wife of the King of Cyprus, who poisoned her husband so that Venice would gain Cyprus. Cardinal Pietro Bembo, a poet, coined the verb *asolare* to describe the bittersweet life of enforced idleness she endured in exile here. Among others who fell in love with the narrow streets and grand houses was poet Robert Browning, who named a volume of poems *Asolanda* (1889) after Asolo.

Environs

At Maser, 6 miles (10 km) east of the town, stands the magnificent **Villa Barbaro** *(see pp84–5)*. It was designed by Palladio in about 1555, in conjunction with the artist Veronese, and perfectly blends symmetry and light, airy rooms with sumptuous *trompe l'oeil* frescoes.

🏛 **Villa Barbaro**
Maser. **Tel** 0423 92 30 04. **Open** opening times vary; check website for details. **Closed** Jan 1, Easter, Dec 25. 🗓 🌐 **villadimaser.it**

❺ Castelfranco Veneto

Treviso. 🚐 30,000. 🚆 🚌 **ℹ** Via Francesco M Preti 66 (0423 49 50 00). 🗓 Tue am & Fri am.

Fortified in 1199 by rulers of Treviso as a defense against the neighboring Paduans, the historic core of this town lies within well-preserved walls. In the **Casa di Giorgione**, said to be the birthplace of the painter Giorgione (1478–1511), about whom little is known, there is a museum devoted to his life. Giorgione innovatively used landscape to create mood, adding figures to intensify the atmosphere – for instance in his most famous work, the brooding-ly mysterious but evocative *The Tempest (see p110)*. Another of his few directly attributable works hangs here in the **Duomo**: the *Madonna and Child with Saints Liberal and Francis* (1504).

Environs

About 5 miles (8 km) northeast of the town, at Fanzolo, lies the **Villa Emo** (c.1555). Designed by Palladio, it is a typical example of his work: a cube flanked by two symmetrical wings. Inside there are lavish frescoes by Zelotti.

🏛 **Casa di Giorgione**
Piazza San Liberale. **Tel** 0423 72 50 22. **Open** Tue–Sun. **Closed** pub hols. 🗓

🏛 **Villa Emo**
Via Stazione 5, Fanzolo. **Tel** 0423 47 63 34. **Open** May–Oct: daily (pm only Mon–Sat); Nov–Apr: daily. **Closed** Jan 1, Dec 25, 26, & 31. 🗓 🗓

Fresco (c.1561) by Veronese adorning the Villa Barbaro near Asolo

❻ Street by Street: Vicenza

Vicenza is known as the adoptive city of
Andrea Palladio (1508–80), who started
out as a stonemason and became the most
influential architect of his time. The evolution
of his distinctive style is visible all around the
city. In the center is the monumental basilica
he adapted to serve as the town hall, nearby
is the Teatro Olimpico, and all around are the
palaces he built for Vicenza's wealthy citizens.

Contrà Porti is
bordered by some
of the most elegant
palazzi in Vicenza.

Loggia del Capitaniato
This covered arcade
was designed by
Palladio in 1571.

Palazzo Valmarana Braga
Palladio's impressive building of 1566 is
decorated with giant pilasters and sculpted
scenes. It was not completed until 1680,
100 years after the architect's death.

San Lorenzo

Piazza Stazione

CORSO ANDREA PALLADIO

CONTRA CAVOUR

PIAZZA DE SIGNO

PALLADIO

VIA BATTISTI

C MUSCHERIA

CONTRA PESCHERIE VECCHIE

CONTRA GARIBALDI

CONTRA P LAMPERTICO

PIAZZA DEL DUOMO

CONTRA SAN ANTONIO

CONTRA

Duomo
Vicenza's cathedral
was rebuilt after bomb
damage during World
War II left only the façade
and choir entirely intact.

Andrea Palladio
This memorial to
Vicenza's most
famous citizen is
usually surrounded
by market stalls.

0 meters   2
0 miles   1

Key
— Suggested route

A large hall is all that remains of the 15th-century Palazzo della Ragione.

Torre di Piazza, built in the 12th century, is an impressive 269 ft (82 m) high.

Santa Corona

Teatro Olimpico Museo Civico

COVNTRA S BARBARA

★ **Piazza dei Signori**
Palladio's elegant buildings flank the Piazza dei Signori, including the majestic two-tier colonnades of the 16th-century "Basilica," built around the old Palazzo della Ragione.

The Quartiere delle Barche contains numerous attractive palaces built in the 14th-century Venetian Gothic style.

PIAZZA DELLE BIADE
CONTRA CATENA
C GAZZOLE
PIAZZA DELL ERBE
CONTRA SAN PAOLO
CONTRA PONTE SAN MICHELE
CONTRA PIANCOLI
CONTRA PESCARIA
RETRONE

Ponte San Michele
This elegant stone bridge, built in 1620, provides lovely views of the surrounding town.

La Rotonda
Monte Berico
Villa Valmarana ai Nani

Piazza delle Erbe, the city's market square, is overlooked by a 13th-century prison tower.

Casa Pigafetta
This striking 15th-century house was the birthplace of Antonio Pigafetta, who in 1519 set sail around the world with Magellan.

VISITORS' CHECKLIST

Practical Information
🗺 116,000. 🛈 Piazza Matteotti 12 (0444 32 08 54). 🛒 Tue & Thu.
🎭 May–Jun: concert season; Sep–Oct: theater season; end Jun–early Jul: Concerti in Villa.
W vicenzae.org

Transportation
FS 🚌 Piazza Stazione.

The lion of St. Mark gazing down on Piazza dei Signori

🏛 Piazza dei Signori
Basilica: **Tel** 0444 32 36 81.
Open for exhibitions only (call tourist office for schedule). 🖼

This square at the heart of Vicenza is dominated by the Palazzo della Ragione, often referred to as the **Basilica**. Its green, copper-clad roof is shaped like an upturned boat with a balustrade bristling with the statues of Greek and Roman gods. The colonnades were designed by Palladio in 1549 as a facing to support the city's 15th-century town hall, which had begun to subside. The Basilica is now used as an exhibition space. Beside it stands the 12th-century Torre di Piazza.

The **Loggia del Capitaniato**, to the northwest, was built by Palladio in 1571: the Loggia's upper rooms contain the city's council chamber.

🏛 Contrà Porti
Contrà (an abbreviation of *contrada*, or district) is the Vicenza dialect word for street. On one side of the Contrà is a series of pretty Gothic buildings with painted windows and ornate balconies, reminiscent of Venice and a reminder that Vicenza was once part of the Venetian empire.

Several elegant Palladian palazzi stand on this street. Palazzo Porto Barbarano (No. 11), Palazzo Thiene (No. 12), and Palazzo Iseppo da Porto (No. 21) illustrate the variety of Palladio's style – all share Classical elements but each is unique. An intriguing detail is that Palazzo Thiene appears to be of stone, but it is in fact built of cheap brick, rendered to look like masonry.

Exploring Vicenza

Vicenza, the great Palladian city and one of the wealthiest cities in the Veneto, is celebrated the world over for its splendid and varied architecture; it also offers the visitor elegant shops and cafés to visit.

Brusazorzi's ceiling fresco in the large entrance hall of the Museo Civico

🏛 Museo Civico

Piazza Matteotti 37–39.
Tel 0444 22 28 11.
Open 9am–5pm Tue–Sun.
🅿 ♿ 🌐 museicivicivicenza.it

This museum is housed in **Palazzo Chiericati** (see p84) by Palladio. Inside is a fresco by Domenico Brusazorzi of a naked charioteer, representing the Sun, who seems to fly over the entrance hall. Among the Gothic altarpieces from churches in Vicenza is Hans Memling's *Crucifixion* (1468–70), the central panel from a triptych whose side panels are now in New York.

Other rooms contain works by the local artist Bartolomeo Montagna (c.1450–1523).

⛪ Santa Corona

Contrà Santa Corona.
Tel 0444 32 36 44. **Open** Tue–Sun.

This Gothic church was built in 1261 to house a thorn donated by Louis IX of France and said to be from Christ's Crown of Thorns. The Cappella Porto houses the tomb of Luigi da Porto, author of *Giulietta e Romeo*, on which Shakespeare based his famous play. Notable paintings include Giovanni Bellini's *Baptism of Christ* (c.1500) and the *Adoration of the Magi* (1573) by Paolo Veronese.

🎭 Teatro Olimpico

Piazza Matteotti 11. **Tel** 0444 22 28 00.
Open 9am–5pm Tue–Sun. **Closed** during performances, Jan 1, Dec 25.
🅿 ♿ 📷

Europe's oldest surviving indoor theater is a remarkable structure, largely made of wood and plaster, and painted to look like marble. Palladio began work on the design in 1579, but he died the year after. His pupil Vincenzo Scamozzi took over the project, completing the theater in time for its opening performance of Sophocles' tragic drama *Oedipus Rex* on March 3, 1585.

Odeon Frescoes
The gods of Mount Olympus, after which the theater is named, decorate the Odeon, a room used for music recitals.

The Anteodeon contains frescoes depicting the theater's opening performance and oil lamps from the original stage set.

Main ticket office

Stage Set
Scamozzi's scenery represents the Greek city of Thebes. The streets are cleverly painted in perspective and rise at a steep angle to give the illusion of great length.

The Auditorium was designed by Palladio to resemble the outdoor theaters of ancient Greece and Rome, such as the Arena at Verona (see p147), with a semicircle of "stone" benches and a ceiling painted to portray the sky.

⛪ San Lorenzo

Piazza San Lorenzo. **Open** daily.

The portal of this church is a magnificent example of Gothic stone carving, richly decorated with the figures of the Virgin and Child, and St. Francis and St. Clare. Inside there are fine tombs and damaged frescoes. The lovely cloister, north of the church, is an attractive, flower-filled haven of calm.

⛪ Monte Berico

Basilica di Monte Berico. **Tel** 0444 55 94 11. **Open** daily (Sun pm only).

Monte Berico is the green, cypress-clad hill to the south of Vicenza to which wealthy residents once escaped, in the heat of summer, to enjoy the cooler air and pastoral charms of their country estates. Today, shady *portici*, or colonnades, adorned with shrines, line the wide avenue linking central

La Rotonda (1550–52), most famous of all Palladio's works

Vicenza to the basilica on top of the hill. The domed basilica itself, built in the 15th century and enlarged in the 18th, is dedicated to the Virgin, who appeared here during the 1426–8 plague to announce that Vicenza would be spared.

The ornate interior contains a moving *Pietà* fresco (1500) by Bartolomeo Montagna, a fossil collection in the cloister, and Veronese's fine painting *The Supper of St. Gregory the Great* (1572) in the refectory.

The Baroque hilltop church, the Basilica di Monte Berico

🏛 Villa Valmarana ai Nani

Via dei Nani 8. **Tel** 0444 32 18 03. **Open** 10am–12:30pm Tue–Fri, 10am–12:30pm, 3–6pm Sat & Sun. **Closed** Nov 6–Mar 9.

The wall alongside the Villa Valmarana, built in 1688 by Antonio Muttoni, is topped by figures of dwarfs (*nani*) which give the building its name.

Inside, the walls are covered with frescoes by Tiepolo, in which the gods of Mount Olympus float about on clouds watching scenes

from the epics of Homer and Virgil. In the separate Foresteria (guesthouse), the 18th-century frescoes depicting peasant life and the seasons, painted by Tiepolo's son Giandomenico, are imbued with an earthy realism.

The villa can be reached by a 10-minute walk from the basilica on Monte Berico. Head downhill along Via Massimo d'Azeglio to the high-walled convent on the right where the road ends, then take Via San Bastiano.

🏛 La Rotonda

Via Rotonda 45. **Tel** 0444 32 17 93. Villa: **Open** Mar 13–Nov 4: Wed & Sat. Garden: **Open** Tue–Sun. villalarotonda.it

With its perfectly regular, symmetrical forms, this villa, also known as the Villa Capra Valmarana, is the epitome of Palladio's architecture (*see pp84–5*) of which there are several fine examples throughout the Veneto.

The design, consisting of a dome rising above a cube, received immediate acclaim for the way it blends perfectly with its surroundings. A pleasant contrast exists between the terracotta roof tiles, the white walls, and the green lawns.

The villa, built in 1550–52, has inspired many copies in cities as far away as London, St. Petersburg, and Delhi. Fans of *Don Giovanni* will enjoy spotting locations used in Joseph Losey's 1979 film.

La Rotonda can be reached by bus from town, or on foot, following the path alongside the Villa Valmarana ai Nani.

The façade statues of stately toga-clad figures are portraits of sponsors who paid for the theater's construction.

The courtyard giving access to the Teatro is decorated with ancient sculptures. These were donated by members of the Olympic Academy, the learned body that built the theater.

Main entrance

❼ Street by Street: Padua

Padua (Padova) is an old university town with an illustrious academic history. Rich in art and architecture, it has two particularly outstanding sights. The magnificent Cappella degli Scrovegni *(see pp160–1)*, north of the city center, is famous for Giotto's lyrical frescoes. Close to the train station, it forms part of the complex incorporating the Eremitani church and museums. The Basilica di Sant'Antonio, which forms the focal point in the southern part of the city, is one of the most popular pilgrimage destinations in Italy.

Palazzo del Capitanio
Built between 1599 and 1605 for the head of the city's militia, the tower incorporates an astronomical clock made in 1344.

Corte Capitaniato, a 14th-century arts faculty (open for concerts), contains frescoes which include a rare portrait of the poet Petrarch.

Ufficio di Turismo

Loggia della Gran Guardia
This fine Renaissance building dating from 1523 once housed the Council of Nobles. It is now used as a conference center.

PIAZZA CAPITANIATO

VIA MONTE DI PIETÀ

VIA SAN CLEMENTE

PIAZZA DEI SIGNORI

VIA MANIN

PIAZZA DEL DUOMO

V GRITI

VIA SONCIN

VIA VANDELLI

★ **Duomo and Baptistry**
The 12th-century baptistry of the Duomo contains one of the most complete medieval fresco cycles to survive in Italy, painted by Giusto de' Menabuoi in 1378.

Piazza dei Signori is bordered by attractive arcades that house small specialty shops, cafés, and old-fashioned wine bars.

The Palazzo del Monte di Pietà has 16th-century arcades and statues enclosing a medieval building.

Key

— Suggested route

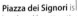

0 meters   75
0 yards   75

Caffè Pedrocchi
Built like a Classical temple, the Caffè Pedrocchi has been a famous meeting place for students and intellectuals since it opened in 1831.

A bronze statue of a woman (1973) by Emilio Greco stands at the center of this largely pedestrianized square.

Stazione Chiesa Degli Eremitiani Cappella Degli Scrovegni Museo Civico

PIAZZA CAVOUR

VIA GORIZIA

PIAZZA DELLE FRUTTA

VIA OBERDAN

PIAZZA DELLE ERBE

VIA VIII FEBBRAIO

PITTA GARZERIA

V SAN CANZIANO

Basilica di Sant'Antonio
Orto Botanico

Padua University
Founded in 1222, this is Italy's second oldest university. Elena Piscopia was the first woman graduate, in 1678.

Palazzo della Ragione, the medieval court of justice, contains magnificent frescoes.

Piazza delle Erbe
There are some excellent views to be had over the marketplace from the 15th-century loggia, which runs alongside the 13th-century Palazzo della Ragione.

🏛 Duomo and Baptistry
Piazza Duomo. Baptistry: **Tel** 049 65 69 14. **Open** 10am–6pm daily. **Closed** Jan 1, Easter, Dec 25. 🚫 ♿

The Duomo was built in 1552, to plans partly by Michelangelo, on the site of an earlier 14th-century cathedral. Beside it stands a domed baptistry (c.1200). The interior is entirely decorated with vibrant frescoes painted by Giusto de' Menabuoi, dating from around 1378. The frescoes depict episodes from the Bible, including scenes of the Creation, the Miracles, the Passion, the Crucifixion, and the Resurrection of Christ.

🏛 Palazzo della Ragione
Piazza delle Erbe (entrance via the town hall). **Tel** 049 820 50 06. **Open** 9am–7pm Tue–Sun (Nov–Jan: to 6pm). **Closed** Jan 1, May 1, Dec 25 & 26. 🚫 ♿

The "Palace of Reason" was built in 1218 to serve as Padua's law court and council chamber. The vast main hall was originally decorated with frescoes by Giotto, but fire destroyed his work in 1420. The Salone is breathtaking in its sheer size. It is the largest undivided medieval hall in Europe, 260 ft (80 m) long, 90 ft (27 m) wide, and 90 ft (27 m) high. Frescoes painted in 1420–25 by Nicola Miretto cover its walls: the 333 panels depict the months of the year, with appropriate gods, signs of the zodiac, and seasonal activities. A 1466 copy of the huge Gattamelata statue *(see p162)* by Donatello stands at one end of the hall.

🏛 Caffè Pedrocchi
Via VIII Febbraio 15. **Tel** 049 878 12 31. **Open** daily. **Closed** Aug. Museum: **Open** Tue–Sun.

Caffè Pedrocchi opened in 1831, and became famous as the café that never closed its doors. Today people come as much to talk, play cards, or watch the world go by as to eat or drink. The upstairs rooms, decorated in Moorish, Egyptian, and other styles, house a museum documenting modern Italian history.

Padua: Cappella degli Scrovegni

Enrico Scrovegni built this chapel in 1303, hoping thereby to spare his dead father, a usurer, from the eternal damnation in hell described by the poet Dante in his *Inferno*. The interior of the chapel is entirely covered with beautiful frescoes of scenes from the life of Christ, painted by Giotto between 1303 and 1305. As works of great narrative force, they exerted a powerful influence on the development of European art.

The Nativity
The naturalism of the Virgin's pose marks a departure from Byzantine stylization, as does the use of natural blue for the sky, in place of celestial gold.

Expulsion of the Merchants
Christ's physical rage, the cowering merchant, and the child hiding his face show an animation that is characteristic of Giotto's style.

The Coretti
Giotto painted the two panels known as the Coretti as an exercise in perspective, creating the illusion of an arch with a room beyond.

View toward altar

| West entrance | North side | Altar | South side | West entrance |

Gallery Guide

Due to the Cappella degli Scrovegni's small size, the number of visitors allowed in at any one time is strictly limited. Prior to entering, visitors are required to spend 15 minutes in a decontamination chamber, where multimedia and multilingual information on the chapel is provided. The visit itself is also restricted to 15 minutes. Advance booking is required, either by phone (049 201 00 20) or online (www. cappelladegliscrovegni.it), with a credit card payment.

Key
- Episodes of Joachim and Anna
- Episodes from the Life of Mary
- Episodes from the Life and Death of Christ
- The Virtues and Vices
- The Last Judgment

For hotels and restaurants in this region see pp562–77 and pp580–605

The Last Judgment
This scene fills the entire west wall of the chapel. Its formal composition is closer to Byzantine tradition than some of the other frescoes, with parts probably painted by assistants. A model of the chapel is shown (center left, at the bottom) being offered to the Virgin by Scrovegni.

View toward entrance

Mary is Presented at the Temple
Giotto sets many scenes against an architectural background, using the laws of perspective to give a sense of three dimensions.

Injustice
The Vices and Virtues are painted in monochrome. Here Injustice is symbolized by scenes of war, murder, and robbery.

Lament over the Dead Christ
Giotto's figures express their grief in different ways: some huddle together, another gestures wildly.

Giotto

The Florentine artist Giotto (1266–1337) is regarded as the father of the Renaissance, the great revival in the Classical traditions of Western art. His work, with its sense of pictorial space, naturalism, and narrative drama, marks a decisive break with the Byzantine tradition of the preceding 1,000 years. Although he was regarded in his lifetime as a great artist, few of the works attributed to him are fully documented. Some may have been painted by others, but his authorship of the frescoes in the Scrovegni Chapel need not be doubted.

Exploring Padua

Padua is a city of many attractions, with a rich history: this is reflected in the major museum complex that occupies a group of 14th-century monastic buildings attached to the church of the Eremitani, a reclusive Augustinian order. Next door is the Cappella degli Scrovegni *(see pp160–1)*. Padua is, in addition, the setting for one of Italy's most important churches – the splendid Basilica di Sant'Antonio – and for one of the earliest universities to be founded in Italy.

15th-century *Angels in Armor* by Guariento, Museo Civico Eremitani

🏛 Chiesa degli Eremitani and Museo Civico Eremitani

Piazza Eremitani 8. **Tel** 049 820 45 50. Museum: **Open** Tue–Sun. 🖼

The Eremitani church, built from 1276 to 1306, contains magnificent roof and wall tombs. Among them is that of Marco Benavides (1489–1582), a professor of law at the city university, whose Renaissance tomb was the work of Florentine architect Ammannati (1511–92). Celebrated frescoes (1454–7) by Mantegna, portraying scenes from the lives of St. James and St. Christopher, were destroyed during a bombing raid in 1944. Two scenes from this magnificent series survive in the Cappella Ovetari, south of the sanctuary: *The Martyrdom of St. James* and *The Martyrdom of St. Christopher*.

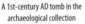

A 1st-century AD tomb in the archaeological collection

The Museo Civico Eremitani comprises a coin collection (which includes rare Roman medallions and an almost complete set of Venetian coinage), an archaeological section, and an art gallery.

The rich archaeological collection contains interesting Roman tombs, fine mosaics, and impressive life-size statues. Renaissance bronzes include the comical *Drinking Satyr* by Il Riccio (1470–1532). The beautiful 14th-century Crucifix from the Cappella degli Scrovegni is in the Quadreria Emo Capodilista, as well as works by Giotto and 15th- to 18th-century paintings from the Venetian and Flemish schools.

🏛 Basilica di Sant'Antonio

Piazza del Santo. **Tel** 049 822 56 52.

This exotic church, with its minaret-like spires and Byzantine domes, is also known as Il Santo. It was built from 1232 to house the remains of St. Anthony of Padua, a preacher who modeled himself on St. Francis of Assisi. Although he was a simple man who rejected worldly wealth, the citizens of Padua built one of the most lavish churches in Christendom to serve as his shrine.

The influence of Byzantine architecture is clearly visible in the basilica's outline: a cone-shaped central dome rises above seven encircling domes; the façade combines Gothic and Romanesque elements.

Inside, the high altar features Donatello's magnificent reliefs (1444–5) on the miracles of St. Anthony, and his statues of the Crucifixion, the Virgin, and Paduan saints. The tomb of St. Anthony, hung with offerings, lies in the north transept; large marble reliefs depicting the saint's life, carved in 1505–77 by various artists, adorn the walls around it. A lively fresco scene of the Crucifixion by Altichiero da Zevio (1380s) adorns the south transept.

🏛 Statue of Gattamelata

Beside the entrance to the basilica stands one of the great works of the Renaissance: a statue of the mercenary soldier Gattamelata. This gritty portrait was created in 1443–52, in honor of a man who during his life did great service to the Venetian Republic. The artist Donatello won fame for the monument, the first equestrian statue made on such a large scale since Roman times.

The Basilica di Sant'Antonio, and Donatello's statue of Gattamelata

⊞ Scuola del Santo and Oratorio di San Giorgio

Piazza del Santo 11. **Tel** 049 822 56 52.
Open daily.

Five excellent frescoes, including the earliest documented paintings by Titian, are to be found in these two buildings. The Scuola del Santo contains two scenes from the life of St. Anthony, which were painted by Titian in 1511. The works in the San Giorgio oratory are by Altichiero da Zevio and Jacopo Avenzo, who painted them in 1378–84.

♣ Orto Botanico

Via Orto Botanico 15. **Tel** 049 827 21 19.
Open daily (Nov–Feb: Mon–Sat am).
ortobotanico.unipd.it

Padua's botanical garden, one of the oldest in Europe (1545), still retains much of its original appearance. The gardens and hothouses were used to cultivate the first lilac trees (1568), sunflowers (1568), and potatoes (1590) to be grown in Italy.

⊞ Palazzo del Bo

Via VIII Febbraio 2. **Tel** 049 827 51 11.
Open for guided tours only. Tue, Thu, Sat am, Mon, Wed, Fri pm. Times vary: call in advance. unipd.it

The historic main university building originally housed the medical faculty, renowned throughout Europe. Among its famous teachers and students was Gabriele Fallopio (1523–62), after whom the Fallopian tubes are named.

Guided tours include the pulpit Galileo used when he taught physics here from 1592 until 1610 and the wooden anatomy theater, built in 1594 and now the oldest surviving medical lecture theater in the world.

The 16th-century anatomy theater in the old medical faculty of the university's Palazzo del Bo, Padua

The Euganean Hills, formed by ancient volcanic activity

❽ Euganean Hills

to Terme Euganee, Montegrotto Terme. Viale Stazione 60, Montegrotto Terme (049 892 83 11).

The conical Euganean Hills, remnants of long-extinct volcanoes, rise abruptly out of the surrounding plain. Hot water springs bubble up out of the ground at Abano Terme and Montegrotto Terme, where scores of establishments offer thermal treatments, ranging from mud baths to immersion in the hot sulfurated waters. Spa cures originated in Roman times; remains of the original baths and theater are still visible at Montegrotto Terme.

⌂ Abbazia di Praglia

Via Abbazia di Praglia 16, Bresseo di Teolo. **Tel** 049 999 93 00. **Open** Tue–Sun (pm only). **Closed** first 2 weeks Jan, religious hols. Donations welcome. praglia.it

The Benedictine monastery at Praglia, 4 miles (6 km) west of Abano Terme, is a peaceful haven in the hills where the monks grow herbs and restore manuscripts. They lead guided tours of parts of the abbey and the church (1490–1548), noted for its beautiful cloister. There are also richly carved stalls in both the choir and the refectory, and paintings and frescoes by Zelotti, a 16th-century painter from Verona.

⊞ Casa di Petrarca

Via Valleselle 4, Arquà Petrarca. **Tel** 0429 71 82 94. **Open** Tue–Sun (also Mon if public hol). **Closed** public hols.

The picturesque town of Arquà Petrarca, on the southern edge of the Euganean Hills, is named after Francesco Petrarca (1304–74). This medieval poet, known in English as Petrarch, spent the final years of his life here, in a house frescoed with scenes from his lyrical poems, overlooking a landscape of olive groves and vineyards. He lies buried in a simple sarcophagus in front of the church.

The Casa di Petrarca (part 14th century) in Arquà Petrarca

⊞ Villa Barbarigo

Valsanzibio. **Tel** 049 805 92 24.
Open Mar–Nov: 10am–1pm, 2pm–sunset daily.

This 18th-century villa north of Arquà boasts one of the finest Baroque gardens in the Veneto, planned by Antonio Barbarigo in 1669. The gardens are a grandiose mix of statuary, fountains, a maze, formal parterres, lakes, and avenues of cypress trees.

The 16th-century Villa Foscari at Malcontenta, beside the Brenta Canal

❾ Brenta Canal

Padua and Venezia. **FS** Venezia Mestre, Dolo, Mira. 🚌 to Mira, Dolo, and Strà. Canal trips on Il Burchiello: Venice. **Tel** 041 241 32 96. **Closed** Jan 25–Feb 7. 🖼
W ilburchiello.it

Over the centuries, in order to prevent the Venetian lagoon silting up, the rivers flowing into it were diverted. The river Brenta was canalized in two sections: the older branch, between Padua and Fusina (just west of Venice), dates back to the 1500s and flows for 22 miles (36 km). Its potential as a transportation route was quickly realized and fine villas were built along its length. Many of these elegant buildings can still be admired today – the S11 road runs alongside most of the canal's length – and several of them are open to the public.

The 18th-century **Villa Nazionale** at Strà has an extravagant frescoed ceiling by Tiepolo. The **Barchessa Valmarana** at Mira (a pretty village) boasts 18th-century decorations. In the village of Malcontenta is **Villa Foscari**, or Villa Malcontenta, one of Palladio's loveliest villas *(see pp84–5)*. It was built in 1560 and the interior decorated with magnificent frescoes by Zelotti.

These villas may also be visited as part of an indulgent 8.5-hour guided tour from Padua, traveling to Venice (or, on alternate days, from Venice to Padua) along the river in a leisurely fashion on board the *Burchiello* motor launch – the cost, however, is fairly prohibitive.

🏛 Barchessa Valmarana

Via Valmarana 11, Mira. **Tel** 041 426 63 87. **Open** Mar–Oct: 10am–6pm Tue–Sun; Nov–Feb: Sat & Sun, groups by appt only. 🖼 🚻 🖂

🏛 Villa Nazionale

Via Pisani, Strà. **Tel** 049 50 20 74. **Open** Tue–Sun. **Closed** Jan 1, May 1, Dec 25. 🖼 🖼 🏠 Fri–Sun (in Italian).

🏛 Villa Foscari

Via dei Turisti 9, Malcontenta. **Tel** 041 547 00 12. **Open** Tue & Sat am. **Closed** Nov–Mar. 🖼

❿ Treviso

🏙 81,700. 🚌 **FS** 🚹 Piazzale Duca D'Aosta 25 (0422 54 76 32). 🚺 Tue & Sat am. **W** turismo.provincia.treviso.it

Despite comparisons with Venice, the lovely fortified city of Treviso has its own very distinctive character.

A good place to start a tour of the streets, some lined with attractive balconied houses, is **Calmaggiore**. The street links the Duomo with the Palazzo dei Trecento, the rebuilt 13th-century town hall. The **Duomo** was founded in the 1100s but rebuilt several times. Inside, Titian's *Annunciation* (1570) vies for attention with the striking *Adoration of the Magi* fresco (1520) by Titian's archrival, Il Pordenone. More paintings by Titian and other artists of the Renaissance may be seen in the **Museo Civico**.

The fish market, which dates from medieval times, is held on an island in the middle of Treviso's river Sile; this allows the remains of the day's trading to be flushed away.

The Dominican church of **San Nicolò**, nestling by the 16th-century city wall, contains interesting tombs and frescoes, including, on a wall of the chapter house, the first-ever depiction of spectacles in art. A magnificent tomb (1500) by Antonio Rizzo is framed by a fresco of pageboys by Lorenzo Lotto.

🏛 Museo Civico

Chiesa di Santa Caterina, Piazzeta Mario Botter 1. **Tel** 0422 54 48 64. **Open** Tue–Sun. **Closed** public hols. 🖼 🚻

The houses of the medieval town of Treviso overlooking ancient canals

The façade and entrance to the Renaissance Palazzo dei Rettori in Belluno

⓫ Conegliano

Treviso. 🚹 35,000. FS 🚌 ℹ️ Via XX Settembre 61 (0438 212 30). 🛍️ Fri.

Conegliano lies among Prosecco-producing vineyards, and wine makers from all over Italy learn their craft at Conegliano's renowned wine school. Via XX Settembre, the arcaded main street, is lined with fine 15th- to 18th-century palazzi, many in the Venetian Gothic style or decorated with fading frescoes. The **Duomo** contains the town's one great work of art, an altarpiece painted by local artist Cima da Conegliano (1460–1518) depicting the *Virgin and Child with Saints* (1493).

Reproductions of Cima's most famous works are on show in the **Casa di Cima**, the artist's birthplace. The detailed landscapes in the background of his paintings were based on the hills around the town; the same views can still be seen from the gardens surrounding the Castelvecchio (old castle).

A mythical statue on Conegliano's theater

🏛️ Casa di Cima
Via Cima 24. **Tel** 0438 21 660. **Open** Sat & Sun, pm only and during temporary exhibitions. 🎨

⓬ Belluno

🚹 36,000. FS 🚌 ℹ️ Piazza Duomo 2 (0437 94 00 83). 🛍️ Sat. 🌐 infodolomiti.it

Picturesque Belluno, capital of Belluno province, serves as a bridge between the two different parts of the Veneto, with the flat plains to the south and the Dolomite peaks to the north. Both are encapsulated in the views to be seen from the 12th-century **Porta Rugo** at the southern end of Via Mezzaterra, the main street of the old town. More spectacular still are the views from the bell tower of the 16th-century **Duomo** (subsequently rebuilt). The nearby baptistry houses a font cover with the figure of John the Baptist carved by Andrea Brustolon (1662–1732). Brustolon's works also grace the churches of San Pietro (on Via San Pietro) and Santo Stefano (Piazza Santo Stefano). North of Piazza del Duomo stands the elegant **Palazzo dei Rettori** (1491) – once home to the town's Venetian rulers – and the 12th-century **Torre Civica**, all that now survives of a medieval castle.

The **Museo Civico** contains paintings by Bartolomeo Montagna (1450–1523) and Sebastiano Ricci (1659–1734), and a notable archaeological section. North of the museum is Belluno's finest square, the **Piazza del Mercato**, with its arcaded Renaissance palaces and its fountain of 1410.

South of the town are the ski resorts of the Alpe del Nevegal; in the summer a chairlift operates from Faverghera up the flank of the mountain to a height of 5,250 ft (1,600 m), offering extensive views.

🏛️ Museo Civico
Piazza Duomo 16. **Tel** 0437 94 48 36. **Open** May–Oct: Tue–Sun; Nov–Apr: Sun–Fri. 🎨 🎥 🏛️

⓭ Cortina d'Ampezzo

Belluno. 🚹 6,800. 🚌 ℹ️ Piazzetta San Francesco 8 (0436 32 31). 🛍️ Tue am & Fri am. 🌐 infodolomiti.it

Italy's top ski resort, much favored by the smart set from Turin and Milan, is well supplied with restaurants and bars. Cortina is set amid the extremely dramatic scenery of the Dolomites (*see pp86–7*), which explains part of the resort's attraction: all around, crags and spires thrust their distinctive weather-beaten shapes above the trees.

Cortina benefits from better-than-average sports facilities, thanks to hosting the 1956 Winter Olympics. In addition to downhill and cross-country skiing, there is also a ski jump and a bobsled run for those who favor something more adventurous than usual, as well as an Olympic ice stadium, several swimming pools, tennis courts, and riding facilities.

During the summer months, Cortina becomes an excellent base for walkers. Useful information on trails and guided walks is available from the tourist office or, during the summer, from the Guides' office opposite.

Corso Italia in Cortina d'Ampezzo, Italy's most important ski resort

Traditional copper pans on display in the Museo Carnico in Tolmezzo

⓮ Tolmezzo

🏠 10,000. 🚌 ℹ️ Via della Vittoria 4 (0433 448 98). 🔵 Mon am.
🌐 turismofvg.it

Tolmezzo is the capital of the Carnia region, named after the Celtic tribe that inhabited the area around the 4th century BC. The town is surrounded by the high peaks of the Carnic Alps, including the pyramidal Monte Amariana (6,253 ft/1,906 m) to the east. The best place to begin a tour of the region is the **Museo delle Arti Popolari**, which has displays of local costumes, crafts, textiles, and agriculture.

Southwest of the town, a scenic road climbs 9 miles (14 km) to the ski resort of **Sella Chianzutan**, a good base for walking in the summer. More resorts line the road, west of Tolmezzo, to **Ampezzo**, at which point a minor road heads north through the gorge of the River Lumiei. Following this road to the Ponte di Buso bridge and the **Lago di**

Sauris is an excellent introduction to the majestic Carnic Alps.

Above this point the road is often impassable in winter, but in summer there are flower-filled meadows all along the road up to Sella di Razzo, and then back along the **Pesarina Valley**, via Comeglians and Ravascletto. Returning south, **Zuglio** was once the Roman town of Forum Iulii Carnicum, guarding the road over the pass. Today it is worth a detour for the remains of its Roman basilica, baths, and forum.

🏛️ **Museo delle Arti Popolari**
Via della Vittoria 2. **Tel** 0433 432 33.
Open Tue–Sun (Aug: daily).
Closed Jan 1, Dec 25. 🎫 ♿ 📷

⓯ Pordenone

🏠 49,000. 🚆 🚌 ℹ️ Via Damiani 2/c (0434 52 03 81). 🔵 Sat am & Wed.
🌐 turismofvg.it

Old Pordenone consists of one long street, the **Corso Vittorio Emanuele**, lined with pretty arcaded houses of pink brick, some with the faded traces of decorative frescoes on their façades. The 13th-century **Palazzo Comunale** forms a striking conclusion to the street, with its eccentrically shaped roofline of curves and minaret-like side towers, and its 16th-century clock tower. Opposite is the **Museo d'Arte**,

housed in the 17th-century Palazzo Ricchieri, where works by the local artist Il Pordenone (1484–1539) are on display.

Around the corner stands the **Duomo**, which contains the lovely altar painting of the *Madonna della Misericordia* (1515) by Il Pordenone. The bell tower beside the Duomo is a fine example of Romanesque decorative brickwork.

🏛️ **Museo d'Arte**
Corso Vittorio Emanuele II 51. **Tel** 0434 39 29 35. **Open** Tue–Sun (pm only Tue–Sat). 🎫 ♿ 📷

⓰ Udine

🏠 99,000. 🚆 🚌 ℹ️ Piazza I Maggio 7 (0432 29 59 72). 🔵 Sat.

Udine is a city of varied and surprising architecture. In the center lies **Piazza della Libertà**, where the Loggia del Lionello (1448–56), built of pink stone in Venetian Gothic style, stands beside the Art Deco Caffè Contarena. Opposite, the Renaissance symmetry of the Porticato di San Giovanni is interrupted by the Torre dell'Orologio (Clock Tower, 1527), crowned by two bronze Moors who strike the hours. Note also the fountain of 1542, the two 18th-century statues, and the column supporting the Lion of St. Mark.

Beyond the **Arco Bollani**, a gateway designed by Palladio in 1556, steps lead up to a 85-ft (26-m) hill that offers sweeping views over the city. On the hill is the 16th-century castle, now the **Musei Civici e Galleria di Storia e Arte Antica**, which houses fine art and archaeology collections.

Southeast of Piazza Matteotti, at the end of Via Savorgnana where a small market is held, stands the **Oratorio della Purità**, and the **Duomo** with its octagonal bell tower. Both contain important paintings and frescoes by Giambattista Tiepolo (1696–1770). More of Tiepolo's work can be seen in the **Palazzo Arcivescovile**, which the artist decorated with frescoes.

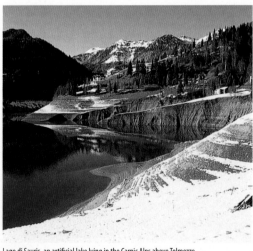

Lago di Sauris, an artificial lake lying in the Carnic Alps above Tolmezzo

The arcaded Porticato di San Giovanni on Piazza della Libertà, Udine

Environs

Outside Codroipo, 15 miles (24 km) west, rises the imposing **Villa Manin**. A road passes through the villa's grounds, so its massive size can be seen even when the house – once the retreat of Ludovico Manin, the last doge of Venice (1725–1802) – and its magnificent gardens are closed to the public.

🏛 Musei Civici e Galleria di Storia e Arte Antica
Castello di Udine. **Tel** 0432 27 15 91. **Open** Tue–Sun. **Closed** Jan 1, Easter, May 1, Dec 25. 🚫 🅰 📷

🏛 Palazzo Arcivescovile
Piazza Patriarcato 1. **Tel** 0432 250 03. **Open** Wed–Sun. **Closed** Jan 1, Easter, Dec 25. 🚫 🅰 📷

🏛 Villa Manin
Passariano. **Tel** 0432 82 12 11. **Open** daily. **Closed** Jan 1, Dec 25. 🚫 for exhibitions only. 🅰

⑰ Cividale del Friuli

🚹 11,000. 🚆 🚌 ℹ Piazza Paolo Diacono 10 (0432 71 04 60). 🚩 Sat. 🌐 cividale.net

A gate in the medieval walls of Cividale leads down the main street and straight to the dramatic ravine of the River Natisone, which is spanned by the arch of the **Ponte del Diavolo** (Devil's Bridge).

Above the river's north bank stands the **Tempietto Longobardo** (Lombardic Chapel), a very rare example of an 8th-century church decorated with reliefs of saints, modeled in stucco. The town's history is traced in the excellent **Museo Archeologico Nazionale**, which contains the excavated remains of buildings from a Roman town, and a collection of Lombardic items including jewelry, ivory, and weapons.

Next door is the **Duomo**, rebuilt in 1453 after a fire, with its beautiful silver altarpiece (13th century). The **Museo Cristiano**, off the south aisle, contains sculptures from the original church: of particular interest is the altar donated by Ratchis, the Lombardic Duke of Friuli and later King of Italy (737–44), which is finely carved with scenes from the Life of Christ. There is in addition the unusual baptismal font of Patriarch Callisto (737–56): this octagonal structure, with a roof supported by pillars, is decorated with symbols of the Evangelists.

⛪ Tempietto Longobardo
Via Monastero Maggiore 34. **Tel** 0432 70 08 67. **Open** daily. 🚫 📷

Interior view of the Tempietto Longobardo in Cividale del Friuli

🏛 Museo Archeologico Nazionale
Palazzo dei Provveditori Veneti, P.za del Duomo 13. **Tel** 0432 70 07 00. **Open** 9am–2pm Mon, 8:30am–7:30pm Tue–Sun. **Closed** Jan 1, Dec 25. 🚫 🅰

🏛 Museo Cristiano
Via Condotti 1. **Tel** 0432 73 04 03. **Open** Jun–Sep daily, Oct–May Wed–Sun. **Closed** Jan 1, Dec 25. 🚫 🅰

⑱ Gorizia

🚹 37,000. 🚆 🚌 ℹ Corso Italia 9 (0481 53 57 64). 🚩 Thu, Fri. 🌐 turismofvg.it

Gorizia was at the center of fierce fighting during both world wars and was split in two by the 1947 Treaty of Paris, leaving part in Italy, part in Yugoslavia (now Slovenia).

The town's arcaded streets and pastel-painted houses have been carefully restored following substantial damage during World War II. The modern Museo Provinciale della Grande Guerra (Museum of the Great War), housed in the basement of the **Museo Provinciale**, provides a fascinating introduction to the realities of war. Videos, photographs, and life-size mock-ups of trenches, latrines, and gun emplacements are used to show the waste, squalor, and heroism of war.

The Lion of Venice above the entrance to Gorizia's castle

Rooms on the upper floor of the museum house temporary exhibitions and items from the town's art collection, which includes works by local artists.

On a mound nearby rises the castle, encircled by 16th-century fortifications. From here there are extensive views stretching over the town.

Environs

Southwest of Gorizia, scenic country roads pass through the foothills of the **Carso**, a limestone plateau stretching down to Trieste. The plateau is dotted with fields enclosed by drystone walls and gouged with tunnels, caves, and underground rivers.

🏛 Museo Provinciale
Borgo Castello 13. **Tel** 0481 53 39 26. **Open** Tue–Sun. **Closed** Dec 25. 🚫 📷

The attractive harborside at Grado, along the coast south of Aquileia

⑲ Aquileia

3,300. Piazza Capitolo 4 (0431 91 087). Tue.

Aquileia, now little more than a village but encircled by the ruins of palatial villas, baths, temples, and market buildings, provides a poignant reminder of the lost splendor of the Roman Empire.

It was here that Emperor Augustus received Herod the Great, King of Judea, in 10 BC, and it was here too, in AD 381, that the early Christian church held a major council attended by the learned saints Ambrose and Jerome to settle doctrinal issues. In the 5th century, however, the town was abandoned following several sackings. Fortunately, substantial parts of the early Christian basilica have survived, which contain the town's particular treasure: ornate floor mosaics.

🏛 Basilica
Piazza Capitolo. **Tel** 0431 910 67. **Open** daily. **Closed** during mass. Crypt

The basilica was founded in about AD 313 and much of the original structure still survives, including the magnificent floor mosaics of the nave and **Cripta degli Scavi** below. The designs are a mixture of geometric patterns, biblical stories, and scenes from everyday life in ancient Aquileia. There is a lively portrayal of the tale of Jonah, who was swallowed by an extraordinary sea monster: the fishing boats are also surrounded by a rich array of creatures from the deep, including wide-eyed dolphins and squid.

🏛 Museo Archeologico Nazionale
Via Roma 1. **Tel** 0431 910 16. **Open** 8:30am–7:30pm Tue–Sun. 🖾 📧 W museoarcheo-aquileia.it

The mosaics in the basilica demonstrate a tradition of craftsmanship that flourished in the city from the 2nd century AD. Additional examples of mosaics and stone carvings from the Classical era (1st to 3rd centuries) are on display in this museum, together with glass, amber, and a collection of flies, beautifully worked in gold, that formed the adornment of a Roman matron's veil.

🏛 Museo Paleocristiano
Località Monastero. **Tel** 0431 911 31. **Open** 8:30am–1:45pm Tue–Sun. **Closed** Jan 1, May 1, Dec 25. 🖾 📧 📧

This museum, which stands not far from Aquileia's ancient harbor beside the once-navigable River Natissa, focuses on the development of art during the early Christian era.

Environs
South of Udine, **Palmanova** is worth a visit for its remarkable octagonal layout and intact walls. The town was built in 1593 by the Venetians to commemorate the Battle of Lepanto.

Grado sits on a group of low islands in the middle of the Adriatic lagoon, attached to the mainland by a narrow causeway. The town grew into a port for Aquileia in the 2nd century and was used as a haven by Aquileia's citizens during the barbarian invasions. Today, Grado is a popular seaside resort. At the center of the old town is the **Duomo**, which contains 6th-century frescoes in the apse, similar to those on the vaults of San Marco in Venice (see pp114–17). Nearby, in the church of **Santa Maria delle Grazie**, there are more 6th-century mosaics.

Symbolism in Early Christian Art

Christians were persecuted until their religion was granted official status by Constantine the Great in AD 313. Prior to this they had developed a language of secret symbols to express their beliefs, many of which can be seen in the mosaics and marble tomb chests of Aquileia. Many of these and other symbols later found their way into popular bestiaries and folk art.

Part of the 4th-century floor mosaic in the basilica at Aquileia

The Winged Figure of Victory holding a laurel wreath was a Classical symbol of triumph and holiness. Later, it came to represent Christ's resurrection, and more generally, victory over death.

⑳ Trieste

🏙 218,000. ✈ 🚉 🚌 ℹ Piazza Unità D'Italia 4/b (040 347 83 12). 📅 Tue–Sat. 🌐 **turismofvg.it**

Trieste is an atmospheric city, tucked up next to Slovenia, with a long, bustling harbor lined with handsome buildings and lapped by the waves of the Adriatic Sea.

🏛 Acquario Marino

Molo Pescheria 2. **Tel** 040 30 62 01. **Open** 9am–7pm Tue–Sun (Nov–Mar: to 1pm). 🚫 ♿

The aquarium, one of Trieste's most popular attractions, contains examples of the fascinating marine life in the Adriatic.

🏰 Castello di San Giusto

Pza Cattedrale 3. **Tel** 040 30 93 62. **Open** daily. Castle: 9am–7pm (Nov–Mar: to 5pm); museums: 9am–1pm. 🚫

Up above the harbor stands a hilltop castle built by Trieste's Venetian governors from 1368. It is set on a terrace that offers sweeping views over the Gulf of Trieste. The castle houses two

The Castello di Miramare on the bay of Trieste

museums containing Roman mosaics, and a collection of weapons and armor.

🏰 Basilica Paleocristiana

Via Madonna del Mare 11. **Tel** 040 436 31. **Open** daily (by appointment only).

Beside the castle lie the substantial ruins of the Roman basilica or law court built around AD 100. Note the stone magistrates' bench and throne.

🏰 Duomo

Pza Cattedrale 2. **Tel** 040 30 96 66. **Open** daily. ♿

In the church of **San Giusto**, the city's Duomo, magistrates' bench and throne of the Roman basilica were reinterpreted to become the seat of the bishop and clergy. Because the building was formed in the 14th century by linking two 5th-century churches that stood side by side, there are two thrones and benches here. The two apses are decorated with very fine 13th-century mosaics in the Venetian style.

🏛 Museo di Storia ed Arte ed Orto Lapidario

Piazza della Cattedrale 1. **Tel** 040 31 05 00. **Open** 10am–5pm Tue–Sun. **Closed** public hols. 🚫

The important archaeological collection here provides fascinating evidence of Trieste's extensive trade links with the ancient Greek world.

13th-century mosaics in the apse of San Giusto, Trieste's Duomo

Environs

From **Villa Opicina**, just north of Trieste, sweeping views may be had over the city, its bay, and south down the coast of Slovenia. A little beyond, at Borgo Grotta Gigante, lies the **Grotta del Gigante**, a huge cavern filled with stunning "organ pipe" formations and tall columns of stalagmites.

At Grignano, 5 miles (8 km) northwest of the city, stands the **Castello di Miramare**, a white castle set in lush green gardens beside the sparkling blue Adriatic. It was built by the Habsburg Archduke Maximilian in 1856–60 as his summer retreat, a few years before he was assassinated in Mexico. It is still furnished in contemporary style.

🕳 Grotta del Gigante

Borgo Grotta Gigante 42a. **Tel** 040 32 73 12. **Open** Tue–Sun (Jul & Aug: daily). 🚫 📷

🏰 Castello di Miramare

Viale Miramare, Grignano. **Tel** 040 22 41 43. **Open** daily. ♿ 🚫 (castle).

The Tortoise hiding in his shell represented darkness and ignorance, while the cockerel, who crows at dawn, signified light and enlightenment.

ICHTHUS, or fish, was an acronym for Iesous CHristos THeou Uios Soter – Jesus Christ, Son of God, Savior, in ancient Greek.

Colorful birds, such as peacocks, symbolized immortality and the glorious transformation of the soul when it arrives in Heaven.

TRENTINO–ALTO ADIGE

The Italian-speaking Trentino – named after Trento, the regional capital – and the German-speaking Alto Adige or Südtirol (South Tyrol, the region bordering the upper reaches of the River Adige) differ dramatically in culture. However, they do share one feature in common: the majestic Dolomites that form the backdrop to every town and village, covered in snow for three months of every year and carpeted with exquisite Alpine plants for another three.

The region's mountains have been cut by glaciers into a series of deep, broad valleys. Many of these face south, so it remains unusually warm and sunny, even in winter. Travelers have passed up and down these valleys for generations – as confirmed by the extraordinary discovery, in 1991, of a 5,000-year-old man's body emerging from the surface of a melting glacier in Alto Adige. The frozen corpse wore leather boots, stuffed with hay for warmth, and was armed with a copper ice pick.

The paths that Neolithic man once trod became major road networks under the Romans, when many of the region's cities were founded. By the Middle Ages, Alto Adige had established its very own distinctive culture under the Counts of Tyrol, whose land (later appropriated by the Habsburgs) straddled both sides of today's Italian/Austrian border. The Tyrolean nobility built the castles that still line the valleys and the mountain passes, in order to protect travelers from brigands.

Another ancient legacy is the tradition of hospitality to be found in the numerous guest houses along the valleys. Many of these are built in the distinctive Tyrolean style, with beautiful timber balconies for making the most of the winter sun, and overhanging roof eaves to keep snow at a distance. Cozy in winter, with log fires and warming food, and offering marvelous views, they make the ideal base for enjoying the region's mountain footpaths and ski slopes.

Skiers enjoying the slopes around Monte Spinale, near Madonna di Campiglio, in Trentino

◀ Trekkers climbing the glowing peaks of the Rosengarten mountain range in the Dolomites, South Tyrol

Exploring Trentino–Alto Adige

Trentino–Alto Adige is a region where unspoiled nature is complemented by a wealth of sporting opportunities. The tributary valleys feeding into the Adige valley contain lakes, rivers, and streams, and also woodland, vineyards, and Alpine pasture full of butterflies, birds, and flowers. Southeast of the region rise the distinctive limestone peaks of the Dolomites, while further north the area becomes more mountainous still, enclosed finally by the splendid heights of the Alps.

Via Ponte Aquila in Bressanone

Sights at a Glance

1 Malles Venosta (Mals im Vinschgau)
2 Merano (Meran)
3 Vipiteno (Sterzing)
4 Brunico (Bruneck)
5 Bressanone (Brixen)
6 Bolzano (Bozen)
7 Ortisei (Sankt Ulrich)
8 Canazei
9 Cavalese
10 San Martino di Castrozza
11 Cembra
12 Madonna di Campiglio
13 Trento
14 Rovereto
15 Castello di Avio

Key

━━ Highway	── Minor railroad
━━ Major road	━━ International border
── Secondary road	── Regional border
┄┄ Minor road	△ Summit
── Scenic route	
┅┅ Main railroad	

For additional map symbols *see back flap*

Landeck
Passo di Resia
Resia
Melago
Moso in Pass
Lago di Resia
Curon Venosta
l'Altissima 3480m
Abbazia di Monte Maria
Alpi Venoste
Senales
MALLES VENOSTA 1
Monte Alto 3260m
Tiro
MERANC
Glorenza
Castel Coira
Silandro
Adige
Prato allo Stelvio
Laces
Guardia Alta 2608m
Lan
Passo dello Stelvio
Trafoi
Solda
TRE
Bormio
Ortles 3899m
Santa Gertrude
Senale
Monte degli 2656m
Monte Cevedale 3757m
Marcena
Malosc
Bagni di Rabbi
Revò
Pejo
ALTC
Dimaro
Cles
Tuenno
Derr
Vermiglio
Noce
Sondrio
MADONNA DI CAMPIGLIO 12
Mezzolombardo
Sarca
Pinzolo
Cima Brenta 3150m
Andalo
Adamello
Cascate di Nardis
Cima Tosa 3159m
Lago di Molvenno
Paganella 2125m
Stenico
Vezzano
TRENTO
Re di Castello 2889m
Tione di Trento
Sarche
Vason
Lardaro
Dro
Calliano
Monte Cadria 2254m
Tenno
Arco
Cas Bese
Tiarno
Valli Giudicarie
Riva del Garda
ROVERETO 14
Storo
Torbole
Ruina Dantesc
Brentonico
S12
Raossi
CASTELLO DI AVIO 15
Ala
A22
Verona

0 kilometers 25
0 miles 10

The Val di Funes, South Tyrol

View of the Dolomites from Madonna di Campiglio

Getting Around

The region's main artery is the Brenner Pass road: it runs from Austria in the north, following the River Adige from Bolzano to Trento, and southward on to Verona. Both the highway and the main road beside it are among the busiest in Europe, and the valley roads can also be congested during the ski season. Winter driving can be hazardous, requiring special tires and snow chains. An excellent railroad and bus network serves the whole area.

Abbazia di Monte Maria, founded in the 12th century, near Malles Venosta

❶ Malles Venosta

Mals Im Vinschgau

🏔 4,600. FS 🚌 *i* Via San Benedetto 1 (0473 83 11 90). 🛍 Wed. **w** altavenosta-vacanze.it

Malles Venosta sits in high border country, close to Switzerland and Austria, and was a customs point during the Middle Ages. The town has several Gothic churches, whose spires and towers create an appealing skyline, mirroring the jagged peaks that rise all around. The oldest is the tiny church of **San Benedetto**, a 9th-century Carolingian building on Via San Benedetto, with frescoes of its patrons.

Environs

The medieval **Castel Coira** (Churburg) rises at Sluderno (Schluderns), 2.5 miles (4 km) southeast of Malles. It contains an excellent collection of weapons and armor.

Clinging to the mountainside above the town of Burgusio (Burgeis), 3 miles (5 km) north of Malles, is the Benedictine **Abbazia di Monte Maria** (Marienberg), founded in the 12th century but enlarged in the 18th and 19th. The church's crypt shelters an outstanding series of 12th-century frescoes.

The glorious medieval town of **Glorenza** lies just 1 mile (2 km) south of Malles.

🏰 Castel Coira
Churburg, Sluderno. **Tel** 0473 61 52 41. **Open** Mar 20–Oct: Tue–Sun (& Mon if pub hol). 📷 compulsory. 🎒

🏰 Abbazia di Monte Maria
Tel 0473 83 13 06. **Open** May–Oct: Mon–Sat; Nov–Apr: groups by appt only. **Closed** public hols. 🎒 🚫

❷ Merano

Meran

🏔 35,000. FS 🚌 *i* Corso della Libertà 45 (0473 27 20 00). 🛍 Tue, Fri. **w** merano.eu

Merano is an attractive spa town popular with Austrians, Germans, and Italians. On Corso Libertà, a street of stylish shops and hotels, stands the **Kurhaus** or Spa Hall built in 1914, now a concert venue. Furnished in period style, the 15th-century **Castello Principesco** was home to the Habsburg Archduke Sigismund. Inviting gardens line the River Passirio, which winds

The Art Nouveau façade of the Kurhaus in Merano

its way through the town. The Passeggiata Lungo Passirio d'Inverno (Winter Walk) follows the north bank to the Roman bridge, Ponte Romano; the Passeggiata d'Estate (Summer Walk) on the south bank leads to the medieval Ponte Passirio.

Environs

The romantic 12th-century **Castel Tirolo** lies 2.5 miles (4 km) to the north. It hosts a museum of Tyrolean history.

The grounds of **Castel Trauttmansdorff** house a fascinating botanical garden.

🏰 Castello Principesco
Via Galilei. **Tel** 3290 18 63 90. **Open** Tue–Sun & public hols. **Closed** Jan–Feb. 🎒 🚫

🏰 Castel Tirolo
Via Castello 24, Tirolo. **Tel** 0473 22 02 21. **Open** mid Mar–Nov: Tue–Sun. **Closed** Dec–mid-Mar. 🎒 ♿ 🏛 💺

🏰 Castel Trauttmansdorff
Via S. Valentino 51a. **Tel** 0473 27 01 72. **Open** Apr 1–Nov 15: daily. 🎒 🔔 🚫 🍴 **w** touriseum.it

❸ Vipiteno

Sterzing

🏔 5,600. FS 🚌 *i* Piazza Città 3 (0472 76 53 25). 🛍 daily.

Surrounded by mineral-rich valleys, Vipiteno is very Tyrolean in feel. On Via Città Nuova, lined with fine mansions, rise the Gothic **Palazzo Comunale**, containing Renaissance sculpture and paintings, and the Torre dei Dodici, the symbol of the town. Wood carvings in the **Museo Multscher** are by Hans Multscher; the Bavarian sculptor came to Vipiteno in 1456–8 to carve the altar for the parish **church**, which lies just south of the town.

To the west, the charming **Val di Racines** includes waterfalls and a natural rock bridge.

🏛 Palazzo Comunale
Via Città Nuova 21. **Tel** 0472 72 37 00. **Open** Mon–Fri. **Closed** Fri pm & public hols.

🏛 Museo Multscher
Via della Commenda 11. **Tel** 0472 76 64 64. **Open** Apr–Oct: Tue–Sat. **Closed** public hols. 🎒

The medieval castle dominating the town of Brunico

❹ Brunico

Bruneck

🏠 13,000. 🚊 🚌 *i* Piazza Municipio 7 (0474 55 57 22). 🛒 Wed. 🌐 **bruneck.com**

This attractive town, overlooked by the imposing form of its medieval **castle**, retains 14th-century fortifications and a network of narrow streets that can only be explored on foot. The church of **St. Ursula**, to the northwest of St. Ursula's Gate, holds a series of outstanding mid-15th-century altar reliefs of the Nativity. The **Museo Etnografico di Teodone** offers displays of traditional agricultural life and local costumes; this folklore museum also provides an ideal opportunity to visit a 16th-century farmhouse and barn.

St. Ursula's Gate sundial, Brunico

🏛 **Museo Etnografico di Teodone**
Via Duca Teodone 24, Teodone. **Tel** 0474 55 20 87. **Open** Easter–Oct: Tue–Sat, Sun, & pm on public hols (Aug: also Mon). 🚗 ♿ 🖊

❺ Bressanone

Brixen

🏠 18,000. 🚊 🚌 *i* Via Ratisbona 9 (0472 83 64 01). 🛒 Mon. 🌐 **brixen.org**

The narrow medieval alleys of Bressanone cluster around the cathedral and the palace of the prince-bishops who ruled the town for much of its history. The **Duomo**, on Piazza del Duomo, was rebuilt in the

18th century but retains its 12th-century cloister, decorated with superb 15th-century frescoes. The lavish interiors of Palazzo Vescovile, the bishops' Renaissance palace, house the **Museo Diocesano**. It contains precious items from the Middle Ages, as well as the **Museo dei Presepi**, with its collection of wooden Nativity figurines that are carved locally.

Environs
At Velturno (Feldthurns), just 5 miles (8 km) southwest, stands the Renaissance **Castello di Velturno**, the summer retreat of the rulers of Bressanone noted for its frescoed rooms. A little over 2 miles (3 km) north of Bressanone lies the **Abbazia di Novacella**,

a picturesque group of fortified monastic buildings with an outstanding series of cloister frescoes. Further north up the valley, at **Rio di Pusteria** (Mühlbach), the remains of a 16th-century fortified barrier can be seen to the east of the town. The barrier funneled ancient travelers through the customs post that divided Tyrol from the Görz district.

High above Rio di Pusteria, to the southeast, looms the massive outline of the **Castello di Rodengo** (Rodeneck). The castle contains wonderful 13th-century frescoes showing battle scenes, the Last Judgment and courtly episodes from the *Iwein* romance by Hartmann von Aue, the medieval poet.

🏛 **Museo Diocesano & Museo dei Presepi**
Piazza Palazzo Vescovile 2. **Tel** 0472 83 05 05. Museo Diocesano **Open** 10am–6pm Tue–Sun (Jul–Sep: 7pm–midnight). **Closed** Nov–mid-Mar. Museo dei Presepi **Open** mid-Mar–Oct: 10am–6pm Tue–Sun (Dec–Jan 6: to 5pm). **Closed** Dec 24 & 25. 🖊

🏰 **Castello di Velturno**
Velturno. **Tel** 0472 85 55 25. **Open** Mar–Nov: Tue–Sun. 🎟 only. 🖊

🏰 **Abbazia di Novacella**
Via Abbazia 1/2b, Varna. **Tel** 0472 83 61 89. **Open** Mon–Sat. **Closed** Mon (Jan–Mar) & public hols. 🎟 only. 🖊

🏰 **Castello di Rodengo**
Rodengo. **Tel** 0472 45 40 56. **Open** May–mid-Oct: Sun–Fri. 🎟 🖊

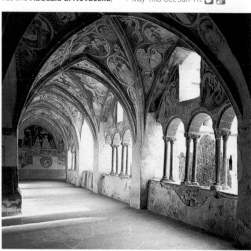

The cloisters of Bressanone Duomo with their 15th-century frescoes

The Baroque interior of the church of St. Ulrich in Ortisei

❻ Bolzano

Bozen

🏛 98,000. FS 🚌 ℹ️ Piazza Walther 8 (0471 30 70 00). 🛒 Sat.
🌐 bolzano-bozen.it

Bolzano, the capital of the Alto Adige, is the gateway between the Italian-speaking Trentino region and the German-speaking Alto Adige, or Südtirol, and has a marked Tyrolean atmosphere. The old center, **Piazza Walther**, is dominated by the 15th-century Gothic **Duomo**, with its multicolored mosaic-patterned roof and elaborate spire.

The "wine door" inside the Duomo is carved with figures at work among vines and reflects the importance of wine to the local economy. In the middle of Piazza Walther is a statue of Walther von der Vogelweide, the 13th-century troubadour – born, according to legend, in this area. North of the square, the streets are lined with houses adorned with intricate gables, balconies, and oriel windows. The outdoor market, starting at Piazza Grano, forms an inviting array of local produce that continues along the arcaded Via dei Portici. The modern **Museo Archeologico** houses impressive finds from the Stone Age, the Bronze Age, the Iron Age, Roman times, and the time of Charlemagne. A key exhibit is

The Duomo spire, Bolzano

Ötzi, the famous 5,000-year-old "Iceman." The **Chiesa dei Domenicani** (Dominican church), on Piazza Domenicani, has 14th-century *Triumph of Death* frescoes and a frescoed cloister.

🏛 Museo Archeologico
Via Museo 43. **Tel** 0471 32 01 00.
Open Tue–Sun (Jul, Aug, & Dec: daily).
Closed Jan 1, May 1, Dec 25. 🚫 📷
📷 🌐 iceman.it

❼ Ortisei

Sankt Ulrich

🏛 4,500. 🚌 ℹ️ Via Rezia 1 (0471 77 76 00). 🛒 Fri. 🌐 valgardena.it

Ortisei is the prosperous main resort for the pretty Val Gardena and Alpe di Siusi region, and a major center for woodcarving; examples of local craftsmanship may be seen in local shops, in the **Museo della Val Gardena** (which also focuses on local

archaeology), and in the church of **St. Ulrich**.

To the south is the **Alpe di Siusi** (Seiser Alm) region, noted for its Alpine meadows, balconied farmsteads, and onion-domed churches. The best way to explore this beautiful area is by cableway from Ortisei: to the northeast another cable car runs to 8,260-ft (2,518-m) high Monte Seceda, and walks from here lead into the Odle Dolomites.

🏛 Museo della Val Gardena
Via Rezia 83. **Tel** 0471 79 75 54.
Open Jan–Mar: Tue–Fri; mid-May–Oct: Mon–Fri; Jul & Aug: daily.
🌐 museumgherdeina.it

❽ Canazei

🏛 1,800. 🚌 ℹ️ Piazza Marconi 5 (0462 60 96 00). 🛒 Sat (Jul–Sep).
🌐 fassa.com

Located at the base of some of the highest and most awe-inspiring groups of peaks, Canazei is a good base for exploring the Dolomites. In summer, chairlifts climb to viewpoints where the beauty of the encircling mountains can be appreciated to the full. The most popular viewpoints are Pecol and Col dei Rossi, reached by the Belvedere cableway from Via Pareda in Canazei: the cliffs of the Sella group are visible to the north, with Sasso Lungo to the west and Marmolada, the highest of the Dolomites at 10,965 ft (3,343 m), to the south.

Skiers enjoying views of the Dolomites above Canazei

Environs

At **Vigo di Fassa**, 8 miles (13 km) southwest, the **Museo Ladino** focuses on the Ladin-speaking people of some of the valleys. Ladin – a Rhaeto-Romance language – is taught in local schools and the ancient traditions still thrive.

🏛 **Museo Ladino**
Località San Giovanni, Vigo di Fassa. **Tel** 0462 76 01 82. **Open** Tue–Sat pm (late Jun–mid-Sep & Dec 20–Jan 6: daily).

The frescoed façade of the Palazzo della Magnifica Comunità

❾ Cavalese

🗺 3,600. 🚍 🛈 Via Fratelli Bronzetti 60 (0462 24 11 11). 🏧 last Tue of month (not Jul). 🖥 **visitfiemme.it**

Cavalese is the chief town in the Val di Fiemme, a pretty region of flower-filled, aromatic pastures, delightful wooded valleys, and Tyrolean architecture. At the center of the town stands the **Palazzo della Magnifica Comunità**. Originally built in the 13th century, this was the seat of the medieval governing council, which ruled the area as a semiautonomous region. Today the paneled interiors contain medieval paintings by local artists and an archaeology collection. Most visitors come for the excellent summer and winter resort facilities, and to climb, by cable car, to the 7,311 ft (2,229 m) top of **Alpe Cermis**, the mountain that rises to the south of the town.

Environs

The church in **Tesero**, the next village east, bears a 15th-century fresco by an unknown painter depicting Sabbath-breakers. The church itself, dating back to 1450, has a flurry of Gothic vaulting and a modern representation of the Crucifixion painted against a background of the village.

At **Predazzo**, about 8 miles (13 km) east, the **Museo di Geologia e Etnografia** explains the local geology.

🚍 **Palazzo della Magnifica Comunità**
Piazza Cesare Battisti 2. **Tel** 0462 34 03 65. **Closed** for restoration. 🎫
🖥 **mcfiemme.eu**

🏛 **Museo di Geologia e Etnografia**
Via Cesare Battisti 4. **Tel** 0462 50 23 92. **Open** 10am–noon & 5–7pm Mon–Sat (mid-Sep–Feb by appt).

❿ San Martino di Castrozza

🗺 470. 🚍 🛈 Via Passo Rolle 165 (0439 76 88 67). 🖥 **sanmartino.com**

The resort of San Martino occupies one of the most scenic and accessible valleys in the southern Dolomites, making it very popular with walkers and skiers. Cable cars rise to the peak of **Alpe Tognola** (7,095 ft, 2,163 m), southwest of the town, and up the **Cima della Rosetta** (8,557 ft, 2,609 m) to the east. Both offer fabulous views of the Pale di San Martino peaks, a stirring sight as the massive rock peaks, split by glaciers, rise above a sea of green meadows and woodland.

Piramidi di Segonzano, near Cembra

Vines growing on the terraced slopes of the Cembra valley

San Martino is almost entirely surrounded by forest, which once supplied the Venetian Republic with timber for ships. The forest is now protected, and as a result it is possible to see Alpine flowers, mushrooms, birds, and other wildlife with relative ease.

⓫ Cembra

🗺 2,500. 🚍 🛈 Piazza San Rocco 10 (0461 68 31 10). 🏧 Wed am.

The wine-producing town of Cembra nestles on the terraced slopes of a scenic valley of flower-filled villages. Some 4 miles (6 km) east of Cembra stand the **Piramidi di Segonzano**, a rare series of erosion pillars, some over 100 ft (30 m) high, each topped by a rock. The footpath to the pillars is well marked, with informative noticeboards along the way explaining the formation of the bizarre columns, which are similar in appearance to giant termites' nests. Their setting amid bird-filled woodland makes the steep climb up to the site well worthwhile. A further reward is the fine view, from the top of the hill, along the Cembra valley and westward as far as the Brenta group of Dolomites.

🏞 **Piramidi di Segonzano**
Strada Statale 612 to Cavalese. **Open** daily.

The impressive falls of the Cascate di Nardis, Madonna di Campiglio

⑫ Madonna di Campiglio

🏔 1,300. 🚌 *i* Via Pradalago 4 (0465 44 75 01). 🗓 Jul–Aug: Tue & Thu. 🖳 campigliodolomiti.it

Madonna di Campiglio is the chief resort in the Val Meledrio. Nestling between the Brenta and Adamello groups of peaks, it makes the perfect base for walking or skiing amid the magnificent mountain terrain. Cableways radiate out from the town in every direction, giving easy access to the peaks.

Environs
The church at **Pinzolo**, 9 miles (14 km) south, has a well-preserved fresco depicting a *Dance of Death* (1539). The inevitable march of the figures, both rich and poor, is underlined by a text written in local dialect.

North of Pinzolo, the road west from Carisolo leads to the verdant and popular, yet unspoiled, **Val Genova**. About 2 miles (4 km) along the valley is the spectacular **Cascate di Nardis**, a waterfall that plunges down 300 ft (90 m). The two masses of rock at the bottom are said to be the forms of petrified demons.

⑬ Trento

🏔 105,000. FS 🚌 *i* Via Manci 2 (0461 21 60 00). 🗓 Thu am.

Trento, the capital of the region to which it gave its name, is also the most attractive town in Trentino: it has a fine Romanesque cathedral, a richly decorated castle, and streets lined with handsome Renaissance mansions. Trento is noted as the venue for the **Council of Trent** (1545–63), set up by the Catholic Church to consider reforms that might encourage breakaway groups, in particular the German Protestants, to return to the fold. The reforms, which ushered in the period of the Counter-Reformation, were only partly successful.

The **Duomo**, site of some of the Council meetings, was built in robust Romanesque style from the 13th century. It was three centuries before it was completed, in 1515, but the builders maintained architectural harmony by ignoring Gothic and Renaissance styles entirely. The result is a church of unusual integrity. The Duomo stands on **Piazza Duomo**, the city's main square, first laid out by the Romans as their central marketplace or forum. Trento's Roman name, Tridentum, is commemorated in the figure of Neptune who stands holding his trident at the top of the fountain, which stands in the middle of the main square.

Inner courtyard of the Magno Palazzo

🏛 Museo Diocesano Tridentino

Piazza Duomo 18. **Tel** 0461 23 44 19. **Open** Tue–Sun. **Closed** Jan 1, Dec 25. 🖳 museodiocesanotridentino.it

This museum is housed in the **Palazzo Pretorio**, an imposing medieval building that stands on the eastern side of Piazza Duomo. Its contents include early ivory reliquaries, Flemish tapestries, and paintings depicting the Council of Trent.

🏰 Castello del Buonconsiglio

Via Bernardo Clesio 5. **Tel** 0461 23 37 70. **Open** Tue–Sun. **Closed** Jan 1, Dec 25. 🖳 buonconsiglio.it

This large castle, built in the 13th century and later enlarged with additional buildings, is part of the defenses of the town. Trento was an important frontier on the main road linking Italy to northern Europe, and thick walls still encircle the town.

The southern section of the castle consists of the magnificent **Magno Palazzo** (1530), built for the ruling prince-bishops of Trento, who were given extensive powers by the Holy Roman Emperor to foster loyalty and discourage defection to the pope. The lavish decoration (including frescoes of virile satyrs and nymphs by Gerolamo Romanino, 1531–2) speaks of huge wealth and a luxurious lifestyle. The palazzo houses the **Museo Provinciale**, with paintings, ceramics, and 15th-century wood carvings, and prehistoric, Etruscan and Roman items. The **Torre dell' Aquila** (Eagle Tower)

Palazzo Pretorio and the Duomo in Trento's main square

The commanding form of the Ossario del Castel Dante in Rovereto

nearby contains frescoes painted around 1400 that depict the months of the year.

Environs

Immediately to the west of Trento, a scenic round-trip along a winding road leads up the north flank of **Monte Bondone** and back, via **Vezzano**, down the western slopes. The views along the route are magnificent, in particular from Vaneze and Vason. East of Trento, Pergine marks the start of the **Val Sugana**, a broad valley with lakes. In the hills north of Lake Levico lies the spa town of **Levico Terme**, distinguished by elegant Neo-Classical buildings set amid beautifully wooded parkland.

⓮ Rovereto

🏙 33,000. **FS** 🚌 🛈 Corso Rosmini 6 (0464 43 03 63). 🛒 Tue.

Rovereto was at the center of fierce fighting during World War I, after which the Venetian castle (built in 1416) that dominates the town was transformed into the **Museo Storico Italiano della Guerra**, a war museum. The displays include sections on wartime humor, propaganda, and spying. Near the museum entrance, stairs lead out onto the castle roof for a view of the imposing **Ossario del Castel Dante.**

Some distance away is the **Campana dei Caduti** (Bell of the Fallen), which was cast from melted-down cannons at the end of World War II and mounted in an imposing building above the town; it is rung daily at sunset.

Below the war museum is the **Museo Civico**, with its collections on archaeology, art, natural history, and folklore. Another branch of the museo, in Corso Bettini, houses a collection of sculpture by Carlo Fait. The Mario Botta–designed **Museo di Arte Contemporanea di Trento e Rovereto (MART)** showcases 20th-century Italian art. A second site, in Via Portici, holds Italian Futurist art.

Environs

A little over 5 miles (8 km) north of Rovereto is **Castel Beseno**, rising on a hill to the east. This enormous castle was built and rebuilt from the 12th century to the 18th to guard the junction of the three valleys. The ruins are undergoing restoration.

Three miles (5 km) south of Rovereto, the main road passes through a valley littered with massive boulders created by landslides: these are known as Lavini di Marco or **Ruina Dantesca**, because they are mentioned in Dante's *Inferno* (XII, 4–9). Fossilized dinosaur footprints have been discovered there.

🏛 **Museo Storico Italiano della Guerra**
Via Castelbarco 7. **Tel** 0464 43 81 00.

Open Tue–Sun. **Closed** Jan 1, Dec 24, 25, & 31. 🏿

🏛 **Museo Civico**
Borgo Santa Caterina 41.
Tel 0464 45 28 00; Palazzo Alberti, Corso Bettini 41. **Tel** 0464 45 28 30.
Open Tue–Sun. **Closed** Jan 1, Aug 5, Nov 1, Dec 25. 🏿 ♿
🌐 museocivico.rovereto.tn.it

🏛 **MART**
Corso Bettini 43. **Tel** 0464 43 88 87; Casa d'Arte Futurista Depero, Via Portici 38. Tel 0464 43 18 13.
Open Tue–Sun. 🏿 📷 ♿ 🍴 🖥 🚻

🏰 **Castel Beseno**
Besenello. **Tel** 0464 83 46 00.
Open Mar–Nov: Tue–Sun (Mon if public hol); Dec–Feb: Sat & Sun. 🏿

Castello di Avio in its lush setting

⓯ Castello di Avio

Via Castello, Sabbionara d'Avio.
Tel 0464 68 44 53. 🚌 **FS** to Vo, then 2-mile (3-km) walk. Open Mar–Sep: 10am–6pm Tue–Sun; Oct–Feb: 10am–5pm Tue–Sun. 🏿 📷 🖥 🚻

Castles line the Adige valley all the way to the Brenner Pass, but few are as accessible as the Castello di Avio. It was founded in the 11th century, extended in the 13th, and today offers visitors far-reaching views. Among the numerous frescoes with secular themes is a rare series in the Casa delle Guardie (the Sentry House) depicting 13th-century battle scenes.

The extensive walls enclosing Castel Beseno above Rovereto

NORTHWEST ITALY

Introducing Northwest
  Italy   **182–189**

Lombardy   **190–213**

Valle d'Aosta and
  Piedmont   **214–233**

Liguria   **234–247**

Northwest Italy at a Glance

The northwest of Italy is made up of three very different geological characteristics: the jagged Alps, the flat plain, and the undulating shoreline of the Mediterranean. Within this varied landscape, some of it still wild and unspoiled, lie extremely rich and diverse vestiges of the area's substantial cultural heritage. The major sights, in the regions of Valle d'Aosta and Piedmont, Liguria and Lombardy, are shown on this map.

The Parco Nazionale del Gran Paradiso is a beautiful wilderness, and the habitat of rare Alpine fauna and flora *(see pp220–21)*.

The capital of Piedmont is Turin, an elegant and bustling city of splendid Baroque architecture. Its skyline is dramatically dominated by the Mole Antonelliana *(see p228)*.

Aosta

VALLE D'AOSTA

Biella

Ivrea

Nova

Vercelli

Turin

Moncalieri

Po

Pinerolo

VALLE D'AOSTA
AND PIEDMONT
(See pp214–33)

Asti

Alessandr

Alba

Cuneo

LIGURIA
(See pp234–

Savona

Impería

Sanremo

Sanremo is a typical Riviera resort, with palm trees and a casino. The onion-domed outline of the Russian church adds an exotic flavor to the town *(see p238)*.

The Basilica di Sant'Andrea in Vercelli is an important Romanesque building, one of the earliest to use Gothic elements *(see p232)*.

◀ The picturesque Isola San Giulio in the center of Lake Orta, Valle d'Aosta

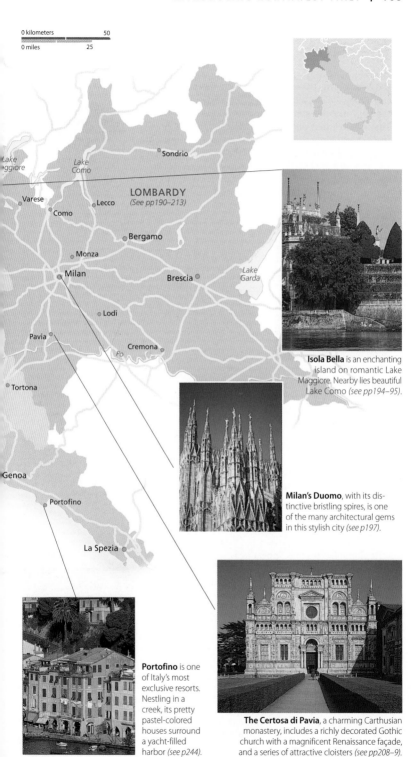

0 kilometers 50

0 miles 25

Sondrio

Lake Maggiore

Lake Como

LOMBARDY
(See pp190–213)

Varese

Lecco

Como

Bergamo

Monza

Milan

Brescia

Lake Garda

Lodi

Pavia

Cremona

Po

Tortona

Genoa

Portofino

La Spezia

Isola Bella is an enchanting island on romantic Lake Maggiore. Nearby lies beautiful Lake Como *(see pp194–95)*.

Milan's Duomo, with its distinctive bristling spires, is one of the many architectural gems in this stylish city *(see p197)*.

Portofino is one of Italy's most exclusive resorts. Nestling in a creek, its pretty pastel-colored houses surround a yacht-filled harbor *(see p244)*.

The Certosa di Pavia, a charming Carthusian monastery, includes a richly decorated Gothic church with a magnificent Renaissance façade, and a series of attractive cloisters *(see pp208–9)*.

The Flavors of Northwest Italy

From Mediterranean Liguria to the Alps, the Lombardy plain, and Piedmont, this diverse area is characterized by its rich yet hearty cuisine. Along with the Veneto, Lombardy and Piedmont are Italy's main rice-growing areas and risotto features widely, especially delicious when made with local wild mushrooms. The white truffles of Alba are the "white gold" of Piedmont, while lush pastures produce some of the country's best meat and many of Italy's finest cheeses. The mild Ligurian climate favors olives and herbs – especially basil, used in pesto sauce. And fish teem in the sparkling Mediterranean.

Fresh basil

A precious haul of aromatic Piedmontese truffles

Lombardy

This is the home of dishes prepared *alla Milanese*, rich in butter, *ossobuco* (shin of veal), vegetable soups, and boiled meats *(bollito misto)*. From veal to beef and from pork to poultry, Lombardy produces some of the country's finest meat, but it is also associated with *cucina povera* (the cuisine of the poor), in which polenta (corn porridge) still features

from its days as the staple diet of impoverished country folk. The other staple food, the short-grained rice that is used in risotto, grows abundantly in the area around Pavia. Lombardy is one of Italy's largest cheese-making regions, the most famous including Gorgonzola, Mascarpone, Bitto, and Grana Padano.

Piedmont & Valle d'Aosta

The "Slow Food" movement was born in Piedmont in 1986. Its mission is "to defend biodiversity in our food supply, spread taste education, and connect producers of excellent food." The movement now has more than 100,000 members in more than 50 countries. Piedmontese flavors are robust,

Grana Padano · Gorgonzola · Fontina · Bitto · Mascarpone · Taleggio

Mouthwatering range of northwest Italy's finest cheeses

Regional Dishes and Specialties

Gianduiotti

Veal is especially popular in Lombardy and Piedmont, and a great favorite with the Milanese is *ossobuco*. Another classic Piedmontese dish, *vitello tonnato* is a surprisingly delicious blend of cold roast veal served with a sauce made with mayonnaise, tuna, gherkins, and capers. As well as pesto, a traditional dish from Genoa is *buridda alla Genovese* – a delicious fish soup or stew containing mussels, shrimps, octopus, squid, and clams. Shavings of truffle in dishes such as risotto and *fagiano tartufato* (pheasant stuffed with white truffle and pork fat) give a taste of sheer luxury, and fortunately, a little of this very expensive delicacy goes a long way. And, for those with a sweet tooth, *panettone* is a soft Christmas cake studded with dried and candied fruit, another Milanese specialty.

Bagna Caôda From Piedmont; a warm mix of olive oil, anchovies, and garlic into which raw vegetables are dipped.

Liguria

The Mediterranean climate is perfect for growing herbs, fruits and vegetables, nuts, and olives. Ligurian olive oil is of the highest quality and is used in the preparation of many dishes. To accompany pasta, pesto is the signature sauce, made from basil, pine nuts, garlic, and olive oil, as well as a mix of Pecorino and Parmesan. This use of aromatic herbs is typical of Ligurian cuisine in general.

Not surprisingly, fish and seafood are as common as meat and dairy in this region, where the vast majority of people live on the coast.

Boxes of fresh fish are unloaded onto a Ligurian quayside

rich, and earthy, and laced with French flair, reflecting a history of French rule and influence.

The paddy fields of Vercelli are the rice capital of Europe and truffle risotto, especially when flavored using the prized white variety from Alba, is truly memorable fare.

The mountains are famous for cow's milk cheese, especially the semisoft Fontina from the Valle d'Aosta, cured meats, salamis, terrines, and game. Piedmont also produces Italy's greatest red wines, and the prized Barolo and Barbaresco often feature as a marinade in beef dishes.

The Turinese are passionate about chocolate, echoing Turin's tradition of chocolate-making originating in the 17th century. Most famous are the sublime ingot-shaped *gianduiotti*, filled with a rich chocolate-hazelnut cream. The

city is also the birthplace of *grissini*, crisp breadsticks that grace every restaurant table. The tradition of the *aperitivo* also originates in Turin. The spread that accompanies a glass of Prosecco or a cocktail in bars throughout the city between 6pm and 8pm is substantial.

Delicious foccacia bread made with Ligurian olive oil

ON THE MENU

Agnolotti Piedmont pasta specialty – crescent-shaped ravioli stuffed with meat or vegetables. Served with *ragù* or a creamy sauce.

Brasato al Barolo Braised beef cooked gently with vegetables in Barolo wine.

Lumache Piedmontese snails, the best of which come from Cherasco, served either in garlic and butter or in a sauce of olive oil, tomatoes, and garlic.

Oca alla Piemontese Goose preserved in fat.

Risotto alla Milanese Rich, saffron-scented dish of rice with white wine, onion, and Parmesan cheese.

Trenette con pesto A Ligurian dish of flat noodles with a sauce of basil, garlic, pine nuts, and olive oil.

Ossobuco Milanese shin of veal, braised slowly in white wine. The bone marrow is considered a delicacy.

Zabaione A frothy dessert of egg yolks, sugar, and Marsala, *zabaione* is a specialty of the Piedmont region.

The Wines of Northwest Italy

Grapes are grown throughout the northwest – from the cliffs of Liguria to the steep mountainsides of Valle d'Aosta. The best wines, however, come from Piedmont, in particular the Langhe hills southwest of Turin, source of two of Italy's finest reds: the rich, powerful, long-lived Barolo and Barbaresco. Both of these are now showing the benefits of modern techniques and a renewed interest in high-quality wine making. Lighter, everyday red wines that go well with the local cuisine include Dolcetto and the popular Barbera. Another Piedmont specialty is sparkling *spumante*, Italians' instinctive choice whenever there is something around to celebrate.

Castiglione Falletto in the heart of Piedmont

Barbera d'Alba comes from the adaptable Barbera grape, which can grow on almost any slope. Its ubiquitous nature means that the wines it yields can be light and full of fruit, as well as dense, strong, and full-flavored. Good producers include Aldo Conterno, Voerzio, Pio Cesare, Altare, Gaja, Vaira, and Vietti.

Dolcetto is grown in seven different areas. Dolcetto d'Alba has a delicious perfume and deep purple color. Best drunk within one or two years, it ranges in flavor from fresh and fruity to the rich, concentrated plumminess of some of the top wines, such as those produced by Giuseppe Mascarello.

Turin
Chieri
Piedmont
MONFERRATO
Canale
Barbaresco
Alba
Bra
Saluzzo
Barolo
Castiglione Falletto
Dogliani
Mondovi
LANGHE
Cuneo

Barolo, prized the world over for its complex array of flavors and firm tannins, is made from the Nebbiolo grape and may take up to 20 years to mature. Vigna Colonnello is a top Barolo from Aldo Conterno, made only in the best years, like 2006, 2005, 2004, and 1993.

Key

- Barolo
- Barbaresco
- Other vineyard areas

| 0 kilometers | 25 |
| 0 miles | 15 |

The white truffle of Alba is an autumn specialty from the Langhe hills. Highly prized for its earthy scent, it is excellent with Barolo.

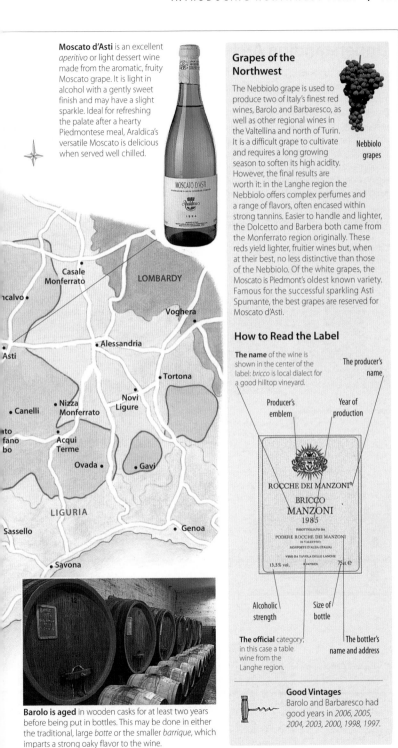

Moscato d'Asti is an excellent *aperitivo* or light dessert wine made from the aromatic, fruity Moscato grape. It is light in alcohol with a gently sweet finish and may have a slight sparkle. Ideal for refreshing the palate after a hearty Piedmontese meal, Araldica's versatile Moscato is delicious when served well chilled.

Grapes of the Northwest

The Nebbiolo grape is used to produce two of Italy's finest red wines, Barolo and Barbaresco, as well as other regional wines in the Valtellina and north of Turin. It is a difficult grape to cultivate and requires a long growing season to soften its high acidity.

Nebbiolo grapes

However, the final results are worth it: in the Langhe region the Nebbiolo offers complex perfumes and a range of flavors, often encased within strong tannins. Easier to handle and lighter, the Dolcetto and Barbera both came from the Monferrato region originally. These reds yield lighter, fruitier wines but, when at their best, no less distinctive than those of the Nebbiolo. Of the white grapes, the Moscato is Piedmont's oldest known variety. Famous for the successful sparkling Asti Spumante, the best grapes are reserved for Moscato d'Asti.

How to Read the Label

The name of the wine is shown in the center of the label: *bricco* is local dialect for a good hilltop vineyard.

The producer's name

Producer's emblem

Year of production

ROCCHE DEI MANZONI®

BRICCO
MANZONI
1985

IMBOTTIGLIATO DA
PODERE ROCCHE DEI MANZONI
IN VALENTINO
MONFORTE D'ALBA (ITALIA)

VINO DA TAVOLA DELLE LANGHE

13.5% vol.   75cl ℮

Alcoholic strength

Size of bottle

The official category; in this case a table wine from the Langhe region.

The bottler's name and address

Barolo is aged in wooden casks for at least two years before being put in bottles. This may be done in either the traditional, large *botte* or the smaller *barrique*, which imparts a strong oaky flavor to the wine.

Good Vintages
Barolo and Barbaresco had good years in *2006, 2005, 2004, 2003, 2000, 1998, 1997.*

Casale Monferrato

LOMBARDY

ncalvo

Voghera

Asti

Alessandria

Tortona

Canelli

Nizza Monferrato

Novi Ligure

ato fano bo

Acqui Terme

Ovada

Gavi

LIGURIA

Sassello

Genoa

Savona

Understanding Architecture in Northwest Italy

Although the buildings of the northwest tend to be solid and imposing – a result partly of the more severe climate – there is no distinctive architectural stamp as there is around Venice, Florence, or even Rome. Instead, a variety of buildings in different styles, many borrowed or reinterpreted from elsewhere, are dotted across the area: enchanting medieval castles, outstanding Romanesque and Gothic buildings, unusual Baroque structures. The northwest is also rich in modern architecture – in terms of both design and materials – influenced by the region's industrial developments and its strong flair for innovative design, which also often draws its inspiration from earlier architectural styles.

Castello Sforzesco, 1451–66
(see p192)

Characteristics of Northwest Italian Architecture

Double row of defensive walls

Wooden balcony

Few windows

Massive square tower

Pointed turret

Battlements

Castello di Fénis, one of the finest castles in the Valle d'Aosta, is a 14th-century fortress with asymmetrical towers, turrets, and crenellated walls. Frescoes adorn the interior (see p215).

Alternating bands of marble

Rose window

Lions support columns and porch above

Elaborate carving

Rose window

Octagonal drum influenced by the Duomo in Florence

Cappella Colleoni, Bergamo (1476), mixes rich, decorative elements in this early Renaissance masterpiece (see p201).

Highly ornate façade

Patterned marble design

Monza's Duomo (1390s) typifies the Lombard style of Romanesque architecture with its marble stripes and ornate carving (see p201).

Massive scale

Ornate window surrounds

Rotunda

Balcony

Curved brickwork

Palazzo Carignano is perhaps the finest product of Turin's idiosyncratic Baroque school. Guarini's masterpiece (1679) boasts an extraordinary undulating brick façade and a fine rotunda (see p223).

Where to See the Architecture

The road to Aosta is flanked by numerous medieval castles (see p214) while inspirational Romanesque and Gothic churches are found in Lombardy – at Monza (p201), Pavia (p203), Milan (pp192–201), and Como (pp190–91). The 15th-century Certosa di Pavia (pp204–5) is a must, as well as the charming city of Mantua (p207). Turin (pp220–24) is famous for its unique Baroque school, and Bergamo for its exuberance. Architecture from the last two centuries is best represented in Milan and Turin, and in Genoa some exciting redevelopment projects are taking place.

Renzo Piano's mast structure (1992) in Genoa's redeveloped port

19th–20th Century Architecture

Top reaches 550 ft (167 m)

Aluminium replaces original granite top

Square-sided dome

The Mole Antonelliana (1863–97), designed by Antonelli, was the tallest building in the world when it was built (see p224).

Galleria Vittorio Emanuele II in Milan, designed by Mengoni in 1865, was the first Italian building to use glass and iron structurally (see p194).

Central dome

Mosaics

Glass balcony

Overhanging upper stories

Struts support the top

Torre Velasca, Milan, is a 26-floor tower south of the Duomo. The design, from the 1950s, was influenced by medieval castles such as the Castello Sforzesco.

Elliptical shape

Taller windows

Tapering struts

Spiral ramps up to roof

Roof served as test track

Reinforced concrete

The Lingotto building, Turin, was built in 1915–18 as FIAT's car factory. Made of advanced materials, it was the first large-scale modern building in Italy. The structure of the ramps up to the roof is similar to the interior of Guarini's Baroque dome for San Lorenzo in Turin.

Milan's Pirelli building, by Ponti and Nervi, is an elegant and innovative skyscraper built in 1959.

LOMBARDY

The region of Lombardy stretches from the Alps, on the border with Switzerland, down through the romantic lakes of Como and Maggiore to the broad, flat plain of the River Po. It is an area of lakeside villas with azalea-filled gardens, of wealthy towns with imposing palazzi and highly decorated churches, and of efficient, modern industry and large-scale agriculture, the financial heart of Italy. At its center stands Milan, the style-conscious capital of Lombardy.

The region was named after the Lombards or Longobards, a Germanic tribe that invaded Italy in the 6th century AD. During the Middle Ages, Lombardy was part of the Holy Roman Empire, but not always loyal to its German emperors. The Lombards, who had a talent for banking and commerce, resented any outside interference with their prosperity.

The 12th century saw the rise of the Lega Lombarda, or Lombard League, a band of forceful separatists founded to counter the brutal imperialism of Frederick Barbarossa (their most modern incarnation being the Lega Nord political party). Power was seized by the region's great families, most notably the Visconti and the Sforza of Milan, from the 14th to the early 16th century. These dynasties also became great patrons of the arts, commissioning exquisite palaces, churches, and artworks, many of which can still be seen. Bergamo, Mantua, and Cremona – not to mention Milan itself – contain a remarkably rich array of art treasures. Here are such pinnacles of European civilization as the charterhouse at Pavia, Leonardo da Vinci's *Last Supper*, and the magnificent paintings of the Pinacoteca di Brera in Milan.

Lombardy – famous as the birthplace of Virgil, Monteverdi, Stradivarius, and Donizetti – today offers visitors the contrasting pleasures of lyrical lakeside landscapes (resorts on lakes Como and Maggiore have attracted poets, aristocrats, and gamblers for centuries) and beautiful, bustling cities.

Strolling through Milan's enormous Galleria Vittorio Emanuele II

◄ The village of Corenno Plinio on the peaceful eastern shores of the beautiful Lake Como

Exploring Lombardy

The enormous plain of the River Po runs through much of
Lombardy, providing a landscape that is flat and perfectly suited to
the consequent expansion of industry in the region. This is, however,
also a region of great contrasts. To the north, in a still unspoiled setting
in the foothills of the mountains, lie the lakes Como and Maggiore, as
well as the dramatic valleys and peaks of the Parco Nazionale dello
Stelvio around Bormio, Sondrio, and Val Camonica. Further south,
busy industrialized areas give way to huge tracts of agriculture
dotted with towns of great beauty such as
Cremona, Mantua, and Pavia, which
offer a rich and splendid array
of artistic pleasures.

A view of Isola Bella on Lake Maggiore

Sights at a Glance

1. Lago di Como
2. Lago Maggiore
3. *Milan (Milano) pp196–205*
4. Monza
5. Bergamo
6. Parco Nazionale dello Stelvio
7. Val Camonica
8. Lago d'Iseo
9. Brescia
10. Lodi
11. Pavia
12. *Certosa di Pavia pp208–9*
13. Cremona
14. Sabbioneta
15. Mantua

The colorful façade of the
Cappella Colleoni in Bergamo

For additional map symbols *see back flap*

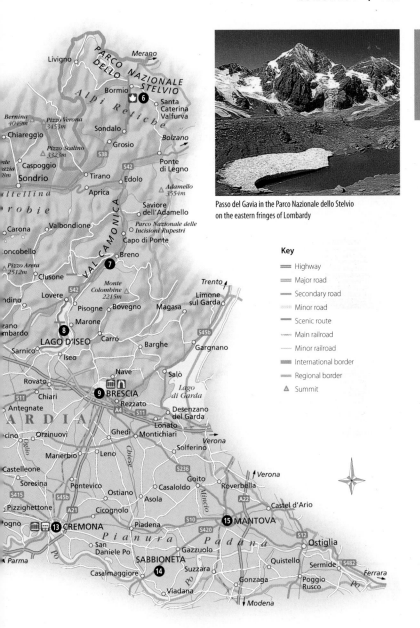

Passo del Gavia in the Parco Nazionale dello Stelvio
on the eastern fringes of Lombardy

Key

═══ Highway
── Major road
── Secondary road
╌╌╌ Minor road
── Scenic route
╌╌╌ Main railroad
── Minor railroad
▬▬▬ International border
── Regional border
▲ Summit

Getting Around

Milan has three international airports, which are
obvious gateways into northern Italy, and the vast and
flat Lombard plain has its advantages when it comes
to transport: roads and railway lines crisscross it and
make trips between the larger towns very easy. The
lakes, however, are better visited by car: only two main
towns are served by trains, though there are bus and
boat services around the shores. The Parco Nazionale
dello Stelvio and the mountains are more remote still,
but offer good tourist facilities.

0 kilometers 25

0 miles 20

❶ Lago di Como

Set in an idyllic landscape of mountains and rugged hillsides, Lake Como has for centuries attracted visitors who come here to go boating, for walks in the hills, or for relaxation and inspiration. The northern stretches, in particular, are shrouded in an almost eerie calm. The long and narrow lake, crafted into a wishbone shape by glacial erosion, offers fine views up to the Alps and down to the towns of Como and Lecco.

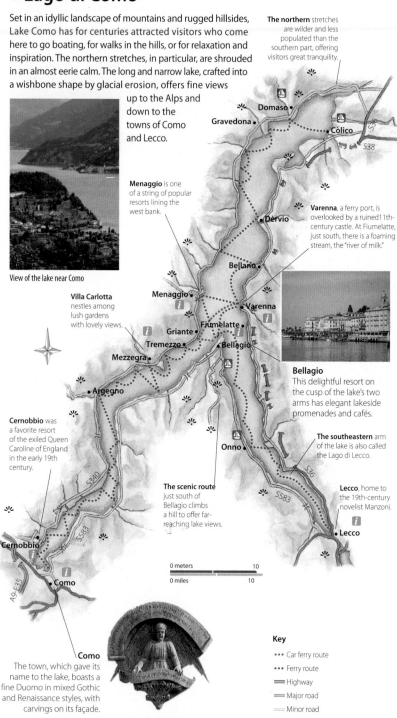

View of the lake near Como

The northern stretches are wilder and less populated than the southern part, offering visitors great tranquility.

Menaggio is one of a string of popular resorts lining the west bank.

Varenna, a ferry port, is overlooked by a ruined 11th-century castle. At Fiumelatte, just south, there is a foaming stream, the "river of milk."

Villa Carlotta nestles among lush gardens with lovely views.

Bellagio
This delightful resort on the cusp of the lake's two arms has elegant lakeside promenades and cafés.

Cernobbio was a favorite resort of the exiled Queen Caroline of England in the early 19th century.

The southeastern arm of the lake is also called the Lago di Lecco.

The scenic route just south of Bellagio climbs a hill to offer far-reaching lake views.

Lecco, home to the 19th-century novelist Manzoni.

Domaso
Gravedona
Còlico
Dèrvio
Bellano
Menaggio
Varenna
Griante
Fiumelatte
Tremezzo
Bellagio
Mezzegra
Argegno
Onno
Lecco
Cernobbio
Como

0 meters   10
0 miles   10

Como
The town, which gave its name to the lake, boasts a fine Duomo in mixed Gothic and Renaissance styles, with carvings on its façade.

Key

••• Car ferry route
••• Ferry route
━━ Highway
━━ Major road
═══ Minor road

Tadoline's copy (1834) of Canova's *Cupid and Psyche* in Villa Carlotta

Exploring Lago di Como

In the heart of **Como** lies the elegant Piazza Cavour. Nearby rises the beautiful 14th-century **Duomo**, with its 15th- and 16th-century reliefs and paintings, and fine tombs. The 18th-century dome is by Turin's famous Baroque architect, Juvarra. Next to the Duomo stand the 13th-century Broletto (town hall), charmingly striped in white, pink, and gray, and the tall Torre del Comune. At Tremezzo, **Villa Carlotta** is an elegant 18th-century summer-house known for its gardens. In springtime, all sorts of flowers burst into color in this pretty setting. The villa houses a collection of sculptures.

Lecco, a small industrial town lying to the south of the lake's eastern arm, is home to Alessandro Manzoni (1785–1873). The writer's childhood home, the **Villa Manzoni**, is devoted to memorabilia of his life and works. A monument in Piazza Manzoni depicts scenes from his most famous novel, *I Promessi Sposi (The Betrothed)* – set in 17th-century Lecco and Milan.

Villa Carlotta
Via Regina 2b, Tremezzo. **Tel** 0344 404 05. **Open** Apr–mid-Oct: 9am–6pm daily (mid-Mar–end Mar & mid-Oct–early-Nov: 10am–5pm daily).

Villa Manzoni
Via Guanella 1, Lecco. **Tel** 0341 48 12 47. **Open** 9.30am–5:30pm Tue–Sun. **Closed** Jan 1, Easter, May 1, Aug 15, Dec 25.

❷ Lago Maggiore

Verbania. **FS** Stresa, Verbania, Baveno & the islands. Piazza Marconi 16, Stresa (0323 301 50). **W** distrettolaghi.it

Lake Maggiore, the second largest Italian lake after Lake Garda, is a long expanse of water nestling right against the mountains and stretching into Alpine Switzerland; it is warmer in atmosphere and more romantic than Lake Como. The gently sloping shores are dotted with camellias, azaleas, and verbena vegetation – from which the ancient lake derived its Roman name, Verbanus.

A huge copper statue of Cardinal San Carlo Borromeo, the chief patron of the lake, stands in **Arona**, the town where he was born in 1538. It is possible to climb up and look out over the lake through his eyes and ears. Arona also boasts a ruined castle and a chapel, Santa Maria, dedicated to the Borromeo family.

Further up the western coast of the lake is **Stresa**, the chief resort and main jumping-off point for visits to the islands; the town boasts many grand hotels, handsome villas, and pleasant gardens. Behind Stresa, a cable car ride away, rises Monte Mottarone, a snowcapped peak offering spectacular panoramic views of the surrounding mountains, including Monte Rosa.

The statue of Carlo Borromeo in Arona

The **Borromean islands**, at the center of the lake near Stresa, are small jewels of natural beauty augmented by artificial grottoes, architectural follies, and landscaped gardens. The **Isola Bella** is home to the 17th-century **Palazzo Borromeo** and its splendid gardens, while Isola Madre is largely given over to a botanical garden. The only island inhabited all year round is Isola dei Pescatori, with a population of 50. The private Isola di San Giovanni is the smallest of the isles, with a villa that once belonged to the great conductor Arturo Toscanini (1867–1957).

The lake becomes quieter toward the Swiss border, but continues to be lined with attractive villas. The **Villa Taranto**, located on the outskirts of Verbania, houses a fine exotic botanical collection.

About 2 miles (3 km) west of **Cannobio**, a market town near Switzerland, is the dramatic gorge and tumbling waterfall of Orrido di Sant'Anna, which can be reached by boat.

Palazzo Borromeo
Isola Bella. from Stresa. **Tel** 0323 305 56. **Open** mid-Mar–Oct: daily. **W** borromeoturismo.it

Villa Taranto
Via Vittorio Veneto 111, Verbania, Pallanza. **Tel** 0323 55 66 67. **Open** mid-Mar–Oct: daily.

Isola Bella's 17th-century Palazzo Borromeo and garden on Lago Maggiore

❸ Milan

Center of fashion, business, and finance, Milan has a bustling, businesslike feel about it. It is stylish rather than attractive – a city of wealth as opposed to imagination, and the heartland of the Italian economy. Its name is thought to come from a composite of the Latin words *medio* and *planum*, meaning "middle of the plain." It has long been an important trading center at the junction of trans-Alpine routes, and a prize for powerful dynasties. Today, it is the best place to see Italy at its most cosmopolitan and stylish.

Portrait of a Young Woman by Pollaiuolo, Museo Poldi-Pezzoli

🏠 Castello Sforzesco

Piazza Castello. **Tel** 02 88 46 37 00. Castello: **Open** daily. Musei del Castello: **Open** 9am–5:30pm Tue–Sun. **Closed** public hols. 🎦 ♿
W milanocastello.it

The first castle on this site was built by the Visconti family, but demolished when their reign ended in the mid-15th century. Milan's new ruler, Francesco Sforza, built in its place this Renaissance palace. The castle is based on a series of courtyards, the most beautiful of which, the Cortile della Rocchetta, is a graceful arcaded square designed by Bramante and Filarete. The palace now contains, together with sections on Applied Arts, Archaeology, and Coins, the **Musei del Castello**. This fine collection of furniture, antiquities, and paintings includes Michelangelo's unfinished sculpture known as the *Rondanini Pietà*. The canvases

in the picture collection, dating from the Renaissance to the 18th century, are particularly impressive.

🏛 Museo Poldi-Pezzoli

Via Alessandro Manzoni 12. **Tel** 02 79 48 89. **Open** 10am–6pm Wed–Mon. 🚇 W museopoldipezzoli.it

Giacomo Poldi-Pezzoli was a wealthy nobleman who, on his death in 1879, bequeathed his magnificent art collection to the state. Its most famous painting is the 15th-century Renaissance *Portrait of a Young Woman* by Antonio Pollaiuolo, though there are also works by Piero della Francesca, Botticelli, and Mantegna, among others. The applied arts section is richly endowed with fascinating items ranging from rugs and lace to glass, enamels, and porcelain, as well as sculpture, jewelry, and sundials.

Sights at a Glance

① Castello Sforzesco
② *Pinacoteca di Brera pp198–9*
③ Museo Poldi-Pezzoli
④ Teatro alla Scala
⑤ Galleria Vittorio Emanuele II
⑥ Duomo)
⑦ Palazzo Reale (Museo della Reggia)
⑧ San Satiro
⑨ Pinacoteca Ambrosiana
⑩ Sant'Ambrogio
⑪ San Lorenzo Maggiore
⑫ Civico Museo Archeologico
⑬ Parco Sempione

Michelangelo's *Rondanini Pietà* (c.1564) in the Castello Sforzesco

🎭 Teatro alla Scala

Pza della Scala. **Tel** 02 887 91. Box
Office **Tel** 02 72 00 37 44. ♿ Museo
Teatrale Largo Ghiringhelli 1 (Piazza
Scala). **Tel** 02 88 79 24 73. **Open** 9am–
noon, 1:30–5pm daily. 🎭♿📷
🌐 teatroallascala.org

This Neo-Classical theater opened
in 1778 and is one of the world's
most prestigious opera houses.
It has one of the largest stages
in Europe and hosts sumptuous
productions. Two hours before
each performance the box office

The façade of the world-famous
Teatro alla Scala

🏛 Duomo

Piazza del Duomo. **Tel** 02 72 02 26 56.
Open daily. Baptistry digs:
Open 9:30am–5:30pm. Treasury:
Open 9:30am–5:30pm Mon–Fri (to
5pm Sat), 1:30–3:30pm Sun & public
hols. Roof: **Open** 9am–9:30pm (to
7pm Nov–Feb). 📷 for roof. ♿
🌐 duomomilano.it

Milan's cathedral is one of the
largest Gothic churches in the
world. It was begun in the 14th
century under Prince Gian
Galeazzo Visconti but not
completed until more than
500 years later. The building's
most startling feature is the
extraordinary roof, with its
135 spires and innumerable
statues and gargoyles, and
from which, on a clear day, there
are views of the Alps. Below, the
façade boasts an assortment of
styles from Gothic through to
Renaissance and Neo-Classical.
The bronze doors are faced with
bas-reliefs recounting episodes
from the life of the Virgin and
of Sant'Ambrogio, and scenes
retelling the history of Milan.

The aisles are divided by 52
giant pillars and well
lit by stained-glass
windows. Look out for
the Visconti family
symbol – a serpent
swallowing a man – in
the fine tracery of the
apse windows. Among
the many statues is a
depiction of the flayed
San Bartolomeo
carrying his own skin.
The treasury, beneath
the main altar, contains
much medieval gold
and silverwork, and
the remains of a
4th-century baptistry.

opens to sell tickets at discount
prices. The **Museo Teatrale**
houses sets and costumes of
past productions, portraits of
conductors, and theatrical items
dating back to Roman times.
There is also a good view of the
auditorium, with its gilded box
galleries, *trompe-l'oeil* effects,
and huge chandelier.

The Gothic Duomo, crowned with spires

For keys to map symbols *see back flap*

Exploring Milan

In addition to the great monuments in Milan, such as the cathedral and the castle, there is a host of varied and interesting museums, churches, and civic buildings that provide an enthralling mix of old and new. This chic and busy metropolis offers plenty of opportunities for cultural activities, gastronomic adventures, designer-fashion shopping, or just strolling about, Milan-style.

The glass ceiling and dome covering the Galleria Vittorio Emanuele II

🖼 Galleria Vittorio Emanuele II

Main entrances on Piazza del Duomo and Piazza della Scala.

This ornate shopping arcade, known as *il Salotto di Milano* (Milan's drawing room), was designed by the architect Giuseppe Mengoni in 1865. The galleria had a tragic start, however, as Mengoni fell to his death from the scaffolding not long before its inauguration in 1877 (a year before the arcade was actually finished). Tourists are nevertheless attracted to its stylish shops and cafés, as well as Savini, one of Milan's historic restaurants.

The galleria itself has a floorplan in the shape of a Latin cross, with an octagonal center adorned with mosaics representing four continents (Europe, America, Africa, and Asia), together with others representing Art, Agriculture, Science, and Industry. Its finest feature is its metal and glass roof, crowned with a magnificent central dome. The roof was the first structure in Italy to use metal and glass in a structural way, rather than just decoratively. The floors are decorated with mosaics of the signs of the zodiac; tourists may be seen stepping on the genitals of Taurus the Bull, which is said to bring good luck.

🖼 Palazzo Reale

Piazza del Duomo. **Tel** 02 88 46 52 36. **Open** Museo della Reggia. ♿

The former royal palace, for centuries home to the Visconti and other rulers of Milan, houses the **Museo della Reggia**. It displays the sumptuous interiors of the building and showcases the four historic phases of the palace including the Neo-Classical era and the Restoration. Palazzo Reale is also a prestigious venue for temporary art exhibitions. The building abutting it to the west (the Arengario) has been transformed into a Modern Art museum, the **Museo del Novecento**, and many Italian artworks from the 20th century are displayed here.

🖼 Villa Belgiojoso Bonaparte and Galleria d'Arte Moderna

Villa Belgiojoso Bonaparte, Via Palestro 16. **Tel** 02 88 44 59 47. **Open** 9am–1pm, 2–5:30pm Tue–Sun. ♿ 🅦 gam-milano.com

Milan's 19th-century and Modern Art collections are housed in a Neo-Classical villa built by Leopold Pollack in 1790 for Count Ludovico Barbiano di Belgiojoso. It was lived in by Napoleon in 1802 and later by Marshal Radetzky. The villa houses 19th-century Italian art, showing all the major art movements, as well as the Grassi and Vismara collections of 19th- and 20th-century Italian and foreign artists and the Marino Marini Museum. Of particular note are works by Giorgio Morandi (1890–1964) and Carlo Carrà (1881–1966), as well as by Modigliani (1884–1920) and De Chirico (1888–1978). Non-Italian artists include Van Gogh, Cézanne, Gauguin, Picasso, Matisse, Klee, Mondrian, and Kandinsky.

Still Life (1920) by Giorgio Morandi in the Galleria d'Arte Moderna

For hotels and restaurants in this region see pp562–77 and pp580–605

Fruit Basket (c. 1596) by Caravaggio in the Pinacoteca Ambrosiana

Pinacoteca Ambrosiana

Piazza Pio XI 2. **Tel** 02 80 69 21.
Open 10am–6pm Tue–Sun.
ambrosiana.eu

The Ambrosiana is home to Cardinal Federico Borromeo's magnificent library of 36,000 manuscripts. These include a 5th-century illustrated *Iliad*, early manuscripts of Dante's *Divine Comedy* (1353), and the *Atlantic Codex* (1478–1519) by Leonardo da Vinci. In order to exhibit as much of the *Atlantic Codex* as possible, the pages on display are changed every three months.

The building also houses an art gallery, bequeathed by Borromeo in 1618. The collection ranges from 14th-century pieces to works of the early 19th century. Among the canvases are *Portrait of a Musician* by Leonardo, the *Madonna of the Canopy* by Botticelli (15th century), a cartoon version of Raphael's Vatican fresco, *The School of Athens* (16th century), and Caravaggio's *Fruit Basket*. There is also a strong collection of Venetian art, with paintings by Giorgione, Titian, Bassano, and Tiepolo, and panel paintings by the late 15th-century Lombard painter Bergognone.

San Satiro

Via Speronari 3. **Tel** 02 87 46 83.
Open 7:30–11:30am, 3:30–5:30pm daily.

This church, its full title Santa Maria presso San Satiro, is one of the most beautiful Renaissance buildings in Milan. It was built on the site of a 9th-century sanctuary, little of which remains apart from the Cappella della Pietà, beside an 11th-century bell tower.

The interior seems to be in the shape of a Greek cross, but this is an illusion created by *trompe-l'oeil* effects, since space restrictions led Bramante to choose a T-shaped plan. Above the altar is a 13th-century fresco. An octagonal baptistry lies off the right aisle. The church's façade was finished in the 19th century.

Civico Museo Archeologico

Corso Magenta 15. **Tel** 02 88 44 52 08.
1, 2 Cadorna. 16, 19, 27. 50, 58, 94. **Open** 9am–5:30pm Tue–Sun. (phone ahead).

At the entrance to this museum is a model of Roman Milan, which illustrates urban planning and architecture in Milan from the 1st to the 4th century AD. The exhibition begins in a hall on the right, containing clay objects and Roman sculpture. At the end of this room is a huge fragment of a torso of Hercules and 3rd-century AD floor mosaics. Also in this room are two of the most important works in the museum: the Parabiago Patera and the Diatreta Cup. The Patera is a gilded silver plate with a relief of the goddess Cybele (4th century AD). The Diatreta Cup, dating from the same period, is a single piece of colored glass, with finely wrought, intricate decoration.

Parco Sempione

Piazza Castello–Piazza Sempione.
1 Cadorna, Cairoli, 2 Lanza, Cadorna. Ferrovie Nord, Cadorna. 1, 2, 4, 12, 14, 19, 27. 43, 57, 61, 94. **Open** Mar–Apr: 6:30am–9pm; May: 6:30am–10pm; Jun–Sep: 6:30am–11:30pm; Oct: 6:30am–9pm; Nov–Feb: 6:30am–8pm

Although it covers an area of about 116 acres (47 ha), this park occupies only a part of the old Visconti ducal garden, enlarged by the Sforza in the 15th century to make a 740-acre (300-ha) hunting reserve.

The present-day layout was designed by Emilio Alemagna between 1890–93.

Among the trees are monuments to Napoleon III by Francesco Barzaghi, De Chirico's *Mysterious Baths*, the sulfur water fountain, and the Torre Branca, a tower of steel tubes made in 1932 to a design by Gio Ponti.

Gallerie d'Italia

Via Manzoni 10. **Tel** 800 16 76 19.
Open 9:30am–7:30pm Tue–Sun (to 10:30pm Thu).

Housed in the Palazzo Anguissola Antona Traversi and Palazzo Brentani, Gallerie d'Italia has around 200 works of art from the 1800s. This collection offers a fascinating journey through one century of Italian art, with pieces by such artists as Antonio Canova, Angelo Inganni, and Umberto Boccioni.

View of the Parco Sempione with the Arco della Pace in the background

Shopping in Milan

In Milan, one of the most affluent cities in Italy, shopping is synonymous with buying designer apparel. High-fashion flagship stores here are invariably smart and stylish, especially in the city center, and looking is almost as satisfying as making a purchase. However, Milan also has many independent boutiques with a range of styles to suit all tastes. If you are looking for gifts to take home, there are some excellent *pasticcerie* (pastry shops), where you can buy authentic delicacies and traditional local confectionery. Alternatively, a cutting-edge object of design will make for an impressive souvenir of your trip to the city.

Where to Shop

All leading fashion designers have shops in the area between Via Montenapoleone, Via della Spiga, Via Manzoni, and Via Sant'Andrea, the so-called "fashion quadrilateral."

Those interested in interior design will enjoy Via Durini, while lovers of antiques should head to Brera or the Navigli, where antiques markets are held monthly.

If time is of the essence, call ahead to check on opening hours. In Milan generally, non-food shops are closed on Monday mornings, and food shops are closed on Monday afternoons. The largest shops tend to stay open throughout the day, but sometimes a lunch break is taken. Shops are closed on Sundays, except for the run-up to Christmas and during the main fashion shows.

Designer Fashion

Milan is renowned as a world capital of fashion, and most national and international designers have a flagship store here. As well as the designers that you would expect to find in a fashion center, such as **Dolce & Gabbana**, **Giorgio Armani**, **Gucci**, **Prada**, and **Hugo Boss**, there are many smaller designer stores. For an overview of what's new, check out multibrand boutiques such as **Banner**, which features a selection of the best from a wide array of names. For the latest on what the younger set is wearing, go to **Amedeo D** or to the Corso di Porta Ticinese area.

Up-and-coming designers are gathering in the areas around Corso Garibaldi and Corso Como. As well as of-the-moment clothes and accessories, **10 Corso Como** offers a bookstore, record store, art gallery, café, and restaurant, and even a top-class B&B. The **Gianfranco Ferrè** boutique, on the other hand, has a spa attached.

Most designers carry men's as well as women's apparel. Specialized men's stores include **Pal Zileri**, **Ermenegildo Zegna**, and **Corneliani**.

Regular Clothing

Designer outlets sell samples, seconds, and last season's goods at a discount. Among Milan's longest-established outlets are **Salvagente** and **DMagazine**. Many designers also have their own outlets: fans of Max Mara, for example, should head for **Diffusione Tessile**.

Milan's main department stores are **La Rinascente** and **Coin**. The former carries many leading-edge fashion designers, while the latter features smaller fashion labels, handbags, costume jewelry, and housewares. There is more to Milan than upmarket, cutting-edge designer fashion, though. For good-value casualwear for the whole family, try **Oviesse**.

Many fashion shoppers also scour the stalls at the Saturday market at Viale Papiniano, at the Piazza Sant'Agostino end, which starts at 8:30am and goes on until 5pm. Corso Vercelli is also recommended.

Accessories

Handbags, shoes, hats, and jewelry, real or otherwise, are also worth seeking out. Chains such as **Furla** and **Coccinelle** offer a wide array of bags, while those looking for shoes can head to **René Caovilla** for a pair of stylish heels, or purchase comfortable shoes with a twist from **Tod's** and **Hogan**. **Garlando** carries a number of classic styles in a wide array of colors and sizes, while **Ghigodonna** has elegant shoes in larger sizes. **Borsalino** is synonymous with stylish headwear.

The "fashion quadrilateral" also features many jewelers, such as **Federico Buccellati**, **Bulgari**, and **Pianegonda**.

Food and Wine

Gourmands will have a great time in Milan. **Peck** consists of three floors of the best that Italy can offer, in terms of both food and wine. **Giovanni Galli Marroni e Canditi** offers a different take on chocolate-coated delicacies.

For those who like a hands-on approach to their food, **High Tech** is a gold mine for kitchen tools, including all the top names such as Alessi, as well as plates and cutlery.

Design, Books, and Gifts

Milan is the cradle of designer furniture. Several top stores are around Piazza San Babila. A stroll down Via Durini will reveal, among others, **Cassina** and **B&B**. For lighting, see **Flos** and **Artemide**. Those interested in 20th-century design could visit **Spazio 900**.

If an item of furniture is not an option, the next best thing might be a book on design or architecture. Visit the bookstore of the **Triennale** or that of the art-catalogue publisher **Skira** for the best on the market.

Fabriano, the company that developed the first paper mill in the 1200s, has a store selling handsome writing paper, envelopes, and gift items.

DIRECTORY

Designer Fashion

10 Corso Como
Corso Como 10.
Tel 02 2900 2674.
Tel 02 626 163 (B&B).
Tel 02 2901 3581
(bar & restaurant).
Tel 02 653 531 (gallery).
W **10corsocomo.it**

Amedeo D
Corso Vercelli 23.
Tel 02 4800 4048.
W **amedeod.it**

Banner
Via Sant'Andrea 8.
Tel 02 7600 4609.
W **biffi.com**

Corneliani
Via Montenapoleone 26.
Tel 02 7631 7955.
W **corneliani.com**

Dolce & Gabbana
Via della Spiga 26
(women).
Tel 02 7600 1155.
Corso Venezia 15 (men).
Tel 02 7602 8485.
Via della Spiga 2
(women's accessories).
Tel 02 795 747.
Corso Venezia 7 (D&G).
Tel 02 7600 4091.
W **dolcegabbana.it**

Ermenegildo Zegna
Via Montenapoleone 27.
Tel 02 7600 6437.
W **zegna.com**

Gianfranco Ferrè
Via Sant'Andrea 15.
Tel 02 794 864 or
02 780 406 (spa and
beauty parlor).
W **gianfrancoferre.com**

Giorgio Armani
Via Sant'Andrea 9.
Tel 02 7600 3234.
Via Manzoni 31 (megastore).
Tel 02 7231 8600.
Via Montenapoleone 2
(Collezioni).
Tel 02 7639 0068.
Via Montenapoleone 10
(Armani Junior).
Tel 02 783 196. Via
Manzoni 37 (Armani Casa).
Tel 02 657 2401. Corso di
Porta Ticinese 60 (Armani
Jeans).
Tel 02 8324 1924.
W **armani.com**

Gucci
Via Montenapoleone 5–7.
Tel 02 771 271.
Galleria Vittorio Emanuele
(accessories).
Tel 02 859 7991.
W **gucci.com**

Hugo Boss
Corso Matteotti 11 (men).
Tel 02 7639 4667.
Corso Matteotti 8
(women).
Tel 02 7601 3266.
W **hugoboss.com**

Pal Zileri
Via Manzoni 20.
Tel 02 7639 4680.
W **palzileri.com**

Prada
Galleria Vittorio
Emanuele 63–65.
Tel 02 876 979.
Via Montenapoleone 8
(women).
Tel 02 777 1771.
Via Montenapoleone 6
(men).
Tel 02 7602 0273.
Via della Spiga 18
(accessories).
Tel 02 780 465.
W **prada.com**

Regular Clothing

Coin
Piazza Cinque Giornate.
Tel 02 5519 2083.
Corso Vercelli 30.
Tel 02 4399 0001.
Piazza Cantore 12.
Tel 02 5810 4385.
W **coin.it**

Diffusione Tessile
Galleria San Carlo 6.
Tel 02 7600 0829.

DMagazine
Via Montenapoleone 26.
Tel 02 7600 6027.

Oviesse
Galleria Passarella 2.
Tel 02 7628 1677.
Corso Garibaldi 72.
Tel 02 655 1649.
Corso Buenos Aires 35.
Tel 02 20 40 48 01.
W **oviesse.it**

La Rinascente
Piazza del Duomo.
Tel 02 88 521.
W **rinascente.it**

Salvagente
Via Fratelli
Bronzetti 16.
Tel 02 7611 0328.
W **salvagentemilano.it**

Accessories

Borsalino
Galleria Vittorio
Emanuele.
Tel 02 8901 5436.
W **borsalino.com**

Bulgari
Via Montenapoleone 2.
Tel 02 777 001.
W **bulgari.com**

Coccinelle
Via Manzoni 26.
Tel 02 7602 8161.
Corso Buenos Aires 16.
Tel 02 2040 4755.

**Federico
Buccellati**
Via della Spiga 2.
Tel 02 7600 3867.
W **federicobuccellati.it**

Furla
Piazza Liberty 8.
Tel 02 782 449.
Corso Vercelli 11.
Tel 02 4801 4189.
W **furla.com**

Garlando
Via Madonnina 2.
Tel 02 874 665.
W **alfonsogarlando.it**

Ghigodonna
Viale Tunisia 2.
Tel 02 2940 8414.
W **ghigocalzature.com**

Hogan
Via Montenapoleone 23.
Tel 02 7601 1174.
W **hogan.com**

Pianegonda
Via Montenapoleone 6.
Tel 02 7600 3038.
W **pianegonda.com**

René Caovilla
Via Bagutta 28.
Tel 02 7631 9049.
W **renecaovilla.com**

Tod's
Via della Spiga 22.
Tel 02 7600 0983.
Galleria Vittorio
Emanuele.
Tel 02 877 997.
W **todsgroup.com**

Food and Wine

**Giovanni Galli
Marroni e Canditi**
Via Victor Hugo 2.
Tel 02 8646 4833.

High Tech
Piazza XXV Aprile 12.
Tel 02 624 1101.

Peck
Via Spadari 9.
Tel 02 802 3161.
W **peck.it**

Design, Books, and Gifts

Artemide
Corso Monforte 19.
Tel 02 7600 6930.
W **artemide.com**

B&B
Via Durini 14.
Tel 02 764 4411.
W **bebitalia.it**

Cassina
Via Durini 16.
Tel 02 7602 0745.
W **cassina.it**

Fabriano
Via Ponte Vetero 17.
Tel 02 7631 8754.
W **cartierefabriano.it**

Flos
Corso Monforte 7.
Tel 02 794 559.
W **flos.net**

Skira
Via Torino 61.
Tel 02 724 441.
W **skira.it**

Spazio 900
Viale Campania 51.
Tel 02 7012 5737.
Corso Garibaldi 42.
Tel 02 7200 1775.

Triennale
Viale Alemagna 6.
Tel 02 7201 8128.
W **triennale.it**

Milan: Pinacoteca di Brera

Milan's finest art collection is held in an imposing 17th-century building, the Palazzo di Brera. This is where, in the 18th century, the Accademia di Belle Arti was founded; the picture collection developed alongside the academy. Inside the Brera hang some of the finest examples of Italian Renaissance and Baroque painting, including works by Piero della Francesca, Mantegna, Canaletto, Bellini, Raphael, Tintoretto, Veronese, and Caravaggio. The collection also includes 20th-century works by some of Italy's most famous modern artists.

★ Dead Christ by Mantegna
The subtle lighting and dramatic perspective of this lamentation by Mantegna (1430–1506) make it one of his greatest masterpieces.

Gallery Guide

The collection is displayed in 38 rooms, and was first built up by paintings from churches, later from acquisitions. Not all of it is permanently on view – this is due to restoration work and research.

Twin staircases lead up to the first-floor entrance of the Pinacoteca.

The Kiss *(1859)*
Francesco Hayez's painting is one of the most reproduced works of Italian 19th-century art. Patriotic and sentimental, it became a symbol of the optimism surrounding the unification of Italy.

The bronze statue (1809) by Canova depicts Napoleon as a demigod with Victory wings in his hand.

Works by Rubens and Van Dyck represent some of the non-Italian artists on show.

Key to Floorplan

- 15th- to 16th-century Italian painting
- 16th- to 17th-century Dutch and Flemish painting
- 17th-century Italian painting
- 18th- to 19th-century Italian painting
- 20th-century Italian painting and sculpture and Jesi Collection
- Nonexhibition space

For hotels and restaurants in this region see pp562–77 and pp580–605

Mother and Son
(1917)
The metaphysical paintings of Carlo Carrà show a dream world full of strange and obscure symbols.

Portrait of Moisè Kisling
Modigliani's angular portrait of 1915 reflects his interest in African sculpture.

Twinned columns support the arcades in the courtyard.

The stone façade presents a regular and slightly austere appearance.

Madonna della Candeletta *(c.1490)* This painting by Carlo Crivelli was the central part of a polyptych. It is richly detailed with much distinctive ornamentation.

Main entrance from Via Brera

★ **Marriage of the Virgin by Raphael** This graceful altarpiece was painted in 1504. The circular temple is signed with the artist's name.

Milan: Southwest of the Center

Some of Milan's finest treasures are to be found in its religious buildings: the ancient monasteries and churches make up some very fine architectural ensembles in themselves, as well as incorporating important ruins and relics dating back to Roman times. It is also in Milan that one of the most famous images in the world is to be found: Leonardo's evocative masterpiece, *The Last Supper*.

San Lorenzo Maggiore viewed from the northeast

The entrance to Sant'Ambrogio, flanked by unequal bell towers

🔼 Sant'Ambrogio

Piazza Sant'Ambrogio 15. **Tel** 02 86 45 08 95. Basilica: **Open** 10am–noon, 2:30–6pm Mon–Sat, 3–5pm Sun. Museum: **Open** 9:30am–noon, 2:30–6pm Mon–Sat, 3–5pm Sun. 🔵 W basilicasantambrogio.it

Sant'Ambrogio, or St. Ambrose, Milan's patron saint and its bishop in the 4th century, was so eloquent that bees were said to fly into his mouth, attracted by his honey tongue. This is the basilica that he began in AD 379, though today most of it is 10th-century Romanesque. A gateway leads to the bronze doors of the entrance, flanked by two bell towers. Inside, note the fine rib vaulting and pulpit, and the 9th-century altar decorated with gold, silver, and

gems. In a chapel off the south aisle, fine mosaics line a stunning cupola. In the crypt lies the tomb of Sant'Ambrogio himself.

Above the portico, a small museum contains architectural fragments, tapestries, and paintings relating to the church.

🔼 San Lorenzo Maggiore

Corso di Porta Ticinese 39. **Tel** 02 89 40 41 29. **Open** 7:30am–6:30pm Mon, Fri, & Sat, 7:30am–12:30pm, 2:30–6:30pm Tue–Thu, 9am–7pm Sun. Cappella Sant'Aquilino: **Open** 9am–6:30pm daily. 🔳 for the Cappella.
W sanlorenzomaggiore.com

This church contains a vast collection of Roman and early Christian remains. The octagonal basilica was built in the 4th century, above what was probably a Roman amphi-theater, and was rebuilt in the 12th and 16th centuries.

In front of the church stands a row of 16 Roman columns and a statue of Emperor Constantine. Fine 4th-century mosaics adorn the Cappella di Sant'Aquilino, a Romanesque chapel, with two early Christian sarcophagi. Other Roman architectural elements of this church are in a chamber below the chapel.

🔼 Santa Maria delle Grazie

Piazza Santa Maria delle Grazie 2. **Tel** 02 46 76 111. Cenacolo: **Tel** 02 92 80 03 60 (reservations required – up to 60 days in advance). **Open** 8:15am–6:45pm Tue–Sun. **Closed** public hols. 🔳 🔵 W cenacolovinciano.org

This beautiful 15th-century Renaissance convent, its lovely apse, and calm small cloister designed by Bramante contains one of the key images of western civilization: the *Cenacolo (The Last Supper)* by Leonardo da Vinci. The image captures the moment at which Christ tells his disciples that one of them will betray him. The Christ figure is unfinished: Leonardo did not consider himself worthy enough to complete it.

The artist also spurned the standard fresco technique of painting on wet plaster, apply-ing tempera to the dry wall instead. The result has deterio-rated badly: the paint is flaking off, and restoration has proved difficult. The painting is now protected by a filtering system.

Leonardo da Vinci's *Last Supper* (1494–7) adorning the refectory wall of Santa Maria delle Grazie

For hotels and restaurants in this region see pp562–77 and pp580–605

❹ Monza

Monza. 🚇 120,000. 🚆 🚌 ℹ️ Piazza Carducci 2 (039 32 32 22). **Open** 9am–noon, 3–6pm daily. 🛍️ Thu & Sat.

These days Monza is famous mostly for its international Formula One **Autodromo**, which lies inside a vast park that also has an elegant Rococo hunting lodge, the Villa Reale, and a golf course. At one time, however, Monza was one of the most important towns in Lombardy. Theodolinda, the 6th-century Lombard queen, built its first cathedral and bequeathed her treasure to the town.

In the town center is the **Duomo**, with its notable green and white 14th-century façade and beautiful 15th-century frescoes portraying Theodolinda's life. Behind the high altar is the small Iron Crown, believed to have belonged to Emperor Constantine: it is prized for the iron strip, said to have been one of the nails from the cross of Christ. More local treasures may be found in the Duomo's **Museo e Tesoro del Duomo**, including a silver hen standing over seven tiny chicks – which symbolize Lombardy and the seven provinces it ruled – and a relic said to be John the Baptist's tooth.

🏁 Autodromo
Parco di Monza. **Tel** 039 248 21. **Open** daily. **Closed** public hols. 🅿️ ♿

🏛️ Duomo
Piazza Duomo. **Tel** 039 38 94 20. Museo e Tesoro del Duomo: **Open** 9am–1pm, 2–6pm Tue–Sun. 🅿️

Leonello d'Este (c.1440) by Pisanello in the Accademia Carrara, Bergamo

❺ Bergamo

🚇 120,000. 🚆 🚌 ℹ️ Via Gombito 13 (035 24 22 26). **Open** 9am–12:30pm, 2–5:30pm daily. 🛍️ Mon. 🌐 turismo.bergamo.it

Bergamo owes much of its artistic inspiration and architectural splendor to the influence of Venice, which ruled it from the 15th to the late 18th century. The town is divided into two distinct parts: Bergamo Alta, crowning the hill with its cluster of attractive medieval and Renaissance buildings, and the more modern Bergamo Bassa below.

The jewel of the upper town is **Piazza Vecchia**, containing one of the most appealing architectural ensembles in the region. Its buildings include the 12th-century Torre del Comune with its fine clock and curfew bell that rings daily at 10pm, the late 16th-century Biblioteca Civica, and the attractive 12th-century Palazzo della Ragione, or law courts, adorned with a bass-relief of the Lion of Venice.

The arcades of the Palazzo della Ragione lead to Piazza del Duomo, the square of the Neo-Classical Duomo. The square is dominated by the **Cappella Colleoni** *(see p184)*, a chapel built in 1476 to house the tomb of Bergamo's famous political leader, Bartolomeo Colleoni. It is flanked by two 14th-century buildings: an octagonal baptistry and the porch leading to the Romanesque basilica of Santa Maria Maggiore. The basilica's austere exterior contrasts with its Baroque interior, which contains the tomb of Bergamo-born composer Gaetano Donizetti (1797–1848).

The collection from the **Galleria dell' Accademia Carrara**, a major picture gallery with works by Venetian masters and local artists, as well as masterpieces from the rest of Italy, is housed temporarily in **Palazzo della Ragione** while the building is being restored. It includes 15th- and 16th-century works by Pisanello, Crivelli, Mantegna, Giovanni Bellini, Botticelli, Titian, Raphael, and Perugino, 18th-century canvases by Tiepolo, Guardi, and Canaletto, as well as paintings by Holbein, Dürer, Brueghel, and Velázquez.

🏛️ Palazzo della Ragione
Città Alta. **Tel** 035 39 96 77. **Open** Jun–Sep: 10am–9pm Tue–Sun (to 11pm Sat); Oct–May: 9:30am–5:30pm Tue–Fri, 10am–6pm Sat–Sun. 🅿️ ♿

Emperor Constantine

The Edict of Milan

Milan was colonized by the Romans in 222 BC, and quickly grew to be an important city at the junction of various trading routes. As the Roman Empire grew and then split into two, the emperors began to neglect Rome for the better-placed Mediolanum (literally, city in the middle of the plain). It was here that Emperor Constantine declared his edict of AD 313, in which Christianity was recognized as one of the permitted religions of the empire, ending centuries of persecution. The emperor is said to have converted following a vision, but by the 4th century adopting Christianity was also one way to unite the disparate empire.

Detail from the Cappella Colleoni

A leafy pathway through the Parco Nazionale dello Stelvio

❻ Parco Nazionale dello Stelvio

Trento, Bolzano, Sondrio, & Brescia. 🚌 from Bormio to Santa Caterina Valfurva & Madonna dei Monti. 🛈 Via de Simoni 42, Bormio (0342 90 08 11). 🔳 **stelviopark.it**

The Stelvio, Italy's largest national park, is the gateway from Lombardy to the glacier-strewn Dolomite mountains stretching into Trentino–Alto Adige. The glaciers are dotted with more than 50 lakes, and dominated by craggy peaks such as Gran Zebrù, Cevedale, and Ortles – the tallest mountain here at 12,811 ft (3,905 m).

For walkers, the area offers excellent hiking, and access to remote areas populated by ibexes, marmots, chamois, and eagles. The only real population center in the Lombardy part of the park is at **Bormio**, which boasts plenty of winter and summer sports facilities, and is a good base from which to explore the area. The town's **Giardino Botanico**, a 0.6 mile (1 km) walk from the center, displays some of the species of mountain plants found in the region.

🌿 **Giardino Botanico Alpino Rezia**
Via Sertorelli, Loc. Rovinaccia, Bormio. **Tel** 0342 92 73 70. **Open** Jun–mid-Sep: daily. 🐾 🔳 **stelviopark.it**

❼ Val Camonica

Brescia. 🚊 🚌 Capo di Ponte. 🛈 Via Briscioli, Capo di Ponte (0364 420 80). 🔳 **proloco.capo-di-ponte.bs.it**

This attractive broad valley formed by a glacier is the setting for an extraordinary series of prehistoric rock carvings. These form an astonishing outdoor mural from the Lago d'Iseo to Capo di Ponte and beyond, and the valley is a UNESCO cultural protection zone. More than 180,000 engravings from the Neolithic era until early Roman times have been discovered; the best are in the **Parco Nazionale delle Incisioni Rupestri**. Do not miss the Naquane rock, carved with nearly 1,000 figures from the Ice Age. The **Centro Camuno** focuses on the Roman settlement in the valley.

🏛 **Centro Camuno di Studi Preistorici**
Via Marconi 7, Capo di Ponte. **Tel** 0364 420 91. **Closed** to tourists. ♿

🏛 **Parco Nazionale delle Incisioni Rupestri**
Capo di Ponte. **Tel** 0364 421 40. **Open** 8:30am–7:30pm Tue–Sun (mid-Oct–Feb to 4:30pm). **Closed** Jan 1, May 1, Dec 25.

❽ Lago d'Iseo

Bergamo & Brescia. 🚊 🚌 🚢 Iseo. 🛈 Lungolago Marconi 2, Iseo (030 98 02 09). 🔳 **lagodiseo.org**

This glaciated lake is surrounded by tall mountains and waterfalls and boasts a mini-mountain of its own, in the form of the island of Monte Isola. Along the shores of the lake are a clutch of fishing villages such as Sale Marasino and Iseo itself. From Marone, on the east bank of the lake, a road leads to the village of **Cislano**, about 3 miles (5 km) away. Here, extraordinary spire-like rock formations rise from the ground, each spire topped by a boulder. These distinctive erosion pillars, one of the strangest natural wonders in Lombardy, are known as the "Fairies of the Forest."

Prehistoric engraving of a mounted hunter and stag in the Val Camonica

The partly Renaissance Ponte Coperto, straddling the River Ticino at Pavia

9 Brescia

195,000. FS ☐ 🛈 Via Musei 32 (030 374 96 16). ☐ Sat.

Lombardy's second city after Milan boasts a rich artistic heritage, ranging from Roman temples to the triumphalist Mussolini-era architecture of Piazza Vittoriale. The major sights, which are on the UNESCO World Heritage list, include the Roman ruins around Piazza del Foro, consisting of the **Tempio Capitolino** – a three-part temple incorporating the **Museo di Santa Giulia**, Brescia's main gallery – and a theater. The **Pinacoteca Civica Tosio Martinengo** has masterpieces by Raphael, Lorenzo Lotto, and Tintoretto. The **Duomo** on Piazza Paolo VI, with its 11th-century core and 17th-century exterior, is another main attraction. One of the relics in the Duomo is the banner from the *Carroccio*, or sacred ox cart, which served as a symbol for the medieval Lega Lombarda. **Piazza della Loggia**, where the market is held, is named after the Renaissance loggia, built in Palladian style. The 18th-century church of San Nazaro e San Celso on Via Bronzoni contains an altarpiece by Titian.

🏛 **Tempio Capitolino**
Via Musei 57a. **Open** 11am–4pm Tue–Sun. 🎟

🏛 **Museo di Santa Giulia**
Via Musei 81b. **Tel** 030 297 78 34. **Open** Tue–Sun. 🎟 🚻

🏛 **Pinacoteca Civica Tosio Martinengo**
Via Martinengo da Barcol. **Tel** 030 377 49 99. **Open** daily.

10 Lodi

Lodi. 44,000. FS ☐ 🛈 Via Fanfulla 14 (0371 44 27 11). ☐ Tue, Thu, Sat, & Sun. 🖵 turismo. provincia.lodi.it

This is a charming medieval town of pastel-colored houses, pretty courtyards, and gardens. Just off Piazza della Vittoria, the arcaded square on which the 12th-century Duomo stands, is the fine Renaissance church of the **Incoronata**. The magnificent octagonal interior is entirely decorated with wall paintings and gilding, and crowned with a dome. One of the chapels has 15th-century works by Bergognone.

11 Pavia

71,000. FS ☐ 🛈 Palazzo del Broletto, Piazza della Vittoria (0382 07 99 43). ☐ Wed & Sat. 🖵 turismo. provincia.pv.it

During Pavia's golden age, the city was the Lombards' capital, and later witnessed coronations of Charlemagne and Frederick

The Roman Tempio Capitolino in Brescia

Barbarossa. Even after it lost its status to Milan in 1359, Pavia remained an important city, and great Romanesque churches, tall towers, and other monuments still reflect this.

As well as the Charterhouse (Certosa) *(see pp204–5)*, there is the sandstone **Basilica di San Michele** off Corso Garibaldi. The building was founded in the 7th century but largely rebuilt in the 12th. Its façade is decorated with symbols and friezes of fantastic animals, and inside there are intricate carvings on the columns; a chapel to the right of the main altar contains a 7th-century silver crucifix.

In the town center, around Piazza della Vittoria, are several ancient monuments, such as the medieval **Broletto** (town hall), with its 16th-century façade, and the **Duomo**, originally begun in 1488 and worked on in turn by Amadeo, Leonardo, and Bramante. The dome was added in the 1880s. The 11th-century tower that stood next to it collapsed suddenly in 1989. Crossing the river is the **Ponte Coperto**, a Renaissance covered bridge with a consecrated chapel halfway along it. The bridge was rebuilt after World War II.

Pavia is also the site of one of Europe's oldest (1361) and most respected universities, now residing around a series of Neo-Classical courtyards off Strada Nuova. This road continues northward to the 14th-century castle, now home to the **Museo Civico**.

Northwest of Piazza Castello is the 12th-century church **San Pietro in Ciel d'Oro**. It no longer boasts the fine gilded ceiling after which it is named, but does still contain a magnificent shrine to St. Augustine, whose bones were allegedly brought to Pavia in the 8th century. The body of the philosopher Boëthius (c.480–524) is buried down in the crypt.

🏛 **Museo Civico**
Castello Visconteo, Viale 11 Febbraio. **Tel** 0382 338 53. **Open** 10am–5:50pm Tue–Sun (Jan, Jul, Aug, & Dec: 9am–1:30pm). **Closed** public hols. 🎟 🚻

⑫ Certosa di Pavia

The Charterhouse 5 miles (8 km) north of Pavia is the pinnacle of Renaissance architecture in Lombardy, a gloriously decorated Carthusian monastery built over 200 years. Conceived as a monument to Gian Galeazzo Visconti, the Milanese ruler who founded the complex in 1396, this shrine was created by the great 15th-century craftsman Giovanni Antonio Amadeo, among others, who used innovative techniques of relief work and multicolored decoration. The Certosa is still home to Carthusian monks, who are under a strict vow of silence.

Pietra Dura Altar
Several of the 17th-century altars in the chapels have lavish designs worked in semiprecious stones ("pietra dura").

KEY

① **The side chapels** are richly decorated with marble, *trompe l'oeil* frescoes, and ornate altars and altarpieces.

② **The interior** of the church is largely Gothic.

③ **The grilles** date from c.1660.

④ **The choir stalls** (15th century) are deeply carved and inlaid with intricate marquetry

⑤ **The tomb** of Gian Galeazzo Visconti (1351–1402) is in the south transept.

⑥ **The New Sacristy** is painted with colorful ceiling frescoes.

⑦ **Monk's cell**

⑧ **This delightful**, arcaded Small Cloister, with fine terra-cotta ornamentation, contains a small garden, planted in formal designs.

⑨ **Main entrance** to the Certosa

Tomb of Ludovico il Moro and Beatrice d'Este
This realistic marble portrait of Ludovico and his child bride was begun by Cristoforo Solari in 1497, some 11 years before Ludovico's death.

★ Frescoes by Bergognone *(c.1488–93)*
This striking portrait of Christ is one of several frescoes by Bergognone in the transept and chapels, together with an altar painting of Sant'Ambrogio.

Great Cloister
This huge cloister is reached through the Small Cloister. It is framed on three sides by the two-story monks' cells, each backed by a small garden. A hatch beside the door permits food to be delivered without any communication.

VISITORS' CHECKLIST

Practical Information
Viale del Monumento, Pavia.
Tel 0382 92 56 13. from Pavia & Milan. **Open** 9–11:30am, 2:30–4:30pm Tue–Sun & pub hols (Mar, Oct: to 5pm; Apr, Sep: to 5:30pm; May–Aug: to 6pm). (Last adm: 30 mins before closing.) Donation to guide.

Transportation
Certosa. Followed by 0.5 mile (1 km) walk.

★ **Altarpiece by Perugino**
The six-panel altarpiece was painted in 1499, but now only one panel – that depicting God the Father – is original; it is flanked by two paintings by Bergognone.

★ **Renaissance Façade**
The 15th-century lower part of the façade is profusely decorated with statues and carvings of Roman emperors, saints (here St. Peter), apostles, and prophets. The upper part dates from 1500.

The Duomo on Piazza del Comune, Cremona

⑬ Cremona

🏙 72,000. 🚆 🚌 ℹ Piazza del Comune 5 (0372 40 63 91). 📅 Wed & Sat. 🌐 **turismocremona.it**

Cremona, a major agricultural market, is most famous for music, thanks to native sons such as the composer Claudio Monteverdi (1567–1643) and the violin-maker Stradivarius (1644–1737). The town itself is dominated by the beautiful Piazza del Comune.

The main attraction is the exuberant part-Romanesque **Duomo** and its bell tower – said to be the tallest medieval tower in Italy – known as the **Torrazzo**; the two are linked by a Renaissance loggia. The wonderful façade is dominated by the large 13th-century rose window and by a number of intricate touches, including a small portico with statues of the Virgin and saints. Inside, the Duomo is sumptuously decorated with magnificent early 16th-century frescoes and Flemish tapestries, as well as paintings in the side chapels. The top of the Torrazzo offers sweeping views. Outside the Duomo, note the pulpit where itinerant preachers, including San Bernardino of Siena, spoke.

Next to the Duomo stands an octagonal 12th-century baptistry, while on the other side of the piazza rise the arcades of the late 13th-century **Loggia dei Militi** where the town's lords once met, now a war memorial.

The **Palazzo del Comune** is the other major building on the square. It was rebuilt in the 1200s and houses the Stradivari family collection of violins and masterpieces by Amati and Guarnieri.

The **Museo Civico**, in a 16th-century palazzo, houses the Pinacoteca, containing paintings, wood carvings, the cathedral's treasure, and ceramics. The building also houses the **Museo Stradivariano**, which displays drawings, models, and tools from Stradivarius's workshop.

On the eastern outskirts of the town, on the road to Casalmaggiore, lies the Renaissance church of **San Sigismondo** (closed at lunchtime). It was here in a small chapel that Francesco Sforza married Bianca Visconti in 1441. The interior is richly decorated with 16th-century paintings, altarpieces, and frescoes by artists of the Cremona school (Campi family, Gatti, and Boccaccino).

🏰 **Torrazzo**
P. del Comune. **Tel** 0372 49 50 29.
Open 10am–1pm, 2:30–6pm Tue–Sun. 🏷

🏛 **Palazzo del Comune**
Piazza del Comune. **Tel** 0372 80 36 18.
Open 9am–6pm Tue–Sat; 10am–6pm Sun. **Closed** public hols. 🏷 ♿

🏛 **Museo Stradivariano & Museo Civico**
Via Ugolani Dati 4. **Tel** 0372 80 36 22.
Open 10am–5pm Tue–Sun.
Closed public hols. 🏷 ♿

⑭ Sabbioneta

Mantua. 🏙 4,400. 🚌 from Mantua.
ℹ Piazza d'Armi 1 (0375 520 39).
📅 Wed am. 🎫 apply at tourist office.
🏷 🌐 **iatsabbioneta.org**

Sabbioneta is the result of a delightful experiment in the theory of Renaissance architecture. It was built by Vespasiano Gonzaga Colonna (1531–91) as an ideal city, and within its hexagonal walls is a perfect gridwork arrangement of streets and buildings designed on a human scale. The finest buildings include the splendid Teatro All'Antica designed by Scamozzi, the Palazzo Ducale, and the frescoed Palazzo del Giardino, which may be visited as part of a tour of the town.

Antonio Stradivari and His Violins

The city of Cremona has been synonymous with violin-making since the 1530s, when Andrea Amati's instruments became sought after at the royal courts throughout Europe because of their superior tone to the medieval fiddle.

However, it was Antonio Stradivari, known as Stradivarius (1644–1737) – the pupil of Andrea Amati's grandson Niccolò – who raised the level of violin craftsman-

19th-century engraving of Antonio Stradivari

ship to genius. He went walking in the forests of the Dolomites in search of the perfect wood for his instruments. Stradivarius produced more than 1,100 violins in his workshop, of which more than 400 exist today. The main stopping-off points on a Stradivarius tour of Cremona are the Museo Stradivariano in the Museo Civico, the string collection in the Palazzo del Comune, and the great man's tombstone in the public gardens in Piazza Roma.

The ceiling of the Camera degli Sposi, by Mantegna, in the Palazzo Ducale

⓯ Mantua

🏙 49,000. 🚆 🚌 ℹ️ Piazza Andrea Mantegna 6 (0376 43 24 32). 🛍 Thu.
🌐 **turismo.mantova.it**

Mantua (Mantova in Italian) is a striking place of fine squares and aristocratic architecture, bordered on three sides by lakes formed by the River Mincio. The climate can be humid as a result, but the city makes up for it with its cultural history: it was the birthplace of the poet Virgil and the playground of the Gonzaga dukes for three centuries. It was also the refuge where Shakespeare sent Romeo into exile from Verona, and the setting for Verdi's opera *Rigoletto*. These links are all celebrated in street names, signposts, and monuments around the town. The theatrical connections are enhanced by the 18th-century **Teatro Accademico Bibiena**, on Via Accademia, which Mozart's father claimed was the finest he had ever seen.

Mantua is focused on three attractive main squares: Piazza delle Erbe, Piazza Broletto, named after the 13th-century building adorned with a statue of the poet Virgil, and the cobbled Piazza Sordello. On one side of Piazza Sordello is the **Duomo**, with an 18th-century façade and fine interior stuccoes by Giulio Romano (c.1492–1546); on another side, the forbidding façade of the Palazzo Bonacolsi, with its tall prison tower. Piazza delle Erbe is dominated by the **Basilica di Sant'Andrea**

(15th century), designed largely by Leon Battista Alberti, the early Renaissance architect and theorist, and now flanked by an arcade of shops. The square is also notable for the appealing 11th-century Rotonda di San Lorenzo, and the part-13th-century Palazzo della Ragione with its 15th-century clock tower.

Detail from the 15th-century clock tower on Piazza delle Erbe

🏛 Palazzo Ducale

Piazza Sordello 40. **Tel** 0376 22 48 32. **Open** 8:15am–7:15pm (last adm: 6pm) Tue–Sun. **Closed** Jan 1, Dec 25. 📷 📹 Camera degli Sposi Make advance reservations at **Tel** 041 241 18 97 or 🌐 **ducalemantova.org**

The vast, 500-room home of the Gonzaga family covers the northeastern corner of the town and incorporates Castello San Giorgio (a 14th-century fortress), a basilica, and the palace proper. The many works of art include an unfinished series of 15th-century frescoes by Pisanello, retelling episodes from the Arthurian legends; a large portrait by Rubens (17th century) of the ducal family in the Salone degli Arcieri; and – most absorbing of all – the frescoes by Mantegna in the **Camera degli Sposi** (1465–74). These portray Lodovico Gonzaga and members of his family and court in all their magnificence *(pp208–9)*. The entire room is decorated with images of people, animals, and fantastic landscapes, and is completed by a lighthearted *trompe l'oeil* ceiling of figures, *putti*, and a blue sky.

🏛 Palazzo Tè

Viale Tè. **Tel** 0376 32 32 66. **Open** 1–6pm Mon, 9am–6pm Tue–Sun. **Closed** Jan 1, May 1, Dec 25. 📷 ♿
🌐 **palazzote.it**

At the other end of town stands the early 16th-century Palazzo Tè, built by Giulio Romano for the Gonzaga family as a base from which they could go horseback riding. Here the artworks conspire with the architecture to produce striking effects: in the **Sala dei Giganti**, for instance, the frescoed Titans seem to be tearing down the very pillars of the room. Also remarkable is the **Sala di Amore e Psiche**, decorated with erotic scenes from Apuleius' *Golden Ass* and said to celebrate Federico II's love for his mistress. Other rooms are lavishly painted with horses and signs of the Zodiac.

The 13th-century façade of Palazzo Ducale overlooking Piazza Sordello

Late Renaissance fresco, by Romano, in the Duomo di Mantua, Mantua ▶

VALLE D'AOSTA AND PIEDMONT

Piedmont and the neighboring Valle d'Aosta are – apart from Turin and its cultural splendors – essentially countryside. To the north lie the Alps, with ski resorts such as Courmayeur, and the wild stretches of the Parco Nazionale del Gran Paradiso. To the south lie the vineyard-clad hills around Barolo, and seemingly endless fields of grain and rice, used in the local dish, risotto.

The northwest is also rich in culture. From the 11th century to the 18th, both the verdant Valle d'Aosta and Piedmont were part of the French-speaking principality of Savoy and enjoyed the influences of both sides of the Alpine divide. Even today, French and dialectal variants are still spoken in the remote valleys of Piedmont and in much of the Valle d'Aosta. It was only under Duke Emanuele Filiberto in the 16th century that the region was brought definitively into the Italian sphere of influence, and later it was to play the key role in the Risorgimento *(see pp66–7)*, the ambitious movement that united Italy under a king from Piedmont. The vestiges of this history are to be found in the medieval castles of the Valle d'Aosta and the clusters of

chapels known as *sacri monti* (sacred mountains) built into the foothills of the Alps. Piedmont also spawned a school of painting, which is in evidence in the small parish churches and excellent fine art collections in the region. The most impressive architecture in the northwest, however, is undoubtedly to be found in Turin, a much underrated and surprisingly elegant Baroque city that boasts, among other things, one of the best Egyptian museums in the world. Piedmont is also known for its industry – FIAT in Turin, Olivetti in Ivrea, Ferrero in Alba – but it has not forgotten its agricultural roots, and food and drink play an important role in the life of the region: the hills of southern Piedmont produce many of the great Italian red wines.

Traditional sidewalk café in the heart of Turin

◀ Banners hanging outside of the Gothic Duomo in Asti, Piedmont

Exploring Valle d'Aosta and Piedmont

The vast flat plain of the Po, covered with the watery expanse of rice fields around Vercelli and Novara, eventually gives way, in the west, to the majestic heights of the Alps. Turin, the largest city in the area and the capital of Piedmont, stands at the edge of the plain, nestling almost in the shadow of the mountains. Further northwest, attractive Alpine valleys headed by dramatic peaks provide the setting for the traditional villages, ancient towns, and castles around Aosta. The Parco Nazionale del Gran Paradiso is an unspoiled tract of breathtaking scenery.

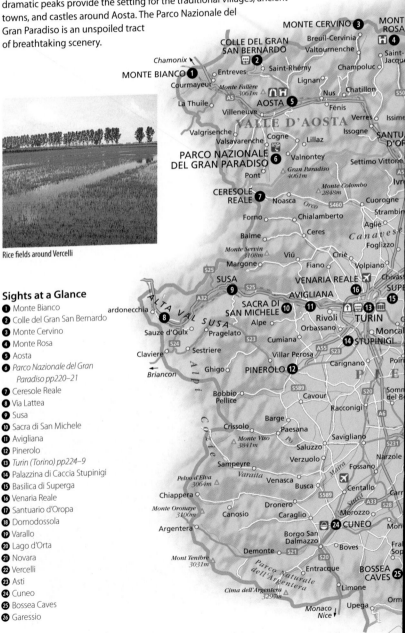

Rice fields around Vercelli

Sights at a Glance

1 Monte Bianco
2 Colle del Gran San Bernardo
3 Monte Cervino
4 Monte Rosa
5 Aosta
6 Parco Nazionale del Gran Paradiso pp220–21
7 Ceresole Reale
8 Via Lattea
9 Susa
10 Sacra di San Michele
11 Avigliana
12 Pinerolo
13 Turin (Torino) pp224–9
14 Palazzina di Caccia Stupinigi
15 Basilica di Superga
16 Venaria Reale
17 Santuario d'Oropa
18 Domodossola
19 Varallo
20 Lago d'Orta
21 Novara
22 Vercelli
23 Asti
24 Cuneo
25 Bossea Caves
26 Garessio

For additional map symbols *see back flap*

Turin, the capital of Piedmont, in the valley of the Po

Getting Around

The Fréjus Pass and the Mont Blanc Tunnel link France with northwest Italy, while the tunnel under the Simplon or Sempione Pass provides a direct rail route from Switzerland. From the rest of Italy there are excellent highway connections across the plain to Turin and up to Aosta. The region is well served with railroad links, and buses connect the main towns and outlying resorts. Getting around the mountains is more difficult, making the car the best method of transportation.

St. Pierre castle in the Valle d'Aosta

0 kilometers 25

0 miles 20

Key

- ▬▬ Highway
- ▬▬ Major road
- ▬▬ Secondary road
- ⋯⋯ Minor road
- ▬▬ Scenic route
- ⌐⌐⌐ Main railroad
- ─── Minor railroad
- ▬▬ International border
- ▬▬ Regional border
- △ Summit

❶ Monte Bianco

Aosta. **FS** Pré-St-Didier. 🚌 Courmayeur. 🛈 Piazzale Monte Bianco 13, Courmayeur (0165 84 20 60).

Monte Bianco (Mont Blanc), the tallest mountain in the Alps at 15,780 ft (4,810 m), dominates the western Aosta valley and its attractive all-year resort, **Courmayeur**. A series of cable car rides from Entrèves, 3 miles (5 km) further north, leads to Chamonix. Passing its highest point (12,606 ft, 3,842 m) at Aiguille du Midi, it offers a spectacular view. From Pré-St-Didier, below Courmayeur, the **Little St. Bernard Pass**, with its small glaciers, forests, and ravines, can be explored.

❷ Colle del Gran San Bernardo

Aosta. **FS** 🚌 Aosta. 🛈 Strada Nazionale Gran San Bernardo 13, Etroubles (0165 785 59). **Open** daily.

The Great St. Bernard pass is synonymous with the hardy mountain rescue dogs that have been trained locally by Catholic monks since the 11th century.

The **Monks' Hospice**, founded around 1050 by St. Bernard of Aosta, lies just over the Swiss border (bring your passport), on the shores of a lovely lake; the dogs are still being trained here. The pretty Great St. Bernard valley itself includes the town of Etroubles, set in a forest of conifers, the hamlet of St-Oyen with its pretty parish church, and the resort of St-Rhémy-en-Bosses.

A St. Bernard dog

🏠 **Monks' Hospice**
Colle San Bernardo, Switzerland.
Tel 00 41 277 87 12 36. **Open** daily.

❸ Monte Cervino

Aosta. **FS** 🚌 Breuil-Cervinia. 🛈 Piazza Rey Guido, Breuil-Cervinia (0166 94 91 36).

The distinctive triangular peak of Monte Cervino (the Matterhorn) rises to 14,691 ft (4,478 m) and is easily recognizable. Below the mountain lies a scattering of attractive villages like Antey-St-André, Valtournanche (which gave its name to the valley), and the resort of **Breuil-Cervinia**.

From Breuil a cable car rises to the Plateau Rosa (11,418 ft, 3,480 m), offering dramatic views of the surrounding mountains. This entire area is a paradise for both skiers and walkers.

❹ Monte Rosa

Aosta. **FS** Verrès. 🚌 St-Jacques. 🛈 Route Varasc, Champoluc/Ayas (0125 30 71 13).

Monte Rosa, Italy's second-highest mountain, overlooks the picturesque Ayas and Gressoney valleys. The rolling lower Ayas valley is dominated by the ruins of the 11th-century **Castello di Graines**. Higher up, the resort of Champoluc has a cable car connection with the striking **Testa Grigia** (10,877 ft/3,315 m). The Gressoney valley is home to the Walser people, who speak a German dialect. At the bottom of the valley, north of Pont-St-Martin, lies **Issime**: the 16th-century church here has a fresco of the Last Judgment on its façade.

🏠 **Castello di Graines**
Graines, Strada Statale 506.

Medieval Castles and Forts in the Valle d'Aosta

The mountains alone provided insufficient protection to the fragmented fiefs that covered the Valle d'Aosta in the Middle Ages. The medieval lords, who ruled ruthlessly over their small domains, built castles to enforce their often fragile power. Of the many built, 70 castles survive in some form to this day. You will pass a number of them if you drive into Italy by the Mont Blanc tunnel; they stretch from Aosta to Pont-St-Martin.

Originally, Aosta castles were designed to be defensive and threatening, such as the looming tower of **Montmayer**, perched high on a huge rock by the Valgrisenche valley. Nearby, the equally forbidding dark tower of **Ussel** throws a melancholy, brooding watchfulness over the valley.

Fénis and **Verrès** represent an important shift in the function of the feudal castle. Both Fénis, a splendid 14th-century showpiece *(see p184)*, and Verrès were not just important military outposts but also examples of palatial opulence and good living. **Issogne** too furthered this luxurious trend with its elaborate frescoes, loggias, and fountains. Decoration was also important to Vittorio Emanuele II, owner of **Sarre**, who turned the halls of his fortress into a plush hunting lodge. The owners of **Châtelard**, set in some of the highest vineyards in Europe, placed fine wine production alongside military aims.

The strategically sited 14th-century castle at Verrès

The 12th-century cloister, with 40 carved columns of darkened marble, in Sant'Orso

❺ Aosta

🏙 35,000. 🚉 🚌 ℹ️ Porta Pretoria 3 (0165 23 66 27). 🗓 Tue. 🌐 **lovevda. it**

Lying on a plain surrounded by dramatic mountains, the town of Aosta provides a remarkable mixture of ancient culture and spectacular scenery. The Romans captured it from the Salassian Gauls in 25 BC, and Aosta is still dotted with fine Roman architecture built in honor of Emperor Augustus – indeed the town was once called *Augusta Praetoria*, its name only evolving into Aosta over the centuries. The medieval town was later fortified by the Challant family and then by the Dukes of Aosta, who added towers to the old Roman walls.

Modern Aosta is a bustling crossroads for local industries and tourists on their way to the mountains. The center, however, still consists of a delightful grid of large squares and surprising architectural treasures, which justify Aosta's nickname of "Rome of the Alps."

🏛 Roman Ruins

Roman Theater, Via Baillage. **Open** 9am–8pm daily (to 7pm Sep–Mar, to 6:30pm Oct & Feb, to 5pm Nov–Jan). **Roman Forum**, Piazza Giovanni XXIII. **Open** daily.

In Roman times, entry to Aosta was over the **bridge** to the east of the town (beyond the modern bridge) and through the **Arch of Augustus**. This triumphal arch is today marred by a roof added in the 18th century. Ahead stands the **Porta Pretoria**, its double row of stone arches flanked by a medieval tower; the gateway originally stood about 8 ft (2.5 m) higher than at present. Also worth a look is the 65-ft (20-m) high façade of the **Roman Theater**. A little to the north is the elliptical amphitheater, although this is buried apart from three columns that form part of the convent of San Giuseppe. In the old town, next to the cathedral, lies the **Roman Forum**, or marketplace, with its huge cryptoporticus: the function of this impressive underground gallery remains the subject of speculation.

Detail of a medieval mosaic on the floor of Aosta's Cattedrale

🏛 Cattedrale

Piazza Giovanni XXIII. **Open** 6:30am–12:30pm, 2–7:30pm Mon–Fri, 7am–noon, 2–6pm Sat & Sun (early Sep–Easter: 6:30am–noon, 3–7pm). **Museo del Tesoro Tel** 0165 404 13. **Open** 3–5:30pm Sat & Sun. **Closed** during religious services. 📷

This relatively modest shrine to St. John the Baptist was first built in the 12th century, but has been altered many times since. The interior is Gothic, with finely carved 15th-century choir stalls and floor mosaics. Next door, the **Museo del Tesoro** contains a rich collection of statuettes and reliquaries, and a number of impressive medieval tombs.

🏛 Sant'Orso

Via Sant'Orso. **Open** daily. ♿

East of the town walls is the architectural highlight of Aosta: a medieval complex of church buildings. Sant'Orso itself has an unusual Gothic façade with a narrow, tall portal. The interior has 11th-century frescoes, a crypt holding the tomb of St. Orso, patron saint of Aosta, and a beautiful **cloister** with carved columns and capitals.

Environs

The castle at **Fénis** *(see p218)*, 8 miles (12 km) east, is one of the few castles in the Aosta valley with a well-preserved interior, including beautiful frescoes and wooden galleries. **Issogne**, 23 miles (38 km) southeast, is the setting for another highly decorated castle, remodeled around 1490. It has many frescoes and decorative motifs, including an octagonal fountain with a centerpiece in the shape of a pomegranate tree.

🏰 Castello di Fénis

Fénis. **Tel** 0165 76 42 63. **Open** daily. **Closed** Tue (Oct–Feb); Jan 1, Dec 25. 📷

🏰 Castello di Issogne

Issogne. **Tel** 0125 92 93 73. **Open** daily. **Closed** Wed (Oct–Feb); Jan 1, Dec 25. 📷

Some of the impressive ruins standing in the Roman Forum in Aosta

⊙ Parco Nazionale del Gran Paradiso

A breathtaking wilderness of dramatic mountains and lush meadows, the Gran Paradiso is Italy's foremost national park, created in 1922 from part of a former royal hunting reserve of the House of Savoy. It is mainly a summer resort for walkers due to its unspoiled scenery, rare wildlife, and unusual Alpine flowers, though there is also cross-country skiing during the winter months. The king of the park is the ibex, a relative of the goat family all but extinct in the rest of Europe. The park is also prized by naturalists for its chamois, ptarmigan, golden eagles, rare butterflies, and marmots.

Castello di Aymavilles
The 18th-century core of this castle is framed by medieval corner towers.

Val di Rhêmes-Notre-Dame
This peaceful and broad valley offers magnificent scenery with waterfalls and fast-flowing streams running from the glacier at its head.

AOSTA

ARVIER · VILLENEUVE · Aymavilles

Pondel

Rhêmes-St-George

Val di rhêmes

Val di savarenche

Valsavarenche

Rhêmes-Notre-Dame

COL LAUSO

Eaux-Rousses

PICCO PARAD

Pont

GRAN PARADISO,
4,061 m
(13,320 ft)

No

Ceresole Reale

KEY

① **Goletta Waterfall** is an impressive cascade near the Lago di Goletta.

② **Cogne** is the main resort and a good base from which to explore the park. Maps of the park's routes and hiking trails are available here.

③ **Lillaz** is sedate and off the beaten track, while Valnontey and Cogne are two of the busiest resorts.

★ Paradisia Alpine Garden
The botanic garden contains a collection of Alpine plants, including the delicate "twinflower."

Cascata di Lillaz
This tall, dramatic waterfall, situated a little to the east of the rustic village of Lillaz, is best observed after the spring snowmelt.

★ Valnontey
This lovely valley, after which the resort is named, provides dramatic views of glaciers and easy access to various hiking trails.

• Épinel

② Cogne Lillaz
③

Valnontey

Pont Canavese
Cuorgne

Pont Canavese
Cuorgne

S460

Pont Canavese
Cuorgne

Key

═ Main road

0 kilometers 5

0 miles 5

Male Ibex
The ibex lives largely above the tree line. Groups are often seen around Col Lauson at dawn and dusk, and also around Pont in June.

The small resort of Ceresole Reale under winter snow

⑦ Ceresole Reale

Turin. 🚌 to Ceresole Reale.
ℹ️ Palazzo Comunale, Ceresole
Reale (0124 95 32 00).
🌐 turismotorino.org

On the southern, Piedmont side of the extensive Parco Nazionale del Gran Paradiso (see pp216–17) lies the small resort of Ceresole Reale. The route from Cuorgnè traverses rolling countryside and follows the S460 along a narrow gorge with a cascading stream. At **Noasca**, a spectacular waterfall may be seen high above the houses.

Ceresole Reale lies in a basin surrounded by meadows and forests of larch, and framed by mountains – the Gran Paradiso range to the north, Levanna to the southwest – which are reflected in the clear waters of a spectacular artificial mountain lake, which is actually a dammed reservoir, providing energy to supply Turin with electricity. This nevertheless unspoiled corner of the country is a good base for walking, climbing, and hiking, and also offers facilities for skiing during the winter.

⑧ Alta Val Susa

Turin. 🚆 Oulx. 🚌 to Sauze d'Oulx.
ℹ️ Via Louset, Sestriere (0122 75 54 44). 🌐 **vialattea.it**

The closest ring of mountain resorts to Turin, and as a consequence popular for weekend excursions, is also known colloquially as the Via Lattea or "Milky Way." Villages such as **Bardonecchia** and **Sauze d'Oulx** preserve traditional old stone and wood buildings that have been a feature of the region for centuries. The small church in Bardonecchia has, in addition, a fine 15th-century carved choir. In contrast, the supermodern complex at **Sestriere** was purpose-built to accommodate skiers in winter and hikers in summer.

From Bardonecchia a chairlift operates some of the way up **Punta Colomion**, which rises immediately to the south of the resort. The summit, at 6,738 ft (2,054 m), offers fine views, and numerous hiking and walking possibilities.

⑨ Susa

Turin. 🗻 6,500. 🚆 🚌 ℹ️ Corso Inghilterra 39 (0122 62 24 47). 🛒 Tue.
🌐 **turismotorino.org**

This attractive mountain town flourished in Roman times: the **Arch of Augustus**, built in 8 BC, commemorates the alliance between the local Gaulish

The impressive part-Roman gateway, Porta Savoia, in Susa

chieftain and the Emperor Augustus. Other relics from the Roman period include two arches of an aqueduct, sections of an amphitheater, and traces of the old town walls. **Porta Savoia**, an imposing Roman gateway dating from the 4th century, was remodeled in the Middle Ages.

Most of the historic center of the town is medieval, including the castle of Countess Adelaide and the **Duomo**, both originally 11th century. The Duomo, much altered since then, houses a polyptych (c.1500) attributed to Bergognone, and a copy of a precious 14th-century Flemish triptych portraying the Virgin and Saints. South of the town lies the Gothic church of **San Francesco**, surrounded by an area of early medieval houses.

A street in the traditional village of Bardonecchia, in Alta Val Susa

Carved capitals on the Porta dello Zodiaco at the Sacra di San Michele

⑩ Sacra di San Michele

Strada Sacra San Michele. **Tel** 011 93 91 30. 🚌 May–Sep: Sun pm from Avigliana & Turin. **Open** 9:30am–noon, 2:30–6pm Tue–Sun (mid-Oct–mid-Mar: to 5pm). Call ahead to arrange group visits. ♿ **w** **sacradisanmichele.com**

This somewhat forbidding abbey complex is perched on a ridge halfway up Monte Pirchiriano, at 3,156 ft (962 m). Its monastic community was founded around the year 1000, possibly on the site of a previous sanctuary, though the exterior looks every bit as much a fortress as the spiritual refuge that it was for 600 years.

During its prime, the abbey attracted pilgrims on their way to Rome, and as a result it grew enormously wealthy and powerful, controlling over 100 other abbeys in Italy, France, and Spain. It was subsequently looted several times, despite being fortified, before falling into decline and eventually being suppressed in 1662.

The sanctuary is reached by climbing 154 steep steps hewn out of the rock, which offer wonderful views over the surrounding countryside and up to the Alps. At the very top of this stairway, known as the Scalone dei Morti (Stairway of the Dead), is the Romanesque Porta dello Zodiaco, a doorway carved with creatures and symbols relating to the signs of the Zodiac. Beyond the doorway a few more steps lead into the church itself, which dates from the 12th–13th centuries and incorporates traces of an earlier building. The interior houses 15th- and

16th-century paintings and frescoes, and a 16th-century triptych by the Piedmontese artist Defendente Ferrari. The crypt holds the tombs of the early dukes and princes of the House of Savoy-Carignano.

⑪ Avigliana

Turin. 🏘 12,000. 🚉 🚌 **i** Piazza Conte Rosso 17 (011 97 69 111). 🗓 Thu. **w** **comune.avigliana.to.it**

On a fine day, this small town perched beside two glacier-fed lakes and encircled by tall mountains looks breathtakingly beautiful. Avigliana is overlooked by a castle, first erected in the mid-10th century but now in ruins, which was once the home of the Counts of Savoy. Until the early 15th century the town was one of their favorite bases.

The medieval houses here are largely unspoiled, particularly in the two main *piazzas*, Santa Maria and Conte Rosso. Other buildings of note are the Casa della Porta Ferrata and the 15th-century Casa dei Savoia, both on Via XX Settembre. The church of San Giovanni

(13th–14th century) contains early 16th-century paintings by Defendente Ferrari.

⑫ Pinerolo

Turin. 🏘 36,000. 🚉 🚌 **i** Viale Giolitti 7/9 (0121 79 55 89). 🗓 Wed & Sat. **w** **turismotorino.org**

Pinerolo lies in an attractive setting beside hills at the confluence of the Lemina and Chisone valleys. The town was the capital of the Acaia family, a branch of the House of Savoy, and in the 14th and 15th centuries it was known for the cultural atmosphere that prevailed here under the family's patronage. However, the town enjoyed none of the stability of Turin: it was occupied by the French five times between the 15th and 18th centuries. During the 17th century the French demolished many of the town's ancient buildings in order to make Pinerolo a defensive stronghold; among the political prisoners allegedly held here was the notorious "Man in the Iron Mask." Today the town is a busy center of commerce.

A number of monumental buildings do remain, however. The **Duomo**, at the center of the town, was remodeled in Gothic style in the 15th–16th centuries and has a fine portal and an impressive bell tower. Via Principi d'Acaia climbs up to the 14th-century palace of the Princes of Acaia, and to the 15th-century church of **San Maurizio**, where the Acaia princes are buried; beside it rises a 14th-century bell tower.

The medieval arcades surrounding Piazza Conte Rosso in Avigliana

Turin ⑬

Mention Turin (Torino) and most people will think of industry and prosperity. It is certainly an economic powerhouse, but it is also a town of grace and charm, with superb Baroque architecture, elegant arcades of shops, and excellent museums, set against the dramatic scenery of the foothills of the Alps. Turin is also, of course, home to the famous Turin Shroud, the FIAT car company, and the Juventus soccer team.

Exploring Turin

Though settled by the Romans (**Porta Palatina** is an impressive 1st-century AD relic), and the seat of a university since the Middle Ages, Turin came into its own only after 1563, when Emanuele Filiberto of Savoy moved his capital here. Three centuries of prosperity ensued. Turin then became the base for Italy's unification movement and, from 1861 to 1865, the first capital of the newly united country. Subsequently its main power

The FIAT car factory logo

was economic. In 1899 the Agnelli family created the car company **FIAT** (Fabbrica Italiana Automobili Torino), which grew to be one of the biggest in Europe. After World War II, Turin attracted thousands of poor Italians from the south who came to work in its factories. Though there have been social conflicts and labor disputes as a result, managers and workers unite over soccer: the Juventus team is owned by the Agnelli family.

Statue of Emperor Augustus in front of the Roman Porta Palatina

🏛 Duomo

Piazza San Giovanni. **Tel** 011 436 15 40.
Open daily. ♿

The cathedral, which was built in 1491–8 and dedicated to St. John the Baptist, is the only

Turin Town Center

① Porta Palatina
② Duomo
③ San Lorenzo
④ Palazzo Reale
⑤ Armeria Reale
⑥ Palazzo Madama
⑦ Museo Egizio and Galleria Sabauda
⑧ Palazzo Carignano
⑨ Mole Antonelliana

0 meters 500
0 yards 500

For keys to map symbols see back flap

The 15th-century Duomo, with the Cappella della Sacra Sindone beyond

VISITORS' CHECKLIST

Practical Information

🏛 910,000. ℹ️ Piazza Castello 161 *(011 53 51 81)*, also at Stazione Porta Nuova. 🚇 Sat. 🎉 Jun 24: Festa di San Giovanni. 🌐 turismotorino.org

Transportation

✈️ Caselle 9 miles (15 km) N. 🚆 Porta Nuova, Piazza Carlo-Felice. Porta Susa, Piazza XVIII Dicembre. 🚌 Corso Vittorio Emanuele II 131.

example of Renaissance architecture in Turin. The sober square bell tower, which predates the rest of the church by 30 years, stands in refreshing contrast to Turin's sumptuous Baroque buildings; its top was designed by Filippo Juvarra in 1720. Inside, the Duomo is heavy with statuary and paintings. On the right side of the church is the **Cappella della Sacra Sindone** (Chapel of the Holy Shroud), which is incorporated into the Palazzo Reale *(see p224)*. The chapel is a remarkable feat, designed by Guarino Guarini (1624–83), with an extraordinary meshlike cupola; the exterior view is equally eccentric.

🏛 Palazzo Madama

Piazza Castello. **Tel** 011.443.3501. **Open** 10am–6pm Tue–Sat, 10am–7pm Sun (last adm: 1 hour before closing). 🎟 🌐 palazzomadamatorino.it

Turin's main square once contained a medieval castle that incorporated elements of the original Roman city walls. The castle was later enlarged and remodeled, and a new façade by Juvarra was added, at the request of a royal widow, in the 18th century. The Palazzo Madama – as it was renamed – sits in the center of the square with a stately façade. The interior, with its grand staircase and first floor,

both designed by Juvarra, houses the **Museo Civico d'Arte Antica**. This collection contains treasures ranging from the Graeco-Roman era to the 19th century. The display includes *Portrait of an Unknown Man* by Antonello da Messina (15th century) among the paintings and sculptures, and reproductions of the Duc de Berry's *Book of Hours* from c.1420. Glass, jewelry, textiles, and furniture are also on display.

The façade of the Palazzo Madama, designed by Filippo Juvarra in 1718–21

Detail of the mysterious 12th-century Holy Shroud

The Holy Shroud

The most famous – and most dubious – holy relic of them all is kept in Turin's Duomo. The Shroud, said to be the winding-sheet in which the body of Christ was wrapped after his crucifixion, owes its fame to the fact that the Shroud bears the imprint of a crucified man with a wound in his side, and bruises from what might have been a crown of thorns.

The Shroud is one of the most famous medieval relics. Its early history is unclear, but the House of Savoy was in possession of it around 1450, and had it displayed in Guarini's chapel from 1694. The "original" Shroud – which sits in a silver casket inside an iron box within a marble coffer – is not on display, though a replica is, together with a welter of scientific explanations as to the Shroud's possible origins. In 1988, however, the myth of the Shroud was exploded: a carbon-dating test showed that it dates back no further than the 12th century. The Shroud nevertheless remains an object of religious veneration.

Exploring Turin

The city of Turin is blessed with numerous interesting museums, which are housed in splendid palazzi and civic buildings. The center itself is relatively small, with broad, straight streets, often bordered with historic cafés and shops, which are pleasant places to stroll along. The city is also famous for its innovative cuisine and boasts some of the country's finest restaurants.

Granite statue of Ramses II (13th century BC) in the Museo Egizio

🏛 Museo Egizio
Via Accademia delle Scienze 6. **Tel** 011 561 77 76. **Open** 8:30am–7:30pm Tue–Sun (last adm: 6:30pm). 🖼 ♿
W **museoegizio.it**

Turin owes its magnificent Egyptian Museum – one of the most important in the world – largely to the Piedmont-born Bernardo Drovetti, who was stationed in Egypt as French Consul General at the time of the Napoleonic Wars. It was the booty he brought back that formed the basis of this very fine collection of Egyptian artifacts. On the ground floor, items on display include monumental sculptures and reconstructed temples; upstairs, there are collections of papyrus and everyday objects. Among the most impressive sculptures are a black granite Ramses II (13th century BC, or 19th dynasty), the slightly earlier Amenophis II, and the basalt figure of Gemenef-Har-Bak, a vizier from the 26th dynasty. The Sala della Nubia contains a reconstruction of the 15th-century BC **Rock Temple of Ellesija**.

Extraordinary wall and tomb paintings are displayed on the upper floor, together with items of daily use such as the tools used for measuring, weaving, fishing, and hunting. The 14th-century BC Tomb of Kha and Merit, complete with the food, tools, and ornaments buried with them for the afterlife, is particularly fascinating. The papyrus collection is beautiful and of enormous interest to scholars: these documents have been vital to modern understanding of Egyptian language, customs, and history – one document, the *Papiro dei Re* (Royal Papyrus), lists all the pharaohs up to the 17th dynasty, with their dates.

G. Ferrari's *St. Peter and a Donor* (16th century), Galleria Sabauda

🏛 Galleria Sabauda
Via Accademia delle Scienze 6. **Tel** 011 56 41 749. **Open** 8:30am–7:30pm Tue–Sun (2–7:30pm Wed & Thu). 🖼 ♿
W **artito.arti.beniculturali.it**

The Palazzo dell'Accademia delle Scienze, the building by Guarini in which the Egyptian Museum is housed, is also home to the House of Savoy's main painting collection. The top two floors are the setting for a stunning array of works by Italian, French, Flemish, and Dutch masters.

The collection was originally begun in the mid- to late-1400s, and has been expanded over the centuries. It is grouped in regional schools. The Piedmontese section includes masterpieces by Gaudenzio Ferrari (c.1480–1546) and two early 16th-century paintings by Defendente Ferrari. Among works of particular interest from other Italian schools are Antonio and Piero Pollaiolo's 15th-century

Detail from an 18th-dynasty papyrus Book of the Dead, Museo Egizio

For hotels and restaurants in this region see pp562–77 and pp580–605

Spacious arcades on Turin's Via Roma

Tobias and the Archangel Raphael, and the *Ritratto di Gentiluomo* by Bronzino. Bellini, Mantegna, and Veronese are among other Italian artists represented.

The section on Dutch and Flemish art includes important works such as Jan Van Eyck's *St. Francis* (15th century) and Rembrandt's *Old Man Sleeping* (17th-century), as well as several portraits by Van Dyck, which include his *Principe Tommaso di Savoia-Carignano* (1634). Among the French works here are 17th-century landscape paintings by Claude Lorrain and Poussin. Plans are underway to move the Galleria Sabauda collection to the Palazzo Reale by 2015.

🏛 Palazzo Carignano

Via Accademia delle Scienze 5. **Tel** 011 562 11 47. **Open** 9am–7pm Tue–Sun. 🅿 ♿

This Baroque palazzo is not only Guarini's masterpiece, it is arguably the finest building in Turin, with its magnificent façade and ornate rotunda. It was built in 1679 for the Carignano family – an offshoot of the main House of Savoy and ancestors of the Italian kings – but came into its own in the 1800s. The first king of Italy, Vittorio Emanuele II, was born here in 1829. After Italy was unified in 1861 by a series of referenda, the former royal residence was used as the first national parliament building.

The palazzo is home to the **Museo Nazionale del Risorgimento**, which, through paintings and a collection of artifacts (housed in the rooms where history was made), tells the story of unification. It introduces Mazzini, Cavour, and Garibaldi – key figures in the Risorgimento (*see pp66–7*).

🚇 Via Roma

Running through the historic center, Turin's main street Via Roma leads from Piazza Castello (north) through Piazza San Carlo to the distinctive arched façade of Stazione Porta Nuova (south). Via Roma is a magnificent concourse lined with stylish shops and shaded arcades, interrupted only by cobbled squares.

A grid pattern of side streets branches off either side of Via Roma, revealing additional shopping arcades.

🚇 Piazza San Carlo

The ensemble of Baroque architecture on this square, now a pedestrian zone, has earned it the nickname of "Turin's drawing room." At its southern end are the twin churches of Santa Cristina and San Carlo; both were built in the 1630s, though **Santa Cristina** has a Baroque façade, crowned with statues, which was designed by Juvarra in the early 18th century.

At the center of the square stands a 19th-century statue of Duke Emanuele Filiberto. The work, by Carlo Marocchetti, has become an emblem of the city.

At the corners of the square, frescoes depict the Holy Shroud. The **Galleria San Federico**, in the square's northwestern corner, is a stylish shopping arcade.

Piazza San Carlo is known for its society cafés. In one such establishment, in 1786, Antonio Benedetto Carpano invented the drink known as vermouth, which is still very popular all over Italy today.

🏛 Pinacoteca Giovanni e Marella Agnelli

Lingotto, Via Nizza 230. **Tel** 011 00 62 713. **Open** 10am–7pm Tue–Sun (last adm: 6:15pm). 🅿 ♿ 🎫 🖾 ⊘
W pinacoteca-agnelli.it

Located on the roof of the former FIAT factory redesigned by architect Renzo Piano, this museum holds paintings by Modigliani and Canaletto, as well as two statues by Canova.

🌳 Parco del Valentino

Corso Massimo D'Azeglio. **Open** daily. Borgo Medioevale: Viale Virgilio 107. **Tel** 011 443 17 01. **Open** 9am–7pm daily (to 8pm Apr–Oct). Orto Botanico: **Tel** 011 670 59 85. **Open** Apr–Sep: Sat & Sun. 🅿 ♿
W borgomedievaletorino.it

This park contains the **Borgo Medioevale**, a complex of medieval buildings erected for an exhibition in the late 1880s. The edifices show different types of design and construction, based on traditional houses and castles found throughout the region.

The **Orto Botanico**, beside the medieval complex, is an impressive botanical garden in a pleasant setting.

Looking south across the elegant Piazza San Carlo, "Turin's drawing room"

Turin: Symbols of the City

Turin's architecture mirrors the city's transition from monarchic power to industrial power. Witness the ostentation of the Baroque apartments of the Savoy family in Palazzo Reale, and contrast them with the futuristic Mole Antonelliana, a tall structure that heralded the dawn of the modern industrial age. Much of Turin's history in the 20th century has been dominated by the automobile: FIAT is synonymous with Turin. For the curious, the city's extensive motor museum is worth a visit, since it maps out the history of Italian car design.

The 19th-century tower, Mole Antonelliana, dominating Turin

🏛 Mole Antonelliana
Via Montebello 20. **Tel** 011 813 85 61. Panoramic elevator **Open** 10am–8pm Tue–Sun (to 11pm Sat). 🎬 Museo del Cinema: **Tel** 011 813 85 64. **Open** 9am–8pm Tue–Sun (to 11pm Sat) (last adm: 45 mins before closing). 🎬 ♿
W museocinema.it

This building is the Turin equivalent of the Eiffel Tower in Paris: an unmissably tall landmark that is a signature for the city. It looks like a glorified lightning conductor: indeed in 1954 an electric storm struck down the top 155 ft (47 m), which was later replaced. The 550-ft (167-m) Mole, by Alessandro Antonelli (1798–1888), was meant to be a synagogue, but upon its completion in 1897, the city used it to house the Risorgimento museum. The Mole ("massive structure") – for

a time the world's tallest brick building – provides panoramic views from its elevator and now houses the Cinema Museum.

🏛 Palazzo Reale
Piazzetta Reale. **Tel** 011 436 14 55. **Open** 8:30am–7:30pm Tue–Sun (last adm: 6:20pm). 🎬 📷 ♿
W piemonte.beniculturali.it

This palace was the seat of the Savoy royal family from 1660 until the unification of Italy in 1861. Behind the austere façade, designed by Amedeo di Castellamonte, lie richly decorated state apartments; the ceilings were painted by Morello, Miel, and Seyter in the 17th century. The many splendid furnishings, tapestries, and ornaments date from the 17th to the 19th centuries; they include the elaborate Chinese Cabinet, the Alcove Room, the lavishly decorated Throne Room, and the innovative Scala delle Forbici, or Scissor Stairs, created by Juvarra in 1720. Behind the palace are extensive gardens, which extend northward.

To the left of the main entrance is the church of **San Lorenzo**. This fine Baroque building, begun in 1634, is by architect Guarino Guarini, its ornate interior boasting another of his extraordinary geometric domes.

The interior of San Lorenzo's dome

🛡 Armeria Reale
Piazza Castello 191. **Tel** 011 54 38 89. **Open** 8:30am–7:30pm Tue–Sun (last adm: 30 mins before closing). **Closed** Jan 1, Dec 25. 🎬 ♿
W artito.arti.beniculturali.it

One wing of the Palazzo Reale, on the northern side of the main square, provides the splendid setting for one of the most extensive and breathtaking collections of arms and armory in the world.

Opened to the public in 1837, the armory originally belonged to the House of Savoy. The fine rooms, such as the splendid Galleria Beaumont, designed by Juvarra in 1733, hold treasures ranging from Roman and Etruscan times to the 1800s. The collection has magnificent medieval and Renaissance items from some of the world's greatest armorers and gunsmiths, including a pistol that belonged to Emperor Charles V. One section is devoted largely to Oriental arms and armor.

The Royal Library contains a collection of drawings, including a self-portrait by Leonardo da Vinci on display during special exhibitions only.

Environs
About 2 miles (3 km) out of the city center is the vast **MAUTO – Museo dell'Automobile di Torino**. Founded in 1933, and

A lavishly decorated gallery in the 17th-century Palazzo Reale, a royal residence until unification since renovated by the architect Cino Zucchi, it now houses over 150 veteran, vintage, and classic cars. The collection includes glorious Bugattis, Maseratis, Lancias, FIATs, and some fine foreign cars. The first gas-driven car made in Italy (1896) is kept here, as well as the first FIAT (1899) and the 1929 Isotta Fraschini *coupé de ville* used to transport Gloria Swanson in the film *Sunset Boulevard*. Note also that a large number of the sports cars from the 1950s are right-hand drive in deference to the great British car-makers such as Aston Martin.

🏛 MAUTO – Museo dell'Automobile di Torino
Corso Unità d'Italia 40. **Tel** 011 67 76 66. **Open** daily. 🅿 ♿ **w** museoauto.it

An interior view of the 18th-century Palazzina di Caccia di Stupinigi

⓮ Palazzina di Caccia di Stupinigi

Piazza Principe Amedeo 7, Stupinigi. **Tel** 011 358 12 20. 🚌 4 to Piazza Caio Mario, then 41. **Open** times vary, so call ahead. 🅿 📷 ♿

In 1729–30 the architect Filippo Juvarra (1676–1736) designed a magnificent hunting lodge at Stupinigi, a beautiful location 5 miles (9 km) southwest of Turin. Known as the Palazzina di Caccia di Stupinigi, the building was created for Duke Vittorio

Designs from 1949 for the Ferrari 166 MM

Amedeo II of Savoy and is one of the very finest hunting lodges, built on an impressive scale, reminiscent of the palace of Versailles in France.

The dynamic and complex plan incorporates semicircles and an octagon, with the main block consisting of a dome rising above a circular building from which wings jut out, not unlike the arms of a windmill.

The mass of the central section is lightened by balus-trading topped with urns and figures, while the dome is crowned with an 18th-century bronze figure of a stag.

The huge interior includes rooms sumptuously decorated with *trompe l'oeil* paintings and frescoes on a hunting theme – the 18th-century *Triumph of Diana*, for instance, in the main *salone*. About 40 of those rooms house the interesting **Museo d'Arte e di Ammobiliamento**, a museum specializing in 17th- and 18th-century furniture and furnishings. Many of the ornate items on display in these rooms were originally kept in other former royal residences.

Outside there are extensive grounds, which feature an elegant combination of spectacular broad avenues, parkland, and colorful formal parterres.

⓯ Basilica di Superga

Strada Basilica di Superga 75, Comune di Torino. 🚌 15, 61, 68 from city center. **Open** daily. **Closed** Sep 8. Tombs **Tel** 011 899 74 56. **Open** daily; times vary so call ahead. **Closed** public hols. **w** basilicadisuperga. com

On a hill to the east of Turin, accessible by car, Tram-Track, and bus 79, stands the superb Baroque Basilica of Superga, built by Juvarra in 1717–31. The commission came from Duke Vittorio Amedeo II, in fulfillment of a vow made to the Virgin Mary in 1706 while the French were besieging the duke and his army in Turin.

The beautiful yellow and white façade is dominated by a large portico designed like a Classical temple, with a 213-ft (65-m) high dome immediately beyond. It is flanked by twin bell towers. The interior is magnificent, decorated in light blue and yellow, and contains fine paintings and carvings.

Underneath the Basilica lies the great mausoleum that houses the tombs of the kings, princes, and princesses of Savoy from the 18th and 19th centuries. The victims of the 1949 aircrash, including the Turin soccer team, are commemorated on a plaque behind the Basilica.

One other benefit of visiting the basilica is seeing the views over Turin.

The imposing façade of the 18th-century Baroque Basilica di Superga designed by Filippo Juvarra

The 17th-century Basilica dell'Assunta dominating Sacro Monte, Varallo

⑯ Venaria Reale

Piazza della Repubblica 4. **Tel** 011 499 23 33. **FS** 🚌 **Open** 9am–6pm Tue–Sun (to 8pm Sat & Sun). 🏛
W lavenaria.it

This grandiose complex dates from the mid-17th century, when Charles Emanuel II of Savoy decided to build a royal hunting lodge on the site of the existing town of Altessano Superiore. Venaria Reale incorporates the **Reggia di Diana**, a formal palace and garden built between 1660 and 1671, as well as **La Mandria**, the 3,000-hectare (7,413-acre) park surrounding it.

Venaria's historical center was designed by Amadeo di Castellamonte between 1667 and 1690; its focal point is the Piazza dell'Annunziata, with statues depicting the Angel Gabriel and the Virgin Mary.

⑰ Santuario d'Oropa

Via Santuario d'Oropa 480, Comune di Biella. **Tel** 015 255 512 00. **FS** Biella. 🚌 from Biella. 🏛 **Basilica Antica Open** 7:30am–7pm daily. **Basilica Superiore Open** 8:30am–4:30pm daily. **W** santuariodioropa.it

Perched above the wool town of Biella stands the tranquil church and hospice complex of Oropa, comprised of a series of three squares surrounded by pale buildings with stone-shingled roofs, cut into the hillside. The sanctuary was founded in the 4th century by Sant'Eusebio, Bishop of Vercelli. It was intended as a hospice for the poor, and to honor the "Black Madonna," which he had brought back from the Holy Land. The Madonna, said to be the work of St. Luke himself, is the object of some of the most important pilgrimages in the region.

The statue of the Madonna is kept in the restored **Basilica Antica** (Old Church). Beyond it, at the top of the complex, is the imposing Neo-Classical **Basilica Superiore** (Upper Church), which was begun in 1885 but completed only in 1960.

⑱ Domodossola

Verbania. 🚠 19,000. **FS** 🚌 **i** Stazione entrance, Pza Matteotti 24 (0324 24 82 65). 🏛 Sat.
W prodomodossola.it

At the center of this pretty mountain town of Roman origin lies the **Piazza Mercato**, or market square, framed by attractive arcades and houses from the 15th and 16th centuries. The Ossola valley, where the town lies, sits in an Alpine landscape of pasture and forest sliced by rivers and streams. Pretty villages north of the town include **Crodo**, with its cold-water mineral spas, and **Baceno**, where the 14th–16th-century church contains fine frescoes and wood carvings.

⑲ Varallo

Vercelli. 🚠 7,500. **FS** 🚌 **i** Corso Roma 38 (0163 56 44 04). 🏛 Tue.
W atlvalsesiavercelli.it

The small town and tourist resort of Varallo lies halfway up the attractive Sesia valley, and boasts a remarkable church, **Santa Maria delle Grazie**. The late 15th-century church is notable for its beautiful frescoed wall depicting the Life of Christ and *trompe l'oeil* architectural elements; the paintings are the work of Gaudenzio Ferrari (1484–1546).

A long stairway behind the church (and also a cableway) climbs up to the extraordinary **Sacro Monte**, a religious community built at an altitude of about 2,000 ft (610 m). This "Sacred Mount" was founded as a sanctuary of the New Jerusalem in 1486 under the patronage of the Archbishop of Milan, San Carlo Borromeo.

The Basilica dell'Assunta, with a 19th-century façade, is set in a tranquil courtyard with palm trees and a fountain; the interior is a riot of ornate Baroque architecture. Dotted around it are over 40 chapels representing the sacred sites of Jerusalem, with statues and painted figures positioned in front of frescoed backdrops painted by Gaudenzio Ferrari, Tanzio da Varallo, and others.

Christ Condemned (16th century) in a chapel at Varallo's Sacro Monte

The interior of the church of San Giulio in the center of Lago d'Orta

⑳ Lago d'Orta

Novara. **FS** 🚌 ⛴ Orta. **i** Via Panoramica, Orta San Giulio (0322 90 56 14). **W** distrettolaghi.it

Lago d'Orta is one of Italy's least visited lakes – unjustly, as it is delightfully set among the foothills of the Alps.

The lake's main resort is **Orta San Giulio**, a small town containing handsome palazzi, and houses decorated with wrought iron balconies. In the lakeside **Piazza Principale** stands the Palazzo della Comunità, a frescoed building of 1582 resting on arcades. A cobbled pathway leads up to the 15th-century church of **Santa Maria Assunta** (rebuilt in the 17th century), with a Romanesque doorway and an interior that is richly decorated with 17th-century frescoes and paintings.

Above Orta San Giulio is the sanctuary of **Sacro Monte**, a UNESCO World Heritage site built from 1591 to 1770 and dedicated to St. Francis of Assisi. A winding path, offering lovely views of the lake, climbs to the church. The path is lined by 21 chapels, most of them Baroque, in which frescoes and life-size figure groups by various artists depict scenes from the life of St. Francis.

In the center of the lake rises the picturesque **Isola San Giulio**. The island was said to have been liberated from snakes and monsters by the 4th-century Christian preacher Julius, from whom the island's name derives. The basilica here is notable for its 12th-century black marble pulpit and for the 15th-century frescoes – including one attributed to Gaudenzio Ferrari, of the *Virgin and Child Enthroned*.

Fresco detail of a horseman (17th century) by Morazzone in San Gaudenzio, Novara

㉑ Novara

🏘 105,000. **FS** 🚌 **i** Baluardo Quintino Sella 40 (0321 39 40 59). 🛒 Mon, Thu, & Sat. **W** turismonovara.it

Novara has distant origins as the Roman city of Nubliaria – meaning "surrounded in mist." Nowadays its delightful arcaded streets and squares, and historic buildings, exude a quiet affluence. Many of the most important buildings stand around Piazza della Repubblica. They include the beautiful Renaissance courtyard of the **Broletto** (town hall), with its graceful 15th-century red-brick arcades and covered stairway.

Across the piazza rises the **Duomo**, rebuilt by the architect Alessandro Antonelli in around 1865 in Neo-Classical style, with a huge central doorway. The interior contains dramatic Renaissance paintings of the Vercelli school and Flemish tapestries, as well as the remains of an earlier sanctuary on this site: these include the frescoed 12th-century chapel of San Siro and the 15th-century cloisters. The octagonal **Baptistry** next door dates in part from the 5th century and is painted with medieval scenes of the Apocalypse. The **Museo della Canonica del Duomo** beside the Duomo has tombstones and inscriptions from the Roman and early Christian eras.

A few streets away stands the **Basilica di San Gaudenzio**. It is strikingly crowned by an elongated four-tiered dome and spire. Designed by Antonelli, it is reminiscent of his Mole Antonelliana in Turin (224). At the top of the spire, which is 400 ft (121 m) high, is a statue of San Gaudenzio himself. Inside, the late 16th-century church contains a fine collection of Renaissance and Baroque paintings by artists from Piedmont: these include a notable 17th-century battle scene by Tanzio da Varallo, a 16th-century altarpiece by Gaudenzio Ferrari, and a fresco painting by Pier Francesco Morazzone (c.1572–1626).

🔒 Baptistry
Piazza della Repubblica. **Tel** 0321 66 16 35. **Open** to book visit the Curia Arcivescovile.

🏛 Museo della Canonica del Duomo
Vicolo della Canonica 9. **Tel** 0321 66 16 35. **Open** 3–6pm Sat–Sun.

View across Lago d'Orta to the Isola San Giulio

㉒ Vercelli

🏙 47,000. 🚉 🚌 🛈 Viale Garibaldi 90 (0161 58 002). 🗓 Tue & Fri.
🌐 atlvalsesiavercelli.it

Vercelli is the rice capital of Europe, set in a vast plain of paddy fields that provide a sight of shimmering sheets of water stretching far into the distance. Vercelli itself also developed its own school of painting in the 16th century, and has one major architectural treasure, the 13th-century **Basilica di Sant'Andrea**.

The Basilica, standing just across from the train station, is famous as the first example of Italian architecture to be influenced by the Gothic style of northern France – note the beautiful vaulted nave and the flying buttresses, typical Gothic elements. Overall, however, the Basilica remains a stunning achievement in Romanesque architecture, built from 1219 to 1227 as part of an abbey for the papal legate Cardinal Guala Bicheri. The façade, curiously, changes color halfway up, the blue-gray of the lower part turning to red and white in the twin towers; these are linked by a double arcade. A carving attributed to Antelami (12th century) adorns the central lunette.

The three-aisled interior is gently illuminated through rose windows. The muted decoration is largely focused on the vaulting, which is supported by tall, slender shafts. Off the north side is the simple 13th-century cloister, beautifully framed by arcades rising from clustered columns.

Vercelli's other important historic buildings are not far away, including the imposing 16th-century **Duomo**, the church of **San Cristoforo**, with frescoes and a particularly fine Madonna degli Aranci (both c.1529) painted by Gaudenzio Ferrari, and the **Piazza Cavour** with its medieval arcades. The **Museo Borgogna** is the best place to admire the masterpieces of the Vercelli school. The main shopping street, Corso Libertà, has a handful of attractive 15th-century houses and courtyards.

🏛 **Museo Borgogna**
Via A. Borgogna 4/6. **Tel** 0161 25 27 76.
Open Tue–Fri pm, Sat am, Sun am & pm. **Closed** Jan 1, Aug 15, Nov 1, Dec 25. 🗓 📷 🌐 **museoborgogna.it**

The 13th-century cloisters of the Basilica di Sant'Andrea in Vercelli

㉓ Asti

🏙 77,000. 🚉 🚌 🛈 Piazza Alfieri 29 (0141 53 03 57). 🗓 Wed & Sat.
🌐 astiturismo.it

Renowned for its *spumante* (sparkling) wine, Asti is at the center of Italy's most prestigious wine region (*see pp186–7*) and is

Detail of the carving on the 15th-century porch at the entrance to the Duomo in Asti

also a tranquil and noble city of medieval towers, elegant churches, and warm red roofs.

Just north of the main train station lies the Piazza del Campo del Palio, the largest square in Asti and formerly the site of its annual horse race, now in Piazza Alfieri. The race, held on the third Sunday of September to coincide with the local wine fair, rivals the Palio in Siena (*see p345*) for outrageous horsemanship and medieval pageantry.

Beyond this square lies the triangular-shaped **Piazza Alfieri**. A statue here commemorates the local poet and dramatist Vittorio Alfieri (1749–1803), in whose honor both this square and the main street were renamed.

Corso Alfieri runs the entire length of the old city center. At its eastern end stands the 15th-century church of **San Pietro in Consavia**, with its terracotta decoration, 17th-century frescoes, and attractive cloister. Beside it is the circular Romanesque **baptistry** which dates from the 10th–12th centuries; it was once the church of the knights of the Order of St. John of Jerusalem, who had their headquarters here.

West of Piazza Alfieri is the **Collegiata di San Secondo** (13th–15th century), named after Asti's patron saint, which houses a Renaissance polyptych by Gandolfino d'Asti and 15th-century frescoes. The area around the western section of Corso Alfieri contains a few of the medieval towers for which the town was once famous; they include the Torre dei Comentini, the very elegant

The watery expanses of the rice fields around Vercelli

Torre Troyana, and, at the far end, the Torre Ropa. This was built on the ruins of a tower in which San Secondo, a Roman soldier, was held. The nearby 14th-century Gothic **Duomo** has a 15th-century porch and, inside, 18th-century frescoes and two 12th- to 13th-century carvings on the west corner of the transept.

❷❹ Cuneo

🗺 55,000. 🚉 🚌 ℹ Via Amedeo II 8a (0171 69 02 17). 🛒 Tue, Fri.
🌐 cuneoholiday.com

"Cuneo" in Italian means wedge-shaped, and this perfectly describes the sliver of land that the town occupies at the confluence of two rivers, the Gesso and the Stura di Demonte. In early November the town hosts the regional cheese fair, with unusual local cheese varieties.

The town centers on a large square, **Piazza Galimberti**, with its old arcades, where the traders come to hawk their wares every Tuesday. Much of the town was rebuilt in the 18th and 19th centuries, providing Cuneo with wide, tree-lined boulevards, though the impressive viaduct that takes the railroad line into town dates from the 1930s. The deconsecrated 13th-century church of **San Francesco** has a fine 15th-century portal. The

Market day in the enormous Piazza Galimberti at the center of Cuneo

The Castello di Casotto in the hills above the resort of Garessio

18th-century church of **Santa Croce** has a concave façade by Francesco Gallo.

Cuneo is a good base for exploring the pretty local valleys, such as the Valle Stura, where rare flowers grow.

❷❺ Bossea Caves

Località Bossea, Comune Frabosa Soprana. **Tel** 0174 34 92 40.
🚉 Mondovì. 🚌 from Mondovì.
Open daily for guided tours only. 🎫
🌐 grottadibossea.com

Some 16 miles (25 km) south of Mondovì, near the end of a scenic route that follows the valley of the Torrente Corsaglia up into the Maritime Alps, are the caves of Bossea, some of the finest in Italy. The series of caves contains remarkable stalactite columns and shapes that have formed over many hundreds of thousands of years. Guided tours lead through different chambers – some of them surprisingly vast – following the underground rivers and lakes. The skeleton of a prehistoric bear, *Ursus spelaeus*, which was discovered here, is also on display.

Bring a sweater – the temperature rarely rises above 50°F (9°C).

❷❻ Garessio

Cuneo. 🗺 3,400. 🚉 🚌 ℹ Corso Statuto 1 (0174 80 31 45). 🛒 Fri.
🌐 garessio.net

One of the prettier resorts of the Maritime Alps, Garessio is no more than a sprinkling of houses spread out over the hills, surrounded by woods of chestnut trees. It is also a popular spa.

According to legend, the waters here have miraculous powers: in about AD 980 an octogenarian nobleman found instant relief from his kidney and circulatory problems by drinking the mineral-rich water. Since then, the waters have been drunk for their remedial properties – linked in particular with the relief of diuretic and digestive problems – and for their refreshing taste.

Environs

About 4 miles (10 km) west of Garessio stands the **Castello di Casotto**, the dramatically sited summer palace used by the House of Savoy. The royal family used to come here to enjoy the local mineral water, the attractive scenery and the exceptionally pure air of the hills.

The town of **Ormea**, 7 miles (12 km) southwest, is interesting for its ruined 11th-century castle, its church with late 14th-century Gothic frescoes, and its attractive houses.

🏰 **Castello di Casotto**
Garessio. **Tel** 0174 80 31 45. **Open** call ahead for opening times. 🎫

LIGURIA

Liguria is a long, thin coastal strip nestling at the foot of vine-covered mountains. Here pastel-colored houses bask in the Mediterranean sun, while their gardens, flourishing in the mild climate, are a riot of colorful plants. In contrast with resorts like Portofino and even Sanremo, the bustling city of Genoa, for centuries a trading port of immense power, is the only major population center.

Genoa has a long history as a seafaring power, achieving greatness first as a trading post with ancient Greece and Phoenicia, and later as the capital of a small commercial empire that at one stage eclipsed even Venice. The great sea admiral Andrea Doria came from Genoa, as did the 15th-century explorer of the Americas, Christopher Columbus.

Genoa's rise began in the 12th century, when it succeeded in beating the Saracen pirates who plagued the Ligurian coast. Thereafter, the maritime republic prospered, profiting from the Crusades to set up trading posts in the Middle East and marshaling its naval might to humble its rivals. The golden age lasted from the 16th to the mid-17th century, and included the glorious reign of Andrea Doria, who enriched the city by financing the wars of Genoa's European allies through the offices of the city's bank. Factionalism among the ruling aristocracy, however, and foreign conquest, by the French in 1668 and the Austrians in 1734, led to the region's decline. It was only in the early 19th century, with unification fervor spreading thanks to native son Giuseppe Mazzini and the revolutionary Garibaldi, that Liguria ever recaptured a glimpse of its former prominence. Today, sheltered by the steep slopes that rise from the sea, faded, elegant mansions lie along the coast, particularly in Sanremo, where aristocrats came to spend the winter at the end of the 19th century.

Green shutters and rich ocher walls characterize the houses of Portofino

◀ The sunlit harbor of Riomaggiore, one of the Cinque Terre

Exploring Liguria

Liguria divides neatly into two parts. The western coastline, known as the Riviera Ponente, is a thin strip of coastal plain stretching across to the French border, while the eastern coastline, or Riviera Levante, is more rugged and picturesque, descending directly into the sea. Between the two lengths of coast lies the region's capital and biggest port, Genoa (Genova). The faded elegance of the tranquil coastal villages contrasts with this cramped and busy port that snakes along the coast, hemmed in between the sea and the mountains rising steeply behind it.

Stag motif of the city of Cervo, above the cathedral doors

Genoese street market selling fruit and vegetables

Sights at a Glance

1. Balzi Rossi
2. Villa Hanbury
3. Dolceacqua
4. Sanremo
5. Bussana Vecchia
6. Cervo
7. Albenga
8. Grotte di Toirano
9. *Genoa (Genova) pp240–41*
10. Camogli
11. Portofino Peninsula
12. Rapallo
13. Cinque Terre
14. Portovenere
15. Lerici

Key

═══ Highway

═══ Major road

─── Secondary road

···· Minor road

─── Scenic route

⌁⌁ Main railroad

---- Minor railroad

▬▬▬ International border

═══ Regional border

△ Summit

For additional map symbols *see back flap*

The stylish resort of Sanremo on the Riviera Ponente, west of Genoa

Milano

nco
ivia
lla

Vobbia

Monte Antola
△ *1597m*

Santo
Stefano d'Aveto

Monte Maggiorasca
△ *1799m*

Casella

Montebruno

Torriglia

Pontedecimo

S45

Rezzoaglio

Monte Còllere
△ *1288m*

A7

L I G U R I A

Doria

Cicagna

Taro

Uscio

Borzonasca

Varese Ligure

9 GENOA

Nervi

A12

RAPALLO

San Pietro Vara

CAMOGLI 10

12

S. Margherita Ligure

enova

Chiavari

Sesta Godano

PORTOFINO PENINSULA 11

Lavagna

S1

S523

Castiglione Chiavarese

Vara

Sestri Levante

Moneglia

A12

0 kilometers   25

0 miles   10

I G U R E

R i v i e r a

Deiva Marina

Bonassola

Borghetto
di Vara

Parma

A15

d i

Monterosso al Mare

13

CINQUE TERRE

La Spezia

Sarzana

L e v a n t e

Corniglia

Riomaggiore

PORTOVENERE 14

15 LERICI

Isola Palmaria

Bocca di
Magra

Pisa

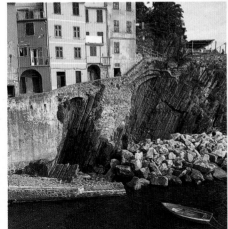

Houses wedged into the cliffs in Riomaggiore, Cinque Terre

Getting Around

If you keep to the coast, transportation
in Liguria is straightforward. Both the
A10–E80 highway, becoming the A12–
E80 at Genoa, and a mainline railroad
hug the shore from the French border
to Tuscany. The main stations along
the route are at Ventimiglia, Sanremo,
Imperia, Savona, Genoa, and La Spezia.
There are good road and railroad links
between Genoa and Milan and Turin.
Access to inland Liguria is harder
because of the mountains. Bus services
link many of the coastal towns with the
prettiest hill villages. You can explore
some of the countryside by car by
following the smaller routes, such as
the S28 from Imperia toward Garessio
in Piedmont, the S334 from Albisola,
or the S456 from Voltri toward Milan.

The spectacular gardens of the Villa Hanbury near Ventimiglia

❶ Balzi Rossi

Imperia. 🚉 Ventimiglia & Menton. 🚌 from Ventimiglia to Ponte San Luigi & then a 10-minute walk. 🌐 archeoge.arti.beniculturali.it

An unassuming promontory is the setting for some of the most important caves in northern Italy. Guided tours lead through the traces of the cave-dwelling civilization of pre-Iron Age Liguria. The caves contain excavated burial sites where the dead were adorned with sea-shells. The **Museo Nazionale dei Balzi Rossi** contains tools, weapons, and stone-etched female figures dating from 100,000 years ago. There is also a reproduction of an etching of a horse.

🏛 **Museo Nazionale dei Balzi Rossi**
Via Balzi Rossi 9. **Tel** 0184 381 13. **Open** Tue–Sun. **Closed** Jan 1, May 1, Dec 25. 📷

❷ Villa Hanbury

Corso Monte Carlo 43, Località La Mortola. **Tel** 0184 22 95 07. 🚉 Ventimiglia. 🚌 from Ventimiglia. **Open** 9:30am–5pm (Mar–mid-Jun & mid-Sep–mid-Oct: to 5pm; mid-Jun–mid-Sep: to 6pm; mid-Oct–Feb: to 4pm) daily. **Closed** Mon Nov–Feb. 📷 🌐 **giardinihanbury.com**

In 1867 the English botanist Sir Thomas Hanbury and his brother bought this villa on the Mortola promontory. They took full advantage of the exceptionally mild Ligurian climate to establish a garden of exotic plants along the sloping pathways of the seaside villa.

The collection, gathered by Hanbury on trips to Africa and Asia, has grown to number more than 3,000 varieties of tropical flora including rubber trees, palms, and wild cacti.

The garden is now run by the state and is one of the most impressive botanical gardens in Italy, even during the winter.

❸ Dolceacqua

Imperia. 🔺 2,000. 🚉 🚌 ℹ Via Barberis Colomba 3 (0184 20 66 66). 🗓 Thu. 🌐 **dolceacqua.it**

This pretty village, 5 miles (8 km) north of Ventimiglia, is built on either side of the churning River Nervia, its two halves joined by an arching 108 ft (33 m) medieval stone bridge. The highlight is the ruined 12th- to 15th-century **castle**, inhabited for a while in the 16th century by the powerful Doria family from Genoa. The two square towers at the front dominate

the village. The terraced vineyards in the surrounding hills produce grapes for general consumption as well as for a robust red wine known as Rossese or vino di Dolceacqua.

The Casinò Municipale in Sanremo, completed in 1906

❹ Sanremo

Imperia. 🔺 57,000. 🚉 🚌 ℹ Largo Nuvoloni 1 (0184 590 59). 🗓 Tue & Sat am. 🌐 **visitrivieradeifiori.it**

Sanremo is a pleasant resort of faded elegance. The composer Tchaikovsky, Alfred Nobel (the father of modern explosives), and the nonsense poet Edward Lear all stayed in the stuccoed mansions of the palm-lined seafront avenue, the Corso Imperatrice. The focus of the town, then as now, is the Casino. A little further down the Corso stands the ornate Russian Orthodox church of San Borilio.

The old town, La Pigna (fir cone), is a huddle of narrow lanes with medieval houses and pastel-colored shutters. A bus service goes from Sanremo to San Romolo, a small village 2,579 ft (786 m) above sea level that offers beautiful views of the area.

A delightful flower market is held in Valle Armea (5–7am, Jun–Oct, by appt, 0184 517 11), while the Italian Song Festival takes place here in February.

❺ Bussana Vecchia

Imperia. Off Sanremo–Arma di Taggia road.

Bussana Vecchia is a marvelously atmospheric ghost town. In February 1887 an earthquake shook the village, reducing its Baroque church and

The village of Dolceacqua with its medieval bridge and ruined castle

surrounding houses to ruins. (One survivor, Giovanni Torre del Merlo, went on to invent the ice-cream cone.)

The town was rebuilt closer to the sea and since then the original village has been taken over by artists, who have restored some interiors, providing a venue for summer concerts and exhibitions.

❻ Cervo

Spectacular rock formations in the grottoes of Toirano

Imperia. 🏔 1,200. 🚊 🚌 🅸 Piazza Santa Caterina 2 (0183 40 81 97). 🍴 Thu. 🆆 cervo.com

Cervo is the prettiest of the many old seafront villages just east of Imperia, with a narrow complex of streets and houses rising dramatically up from the shingle beach. At the top of the village stands the concave Baroque façade of **San Giovanni Battista.** Charming chamber orchestra performances are held in front of the church in July and August. The church is also known as the *"dei corallini,"* after the coral fishing which once brought prosperity to the local people. Now Cervo is an unassuming but

The 5th-century Baptistry at Albenga

characteristic Ligurian vacation resort, with unspoiled hotels near the beach.

San Giovanni Battista at Cervo

❼ Albenga

Savona. 🏔 24,000. 🚊 🚌 🅸 Piazza del Popolo (0182 55 84 44). 🍴 Wed. 🆆 inforiviera.it

Until the Middle Ages, the Roman port of Albium Ingaunum played an important maritime role. The sea, however, gradually moved further out, leaving the town, now called Albenga, stranded on the Centa River. Most striking now is its Romanesque brick architecture, in particular the three 13th-century towers clustered around the cathedral of **San Michele.** The cathedral's interior was restored to its medieval form in the late 1960s. To the south is an intriguing 5th-century **Baptistry** with a ten-sided exterior and octagonal interior. Inside, the original 5th-century blue and white mosaics of doves represent the 12 apostles. To the north of the cathedral is the small Piazza dei Leoni, named after its three stone lions imported from Rome.

In a 14th-century palace on Piazza San Michele is the **Museo Navale Romano**, founded in 1950 following the salvage of a Roman ship that had sunk in the 1st century BC. The museum houses ancient amphorae as well as exhibits salvaged from more recent shipwrecks.

🏛 **Baptistry**
Piazza San Michele. **Tel** 0182 502 88.
Open 10am–noon, 3–6pm Tue–Sun.
Closed Jan 1, Easter, Dec 25. 📷

🏛 **Museo Navale Romano**
Piazza San Michele 12. **Tel** 0182 512 15.
Open 10am–noon, 3–6pm Tue–Sun.
Closed Jan 1, Easter, Dec 25. 📷

❽ Grotte di Toirano

Piazzale delle Grotte, Toirano. **Tel** 0182 980 62. 🚌 from Albenga to Borghetto Santo Spirito. 🚊 to Borghetto Santo Spirito or Loano. **Open** 9:30am–12:30pm, 2–5pm daily. **Closed** Dec 25–Jan 1. 📷 times vary (book ahead).
🆆 toiranogrotte.it

Beneath the delightful medieval town of Toirano lies a series of caves containing relics of Paleolithic life dating from 100,000 years ago.

The **Grotta della Basura** (Witch's Cave) has remarkable prehistoric human and animal footprints, and a collection of ancient bear bones and teeth in the "bear cemetery."

The **Grotta di Santa Lucia** reveals the full beauty of the yellow and gray stalactites and stalagmites that have formed here over hundreds of thousands of years.

The **Museo Etnografico della Val Varatella**, housed in the 16th-century stables of the Palazzo del Marchese, has a collection of agricultural and domestic tools from the 17th to the early 20th century.

🏛 **Museo Etnografico della Val Varatella**
Via Giuseppe Polla, Toirano. **Tel** 0182 98 99 68. **Open** 10am–1pm, 3–8pm daily. 📷

𝟡 Street by Street: Genoa

There is something refreshingly rough-edged about Genoa (Genova in Italian), Italy's most important commercial port. In contrast to the genteel resorts along the neighboring coast, the narrow streets of the old town are the haunts of sailors and streetwalkers.

With its natural harbor and the mountains to protect it, Genoa rose to prominence as a sea-based power. During the 16th century Andrea Doria cemented Genoa's importance, and also proved an astute patron of the arts.

Piazza San Matteo
The houses and church of San Matteo were built by the Doria family in 1278. Palazzo Quartara has a bas relief of St. George above the doorway.

↖ **Musei di Strada Nuova**

← The port and Palazzo Reale

San Lorenzo
The black and white striped Gothic façade of the Duomo dates from the early 13th century.

Palazzo Ducale
Once the seat of the doges of Genoa, this elegant building with its two fine 16th-century courtyards and arcades now contains a major arts and cultural center.

San Donato has a splendid 12th-century octagonal bell tower.

VICO TRE RE MAGI

Sant'Agostino
The 13th-century church and convent were bombed during World War II, but the bell tower remains. The cloisters now house sculpture such as this fragment from the tomb of Margaret of Brabant by Pisano (1312).

Key

— Suggested route

0 meters 100
0 yards 100

Church of Gesù

This Baroque church, built between 1589 and 1606, is also known as the church of Santi Ambrogio e Andrea.

Piazza De Ferrari is the site of the Neo-Classical Banco di Roma and the Accademia, as well as the restored Teatro Carlo Felice.

The bronze fountain in Piazza De Ferrari was constructed in 1936.

Porta Soprana

The eastern gateway to the city has curved outer walls and stands close to the site of Christopher Columbus's house.

Sant'Andrea

The 12th-century cloisters standing in a small garden are all that remain of the convent that once stood here.

🏛️ San Lorenzo (Duomo)

Piazza San Lorenzo. **Tel** 010 254 12 50. **Open** daily. Museo del Tesoro: **Tel** 010 254 12 50. **Open** 9am–noon, 3–6pm Mon–Sat. 📷

The Duomo, with its black and white striped exterior, blends many architectural styles, from the 12th-century Romanesque side portal of San Giovanni to the Baroque touches of some of its side chapels. The three portals at the west end are in French Gothic style.

The most sumptuous of the chapels is dedicated to St. John the Baptist, patron saint of the city; it includes a 13th-century sarcophagus that once held the venerated saint's relics.

Steps lead down from the sacristy to the **Museo del Tesoro di San Lorenzo**. It houses such treasures as the Roman green glass dish said to have been used at the Last Supper, and a blue chalcedony plate on which the head of John the Baptist was allegedly served up to Salome.

🏛️ The Port

Aquarium Ponte Spinola. **Tel** 010 234 56 78. **Open** 9:30am–7:30pm daily (to 8:30pm Sat, Sun, & hols); Jul & Aug: 8:30am–10pm daily. Last adm: 90 mins before closing. 📷🍴♿🎫
🌐 acquariodigenova.it

The port is the heart of Genoa and the origin of its power as a seafaring city state in the 11th and 12th centuries. A workaday place, it is ringed by busy roads and 1960s buildings.

Among the vestiges of its medieval glory is the **Lanterna** lighthouse (restored in 1543) near the Stazione Marittima. In the old days fires would be lit at the top of the Lanterna to guide ships into port. Today, regeneration of the port is in part due to the Renzo Piano–designed conference center (see p189) and the **Aquarium**, one of the largest in Europe and an ideal place to sample the richness of marine life.

Exploring Genoa

Visitors are well rewarded when they explore Genoa – a city proud of its history and legends. The palazzi of Via Balbi and Via Garibaldi, and the paintings and sculptures dotted around the city in churches and museums, are among the finest in northwestern Italy. The environs, too, provide scenic and relaxing locations for excursions along the coast or in the steep hills behind.

The courtyard of the University on Via Balbi

🏛 Sant'Agostino

Piazza Sarzano 35. **Tel** 010 251 12 63.
Museo di Architettura e Scultura Ligure:
Tel 010 251 12 63. **Open** 9am–7pm
Tue–Fri, 10am–7pm Sat & Sun.
Closed public hols. 🅿 ♿

This Gothic church was begun in 1260, but it was bombed to pieces in World War II. It is now deconsecrated and all that remains of the original building is the fine Gothic bell tower, decorated with colored tiles. The monastery, of which the church of Sant'Agostino was once a part, was also bombed. What remained were two ruined cloisters – one of which forms the only triangular building in Genoa. The cloisters have been reconstructed and converted into the **Museo di Architettura e Scultura Ligure**. The museum contains the city's collection of architectural pieces, some dating back to the Roman era, along with fragments of sculpture and frescoes – all salvaged from Genoa's other destroyed churches. The finest piece is a magnificent fragment from the tomb of Margaret of Brabant, who died in 1311. She was the wife of Emperor Henry VII who invaded Italy in 1310. Carved by Giovanni Pisano around 1313, the sculptures from her tomb were restored and repositioned in 1987. The figures, whose garments are arranged in simple folds, seem to be helping Margaret to lie down to rest.

🏛 Palazzo Reale

Via Balbi 10. **Tel** 010 271 02 36.
Open 9am–1:30pm Tue & Wed,
9am–7pm Thu–Sun (last adm: 30 mins
before closing). **Closed** Jan 1, May 1,
Dec 25. 🅿 ♿

This austere-looking residence, used by the Kings of Savoy from the 17th century onward, has a highly ornate Rococo interior – notably its ballroom and its Hall of Mirrors. Among the paintings is a *Crucifixion* by Van Dyck. The garden, which slopes down toward the old port, includes an intriguing cobblestone mosaic around the central fountain, depicting houses and animals.

Opposite the palace is the old **University** (1634) designed by the architect Bartolomeo Bianco, as was much of Via Balbi. The large building brilliantly overcomes Genoa's hilly topography, and is constructed on four levels.

🏛 Palazzo Bianco

Via Garibaldi 11. **Tel** 010 557 21 93.
Open 9am–7pm Tue–Fri (from 10am
Sat & Sun). 🅿 **Palazzo Rosso Tel** 010
557 49 72. **Open** as for Palazzo Bianco.
🅿 **Palazzo Tursi Tel** 010 557 21 93.
Open as for Palazzo Bianco. 🅿 ♿

The Palazzo Bianco is situated on Genoa's most beautiful street, **Via Garibaldi**, where there are numerous fine 16th-century mansions and palazzi. The Palazzo Bianco contains the city's prime collection of paintings, including the works of many Genoese artists such as Luca Cambiaso, Bernardo Strozzi,

Christopher Columbus in Genoa

A portrait of Columbus,
Villa Doria at Pegli

The name of Cristoforo Colombo, or Christopher Columbus, as English speakers know him, is in evidence all over Genoa. A statue of the explorer of the New World greets you as soon as you emerge in Piazza Acquaverde from the Porta Principe train station; various public buildings bear his name; even the airport is named after him. In the 17th-century Palazzo Belimbau, built on top of the old city walls, is a series of frescoes by the local artist Tavarone celebrating the explorer's life, and you can see three of his letters in the Sala del Sindaco in Palazzo Tursi (the city hall) on Via Garibaldi. It is not certain whether Columbus (c.1451–1506) was born in Genoa, in Savona 9 miles (15 km) to the west, or even outside Italy. However, city registers mention his father, a weaver, and various family homes within the city. The small ivy-clad house adjacent to Porta Soprana may have been Columbus's childhood home, where he first discovered his passion for the sea.

The house where Columbus
may have lived

The romantic gardens at Villa Durazzo-Pallavicini in Pegli

Domenico Piola, and Giovanni Benedetto Castiglione. Better-known artists include Filippino Lippi Van Dyck, Veronese, and Rubens. At number 9 Via Garibaldi, **Palazzo Tursi** hosts the Lord Mayor's boardrooms, as well as an extension of the Palazzo Bianco Gallery. Across the street in the **Palazzo Rosso** are more paintings, including works by Dürer and Caravaggio, as well as ceramics and furniture.

Fine tomb architecture from the huge Staglieno Cemetery

🏛 Staglieno Cemetery
Piazzale Resasco, Staglieno. **Tel** 010 87 01 84. **Open** daily. **Closed** pub hols. &

This grandiose cemetery, just over the hills northeast of Genoa along the Bisagno River, is so big (81.5 acres/33 ha) that it has its own internal bus system. Founded in 1844, its tombs and monuments make up an eerie city of miniature cathedrals, Egyptian temples, and Art Nouveau palaces. Its most famous resident is Giuseppe Mazzini, the Genoese revolutionary who died near Pisa in 1872.

Environs
Until World War II, **Pegli**, 4 miles (6 km) west of the city center, was a popular weekend retreat for rich Genoese. Now it forms part of the city, but maintains an air of tranquility thanks to its parks and two villas, the 19th-century **Villa Durazzo-Pallavicini** and the 16th-century **Villa Doria, Museo Navale**. The latter is a naval history museum celebrating Genoa's glorious past: you can see compasses, astrolabes, globes, model ships, and a portrait of Columbus, ascribed to Ghirlandaio, probably dating from 1525. An archaeological museum in the Villa Durazzo-Pallavicini relates the pre-Roman history of the Ligurian coast. The villa's garden is landscaped with romantic grottoes, pavilions, and fountains.

Nervi, 5 miles (8 km) to the east of the city, is another former resort town, famous for its seafront promenade, the **Passeggiata Anita Garibaldi** (named after Garibaldi's wife). The walk follows a route that has been cut into the rock face, giving panoramic views of the coast. The lush **Parco Municipale** is another feature of Nervi. It once formed the grounds of two aristocratic villas – the Villa Serra and the Villa Gropallo. The former, on Via Capolungo, now houses the **Galleria d'Arte Moderna** featuring modern Italian painting. The **Villa Luxoro** on Via Aurelia is notable for its collection of clocks, fabrics, furniture, and lace. The area is also famous as Garibaldi's departure point when he set off for Sicily with his *Mille* (the famous "Thousand" men) to help bring about the unification of Italy. A large monument at Quarto dei Mille, about 2 miles (3 km) back toward the city, marks the place where the volunteers met in May 1860 to follow the intrepid revolutionary (*see pp66–7*). **Villa Grimaldi** houses an art and sculpture collection showing late 18th- and early 19th-century works by Fattori, Boldi, and Messina.

🏛 Galleria d'Arte Moderna
Villa Serra, Via Capolungo 3, Nervi. **Tel** 010 372 60 25. **Open** Tue–Sun. 📷

🏛 Villa Doria, Museo Navale
Piazza Bonavino 7, Pegli. **Tel** 010 696 98 85. **Open** Tue–Sun. **Closed** public hols. 📷 &

🏛 Villa Durazzo-Pallavicini
Via Pallavicini 11, Pegli. **Tel** 010 698 10 48. **Open** 9am–7pm Tue–Fri (from 10am Sat–Sun). **Closed** public hols. 📷 &

🏛 Villa Grimaldi
Via Capolungo 9, Nervi. **Tel** 010 32 23 96. **Open** Tue–Fri.

🏛 Villa Luxoro
Via Mafalda di Savoia 3, Nervi. **Tel** 010 32 26 73. **Open** Tue–Sun am. **Closed** public hols. 📷

Pini (c.1920) by Rubaldo Merello in the Galleria d'Arte Moderna at Nervi

Pastel-colored houses near the pebbly beach at Camogli

⑩ Camogli

Genoa. 🚠 5,500. 🚉 🚌 🚢 ℹ Via XX Settembre 33 (0185 77 10 66). 🚢 Wed. 🔳 **camogli.it**

Built on a pine-wooded slope, Camogli is a fishing village where seashells adorn the pastel-painted house walls, and the smell of frying fish wafts out from the small restaurants into the streets. Near the pebble beach and fishing port is the medieval Castello della Dragonara.

Camogli celebrates its famous festival of the Blessing of the Fish on the second Sunday of May when sardines are fried in a huge pan 13 ft (4 m) in diameter. The fish is distributed free to all comers.

⑪ Portofino Peninsula

Genoa. 🚌 🚢 Portofino. ℹ Via Roma 35 (0185 26 90 24). 🔳 **turismoinliguria.it**

Portofino is the most exclusive harbor and resort town in Italy, crammed with the yachts of the wealthy. You can reach Portofino by road (although cars are not allowed into the village), or by boat, from the resort of Santa Margherita Ligure. Above the town are the church of **San Giorgio**, containing relics said to be those of the dragon-slayer, and a castle.

On the other side of the peninsula, which you have to reach on foot (a two-hour walk) or by boat, is the **Abbazia di San Fruttuoso**, named after a 3rd-century saint whose followers were ship-wrecked here and, according to legend, protected by three lions. The white abbey buildings, set among pines and olive trees, date mostly from the 11th century,

The 16th-century castle jutting into Rapallo harbor

although the imposing Torre dei Doria was added 500 years later. You can take a boat to try to locate the **Cristo degli Abissi**, a bronze statue of Christ that sits on the sea bed near San Fruttuoso, protecting sailors. Further west along the coast is Punta Chiappa, a rocky promontory famous for the changing colors of the surrounding sea.

🔼 **Abbazia di San Fruttuoso**
San Fruttuoso. **Tel** 0185 77 27 03. **Open** Mar–Oct: daily; Nov–Jan: Tue–Sun. **Closed** Feb. 🈲

⑫ Rapallo

Genoa. 🚠 31,000. 🚉 🚌 🚢 ℹ Lungomare Vittorio Veneto 7 (0185 23 03 46). 🚢 Thu. Cable car **Tel** 0185 523 41. 🔳 **turismoinliguria.it**

Historians know Rapallo as the place where two post-World War I treaties were signed, while film buffs might recognize it from the 1954 movie *The Barefoot Contessa*, which was shot here. Rapallo was also a haven for writers such as D.H. Lawrence and Ezra Pound. Its villas still have a patrician feel to them, as do the riding stables, golf course, and tennis courts. The palm-lined esplanade ends in a small 16th-century **castle**, in which art exhibitions are occasionally held. A cable car from the center of the town leads to the 16th-century **Santuario di Montallegro**, which houses a Byzantine icon said to possess miraculous powers.

🔼 **Santuario di Montallegro**
Montallegro. Tel 0185 23 90 00. **Open** daily (**closed** noon–2:30pm).

Large yachts moored in Portofino's famous harbor

The dramatic coastline near Corniglia in the Cinque Terre

⑬ Cinque Terre

La Spezia. 🚉 to all towns.
🚌 Monterosso, Vernazza.
ℹ️ Via Fegina 40, Monterosso
(0187 81 70 59) (summer only);
Piazza Rio Finale 26, Riomaggiore
(0187 92 06 33).
🌐 parconazionale5terre.it

The Cinque Terre are five self-contained villages – Monterosso al Mare, Vernazza, Corniglia, Manarola, and Riomaggiore – located on the rocky coastline of the Riviera di Levante. Clinging dramatically to the steep cliffs, these villages are linked only by an ancient footpath known as the Sentiero Azzurro (Blue Path), which offers spectacular views of the rocky coastlines and terraced vineyards that produce the local dry white Cinque Terre wines. The footpath also provides access to secluded beaches.

These days the five villages suffer from some depopulation. The largest, **Monterosso al Mare**, on the northwestern edge of the Cinque Terre, overlooks a wide bay with its own sandy beach. **Vernazza**, further down the coast, has streets linked by steep steps or *arpaie*. **Corniglia**, perched at the pinnacle of rocky terraces, seems untouched by the passage of time, as does **Manarola**, which is linked by the famous Via dell'Amore, or

Lovers' Lane, to **Riomaggiore**, a 15-minute walk away.

The best way to visit the villages is by boat (from La Spezia, Lerici or Porto Venere) or by train (La Spezia–Genoa railroad line).

⑭ Portovenere

La Spezia. 🚐 3,900. 🚌 🚢 ℹ️ Piazza Bastreri 1 (0187 79 06 91). 🗓️ Mon.
🌐 portovenere.it

Named after the goddess Venus, Portovenere is one of the most romantic villages on the Ligurian coast with its cluster of narrow streets lined with pastel-colored houses. In the upper part of the village is the 12th-century church of **San Lorenzo**. A sculpture over the doorway here depicts the martyrdom of the saint who was roasted alive on a grill. On the stone promontory that curls out into the sea is the

Above the doorway of San Lorenzo in Portovenere

small, black-and-white 13th-century church of **San Pietro**. From here, or from the 16th-century castle on the cliffs on the northwestern side of the village, there are superb views of the Cinque Terre and the small island of Palmaria, about 435 yards (400 m) offshore.

⑮ Lerici

La Spezia. 🚐 10,500. 🚌 🚢 ℹ️ Via Biagini 6, Località Venere Azzurra (0187 96 73 46). 🗓️ Sat am.
🌐 parconazionale5terre.it

This stretch of coast, along the Gulf of La Spezia or Poets' Gulf, was once popular with such literati as Yeats and D.H. Lawrence. The village of San Terenzo, across the bay from Lerici, was where the poet Shelley spent the last four years of his life. It was from his home, the Casa Magni, that he set out in 1822 on a voyage to meet Leigh Hunt in Livorno. Tragically, he was shipwrecked near Viareggio and drowned.

The popular resort of Lerici sits on the edge of a beautiful bay overlooked by pastel-colored houses. The forbidding medieval **Castello di Lerici** (13th century), built by the Pisans and later passed to the Genoese, dominates the vacation villas below. Today it houses a museum of geo-paleontology and hosts art exhibitions and concerts.

🏰 **Castello di Lerici**
Piazza San Giorgio. **Tel** 0187 96 91 14.
Open Tue–Sun. **Closed** Dec 9–26. 📷
🌐 castellodilerici.it

The harbor of Vernazza in the Cinque Terre

Brightly painted buildings in Manarola, one of the villages that make up the Cinque Terre ▶

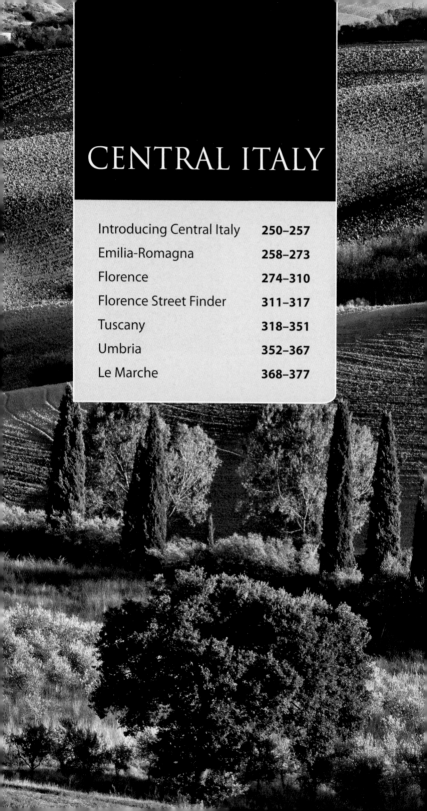

CENTRAL ITALY

Introducing Central Italy	250–257
Emilia-Romagna	258–273
Florence	274–310
Florence Street Finder	311–317
Tuscany	318–351
Umbria	352–367
Le Marche	368–377

Central Italy at a Glance

The central regions of Italy are popular with visitors because they offer a range of beautiful landscapes and towns rich in culture and history, including outstanding churches, towers, and palaces. Emilia-Romagna is home to the impressive Po Delta that provides a haven for wildlife. Tuscany is dominated by Florence, one of Italy's most celebrated centers. Umbria and Le Marche offer gentle pastoral countryside and picturesque hill towns. The major sights of this rewarding area are shown here.

The Leaning Tower of Pisa and the Duomo *(see pp328–30)*, splendid examples of 12th- and 13th-century architecture, are decorated with Arabic-inspired, complex geometric patterns.

Florence
(See pp274–317)

The Duomo and the Baptistry, set in the heart of Florence, dominate the city *(see pp284–6)*. The dome dwarfs many surrounding buildings.

The Uffizi contains a superb collection of Florentine art from Gothic to High Renaissance and beyond *(see pp290–93)*.

The Palazzo Pitti, begun in 1457 for the banker Luca Pitti, became the main residence of the Medici. It now houses their treasures *(see pp306–7)*.

Piacenza
Po
Fiorenzuola d'Arda
Parma
Reggio Emilia
Parma
Massa
Lucca
Pisa
Livorno
Volterra
Campiglia Marittima
Piombino

SAN LORENZO
S. MARIA NOVELLA
CENTRO STORICO
SANTA CROCE
OLTRARNO
Arno
Giardino di Boboli

0 kilometers   50
0 miles   25

0 kilometers   1
0 miles   0.5

◄ Sun setting over a tranquil vineyard in Tuscany

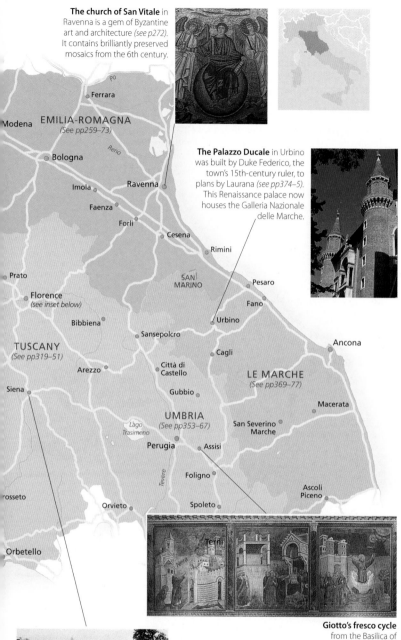

The church of San Vitale in Ravenna is a gem of Byzantine art and architecture *(see p272)*. It contains brilliantly preserved mosaics from the 6th century.

The Palazzo Ducale in Urbino was built by Duke Federico, the town's 15th-century ruler, to plans by Laurana *(see pp374–5)*. This Renaissance palace now houses the Galleria Nazionale delle Marche.

Ferrara

PO

EMILIA-ROMAGNA
(See pp259–73)

Modena

Reno

Bologna

Imola

Faenza

Ravenna

Forlì

Cesena

Rimini

Prato

SAN MARINO

Pesaro

Florence
(see inset below)

Fano

Bibbiena

Urbino

TUSCANY
(See pp319–51)

Sansepolcro

Ancona

Arezzo

Città di Castello

Cagli

LE MARCHE
(See pp369–77)

Siena

Gubbio

Macerata

UMBRIA
(See pp353–67)

Làgo Trasimeno

San Severino Marche

Perugia

Assisi

osseto

Foligno

Orvieto

Spoleto

Ascoli Piceno

Terni

Nera

Tevere

Orbetello

Siena, a medieval town steeped in tradition, centers around the Campo, the large piazza shaped like a scallop shell *(see pp342–7)*. The lively horse race, the Corsa del Palio, is held here in July and August.

Giotto's fresco cycle from the Basilica of San Francesco in Assisi was executed in the 13th century *(see pp358–61)*. The church is visited by thousands of pilgrims each year.

The Flavors of Central Italy

Emilia-Romagna is Italy's gourmet capital, and home to Parmesan, Parma ham, and balsamic vinegar. Bologna has earned the epithet *La Grassa* ("the fat") for rich dishes in which butter, cheese, and velvety sauces feature strongly. The lush lands and rolling hills of Tuscany, Umbria, and Le Marche tend to offer simpler flavors and more rustic, peasant cuisine. Top-quality pork from the Cinta Senese pig, beef from the Chianina cattle of Tuscany, fabulous *fungi* and Umbrian truffles, superb wild boar, and saffron-scented fish soups from the coast of Le Marche are all gastronomic delights of Central Italy.

Italian tomatoes

Tray of perfect, freshly made tortellini pasta

Emilia-Romagna

Not only is this rich, fertile land the home of many of Italy's most classic ingredients, but it has also given the world *bolognese* sauce (*ragù*). The authentic sauce contains some 20 ingredients and is usually served with tagliatelle – never spaghetti. Pasta is an art form here. Legend has it that tagliatelle was invented in honor of Lucrezia Borgia's golden hair, while tortellini pasta is said to be modelled on the shape of Venus's navel.

The region's pork butchers are the most famous in Italy, making excellent sausages, *salumi*, and mortadella, and using every part of the animal including the feet, which are stuffed to form the local specialty *zamponi*. Emilia and coastal Romagna were once two provinces, and there is still a culinary distinction between them. While Emilia's gastronomy is liberally laced with butter, cheese, and mushrooms, Romagna's keynotes tend to be olive oil, garlic, and onions – and fish. The Adriatic in this region teems with life and is an especially good catching ground for turbot (*rombo*) – the "pheasant of the sea."

Nostrano   Milano   Finocchiona   Bococcini
Porchetta
Spianatta romana   Mortadella
Selection of the finest Italian salumi and other cooked meats

Regional Dishes and Specialties

Tuscan olive oil is outstanding in quality. It has many uses and is an integral part of *crostini*, slices of toasted bread smeared with olive oil on which different toppings are spread, such as chicken livers in *crostini alla Toscana*. *Salumi* producers are a great feature of the region and *prosciutto di cinghiale* (wild boar ham) is a rich, gamey delicacy. As well as *tagliatelle al ragù* in Bologna, other very popular pastas include tortellini and tortelloni (the latter being larger than the former), often filled with cheese, butter, and herbs. *Panforte* is the Italian Christmas specialty – a delicious confection of fruits, nuts, honey, sugar, and spices originating in Siena. Try also *ricciarelli*, diamond-shaped almond biscuits, and *torta di riso* – a rich, golden cake made with rice.

Crostini alla Toscana

Cacciucco A fish and seafood soup from Livorno, flavored with herbs and tomatoes and ladled over garlicky toast.

Just part of a gigantic wheel of Parmigiano-Reggiano, or Parmesan

Tuscany

Tuscany is the orchard and vegetable garden of Italy. It is also famous for its red meat, especially from the prized Valdichiana cattle, from south of Arezzo. Pork is also excellent, and the Tuscan passion for hunting ensures that hare, pheasant, and wild boar, often served with local chestnuts, feature prominently on menus.

If there is one staple Tuscan ingredient it is fruity olive oil, liberally used in cooking and for seasoning everything from bread to salads, vegetables, stews and soups.

Broths and soups are very popular, often made with beans, especially white cannellini beans. Not for nothing are Tuscans known as *toscani mangiafagioli* (Tuscan bean-eaters).

Umbria & Le Marche

Umbria, "the green heart of Italy," is the only area outside Piedmont where truffles are found in such high concentration. Norcia is the capital of the black truffle, and shops everywhere

Tuscan market stall piled high with fresh, ripe vegetables

sell truffle paste and truffle oils. Norcia is also famous for its pigs, and a favorite dish is *porchetta* – whole roast suckling pig stuffed with herbs. Wild mushrooms are plentiful in season, in particular *porcini*. Game features too, usually in the form of pheasant, guinea fowl, or pigeon, with the odd songbird thrown in, although it is now illegal to catch wild songbirds. The rural interior of Le Marche also features *porchetta*; lamb and rabbit are popular, too. The long coastline yields a bounty of fish, often made into fish broths, and a specialty of Ancona, *zuppa di pesce*, fish soup with saffron.

ON THE MENU

Baci From Perugia, these are chocolate-coated hazelnuts, their name literally meaning "kisses" in Italian.

Bistecca alla Fiorentina Steak, marinated in herbs, garlic, and finest extra virgin olive oil, rapidly grilled over wood coals. The best meat for this is Chianina beef.

Cinghiale in Umido Traditional Tuscan wild boar stew with red wine, tomatoes, garlic, and vegetables. Usually served with polenta.

Vincisgrassi A baked, layered dish from Le Marche of ham, pasta, and béchamel sauce, often served sprinkled with truffle shavings.

Tagliatelle al ragù Flat strips of pasta are tossed with the quintessential Italian meat sauce from Bologna.

Arista alla Fiorentina Pork loin is roasted in the oven with garlic and rosemary, a specialty of Florence.

Zuccotto A Tuscan specialty of light sponge cake filled with hazelnuts, almonds, chocolate, and cream.

The Wines of Central Italy

Vineyards are seen everywhere in Central Italy, from the rolling cypress-fringed hills of Tuscany to the flatter, Lambrusco-producing plains of Emilia-Romagna. The finest red wines are made in the hills of southeastern Tuscany: Chianti Classico, Brunello di Montalcino, and Vino Nobile di Montepulciano. Today's innovative mix of modern and traditional techniques is steadily improving the quality of much of the region's wine.

Chianti Classico is the heart of the Chianti zone. Chianti may be light and fruity or dense and long-lived – price is the usual guide. Rocca delle Macie is very reasonably priced.

Vernaccia di San Gimignano is a Tuscan white wine with a long, distinguished history. Traditionally a golden, often oxidized wine, it is now also produced in a fresher style, for early drinking. Teruzzi e Puthod make consistently good Vernaccia.

Vino Nobile di Montepulciano is made from the same grapes as Chianti. It can be of superior quality, hence its claim to be a "noble wine." The vineyards are set around the delightful hilltop village of Montepulciano.

Brunello di Montalcino is made from Sangiovese, Brunello being its local name. Its firm tannins may need up to 10 years to soften before the rich, spicy flavors are revealed. Rosso di Montalcino, on the other hand, can be enjoyed much younger.

Parma
Moderna
Bologna

EMILIA-ROMAGNA

Fo

Pistoia
Lucca
Florence
Pisa
Greve
San Gimignano
Are
Siena
TUSCANY
Montepulc
Montalcino

0 kilometers   50
0 miles   25

Super-Tuscans

During the 1970s, innovative wine makers set out to create new, individual wines, even though under the existing rules they would be labeled as simple table wine. A trend which started with Antinori's Tignanello (a Sangiovese–Cabernet Sauvignon blend), this approach has reinvigorated Tuscan wine, to produce some exciting variations.

Sassicaia, a red wine made from the Cabernet Sauvignon grape

Chianti estate at Badia a Passignano in Tuscany

Key

- Chianti
- Chianti Classico
- Vernaccia di San Gimignano
- Brunello di Montalcino
- Vino Nobile di Montepulciano
- Orvieto Classico
- Orvieto
- Verdicchio dei Castelli di Jesi
- Lambrusco

Rimini
an Marino
Pèsaro
Urbino · Ancona
LE MARCHE
Jesi
Gubbio
UMBRIA
Perugia
Assisi
vieto
venna

Grapes of Central Italy

The versatile Sangiovese grape dominates wine making in Central Italy. It is the main grape in Chianti, in Vino Nobile di Montepulciano, in Brunello di Montalcino, and in many of the Super-Tuscan wines. Of the established whites, Trebbiano and Malvasia head the list. Imported varieties such as Chardonnay and Cabernet Sauvignon play a role, often being used to complement and enhance native varieties, of which there has been a resurgence.

Sangiovese grapes

How to Read the Label

The **DOCG name** guarantees the origin of the wine.

Producer's name

Year of production

CASTELGIOCONDO
1998

BRUNELLO DI MONTALCINO
DENOMINAZIONE DI ORIGINE CONTROLLATA E GARANTITA

Castelgiocondo

MARCHESI DE'
FRESCOBALDI

The **bottler's** name and address are given so the region of production is clear.

Alcoholic content

Verdicchio is a dry white wine from Le Marche with a crisp, slightly salty taste. The single-vineyard Verdicchio, such as Umani Ronchi's CaSal di Serra, is winning much acclaim.

Orvieto Classico is a popular Umbrian white wine. This fresh, dry *(Secco)* version from the Antinori estate is a good example of a modern-style Orvieto. The wine also comes in a sweeter form, known as *Abboccato*.

Good Wine Producers

Chianti: Antinori, Badia a Coltibuono, Brolio, Castello di Ama, Castello di Rampolla, Fattoria Selvapiana, Felsina Berardenga, Il Palazzino, Isole e Olena, Monte Vertine, Riecine, Rocca delle Macie, Ruffino, Tenuta Fontodi.
Brunello di Montalcino: Argiano, Altesino, Caparzo, Castelgiocondo, Costanti, Il Poggione, Villa Banfi.
Vino Nobile di Montepulciano: Avignonesi, Le Casalte, Poliziano. In **Umbria**: Adanti, Lungarotti.

Good Chianti Vintages

2008, 2007, 2004, 2003, 2001, 2000, 1999, 1997, 1995, 1993, 1990, 1988.

Understanding Architecture in Central Italy

Central Italy has countless fine Renaissance buildings, many of them concentrated in and around Florence. Their clear lines, elegant simplicity, and harmonious proportions came out of a re-evaluation of the past. Turning their backs on the Gothic style, the architects of the Renaissance returned to Classical Rome for inspiration. Most of the large buildings had been started by the late 15th century, paid for by the Catholic Church or by powerful noble families, such as the Medici of Florence.

The Palazzo Ducale in Urbino (begun 1465)

Religious Buildings

Arched bays trisect the façade.

Pope Pius II's coat of arms

One of 12 roundels by Luca della Robbia

Small circular windows

Square plan topped by small dome

Harmonious proportions

Symmetrical floorplan is based on a Greek cross.

Pienza's Duomo was built by Bernardo Rossellino in *1459* for Pope Pius II as part of his vision of the ideal Renaissance city *(see p337)*.

The Pazzi Chapel of Santa Croce in Florence *(1433)* is one of Brunelleschi's most famous works, decorated with terracotta roundels by Luca della Robbia *(see pp288–9)*.

Santa Maria della Consolazione in Todi, begun in *1508*, owes much to the ideas of the architect Bramante *(see p363)*.

Town and Country Houses

The cornice was designed to cast a shadow over the face of the palace around midday.

Square windows are found only on the ground floor.

Wedge-shaped masonry

Strong horizontal line

The Palazzo Strozzi in Florence *(1489–1536)* is typical of many Tuscan city palaces *(see p332)*. The three storys are given equal importance, and the massive rusticated stonework conveys the impression of strength and power *(see p297)*.

Where to See the Architecture

The simple canons of the Renaissance were interpreted differently away from the hotbed of artistic thought and cultural endeavor of Florence, which has the greatest number of churches and palaces. Alberti's Tempio Malatestiano at Rimini (*see p270*) evokes the sobriety of ancient Roman architecture yet

Vista in the Boboli Gardens, Florence

seeks to reinterpret it in his own unique fashion. Urbino's Palazzo Ducale (*pp374–5*) perfects the grace and polish of the era and is a truly noble period residence. On a smaller scale are the planned Renaissance centers of elegant towns such as Ferrara (*p265*), Pienza (*p337*), and Urbania (*p373*). All three centers are examples of enlightened patronage, and pay homage to the art of antiquity.

The weight of the lantern prevents the dome from springing apart.

Timber ribs provide the main support.

Outer shell

Inner shell

The Duomo in Florence is crowned by the revolutionary dome (*1436*) by Brunelleschi, which had to be built without scaffolding due to its size. The timber structure is covered by an inner and outer shell (*see pp284–5*).

Classical triangular pediment

The top edge of the frieze divides the façade in two.

Volute connects the lower and upper parts.

The façade of Santa Maria Novella in Florence (*1458–70*) was designed by Leon Battista Alberti. He incorporated some of the existing Gothic features into an overall design typical of the Renaissance (*see pp300–1*).

The villa at Poggio a Caiano (*1480*) was redesigned in the Renaissance by Giuliano da Sangallo (*see p332*). The graceful, curved staircase was added around *1802*.

Clock, a later addition

Classical frieze

Colonnade derived from a Classical temple

Classical portico

EMILIA-ROMAGNA

Emilia-Romagna is the heartland of central Italy, a broad corridor through the hills and plains of the Po Valley that marks the watershed between the cold north of the Alps and the hot Mediterranean south. With its rich agricultural land, historical cities, and thriving industry, it is one of the most prosperous areas in Italy.

Most of the major towns in Emilia-Romagna lie near the Via Aemilia, a Roman road built in 187 BC that linked Rimini on the Adriatic coast with the garrison town of Piacenza. Prior to the Romans, the Etruscans had ruled from their capital, Felsina, located on the site of present-day Bologna. After the fall of Rome, the region's focus moved to Ravenna, which became a principal part of the Byzantine Empire administered from Constantinople.

During the Middle Ages, pilgrims heading for Rome continued to use the Via Aemilia. Political power, however, passed to influential noble families – the Malatesta in Rimini, the Bentivoglio in Bologna, the d'Este in Ferrara and Modena, and the Farnese in Parma and Piacenza. Great courts grew up around the families, attracting poets such as Dante and Ariosto, as well as painters, sculptors, and architects whose works still grace the medieval centers of these towns. Cobbled together from separate Papal States in 1860, modern Emilia-Romagna was given its present borders in 1947. Emilia, the western part of the region, is traditionally associated with a more northern outlook and a tendency toward the left in politics. Romagna, on the other hand, has witnessed an increase in the support for right-wing parties calling for political independence from Rome.

The entire region has a reputation as a great gastronomic center. Agriculture has long thrived on the Po's alluvial fringes, earning the Pianura Padana (Po Plain) epithets such as the "bread basket" and "fruit bowl" of Italy. Pigs still outnumber humans in many areas, and some of the country's most famous staples – Parma ham and Parmesan cheese – originate here.

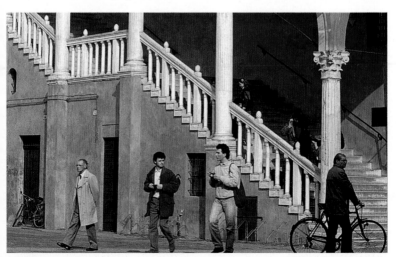

The medieval Palazzo del Comune in Ferrara

◀ The statue of Garibaldi that stands in front of the Palazzo del Governatore, Parma

Exploring Emilia-Romagna

Emilia-Romagna is a checkerboard of fields and plains between the Po river to the north and the forest-covered Apennine mountain slopes to the south. The best place to begin a tour of the region is centrally situated Bologna. Modena, its longtime rival, boasts one of the country's loveliest Romanesque cathedrals. Parma has a more provincial feel and Ferrara, too, has an easygoing air. Castell'Arquato offers a taste of the smaller villages that dot the hills south of the Po.

Piazza Cavalli, Piacenza's central square

Reed-lined shores along the Po Delta

Sights at a Glance

1. Piacenza
2. Castell'Arquato
3. Fidenza
4. Parma
5. Modena
6. Ferrara
7. *Bologna pp266–9*
8. Faenza
9. Rimini
10. Po Delta
11. *Ravenna pp271–3*

For additional map symbols *see back flap*

Getting Around

Excellent road and railroad links, aided by mostly flat terrain, make this region quick and easy to get around. Bologna is connected by the A1–E35 to Florence and by the A13 to Ferrara and Venice. The busy A1–E35 links Bologna to Milan via Piacenza, Fidenza, and Parma. The A15–E31 connects Parma with La Spezia, and the A21–E70 joins Piacenza and Cremona. Fast, frequent train services run along almost parallel routes.

The beach at Cesenatico, north of Rimini on the Adriatic coast

Key

━━━ Highway
━━━ Major road
━━━ Secondary road
┄┄┄ Minor road
━━━ Scenic route
╍╍╍ Main railroad
─── Minor railroad
▬▬▬ International border
━━━ Regional border
△ Summit

The 13th-century Palazzo Pretorio in Castell'Arquato

❶ Piacenza

🏛 105,000. 🚉 FS 🚌 🛈 Piazza Cavalli 7 (0523 32 93 24). 🛒 Wed & Sat.

Piacenza traces its history back to Roman times. Located near the Po, it served as a fortified camp protecting the Emilian plain from invasion. The center is still based on the Roman plan.

Piacenza has a pleasantly understated old center full of fine medieval and Renaissance buildings. Pride of place goes to two bronze equestrian **statues** in the central Piazza Cavalli, the work of the 17th-century sculptor Francesco Mochi, a pupil of Giambologna. Lauded as masterpieces of Baroque sculpture, the statues represent Alessandro Farnese, a soldier of fortune, and his son, Ranuccio: both were rulers of 16th-century Piacenza.

Behind the statues is the redbrick **Palazzo del Comune**, also known as "Il Gotico," an evocatively battlemented Lombard-Gothic palace begun at the end of the 13th century. It is one of Italy's most beautiful medieval buildings. The **Duomo**, at the end of Via XX Settembre,

has a rather leaden Lombard-Romanesque exterior (begun in 1122) and a 14th-century campanile. The interior features Guercino's painted cupola and medieval frescoes. There are also frescoed saints near the main door, painted to resemble members of the congregation.

The **Museo Civico** offers an eclectic mixture of sculpture and paintings – the star among these is the *Madonna and Child with John the Baptist* by Botticelli (1444–1510). There is also an armory and archaeology section. The highlight here is the so-called *Fegato di Piacenza*, an Etruscan bronze representation of the sheep livers once used by priests for divination, inscribed with deities' names.

🏛 Museo Civico

Palazzo Farnese, Piazza Cittadella. **Tel** 0523 49 26 58. **Open** Tue–Sun (Tue–Thu am only). **Closed** public hols. 🅿

❷ Castell'Arquato

Piacenza. 🏛 4,500. 🚌 🛈 Piazza Municipio 1 (0523 80 32 15). 🛒 Mon.

Tucked into the folded hills between Fidenza and Piacenza, Castell'Arquato is one of the prettiest villages in the countryside south of the Po. Day visitors come on weekends to escape Emilia's larger cities, thronging the restaurants and bars around the beautiful **Piazza Matteotti**. The best medieval building on the piazza is the 13th-century **Palazzo Pretorio**, a Romanesque basilica. The impressive **Rocca Viscontea** (14th century), a former fortress, is on Piazza del Municipio. The village's hilltop site offers good views, particularly over the verdant Arda valley to the east.

❸ Fidenza

Parma. 🏛 25,000. 🚉 FS 🚌 🛈 Piazza Duomo 16 (0524 833 77). 🛒 Wed & Sat.

Like many towns hugging the line of the Po, Fidenza owed its early prominence to the Via Aemilia (the old Roman road). The town assumed greater importance as a medieval way station for pilgrims en route to Rome. Today Fidenza is visited for its superb **Duomo** on Piazza Duomo (13th century), a composite piece of architecture that embraces Lombard, Gothic, and transitional Romanesque elements. The most immediately eye-catching feature is the opulent façade, most probably created by the craftsmen who worked with Benedetto Antelami on Parma's Duomo. Inside, the walls are dotted with fragments of medieval frescoes, while the crypt contains the relics of San Donnino, the Duomo's patron.

Detail from façade of Duomo in Fidenza

Interior of Parma Baptistry

❹ Parma

🅼 190,000. 🚆 🚌 ℹ️ Via Melloni 1a (0521 21 88 89). 🅰️ Wed & Sat; Thu (flea market). 🆆 turismo.comune.parma.it

Few Italian towns are as prosperous as Parma, not only a byword for fine food and good living but also a treasure trove of excellent paintings, superlative sculpture, and fine medieval buildings. It boasts one of Italy's top opera houses and a panoply of elegant shops and first-rate bars and restaurants.

The Lombard-Romanesque **Duomo** on Piazza Duomo, among the greatest in northern Italy, is renowned for the painting that fills its main cupola, the *Assumption* (1526–30) by Antonio da Correggio. The nave is adorned with the work of Correggio's pupils. The

south transept features a carved frieze of *The Deposition* (1178) by Benedetto Antelami, who was also responsible for much of the exquisite **Baptistry** (1196) just south of the cathedral. The reliefs inside and outside the latter – particularly those describing the months of the year – are among the most important of their age in Italy.

East of the Duomo is the church of **San Giovanni Evangelista** (rebuilt 1498–1510) whose dome features a fresco (c.1520) of the *Vision of St. John at Patmos* by Correggio. Frescoes by Parmigianino can be seen here and in the 16th-century church of **Madonna della Steccata** on Via Dante.

🏛️ Palazzo Pilotta

Piazzale della Pilotta 15. Galleria: **Tel** 0521 23 33 09. **Open** Tue–Sun am. 🎟️ 🚻 Museo: **Tel** 0521 23 37 18. **Open** Tue–Sat am, Sun pm. 🎟️ 🚻

This vast palace was built for the Farnese family during the 1500s and rebuilt after bomb damage from World War II. It comprises several parts, including the **Teatro Farnese** (1628), a copy of Palladio's ravishing theater in Vicenza, built entirely of wood.

Both Correggio and Parmigianino are represented in the palace's **Galleria Nazionale**, which also houses works by Fra Angelico, El Greco, and Bronzino, and two paintings by Ludovico Carracci: the *Apostles at the Sepulchre* and the *Funeral of the Virgin* (both late 16th century).

The **Museo Archeologico Nazionale**, on the lower floor, has exhibits from Velleia, an Etruscan necropolis, and from prehistoric sites in the hills around Parma.

🏛️ Camera di Correggio

Via Melloni. **Tel** 0521 23 33 09. **Open** Tue–Sun (am only). 🎟️ 🚻
Originally the refectory of the Benedictine convent of San Paolo, this room was frescoed by Correggio in 1518 with mythological scenes.

Campanile and Baptistry in Parma

The Making of Parmesan Cheese and Parma Ham

No cheese is as famous or as vital to Italy's cuisine as Parmesan *(Parmigiano)*. There are two types: the superior Parmigiano-Reggiano and the lower-quality Grana. The cheese is made using techniques that have barely altered in centuries. Partially skimmed milk is added to whey, to promote fermentation, and rennet is used to curdle the milk. The cheese is then salted and shaped. Parmesan is not only used in cooking but is delicious eaten on its own, or with pears – an Italian specialty.

Shop selling Parmesan cheese and Parma ham

Parma ham owes its excellence to techniques perfected over many years and to the special conditions in which it is cured. It is made from pigs fattened on whey left over from the making of Parmesan cheese. The meat has a character that requires little more than salt and pepper to produce the famous *prosciutto crudo*. The breezy hills of Langhirino, south of Parma, are ideal for curing the hams, which are aged for up to 10 months. Each ham is branded with the five-pointed crown of the old Duchy of Parma.

Flora by Carlo Cignani (1628–1719) in the Galleria Estense in Modena

❺ Modena

🏛 185,000. 🚉 🚌 ℹ Piazza Grande 14 (059 203 26 60). 🗓 Mon.
🌐 turismo.comune.modena.it

To most Italians Modena means fast cars, for both Ferrari and Maserati have factories in its industrial outskirts, and opera, since this is the birthplace of Luciano Pavarotti. Monuments to an earlier age, however, make this one of Emilia's most enticing historic destinations. A thriving colony since Roman times, the city rose to medieval prominence on the back of its broad agricultural hinterland and the arrival in 1598 of the d'Este nobles from Ferrara. This family continued to rule the city until the 18th century.

🏠 Duomo
Corso Duomo. **Tel** 059 21 60 78. **Open** daily. Torre Ghirlandina: **Open** Apr–Oct: 9:30am–12:30pm, 3–7pm Sun. **Closed** Aug. 🎨

Modena's superlative **Duomo** rises alongside the old Roman Via Emilia. One of the region's greatest Romanesque buildings, it was founded by Countess Matilda of Tuscany, ruler of Modena in the 11th century. It was designed by Lanfranco and dedicated to San Geminiano, the city's patron saint, whose stone coffin lies under the

choir. Its most noticeable feature is the **Torre Ghirlandina**, a perilously leaning tower begun at the same time as the Duomo and completed two centuries later. It once housed the *Secchia*, a wooden bucket whose 1325 theft from Bologna allegedly sparked a war between the two cities. It also inspired Tassoni's 17th-century mock epic poem *La Secchia Rapita* (The Stolen Bucket), and became the symbol of a rivalry between the cities.

The large reliefs on the Duomo's main (west) façade are the work of the 12th-century sculptor Wiligelmus. The highlight of the rather severe interior is a large carved *tribuna* (rood screen) decorated with 12th-century scenes from the Passion.

🏛 Palazzo dei Musei
Largo di Porta Sant'Agostino 337. Galleria Estense: **Tel** 059 439 57 11. **Open** Call for opening times. 🎨 ♿ Biblioteca Estense: **Tel** 059 22 22 48. **Open** Tue–Thu (Mon, Fri, & Sat am). **Closed** public hols. 🎨

Northwest of the Duomo, and reached through an attractive warren of old streets, is the Palazzo dei Musei. Formerly an arsenal and workhouse, it is now home to the city's best museums and galleries. Its finest section is the **Galleria Estense**, given over to the d'Este private art collection, which was transferred here when the city of Ferrara, the family's former dominion, became part of the Papal States. Most of the paintings are by Emilian and Ferrarese artists (notably Reni and the Carracci) but there are also works by Velázquez, Tintoretto, Bernini, and Veronese.

Among the permanent displays in the **Biblioteca Estense**, the d'Este Library, are a 1481 edition

of Dante's *Divine Comedy* and dozens of fascinating maps and diplomatic letters, many dating back centuries. A map dated 1501 was among the first to show the 1492 voyage by Columbus to the New World. The jewel of the collection is the magnificent illuminated Borso d'Este Bible, with gloriously decorated pages containing over 1,200 miniatures by 15th-century artists of the Ferrara school, most notably Taddeo Crivelli and Franco Russi. Certain sections of the museum are closed due to damage caused by an earthquake, but are due to reopen in late 2013.

Environs
The **Ferrari** factory, 12 miles (20 km) to the south, was founded by Enzo Ferrari in 1945. The FIAT-owned manufacturer now produces around 2,500 cars annually. The **Galleria Ferrari** has an excellent exhibition featuring memorabilia, classic engines, and many vintage cars.

🏛 Galleria Ferrari
Via Dino Ferrari 43, Maranello. **Tel** 0536 94 97 13. **Open** 9:30am–6pm daily (to 7pm summer). **Closed** Jan 1, Dec 25. 🎨 ♿

❻ Ferrara

🏛 135,000. 🚉 🚌 ℹ Castello Estense, Largo Castello (0532 20 93 70). 🗓 Mon & Fri.

The d'Este Dynasty has left an indelible mark on Ferrara, one of the region's greatest walled towns. The noble family took control of the town under Nicolò II in the late 13th century, holding power until 1598, when the family was forced by the papacy to move to Modena.

Ferrari 250 SWB, produced between 1959 and 1962

For hotels and restaurants in this region see pp562–77 and pp580–605

🏰 Castello Estense

Largo Castello. **Tel** 0532 29 92 33.
Open Tue–Sun (Mar–May: daily).
Closed public hols.

With its towers and battlements, the Este family's dynastic seat (begun 1385) looms over the town center. Ferrante and Giulio d'Este were incarcerated in its dungeons for plotting to overthrow Alfonso I d'Este. Parisina d'Este, wife of Nicolò III, was executed here for having an affair with Ugo, her illegitimate stepson.

🏛 Palazzo del comune

Piazza Municipale.
Bronze statues of Nicolò III and Borso d'Este, one of Nicolò's reputed 27 children, adorn this medieval palace (begun 1243). Both are copies of the 15th-century originals by Leon Battista Alberti.

The impressive medieval Castello Estense in Ferrara

Façade of the Duomo in Ferrara

🏛 Museo della Cattedrale

Via San Romano. **Tel** 0532 76 12 99.
Open Tue–Sun. **Closed** Jan 1 & 6, Easter, Dec 25 & 26.

Ferrara's 12th-century Duomo is a Romanesque-Gothic hybrid designed by Wiligelmus, who is widely regarded as the first great Italian sculptor. Fine reliefs on the façade depict scenes from the Last Judgment. The excellent **museum** (in a deconsecrated church opposite the cathedral) contains a fine set of marble reliefs of the *Labors of the Months* (late 1100s), two painted organ shutters (1469) of *St. George* and the *Annunciation* by Cosmè Tura, and the *Madonna of the Pomegranate* (1408) by Jacopo della Quercia.

🏛 Palazzo Schifanoia

Via Scandiana 23. **Tel** 0532 24 49 49.
Open Tue–Sun. **Closed** public hols.

Building work in the d'Este summer retreat begun in 1385. The estate is famous for its Salone dei Mesi (Room of the Months), decorated with beautiful 15th-century murals by Tura and other Ferrarese painters with detailed scenes depicting the different months of the year.

🏛 Museo Archeologico Nazionale

Palazzo di Ludovico il Moro, Via XX Settembre 122. **Tel** 0532 662 99.
Open 9:30am–5pm Tue–Sun. **Closed** May 1, Dec 25.

The most interesting exhibits in the Museo Archeologico Nazionale are artifacts that were excavated from Spina, a Greco-Etruscan trading post near Comacchio on the Po Delta.

🏛 Palazzo dei Diamanti

Corso Ercole d'Este 21.
Tel 0532 24 49 49. **Open** 9am–7pm daily.

Named after the diamond motifs on its façade, the Palazzo dei Diamanti houses a modern art gallery, an interesting museum devoted to the Risorgimento, and the Pinacoteca Nazionale, which contains works from leading exponents of the local Renaissance school.

The d'Este Family Dynasty

During their medieval heyday, the d'Este family presided over one of Europe's leading courts, combining the roles of blood-crazed despots with enlightened Renaissance patrons. Nicolò III, for example, had his wife and her lover brutally murdered. Alfonso I (1503–34) married Lucrezia Borgia, descendant of one of Italy's most notorious families, while Ercole I (1407–1505) attempted to poison a nephew who tried to usurp him (and eventually had him executed). At the same time the d'Este court attracted writers like Petrarch, Tasso, and Ariosto, and painters such as Mantegna, Titian, and Bellini. Ercole I also rebuilt Ferrara, creating one of Europe's finest Renaissance cities.

Portrait of Alfonso I d'Este by Titian (c.1485–1576)

❼ Street by Street: Bologna

The historic city center of Bologna is a handsome ensemble of brick buildings and charming porticoed streets. Medieval palaces are clustered around the two central squares, Piazza Maggiore and Piazza del Nettuno, flanked to the south by the churches of San Petronio and San Domenico. The university of Bologna is the oldest in Europe and the venerable Archiginnasio was its first official building. Further afield, the skyline is etched by the Asinelli and Garisenda towers, and by the campanile of Santo Stefano.

Fontana di Nettuno
The famous Neptune fountain (1566) was designed by Tommaso Laureti and decorated with magnificent bronze figures by Giambologna.

Train station

The Palazzo del Podestà (13th century) was remodeled in 1484.

Modena ◄

VIA UGO BASSI

VIA RIZZOLI

VIA OREFIC

VIA IV NOVEMBRE

PIAZZA MAGGIORE

VIA DELL'ARCHIGINNASIO

★ San Petronio
The Martyrdom of St. Sebastian (15th century) in the Cappella di San Sebastiano is by Lorenzo Costa of the Ferrarese School.

Archiginnasio

VIA FARINI

Piazza Cavour
The flagged medieval streets and shady porticoed buildings found in this pleasant piazza are typical of Bologna's elegant city center.

PIAZZA CAVOUR

VIA GARIBALDI

Key

— Suggested route

| 0 meters | 150 |
| 0 yards | 150 |

San Domenico
(1251) is dedicated to St. Dominic, who is buried here in a magnificent tomb.

San Giacomo Maggiore
The *Triumph of Death* fresco by Costa (1483–6) adorns the Cappella Bentivoglio.

Pinacoteca Nazionale
Museo di Anatomia
Umana Normale

V I A   Z A M B O N I

V I A   S A N   V I T A L E
Ravenna

S T R A D A   M A G G I O R E

P I A Z Z A   D I
P O R T A
R A V E G N A N A

V I A   S A N T O   S T E F A N O

V I A   C A S T I G L I O N E

Firenze

Torri degli Asinelli e Garisenda
The colossal towers are two of the few remaining towers begun by Bologna's important families in the 12th century.

Abbazia di Santo Stefano
The Fontana di Pilato, or Pilate's fountain, in the courtyard features a basin with Lombard inscriptions from the 8th century.

🔵 San Giacomo Maggiore
Piazza Rossini. **Open** daily.

This Romanesque-Gothic church, begun in 1267 but altered substantially since, is visited mainly for the Cappella Bentivoglio, a superb family chapel founded by Annibale Bentivoglio in 1445 and consecrated in 1486. Pride of place naturally goes to a portrait with subtle characterization of the patrons by Lorenzo Costa (1460–1535), who was also responsible for the frescoes of the *Apocalypse*, the *Madonna Enthroned*, and the *Triumph of Death*. The chapel's altarpiece, depicting the *Virgin and Saints with Two Angel Musicians* (1488), is the work of Francesco Francia. The Bentivoglio family is further glorified in the tomb of Anton Galeazzo Bentivoglio (1435) opposite the chapel. It was among the last works of the noted Sienese sculptor, Jacopo della Quercia. The Oratory of Santa Cecilia features frescoes on the lives of Santa Cecilia and San Valeriano by Costa and Francesco Francia (1504–6).

The Bentivoglio tomb (1435) by Jacopo della Quercia

Exploring Bologna

Monuments to Bologna's rich cultural heritage are scattered across the city, from the leaning towers and the church of San Petronio in the old center to the Pinacoteca Nazionale in the university district.

⊞ Torri degli Asinelli e Garisenda

Piazza di Porta Ravegnana. Torre degli Asinelli: **Open** daily.

The famous leaning towers – Torre degli Asinelli and Torre Garisenda – are among the few survivors of the original 200 that once formed the skyline of Bologna. Both were begun in the 12th century, though there were probably earlier towers on the site – Dante mentioned a pair of towers here in his *Inferno*. Torre Garisenda was shortened as a safety measure within only a few years of its construction,

and still leans some 10 ft (3 m) from the vertical. At 318 ft (97 m) tall, Torre Asinelli is the fourth highest tower in Italy after those in Cremona, Siena, and Venice. Its 500-step ascent offers fine views over the city's rooftops to the hills beyond.

Exterior of the Abbazia di Santo Stefano

⛪ Abbazia di Santo Stefano

Via Santo Stefano 24. **Tel** 051 22 32 56. **Open** 9am–noon, 3:30–6:30pm daily.

Santo Stefano is a curious collection of four medieval churches (originally seven) jumbled together under one roof. The 11th-century church of the Crocifisso provides little more than a corridor to

⛪ San Petronio

Piazza Maggiore. **Tel** 051 23 14 15. **Open** daily.

Dedicated to the city's 5th-century bishop, this church ranks among the greatest of Italy's brick-built medieval buildings. Founded in 1390, it was originally intended to be larger than St. Peter's in Rome, but its size was scaled down when the church authorities diverted funds to the nearby Palazzo Archiginnasio. The resulting financial shortfall left the church decidedly lopsided, with a row of columns on its eastern flank that were intended to support an additional internal aisle. The project's financial profligacy, nonetheless, was said to have been instrumental in turning Martin Luther against Catholicism.

The altarpiece of the *Martyrdom of St. Sebastian* is from the late Ferrarese School.

The pink and white interior adds to the overall light and airy effect.

The canopied main portal features beautiful biblical reliefs (1425–38) by Jacopo della Quercia.

Gothic Interior
The interior is airy, with graceful pillars supporting the roof. Twenty-two chapels, shielded by screens, open off the nave. In 1547 the Council of Trent (174) was temporarily moved here due to the plague.

Entrance

Unfinished upper façade

The meridian line was traced in 1655 by the astronomer Gian Domenico Cassini. It is 219 ft (67 m) long.

The stained-glass windows (1464–6) in this chapel are by Jacob of Ulm.

polygonal San Sepolcro, the most appealing of the quartet. Also dating from the 11th century, its centerpiece is the tomb of St. Petronius, a marvelously overstated affair modeled on the Holy Sepulchre of Jerusalem. The courtyard contains the so-called Fontana di Pilato, an 8th-century basin.

The 5th-century Santi Vitale e Agricola is the oldest church in the city. It was rebuilt in the 8th and 11th centuries. Inside are the sarcophagi of Saints Vitalis and Agricola, martyred in the 4th century. Santa Trinità features a small museum of minor paintings and religious artifacts, including wooden statues of the *Adoration of the Magi* painted by Simone dei Crocifissi (c.1370).

Bell tower

Choir Stalls The exquisite inlaid choir stalls of the Chapel of the Holy Sacrament were made by Raffaello da Brescia in 1521.

🏛 Pinacoteca Nazionale

Via delle Belle Arti 56. **Tel** 051 420 94 11. **Open** Tue– Sun. **Closed** Jan 1, May 1, Aug 15 Dec, 25. 🎨 ♿

Bologna's principal art gallery, and one of northern Italy's most important collections, stands on the edge of the city's university district, a bustling area of bars, bookstores, and cheap restaurants. The gallery is mainly dedicated to work by Bolognese painters, notably Vitale da Bologna, Guido Reni, Guercino, and the Carracci family. Members of the Ferrarese School are also represented, in particular Francesco del Cossa and Ercole de' Roberti. The two highlights are Perugino's *Madonna in Glory* (c.1491) and Raphael's famous *Ecstasy of St. Cecilia*, painted around 1515, both artists having worked in Bologna.

The Ecstasy of St. Cecilia (c.1515) by Raphael in Bologna's Pinacoteca Nazionale

🏛 Museo delle Cere Anatomiche

Via Irnerio 48. **Tel** *051 24 42 15/051 24 22 17*. **Open** 9am–1pm Mon–Fri. **Closed** Jan 1, Easter, May 1, Dec 25, public hols. 📷

The Museum of Anatomical Waxworks is one of the more memorable of Bologna's smaller museums, featuring occasionally gruesome visceral waxworks and numerous models of organs, limbs, and flayed bodies. Sculpted rather than made from casts, they have an artistic as well as scientific appeal. The models were used as medical teaching aids until the 19th century. Exhibits from the 18th century are in Palazzo Poggi, which also contains the Museo Cartageographica.

🏛 San Domenico

Piazza di San Domenico 13. **Tel** 051 640 04 11. **Open** daily. ♿

Bologna's San Domenico can lay claim to being the most important of Italy's many Dominican churches. Begun in 1221, after St. Dominic's death, it was built to house the body of the saint, who died here and lies buried in a tomb known as the Arca di San Domenico. A magnificent composite work, the tomb's statues were executed by Nicola Pisano; the reliefs of scenes from the *Life of St. Dominic* were the work of Nicola Pisano and his assistants; the canopy (1473) is attributed to Nicola di Bari; while the figures of the angels and Saints Proculus and Petronius are early works by Michelangelo. The reliquary (1383) behind the sarcophagus contains St. Dominic's head.

Arca di San Domenico in the Basilica di San Domenico

Fresco of Malatesta and St. Sigismund (1451) by Piero della Francesca in the Tempio Malatestiano, Rimini

❽ Faenza

Ravenna. 🚗 54,000. 🚆 🚌
ℹ️ Voltone Molinella 2 (0546 252 31).
🏛️ Tue, Thu, & Sat.

Faenza is synonymous with the *faïence* ceramic-ware to which it gave its name. Renowned across Europe for over 500 years, the pottery, with its distinctive blue and ocher coloring, is still made in countless small factories around the town.

The highlight of Faenza is the **Museo Internazionale delle Ceramiche**, one of the largest ceramic collections in Italy. Its exhibits feature not only examples of local ware, but also pottery from other countries and other periods, including Roman ceramics and medieval majolica. There is also a section devoted to the modern ceramic art of Picasso, Matisse, and Chagall.

🏛️ **Museo Internazionale delle Ceramiche**
Viale Baccarini 19. **Tel** 0546 69 73 11.
Open Apr–Oct: Tue–Sun; Nov–Mar: Tue–Sun (Tue–Thu am only). **Closed** Jan 1, May 15, Aug 15, Dec 25. 🦽 📷

❾ Rimini

🚗 140,000. 🚆 🚌 ℹ️ Piazzale Fellini 3 (0541 533 99). 🏛️ Wed & Sat.
🌐 **riminiturismo.it**

Rimini was once a quaint seaside resort, whose charms were celebrated in the early films of Federico Fellini (1920–93), the

director born and raised here. Today it is the largest beach resort in Europe. The seafront, which stretches unbroken for almost 9 miles (15 km), is lined with clubs, bars, and restaurants. The crowded beaches are clean and well groomed, though entrance fees are charged at private beaches.

The town's old quarter, by contrast, is pleasantly quiet. Its charming cobbled streets gather around **Piazza Cavour**, dominated by the 14th-century **Palazzo del Podestà**. Rimini's finest building is the **Tempio Malatestiano**, built as a Franciscan church but converted in 1450 by Leon Battista Alberti, the great Florentine architect, into one of Italy's great Renaissance monuments. The work was commissioned by Sigismondo Malatesta (1417–68), a descendant of Rimini's ruling medieval family, and reputedly one of the most evil and debauched men of his time. Ostensibly designed as a chapel, the Tempio became little more than a monument to Malatesta. Inside are sculptures by Agostino di Duccio and a fresco (1451) by Piero della Francesca of Malatesta kneeling before St. Sigismund (1451).

The entwined initials of Malatesta and his fourth wife, Isotta degli Atti, provide a recurring decorative motif, and there are reliefs depicting scenes of bacchanalian excess and oddities such as strangely posed elephants (a Malatesta family emblem). All this led Pope Pius II to condemn the building as "a temple of devil-worshippers," and to burn Malatesta's effigy for acts of "murder, violation, adultery, incest, sacrilege, and perjury."

Environs
Further along the coast, the resorts become relatively quieter. **Cesenatico**, 11 miles (18 km) north, offers all the usual facilities yet the beaches are less crowded.

🏛️ **Tempio Malatestiano**
Via IV Novembre. **Tel** 0541 511 30.
Open 8:30am–12:30pm, 3:30–7pm daily (9am–1pm, 3:30–7pm Sun). 🦽

❿ Po Delta

Ferrara. 🚆 Ferrara Ostellata. 🚌 to Goro or Gorino. ⛴️ from Porto Garibaldi, Goro, & Gorino. ℹ️ Via Mazzini 4, Comacchio (0533 31 41 54). Parco Delta del Po: **Tel** 0533 31 40 03.
🌐 **parcodeltapo.it**

The Po is Italy's longest river. Its vast basin covers some 15 percent of the country and

Façade of the Renaissance Tempio Malatestiano in Rimini

supports around a third of the nation's population. Although ravaged in many places by industrial pollution, at its finest it offers beautifully subtle landscapes – rows of poplar trees across misty fields and vistas over the shifting sands of its vast delta, an estuary of marshes, dunes, and islands.

The immense **Parco Delta del Po** is a national park stretching for 234 sq miles (600 sq km), all the way to the Veneto. Wetland areas such as the **Valli di Comacchio** north of Ravenna have long been nature reserves, a winter home to thousands of breeding and migrating birds. Ornithologists gather here to see gulls, coots, bean geese, and black terns, and far rarer species such as the white egret, hen harrier, and pygmy cormorant. **Comacchio,** the nearest settlement, comprises 13 tiny islands connected by bridges. It is one of several fishing villages in the area, and its most famous catch is eels, often caught using methods, like water gates, that date back as far as Roman times.

Hen harrier, found in the Po Delta

Other nature reserves include the **Bosco della Mesola,** a tract of ancient woodland planted by the Etruscans and cared for by generations of monks. You can either walk or cycle through it, with excellent opportunities for seeing large herds of deer.

For a good look at the entire region, follow the S309 – part of the old Via Romea pilgrimage trail to Rome – that runs north to south through some 62 miles (100 km) of the park. A number of smaller lanes branch off into the wilderness. There are also boat trips to some of the delta's more remote corners: key departure points include the villages of Ca'Tie-polo, Ca'Vernier, and Taglio di Po. Most areas also offer the possibility of hiring bicycles. The 78-mile (125-km) ride along the right bank of the Po is very popular with cyclists.

Piazza del Popolo, Ravenna's central square

⑪ Ravenna

🏙 160,000. 🚉 🚌 *i* Via Salara 8–12 (0544 354 04). 🛒 Wed & Sat; antiques on 3rd weekend of each month. 🌐 turismo.ravenna.it

Most people visit Ravenna for its superb mosaics from the Byzantine period *(see pp22–3),* but the town itself is a surprisingly pleasant medley of old streets, fine shops, and peaceful piazzas. The **Museo Nazionale** has a wide range of icons, paintings, and archaeological displays. The best place to take a break from sightseeing is Piazza del Popolo, a lovely ensemble of medieval buildings.

🏛 Museo Nazionale
Via Fiandrini. **Tel** 0544 21 56 18. **Open** Tue–Sun. **Closed** Jan 1, May 1, Dec 25. 🚫 🚻

The peaceful landscape along the banks of the river in the Po Delta

A Tour of Ravenna

Ravenna rose to power in the 1st century BC under the Emperor Augustus, who built a port and naval base at nearby Classe, currently the site of a major excavation project. As Rome's power declined, Ravenna was made the capital of the Western Empire (AD 402), a role it retained during the Ostrogoth and Byzantine rule in the 5th and 6th centuries. Ravenna is renowned for its early Christian mosaics – the town had converted to Christianity in the 2nd century AD. The mosaics span the years of Roman and Byzantine rule, offering comparisons between Classically inspired designs and later Byzantine motifs.

② **The Good Shepherd**
This mosaic adorns the tiny Mausoleo di Galla Placidia. Begun in 430, this exquisite building probably never received the remains of Placidia, wife of a barbarian emperor.

① **San Vitale**
San Vitale's apse mosaics (526–547) show Christ, San Vitale (being handed a martyr's crown), two angels, and Bishop Ecclesius, who began the church *(see pp54–5)*.

③ **Baptism of Jesus**
The 5th-century Battistero Neoniano (Neonian Baptistry) is named after the bishop who may have commissioned its decoration, including this beautiful mosaic. It was built near the remains of a Roman bathhouse and is Ravenna's oldest monument.

⑤ Battistero degli Ariani
The cupola of this late 5th-century baptistry has a mosaic showing the Apostles ringed around a centerpiece depicting the Baptism of Christ.

⑥ Sant'Apollinare Nuovo
This glorious 6th-century church, named after Ravenna's first bishop, is dominated by two rows of mosaics. Both show processions of martyrs and virgins bearing gifts for Christ and the Virgin.

④ Tomba di Dante
Dante's wanderings around Italy after his exile from Florence eventually brought him to Ravenna, where he died in 1321. A lamp in his sepulchre (1780) is fed by oil given by the city of Florence.

Key
— Suggested route

0 meters 200
0 yards 200

FLORENCE

Florence is a vast and beautiful monument to the Renaissance, the artistic and cultural reawakening of the 15th century. Writers such as Dante, Petrarch, and Machiavelli contributed to its proud literary heritage, though it was the paintings and sculptures of artists such as Botticelli, Michelangelo, and Donatello that turned the city into one of the world's greatest artistic capitals.

While the Etruscans had long settled the hills around Fiesole, Florence first sprang to life as a Roman colony in 59 BC. Captured by the Lombards in the 6th century, the city later emerged from the Dark Ages as an independent city-state. By the 13th century a burgeoning trade in wool and textiles, backed by a powerful banking sector, had turned the city into one of Italy's leading powers. Political control was wielded first by the guilds, and later by the Florentine Republic. In time, power passed to leading noble families, of which the most influential were the Medici, a hugely wealthy banking dynasty. Florence, and later Tuscany, remained under the family's

almost unbroken sway for three centuries. During this time the city was at the cultural and intellectual heart of Europe, its cosmopolitan atmosphere and wealthy patrons providing the impetus for a period of unparalleled artistic growth. Artists, sculptors, and architects flocked to the city, filling its streets, churches, and palaces with some of the world's greatest Renaissance works. By 1737 the Medici had died out, leaving the city under Austrian (and briefly Napoleonic) control until Italian Unification in 1860. Between 1865 and 1871 Florence was the capital of the new Kingdom of Italy. The historic streets and artistic heritage were ravaged by the Arno floods of November 1966.

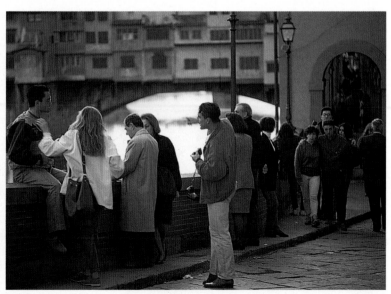

Florentines strolling in front of Ponte Vecchio (1345), the old bridge lined with shops spanning the Arno

◀ A replica of Michelangelo's *David* in Piazza della Signoria

Exploring Florence

Historic Florence is a surprisingly compact area, and the majority of the sights described on the following pages can easily be reached on foot. Most visitors head for the Duomo, the city's geographical and historical focus, ideally placed to explore the Campanile, Baptistry, and Museo dell'Opera del Duomo. To the south is Piazza della Signoria, long the city's political heart, flanked by the Palazzo Vecchio, Florence's town hall, and the Uffizi, one of Italy's leading art galleries. To the east lies the church of Santa Croce, home to frescoes by Giotto and the tombs of some of Florence's greatest men. To the west stands Santa Maria Novella, the city's other great church, also adorned with fresco-filled chapels. Across the Ponte Vecchio and the Arno – the river that bisects the city – is the district of Oltrarno, dominated by Santo Spirito and the vast Pitti Palace, containing galleries with works by great Renaissance artists including Raphael and Titian.

Getting Around

Florence has excellent bus service. Three streetcar lines operate in the city; one links the city center to the outskirts. The compact city center, a restricted traffic area, is best negotiated on foot.

Key

- Major sight
- Place of interest
- Pedestrian street
- City walls

Ponte Vecchio with Ponte Santa Trinità in the foreground

For additional map symbols see back flap

Sights at a Glance

Churches

- **2** Convento di San Marco
- **3** Santissima Annunziata
- **7** Duomo and Baptistry pp280–82
- **8** Orsanmichele
- **10** Santa Croceg Ognissanti
- **18** San Lorenzo
- **19** Cappelle Medicee
- **21** Santa Maria Novella
- **25** *Ognissanti*
- **26** *Cappella Brancacci pp298–9*
- **27** Santo Spirito
- **29** Santa Felicita
- **31** San Miniato al Monte

Buildings, Monuments, and Squares

- **5** Spedale degli Innocenti
- **12** Ponte Vecchio
- **14** Piazza della Signoria
- **15** Palazzo Vecchio
- **16** Palazzo Davanzati
- **17** Palazzo Strozzi
- **20** Mercato Centrale
- **22** Palazzo Antinori
- **23** Palazzo Rucellai
- **30** Piazzale Michelangelo

Museums and Galleries

- **1** Galleria dell'Accademia
- **4** Museo Archeologico
- **6** Museo dell'Opera del Duomo
- **9** Bargello
- **11** Museo Galileo
- **13** *Uffizi pp286–9*
- **24** Museo Nazionale Alinari della Fotografia
- **28** *Palazzo Pitti pp302–3*

Bell tower, Palazzo Vecchio

0 meters	500
0 yards	500

Street by Street: Around San Marco

The buildings in this part of Florence once stood on the fringes of the city, serving as stables and barracks. The Medici menagerie of lions, elephants, and giraffes was housed here. Today it is a student quarter and the streets are often busy with young people attending the university or the Accademia di Belle Arti, the world's oldest art school, founded in 1563.

Palazzo Pandolfini was designed by Raphael in 1516.

❸ Santissima Annunziata
This Renaissance church has an opulent Baroque interior.

❷ ★ Convento di San Marco
The Annunciation (c.1445) is an example of Fra Angelico's exquisite fresco decoration.

Sant'Apollonia features a fresco of the *Cenacolo* (Last Supper) by Andrea del Castagno (1450).

Luigi Cherubini *(1760–1842)*, the Florentine composer, trained at the Conservatorio.

❶ ★ Galleria dell'Accademia
This detail is from a 14th-century altarpiece, the *Madonna and Saints*, by an unnamed master.

Giambologna's statue of Duke Ferdinando I was cast by Tacca in 1608.

For hotels and restaurants in this region see pp562–77 and pp580–605

Locator Map
See Florence Street Finder map 2

0 meters 50
0 yards 50

Key

— Suggested route

The Giardino dei Semplici was opened in 1543.

❹ Museo Archeologico
Many of the Etruscan objects in the museum were originally in the Medici collections.

❺ Spedale degli Innocenti
Opened in 1444, the city orphanage by Brunelleschi was decorated with cameos by Andrea della Robbia.

Part of the 15th-century *Cassone Adimari* by Lo Scheggia in the Accademia

❶ Galleria dell'Accademia

Via Ricasoli 60. **Map** 2 D4. **Tel** 055 238 86 12 (information); 055 29 48 83 (reservations). **Open** 8:15am– 6:50pm Tue–Sun (occasional extended hours in the summer). **Closed** public hols.

The Academy of Fine Arts, founded in 1563, was the first school established in Europe specifically to teach the techniques of drawing, painting, and sculpture. The art collection displayed here was formed in 1784 to provide material for students to study and copy.

The most famous work is Michelangelo's *David* (1504), a colossal (17 ft/5.2 m) nude of the biblical hero who killed the giant Goliath. The sculpture was commissioned by the city for Piazza della Signoria, but it was moved to the Accademia for safe-keeping in 1873. One copy now stands in its original position *(see pp294–5)* and a second is on Piazzale Michelangelo. The *David* established Michelangelo, at the age of 29, as the foremost sculptor of his time.

Michelangelo's other master-pieces in the Accademia include the *Quattro Prigionieri* (the Four Prisoners), sculpted between 1521 and 1523 and intended to adorn the tomb of Pope Julius II. The muscular figures struggling to free themselves from the stone are among the most dramatic of Michelangelo's works. The statues were presented to the Medici family in 1564 by the artist's nephew, Leonardo. They were then moved to the Grotta Grande in the Boboli Gardens, where casts of the originals can now be seen.

The Accademia also contains an important collection of paintings by 15th- and 16th-century Florentine artists, among them Filippino Lippi, Fra Bartolomeo, Bronzino, and Ridolfo del Ghirlandaio. The major works include the *Madonna del Mare* (Madonna of the Sea), attributed to Botticelli (1445–1510), and *Venus and Cupid* by Jacopo Pontormo (1494–1556), based on a preparatory drawing by Michelangelo. Also here is an elaborately painted wooden chest, the *Cassone Adimari* (1440–45) by Lo Scheggia, the step-brother of Masaccio. Originally part of a wealthy bride's trousseau, it is decorated with details of Florentine life, clothing and architecture. A scene of the bridal party appears on the chest in front of the Baptistry.

The Salone della Toscana (Tuscany Room) features modest paintings and sculptures by 19th-century members of the Accademia and plaster models by sculptor Lorenzo Bartolini.

Michelangelo's *David*

The light and airy former library, designed by Michelozzo

❷ Convento di San Marco

Piazza di San Marco. **Map** 2 D4. **Tel** 055 28 76 28 (information). **Open** 7am–noon, 4–8pm. 🏛 Museo di San Marco: **Tel** 055 238 86 08; 055 29 48 83 (reservations). **Open** 8:15am–1:50pm (to 4:50pm Sat, Sun). **Closed** Jan 1, May 1, Dec 25, 2nd & 4th Mon and 1st, 3rd, & 5th Sun of each month. 🎫 ♿ 📷

The Convent of San Marco was founded in the 13th century and enlarged in 1437 when Dominican monks from nearby Fiesole moved there at the invitation of Cosimo il Vecchio. He paid a considerable sum to have the convent rebuilt by his favorite architect, Michelozzo, whose simple cloisters and cells provide the setting for a remarkable series of devotional frescoes (c.1438–45) by Florentine painter and Dominican friar Fra Angelico. The convent and art collections form the **Museo di San Marco**.

Michelozzo's magnificent **Chiostro di Sant'Antonino** was named after the convent's first prior, Antonino Pierozzi (1389–1459), who later became the Archbishop of Florence. Most of the faded frescoes in this cloister describe scenes from the saint's life by Bernardino Poccetti. The panels in the corner are by Fra Angelico. A door in the right side of the cloister leads to the **Ospizio dei Pellegrini** (Pilgrims' Hospice). Today it houses the museum's free-standing paintings, including two famous masterpieces: Fra Angelico's

A detail from Fra Angelico's poignant *Deposition* (c.1440)

moving *Deposition* (c.1435–40), an altarpiece painted for the church of Santa Trinità, and the *Madonna dei Linaiuoli*, commissioned by the Linaiuoli (flaxworkers' guild) in 1433.

In the courtyard, right of the convent's former bell, is the vaulted **Sala Capitolare** (Chapter House), decorated with a noted but over-restored *Crucifixion and Saints* (1440) painted by Fra Angelico.

Covering one wall of the small **Refettorio** (refectory) is a fresco of the *Last Supper* (c.1480) by Domenico Ghirlandaio. Stairs from the courtyard lead to the first floor, where you suddenly see Fra Angelico's *Annunciation* (c.1440), thought by many to be among the city's most beautiful Renaissance paintings.

Beyond, ranged around three sides of the cloister, are the **Dormitory Cells**. These 44 tiny monastic cells are frescoed with scenes from *The Life of Christ* by Fra Angelico and assistants (1439–45). The cells numbered 1 to 11 are generally attributed to Fra Angelico personally, as is the lovely fresco of the *Madonna and Saints* on the right of the corridor (*see p36*).

Cells 12–14 were once occupied by Savonarola, the zealous Dominican monk who became Prior of San Marco in 1491. Among other deeds, Savonarola incited Florentines to rebel against the Medici and was responsible for the burning of many works of art. Denounced as a heretic, he was burned at the stake in Piazza della Signoria in 1498.

Along the third corridor lies an airy colonnaded hall, formerly a public **library** designed by Michelozzo in 1441 for Cosimo il Vecchio. Beyond it lie two cells (38 and 39) which were used by Cosimo when he went on retreat here. Each is decorated with two frescoes (the other cells have only one), and they are both larger than any of the neighboring rooms.

Fra Angelico's allegorical fresco, the *Mocking of Christ* (c.1442), showing Jesus blindfolded and being struck by a Roman guard

The Birth of the Virgin (1514) by del Sarto in Santissima Annunziata

❸ Santissima Annunziata

Piazza della Santissima Annunziata. **Map** 2 E4. **Tel** 055 26 61 81. **Open** 7:30am–12:30pm, 4pm–6:30pm daily.

Founded by the Servite order in 1250, the church of the Holy Annunciation was later rebuilt by Michelozzo between 1444 and 1481. Its atrium contains frescoes by the Mannerist artists Rosso Fiorentino, Andrea del Sarto, and Jacopo Pontormo. Perhaps the finest of its panels are *The Journey of the Magi* (1511) and *The Birth of the Virgin* (1514) by Andrea del Sarto.

The heavily decorated, dark interior has a frescoed ceiling completed by Pietro Giambelli in 1669. Here is one of the city's most revered shrines, a painting of the Virgin Mary begun by a monk in 1252 but miraculously completed by an angel, according to devout Florentines. Newlywed couples traditionally visit the shrine (on the left as you enter the church) to present a bouquet of flowers to the Virgin and to pray for a long, fruitful, and fecund marriage.

A door from the north transept leads to the **Chiostrino dei Morti** (Cloister of the Dead), so called because it was originally used as a burial ground. Today it is best known for del Sarto's beautiful fresco, *The Madonna del Sacco* (1525). The church is situated on the northern flank of **Piazza della Santissima Annunziata**, one of the finest Renaissance squares in Florence. Designed by Brunelleschi, the delicate nine-bay arcade fronts the Spedale degli Innocenti to its right, while at the center of the square stands a bronze equestrian statue of Duke Ferdinando I. Started by Giambologna, it was finished in 1608 by his assistant Pietro Tacca (who designed the square's bronze fountains).

❹ Museo Archeologico

Via della Colonna 36. **Map** 2 E4. **Tel** 055 235 75. **Open** 8:30am–7pm Tue–Fri, 8:30am–2pm Sat & Sun. **Closed** Jan 1, May 1, Dec 25. 🔖 🖼

The Archaeological Museum in Florence is in a palazzo built by Giulio Parigi for the Princess Maria Maddalena de' Medici in 1620. It now exhibits an outstanding collection of Etruscan, Greek, Roman, and Egyptian artifacts, although parts of the collection are being restored following the flood in 1966. The first floor contains a splendid series of Etruscan bronzes as well as the famous *Chimera* (4th century BC), a mythical lion with a goat's head imposed on its body and a serpent for a tail. Equally impressive is the 1st-century *Arringatore* bronze found near Lake Trasimeno in

Etruscan warrior, Museo Archeologico

Umbria. It is inscribed with the name of Aulus Metellus. A large section on the second floor is dedicated to Greek vases, notably the famed François Vase, found in an Etruscan tomb near Chiusi.

❺ Spedale degli Innocenti

Piazza della Santissima Annunziata 12. **Map** 2 E4. **Tel** 055 203 73 08. **Open** 10am–7pm daily. **Closed** Jan 1, Easter, Dec 25. 🖼

Named after Herod's biblical Massacre of the Innocents, the "Hospital" opened in 1444 as Europe's first orphanage. Part of the building is still used for this purpose. Brunelleschi's arcaded loggia is decorated with glazed terracotta roundels, added by Andrea della Robbia around 1498, showing babies wrapped in swaddling bands. At the left end of the portico you can see the *rota*, a rotating stone cylinder on which anonymous mothers could place their unwanted children and ring the bell for them to be admitted to the orphanage.

Within the building lie two elegant cloisters: the **Chiostro degli Uomini** (Men's Cloister), built between 1422 and 1445 and decorated with *sgraffito* roosters and cherubs, and the smaller Women's Cloister (1438). A small upstairs gallery contains a handful of fine works, including terracottas by della Robbia and pictures by Botticelli, Piero di Cosimo, and Domenico Ghirlandaio.

Part of Brunelleschi's arcaded loggia, Spedale degli Innocenti

Street by Street: Around the Duomo

While much of Florence was rebuilt during the Renaissance, the eastern part of the city retains a distinctly medieval feel. With its maze of tiny alleys, it is an area that would still be familiar to Dante (1265–1321), whose birthplace allegedly lay somewhere among these lanes. The poet would recognize the church of Santa Maria de' Cerchi, where he first glimpsed Beatrice, as well as the gaunt outlines of the Bargello. He would also be familiar with the Baptistry, one of the city's oldest buildings, though he would not know the Campanile nor the Duomo, whose foundations were laid in the poet's old age.

PIAZZA DI SAN GIOVANNI

PIAZZA DEL DUOMO

VIA DELL'OCHE

VIA D. STUDIO

VIA DE' MEDICI

VIA ROMA

VIA D. SPEZIALI

VIA DEI CALZAIUOLI

VIA DE' CERCHI

V.D. TAVOLINI

V.D. CIMATORI

V. DE' LAMBERTI

CALIMALA

VIA PORTA ROSSA

Piazza della Signoria

❼ ★ Duomo and Baptistry
The exteriors of the Duomo and Baptistry are richly decorated with marbles and reliefs, such as this detail from the Duomo's façade.

Key

— Suggested route

The Loggia del Bigallo *(1358)* is where abandoned children were once left. They were then sent to foster homes if they remained unclaimed.

```
0 meters        100
0 yards         100
```

❽ Orsanmichele
The church's niche carvings depict patron saints of trade guilds, such as this copy of Donatello's *St. George.*

Via dei Calzaiuoli, lined with stylish shops, is the city's liveliest street.

6 Museo dell'Opera del Duomo

Works from the Duomo, Campanile, and Baptistry are displayed in this museum.

Pegna sells a range of fine wines, oil, and honey.

Locator Map
See Florence Street Finder map 6

Carving from Luca della Robbia's choir loft in the Museo dell'Opera

Badia Fiorentina, the abbey church founded in 978, is home to *The Virgin Appearing to St. Bernard* (1485) by Filippino Lippi.

Casa di Dante, a restored medieval house, is reputedly Dante's birthplace.

9 ★ Bargello
The city's old prison is home to a rich collection of applied arts and sculpture, including this figure of *Mercury* by Giambologna (1564).

6 Museo dell'Opera del Duomo

Piazza del Duomo **Map** 2 D5 (6 E2).
Tel 055 230 28 85. **Open** 9am–7:30pm daily (to 1:40pm Sun & public hols) (last adm: 40 mins before closing).
Closed Jan 1, Easter, Dec 25.

The Cathedral Works Museum has reopened after extensive remodeling, and now a series of rooms is dedicated to the history of the Duomo. The main ground-floor room holds statues from Arnolfo di Cambio's workshop that were once placed in the cathedral's niches. Nearby is Donatello's *St. John*. Another room contains 14th- and 15th-century religious paintings and reliquaries.

Michelangelo's *Pietà* has pride of place on the staircase. The hooded figure of Nicodemus is widely believed to be a self-portrait.

The first room on the upper floor contains two choir lofts, dating to the 1430s, by Luca della Robbia and Donatello. Carved in crisp white marble and decorated with colored glass and mosaic, both depict children playing musical instruments and dancing. Other works by Donatello in this room are his statue of *La Maddalena* (1455) and several Old Testament figures.

The room to the left contains an exhibition of the tablets that used to decorate the bell tower. A lower level houses examples of the tools used by Brunelleschi's workmen and a copy of di Cambio's original cathedral façade.

❼ Duomo and Baptistry

Rising above the heart of the city, the richly decorated Duomo – Santa Maria del Fiore – and its orange-tiled dome have become Florence's most famous symbols. Typical of the Florentine determination to lead in all things, the cathedral is Europe's fourth largest church, and to this day it still remains the city's tallest building. The Baptistry, with its celebrated bronze doors, may date back to the 4th century, making it one of Florence's oldest buildings. The Campanile, designed by Giotto in 1334, was completed in 1359, 22 years after his death.

Campanile
At 276 ft (85 m), the Campanile is 20 ft (6 m) shorter than the dome. It is clad in white, green, and pink Tuscan marble.

Dante Explaining the Divine Comedy (1465)
This painting by Michelino shows the poet outside Florence against a backdrop of Purgatory, Hell, and Paradise.

★ **Baptistry**
Colorful 13th-century mosaics illustrating the *Last Judgment* decorate the ceiling above the octagonal font, where many famous Florentines, including Dante, were baptized. The doors are by Andrea Pisano (south) and Lorenzo Ghiberti (north, east).

Main entrance

North Doors

East Doors
(see p286)

South Doors

KEY

① **The Neo-Gothic marble façade** echoes the style of Giotto's Campanile but was only added in 1871–87.

② **Gothic windows**

③ **The top of the dome** offers spectacular views over the city.

④ **The *Last Judgment*** frescoes (1572–4) by Vasari were completed by Zuccari.

⑤ **Bricks were set** between marble ribs in a self-supporting herringbone pattern – a technique Brunelleschi copied from the Pantheon in Rome.

⑥ **The marble sanctuary** around the High Altar was created by Baccio Bandinelli in 1555.

★ Dome by Brunelleschi
Brunelleschi's dome, finished in 1463, was the largest of its time to be built without scaffolding. The outer shell is supported by a thicker inner shell that acts as a platform for it.

Entrance leading to the dome

VISITORS' CHECKLIST

Practical Information
Piazza del Duomo. **Map** 2 D5 (6 E2). **Tel** 055 230 28 85. Cathedral: **Open** 10am–5pm Mon–Sat (4:30pm Thu, 4:45pm Sat), 1:30–4:45pm Sun. 🚻 ♿ Crypt: **Open** 10am–5pm Mon– Sat (4:45pm Sat). 🖼 Baptistry: **Open** 12:15–7pm Mon–Sat, 8:30am–2pm Sun. 🖼 🚻 Dome: **Open** 8:30am–7pm Mon–Sat (5:40pm Sat). 🖼 Campanile: **Open** 8:30am–7:30pm daily. 🖼 All buildings: **Closed** Jan 1, Easter, Aug 15, Sep 8, Dec 25.
W operaduomo.firenze.it

Transportation
🚌 1, 6, 14, 17, 23

Chapels at the East End
The three apses, crowned by smaller copies of the dome, have five chapels each. The 15th-century stained glass is by Ghiberti.

Campanile Reliefs
Copies of reliefs by Andrea Pisano on the Campanile's first story depict the Creation of Man, and the Arts and the Industries. The originals are kept in the Museo dell'Opera del Duomo *(see p283)*.

Marble Pavement
The colorful, intricately inlaid pavement (16th century) was designed in part by Baccio d'Agnolo and Francesco da Sangallo.

The East Doors of the Baptistry

Lorenzo Ghiberti's famous bronze Baptistry doors were commissioned in 1401 to mark the city's deliverance from the plague. Ghiberti was chosen to make a set of new doors after a competition that involved seven leading artists, including Donatello, Jacopo della

Ghiberti's winning panel

Quercia, and Brunelleschi. The trial panels by Ghiberti and Brunelleschi are so different from Florentine Gothic art of the time, notably in the use of perspective and individuality of figures, that they are often regarded as the first works of the Renaissance.

"Gate of Paradise"

Having spent 21 years working on the North Doors, Ghiberti was commissioned to make the East Doors (1424–1452). Michelangelo enthusiastically dubbed them the "Gate of Paradise." The original 10 relief panels showing scriptural subjects are now exhibited in the Museo dell'Opera del Duomo (*see p283*); those on the Baptistry are copies.

Abraham and the Sacrifice of Isaac
The jagged modeled rocks symbolizing Abraham's pain are carefully arranged to emphasize the sacrificial act.

Joseph Sold into Slavery
Ghiberti, a master of perspective, formed the architectural elements in shallower relief behind the figures to create the illusion of depth in the scene.

Key to the East Doors

1	2
3	4
5	6
7	8
9	10

1   Adam and Eve Are Expelled from Eden
2   Cain Murders His Brother, Abel
3   The Drunkenness of Noah and His Sacrifice
4   Abraham and the Sacrifice of Isaac
5   Esau and Jacob
6   Joseph Sold into Slavery
7   Moses Receives the Ten Commandments
8   The Fall of Jericho
9   The Battle with the Philistines
10   Solomon and the Queen of Sheba

Detail of carvings by Donatello on the wall of Orsanmichele

❽ Orsanmichele

Via dell'Arte della Lana. **Map** 3 C1 (6 D3). **Tel** 055 28 49 44. **Open** 10am–5pm daily. **Closed** Jan 1, May 1, Mon in Aug, Dec 25.

Built in 1337 as a grain market, Orsanmichele was later converted into a church which took its name from *Orto di San Michele*, a monastic garden long since vanished. The arcades of the market became windows, which are today bricked in, but the original Gothic tracery can still be seen. The decoration was entrusted to Florence's major *Arti* (guilds). Over 60 years they commissioned sculptures of their patron saints to adorn the 14 exterior niches; however today many of the figures are copies. Among the sculptors were Lorenzo Ghiberti, Donatello, and Verrocchio.

The beautifully tranquil interior contains an opulent 14th-century altar by Andrea Orcagna, a *Virgin and Child* by Bernardo Daddi (1348), and a statue of the *Madonna and Child with St. Anne* by Francesco da Sangallo (1522).

❾ Bargello

Via del Proconsolo 4. **Map** 4 D1 (6 E3). **Tel** 055 238 86 06. 🚌 14, A. **Open** 8:15am–1:50pm daily. **Closed** 2nd & 4th Mon, 1st, 3rd, & 5th Sun of each month; Jan 1, May 1, Dec 25. 🅿 ♿ &

Florence's second-ranking museum after the Uffizi, the Bargello contains a wonderful medley of applied arts and Italy's finest collection of Renaissance sculpture. Begun in 1255, the fortresslike building was initially the town hall (making it the oldest seat of government in the city), but later became a prison and home to the chief of police (the *Bargello*). It also became known for its executions, which took place in the main courtyard until 1786, when the death sentence was abolished by Grand Duke Pietro Leopoldo. Following extensive renovation, the building opened as one of Italy's first national museums in 1865.

The key exhibits range over three floors, beginning with the Michelangelo Room, superbly redesigned after extensive damage during the 1966 flood. Three contrasting works by Michelangelo lie dotted around the room, the most famous a tipsy-looking *Bacchus* (1497), the sculptor's first large freestanding work. Close by is a powerful bust of *Brutus* (1539–40), the only known portrait bust by Michelangelo, and a beautifully delicate circular relief depicting the *Madonna and Child* (1503–5). Countless works by other sculptors occupy the same room. Among them is an exquisite *Mercury* (1564) by the Mannerist genius, Giambologna, as well as several virtuoso bronzes by the sculptor and goldsmith Benvenuto Cellini (1500–71).

Donatello's *David* (c.1430) in the Bargello

Across the courtyard, full of fragments and the coats of arms of the Bargello's various incumbents, two more rooms contain exterior sculptures removed from sites around the city. The courtyard's external staircase leads to the first floor, which opens with a wonderfully eccentric bronze menagerie by Giambologna. To the right is the Salone del Consiglio Generale, a cavernous former courtroom that contains the cream of the museum's Early Renaissance sculpture. Foremost among its highlights is Donatello's heroic *St. George* (1416) – the epitome of "youth, courage, and valor of arms" in the words of Vasari. Commissioned by the Armorers' Guild, the statue was brought here from Orsanmichele in 1892. At the center of the room, in direct contrast, is Donatello's androgynous *David* (c.1430), famous as the first freestanding nude by a Western artist since antiquity. Among the room's more easily missed works, tucked away on the right wall, are two reliefs depicting *The Sacrifice of Isaac* (1402). Created by Brunelleschi and Lorenzo Ghiberti respectively, both were entries in the competition to design the Baptistry doors.

Beyond the Salone, the Bargello's emphasis shifts to the applied arts, with room after room devoted to rugs, ceramics, silverware, and a host of other beautiful *objets d'art*. The most celebrated of these rooms is the Salone del Camino on the second floor, which features the finest collection of small bronzes in Italy. Some are reproductions of antique models, others are small copies of Renaissance statues. Giambologna, Cellini, and Antonio del Pollaiuolo are among those represented.

Brunelleschi's *Sacrifice of Isaac* (1402) in the Bargello

Bacchus (1497) by Michelangelo

⑩ Santa Croce

Work began around 1294 on the Gothic church of Santa Croce, which contains tombs and monuments of famous Florentines, such as Michelangelo, Galileo, and Machiavelli, as well as radiant early 14th-century frescoes by Giotto and his pupil Taddeo Gaddi. In the cloister alongside the church stands the Cappella de' Pazzi (Pazzi Chapel), a Renaissance masterpiece designed by Filippo Brunelleschi.

Tomb of Leonardo Bruni (1447) Rossellino's effigy of this great humanist was unusual in its sensitive realism and lack of monumental pomp.

KEY

① **The Neo-Gothic façade** by Niccolò Matas was added in 1863.

② **The Neo-Gothic campanile** was added in 1842, after the original was destroyed in 1512 by lightning.

③ **The Cappella Baroncelli**, frescoed by Taddeo Gaddi between 1332 and 1338, contains the first true night scene in Western art.

④ **Vasari's Tomb of Michelangelo** is decorated with figures representing sculpture and architecture.

Annunciation by Donatello (15th century)

Tomb of Machiavelli

Ticket booth and entrance

Tomb of Galileo

Exit

Tree of Life by Taddeo Gaddi

Refectory

Cimabue's Crucifixion
Badly damaged in the flood of 1966, this 13th-century masterpiece is among the highlights of the collection, as is Taddeo Gaddi's magnificent *Last Supper* (c.1355–60).

★ **Cappella de' Pazzi**
Brunelleschi's domed chapel with Classical proportions was begun in 1443. The roundels (c.1442–52) are by Luca della Robbia.

Sacristy

★ **Cappella Bardi Frescoes**
Giotto frescoed the Bardi and
Peruzzi chapels to the right of
the high altar between 1315
and 1330. This touching scene
from the left-hand wall of the
chapel shows *The Death of
St. Francis* (1317).

⓫ Museo Galileo

Piazza de' Giudici 1. **Map** 4 D1 (6 E4).
Tel 055 26 53 11. **Open** 9:30am–6pm
daily (to 1pm Tue). **Closed** Jan 1 & 6,
May 1, Easter, Jun 24, Aug 13, Nov 1,
Dec 8, 25, & 26. 📷 📷

This lively and superbly
presented museum devotes
two floors to various scientific
themes, illustrating each with
countless fine displays and a
panoply of old and beautifully
made scientific instruments. It
is also something of a shrine to
the Pisa-born scientist Galileo
Galilei (1564–1642), and
houses the only
surviving instruments
he designed and
built, including
two telescopes
and the
objective lens
from the
telescope with
which he
discovered Jupiter's
moons.

A number of rooms
are devoted to
astronomical, mathematical,
and navigational instruments,
with galleries concentrating on
Galileo, telescopes and optical
games. The museum also
houses the scientific collections
of the two dynasties that once
ruled Florence: the Medici and
the House of Lorraine.

Some of the best exhibits on
display are early maps, globes,
and astrolabes, antique
microscopes, thermometers, and
barometers. There are also some
fine old clocks, mathematical
instruments, calculators, a horri-
fying collection of 19th-century
surgical instruments, and some

Astrolabe, Museo Galileo

graphic anatomical models. The
museum has installed a large
bronze sundial outside the
entrance that can be used to
read the hour and the date.

⓬ Ponte Vecchio

Map 4 D1 (6 E4).

Ponte Vecchio, the oldest
surviving bridge in the city,
was built in 1345, the last in a
succession of bridges and fords
on the site that dated back to
Roman times. Designed by
Giotto's pupil Taddeo
Gaddi, it was originally
the domain of
blacksmiths,
butchers, and
tanners (who
used the river
for disposing
of waste). They
were reviled for
their noise and
stench and were
evicted in 1593 by
Duke Ferdinando I –
replaced by jewelers
and goldsmiths. The elevated
Corridoio Vasariano runs along
the eastern side of the bridge,
above the shops. Giorgio Vasari
designed the corridor in 1565 to
allow the Medici family to move
about their residences without
having to mix with the public.
This was the city's only bridge
to escape destruction during
World War II and visitors today
come as much to admire the
views as to browse among the
antique shops and specialized
jewelry stores. A bust of the
famous goldsmith Benvenuto
Cellini stands in the middle
of the bridge.

Ponte Vecchio viewed from the Ponte Santa Trinità

⓲ Uffizi

The Uffizi, Italy's greatest art gallery, was built in 1560–80 to house offices *(uffici)* for Duke Cosimo I. The architect Vasari used iron as reinforcement, enabling his successor, Buontalenti, to create an almost continuous wall of glass on the upper story. This was used as a gallery for Francesco I to display the Medici art treasures. In the 19th century the collection's ancient objects were moved to the archaeological museum and sculpture to the Bargello, leaving a priceless collection of paintings. Building work to double the gallery's exhibition space should end late 2013.

Bacchus *(c.1589)*
Caravaggio's early work depicting the god of wine can be found in the first floor exhibition rooms. The mood of dissipation is echoed in the foreground in the decaying fruit.

Main staircase

Entrance hall

Entrance

Corridor ceilings are frescoed with 1580s "grotesques" inspired by Roman grottoes.

Annunciation *(1333)*
The Sienese painter Simone Martini was strongly influenced by French Gothic art, and this is one of his masterpieces. The two saints are by Martini's pupil and brother-in-law, Lippo Memmi.

Buontalenti staircase

Gallery guide

Ancient Greek and Roman sculptures are in the second floor corridor around the inner side of the horseshoe-shaped building. The paintings are hung in a series of rooms off the main corridor, in chronological order, to show the development of Florentine art from Gothic to Renaissance and beyond. Many well-known paintings are in rooms 7–18. Due to planned building work during 2013, there may be disruptions, such as room closures, artworks moved, and changes to opening times.

Ognissanti Madonna *(c.1310)*
Giotto's grasp of spatial depth and substance in this altarpiece was a milestone in the mastery of perspective.

Key to Floorplan

- ☐ East Corridor
- ☐ West Corridor
- ☐ Arno Corridor
- ☐ Gallery rooms 1–45
- ☐ Nonexhibition space

The Duke and Duchess of Urbino *(c.1465–70)*
Piero della Francesca's portraits of Federico da Montefeltro
and his wife Battista Sforza were painted after Battista died at
age 26. Her portrait was probably based on her death mask.

The Tribune,
decorated in
red and gold,
contains the
works most
valued by
the Medici.

The Birth of Venus *(c.1485)*
Botticelli shows the goddess of love flanked by Zephyrus, god of the
west wind, who blows the risen Venus to shore on a half-shell. The
myth may symbolize the birth of beauty through the divine
fertilization of matter.

The Holy Family
(1507)
Michelangelo's
painting, the first
to break with the
convention of
showing Christ
on
the Virgin's
lap, inspired
Mannerist
artists through
its expressive
handling of color
and posture.

Vasari's Classical Arno façade
(begun 1560)

**The Vasari
Corridor** is a
passageway
across the Arno
to the Pitti
Palace.

The Venus of Urbino *(1538)*
Titian's sensuous nude,
inspired by Giorgione's
Sleeping Venus, may in fact be
a portrait of a courtesan
deemed sufficiently beautiful
to represent a goddess.

Exploring the Uffizi

The Uffizi offers not only the chance to see the world's greatest collection of Italian Renaissance paintings, but also the opportunity to enjoy masterpieces from as far afield as Holland, Spain, and Germany. Accumulated over the centuries by the Medici, the collection was first housed in the Uffizi in 1581, and eventually bequeathed to the Florentine people by Anna Maria Lodovica, the last of the Medici.

Madonna and Child with Angels (1455–66) by Fra Filippo Lippi

Gothic Art

Past the statues and antiquities of room 1, the Uffizi proper opens in style with three altarpieces of the *Maestà*, or *Madonna Enthroned*, by Giotto, Duccio, and Cimabue, some of Italy's greatest 13th-century painters. Each work marks a stage in the development of Italian painting away from the stilted conventions of Byzantium to the livelier traditions of Gothic and Renaissance art. The shift is best expressed in Giotto's version of the subject (known as the *Ognissanti Madonna*), where new feeling for depth and naturalistic detail is shown in the range of emotion displayed by the saints and angels, and by the carefully evoked three-dimensionality of the Virgin's throne.

Giotto's naturalistic influence can also be seen among the paintings of room 4, which is devoted to the 14th-century Florentine School, an interesting counterpoint to the Sienese paintings of Duccio and his followers in room 3. Among the many fine paintings here are works by Ambrogio and Pietro Lorenzetti, and Simone Martini's *Annunciation*.

Room 6 is devoted to International Gothic, a highly decorative style that represented the height of Gothic expression. It is exemplified by Gentile da Fabriano's exquisite, glittering *Adoration of the Magi* painted in 1423.

Early Renaissance

A new understanding of geometry and perspective during the 15th century increasingly allowed artists to explore the complexities of space and depth. None became more obsessed with these new compositional possibilities than Paolo Uccello (1397–1475), whose picture of *The Battle of San Romano* (1456) in room 7 is one of the gallery's most fevered creations.

Room 7 also contains two panels from 1460 by Piero della Francesca, another artist preoccupied with the art of perspective. The panels, which are among the earliest Renaissance portraits, depict the Duke and Duchess of Urbino on one side and representations of their virtues on the other.

While such works can seem coldly experimental, Fra Filippo Lippi's *Madonna and Child with Angels* (1455–66), in room 8, is a masterpiece of warmth and humanity. Like many Renaissance artists, Lippi uses

Sandro Botticelli's allegorical painting, *Primavera* (1480)

a religious subject to celebrate earthly delights such as landscape and feminine beauty. A similar approach is apparent in the works of Botticelli, whose famous paintings in rooms 10–14 are for many the highlight of the gallery. In *The Birth of Venus*, for example, Venus takes the place of the Virgin, expressing a fascination with Classical mythology common to many Renaissance artists. The same is true of the *Primavera* (1480), which breaks with Christian religious painting by illustrating a pagan rite of spring.

Detail from *The Annunciation* (1472–5) by Leonardo da Vinci

High Renaissance And Mannerism

Room 15 features works attributed to the young Leonardo da Vinci, notably a sublime *Annunciation* (1472–5), which reveals hints of his still emerging style, and the *Adoration of the Magi* (1481), which remained unfinished when he left Florence for Milan to paint *The Last Supper* (1495–8).

Room 18, better known as the Tribune, was designed in 1584 by Buontalenti in order to accommodate the best-loved pieces of the Medici collection. Its most famous work is the so-called Medici Venus (1st century BC), a Roman copy of a Greek statue deemed to be the most erotic in the ancient world. The copy proved equally salacious and was removed from Rome's Villa Medici by Cosimo III to keep it from corrupting the city's art students. Other highlights in room 18 include

Agnolo Bronzino's portraits of *Cosimo I* and *Eleonora di Toledo*, both painted around 1545, and Pontormo's *Charity* (1530) and the portrait of *Cosimo il Vecchio* (1517).

Rooms 19 to 23 depart from the gallery's Florentine bias, demonstrating how rapidly Renaissance ideas and techniques spread beyond Tuscany. Painters from the German and Flemish schools are well represented, together with painters from Umbria like Perugino, but perhaps the most captivating works are the paintings by Venetian and northern Italian artists such as Mantegna, Carpaccio, Correggio, and Bellini.

Room 25, which returns to the Tuscan mainstream, is dominated by Michelangelo's *Holy Family* or Doni Tondo (1456), notable for its vibrant colors and the Virgin's unusually twisted pose. The gallery's only work by Michelangelo, it was to prove immensely influential with the next generation of painters, especially Bronzino (1503–72), Pontormo (1494–1556), and Parmigianino (1503–40). The last of these was responsible for the *Madonna of the Long Neck* (c.1534) in room 29. With its contorted anatomy, unnatural colors and strange composition, this painting is a masterpiece of the style that came to be called Mannerism. Earlier, but no less remarkable masterpieces in rooms 26 and 28 include

Madonna of the Goldfinch (1506) by Raphael

Madonna of the Long Neck (c.1534) by Parmigianino

Raphael's sublime *Madonna of the Goldfinch* (1506) and Titian's notorious *Venus of Urbino* (1538), censured by Mark Twain as the "foulest, the vilest, the obscenest picture the world possesses." Others hold it to be one of the most beautiful nudes ever painted.

Later Paintings

Visitors, already sated by a surfeit of outstanding paintings, are often tempted to skim through the Uffizi's final rooms. The paintings in rooms 30 to 35 – which are mainly from the Veneto and Emilia-Romagna – are mostly unexceptional, but the gallery's last rooms (41–45) contain important paintings. Rooms 41 and 42 have works by Rubens and Van Dyck. Room 44, dedicated to Rembrandt and northern European painting, features Rembrandt's *Portrait of an Old Man* (1665) and two self-portraits of the artist as a young and old man (painted in 1634 and 1664, respectively). Rooms on the first floor hold works by Caravaggio. These include *Medusa* (1596–8), painted for a Roman cardinal; *Bacchus* (c.1589), one of the artist's earliest works; and the *Sacrifice of Isaac* (c.1590), whose violent subject is belied by the painting's gentle background landscape. These rooms also hold works by Guido Reni.

⑭ Piazza della Signoria

Piazza della Signoria and Palazzo Vecchio have been at the heart of Florence's political and social life for centuries. The great bell was once used to summon citizens to *parlamento* (public meetings) here, and the square has long been a popular promenade for both visitors and Florentines. The piazza's statues (some are copies) commemorate the city's major historical events, though its most famous episode – the execution of the religious leader Girolamo Savonarola, who was burned at the stake – is celebrated by a simple pavement plaque near the loggia.

David
This copy of the famous Michelangelo statue symbolizes triumph over tyranny. The original *(see p279)* stood in the piazza until 1873.

Heraldic Frieze
The crossed keys on this shield represent Medici papal rule.

KEY

① **Fontana di Nettuno**, created by Ammannati *(1575)*, is of the Roman sea god surrounded by water nymphs and commemorates Tuscan naval victories.

② **Sala dei Gigli**

③ **The Uffizi**

④ **The Loggia dei Lanzi** *(1382)*, designed by Orcagna, is named after the Lancers, the bodyguards of Cosimo I who were billeted here.

⑤ **Roman statues**, possibly of emperors, line the Loggia.

⑥ **The Marzocco** is a copy of the heraldic lion of Florence carved by Donatello in 1420. The original is in the Bargello *(see p287)*.

Salone dei Cinquecento *(1495)*
This vast chamber contains a statue of Victory by Michelangelo and frescoes by Vasari describing Florentine triumphs over Pisa and Siena.

★ **Palazzo Vecchio** (completed 1332)
This Republican frieze over the palace entrance is inscribed with the words, "Christ is King," implying that no mortal ruler has absolute power.

★ **The Rape of the Sabine Women by Giambologna** (1583)
The writhing figures in Giambologna's famous statue were carved from a single block of flawed marble.

★ **Perseus by Cellini**
This bronze statue (1554) of Perseus beheading Medusa was intended to warn Cosimo I's enemies of their probable fate.

⓯ Palazzo Vecchio

Piazza della Signoria (entrance on via della Ninna). **Map** 4 D1 (6 D3). **Tel** 055 276 83 25. 🚌 A, B. **Open** 9am–7pm daily (to 2pm Thu). Last adm: 1 hour before closing. **Closed** Jan 1, Easter, May 1, Aug 15, Dec 25. 📷 ♿ Secret Itineraries & Children's Museum (by reservation only). **Tel** 055 276 83 25.

The "Old Palace" still fulfills its original role as town hall.

It was completed in 1322 when a huge bell, used to call citizens to meetings or warn of fire, flood, or enemy attack, was hauled to the top of the imposing bell tower. While retaining much of its medieval appearance, the interior was remodeled for Duke Cosimo I in 1540. The redecoration was undertaken by Vasari, who incorporated bombastic frescoes (1563–5) of Florentine achievements. Michelangelo's *Victory* statue (1525) graces the Salone dei Cinquecento, which also has a tiny study decorated by Florence's leading Mannerist painters in 1569–1573. Other highlights include the Cappella di Eleonora, painted by Bronzino (1540–45); the loggia, with its views over the city; the Sala dei Gigli (Room of Lilies), with Donatello's *Judith and Holofernes* (c.1455) and frescoes of Roman heroes by Ghirlandaio (1485); as well as the excellent museum for children and the secret rooms and passageways.

A copy of Verrocchio's Putto fountain in Vasari's courtyard

Street by Street: Around Piazza della Repubblica

Underlying the street plan of modern Florence is the far older pattern of the ancient Roman city. Nowhere is this more evident than in the grid of narrow streets around Piazza della Repubblica, site of the old Roman forum. This pivotal square housed the city's main food market until the 1860s, when redevelopment tidied up the area, and added the triumphal arch that now stands in today's café-filled square.

Santa Trìnita has frescoes by Ghirlandaio on the Life of St. Francis (1486), depicting events that took place in this area. Here, a child is revived after falling from the Palazzo Spini-Ferroni.

Palazzo Spini-Ferroni

Ponte Santa Trìnita was built in wood in 1290 and then rebuilt by Ammannati in 1567 to celebrate the defeat of Siena.

Key

— Suggested route

0 meters 200
0 yards 200

⓱ Palazzo Strozzi
This monumental palazzo dominates the square.

Santi Apostoli
was reputedly founded by Charlemagne.

⓰ Palazzo Davanzati
Frescoes with exotic birds decorate the Sala dei Pappagalli, which was once the dining room of this 14th-century palazzo.

VIA DEL CAMPIDOGLIO
VIA DÉ PESCIONI
VIA DÉ VECCHIETTI
VIA DÉ BRUNELLESCHI
PIAZZA
REPUBB
VIA DEGLI STROZZI
VIA DÉ TORNABUONI
VIA DÉ SASSETTI
ANSELMI
PIAZZA DEGLI STROZZ
VIA DEGLI
PELLICCERIA
PIAZZA DÉ DAVANZATI
VIA MONALDA
VIA PORTA ROSSA
VIA PARIONE
PIAZZA DI S. TRINITA
VIA DELLE TERME
V. D FIORDALISO
CORSO CORNINO
BORGO SS. APOSTOLI
LUNGARNO DEGLI ACCIAIUOLI

Locator Map
See Florence Street Finder maps 5, 6

Piazza della Repubblica, which dates from the 19th century, is lined by some of Florence's oldest and best known cafés.

Mercato Nuovo, the "New Market" (1547), now deals mainly in souvenirs.

Palazzo di Parte Guelfa was the headquarters of the Guelphs, the dominant political party of medieval Florence.

Ponte Vecchio
(See p289)

Detail of a frieze illustrating a medieval romance in Palazzo Davanzati

⓰ Palazzo Davanzati

Via Porta Rossa 13. **Map** 3 C1 (5 C3). **Tel** 055 238 86 10. **Open** 8:15am–1:50pm daily. **Closed** 1st, 3rd, & 5th Mon and 2nd and 4th Sun of the month, Jan 1, May 1, Dec 25. 🖼 10am, 11am, noon (2nd floor only).

This wonderful museum, also known as the Museo dell'Antica Casa Fiorentina, uses original fittings and furniture to recreate a typical well-to-do 14th-century town house. Among the highlights are the Salone Madornale, where large gatherings would have been held, and the Sala dei Pappagalli (Parrots Room), with its frescoes and rich tapestries.

Pelting holes in the vaulted ceiling of the entrance courtyard were for dropping missiles on unwanted visitors. In one corner of the inner courtyard is a well and a pulley system to raise pails of water to each floor – a real luxury since most medieval households had to fetch water from a public fountain.

⓱ Palazzo Strozzi

Piazza degli Strozzi. **Map** 3 C1 (5 C3). **Tel** 055 264 51 55. 🖼 🖼 for exhibitions. 🌐 **palazzostrozzi.org**

Sheer size accounts for the impact of the Palazzo Strozzi, and although it is only three stories high, each floor exceeds the height of a normal palazzo. It was commissioned by the wealthy banker Filippo Strozzi, who had 15 buildings demolished to make way for the palazzo. He hoped it would rival the Medici palaces elsewhere in the city. Strozzi died in 1491, just two years after the first stone was laid.

Work on the building continued until 1536, with three major architects contributing to its design – Giuliano da Sangallo, Benedetto da Maiano, and Simone del Pollaiuolo (also known as Cronaca). The exterior, built of huge rusticated masonry blocks, remains unspoiled. Look out for the original Renaissance torch-holders and lamps and the rings for tethering horses that still adorn the corners and façades. The palace is now primarily used as an exhibition venue. During exhibitions, visitors can also access "La Strozzina," a vaulted gallery space in the basement, where small temporary exhibitions are held.

Exterior of Palazzo Strozzi, with masonry block rustication

⑱ San Lorenzo

San Lorenzo was the parish church of the Medici family, and in 1419 Brunelleschi was commissioned to rebuild it in the Classical style of the Renaissance. Almost a century later, Michelangelo submitted some plans for the façade and began work on the Medici tombs in the Sagrestia Nuova. He also designed a library, the Biblioteca Mediceo-Laurenziana, to house the family's collection of manuscripts. The lavish family mausoleum, the Cappella dei Principi, was started in 1604.

Cappella dei Principi
The Medici mausoleum, behind the high altar, was begun in 1604 by Matteo Nigetti, and forms part of the Cappelle Medicee.

Biblioteca Staircase
Michelangelo's Mannerist staircase, one of the artist's most innovative designs, was built by Ammannati in 1559.

KEY

① **St. Joseph and Christ in the Workshop**, a striking work showing the young Christ with his father, is by Pietro Annigoni (1910–88), one of the few modern artists whose work is seen in Florence.

② **The cloister garden** is planted with box hedges, pomegranate, and orange trees.

③ **Michelangelo** designed the desks and ceiling of the Biblioteca, where exhibitions of Medici manuscripts are often held.

④ **The Old Sacristy** was designed by Brunelleschi and decorated by Donatello.

⑤ **The huge dome** by Buontalenti echoes that of the Duomo (see pp284–6).

⑥ **Campanile**

⑦ **The Cappelle Medicee** complex comprises the Cappella dei Principi and its crypt, the Sagrestia Nuova (see p299).

⑧ **Michelangelo** submitted several designs for the façade of San Lorenzo, but it remains unfinished.

⑨ **A simple stone** slab marks the unostentatious grave of Cosimo il Vecchio (1389–1464), founder of the Medici dynasty.

Entrance to church

VISITORS' CHECKLIST

Practical Information
Piazza San Lorenzo 9.
Map 1 C5 (6 D1).
Basilica: Tel 055 21 40 42.
Open 10am–5pm Mon–Sat
(Mar–Oct: also Sun pm). 🎧 ✝
Biblioteca: Tel 055 21 07 60.
Open only to scholars.

Transportation
🚌 C1, C2

The Tomb of the Duke of Nemours (1520–34)
by Michelangelo in the Cappelle Medicee's
New Sacristy

🄳 Cappelle Medicee

Piazza di Madonna degli Aldobrandini. **Map** 1 C5 (6 D1). **Tel** 055 238 86 02; 055 29 48 83 (reservations). 🚌 many routes. **Open** 8:15am–1:50pm daily. Last adm: 30 mins before closing. **Closed** 1st, 3rd, & 5th Mon of each month, 2nd & 4th Sun, Jan 1, May 1, Dec 25. 🎧 ♿

The Medici Chapels divide into three distinct areas. Beyond the entrance hall lies a low-vaulted crypt, a suitably subdued space for the brass-railed tombs of many lesser members of the Medici family. From here steps lead to the octagonal **Cappella dei Principi** (Chapel of Princes), a vast family mausoleum begun by Cosimo I in 1604. The ceiling is garishly frescoed and the walls are smothered in huge swathes of semiprecious *pietre dure* (inlaid stone). Spaced around the walls are the tombs

of six Medici Grand Dukes. A corridor leads to Michelangelo's **New Sacristy**, designed as a counterpoint to Brunelleschi's Old Sacristy in San Lorenzo. Three groups of statues, all carved by Michelangelo between 1520 and 1534, stand around the walls: that on the near left-hand wall is *The Tomb of the Duke of Urbino* (grandson of Lorenzo the Magnificent). Opposite is *The Tomb of the Duke of Nemours* (Lorenzo's third son). Close to the unfinished *Madonna and Child* (1521) is the simple tomb containing Lorenzo the Magnificent and his murdered brother, Giuliano (died 1478).

🄴 Mercato Centrale

Piazza del Mercato Centrale. **Map** 1 C4 (5 C1). **Open** 7am–2pm Mon–Sat.

At the heart of the San Lorenzo street market is the bustling Mercato Centrale, Florence's busiest food market. It is housed in a vast two-story building of cast-iron and glass, built in 1874 by Giuseppe Mengoni.

The ground floor stalls sell meat, poultry, fish, hams, cheeses, and olive oils. There are also Tuscan takeout foods such as *porchetta* (roast suckling pig), *lampredotto* (pig's intestines), and *trippa* (tripe). Fresh fruit, vegetables, and flowers are sold on the top floor: look out for wild mushrooms and truffles in the autumn, and broad beans and baby artichokes in early spring.

Pulpits by Donatello
The bronze pulpits in the nave were Donatello's last works. Completed by his pupils in 1460, the reliefs capture the flinching pain of Christ's Passion and the glory of the Resurrection.

The Martyrdom of St. Lawrence
Bronzino's vast Mannerist fresco of 1569 is a bravura, choreographed study of the human form, rather than a reverential response to the agony of the saint.

Yellow zucchini flowers and other vegetables in the Mercato Centrale

㉑ Santa Maria Novella

The Church of Santa Maria Novella was built by the Dominicans between 1279 and 1357. The lower Romanesque part of its façade was incorporated into one based on Classical proportions by the pioneering Renaissance architect Leon Battista Alberti in 1456–70. The Gothic interior contains superb frescoes, including Masaccio's powerful Trinity. The famous Green Cloister, frescoed with perspective scenes by Paolo Uccello, and the dramatically decorated Spanish Chapel now form a museum.

The Nave
The piers of the nave are spaced closer together at the altar end. This trick of perspective creates the illusion of an exceptionally long church.

Trinity by Masaccio
This pioneering fresco (c.1428) is renowned as a masterpiece of perspective and portraiture. The kneeling figures flanking the arch are the painting's sponsors, judge Lorenzo Lenzi and his wife.

KEY

① **Chiostro Verde** takes its name from the green base used in Uccello's frescoes, which were sadly damaged by the 1966 floods.

② **Cappellone degli Spagnuoli**, the chapel used by the Spanish courtiers of Eleonora of Toledo, has frescoes of salvation and damnation.

③ **Monastic buildings**

④ **The arcade arches** are emphasized by gray and white banding.

⑤ **The Strozzi Tomb** is by Benedetto da Maiano (1493).

⑥ **Cappella di Filippo Strozzi** features Filippino Lippi's frescoes of St. John raising Drusiana from the dead and St. Philip slaying a dragon.

Main door

Entrance to museum

Entrance (via courtyard)

Cappella Strozzi
The 14th-century frescoes by Nardo di Cione and his brother Andrea Orcagna were inspired by Dante's epic poem, *The Divine Comedy*.

Ghirlandaio's *Madonna della Misericordia* (1472) in Ognissanti

Cappella Tornabuoni
Ghirlandaio's famous fresco cycle,
The Life of John the Baptist (1485),
peoples the biblical episodes
with Florentine aristocrats in
contemporary dress.

㉒ Palazzo Antinori

Piazza Antinori 3. **Map** 1 C5 (5 C2).
Closed to the public. Cantinetta
Antinori: **Tel** 055 29 22 34. **Open**
12:30–2:30pm, 7–10:30pm Mon–Fri.

Palazzo Antinori was built in
1461–6 and is one of the finest
small Renaissance palazzi in
Florence. It was acquired by the
Antinoris in 1506 and has
remained with the family ever
since. The dynasty produces a
range of wines, oils, and liqueurs
that can be sampled – along
with fine Tuscan dishes – in the
Cantinetta Antinori, the wine
bar off the main courtyard.

㉓ Palazzo Rucellai

Via della Vigna Nuova 16. **Map** 1 C5
(5 B2). **Closed** to the public.

Built in 1446–51, this is one of
the most ornate Renaissance
palaces in the city. It was
commissioned by Giovanni
Rucellai, whose enormous
wealth derived from the import
of a rare and costly red dye
made from lichen found
only on the Spanish island
of Majorca. The precious
dye was called *oricello*, from
which the name Rucellai
is derived. Giovanni
commissioned several
buildings from the architect
Leon Battista Alberti, who
designed this palace as a
virtual textbook illustration
of the major Classical
orders. The palazzo used to
house the Museo Alinari but
the collection has now
moved to Piazza Santa
Maria Novella.

㉔ Museo Nazionale Alinari della Fotografia

Piazza Santa Maria Novella 14ar.
Map 1 B5 (5 B2). **Tel** 055 21 63 10.
Open 10am–7:30pm Thu–Tue.
mnaf.it

The Alinari brothers began
taking pictures of Florence in
the 1840s. They supplied high-
quality postcards and prints
to visitors to Florence in the
19th century. The exhibits offer
a vivid insight into the social
history of Florence at that time.
The museum also houses
a collection of cameras,
documents, and objects that
illustrate the history
of photography.

㉕ Ognissanti

Borgo Ognissanti 42. **Map** 1 B5 (5 A2).
Tel 055 239 87 00. Church: **Open**
7am–12:30pm, 4–8pm daily.
Ghirlandaio's The Last Supper
Open 9am–noon Mon, Tue, Sat.

Ognissanti, or All Saints, was the
parish church of the Vespucci,
one of whose members, the
15th-century navigator
Amerigo, gave his name to the
New World. The young Amerigo
is depicted in Ghirlandaio's
fresco of the *Madonna della
Misericordia* (1472) in the
second chapel on the right;
Ghirlandaio's *The Last Supper*
(1480) can be seen in the
convent next door.
  In a chapel to the left of the
transept hangs the 14th-century,
16 ft- (5 m-) high Ognissanti
Crucifix by Giotto di Bondone.

㉖ Cappella Brancacci

The Church of Santa Maria del Carmine is famous for the Brancacci Chapel, which contains frescoes on *The Life of St. Peter* commissioned by the Florentine merchant Felice Brancacci around 1424. Although the paintings were begun by Masolino in 1425, many of the scenes are by his pupil Masaccio (who died before completing the cycle) and by Filippino Lippi, who completed the work in 1480. Masaccio's revolutionary use of perspective, his narrative drama, and the tragic realism of his figures placed him in the vanguard of Renaissance painting. Many great artists, including Michelangelo, later visited the chapel to study his pioneering work.

St. Peter Healing the Sick
Masaccio's realistic portrayal of cripples and beggars was revolutionary in his time.

KEY

① **Masaccio's simple style** allows us to focus on the figures central to the frescoes without distracting detail.

② **In every scene**, St. Peter is distinguished from the crowds as the figure in the orange cloak.

③ **St. Peter** is depicted against a background of Florentine buildings.

④ **Masolino's Temptation of Adam and Eve** is gentle and decorous, in contrast with the emotional force of Masaccio's painting on the opposite wall.

⑤ **The grouping** of stylized figures in Masaccio's frescoes reflects his interest in the sculpture of Donatello.

Expulsion of Adam and Eve
Masaccio's ability to express emotion is well illustrated by his harrowing portrait of Adam and Eve being driven out of the Garden of Eden, their faces wracked by misery, shame, and the burden of self-knowledge.

Key to the Frescoes: Artists and Subjects

☐ Masolino
☐ Masaccio
☐ Lippi

1 Expulsion of Adam and Eve
2 The Tribute Money
3 St. Peter Preaching
4 St. Peter Visited by St. Paul
5 Raising the Emperor's Son;
   St. Peter Enthroned
6 St. Peter Healing the Sick

7 St. Peter Baptizing the Converts
8 St. Peter Healing the Cripple;
   Raising Tabitha
9 Temptation of Adam and Eve
10 St. Peter and St. John Giving Alms
11 Crucifixion; Before the Proconsul
12 The Release of St. Peter

VISITORS' CHECKLIST

Practical Information
Piazza del Carmine.
Map 3 A1 (5 A4).
Tel 055 238 21 95; 055 276 82 24
(reservation required).
Open 10am–5pm Mon, Wed–Sat;
1–5pm Sun.
Closed public hols. 🖼

Transportation
🚌 D.

Woman in a Turban
The freshness of Masaccio's original colors is seen in this rediscovered roundel, hidden behind the altar for 500 years.

Two Figures
Masolino's work tends to be more formal, less naturalistic, and less animated than that of Masaccio.

Before the Proconsul
Filippino Lippi was called in to complete the cycle of frescoes in 1480. He added this emotional scene showing the Proconsul sentencing St. Peter to death.

Street by Street: Oltrarno

For the most part, the Oltrarno is a homely area of small houses, quiet squares, and shops selling antiques, bric-a-brac, and foodstuffs. The Via Maggio, a busy thoroughfare, breaks this pattern, but step into the side streets and you escape the bustle to discover a corner of old-world Florence. The restaurants serve authentic, reasonably priced food, and the area is full of studios and workshops restoring antique furniture. Among the things to see are Santo Spirito and Palazzo Pitti, one of the city's largest palaces, whose medley of museums contains an art collection second only to that of the Uffizi.

㉗ Santo Spirito
Brunelleschi's simple church was completed after the architect's death.

Ponte Santa Trinità

Cenacolo di Santo Spirito, the old refectory of a monastery that once stood here, contains a dramatic fresco attributed to Orcagna (c.1360).

★ **Palazzo Guadagni**
(1500) was the first in the city to be built with a rooftop loggia, setting a trend among the aristocracy.

★ **Palazzo di Bianca Cappello**
(1579) is covered in ornate *sgraffito* work and was the home of the mistress of Grand Duke Francesco I.

Masks and murals are handmade at this shop, Frieze of Papier Mâché.

For hotels and restaurants in this region see pp562–77 and pp580–605

Locator Map
See Florence Street Finder maps 3, 5

The 16th-century fountain and gargoyle in Piazza de' Frescobaldi were designed by Buontalenti, as was the façade (1593–4) of the nearby church of Santa Trinità.

Ponte Vecchio
(see p289)

BORGO SAN JACOPO

VIA TOSCANELLA

V.D RAMAGLIANTI

VIA DE' GUICCIARDINI

Palazzo Guicciardini
was the birthplace of historian Francesco Guicciardini.

㉘ ★ Palazzo Pitti
Several museums are contained in this massive palazzo, including an outstanding collection of paintings. This painting of Palazzo Pitti was made by Giusto Utens in 1599.

Key

— Suggested route

0 meters   100
0 yards   100

㉗ Santo Spirito

Piazza di Santo Spirito 30. **Map** 3 B2 (5 B4). 🚌 D. **Tel** 055 21 00 30. **Open** 9:30am–12:30pm, 4–5:30pm Mon–Sat; 11:30am–12:30pm & 4–5:30pm Sun. **Closed** Wed.

The Augustinian foundation of this church dates from 1250. The present building, dominating the northern end of the pretty Piazza di Santo Spirito, was designed by the architect Brunelleschi in 1435, but not completed until the late 15th century. The unfinished, modest façade was added in the 18th century.

Inside, the harmony of the proportions has been somewhat spoiled by the elaborate Baroque baldacchino and the High Altar, which was finished in 1607 by Giovanni Caccini. The church has 38 side altars, decorated with 15th- and 16th-century Renaissance paintings and sculpture, among them works by Cosimo Rosselli, Domenico Ghirlandaio, and Filippino Lippi. The latter painted a magnificent *Madonna and Child* (1466) for the Nerli Chapel in the south transept.

In the north aisle, a door beneath the organ leads to a vestibule with an ornate coffered ceiling. It was designed by Simone del Pollaiuolo, more commonly known as Cronaca, in 1491. The sacristy adjoining the vestibule, in which 12 huge columns are crammed into a tiny space, was designed by Giuliano da Sangallo in 1489.

Interior of Santo Spirito with colonnaded aisle

㉘ Palazzo Pitti

The Palazzo Pitti was originally built for the banker Luca Pitti. The huge scale of the building, begun in 1457 and attributed to Brunelleschi, illustrated Pitti's determination to outrival the Medici family through its display of wealth and power. Ironically, the Medici later purchased the palazzo when building costs bankrupted Pitti's heirs. In 1550 it became the main residence of the Medici, and subsequently all the rulers of the city lived here. Today the richly decorated rooms exhibit countless treasures from the Medici collections.

Judith (1620–30) by Artemisia Gentileschi

The Three Ages of Man (c.1510), attributed to Giorgione

Galleria Palatina

The Palatine Gallery, which forms the heart of the Pitti museum complex, contains countless masterpieces by artists such as Botticelli, Titian, Perugino, Andrea del Sarto, Tintoretto, Veronese, Giorgione, and Gentileschi. The works of art, accumulated by the Medici family and the house of Habsburg-Lorraine, are still hung much as the grand dukes wished, regardless of subject or chronology. The gallery consists of 11 main salons, the first 5 of which are painted with allegorical ceiling frescoes glorifying the Medici. Begun by Pietro da Cortona in 1641, they were completed in 1665 by his pupil Ciro Ferri. Room 1 (Sala di Venere) contains Antonio Canova's statue of the *Venus Italica* (1810), commissioned by Napoleon to replace the *Venus de' Medici* (which was to be taken to Paris). Room 2 (Sala di Apollo) features Titian's *Portrait of a Gentleman* (1540), perhaps the finest of several paintings by the artist in the gallery. Still finer pictures adorn rooms 4 and 5, including some by Perugino and Andrea del Sarto and a host of paintings by Raphael. The most beautiful of the last group are Raphael's High Renaissance *Madonna della Seggiola* or Madonna of the Chair (c.1514–15) and the *Donna Velata* or Veiled Woman (c.1516), whose model was reputedly the artist's mistress. Other paintings in the remaining gallery rooms include Fra Filippo Lippi's lovely *Madonna and Child*, painted in the mid-15th century, and Caravaggio's *The Sleeping Cupid* (1608).

Madonna of the Chair (c.1515) by Raphael

Galleria Palatina

The Museo degli Argenti, or the silverware museum, also displays precious *objets d'art*.

The Boboli Gardens

Entrance to museums and galleries

Brunelleschi designed the palace façade, which was eventually extended to three times its original length.

Appartamenti Reali

The Galleria d'Arte Moderna is a 30-room gallery featuring paintings from the years 1784 to 1924.

The Palmieri Rotonda by Giovanni Fattori (1825–1908)

Appartamenti Reali

The Royal Apartments on the first floor of the south wing of the palazzo were built in the 17th century. They are decorated with frescoes by various Florentine artists, a series of portraits of the Medici by the Flemish painter Justus Sustermans, who worked at the court between 1619 and 1681, and a group of 18th-century Gobelins tapestries. In the late 18th and early 19th centuries, the apartments were revamped

The Throne Room of the Appartamenti Reali

in Neo-Classical style by the Dukes of Lorraine when they succeeded the Medici dynasty as the rulers of Florence.

The apartments are lavishly appointed with ornate gold and white stuccoed ceilings and rich decoration, notably the walls of the Parrot Room, which are covered with an opulent crimson fabric detailed with a bird design. The Tapestry Rooms are hung with 17th- and 18th-century tapestries of French, Belgian, and Italian manufacture. The apartments reflect the tastes of three distinct historical periods.

Other Collections

The Museo degli Argenti (Silverware Museum) is housed in rooms formerly used by the Medici as summer apartments. The family's lavish taste is reflected in the vast array of precious objects on display. These embrace beautiful examples of Roman glassware, ivory, carpets, crystal, amber, and fine works by Florentine and German goldsmiths. Pride of place goes to 16 *pietre dure* vases (decorated with hard or semiprecious inlaid stones), once owned by Lorenzo the Magnificent.

The Galleria del Costume, which opened in 1983, reflects the changing taste in the courtly fashion of the late 18th century up to the 1920s.

The highlights of the Galleria d'Arte Moderna (Modern Art Gallery) are the wonderful paintings of the *Macchiaioli* (spot-makers), who were a group of Tuscan artists with a style very similar to that of the French Impressionists.

Galleria del Costume

Piazza della Signoria depicted in precious stones

VISITORS' CHECKLIST

Practical Information
Piazza de' Pitti.
Map 3 C2 (5 B5).
Tel 055 29 48 83 (info & booking).
Galleria Palatina & Royal
Apartments: **Open** 8:15am–
6:50pm Tue–Sun.
Closed Jan 1, May 1, Dec 25.
Boboli Gardens: **Open** 8:15am–
6:30pm daily (Mar: to 5:30pm;
Jun–Aug: to 7:30pm; Nov–Feb:
to 4:30pm).
Closed 1st & last Mon.
Other collections:
Open & **Closed** same as Boboli
Gardens.
Transportation
D.

A copy of Giambologna's *Oceanus Fountain* (1576)

The Boboli Gardens

The Boboli Gardens, a lovely place to escape the rigors of sightseeing, were laid out for the Medici after they bought the Palazzo Pitti in 1549. An excellent example of stylized Renaissance gardening, they were opened to the public in 1766. The more formal parts of the garden, nearest the palazzo, consist of box hedges clipped into symmetrical geometric patterns. These lead to wilder groves of ilex and cypress trees, planted to create a contrast between artifice and nature. Countless statues adorn the gardens, particularly along the Viottolone, an avenue of cypress trees planted in 1637. High above the gardens stands the Forte di Belvedere, designed by Buontalenti in 1590 for the Medici Grand Dukes.

The Virgin from *The Annunciation*
(1528) by Pontormo

㉙ Santa Felicità

Piazza di Santa Felicita. **Map** 3 C2 (5 C5).
D. **Tel** 055 21 30 18.
Open 9:30am–noon, 3:30–6:30pm
daily (only am Sun).

There has been a church on this
site since the 4th century. The
present structure, begun in the
11th century, was remodeled in
1736–9 by Ferdinando Ruggieri,
who retained Vasari's earlier
porch (added in 1564) as well
as many of the church's original
Gothic features.

The Capponi family chapel
to the right of the entrance
contains two works by Jacopo
da Pontormo: *The Deposition*
and *The Annunciation* (1525–28).
Their strange composition and
remarkable coloring make them
two of Mannerism's greatest
masterpieces.

㉚ Piazzale Michelangelo

Piazzale Michelangelo. **Map** 4 E3.
12, 13.

Of all the great Florentine
viewpoints – such as the
Duomo and Campanile – none
offers such a magnificent
panorama of the city as Piazzale
Michelangelo. Laid out in the

1860s by Giuseppe Poggi,
and dotted with copies of
Michelangelo's statues, its
balconies attract many visitors
and the inevitable massed ranks
of souvenir sellers. However, this
square remains an evocative
spot, especially when the sun
sets over the Arno and distant
Tuscan hills.

㉛ San Miniato al Monte

Via del Monte alle Croci. **Map** 4 E3.
Tel 055 234 27 31. 12, 13.
Open 8am–1pm, 3:30–7pm daily.
Closed public hols.

San Miniato is one of the most
beautiful Romanesque churches
in Italy. Begun in 1018, it was
built over the shrine of San
Miniato (St. Minias), a rich
Armenian merchant beheaded
for his beliefs in the 3rd century.
The façade, begun around
1090, has the geometric
marble patterning typical of
Pisan-Romanesque architecture.
The statue on the gable shows
an eagle carrying a bale of
cloth, the symbol of the
powerful Arte di Calimala
(guild of wool importers), who
financed the church in the
Middle Ages. The 13th-century
mosaic shows Christ, the Virgin,
and St. Minias. The same

The façade of the church of San Miniato
al Monte

protagonists appear in the
apse mosaic inside the church,
which sits above a crypt
supported by columns
salvaged from ancient Roman
buildings. The floor of the nave
is covered with seven mosaic
panels of animals and signs of
the Zodiac. These mosaics date
back to 1207.

Other highlights include
Michelozzo's freestanding
Cappella del Crocifisso (1448)
and the Renaissance Cappella
del Cardinale del Portogallo
(1480) with terracotta roundels
(1461) on the ceiling by Luca
della Robbia. There is a fresco
cycle of *Scenes from the Life of
St. Benedict* by Spinello Aretino
in the sacristy, which was
completed in 1387.

Ponte Vecchio and the Arno from the heights of Piazzale Michelangelo

Shopping in Florence

Few cities of comparable size can boast such a profusion and variety of high-quality shops as Florence. As you wander through its medieval streets, you will find all the big names in Italian fashion and jewelry alongside artisan workshops and family-run businesses. The city has translated its reputation as a center of artistic excellence into a wealth of antiques and fine-art shops. Tuscan tanneries are justifiably renowned, and there is nowhere better than Florence to buy shoes, bags, and other leather goods. Those searching for unusual gifts and souvenirs – from handmade stationery to delicious foodstuffs – will also be spoiled for choice.

Where to Shop

The center of Florence is packed with all sorts of shops, from fashion designer flagships to secondhand bookstores. The tiny jewelry shops on the Ponte Vecchio sell both antique items and high-quality new gold pieces. Antiques shops are mostly clustered around Via dei Fossi, Via dei Serragli, and Via Maggio. The best bargains can be found in the January and July sales.

Clothing

Most leading Italian designer names – **Gucci**, **Armani**, **Versace**, and **Prada**, for example – can be found on Via de' Tornabuoni. Opposite Palazzo Strozzi is **Louis Vuitton**, with its collections of footwear, clothing, and luggage. **Dolce & Gabbana** is nearby, as is **Patrizia Peppe**, while **Valentino** is in Via dei Tosinghi. **La Perla**, specializing in sophisticated lingerie, is located in Via della Vigna Nuova, but more affordable lingerie styles can be found at **Intimissimi**.

Most department stores sell clothing. For mid-range fashion, try **Coin**. The more upmarket **La Rinascente** has designer clothing, lingerie, and a great rooftop bar.

For discounts on designer fashion, visit **The Mall** or **Barberino Designer Outlet**, both about 30 minutes away from Florence.

There are fine silks and handwoven fabrics at **Casa dei Tessuti**.

Shoes and Leather Goods

The main meccas for fans of designer Italian shoes are **Ferragamo**, **Gucci**, and **Prada**. For more classic styles, head to **Quercioli**, which stocks handmade leather footwear. The mid-priced range is well represented by **Peppe Peluso** and the chain store **Bata**.

The streets around Piazza di Santa Croce are filled with leather shops. Inside the cloisters of the church itself is the **Scuola del Cuoio**, where customers can watch the leather craftsmen at work.

Classic leather bags are sold at **Il Bisonte** and **Beltrami**; for more contemporary styles head to **Coccinelle** and **Furla**.

Bound leather books, leather boxes, and leather-covered wooden desk objects are sold at **Scriptorium**.

Jewelry

Florence has always been noted for its gold- and silversmiths. Visit **Torrini**, whose family has produced jewelry for six centuries, and **Pomellato**'s stunning shop for its chunky white gold rings with huge semi-precious gems. **Bulgari** is on the same street, and so is **Parenti**, which has unique antique jewels. Try **Aprosio & Co** for decorative jewelry made from precious metals and tiny glass stones.

Art and Antiques

Galleria Romanelli has bronze statuary and works encrusted in semiprecious stones. The gallery also stocks marble sculptures and statues. It was established in 1860 and is still run by the same founding family. For lovers of Art Nouveau and Art Deco, there is **Galleria Tornabuoni**, while **Ugo Poggi** has a selection of elegant porcelain. **Ugolini** and **Mosaico di Pitti** create tables and framed pictures using the age-old technique of marble inlay.

Books and Gifts

Feltrinelli International and **Edison** sell publications in several languages, while **Paperback Exchange** has a wide selection of new and secondhand books in English.

Typical Florentine crafts include bookbinding and handmade marbled paper, used to decorate a variety of objects. These are available at **Il Torchio** and **Il Papiro**.

For terracotta and ceramics, try **Sbigoli Terracotte**; for chandeliers and decorative glass objects head to **La Bottega dei Cristalli**.

Signum sells postcards, posters, and prints, while **Mandragora** has a wide range of gifts based on famous artworks in the city.

Food and Markets

Florence's main food market is the covered **Mercato Centrale** (*see p295*), but fruit and vegetable stalls can also be found at the **Mercato di Sant'Ambrogio**. On Tuesday mornings, there is a large market at the **Parco delle Cascine** with food, affordable clothing, and shoes.

Pegna is a mini-supermarket that stocks fresh foods, as well as a range of gourmet items. The **Bottega dell'Olio** sells extra virgin Tuscan olive oils, and **Grom** is famous for its artisan gelato.

Dolceforte sells chocolate souvenirs in the shape of the Duomo and the statue of *David*. Biscuits and chocolates fill the front half of **Alessi**, while at the back are fine wines, spirits, and liqueurs. At **Procacci**, you can stop for a glass of Italian wine while choosing between pots of black or white truffles and other delicacies to buy.

DIRECTORY

Clothing

Armani
Via de'Tornabuoni 48–50r.
Map 1 C5 & 5 C2.
Tel 055 21 90 41.

Barberino Designer Outlet
A1 Firenze-Bologna, Exit Barberino di Mugello.
Tel 055 84 21 61.

Casa dei Tessuti
Via dei Pecori 20–24r.
Map 1 C5 & 6 D2.
Tel 055 21 59 61.

Coin
Via dei Calzaiuoli 56r.
Map 6 D3.
Tel 055 28 05 31.

Dolce & Gabbana
Via dei Strozzi 12–18r.
Map 1 C5 & 5 C3.
Tel 055 28 10 03.

Gucci
Via de'Tornabuoni 73r.
Map 1 C5 & 5 C2.
Tel 055 26 40 11.

Intimissimi
Via dei Calzaiuoli 99r.
Map 3 C1 & 6 D3.
Tel 055 230 26 09.

Louis Vuitton
Piazza degli Strozzi 1.
Map 1 C5 & 5 C3.
Tel 055 26 69 81.

The Mall
Via Europa 8,
Leccio Reggello.
Tel 055 865 77 75.

Patrizia Peppe
Via degli Strozzi 11/19r.
Map 3 C1 & 6 D2.
Tel 055 230 25 18.

La Perla
Via Strozzi 24r.
Map 1 C5 & 5 C3.
Tel 055 21 52 42.

Prada
Via de'Tornabuoni 67r.
Map 1 C5 & 5 C2.
Tel 055 26 74 71.

La Rinascente
Piazza della Repubblica 1.
Map 1 C5 & 6 D3.
Tel 055 21 91 13.

Valentino
Via dei Tosinghi 52r.
Map 1 C5 & 6 D2.
Tel 055 29 31 42.

Versace
Via de'Tornabuoni 13–15r.
Map 1 C5 & 5 C2.
Tel 055 28 26 38.

Shoes and Leather Goods

Bata
Via dei Calzaiuoli 110r.
Map 3 C1 & 6 D2.
Tel 055 21 16 24.

Beltrami
Via della Vigna Nuova 70r.
Map 1 C5 & 5 C3.
Tel 055 28 77 79.

Il Bisonte
Via del Parione 31r.
Map 1 C5 & 5 C3.
Tel 055 21 57 22.

Coccinelle
Via Por Santa Maria 49r.
Map 3 C1 & 6 D4.
Tel 055 239 87 82.

Ferragamo
Via de'Tornabuoni 14r.
Map 1 C5 & 5 C2.
Tel 055 29 21 23.

Furla
Via de'Calzaiuoli 47r.
Map 3 C1 & 6 D3.
Tel 055 23.8 28 83.

Peppe Peluso
Via del Corso 5–6r.
Map 3 C1 & 6 D3.
Tel 055 26 82 83.

Quercioli
Via Calzaiuoli 18/20r.
Map 3 C1 & 6 D2.
Tel 055 21 39 41.

Scriptorium
Via dei Servi 5–7r.
Map 2 D5 & 6 E2.
Tel 055 21 18 04.

Scuola del Cuoio
Piazza di Santa Croce 16.
Map 3 C1 & 6 F4.
Tel 055 24 45 33.

Jewelry

Aprosio & Co
Via della Spada 38/r.
Map 3 B1 & 5 B4.
Tel 055 265 40 77.

Bulgari
Via de'Tornabuoni 61r.
Map 1 C5 & 5 C3.
Tel 055 239 67 86.

Parenti
Via de'Tornabuoni 93r.
Map 1 C5 & 5 C2.
Tel 055 21 44 38.

Pomellato
Via de'Tornabuoni 89–91r.
Map 1 C5 & 5 C2.
Tel 055 28 85 30.

Torrini
Piazza del Duomo 10r.
Map 2 D5 & 6 D2.
Tel 055 230 24 01.

Art and Antiques

Galleria Romanelli
Borgo San Frediano 70.
Map 3 C1 & 5 C4.
Tel 055 239 60 47.

Galleria Tornabuoni
Borgo San Jacopo 53r.
Map 3 C1 & 5 C4.
Tel 055 28 47 20.

Mosaico di Pitti
Piazza de'Pitti 16–18r.
Map 3 B2 & 5 B5.
Tel 055 28 21 27.

Ugo Poggi
Via degli Strozzi 26r.
Map 1 C5 & 5 C3.
Tel 055 21 67 41.

Ugolini
Lungarno degli Acciaiuoli 66–70r.
Map 3 C1 & 5 C4.
Tel 055 28 49 69.

Books and Gifts

La Bottega dei Cristalli
Via dei Benci 51r.
Map 3 C1 & 6 F4.
Tel 055 234 48 91.

Edison
Piazza della Repubblica 27r.
Map 1 C5 & 6 D3.
Tel 055 21 31 10.

Feltrinelli International
Via dè Cerretani 30/32r.
Map 2 D4.
Tel 055 238 26 52.

Mandragora
Piazza del Duomo 9r.
Map 2 D5 & 6 D2.
Tel 055 29 25 59.

Paperback Exchange
Via delle Oche 4r.
Map 2 D5 & 6 E2.
Tel 055 29 34 60.

Il Papiro
Piazza del Duomo 24r.
Map 2 D5 & 6 D2.
Tel 055 649 91 51.

Sbigoli Terracotte
Via Sant'Egidio 4r.
Map 6 F2.
Tel 055 247 97 13.

Signum
Borgo dei Greci 40r.
Map 3 C1 & 6 E4.
Tel 055 28 06 21.

Il Torchio
Via de'Bardi 17.
Map 3 C2 & 6 D5.
Tel 055 234 28 62.

Food and Markets

Alessi
Via delle Oche 27r.
Map 3 C1 & 6 D2.
Tel 055 21 49 66.

Bottega dell'Olio
Piazza del Limbo 2r.
Map 3 C1 & 6 D4.
Tel 055 267 04 68.

Dolceforte
Via della Scala 21.
Map 1 C5 & 5 B2.
Tel 055 21 91 16.

Grom
Via del Campanile (on the corner of Via delle Oche).
Map 2 D5 & 6 D2.
Tel 055 21 61 58.

Mercato Centrale
Via dell'Ariento 10–14.
Map 1 C4 & 5 C1.

Mercato di Sant'Ambrogio
Piazza Sant'Ambrogio.
Map 4 F1. **Open**
7am–2pm Mon–Sat.

Parco delle Cascine
Piazza Vittorio Veneto.
Open 8am–2pm Tue.

Pegna
Via dello Studio 26r.
Map 6 E2.
Tel 055 28 27 01.

Procacci
Via de'Tornabuoni 64r.
Map 1 C5 & 5 C2.
Tel 055 21 16 56.

FLORENCE STREET FINDER

Map references given for sights in the Florence section refer to the maps on the following pages. Where two references are provided, the one in brackets relates to the large-scale maps, 5 and 6. References are also given for Florence hotels *(see pp562–77)* and restaurants *(see pp580–605)*, and for useful addresses in the *Travelers' Needs* and *Survival*

Guide sections at the back of the book. The map below shows the area of Florence covered by the *Street Finder*. The symbols used for sights and other features on the *Florence Street Finder* maps are listed below. Streets in Florence have double sets of numbers: red numbers are for businesses, and black or blue for domestic residences.

Scale of Maps 1–2 & 3–4

| 0 meters | 200 |
| 0 yards | 200 |

1:11,000

Scale of Maps 5–6

| 0 meters | 125 |
| 0 yards | 125 |

1:6000

Key to Street Finder

Major sight
Place of interest
FS Train station
Bus station
Streetcar stop

i Tourist information
+ Hospital with emergency room
Police station
✡ Synagogue
✝ Church

Railroad line
City walls
Pedestrianized street

TUSCANY

Renowned for its art, history, and evocative landscape, Tuscany is a region where the past and present merge in pleasant harmony. Hill towns gaze across the countryside from on high, many encircled by Etruscan walls and slender cypress trees. Handsome palaces testify to the region's wealth while medieval town halls indicate a long-standing tradition of democracy and self-government.

In the countryside, among the vineyards and olive groves, there are hamlets and farmhouses, as well as fortified villas and castles that symbolize the violence and intercommunal strife that tore Tuscany apart during the Middle Ages. Several imposing castles and villas were built for the Medici family, the great patrons of the Renaissance who supported eminent scientists, such as Galileo.

Northern Tuscany, and the heavily populated plain between Florence and Lucca, is dominated by industry, with intensively cultivated land between the cities and the wild mountainous areas.

The area centerd around Livorno and Pisa is now the region's economic hub. Pisa, at the height of its powers, dominated the western Mediterranean from the 11th to the 13th centuries.

Its navy opened up extensive trading routes with North Africa, and brought to Italy the benefits of Arabic scientific and artistic achievement. During the 16th century the Arno estuary began to silt up, ending Pisan power.

At the heart of central Tuscany lies Siena, which was involved in a long feud with Florence. Its finest hour came with its victory in the Battle of Montaperti in 1260, but it was devastated by the Black Death in the 14th century and finally suffered a crushing defeat by Florence in the siege of 1554–5.

Northeastern Tuscany, with its mountain peaks and woodland, provided refuge for hermits and saints, while the east was home to Piero della Francesca, the early Renaissance painter whose timeless and serene works are imbued with an almost religious perfection.

A timeless view and way of life in Casole d'Elsa, near San Gimignano in central Tuscany

◀ The picturesque farmlands of Pienza in Tuscany

Exploring Tuscany

Tuscan cities such as Florence, Siena, and Pisa, together with smaller towns like Lucca, Cortona, and Arezzo, contain some of Italy's most famous artistic treasures. Medieval villages such as San Gimignano, with its famous towers, or Pienza, a tiny Renaissance jewel, sit at the heart of the glorious pastoral countryside for which the region is equally renowned. Elsewhere landscapes range from the spectacular mountains of the Alpi Apuane to the gentle hills of Chianti.

Sights at a Glance

1. Carrara
2. Garfagnana
3. Bagni di Lucca
4. Viareggio
5. Torre del Lago Puccini
6. Lucca *pp324–7*
7. Pisa *pp328–30*
8. Vinci
9. Pistoia
10. Prato
11. Artimino
12. San Miniato
13. Fiesole
14. Arezzo *pp333–5*
15. Sansepolcro
16. Cortona
17. Chiusi
18. Montepulciano
19. Pienza
20. Montalcino
21. Crete Senesi
22. Siena *pp342–7*
23. Monteriggioni
24. San Gimignano *pp348–9*
25. Volterra
26. San Galgano
27. Massa Marittima
28. Elba
29. Sovana
30. Pitigliano
31. Maremma
32. Monte Argentario

Florence (see *pp274–317*)

View of Cortona in eastern Tuscany

For additional map symbols *see back flap*

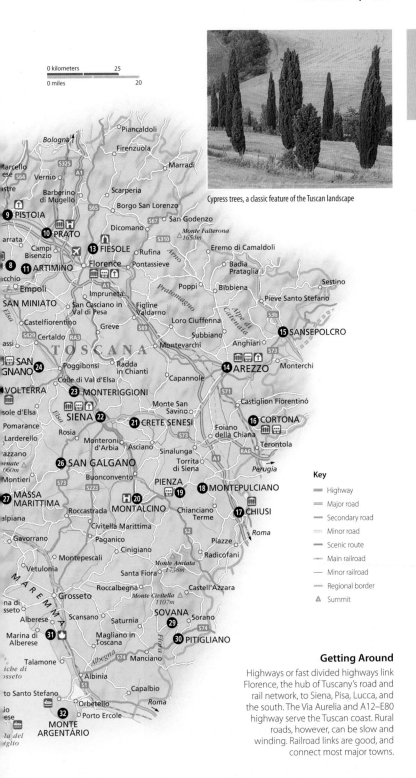

Cypress trees, a classic feature of the Tuscan landscape

0 kilometers 25
0 miles 20

Piancaldoli
Bologna
Firenzuola
Marradi
Marcello
ese
S64
Vernio
S325
astre
A1
Barberino
di Mugello
Scarperia
San Godenzo
S65
Borgo San Lorenzo
S67
9 PISTOIA
10 PRATO
Dicomano
S310
Monte Falterona
△ *165 m*
arrata
13 FIESOLE
Rufina
Eremo di Camaldoli
Campi
Bisenzio
Florence
Pontassieve
Badia
Pratáglia
ecchio
8
11 ARTIMINO
Poppi
Bibbiena
Sestino
Empoli
Imprunéta
Pratomagno
Pieve Santo Stefano
SAN MINIATO
San Casciano in
Val di Pesa
Figline
Valdarno
Alpe di
Catenaia
S3b
Castelfiorentino
Greve
Loro Ciuffenna
15 SANSEPOLCRO
assi
S429
Certaldo
RA3
Subbiano
Anghiari
S73
T O S C A N A
Montevarchi
Monterchi
SAN
GNANO
24
Poggibonsi
Radda
in Chianti
Capannole
14 AREZZO
Colle di Val d'Elsa
571
VOLTERRA
23 MONTERIGGIONI
Monte San
Savino
Castiglion Fiorentino
sole d'Elsa
SIENA
22
21 CRETE SENESI
S73
16 CORTONA
Pomarance
Rosia
Foiano
della Chiana
Larderello
Monteroni
d'Arbia
Asciano
Sinalunga
RA6
Terontola
azzano
rnate
060 m
26 SAN GALGANO
Torrita
di Siena
A1
Perugia
Montieri
Buonconvento
PIENZA
18 MONTEPULCIANO
S73
S223
20
19
27 MASSA
MARITTIMA
MONTALCINO
Chianciano
Terme
17 CHIUSI
alpiana
Roccastrada
Civitella Marittima
S2
Roma
Gavorrano
Paganico
Piazze
Cinigiano
Radicofani
Montepescali
Monte Amiata
△ *1738 m*
Vetulonia
Santa Fiora
na di
sseto
Grosseto
Roccalbegna
Castell'Azzara
Alberese
Scansano
Monte Civitella △
1107 m
SOVANA
Marina di
Alberese
31
Saturnia
Sorano
574
Magliano in
Toscana
29
30 PITIGLIANO
Talamone
iche di
osseto
Albinia
Albegna
S74
Manciano
to Santo Stefano
Capalbio
S1
Roma
io
ese
32
Orbetello
Porto Ercole
MONTE
ARGENTÁRIO
la del
iglio

Key

═══ Highway
─── Major road
─── Secondary road
∷∷∷ Minor road
─── Scenic route
╍╍╍ Main railroad
─── Minor railroad
─── Regional border
△ Summit

Getting Around

Highways or fast divided highways link Florence, the hub of Tuscany's road and rail network, to Siena, Pisa, Lucca, and the south. The Via Aurelia and A12–E80 highway serve the Tuscan coast. Rural roads, however, can be slow and winding. Railroad links are good, and connect most major towns.

● Carrara

Massa Carrara. 🚗 200,000. FS 🚌
ℹ️ Lungomare Vespucci 24 (0585 24 00 63). 🏛 Mon.

Internationally renowned for its marble quarries, Carrara's almost flawless white stone has been prized for centuries by famous sculptors from Michelangelo to Henry Moore (the stone for Michelangelo's *David* came from Carrara). The region's 300 or more quarries date back to Roman times, making this one of the oldest industrial sites in continuous use in the world. Many of the town's marble-sawing mills and workshops welcome visitors, offering them the chance to see the ways in which marble and quartz are worked. These techniques – along with marble artifacts old and new – can be seen at the **Museo Civico del Marmo**.

   Local marble is put to good use in the town's **Duomo** in Piazza del Duomo, particularly in the fine Pisan-Romanesque façade with its delicate rose window. The cathedral square also contains Michelangelo's house, used by the sculptor

A quarry in the marble-bearing hills around Carrara

during his visits to select blocks of marble. The town has some lovely corners to explore, in particular the elegant Piazza Alberica. Most visitors head for the stone quarries that are open to the public at nearby **Colonnata** and at **Fantiscritti** (take one of the regular town buses or follow the signs to the "Cave di Marmo"). The latter features a small museum with displays of various marble quarrying techniques.

🏛 **Museo Civico del Marmo**
Viale XX Settembre. **Tel** 0585 84 57 46.
Open Mon–Sat.

❷ Garfagnana

Lucca. FS 🚌 Castelnuovo di Garfagnana. ℹ️ Piazza delle Erbe, Castelnuovo di Garfagnana (0583 651 69).

A verdant, silent valley wedged between the Orecchiella mountains and the Alpi Apuane, the Garfagnana region can be explored from **Seravezza**, **Barga**, or **Castelnuovo di Garfagnana**. While the town of Barga makes the prettiest base, thanks to its tawny stone cathedral and charming streets, Castelnuovo is more convenient for drives and walks in the surrounding mountains. **San Pellegrino in Alpe** in the Orecchiella has a fascinating folklore museum, the **Museo Etnografico**. It is easily seen in conjunction with the **Orto Botanico Pania di Corfino** at the headquarters of the **Parco dell'Orecchiella** at Pania di Corfino, with its collection of local Alpine trees.

   To the west is the Parco Naturale delle Alpi Apuane, an area whose spectacular jagged peaks and wooded valleys are crisscrossed by hiking trails and scenic mountain roads.

🏛 **Museo Etnografico**
Via del Voltone 15, San Pellegrino in Alpe. **Tel** 0583 64 90 72. **Open** Tue–Sun (Jul–Aug: daily). 🖼

🌿 **Parco dell'Orecchiella**
Centro Visitatori, Orecchiella. **Tel** 0583 61 90 02. **Open** Jun & Sep: 10am–5pm daily; Jul & Aug: 9am–7pm daily. ♿

🌿 **Orto Botanico Pania di Corfino**
Parco dell'Orecchiella. **Tel** 0583 64 49 11. **Open** May–Sep: daily.

The Parco Naturale delle Alpi Apuane on the edge of the Garfagnana

One of many seaside cafés lining the waterfront in the popular beach resort of Viareggio

❸ Bagni di Lucca

Lucca. 🚹 7,400. 🚌 ℹ️ Viale
Umberto I 97 (0583 80 57 45).
🗓 Sat.

All over Tuscany there are hot
springs of volcanic origin, like
Bagni di Lucca. The Romans
first exploited the springs and
built bath complexes where
army veterans who settled in
the area could relax. More
spas came into prominence
in the Middle Ages and the
Renaissance, and they have
continued to be recommended
for relieving a variety of ailments,
such as arthritis.

Tuscan spas really came into
their own in the early 19th
century when Bagni di Lucca
reached its heyday as one of
Europe's most fashionable spas,
frequented by emperors, kings,
and aristocrats. Visitors came
not only for thermal cures, but
also for the **Casino** (1837), one
of Europe's first licensed
gambling houses. These days
the town is rather sleepy, and
its main sights are the 19th-
century monuments, including
the Neo-Gothic **English Church**
(1839) on Via Crawford and the
Cimitero Anglicano (Protestant
Cemetery) on Via Letizia.

Environs

Southeast of Bagni di Lucca lies
another popular spa town,
Montecatini Terme. Developed

in the 18th century, this town is
one of the most interesting, with
a wide range of spa architecture,
from Neo-Classical to Art
Nouveau spa establishments.

❹ Viareggio

Lucca. 🚹 65,000. 🚉 🚌 ℹ️ Viale
Carducci 10 (0584 96 22 33). 🗓 Thu.

Known for its carnival, held in
January and early February, this
is also the most popular of the
resorts on the Versilia coast. Its
famous "Liberty" (Art Nouveau)
style of architecture can be seen
in the grand hotels, villas, and
cafés built in the 1920s after
the resort's original boardwalk
and timber chalets went up
in flames in 1917. The finest
example of the architecture
is the **Gran Caffè Margherita**
at the end of Passeggiata
Margherita, designed by the
prolific father of Italian Art
Nouveau, Galileo Chini.

❺ Torre del Lago Puccini

Lucca. 🚹 11,000. 🚉 🚌 ℹ️ Viale
Kennedy 2 (0584 35 98 93). 🗓 Fri.

A glorious avenue of lime trees,
the Via dei Tigli, connects
Viareggio with Torre del Lago
Puccini, once the home of the
opera composer Giacomo

Puccini (1858–1924). He and his
wife are buried in their former
home, now the **Museo Villa
Puccini**, a small museum that
features the piano on which the
maestro composed many of his
works. Equal prominence is given
to the villa's original fittings,
including the gun room that
housed Puccini's hunting rifle.
Lago Massaciuccoli, a nature
reserve for rare and migrant
birds, provides a pretty backdrop
for open-air performances of
Puccini's works.

🏛 Museo Villa Puccini
Piazzale Belvedere Puccini 226.
Tel 0584 34 14 45. **Open** Tue–Sun.
Closed Nov, Dec 25. 🅿️ ♿

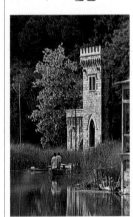

Near Puccini's lakeside home at Torre del
Lago Puccini

❻ Street by Street: Lucca

Lucca's regular grid of streets still follows the pattern of the former Roman colony founded in 180 BC. Great, solid ramparts, built in the 16th to 17th century, help to shut out traffic, making the city a pleasant place to explore on foot. San Michele in Foro – one of the town's many fine Pisan-Romanesque churches – stands on the site of the Roman forum (foro), the city's main square laid out in ancient times. It is still Lucca's main square today.

San Frediano
Palazzo Pfanner

In Via Fillungo, Lucca's main shopping street, several storefronts are decorated with Art Nouveau details.

Casa Natale di Puccini
Giacomo Puccini (1858–1924), composer of hugely popular operas, including *La Bohème*, was born in this house.

Piazza Napoleone
This sprawling square is named after Napoleon, whose sister, Elisa Baciocchi, ruled Lucca from 1805 to 1815.

Train station

★ San Michele in Foro
The extraordinary Pisan-Romanesque façade (11th to 14th century) has three tiers of twisted or carved columns, each one different from the rest.

San Giovanni

The Museo dell'Opera del Duomo features treasures removed from San Martino.

Key

— Suggested route

| 0 meters | | 300 |
| 0 yards | | 300 |

For hotels and restaurants in this region see pp562–77 and pp580–605

VISITORS' CHECKLIST

Practical Information
85,000. Piazza Santa Maria 35 (0583 91 99 31). 3rd Sun of month (antiques), Wed, Sat. Jul 12: Palio della Balestra; Jul: Lucca Summer Festival; Sep 13: Luminara di Santa Croce.
luccaturismo.it

Transportation
Piazza Ricasoli.
Piazzale Verdi.

Anfiteatro Romano and tourist information

Torre dei Guinigi

Villa Bottoni Pinacoteca Nazionale

Giardino Botanico

★ **San Martino**
Lucca's beautiful 11th-century Duomo is one of the outstanding examples of the exuberant Pisan-Romanesque style.

Apostles from the mosaic on the façade of San Frediano in Lucca

San Frediano
Piazza San Frediano. **Open** daily.
San Frediano's striking façade features a colorful 13th-century mosaic, *The Ascension*, a fine prelude to the church's wonderfully atmospheric interior. Pride of place goes to a splendid Romanesque font on the right, its sides carved with scenes from the Life of Christ and the story of Moses. Note the scene of Moses and his followers (dressed as medieval knights) as they pass through the divided Red Sea. In the second chapel in the north aisle, Aspertini's frescoes (1508–9) tell the story of Lucca's precious relic, the Volto Santo – a carving said to date from the time of the Crucifixion. The fine altarpiece (1422) in the fourth chapel of San Frediano's north aisle is by Jacopo della Quercia.

San Michele in Foro
Piazza San Michele. **Open** daily.
Built on the site of the old Roman forum (*foro*), San Michele's rich mixture of twisted marble columns and Cosmati work (inlaid marble) adorns one of the most exuberant Pisan-Romanesque façades in Tuscany. Built between the 11th and 14th centuries, its decoration is overwhelmingly pagan. Only the huge winged figure of St. Michael on the pediment marks this out as a church. The interior has little of interest except for the beautiful

painting of *Saints Helena, Jerome, Sebastian, and Roch* by Filippino Lippi (1457–1504).

Casa Natale di Puccini
Corte San Lorenzo 9. **Tel** 0583 58 40 28. **Open** Apr–Oct: 10am–6pm daily; Nov–Mar: 11am–5pm. **Closed** Tue, Jan 1, Dec 25.

The fine 15th-century house in which Giacomo Puccini (1858–1924) was born is now a shrine to the great opera composer. It contains portraits of Puccini, costume designs for his operas, and the piano he used when composing his last opera, *Turandot*.

Via Fillungo
Lucca's principal shopping street winds its way through the heart of the city toward the Anfiteatro Romano. Its northern end has several shops with Art Nouveau ironwork; halfway down lies the deconsecrated church of San Cristoforo, built in the 13th century, with a lovely interior.

One of the many bars and shops along Via Fillungo

Exploring Lucca

Lucca's peaceful narrow lanes wind among the medieval buildings, opening suddenly to reveal churches, tiny piazzas, and many other reminders of the city's long history, including a Roman amphitheater.

Medieval buildings mark the outline of Lucca's old Roman amphitheater

🏛 Anfiteatro Romano
Piazza del Mercato.
Roman *Luca* was founded in 180 BC, and stones from the ancient Roman amphitheater have been ransacked over the centuries to build churches and palaces, leaving only a handful of original fragments studded into today's arena-shaped Piazza del Mercato. Slum housing clogged the piazza until 1830, when it was cleared on the orders of Marie Louise, the city's Bourbon ruler of that time. It was then that the amphitheater's original shape was revealed, a graphic and evocative reminder of Lucca's rich Roman heritage. Low archways at the piazza's cardinal points mark the gates through which beasts and gladiators would once have entered the arena.

🏛 Museo dell'Opera del Duomo
Piazza Antelminelli 5. **Tel** 0583 49 05 30. **Open** daily. **Closed** Jan 1, Easter (am), Dec 25. 🅿 ♿

The museum, housed in the former Archbishop's Palace (14th century), displays the treasures of the Duomo of San Martino. These include the 11th-century carved stone head of a king and a rare

🏛 San Martino
Piazza San Martino. **Tel** 0583 95 70 68. **Open** daily. 📷 for sacristy.

Lucca's cathedral was built after the campanile, hence the façade's cramped and asymmetric appearance. The main portals contain remarkable 13th-century carvings by Nicola Pisano and Guidetto da Como. The Tempietto inside houses a painting by Tintoretto and the Volto Santo, a revered 13th-century effigy once believed to have been carved at the time of the Crucifixion.

Façade
The cathedral façade is decorated with Romanesque sculptures and colonnading (1204).

The campanile was begun in 1060 as a defensive tower.

Ghirlandaio's painting of *The Madonna and Saints* (1449–94) is in the Sacristy.

Domed chapels encircling the apse

Romanesque blind arcades and carved capitals

Tomb of Ilaria del Carretto
This beautiful portrait in marble by Jacopo della Quercia (1405–6) is of the youthful bride of Paolo Guinigi.

Matteo Civitali's marble Tempietto (1184)

Circular clerestory windows, in the nave and above the aisle roof, illuminate the church's unusually tall nave.

Nicola Pisano (1200–78) carved the *Journey of the Magi* and *Deposition* on the left portal.

Baroque gods and goddesses in the garden of the Palazzo Pfanner

12th-century Limoges casket, possibly created for a relic of St. Thomas à Becket. The Croce dei Pisani, made by Vincenzo di Michele in 1411, is a sublime masterpiece of the goldsmith's art. It shows Christ on the Tree of Redemption, surrounded by angels, the Virgin, St. John, and the other Evangelists.

🏛 Palazzo Pfanner

Via degli Asili 33. **Tel** 0583 954 029.
Open Apr–Oct: 10am–6pm; Nov–Mar: by appt. 🖼

This elegant, imposing house (1667) has a beautiful outside staircase. It also boasts one of Tuscany's most delightful formal gardens. Laid out in the 18th century, the garden's central avenue is lined with Baroque statues of the gods and goddesses of ancient Roman mythology. The garden can also be viewed while walking along the ramparts.

The house itself contains an interesting collection of furniture, antiques, and medical instruments.

🏛 Ramparts

One of the pleasures of visiting Lucca is strolling along the ramparts – the magnificent city walls, whose tree-lined promenade offers some entrancing views of the city. Work on the ramparts began around 1500, when advances in military technology made the old medieval defenses ineffective. On their completion in 1645, the walls were some of the most advanced of their time. One of their most curious features was the open space that lay beyond them, and which survives to this day, cleared to prevent the enemy taking cover in trees and undergrowth. Ironically, the walls never actually had to be defended, and they were eventually converted into a public park in the early 19th century.

Part of the imposing 17th-century ramparts that encircle Lucca

🏛 Santa Maria Forisportam

Piazza di Santa Maria Forisportam.
Open daily.

This church was built at the end of the 12th century, beyond the Roman walls of Lucca. Its name, Forisportam, means "outside the gate." The unfinished marble façade, in Pisan-Romanesque style, has blind arcading. Above the central portal is a relief of the *Coronation of the Virgin* (17th century). The interior was redesigned in the early 16th century, resulting in the nave and transepts being raised. The fourth altar of the south aisle contains a painting of *St. Lucy,* and the north transept has an *Assumption,* both by Guercino (1591–1666).

🏛 Museo Nazionale di Villa Guinigi

Via della Quarquonia. **Tel** 0583 49 60 33.
Open Tue–Sat. **Closed** Jan 1, May 1, Dec 25. 🖼 🖼

This massive Renaissance villa was built in 1418 for Paolo Guinigi, leading light of the noble family who ruled Lucca in the early 15th century. A familiar landmark of the city is the battlemented tower, the Torre dei Guinigi, with oak trees growing at the top. It offers good views over the city and the Apuan Alps. The garden features traces of a Roman mosaic, together with a pride of Romanesque lions removed from the city's walls.

Romanesque lion in the Museo Nazionale Guinigi

Inside, the museum's first floor is devoted to sculptures and archaeological displays. The highlights are works by Matteo Civitali and Jacopo della Quercia and fine Romanesque reliefs removed from several of Lucca's churches. Most of the paintings in the gallery on the floor above are by minor local artists, with the exception of two by Fra Bartolomeo (c.1472–1517): *God the Father with Saints Catherine and Mary Magdalene* and the *Madonna della Misericordia.* The floor also has furnishings, church vestments, and choir stalls from Lucca's cathedral, inlaid with marquetry views of the city carved in

❼ Pisa

For much of the Middle Ages, Pisa's powerful navy ensured its dominance of the western Mediterranean. Trading links with Spain and North Africa in the 12th century brought vast mercantile wealth and formed the basis of a cultural revolution that is still reflected in Pisa's splendid buildings – especially the Duomo, Baptistry, and Campanile (Leaning Tower). Pisa's decline began in 1284, with its defeat by Genoa, and was hastened by the silting up of the harbor. The city fell to the Florentines in 1406, but suffered its worst crisis in 1944 when it fell victim to Allied bombing.

A detail from the Duomo pulpit

da Camaino, and a mosaic of *Christ in Majesty* in the apse, completed by Cimabue in 1302.

The circular Baptistry was begun in 1152 along Roman-esque lines, and finished a century later (the delay caused by a shortage of money) in a more ornate Gothic style by Nicola and Giovanni Pisano. The former was responsible for the marble pulpit (1260) in the interior, carved with reliefs of the *Nativity*, the *Adoration of the Magi*, the *Presentation*, the *Crucifixion*, and the *Last Judgment*. The pillars that support the pulpit feature statues of the Virtues. The inlaid marble font (1246) is by Guido da Como.

✝ Camposanto

Piazza dei Miracoli. **Tel** 050 83 50 11. **Open** daily. **Closed** Jan 1, Dec 25.

The Camposanto (cemetery) is the fourth element in the Campo dei Miracoli's lovely ensemble. Begun in 1278 by Giovanni di Simone, the vast marble arcades of this long, rectangular building are said to enclose soil from the Holy Land. Bombs in World War II all but destroyed its once famous frescoes, leaving only traces of *The Triumph of Death* (1360–80). Nearby is the Orto Botanico, one of Europe's oldest botanical gardens.

The Baptistry, Duomo, and Leaning Tower in Pisa's Campo dei Miracoli

⊞ Leaning Tower

See p330. **Open** daily. 🕐 Visits last 30 mins. No children under 8 allowed. 🐾 🌐 **opapisa.it** (reservations).

⚑ Duomo and Baptistry

Piazza Duomo. **Tel** 050 83 50 11. **Open** daily (Duomo: pm only on Sun). 🌐 **opapisa.it**

Pisa's famous Leaning Tower is now the best-known building in the Campo dei Miracoli (Field of ... lly, however, it ... a campanile to ... Duomo, which ... scheto in 1064. ... o stands as one

of the finest Pisan-Romanesque buildings in Tuscany, its wonderful four-tiered façade a medley of creamy colonnades and intricate blind arcades. Buscheto's tomb is in the left arch of the façade. Other important features of the exterior include the Portale di San Ranieri (leading to the south transept) and the bronze doors (1180), decorated with reliefs cast by Bonanno Pisano, the first architect of the Leaning Tower. Inside, the highlights are the carved pulpit (1302–11) by Giovanni Pisano, the *Tomb of Emperor Henry VII* (1315) by Tino

A fresco from the *Triumph of Death* cycle in the Camposanto

Santa Maria della Spina alongside the River Arno in Pisa

🏛 Museo dell'Opera del Duomo

Piazza del Duomo 6. **Tel** 050 83 10 11.
Open daily. 🎫 ♿

Housed in the cathedral's 13th-century former Chapter House, this excellent modern museum displays exhibits removed over the years from the Duomo, Baptistry, and Camposanto. Among the highlights is an imposing 10th-century hippogriff (half horse, half griffin). Cast in bronze by Moorish craftsmen, this statue was looted by Pisan adventurers during the wars against the Saracens. There are also works by both Nicola and Giovanni Pisano, notably Giovanni's ivory *Virgin and Child* (1300), carved for the Duomo's high altar. Other exhibits include paintings, Roman and Etruscan remains, and ecclesiastical treasures.

10th-century bronze hippogriff

🏛 Museo Nazionale di San Matteo

Lungarno Mediceo, Piazza San Matteo
1. **Tel** 050 54 18 65. **Open** 9am–7pm Tue–Sun (Sun: am only). 🎫 📷

This museum is located on the banks of the Arno in San Matteo, an elegantly fronted medieval convent that in the 1800s also served as a prison. Much of the building has been closed for years – several of the rooms have no numbers and some of the exhibits are poorly labeled. Nevertheless, the museum presents a unique opportunity to examine the complete sweep of Pisan and Florentine art from the 12th to the 17th centuries.

The first rooms are devoted to sculpture and early Tuscan paintings. The best exhibits include a 14th-century polyptych by Francesco Traini of *Scenes from the Life of St. Dominic*, Simone Martini's fine polyptych of *The Madonna and Saints* (1321), and a 14th-century statue of the *Madonna del Latte* attributed to Andrea Pisano, another member of Pisa's talented school of medieval sculptors. The half-length statue, in gilded marble, shows Christ feeding at his mother's breast. In room 6 are some of the highlights of the museum, including Masaccio's *St. Paul* (1426), Gentile da Fabriano's radiant 15th-century *Madonna of Humility*, and Donatello's reliquary bust of *San Rossore* (1424–7). Additional rooms contain paintings by Guido Reni, Benozzo Gozzoli, and Rosso Fiorentino, and an important picture of *Christ* attributed to Fra Angelico (c.1395–1455).

🏛 Santa Maria della Spina

Lungarno Gambacorti. **Tel** 055 12 19 19. **Open** Tue–Sun.

The roofline of this tiny church, located just beyond the Ponte Solferino, bristles with spiky Gothic pinnacles, spires, and niches sheltering statues of apostles and saints. The decoration reflects the history of the church, which was built between 1230 and 1323 to house a thorn *(spina)* from Christ's Crown of Thorns, the gift of a Pisan merchant. The church was once even closer to the Arno, but was rebuilt on the present site in 1871 to protect it from flooding.

🏛 Piazza dei Cavalieri

The huge building on the north side of this square is the Palazzo dei Cavalieri, home to one of Pisa University's most prestigious colleges: the Scuola Normale Superiore. Designed by Vasari in 1562, the building, which is covered in exuberant black and white *sgraffito* decoration (designs scratched into wet plaster), served as the headquarters of the Cavalieri di Santo Stefano, an order of knights created by Cosimo I in 1561.

The Virgin and Child (1321) by Simone Martini in the Museo Nazionale

The Leaning Tower of Pisa

Begun in 1173 on sandy silt subsoil, the Leaning Tower (Torre Pendente) started to tilt even before the third story was finished in 1274. Despite the shallow foundations, construction continued, and the structure was completed in 1350. The tower's apparent flouting of the laws of gravity has attracted many visitors over the centuries, including the Pisan scientist Galileo, who climbed to the top to conduct his experiments on the velocity of falling objects. After several engineering interventions that decreased the lean by 14 inches (38 cm), the tower is once again safe and open to the public.

Galileo Galilei
(1564–1642)

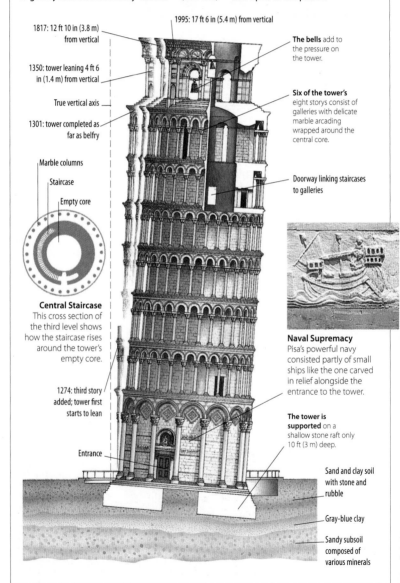

1995: 17 ft 6 in (5.4 m) from vertical

1817: 12 ft 10 in (3.8 m) from vertical

1350: tower leaning 4 ft 6 in (1.4 m) from vertical

True vertical axis

1301: tower completed as far as belfry

Marble columns

Staircase

Empty core

Central Staircase
This cross section of the third level shows how the staircase rises around the tower's empty core.

1274: third story added; tower first starts to lean

Entrance

The bells add to the pressure on the tower.

Six of the tower's eight storys consist of galleries with delicate marble arcading wrapped around the central core.

Doorway linking staircases to galleries

Naval Supremacy
Pisa's powerful navy consisted partly of small ships like the one carved in relief alongside the entrance to the tower.

The tower is supported on a shallow stone raft only 10 ft (3 m) deep.

Sand and clay soil with stone and rubble

Gray-blue clay

Sandy subsoil composed of various minerals

❽ Vinci

Florence. 🚈 15,000. 🚌 🚆 Wed.

Famous as the birthplace of Leonardo da Vinci (1452–1519), this hilltop town celebrates the genius in the **Museo Leonardiano**, housed in the 13th-century castle. Among the displays are wooden models of Leonardo's machines and inventions – most are based on drawings from his notebooks, copies of which are shown alongside. These include a bicycle, his conception of a car, an armored tank, and even a machine gun.

🏛 Museo Leonardiano
Castello dei Conti Guidi. **Tel** 0571 93 32 51. **Open** daily. 📷

Model bicycle based on designs by Leonardo, Museo Leonardiano

❾ Pistoia

🚈 93,000. 🚆 🚌 👤 Palazzo dei Vescovi, Piazza del Duomo (0573 216 22). 🚆 Wed & Sat.

Pistoia's citizens were once known for violence and intrigue, a reputation grounded in the medieval disputes between the city's rival factions, the Bianchi and Neri (Whites and Blacks). Their favored weapon was a tiny, locally made dagger known as a *pistola*. Long a center of metalwork, everything from buses to mattress springs are now made here. In the center, several fine historic buildings are preserved.

🏛 Duomo
Piazza del Duomo. **Open** daily.
Piazza del Duomo, Pistoia's main square, is dominated by the Duomo (San Zeno) and its bulky 12th-century campanile, originally built as a watchtower in the city walls. The interior of the Duomo is rich in funerary

Detail of frieze (1514–25) by Giovanni della Robbia, Ospedale del Ceppo

monuments. The finest of these, in the south aisle, is the tomb of Cino da Pistoia. He was a friend of Dante and fellow poet, and is depicted in a relief (1337) lecturing to a class of young boys.

Nearby is the chapel of St. James and its extraordinary silver altar decorated with more than 600 statues and reliefs. Although the earliest of these dates from 1287, the altar was not completed until 1456. One of the craftsmen involved was Brunelleschi, who began his career as a silversmith before turning to architecture. Also in the Piazza del Duomo is the octagonal Baptistry, completed in 1359.

🏛 Ospedale del Ceppo
Piazza Giovanni XXIII.
This hospital and orphanage, founded in 1277, was named after the *ceppo* (hollowed-out tree trunk) that was used to collect donations for its work. The main façade features colored terracotta panels (1514–25) by Giovanni della Robbia illustrating the *Seven Works of Mercy*. The portico is by Michelozzo.

The Pisan-Romanesque façade of Pistoia's Duomo (San Zeno)

🏛 Cappella del Tau
Corso Silvano Fedi 70. **Tel** 0573 322 04. **Open** 8:30am–1:30pm Mon–Sat.
The Cappella del Tau (1360) is so called because the monks who built it wore on their cloaks the letter T (*tau* in Greek), symbolizing a crutch and their work with the sick and disabled. Inside there are frescoes by Niccolò di Tommaso on *The Creation* and the *Life of St. Anthony Abbot* (1370). Two doors down, the **Palazzo Tau** has work by Marino Marini, Pistoia's best-known 20th-century artist.

The Fall (1372) by Niccolò di Tommaso in the Cappella del Tau

🏛 San Giovanni Fuorcivitas
Via Cavour. **Open** daily.
Built in the 12th to 14th centuries, the striking church of San Giovanni Fuorcivitas (literally "St. John Outside the City") once stood beyond the city walls. Its north flank is clad in banded marble and there is a Romanesque relief of the Last Supper over the portal. Inside, the holy water stoup, carved in marble with figures of the Virtues, is by Giovanni Pisano (1245–1320). A masterly pulpit, carved in 1270 with scenes from the New Testament, is by Gugliemo da Pisa. Both are among the finest works of this period, when artists were reviving the art of carving.

⑩ Prato

🏛 190,000. 🚍 ℹ Piazza Duomo 8 (0574 241 12). 🛍 Mon.

While textile factories gird Prato's outskirts, the city center retains several important churches and museums. The **Duomo** (begun 1211) is flanked by the Pulpit of the Holy Girdle (1434–8), designed by Donatello and Michelozzo, used once a year to display a girdle, reputedly given to Thomas the Apostle before the Assumption of the Virgin. Inside the Duomo is *The Life of John the Baptist* (1452–66) by Fra Filippo Lippi, and a fresco cycle (1392–5) by Agnolo Gaddi.

Other sights include the **Museo Civico**; **Santa Maria delle Carceri**, a Renaissance church in Piazza delle Carceri; the **Castello dell'Imperatore**, a fortress built by Emperor Frederick II in 1237; the **Centro per l'Arte Contemporanea Pecci**; and the **Museo del Tessuto**, which traces the history of Prato's textile industry.

🏛 **Museo Civico**
Palazzo Pretorio, Piazza del Comune. **Tel** 0574 183 61. **Closed** for restoration.

🏰 **Castello dell'Imperatore**
Piazza delle Carceri. **Open** Wed–Mon.

🏛 **Centro per l'Arte Contemporanea Pecci**
Viale della Repubblica 277. **Tel** 0574 53 17. **Open** Wed–Mon. 🎨

🏛 **Museo del Tessuto**
Via Santa Chiara 24. **Tel** 0574 61 15 03. **Open** Tue–Sun. 🎨 free Sun.

Madonna del Ceppo by Fra Filippo Lippi in Prato's Museo Civico

Buontalenti's Villa di Artimino, or "Villa of a Hundred Chimneys"

⑪ Artimino

Prato. 🏛 400. 🚍

A small fortified hamlet, Artimino is remarkable for the unspoiled Romanesque church of **San Leonardo**. Outside the walls lies the **Villa di Artimino**, designed by Buontalenti in 1594 for Grand Duke Ferdinando I. Also known as the "Villa of a Hundred Chimneys" – after the chimney pots crowding the roofline – it houses the **Museo Archeologico Etrusco**, a collection of beautiful archaeogical exhibits.

Environs
For lovers of Pontormo's paintings, the church of **San Michele** in Carmignano, 3 miles (5 km) north of Artimino, contains *The Visitation* (1530). East of here lies the villa of **Poggio a Caiano**. Built in 1480 by Giuliano da Sangallo for Lorenzo de' Medici *(see p257)*, it was the first Italian villa to be designed in the Renaissance style.

🏛 **Villa di Artimino**
Viale Papa Giovanni 23. Villa: **Tel** 055 875 14 27. **Open** Tue am by appt. **Museum: Tel** 055 871 81 24. **Open** 9:30am–1:30pm daily. **Closed** Wed. 🎨

🏛 **Poggio a Caiano**
Piazza Medici. **Tel** 055 87 70 12. **Open** Tue–Sun; also 1st & 4th Mon of month. 🎨 ♿

⑫ San Miniato

Pisa. 🏛 3,900. 🚍 ℹ Piazza del Popolo (0571 427 45). 🛍 Tue.

This hilltop town manages to remain aloof from the vast industrial sprawl of the Arno

valley. Its key building is the semi-derelict Rocca (castle), built for Frederick II, German Holy Roman Emperor, in the 13th century. Close by stands the **Museo Diocesano**, which is home to a *Crucifixion* (c.1430) attributed to Filippo Lippi, a terracotta bust of Christ attributed to Verrocchio (1435–88), and the *Virgin of the Holy Girdle* by Andrea del Castagno (c.1417–57). Next door, the red-brick Romanesque façade of the **Duomo** dates from the 12th century. Its strange inset majolica plates, evidence of trade with Spain or North Africa, probably represent the North Star and the constellations of Ursa Major and Minor (all three were key points of reference for early navigators).

🏛 **Museo Diocesano**
Piazza Duomo. **Tel** 0571 41 80 71. **Open** 10am–1pm, 2–5pm Thu–Sun (Apr–Sep: 10am–6pm). 🎨

Façade of the Duomo in San Miniato

⑬ Fiesole

Florence. 🏛 15,000. 🚍 ℹ Via Portigiani 3 (055 596 13 23). 🛍 Sat.

Fiesole stands in rolling hilly countryside 5 miles (8 km) north of Florence. Idyllically situated among olive groves, it is a popular retreat from the city thanks to its hilltop position which attracts cool breezes. Founded in the 7th century BC, the original Etruscan colony was a powerful force in central Italy,

A view over the hills and rooftops of Fiesole from Via di San Francesco

only surrendering its supremacy after the foundation of Florence (1st century BC).

The restored **Duomo** of San Romolo in Piazza Mino da Fiesole was begun in 1028. It has a massive bell tower and a bare Romanesque interior. Behind the Duomo, an archaeological area contains the remains of a 1st-century BC **Roman theater**, traces of **Etruscan walls** from the 4th century BC, and the **Museo Faesulanum**, with a collection of bronzes, ceramics, and jewelry dating from the Bronze Age.

Via di San Francesco, a steep lane offering lovely views, leads to the Franciscan friary of **San Francesco** (14th century) and the interesting 9th-century church of **Sant'Alessandro**, with a Neo-Classical façade.

Via Vecchia Fiesolana leads to the hamlet of **San Domenico**, where the 15th-century church of the same name contains a painting of the *Madonna with Angels and Saints* (c.1430) by Fra Angelico and the Chapter House contains a fresco of *The Crucifixion* (c.1430), also by him. Close by, on the Via della Badia dei Roccettini, is the **Badia Fiesolana**, a pretty Romanesque church with a striped marble façade and interior of local gray sandstone, *pietra serena*.

🏛 Museo Faesulanum
Via Portigiani 1. **Tel** 055 596 12 93. **Open** daily (Oct–Mar: Wed–Mon). 🎫

⑭ Arezzo

🏙 100,000. 🚇 ℹ Piazza della Repubblica 28 (0575 377 678). 📅 Sat.

Arezzo is one of Tuscany's wealthiest cities, its prosperity based on a thriving jewelry industry. Although much of its medieval center was destroyed during World War II, resulting in extensive rebuilding and many medieval alleys being replaced by broad avenues, the city preserves some outstanding sights: foremost are Piero della Francesca's famous frescoes in the church of **San Francesco** (*see pp334–5*). Close to the church on Corso Italia, the main street, stands the **Pieve di Santa Maria**, which boasts one of the most ornate Romanesque façades in the region. To its rear stretches the steeply sloping **Piazza Grande**, flanked by an arcade (1573) designed by Vasari, and by the **Palazzo della**

Fraternità dei Laici (1377–1552). The latter features a *Madonna* relief by Bernardo Rossellino. The huge **Duomo** to the north is best known for its 16th-century stained glass and a small fresco of *Mary Magdalene* by Piero della Francesca (1416–92). The **Museo Diocesano (Mudas)** features three wooden crucifixes dating from the 12th and 13th centuries, a bas relief of *The Annunciation* (1434) by Rossellino, and paintings by Vasari. More works by Vasari can be seen in the **Casa di Vasari**, a house built by the artist in 1540. Still more frescoes by him are displayed in the **Museo d'Arte Medioevale e Moderna**, a museum that is famed for its excellent collection of majolica pottery.

The **Fortezza Medicea**, a ruined Medici castle built by Antonio da Sangallo during the 16th century, has fine views.

🏛 Museo Diocesano (Mudas)
Piazzetta Dietro il Duomo 12. **Tel** 0575 402 72 68. **Open** daily. 🎫

🏠 Casa di Vasari
Via XX Settembre 55. **Tel** 0575 40 90 40. **Open** Wed–Mon. 🎫

🏛 Museo d'Arte Medioevale e Moderna
Via di San Lorentino 8. **Tel** 0575 40 90 50. **Open** Tue–Sun. 🎫

🏰 Fortezza Medicea
Parco il Prato. **Tel** 0575 37 76 78. **Open** daily.

The monthly antiques market held in Arezzo's Piazza Grande

Arezzo: San Francesco

The 13th-century Church of San Francesco houses one of Italy's greatest fresco cycles, the *Legend of the True Cross* (1452–66), Piero della Francesca's masterpiece. The scenes, on the walls of the choir, are now visible again after a long restoration. They describe the history of the Cross used to crucify Christ, from sprig to Tree of Knowledge, to its use as a bridge during the reign of Solomon, and ultimately its discovery by Helena, mother of Constantine, the first Christian emperor.

A Group of Onlookers
These figures kneel in wonder while Heraclius returns the True Cross to Jerusalem.

Excavation of the Cross
The town, meant to be Jerusalem, gives a fair representation of 15th-century Arezzo.

KEY

① **The Defeat of Chosroes** depicts the defeat of a Persian king who had stolen the Cross.

② **The Cross** returns to Jerusalem.

③ **Judas reveals** where the Cross is hidden.

④ **The 13th-century Crucifix** forms the focal point of the fresco cycle. The figure at the foot of the Cross represents St. Francis, to whom the church is dedicated.

⑤ **The prophets** appear to play no part in the narrative cycle; their presence may be for purely decorative reasons.

⑥ **The wood** of the Cross is buried in a pit.

⑦ **The Queen of Sheba** recognizes the wood of the Cross.

⑧ **The buildings** in the fresco reflect the newly fashionable styles of Renaissance architecture.

⑨ **Constantine leads** his cavalry into battle.

⑩ **Constantine dreams** of the Cross on the eve of battle against rival emperor Maxentius.

Key to Frescoes

1 The Death of Adam; a sprig from the Tree of Knowledge is planted over his grave.

2 The Queen of Sheba visits Solomon and foresees that a bridge made from the Tree will be used to crucify the greatest king in the world.

3 Solomon, assuming he is the greatest king in the world, orders the bridge to be buried.

4 The Annunciation: Christ's death is foreshadowed in the panel's cruciform structure.

The Death of Adam
Piero's vivid portrayal of Adam and Eve in old age shows an adept treatment of anatomy. He was one of the first Renaissance artists to paint nude figures.

VISITORS' CHECKLIST

Practical Information
P. San Francesco.
Tel 0575 35 27 27
(reservations mandatory).
Open 8:30am–noon,
2pm–6:30pm daily.
Closed Jan 1, Dec 25.

5 Constantine has a vision of the Cross and hears a voice saying "In this sign you shall conquer."
6 Constantine defeats his rival Maxentius.
7 The Levite Judas is tortured and reveals the location of the True Cross.
8 Three crosses are dug up; Constantine's mother Helena recognizes the True Cross.
9 The Persian king Chosroes is defeated after stealing the Cross.
10 The True Cross is returned to Jerusalem.

Solomon's Handshake
The handshake between the Queen of Sheba and Solomon, King of Israel, portrays 15th-century hopes for a union between the Orthodox and Western churches.

Piero's *The Resurrection* (1463) in Sansepolcro

⓯ Sansepolcro

Arezzo. 🚗 16,000. 🚌 𝒊 Via Matteotti 8 (0575 74 05 36). 🛒 Tue, Sat.

Sansepolcro is the birthplace of Piero della Francesca (1410–92). The town's **Museo Civico** contains two of his masterpieces: *The Resurrection* (1463) and the *Madonna della Misericordia* (1462). It also has a 15th-century *Crucifixion* by Luca Signorelli. In the church of **San Lorenzo** on Via Santa Croce there is a *Deposition* in the Mannerist style by Rosso Fiorentino (1494–1541).

Another renowned painting by Piero della Francesca, the *Madonna del Parto*, can be seen at Via Reglia 1 in Monterchi, 8 miles (13 km) southwest of Sansepolcro.

🏛 **Museo Civico**
Via Aggiunti 65. **Tel** 0575 73 22 18. **Open** daily. **Closed** public hols. 🗺 📷

⓰ Cortona

Arezzo. 🚗 23,000. 🚆 🚌 𝒊 Via Nazionale 42 (0575 63 03 52). 🛒 Sat.

Cortona was founded by the Etruscans and apart from being one of the oldest hill towns in Tuscany, it is also one of the most scenic. A major power in the Middle Ages, it was able to hold its own against Siena and Arezzo. Today it is a charming maze of old streets and medieval buildings, like the **Palazzo Comunale** on Piazza della Repubblica. The town's early history is traced in the **Museo dell'Accademia Etrusca**, which contains Etruscan artifacts and a wide variety of Egyptian and Roman remains. The small **Museo Diocesano** features several fine paintings, in particular a *Crucifixion* by the Renaissance artist Pietro Lorenzetti, a *Deposition* (1502) by Luca Signorelli, and a sublime *Annunciation* (c.1434) by Fra Angelico. Signorelli, born in Cortona, is buried in the church of **San Francesco** (built in 1245), which contains an *Annunciation* painted in Baroque style by Pietro da Cortona, another native artist. The **Madonna del Calcinaio** (1485), a gem of Renaissance architecture, is located on the southern outskirts of town.

The 13th-century Palazzo Comunale in Cortona

🏛 **Museo dell'Accademia Etrusca**
Palazzo Casali, Piazza Signorelli 9. **Tel** 0575 63 72 35. **Open** daily (Tue–Sun in winter). 🗺

🏛 **Museo Diocesano**
Piazza del Duomo 1. **Tel** 0575 628 30. **Open** daily (Tue–Sun in winter). 🗺

⓱ Chiusi

Siena. 🚗 10,000. 🚆 🚌 𝒊 Via Porsenna 79 (0578 22 76 67). 🛒 Tue.

Chiusi is now a largely modern town, but in the past it was one of the most powerful cities in the Etruscan league, reaching the height of its influence in the 7th and 6th centuries BC *(see p45)*. Numerous Etruscan tombs lie dotted in the surrounding countryside, the source of the exhibits in the town's **Museo Nazionale Etrusco**. Founded in 1871, the museum is packed with cremation urns, vases decorated with black figures, and Bucchero ware, burnished to resemble bronze.

The Romanesque **Duomo** in Piazza del Duomo incorporates recycled Roman pillars and capitals. The wall decorations in the nave, resembling frescoes, were painted by Arturo Viligiardi in 1887. There is a Roman mosaic underneath the high altar. Visits can be made to several Etruscan tombs under the town from the **Museo della Cattedrale**, a museum in the cloister of the Duomo that has displays of Roman, Lombardic, and medieval sculpture.

🏛 **Museo Nazionale Etrusco**
Via Porsenna 93. **Tel** 0578 201 77. **Open** 9am–8pm daily (to 2pm Sun & public hols). 🗺 📷

🏛 **Museo della Cattedrale**
P. del Duomo. **Tel** 0578 22 64 90. **Open** daily (Jan–Mar: Tue, Thu, Sat, Sun). 🗺

Etruscan frieze in the Museo Nazionale Etrusco in Chiusi

Pienza's Piazza Pio II, designed by Bernardo Rossellino (1459)

⑱ Montepulciano

Siena. 🚗 14,000. 🚌 🛈 Piazza Don
Minzoni ⅃ (0578 75 73 41). 🛒 Thu.
🌐 prolocomontepulciano.it

This is one of Tuscany's highest
hill towns, its walls and
fortifications offering broad
views over Umbria and
southern Tuscany, and the
vineyards providing the Vino
Nobile wine that has made its
name famous. The streets are
brimming with Renaissance
palazzi. The main street, the
Corso, climbs to the **Duomo**
(1592–1630), the setting for
one of the masterpieces of the
Sienese School, the *Assumption*
(1401) by Taddeo di Bartolo.
The High Renaissance church,
Tempio di San Biagio (1518–
34), lies off the road to Pienza.

⑲ Pienza

Siena. 🚗 2,300. 🚌 🛈 Piazza Dante
Alighieri 18 (0578 74 83 59). 🛒 Fri.

Pienza is a delightful village
whose intimate little center was
almost completely redesigned
in the 15th century by Pope Pius
II. Born as Aeneas Sylvius
Piccolomini in 1405, when the
village was known as
Corsignano, he became a
leading Humanist scholar and
philosopher. Elected pope in
1458, he decided to rebuild his
birthplace, renaming it Pienza in
his own honor. The Florentine
architect and sculptor Bernardo
Rossellino was commissioned to
build a cathedral, papal palace,
and town hall (all completed in

the three years from 1459 to
1462), but the grander scheme
for a planned model
Renaissance town was never
realized. Some idea of what
might have been, however, can
still be gained from the **Palazzo
Piccolomini**, the former papal
palace, which continued to be
inhabited by Pius's descendants
until 1968. The rooms open to
the public include Pius's
bedroom and library, though
the highlight of a visit is the
superb panorama from the
loggia and arcaded courtyard at
the palace's rear.

Pleasant walks and more
great views can be had from
the village walls. The airy
Duomo *(see p256)* next door
contains six altarpieces of the
Madonna and Child, each
commissioned from the
leading Sienese painters of
the day. Rossellino was
forced to build the
Duomo on a cramped
site with poor found-
ations, and cracks
appeared in the

building before it was even
completed. Today the church's
eastern end suffers from severe
subsidence.

🏛 **Palazzo Piccolomini**
Piazza Pio II. **Tel** 0577 28 63 00.
Open 10am–6:30pm Tue–Sun (to
4:30pm mid-Oct–mid-Mar). **Closed**
Jan–mid-Feb, mid-end Nov. 🪧 🎫

⑳ Montalcino

Siena. 🚗 5,100. 🚌 🛈 Costa del
Municipio 1 (0577 84 93 31). 🛒 Fri.

Hilltop Montalcino sits at the
heart of vineyards that produce
Brunello, one of Italy's finest red
wines. It can be sampled in the
Enoteca (wine shop) situated in
the 14th-century **Fortezza** with
its impressive ramparts. The
town's timeless streets are a
pleasure to wander, and there
are some buildings of interest.
On the way from the fortress
into town is the monastery
of Sant' Agostino and its
14th-century church, and, just
beyond, the Palazzo Vescovile.
On Piazza del Popolo the slim
tower of the Palazzo Comm-
unale, constructed in the 13th
and 14th centuries, stands tall
above the town.

🏰 **Fortezza**
Piazzale della Fortezza. **Tel** 0577 84 92
11. 🪧 for ramparts. Enoteca: **Open**
9am–8pm daily (to 7:30pm Sat, Sun;
Nov–Mar: 9am–6pm Tue–Sun).

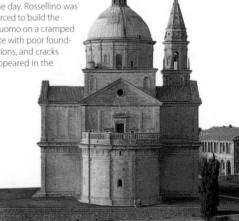

The Tempio di San Biagio on the outskirts of Montepulciano

The landscape of the Crete Senesi

㉑ Crete Senesi

Asciano. **FS** 🚍 **i** Via delle Fonti (0577 71 88 11).

To the south of Siena and central Tuscany is the area known as the Crete Senesi, which is characterized by round clay hillocks eroded by heavy rain over the centuries. Dubbed the "Tuscan desert," it is almost completely barren. Cypress and pine trees, planted to provide windbreaks along roads and around isolated farmhouses, are an important feature in this empty, primeval landscape. Shepherds tend flocks of sheep here; the milk is used to produce the strongly flavored *pecorino* cheese that is popular throughout Tuscany.

㉒ Siena

See pp342–7.

㉓ Monteriggioni

Siena. 🗺 99,000. 🚍 **i** Piazza Roma (0577 30 48 34).
W monteriggioniturismo.it

Monteriggioni is a gem of a medieval hilltop town. It was built in 1203 and 10 years later became a garrison town. It is completely encircled by high walls with 14 heavily fortified towers, built to guard the northern borders of Siena's territory against invasion by Florentine armies.

Dante used Monteriggioni as a simile for the deepest abyss at the heart of his *Inferno*, which compares the town's "ring-shaped citadel … crowned with

towers" with giants standing in a moat. The perfectly preserved walls are best viewed from the Colle di Val d'Elsa road. Within the walls, the sleepy town consists of a large piazza, a pretty Romanesque church (on the piazza), a few houses, a couple of craft shops, restaurants, and shops selling many of the locally produced Castello di Monteriggioni wines.

Environs
West of Monteriggioni by 2 miles (3 km) lies the former Cistercian Abbey of **Abbadia dell' Isola** (12th century). This Romanesque church was largely rebuilt in the 18th century, after the cupola fell apart. It contains frescoes by Taddeo di Bartolo and Vincenzo Tamagni.

Detail from the pulpit in Volterra's Duomo

㉔ San Gimignano

See pp348–9.

㉕ Volterra

Pisa. 🗺 13,000. 🚍 **i** Piazza dei Priori 20 (0588 872 57). 🛒 Sat.
W volterratur.it

Like many Etruscan cities, Volterra is situated on a high plateau, offering fine views over the surrounding hills. In many places the ancient Etruscan

walls still survive. The **Museo Guarnacci** contains one of the best collections of Etruscan artifacts in Italy. Of special interest is the group of over 600 cinerary urns, made from alabaster or terracotta, many of which were gathered from local tombs.

The **Palazzo dei Priori**, the medieval seat of government on Piazza dei Priori, is the oldest of its kind in Tuscany. It was begun in 1208 and there are 14th-century frescoes inside. The Pisan-Romanesque **Duomo**, located on Piazza San Giovanni, has a fine 13th-century pulpit with sculptured panels. Volterra's excellent art gallery and museum, the **Pinacoteca e Museo Civico**, features works by Florentine artists. *Christ in Majesty* (1492) by Ghirlandaio shows Christ hovering above an idealized Tuscan landscape. Luca Signorelli's *Virgin and Child with Saints* (1491) states his debt to Roman art through the reliefs on the base of the Virgin's throne. Painted in the same year, his *Annunciation* is a beautifully balanced composition. Another highlight is Rosso Fiorentino's Mannerist painting, *The Deposition* (1521).

The city is famous for its craftsmen, who have been

The beautifully preserved walls of Monteriggioni in central Tuscany

The ruined abbey at San Galgano, surrounded by dense woodland

carving elaborate statues and *objets d'art* from locally mined alabaster for 2,500 years.

🏛 Museo Guarnacci
Via Don Minzoni 15. **Tel** 0588 863 47.
Open daily. **Closed** Jan 1, Dec 25. 🖉

🏛 Pinacoteca e Museo Civico
Via dei Sarti 1. **Tel** 0588 875 80.
Open daily. **Closed** Jan 1, Dec 25. 🖉

㉖ San Galgano

Siena. 🚌 from Siena. Abbey & oratory: **Open** daily.
W sangalgano.org

The remote Cistercian abbey at San Galgano lies in a superb setting. San Galgano (1148–81) was a brave but dissolute knight who turned to God, renouncing the material world. When he tried to break his sword against a rock as a symbol of his rejection of war, it was swallowed by the stone. This he interpreted as a sign of God's approval. He built a hut on a hill above the abbey (the site of today's beehive-shaped chapel at **Montesiepi**, built c.1185). Here he later died a hermit. Pope Urban III declared him a saint.

The abbey, begun in 1218, is Gothic in style, reflecting the French origins of the Cistercian monks who designed it. They avoided contact with the outside world and divided their lives between prayer and labor. Despite an emphasis on poverty, the monks became wealthy from the sale of wood, and by the

middle of the 14th century the abbey was corruptly administered and gradually fell into decline.

In the late 14th century, the English mercenary Sir John Hawkwood sacked the abbey, and by 1397 the abbot was its sole occupant. It was eventually dissolved in 1652.

St. Galgano's sword stands embedded in a stone just inside the door of the circular **oratory**. The 14th-century stone walls of the side chapel are covered with worn frescoes showing scenes from Galgano's life by Ambrogio Lorenzetti (1344).

㉗ Massa Marittima

Grosseto. 🏘 9,500. 🚌 🚉 Amatur, Via Todini 3–5 (0566 90 27 56). 🛒 Wed.

Set in the Colline Metallifere (metal-bearing hills), where lead, copper, and silver ores were mined as early as Etruscan times, Massa Marittima is far from being a grimy industrial town. Examples of Romanesque architecture survive from the time when the town became an independent republic (1225–1335). The Romanesque-Gothic **Duomo** in Piazza Garibaldi is dedicated to

St. Cerbone, a 6th-century saint whose story is sculpted in stone above the main portal. Inside the building, the *Maestà* is attributed to Duccio (c.1316).

The **Museo della Miniera** (museum of mining) is located partially inside a former mine shaft and has exhibits that explain mining techniques, tools, and minerals.

The **Museo Archeologico e Museo d'Arte Sacra** has material from Paleolithic to Roman times. Other attractions are the Fortezza Senese and the Torre della Candeliera.

🏛 Museo della Miniera
Via Corridoni. **Tel** 0566 90 22 89.
Open Tue–Sun.
🎦 compulsory. 🖉

🏛 Museo Archeologico e Museo d'Arte Sacra
Palazzo del Podestà, Pza Garibaldi.
Tel 0566 90 22 89. **Open** Tue–Sun. 🖉

View across the rooftops of Massa Marittima

Denuded hillocks of clay in the Crete Senesi area southeast of Siena ▶

㉒ Street by Street: Siena

Siena's principal sights cluster in the maze of narrow streets and alleys around the fan-shaped Piazza del Campo. One of Europe's greatest medieval squares, the piazza sits at the heart of the city's 17 *contrade*, a series of parishes whose ancient rivalries are still acted out in the twice-yearly Palio *(see p341)*. Loyalty to the *contrada* of one's birth is fierce, and as you wander the streets you will see the parishes' animal symbols repeated on flags, plaques, and carvings. Siena's hilly position also means that city walks offer delightful hidden corners and countless sudden views.

The Duomo dominating Siena's skyline

Bus station

Train station

Via della Galluzza leads to the house of St. Catherine.

The Baptistry has fine frescoes and a font with reliefs by Donatello, Jacopo della Quercia, and Ghiberti.

VIA D. GALLUZZA

PIAZZA INDIPENDENZA

VIA DI DIACCETO

VIA DI CITTÀ

VIA DI FONTEBRANDA

VIA DEI PELLEGRINI

VIA FRANCIOSA

PIAZZA SAN GIOVANNI

VIC. D. CAMPANE

★ **Duomo**
Striped black and white marble pillars, surmounted by a carved frieze of the popes, support the Duomo's vaulted ceiling, painted blue with gold stars to resemble the night sky.

VIA DEL FUSARI

VIA DEL POGGIO

VIA DI CITTÀ

Each tier of the Duomo's bell tower has one more window than the floor below.

PIAZZA DEL DUOMO

VIA DEL CAPITANO

Museo dell'Opera del Duomo
Duccio's *Maestà*, one of the greatest Sienese paintings, was paraded around Siena's streets on its completion in 1311, and influenced the city's painters for decades to come.

Key

— Suggested route

0 meters   300
0 yards   300

Loggia della Mercanzia
Built in 1417, the arcade is where Siena's medieval merchants and money dealers carried out their business.

VISITORS' CHECKLIST

60,000. **FS** Piazzale Rosselli Piazza S. Domenico. *i* Piazza del Campo 56 (0577 28 05 51). Wed. Jul 2, Aug 16: Palio; Jul: Settimana Musicale Chigiana (classical music). **W** terresiena.it

The Logge del Papa, or Pope's colonnade, was built in honor of Pius II in 1462.

Drummer in Siena's Palio

Tourist information

Fonte Gaia
These reliefs are 19th-century copies of originals by Jacopo della Quercia.

Piazza del Campo
Italy's loveliest piazza occupies the site of the old Roman forum, and for much of Siena's early history was the city's principal marketplace. It began to assume its present shape in 1293, when the Council of Nine, Siena's ruling body at the time, began to acquire land with a view to creating a grand civic piazza. The red brick paving was begun in 1327 and completed in 1349, its distinctive nine segments designed to reflect the authority of the Council of Nine and to symbolize the protective folds of the Madonna's cloak. The piazza has been the focus of city life ever since, a setting for executions, bullfights, and the twice-yearly drama of the Palio *(see p341)*, a festival centered around a bareback horse race. Cafés, restaurants, and fine medieval palazzi now line the Campo's fringes, dominated by the **Palazzo Pubblico** (1297–1342) and **Torre del Mangia**, built in 1348 *(see p340)*. This imposing ensemble tends to overshadow the little **Fonte Gaia** on the piazza's northern edge. The fountain is a 19th-century copy of an original carved by Jacopo della Quercia in 1409–19. Its reliefs depict the *Virtues, Adam and Eve*, and the *Madonna and Child* (the originals are on the rear loggia of the Palazzo Pubblico). The fountain's water is still supplied by a 500-year-old aqueduct.

The Piazza del Campo and Fonte Gaia from the Torre del Mangia

★ **Palazzo Pubblico**
The graceful Gothic town hall was completed in 1342. At 330 ft (102 m), the bell tower, Torre del Mangia, is the second highest medieval tower ever built in Italy.

Exploring Siena

Once a capital to rival Florence, Siena is Italy's prettiest medieval town, still endowed with the grandeur of the age in which it was at its peak (1260–1348). Begin an exploration of its historic center in Piazza del Campo and the surrounding maze of medieval alleys.

Lorenzetti's *Allegory of Good Government* (1338), Palazzo Pubblico

🏛 Palazzo Pubblico

Piazza del Campo 1. **Tel** 0577 22 62 30. Museo Civico & Torre del Mangia: **Open** daily. 🎨

Although it continues in its ancient role as Siena's town hall, the Palazzo Pubblico's medieval rooms, some decorated with paintings of the Sienese School, are open to the public. The **Museo Civico** is housed here. The main council chamber, or Sala del Mappamondo, is named after a map of the world painted by Ambrogio Lorenzetti in the early 14th century. One wall is covered by Simone Martini's fresco of the *Maestà* (1315), which depicts the Virgin in Majesty as the Queen of Heaven, attended by the Apostles, saints, and angels. Opposite is a fresco (attributed to Simone Martini, but possibly later) of the mercenary *Guidoriccio da Fogliano* (1330). The walls of the chapel alongside are covered with frescoes of the *Life of the Virgin* (1407) by Taddeo di Bartolo, and the choir stalls (1428) are decorated with wooden panels inlaid with biblical scenes. The Sala della Pace contains the famous *Allegory of Good and Bad Government* (1338–40), a pair of frescoes by Ambrogio Lorenzetti. They form one of the most important series of secular paintings from the Middle Ages. In the *Good Government* fresco civic life flourishes, while the *Bad Government*, presided over by a demon, reveals rubbish-strewn streets and ruins.

The Sala del Risorgimento is covered with late 19th-century frescoes illustrating the events leading up to the unification of Italy under King Vittorio Emanuele II.

In the palace courtyard is the entrance to the magnificent **Torre del Mangia**, the palace's huge bell tower. Rising 330 ft (102 m), it is a prominent feature of Siena's skyline. Built by the brothers Muccio and Francesco di Rinaldo between 1338 and 1348, it was named after the first bellringer, whose idleness led to the nickname *Mangiaguadagni* (literally "eat the profits"). There are 505 steps to the top of the tower, which has wonderful views.

🏛 Santuario e Casa di Santa Caterina

Costa di Sant'Antonio. **Tel** 0577 28 81 75. **Open** daily.

Siena's patron saint, Catherine Benincasa (1347–80), was the daughter of a tradesman. At the age of eight she devoted herself to God and had many visions, as well as later receiving the stigmata (wounds of Christ). Like her namesake, St. Catherine of Alexandria, she was believed to have been betrothed to the Christ child in a vision – a scene which inspired many artists. Her eloquence persuaded Pope Gregory XI to return the seat of the papacy to Rome in 1376, after 67 years of exile in Avignon. St. Catherine died in Rome and was canonized in 1461.

Today Catherine's house is surrounded by chapels and cloisters. Among them is the Church of the Crucifixion, which was built in 1623 in her orchard to house the late 12th-century Crucifixion, in front of which she received the stigmata in 1375. The house is decorated with paintings of events from her life by artists including her contemporaries Francesco Vanni and Pietro Sorri.

Cloister of Santuario e Casa di Santa Caterina, birthplace of Siena's patron saint

🏛 Palazzo Piccolomini

Via Banchi di Sotto 52. **Tel** 0577 24 71 45. **Open** Mon–Sat am. **Closed** Aug 1–15.

Siena's most imposing private palazzo was built for the wealthy Piccolomini family in the 1460s by the Florentine architect and sculptor Bernardo Rossellino. It now contains the Sienese state archives, account books, and taxation documents dating back to the 13th century. Some of the leading artists of their day were employed to paint the wooden bindings used to enclose the tax and account records. The paintings, now on display in the Sala di Congresso, often show scenes of Siena itself, bristling with towers, or episodes from the city's past.

Other records include a will attributed to Boccaccio and the council's contract with Jacopo della Quercia for the Fonte Gaia (see p343).

A detail from Martini's *Blessed Agostino Novello* (c.1330)

🏛 Pinacoteca Nazionale

Via San Pietro 29. **Tel** 0577 28 61 43. **Open** daily (Sun & Mon am only).

This fine gallery, which is housed in the 14th-century Palazzo Buonsignori, contains an unsurpassed collection of paintings by artists of the Sienese School. Arranged in chronological order, from the 13th century through to the Mannerist period (1520–1600), highlights include Duccio's *Madonna dei Francescani* (1285) and Simone Martini's masterpiece *The Blessed Agostino Novello and Four of His Miracles* (c.1330). Pietro Lorenzetti's *Two Views*, from the 14th century, are early examples of landscape painting, and Pietro da Domenico's *Adoration of the Shepherds* (1510) shows

The austere exterior of the church of San Domenico (begun 1226)

how the art of Siena remained visibly influenced by its Byzantine roots long after the naturalism of the Renaissance had reached across the rest of Europe.

🏛 San Domenico

Piazza San Domenico. **Open** daily.

The preserved head of the city's patroness, St. Catherine of Siena (1347–80), can be seen in a gilded tabernacle on the altar of a chapel dedicated to her in the huge, barnlike Gothic church of San Domenico (begun 1226). The chapel itself was built in 1460 for this purpose and is dominated by Sodoma's frescoes (1526), to the right and left of the altar, which show Catherine in states of religious fervor and her early life. The church has the only portrait of St. Catherine considered authentic, painted by her friend Andrea Vanni. The fresco by Vanni can be found in the Chapel of the Vaults.

The Sienese Palio

The Palio is Tuscany's most celebrated festival and it occurs in the Campo each year on July 2 and August 16 at 7pm. This special event is a bareback horse race first recorded in 1283, but it may have had its origins in Roman military training. The jockeys represent 10 of Siena's 17 *contrade* (districts); the horses are chosen by the drawing of lots and are blessed at the local *contrada* churches. Preceded by days of colorful pageantry, costume processions, and heavy betting, the races themselves last only 90 seconds each. Thousands of spectators crowd into the piazza to watch the race, and rivalry between competitors is intense. The winner is rewarded with a silk *palio* (banner). Festivities for the winners can last for weeks.

A *contrada* symbol

The Sienese displaying their flag-throwing skills before the Palio

Siena: Duomo

Siena's Duomo (1136–1382) is one of Italy's greatest cathedrals, a spectacular mixture of sculpture, paintings, and Pisan-influenced Romanesque-Gothic architecture. Had 14th-century plans to create a new nave come to fruition, the building would have become the largest church in Christendom. As it happened, the plan came to nothing, abandoned when the plague of 1348 virtually halved the city's population. Among the Duomo's treasures are sculptural masterpieces by Nicola Pisano, Donatello, and Michelangelo, a fine inlaid pavement, and a magnificent fresco cycle by Pinturicchio.

Baptismal Font
This Renaissance font by della Quercia, Ghiberti, and Donatello stands in the Baptistry.

Pulpit Panels
Carved in 1265–8 by Nicola Pisano, with help from Arnolfo di Cambio and his son Giovanni, the panels on the octagonal pulpit depict scenes from the *Life of Christ*.

KEY

① **In the nave** black and white marble pillars support the vault.

② **The Campanile** was added in 1313.

③ **Archway** leading to the Baptistry.

④ **The Museo dell'Opera del Duomo** occupies the side aisle of the unfinished nave, which was roofed over to house the museum.

⑤ **The façade** gives indication of planned size of nave.

⑥ **The unfinished nave**, if completed, would have measured 162 ft (50 m) in length and 97 ft (30 m) in breadth.

⑦ **The doors** were built in 1284–97, the rest of the façade a century later.

⑧ **The north aisle** contains sculptures by Michelangelo of Saints Peter, Pius, Gregory, and Paul (1501–4).

⑨ **Chapel of St. John the Baptist**.

Piccolomini Library
Pinturicchio's frescoes (1509) portray the life of the Piccolomini pope, Pius II. Here he presides at the betrothal of Frederick III to Eleonora of Portugal.

Inlaid Marble Floor
The Massacre of the Innocents is
one of a series of scenes in the
inlaid marble floor. The marble is
usually uncovered during
September each year.

Museo dell'Opera del Duomo

Piazza del Duomo 8. **Tel** 0577 28 63 00.
Open daily; call for opening times.
Part of this museum is devoted
to items removed from the
Duomo, including a tondo of
a *Madonna and Child*, probably
by Donatello, as well as several
badly eroded Gothic statues by
Giovanni Pisano and Jacopo
della Quercia. The highlight
is Duccio's huge *Maestà*
(1308–11), one of the Sienese
School's finest works. It depicts
the Madonna and Child on one
side, and scenes from the Life
of Christ on the other. It was
originally placed on the
Duomo's high altar, where it
replaced the striking *Madonna
of the Large Eyes* (1220–30) by
an anonymous Sienese painter,
also in the museum.

Statues from the Duomo now on show
in the Museo dell'Opera

Fortezza Medicea

Piazza Libertà 1 **Open** daily.
Enoteca: **Tel** 0577 22 88 43.
Open noon–1am Mon–Sat.
This huge red-brick fortress was
built for Cosimo I by Baldassarre
Lanci in 1560, following Siena's
defeat by the Florentines in the
1554–5 war. After an 18-month
siege, during which more than
8,000 Sienese died, the town's
banking and wool industries
were suppressed by the
Florentine masters and all
major building work ended.

The fortress now houses the
Enoteca Italica, offering visitors
the chance both to taste and to
buy quality wines from all over
Italy. There is also a restaurant
on the site.

Entrance to
Duomo

Façade Statues
Many façade statues have been
replaced by copies; the originals
are in the Museo dell'Opera
del Duomo.

⚫ Street by Street: San Gimignano

The 13 towers that dominate San Gimignano's skyline were built by noble families in the 12th and 13th centuries, when the town's position – on the main pilgrim route from northern Europe to Rome – brought it great prosperity. The plague of 1348, and the diversion of the pilgrim route, led to its decline as well as its preservation. Today only one of the towers, the Torre Grossa, is open. San Gimignano is rich in works of art as well as good shops and restaurants, although many close from November to March.

San Gimignano's famous skyline, almost unchanged since the Middle Ages

The Museo Civico provides access to the tallest of the town's 13 remaining towers.

Collegiata
This 11th-century church's interior is full of frescoes, including *The Creation* (1367) by Bartolo di Fredi.

Palazzo del Popolo
The council chamber of the town hall (1288–1323) features a large *Maestà* (1317) by Lippo Memmi.

The Annunciation by Ghirlandaio
This painting, completed in 1482, is located in a courtyard loggia alongside the Collegiata.

Via San Giovanni is lined with shops selling local goods.

Bus station
Museo San Gimignano 1300

VISITORS' CHECKLIST

Practical Information
Siena. 7,000. Piazza del
Duomo 1 (0577 94 00 08).
Thu. Patron saints' festivals:
Jan 31 San Gimignano & Mar 12
Santa Fina; varying dates in Feb:
Carnival; 1st Sun in Aug: Fiera
di Santa Fina; Aug 29: Fiera di
Sant'Agostino; Sep 8: Festa della
Madonna di Panacole.
W sangimignano.com

Transportation
Porta San Giovanni.

Among the **Piazza del Duomo's**
historic buildings is the Palazzo
Vecchio del Podestà (1239),
whose tower is probably the
town's oldest.

Piazza della Cisterna
This square
is named after
the well at
its center and is
the heart of
the old town.

Key
— Suggested route

0 meters   250
0 yards   250

🏛 Museo Civico
Palazzo del Popolo, Piazza del Duomo.
Tel 0577 99 03 12. Museum & tower:
Open daily. **Closed** Jan 1, Jan 31,
Dec 25.

Frescoes in the courtyard of
this museum feature the coats
of arms of city mayors and
magistrates, as well as a
14th-century *Virgin and Child*
by Taddeo di Bartolo.
   The first room is the Sala di
Dante, where an inscription
recalls a visit by the poet in
1300. The floor above has an
art collection, which includes
excellent works by Pinturicchio,
Bartolo di Fredi, Benozzo
Gozzoli, and Filippino Lippi. The
famous *Wedding Scene* frescoes
by Memmo di Filippucci (early
14th century) show a couple
sharing a bath and going to
bed – an unusual record of life
in 14th-century Tuscany.

🏛 Collegiata
Piazza del Duomo. **Open** daily.
This 12th-century Romanesque
church contains a feast of
frescoes. In the north
aisle the frescoes
comprise 26 episodes
from the Old
Testament (1367) by
Bartolo di Fredi.
The opposite wall
features scenes from
the *Life of Christ* (1333–
41) by Lippo Memmi,
while at the back of the church
there are scenes from the
Last Judgment painted by
Taddeo di Bartolo.

Bartolo di Fredi's *Christ*,
Sant'Agostino

The ceiling of the Collegiata, painted
with gold stars

🏛 Sant'Agostino
Piazza Sant'Agostino. **Open** daily.
Consecrated in 1298, this
church has a simple façade,
contrasting markedly with the
heavily decorated Rococo
interior (c.1740) by Vanvitelli.
Above the main altar is the
Coronation of the Virgin by
Piero del Pollaiuolo, dated
1483. The choir is covered in
a cycle of frescoes of *The Life
of St. Augustine* (1465) executed
by the Florentine artist
Benozzo Gozzoli.

🏛 Museo San
Gimignano 1300
Via San Giovanni 50.
Tel 0577 94 10 78. **Open**
9am–7pm daily.

This museum houses
a reconstruction of
San Gimignano as
it was during the 13th
and 14th centuries. The
exhibits have been made entirely
by hand and include 72 "tower
houses," symbols of the city's
power during the Middle Ages.

Fresco from the early 14th-century *Wedding Scene* cycle by Memmo di Filippucci
in the Museo Civico

㉘ Elba

Livorno. 🔼 30,000. 🚢 Portoferraio.
🚌 *i* Calata Italia 26 (0565 91 46 71).
🍴 Portoferraio: Fri.

Elba's most famous resident was Napoleon, who spent nine months here after the fall of Paris in 1814. Today Italy's third largest island is mainly populated by vacationers, who come by ferry from Piombino, 6 miles (10 km) away on the mainland. The main town is Portoferraio, with an old port and a modern seafront of hotels and fish restaurants.

The landscape of the island is varied. On the west coast, which tends to be a little quieter, there are sandy beaches suitable for all water sports. The east coast, centered on the town of Porto Azzurro, the island's second port, is more rugged, with high cliffs and stony beaches. Inland, olive groves and vineyards line hillsides, and vegetation covers the mountains. A good way to see the interior is to take the road from Marciana Marina to the old medieval village of Marciana Alta. Close by, a minor road leads to a cable car that runs to Monte Capanne (3,300 ft/1,018 m), a magnificent viewpoint.

Marciana Marina on Elba

㉙ Sovana

Grosseto. 🔼 100. *i* Piazza Busatti 8 (0564 63 30 99).

Sovana is one of southern Tuscany's prettiest villages. Its single little street ends in Piazza del Pretorio, home to the ancient church of Santa Maria,

View over Pitigliano and the town's dramatic cliffs and caves

which contains frescoes and a 9th-century altar canopy. A lane beyond leads through olive groves to the Romanesque Duomo, filled with reliefs and carvings from an earlier church on the site. Some fine Etruscan tombs lie in the surrounding countryside, many of them clearly marked and easily visited from the village.

㉛ Maremma

Grosseto. *i* Maremma Centro Visite, Alberese (0564 40 70 98). Marginal Areas: 🚌 to entrances from Alberese. **Open** daily. 🎫 🅿️ Inner Park Areas: 🚌 from Alberese to tour departure point. **Open** 8:30am–2pm daily. 🅿️
🌐 **parcomaremma.it**

The Etruscans, followed by the Romans, were the first to cultivate the marshes and low hills of the Maremma. Following the collapse of the Roman Empire, however, the area fell prey to flooding and malaria, twin scourges that left it virtually uninhabited until the 18th century. The land has since been reclaimed, the irrigation canals unblocked, and farming developed on the fertile soil. The stunning Parco Naturale della Maremma was set up in 1975 to preserve the area's native flora and fauna, and to prevent development on one of Italy's few pristine stretches of coastline. Entrance to much of the park is restricted to access on foot or by a park bus from Alberese. Other areas more on the borders of the park, however, such as the excellent beach at Marina di Alberese and the countryside around Talamone in the south, are easier to see.

㉚ Pitigliano

Grosseto. 🔼 4,400. 🚌 *i* Piazza Garibaldi 51 (0564 61 71 11). 🍴 Wed.

Pitigliano is spectacularly situated high above the cave-riddled cliffs of the Lente valley. Its maze of tiny medieval streets includes a small Jewish ghetto, formed in the 17th century by Jews fleeing from Catholic persecution.

Irrigated salt marsh

Beaches

The Ombrone estuary is a mixture of pines, marsh, and dunes and is home to birds such as the flamingo, sea eagle, roller, and bee-eater.

Key

══ Roads
══ Paths
══ Canals and rivers
── Itineraries

0 kilometers   2
0 miles   1

The **Palazzo Orsini** has its water supply brought in by an impressive aqueduct, built in 1545. It houses the **Museo di Palazzo Orsini** with its exhibit of painted, engraved, and sculptured works dating from the 14th century. Within the display are pieces by local artist Francesco Zuccarelli (1702–88). He also painted two of the altarpieces in the **Duomo** in Piazza San Gregorio. The **Museo Etrusco** contains finds from ancient local settlements.

🏛 **Museo di Palazzo Orsini**
Piazza della Fortezza Orsini 4. **Tel** 0564 78 85 20. **Open** 10am–1pm, 3–7pm Tue–Fri (to 5pm in winter). 🎫
🏛 **Museo Etrusco**
Piazza della Fortezza Orsini 59. **Tel** 0564 61 40 67. **Open** 10am–6pm daily (call for winter times). 🎫

𝟛𝟚 Monte Argentario

Grosseto. 🏔 13,000. 🚌 🛈 Piazzale Sant'Andrea, Porto Santo Stefano (0564 81 42 08). 📅 Tue.

Monte Argentario was an island until the early 1700s, when the shallow waters separating it from the mainland began to silt up, creating two sandy spits of land, known as *tomboli*, which enclose the Orbetello lagoon. Today the lagoon hosts a beautiful nature reserve. **Orbetello** itself, a lively and relatively unspoiled little town, was linked to the island in 1842, when a dyke was constructed from the mainland. The harbor towns of **Porto Ercole** and **Porto Santo Stefano** are upmarket resorts, busy with

Porto Ercole, Monte Argentario

visitors in summer. Interior roads – notably the Strada Panoramica – offer peaceful drives past rocky coves and bays.

Entry tickets are sold at Alberese's park headquarters.

Wild Boar
The most impressive of the Maremma's many wild animals is the indigenous wild boar, a smaller creature than the Eastern European boar found elsewhere in Tuscany.

San Rabano, a ruined Cistercian abbey (12th century), is close to the park's highest point.

Pine nuts for cooking are still collected from the park's woodlands.

The Uccellina Hills are crowned by old Spanish watchtowers, pinewoods, and scented *macchia*.

Birds of prey, such as the hobby and peregrine, hunt in more remote parts of the park.

Unspoiled coastline

Marked Footpaths
Several gentle footpaths are marked around the park, but in practice you can wander almost at will among most of its dunes and pinewoods.

This fishing village is set against pretty countryside.

UMBRIA

Long dismissed as Tuscany's "gentler sister," Umbria has finally emerged from the shadow of its more famous western neighbor. Forming an expanse of gentle pastoral countryside and high mountain wilderness, the picturesque region has been dubbed the "Green Heart of Italy." Umbria is also well-known for the beauty and profusion of its medieval hill towns.

The region was inhabited in the 8th century BC by the Umbrians, a peaceable farming tribe, and later colonized by the Etruscans and Romans. In the Middle Ages, the Lombards established a dukedom centered around Spoleto. By the 13th century much of the region was scattered with independent city-states, most of them eventually absorbed by the Papal States, where they remained until Italian unification in 1860.

Today the old towns are Umbria's chief glory. In Perugia, the region's capital, and the smaller centers of Gubbio, Montefalco, and Todi, there are numerous Romanesque churches, civic palaces, vivid fresco cycles, and endless medieval nooks and crannies. Spoleto, renowned for its summer arts festival, blends grandiose medieval monuments with Roman remains and some of Italy's oldest churches. The surrounding Vale of Spoleto is a checkerboard of agricultural countryside and fascinating traditional villages.

Assisi, the birthplace of St. Francis, contains the Basilica di San Francesco, frescoed in part by Giotto. At Orvieto, magnificently situated on its volcanic crag, there are Etruscan remains and one of Italy's finest Romanesque-Gothic cathedrals.

Umbria's oak woods, ice-clear streams, and rich soils yield many delicacies. Chief among these are trout and truffles, olive oils to rival those of Tuscany, prized lentils from Castelluccio, cured meats from Norcia, and tangy mountain cheeses. A variety of well-regarded wines are produced from the vineyards of Torgiano and Montefalco.

A shop in Norcia selling a selection of Italy's finest hams, sausages, and salamis

◄ One of the ceilings in the Palazzo Pianetti, a flamboyant building in the town of Jesi

Exploring Umbria

Assisi and Spoleto, Umbria's loveliest towns, are the most convenient and charming bases for exploring the region. Both these medieval gems are unmissable, as is the old center of Perugia, the region's capital, and the alluring hill towns of Orvieto, Gubbio, Spello, Montefalco, and Todi. Umbria's landscapes are as compelling as its towns, from the eerie wastes of the Piano Grande and the mountain splendor of the Monti Sibillini national park (best reached from Norcia) to the gentler countryside of the Valnerina and the beach-fringed shores of Lake Trasimeno.

Sights at a Glance

- ❶ Gubbio
- ❷ *Assisi pp358–9*
- ❸ Perugia
- ❹ Lake Trasimeno
- ❺ Orvieto
- ❻ Todi
- ❼ Spoleto
- ❽ Montefalco
- ❾ Spello
- ❿ Monti Sibillini
- ⓫ Norcia
- ⓬ Valnerina

Olive harvest in the Umbrian countryside near Orvieto

Getting Around

Excellent road, railroad, and bus links exist in the region. The A1 from Florence passes Orvieto, which is linked to Todi by the S448. The S75 connects Perugia, Assisi, and Spello, then the S3 continues to Trevi, Spoleto, and Terni. Rome–Florence trains serve Orvieto, and Rome–Ancona trains serve Spoleto, with branch lines connecting Perugia, Spello, and Assisi.

For additional map symbols *see back flap*

The hill town of Castelluccio, east of Norcia, and the Monti Sibillini

A side street in the medieval town of Gubbio in northern Umbria

Key

━━━ Highway

━━━ Major road

━━ Secondary road

⋯⋯ Minor road

━━ Scenic route

┅┅ Main railroad

── Minor railroad

── Regional border

△ Summit

0 kilometers 25

0 miles 15

❶ Gubbio

Perugia. 🚹 33,000. 🚆 Fossato di Vico-Gubbio. 🚌 ℹ️ Via della Repubblica 15 (075 922 06 93). 🛒 Tue.

Gubbio vies with Assisi for the title of Umbria's most medieval town. The beauty of its twisting streets and terracotta-tiled houses is enhanced by the forest-swathed Apennines. Founded by the Umbrians in the 3rd century BC as Tota Ikuvina, it assumed greater prominence in the 1st century AD as a Roman colony (Eugubium). It emerged as an independent commune in the 11th century, having spread up the slopes of Monte Ingino. From 1387 to 1508 Gubbio was ruled from Urbino by the Dukes of Montefeltro.

The 13th-century **Duomo** is distinguished by a wagon-vaulted ceiling whose curved arches symbolize hands in prayer. Medieval Via dei Consoli leads to the 13th-century **Palazzo del Bargello** – a stone-faced building formerly the headquarters of the chief of police. Also here is the **Fontana dei Matti** (Fountain of the Mad), named after the idea that anyone who walks around it three times will go insane.

Macabre legends surround the walled-up **Porte della Morte** (Doors of Death) that can be seen in Via dei Consoli and elsewhere in the town. Reputedly used for the passage of coffins from houses, the doors, once tainted, were sealed and never used again. Their purpose was probably defensive. In the lower town, the church of **San Francesco** (1259–82) is known for 17 faded frescoes showing scenes from the *Life of the Virgin* (1408–13) by Ottaviano Nelli. Opposite is the **Tiratoio** (Weavers' Loggia). Wool was stretched out to dry in its shady arcade. West of here are the ruins of a 1st-century AD Roman amphitheater.

🏛 Palazzo dei Consoli

Piazza Grande. **Tel** 075 927 42 98. **Open** 10am–1pm, 3–6pm daily (Nov–Mar: 10am–1pm, 2:30–5:30pm). **Closed** Jan 1, May 13–15, Dec 25. 🖼

Dominating the skyline of Gubbio is this mighty civic palace, begun in 1332 by Gattapone. Its Salone dell'Arengo houses the Museo Civico, best known for the Eugubine Tablets (250–150 BC). Discovered in 1444, the seven bronze slabs are inscribed with Etruscan and Roman characters, probably a phonetic translation of prayers and rituals from the ancient Umbrian and Etruscan languages. Upstairs, a small art gallery contains works by local painters.

One of the Eugubine Tablets in Gubbio

🏛 Palazzo Ducale

Via Federico da Montefeltro. **Tel** 075 927 58 72. **Open** 8:30am–7pm Tue–Sun. **Closed** Jan 1, Dec 25. 🖼 ♿

Attributed to Francesco di Giorgio Martini, this palace was built in 1470 for the Montefeltro as a copy of the family home in Urbino (*see pp374–5*). It also has a pretty Renaissance courtyard.

Façade of the Palazzo dei Consoli in Gubbio

The interior of Perugia's San Pietro, rebuilt in the 15th century

❷ Assisi

See pp358–9.

❸ Perugia

🚹 160,000. 🚆 🚌 Piazza Vittorio Veneto. ℹ️ Piazza Matteotti 18 (075 573 64 58). 🛒 Tue, Sat. 🌐 turismo. comune.perugia.it

Perugia's old center hinges around the pedestrianized Corso Vannucci, named after the local painter Pietro Vannucci (Perugino). At its northern end is Piazza IV Novembre, dominated by the **Fontana Maggiore**, a 13th-century fountain by Nicola and Giovanni Pisano. To the rear rises the 15th-century **Duomo**, its entrance flanked by a statue of Pope Julius II (1555) and a pulpit built for Siena's San Bernardino (1425). Its Cappella del Santo Anello contains the Virgin's "wedding ring," a weighty piece of agate said to change color according to the character of the person wearing it. The third pillar in the south nave holds a Renaissance painting of the *Madonna delle Grazie* by Giannicola di Paolo. The figure is credited with miraculous powers, and mothers bring newly baptized children to kneel before it. Buried in the transepts are Popes Urban IV and Martin IV.

Away from the Corso is the **Oratorio di San Bernardino** (1457–61) on Piazza San Francesco, with a colorful façade by Agostino di Duccio.

Beyond the old city walls on Borgo XX Giugno stands **San Pietro**. Founded in the 10th century and rebuilt in 1463, the best feature of the fine interior is the wooden choir (1526).

Piazza Giordano Bruno is home to **San Domenico** (1305–1632), Umbria's largest church, which is known for the Gothic tomb of Benedict XI (c.1304) and decoration by Agostino di Duccio.

🏛 Museo Archeologico Nazionale dell'Umbria

San Domenico, Piazza Giordano Bruno 10. **Tel** 075 572 71 41. **Open** daily. **Closed** Jan 1, May 1, Dec 25. 🅿 ♿

Housed in the cloisters of San Domenico, this museum exhibits prehistoric, Etruscan, and Roman artifacts.

🏛 Palazzo dei Priori

Corso Vannucci 19. **Tel** 075 573 64 58. **Open** daily (Sun: am only). **Closed** Jan 1, May 1, Dec 25, & 1st Mon each month. ♿ Collegio del Cambio: **Open** daily.

The monumental walls and bristling crenellations of this palace mark it as Umbria's finest public building (*see pp58–9*). Among its fine rooms is the Sala dei Notari (c.1295), the former lawyers' hall, vividly frescoed with scenes from the Old Testament – the work of a follower of Pietro Cavallini. The doorway is guarded by a pair of large bronzes made in 1274: a Guelph lion, and a griffin, the medieval emblem of

Medieval street in Perugia

Perugia. The Sala di Udienza del Collegio della Mercanzia, built around 1390, was formerly used by the Merchants' Guild. This room is late Gothic in style, with exquisite paneling and 15th-century inlaid wood.

Also in the palace is the **Collegio del Cambio**, Perugia's former money exchange, which was begun in 1452. This room was used by the Bankers' Guild. Its walls are covered with superlative frescoes (1498–1500) by Perugino, works devoted to Classical and religious scenes. A glum self-portrait scowls down from the center of the left wall, while the hand of Perugino's pupil Raphael may be evident in some panels on the right wall.

Colorful façade of Perugia's Oratorio di San Bernardino

Entrance of Palazzo dei Priori, Perugia

🏛 Galleria Nazionale dell'Umbria

Palazzo dei Priori, Corso Vannucci 19. **Tel** 075 58 66 84 10. **Open** Tue–Sun. **Closed** Jan 1, May 1, Dec 25. 🅿 ♿

Umbria's greatest collection of paintings is displayed here on the third floor of the palace. Most of the works are 13th- to 18th-century paintings by local artists, but the highlights are altarpieces by Piero della Francesca and Fra Angelico.

❹ Lake Trasimeno

Perugia. 🚆 🚌 Castiglione del Lago. ℹ Piazza Mazzini 10, Castiglione del Lago (075 965 24 84). 🆆 regioneumbria.eu

Edged with low hills, this is Italy's fourth-largest lake. Its miles of placid water and reed-lined shores have a tranquil, melancholy beauty.

Drainage of the lake began under the Romans, but today the lake is gently drying up of its own accord. The town of **Castiglione del Lago**, jutting out on a fortified promontory, has an easygoing atmosphere and small sandy beaches. The 16th-century **castle** is used for summer concerts. The church of **Santa Maria Maddalena**, begun in 1836, has a fine *Madonna and Child* (c.1500) by Eusebio di San Giorgio.

Like Castiglione, **Passignano sul Trasimeno** offers boat trips to **Isola Maggiore**. The island's charming village is known for lace-making.

The battle of Lake Trasimeno

In 217 BC the Romans suffered one of their worst ever military defeats on the shores of Lake Trasimeno. The Carthaginian general, Hannibal, lured the Romans (who were led by the consul Flaminius) into a masterful ambush close to present-day Ossaia (Place of Bones) and Sanguineto (Place of Blood). Some 16,000 legionaries perished, hacked down on the lake's marshy fringes. Hannibal, by contrast, lost only 1,500 men. Today you can explore the battlefield, which includes over 100 mass graves found near Tuoro sul Trasimeno.

19th-century engraving of General Hannibal

Assisi: Basilica di San Francesco

The burial place of St. Francis, this basilica was begun in 1228, two years after the saint's death. Over the next century its Upper and Lower Churches were decorated by the foremost artists of their day, among them Cimabue, Simone Martini, Pietro Lorenzetti, and Giotto, whose frescoes on the *Life of St. Francis* are some of the most renowned in Italy. The basilica, which dominates Assisi, is one of the great Christian shrines and receives vast numbers of pilgrims throughout the year.

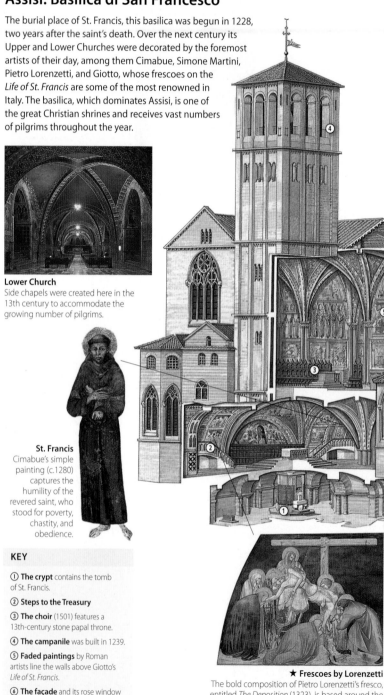

Lower Church
Side chapels were created here in the 13th century to accommodate the growing number of pilgrims.

St. Francis
Cimabue's simple painting (c.1280) captures the humility of the revered saint, who stood for poverty, chastity, and obedience.

KEY

① **The crypt** contains the tomb of St. Francis.

② **Steps to the Treasury**

③ **The choir** (1501) features a 13th-century stone papal throne.

④ **The campanile** was built in 1239.

⑤ **Faded paintings** by Roman artists line the walls above Giotto's *Life of St. Francis*.

⑥ **The façade** and its rose window are early examples of Italian Gothic.

★ **Frescoes by Lorenzetti**
The bold composition of Pietro Lorenzetti's fresco, entitled *The Deposition* (1323), is based around the truncated Cross, focusing attention on the twisted figure of Christ.

Upper Church
The soaring Gothic lines of the 13th-century Upper Church symbolized the heavenly glory of St. Francis. This style also influenced later Franciscan churches.

VISITORS' CHECKLIST

Practical Information
Piazza San Francesco. **Tel** 075 819 00 84. **Open** 6am–5:45pm daily (Lower Church: from 8:30am). Longer hours Sun & summer.
🚻 ♿ 🌐 sanfrancescoassisi.org

Transportation
🚌 FS

Entrance to Upper Church

Entrance to Lower Church

★ **Frescoes by Giotto**
The Ecstasy of St. Francis is one of 28 panels that make up Giotto's cycle on the *Life of St. Francis* (c.1290–95).

★ **Cappella di San Martino**
The frescoes in this chapel on the *Life of St. Martin* (1315) are by the Sienese painter Simone Martini. This panel shows the *Death of the Saint*. Martini was also responsible for the fine stained glass in the chapel.

❷ Assisi

Perugia. 🅰 25,000. FS 🚌 ℹ Piazza del Comune 22 (075 81 25 34). 🗓 Sat. 🌐 conoscerelumbria. regioneumbria.eu

This beautiful medieval town, with its geranium-hung streets, lovely views, and fountain-splashed piazzas, is heir to the legacy of St. Francis (c.1181–1226), who is buried in the **Basilica di San Francesco**. Sadly, the town suffered serious damage during the earthquake of September 1997, but restoration was relatively swift – completed in approximately two years. The tourist office can give information on which sights are open to visitors.

Piazza del Comune, Assisi's main square, is dominated by the columns of the **Tempio di Minerva**, a Roman temple-front from the Augustan age. The Palazzo Comunale, opposite, is home to the **Pinacoteca Comunale**, an art gallery with works by local medieval artists.

Down Corso Mazzini lies the **Basilica di Santa Chiara**, the burial place of St. Clare – Francis's companion and the founder of the Poor Clares (an order of nuns). One of its chapels contains the crucifix that is said to have bowed its head and ordered Francis to "Repair God's church." It came from **San Damiano**, a sublime church set amid olive groves south of the Porta Nuova.

The **Duomo (San Rufino)**, built during the 12th and 13th centuries, has a superb Romanesque façade. Inside is a small museum of paintings, and there are archaeological items in the crypt. From the Duomo, Via Maria delle Rose leads to the **Rocca Maggiore** (rebuilt in 1367), an evocative if much-restored castle.

Thirteenth-century **San Pietro**, on Piazza San Pietro, is a simple and carefully restored Romanesque church. The nearby **Oratorio dei Pellegrini**, a 15th-century pilgrims' hospice, contains well-preserved frescoes by Matteo da Gualdo.

Giotto's fresco, *St. Francis Appearing to the Friars at Arles* (c.1295), in the Basilica di San Francesco, Assisi ▶

⑤ Orvieto

Terni. 🚗 22,000. 🚈 🚌 ℹ️ Piazza Duomo 24 (0763 34 17 72). 🕑 Thu & Sat. 🌐 orvietoonline.com

Perched on a a 984-ft (300-m) plateau, Orvieto looks down over a vineyard-spotted plain. Visitors flood into the town to admire the **Duomo**, among the greatest of Italy's Romanesque-Gothic cathedrals.

The tiny 14th-century church of **San Lorenzo in Arari** is at the end of Via Scalza. Its walls feature frescoes describing the martyrdom of St. Lawrence, who was grilled to death. The altar is made from an Etruscan sacrificial slab. Via Malabranca leads to **San Giovenale** at Orvieto's western tip, a church that is beautifully and almost completely covered in detailed frescoes from the 15th and 16th centuries. It offers broad views over the surrounding countryside. **Sant'Andrea**, in Piazza della Repubblica, is distinguished by a curious 12-sided campanile, part of the original 12th-century building.

🏛️ Museo dell' Opera del Duomo & Museo d'Arte Moderna "Emilio Greco"

Piazza Duomo. **Tel** 0763 34 35 92. **Open** Apr–Oct: 9:30am–7pm daily; Nov–Mar: 9:30am–1pm, 2:30–5pm Wed–Mon. 🔲 🌐 opsm.it

The Museo dell'Opera del Duomo is an interesting little museum containing an eclectic collection of treasures given to the Duomo. Among the highlights are paintings by Lorenzo Maitani (died 1330) and sculptures by Andrea Pisano (c.1270–1348).

The "Emilio Greco" museum is devoted to the modern Sicilian sculptor Emilio Greco, who made the bronze doors (1964–70) of the Duomo in Orvieto.

View into the Pozzo di San Patrizio in Orvieto

🏛️ Museo Archeologico Faina & Museo Civico

Piazza Duomo 29. **Tel** 0763 34 10 39. **Open** daily. **Closed** Mon am, Jan 1, Dec 24–26. 🔲 🎫 ♿

The first of these two museums has a well-known, low-key collection of Etruscan remains, including many Greek vases that were found in Etruscan tombs in the surrounding area. The Museo Civico contains ancient Greek artifacts and Etruscan copies of Greek works.

🏛️ Duomo of Orvieto

Piazza Duomo. **Tel** 0763 34 11 67. **Open** daily. ♿

Some 300 years in the building, Orvieto's Duomo (begun 1290), with its breathtaking façade, is one of Italy's greatest cathedrals. It was inspired by the Miracle of Bolsena in which real blood from a consecrated host supposedly fell on the altar cloth of a church in nearby Bolsena.

Carved choir stalls

The exterior is characterized by horizontal bands of white travertine and blue-gray basalt.

Cappella Nuova

14th-century rose window by Orcagna

The reliquary of the Corporal contains the altar cloth from Bolsena.

Cappella del Corporale
This chapel contains Lippo Memmi's *Madonna dei Raccomandati* (1320). There are also frescoes (1357–64) by Ugolino di Prete Ilario of the *Miracle of Bolsena* and *Miracles of the Sacrament.*

Bronze doors (1964–70) by Emilio Greco

⊞ Pozzo di San Patrizio

Viale San Gallo. **Tel** 0763 34 37 68.
Open daily. 🖼 allows entry at Museo
d'Arte Moderna.

This well was commissioned in
1527 by Pope Clement VII and
designed by the Florentine
architect Antonio da Sangallo to
provide the town with a water
supply in case of attack. Two
248-step staircases drop into its
dank interior, cleverly arranged
as a double helix (spiral) so as
not to intersect. The 203-ft (62-m)
shaft took 10 years to complete.

⋒ Necropoli Etrusca – Crocefisso del Tufo

Strada Statale 71 to Orvieto Scalo,
km 1,600. **Tel** 0763 34 36 11. **Open**
8:30am–7pm (Oct–Mar: to 5pm) daily.
Closed Jan 1, May 1, Dec 25. 🖼 ♿

This Etruscan necropolis from
the 6th century BC has burial
chambers built of blocks of tufa.
Etruscan letters, thought to be
the names of the deceased, are
inscribed on the tombs.

Cappella Nuova

Luca Signorelli's great fresco cycle
of the *Last Judgment* (1499–1504)
features prominently in this chapel.
Fra Angelico and Benozzo Gozzoli
worked here before Signorelli.

The Façade

There are detailed carvings
(c.1320–30) at the base of its four
main pilasters. By Lorenzo Maitani,
they depict scenes from the Old
and New Testaments, including
hell and damnation.

View of the hill town of Todi in
southern Umbria

❻ Todi

Perugia. 🗺 17,000. 🚉 🚌 🈺 Piazza
del Popolo 38 (075 894 54 16). 🛒 Sat.

Looking down over the Tiber
valley from its hilltop eyrie, Todi
is one of the most strikingly
situated of Umbria's famous
hill towns. An ancient Etruscan,
and then Roman, settlement,
it still preserves an uncorrupted
medieval air, with several tiny
churches, three austere
public palaces, and many
sleepy corners.

Most people are drawn here
by the **Piazza del Popolo**, the
main square, flanked by the
lovely plain-faced **Duomo**. Built
in the 13th century on the site
of a Roman temple to Apollo, it
has a dusky interior and one of
Umbria's finest choirs (1521–30).
Note Ferraù da Faenza's
huge painting (1596) on
the rear wall, a less than
totally successful copy of
Michelangelo's *Last Judgment*,
and the altarpiece at the end of
the right aisle by Giannicola di
Paolo (a follower of Perugino).

Also flanking the piazza are
the **Palazzo dei Priori** (1293–
1337) and the linked **Palazzo
del Capitano** (1290) and
Palazzo del Popolo
(1213). In the
Palazzo del Capitano,
distinguished by
its redoubtable
medieval interior, lies
the **Museo Etrusco-
Romano**. The
museum contains a
collection of local
Etruscan and Roman
artifacts. There are

altarpieces and sacred objects
in the **Pinacoteca Comunale**,
also housed in the palace.

A few steps from the piazza
rises **San Fortunato** (1292–
1462), named after Todi's first
bishop, with a florid Gothic
doorway (1415–58). The high
vaulted plan is based on
German Gothic "hall" churches
and the "barn" churches of
Tuscany, characterized by a low-
pitched vault, polygonal apse
and naves, and aisles of equal
height. The choir (1590) is
superb, but the church's most
famous work is a *Madonna and
Child* (1432) by Masolino da
Panicale (fourth chapel on the
right). The crypt contains the
tomb of Jacopone da Todi
(c.1228–1306), a noted medieval
poet and mystic.

To the right of the church are
some shady gardens, from
which a path (past the tiny
castle) drops through the trees
to emerge in front of **Santa
Maria della Consolazione**
(1508–1607), near the N79.
One of central Italy's finest
Renaissance churches, and
based on a Greek cross, it may
have been built to a plan by
Bramante. The stark, chill interior
is overshadowed by the
harmonious exterior.

⊞ Museo Etrusco-Romano and Pinacoteca Comunale

Palazzi Comunali. **Tel** 075 895 61.
Open Tue–Sun. 🖼 ♿

Santa Maria della Consolazione in Todi

❼ Spoleto

Perugia. 🚶 38,000. 🚆 🚍 🛈 Piazza della Libertà 7 (0743 21 86 20 or 21 86 21). 🗓 Fri. 🌐 regioneumbria.eu

Founded by the Umbrians, Spoleto was one of central Italy's most important Roman colonies, a prominence maintained by the Lombards, who in the 7th century made it the capital of one of their three Italian dukedoms. After a spell as an independent city-state, in 1354 Spoleto fell to the papacy.

Spoleto, within its wooded setting, is the loveliest of the Umbrian hill towns. Its urbane atmosphere is enhanced by its superb monuments and by the Festival dei Due Mondi, one of Europe's leading arts festivals, held annually in June and July.

At the southern end of Piazza del Mercato is the **Arco di**

Druso, a 1st-century AD Roman arch. It is flanked by the church of **Sant'Ansano**, whose crypt is covered in frescoes that may date from the 6th century. Via Aurelio Saffi, at the piazza's northern end, leads to **Sant'Eufemia**. This utterly simple 10th-century Romanesque church is known for its *matroneum* (women's gallery), once used to segregate the congregation.

A short way beyond, the fan-shaped Piazza del Duomo opens out to reveal Spoleto's 12th-century **Duomo**, graced with an elegant Romanesque façade. Filling the apse of the Baroque interior is a great fresco cycle. The final work of Fra Lippo Lippi, from 1467–9, it describes episodes from the *Life of the Virgin*. The Cappella Erioli is adorned with Pinturicchio's unfinished *Madonna and Child* (1497).

The best of the exceptional churches in the lower town is 4th-century **San Salvatore**, located in the main cemetery, a spot suited to the church's eerie sense of antiquity. Nearby stands **San Ponziano**, fronted by a captivating three-tiered Romanesque façade typical of Umbria.

Façade of San Pietro in Spoleto

It has a 10th-century crypt, supported by odd little columns and decorated with Byzantine frescoes.

Romanesque **San Gregorio** in Piazza Garibaldi dates from 1069, but its cramped façade and stolid campanile incorporate fragments of Roman buildings. Inside is a raised presbytery and a lovely multi-columned crypt. Well-preserved patches of fresco dot the walls. Some 10,000 Christian martyrs are supposedly buried near the church. They were reputedly slaughtered in the town's Roman **amphitheater**, traces of which can be seen in the barracks on Via del Anfiteatro.

🌉 Ponte delle Torri

This magnificent 14th-century aqueduct, the "bridge of towers," is 262 ft (80 m) high. Designed by Gattapone (from Gubbio), it is the town's single most famous monument.

Ponte delle Torri, Spoleto

Romanesque churces in Umbria

Umbria's church-building tradition had its roots in ancient Roman basilicas and in the chapels built over the shrines of its many saints and martyrs. The region's Romanesque façades are usually divided into three tiers, often with three rose windows arranged above a trio of arched portals. The three doors usually correspond to the interior's nave and two aisles, which derive from the simple barnlike plan of Roman basilicas. Inside, the presbytery is often raised in order to allow for the building of a crypt, which usually contained the relics of a saint or martyr. Many of the churches took centuries to build, or were repeatedly modified over time, often acquiring elements of Gothic, Baroque, or Renaissance styles.

San Lorenzo di Arari in Orvieto takes its name from an Etruscan altar (*arari*). This 14th-century church has a very simple façade (*see p362*).

12th-century campanile

Renaissance portico

Spoleto's Duomo (1198) has eight rose windows, a mosaic (1207), and a Renaissance portico (1491). The tower was built from old Roman remains.

From the bridge, there are views of the bastions of the **Rocca Albornoz**, a huge papal fortress built in 1359–64, also by Gattapone. Across the bridge a path leads to the Strada di Monteluco and the church of **San Pietro**, famous for the fascinating 12th-century carvings on its façade.

Rocca Albornoz
Piazza Campello 1. **Tel** 0743 22 49 52.
Open daily. required.

Museo del Tessile e del Costume
Via delle Terme. **Tel** 0743 459 40.
Open Thu–Sun (Sat–Sun in winter).
Closed Jan 1, Dec 25.

Among the exhibits in this exquisite collection are sacred vestments complete with headgear, ties, and gold chains, and a series of 17th-century tapestries that once belonged to Queen Christina of Sweden.

❽ Montefalco

Perugia. 4,900. Mon.

Montefalco, whose name (Falcon's Mount) draws inspiration from its lofty position and sweeping views, is the best of the fascinating villages in the Vale of Spoleto. Crisscrossed by streets almost too narrow for cars, it takes less than five minutes to walk through the village. Yet you might happily spend a morning here, most of it in the polished **Museo Civico** housed

A panel from Gozzoli's fresco cycle (1452) in Montefalco's Museo Civico

in the former church of San Francesco. Its highlight is Benozzo Gozzoli's *Life of St. Francis* (1452), a radiant fresco cycle that borrows heavily from Giotto's cycle in Assisi *(see pp358–61)*. Other painters represented here are Perugino, Tiberio d'Assisi, and Nicolò Alunno, all leading medieval Umbrian artists.

The simple Gothic church of **Sant'Agostino** (begun 1279) on Corso Mameli is dotted with frescoes from the 14th–16th centuries. The church also contains three mummies.

In the main square local wines on sale include the rich, red Sagrantino di Montefalco. Just outside the town walls, the church of **Sant'Illuminata** is covered with charming frescoes, the work of the local 16th-century artist

Francesco Melanzio. About 1 mile (2 km) beyond, the prettily situated church of **San Fortunato** is decorated with frescoes by Gozzoli and Tiberio d'Assisi.

Environs
The village in the Vale of Spoleto with the most spectacular setting is **Trevi**. The churches of **San Martino** (16th century), on Passeggiata di San Martino, and **Madonna delle Lacrime** (1487–1522), south of Trevi on the road into the village, contain paintings by Perugino and Tiberio d'Assisi, among others.

Museo Civico di San Francesco
Via Ringhiera Umbra 9. **Tel** 0742 37 95 98. **Open** daily (Nov–Feb: Tue–Sun). **Closed** Jan 1, Dec 25.

The Duomo (1253) in Assisi is a fine example of the three-tiered façades found across central Italy *(see p359)*. It has a pointed arch and a row of arcading.

11th-century campanile
Carved figures

Rose window
Rounded portal

Todi's Duomo was begun in the 12th century, but work on its windows and portals continued until the 17th century *(see p363)*.

18th-century rose window

San Michele (c.1195) in Bevagna has a beautiful portal that combines both Romanesque and old Roman fragments *(see p366)*.

❾ Spello

Perugia. 🚹 8,000. 🚉 🚌 ℹ️ Piazza Matteotti 3 (0742 30 10 09). 🗓️ Wed.

Spello is one of the better known villages in the Vale of Spoleto. It is renowned for a fresco cycle by Pinturicchio in the Cappella Baglioni of the church of **Santa Maria Maggiore** (12th–13th century) on Via Consolare. Executed around 1500, the frescoes depict scenes from the New Testament. Toward the center of the village is the Gothic church of **Sant'Andrea** (13th century) on Via Cavour. This road becomes Via Garibaldi, which leads to **San Lorenzo**, a Baroque gem of a church dating from the 12th century.

Spello also boasts Roman ruins from the age of Augustus: the **Porta Consolare** at the end of Via Consolare, and the twin-towered **Porta Venere** by Via Torri di Properzio.

The road to Assisi over **Monte Subasio** offers stunning views from the top of the mountain above Spello.

Environs

The least known village in the Vale of Spoleto is **Bevagna**. Like Spello, it sprang to life as a way-station on the Via Flaminia (the Roman road that ran through this part of Umbria). The medieval Piazza Silvestri is the setting for two Romanesque churches.

The lofty peaks of the Monti Sibillini in eastern Umbria

San Silvestro (1195) is the more atmospheric of the pair, thanks to its shadowy interior and ancient crypt, but **San Michele** (late 12th century) has an elegant portal, famed for the little gargoyles on either side. Both churches are the work of Maestro Binello.

❿ Monti Sibillini

Macerata. 🚉 Spoleto. 🚌 Visso. ℹ️ Piazza del Forno 1, Visso (0737 97 27 11). 🌐 sibillini.net

The national park of the Monti Sibillini in eastern Umbria provides the region's wildest and most spectacular scenery. A range 25 miles (40 km) long, the mountains form part of the Apennines, a chain that runs the length of the Italian peninsula. **Monte Vettore** is the loftiest point, and the peninsula's third highest; it stands at 8,123 ft (2,476 m), a great whale-backed peak close to the cave of the mythical sybil that gave the region its name.

Good maps and trails make this a superb walking area, while drivers can follow hairpin roads to some of Italy's most magical landscapes. Chief of these is the **Piano Grande**, a huge upland plain surrounded by a vast amphitheater of mountains. Bare but for flocks of sheep and bedraggled haystacks, the plain blazes with wildflowers in spring and with lentils later in the year. The only habitation is **Castelluccio**, a beautiful, neglected mountain village now being restored. It can be reached by road from Norcia and Arquata del Tronto.

Storefront in Norcia displaying the town's varied meats

⓫ Norcia

Perugia. 🚹 4,700. 🚌 ℹ️ Piazza San Benedetto (0743 82 49 11). 🗓️ Thu.

The birthplace of St. Benedict, Norcia is a robust mountain town and an excellent base for exploring Valnerina and Monti Sibillini. One of Italy's culinary capitals, it is renowned for truffles and for some of Italy's best hams, sausages, and salamis. Indeed, the Italian word for a pork butcher's (*norcineria*) derives from the name of the town.

Norcia's main sights are in **Piazza San Benedetto**. On the eastern flank, the church of **San Benedetto** has a 14th-century portal adorned with statues of Benedict and his sister (Santa Scolastica). Legend claims that the church marks the site of Benedict's birth – indeed there are the remains of a 5th-century building in the crypt. However,

Pinturicchio's *Annunciation* (c.1500) in Spello's Santa Maria Maggiore

The 8th-century monastery of San Pietro in Valle, set in the beautiful Valnerina

the church was more likely to have been built over the site of an old Roman temple, since the forum of the Roman colony of Nursia once occupied this spot.

Left of the church stands the **Palazzo Comunale**, a monument to the town's period as a free commune during the 13th and 14th centuries. On the opposite side of the square rises the **Castellina** (1554), a blunt papal fortress designed by Vignola to help impose order on an unruly mountain district. The **Duomo** (1560), to the left of the Castellina, has been ravaged by earthquakes over the centuries. Indeed, Norcia has been the victim of successive earthquakes, and its houses are low and heavily buttressed with thick walls to protect them from further

damage. **Sant'Agostino** on Via Anicia features a range of good 16th-century frescoes. A little way beyond, the **Oratorio di Sant'Agostinaccio** in Piazza Palatina contains a superb 17th-century ceiling. Via Umberto shelters the **Edicola** (1354), a strange tabernacle believed to have been carved for a Holy Week procession.

⑫ Valnerina

Perugia. **FS** Spoleto, then bus. **i** Piazza Garibaldi 1, Cascia (0743 711 47).

The Valnerina (Little Valley of the River Nera) curves through a broad swath of eastern Umbria, draining the mountains around Norcia and the Sibillini before emptying into the Tiber.

It is edged with craggy, tree-covered slopes and dotted with upland villages and fortified hamlets.

The high spot is **San Pietro in Valle**, an idyllically situated monastery in the hills above the village of Colleponte. Founded in the 8th century, it is one of the few surviving memorials to the Lombards, whose central Italian duchy had its capital in Spoleto. The main body of the monastery church dates from this period, as does the high altar. The nave walls are covered in a wealth of 12th-century frescoes. Some of the best Romanesque carvings in Umbria can be found here.

More popular than the monastery are the **Cascate delle Marmore** near Terni, among Europe's highest waterfalls at 541 ft (165 m). Created by the Romans during drainage work, their waters are now diverted to produce hydroelectric power on all but a few special days. You can view the falls from Marmore village or the S209.

🏠 **San Pietro in Valle**
Località Ferentillo, Terni. **Tel** 0744 78 01 29. **Open** daily (Sat & Sun in winter).

🌊 **Cascate delle Marmore**
4 miles (7 km) along S209 Valnerina, Terni. **Open** daily. Visit the website for opening hours. **W** marmorefalls.it

Piazza San Benedetto and the church of San Benedetto in Norcia

LE MARCHE

Tucked away in a remote corner between the Adriatic Sea and the Apennine mountains, Le Marche (the Marches) is an enchanting rural patchwork of old towns, hill country, and long, sandy beaches. In pre-Christian times the area was settled by the Piceni, a tribe eventually assimilated by the Romans.

In the 4th century BC, exiles from Magna Graecia colonized much of the region. The most notable town was Ancona, also the northernmost point of Greek influence on the Italian peninsula. During the early Middle Ages the region marked the edge of the Holy Roman Empire, giving rise to its present name (*march* meant border area).

The region's historical peak was reached in the 15th century under Federico da Montefeltro, whose court at Urbino became one of Europe's leading cultural centers. Much of Urbino's former grandeur survives, particularly in Federico's magnificent Renaissance Palazzo Ducale, now home to a regional art collection. Ascoli Piceno is almost as enchanting as Urbino, its central Piazza del Popolo among the most evocative old squares in Italy. Smaller towns like San Leo and Urbania and the republic of San Marino also boast fine medieval monuments.

Today probably as many people come to Le Marche for its beaches and towns as for its hilly, unspoiled interior. Especially beautiful are the snowcapped peaks of the Monti Sibillini, situated in magnificent walking and skiing country.

Regional cuisine encompasses the truffles and robust cheeses of the mountains, tender hams and salamis, *olive ascolane* (olives stuffed with meat and herbs), and *brodetto*, fish soup made in several versions up and down the coast. Dry, white Verdicchio is the best known wine, although more unusual names, such as Bianchello del Metauro, are gaining in popularity.

A field of poppies and olive trees in the heart of Le Marche's countryside

◄ A view of the Piazza del Popolo, built in traventine marble, in the town of Ascoli Piceno

Exploring Le Marche

The medieval towns of Urbino and Ascoli Piceno are the highlights of
the region, but the rolling hills of the interior contain an abundance of
smaller towns and all-but-undiscovered villages. San Leo, with its
dramatic fortress, is one of the best. Most of the countryside is a pretty
mixture of woods and remote hills,
rising in the west to the majestic
Monti Sibillini. Ancona and the
attractive town of Pèsaro are
the pivotal points of the
vast coastline.

Rolling countryside between Loreto
and Ascoli Piceno

Key

🚃 Highway

Major road

Secondary road

Minor road

Scenic route

Main railroad

Minor railroad

International border

Regional border

△ Summit

View of Ascoli Piceno, one of the prettiest towns in Le Marche

For additional map symbols *see back flap*

Sights at a Glance

1. San Leo
2. San Marino
3. Pèsaro
4. Fano
5. *Urbino pp374–5*
6. Urbania
7. Grotte di Frasassi
8. Jesi
9. Ancona
10. Conero Peninsula
11. Loreto
12. Ascoli Piceno

The rocky reef near Portonovo on the Conero Peninsula

Getting Around

The A14–E55 provides easy access to the coastal resorts. Divided highway spurs from the A14–E55 lead to Jesi, Urbino, and Ascoli Piceno, but north-south roads in the interior can be slow. Bus services are generally good, but in the interior can be infrequent. The train service along the coast is excellent, with a good service through the heart of the region, though it can be slow.

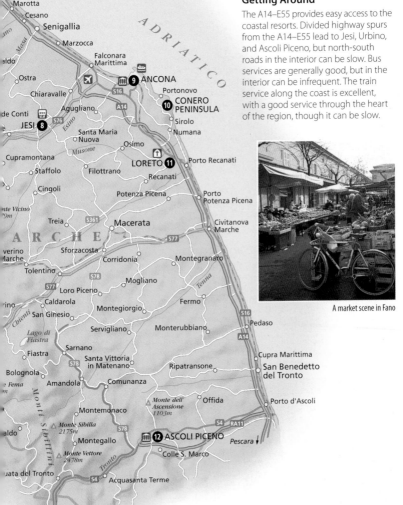

A market scene in Fano

The bell tower of the Duomo rising above the village of San Leo

● San Leo

Pèsaro. △ 3,000. *i* Piazza Dante
Alighieri 14 (0541 91 63 06).
▣ from Rimini, change at Villanova.
▣ **san-leo.it**

Few castles are as impressive as
the great **fortress** that towers
over the village of San Leo. Dante
used this crag-top site as a model
for the landscapes of *Purgatorio*,
while Machiavelli considered the
citadel to be the finest piece of
military architecture in Italy. Its
rocky ramparts once contained
the Mons Feretrius, a Roman
temple dedicated to Jupiter.

An earlier Roman fortress on
the site became a papal prison
in the 18th century. Its most
famous inmate was the larger-
than-life Conte di Cagliostro.
A swindler, womanizer, necro-
mancer, quack, and alchemist,
Cagliostro was imprisoned for
heresy in the 1790s. His cell was
specially built so that its window
faced the village's two churches.
It is still visible, together with a
small picture gallery, state rooms,
and the majestic Renaissance
ramparts, built by Francesco di
Giorgio Martini for the dukes of
Montefeltro in the 15th century.

The captivating village has
a quaint cobbled square with
a superb 9th-century **Pieve**
(parish church). Built partly
with stone from the ruined
Mons Feretrius, the church was
raised over the site of a
6th-century chapel.

Just behind lies the
12th-century **Duomo**, a fine
Romanesque building with
Corinthian capitals and Roman
columns from the Mons Feretrius.
The lid of St. Leo's sarcophagus
is in the crypt. Ancient pagan
carvings can be seen on the
wall behind the altar.

⊞ Fortress
Via Leopardi. **Tel** 0541 91 63 06.
Open daily. **Closed** lunch Oct–Mar. ◪

❷ San Marino

△ 26,000. ▣ San Marino
Città (fr Rimini). *i* Contrada
Omagnano (0549 88 29 14).
▣ **visitsanmarino.com**

Europe's oldest republic, tiny
San Marino was reputedly
founded by St. Marinus, a
4th-century monk and stonemason forced to flee the
religious persecution of
the Emperor Diocletian.
With him was St. Leo,
founder of the nearby
town of San Leo.
Situated on the slopes
of Monte Titano, the
country has its own
mint, stamps, soccer
team – even its own
1,000-strong army.
It is also famous for
Formula One racing.

Duty-free shop in San Marino

There are no customs formalities
in this country, whose borders are
just 7 miles (12 km) apart at the
widest point. Sadly, the capital,
San Marino, is overrun with
visitors and souvenir stalls
throughout the year. Garibaldi
sought shelter here after fleeing
Venice in 1849 and is honored by
a monument in Piazza Garibaldi.
The town of **Borgomaggiore** lies
at the foot of Monte Titano, with
a cable car to the capital above.

❸ Pèsaro

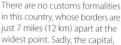
△ 110,000. ⒻⓈ ▣ *i* Viale Trieste
164 (0721 693 41). ▤ Tue & 1st Thu
of month.

One of the Adriatic's larger seaside resorts, Pèsaro has managed
to retain a stylish air. Behind the
promenade and the wall of white
stucco hotels is a lively, attractive
medieval area.

The art gallery of the **Musei
Civici** contains Giovanni Bellini's
sumptuous polyptych, the
Coronation of the Virgin (c.1470).
The museum also features
Renaissance ceramics.

The **Museo Archeologico
Oliveriano** presents historical
displays from Roman remains to
Iron Age artifacts from the
necropolis of nearby Novilara.

The best of the town's churches
is **Sant'Agostino** on Corso XI
Settembre, remarkable for its
choir stalls, each a patchwork
of inlaid landscapes and
narrative scenes.

Pèsaro is also a point of
musical pilgrimage because the
composer Gioacchino Rossini
was born here in 1792. His home,
Casa Rossini, contains memorabilia, while his piano and some

Detail of the *Coronation of the Virgin* by
Bellini (c.1470) in the Musei Civici

original manuscripts lie in the **Conservatorio Rossini**. His operas are performed in **Teatro Rossini** in Piazza Lazzarini during the annual August music festival.

🏛 Musei Civici
Piazza Mosca 29. **Tel** 0721 38 72 95. **Open** Tue–Sun. **Closed** Jan 1, Dec 25. 🖼

🏛 Museo Archeologico Oliveriano
Via Mazza 97. **Tel** 0721 333 44. **Open** Mon–Sat. ♿

🏠 Casa Rossini
Via Rossini 34. **Tel** 0721 38 73 57. **Open** Tue & Wed am, Thu–Sun. 🖼

🏠 Conservatorio Rossini
Piazza Olivieri 5. **Tel** 0721 336 71. **Open** Mon–Sat, but call ahead to arrange. **Closed** public hols.

❹ Fano

Pèsaro. 🚶 65,000. 🚆 🚌 🚢 ℹ Via Cesare Battisti 10 (0721 80 35 34). 🛒 Wed & Sat.

Ancient Fano stands out from the string of beach resorts south of Pèsaro, thanks to its fine old center and historic monuments. Named after Fanum Fortunae, a pagan temple to the goddess Fortuna, it became the terminus of the Via Flaminia (an important consular road from Rome) and the largest Roman colony on the Adriatic coast. The **Arco d'Augusto** (AD 2), on Via Arco d'Augusto, is Fano's most significant ancient monument, having narrowly escaped destruction at the hands of Federico da Montefeltro in 1463. He destroyed its upper section while besieging the town as a papal *condottiere*.

The 16th-century **Fontana della Fortuna**, in Piazza XX Settembre, is dedicated to the goddess Fortuna. The large **Palazzo Malatesta** that rises up to its rear was built around 1420 and enlarged in 1544 for Fano's rulers, the Rimini-based Malatesta family. Inside is the small **Museo Civico** and the **Pinacoteca Malatestiana**, with works by Guercino, Guido Reni, and the Venetian artist Michele Giambono.

🏛 Museo Civico and Pinacoteca Malatestiana
Piazza XX Settembre. **Tel** 0721 82 83 62. **Open** Tue–Sun. **Closed** Jan 1, Dec 25 & 26. 🖼

Entrance to the Palazzo Ducale in Urbania

❺ Urbino

See pp374–5.

❻ Urbania

Pèsaro. 🚶 7,200. 🚌 ℹ Corso Vittorio Emanuele 21 (0722 31 31 40). 🛒 Thu.

Urbania, with its elegant arcaded center, takes its name from Pope Urban VIII (1623–44), who entertained the notion of converting the old medieval village known as Castel Durante into a model Renaissance town.

Its chief attraction is a monument from an earlier age, the huge **Palazzo Ducale**, built by the dukes of Montefeltro as one of several residential alternatives to the Palazzo Ducale in nearby Urbino. It was begun in the 13th century and then rebuilt in the 15th and 16th centuries. Beautifully situated alongside the Metauro river, it houses a small art gallery, a modest museum, old maps and globes, and the remnants of Duke Federico's famous library.

🏛 Palazzo Ducale
Palazzo Ducale. **Tel** 0722 31 31 51. **Open** Tue–Sun. **Closed** public hols. 🖼

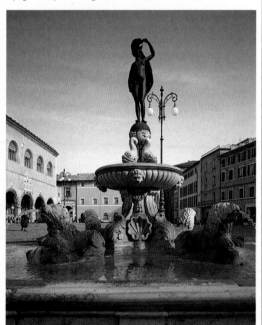

Fontana della Fortuna in Fano

Urbino: Palazzo Ducale

Italy's most beautiful Renaissance palace was built for Duke Federico da Montefeltro, ruler of Urbino (1444–82). He was a soldier, but also a man of the arts, and his palace, with its library, paintings, and refined architecture, is a tribute to courtly life and to the artistic and intellectual ideals of the Renaissance. The Palazzo Ducale houses the Galleria Nazionale delle Marche.

★ The Flagellation by Piero della Francesca
Dramatic perspective creates an unsettling effect in this 15th-century painting of the scourging of Christ.

The palace rising above Urbino

KEY

① **The Library** was one of Europe's largest in its day.

② **The simple east side** of the palace was designed by Maso di Bartolomeo before 1460.

③ **Towers attributed to Laurana**

④ **The Ideal City**, attributed to Luciano Laurana, is a 15th-century painting of an imaginary Renaissance city. The piece is notable for its measured perspective and lack of people.

⑤ **Hanging garden**

⑥ **The rooms** in this wing are known as the Appartamento della Duchessa.

Cortile d'Onore
This early Renaissance courtyard was designed by the Dalmatian-born artist Luciano Laurana (1420–79).

★ Studiolo
The former study of Federico da Montefeltro is decorated with intarsia (inlaid wood), some of it designed by Botticelli.

Duke Federico by Pedro Berruguete
The duke, shown here with his son in this 15th-century painting, was always portrayed in left profile after an injury to his face.

Main entrance

★ La Muta by Raphael
The Mute Woman may be a portrait of Maddalena Doni, a Florentine noblewoman.

⑤ Urbino

Pèsaro. 🏘 16,000. 🚌 ℹ Piazza
Rinascimento (0722 26 13). 🛍 Sat.
🌐 turismo.pesarourbino.it

Amid Urbino's tangle of medieval and Renaissance streets stands the Neo-Classical **Duomo**, on Piazza Federico, built in 1789. Of special interest is the painting of the *Last Supper* by Federico Barocci (c.1535–1612). The **Museo Diocesano** contains a collection of ceramics, glass, and religious artifacts.

Urbino's famous son, the painter Raphael (1483–1520), lived in the **Casa Natale di Raffaello**. It has a highly evocative interior, especially the kitchen and courtyard.

In Via Barocci is the medieval **Oratorio di San Giuseppe**, known for its *presepio* (Christmas crib), and the 14th-century **Oratorio di San Giovanni Battista**, whose interior is smothered in 15th-century frescoes of the *Crucifixion* and the *Life of John the Baptist* by Giacomo and Lorenzo Salimbeni.

The 15th-century **Fortezza dell'Albornoz** on Viale Bruno Buozzi is the defensive focus of Urbino's surviving 16th-century walls and bastions.

🏛 **Museo Diocesano**
Piazza Pascoli 2. **Tel** 0722 48 18. **Open**
9:30am–1pm, 2:30–6:30pm daily. 📷

🏠 **Casa Natale di Raffaello**
Via di Raffaello 57. **Tel** 1991 511 23.
Open daily (Sun am only).
Closed Jan 1, Dec 25. 📷

A street scene in the medieval town of Urbino

Fresh seafood and fishing boats in the harbor at Ancona

❼ Grotte di Frasassi

Ancona. **Tel** 0732 97 21 66. Genga San Vittore Terme. **Open** daily. Guided tours only (70 mins). **Closed** Jan 1, Jan 10–30, Dec 4, Dec 25.
W frasassi.com

Some of Europe's largest publicly accessible caverns lie in the cave network gouged out by the River Sentino southwest of Jesi. Of the vast network of 11 miles (18 km), an area of about 3,281 ft (1,000 m) is open to the public. The colossal **Grotta del Vento** is large enough to contain Milan cathedral – its ceiling extends to a height of 787 ft (240 m). This cavern has been used for a range of experiments, from sensory deprivation to an exploration of the social consequences of leaving a group of people alone in its depths for long periods.

❽ Jesi

Ancona. 41,000. Piazza della Repubblica 11 (0731 53 84 20). Wed & Sat. **W** comune.jesi.an.it

Perched on a long, rocky ridge, Jesi lies in the heart of the verdant hill country where Verdicchio is produced. A crisp, white wine, Verdicchio is bottled in unique containers – glass models of the terracotta amphorae once used to export the wine to ancient Greece. There are many vineyards in the surrounding countryside.

Housed in the town's 18th-century Palazzo Pianetti is the **Pinacoteca e Musei Civici**, which contains fine late-period paintings by Lorenzo Lotto. Almost as alluring as the gallery's paintings, however, is the great central salon – an orgy of Rococo decoration that once formed the centerpiece of the Palazzo Pianetti. The nearby **Palazzo della Signoria** features an interesting collection of archaeological finds, while beyond the old town's Renaissance walls stands the 14th-century church of **San Marco**, known for its collection of well-preserved Giottesque frescoes.

Pinacoteca e Musei Civici
Via XV Settembre. **Tel** 0731 53 83 42.
Open Tue–Sun.

Palazzo della Signoria
Piazza Colocci. **Tel** 0731 53 83 45.
Open Mon–Sat. **Closed** Mon am & Sat pm.

❾ Ancona

98,000. Via della Loggia 50 (071 35 89 91). Tue & Fri.
W turismo.marche.it

The capital of Le Marche and its largest port (with ferries to and from Greece and Croatia), Ancona dates back to at least the 5th century BC, when it was settled by Greek exiles from Siracusa. Its name derives from *ankon* (Greek for elbow), a reference to the rocky spur that juts into the sea to form the town's fine natural harbor.

Heavy bombing during World War II destroyed much of the medieval town. The 15th-century **Loggia dei Mercanti** (merchants' exchange) on Via della Loggia survives as a monument to the town's medieval heyday.

Just north of the loggia is the Romanesque church of **Santa Maria della Piazza**, with a lovely façade. The nearby **Pinacoteca Comunale F Podesti e Galleria d'Arte Moderna** includes canvases by Titian and Lorenzo Lotto. In the **Museo Archeologico Nazionale delle Marche** there are displays of Greek, Gallic, and Roman art. The **Arco di Traiano**, by the harbor, was erected in AD 115 and is one of Italy's better preserved Roman arches.

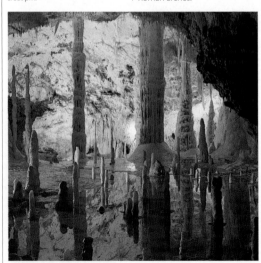

An impressive cavern in the cave system of the Grotte di Frasassi

The beach at the village of Sirolo on the Conero Peninsula

**🏛 Pinacoteca Comunale F
Podesti e Galleria d'Arte Moderna**
Via Pizzecolli 17. **Tel** 071 222 50 41.
Open Tue–Sat daily (Sun pm).
Closed public hols. 🖼 ♿

**🏛 Museo Archeologico
Nazionale delle Marche**
Via Ferretti 1. **Tel** 071 20 26 02.
Open Tue–Sun. **Closed** Jan 1, May 1,
Aug 15, Dec 25. 🖼 ♿

⓾ Conero Peninsula

Ancona. 🚆 🚌 Ancona. 🚌 from
Ancona to Sirolo or Numana. 🛈 Via
della Loggia 50, Ancona (071 35 89 91).
🌐 parcodelconero.eu

The beautiful, cliff-edged Conero
Peninsula is the only natural
feature to disturb the almost
unbroken line of beaches along
the coast of Le Marche. Easily
accessible from Ancona to the
north, it is a semi-wild area
known for its scenery, its wines
(notably Rosso del Conero),
and for a collection of coves,
beaches, and little resorts.

The best of these resorts is
Portonovo, above whose
beach stands **Santa Maria
di Portonovo**, a pretty
11th-century Romanesque
church mentioned by Dante in
Canto XXI of *Paradiso*. **Sirolo** and
Numana are busier and more
commercialized, but you can
escape the crowds by hiking the
flower-swathed slopes of Monte
Conero, which stands at 1,877 ft
(572 m), or by taking a boat trip
to the smaller beaches beyond
the resorts.

⓫ Loreto

Ancona. 🚹 11,000. 🚆 🚌 🛈 Via
Solari 3 (071 97 02 76). 🖐 Fri.

Legend has it that in 1294,
the house of the Virgin
Mary (**Santa Casa**)
miraculously
uprooted itself from
the Holy Land and
was brought by
angels to a laurel
grove *(loreto)* south
of Ancona. Each year
several million
pilgrims visit the **Santa
Casa** in Loreto and its **Basilica**.
Begun in 1468, the latter was
designed and built in part by
Renaissance architects Bramante,
Sansovino, and Giuliano da
Sangallo. Its paintings include
works by Luca Signorelli.
The **Museo-Pinacoteca** has
16th-century paintings by
Lorenzo Lotto.

Santa Casa in Loreto

⛪ Basilica and Santa Casa
Piazza Santuario. **Tel** 071 97 01 04.
Open daily. ♿

🏛 Museo-Pinacoteca
Palazzo Apostolico. **Tel** 071 974 71 98.
Open Apr–Oct: Tue–Sun; Nov–Mar:
Fri–Sun. 🖼

⓬ Ascoli Piceno

🚹 54,000. 🚌 🛈 Palazzo Comunale,
Piazza Arringo (0736 25 30 45).
🖐 Wed & Sat.

This alluring town takes its name
from the Piceni, a tribe eventually
conquered by the Romans in
89 BC. The gridiron plan of
Roman Asculum Picenum is
visible in the streets today, but it
is the town's medieval heritage
that attracts most visitors.

The enchanting **Piazza del
Popolo** is dominated by the
13th-century **Palazzo dei
Capitani del Popolo**, whose
façade was designed by Cola
dell'Amatrice, and the church of
San Francesco, a large and
faintly austere Gothic ensemble
built between 1262 and 1549.

Via del Trivio leads north to a
medieval district overlooking the
River Tronto. Along Via Cairoli lies
the 13th-century church of **San
Pietro Martire**. Opposite is the
church of **Santi Vincenzo e
Anastasio** (11th century), with
an ancient crypt built over a
spring said to cure leprosy.

Around Piazza dell'Arringo is
the 12th-century **Duomo**,
spoiled by a Baroque overlay.
Its Cappella del
Sacramento contains
a polyptych by the
15th-century artist
Carlo Crivelli. The
Pinacoteca Civica
has more works by
Crivelli and by Guido
Reni, Titian, and
Alemanno. The **Museo
Archeologico** contains Roman,
Piceni, and Lombard artifacts.

🏛 Pinacoteca Civica
Palazzo Comunale, Piazza Arringo.
Tel 0736 29 82 13. **Open** Tue–Sun.
🖼 ♿

🏛 Museo Archeologico
Palazzo Panighi, Piazza Arringo.
Tel 0736 25 35 62. **Open** Tue–Sun.
Closed Jan 1, May 1, Dec 25. 🖼 ♿

A view of the medieval town of Ascoli Piceno

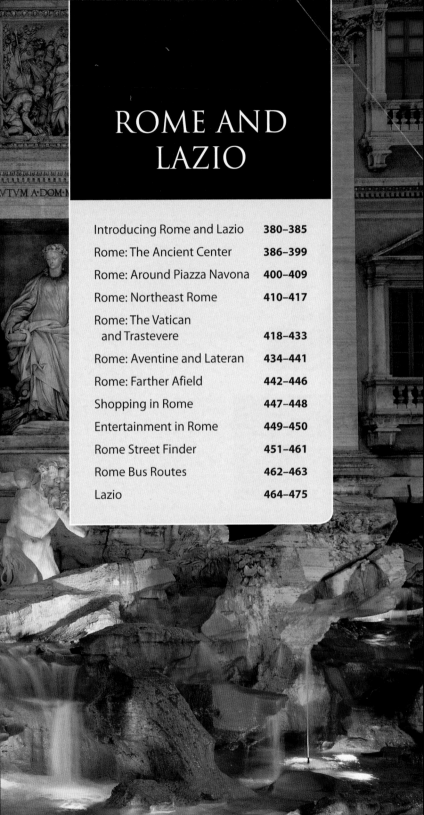

ROME AND LAZIO

Introducing Rome and Lazio   380–385

Rome: The Ancient Center   386–399

Rome: Around Piazza Navona   400–409

Rome: Northeast Rome   410–417

Rome: The Vatican
  and Trastevere   418–433

Rome: Aventine and Lateran   434–441

Rome: Farther Afield   442–446

Shopping in Rome   447–448

Entertainment in Rome   449–450

Rome Street Finder   451–461

Rome Bus Routes   462–463

Lazio   464–475

Rome and Lazio at a Glance

The first settlements in the region can be traced back to the early Etruscan civilization in northern Lazio. Rome grew to rule a vast empire, and as the empire began to divide, the region became the center of the Christian world. Artists and architects flocked to work for the popes and their families, notably in the Renaissance and Baroque periods when some magnificent architectural works were created. The legacy of this uninterrupted history can be seen all over the city and the surrounding area.

St. Peter's, with its majestic dome by Michelangelo, is a magnificent and sumptuous 16th-century basilica *(see pp422–3).*

Piazza Navona, flanked by cafés, contains three Baroque fountains, including the colossal Fontana dei Quattro Fiumi, one of Bernini's finest works *(see p403).*

Santa Maria in Trastevere, probably the first Christian church in Rome, holds some remarkable mosaics, such as this detail from Cavallini's *Life of the Virgin* which dates from 1291 *(see p432).*

PIAZ.
NAVC
(See pp4

THE VATICAN AND TRASTEVERE
(See pp418–33)

Lazio
(See pp464–75)

Viterbo

Rieti

Tarquinia

Magliano
Sabina

Civitavecchia

Tivoli

ROME
(See main map)

Velletri

Anagni

Sermoneta

Anzio

Terracina

Sperlonga

0 kilometers 15
0 miles 10

Cerveteri is one of the many necropolises left by the Etruscan civilization in northern Lazio. The larger tumulus tombs often contained frescoes and utensils useful for the afterlife *(see p470).*

◄ The famous Trevi Fountain, designed by Nicola Salvi

The Pantheon, built between AD 118–125, is a marvel of Roman engineering with its huge dome hidden behind the Classical portico *(see p408)*.

Santa Maria Maggiore's richly decorated interior blends different architectural styles, such as this baldacchino from the 18th century *(see p417)*.

NORTHEAST ROME
(See pp410–17)

San Giovanni in Laterano, the Cathedral of Rome, incorporates the elaborate Corsini Chapel built in the 1730s *(see p440)*.

THE ANCIENT CENTRE
(See pp386–99)

AVENTINE AND LATERAN
(See pp434–41)

The Capitoline Museums have held treasures of the Classical world since the Renaissance, including this colossal 4th-century head of Constantine *(see pp390–91)*.

| 0 meters | | 750 |
| 0 yards | | 750 |

The Colosseum was constructed in AD 80 by Emperor Vespasian. His aim was to gain popularity by staging deadly gladiatorial combats and wild animal fights for public viewing *(see p397)*.

The Flavors of Rome and Lazio

The countryside of Lazio varies from gently rolling hills to mountains to shimmering coast. Olive groves and vineyards cloak this fertile area, where wild boar roam and many other kinds of game find their way onto the table. But authentic Roman cuisine takes its origins from offal, and slow, inventive cooking transforms these traditionally "poor" cuts into flavorsome dishes. Pasta is still the vital ingredient in any meal, and several well-known dishes originate from Rome. Many of the capital's top restaurants are dedicated to fish and seafood, and as home of *la dolce vita*, there is a long tradition of delicious pastries, cakes, and ice cream.

Globe artichokes

A stall of Lazio vegetables, fresh from field to market

Traditional Roman cuisine originated in the Testaccio area, near the old slaughterhouse whose butchers *(vaccinari)* were paid partly in meat, generally offal. The "fifth quarter" *(quinto quarto)* included head, feet, tail, intestines, brain, and other bits of the beast not for the squeamish, but which, when cooked slowly and richly flavored with herbs and spices, became a culinary delight.

These robust dishes, such as the signature dish *coda alla vaccinara* (literally, oxtail in the style of the slaughterhouse butcher) still feature on many menus.

Cucina Romana

Authentic *cucina romana* also has its roots in Jewish cuisine of the atmospheric Ghetto area, whose origins date back over 400 years. Plump,

locally grown globe artichokes are fried whole in olive oil *(carciofi alla giudia)* or served *alla romana*, with oil, garlic, and Roman mint. Just as popular are salt cod fillets *(filetti di baccalà)* deep fried, Jewish-style.

Seafood and fish restaurants are among the best in Rome, and while not cheap, many are temples of gastronomy. It was in response to the launch of

Fusilli   Tagliatelle   Spaghettini   Lumaconi
Ravioli
Tortellini
Orecchiette

Just a few of the hundreds of types of pasta available in Italy

Regional Dishes and Specialties

Crispy fried vegetables, especially artichokes and zucchini flowers, are often served as an *antipasto*. For the *primo* course, pasta dishes include *bucatini all'amatriciana* – long, thin pasta tubes in a spicy tomato and bacon sauce, sprinkled with grated Pecorino cheese made from tangy ewe's milk. Veal is a great favorite and delicacies include *rigatoni alla pajata* (pasta with milk-fed veal intestines). Lamb is also very popular, such as *abbacchio al forno* (roasted milk-fed lamb) or *alla cacciatore* ("huntsman's style" with anchovy sauce). Offal is very common in traditional *trattorie*, and delicacies include *cervelle* (calves' brains), *ossobuco* (beef shins with marrow jelly), *pajata* (veal intestines), and *trippa* (tripe).

Bruschetta

Gnocchi alla romana Little dumplings, made with semolina flour, are usually served with a tomato or meat *ragù*.

Sumptuous Roman pizzas, sizzling hot from the wood-fired oven

the first McDonald's in Rome in 1986 that the Slow Food Movement started in Piedmont (see p178), but more typical Roman fast food includes *bruschetta* ("lightly burnt bread" in Roman dialect) rubbed with garlic, sea salt, and olive oil and topped with a selection of intense flavors. There's also authentic thin and crispy *pizza romana* from wood-fired ovens, often served *al taglio* – by the slice.

Pasta, Pasta

Pasta is still the mainstay of the Roman meal, especially spaghetti. *Spaghetti alla carbonara*, made with *pancetta* (cured bacon) or *guanciale* (pig's cheek), egg yolks, and cheese, is a classic Roman dish, as is *spaghetti alle vongole*, with garlic and clams. At a conservative estimate, there is one type of pasta for every day of the year, many of which have wonderfully descriptive or poetic names, such as *capelli d'angelo* (angel's hair) or *ziti* (bridegrooms), whose shape is best left to the imagination.

An array of mouthwatering *gelati* in a Roman ice-cream parlor

La Dolce Vita

For those with a taste for "the sweet life," nuts, fruits, and versatile ricotta cheese are often combined in mouth-wateringly delicious sweets.

Ice cream is an art form in Rome, where some parlors offer over 100 flavors of homemade *gelati*. Types vary from the classic *crema* and *frutta* to *grattachecca* (water ice), from *semifreddo* (a half-frozen sponge pudding, similar to *tiramisù* in consistency) to *granità* (ice shavings flavored with fruit syrups). Glorious *gelato* is one of the great pleasures here, to be enjoyed at any time of the day – or night.

ON THE MENU

Abbacchio alla cacciatore Baby lamb cooked with anchovies, garlic, Castelli Romani wine, rosemary, and olive oil.

Coda alla vaccinara Oxtail braised in herbs, tomato, and celery.

Fave al guanciale Young spring broad (fava) beans simmered in olive oil with pig's cheek and onion.

Filetti di baccalà Salt cod fillets in batter – once a Jewish specialty, now a feature of Roman cuisine.

Spigola alla romana Sea bass with porcini mushrooms, Roman-style.

Spaghetti alle vongole The classic Italian pasta is here served with a sauce made of baby clams and tomatoes.

Saltimbocca alla romana Veal slices are rolled with prosciutto and sage. *Saltimbocca* means "jump in the mouth."

Torta di ricotta Ricotta cheese is baked in a tart with sugar, lemon, brandy, eggs, and cinnamon.

Understanding Architecture in Rome and Lazio

The architecture of Imperial Rome, a combination of Etruscan and Classical Greek styles, gradually developed new and uniquely Roman forms based on the arch, the vault, and the dome. During the early Christian period, simple, rectangular basilicas were built, forms which by the 12th century had been incorporated into the stark Romanesque style. The Renaissance, inspired by the example of Florence, saw a return to Classical ideals of simplicity and harmonious proportions, though it was to be in the flamboyance of the 17th-century Baroque that Rome once again found great architectural expression.

The extravagant Baroque style of the Fontana di Trevi, Rome

From Etruscan to Classical Rome

The Podium made the temple more prominent.

A portico was a porch with columns.

Etruscan temples, based on Greek models, inspired early Roman architecture. A front portico was the only entrance.

The arch became a feature of Roman architecture.

Reliefs were scavenged from earlier monuments.

The Arch of Constantine (AD 315) is typical of triumphant Imperial Roman architecture *(see p393)*. It stands at a colossal 82 ft (25 m).

Three naves divided the interior of the basilica.

Early Christian basilicas (4th century) were based on a rectangular floorplan.

From Renaissance to Baroque

Doric columns recall Classical architecture.

Bramante adopted the circular form of ancient temples.

The Tempietto at San Pietro in Montorio, Rome, (1502) is a model of Renaissance architecture: simple and perfectly proportioned *(see p433)*.

Rustication, massive blocks divided by deep joints, was used for palazzi.

Ionic pilasters lend an air of elegance to the imposing upper stories.

The elliptical staircase was a typical feature of Mannerist houses.

Palazzo Farnese at Caprarola, a pentagonal building completed in 1575 *(see p469)*, combines some Mannerist tricks of architecture with the strict geometric proportions characteristic of the Renaissance.

Where to See the Architecture

A walk through the back streets of the center of Rome will reveal masterpieces of virtually every architectural age. The most ancient treasures are seven obelisks stolen from Egypt. One stands on the back of Bernini's elephant (see p408). Highlights from Ancient Rome include triumphal arches and temples such as the Pantheon (see p408). Romanesque elements survive in the church of San Clemente (see p439), while the Renaissance finds expression in the dome of St. Peter's (see pp422–3). Magnificent Baroque treasures dot the entire city, in particular flamboyant fountains that adorn the squares. Outside the city the outstanding sights are the late Renaissance villas such as Caprarola (see p469).

Part of Bernini's elephant supporting an ancient Egyptian obelisk

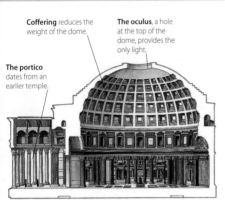

Coffering reduces the weight of the dome.

The oculus, a hole at the top of the dome, provides the only light.

The portico dates from an earlier temple.

The Pantheon (see p408) is one of the cardinal buildings of late Roman architecture. Completed in AD 125, it reveals how the form of the Greek temple was elaborated upon to create a masterpiece of perfect proportions.

Corinthian capitals were decorated with acanthus leaves.

Doric columns had straight capitals.

Ionic columns had scrolled capitals.

The orders of Classical architecture were building styles based on ancient Greek models, identified by the column capitals.

Columns around the altar draw attention away from the prominent lateral axis.

A concave portico reflects the oval body of the church.

The oval floorplan of the Baroque Sant'Andrea al Quirinale (see p415) makes ingenious use of restricted space.

Deep recesses create complex effects of light and shade.

Engaged pillars replace the flat pilasters of the Renaissance.

The Gesù façade (1584) epitomizes Counter-Reformation architecture and has been imitated throughout the Catholic world (see p407).

Two superimposed equilateral triangles form the complex hexagonal floorplan.

Sant'Ivo alla Sapienza's floorplan (1642) favored grandiose design over Classical form (see p404).

THE ANCIENT CENTER

The Capitol, the southern summit of the Capitoline Hill, was the symbolic center of the Roman world and home to the city's three most important temples. These were dedicated to the god Jupiter Optimus Maximus, protector of Rome, Minerva, goddess of wisdom and war, and Juno Moneta, a guardian goddess. Below the Capitol lies the Forum, once the focus of political, social, legal, and commercial life; the Imperial Fora, built when Rome's population grew; and the Colosseum, the center of entertainment. Overlooking the Forum is the Palatine Hill, where Romulus is said to have founded Rome in the 8th century BC, and emperors lived for over 400 years.

Sights at a Glance

Churches
❸ Santa Maria in Aracoeli

Museums and Galleries
❶ Capitoline Museums pp390–91

Historic Piazzas
❷ Piazza del Campidoglio

Ancient Sites and Buildings
❹ Trajan's Forum and Markets
❺ Forum of Augustus

❼ Forum of Caesar
❽ Roman Forum pp394–5
❾ Colosseum p397
❿ Arch of Constantine
⓫ Palatine pp398–9

0 meters 250
0 yards 250

See also Rome Street Finder
maps 3, 6, 7, 10

◀ View of the Colosseum's Ionic and Corinthian tiers

For keys to symbols see back flap

Street by Street: The Capitoline Hill

The Capitol, citadel of ancient Rome, was redesigned by Michelangelo in the 16th century. He was responsible for the trapezoid Piazza del Campidoglio as well as the Cordonata, the broad flight of steps leading up to it. The piazza is flanked by Palazzo Nuovo and Palazzo dei Conservatori, housing the Capitoline Museums, with their fine collections of sculpture and paintings. It is also well worth walking behind the museums to the Tarpeian Rock, for a fine view of the Forum lying below.

The Victor Emmanuel Monument was begun in 1885 and inaugurated in 1911 in honor of Victor Emmanuel II, the first king of unified Italy.

PIAZZA VENEZIA

San Marco, dedicated to the patron saint of Venice, has splendid 9th-century mosaics in the apse.

Palazzo Venezia, once the home of Mussolini, now holds a museum of fine and decorative arts. Exhibits include this medieval gilt and enamel angel.

The Aracoeli Steps were completed in 1348 to commemorate the end of the plague.

VIA DEL TEATRO DI MARCELLO

The Cordonata is presided over by the colossal statues of Castor and Pollux.

❶ ★ Capitoline Museums
The collections of art and ancient sculpture include this statue of the Emperor Marcus Aurelius, a replica of which stands in the center of the piazza.

Key

— Suggested route

0 meters   75
0 yards   75

❸ Santa Maria in Aracoeli
The brick façade hides treasures such as this 15th-century fresco of *The Funeral of San Bernardino* by Pinturicchio.

Locator Map
See Rome Street Finder map 3

Palazzo Nuovo was made into a public museum in 1734.

Palazzo Senatorio, the splendid Renaissance seat of the city government, is built on the ruins of the ancient Tabularium.

❷ Piazza del Campidoglio
Michelangelo designed the geometric paving and the façades of the buildings.

Palazzo dei Conservatori

The Temple of Jupiter, represented on this coin, was dedicated to Jupiter Optimus Maximus, the most important of the Roman gods. He was believed to have the power to protect or destroy the city.

The Tarpeian Rock is a cliff from which traitors were believed to have been thrown to their death in ancient Rome.

Steps to the Capitoline

SAN PIETRO IN CARCERE

VIA DEL TEMPIO DI GIOVE

❶ Capitoline Museums

See pp390–91.

❷ Piazza del Campidoglio

Map 3 A5. 🚌 40, 63, 70, 81.

When Emperor Charles V announced he was to visit Rome in 1536, Pope Paul III Farnese asked Michelangelo to give the Capitoline a facelift. He redesigned the piazza, renovated the façades of its palaces, and built a new flight of steps, the Cordonata. This gently rising ramp is now crowned with the massive statues of Castor and Pollux.

❸ Santa Maria in Aracoeli

Piazza d'Aracoeli. **Map** 3 A5. **Tel** 06 69 76 38 39. 🚌 63, 70, 81. **Open** 7:30am–12:30pm, 3–6:30pm daily (2:30–5:30pm in winter).

This church stands on the site of the temple of Juno on the northern summit of the Capitoline Hill, and dates back at least to the 6th century. The church is famous for its ornate gilded ceiling and a very fine series of frescoes by Pinturicchio, dating from the 1480s. They depict scenes from the life of San Bernardino of Siena. The miracle-working *Santo Bambino* figure, stolen in 1994, has been replaced by a replica.

The marble steps and austere façade of Santa Maria in Aracoeli

❶ Capitoline Museums:
Palazzo Nuovo

A collection of Classical sculptures has been kept on the Capitoline Hill since Pope Sixtus IV donated a group of bronze statues to the city in 1471. Paintings as well as sculpture are now housed in two palaces designed by Michelangelo. The Palazzo Nuovo contains a fine selection of Greek and Roman sculptures. Access is via the Palazzo dei Conservatori *(opposite)*.

Locator Map
See Rome Street Finder map 10

Discobolus
The twisted torso was part of a Greek statue of a discus thrower. An 18th-century sculptor turned him into a wounded warrior.

Mosaic of the Doves
This 1st-century AD naturalistic mosaic once decorated the floor of Hadrian's Villa at Tivoli *(see p472)*.

Alexander Severus as Hunter
In this marble of the 3rd century AD, the emperor's pose is a pastiche of the mythical hero, Perseus, holding up the head of Medusa the Gorgon after he had killed her.

Hall of the Philosophers
The hall contains Roman copies of portrait busts of Greek politicians, scientists, and poets. These adorned the homes of wealthy Romans.

Stairs to ground floor

Stairs to first floor

Courtyard

Exit

Dying Galatian
Great compassion is conveyed in this Roman copy of a Greek work of the 3rd century BC.

Key to Floor Plan

- Ground floor
- First floor
- Second floor
- Nonexhibition space

Palazzo dei Conservatori

The Palazzo dei Conservatori was the seat of the city's magistrates during the late Middle Ages. Its frescoed halls are still used occasionally for political meetings and the ground floor houses the municipal registry office. While much of the palazzo is given over to sculpture, including fragments of a huge sculpture of Constantine, the art galleries on the second floor hold works by Veronese, Tintoretto, Caravaggio, Van Dyck, and Titian.

VISITORS' CHECKLIST

Practical Information
Musei Capitolini, Piazza del Campidoglio.
Map 3 A5. **Tel** 06 06 08.
W museicapitolini.org
Open 9am–8pm Tue–Sun.
Closed Jan 1, May 1, Dec 25.
Entrance ticket is valid for both museums.

Transportation
40, 63, 70, 81, 87, and many other routes through Piazza Venezia.

St. John the Baptist
Caravaggio's sensual portrait (1595–6) of the young saint caressing a sheep is a highly unorthodox image of Christ's forerunner.

Medusa
This bust by Bernini of the mythological Medusa is in Room 8.

To temporary exhibition space

32

18

33

20A

17

30

31

28

20

29

26

24

19

Portico of Marcus Aurelius

26A

25

22B

16

24

22A

First floor

Second-floor art gallery

34

22

21

21B

15

14

21A

13

22C

Courtyard

12

Stairs to first floor

22D

11

10

Stairs to ground floor

6

9

22E

7

The Rape of the Sabine Women
Pietro da Cortona glamorized the mass abduction of Sabine women by the Romans in this painting of 1629.

4

5

8

Main entrance

Spinario
This is a charming bronze sculpture from the 1st century BC of a boy trying to remove a thorn from his foot.

❹ Trajan's Forum and Markets

Map 3 B4. Trajan's Forum, Via dei Fori Imperiali. **Closed** to the public. Trajan's Markets, Via IV Novembre. **Tel** 06 06 08. **Open** 9am–7pm Tue–Sun (last adm: 6pm). 🅿 🔊 👜 ♿

Trajan began to build his forum in AD 107 to commemorate his final conquest of Dacia (present day Romania) after successful campaigns in AD 101–2 and 105–6. His new forum was the most ambitious yet, with a vast colonnaded open space centering on an equestrian statue of the emperor, a huge basilica, and two big libraries. Dominating the ruins today is **Trajan's Column**, which

Trajan's Column

originally stood between the two libraries. Spiraling up its 98 ft (30 m) high stem are minutely detailed scenes from the Dacian campaigns, beginning with the Romans preparing for war and ending with the Dacians being ousted from their homeland. The subtly modeled reliefs were designed to be seen from viewing platforms on the libraries, and are consequently difficult to interpret from ground level. If you want to examine the scenes in detail there are casts in the Museo della Civiltà Romana (see p446). The **market** complex, which is situated directly behind the forum, was begun slightly earlier. Like the forum it was probably designed by Apollodorus of Damascus, and was the ancient Roman

Via Biberatica, the main street through Trajan's Markets

equivalent of the modern shopping center. There were around 150 shops selling everything from oriental silks and spices to fruit, fresh fish, and flowers. It was also here that the *annone*, or corn dole, was distributed. This was a free ration of corn given to Roman men, a practice that was introduced in the Republic by politicians who wanted to buy votes and prevent unrest during periods of famine.

Reconstruction of Trajan's Markets

Cross vaulting

The Main Hall had 12 shops on two stories. The corn ration was distributed from the upper floor.

Amphorae, used for storing wine and oil, were discovered on the upper corridor.

The terrace has a good view of Trajan's Forum.

The shops on the ground floor were cool, and probably sold vegetables, fruit, and flowers.

Staircase

Via Biberatica is named after the drinking inns that once lined it.

Large hall with semidomed ceiling

❺ Forum of Augustus

Piazza del Grillo 1. **Map** 3 B5. **Tel** 06 06 08. 87, 186. **Open** to research scholars by appt.

The Forum of Augustus, which once stretched from the foot of sleazy Suburra to the edge of Caesar's Forum, was built to celebrate Augustus's victory in 41 BC over Brutus and Cassius, the assassins of Julius Caesar. Consequentially, the temple in its center was dedicated to Mars the Avenger. The temple, with its cracked steps and four Corinthian columns, is easily identified. Originally it had a statue of Mars that looked very like Augustus, but in case anyone failed to notice the resemblance, a colossal statue of the emperor himself was placed against the wall of the Suburra quarter.

19th-century engraving of the Mamertine Prison

❻ Mamertine Prison

Clivo Argentario 1. **Map** 3 A5. **Tel** 06 69 89 63 80. 80, 85, 87, 175, 186. **Open** 9am–7pm daily. every 20 mins.

Below the 16th-century church of San Giuseppe dei Falegnami is a dank dungeon in which, according to Christian legend, St. Peter and St. Paul were imprisoned. They are said to have caused a spring to bubble up

Podium of the Temple of Mars the Avenger, Forum of Augustus

into the cell, and to have used the water to baptize two prison guards. The prison was in an old cistern with access to the city's main sewer (the Cloaca Maxima). The lower cell was used for executions, and corpses were thrown into the sewer. However, the inmates, who received no food, often died of starvation.

❼ Forum of Caesar

Via del Carcere Tulliano. **Map** 3 A5. **Tel** 06 06 08. 80, 85, 87, 175, 186, 810. **Open** to research scholars by appt only.

The first of Rome's Imperial fora was built by Julius Caesar to relieve congestion in the Roman Forum when Rome's population boomed. He spent a fortune – most of it booty from his recent conquest of Gaul – buying up and demolishing houses on the site. Pride of place went to a temple dedicated in 46 BC to Venus Genetrix (Venus the Ancestor), as Caesar claimed to be descended from the goddess. The temple contained statues of Caesar and Cleopatra as well as of Venus, but all that remains today is a platform and three Corinthian columns. The forum was once enclosed by a double colonnade, under which was sheltered a row of shops. However, this burned down in AD 80 and was rebuilt by Domitian and Trajan. The latter also added the Basilica

Argentaria – which became an important financial exchange – as well as shops and a heated public lavatory.

❽ Roman Forum

See pp394–5.

❾ Colosseum

See p397.

❿ Arch of Constantine

Between Via di San Gregorio and Piazza del Colosseo. **Map** 6 F1. 75, 85, 87, 175, 673, 810. 3. Colosseo.

This triumphal arch is one of Imperial Rome's last monuments, built in AD 315, a few years before Constantine moved the capital of the Empire to Byzantium. It was built to celebrate Constantine's victory in AD 312 over his co-emperor Maxentius at the Battle of the Milvian Bridge. Constantine attributed the victory to a dream in which he was told to mark his men's shields with *chirho*, the first two Greek letters of Christ's name. Christian tradition prefers a version in which the emperor has a vision of the Cross, mid-battle. There is nothing Christian about the arch: most of the reliefs were from earlier pagan monuments.

⓫ Palatine

See pp398–9.

The north side of the Arch of Constantine

❽ Roman Forum

In the early Republic, the Forum was a chaotic place, with food stalls and brothels as well as temples and the Senate House. By the 2nd century BC it was decided that Rome required a more salubrious center, and the food stores were replaced by business centers and law courts. The Forum remained the ceremonial center of the city under the Empire, with emperors renovating old buildings and erecting new temples and monuments.

Arch of Septimius Severus
This triumphal arch was erected in AD 203, the 10th anniversary of Emperor Septimius Severus' accession.

The Temple of Antoninus and Faustina is now incorporated into the church of San Lorenzo in Miranda.

VIA DELLA CURIA

The Rostra was the orator's tribune from which speeches were made.

Temple of Saturn

VIA SACRA

The Curia, or ancient Roman Senate House, has been reconstructed.

Basilica Julia
Named after Julius Caesar, who began its construction in 54 BC, this was the seat of the civil magistrates' court.

Basilica Aemilia was a meeting hall for business and money exchange.

Temple of Vesta

Temple of Castor and Pollux
Although there has been a temple here since the 5th century BC, the columns and elaborate cornice date from AD 6, when the temple was rebuilt.

0 meters 500
0 yards 500

★ **House of the Vestal Virgins**
The priestesses who tended the sacred flame in the Temple of Vesta lived here. The house was a large rectangular building around a central garden.

★ Basilica of Constantine and Maxentius
The basilica's three vast barrel vaults are all that remain of the Forum's largest building. Like other basilicas, it was used for the administration of justice and conducting business.

The Temple of Romulus, now part of the church of Santi Cosma e Damiano that stands behind it, retains its original 4th-century bronze doors.

Arch of Titus
This arch was erected by Emperor Domitian in AD 81 to commemorate the sack of Jerusalem by his father Vespasian and brother Titus, 13 years earlier.

VIA DEI FORI IMPERIALI

VIA SACRA

Antiquarium Forense
This small museum contains finds from the Forum. Exhibits range from Iron Age burial urns to this frieze of Aeneas from the Basilica Aemilia.

VIA SACRA

Colosseum

Palatine

The Temple of Venus and Rome
was built in AD 135, and was largely designed by Hadrian.

Santa Francesca Romana
The Romanesque bell tower of Santa Francesca Romana towers over one of a number of churches built among the ruins of the Forum.

The Vestal Virgins
The cult of Vesta, the goddess of fire, dates back to at least the 8th century BC. Romulus and Remus were allegedly born of the Vestal priestess Rhea and the god Mars. Six virgins kept the sacred flame of Vesta burning in her circular temple. The girls, who came from noble families, were selected when they were between 6 and 10 years old, and served for 30 years. They had high status and financial security, but were buried alive if they lost their virginity and were whipped by the high priest if the sacred flame died out. Although they were permitted to marry after finishing their service, few did so.

Honorary statue of a Vestal Virgin

Exploring the Roman Forum

To appreciate the layout of the Roman Forum before wandering through its confusing patchwork of ruined temples, triumphal arches, and basilicas, it is best to view the whole area from the Capitoline Hill above. From there you can make out the more substantial ruins, and the course of the Via Sacra (Sacred Way), the route followed through the Forum by religious and triumphal processions making their way up to the Capitol to give thanks at the Temple of Jupiter *(see p389)*.

Corinthian columns of the Temple of Castor and Pollux

The Main Sights

The first building you come to on entering the Forum is the **Basilica Aemilia**. A rectangular hall built in 179 BC, it was a meeting place for moneylenders, businessmen, and tax collectors. Although little more remains of it than a pastel marble pavement fringed with column stumps, you can still find splashes of verdigrised bronze, reputedly the remains of coins that melted when the Visigoths invaded Rome and burned down the basilica in the 5th century.

Inside the Curia – the stark brick building next to the basilica – are the **Plutei of Trajan**, relief panels commissioned by either Trajan or Hadrian to decorate the Rostra, the public oratory platform. On one panel are piles of books holding tax records, which Trajan had destroyed in order to free citizens from debts. The **Arch of Septimius Severus** is the best preserved of the Forum's monuments. The marble relief panels depict the military triumphs of the emperor in Parthia (modern-day Iran and Iraq) and Arabia. The **Temple of Saturn** was the

focus of the annual Saturnalia celebrations, when, for up to a week in December, schools closed, slaves dined with their masters, presents were exchanged, and a fair and market were held.

Soaring above the remains of the Basilica Julia are three delicately fluted columns and a finely carved slab of entablature taken from the **Temple of Castor and Pollux**. This striking relic is dedicated to the twin brothers of Helen of Troy, who were supposed to have appeared at the battle of Lake Regillus in 499 BC, aiding the Romans in their defeat of the Etruscans.

Restored section of Temple of Vesta

The elegant circular **Temple of Vesta** was one of ancient Rome's most sacred shrines and was dedicated to the goddess of the hearth. The flame, kept alive by the Vestal Virgins, symbolized the perpetuity of the state and its extinction prophesied doom for the city. The building was partly reconstructed in 1930, but the circular form goes back to the

Latin mud huts that originally occupied the site. Just behind is the **House of the Vestal Virgins**, the living quarters of the priestess and the Vestals. This enormous complex of 50 rooms was once annexed to the Temple. Best preserved are the rooms overlooking a pretty courtyard, ornamented with statues of Vestals, ponds of waterlilies, and rose trees.

On the other side of the Forum lie the impressive remains of the **Basilica of Constantine**. It was begun in AD 308 by Maxentius, and is therefore also known as the Basilica of Maxentius. Constantine completed it after he defeated his rival at the battle of Milvio in AD 312. The stark remains of the huge arches and ceilings give an indication of the original scale and grandeur of the forum's public buildings. Three enormous coffered vaults remain, which originally measured up to 115 ft (35 m) and were faced with marble.

The interior walls, which held niches for statues, were also covered with marble below and stucco above. Remains of a spiral staircase that once led to the roof can be found scattered on the ground.

The basilica's apse and hexagonal arches were often used as models by Renaissance architects striving to re-create a Classical symmetry and nobility in their work. They include Michelangelo, who allegedly studied the basilica's architecture when working on the dome of St. Peter's.

Central courtyard of the House of the Vestal Virgins

❷ Colosseum

Rome's greatest amphitheater was commissioned by Emperor Vespasian in AD 72. Deadly gladiatorial combats and wild animal fights were staged by emperors and wealthy citizens, largely to gain popularity. Slaughter was on a huge scale: at the inaugural games in AD 80, over 9,000 wild animals were killed. The Colosseum could hold up to 55,000 people, who were seated according to rank.

Internal Corridors
These allowed the large and often unruly crowd to move freely and be seated quickly.

The Velarium, a huge sailcloth awning that sheltered spectators from the sun, was supported by poles on the upper story.

The Colossus of Nero
This gilt bronze statue from Nero's palace, over which the Colosseum was built, may have given the amphitheater its name.

Entry routes
and stairs led to seats at the various levels. The emperor and consul had their own, separate entrances.

Corinthian columns

Ionic columns

The arena floor covered a network of lifts and cages for wild animals.

Doric columns

Entrances

Doric, Ionic, and Corinthian Tiers
The tiers inspired many Renaissance architects, who also plundered the building, using its travertine to build palaces and part of St. Peter's.

Roman Gladiators
These were originally soldiers in training. Their combat became a sport, and slaves, prisoners of war, and criminals were forced to fight men or wild animals to the death.

Emperor Vespasian
He ordered the Colosseum to be built on the site of Nero's palace, to dissociate himself from the hated tyrant.

⑪ Palatine

The Palatine, once the residence of emperors and aristocrats, is the most pleasant of Rome's ancient sites. The ruins range from the simple house in which Augustus is thought to have lived to the Domus Flavia and Domus Augustana, the public and private wings of a luxurious palace built by Domitian.

Cryptoporticus

★ House of Augustus
This building boasts four rooms with magnificent frescoes.

★ House of Livia
Many of the wall paintings have survived in the private quarters of the house where Augustus is believed to have lived with his wife Livia.

KEY

① **Domus Augustana** was the private home of the emperors.

② **The Huts of Romulus**, indicated by holes left by the supporting posts, were reputedly founded by Romulus in the 9th century BC.

③ **Temple of Cybele, goddess of fertility**

④ **The courtyard** of the Domus Flavia was lined by Domitian with mirrorlike marble, so he could spot would-be assassins.

⑤ **The exedra** of the stadium may have housed a balcony.

★ Domus Flavia
The courtyard of the Domus Flavia was lavishly paved with colored marble. The Roman poets praised this villa as the most splendid.

Emperor Septimius Severus
During his reign (AD 193–211), he extended the Domus Augustana and built an impressive bath complex.

Cryptoporticus
This underground gallery, elaborately decorated with stuccoed walls, was built by Emperor Nero.

↗ Forum entrance

The Palace of Septimius Severus
This extension of the Domus Augustana projected beyond the hillside, supported on giant arches.

⑤

0 meters   75
0 yards   75

Stadium
Part of the Imperial palace, this enclosure may have been used by the emperors as a private garden.

A History of the Palatine Hill

Romans of the Decadence by Thomas Couture (1815–79)

The Founding of Rome
According to legend, the twins Romulus and Remus were brought up on the Palatine by a wolf. Here Romulus, having killed his brother, is said to have founded the village that was destined to become Rome. Traces of mud huts dating back to the 8th century BC have been found on the hill, lending archaeological support to the legend.

The Republic
By the 1st century BC, the Palatine was the most desirable address in Rome and home to the leading citizens of the Republic. Its residents, including the erotic poet Catullus and the orator Cicero, were notoriously indulgent, and their villas were magnificent dwellings with doors of ivory, floors of bronze, and frescoed walls.

The Empire
Augustus was born on the Palatine in 63 BC, and lived there in a modest house after becoming emperor. The hill was therefore an obvious choice of abode for future emperors. Domitian's ambitious house, the Domus Flavia (1st century AD), and its private quarters, the Domus Augustana, remained the official residence of future emperors (who were referred to as *Augustus*) for more than 300 years.

AROUND PIAZZA NAVONA

The area around Piazza Navona, known as the *centro storico*, has been inhabited for at least 2,000 years. Piazza Navona stands above an ancient stadium; the Pantheon has been a temple since AD 27; and the theater of Marcellus in the Ghetto has been converted into exclusive flats. The area's heyday began in the 15th century, when the papacy returned to Rome. Throughout the Renaissance and Baroque eras princes, popes, and cardinals settled here, as did the artists and artisans they commissioned to build and adorn lavish palaces, churches, and fountains.

Sights at a Glance

Churches and Temples
❷ Sant'Ivo alla Sapienza
❸ San Luigi dei Francesi
❺ Santa Maria della Pace
❻ Chiesa Nuova
⓭ Gesù
⓯ Santa Maria sopra Minerva
⓱ Sant'Ignazio di Loyola
⓴ La Maddalena

Ancient Sites and Buildings
❹ Palazzo Altemps
❼ Palazzo della Cancelleria
❾ Palazzo Farnese
⓬ Area Sacra di Largo Argentina
⓲ Pantheon
㉒ Historic Building

Museums and Galleries
❿ Palazzo Spada
⓮ Palazzo Doria Pamphilj

Historic Piazzas and Areas
❶ Piazza Navona
❽ Campo de' Fiori
⓫ Ghetto and Tiber Island
⓳ Piazza Colonna
⓳ Piazza di Montecitorio

See also Rome Street Finder maps 9, 10

◀ The starry blue vault of the nave in Santa Maria sopra Minerva, Piazza della Minerva

For keys to symbols *see back flap*

Street by Street: Around Piazza Navona

No other piazza in Rome can rival the theatricality of Piazza Navona. The luxurious cafés are the social center of the city, and day and night there is always something going on in the pedestrian area around the three flamboyant Baroque fountains. The Baroque is also represented in many of the area's churches. To discover an older Rome, walk along Via del Governo Vecchio to admire the façades of Renaissance buildings, browse in the fascinating antiques shops, and lunch in one of the many trattorias.

↖ The Vatican

The Torre dell'Orologio by Borromini (1648) formed part of the Oratorio dei Filippini.

❻ Chiesa Nuova
This church was rebuilt in 1575 for the order founded by San Filippo Neri.

VIA DEL CORALLO

VIA DEL GOVERNO VECCHIO

VIA DI PARIONE

VIA DI SAN

At the Oratorio dei Filippini (1637) biblical stories were sung and the congregation responded with a chorus: the origin of the oratory.

Via del Governo Vecchio preserves a large number of fine Renaissance houses.

CORSO VITTORIO EMANUELE II

PIAZZA DI PASQUINO

❺ Santa Maria della Pace
This Renaissance church has frescoes of the Four Sibyls by Raphael and a refined courtyard by Bramante. The Baroque portico is by Pietro da Cortona.

Pasquino is a 3rd-century BC Hellenistic statue of Menelaus. Romans have been hanging satirical verses at its feet since the 16th century.

Palazzo Braschi, a late 18th-century building designed by Cosimo Morelli, has a splendid balcony overlooking the piazza.

Palazzo Pamphilj

Fontana del Moro

Campo de' Fiori

| 0 meters | | 75 |
| 0 yards | | 75 |

Key

— Suggested route

Sant'Andrea della Valle, begun in 1591, has a flamboyant Baroque façade flanked by angels with outstretched wings by Ercole Ferrata. The church is the setting of the first act of Puccini's *Tosca*.

Sant'Agnese in Agone by Borromini (1657) is allegedly built on the site where, in AD 304, the young St. Agnes was exposed naked to force her to renounce her faith.

Locator Map
See Rome Street Finder map 2

Fontana dei Quattro Fiumi

❸ **San Luigi dei Francesi**
This church, which was completed in 1589, is best known for three paintings by Caravaggio.

Palazzo Madama, the seat of the Italian Senate, was originally built for the Medici family in the 16th century, on the site of one of their banks.

❷ **Sant'Ivo alla Sapienza**
This tiny domed church is one of Borromini's most original creations. He worked on it between 1642 and 1650.

Largo di Torre Argentina

❶ ★ **Piazza Navona**
The piazza is lined with palaces and sidewalk cafés, and punctuated by flamboyant Baroque fountains.

❶ Piazza Navona

Map 2 E4. 🚌 30, 70, 81, 87, 130, 186, 492, 628.

Rome's most beautiful Baroque piazza follows the shape of a 1st-century AD stadium built by Domitian, which was used for athletic contests *(agones)*, chariot races, and other sports. Traces of the stadium are still visible below the church of Sant'Agnese in Agone, which is dedicated to a virgin martyred on the site for refusing to marry a pagan.

The piazza began to take on its present appearance in the 17th century, when Pope Innocent X, whose family palazzo was on the piazza, commissioned a new church, palace, and fountain. The fountain, the Fontana dei Quattro Fiumi, is Bernini's most magnificent, with statues of the four great rivers of the world at that time (the Nile, the Plate, the Ganges, and the Danube) sitting on rocks below an obelisk. Bernini also designed the muscle-bound Moor in the Fontana del Moro, though the present statue is a copy. Until the 19th century, the piazza was flooded in August by stopping the fountain outlets. The rich would splash around in carriages, while street urchins paddled. Even today the piazza remains the social center of the city.

Symbolic figure of the River Nile on Bernini's Fontana dei Quattro Fiumi

❷ Sant'Ivo alla Sapienza

Corso del Rinascimento 40. **Map** 2 F4. **Tel** 06 686 49 87. 30, 70, 81, 87, 116, 186, 492, 628. **Open** 9am–noon Sun.

Hidden in the courtyard of Palazzo della Sapienza, seat of the old University of Rome, Sant'Ivo's spiral belfry is nevertheless a distinctive landmark on Rome's skyline. Built by Borromini in 1642–60, the church is astonishingly complex, an ingenious combination of concave and convex surfaces. The work spanned the reigns of three popes, and incorporated in the design are their emblems: Urban VIII's bee, Innocent X's dove and olive branch, and the star and hills of Alexander VII.

❸ San Luigi dei Francesi

Piazza di San Luigi de' Francesi 5. **Map** 2 F4 & 12 D2. **Tel** 06 68 82 71. 70, 81, 87, 116, 186, 492, 628. **Open** 10am–12:30pm, 3–7pm daily. **Closed** Thu pm.

The French national church in Rome, San Luigi is a 16th-century building, best known for three magnificent canvases by Caravaggio in the Cerasi chapel. Painted between 1597 and 1602, these were Caravaggio's first significant religious works: *The Calling of St. Matthew*, *Martyrdom of St. Matthew*, and *St. Matthew and the Angel*. The first version of this last was initially rejected because it depicted the saint as an old man with dirty feet.

Detail from Caravaggio's *The Calling of St. Matthew* (1597–1602) in San Luigi dei Francesi

Side relief of the Ludovisi Throne, on display in the Palazzo Altemps

❹ Palazzo Altemps

Via di Sant'Apollinare 46. **Map** 2 E3. **Tel** 06 39 96 77 00. 70, 81, 87, 115, 280, 628. **Open** 9am–7:45pm Tue–Sun. **Closed** Jan 1, Dec 25.

An extraordinary collection of Classical sculpture is housed in this branch of the Museo Nazionale Romano (*see p416*). Restored as a museum during the 1990s, the palazzo was originally built for Girolamo Riario, nephew of Pope Sixtus IV, in 1480. In the popular uprising that followed the pope's death in 1484, the building was sacked and Girolamo fled the city. In 1568 Cardinal Marco Sittico Altemps bought the palazzo; it was renovated in the 1570s by Martino Longhi the Elder, who added the obelisk-crowned belvedere and marble unicorn. The Altemps family were avid collectors; the courtyard and its staircase are lined with ancient sculptures, which complement the Ludovisi sculptures. One of the highlights is the marble statue *Galata's Suicide*, a copy of the original, in the Salone del Camino. On the first floor is the Greek, 5th-century BC Ludovisi Throne, a carved relief shows Aphrodite.

Galata's Suicide in the Palazzo Altemps

❺ Santa Maria della Pace

Vicolo del Arco della Pace 5. **Map** 2 E3. **Tel** 06 686 11 56. 70, 81, 87, 116, 492, 628. **Open** 9am–noon Mon, Wed, Sat.

Named by Pope Sixtus IV to celebrate the peace he hoped to bring to Italy, this church dates from the 1480s and contains a beautiful fresco by Raphael. Bramante's refined cloister was added in 1504, while the façade was designed in 1656 by Pietro da Cortona.

❻ Chiesa Nuova

Piazza della Chiesa Nuova. **Map** 2 E4. **Tel** 06 687 52 89. 46, 64. **Open** 7:30am–noon, 4:30–7pm daily.

San Filippo Neri commissioned this church in 1575 to replace the dilapidated one given to his Order by Pope Gregory XIII. Neri required his followers to humble themselves, and set aristocratic young men to work as laborers on the church. Against his wishes, the nave, apse, and dome were richly frescoed after his death by Pietro da Cortona. There are three paintings by Rubens around the altar. The first versions were rejected, so Rubens repainted them on slate, placing the originals above his mother's tomb.

❼ Palazzo della Cancelleria

Piazza della Cancelleria. **Map** 2 E4. **Tel** 06 69 89 34 05. 46, 62, 64, 116, 916. **Open** 7:30am–2pm, 4pm–8pm. **Closed** Sun.

A supreme example of the confident delicacy of early Renaissance architecture, this palazzo was begun in 1485, and was allegedly financed by the gambling proceeds of Raffaele Riario, a nephew of Pope Sixtus I. In 1478 Riario was involved in the Pazzi conspiracy against the Medici, and when Giovanni de' Medici became Pope Leo XIII in 1513, he took belated revenge, seizing the palace and turning it into the papal chancellery.

Tiber Island, with Ponte Cestio, built in 46 BC, linking it to Trastevere

❽ Campo de' Fiori

Map 2 E4. 🚌 116 & routes to Corso Vittorio Emanuele II.

Campo de' Fiori (field of flowers) was one of the liveliest and roughest areas of medieval and Renaissance Rome. Cardinals and nobles mingled with fishmongers and foreigners in the piazza's market; Caravaggio killed his opponent after losing a game of tennis on the square; and the goldsmith Cellini murdered a business rival nearby. Today, the area continues to be a hub of secular activity. The colorful market, trattorias, and down-to-earth bars retain the original animated atmosphere.

In the Renaissance the piazza was surrounded by inns, many of which were owned by the 15th-century courtesan Vannozza Catanei, mistress of Pope Alexander VI.

The square was also a place of execution. The statue in its center is the philosopher Giordano Bruno, burned at the stake for heresy on this spot in 1600 for suggesting the earth moved around the sun.

❾ Palazzo Farnese

Piazza Farnese. **Map** 2 E5. 🚌 23, 116, 280 & routes to Corso Vittorio Emanuele II. 🎫 book in advance. 🌐 **inventerrome.com**

Originally constructed for Cardinal Alessandro Farnese, who became Pope Paul III in 1534, this palazzo was started by Antonio da Sangallo the Younger, and continued after his death by Michelangelo, who created the cornice on the façade and the courtyard's third story.

The palace, now the French Embassy, is closed to the public, but when the chandeliers are lit at night you may be able to glimpse the ceiling of the Galleria, an illusionistic masterpiece (1597–1603) by Annibale Carracci based on Ovid's *Metamorphoses*.

❿ Palazzo Spada

Piazza Capo di Ferro 13. **Map** 2 E5. **Tel** 06 686 11 58. 🚌 23, 116, 280, & routes to Largo di Torre Argentina. **Open** 8:30am–7:30pm Tue–Sun (last adm: 7pm). **Closed** Jan 1, Dec 25.
🎟 🎦 🎭 ♿

A stucco extravaganza studded with reliefs of illustrious Romans, this palazzo was built in 1550, but bought in 1637 by Cardinal Bernardino Spada. A keen patron of the arts, he commissioned Borromini to create an illusionistic tunnel that appears four times longer than it is. The cardinal's art collection, in the Galleria Spada, includes works by Guercino, Dürer, and Artemisia Gentileschi.

⓫ Ghetto and Tiber Island

Map 2 F5 & 6 D1. 🚌 23, 63, 280, 780 and routes to Largo di Torre Argentina.

The first Jews came to Rome as traders in the 2nd century BC and were greatly appreciated for their financial and medical skills during the Roman Empire. Persecution began in the 16th century, when Pope Paul IV forced all of the Jews to live within a walled enclosure, an area later to form the hub of the present-day Ghetto.

Today Via del Portico d'Ottavia, the district's main street, leads to Rome's central synagogue, passing restaurants and shops selling Roman Jewish food. Ponte Fabricio links the Ghetto with Tiber Island, a center of healing since 293 BC when a Temple to Aesculapius was founded. The island is now home to a hospital.

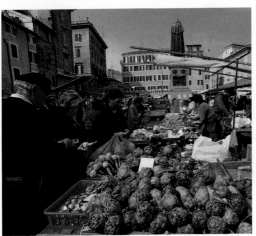

Fruit stalls at Campo de' Fiori's lively morning market

Street by Street: Around the Pantheon

The maze of narrow streets around the Pantheon is a mixture of lively restaurants and cafés, and some of Rome's finest sights. This is also the city's financial and political district, home to Parliament, government offices, and the stock exchange. The Pantheon itself, with its awe-inspiring domed interior, has long been a symbol of the city.

⑰ Sant'Ignazio di Loyola
This church has a superb illusionistic ceiling painted by Andrea Pozzo in 1685.

The Temple of Hadrian now forms the façade of the Stock Exchange.

Piazza della Minerva centers on Bernini's outlandish sculpture of an elephant supporting an Egyptian obelisk.

⑭ ★ Palazzo Doria Pamphilj
Among the masterpieces in the art gallery of this vast family palazzo is this Salomé by Titian, painted in 1516.

⑯ ★ Pantheon
The Pantheon, a temple to "all the gods," is Rome's best-preserved ancient building. It was built in the 1st century AD, probably to a design by Emperor Hadrian.

The Pie' di Marmo

Santa Maria sopra Minerva

Palazzo Altieri incorporates the hovel of an old woman who refused to allow her house to be demolished when this palace was built in the 17th century.

⑬ Gesù
Built in the late 16th century, this Jesuit church served as a model for the Order's churches throughout the world.

Map labels: PIAZZA DI SANT' IGNAZIO · VIA DI SANT' IGNAZIO · VIA DEL SEMINARIO · PIAZZA DEL COLLEGIO ROMANO · VIA DELLA GATTA · Via della Gatta · PIAZZA DELLA ROTONDA · VIA DEL PIE' DI MARMO · PIAZZA DELLA MINERVA · VIA DEL GESÙ · VIA DEL PLEBISC...

Locator Map
See Rome Street Finder map 3

Via della Gatta is overlooked by this marble statue of a cat *(gatta)* that gives the narrow street its name.

The Pie' di Marmo, an ancient marble foot, is probably part of a giant statue from the temple to the Egyptian goddess Isis.

⑮ Santa Maria sopra Minerva
This is one of Rome's few Gothic churches, with works by Michelangelo, Bernini, and Filippino Lippi.

Key

— Suggested route

| 0 meters | 75 |
| 0 yards | 75 |

⑫ Area Sacra di Largo Argentina

Largo di Torre Argentina. **Map** 2 F5.
🚌 40, 46, 62, 64, 70, 81, 87, 186, 492.
Closed to the public.

The remains of four temples were discovered in the 1920s at the center of Largo Argentina, now a busy bus terminal and traffic junction. They date from the era of the Republic, and are among the oldest found in Rome. For the purpose of identification, they are known as A, B, C, and D. The oldest (temple C) dates from the early 3rd century BC. It was placed on a high platform preceded by an altar and is typical of Italic temple plans as opposed to the Greek model. Temple A is from the 3rd century BC, but in medieval times the small church of San Nicola di Cesarini was built over its podium and the remains of its two apses are still visible. The column stumps to the north belonged to a great portico, known as the Hecatostylum (portico of 100 columns). In Imperial times two marble latrines were built here – the remains of one are visible behind temple A. Behind temples B and C, near Via di Torre Argentina, are the remains of a great platform of tufa blocks. These have been identified as part of the Curia of Pompey, a rectangular building where the Senate met, and where Julius Caesar was assassinated by Brutus, Cassius, and their followers on March 15, 44 BC.

Area Sacra, with the ruins of circular temple B

Baroque *Triumph of Faith over Idolatry* by Pierre Legros, Gesù

⑬ Gesù

Piazza del Gesù. **Map** 3 A4. **Tel** 06 69 70 01. 🚌 H, 46, 62, 64, 70, 81, 87, 186, 492, 628, & other routes. **Open** 7am–12:30pm (7am–1pm Sun), 4–7:30pm daily.

Built between 1568 and 1584, the Gesù was Rome's first Jesuit church. The Jesuit order was founded in Rome in 1537 by a Basque soldier, Ignatius Loyola, who became a Christian after he was wounded in battle. The order was austere, intellectual, and heavily engaged in missionary activity and religious wars.

The much-imitated design of the Gesù typifies Counter-Reformation architecture, with a large nave with side pulpits for preaching to crowds, and a main altar as the centerpiece for the mass. The illusionistic decoration on the nave ceiling and dome was added by Il Baciccia in the 17th century.

The nave depicts the *Triumph of the Name of Jesus* and its message is clear: faithful, Catholic worshippers will be joyfully uplifted to heaven while Protestants and heretics are flung into the fires of hell. The message is reiterated in the Cappella di Sant'Ignazio, a rich display of lapis lazuli, serpentine, silver, and gold. The Baroque marble by Legros, *Triumph of Faith over Idolatry*, shows a female "Religion" trampling on the head of the serpent Idolatry, while in Théudon's *Barbarians Adoring the Faith*, an angel aims a kick toward a decrepit old barbarian couple entangled with a snake.

⑭ Palazzo Doria Pamphilj

Via del Corso 305. **Map** 3 A4.
Tel 06 679 73 23. 🚌 64, 81, 119, 492.
Open 10am–5pm daily. **Closed** Jan 1,
Easter Sun, May 1, Dec 25. 🏛 ♿ 🛍
📷 🖼 by appt for private apartments.

Palazzo Doria Pamphilj is a vast
edifice whose oldest parts date
from 1435. When the Pamphilj
family took over in 1647 they
built a new wing, a splendid
chapel, and a theater.

The family art collection has
over 400 paintings dating from
the 15th–18th centuries,
including a portrait of Pope
Innocent X by Velázquez and
works by Titian, Guercino,
Caravaggio, and Claude Lorrain.
The opulent rooms of the
private apartments retain many
of their original furnishings,
including Brussels and Gobelins
tapestries, Murano chandeliers,
and a gilded crib.

Velázquez's *Pope Innocent X* (1650)

⑮ Santa Maria sopra Minerva

Piazza della Minerva 42. **Map** 2 F4.
Tel 06 679 39 26. 🚌 116 & many
other routes. **Open** 8am–7pm Mon–
Sat, 8am–1pm, 4–7pm Sun.

One of Rome's rare Gothic
buildings, this church was built in
the 13th century over what were
thought to be the ruins of a
Temple of Minerva. It was a
stronghold of the Dominicans,
who produced some of the
Church's most infamous inquisitors, and who tried the scientist
Galileo in the adjoining monastery.

Inside, the church has a superb
collection of art and sculpture,
ranging from 13th-century
Cosmatesque tombs to a bust

Interior of the Pantheon, burial place for Italian monarchs

by Bernini. Highlights include
Antoniazzo Romano's
Annunciation featuring Cardinal
Juan de Torquemada, uncle of
the vicious Spanish Inquisitor,
and the Carafa Chapel's frescoes
by Filippino Lippi.

In the Aldobrandini Chapel
are the tombs of the 16th-
century Medici popes,
Leo X and his cousin Clement
VII, and near the steps of the
choir is a stocky *Risen Christ*,
begun by Michelangelo.

The church also contains the
tombs of many famous Italians,
such as St. Catherine of Siena,
who died in 1380, and Fra
Angelico, the Dominican friar
and painter, who died in 1455.
Outside, Bernini's spectacular
sculpture of an elephant holds
an obelisk on its back.

Simple vaulted nave of Santa Maria
sopra Minerva

⑯ Pantheon

Piazza della Rotonda. **Map** 2 F4.
Tel 06 68 30 02 30. 🚌 116 & many
routes. **Open** 8:30am–7:30pm daily
(9am–6pm Sun). **Closed** Jan 1, May 1,
Dec 25. ♿

The Pantheon, the Roman
"temple of all the gods," is the
most extraordinary and best
preserved ancient building
in Rome. The first temple on
the site was a conventional
rectangular affair erected by
Agrippa between 27 and 25 BC;
the present structure was built
and possibly designed by
Emperor Hadrian in AD 118.

The temple is fronted by a
massive pedimented portico
screening what appears to be
a cylinder fused to a shallow
dome. Only from the inside can
the true scale and beauty of this
building be appreciated: a vast
hemispherical dome equal in
radius to the height of the
cylinder giving perfectly
harmonious proportions to the
building. A circular opening,
the *oculus*, lets in the only light.

In the 7th century, Christians
claimed to be plagued by
demons as they passed by, and
permission was given to make
the Pantheon a church. Today
it is lined with tombs, ranging
from a restrained monument to
Raphael to huge marble and
porphyry sarcophagi holding
the bodies of Italian monarchs.

⓱ Sant'Ignazio di Loyola

Piazza di Sant'Ignazio. **Map** 2 F4.
Tel 06 679 44 06. 🚌 117, 119, 492.
Open 7:30am–12:20pm, 3pm–7:20pm
daily (from 9am Sun). 🚻

This church was built by Pope Gregory XV in 1626 in honor of St. Ignatius of Loyola, founder of the Society of Jesus (Jesuits) and the man who most embodied the zeal of the Counter-Reformation.

Together with the Gesù (see p407), Sant'Ignazio forms the nucleus of the Jesuit area of Rome. It is one of the most extravagant Baroque churches and its vast interior is plated with precious stones, marble, stucco, and gilt, creating a thrilling sense of theater. The church has a Latin-cross plan, with an apse and many side chapels. A cupola was planned but never built, as the nuns from a nearby convent objected that it would obscure the view from their roof garden. Instead the space was filled by a perspective painting of a dome on a flat disc.

Even more striking is the illusionistic ceiling created by the Jesuit artist Andrea Pozzo in 1685, a propagandist extravaganza extolling the success of Jesuit missionaries throughout the world. Above four women – representing Asia, Europe, America, and Africa – lithe angels, and beautiful youths are sucked into a heaven of fluffy clouds.

Detail from the AD 180 Column of Marcus Aurelius, Piazza Colonna

⓲ Piazza Colonna

Map 3 A3. 🚌 116, 117, 492.

Home to Palazzo Chigi, official residence of the prime minister, Piazza Colonna is dominated by and named after the majestic Column of Marcus Aurelius. This was erected after the death of Marcus Aurelius in AD 180 to commemorate his victories over the barbarian tribes of the Danube. It is clearly an imitation of Trajan's Column (see p392) with scenes from the emperor's wars spiraling in reliefs up the column. The 80-year lapse between the two works produced a great artistic change: the wars of Marcus Aurelius are rendered in simplified pictures in stronger relief, sacrificing Classical proportions for the sake of clarity and immediacy.

⓳ Piazza di Montecitorio

Map 2 F3. Palazzo di Montecitorio
Tel 06 676 01. 🚌 116. **Open**
10am–5:30pm 1st Sun of month.

The obelisk in the center of Piazza di Montecitorio formed the spine of a giant sundial brought back from Egypt by Augustus. It vanished in the 9th century, and was rediscovered under medieval houses during the reign of Julius II (1503–13).

The piazza is dominated by the rugged façade of Palazzo di Montecitorio, designed by Bernini and completed in 1697, after his death, by Carlo Fontana. It has been the seat of Italy's Chamber of Deputies since the late 19th century.

La Maddalena's stuccoed façade

⓴ La Maddalena

Piazza della Maddalena. **Map** 2 F3.
Tel 06 899 281. 🚌 116 & many other
routes. **Open** 8:30–11:30am,
5–6:30pm daily (Sat am only).

Situated in a small piazza near the Pantheon, the Maddalena's Rococo façade, built in 1735, epitomizes the love of light and movement of the late Baroque. The façade has been restored, despite the protests of Neo-Classicists who dismissed its painted stucco as icing sugar.

The diminutive dimensions of the church did not deter 17th- and 18th-century decorators from filling the interior with paintings and ornaments from the floor to the top of the elegant cupola.

Baroque illusionistic ceiling by Andrea Pozzo in Sant'Ignazio di Loyola

NORTHEAST ROME

This area stretches from the exclusive shopping streets around Piazza di Spagna to the Esquiline Hill, once bourgeois, but now a poor, often seedy area full of early Christian churches. The Piazza di Spagna and Piazza del Popolo district grew up in the 16th century, when the increase in the influx of pilgrims was such that

a road was built to channel them as quickly as possible to the Vatican. About the same time, the Quirinal Hill became the site of a papal palace. When Rome became capital of Italy in 1870, Via Veneto became a lavish residential area, and the Esquiline was covered with apartments for the new civil servants.

Sights at a Glance

Churches
❸ Santa Maria del Popolo
❼ Sant'Andrea al Quirinale
❽ San Carlo alle Quattro Fontane
❿ Santa Maria della Concezione
⓫ Santa Maria della Vittoria
⓭ Santa Prassede

⓮ San Pietro in Vincoli
⓯ Santa Maria Maggiore

Museums and Galleries
❾ Palazzo Barberini
⓬ Museo Nazionale Romano

Ancient Sites and Buildings
❹ Ara Pacis

❺ Mausoleum of Augustus

Historic Buildings
❷ Villa Medici

Piazzas and Fountains
❶ Piazza di Spagna and
the Spanish Steps
❻ Trevi Fountain

See also Rome Street Finder maps 2, 3, 4, 7

◀ The Spanish Steps leading up to the Church of the Santissima Trinità dei Monti

For keys to symbols *see back flap*

Street by Street: Piazza di Spagna

The network of narrow streets around Piazza di Spagna forms one of the most exclusive areas in Rome, drawing droves of tourists and Romans to the elegant shops around Via Condotti. The square and its nearby coffeehouses have long attracted those who want to see and be seen. In the 18th century the area was full of hotels for frivolous aristocrats doing the Grand Tour, as well as artists, writers, and composers, who took the city's history and culture more seriously.

Caffé Greco is an 18th-century café once frequented by writers and musicians such as Keats, Goethe, Byron, Liszt, and Wagner.

ANTICO CAFFÉ GRECO

Spagna

Trinità dei Monti is a 16th-century church at the top of the Spanish Steps. There are fine views of Rome from the stairway.

Babington's Tea Rooms, founded by two English spinsters in 1896, still serves English teas.

The Keats-Shelley Memorial House, where the poet Keats died in 1821, is now a museum honoring English Romantic poets.

The Collegio di Propaganda Fide, built for the Jesuits in 1662, has a superb façade designed by Francesco Borromini.

The Colonna dell' Immacolata, erected in 1857, commemorates Pope Pius IX's doctrine of the Immaculate Conception.

❶ ★ Piazza di Spagna and the Spanish Steps
These have been at the heart of tourist Rome since the 18th century.

Locator Map
See Rome Street Finder map 3

Sant'Andrea delle Fratte
contains two angels by Bernini (1669) made for Ponte Sant'Angelo, which Pope Clement X thought too lovely to expose to the weather.

Key

— Suggested route

0 meters 75
0 yards 75

The Fontana della Barcaccia at the foot of the Spanish Steps

❶ Piazza di Spagna and the Spanish Steps

Map 3 A2. 🚌 116, 117. Ⓜ Spagna.

Shaped like a crooked bow tie, and surrounded by muted, shuttered façades, Piazza di Spagna is crowded all day and (in summer) most of the night. The most famous square in Rome, it takes its name from the Palazzo di Spagna, built in the 17th century to house the Spanish Embassy to the Holy See.

The piazza has long been the haunt of foreign visitors and expatriates. In the 18th and 19th centuries the square stood at the heart of the city's main hotel district. Some of the travelers came in search of knowledge and inspiration, although most were more interested in collecting statues to adorn their family homes.

When the Victorian novelist Charles Dickens visited, he reported that the Spanish Steps were crowded with models dressed as Madonnas, saints, and emperors, hoping to attract the attention of foreign artists.

The steps were built in the 1720s to link the square with the French church of Trinità dei Monti above. The French wanted to place a statue of Louis XIV at the top, but the pope objected, and it was not until the 1720s that the Italian architect Francesco de Sanctis produced the voluptuous Rococo design that satisfied both camps. The Fontana Barcaccia, sunk into the paving at the foot of the steps due to low water pressure, was designed by Bernini's less famous father, Pietro.

❷ Villa Medici

Accademia di Francia a Roma, Viale Trinità dei Monti 1. **Map** 3 A2. **Tel** 06 67 611. 🚌 117. Ⓜ Spagna. **Open** garden visits: 10:30am–12:30pm, 2–5:30pm Tue–Sun, (Cardinal's apartments: Wed only). 🚫 📷 ✏️ only (at noon in English).

Superbly positioned on the Pincio Hill, this 16th-century villa has retained the name that it assumed when Cardinal Ferdinando de' Medici bought it in 1576. It is now home to the French Academy, founded in 1666 to give artists the chance to study in Rome. From 1803 musicians were also allowed to study here: both Berlioz and Debussy were students.

The villa is open only for exhibitions, but the formal gardens, with a gorgeously frescoed pavilion and copies of ancient statues, can be visited in certain months.

19th-century engraving of the inner façade of the Villa Medici

Pinturicchio's fresco of the *Delphic Sibyl* (1509) in Santa Maria del Popolo

❸ Santa Maria del Popolo

Piazza del Popolo 12. **Map** 2 F1. **Tel** 06 361 08 36. 🚌 117, 119, 490, 495, 926. Ⓜ Flaminio. **Open** 7am–noon, 4–7pm Mon–Sat; 7am–1:30pm, 4:30–7:15pm Sun.

Santa Maria del Popolo was one of the first Renaissance churches in Rome, commissioned by Pope Sixtus IV della Rovere in 1472. Lavish endowments by Sixtus's descendants and other powerful families have made it one of Rome's greatest artistic treasures.

Shortly after Sixtus died in 1484, Pinturicchio and his pupils frescoed two chapels (first and third right) for the della Rovere family. On the altar of the first chapel there is a lovely *Nativity* from 1490 that depicts a stable at the foot of a Classical column.

In 1503 Sixtus IV's nephew Giuliano became Pope Julius II and had Bramante build a new apse. Pinturicchio was called in again to paint its vaults with Sibyls and Apostles framed in an intricate tracery of freakish beasts.

In 1513 Raphael created the Chigi chapel (second left) for the wealthy banker Agostino Chigi. The design is an audacious Renaissance fusion of the sacred and profane; there are pyramid-like tombs and a ceiling mosaic of God holding the signs of the zodiac describing Chigi's horoscope. Raphael died before the chapel was finished and it was completed by Bernini, who added the dynamic statues of Daniel and Habakkuk. In the Cerasi chapel, left of the altar,

there are two realistic works painted by Caravaggio in 1601: the *Conversion of St. Paul* and the *Crucifixion of St. Peter*. The artist uses daringly exaggerated lighting effects and foreshortening techniques to intensify the dramatic effect.

Detail of the Ara Pacis frieze

❹ Ara Pacis

Lungotevere in Augusta. **Map** 2 F2. **Tel** 06 06 08. 🚌 70, 81, 117, 119, 186, 628. **Open** 9am–7pm Tue–Sun (last adm: 6pm). **Closed** Jan 1, Dec 25. 📶 **W** arapacis.it

Painstakingly reconstructed over many years from scattered fragments, the exquisitely carved Ara Pacis (Altar of Peace) celebrates the peace created by Emperor Augustus throughout the Mediterranean. Commissioned by the Senate in 13 BC and completed four years later, the altar stands in a square enclosure of Carrara marble, carved with realistic reliefs of such quality that experts think the craftsmen may have been Greek.

The reliefs on the north and south walls depict a procession that took place on July 4, 13 BC, in which the members of the

emperor's family can be identified, including Augustus's grandson, Lucius, clutching at the skirt of his mother, Antonia. The site is housed in a building by architect Richard Meier.

❺ Mausoleum of Augustus

Piazza Augusto Imperatore. **Map** 2 F2. **Tel** 06 06 08. 🚌 81, 117, 492, 628, 926. **Closed** for restoration. 📶 ♿

Now just a weedy mound ringed with cypresses and strewn with litter, this was once the most prestigious burial place in Rome. Augustus had the mausoleum built in 28 BC, the year before he became sole ruler, as a tomb for himself and his descendants. The circular building was 270 ft (87 m) in diameter with two obelisks (now in Piazza del Quirinale and Piazza dell'Esquilino) at the entrance. Inside were four concentric passageways linked by corridors where urns holding the ashes of the Imperial family were placed, including those of Augustus who died in AD 14.

❻ Trevi Fountain

Piazza di Trevi. **Map** 3 B3. 🚌 116 & many other routes.

Nicola Salvi's theatrical design for Rome's largest and most famous fountain was completed in 1762. The central figures are Neptune, flanked by two Tritons, one trying to master an unruly sea horse, the other leading a

Rome's largest and most famous fountain, the Trevi

quieter beast, symbolizing the two contrasting moods of the sea.

The site originally marked the terminal of the Aqua Virgo aqueduct, built by Augustus's right-hand man and son-in-law, Agrippa, in 19 BC to channel water to Rome's new bath complexes. One of the reliefs on the first story shows a young girl, Trivia, after whom the fountain may have been named. She is said to have first shown the spring, 14 miles (22 km) from the city, to thirsty Roman soldiers.

Interior, Sant'Andrea al Quirinale

❼ Sant'Andrea al Quirinale

Via del Quirinale 29. **Map** 3 B3. **Tel** 06 474 48 72. 🚌 116, 117. **Open** 8:30am–noon, 3:30–6pm Mon–Sat; 9am–noon, 4–7pm Sun. 🗿

Sant'Andrea was designed for the Jesuits by Bernini and executed by his assistants between 1658 and 1670. The site was wide but shallow, so Bernini took the radical step of pointing the long axis of his oval plan toward the sides, and leading the eye round to the altar by means of a strong horizontal cornice. At the altar he combined sculpture and painting to create a theatrical crucifixion of Sant'Andrea (St. Andrew); the diagonally crucified saint on the altarpiece looks up at a stucco effigy of himself ascending to the lantern, where the Holy Spirit and cherubs await him in heaven.

The dome of San Carlo alle Quattro Fontane, by Borromini

❽ San Carlo alle Quattro Fontane

Via del Quirinale 23. **Map** 3 B3. **Tel** 06 488 31 09. 🚌 116 & routes to Piazza Barberini. Ⓜ Barberini. **Open** 10am–1pm, 3–6pm daily (only am Sat & Sun).

In 1638, Borromini was commissioned by the Trinitarians to design a church and convent on a tiny cramped site at the Quattro Fontane crossroads. The church, so small that it is said it would fit inside one of the piers of St. Peter's, is designed with bold, fluid curves on both the façade and interior to give light and life to the diminutive building. The dome, with its concealed windows, illusionistic coffering, and tiny lantern designed to make it look higher than it really is, is a cunning feature.

❾ Palazzo Barberini

Via delle Quattro Fontane 13. **Map** 3 B3. **Tel** 06 328 10. 🚌 52, 53, 61, 62, 63, 80, 116, 175, 492, 590. Ⓜ Barberini. **Open** 8:30am–7pm Tue–Sun (last adm: 6:30pm). **Closed** Jan 1, Dec 25. 🗿 🗿 🗿 🗿 🗿 🗿 (lift). 🆆 galleriaborghese.it

When Maffei Barberini became Pope Urban VIII in 1623, he decided to build a grand family palazzo. Designed by Carlo Maderno as a typical country villa on the fringes of the city, it

now overlooks Piazza Barberini, where traffic hurtles around Bernini's Triton fountain. Maderno died shortly after the foundations had been laid, and Bernini and Borromini took over.

The most dazzling room is the Gran Salone, with an illusionistic ceiling frescoed by Pietro da Cortona in 1633–9. The palazzo also houses part of the Galleria Nazionale d'Arte Antica with works by Titian, Filippo Lippi, Caravaggio, and Artemisia Gentileschi. The most famous is a portrait of a courtesan, reputedly Raphael's lover, *La Fornarina*, said to be a baker's daughter, although not painted by the artist himself.

Ceiling fresco detail in Palazzo Barberini (1633)

❿ Santa Maria della Concezione

Via Veneto 27. **Map** 3 B2. **Tel** 06 487 11 85. 🚌 52, 53, 61, 62, 63, 80, 116, 175. Ⓜ Barberini. Crypt **Open** 9am–noon, 3–6pm daily.

Below this unassuming church on Via Veneto is a crypt decked with the dismembered skeletons of 4,000 Capuchin monks. They form a macabre reminder of the transience of life, with vertebrae wired together to make sacred hearts and crowns of thorns, and, in one chapel, the poignant skeleton of a tiny Barberini princess.

⓫ Santa Maria della Vittoria

Via XX Settembre 17. **Map** 3 C2.
Tel 06 42 74 05 71. 🚌 61, 62, 175, 910.
Ⓜ Repubblica. **Open** 9am–noon,
3:30–6:30pm daily.

Santa Daria della Vittoria is an intimate Baroque church with a lavish, candlelit interior. Inside the Cornaro chapel is one of Bernini's most ambitious sculptures, the *Ecstasy of St. Teresa* (1646). The physical nature of St. Teresa's ecstasy is apparent as she appears collapsed on a cloud with her mouth half open and eyes closed, struck by the arrow of a smiling angel. Ecclesiastical members, past and present, of the Venetian Cornaro family, who commissioned the chapel, sit in boxes as if watching and discussing the scene being played out in front of them.

Bernini's *Ecstasy of St. Teresa* in Santa Maria della Vittoria

⓬ Museo Nazionale Romano

Palazzo Massimo, Largo di Villa Peretti 1 (1 of 5 sites). **Map** 4 D3. **Tel** 06 39 96 77 00. 🚌 all routes to Termini.
Ⓜ Repubblica. **Open** 9am–7:45pm Tue–Sun. 🎟 ticket valid for all sites.
🔲 ♿ 🎧 🛈 📷

Founded in 1899, the Museo Nazionale Romano – one of the world's leading museums of Classical art – houses most of the antiquities found in Rome since 1870, as well as important older collections. During the 1990s it underwent a major reorganization and now has five branches: the Palazzo Altemps (see p404); the Baths of Diocletian; the Aula Ottagona, the Crypta; Balbi, and the Palazzo Massimo. In the latter, exhibits dating from the 2nd century BC to the late 4th century AD are displayed in a series of rooms over three floors. Highlights include the *Quattro Aurighe* mosaics from a villa in northern Rome, the breathtaking series of frescoes from Livia's summer villa, and the famous statue of her husband, the Emperor Augustus.

One of the finely detailed Quattro Aurighe mosaics on display at the Museo Nazionale Romano

⓭ Santa Prassede

Via Santa Prassede 9a. **Map** 4 D4.
Tel 06 488 24 56. 🚌 16, 70, 71, 75, 714. Ⓜ Vittorio Emanuele. **Open** 7:30am–12:30pm, 4–6:30pm daily. ♿

The church was founded by Pope Paschal II in the 9th century and decorated by Byzantine artists with the most important, glittering mosaics in Rome. In the apse Christ stands between Santa Prassede and her sister, dressed as Byzantine empresses, among white-robed elders, lambs, feather-mop palms, and bright red poppies. The Cappella di San Zeno is even lovelier, a jewel box of a

9th-century mosaic, Santa Prassede

mausoleum, built by Pope Paschal II for his mother, Theodora. Her square halo shows that she was still alive when the mosaic was created.

⓮ San Pietro in Vincoli

Piazza di San Pietro in Vincoli. **Map** 3 C5. **Tel** 06 97 84 49 50. 🚌 75, 85, 117.
Ⓜ Colosseo. **Open** 8am–12:30pm, 3–7pm daily (Oct–Mar: to 6pm). ♿

The church's name means St. Peter in Chains, so called because it houses what are said to be the chains with which St. Peter was shackled in the Mamertine Prison (see p393). According to tradition, one set of chains was sent to Constantinople by Empress Eudoxia; when it was returned to Rome some years later it miraculously fused with its partner.

San Pietro is now best known for the Tomb of Julius II, commissioned from Michelangelo by the pope in 1505. Much to the artist's chagrin, Julius soon became more interested in the building of a new St. Peter's, and the tomb project was laid to one side. After the pope died in 1513, Michelangelo resumed work on the tomb, but had only completed the statues of the *Dying Slaves* (now found in Paris and Florence) and *Moses* when he was called away to paint the *Last Judgment* in the Sistine Chapel.

⓯ Santa Maria Maggiore

A confident blend of architectural styles, ranging from Early Christian to late Baroque, Santa Maria is also famous for its superb mosaics. Founded in about AD 420, it retains the original colonnaded triple nave, lined with panels of rare 5th-century mosaics. The Cosmatesque marble floor and bell tower are medieval, as are the spectacular mosaics on the triumphal arch and in the loggia. The lavish coffered ceiling is Renaissance; the façades, domes, and chapels Baroque.

VISITORS' CHECKLIST

Practical Information
Piazza di Santa Maria Maggiore.
Map 4 D4.
Tel 06 69 88 68 00.
Open 7am–6:45pm daily. 🕈 ♿

Transportation
🚌 16, 70, 71, 714. 🚊 14. Ⓜ
Termini, Cavour.

Coronation of the Virgin
This is one of the wonderful 13th-century mosaics in the apse by Jacopo Torriti.

5th-century mosaics

Bell tower

Tomb of Cardinal Rodriguez
This Gothic tomb, which dates from 1299, contains magnificent marblework by the Cosmati.

18th-century façade by Ferdinando Fuga

13th-century mosaics

Cappella Paolina
Flaminio Ponzio, architect of the Villa Borghese, designed this sumptuous chapel in 1611 for Pope Paul V, who is buried here.

Column in Piazza Santa Maria Maggiore
In 1611 a bronze of the Virgin and Child was added to this ancient marble column, which came from the Basilica of Constantine.

Cappella Sistina
This chapel was built for Pope Sixtus V (1584–7) by Domenico Fontana and was opulently covered with ancient marble. It houses the pope's tomb.

THE VATICAN AND TRASTEVERE

Vatican City, the world capital of Catholicism, is the world's smallest state. It occupies 106 acres (43 ha) within high walls watched over by the Vatican guard. It was the site where St. Peter was martyred (c.AD 64) and buried, and it became the residence of the popes who succeeded him. The papal palaces, next to the great basilica of St. Peter's, are home to the Sistine Chapel and the eclectic collections of the Vatican Museums, as well as being the residence of the pope. Neighboring Trastevere is quite different, a picturesque old quarter, whose inhabitants consider themselves to be the only true Romans. Sadly, the proletarian identity of the place is in danger of being destroyed by the proliferation of trendy restaurants, clubs, and shops.

Sights at a Glance

Churches
② St. Peter's pp422–3
⑦ Santa Maria in Trastevere
⑧ Santa Cecilia in Trastevere
⑨ San Francesco a Ripa
⑩ San Pietro in Montorio and the Tempietto

Museums and Galleries
③ Vatican Museums pp424–31
⑤ Palazzo Corsini and Galleria Nazionale d'Arte Antica

Historic Buildings
① Castel Sant'Angelo
④ Villa Farnesina

Parks and Gardens
⑥ Botanical Gardens

See Rome Street Finder maps 1, 2, 5, 6, 9

0 meters 250
0 yards 250

◄ View of St. Peter's with the Ponte Sant'Angelo in the foreground

A Tour of the Vatican

The Vatican, a sovereign state since February 1929, is ruled by the pope, Europe's only absolute monarch. About 500 people live here, and as well as accommodation for staff and ecclesiasts, the city has its own post office, banks, currency, judicial system, radio station, shops, and a daily newspaper, *L'Osservatore Romano*.

★ St. Peter's
Most of the great architects of the Renaissance and Baroque had a hand in the design of the Basilica of St. Peter's, the most famous church in Christendom *(see pp422–3)*.

★ Sistine Chapel
Michelangelo frescoed the ceiling with scenes from Genesis (1508–12), and the altar wall with the *Last Judgment* (1534–41). The chapel is used by cardinals when electing a new pope *(see p428)*.

Raphael Rooms

PIAZZA DEL SANT UFFIZIO

PIAZZA SAN PIETR

PIAZZ

PIO

To Via della Conciliazione

KEY

① **Piazza San Pietro** was laid out by Bernini between 1656 and 1667.

② **Information office**

③ **The Papal Audience Chamber**

④ **Vatican Radio** broadcasts in 20 languages throughout the world from this tower, part of the 9th-century Leonine Wall.

⑤ **The Vatican Gardens**, open for guided tours, make up a third of the Vatican's territory.

Locator Map
See Rome Street Finder map 1

This staircase leading down from the museums, designed in 1932 by Giuseppe Momo, is in the form of a double helix, consisting of two spirals: one to walk up and one to walk down.

Entrance to Vatican Museums

★ **Vatican Museums**
The marble group of the *Laocoön* (AD 1) is one of many prestigious works of art in the Vatican *(see p426)*.

The Cortile della Pigna is named after a bronze pinecone from an ancient fountain.

VIA DI PORTA ANGELICA

★ **Raphael Rooms**
Raphael frescoed this suite in the early 16th century. Works like *The School of Athens* established his reputation, to equal that of his contemporary Michelangelo *(see p431)*.

❶ Castel Sant'Angelo

Lungotevere Castello. **Map** 2 D3.
Tel 06 681 91 11. 34, 280.
Open 9am–7:30pm Tue–Sun (last entry 6:30pm). **Closed** Jan 1, Dec 25.

W castelsantangelo.com

This massive fortress takes its name from the vision of the Archangel Michael by Pope Gregory the Great in the 6th century as he led a procession across the bridge, praying for the end of the plague.

The castle began life in AD 139 as the Emperor Hadrian's mausoleum. Since then it has been a bridgehead in the Emperor Aurelian's city wall, a medieval citadel and prison, and a place of safety for popes during times of political unrest. A corridor links it with the Vatican Palace, providing an escape route for the pope. From dank cells to fine apartments of Renaissance popes, the museums cover all aspects of the castle's history, including the Sala Paolina, with illusionistic frescoes (1546–8) by Pellegrino Tibaldi and Perin del Vaga and the Courtyard of Honor.

Illusionistic frescoes by Pellegrino Tibaldi

View of Castel Sant'Angelo from the Ponte Sant'Angelo

❷ St. Peter's

Catholicism's most sacred shrine, the sumptuous, marble-caked basilica of St. Peter's draws pilgrims and tourists from all over the world. It holds hundreds of precious works of art, some salvaged from the original 4th-century basilica built by Constantine, others commissioned from Renaissance and Baroque artists. The dominant tone is set by Bernini, who created the baldacchino twisting up below Michelangelo's huge dome. Bernini also created the Cathedra in the apse, with four saints supporting a throne that contains fragments once thought to be relics of the chair from which St. Peter delivered his first sermon.

Dome of St. Peter's
The 448 ft (136.5 m) high dome, designed by Michelangelo, was not completed in his lifetime.

KEY

① **Entrance to Historical Artistic Museum and Sacristy**

② **The Monument to Pope Alexander VII** was Bernini's last work in St. Peter's. Completed in 1678, it shows the Chigi Pope among figures of Truth, Justice, Charity, and Prudence.

③ **A staircase** of 537 steps leads to the summit of the dome.

④ **The Baldacchino** was commissioned by Pope Urban VIII in 1624; Bernini's extravagant Baroque canopy stands above St. Peter's tomb.

⑤ **The Papal Altar** stands over the crypt where St. Peter is reputedly buried.

⑥ **The church** is 615 ft (186 m) long.

⑦ **The foot of St. Peter**, sculpted by Arnolfo di Cambio in the 13th century, has worn thin from the touch of pilgrims over the centuries.

⑧ **Two minor cupolas by Vignola** (1507–73)

⑨ **Markings** on the floor of the nave show how other churches compare in length.

⑩ **Façade by Carlo Maderno (1614)**

⑪ **From this Library window** the Pope blesses the faithful gathered in the piazza below.

⑫ **The Holy Door** is used only in Holy Years.

⑬ **Atrium by Carlo Maderno**

Historical Plan of the Basilica of St. Peter's

St. Peter was buried in AD 64 in a necropolis near the site of his crucifixion in the Circus of Nero. In AD 324 Constantine constructed a basilica over the tomb. The old church was rebuilt in the 15th century, and throughout the 16th and 17th centuries various architects developed the existing structure. The new church was inaugurated in 1626.

Key

▢ Circus of Nero
▢ Constantinian
▢ Renaissance
▢ Baroque

The Grottoes
A fragment of this 13th-century mosaic by Giotto, salvaged from the old basilica, is now in the Grottoes, where many popes are buried.

Michelangelo's Pietà
Protected by glass since an attack in 1972, the Pietà was created in 1499 when Michelangelo was only 25.

VISITORS' CHECKLIST

Practical Information
Piazza San Pietro.
Map 1 B3.
Tel 06 69 88 37 12 (sacristy);
06 69 88 16 62 (tourist info).
Basilica: **Open** Apr–Sep:
7am–7pm daily (mid-Oct–Mar:
to 6:30pm). 🚻 ♿ 🗪
Treasury: **Open** Apr–Sep:
8am–7pm daily (Oct–Mar:
to 6pm). 🗪
Grottoes: **Open** Apr–Sep:
7am–4pm daily (Oct–Mar: 6pm).
Dome: **Open** 8am–6pm daily
(Oct–Mar: to 5pm). 🗪
Papal audiences: Usually Wed at
10:30am in Piazza San Pietro or in
the Papal Audience Chamber.
Tickets (free) from Prefecture of
the Pontifical Household. Call 06
69 88 48 57 or check availability at
office through bronze doors on
right of the colonnade
(9am–1pm). The Pope appears
at noon Sun to bless the crowd
in Piazza San Pietro.

Transportation
🚌 23, 49, 70, 180, 492.
Ⓜ Ottaviano San Pietro.

Filarete Doors
These bronze doors from the old basilica were decorated with biblical reliefs by Filarete between 1439 and 1445.

Entrance

Piazza San Pietro
On Sundays, religious festivals, and special occasions such as canonizations, the Pope blesses the crowds from a balcony.

❸ Vatican Museums

Home to the Sistine Chapel and Raphael Rooms as well
as to one of the world's most important art collections,
the Vatican Museums are housed in palaces originally
built for Renaissance popes such as Julius II, Innocent VIII,
and Sixtus IV. Most of the later additions were made
in the 18th century, when priceless works of art
accumulated by earlier popes were first put on show.

Etruscan Museum
The Etruscan collection includes a
woman's gold clasp *(fibula)* from the
7th-century BC Regolini-Galassi tomb
at Cerveteri, north of Rome.

Gallery of Maps
The *Siege of Malta* is one of 40
maps of the Church's territories,
frescoed by the 16th-century
cartographer Ignazio Danti
on the gallery's walls.

Gallery of the
Candelabra

Raphael Rooms
This is a detail of the
*Expulsion of
Heliodorus from the
Temple*, one of many
frescoes painted by
Raphael and his
pupils for Julius II's
private apartments
(see p431).

Gallery of
Tapestries

Stairs
down

Upper
floor

Sala dei Chiaroscuri

Raphael
Loggia

Sistine Chapel
(see p428-30)

Gallery Guide

*The museum complex is vast: the
Sistine Chapel is 20–30 minutes' walk
from the entrance, so allow plenty of
time. There is a strict one-way system,
and it is best to be selective or choose
one of four color-coded itineraries,
which vary from 90 minutes to a
5-hour marathon.*

Borgia Apartment
Pinturicchio and his assistants frescoed
these rooms for Alexander VI in 1492–5.

**Modern religious
art** on view here
was sent to the
popes by artists
worldwide, such
as Bacon, Ernst,
and Carrà.

Pio-Clementine Museum
The finest of the Vatican's Classical statues are on display here, like the *Apollo Belvedere*, a Roman copy in marble of a 4th-century BC Greek bronze.

Gregorian Profane Museum

Stairs up to Etruscan Museum

Entrance

Lower floor

Cortile Ottagonale

Braccio Nuovo

Chiaramonti Museum

The Lapidary Gallery
contains inscriptions from pagan and Christian catacombs, but is closed to the public.

VISITORS' CHECKLIST

Practical Information
Città del Vaticano (entrance in Viale Vaticano).
Map 1 B2.
Tel 06 69 88 46 76.
Open 9am–6pm Mon–Sat (last adm: 4pm); 9am–2pm last Sun of month (last adm: 12:30pm).
Closed religious and public hols. Special permit required for Raphael Loggia, Vatican Library, Lapidary Gallery, & Vatican Archives. 🏛 free last Sun of month. ♿ special routes. 📷 📱
📧 🌐 mv.vatican.va

Transportation
🚌 49 to entrance, 23, 81, 492, 990. Ⓜ Ottaviano San Pietro, Cipro Musei Vaticani.

Egyptian Museum
The collection of Egyptian artifacts includes this painted bas-relief from a 2400 BC tomb. The museum was organized by Father Ungarelli, a 19th-century Egyptologist.

Pio-Christian Museum
Early Christianity adopted Classical images so that its doctrines could be more easily understood. This 4th-century statue of Christ as the Good Shepherd derives from the pastoral figure of the shepherd.

Pinacoteca
The Vatican's art gallery has 15th- to 19th-century works, and is particularly strong on the Renaissance. This unfinished painting of *St. Jerome* by Leonardo da Vinci reveals his mastery of anatomy.

Key to Floor Plan
- ■ Egyptian and Assyrian art
- ☐ Greek and Roman art
- ■ Etruscan art
- ■ Early Christian and medieval art
- ■ 15th- to 19th-century art
- ■ Modern religious art
- ■ Lapidary Gallery
- ☐ Nonexhibition space

Exploring the Vatican's Collections

The Vatican's greatest treasures are its superlative Greek and Roman antiquities, together with the magnificent artifacts excavated from Egyptian and Etruscan tombs during the 19th century. Some of Italy's greatest artists, such as Raphael, Michelangelo, and Leonardo da Vinci, are represented in the Pinacoteca (art gallery) and parts of the former palaces, where the artists were employed by popes to decorate sumptuous apartments and galleries.

Head of an athlete in mosaic from the Baths of Caracalla, AD 217

Egyptian and Assyrian Art

The Egyptian collection contains finds from 19th- and 20th-century excavations in Egypt, as well as statues that were brought to Rome in Imperial times. There are also Roman imitations of Egyptian art from Hadrian's Villa (*see p472*) and from temples in Rome devoted to Egyptian gods and goddesses, such as Isis and Serapis.

The genuine Egyptian works, displayed on the lower floor next to the Pio-Clementine Museum, include statues, mummies, mummy cases, and a Book of the Dead. One of the main treasures is a colossal 13th-century granite statue of Queen Mutuy, the mother of Rameses II, which was found on the site of the Horti Sallustiani gardens near Via Veneto. Also noteworthy are the head of a statue of Montuhotep IV (20th century BC), the beautiful mummy case of Queen Hetepheres, and the tomb of Iri, who was the guardian of the Pyramid of Cheops. This dates back to the 22nd century BC.

Roman copy of the Greek *Doryphoros*

Here, the most famous exhibits are the gold jewelry and bronze throne, bed, and funeral cart, found in the 650 BC Regolini-Galassi tomb in Cerveteri (*see p470*).

Prize Greek and Roman pieces form the nucleus of the Pio-Clementine Museum. These include high-quality Roman copies of 4th-century BC Greek statues, such as the *Apoxyomenos* (an athlete wiping his body after a race) and the *Apollo del Belvedere*. The splendid *Laocoön* (1st century AD), originally from Rhodes, was found in 1506 in the ruins of Nero's Golden House. Works such as these inspired Michelangelo and other Renaissance artists. The much smaller Chiaramonti Museum is lined with ancient busts, and its extension, the Braccio Nuovo, has a 1st-century BC statue of Augustus from the villa of his wife Livia. It is based on the *Doryphoros* (spear-carrier) by

the 5th-century BC Greek sculptor Polyclitus. There is also a Roman copy of this on display opposite. The Gregorian Profane Museum, housed in a separate wing, follows the evolution of Roman art from reliance on Greek models to a recognizably Roman style.

In this museum, original Greek works include large marble fragments from the Parthenon in Athens. Among the Roman pieces are two reliefs, the *Rilievi della Cancelleria*, commissioned by Domitian in AD 81 to glorify the military parades of his father, Emperor Vespasian. There are also fine Roman floor mosaics, two from the Baths of Caracalla (*see p441*), and one, in the Round Room, dated 3rd century AD, from the Baths of Otricoli in Umbria.

In the Vatican Library is the 1st-century AD *Aldobrandini Wedding*, a beautiful Roman fresco depicting a bride being prepared for her marriage.

Greek, Etruscan, and Roman Art

The greater part of the Vatican Museums is dedicated to Greek and Roman art. However, the Etruscan Museum houses a superb collection of Etruscan (*see p48*) and pre-Roman artifacts from Etruria and the Greek colonies of southern Italy.

Roman mosaic from the Baths of Otricoli, Umbria, in the Round Room

Early Christian and Medieval Art

The main collection of early Christian antiquities is in the Pio-Christian Museum, which contains inscriptions and sculpture from catacombs and early Christian basilicas. The sculpture consists chiefly of reliefs from sarcophagi, though the most striking work is a freestanding 4th-century statue of the *Good Shepherd*. The sculpture's chief interest lies in the way it blends Biblical episodes with pagan mythology. The idealized pastoral figure of the shepherd became Christ himself, while bearded philosophers turned into the Apostles.

The first two rooms of the Pinacoteca are dedicated to late medieval art, mostly wooden altarpieces painted in tempera. The outstanding work is Giotto's *Stefaneschi Triptych* of about 1300 which decorated the main altar of the old St. Peter's.

The Vatican Library has a number of medieval treasures including reliquaries, textiles, enamels, and icons.

Pietà (c.1471–4) by the Venetian artist Giovanni Bellini in the Pinacoteca

Detail of Giotto's *Stefaneschi Triptych* (1330) in the Pinacoteca

15th- to 19th-Century Art

Many Renaissance popes were connoisseurs of the arts who considered it their duty to sponsor the leading painters, sculptors, and goldsmiths of the age. The galleries around the Cortile del Belvedere were decorated by great artists between the 16th and the 19th centuries.

The Gallery of Tapestries is hung with tapestries woven in Brussels to designs by students of Raphael. The Apartment of Pope Pius V has beautiful 15th-century Flemish tapestries, and the Gallery of Maps is frescoed with 16th-century maps of ancient and contemporary Italy.

Alongside the Raphael Rooms *(see p431)* are the Room of the Chiaroscuri and Pope Nicholas V's private chapel. This was frescoed between 1447 and 1451 by Fra Angelico. Also worth seeing is the Borgia Apartment, decorated in the 1490s by Pinturicchio and his pupils for the Borgia Pope, Alexander VI. Another set of fascinating frescoes can be found in the Loggia of Raphael, but a visit here requires special permission.

The Pinacoteca has many important Renaissance works. Highlights from the 15th century are a fine *Pietà* by Giovanni Bellini, part of his *Coronation of the Virgin* altarpiece in Pèsaro *(see p372)*; and Leonardo da Vinci's unfinished *St. Jerome*, discovered, after being long lost, in two halves. One was being used as a coffer lid in an antique shop, the other as the seat of a stool in a shoemaker's. Exceptional pieces from the 16th century include eight tapestry cartoons, the *Transfiguration*, and *Madonna of Foligno* by Raphael, in a room devoted to the artist; a *Deposition* by Caravaggio; an altarpiece by Titian; and *St. Helen* by Veronese, which shows the saint as a gorgeously dressed aristocrat.

Pinturicchio's *Adoration of the Magi* (1490), Borgia Apartment

Sistine Chapel: The Ceiling

Michelangelo frescoed the ceiling for Pope Julius II between 1508 and 1512, working on specially designed scaffolding. The main panels, which chart the Creation of the World and Fall of Man, are surrounded by subjects from the Old and New Testaments – except for the Classical Sibyls who are said to have foreseen the birth of Christ. In the 1980s the ceiling was restored, revealing colors of an unsuspected vibrancy.

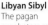

Libyan Sibyl
The pagan prophetess reaches for the Book of Knowledge. Like most female figures Michelangelo painted, the beautiful Libyan Sibyl was probably modeled on a man.

① ← Creation of the Sun and Moon

KEY

① **Illusionistic architecture**

② **The lunettes** are devoted to frescoes of the ancestors of Christ, like Hezekiah.

③ **The Ignudi** are athletic male nudes whose significance is uncertain.

Key to Ceiling Panels

Genesis: 1 God Dividing Light from Darkness; **2** Creation of the Sun and Moon; **3** Separating Waters from Land; **4** Creation of Adam; **5** Creation of Eve; **6** Original Sin; **7** Sacrifice of Noah; **8** The Deluge; **9** Drunkenness of Noah.

Ancestors of Christ: 10 Solomon with His Mother; **11** Parents of Jesse; **12** Rehoboam with Mother; **13** Asa with Parents; **14** Uzziah with Parents; **15** Hezekiah with Parents; **16** Zerubbabel with Parents; **17** Josiah with Parents.

Prophets: 18 Jonah; **19** Jeremiah; **20** Daniel; **21** Ezekiel; **22** Isaiah; **23** Joel; **24** Zechariah.

Sibyls: 25 Libyan Sibyl; **26** Persian Sibyl; **27** Cumaean Sibyl; **28** Erythrean Sibyl; **29** Delphic Sibyl.

Old Testament scenes of salvation: 30 Punishment of Haman; **31** Moses and the Brazen Serpent; **32** David and Goliath; **33** Judith and Holofernes.

Original Sin
This shows Adam and Eve tasting the forbidden fruit from the Tree of Knowledge, and their expulsion from Paradise. Michelangelo represents Satan as a snake with the body of a woman.

Creation of the Sun and Moon
Michelangelo depicts God as a dynamic but terrifying figure commanding the sun to shed light on the earth.

Restoration of the Sistine Ceiling

The restorers of the Sistine Chapel used computers, photography, and spectrum technology to analyze the fresco before cleaning began. They separated Michelangelo's work from that of later restorers and discovered that the restorers had attempted to clean the ceiling with materials ranging from bread to retsina wine. The new restoration revealed the familiarly dusky, eggshell-cracked figures to have creamy skins and lustrous hair, and to be dressed in brightly colored, luscious robes: "a Benetton Michelangelo," mocked one critic, claiming that a layer of varnish that the artist had added to darken the colors had been removed. However, after examining the work, most experts agreed that the new colors probably matched those painted by Michelangelo.

A restorer cleaning the Libyan Sibyl

Sistine Chapel: The Walls

The massive walls of the Sistine Chapel, the main chapel in the Vatican Palace, were frescoed by some of the finest artists of the 15th and 16th centuries. The 12 paintings on the side walls, by artists including Perugino, Ghirlandaio, Botticelli, and Signorelli, show parallel episodes from the life of Moses and of Christ. The decoration of the chapel walls was completed between 1534 and 1541 by Michelangelo, who added the great altar wall fresco, the *Last Judgment*.

Key to the Frescoes: Artists and Subjects

The Last Judgment

☐ Perugino   ☐ Botticelli   ☐ Ghirlandaio

☐ Rosselli   ☐ Signorelli   ☐ Michelangelo

1 Baptism of Christ in the Jordan
2 Temptations of Christ
3 Calling of St. Peter and St. Andrew
4 Sermon on the Mount
5 Handing over the Keys to St. Peter
6 Last Supper
7 Moses's Journey into Egypt
8 Moses Receiving the Call
9 Crossing of the Red Sea
10 Adoration of the Golden Calf
11 Punishment of the Rebels
12 Last Days of Moses

The Last Judgment by Michelangelo

Revealed in 1993 after a year's restoration, the *Last Judgment* is considered to be the masterpiece of Michelangelo's mature years. It was commissioned by Pope Paul III Farnese, and required the removal of some earlier frescoes and two windows over the altar. A new wall was erected that slanted inward to stop dust from settling on it. Michelangelo worked alone on the fresco for seven years, until its completion in 1541.

The painting depicts the souls of the dead rising up to face the wrath of God, a subject that is rarely used for an altar decoration. The Pope chose it as a warning to Catholics to adhere to their faith in the turmoil of the Reformation. In fact the work conveys the artist's own tormented attitude to his faith. It offers neither the certainties of Christian orthodoxy, nor the ordered view of Classicism.

In a dynamic, emotional composition, the figures are caught in a vortex of motion. The dead are torn from their graves and hauled up to face Christ the Judge, whose athletic, muscular figure is the focus of all the painting's movement.

Christ shows little sympathy for the agitated saints around him, clutching the instruments of their martyrdom. Neither is any pity shown for the damned, hurled down to the demons in hell. Here Charon, pushing people off his boat into the depths of Hades, and the infernal judge Minos, are taken from Dante's *Inferno*. Minos has ass's ears, and is a portrait of courtier Biagio da Cesena, who had objected to the nude figures in the fresco. Michelangelo's self-portrait is on the skin held by the martyr St. Bartholomew.

Souls meeting the wrath of Christ in Michelangelo's *Last Judgment*

Raphael Rooms

Pope Julius II's private apartments were built above those of his hated predecessor, Alexander VI, who died in 1503. Julius was impressed with Raphael's work and chose him to redecorate the four rooms (stanze). Raphael and his pupils began in 1508, replacing works by better-known artists, including Raphael's teacher, Perugino. The new frescoes quickly established the young artist's reputation in Rome, but the project took 16 years to complete and he died before it was finished.

Key to floorplan

① Hall of Constantine
② Room of Heliodorus
③ Room of the Segnatura
④ Room of the Fire in the Borgo

Detail from Raphael's *The Mass of Bolsena* (1512)

Hall of Constantine

The frescoes in this room were started in 1517 and completed in 1525, five years after Raphael's death, and are largely the work of the artist's pupils. The theme of the decoration is the triumph of Christianity over paganism, and the four major frescoes show scenes from the life of Constantine, the first Christian emperor. These include the *Vision of the Cross* and the emperor's victory over his rival, Maxentius, at *The Battle of the Milvian Bridge*, for which Raphael had provided a preparatory sketch.

Room of Heliodorus

Raphael decorated this private antechamber between 1512 and 1514. The main frescoes all contain thinly veiled references to the protective powers of the papacy. The room's name refers to the fresco on the right, *The Expulsion of Heliodorus from the Temple*, showing Heliodorus felled by a horseman as he tries to rob the Temple in Jerusalem. It alludes to Pope Julius II's victory over foreign armies in Italy. *The Mass of Bolsena* on the left wall refers to a miracle that occurred in 1263, in which a priest who doubted the doctrine of the Holy Host was said to have seen blood issue from it at the moment of sacrifice.

Room of the Segnatura

Completed between 1508 and 1511, the frescoes here are the most harmonious in the series. The scheme followed by Raphael, dictated by Pope Julius II, reflected the Humanist belief that there could be perfect harmony between Classical culture and Christianity in the search for truth. The most famous work, *The School of Athens*, centers on the debate about truth between the Greek philosophers Plato and Aristotle. Raphael depicted some of his contemporaries as philosophers, including Leonardo da Vinci, Bramante, and Michelangelo.

Room of the Fire in The Borgo

This was originally the dining room, but when the decoration was completed under Pope Leo X, it became a music room. All the frescoes exalt the reigning pope by depicting events in the lives of his 9th-century namesakes, Leo III and IV. The main frescoes were designed by Raphael, but finished by his assistants between 1514 and 1517. The most famous, *The Fire in the Borgo*, shows a miracle of 847, when Pope Leo IV put out a fire by making the sign of the cross. Raphael draws a parallel between this and the legendary flight of Aeneas from Troy, recounted by Virgil. Aeneas appears in the foreground, carrying his father Anchises on his back.

The School of Athens (1511) showing philosophers and scholars

❹ Villa Farnesina

Via della Lungara 230. **Map** 2 E5.
Tel 06 68 02 72 68. ▦ 23, 280.
Open 9am–2pm Mon–Sat. 🖼 🖾

The fabulously wealthy Sienese banker Agostino Chigi commissioned this villa in 1508 from his fellow Sienese Baldassare Peruzzi. Chigi's main home was across the Tiber, and the villa was designed purely for lavish banquets. Artists, poets, cardinals, princes, and the pope himself were entertained here in magnificent style. Chigi also used the villa for sojourns with the courtesan Imperia, who allegedly inspired one of the *Three Graces* painted by Raphael in the Loggia of Cupid and Psyche.

The simple, harmonious design of the Farnesina, with a central block and projecting wings, made it one of the first true villas of the Renaissance. Peruzzi decorated some of the interiors himself, such as the Sala della Prospettiva upstairs, in which the illusionistic frescoes create the impression of looking out over 16th-century Rome through a marble colonnade.

Other frescoes, by Sebastiano del Piombo and Raphael and his pupils, illustrate Classical myths, while the vault of the main hall, the Sala di Galatea, is adorned with astrological scenes showing the position of the stars at the time of Chigi's birth. After his death the business collapsed, and in 1577 the villa was sold off to the Farnese family.

Raphael's *Three Graces* in the Villa Farnesina

Queen Christina of Sweden's bedroom in the Palazzo Corsini

❺ Palazzo Corsini and Galleria Nazionale d'Arte Antica

Via della Lungara 10. **Map** 2 D5.
Tel 06 68 80 23 23. ▦ 23, 280.
Open 8:30am–7:30pm Tue–Sun.
Closed Jan 1, Dec 25. 🖼 🖿 ♿ 🖾
📷 🖥 **galleriaborghese.it**

Built for Cardinal Domenico Riario in 1510–12, the Palazzo Corsini has numbered Bramante, the young Michelangelo, Erasmus, and the mother of Napoleon among its guests. Queen Christina of Sweden died here in 1689. The palazzo was rebuilt by Ferdinando Fuga, who planned the façade to be viewed from an angle, as Via della Lungara is too narrow for a full frontal view.

When the palazzo was bought by the state in 1893, the Corsini family donated their collection of paintings, which formed the core of the national art collection and was soon augmented. The collection is now split between Palazzo Barberini and Palazzo Corsini. Although the best works are in the Barberini, there are paintings by Van Dyck, Rubens, Murillo, and, notably, an androgynous *St. John the Baptist* (c.1604) by Caravaggio and a *Salome* (1638) by Reni. The strangest work is a portrait of the rotund Queen Christina as the goddess Diana by J. Van Egmont.

❻ Botanical Gardens

Largo Cristina di Svezia 24. **Map** 2 D5.
Tel 06 49 91 71 07. ▦ 23, 280. **Open** 9am–6:30pm (Oct–Mar: 5:30pm) Mon–Sat. **Closed** public hols. 🖼 📷

Sequoias, palm trees, orchids, and bromeliads are among the 7,000 plants from all over the world represented in the Botanical Gardens (Orto Botanico). Indigenous and exotic species are grouped to illustrate their botanical families and their adaptation to different climates and ecosystems. There are also some curious plants like the ginkgo that have survived almost unchanged from earlier eras.

Palm trees in the Botanical Gardens, Trastevere

❼ Santa Maria in Trastevere

Piazza Santa Maria in Trastevere.
Map 5 C1. **Tel** 06 581 48 02. ▦ H, 23, 280. **Open** 7:30am–9pm daily. ♿ 📷

Santa Maria in Trastevere was probably the first Christian place of worship in Rome, founded by Pope Callixtus I in the 3rd century, when emperors were still pagan and Christianity a minority cult. According to legend, it was built on the site where a fountain of oil had miraculously sprung up on the day that Christ was born. The basilica became the focus of devotion to the Madonna, and although today's church, and its remarkable mosaics, date largely from the 12th and 13th centuries, images of the Virgin continue to dominate. The façade mosaics probably date

Apse mosaic of the *Coronation of the Virgin*, Santa Maria in Trastevere

from the 12th century, and show Mary, Christ, and ten lamp-bearing women. Inside in the apse is a stylized 12th-century *Coronation of the Virgin*, and below, a series of realistic scenes from the life of the Virgin by the 13th-century artist Pietro Cavallini. The oldest image of the Virgin is a 7th-century icon, the *Madonna di Clemenza*, which depicts her as a Byzantine empress flanked by a guard of angels. It sits above the altar in the Cappella Altemps.

8 Santa Cecilia in Trastevere

Piazza di Santa Cecilia. **Map** 6 D1. **Tel** 06 589 92 89. H, 23, 44, 280. **Open** 9:30am–12:30pm, 4–6:30pm daily. Cavallini fresco **Open** 10am–12:30pm Mon–Fri.

St. Cecilia, aristocrat and patron saint of music, was martyred here in AD 230. After an unsuccessful attempt to suffocate her by locking her in the hot steam bath of her house for three days, she was beheaded. A church was built, possibly in the 4th century, on the site of her house (still to be seen beneath the church, along with the remains of a tannery). Her body was lost, but it turned up again in the Catacombs of San Callisto *(see p446)*. In the 9th century it was reburied here by Pope Paschal I, who rebuilt the church.

A fine apse mosaic survives from this period. The altar canopy by Arnolfo di Cambio

and the fresco of *The Last Judgment* by Pietro Cavallini can be reached through the adjoining convent; they date from the 13th century, one of the few periods when Rome had a distinctive artistic style.

In front of the altar is a delicate statue of St. Cecilia by Stefano Maderno, which is based on sketches made of her perfectly preserved relics when they were briefly disinterred in 1599.

9 San Francesco a Ripa

Piazza San Francesco d'Assisi 88. **Map** 5 C2. **Tel** 06 581 90 20. H, 23, 44, 75, 280. **Open** 7am–1pm, 2–7:30pm daily.

St. Francis of Assisi lived here in a hospice when he visited Rome in 1219, and his stone pillow and crucifix are preserved in his cell. The church was built by a follower, a local nobleman called Rodolfo Anguillara, who is portrayed on his tombstone wearing the Franciscan habit.

Entirely rebuilt in the 1680s by Cardinal Pallavicini, the church is rich in 17th- and 18th-century sculptures. Not to be missed in the Altieri chapel (fourth left, along the nave) is Bernini's exquisite late work, the *Ecstasy of Beata Ludovica Albertoni* (1674).

Bramante's circular Tempietto at San Pietro in Montorio

10 San Pietro in Montorio and the Tempietto

Piazza San Pietro in Montorio 2. **Map** 5 B1. **Tel** 06 581 39 40. 44, 75, 115. **Open** 8:30am–noon daily, 3–4pm Mon–Fri. Tempietto **Open** 9:30am–12:30pm, 3–4pm Tue–Sat.

The Tempietto, a diminutive masterpiece of Renaissance architecture completed by Bramante in 1502, stands in the courtyard of San Pietro in Montorio. The name means "little temple," and its circular shape echoes early Christian *martyria*, chapels built on the site of a saint's martyrdom. This was erroneously thought to be the spot in Nero's Circus where St. Peter was crucified. Bramante ringed the chapel with Doric columns, a Classical frieze, and a fine balustrade.

Bernini's *Ecstasy of Beata Ludovica Albertoni*, San Francesco a Ripa

AVENTINE AND LATERAN

This is one of the greenest parts of the city, taking in the Celian and Aventine Hills as well as the very congested area around San Giovanni in Laterano. The Celian, now scattered with churches, was a fashionable place to live in Imperial Rome. Some of the era's splendor is still apparent in the ruins of the Baths of Caracalla. Behind the Baths rises the Aventine Hill, a peaceful, leafy area, with the superb basilica of Santa Sabina, and lovely views across the river to Trastevere and St. Peter's. In the valley below, cars and Vespas skim around the Circus Maximus, following the ancient charioteering track, while to the south lies Testaccio, a lively working-class district.

Sights at a Glance

Churches
2 Santa Maria in Cosmedin
3 Santa Maria in Domnica
4 Santo Stefano Rotondo
5 Santi Quattro Coronati
6 *San Clemente see p439*
7 San Giovanni in Laterano
11 Santa Sabina

Ancient Sites and Building
1 Temples of the Forum Boarium
8 Baths of Caracalla

Monuments and Tombs
9 Pyramid of Caius Cestius
10 Protestant Cemetery

See Rome Street Finder maps 6, 7, 8

0 meters 250
0 yards 250

◀ One of the mosaics in the Baths of Caracalla

Street by Street: Piazza della Bocca della Verità

The site of Rome's first port and its busy cattle market, this is an odd little corner of the city, stretching from the heavily trafficked road running along the Tiber to the southern spur of the Capitoline Hill, a place of execution from ancient times until the Middle Ages. Although best known for the Bocca della Verità (Mouth of Truth) in Santa Maria in Cosmedin, which is supposed to snap shut on the hands of liars, there are many other sites in the area, notably two temples from the Republican era. In the 6th century the area became home to a Greek community who founded the churches of San Giorgio in Velabro and Santa Maria in Cosmedin.

The Casa dei Crescenzi, studded with ancient fragments, incorporates the ruins of a 10th-century tower built by the powerful Crescenzi family to guard the river Tiber.

Sant'Omobono stands on an archaeological site where finds date back to the 6th century.

❶ ★ Temples of the Forum Boarium
These two buildings are the best preserved of Rome's Republican temples.

Ponte Rotto, as this forlorn ruined arch in the Tiber is called, simply means "broken bridge." Built in the 2nd century BC, its original name was the Pons Aemilius.

The Fontana dei Tritoni, built by Carlo Bizzaccheri in 1715, shows the strong influence of Bernini.

❷ ★ Santa Maria in Cosmedin
The *Bocca della Verità*, a medieval drain cover, is set into the portico.

San Giovanni Decollato belonged to a confraternity that encouraged condemned prisoners to repent.

LUNGOTEVERE DEI PIERLEONI

TEVERE

PONTE PALATINO

PIAZZA DELLA BOCCA DELLA VERITÀ

VIA DI SAN GIOVANNI DECOLLATO

VIA DELLA GR

Key

— Suggested route

0 meters   75
0 yards   75

Santa Maria della Consolazione
was named after an image of the
Virgin placed here in 1385 to give
consolation to the
condemned.

Locator Map
See Rome Street Finder map 6

San Teodoro is a
circular church on the
edge of the Palatine with
exceptional 6th-century
apse mosaics.

San Giorgio in Velabro,
a 7th-century basilica, was
damaged in an explosion in
1994, and has now been restored.

Arco degli Argentari

**The 4th-century Arch of
Janus,** a four-
faced marble-plated arch at
the edge of the Forum
Boarium market, was
an ideal place for merchants
and customers to do
business in the shade.

**❶ Temples of the
Forum Boarium**

Piazza della Bocca della Verità.
Map 6 E1. **Bus** 23, 44, 81, 160, 170,
280, 628, 715, 716.

These wonderfully well-
preserved Republican-era
temples are at their best in
moonlight, standing in their
grassy enclave beside the Tiber
sheltered by umbrella pines.
During the day, they look
less romantic, stranded in a
sea of traffic. They date
from the 2nd century BC,
and were saved from ruin
by being consecrated as
Christian churches in the
Middle Ages by the Greek
community then living in
the area. The rectangular
temple, formerly known as
the Temple of Fortuna Virilis,
was probably dedicated to
Portunus, the god of rivers and
ports. Set on a podium, it has
four Ionic travertine columns
fluted at the front and 12 half-
columns embedded in the tufa
wall of the *cella* – the room that
housed the image of the god.
In the 9th century the Temple
was converted into the church
of Santa Maria Egiziaca, after
a 5th-century prostitute who
reformed and became a hermit.
The smaller circular Temple,
which is made of solid marble
and surrounded by 20 fluted
columns, was dedicated to
Hercules, though it was long
believed to be a Temple of Vesta
because of its similarity to the
one in the Forum.

The Ionic façade of the Republican era
Temple of Portunus

Apse mosaic from the 9th century of the Virgin and Child in Santa Maria in Domnica

❷ Santa Maria in Cosmedin

Piazza della Bocca della Verità. **Map** 6 E1. **Tel** 06 678 77 59. 🚌 23, 44, 81, 160, 170, 280, 628, 715, 716. **Open** 10am–5pm daily. 🚻 ♿ 📷

This beautiful church was built in the 6th century on the site of the ancient city's food market. The Romanesque bell tower and portico were added during the 12th century. In the 19th century a Baroque façade was removed and the church was restored to its original simplicity. It contains many fine examples of Cosmati work, in particular the mosaic sidewalk, the raised choir, the bishop's throne, and the canopy over the main altar.

Set into the wall of the portico is the Bocca della Verità (Mouth of Truth), a grotesque marble face, thought to have been an ancient drain cover.

The nave of Santa Maria in Cosmedin with its Cosmati floor

Medieval tradition had it that the jaws would snap shut on liars – a useful way of testing the faithfulness of spouses.

❸ Santa Maria in Domnica

Piazza della Navicella 12. **Map** 7 A2. **Tel** 06 772 02 685. 🚌 81, 117, 673. Ⓜ Colosseo. **Open** 8am–noon, 3:30–7pm daily (to 6pm in winter). ♿

Santa Maria in Domnica was probably founded in the 7th century, and renovated in the 9th century. By this time the Romans had lost the art of making mosaics, so Pope Paschal I imported mosaicists from Byzantium. They created an exquisite apse mosaic showing the Virgin, Child, and angels in a delicate garden of paradise. Paschal I is kneeling at the Virgin's feet wearing a square halo, indicating that he was alive when it was made.

In 1513 Andrea Sansovino added a portico decorated with lions' heads, a punning homage to Pope Leo X.

❹ Santo Stefano Rotondo

Via di Santo Stefano Rotondo 7. **Map** 7 B2. **Tel** 06 42 11 91 30. 🚌 81, 117, 673. **Open** 9:30am–12:30pm, 3–6pm (2–5pm in winter) Tue–Sun. ✉

Santo Stefano Rotondo was built between 468 and 483 on a circular plan with four chapels in a cruciform shape. Its circular inner area is enclosed by

two concentric corridors. A third, outer corridor was demolished on the orders of Leon Battista Alberti in 1453. In the 1500s Niccolò Pomarancio, Antonio Tempesta, and others covered the walls with 34 frescoes detailing the martyrdoms of saints.

Cloister of Santi Quattro Coronati

❺ Santi Quattro Coronati

Via dei Santi Quattro Coronati 20. **Map** 7 B1. **Tel** 06 70 47 54 27. 🚌 85, 117, 810. 🚋 3. **Open** 6:30am–12:45pm, 3–7:45pm daily. Cloister & Chapel of St. Sylvester **Open** 10–11:45am, 4–5:45pm daily. ♿

This fortified convent was built in the 4th century to house the relics of four Persian stonemasons, martyred after they refused to make a statue of the pagan god Aesculapius. It was rebuilt after invading Normans set fire to it in 1084.

Highlights are a delightful garden cloister and the Chapel of St. Sylvester, where 12th-century frescoes recount the legend of Emperor Constantine's conversion to Christianity.

❻ San Clemente

In 1857 Father Mullooly, the Irish Dominican prior of San Clemente, began excavations beneath the existing 12th-century basilica. Directly underneath, he and his successors discovered a 4th-century church, and below that a number of ancient Roman buildings. Both basilicas are dedicated to St. Clement, the fourth Pope. On the lowest level is a temple devoted to the cult of Mithras, a mystical all-male religion imported from Persia which rivaled Christianity for popularity.

Cappella di Santa Caterina
Restored frescoes by the 15th-century artist Masolino da Panicale show scenes from the life of St. Catherine of Alexandria.

Entrance

Apse Mosaic
The 12th-century *Triumph of the Cross* includes finely detailed animals and acanthus leaves.

Paschal Candlestick
This splendid 12th-century spiraling candlestick, striped with glittering multicolored mosaic, is the work of the Cosmati.

12th-century basilica

18th-century façade

Piscina

Schola Cantorum

4th-century basilica

Life of San Clemente
Faded frescoed episodes from the life of the fourth Pope decorate the lower church. This one tells the story of a boy found alive in his tomb under the sea.

Temple of Mithras

Triclinium
An altar to the god Mithras, showing him slaying a bull, stands in the dank triclinium, a room used for ritual banquets by cult members.

❼ San Giovanni in Laterano

San Giovanni, the cathedral of Rome, was founded by Emperor Constantine in the early 4th century. It has been rebuilt several times, notably in 1646 when Borromini restyled the interior, but retains its original basilica form. Before the papacy moved to Avignon in 1309, the adjoining Lateran Palace was the official papal residence. The present structure dates from 1589, but older parts survive, like the Scala Santa (Holy Staircase), which Christ is said to have climbed at his trial.

VISITORS' CHECKLIST

Practical Information
Piazza di San Giovanni in Laterano. **Map** 8 D2. **Tel** 06 69 88 64 93. Cathedral: **Open** 7am–6:30pm daily.
Cloisters: **Open** 9am–6pm daily.
Museum: **Open** 10am–5:30pm.
Baptistry: **Open** 7:30–12:30pm, 4–6:30pm.

Transportation
🚌 16, 81, 85, 87, 650. 🚊 3.
Ⓜ San Giovanni.

North façade

Baptistry
Though much restored, the octagonal baptistry contains some beautiful 5th-century mosaics.

East Façade
The main entrance, on the east façade (1735), is adorned with statues of Christ and the Apostles.

Museum entrance

Apse

Lateran Palace

Papal Altar
The Gothic baldacchino, which rises over the papal altar, is decorated with 14th-century frescoes.

On Maundy Thursday the Pope as Bishop of Rome, gives a blessing from the loggia of the city's main cathedral.

Cloisters
Built by the Vassalletto family in about 1220, the cloisters are remarkable for their twisted columns and inlaid marble mosaics.

The Corsini Chapel was built in the 1730s for Pope Clement XII Corsini, who lies buried in a porphyry tomb from the Pantheon.

Main entrance

Boniface VIII Fresco
Possibly by Giotto, this fragment shows the Pope announcing the Holy Year of 1300, which attracted around two million pilgrims.

Part of one of the gymnasia in the Baths of Caracalla

❽ Baths of Caracalla

Viale delle Terme di Caracalla 52. **Map**
7 A3. **Tel** 06 39 96 77 00. 🚌 160, 628.
🚃 3. **Open** 9am–1 hr before sunset
Tue–Sun, 9am–2pm Mon. **Closed**
Jan 1, Dec 25. 🗞 🔲 📷

Rearing up at the foot of the
Aventine Hill are the monolithic
red-brick ruins of the Baths of
Caracalla. Begun by Emperor
Septimius Severus in AD 206,
and completed by his son
Caracalla in AD 217, they
remained in use until the 6th
century, when the Goths
sabotaged the city's aqueducts.

Going for a bath was one of
the social events of the day in
ancient Rome. Large com-
plexes such as Caracalla, with
a capacity for 1,600 bathers,
were not simply places to have
a chat and get washed, but
also areas which offered an
impressive array of facilities: art
galleries, gymnasia, gardens,
libraries, conference rooms,
lecture rooms, and shops
selling food and drink.

A Roman bath was a long
and complicated business,
beginning with a form of
Turkish bath, followed by a
spell in the *caldarium*, a large
hot room with pools of water
to moisten the atmosphere.
Then came the lukewarm
tepidarium, followed by a visit
to the large central meeting
place known as the *frigidarium*,
and finally a plunge into the
natatio, an outdoor swimming
pool. For the rich, this was
followed by a rubdown with
scented woolen cloth.

Most of the rich marble
decorations of the baths were
scavenged by the Farnese
family in the 16th century to
adorn the rooms of Palazzo
Farnese *(see p405)*. There are,
however, statues and mosaics
from the Baths in the Museo
Nazionale Archeologico in
Naples *(see pp494–5)* and in
the Vatican's Gregorian Profane
Museum *(see p426)*.

So dramatic is the setting
that it is the regular venue for
the outdoor opera season in
summer.

❾ Pyramid of Caius Cestius

Piazzale Ostiense. **Map** 6 E4. 🚌 23,
280. 🚃 3. Ⓜ Piramide.

Caius Cestius was a wealthy but
unimportant 1st-century BC
praetor, or senior magistrate.
At the time, inspired by the
Cleopatra scandals, there was a
craze for all things Egyptian, and
Caius decided to commission
himself a pyramid as a tomb.
Set into the Aurelian Wall near
Porta San Paolo, it is built of brick
and faced with white marble;
according to an inscription, it took
just 330 days to build in 12 BC.

The Pyramid of Caius Cestius on Piazzale
Ostiense

❿ Protestant Cemetery

Cimitero Acattolico, Via di Caio Cestio.
Map 6 D4. **Tel** 06 574 19 00. 🚌 23,
280. 🚃 3. **Open** 9am–5pm Mon–Sat,
9am–1pm Sun. Last adm: 30 mins
before closing. Donation.

Non-Catholics have been buried
in this cemetery behind the
Aurelian Wall since 1738. In the
oldest part (on the left as you
enter) is the grave of the poet
John Keats, who died in 1821 in
a house on Piazza di Spagna *(see
p412)*. He wrote his own epitaph:
"Here lies one whose name was
writ in water." Close by rest the
ashes of Percy Bysshe Shelley,
who drowned in 1822.

The interior of Santa Sabina

⓫ Santa Sabina

Piazza Pietro d'Illiria 1. **Map** 6 D2. **Tel**
06 57 94 06 00. 🚌 23, 44, 170, 781.
Open 8:15am–12:30pm, 3:30–6pm
daily. ♿

High on the Aventine stands an
early Christian basilica, founded
by Peter of Illyria in AD 425 and
later given to the Dominican
order. It was restored to its
original simplicity in the early
20th century. Light filters
through 9th-century windows
onto a nave framed by pale
Corinthian columns. Above the
main door is a blue and gold
5th-century mosaic inscription
to Peter. In the side portico
outside is a 5th-century paneled
door carved with biblical scenes,
notably one of the oldest
images of the Crucifixion (top
left-hand corner).

Farther Afield

It is well worth making the effort to see some of Rome's outlying sights. Highlights are the Villa Giulia, home to a magnificent Etruscan museum, and the Museo Borghese on the splendid Villa Borghese estate, with its extraordinary collection of virtuoso statues by Bernini. Other sights range from ancient churches and catacombs to the more modern suburb of EUR, a strange architectural medley begun by Mussolini in the 1930s.

Sights at a Glance

Churches and Temples
- ⑤ Sant'Agnese fuori le Mura
- ⑥ Santa Costanza
- ⑩ San Paolo fuori le Mura

Museums and Galleries
- ② Museo e Galleria Borghese
- ③ Villa Giulia
- ④ MAXXI

Parks and Gardens
- ① Villa Borghese

Ancient Roads and Sites
- ⑦ Via Appia Antica
- ⑧ Catacombs

City Districts
- ⑨ EUR

Key
- Central Rome
- Suburbs
- Highway
- Major road
- Minor road
- City walls

❶ Villa Borghese

Map 3 B1. 🚍 52, 53, 88, 116, 490. 🚊 3, 19. **Park Open** dawn–sunset daily.

The villa and its park were designed in 1605 for Cardinal Scipione Borghese, the sybaritic nephew of Pope Paul V. An extravagant patron of the arts, he amassed one of Europe's finest collections of paintings, statues, and antiquities, many of which are still displayed in the villa that he built especially to house his antique sculptures.

The **park** was one of the first of its kind in Rome, its formal gardens divided by avenues and graced with statues. It contained 400 newly planted trees, garden sculpture by Bernini's father, Pietro, along with many ingenious fountains, "secret" flower gardens, enclosures of exotic animals and birds, and even a grotto with artificial rain. There was also a speaking robot and a trick chair, which trapped

anyone who sat in it. At first the grounds were open to the public, but after a visitor was shocked by the collection of erotic paintings, Paul V decided to keep the park private.

In 1773 work began on redesigning the park in the wilder, Romantic style made fashionable by landscape artists like Claude Lorrain and Poussin. Over the next few years, mock-

Temple of Aesculapius, an 18th-century folly, at the Villa Borghese

Classical temples, fountains, and *casine* (summerhouses) were added. In 1901, the park and villa were acquired by the state, and in 1911 the area was chosen as the site for the International Exhibition. Pavilions were built by many of the world's nations, the most impressive of which is the **British School at Rome** by Edwin Lutyens. In the north-eastern corner of the park lie the Museo Zoologico and a small redeveloped zoo, known as the Bioparco, where the emphasis is on conservation. Today the estates of the Villa Borghese, Villa Giulia, and the Pincio gardens form one vast park, with the **Giardino del Lago**, at its center, named after an artificial boating lake. Its main entrance is marked by an 18th-century copy of the Arch of Septimius Severus, while on the lake's island is a fake Ionic temple to the Greek god of health, Aesculapius, designed by the 18th-century architect Antonis Aspurucci. A circular Temple of Diana folly lies between the Porta Pinciana, at the top of Via Veneto, and Piazza di Siena, a grassy amphitheater that hosts Rome's international horse show in May. Its umbrella pines inspired the composer Ottorino Respighi to write *The Pines of Rome* (1924). The outdoor opera season is also held in the park.

To the northwest of the park is the Galleria Nazionale d'Arte Moderna, and the Orangery is now home to the Carlo Bilotti museum.

Sacred and Profane Love by Titian (1514), in the Galleria Borghese

❷ Museo e Galleria Borghese

Villa Borghese, Piazzale Scipione Borghese 5. **Tel** 06 328 10. 🚌 52, 53, 116, 910. 🚋 3, 19. **Open** 8:30am–7:30pm Tue–Sun (reservations recommended). **Closed** Jan 1, Dec 25. 🐾 📷 🍴 📷 🍴 ♿ 🆔 **galleriaborghese.it**

Cardinal Scipione Borghese's villa was designed in 1605 as a typical Roman country house, with its wings projecting into the surrounding gardens. It was built by Flaminio Ponzio, Pope Paul V's architect, and was used by Scipione for entertaining guests and for displaying his impressive collection of paintings and sculpture. Between 1801 and 1809 Prince

Camillo Borghese, husband to Napoleon's sister Pauline, unfortunately sold many of the family paintings to his brother-in-law, and swapped 200 of Scipione's Classical statues for an estate in Piedmont. These statues are still in the Louvre, and as a consequence, the remaining antique Classical collection is less interesting than it might once have been. However, the hedonistic cardinal was an enthusiastic patron of the arts and the sculptures he commissioned from artists such as the young Bernini rank among their most famous works.

The eight rooms of the ground floor of the Villa Borghese are set around a central hall, the Salone. The most famous statue is one of Bernini's finest works, *Apollo and Daphne* (1624) in room 3, which shows the nymph Daphne with bay leaves sprouting from her outstretched fingers, roots growing from her toes, and rough bark enfolding her smooth body, as she begins to metamorphose into a laurel tree to escape being abducted by the god Apollo. Abduction is also the theme of *The Rape of Proserpina*, again by Bernini, in room 4. Depicting Pluto, the god of the underworld, carrying Proserpina, daughter of Ceres, off to be his bride, the sculpture is a virtuoso piece in which Bernini contrasts the taut musculature of Pluto with the soft, yielding flesh of Proserpina, whose thigh dimples in his iron grip.

The third famous Bernini piece, which dates from 1623, is *David* in room 2. The artist captures the tensed, grimacing youth the moment before he releases the stone that slew Goliath. It is said that Pope Urban VIII held a mirror up to Bernini so that the sculptor could model David's face on his own. In the next alcove is the

Detail of *Rape of Proserpina* by Bernini (1622), Museo Borghese

Villa Borghese's most infamous work – a sculpture, executed in 1805 by Canova, of Pauline Borghese as *Venus Victrix* (Venus the Conqueror). The semi-naked Pauline reclining on a chaise longue shocked those who saw it, and Pauline's husband kept the statue locked away, even denying Canova access to it.

The next room holds a selection of antiquities, notably a Roman copy of a plump *Bacchus* by the 4th-century BC Greek sculptor Praxiteles, and fragments of a 3rd-century AD mosaic found on one of the Borghese estates in Torrenova, showing gladiators battling with wild animals.

The Galleria Borghese, on the upper floor, houses some magnificent Baroque and Renaissance paintings. Works on display include Raphael's masterpiece, the *Deposition*, various works by Caravaggio, the graceful *Danäe* by the 16th-century artist Correggio, as well as works by Pinturicchio, Barocci, Rubens, and Titian.

Bernini's *Apollo and Daphne* (1624)

❸ Villa Giulia

This villa was built in 1550 as a country retreat for Pope Julius III. Designed by Vignola and Ammannati, with contributions by Michelangelo and Vasari, it was intended for entertaining guests of the Vatican, such as Queen Christina of Sweden, rather than as a permanent home. The gardens were planted with 36,000 trees and peppered with pavilions and fountains. Villa Giulia also used to house an outstanding collection of sculptures: 160 boats filled with statues and ornaments were sent to the Vatican after the death of Pope Julius III in 1555.

Since 1889 the villa has been home to the Museo Nazionale Etrusco, an impressive collection of pre-Roman antiquities from central Italy.

Rooms 14–21, the Antiquarium collection, display domestic and votive objects and ceramics, including the Cima-Pesciotti collection.

Ficoroni Cist
Engraved and beautifully illustrated, this 4th-century BC bronze marriage coffer held mirrors and other body care implements.

Rooms 22–24 exhibit finds from the Castellani collection, including early 6th-century ceramics and bronzes.

Rooms 31–36 contain finds from the Ager Faliscus, an area between the Tiber and Lake Bracciano.

Spiraled Faliscan Crater
Painted in the free style of the 4th century BC, this spiral-handled vase was used to hold wines or oil. The Falisci were an Italic tribe influenced by the Etruscans.

Husband and Wife Sarcophagus
This 6th-century BC tomb from Cerveteri shows a deceased couple banqueting in the afterlife. Their tender expression bears witness to the skill of Etruscan artists.

Ninfeo (Nympheum)

Rooms 1–13b are arranged by site, starting with Vulci (most importantly articles from the Warrior's Tomb) and including finds from Cerveteri.

Key to Floor Plan

- Lower ground floor
- Ground floor
- First floor
- Nonexhibition space

Rooms 37–40 exhibit finds from Veio, including the stunning Etruscan statue Apollo of Veii.

Entrance

VISITORS' CHECKLIST

Practical Information
Piazzale di Villa Giulia 9.
Tel 06 322 65 71.
Open 8:30am–7:30pm Tue–Sun (last adm: 6:30pm).
Closed Jan 1, Dec 25. ◻ with seven days' notice. ◻ ◻ ◻ ◻ ◻

Transportation
▥ 52. ▤ 3, 19.

MAXXI, the National Museum of 21st Century Arts, designed by Zaha Hadid

❹ MAXXI (National Museum of 21st Century Arts)

Villa Guido Reni 4A. **Tel** 06 399 673 50. 🚍 53, 217, 910. 🚋 2. **Open** 11am–7pm Tue–Sun (11am–10pm Sat). **Closed** May 1, Dec 25. 👪 🚳 🖭 📷 📷 (free up to age 14). 🔎 **w** fondazionemaxxi.it

Along with the nearby Parco della Musica *(see p449)*, MAXXI, the National Museum of 21st Century Arts, has put Rome on the contemporary arts map. Completed in 2009, it is located in a stunning building designed by architect Zaha Hadid. The museum showcases emerging Italian and international artists. An impressive amount of space is also given over to architecture.

❺ Sant'Agnese fuori le Mura

Via Nomentana 349. **Tel** 06 862 054 56. 🚍 60, 82, 90. **Open** 7:30am–noon, 4–7:45pm daily. **Closed** late Oct–late Nov. 🚳 to catacombs. 👪 📷

Sant'Agnese fuori le Mura was built in the 4th century above the crypt of the 13-year-old martyr St. Agnes, and although much altered, it retains the form of the original basilica. According to legend it was founded by Constantine's daughter Constantia, who was cured from leprosy after sleeping beside Agnes's tomb.

In the 7th-century apse mosaic, St. Agnes appears as a bejeweled Byzantine empress

in a stole of gold and a violet robe. Tradition has it that she appeared like this eight days after her death, holding a white lamb. On January 21, two lambs are blessed in the church and a vestment called a *pallium* is woven from their wool, to be given to a new archbishop.

Apse mosaic in Sant'Agnese, showing the saint flanked by popes

❻ Santa Costanza

Via Nomentana 349. **Tel** 06 862 054 56. 🚍 60, 82, 90. **Open** 9am–noon, 4–6pm daily (Sun pm only). **Closed** late Oct–late Nov. 🚳 👪 📷

This circular church was built in the early 4th century as a mausoleum for Emperor Constantine's daughters, Constantia and Helena. The dome and its drum are supported by an arcade that rests on 12 magnificent pairs of granite columns. The encircling ambulatory has a barrel-vaulted ceiling decorated with the world's earliest surviving Christian mosaics, which date from the 4th century.

In a niche on the far side of the church is a replica of Constantia's ornate porphyry sarcophagus, carved with cherubs crushing grapes. The

original was moved to the Vatican Museums in 1790. The sanctity of Constantia is somewhat debatable. Described by the historian Marcellinus as a fury incarnate, constantly goading her equally unpleasant husband, Hannibalianus, to violence, her canonization was probably the result of some confusion with a saintly nun of the same name.

❼ Via Appia Antica

🚍 118, 218.

The first part of the Via Appia was built in 312 BC by Appius Claudius Caecus. In 190 BC, when it was extended to the ports of Taranto and Brindisi, the road became Rome's link with its empire in the East. It was the route taken by the funeral processions of the dictator Sulla (78 BC) and Emperor Augustus (AD 14), and it was along this road that St. Paul was led as a prisoner to Rome in AD 56. The church of Domine Quo Vadis? marks the spot where St. Peter is said to have met Christ when fleeing Rome. The road is lined with ruined family tombs, decaying monuments, and collective burial places *(columbaria)*. Beneath the fields on either side lies a maze of catacombs, including those of San Callisto and San Sebastiano.

Cypresses lining the Roman road, Via Appia

❽ Catacombs

Via Appia Antica 126. 🚌 118, 218. San Callisto **Tel** 06 513 01 51. **Open** 9am–noon, 2–5pm Thu–Tue. **Closed** Jan 1, late Jan–late Feb, Easter Sun, Dec 25.

In burying their dead in underground cemeteries outside the city walls, the early Christians were simply obeying the laws of the time. They were not forced to use them because of persecution, as later popular myth has suggested. Many saints were buried here, and the catacombs later became shrines and places of pilgrimage.

Today several catacombs are open to the public. The vast Catacombs of San Callisto, hewn from volcanic tufa, contain niches, or *loculi*, which held two or three bodies, as well as the burial places of several early popes. Close by, walls in the Catacombs of San Sebastiano are covered in graffiti invoking St. Peter and St. Paul, whose remains may once have been moved here.

Engraving of Christian ceremony in Catacombs of San Callisto (AD 50)

❾ EUR

🚌 170, 671, 714. Ⓜ EUR Fermi, EUR Palasport. Museo della Civiltà Romana Piazza G. Agnelli 10. **Tel** 06 06 08. **Open** 9am–2pm Tue–Sun. Last adm 1 hr before closing. **Closed** Jan 1, May 1, Dec 25.

The Esposizione Universale di Roma (EUR), a suburb to the south of the city, was originally built for an international exhibition, a kind of "Work Olympics," that was planned

EUR's Palazzo della Civiltà del Lavoro, the "Square Colosseum"

for 1942, but never took place because of the outbreak of war. The architecture was intended to glorify Fascism, and as a result the bombastic style of the buildings can look overblown and rhetorical to modern eyes. Of all the buildings the best known is probably the Palazzo della Civiltà del Lavoro (the Palace of the Civilization of Work), an unmistakable landmark for people arriving from Fiumicino airport.

The scheme was eventually completed in the 1950s. Despite the area's dubious architecture, EUR has been a planning success, and people are still keen to live here. As well as residential housing, the vast marble halls along the wide boulevards are also home to a number of government offices and museums. Best among the latter is the Museo della Civiltà Romana, famous for its casts of the reliefs from the Column of Trajan, and for a large-scale

model depicting 4th-century Rome with all the buildings which then stood within the Aurelian walls. The south of the suburb features a lake and shady park, and the huge domed Palazzo dello Sport, built for the 1960 Olympics.

❿ San Paolo fuori le Mura

Via Ostiense 186. 🚌 23, 128, 170, 670, 761, 766, 769. Ⓜ San Paolo. **Tel** 06 541 03 41. **Open** 7am–6:30pm daily. Cloister **Open** 9am–6pm daily.

Today's church is a faithful if soulless reconstruction of the great 4th-century basilica destroyed by fire in 1823. Only a few fragments of the earlier church survived, most notably the cloister (1241), with its pairs of colorful inlaid columns, considered one of the most beautiful in Rome.

Elsewhere, the church's triumphal arch is decorated on one side with heavily restored 5th-century mosaics, and on the other with mosaics by Pietro Cavallini originally on the façade. The equally fine mosaics (1220) in the apse represent the figures of Christ with St. Peter, St. Andrew, St. Paul, and St. Luke.

The single most outstanding work of art is the fine marble canopy over the high altar, the work of Arnolfo di Cambio (1285), with the possible assistance of Pietro Cavallini. Below the altar is the *confessio* where it is alleged St. Paul was once buried. To its right is an impressive Paschal candlestick dating from the 12th century by Nicolò di Angelo and Pietro Vassalletto.

19th-century mosaic on façade of San Paolo fuori le Mura

Shopping in Rome

Rome has always been a thriving center for design and shopping. In ancient times, the finest craftsmen were drawn to the city, and artifacts and products of all kinds, including gold, furs, and wine, were imported from far-flung corners of the Empire to satisfy the needs of the wealthy local population. Shopping in Rome today in many ways reflects this diverse tradition. Italian designers have a well-deserved reputation for their luxuriously chic style in fashion, knitwear, and leather goods (especially shoes and handbags), as well as in interior design, fabrics, ceramics, and glass. The artisan tradition is strong, and the love of good design filters through into the smallest items. Rome is not a city for bargains (although it is often better value than Florence or Milan), but the joys of window shopping here will offer plenty of compensation.

Fashion

Italy is one of the leading lights in high fashion, or *alta moda*. Many famous designers may be based in Milan, but Rome is home to a cluster of sophisticated and internationally distinguished fashion houses. The most notable among them are probably **Fendi**, **Laura Biagiotti**, **Prada**, and **Valentino**, whose studio dominates Piazza Mignanelli.

But even for those unable to splash out on genuine designer gear, much fun can be gained from a stroll down the streets that radiate out from the Piazza di Spagna: some of the window displays here are truly spectacular.

Rome is not a good place to buy everyday wear, since there is a distinct lack of mid-price shops bridging the gap between the dazzlingly priced *alta moda* designer exclusives and the ultracheap goods sold in markets. However, at **Discount dell'Alta Moda** you can find end-of-season designer labels at 50 percent less than the boutique prices.

Books and Gifts

Rome offers huge scope for gift buying, both in the well-established tourist stores in the historic center and in smaller shops located in less frequented parts of the city that might not feature in your planned itinerary.

The central Via del Pellegrino is a street crammed with small specialist outlets, such as **Le Tre Ghinee**, which sells ceramics and glass objects. If you are more interested in contemporary design, visit the **Palazzo delle Esposizioni**, where a wide range of objects by famous designers is available.

The **Feltrinelli International** bookstore has an excellent range of foreign-language fiction, as well as nonfiction covering various subjects, including Italian art and architecture, cooking, travel, and history. It also stocks some superb photographic, art, and film posters. For cut-price deals on books try the secondhand stalls in Via delle Terme di Diocleziano and in Largo della Fontanella di Borghese.

Near the Pantheon, the Florentine **Il Papiro** sells a great range of illustrious paper-based products, including diaries, notebooks, envelopes, and beautiful seal-and-wax sets that make ideal gifts.

Religious artifacts are readily available in bookstores near the main basilicas, such as the **Libreria Belardetti** near St. Peter's. Other shops specialize in religious items for both the clergy and the layperson. Facing the Vatican gates, in Via di Porta Angelica, there are several shops, including **Al Pellegrino Cattolico**, that sell mementos to visiting pilgrims.

Food and Drink

If you are tempted to take home some irresistible Italian delicacies, such as pecorino romano cheese, Parma ham, extra virgin olive oil, dried porcini mushrooms, sun-dried tomatoes, olives, and grappa, as well as superb wines from Lazio and elsewhere, then the traditional food stores, *alimentari*, are a great place to start. Try the well-stocked **Fratelli Fabbi**, near Piazza di Spagna, with its exceptional selection of delicious cold meats and cheeses from every corner of Italy, as well as quality wines and champagnes. A few doors down on the same street is **Focacci**, with its wonderful array of Italian delicacies. The historic but expensive **Volpetti** in Testaccio is synonymous with great service and uncompromising quality. Aside from specializing in unusual cheeses, olive oils, vinegars, and a fabulous selection of food baskets, Volpetti also stocks a variety of Italian lard and caviar – you can even try before you buy.

In Pinciano, **Casa dei Latticini Micocci** sells a comprehensive range of cheeses from even the most remote regions of Italy, while in Trastevere, the family-run **Antica Caciara Trasteverina** has a vast assortment of local and regional dairy products, which include sheep's ricotta and the Piedmontese *toma del fen*. More local, reasonably priced cheeses are available at **Cisternino**.

If cakes and chocolate feature on your list, then there is plenty of opportunity to satisfy those cravings too. **Chocolat**, in the historic center, sells brand-name and homemade chocolate and organizes occasional tastings and dinners for connoisseurs, while **Moriondo e Gariglio** specializes in chocolate delights made to traditional Piedmontese recipes. **La Deliziosa**, near Piazza Navona, offers a great range of Italian desserts and cakes; the ricotta-based variety deserves a special mention.

Bear in mind that customs restrictions can apply to certain foodstuffs.

Markets

Rome's outdoor markets are quintessential examples of the bubbling exuberance and earthiness for which Romans are renowned. They are wonderfully vivid experiences, too, since Italian stallholders have raised the display of even the humblest vegetable to an art form.

The city is dotted with small local food markets, and there are several fascinating well-established markets near the center. These include **Campo de' Fiori** for foodstuffs, the **Mercato delle Stampe** for old prints, books, and magazines, and the **Nuovo Mercato Esquilino** for international foods.

Trastevere's famous flea market, **Porta Portese**, was established shortly after the end of World War II and is said to have grown out of the thriving black market that operated at Tor di Nona, opposite Castel Sant'Angelo, during those lean years. Anything and everything seems to be for sale, piled high on stalls in carefully arranged disorder – clothes, shoes, bags, linen, luggage, camping equipment, towels, pots, pans, kitchen utensils, plants, pets, cassettes and CDs, old LPs, and 78s.

If you are looking for a traditional food market in the heart of the old city, Rome's most picturesque market is also its most historical. Its name, Campo de' Fiori (*see p405*), which translates as "field of flowers," sometimes misleads people into expecting a flower market. In fact, the name is said to derive from *Campus Florae* (Flora's square) – Flora being the lover of the great Roman general Pompey. A market has been held in this beautiful central piazza for many centuries. Every morning, except Sunday, the piazza is transformed by an array of stalls selling fruit and vegetables, meat, poultry, and fish. One or two stalls also specialize in legumes, rice, and dried fruits and nuts.

Throughout the year Rome also plays host to many street fairs. If they coincide with your visit, these are fun to go to, because they normally sell a good variety of local produce, handicrafts, and clothes. Seasonal fairs also occur, especially around Christmas; among them is **Mercatino di Natale** in Piazza Navona, where you can stock up on toys and Nativity figurines.

Be sure to keep your wits about you at markets: pickpockets work with lightning speed in the bustling crowds.

DIRECTORY

Fashion

Discount dell'Alta Moda
Via de Pretis 88.
Map 3 C4.
Tel 06 47 82 56 72.
Also: Via di Gesù e Maria 14 & 16A. **Map** 2 F2.
Tel 06 322 50 06.

Fendi
Largo Goldoni 419.
Map 10 E3.
Tel 06 33 45 01.

Laura Biagiotti
Via Mario de' Fiori 26.
Map 10 F1.
Tel 06 679 12 05.

Prada
Via Condotti 92–95.
Map 3 A2.
Tel 06 679 08 97.

Valentino
Via Condotti 15.
Map 3 A2.
Tel 06 673 94 20.

Books and Gifts

Al Pellegrino Cattolico
Via di Porta Angelica 83.
Map 1 C2.
Tel 06 68 80 23 51.

Feltrinelli International
Via VE Orlando 84–86.
Map 3 C3.
Tel 06 487 01 71.

Libreria Belardetti
Via della Conciliazione 4A.
Map 1 C3.
Tel 06 686 55 02.

Palazzo delle Esposizioni
Via Milano 15–17.
Map 3 B4.
Tel 06 48 91 33 61.

Il Papiro
Via del Pantheon 50 (leading to Via degli Orfani).
Map 10 D2.
Tel 06 679 55 97.

Le Tre Ghinee
Via del Pellegrino 90.
Map 2 E4.
Tel 06 687 27 39.

Food and Drink

Antica Caciara Trasteverina
Via San Francesco a Ripa 140A/B.
Map 5 C1.
Tel 06 581 28 15.

Casa dei Latticini Micocci
Via Collina 14. **Map** 4 D2.
Tel 06 474 17 84.

Chocolat
Via del Teatro Valle 54.
Map 10 D3.
Tel 06 68 13 55 45.

Cisternino
Vicolo del Gallo 18–19.
Map 9 C4.
Tel 06 687 28 75.

La Deliziosa
Vicolo Savelli 50.
Map 9 B3.
Tel 06 68 80 31 55.

Focacci
Via della Croce 43.
Map 2 F2.
Tel 06 679 12 28.

Fratelli Fabbi
Via della Croce 28.
Map 2 F2.
Tel 06 679 06 12.

Moriondo e Gariglio
Via del Piè di Marmo 21.
Map 10 E3.
Tel 06 699 08 56.

Volpetti
Via Marmorata 47.
Map 6 D2.
Tel 06 574 23 52.

Markets

Campo de' Fiori
Piazza Campo de' Fiori.
Map 2 E4 & 9 C4.
Open 7am–1:30pm Mon–Sat.

Mercatatino di Natale
Piazza Navona.
Map 9 C4.
Open end Nov–early Jan: daily.

Mercato delle Stampe
Largo della Fontanella di Borghese.
Map 2 F3 & 10 D1.
Open 9am–1pm Mon–Sat.

Nuovo Mercato Esquilino
Via Principe Amedeo.
Map 4 E4.
Open 9am–2pm Mon–Fri.

Porta Portese
Via Portuense & Via Ippolito Nievo.
Map 5 C3.
Open 6:30am–2pm Sun.

Entertainment in Rome

There's a particular excitement attached to entertainment in Rome. Soccer and opera, for example, are worth experiencing for sheer atmosphere alone, whether or not you are a fan. There is also a good jazz scene, with international stars appearing alongside local talent. Unexpectedly, given the general shutdown among shops and restaurants, the summer is Rome's liveliest time in terms of entertainment and cultural events, with the city's Renaissance squares, vast parks, villa gardens, Classical ruins, and other open spaces hosting various arts festivals. Concerts and films take on an added dimension when performances take place beneath the stars in the many outdoor arenas across the city. Rome also has plenty of nightclubs to choose from.

Practical Information

Good sources of information about what's happening are the listings in the magazine *Roma c'è* and in *Trovaroma*, the weekly Thursday supplement to *La Repubblica* newspaper. Also worth getting hold of is *L'Evento*, available from the Rome Tourist Office *(see p617)*, which gives details in English for cultural events in the city.

Booking Tickets

Among the ticket agencies that will book seats for some performances for you (for a small fee) are **Orbis** and **Box Office**. Many theaters do not accept telephone reservations – you have to visit the box office in person. They will charge you a *prevendita* supplement (about 10 percent of the normal price) for any tickets sold in advance. The **Teatro dell'Opera** box office handles sales for both summer and winter seasons. Tickets for most big rock and jazz events can be bought at Orbis and at larger record stores, such as **Ricordi Media Store**. Look out for *due per uno* coupons in local bars – these allow two people entrance for the price of one.

Outdoor Entertainment

Outdoor opera, movies, classical music, and jazz concerts fill the Roman calendar from late June until the end of September. Both the **Cineporto**, a festival held along the Tiber, at the Ponte Milvio, and the **Festival di Massenzio**, at the Forum, offer films, live music, food, and small exhibitions in July and August. The summer months also bring excellent outdoor rock, jazz, and world-music festivals, while Rome's main autumn performing-arts festival, **RomaEuropa**, has occasional performances on the grounds of the Villa Medici. Theater also moves outside in the summer months, and some movie theaters roll back their ceilings for open-air screenings.

More traditional is Trastevere's community festival, the **Festa de Noiantri** *(see p71)*, with music, processions, and fireworks. This religious festival begins on the Saturday after July 16, and celebrations continue until the end of the month.

Classical Music and Dance

Classical concerts take place in a surprising number of venues. Tickets for opera premieres may be hard to find, but soloists, groups, or orchestras playing in gardens, churches, villas, or ancient ruins are more accessible.

World-renowned soloists and orchestras make appearances throughout the year in venues such as the Renzo Piano–designed **Parco della Musica** and the **Accademia Filarmonica Romana**. Past visitors have included Luciano Pavarotti and Placido Domingo, the Berlin Philharmonic, and prima ballerina Sylvie Guillem. One of the most innovative programs of classical and contemporary music is provided by the **Aula Magna dell'Università La Sapienza**. The opera season starts late at the **Teatro dell'Opera**, between November and January. The great ballet classics are also staged at this venue. The **Equilibrio Festival** in February brings contemporary dance to the city; performances take place mainly at the Parco della Musica.

Rock, Jazz, and World Music

Rome's nonclassical music scene is unpredictable and subject to vast seasonal changes. However, there is a huge variety of music at the many clubs and stadiums, such as the **Palalottomatica** and the **Stadio Olimpico**, which attract foreign and homegrown stars. The best jazz musicians play at the splendid **Casa del Jazz**, and at **Alexanderplatz**. Trastevere's **Big Mama** is one of the city's legendary addresses for important jazz names, while world music is well served at the aptly named **Villaggio Globale**.

For smaller venues you might need to buy a monthly or annual membership card (between €2 and €11), which often includes the entrance fee for smaller bands.

Film and Theater

Moviegoing is a popular pastime in Rome, with around 40 films showing on an average weekday. Most Roman movie theaters are *prima visione* (first run) and show the latest international films in dubbed versions. The best theaters for decor and comfort are the **Fiamma** (two screens) and the **Barberini** (three screens). Films in their original language are often shown at the excellent **Casa del Cinema** and at the **Nuovo Olimpia**. Smaller art cinemas, such as the **Azzurro Scipioni**, are more likely to show subtitled versions of foreign films.

Theater productions are performed in Italian whether the plays are national classics or by foreign playwrights. The main theaters – **Teatro Argentina**, **Teatro Quirino**, and the **Eliseo** – offer a selection by great Italian playwrights. There are also performances of traditional cabaret, dance, and avant-garde theater at the **Teatro India**. Theater tickets cost between €8 and €50 and can generally be booked only in advance, by visiting the theater box office in person or through agencies such as Box Office.

Nightlife

Rome's nightlife has never been as vibrant as it is today, with a sharp rise in the number of bars and clubs, all catering for an ever more demanding clientele.

Once the choice was limited to a few well-established bars in the center and the hugely popular clubs in the Ostiense area and in San Lorenzo, such as the unashamedly commercial **Goa** or the more cutting-edge **Locanda Atlantide**, which hosts a whole range of DJs from funk to reggae. Now, though, the capital offers a wide range of options designed to satisfy all tastes and budgets.

Head first to a stylish pre-clubbing venue such as **'Gusto**, where you can rub shoulders with out-on-the-town locals taking advantage of the range of facilities – on three sites there is a restaurant, a pizzeria, a wine bar, and live music. Alternatively, for a more leisurely start to your evening, simply relax in a wine bar in one of the historic center's breathtaking squares.

If you are looking for a gay venue, **Coming Out**, near the Colosseum, attracts both gay and straight drinkers, and **Alpheus** just off Via Ostiense regularly hosts gay nights.

For an alternative edge to Rome's vivacious nightlife, try out the *centri sociali*, illegally occupied buildings that have been converted into arts and entertainment centers. Top billing goes to **Brancaleone**, which features Italian and international DJs for the best in electronic and house tunes.

A night out in Rome can be expensive – you can be charged as much as €10 for a cocktail in the bars around the central parts of Rome. For a cheaper alternative, visit one of the many bars in the area around San Lorenzo.

DIRECTORY

Booking Tickets

Box Office
Largo Argentina 11 (inside Feltrinelli bookshop). **Map** 10 D4. **Tel** 06 68 30 85 96.

Orbis
Piazza dell'Esquilino 37. **Map** 4 D4. **Tel** 06 482 74 03.

Ticketeria
W ticketeria.it

Classical Music and Dance

Accademia Filarmonica Romana
Via Flaminia 118. **Tel** 06 320 17 52. W filarmonicaromana. org

Aula Magna dell'Università La Sapienza
Piazzale Aldo Moro 5. **Map** 4 F3. **Tel** 06 361 00 51. W concertiiuc.it

Parco della Musica
Viale de Coubertin 30. **Tel** 06 80 24 12 81 (info); 89 29 82 (credit card sales). W auditorium.com

RomaEuropa
Via dei Magazzini Generali 20a. **Tel** 06 45 55 30 50. W romaeuropa.net

Teatro dell'Opera
Piazza Beniamino Gigli 1. **Map** 3 C3. **Tel** 06 48 16 01. W operaroma.it

Rock, Jazz, and World Music

Alexanderplatz
Via Ostia 9. **Map** 1 B1. **Tel** 06 39 74 21 71.

Big Mama
Vicolo San Francesco a Ripa 18. **Map** 5 C2. **Tel** 06 581 25 51.

Casa del Jazz
Viale di Porta Ardeatina 55. **Map** 7 A4. **Tel** 06 70 47 31. W casajazz.it

Palalottomatica
Piazzale dello Sport. **Tel** 199 128 800.

Stadio Olimpico
Viale dei Gladiatori (north-west of city center, across the Tiber by Monte Mario).

Villaggio Globale
Ex-Mattatoio, Lungotevere Testaccio 1. **Map** 6 D4. **Tel** 347 413 12 05.

Film and Theater

Azzurro Scipioni
Via degli Scipioni 82. **Map** 1 C2. **Tel** 06 39 73 71 61.

Barberini
Piazza Barberini 24. **Map** 3 B3. **Tel** 06 86 39 13 61.

Casa del Cinema
Largo Mastroianni 1. **Map** 3 B1. **Tel** 06 06 08. W casadelcinema.it

Eliseo
Via Nazionale 183. **Map** 3 B4. **Tel** 06 488 21 14.

Fiamma
Via Bissolati 47. **Map** 3 C2. **Tel** 06 48 55 26.

Nuovo Olimpia
Via in Lucina 16. **Map** 10 E1. **Tel** 06 686 10 68.

Teatro Argentina
Largo Argentina 56. **Map** 2 F4. **Tel** 06 684 00 03 11. W teatrodiroma.net

Teatro India
Via L Pierantoni 6. **Map** 5 C5. **Tel** 06 684 00 03 11.

Teatro Quirino
Via delle Vergini 7. **Map** 3 B3 & 10 F2. **Tel** 06 679 45 85. W teatroquirino.it

Nightlife

Alpheus
Via del Commercio 36–8. **Map** 8 D5. **Tel** 06 574 78 26.

Brancaleone
Via Levanna 13 (in Montesacro). **Tel** 06 82 00 43 82.

Coming Out
Via San Giovanni in Laterano 8. **Map** 7 B1. **Tel** 06 700 98 71.

Goa
Via Libetta 13 (in Ostiense) **Tel** 06 574 82 77.

'Gusto
Piazza Augusto Imperatore 9. **Map** 2 F2. **Tel** 06 322 62 73.

Locanda Atlantide
Via dei Lucani 22b (San Lorenzo district). **Tel** 06 99 93 86 92.

ROME STREET FINDER

Map references given with sights described in the Rome chapters relate to the maps on the following pages. Map references are also given for hotels *(see pp562–77)* and restaurants *(see pp580–605)* and for useful addresses in the *Travelers' Needs* and *Survival Guide* sections at the back of the book. The first figure in the map reference tells you which Street Finder map to turn to, and the letter and number that follow refer to the grid reference on that map. The small map below shows the area of Rome covered by each of the eight maps, and the corresponding map number is given in black. All the major sights are sketched out on the maps, and symbols, listed in the key below, are used to indicate the location of other important buildings.

0 kilometers   2
0 miles   1

Key and Scale for Street Finder Pages

Major sight	✡ Synagogue
Place of interest	⚊ Railroad line
FS Train station	— City walls
M Metro station	Pedestrian street
Streetcar stop	
i Tourist information	
Hospital with emergency room	
Police station	
Church	

Scale of Maps 1–8

0 meters   250
0 yards   250   1:12,000

Scale of Maps 9–10

0 meters   150
0 yards   150   1:7600

3

A　　**B**　　**C**

VILLA BORGHESE

VIALE DEI PUPAZZI

VIALE S. PAOLO DEL BRASILE

VIALE DELLA PINETA

VIALE DI CAVALLI MARINI

VIALE DEL MUSEO BORGHESE

VIA PINCIANA

VIALE DELLE MAGNOLIE

VIALE S. GOETHE

VIA PO

VIA DI S. TERESA

ISONZO

1

GALOPPATOIO

VIALE DEL GALOPPATOIO

VIA DEL MURO TORTO

PORTA PINCIANA

D'ITALIA

VIA CORSO

CAMPANIA

LUDOVISI

VIA SARDEGNA

VIA ABRUZZI

VIA TOSCANA

VIA PIEMONTE

VIA SICILIA

VIA ROMAGNA

VIA QUINTINO

BONCOM

PUGLIE

2

VIA TRINITA DEI

Villa Medici

VIA DI PORTA PINCIANA

VIA VITTORIO VENETO

VIA LAZIO

VIA MARCHE

VIA SICILIA

SALLUSTIANO

VIA MARGUTTA

V. DEL BABUINO

V. ALBERTO

CAMPO MARZIO

Spagna Ⓜ

VIA LOMBARDIA

VIA EMILIA

VIA FRIULI

VIA SALLUSTIANA

VIA LUCULLO

VIA AURELI

VIA CARDUCCI

VIA PASTRENGO

VIA SALANDRA

2

VIA D. CROCE

PIAZZA DI SPAGNA

Babington's Tea Rooms

Trinità dei Monti

Casino dell'Aurora

VIA DI PORTA PINCIANA

VIA LIGURIA

VIA L. BISSOLATI

Ministero dell'Agricoltura e delle Foreste

V. DELLE CARROZZE

Scalinata della Trinità dei Monti

Museo Keats-Shelley

VIA FRANCESCO CRISPI

VIA AURORA

VIA LUDOVISI

VIA UMBRIA

Palazzo Margherita

Santa Maria della Vittoria

SETTEM

V. BOCCA

V. MARIO

Caffè Greco

PIAZZA MIGNANELLI

VIA VITTORIO VENETO

VIA L. MOUSE

Fontana del Mosè

Colonna dell'Immacolata

VIA D. ARTISTI

Santa Maria della Concezione

VIA SALITA DI S. NICOLA DA TOLENTINO

Santa Susanna

SEE PAGES 9–10 FOR ENLARGEMENT OF THIS AREA

VIA FRATTINA

VIA DUE

VIA PURIFICAZIONE

Fontana delle Api

VIA S. NICOLA DA TOLENTINO

PIAZZA S. BERNARDO

San Bernardo alle Terme

Rep

10

VIA D. MERCEDE

VIA GREGORIANA

SISTINA

Ⓜ Barberini

PIAZZA BARBERINI

VIA V. E. ORLANDO

VIA CAPO LE CASE

Sant'Andrea delle Fratte

VIA ZUCCHELLI

Fontana del Tritone

Palazzo Barberini

XX

Ministero della Difesa Esercito

PIA

PIAZZA SAN SILVESTRO

VIA D. TRITONE

VIA DEL TRAFORO

VIA DELLE QUATTRO

Le Quattro Fontane

Teatro dell'Opera

TREVI

VIA S. CLAUDIO

VIAS. POZZETTO

VIA DEI MARONI

VIA RASELLA

FONTANE

VIA MODENA

VIA FIRENZE

3

LARGO CHIGI

Palazzo Chigi

Accademia di San Luca

GIARDINI DEL QUIRINALE

San Carlo alle Quattro Fontane

VIA NAZIONALE

B. GIGLI

PIAZZA COLONNA

Santa Maria in Trivio

Fontana di Trevi

(TRAFORO UMBERTO I)

Sant'Andrea al Quirinale

VIA GENOVA

PIAZZA A. DEPR

Colonna di Marco Aurelio

Santi Vincenzo Anastasio

Palazzo del Quirinale

VIA DEL QUIRINALE

VIAS. VITALE

PIAZZA D. VIMINALE

ℹ️

PIAZZA DEL QUIRINALE

Castore e Polluce

Palazzo della Esposizioni

PIGNA

San Marcello al Corso

VIA DELL'UMILTA

Università Gregoriana

SS. Apostoli

VIA XXIV MAGGIO

VIA D. CONSULTA

MONTI

Santa Pudenziana

Palazzo del Collegio Romano

VIA S. PILOTTA

Palazzo Odescalchi

Palazzo Colonna

10

Banca d'Italia

VIA S. M. MAGGIORE

4

Palazzo Doria Pamphilj

PIAZZA DEI SS. APOSTOLI

Sant'Agata dei Goti

VIA PANISPERNA

VIA CAPOCI

V. D. PLEBISCITO

V. IV NOVEMBRE

Villa Aldobrandini

VIA MAZZARINO

VIA CIMARRA

VIA URBANA

Palazzo Venezia

PIAZZA VENEZIA

Torre delle Milizie

Santi Domenico e Sisto

VIA D. ZINGARI

Gesù

San Marco

Mercati Traianei

Santa Maria dei Monti

Ⓜ Cavour

PIAZZA S. MARCO

Colonna Traiana

Casa dei Cavalieri di Rodi

VIA LEONINA

LARGO VENOSTA

VIA GIOVA

2

VIA S. MARCO

Il Vittoriano

VIA DEI FORI IMPERIALI

Foro di Augusto

VIA BACCINA

VIA MADONNA DEI MONTI

CAVOUR

VIA IN SE

PIAZZA D'ARACOELI

Santa Maria in Aracoeli

Foro di Cesare

Foro di Nerva

San Pietro in Vincoli

VIA D. SETT

5

Palazzo Nuovo

PIAZZA DEL CAMPIDOGLIO

Carcere Mamertino

LARGO CORRADO RICCI

VIA EUDOSSIANA

Musei Capitolini

Palazzo Senatorio

Curia

Tempio di Antonino e Faustina

Basilica di Romolo

Basilica di Costantino e Massenzio

ℹ️

VIA D. TEATRO DI MARCELLO

Palazzo dei Conservatori

Colonna di Foca

Basilica Aemilia

Foro Romano

S. Francesca Romana

Tempio di Venere e Roma

VIA N. SALVI

VIALE

Domus A

Tempio di Giove

Tempio di Saturno

Basilica Giulia

Tempio di Castore e Polluce

Tempio di Vesta

Antiquarium Forense

Ⓜ Colosseo

PIAZZA DEL COLOSSEO

Rupe Tarpea

V. D. CONSOLAZIONE

S. M. della Consolazione

Casa delle Vestali

Colosseo

A　　**B**　　**C**

6

Exploring Lazio

Much of Lazio's landscape was formed by the eruption of four volcanoes that showered the area with lava. Lakes formed in the craters, and the soil, rendered fertile by the lava, nourished vines, olives, and fruit and nut trees. The volcanic activity also left Lazio with hot springs, notably around Tivoli, Viterbo, and Fiuggi. Rome dominates the area, dividing the wooded hills of the north from the reclaimed Pontine marshes in the south. Swimming and sailing are possible in lakes Bracciano, Bolsena, and Albano, while Lazio's best beaches lie between Gaeta and Sabaudia in the Parco Nazionale del Circeo.

Sights at a Glance

1. Tuscania
2. Viterbo
3. Montefiascone
4. Bomarzo
5. Caprarola
6. Tarquinia
7. Cerveteri
8. Lake Bracciano
9. Ostia Antica
10. Frascati and the Castelli Romani
11. Tivoli
12. Palestrina
13. Subiaco
14. Montecassino
15. Anagni
16. Sermoneta and Ninfa
17. Terracina
18. Sperlonga
19. Gaeta

ROME pp387–463

The Tolfa hills southwest of Lake Bracciano

Key

▬▬	Highway
▬▬	Major road
▪ ▪	Road under construction
▬	Secondary road
▪▪▪▪	Minor road
▬	Scenic route
▬	Main railroad
▬	Minor railroad
▬	Regional border
△	Summit

For additional map symbols *see back flap*

The old quarter overlooking the beach at Sperlonga

Getting Around

Rome's two international airports at Fiumicino and Ciampino serve the region. The main highways are the *Autostrada del Sole* Firenze–Roma (A1) and Roma–Napoli (A1–E45), and the Roma–L'Aquila (A24–E80). Rome's beltway *(raccordo anulare)* connects the highways and main roads.

The Lazio bus service, COTRAL, serves all the main towns with transfer points for the smaller locations in Rome and at Latina, Frosinone, Viterbo, and Rieti. Train routes into the region from other Italian cities are efficient, although within Lazio the services are slower and less frequent.

Palestrina's terraces climbing up the hill

Carved loggia of the Palazzo Papale, Viterbo

❶ Tuscania

Viterbo. 🚍 8,200. 🚌 ℹ️ Piazzale
Trieste (0761 43 63 71). 🛒 Fri am.

Tuscania's trim walls and towers
are visible from afar on the
empty, low-lying plains
between Viterbo and Tarquinia.
Although shaken by
an earthquake in 1971,
its medieval and
Renaissance
buildings have since
been carefully re-
constructed. Just
outside the city
walls, on the rocky
Colle San Pietro, two
remarkable
churches dating
from the Lombard-
Romanesque period occupy
the site of Tuscana, a major
Etruscan center conquered by
Rome in 300 BC.

Santa Maria Maggiore, at the
foot of the hill, has a typically
Lombard-Romanesque
asymmetric façade with blind

Façade of San Pietro, Tuscania

arcades and a bold rose window.
Over the central door lies a
simple marble Madonna and
Child, framed by abstract motifs
and biblical scenes. Inside, a rare
12th-century full-immersion
baptism font stands in the aisle.
The Lombard-Romanesque
church of **San Pietro**, on
top of the hill, is a striking
building of ocher-hued
tufa and white
marble details. It
stands on a grassy
piazza, along with
two medieval
towers and a bishop's
palace. The façade
features an intric-
ately inlaid rose
window flanked by
strange reliefs, including three-
headed bearded demons. The
interior is true to its 8th-century
form, with squat columns,
toothed arches, capitals carved
with stylized plants, and a
Cosmati floor. Below the church
lies a strange mosquelike crypt.

❷ Viterbo

🚍 63,000. 🚉 🚌 ℹ️ Piazza S
Carluccio, 5. (0761 30 47 95). 🛒 Sat.

Viterbo was an important
Etruscan center before falling to
the Romans in the 4th century
BC. Its heyday, however, came in
the 13th century when it briefly
became the papal seat (1257–
81). During World War II it was
devastated, but the austere
gray stone medieval core, still
encircled by walls, and many of
the town's churches, have been
carefully restored.

In **San Pellegrino**, Viterbo's
oldest and best preserved
quarter, medieval houses with
towers, arches, and external
staircases line narrow streets
running between little piazzas
decorated with fountains.

On Piazza San Lorenzo, the
12th-century **Duomo** boasts an
elegant black and white striped
bell tower, a solemn 16th-century
façade, and a stark Romanesque
interior. The adjacent 13th-century
Palazzo Papale, with a finely
carved loggia, was built for
popes on their visits to the city.

The town's civic buildings
border the main square, Piazza
del Plebiscito. The most
interesting is the 15th-century
Palazzo dei Priori, frescoed
inside by Baldassare Croce with
scenes from the town's history
and mythological past.

Outside the city walls, on Viale
Capocci, the Romanesque
Santa Maria della Verità has
wonderful 15th-century frescoes
by Lorenzo da Viterbo.

Villa Lante's small but splendid Renaissance gardens, considered Vignola's masterpiece

Environs
The **Villa Lante**, northeast of Viterbo, was begun in 1562 by Vignola for Cardinal Gambara. The main attractions are the outstanding Renaissance gardens and fountains. Be careful not to be a victim of a 16th-century practical joke: many of the fountains will sprinkle people without warning.

🏛 **Palazzo dei Priori**
Piazza Plebiscito. **Tel** 0761 32 59 92.
Open daily. ♿ 📷

🏛 **Villa Lante**
Bagnaia. **Tel** 0761 28 80 08.
Open 8:30am–4:30pm Tue–Sun.
Closed Jan 1, May 1, Dec 25. 📷
♿ to gardens.

Carved 11th-century capital in San Flaviano, Montefiascone

❸ Montefiascone

Viterbo. 🗺 13,000. 🚆 🚌 ℹ️ Piazza V. Emanuele (0761 83 20 60). 🛒 Wed.

This pretty town is perched on the edge of a defunct volcanic crater between the shores of Lake Bolsena, over which there are splendid views, and the Via Cassia. It is dominated by the octagonal bulk of its cathedral, **Santa Margherita**, whose dome, created in the 1670s by Carlo Fontana, is second only in size to St. Peter's.

On the town's outskirts, along the Via Cassia toward Orvieto, lies **San Flaviano**, a lovely double-decker building with a 12th-century church oriented east over an 11th-century church pointing west. Inside are some fine 14th-century frescoes and freely carved capitals, thought to have been inspired by the traditions of Etruscan art.

The main façade of the pentagonal Palazzo Farnese at Caprarola

Environs
The popular lakeside beach resort of **Bolsena**, 9 miles (15 km) north on Lake Bolsena, has a medieval castle, as well as boats to the islands of Bisentina and Martana.

❹ Bomarzo

Parco dei Mostri, Bomarzo. **Tel** 0761 92 40 29. 🚆 to Viterbo. 🚌 from Viterbo (not Sun or public hols).
Open 8:30am–sunset in winter (8:30am–7pm in summer). 📷
♿ 🌐 parcodeimostri.com

The Sacro Bosco beneath the town of Bomarzo was created between 1522 and 1580 by Duke Vicino Orsini as a bizarre memorial to his late wife. Far from designing a meticulous Renaissance garden, Orsini embraced the artificiality and distortion of the Mannerist period by creating lopsided buildings and sculpting huge boulders of stone into fantastic creatures and vast allegorical monsters.

One of the bizarre stone monsters in Bomarzo's Sacro Bosco

❺ Caprarola

Viterbo. 🗺 5,700. 🚌 ℹ️ Via Filippo Nicolai 2 (0761 64 61 57). 🛒 Tue.

Perhaps the grandest of the country villas created during the 17th century by the wealthy families of Rome, **Palazzo Farnese** *(see p384)* is the focal point of the medieval village of Caprarola. Designed by Vignola, it was built between 1559 and 1575 and takes its star shape from the foundations of a large pentagonal fortress designed by Antonio da Sangallo the Younger half a century earlier. On the main floor, reached by an elaborately stuccoed spiral staircase, the rooms were frescoed, largely by the Zuccari brothers in 1560, with scenes depicting heroic episodes from the life of Hercules and the Farnese family.

Environs
Created, according to legend, by the god Hercules ramming his club into the ground, **Lago di Vico**, 3 miles (4 km) west of Caprarola, in fact occupies the remnants of a volcanic crater. An idyllic enclave, the lake is encircled by the wooded slopes of the Cimini Hills (much of which is a nature reserve). A scenic road runs around the lake, and the best place for swimming is on the southeast shore.

🏛 **Palazzo Farnese**
Caprarola. **Tel** 0761 64 60 52. **Open** Tue–Sun. **Closed** Jan 1, Dec 25. 📷

Etruscan tumulus tombs from the necropolis at Cerveteri

necropolis are in museums such as the Vatican Museums, Villa Giulia, and the British Museum in London, some can be seen in the small **Museo Nazionale Cerite** in the center of town.

Environs
There are more traces of the Etruscans to be seen at **Norchia**, where the tombs are carved out of a rock face, and **Sutri**, whose amphitheater is one of the few relics of the living Etruscans.

Necropolis
Via Necropoli. **Tel** 06 994 00 01. **Open** Tue–Sun. **Closed** some pub hols.

Museo Nazionale Cerite
Piazza Santa Maria. **Tel** 06 994 13 54. **Open** Tue–Sun. **Closed** pub hols.

❻ Tarquinia

Viterbo. 15,000. Piazza Cavour (0766 84 92 82). Wed.

Ancient Tarquinia (Tarxuna) was one of Etruria's most important centers. It occupied a strategic position to the northeast of the present town, on a ridge dominating the coastal plain, until the 4th century BC when it fell to Rome.

Tarquinia itself is worth a wander for its crumbling medieval churches and spacious main square, though the main reason to visit is the **Museo Archeologico e Necropoli**, which has one of Italy's better collections of Etruscan finds. Reclining statues of the deceased adorn the sarcophagi on the ground floor, but the star attraction is a group of terracotta winged horses dating from the 4th century BC.

On a hilltop 1 mile (2 km) southeast of town are the frescoed tombs of the **necropolis** dug into the soft volcanic tufa. There are almost 6,000 tombs but only about 15 can be

visited at a time. The frescoes that decorate them, designed to remind the dead of life, range from frenetic dancing figures in the Tomba delle Leonesse to the diners reclining in the Tomba dei Leopardi.

Museo Archeologico e Necropoli
Piazza Cavour. **Tel** 0766 85 60 36; 85 63 08 (necropoli). **Open** Tue–Sun. **Closed** Jan 1, May 1, Dec 25.

❼ Cerveteri

Roma. 36,000. Pza Risorgimento 19 (06 99 55 19 71). Fri.

In the 6th century BC, Cerveteri (ancient Kysry) was one of the largest and most culturally rich towns of the Mediterranean, trading with Greece and controlling a large area along the coast. The **necropolis**, a city of the dead 1 mile (2 km) outside town, is a network of streets lined with tombs dating from the 7th to the 1st century BC. Some of the larger tumulus tombs, like the Tomba degli Scudi e delle Sedie, are arranged like houses with rooms, doors, and corridors. The Tomba dei Rilievi is decorated with plaster reliefs of tools, pets, and mythological figures. Although the best finds from the

Dancers from the 4th-century BC frescoed Tomba del Triclinio in the Museo Archeologico, Tarquinia

Medieval Anguillara on Lake Bracciano

❽ Lake Bracciano

Roma. Bracciano. Piazza Mazzini 5, Bracciano (06 60 65 78 83).

Bracciano is a large lake famous for its fish, and popular for water sports and lakeside lunches.

Medieval **Anguillara**, to the south, is the prettiest of the lakeside towns, with romantic views over the water. The main town, **Bracciano**, on the east shore, is dominated by the Orsini-Odescalchi fortress, a pentagonal 15th-century structure with frescoes by Antoniazzo Romano and other Tuscan and Umbrian artists.

Castello Orsini-Odescalchi
Piazza Mazzini 14. **Tel** 06 99 80 43 48. **Open** Tue–Sun. **Closed** Jan 1, Dec 25.

❾ Ostia Antica

Viale dei Romagnoli 717, Ostia. **Tel** 06
56 35 28 30. Ⓜ Piramide, then
Ⓕ from Porta San Paolo to Ostia
Antica. Excavations & Museum:
Open 8:30am–7:30pm Tue–Sun.
Closed Jan 1, May 1, Dec 25. 🅿

For over 600 years Ostia
was Rome's main port
and a busy trading
center, until the 5th
century AD when a
disastrous combination
of malaria and
commercial
competition brought
the town into decline. Silt
preserved its buildings
and it now lies 3 miles
(5 km) inland.

The ruins of Ostia give a
vivid idea of life in Classical
times. The main thoroughfare,
the **Decumanus Maximus**, runs
through the Forum, which
houses Ostia's largest temple,
the **Capitol**, and past the
restored **theater**, still used for
outdoor concerts in summer.
The road is lined with baths,
shops, and multistory buildings.
There is even a **Thermopolium**,
or bar, with a marble counter
and paintings advertising food
and drink.

**The building
material** for the
houses was brick,
left plain or
covered in mural
decoration.

**The internal
courtyard** has
remained a feature
of Italian housing.

Ruins of shops and offices along
the Decumanus Maximus

Balcony

Apartments or
single rooms were
rented out.

Shops
occupied the
ground floor of
the building.

Ostia Apartments

*Much of Ostia's population
lived in apartment buildings,
such as this one, based on the
Casa di Diana (2nd century AD).*

The bar served wine
and snacks.

❿ Frascati and the Castelli Romani

Roma. Ⓕ 🚌 Frascati. 🛈 Frascati
Point, Piazza Marconi (06 683 37 85).
Villa Aldobrandini Gardens:
Tel 06 942 14 34. **Open** Mon–Fri. 🅿

The Alban hills have long been a
country retreat for Romans. In
Classical times they were scattered with villas; in the Middle
Ages with fortified castles
(hence the name); and in the
16th and 17th centuries with
luxurious residences and their
spectacular parks. During World
War II German defenses were
based in the Alban hills and
many Castelli towns were
damaged by Allied bombs.
Although partly protected by a
nature reserve, the hilltop towns
are popular day-trip destinations
as well as being famous for their
white wine. **Frascati**'s central
piazza is a belvedere overlooked

by the Villa Aldobrandini, a
majestic 17th-century building
set in a splendid park of secret
grottoes, fountains, and statues.

The fortified Abbazia di San
Nilo in **Grottaferrata**, 2 miles
(3 km) south, was founded in
1004 and contains some lovely
17th-century frescoes by
Domenichino in the chapel.
Overlooking Lake Albano,

4 miles (6 km) south, **Castel
Gandolfo** is the site of the
pope's summer palace. When in
residence, the pope addresses
the crowd from the balcony.

Gathered around a sturdy
9th-century castle, and famed
for its strawberries, **Nemi**, 6
miles (10 km) southeast, looks
down onto the glassy dark-blue
waters of Lake Nemi.

The forested shores around the small, volcanic Lake Nemi

Tivoli, a favorite place to escape the heat of the Roman summer

⑪ Tivoli

Roma. 🚇 57,000. 🚊 🚌 ℹ️ Piazzale Nazioni Unite (0774 31 35 36). 🛒 Wed.

Hill town Tivoli, a popular excursion from Rome, was once a favored resort of the ancient Romans, attracted by its fresh water and sulfur springs, and by the beautiful countryside. The temples that once covered Tivoli's hilltop are still visible in places. Some are half buried in medieval buildings, others, such as the Temples of Sibyl and Vesta, inside the gardens of the Sibilla restaurant (on Via Sibilla), are relatively intact.

The town's most famous sight is the **Villa d'Este**, a sumptuous

Splendors from around the world reproduced in Hadrian's Villa

country residence created in the 16th century by Pirro Ligorio for Cardinal Ippolito d'Este from the shell of a Benedictine monastery. It is known primarily for its gardens, steeply raked on terraces, and studded with spectacular, if somewhat faded and moss-hung, fountains. Although suffering from reduced water pressure and polluted water due to centuries of neglect, the gardens give a vivid impression of the frivolous luxury enjoyed by the papal families. Highlights include the Viale delle Cento Fontane and the Fontana dell'Organo Idraulico, which, thanks to a hydraulic system, can play music. At the other end of town, the **Villa Gregoriana**, now a hotel, is set in a lush wooded valley where paths wind down into a deep ravine.

Environs
About 3 miles (5 km) west of Tivoli are the ruins of **Hadrian's Villa**. Easily seen in conjunction with a visit to the town, this is one of the largest and most spectacular villas ever built in the Roman Empire (it once covered an area greater than the center of Imperial Rome).

Hadrian was an inveterate traveler and his aim in creating the villa was to reproduce some of the wonders he had seen around the world. The Stoa Poikile, for example, a walkway around a rectangular pool and garden, recalls the painted colonnade of the Stoic philosophers in Athens, while the Canopus evokes the grand sanctuary of Serapis in

Alexandria. There are also ruins of two bath complexes, a Latin and a Greek library, a Greek theater, and a private study on a little island known as the Teatro Marittimo.

Today the rambling ruins, full of shady nooks and hidden corners, make a lovely place to relax, picnic, or explore.

🏛️ **Villa d'Este**
Pza Trento 1. **Tel** 0774 31 20 70. **Open** Tue–Sun. **Closed** Jan 1, Dec 25. 🗺️

🏛️ **Villa Gregoriana**
Largo Sant'Angelo. **Tel** 06 39 96 77 01. **Open** Tue–Sun. **Closed** Dec–Feb.

🏛️ **Hadrian's Villa**
Tel 0774 53 02 03. **Closed** pub hols. 🗺️

Mosaic fragment of Nile in flood, Archaeological Museum, Palestrina

⑫ Palestrina

Roma. 🚇 18,000. 🚌 ℹ️ Piazza Santa Maria degli Angeli 2 (06 957 31 76). 🛒 Sat.

Medieval Palestrina grew up over the terraces of a huge temple dedicated to the goddess Fortuna Primigenia, the mother of all gods. The temple, founded in the 8th century BC and rebuilt in the 2nd century BC by Sulla, housed one of the most important oracles of ancient times. The terraces of the sanctuary, littered with fragments of columns and porticoes, lead up to the curved **Palazzo Barberini**. Built over the site of a circular temple, it now houses the **Museo Nazionale Archeologico**, best known for a 1st-century BC mosaic of the Nile in flood.

🏛️ **Museo Nazionale Archeologico**
Via Barberini. **Tel** 06 953 81 00. **Open** daily. **Closed** Jan 1, May 1, Dec 25. 🗺️

⑬ Subiaco

Roma. 🚠 9,000. 🚌 ℹ️ Town Library, Viale della Repubblica 26 (0774 81 64 07). 🛒 Sat.

In the 6th century, weary of the decadence of Rome, St. Benedict left the city to become a hermit in a cave above Subiaco. Others joined him, and eventually there were 12 monasteries in the area.

Only two now survive: **Santa Scolastica**, dedicated to Benedict's sister, is organized around three cloisters, one Renaissance, one early Gothic, and the third Cosmatesque. Higher up, the 12th-century **San Benedetto** is a more rewarding destination. Overhanging a deep gorge, it comprises two churches built on top of each other. The upper is decorated with 14th-century Sienese frescoes; the lower, built over several levels, incorporates the original cave where Benedict spent three years after fleeing Rome.

🏛 **Santa Scolastica**
2 miles (3 km) east of Subiaco. **Tel** 0774 824 21. **Open** daily. 📷

🏛 **San Benedetto**
2 miles (3 km) east of Subiaco. **Tel** 0774 850 39. **Open** daily. 📷 ♿ (upper church only).

⑭ Montecassino

Cassino. **Tel** 0776 31 15 29. 🚆 Cassino then bus. **Open** 9am–12:30pm, 3:30–6pm daily (Nov–Mar: to 5pm).

The Abbey of Montecassino, mother church of the Benedictine order and a center of medieval art, was founded in 529 by St. Benedict. By the 8th century it was an important center of learning, and by the 11th century had become one of the richest monasteries in Europe.

In 1944 it was a German stronghold and a target for Allied bombs. Most of the complex was devastated, including the lavish Baroque church, but the walls remained intact and the abbey withstood for three months before falling to the Allies. The adjoining war cemeteries commemorate the 30,000 soldiers killed.

Rose window, Fossanova

The Monasteries of Lazio

St. Benedict founded the Abbey of Montecassino around 529 and there wrote his famous Rule. Based on the principles of prayer, study, and manual labor, this became the fundamental monastic code of western Europe. The Cistercian Order, an offshoot of the Benedictines, came to Italy from Burgundy in the 12th century. The Cistercians were followers of St. Bernard, whose creed was based on austerity and self-sufficiency, qualities that were reflected in the simple, early Gothic architecture of their monasteries. Their first abbey was at Fossanova. Other Cistercian abbeys in Lazio include Valvisciolo (northeast of Sermoneta) and San Martino in Cimino (near Lago di Vico).

The Abbey of Montecassino, destroyed during World War II, was rebuilt as a replica of its 17th-century predecessor.

The Abbey of San Benedetto, Subiaco, was founded in the 11th century over St. Benedict's cave. A staircase carved in the rock leads to the grotto where he preached to shepherds.

The Abbey of Casamari, 8 miles (14 km) east of Frosinone, was founded by Benedictine monks in 1035 and handed over to the Cistercians who rebuilt it in 1203.

The abandoned medieval village of Ninfa, now a beautiful garden

⓫ Anagni

Frosinone. 🅼 20,000. 🄵🅂 🚌
🛈 Piazza Innocenzo III (0775 72 78 52). 🅆 Wed.

According to legend, Saturn founded five towns in southeast Lazio, including Anagni, Alatri, and Arpino. This area is now known as La Ciociaria, from *ciocie*, the bark clogs worn in the area until about 30 years ago.

Before the Romans conquered this part of Lazio it was inhabited by several different tribes: the Volsci, the Sanniti, and the Hernici. Little is known of them, apart from the extraordinary walls with which they protected their settlements. In later years these were believed to have been built by the Cyclops, a mythical giant, which gave them their present name of Cyclopean walls.

Anagni was the most sacred Hernician center until its destruction by the Romans in 306 BC. In the Middle Ages it was the birthplace and family seat of several popes, an era from which many buildings survive, most notably Boniface VIII's 13th-century mullion-windowed palace.

The beautiful Romanesque **Duomo**, Santa Maria, built over the ancient Hernician acropolis, boasts a fine Cosmati mosaic floor from the 13th century as well as 14th-century Sienese frescoes. The crypt of San Magno is frescoed with one of the most complete surviving cycles of the 12th and 13th centuries.

Environs
Alatri, perched on an olive-covered slope 17 miles (28 km) east of Anagni, was an important Hernician town. It preserves an impressive double set of Cyclopean walls, 1 mile (2 km) long and 10 ft (3 m) high, from its 7th-century BC acropolis. In the medieval town below the walls is the Romanesque church of Santa Maria Maggiore, greatly restored in the 13th century.

Arpino, 25 miles (40 km) east of Alatri, is a bustling town with a medieval core, and was the birthplace of the Roman orator,

An unusual pointed arch in the Cyclopean walls at Arpino

Cicero. About 2 miles (3 km) above Arpino, at the site of the ancient town of Civitavecchia, is a tremendous stretch of Cyclopean walls that includes a rare gateway with a pointed arch.

⓬ Sermoneta and Ninfa

Latina. 🄵🅂 Latina Scalo. 🚌 from Latina. 🛈 Via Duca di Mare 19, Latina (0773 69 54 04). Ninfa **Tel** 0773 63 22 31 (call for group reservations). **Open** Apr–Oct: 1st Sat & Sun of the month. 🅿

Sermoneta is a lovely hilltop town overlooking the Pontine Plains, with narrow cobbled streets winding around medieval houses, palaces, and churches. The **Duomo** has a fine 15th-century panel by Benozzo Gozzoli showing the Virgin cradling Sermoneta in her hands. At the top of the town rises the moated fairy-tale Castello Caetani, frescoed with mythological scenes by a pupil of Pinturicchio.

In the valley below lies the abandoned medieval village of **Ninfa**, converted into lush gardens by the Caetani family in 1921. Streams and waterfalls punctuate the picturesque garden laid out among the crumbling buildings.

⑰ Terracina

Latina. 🚉 44,000. 🚆 🚌 🛈 Via Leopardi (0773 72 77 59). 🛒 Thu.

Roman Terracina was a commercial center on the Via Appia (the Appian Way). Today it is a popular seaside resort, with a fascinating collage of medieval buildings and Roman ruins in its historic center, perched on the slopes of the Ausonian Hills. The more modern part of town by the sea is full of restaurants, bars, and hotels.

Bombing during World War II uncovered many of the town's ancient structures, notably a stretch of the Appian Way and the original paving of the Roman Forum in Piazza del Municipio. The 11th-century **Duomo** was built in the shell of a Roman temple, and is still entered by the temple's steps. The medieval portico is adorned with a lovely 12th-century mosaic and the interior preserves the 13th-century mosaic sidewalk. Next door, the modern town hall houses the **Museo Archeologico**, devoted to local Greek and Roman finds.

Duomo at Terracina with original Roman steps

About 2 miles (3 km) above the town are the podium and foundations that once supported the Temple of Jove Anxur, dating back to the 1st century BC. This huge arcaded platform is illuminated at night and offers vertiginous views of Terracina and its bay.

🏛 Museo Archeologico
Piazza del Municipio. **Tel** 0773 70 73 13. **Open** daily. **Closed** Mon pm, some public hols. 📷

⑱ Sperlonga

Latina. 🚉 4,000. 🚌 🛈 Corso San Leone 22 (0771 55 70 00). 🛒 Sat.

Sperlonga is a seaside resort surrounded by sandy beaches. The old town sits on a rocky promontory, a picturesque labyrinth of whitewashed buildings, narrow alleyways, piazzettas, and balconies offering an occasional glimpse of the sea below. It is now full of bars, restaurants, and boutiques. The modern part of town lies down on the seafront.

The area around Sperlonga was a favorite retreat for the ancient Romans during the summer months. They built villas along the coast, and converted the natural caves in the nearby cliffs into places to dine and relax.

In 1957, archaeologists excavating the complex of Tiberius's luxury villa, half a mile (1 km) on the southern outskirts of town, found some marvelous 2nd-century BC Hellenistic sculptures in a large cave open to the sea. These sculptures, representing

12th-century bell tower at Gaeta

incidents from Homer's *Odyssey*, are thought to be by the same artists from Rhodes (where the Emperor Tiberius once lived) who were responsible for the Laocoön *(see p421)*. They are displayed, along with other local finds, in the **Museo Archeologico Nazionale**, which is part of the archaeological zone.

🏛 Zona Archeologica
Via Flacca. **Tel** 0771 54 80 28. **Open** daily. **Closed** Jan 1, Dec 25. 📷

⑲ Gaeta

Latina. 🚉 22,000. 🚌 🛈 Via Emanuele Filiberto 5 (0771 46 11 65). 🛒 Wed.

According to Virgil, Gaeta was named after Aeneas's wet nurse Caieta, who was allegedly buried here. The town sits on the southern headland of the gulf of Gaeta, under Monte Orlando. The historic center is dominated by a mighty Aragonese castle and the pinnacles of mock-Gothic San Francesco. To the north, the modern quarter links Gaeta to the bay of Serapo, a picturesque beach resort.

Gaeta's most beautiful feature is the **Duomo**'s elegant late-Romanesque bell tower, its lofty summit topped by a roof of colored ceramic tiles. On the seafront lies the tiny 10th-century church of **San Giovanni a Mare**, with faded frescoes, a hemispherical dome, and a sloping floor to let the sea flow out after flooding.

Stretches of sandy beach along the coast between Gaeta and Terracina

Southern Italy at a Glance

Visitors to southern Italy find a rich array of archaeological remains. Although those of the Romans at Pompeii are high on everyone's list, Greek ruins are found in Sicily and the southern coast, and there are mysterious ancient structures, called *nuraghe*, in Sardinia. Campania, Puglia, and Sicily are admired for their architecture, while across the south there are magnificent landscapes, abundant wildlife, and endless opportunities for outdoor activities. The cuisine alone, with its eclectic heritage and diversity of tastes, provides the excuse to dawdle on the coast or in the mountain villages.

The Parco Nazionale d'Abruzzo, a vast, unspoiled wilderness, is home to wolves, bears, and many species of birds (*see pp506–7*).

Su Nuraxi at Barumini, built around 1500 BC, is the most celebrated of Sardinia's mysterious stone *nuraghe* sites (*see p549*).

The cloister decoration at Monreale cathedral is a legacy of Sicily's Arabic past, with elaborate columns adorned with fine mosaics and splendid sculpted capitals (*see pp530–31*).

Sicily's Valley of the Temples at Agrigento contains some of the best-preserved Greek ruins outside Greece. Mostly Doric in style, they date from the 5th and 6th centuries BC (*see p536*).

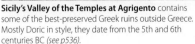

◄ Colorful terraced villas scaling down to the beach in Positano on the Amalfi Coast

The Museo Archeologico Nazionale in Naples is one of Italy's most important museums. It houses the treasures of Pompeii, including sculptures, vases, and everyday artifacts that provide a detailed glimpse of Roman life *(see pp490–91)*.

Pescara

Chieti

RUZZO

Termoli

MOLISE

pobasso

Foggia

ABRUZZO, MOLISE AND PUGLIA *(See pp504–17)*

Bari

NAPLES AND CAMPANIA *(See pp486–503)*

Naples

Pompeii

Potenza

Matera

PUGLIA

Fasano

Brindisi

Taranto

BASILICATA

Lecce

Otranto

Pompeii's Roman ruins include streets, houses, and an amphitheater *(see pp494–5)*.

Cassano allo Ionio

Rossano

BASILICATA AND CALABRIA *(See pp518–25)*

kilometers   100

miles   50

Catanzaro

Crotone

Tropea

Vibo Valentia

Isole Eolie

CALABRIA

Messina

Reggio di Calabria

The church of Santa Croce in Lecce is an excellent example of the exuberant Lecce Baroque style, from its elaborate rose window to the intricately carved capitals *(see pp512–13)*.

Catania

Mount Etna, one of the world's largest volcanoes, is still active, with lava erupting from fissures that dot its flanks. The nearby city of Catania has suffered repeatedly from volcanic damage *(see p539)*.

Siracusa

Scicli

The Flavors of Southern Italy

The "land of the midday sun," the *Mezzogiorno* is majestic and fertile, yet in places barren and achingly poor. This is the land of the Mediterranean diet, which relies heavily on bright vegetables, fresh seafood, aromatic herbs, and fruity olive oil. Puglia produces more grapes and olives than any other region in Italy, while the fertile volcanic soil around Vesuvius and Etna is ideal for growing plump vegetables, juicy fruits, and vines. Naples is the birthplace of the pizza, and the region of Campania also produces the best buffalo mozzarella in the country.

Mixed herbs

Sicilian cheesemaker with a basket of fresh ricotta

Campania

Naples is famous for pizza, but it's also the home of the tomato-based pasta sauce. Especially prized are the distinctive long, tapered tomatoes from San Marzano in Salerno. The tradition of combining mozzarella and tomato originates here. Pasta is generally tubular (in the north it tends to be ribbonlike). Other staple Campanian ingredients are olive oil, garlic, basil, chilies, and lemons. Excellent seafood includes octopus and squid, anchovies, mussels, and clams, most of which are prepared simply, using lemon, garlic, and pepper. Lamb, kid, and buffalo are the most popular meats. There is also a long tradition of making pastries and ice cream.

Puglia

This region is responsible for producing 80 percent of Italy's pasta, as well as being the source of most of the country's fish. As in the rest of Southern Italy, meats such as poultry, pork, and kid are often roasted over aromatic herbs. The distinctive local ear-shaped pasta, *orecchiette*, is popular, and fruits and vegetables,

Tuna   Lobster   Squid   Sardines

Mussels   Clams

Display of the superb seafood caught along the coastline of the south

Regional Dishes and Specialties

Some of Italy's classic sauces originated in the South, such as the powerful *puttanesca* with tomatoes, anchovies, chilies, capers, and olives. Along the Campanian coast, *zuppa di cozze* (mussels in hot pepper sauce) is a specialty. Octopus is particularly good served in dishes such as *polpo alla luciana*, where it is gently cooked in tomatoes and olive oil with parsley and garlic. *Orecchiette con cime di rapa* (ear-shaped pasta with turnip tops) is a signature dish from Puglia, as is *agnello allo squero* – lamb, spit-roasted over a fire scented with thyme and herbs. For those with a sweet tooth, mouthwatering *cassata Siciliana* is a rich sponge cake layered with ricotta cheese, liqueur, candied fruits, and pistachio nuts.

Figs

Maccheroncini con le sarde
Sicilian macaroni with sardines, fennel, pine nuts, raisins, breadcrumbs, and saffron.

Tresses of vine-ripened tomatoes hanging on a southern market stall

especially figs and quinces, are abundant.

A bounty of fish and shellfish is caught along the 250-mile (400-km) coastline. As well as mozzarella, other good cheeses include ricotta, goat's, and smoked cheeses.

Sicily

The island's long list of invasions is reflected in its varied cuisine. Greek colonists in the 8th century BC were amazed at the fertility of the volcanic soil. Rice was introduced to the area by the Arabs, while the influence of North African cuisine is shown in *cuscusu* (couscous) and other Arab flavors that appear in sweet and spicy dishes.

The lamb and pork raised in mountain pastures and oak forests is exceptional. Fish is excellent, especially sardines, tuna, anchovies, and swordfish. Vegetables are plump and delicious and eggplant (aubergine) is a firm favorite. Sheep's milk ricotta cheese features in many delicious

Newly harvested olives, ready to be pressed into olive oil

pastries and puddings, such as the sinfully rich Sicilian *cassata*.

Other Regions

Mountainous Abruzzo and Molise are good sheep-rearing territory, so lamb is a specialty here, as is guitar-shaped pasta (*maccheroni alla chitarra*). Food in Calabria and Basilicata is strong on spices, especially chili peppers, which are considered a cure-all. Sardinia bakes wafer-thin unleavened bread – *carta da musica* (music paper). Honey, wild boar ham, and thrushes are popular, as is *torrone*, a delicious almond nougat.

ON THE MENU

Arancini Sicilian rice balls, usually stuffed with a meat, cheese, or vegetable filling.

Caciocavallo Spun cow's milk cheese, especially good from Avellino in Campania.

Insalata caprese Salad from Campania with mozzarella, tomato, basil, olives, and oregano.

Maccheroni di fuoco Pasta dish from Basilicata with large quantities of garlic and chili.

Seadas A kind of doughnut from Sardinia, fried and covered with honey.

Soppressata A spicy, dry-cured salami from Calabria.

Pizza Napoletana This thin-crusted pizza is topped simply with tomato, garlic, oregano, basil, and anchovies.

Pesce spada In Campania, Puglia, Calabria, and Sicily, swordfish steak is grilled with lemon and oregano.

Sfogliatella Paper-thin layers of pastry ooze with butter, sugar, cinnamon, orange peel, and ricotta.

Understanding the Architecture of Southern Italy

The Romanesque style of southern Italy owes much to the Normans, who in the 11th century brought from France both form and style in architecture and sculpture. In the southeast, the style has hefty Byzantine overtones; in Sicily it is characterized by strong traditional Islamic motifs and a love of rich color, pattern, and ornamentation. These

Baroque carving on Bagheria's Villa Palagonia

elements surface later in Sicily's Baroque style and are allied to a dynamism that originates in the Baroque of Rome – though in Sicily it is more vivacious. Neapolitan Baroque is more sophisticated and displays a greater interest in the creative use of space.

Byzantine and Romanesque Features

Lateral towers

Multicolored marble

Interlacing arches

Glass and plaster mosaics on gold

Rich ornamentation

Interlacing arches

Cefalù, begun in 1131 by Roger II, is one of Sicily's great Norman cathedrals *(see p539)*. Its west front exhibits many northern Romanesque features, such as the massive towers.

Christ Pantocrator, a Byzantine apse mosaic (c.1132), adorns the Cappella Palatina *(see p530)*.

The east end of the Norman cathedral of Monreale, founded in 1172 by William II, is built of multicolored materials with interlacing arches *(see pp534–5)*.

Baroque Features

Massive scale of stairway

Sweeping view down corridor

Bold statue of lion

Lifelike putti

Brilliant realism of drapery

Caserta's Palazzo Reale, a sumptuous royal palace begun by Charles III in 1752, is characterized by its monumental scale *(see p500)*. The richly decorated interior is prefaced by several huge entrances and impressive staircases offering views. The enormous building was designed by Luigi Vanvitelli.

Giacomo Serpotta's stucco reliefs (c.1690) in Palermo's Oratorio di Santa Zita illustrate Sicilians' love of exuberant decoration *(see p533)*.

Where to See the Architecture

The best places to see Romanesque architecture are Puglia and the cathedral cities of northwestern Sicily. Puglia's best churches are those at Trani (see p513) and nearby Canosa, Molfetta, and Bitonto; Ruvo di Puglia (p514), San Leonardo di Siponto on the Gargano Peninsula, and Martina Franca, near Alberobello. The Baroque style of the south is epitomized by the villas, palaces,

The Duomo portal in Ruvo di Puglia

and churches of Naples and Sicily, and by the deeply encrusted ornamentation found on church façades in Lecce (pp516–17), in Puglia. In Sicily, the Baroque of Palermo (pp530–31), Bagheria (p536), Noto, Modica, and Ragusa (p547), and Siracusa (pp546–7) is well known. Less so are churches at Piazza Armerina (p541), Trapani (p536), Palazzolo Acreide, close to Siracusa, and Acireale, near Catania.

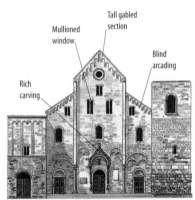

Rich carving — Mullioned window — Tall gabled section — Blind arcading

Bari's Basilica di San Nicola (founded 1087) was the model for subsequent churches in Puglia (see p514). Based on Norman architecture, its façade is flanked by towers and divided vertically into three, reflecting the tripartite nature of its plan.

Half columns — Rose window — Blind arcading

The façade of Troia cathedral (1093–1125) owes its design to Pisan architecture and its rich ornamentation to Byzantine and Arab models (see pp512–13).

Carved scroll — Protruding columns

The façade of Siracusa's Duomo, begun in 1728 by Andrea Palma, is animated by broken or curved elements (see pp546–7).

Three-tiered structure — Central bell tower — Curved surface

San Giorgio in Ragusa (1744) has a façade by Gagliardi with layers of ornamentation culminating in the tower (see p547).

Stone-carved decoration

Lecce's Chiesa del Rosario (begun 1691) was built by Lo Zingarello of soft local sandstone in the Lecce Baroque style of profuse carving (see pp516–17).

The Ancient Greeks in Southern Italy

Some of the best ruins of the ancient Greek world are in Southern Italy. Syracuse, Selinunte, Segesta, and Gela are among the better known Sicilian sites, while those on the mainland include Crotone, Locri, and Paestum. Magna Graecia is the collective name given to these scattered colonies of ancient Greece, the earliest of which were founded in the Naples area between the 8th and 6th centuries BC. Many great figures of the age – including Pythagoras, Archimedes, and Aeschylus – lived in these settlements, and it was here that wine making flourished. Artifacts from this age are exhibited in the excellent archaeological museums of Naples, Syracuse, and Taranto.

KYME
Cuma

NEAPOLIS
Napoli

HERAKLE
Ercolano

Ancient Herakleia
(Herculaneum) was named after its patron deity, the mighty Hercules. It was buried by the eruption of Mount Vesuvius in AD 79 (see p499).

POSEIDONIA
Paestum

EL
Ve

Poseidonia (today's Paestum), was the city of Poseidon, God of the Sea. Its ruins, dating from the 6th century BC, include the hulks of two of the finest Doric temples in Europe (see pp502–3).

Mount Etna was believed to be the forge of Hephaistos (Vulcan) – God of Fire – and the Cyclops, the one-eyed giant (see p543).

Tyndaris was one of the last Greek cities founded on Sicily.

LIPARA
Lipari

TYNDAR
Tindar

PANORMOS
Palermo

SOLUS
Soluto

HIMERA
Himera

ERYX
Erice

EGESTA
Segesta

Eryx, founder of the town, was the son of Aphrodite and Poseidon.

Valley
of the
Selinunte Temples

SELINUS

Belice

HENNA
Enna

KATA
Gatar

MEGARA HYBLA
Megara

The legendary founder of Agrigento was Daedalus, who created wings for himself and his son, Icarus, so they could fly.

AKRAGAS
Agrigento

GELA
Gela

Gelo

Mus
Archeolog
Region
Paolo (

Gela was prosperous under the rule of Hippocrates in the 5th century BC.

Egesta (built 426–416 BC) was colonized by the Elymians, who may have originated at Troy. Among the ruins of this town are a half-completed temple and a theater (see p538). Ancient Greeks used theaters for plays and cultural entertainment rather than combat.

0 kilometers 100
0 miles 50

Aeschylus, the dramatist, died in Gela in 456. Considered the father of Greek tragedy, his plays include *Seven Against Thebes, Women of Aetna,* and *Prometheus Bound*.

Metapontion (Metapontum) was home to Pythagoras after his expulsion from Crotone. Its ruins include Doric temples, the Tavole Palatine, and a theater *(see p523)*.

Taras was home to the philosopher and scientist Archytas, and to Aristoxenes, author of the earliest treatise on music.

Founded by Spartan Greeks (8th century BC), Taras was a rich and powerful city.

Greece and its Colonies

7th–5th century BC

The Sybarites were famed for their luxurious lifestyle, hence the word *sybaritic*. The wealth of Sybaris resulted from trade with the Etruscans.

In about 540 BC Crotone became the chief school of Pythagoras's philosophy. Here the great thinker and mathematician remained for 30 years until the government (which he supported) was overthrown, and he was expelled.

Museo Nazionale di Metaponto

Museo Archeologico Nazionale

• TARAS
Taranto

Basento

METAPONTION •
Metaponto

SIRIS •
Nova Siri

SYBARIS •
Sibari   • THURII
Thuri

KROTON
Crotone •

Locri Epizefiri was the first Greek city to have a written code of law.

ZANKLE-
MESSENE
Messina

• LOKROI
Locri Epizefiri

RHEGION
Reggio di Calabria

OS
dini Naxos

The Straits of Messina vexed Odysseus, the hero of Homer's Odyssey. Here at the meeting of two seas the currents created a "whirlpool" – Charybdis – which posed a threat to safe entry of Messina *(see p542)*. Another threat were the Sirens, who lured voyagers onto rocks with their singing. Odysseus is seen here tied to a mast, so he can hear their song, but resist its call.

Plato the philosopher visited Syracuse and advised the ruler, Dionysius II, how to govern.

KOUSAI
cusa

The mathematician and inventor Archimedes was born in Syracuse c.287 BC. His inventions included the famous Archimedean screw, and various weapons to stave off the Romans *(see pp546–7)*.

Demeter and Persephone

The complex web of Greek mythology was part of the daily life of the ancients. Enna was once the seat of the cult of Demeter, the earth goddess, and between 480 and 460 BC a temple was erected there in her honor. According to the legend, Persephone, the daughter of Demeter and Zeus, was abducted in the nearby fields by Hades, who carried her off into the Underworld. Demeter then left Olympus and wandered the world searching in vain for her daughter. Discovering that Zeus had allowed the abduction to happen, Demeter put a blight on Sicily: it would remain barren until Persephone returned. Finally Hades allowed her return from the Underworld, but only for a few months of each year – from spring to autumn. Demeter, satisfied with the result, ensured that Sicily became the most fertile place on earth.

Sculpture of Persephone

NAPLES AND CAMPANIA

The capital of Campania, Naples is one of the few European cities of the ancient world that has never been completely extinguished. Founded by Greeks, it was embellished and enlarged by the Romans and in subsequent centuries was the much-prized booty of foreign invaders and Imperialists – most prominently the Normans, Hohenstaufen, French, and Spanish.

Naples today is a chaotic yet spectacular metropolis sprawling noisily and dirtily around the edge of the Bay of Naples. To one side is Mount Vesuvius; facing from the sea are the islands of Capri, Ischia, and Procida. Pompeii and Herculaneum, lying in the shadow of the volcano that destroyed them, contain the most revealing Roman ruins in Italy.

For centuries Naples dominated the Italian south, or *Mezzogiorno* (land of the midday sun). Unemployment, poverty, and crime are a problem – the Camorra is as deep-seated here as the Mafia is in Sicily – but there is also an attractive, rude ebullience to the city.

The ancient history of Campania is linked to the Etruscans and the Greeks, whose massive ruins can be seen at Paestum. Next came a time of great prosperity under the Romans; archaeological evidence of this still exists at Benevento, Santa Maria Capua Vetere, and Pozzuoli.

The hinterland, with its rich, well-cultivated plains, is eclipsed by the Amalfi coastline, with its breathtaking views, and the terrific seaboard of the Cilento. The mountainous interior, remote and unvisited, contains small towns that were settled by the Greeks, developed by the Romans, and often abandoned in the wake of malaria and Saracen attacks.

A glimpse into the narrow streets of Naples' Quartieri Spagnoli (Spanish Quarter)

◀ Picturesque beach and town of Amalfi, the largest town on the Amalfi Coast

aples and Campania

hich to explore Campania is the city of
orth, verdant plains sweep down to Santa
he east, the mountainous
verlooks the valley, while
earthquake-ravaged Avellino and its
province lurk on a plain beyond
Vesuvius. The Campi Flegrei area,
west of Naples, is famous for the
Roman ruins at Cuma. Further
south is the splendid, rugged
Amalfi Coast. Clean sandy
beaches lie beyond the tip
of the Sorrentine Peninsula
and along the Cilento coast
as well as on Capri, Ischia, and
Procida in the Gulf of Naples.

Sights at a Glance

1. Naples (Napoli) pp490–97
2. Pompeii pp498–9
3. Santa Maria Capua Vetere
4. Caserta
5. Benevento
6. Amalfi Coast
7. Salerno
8. Paestum
9. Capri
10. Ischia and Procida

Typical Naples street viewed from Santa Maria Maggiore

For additional map symbols see back flap

*Map labels:*

Isernia
Iser
Iser
Monti del Matese
Roma
S6
Pratella
S85
Piedimonte Matese
Morco
Galluccio
S372
Monte Santa Croce 1005m △
A1
Ponteland
Monte Maggiore 1037m △
Sessa Aurunca
Teano
Alvignano
Carinola
S7
Caiazzo
Solo
Volturno
Frasso Telesino
Mondragone
S7q
Capua
San Leucio
Caserta Vecchia
MAR TIRRENO
SANTA MARIA CAPUA VETERE ③
④ CASERTA
Montesarc
S7
Casa di Principe
A30
Cervinara
S7b
Aversa
Cicciano
Acerra
Nola
Marano di Napoli
Casoria
Pomigliano d'Arco
NAPLES ①
A3
Ottaviano
Pozzuoli
Portici
Vesuvio 1277m
Bacoli
Torre del Greco
POMPEII ②
ISOLA DI PROCIDA ⑩
Procida
Torre Annunziata
Noce Inferic
ISOLA D'ISCHIA ⑩
Ischia
Castellammare di Stabia
Sant'Angelo
Vico Equense
Golfo di Napoli
Sorrento
Ravell
Penisola Sorrentina
S163
Positano
⑥
ISOLA DI CAPRI ⑨
Capri
Praiano
A
COSTIERA AMALFITAN

Key

— Highway
— Major road
— Secondary road
⋯ Minor road
— Scenic route
— Main railroad
— Minor railroad
— Regional border
△ Summit

0 kilometers 25
0 miles 20

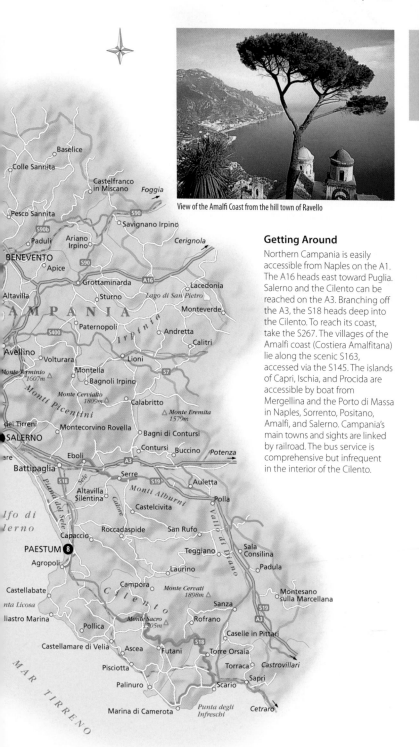

View of the Amalfi Coast from the hill town of Ravello

Getting Around

Northern Campania is easily accessible from Naples on the A1. The A16 heads east toward Puglia. Salerno and the Cilento can be reached on the A3. Branching off the A3, the S18 heads deep into the Cilento. To reach its coast, take the S267. The villages of the Amalfi coast (Costiera Amalfitana) lie along the scenic S163, accessed via the S145. The islands of Capri, Ischia, and Procida are accessible by boat from Mergellina and the Porto di Massa in Naples, Sorrento, Positano, Amalfi, and Salerno. Campania's main towns and sights are linked by railroad. The bus service is comprehensive but infrequent in the interior of the Cilento.

❶ Naples

The compact center of Naples, filled with palaces, churches, convents, and monasteries, revolves around just a few streets. From the Piazza del Plebiscito, Via Toledo (also called Via Roma) proceeds north toward Piazza Dante. To the east, narrow Via dei Tribunali and Via San Biagio dei Librai penetrate the historic and noisy heart of the city, the *Spaccanapoli* (split Naples). South of Palazzo Reale is the Santa Lucia district. To the west is the port of Mergellina, and overlooking the city is the Vomero district.

View of the Bay of Naples and Mount Vesuvius

Exploring Northeast Naples

Much of the city's most interesting art and architecture can be found here, including the Museo Archeologico Nazionale and its Roman treasures from Herculaneum and Pompeii. The buildings provide a wide range of architectural styles from the French-Gothic of the Duomo to the Florentine-Renaissance style of the Porta Capuana.

🏛 MADRE

Via Settembrini 79. **Tel** 081 193 13 016. **Open** 10am–7pm Mon, Wed–Sun. 🎫 (free Mon). ▫ 📷
🌐 **museomadre.it**

Opened in 2005, the Museo d'Arte Contemporanea Donna Regina Napoli (MADRE) is located in the Palazzo Donnaregina, from which it gets its name. The museum houses a remarkable collection by well-known artists such as Andy Warhol, Robert Rauschenberg, Mimmo Paladino, Claes Oldenburg,

The beautiful Renaissance gate of Porta Capuana

Robert Mapplethorpe, and Roy Lichtenstein among others. On the first floor is a library and a children's area, while the third floor is used for temporary exhibitions. The museum often hosts special events such as film screenings, concerts, and theatrical performances. The church of Santa Maria Donnaregina, at the back of the museum, provides additional exhibition space in a beautiful setting.

🏛 Castel Capuano and Porta Capuana

Piazza Enrico de Nicola.
Begun by Norman King William I and completed by Frederick II, Castel Capuano was a royal palace until 1540, when it became the Court of Justice. Today it is a courthouse.

Nearby, between the Aragonese towers of the Capua Gate and facing a market, is a rare sculpture in the Florentine-Renaissance manner. Created by Giuliano da Maiano (and finished in 1490 by Luca Fancelli) as a defensive gate, Porta Capuana is perhaps Italy's finest Renaissance gateway.

Sights at a Glance

① Museo Archeologico Nazionale
   pp494–5
② MADRE
③ Castel Capuano and Porta
   Capuana
④ Duomo
⑤ Pio Monte della Misericordia
⑥ Cappella Sansevero
⑦ San Lorenzo Maggiore

Interior of the Duomo

🏛 Duomo

Via Duomo 147. **Tel** 081 44 90 97.
Open 8am–12:30pm, 4:30–7pm
daily. **Closed** public hols. 🚹

Built between 1294 and
1323, the Cattedrale di
Santa Maria Assunta, or
Duomo, lies behind a
mostly 19th-century façade.
The nave is lined with ancient
columns, and there is an array
of monuments to past rulers,
along with paintings by
Lanfranco and Domenichino.

The Duomo houses the relics
of San Gennaro, Naples' patron
saint (martyred AD 305). The
Cappella San Gennaro holds
phials of his congealed blood,
which miraculously liquefies
three times a year (the Saturday
before the first Sunday in May,
Sep 19, and Dec 16). The
Cappella Carafa, a Renaissance
masterpiece built from 1497 to
1506, contains the saint's tomb.

Accessible from the Duomo's
north aisle is the Cappella di
Santa Restituta, founded in the
4th century on the site of a
former Temple of Apollo, and
rebuilt in the 1300s. It has ceiling
paintings by Luca Giordano
(1632–1705) and a 5th-century
baptistry. The nearby Museo del
Tesoro di San Gennaro (Tel: 081
29 49 80) exhibits a fine range
of gold, silverware, jewels,
statues, and art.

VISITORS' CHECKLIST

Practical Information
🗺 1,300,000. ℹ P. del Gesù
Nuovo (081 551 27 01), Via San
Carlo (081 40 23 94). 🖴 daily.
🎎 San Gennaro: Sep 19.
🌐 **inaples.it**

Transportation
✈ Capodichino 2.5 miles (4 km)
NW. 🚆 Centrale, P. Garibaldi. 🚌
P. Garibaldi. ⛴ Stazione Marittima,
Molo Beverello, & Mergellina.

🏛 Pio Monte della Misericordia

Via dei Tribunali 253. **Tel** 081 44 69 44.
Church & gallery **Open** 9am–2:30pm
Mon–Tue, Thu–Sun. **Closed** public
hols. 🎫 Gallery only.

The octagonal church
belonging to this charitable
foundation houses Caravaggio's
Seven Acts of Mercy (1607). The
art gallery has paintings by Luca
Giordano and Mattia Preti.

🏛 Cappella Sansevero

Via F. de Santis 19. **Tel** 081 551 84 70.
Open 10am–5:40pm Wed–Mon (to
1:10pm Sun & public hols). 🎫 🚫
🚹 (church).

This tiny 16th-century chapel
is the burial sepulchre of the
Princes of Sangro di Sansevero.
Featuring both Christian and
Masonic symbolism, the chapel
has an unusual character.

Remarkable 18th-century
sculpture fills the chapel. *The
Resurrection of the Prince*, by an
unknown artist, is mirrored by
that of Christ, above the altar.
Giuseppe Sammartino's *Veiled
Christ* is an alabaster figure
beneath a marble veil, and is
a work of technical virtuosity.

Prince Raimondo, an 18th-
century alchemist, is associated
with the chapel. He performed
gruesome experiments on
human bodies, for which he was
excommunicated. The results of
some of his experiments can be
seen in the crypt.

⑧ San Gregorio Armeno
⑨ Museo Filangieri
⑩ Sant'Angelo a Nilo
⑪ San Domenico Maggiore
⑫ Santa Chiara
⑬ Gesù Nuovo
⑭ Sant'Anna e San Bartolomeo
   dei Lombardi
⑮ Castel Nuovo
⑯ Quartieri Spagnoli
⑰ Galleria Umberto I and Teatro
   San Carlo
⑱ Palazzo Reale

Sammartino's Veiled Christ (1753) in the Cappella Sansevero

For keys and symbols *see back flap*

Exploring Central Naples

The part of Santa Lucia bordered by Via Duomo to the east, Via Tribunali to the north, Via Toledo (Roma) to the west, and the water to the south is the old heart of Naples. Especially rich in 14th- and 15th-century churches, the area offers visitors an abundance of sights.

Interior of San Gregorio Armeno

⬆ San Lorenzo Maggiore

Via dei Tribunali 316. **Tel** 081 211 08 60. Church & Excavations: **Open** 9:30am–5:30pm daily (to 1:30pm Sun). 📷 excavations. ♿ church.

This mainly 14th-century Franciscan church (with an 18th-century façade) was built during the reign of Robert the Wise of Anjou. The storyteller Giovanni Boccaccio (1313–75) reputedly based the character Fiammetta on King Robert's

daughter Maria, whom he saw here on Easter Eve, 1334. For Naples, San Lorenzo Maggiore is a rare Gothic edifice. Its nave and the apse ambulatory have a magnificent period simplicity. The church houses medieval tombs including the Gothic tomb of Catherine of Austria, who died in 1323, by a pupil of Giovanni Pisano. Excavations in the monastic cloister, where the lyric poet and scholar Petrarch *(see p163)* once stayed, have found the remains of a Roman basilica. There are also important Greek and medieval excavations.

⬆ San Gregorio Armeno

Piazza San Gaetano 1. **Tel** 081 551 70 76. **Open** am daily. 📷 cloister.

Benedictine nuns still preside over this church. The convent attached to it earned a reputation for luxury since the nuns, traditionally from noble families, were accustomed to lavish living, which continued here.

The sumptuous Baroque interior of the church sports frescoes

The simple Gothic interior of San Lorenzo Maggiore, looking down the nave to the apse

by Luca Giordano. Via San Gregorio Armeno is lined with the workshops of vendors of Nativity figures *(presepi)*.

🏛 Museo Filangieri

Palazzo Cuomo, Via Duomo 288. **Tel** 081 20 31 75. **Open** 9:30am–2pm, 3:30–7pm Mon–Sat; 9:30am–1:30pm Sun and public hols. 📷

The 15th-century Renaissance Palazzo Cuomo houses the Museo Filangieri. Founded in 1881, the original museum collections put together by Prince Gaetano Filangieri were destroyed during World War II. The current collection contains interesting and varied objects, including porcelain, embroidery, manuscripts, Italian and Spanish arms, objects from local archaeological excavations, and paintings by such artists as Luca Giordano, Ribera, and Mattia Preti. There is also an important bust by Antonio Canova.

Renaissance tomb of Cardinal Brancaccio, Sant'Angelo a Nilo

⬆ Sant'Angelo a Nilo

Piazzetta Nilo. **Tel** 081 211 08 60. **Open** 8am–1pm, 4:30–7:30pm daily. ♿

This 14th-century church contains a fine work of Renaissance sculpture: the Tomb of Cardinal Rinaldo Brancaccio. Designed by Michelozzo, it was sculpted in Pisa, and then shipped to Naples upon completion in 1428. Donatello reputedly carved the right-hand angel drawing back the curtain, the shallow relief Assumption, and the cardinal's head.

⬆ San Domenico Maggiore

Piazza San Domenico Maggiore. **Tel** 081 45 91 88. **Open** 8:30am–1pm, 4–7pm Tue–Sun. ♿ Treasury: **Open** same as church. 📷

This Gothic church (1289–1324) contains some of the finest Renaissance monuments and sculpture in Naples. The tomb slab of John of Durazzo (died 1335), by Tino da Camaino, is in the south transept. In the sacristy are the *Apotheosis of Faith* ceiling frescoes by Solimena (18th century). The choir features a paschal candlestick (1585) supported by figures by da Camaino. The Cappellone del Crocifisso contains a medieval painting of the *Crucifixion*, which supposedly spoke to St. Thomas Aquinas. The grand Brancaccio tomb by Jacopo della Pila (1492) is in the Chiesa Antica.

Detail of the embossed façade of Gesù Nuovo

⬆ Santa Chiara

Via Benedetto Croce. Church: **Tel** 081 552 62 80. **Open** 7:30am–1pm, 4:30–8pm daily. ♿ 📷 Cloister: **Tel** 081 797 12 35. **Open** 9:30am–5:30pm Mon–Fri, 10am–2:30pm Sat, Sun, & public hols.

This 14th-century church was bombed in World War II, but a reconstruction uncovered the original Provençal-Gothic structure. The tombs of the Angevin monarchs are housed here. The tomb of Robert the Wise (died 1343) is by Giovanni and Pacio Bertini; that of Robert's son, Charles of Calabria (died 1328), is by Tino da Camaino; and the tomb of Charles's wife, Mary of Valois (died 1331), is by da Camaino and his followers. Adjacent is a convent with a cloister designed by Vaccaro (1742). There is also a museum and a Roman bath house (AD 1).

⬆ Gesù Nuovo

Piazza del Gesù Nuovo 2. **Tel** 081 557 81 11. **Open** daily.

The 16th-century Jesuit church was constructed by Valeriano (and later Fanzago and Fuga) from the Severini palace (15th century), of which only a façade survives. The ebullient decoration of the interior (1600s) is fully in accordance with the needs of the Jesuits, who used drama and direct appeal to the emotions to draw the faithful. It is resplendent with colored marble and paintings, including works by Ribera and Solimena. In 1688 an earthquake destroyed the dome – the present one is 18th-century.

⬆ Sant'Anna e San Bartolomeo dei Lombardi

Via Monteoliveto. **Tel** 081 551 33 33. **Open** 9am–noon Tue–Sat.

Mazzoni's *Pietà* (1492) in Sant'Anna e San Bartolomeo dei Lombardi

Also known as Santa Maria di Monteoliveto, this church was built in 1411 and restored after World War II. It is a repository of Renaissance art. Entering, past the tomb (1627) of Domenico Fontana (who completed the dome of St. Peter's in Rome after Michelangelo's death), the richness of the interior unfolds.

The Cappella Mastrogiudice contains an *Annunciation* panel by Florentine sculptor Benedetto da Maiano (1489) and the Cappella Piccolomini contains Antonio Rossellino's monument (c.1475) to Maria d'Aragona (completed by da Maiano). The Cappella del Santo Sepolcro houses a *Pietà* by Guido Mazzoni (1492). Its eight terracotta figures are considered life-size portraits of the artist's contemporaries. The old Sacristy, frescoed by Vasari (1544), has inlaid stalls by Giovanni da Verona (1510).

Majolica tiles decorated with scenes of rural life in the cloisters of Santa Chiara

Naples: Museo Archeologico Nazionale

This building, housing one of the world's most important archaeological museums, started life in the late 1500s as the home of the royal cavalry and was rebuilt in the early 17th century as the seat of Naples university. In 1777, when Ferdinand IV transferred the university to the former monastery of Gesù Vecchio, the building was again adapted to house the Real Museo Borbonico and library. In 1860 it became public property. The 1980 earthquake caused much damage to the collections. Major restoration and reorganization of exhibits continue but most areas of the museum are open on Sundays.

Spring Fresco
The fresco removed from the Villa Stabia in the Varano plain is a masterpiece of grace and elegance; the female figure rendered with soft, delicate colors.

Villa of the Papyri

Bust of "Seneca"
Found in the Villa dei Papiri in Herculaneum, this 1st-century BC bronze head was long thought to represent the philosopher Seneca the Elder (c.55 BC–AD 39). Today, however, its identity is less certain.

★ The Battle of Alexander
The splendid mosaic from the House of the Faun in Pompeii *(see p498)* depicts Alexander the Great's victory over Persian emperor Darius III (333 BC).

Key to Floor Plan

- Epigraphs
- Egyptian collection
- Engraved gems
- Sculptures
- Mosaics
- Numismatics
- Didactics
- Herculaneum & Pompeii
- Hall of the Sundial
- Prehistoric, Greek, and Etruscan collections
- Nonexhibition space

The Secret Cabinet
The erotic works from Pompeii and Herculaneum housed here caused embarrassment at the time of the Bourbons. Today, however, they are available for public viewing (book ahead).

Blue Vase
This wine vessel found in a Pompeii tomb was made with the so-called glass-cameo technique: a layer of opaque white paste was placed over colored glass and then engraved with decorative motifs.

Temple of Isis

Sacrifice of Iphigenia
In this Pompeiian fresco, Iphigenia, daughter of Agamemnon, is about to be sacrificed to Artemis, who saves her by taking a deer instead.

Entrance

Stairs down to Egyptian Collection

★ Farnese Bull
Excavated in the Baths of Caracalla in Rome (see p441), this is the largest sculptural group (c.150 BC) to have survived from antiquity. The best-known piece in the Farnese Collection, it shows the punishment of Dirce who, having ill-treated Antiope, was tied to an enraged bull by the latter's sons.

VISITORS' CHECKLIST

Practical Information
Piazza Museo Nazionale 19.
Tel 081 44 22 149.
Open 9am–7:30pm Wed–Mon.
🅿 ♿ 🎫 🌐 museo
archeologiconazionale.
campaniabeniculturali.it

Transportation
Ⓜ Piazza Cavour-Museo. 🚌 C64, C83, E1, R1, R4, 24, 47, 110, 135.

★ Farnese Hercules
Made by Glykon of Athens, this statue is an enlarged copy of a sculpture by the Greek master Lysippus. Napoleon is said to have regretted leaving it behind when he removed his booty from Italy in 1797.

Exploring Southeast Naples

The area south of Via A. Diaz is home to Naples' castles and royal palace as well as the densely populated Spanish Quarter. On the outskirts of the old town are a number of museums in historic buildings.

🏰 Castel Nuovo

Piazza Municipio. **Tel** 081 795 20 03.
Open 9am–6pm Mon–Sat. Last adm: 6pm. **Closed** some public hols. ♿
Museo Civico: **Tel** 081 795 58 77.
Open 9am–6pm Mon–Sat. ⚜

Also known as the Maschio Angioino, this Angevin fortress was built for Charles of Anjou in 1279–82. However, apart from the squat towers and the Cappella Palatina (with Francesco Laurana's *Madonna* of 1474 above the portal), most of the structure is Aragonese.

The castle was the main royal residence. In the Sala dei Baroni, Ferdinand I of Aragon brutally suppressed the ringleaders of the Baron's revolt of 1486.

The Aragonese were capable of violence, but they were also patrons of the arts. The triumphal arch of the castle's entrance (begun 1454) is theirs. Commemorating Alfonso of Aragon's entry to Naples in 1443, this ingenious application of the ancient triumphal arch design was worked on, in part, by Laurana. The original bronze doors by Guillaume le Moine (1468) are in the Palazzo Reale. Part of the castle houses the **Museo Civico**.

The colorful and compact
Quartieri Spagnoli

🏘 Quartieri Spagnoli

Via Toledo (Roma) to Via Chiaia.
The Spanish Quarter – the neighborhood west of Via Toledo, sloping up to San Martino and Vomero – is one of the city's most densely populated areas. It was named after the Spanish troops who laid out its grid of narrow streets in the 17th century. This is where the archetypal Neapolitan scene comes to life, in which laundry hung above the streets crowds out the sun. This area is lively by day, sinister by night.

🏛 Museo Nazionale di San Martino

Largo di San Martino 5. **Tel** 081 229 45 02. Museo **Open** 8:30am–7pm Thu– Tue. ⚜ ♿ Castel Sant'Elmo: **Open** 8:30am–6:30pm Wed–Mon.

High above Santa Lucia, the Baroque Certosa di San Martino, founded in the 1300s as a Carthusian monastery, has great views of the Bay of Naples. It houses a museum featuring a variety of *presepi*, Nativity figurines of Neapolitan tradition. The cloister was completed in 1623–9 by Cosimo Fanzago (the creator of Neapolitan Baroque) to the 16th-century designs of Dosio. The church and choir are other examples of his virtuosity.

Next to the Certosa, **Castel Sant'Elmo**, built from 1329–43 and rebuilt in the 1500s, offers stunning views over the bay.

🏛 Museo Diego di Aragona Pignatelli Cortes

Riviera di Chiaia 200. **Tel** 081 66 96 75. **Open** 9am–2pm Wed–Mon. **Closed** Jan 1, May 1, Aug 15. ⚜

The Neo-Classical Villa Pignatelli, once home to the Rothschilds, houses this museum and its interesting collection of porcelain, period furniture, paintings, and sculpture.

The bold Castel Nuovo, with the triumphal arch entrance

🚇 Galleria Umberto I

Via Toledo. **Open** daily. Teatro San Carlo: **Tel** 081 797 23 31. **Open** Aug, rehearsals and performances. 🎟 9am–5:30pm daily (081 66 45 45 to book). 🎭 ♿ 🆆 **teatrosancarlo.it**

Once a focus for fashionable Neapolitans, the handsome arcades of the Galleria Umberto I were built in 1887 and rebuilt after World War II. They face Italy's largest and oldest opera house: the **Teatro San Carlo**. Built for Charles of Bourbon in 1737, and later rebuilt, its fine auditorium once aroused envy in the courts of Europe.

Magnificent glass-roofed interior of the Galleria Umberto I

🚇 Palazzo Reale

Piazza Plebiscito. Museo **Tel** 081 40 05 47. **Open** 9am–8pm Thu–Tue (last adm: 1 hr before closing). **Closed** Jan 1, May 1, Dec 25. 🎟 🎭 Biblioteca: **Tel** 081 781 92 31. **Open** 8:30am–7:30pm Mon–Fri (to 1:30pm Sat). Bring ID.

Begun by Domenico Fontana for the Spanish Viceroys in 1600, and expanded by subsequent residents, Naples' royal palace is a handsome edifice with great halls filled with furniture, tapestries, paintings, and porcelain. The small, private Teatro di Corte (1768) was built by Ferdinando Fuga. The building houses the

Danaë and the Shower of Gold by Titian in the Museo di Capodimonte

riches of the Biblioteca Nazionale (library). The exterior of the palace has been partly restored and the huge Piazza del Plebiscito facing it has been cleaned up. The great colonnades sweep toward 19th-century **San Francesco di Paola**, modeled on Rome's Pantheon.

🚇 Villa Floridiana

Via Aniello Falcone 171. **Tel** 081 578 84 18. **Open** 8:30am–4pm Wed–Mon. 🎟 ♿ Park: **Open** daily. **Closed** Jan 1, May 1, Aug 15, Dec 25. 🎭 Museum: **Open** 8:30am–2pm Wed–Mon.

Set in handsome gardens, this Neo-Classical villa houses the **Museo Nazionale della Ceramica Duca di Martina**, famous for its ceramics collection, including porcelain and majolica.

🏛 Museo di Capodimonte

Parco di Capodimonte. **Tel** 081 749 91 11. **Open** 8:30am–7:30pm Thu–Tue. 🎭 🆆 **museo-capodimonte.it**

Begun in 1738 by the Bourbon king Charles III as a hunting lodge, the **Palazzo Reale di Capodimonte** houses this museum and its magnificent collections of Italian paintings. Included are works by Titian,

Botticelli, Raphael, and Perugino, much of it originating in the Farnese family collections. There is also a gallery of 19th-century art, largely from southern Italy.

🏛 Catacombs of San Gennaro

Via di Capodimonte 13. **Tel** 081 744 37 14. **Open** 10am–5pm daily (to 1pm Sun). 🎟 call to arrange a visit. 🎭

These catacombs – the original burial ground of San Gennaro – are located near the church of San Gennaro in Moenia. The small church was founded in the 8th century, and is adjoined by a 17th-century workhouse. Two tiers of catacombs dating from the 2nd century penetrate the tufa, and there are mosaics and early Christian frescoes. Farther along the street, the Catacombs of San Gaudioso commemorate the 5th-century saint who founded a monastery on the spot. Above is the 17th-century church of Santa Maria della Sanità.

🏰 Castel dell'Ovo

Borgo Marinari. **Tel** 081 795 45 93. **Open** 9am–5:30pm daily (to 2pm Sun & hols). 🎭 for exhibitions.

This castle, begun in 1154, occupies a small island facing, and joining, the Santa Lucia district – once the site of the city's shellfish market. A royal residence under the Normans and Hohenstaufen, today it belongs to the army. Interesting exhibitions are held here.

Beneath its ramparts, tiny Porta Santa Lucia is filled with seafood restaurants, and the Via Partenope running past it is a lovely promenade.

The façade of the Palazzo Reale, Naples' royal palace

❷ Pompeii

An earthquake in AD 62, which shook Pompeii and damaged many buildings, was merely a prelude to the tragic day in AD 79 when Mount Vesuvius erupted, burying the town in 20 ft (6 m) of pumice and ash. Although it was discovered in the 16th century, serious excavation began only in 1748, revealing a city petrified in time. In some buildings paintings and sculpture have survived, and graffiti is still visible on street walls.

★ **House of the Vetti**
The villa of the wealthy merchants Aul
Vettius Conviva and Aulus Vetti
Restitutus contains frescoes (see pp48–S
It is currently closed for renovatio

Villa of the Mysteries

Forum Baths

★ **House of the Faun**
This famous villa of the wealthy patrician Casii is named after its bronze statuette. Make advance reservations to visit this and the other private houses on site.

| 0 meters | 100 |
| 0 yards | 100 |

In the bakery
of Modestus, carbonized loaves of bread were found.

Forum

Sacrarium of the Lares
Close to the Temple of Vespasian, this building housed the statues of Pompeii's guardian deities, the Lares Publici.

Macellum
Pompeii's market-place was fronted by a portico with two money-changers' kiosks.

Plan of Pompeii

VIA DI NOLA
VIA DELL'ABBONDANZA
WESTERN POMPEII

Porta Marina
entrance

Piazza Esedra
entrance

Piazza
Anfiteatro entrance

Area illustrated below

VISITORS' CHECKLIST

Practical Information
Piazza Esedra 5. **Tel** *081 857 53 47*.
Open 8:30am–7:30pm (last adm:
6pm) (Nov–Mar: to 5pm, last adm:
3:30). **Closed** Jan 1, Dec 25.
pompeiisites.org
arethusa.net for reservations

Transportation
FS Naples–Salerno: station
Pompei Scavi; Circumvesuviana
Naples–Sorrento: station Pompei
Villa dei Misteri.

Western Pompeii

*This detailed illustration is of the
western area, where the most
impressive and intact Roman
ruins are located. There are
several large patrician villas in
the eastern section, as wealthy
residents built their homes
outside the town center.
However, much of eastern
Pompeii awaits excavation.*

Amphitheater and
sports ground

Teatro
Grande

Via dell'Abbondanza
This was one of the original and
most important roads through
ancient Pompeii. Many inns
lined the route.

Vesuvius and the Campanian Towns

Nearly 2,000 years after the
eruption of Mount Vesuvius, the
Roman towns in its shadow are
still being released from the
petrification that engulfed
them. Both Pompeii and Stabiae
(Castellammare di
Stabia), to the
southeast of Naples
and the volcano,
were smothered by
hot ash and pumice
stone blown there by
the wind. The roofs of
the buildings
collapsed under the
weight of the volcanic
debris. To the west,
Herculaneum (Ercolano)
vanished under a sea of
mud. A large number
of its buildings have
survived, their roofs
intact, and many
domestic items
were preserved by
the mud. In all,
about 2,000
Pompeiians
perished but few, if
any, of the residents of
Herculaneum died.

In AD 79 Pliny the Elder,
the Roman soldier, writer,
and naturalist, was the
commander of a fleet
stationed off Misenum
(present-day Miseno,
west of Naples), and with
his nephew Pliny the
Younger observed the
impending eruption from
afar. Eager to see this
natural catastrophe closer
at hand, Pliny the Elder
proceeded to Stabiae,
but was overcome by
fumes and died. Based
on reports by survivors,

Pompeiian vase in Museo
Nazionale Archeologico

Pliny the Younger related the
first hours of the eruption
and his uncle's death in detail
in two letters to the Roman
historian Tacitus.

Much of our knowledge of
the daily lives of
the ancient
Romans derives
from the
excavations of
Pompeii and
Herculaneum. Most
of the artifacts from
them as well
as Stabiae are now
in Naples' Museo
Archeologico
Nazionale (*see pp494–5*),
creating an outstanding
collection.

Mount Vesuvius has not
erupted since 1944, but
occasional rumbles have
caused minor earthquakes.
Visitors can reach it by train to
Castellammare di Stabia, or by
car. A useful website is
www.guidevesuvio.it.

Casts of a dying mother and child seen at Pompeii

❸ Santa Maria Capua Vetere

Caserta. ⚐ 34,000. **FS** 🚌 **ℹ** Palazzo Reale, Caserta (0823 32 22 33). 🔄 Thu & Sun.

This town boasts a 1st-century AD Roman **amphitheater**, once Italy's largest after the Colosseum, with well-preserved tunnels beneath it. The town occupies the site of ancient Capua, an Etruscan city and then a flourishing center during the Roman Empire. It was the scene of the revolt of the gladiators, led by Spartacus in 73 BC. The on-site **Gladiator Museum** re-creates the history of the gladiators. Nearby is a **Mithraeum** (2nd–3rd century) with well-preserved frescoes. Finds from the sites are shown in the **Museo Archeologico dell'Antica Capua** in Capua.

⌂ Amphitheater

P.za 1 Ottobre. **Tel** 0823 84 42 06. **Open** 9am–1 hr before sunset Tue–Sun. 🏛 valid for Mithraeum:. **Open** Tue–Sun.

⊞ Museo Archeologico dell'Antica Capua

Via Roberto d'Angio 48, Capua. **Tel** 0823 84 42 06. **Open** 9am–7pm Tue–Sun. 🏛

Tunnels under the amphitheater in Santa Maria Capua Vetere

❹ Caserta

⚐ 79,000. **FS** 🚌 **ℹ** Palazzo Reale (0823 32 22 33). 🔄 Wed & Sat. **W** casertaturismo.it

Magnificently opulent, the vast **Palazzo Reale** dominates Caserta. Built for the Bourbon King Charles III, Italy's largest royal palace boasts over 1,000 rooms, grand staircases, and richly adorned

A fountain in the gardens of the Palazzo Reale at Caserta

apartments. It was designed by Luigi Vanvitelli and construction started in 1752. The surrounding park boasts fountains, ornamental waterworks, statuary, and an English Garden. Sound and light shows, in English and Italian, take place in summer.

Environs

The medieval town of **Caserta Vecchia** lies 6 miles (10 km) to the northeast. Its 12th-century cathedral is a fine example of southern Norman architecture. **San Leucio**, 2 miles (3 km) northwest of Caserta, is a model town built by Ferdinand IV, who also founded its silk industry.

⊞ Palazzo Reale

Piazza Carlo III. **Tel** 0823 44 80 84. **Open** 8:30am–7:30pm Wed–Mon. **Closed** public hols. 🏛 ♿ Park: **Open** 8:30am–1 hr before sunset daily.

❺ Benevento

⚐ 62,000. **FS** 🚌 **ℹ** Via Sala 31 (0824 31 99 11/38). 🔄 Mon & Wed–Sat. **W** comune.benevento.it

Benevento, set in a lonely, mountainous province, is home to one of southern Italy's most interesting ancient Roman monuments: the **Arch of Trajan** on Via Traiano. The Roman city, Beneventum, was an important center. It stood at the end of the first extension of the Via Appia from Capua, and the Arch was erected across the old road in honor of Trajan. Built from AD 114–166 of marble, it is extremely well preserved. The relief sculpture adorning it – scenes from the life of Trajan and mythological subjects – is in excellent condition.

Elsewhere, evidence of the Romans is to be found in the ruined **Roman theater**, built during Hadrian's reign, and in the **Museo del Sannio**, which contains artifacts from the region, from ancient Greek finds to modern art.

During World War II, the city stood directly in the way of the Allied advance from the south. It was heavily bombed, hence its largely modern appearance today. The Duomo, a 13th-century building reconstructed after the war, has a sculpted façade that, though badly damaged, has since been restored. The remains of its Byzantine bronze doors are

The ornate 2nd-century Roman arch in Benevento, built to honor Trajan within. The town has centuries-old associations with pagan worship, and a liqueur called *Strega* (witch) is made here.

🏛 Roman Theater
Piazza Caio Ponzio Telesino. **Tel** 0824 47 213. **Open** 9am–1 hr before sunset daily. **Closed** public hols. 🚫 ♿

🏛 Museo del Sannio
Piazza Santa Sofia. **Tel** 0824 218 18. **Open** 9am–7pm Tue–Sun. **Closed** Jan 1, Dec 25. 🚫 ♿

❻ The Amalfi Coast

Salerno. 🚌 ⛴ Amalfi. 🛈 Corso delle Repubbliche Marinare 27, Amalfi (089 87 11 07). 🆆 **amalfitourist office.it**; 🆆 **ravellotime.it**; 🆆 **aziendaturismopositano.it**

The most enchanting route in Campania is that skirting the southern flank of Sorrento's peninsula: the Amalfi Coast (Costiera Amalfitana). Popular pleasures here include dining on grilled fish and sipping Lacrima Christi from the vineyards on the slopes of Vesuvius, beach-hopping, and trips to coastal summits to admire the breathtaking views.

From **Sorrento**, a well-developed holiday resort, the road winds down to **Positano**, a village clambering down a

The small town of Atrani on the Amalfi Coast

vertiginous slope to the sea. A top spot for the jet set, it is nonetheless a good place to swim, or to catch the hydrofoil or ferry to Capri. Further on, **Praiano** is just as fashionable.

Amalfi is the coast's largest town and a popular resort. It was a maritime power before being subdued in 1131 by King Roger of Naples. The world's oldest maritime code, the *Tavole Amalfitane*, originated here. The 13th-century Chiostro del Paradiso flanks the Duomo, a magnificent 9th-century structure fronted by a rich 13th-century façade, and facing the town from the top of a long flight of steps. The style is Lombard-Norman, though

the cloisters have a Saracenic-inspired appearance.

Ravello has the best views on this coast, the prime vantage points being the gardens of Villa Cimbrone and Villa Rufolo. Views from the latter provided inspiration for Wagner's *Parsifal*. The 11th-century Duomo has entrance doors by Barisano da Trani (1179) and an ornate 13th-century ambo (pulpit) held aloft by six spiral columns. The chapel of San Pantaleone contains the blood of its 4th-century namesake, which liquefies annually in May and August.

Beyond **Atrani**, the ruins of a Roman villa at **Minori** show that this coastline has always been a popular holiday spot.

A breathtaking view of the steep village of Positano on the Amalfi Coast

❼ Salerno

Salerno. 🚆 🚌 ⛴ Salerno. 🛈 Piazza Vittorio Veneto 1 (089 23 14 32); Lungomare Trieste (089 22 47 44).

Salerno is a big, busy port. Here the Allies landed in 1943, leaving in their wake a much-bombed city. Once famous for its School of Medicine (12th century), it is visited today for its **Duomo**, an 11th-century structure built on an earlier foundation. Its best feature is the Atrium, whose columns came from nearby Paestum. In the crypt is the Tomb of St. Matthew, brought here in 954.

The **Museo Diocesano** is home to most of the cathedral treasures, including an 11th-century ivory altar-front called the Paliotto. Before wandering off down the bustling Corso Vittorio Emanuele, visit the **Museo Provinciale** for local archaeological finds.

Environs

The **Cilento** is a mountainous region south of Salerno with a remote interior and a lovely, quiet coastline that is only slightly more populous. Among the towns along the coast, **Agropoli** is a busy little seaside resort 25 miles (42 km) south of Salerno. Outside Castellammare di Velia, a further 17 miles (28 km) to the southeast, are the ruins of the Greek town of **Elea** (founded 6th century BC). It was much visited by the Romans – Cicero was here, and Horace came on his doctor's orders to undergo a treatment of sea bathing. Excavations have revealed a magnificent

The Temple of Hera I (left) and the Temple of Neptune at Paestum

4th-century Roman gateway: the Porta Rosa, Roman baths, the foundations of a temple, and the remains of the acropolis.

🏛 **Museo Diocesano**
Largo Plebiscito. **Tel** 089 23 91 26. **Open** 8:30am–7pm Wed–Mon (Sun also 3–7pm).

🏛 **Museo Provinciale**
Via San Benedetto. **Tel** 089 23 11 35. **Closed** closed for renovation; call ahead to check.

❾ Capri

Napoli. ⛴ Capri. 🛈 Piazza Umberto I, Capri (081 837 06 86). Grotta Azzurra ⛴ from Marina Grande; 🚌 from Anacapri. **Open** in calm sea. Certosa: Via Certosa, Capri. **Tel** 081 837 62 18. **Open** 9am–2pm Tue–Sun. 🚶 Villa Jovis: Via Tiberio. **Open** daily. 🚶
🌐 **capritourism.com**

Capri's reputation as a sybaritic paradise is nearly eclipsed by its notoriety as a tourist trap. However, the views are unmarred by the throng.

❽ Paestum

Zona Archeologica. 🛈 Via Magna Grecia 887. **Tel** 0828 81 10 16. 🚌 from Salerno. 🚆 Paestum. **Open** 9am–1hr before sunset daily. Museum: **Tel** 0828 72 26 54. **Open** 8:30am–7:45pm daily (to 2pm Sun & hols). **Closed** 1st & 3rd Mon of month, Jan 1, Dec 25. 🚶 ♿

This is the most important ancient Greek site south of Naples in Campania. The Greeks founded this city on the edge of the Piana

The home of emperors, seat of monasteries, place of exile, its fortunes changed during the 19th century when English and German expatriates discovered its charms. Today it barely has a "low season"; farmers run little hotels, and fishermen rent pleasure boats. Capri enjoys its well-deserved reputation as a Garden of Eden.

The Grotta Azzurra, or the Blue Grotto, is a cave bathed in iridescent blue light, which can be reached by tour boat from Marina Grande.

Anacapri is Capri's second town.

0 kilometers		1
0 miles	0.5	

The busy port of Salerno

For hotels and restaurants in this region see pp562–77 and pp580–605

del Sele in the 6th century BC and called it Poseidonia, the City of Poseidon. The Romans renamed it in 273 BC. It fell into decline and was abandoned in the 9th century due to malaria and a Saracen assault and was rediscovered in the 18th century.

Paestum has three massive Doric temples in an excellent state of repair: the **Basilica** or **Temple of Hera I** (mid-6th century BC); the **Temple of Neptune** (5th century BC), the largest and most complete at Paestum; and the **Temple of Ceres**, thought to date between its two neighbors.

Excavations have revealed the remains of the ancient city, its public and religious buildings, roads and protective walls. A **museum** contains the extensive finds from the site, including tomb paintings, tomb treasures, some terracotta votive offerings, architectural fragments, and sculpture.

A view from the highest point of Procida, called Terra Murata

⑩ Ischia and Procida

Napoli. 🚢 Ischia & Procida. 🛈 Via Sogliuzzo 72, Ischia (081 507 42 11); Via V. Emanuele 168 (081 810 19 68). La Mortella: **Tel** 081 98 62 20. **Open** Apr–Oct: 9am–7pm Tue, Thu, Sat–Sun. 🅿 🌐 **infoischiaprocida.it**

Ischia is the biggest island in the Bay of Naples and, with its beach resorts, thermal springs,

and therapeutic mud baths, it is nearly as popular as Capri. Ferries dock at **Ischia Porto**, the harbor and modern part of the main town, **Ischia. Ischia Ponte**, the older part, is a short walk away. The northern and western shores are developed; the southern flank of the island is the quietest. Here, the village of **Sant' Angelo** is dominated by a long-extinct volcano, **Monte Epomeo**, whose summit of 2,585 ft (788 m) offers terrific views across the bay. Also worth a visit are the gardens of **La Mortella** in Forio.

The tiny, picturesque island of Procida is less visited and very tranquil. The swimming is good at **Chiaiolella**, and as at Ischia, there are inexpensive places to stay. The main town, also called **Procida**, is home to the main ferry port – the **Marina Grande**.

There are views toward Vesuvius and the Bay of Naples from the north of the island.

Capri is the main town on the island.

Marina Grande
This is Capri's main port of call for ferries from Naples and other ports on the Tyrrhenian coast. An array of colorful houses overlooks the harbor.

I Faraglioni

Marina Piccola is reached by dramatic Via Krupp.

Villa Jovis
Covering an enormous area, this was the Imperial villa from which Tiberius ruled the Roman Empire during his final years.

Certosa di San Giacomo
Founded in 1371 on the site of one of Tiberius's villas, this Carthusian monastery was suppressed in 1808 and is now in part a school. The distant rocks are I Faraglioni.

ABRUZZO, MOLISE, AND PUGLIA

Puglia is the "heel" of the Italian boot, the Gargano Peninsula is its "spur," and Abruzzo and Molise together form the "ankle." Hugging the southeastern seaboard of Italy and looking toward the Balkans, the mountainous regions of Abruzzo and Molise, united until 1963, differ considerably from Puglia, the richest of the three.

Abruzzo and Molise are sparsely populated, quiet places where the wild landscape exerts a strong influence. Settled by various Apennine tribes in the Middle Bronze Age, the areas were later subdued by the Romans, united under the Normans in the 12th century, and thereafter ruled by a succession of dynasties based in Naples. Abruzzo, dominated by the Apennines, is a brooding, introspective land of shepherds. Vertiginous drops preface the ascent to ramshackle hill towns clinging to the sides of high mountains, semi-abandoned and poor. Molise's landscape is less dramatic. Legends of witches persist in both regions, as do strange fertility rites and rituals celebrating the changing seasons.

Puglia's advantage over its poverty-stricken neighbors is that it is nearly all flat and highly fertile. It produces the largest amount of olive oil in Italy, and its big cities – Lecce, Bari, and Taranto – are lively commercial centers. The region experienced a long-lasting Greek influence, though the golden age of Puglia's past was under the rule of the Normans, followed by Frederick II, who, between his return from Germany as emperor in 1220 and his death 30 years later, spent only four years away from here.

Puglia has glorious architecture, particularly in the churches and castles of the north. The curious *trulli* houses in central Puglia, the florid Baroque of Lecce, and the Levantine atmosphere of its merchant cities complete the picture of an ancient land subject to more influences from outside the Italian peninsula than from within it.

Traditional dress worn in the town of Scanno in Abruzzo

◀ A row of *trulli* houses in the town of Alberobello, Puglia

Exploring Abruzzo, Molise, and Puglia

Dominated by the Apennine mountain range, the hinterland of Abruzzo and Molise forms one of Italy's last wildernesses. At 9,554 ft (2,912 m), the highest peak is the Gran Sasso. Parts of Abruzzo are covered in tracts of forest, while Molise features high plains, gentle valleys, and lonely peaks. The coastline of the Gargano Peninsula in Puglia (Apulia) is packed with cliffs, caves, and islets. Reaching south is the fertile Tavoliere plain, and further south a series of upland plateaus (the Murge) descends toward the dry Salentine Peninsula and the Adriatic.

The exotic *trulli* houses in Alberobello in central Puglia

San Benedetto del Tronto
Bellante
Giulianova
Teramo
Crognaleto
Pineto
Montereale
Corno Grande 2912m
ATRI **2**
Penne
Montesilvano Marina
Pescara
Pizzoli
Loreto Aprutino
Francavilla al Mare
L'AQUILA **1**
Ortona
Capestrano
Chieti
Monte Velino 2487m
Popoli
Celano
LANCIANO **6**
Punta della Penna
Carsoli
Coculla
Casoli
Vasto
Isola Nicol
Roma
Avezzano
SULMONA **3**
San Salvo
Capistrello
Termoli
Campomarino
SCANNO **4**
Palata
PARCO NAZIONALE **5**
D'ABRUZZO Opi
Capracotta
Trivento
Rotello
Apricena
Carovilli
San Severo
Isernia
MOLISE
Colletorto
Cassino
Campobasso
LUCERA **9**
Venafro
Bojano
Alberona
Fogg
Sepino
TROIA **10**
Bovino
Candela
Napoli

Getting Around

Northern Abruzzo is well served by the A24 and A25–E80, and the S17 traverses the interior of Abruzzo and Molise. The coastal highway (A14–E55) heads south through Abruzzo and Molise into Puglia. Beyond Foggia, it joins the S16 to Taranto. Brindisi, the main port for Greece, is accessible from Bari or Taranto. The roads throughout are good. Train and bus services go to the major centers, with buses only to more remote parts.

Key

— Highway
— Major road
— Secondary road
-- Road under construction
=== Minor road
— Scenic route
— Main railroad
— Minor railroad
— Regional border
△ Summit

The coast at Vieste on the beautiful Gargano Peninsula in Puglia

For additional map symbols *see back flap*

Sights at a Glance

1 L'Aquila
2 Atri
3 Sulmona
4 Scanno
5 *Parco Nazionale d'Abruzzo, Lazio e Molise pp510–11*
6 Lanciano
7 Isole Tremiti
8 Gargano Peninsula
9 Lucera
10 Troia
11 Trani
12 Castel del Monte
13 Ruvo di Puglia
14 Bari
15 Alberobello
16 Taranto
17 *Lecce pp516–17*
18 Galatina
19 Otranto

The high peaks of the Gran Sasso, north of L'Aquila in Abruzzo

Lecce's exuberant Baroque architecture, epitomized in Santa Croce's rose window

The pink and white stone façade of Santa Maria di Collemaggio in L'Aquila

❶ L'Aquila

🏛 73,000. FS 🚌 *i* Via XX
Settembre 10 (0862 223 06). 🛒 daily.
W abruzzoturismo.it

Abruzzo's capital lies at the foot of the **Gran Sasso**, at 9,554 ft (2,912 m) the highest point of the Italian mainland south of the Alps (and good for skiing). Its ancient streets are peppered with churches. In April 2009 an earthquake, measuring 6.3 in magnitude, struck central Italy with the epicenter close to L'Aquila. Many of the historical churches and buildings described below have been seriously damaged by the quake. Restoration work is being carried out on many buildings, so do check with the tourist office before visiting.

The domed **Santa Giusta** (1257), off Via Santa Giusta, has a rose window and a *Martyrdom of St. Stephen* (1615) by Cavalier d'Arpino. **Santa Maria di Paganica**, off Via Paganica, has a 14th-century façade and a carved portal. The **Duomo** (1257) in Piazza del Duomo was rebuilt in the 18th century. The massive church of **Santa Maria di Collemaggio**, on Piazza di Collemaggio, has a façade of pink and white stone. It was built in the 13th century by Pietro dal Morrone, who later became Pope Celestine V.

Detail of Fontanelle delle Novantanove Cannelle in L'Aquila

San Bernardino, on Via di San Bernardino, houses the tomb (1505) of San Bernardino of Siena. The church (built 1454–1472), has a façade (1527) by Cola dell'Amatrice and an 18th-century carved ceiling by Ferdinando Mosca. The bell tower collapsed in the 2009 earthquake. The second chapel in the south aisle has an altarpiece by Andrea della Robbia, the Renaissance artist.

The medieval **Fontanelle delle Novantanove Cannelle** at the end of Via San Iacopo is a fountain commemorating the 99 villages that Frederick II supposedly united when he founded L'Aquila in 1240.

The **Museo Nazionale d'Abruzzo**, in the 16th-century castle, contains the remains of a prehistoric elephant, Roman artifacts, and religious works.

🏛 **Museo Nazionale d'Abruzzo**
Castello Cinquecentesco. **Tel** 0862 63 32 29. **Closed** for restoration – call for details. 📷 ♿

❷ Atri

Teramo. 🏛 12,000. 🚌
i 0861 24 42 22. 🛒 Mon.
W comune.atri.te.it

The prettiest in a series of small hill towns in Abruzzo, Atri is a warren of stepped streets, alleys, and passages bound by mostly brick and stone churches and houses.

The 13th-century **Duomo** occupies the site of a Roman bath; the crypt was once a swimming pool; and fragments of the original mosaic floor are visible in the apse. Also in the apse is Andrea Delitio's beautiful 15th-century fresco cycle, in which he combined landscape and architecture in a variety of religious scenes from the Old and New Testaments. The cloister has views of the 15th-century brick campanile.

Environs
South of Atri is the hill town of **Penne**, with its homogeneous buildings of reddish brick, which give it a wonderful, warm glow. East of Atri, **Loreto Aprutino** is known for the *Last Judgment* fresco (14th century) in Santa Maria in Piano.

Detail from 15th-century fresco by Andrea Delitio in Atri's Duomo

❸ Sulmona

L'Aquila. 🏛 26,000. FS 🚌 *i* Corso Ovidio 208 (0864 532 76). 🛒 Wed & Sat. 🎭 Sep: International Exhibition of Contemporary Art. W sulmona.org

This town is famous as the home of both Ovid and *confetti* (sugared almonds). After a wedding, guests are given *confetti* as a good luck token. Sulmona is filled with ancient buildings, especially along medieval **Via dell'Ospedale**. The **Palazzo dell'Annunziata** was founded in 1320 and combines Gothic and Renaissance styles.

The **Museo Civico** holds a collection of local antiquities, costumes, paintings, and the work of goldsmiths formerly housed in the palace. The adjacent church of the **Annunziata**, with a Baroque façade, was rebuilt in the 18th century. Behind the church are 1 BC–AD 2 ruins of a Roman house.

At the end of Viale Matteotti is the cathedral of **San Panfilo**, built over a Roman temple. **San Francesco della Scarpa**, in Piazza del Carmine, has a 13th-century portal. Winding past it to the **Fontana del Vecchio** (1474) is an aqueduct that once fueled local industry.

Environs

East of Sulmona is the Maiella National Park, a massif of 61 peaks and forested valleys offering walking, bird-watching, climbing, and skiing. To the west, Cocullo hosts the May Processione dei Serpari (Festival of Snakes) in which a statue of the patron saint, Domenico Abate, is draped with snakes and carried through the town. In the 11th century he is said to have rid the area of venomous snakes.

▥ Museo Civico
Palazzo dell'Annunziata, Corso Ovidio. **Tel** 0864 21 02 16. **Open** 9am–7pm Mon–Fri, 9am–1pm Sat & Sun.

Ovid, the Latin Poet

Born in 43 BC, Ovid (Publius Ovidius Naso) was Sulmona's most illustrious son. Not much survives here to remind you of his presence, however, apart from a **Corso Ovidio**, a 20th-century statue of him in Piazza XX Settembre, and, just outside the town, a ruin traditionally known as **Ovid's Villa**. Known as one of the greatest poets of Classical Rome, his subjects included love (*Ars Amatoria*) and mythology (*Metamorphoses*). In AD 8 he was banished into exile on the Black Sea, the far edge of the Roman Empire, after being implicated in a scandal of adultery with Julia, the granddaughter of Emperor Augustus (*see pp52–3*). Ovid continued to write of his hardships, and died in exile in AD 17.

---

❹ Scanno

L'Aquila. ▥ 2,400. ▦ ⓘ Piazza Santa Maria della Valle 12 (0864 743 17). ▧ Tue. ⓦ **scanno.org**

Wonderfully well-preserved, this medieval hill town set in beautiful, wild countryside is one of Abruzzo's most popular attractions. There are alleys and narrow flights of steps, oddly-shaped courtyards into which small churches have been pressed, and ancient mansions in whose windows women can be seen making lace or embroidering.

Traditional costume still worn in Scanno

In the shadow of Apennine peaks and beside lovely **Lago di Scanno**, the town is also a favored stop on the way to the Parco Nazionale d'Abruzzo (*see pp510–11*). The summer months are the busiest, with a variety of activities from riding, boating, and camping by the lake, to the August classical music festival. During the January Festa di Sant' Antonio Abate, a large lasagna is cooked outside **Santa Maria della Valle**, which is built on the remains of a pagan temple. The food is doled out on a first-come, first-served basis.

High Apennine peaks looming above the medieval hill town of Scanno in Abruzzo

❺ Parco Nazionale d'Abruzzo, Lazio, e Molise

This vast park, inaugurated in 1922, has a rich landscape of high peaks, rivers, lakes, and forests, and is one of Europe's most important nature reserves. Part of a royal hunting reserve until 1877, today it provides refuge for 66 species of mammal, 52 types of reptile, amphibian, and fish, and 230 species of bird, including the golden eagle and white-backed woodpecker, as well as over 2,000 varieties of flora. The park offers an extensive network of paths, and there are opportunities for riding, trekking, and climbing.

Golden eagles
may be seen near the Sangro river.

Young Chamois
Dense forests of beech and maple hide the Apennine chamois. There are also red and roe deer in the park.

Forests of beech
and black pine provide beautiful scenery.

Pescasseroli
This town is a major center for information on the area. It has good tourist facilities and a small zoological garden with animals living in the region, such as bears and wolves.

Marsican Brown Bear
Once hunted almost to extinction, between 80 and 100 brown bears now roam in the park.

Apennine Wolves
The park guarantees protection for the Apennine wolf, and about 60 wolves survive here. The chances of seeing one, however, are fairly remote.

Horse Riding
Trekking is an excellent way to explore more remote areas of the park.

❻ Lanciano

Chieti. [A] 35,000. [FS] [bus] [i] Piazza
Plebiscito 50 (0872 71 91 27). [calendar] Wed
& Sat. [w] **lanciano.it**

Large parts of Lanciano's old nucleus remain from the Middle Ages. In the crumbling Civitanova quarter is the 13th-century church of **Santa Maria Maggiore**, with a magnificent 14th-century portal and a silver processional cross (1422). Also in this area is the now disused **San Biagio** (begun c.1059), near the 11th-century **Porta San Biagio** – a rare surviving town gate. The **Duomo** stands on the remains of a Roman bridge dating from the time of Diocletian. An underground passage links the bridge to the **Sanctuary of the Eucharistic Miracle**, where a host and wine that turned into live Flesh and Blood in the 8th century are kept. The Ripa Sacca (Jewish ghetto) was a busy commercial center in the Middle Ages – the period of Lanciano's greatest prosperity. The hefty walls of the **Torri Montanara** were built then by the Aragonese as a bulwark against attack.

Lake Barrea
Created by the artificial damming of the River Sangro, this lake is surrounded by valleys and forests offering walking and pony trekking.

❼ Isole Tremiti

Foggia. [A] 400. [boat] San Nicola. [i] Via
Perrone 17, Foggia (0881 72 31 41);
Via Sant'Antonio Abate 21, Monte
Sant'Angelo (0884 56 89 11).
[w] **lecinqueisole.it**

Off the Gargano coast, the Tremiti are the Italian islands least visited by foreigners. **San Domino** is the largest, with a sandy beach and coves. Julia, granddaughter of Augustus, was exiled here for adultery from AD 8 until her death in AD 28. The poet Ovid was allegedly involved (see p509).

Santa Maria a Mare, in **San Nicola**, the administrative center of the islands, is an abbey fortress founded in the 8th century. It was turned into a prison in the late 1700s, a role it maintained until 1945.

Both the islands of San Domino and Santa Maria a Mare are popular with Italians. The swimming is good, though the coastline of San Nicola is rocky.

Dense Forests
Beech and maple forests, dotted with black hornbeam, ash, hawthorn, cherry, wild apple, and pear, protect the once persecuted bears and wolves.

The Camosciara is a spectacular area, home to many wild animals.

Key

Major road

Minor road

Walking path

Viewpoint

Tourist information

0 kilometers   5

0 miles   5

The coast near Peschici on the Gargano Peninsula

❽ Gargano Peninsula

Foggia. **FS** 🚌 ℹ Piazza del Popolo 10, Manfredonia (0884 58 19 98); Via Sant'Antonio Abate 21, Monte Sant'Angelo (0884 56 89 11).
W parcogargano.it

A rocky spur jutting into the Adriatic Sea, the Gargano is dotted with coves and cliffs. Its coastal towns of **Manfredonia**, **Rodi Garganico**, **Peschici**, and **Vieste** are popular with vacationers. To the east lies the **Foresta Umbra**, a vast woodland of beech, oak, yew, and pine, and to the north the salt lakes of

Typical street scene in the town of Vieste on the Gargano Peninsula

Lesina and **Varano**, havens for waterfowl. Plunging through the Gargano is an old pilgrim route (S272) from **San Severo** in the west to the shrine at **Monte Sant'Angelo** in the east. The first stop is **San Marco in Lamis**, dominated by a huge 16th-century convent. Further along, **San Giovanni Rotondo** is a focus for pilgrims visiting the tomb of Padre Pio (1887–1968), a beatified miracle worker. The last stop is **Monte Sant'Angelo** with its grotto where the Archangel Michael is said to have appeared to the Bishop of Sipontum in 493.

To the south of Manfredonia, beside the ruins of ancient Siponto, is the Oriental-inspired 12th-century church of **Santa Maria di Siponto**.

❾ Lucera

Foggia. 🏚 35,000. 🚌 ℹ Piazza Nocelli 6 (0881 52 27 62). 🛒 Wed.
W comune.lucera.fg.it

On the northeast edge of town, once a prosperous Roman colony, are the ruins of a Roman **amphitheater** (closed for renovation). Lucera was rebuilt in the 13th century by Frederick II, who peopled it with 20,000 Sicilian Muslims. It became one of the strongest fortresses in southern Italy, and its **castle** is one of Puglia's most magnificent. Built in 1233 by

Frederick II, and enlarged after 1269, its fortified wall of 2,953 ft (900 m) is interspersed with 24 towers. Of Frederick's original palace, only the base and some vaulting remains.

In 1300 Charles II, who killed most of Lucera's Muslim population, began the **Duomo** on the site of their main mosque. The high, soaring nave is filled with 15th- and 16th-century frescoes and carvings.

The **Museo Civico Fiorelli** has displays of episodes from throughout Lucera's history.

🏛 **Museo Civico Fiorelli**
Via de Nicastri 44. **Tel** 0881 54 70 41.
Open Tue–Sat.

The remains of Lucera castle

❿ Troia

Foggia. 🏚 33,000. 🚌 ℹ 0881 97 82 41. 🛒 1st & 3rd Sat of month.
W comune.troia.fg.it

Founded in 1017 as a Byzantine fortress against the Lombards, Troia fell to the Normans in 1066. Until Frederick II destroyed it in 1229, the town had been ruled by a succession of powerful bishops who were responsible for producing many remarkable buildings, including Troia's **Duomo** (see pp482–3).

Begun in 1093 and constructed over the following 30 years, it exhibits an extraordinary diversity of styles. It successfully blends elements of Lombard, Saracenic, and Byzantine style with that of the Pisan-Romanesque.

Elegant blind arcading distinguishes the Duomo's lower story. The upper sections are characterized by powerfully carved sculpture – projecting lions and bulls. The upper façade displays a rose window with Saracenic-style detailing.

The main entrance, with bronze doors by Oderisio da Beneventano (1119), is dominated by carved capitals and an architrave, both Byzantine in style. Within the Duomo is a Romanesque pulpit (1169).

⓫ Trani

Bari. 55,000. Piazza Sacra Regia Udienza II (0883 58 88 30). Tue. traniweb.it

During the Middle Ages this small, lively, whitewashed port of Jewish origin bustled with mercantile activity and was filled with merchants and traders from Genoa, Amalfi, and Pisa. It reached its peak of prosperity under Frederick II.

Today it is visited for its Norman **Duomo** in Piazza Duomo, built mainly from 1159

The façade of Trani's Duomo

to 1186 over an earlier church, whose predecessor, the Ipogei di San Leucio, dates from the 7th century. It is dedicated to St. Nicholas the Pilgrim, a little-remembered miracle worker (died 1094) who was canonized as an act of rivalry against the town of Bari, which possessed the bones of another, more memorable St. Nicholas. The

Duomo's most notable external features are its sculptures, particularly surrounding the rose window and the arched window below it, and the entrance portal with bronze doors (1175–9) by Barisano da Trani. The vigor of the interior has been revealed following restoration.

Next to the Duomo is the **castle** (1233–49) founded by Frederick II. Rebuilt in the 14th and 15th centuries, it is a well-preserved edifice with one wall dropping sheer into the sea.

The 15th-century Gothic-Renaissance **Palazzo Caccetta**, in Piazza Trieste, is a rare survival. Nearby, on Via Ognissanti, the 12th-century Romanesque church of the **Ognissanti**, the chapel of the Knights Templar erected in the courtyard of their hospital, is notable for its original portico. Other churches worth a visit are Santa Teresa and the monastery of La Colonna.

⓬ Castel del Monte

Località Andria, Bari. Beni Culturali (0883 56 99 97). **Open** Mar–Sep: 10:15am–7:45pm daily; Oct–Feb: 9am–6pm daily. **Closed** Jan 1, Dec 25. casteldel monte.beniculturali.it

Frederick II

Remote in the endless plains near Ruvo di Puglia, Castel del Monte, built in the mid-13th century, out-classes every other castle associated with Frederick II. It is also one of the most sophisticated secular buildings of the Middle Ages. The emperor had broad intellectual interests,

and he used his castles as hunting lodges where he could retire from court life with his falcons and books. Inside there are two floors, each with eight rib-vaulted rooms, some still lined with marble. This, and the marble moldings on the entrance and the upper floor, as well as sophisticated lavatory arrangements, mark the castle as a palace.

Thick and impenetrable walls

Octagonal satellite tower

Graceful, arched windows

Octagonal courtyard

The main entrance portal is in the style of a Roman triumphal arch.

Floorplan of the Castle

The building is a harmonious geometrical study with two stories of eight rooms each. The reasons for such precise planning of this giant octagon remain a mystery to this day.

The castle standing alone on the summit of a low hill

⑬ Ruvo di Puglia

Bari. 24,000. FS Piazza Matteotti 31 (080 950 71 11). Sat.
w ruvodipugliaweb.it

Once celebrated for its vases, Ruvo di Puglia's ceramics industry, producing "Apulian" ware, flourished until the 2nd century BC. The style was inspired by the striking red and black colors of Attic and Corinthian models. The **Museo Archeologico Nazionale Jatta** has a good overview.

The 13th-century **Cattedrale** is a bold example of the Apulian-Romanesque style with a portal that blends Byzantine, Saracenic, and Classical motifs.

🏛 Museo Archeologico Nazionale Jatta

Piazza Bovio 35. **Tel** 080 361 28 48.
Open 8:30am–1:30pm daily (to 7:30pm Thu–Sat). **Closed** Jan 1, May 1, Dec 25.
w palazzojatta.org

⑭ Bari

321,000. FS Piazza Aldo Moro 33a (080 524 23 61). daily.
w comune.bari.it

Roman Barium was simply a commercial center, but the city became the regional capital under the Saracens in 847, and was later the seat of the *catapan*, the Byzantine governor of southern Italy. Under the Normans, to whom it fell in 1071, Bari became a center of maritime significance. Today it is Puglia's lively capital and an important port with ferries to and from Croatia and Greece.

The **Basilica di San Nicola**, one of Puglia's first great Norman churches (begun 1087), has a plain exterior with a tall gabled section flanked by towers. The Apulian-Romanesque portal has carving on the doorjambs and arch in Arabic, Byzantine, and Classical styles. Beyond the choir screen is a fine 12th-century altar canopy and an episcopal throne (c.11th century). The relics of St. Nicholas – patron saint of the city (and also of Russia) – are buried in the crypt.

The late 12th-century Apulian-Romanesque **Cattedrale** is based on San Nicola, with a dome and one surviving tower (the other one collapsed in 1613). The Baroque portals on the façade incorporate 12th-century doorways. The interior has been restored to its medieval simplicity. The canopy over the high altar, the pulpit, and the episcopal throne are reconstructions from fragments of the originals. The sacristy, built as a baptistry, is known as the *Trulla*. The crypt houses the remains of San Sabino, Bari's original patron saint.

The city's **castle**, founded by Roger II, was adapted by Frederick II in 1233–9. In the vaulted hall is a collection of plaster casts of sculpture and architectural fragments from various Romanesque monuments in the region.

Portal detail of Ruvo di Puglia's Duomo

Sculpture at Bari castle

Bari castle, in the old district known as Città Vecchia, where most of the town's sights are clustered

For hotels and restaurants in this region see pp562–77 and pp580–605

⓯ Alberobello

Bari. 🚉 11,000. 🚇 to Alberobello & Ostuni. 🛈 Piazza Ferdinando IV (080 432 51 71). 🗣 in English, French, and German offered by Trulli e Natura (080 432 38 29). 🎉 Oct/Nov: Frantoi Aperti (visits to the major olive-pressing factories). 🌐 **alberobello.net**

The parched landscape of the **Murge dei Trulli** features olive groves, vineyards, and *trulli*. Strange circular buildings with conical roofs and domed within, *trulli* are built from local limestone stacked without using mortar. The walls and openings are generally whitewashed, while the stone roof tiles often have religious, pagan, or magical symbols painted on them. The origins of *trulli* are obscure, though the name is traditionally applied to ancient round tombs found in the Roman countryside. Most *trulli* are souvenir shops.

Alberobello is a UNESCO World Heritage site and the *trulli* capital. Here the strange white buildings crowd the narrow streets, and there are *trulli* restaurants, shops, and even a *trulli* cathedral.

Environs

The pretty white-washed hill town of **Locorotondo** is an important wine center. The elegant streets of **Martina Franca** are enlivened by Rococo balconies. The spectacular **Grotte di Castellana** are caves estimated to be 50 million years old.

Whitewashed and sun-baked *trulli* in Alberobello

⓰ Taranto

🚉 200,000. 🚇 🚌 🛈 Corso Umberto I (099 453 23 92). 🛒 Wed, Fri, & Sat. 🌐 **comune.taranto.it**

Little remains of the old city of Taras, founded by Spartans in 708 BC and at its most prosperous in the mid-4th century BC. The **Museo Archeologico Nazionale**, founded in 1887, has artifacts that shed light on the region's history. The museum has since

been expanded to allow for a growing collection of historically significant pieces. Taranto was heavily bombed in World War II and is garlanded by factories. The picturesque **Città Vecchia**, an island dividing the Mare Grande from the Mare Piccolo, was the site of the Roman citadel of Tarentum. A lively fish market offering the shellfish for which the city is famous, is housed in an Art Nouveau building. Here, too, is the **Duomo**. Founded in 1071, it has been the object of subsequent rebuilding. The most interesting features include the catacomb-like crypt, with its sarcophagi and fragmented frescoes, and the antique marble columns of the nave. Behind it is the 11th-century **San Domenico Maggiore**, which later gained a high double-approach Baroque staircase. The huge **castle** built by Frederick of Aragon (15th century) covers the eastern corner of the Città Vecchia. Now a military area, the castle is strictly off limits.

Aphrodite in museum in Taranto

🏛 **Museo Archeologico Nazionale**
Via Cavour 10. **Tel** 0994 53 21 12.
Open 8:30am–7:30pm daily.

The Tarantella

Italy's lively and graceful folk dance, the Tarantella, grew out of tarantism – the hysteria that appeared in 15th- to 17th-century Italy, and was prevalent in Galatina (*see p517*). Alleged victims of the tarantula spider's bite could supposedly cure themselves through frenzied dancing, which sweated out the poison. The dance is characterized by light, quick steps and a "teasing" flirt. The strange, private ritual takes place annually on June 29 at 6am at the celebrations for the Feast of Saints Peter and Paul in Galatina, the only place on the Salentine Peninsula where tarantism has survived.

⑰ Street by Street: Lecce

Lecce was the site of the Greek Messapi settlement. It became an important center of the Roman Empire, and in the Middle Ages developed a strong tradition of scholarship. Much of the architecture is in the highly decorative Lecce Baroque style, which flourished in the 1600s and earned the city the name of Florence of the South. This style was possible due to the *pietra di Lecce*, an easily carved stone. Giuseppe Zimbalo (Lo Zingarello) was its greatest master. Lecce is also famed for its papier-mâché workshops.

★ **Palazzo Vescovile and Duomo**
The bishop's palace (rebuilt in 1632), the adjoining Duomo by Lo Zingarello (after 1659), and a seminary (1709) enclose the Piazza Duomo.

Key

– – – Suggested route

0 meters — 100
0 yards — 100

Porta Rudiae
This 18th-century city gate leads to the suburbs and to the ruins of Roman Rudiae.

Chiesa del Rosario
Said to be the finest work by Lo Zingarello (begun 1691), the exterior is ornate and idiosyncratic in its detail.

Famous papier-mâché *(carta pesta)* workshops

The Seminary once supplied the Vatican with *castrato* singers – eunuchs noted for their high voices.

Chiesa del Carmine

Tourist information

VIA UMBERTO I
PIAZZA CASTROMEDIANO
VIA RUBICHI
PIAZZA SANT'ORONZO
VIA PALADINI
VIA VITTORIO EMANUELE
PIAZZA DUOMO
VICOLO SANTA VENERA
VIA MARCO BASSEO
VIA GIUSEPPE LIBERTINI
VIA MORELLI
VIA G CINO
VIA R CARACCIOL

★ **Santa Croce**
Built 1549–1679, this church was begun by Gabriele Riccardi; the rose window is by Lo Zingarello. Next door is the ex-convent of the Celestines.

The 16th-century Castello
lies between ancient city and modern suburbs. A 12th-century construction is enclosed by a wall built later by Charles V. Only one floor is open to the public.

Colonna di Sant'Oronzo
St. Oronzo was appointed Bishop of Lecce by St. Paul in AD 57, and later martyred by the Roman emperor Nero. This bronze statue dates from 1739.

Church of San Matteo

A Roman theater
was excavated virtually intact with its orchestra and seats.

Roman Amphitheater
Excavated in 1938, only part of this 1st-century BC amphitheater is visible.

Detail of a 15th-century fresco in Santa Caterina d'Alessandria

⓲ Galatina

Lecce. 28,000. FS ℹ️ Sala dell'Orologio (0836 56 99 84). Thu. Jun 29: Feast of Saints Peter & Paul. 🌐 comune.galatina.le.it

An important Greek colony in the Middle Ages, this *città d'arte* (city of art, a status given by the region) retains its Greek flavor. It is the center of one of Puglia's chief wine-producing regions, although it is more famous for the ritual of tarantism *(see p515)*.

The Gothic church of **Santa Caterina d'Alessandria** (begun 1384) on Piazza Orsini contains early 15th-century frescoes with scenes from the Old and New Testaments that glorify the Orsini, who were feudal lords.

⓳ Otranto

Lecce. 5,500. FS ℹ️ Piazza Castello (0836 84 14 36). Wed. 🌐 comune.otranto.le.it

Otranto was one of Republican Rome's leading ports for trade with Asia Minor and Greece, and under the Byzantines was an important toehold of the Eastern Empire in Italy. In 1070 it fell to the Normans. Turks attacked in 1480 and slaughtered its inhabitants. The 800 survivors were promised their lives if they renounced Christianity: all refused.

The Norman **Duomo** (founded 1080) on Via Duomo houses the bones of the martyrs. There is a 12th-century mosaic floor and a fine crypt. A **castle** (1485–98) built by the Aragonese at the center of town adds to Otranto's charm and there are some fine beaches close by.

BASILICATA AND CALABRIA

Remote and wild, Basilicata is one of the poorest regions in Italy. It is underdeveloped and undervisited, and rural areas remain unspoiled. Neighboring Calabria has been immortalized in the drawings of Edward Lear, who, traveling through on a donkey in 1847, was transfixed by the "horror and magnificence" of its savage landscape.

Today these regions are distinctly separate, but they share a common history and, along with Sicily and Puglia, were part of Magna Graecia. Ancient Metaponto in Basilicata was an important center, as were Crotone and Locri Epizephiri in Calabria. Their ruins evoke an illustrious past.

After the Greeks came the Romans, followed by Basilian monks. These were members of the Greek-Byzantine church who were fleeing their territories that had been invaded by Muslims. Their religious establishments make up a core of interesting monuments, such as the Cattolica at Stilo and Matera, where the monks took refuge in caves.

Many of the historic remains are Norman, but sporadic evidence of Swabian, Angevin, Aragonese, and Spanish occupation still exists.

Centuries of rule by Naples led to the marginalization of Basilicata and Calabria. Nowadays Calabria has an infamous reputation due to the *'ndrangheta*, the ferocious first cousin to the Mafia, whose activities are a constant menace. Banditry exists, but the sensible traveler should have little to fear.

Owing to emigration, Basilicata and Calabria are sparsely populated and have as much to offer in unspoiled countryside as in historic centers. The vast coastline boasts fine beaches, while the interior features the Aspromonte and Sila mountain ranges.

The remote landscape has kept change at bay. Isolated Pentedattilo, for example, preserves customs of Byzantine origin, while around San Giorgio Albanese there live close-knit communities of Albanians, descended from 15th-century refugees.

Sparsely populated, rugged countryside surrounding Stilo in southern Calabria

◄ Traditional white houses nestled among the hills of il Dirupo, Pisticci

Exploring Basilicata and Calabria

Mostly upland country, Basilicata (or Lucania, as it is also
known) is scattered with Greek ruins (like those at
Metaponto), medieval abbeys, and Norman castles (such
as Melfi's). Matera, its most interesting city, stands amid an
arid lunar landscape of denuded valleys. Calabria is often
described as the land between two seas. The lovely
beaches and virgin landscape between Tropea and
Maratea attract many visitors. The Ionian coast's chief
attractions are its Greek ruins, such as Locri Epizephiri,
and the hill towns, like Stilo and Gerace.

Repairing nets in the town of Pizzo,
northeast of Tropea

Key

▬▬ Highway
▬▬ Major road
— Secondary road
═══ Minor road
— Scenic route
— Main railroad
— Minor railroad
▬▬ Regional border
△ Summit

The picturesque hill town of Rivello, north of Maratea in Basilicata

Sights at a Glance

1. Melfi
2. Venosa
3. Lagopesole
4. Matera
5. Metaponto
6. Maratea
7. Rossano
8. Tropea
9. Stilo
10. Gerace
11. Reggio di Calabria

For additional map symbols *see back flap*

Foggia
Lavello
MELFI **1** **2** VEN
Rionero in Vulture
Fore
LAGOPESOLE **3**
Acere
Ruoti
Napoli
Potenza
Tito
Anzi
Marsico Nuovo
BA
Corleto Perti
Grumento Nova
Monte Raparo
1761m
Lagonegro
Monte
2005m
Rivello
Lauria
Latr
MARATEA **6**
Praia a Mare
Scalea
Monte Cara
Diamante
Cittadella del Capo
Cetraro
Serra Pantano
Pae
San Luc
Longobardi Mar
Amar
Campora S. Giov
Golfo
Sant'Eu
TROPEA **8**
Vale
Mil
Nicotera
Golfo
di Gioia
Rosarno
Gioia Tauro
Palmi
Poli
Bagnara Calabra
Messina
Aspromo
Monti Peloritani
REGGIO DI **11**
CALABRIA
Pellaro
Sta
Lazzaro
Stracia

The port of Maratea on the Tyrrhenian coast of Basilicata

Getting Around

Calabria's Tyrrhenian coast is well served by the A3–E45, a spur of which extends to Potenza in Basilicata. To reach the Ionian coast, it is best to skirt the Aspromonte via the S106–E90 from Reggio to Basilicata. Although the mountains can be crossed, namely on the S280–E848 to Catanzaro, the roads are narrow and pass through isolated countryside. Much of Basilicata is even less accessible, and Matera is more easily reached from Puglia. There are airports at Reggio di Calabria, Lamezia Terme (west of Catanzaro), Crotone, Bari, and Brindisi (Puglia). Trains connect the bigger centers and country buses serve the small towns.

The countryside near Miglionico, south of Matera

The impressive castle at Melfi, showing evidence of both Angevin and later construction

❶ Melfi

Potenza. 🏔 18,000. 🚇 🚌 ℹ️ Piazza Umberto I (0972 23 97 51). 🛒 Wed & Sat. 🌐 aptbasilicata.it

A brooding and now almost deserted medieval town, Melfi is crowned by the **castle** where Pope Nicholas II conducted Robert Guiscard's investiture in 1059, thus legitimizing the Normans in the south. Melfi later became the Norman capital. Here Frederick II proclaimed his *Constitutiones Augustales* (1231), which unified his kingdom as a state. In the castle is the **Museo Nazionale del Melfese**, with its collection of Byzantine jewelry. The **Duomo**, off Via Vittorio Emanuele, was begun in 1155 by William the Bad but rebuilt in the 18th century. Only the campanile survives.

🏛 **Museo Archeologico Nazionale del Melfese**
Castello di Melfi, Via Castello. **Tel** 0972 23 87 26. **Open** 9am–Sat (to 2pm Sun). **Closed** Mon am, Jan 1, Dec 25. 🅿 ♿ 📷 (Sat & Sun).

❷ Venosa

Potenza. 🏔 12,200. 🚇 🚌 ℹ️ Piazza Castello 47 (0972 316 09). 🛒 1st & 3rd Thu of month. 🌐 comune.venosa.pz.it

Venosa was one of the most important Roman colonies around 290 BC, and remains of **baths** and an **amphitheater**

survive in the archaeological zone along Via Vittorio Emanuele. It was also the birthplace of the Latin poet Horace (65–8 BC) and the site where the Roman general Marcellus died at the hands of Hannibal in 208 BC. Marcellus's reputed **tomb** is in Via Melfi. For more treasures, visit the **Museo Archeologico Nazionale**.

The **Duomo**, also on Via Vittorio Emanuele, and the huge **castle** in Piazza Umberto I date from the 16th century.

An abbey complex formed by an older, possibly early Christian (5th–6th century) church, **La Trinità** is backed by an unfinished 11th-century construction, in which Robert Guiscard (died 1085) was buried with his half-brothers and Alberada, his first wife. Only her tomb has survived.

🏛 **Museo Archeologico Nazionale**
Piazza Castello. **Tel** 0972 360 95. **Open** 9am–8pm Wed–Mon. 🖼

❸ Lagopesole

Potenza. **Tel** 0971 860 83. 🚇 to Lagopesole Scalo then bus to town. **Open** 9:30am–1pm, 4–7pm daily (3–5pm in winter). 🌐 aptbasilicata.it

Rising dramatically on a hill, Lagopesole's **castle** (1242–50) was the last castle built by Frederick II. The interesting carved heads above the portal of the keep are said to represent

Frederick Barbarossa (grandfather of Frederick II) and Barbarossa's wife, Beatrice. Inside, the royal apartments and chapel can be visited.

The Sassi district of Matera

❹ Matera

🏔 56,900. 🚇 🚌 ℹ️ Via de Viti de Marco 9 (0835 33 19 83). 📞 0835 31 94 58. 🛒 Sat. 🌐 materaturismo.it

Perched on the edge of a deep ravine, this town consists of the bustling upper district and the silent, lower **Sassi** (caves) district, divided into the Sasso Barisano and the more picturesque Sasso Caveoso. The people of Matera once lived here in dwellings scooped out of the rock. The two parts are odd neighbors, making Matera a truly fascinating city.

For the best overview, walk along the **Strada Panoramica dei Sassi** and look down into the caves. From the 8th to the

13th centuries, such caves probably provided refuge for monks from the Byzantine empire. Many chapels, gouged out of the rock, were taken over in the 15th century by peasants. Later, a cave-dwelling Matera evolved and by the 18th century some buildings fronting the caves had become fairly grand mansions and convents. By the 1950s and '60s the Sassi were overtaken by squalor and poverty, and the inhabitants forcibly rehoused. Carlo Levi (1912–75) drew attention to their living conditions in his book *Christ Stopped at Eboli*, comparing the Sassi to Dante's *Inferno*. The area was made a UNESCO World Heritage site in 1993.

Of the 120 *chiese rupestri* (rock-cut churches; **w parco murgia.it**) in the Sassi and the Agri district outside the town, **Santa Maria di Idris** in the Monte Errone area and **Santa Lucia alle Malve** in the Albanian quarter both contain 13th-century frescoes.

The **Museo della Tortura** (torture), in Via San Biagio, has exhibits dating back to the time of the Inquisition, while the **Museo Nazionale Ridola** provides a background to Matera and the Sassi. The artifacts from many Neolithic trench villages, necropolises, and other ancient sites are displayed here.

Church of San Francesco in Matera

The Apulian-Romanesque **Duomo** (13th century) in Piazza Duomo has a 12th-century painting of the *Madonna della Bruna*, the patroness of Matera. Via Duomo leads toward **San Francesco d'Assisi** (13th century with Baroque overlay). Other churches to visit are **San Domenico** and **San Giovanni Battista** on Via San Biagio (both 13th century), and the **Purgatorio** (1770) on Via Ridola.

Matera is where Mel Gibson's *The Passion of the Christ* (2004) was largely filmed.

🏛 **Museo Nazionale Ridola**
Via Ridola 24. **Tel** 0835 31 00 58. **Open** 9am–8pm daily (from 2pm Mon). **Closed** Jan 1, Dec 25. 🚫

The Tavole Palatine in Metaponto

❺ Metaponto

Metaponto Borgo. 🚌 FS to Metaponto. 🅸 Via Apollo Licio (0835 74 52 20). **Open** 9am–1 hr before sunset daily. **Closed** Mon am, Jan 1, Easter, Dec 25. 🚫 ♿ **w** aptbasilicata.it

Founded in the 7th century BC, ancient Metapontum was once the center of a wealthy city-state with a philosophical tradition expounded by Pythagoras, who settled here after his expulsion from Croton. Its ruins include the **Tavole Palatine** (6th century BC) at the Bradano River bridge, 15 columns that are part of a Doric temple, probably dedicated to Hera. The **Museo Nazionale di Metaponto** displays artifacts from the site. The ruins of a theater and the Doric **Temple of Apollo Lycius** (6th century

BC) are in the **Archaeological Zone**. Further south, modern **Policoro** occupies the site of ancient Heraclea (founded 7th–5th century BC). Its **Museo Nazionale della Siritide** has finds from this and other sites.

🏛 **Museo Nazionale di Metaponto**
Via Aristea 21. **Tel** 0835 74 53 27. **Open** 9am–8pm daily. **Closed** Mon am, pub hols. 🚫 includes Archaeological Zone.

🏛 **Museo Nazionale della Siritide**
Via Colombo 8, Policoro. **Tel** 0835 97 21 54. **Open** 9am–7pm daily. **Closed** Tue am, Jan 1, May 1, Dec 25. 🚫

❻ Maratea

Potenza. 🏔 5,200. FS 🚌 🅸 Piazza del Gesù 32 (0973 87 69 08). 🛒 1st & 3rd Sat of month.

A tiny stretch of Basilicata meets the Tyrrhenian Sea in the Gulf of Policastro. This unblemished coast is home to Maratea. Its small port (Maratea Inferiore) is beneath the old center (Maratea Superiore), which straddles the flank of a hill. From here the road climbs Monte Biagio to a summit with breathtaking views where a huge statue of the **Redeemer** stands.

Environs
Dramatically sited **Rivello**, 14 miles (23 km) to the north, once had a largely Greek population. Byzantine influences can be seen in the churches of **Santa Maria del Poggio** and **Santa Barbara**.

The small port of Marina di Maratea with fishing boats

A page from the precious *Codex Purpureus Rossanensis*

❼ Rossano

Cosenza. 🚇 39,000. 🚆 🚌 🛈 Piazza Matteotti (0983 52 09 08). 🍴 2nd & 4th Fri of month.

This pretty hill town was one of the main centers of Byzantine civilization in Calabria. It assumed power when Reggio di Calabria fell to the Saracens (9th–11th centuries). The **Museo Diocesano** houses the *Codex Purpureus Rossanensis*, a rare 6th-century Greek Gospel with silver lettering and splendidly detailed miniatures.

The Baroque **cathedral** contains the *Madonna Acheropita* fresco, a much-venerated Byzantine relic of the 8th or 9th century.

Environs

On a hilltop to the southeast is the five-domed Greek church of **San Marco** (10th century). The 12th-century **Panaghia**, another Greek church, lies off Via Archivescovado. Both contain fragments of early frescoes.

Santa Maria del Patirion, on a hilltop 11 miles (18 km) to the west, is magnificently adorned with colored brickwork, tile, and stone. It offers great views over the Piana di Sibari (Plain of Sibari), the alleged location of the fabled city of Sybaris, destroyed in 510 BC.

🏛 **Museo Diocesano**
Palazzo Arcivescovile, Via Arcivescovado 5. **Tel** 0983 52 52 63. **Open** 9:30am–noon, 3–5pm Tue–Sun; 10am–noon, 4–6pm public hols. 🖼

❽ Tropea

Vibo Valentia. 🚇 6,700. 🚆 🚌 🛈 Piazza Ercole (0963 614 75). 🍴 Sat. 🌐 tropea.biz

One of the most picturesque towns on Calabria's largely built-up Tyrrhenian coast, Tropea offers superb views of the sea and beaches. The old town hangs on to a cliffside facing a large rock, formerly an island. The rock is topped by **Santa Maria dell'Isola**, a former medieval Benedictine sanctuary. The **cathedral** at the end of Via Roma is of Norman origin, although it has been rebuilt several times. Inside is a 14th-century painting, the *Madonna di Romania*, by an unknown artist.

Casa Trampo (14th century) and **Palazzo Cesareo** (early 20th century) in Vicolo Manco are the most interesting of the small palaces in Tropea. The latter has a splendid balcony adorned with carvings.

Below the town are pretty beaches and a good choice of places to eat. Other seaside towns to visit are **Scilla** to the south and **Pizzo** to the north.

❾ Stilo

Reggio di Calabria. 🚇 3,000. 🚌 🛈 Town hall (0964 77 60 06). 🍴 Tue.

A short distance from the coast, Stilo is an earthquake-damaged town clamped to the side of Monte Consolino. Standing on a ledge looking out over the olive trees is the **Cattolica**, which has made Stilo a focus of pilgrimage for lovers of Byzantine architecture. Built in the 10th-century by Basilian monks, the brick building with its terracotta-tiled roof is based on a Greek cross-in-a-square plan. Four antique, mismatched marble columns divide the interior into nine quadrants. The capitals are placed at the base of the columns, instead of on top, to indicate the triumph of Christianity over paganism. The frescoes within, discovered and restored in 1927, date from the 11th century.

The Cattolica dominates the town, but on Via Tommaso Campanella there is a medieval **Duomo** as well as the 17th-century ruins of the **Convent of San Domenico**, where the philosopher and Dominican friar Tommaso Campanella (1568–1639) lived. The church of **San Francesco**, built around 1400, has an ornate carved wooden altar and a lovely 16th-century painting of the *Madonna del Borgo* (unknown origin). Bivongi, northwest of Stilo, has two churches dedicated to St. John: the Byzantine-Norman **San Giovanni Theresti**, and the Norman **San Giovanni Vecchio**.

🏛 **Cattolica**
1 mile (2 km) above Stilo on Via Cattolica. **Tel** 0965 81 22 56. **Open** Mon–Sat. 🖼 ♿

The beautiful and unspoiled coastline at Tropea

The distinctive five-domed Cattolica in Stilo

⑩ Gerace

Reggio di Calabria. 🏠 3,000. 🚌
ℹ️ Pro Loco, Via Regina Margherita
77, Locri (0964 23 27 60). 🔲 comune.
gerace.rc.it

Occupying a crag on the north-eastern flank of the Aspromonte, Gerace was founded by refugees from **Locri Epizephiri** who fled in the 9th century to escape Saracen attack. Its defensive character is reinforced by the medieval town walls and the remains of the castle.

Apart from the slow pace of life here – where you are as likely to meet a flock of sheep in an alley as a Fiat 500 – the main attraction is Calabria's grandest **Duomo**. This large structure indicates the significance of Gerace at least up to the time of the Normans. Constructed around the early 12th century, rebuilt in the 13th century, and restored in the 18th century, the crypt is its chief treasure. Both crypt and church are simple, adorned by a series of antique colored marble and granite columns probably stolen from the site of ancient

Locri Epizephiri. At the end of Via Cavour is 12th-century **San Giovanello**, part Byzantine and part Norman. Nearby is the Gothic church of **San Francesco d'Assisi** which contains a Baroque marble altar (1615) and the Pisan-style tomb of Niccolò Ruffo (died 1372), a member of a prominent Calabrian family.

Environs

The vast site of **Locri Epizephiri**, the first Greek city to have a written code of law (660 BC), was a famous center of the cult of Persephone. There are remains of **temples**, a **theater**, and Greek and Roman **tombs**. The **Museo Nazionale** displays a ground plan of the site, as well as Greek and Roman votive statues, coins, and sculptural fragments.

🏛️ **Locri Epizephiri**
Southwest of Locri on the SS 106, Contrada Marasà. **Open** 9am–7pm Tue–Sun. 🔲 locriantica.it

🏛️ **Museo Nazionale**
Contrada Marasà, SS 106.
Tel 0964 39 00 23. **Open** Tue–Sun.

⑪ Reggio di Calabria

🏠 183,000. ✈️ 🚆 🚌 ⛴
ℹ️ Station (0965 271 20). 🛍️ Fri.
🔲 turismo.reggiocal.it

One reason to visit Reggio di Calabria, which was heavily rebuilt after a major earthquake in 1908, is the **Museo Nazionale della Magna Grecia**. It houses a fine collection of artifacts from ancient Rhegion – a Greek city on the site of the present town – and from other Greek sites.

Chief among its treasures are the Greek bronzes, larger-than-life statues of warriors dredged from the sea off Riace Marina in 1972. Statue A (460 BC) is thought to be by Phidias, the Athenian sculptor and chief exponent of the idealizing, Classical style. If true, it is a rare survivor because his works were hitherto known to us only from Roman copies. Statue B (430 BC) has been attributed to Polyclitus. It is possible that the statues originated from an Athenian shrine at Delphi built to celebrate the victory of Marathon.

🏛️ **Museo Nazionale della Magna Grecia**
Piazza de Nava 26. **Tel** 0965 81 22 55.
Closed for renovations; call 800 98 51 64 to visit Riace bronzes at the Palazzo della Regione. 📷 🎫 ♿
🔲 museonazionalerc.it

Riace Bronzes (6th and 5th century BC) in Reggio's Museo Nazionale

Exploring Sicily

The vast coastline of Sicily (Sicilia) provides hundreds of long, sandy beaches, particularly at Taormina and the Golfo di Castellammare by San Vito Lo Capo – part of a large nature reserve. Sicily's varied interior is characterized by remote hill towns and plains punctuated by mountain ranges known for spring flowers and wildlife. Among the most famous sights is Mount Etna, an active volcano whose lava flows over the centuries have fertilized the land, which supports an abundance of walnut trees, citrus groves, and vineyards.

Fishermen at work in their boats at Siracusa

Sights at a Glance

1 Palermo pp530–33
2 Monreale pp534–5
3 Bagheria
4 Trapani
5 Erice
6 Marsala
7 Segesta
8 Selinunte
9 Cefalù
10 Agrigento
11 Piazza Armerina
12 Enna
13 Tindari
14 Messina
15 Taormina
16 Mount Etna
17 Catania
18 Pantalica
19 Siracusa
20 Noto

Getting Around

The A19–E932 links Palermo and Catania, the A18–E45 Catania and Messina, and the A20–E90 Palermo and Messina. The west is accessible from Palermo on the A29–E90. Ferry routes run from Messina to Reggio di Calabria, and from Palermo to Genoa or Naples. Between the larger towns, train services are efficient, but for smaller towns the buses are better. Catania, Palermo, and Trapani have international airports.

For keys to symbols see back flap

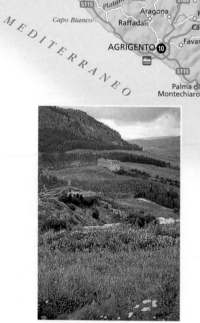

The magnificent temple at Segesta

The Norman Duomo in Palermo

Key

▬ Highway

▬ ▬ Road under construction

▬ Major road

▬ Minor road

═══ Other road

▬ Scenic route

▬ Main railroad

▬ Minor railroad

△ Summit

0 kilometers 50

0 miles 25

❶ Palermo

Nestling on the protective flank of Monte Pellegrino, with Monte Alfano to the east, Palermo lies in a natural amphitheater called the Conca d'Oro (Golden Shell). The city is an eclectic mix of Oriental and old European influences, and it features architectural styles that range from Arabic to Norman, Baroque, and Art Nouveau. This cultural infusion is unmatched in Italy, making this exotic city an exciting place to explore.

🏛 Gesù

Piazza Casa Professa 21. **Tel** 091 607 62 23. **Open** 7–11:30am, 5–6:30pm daily (to 12:30pm Sun; Aug: 7–10am only). **Closed** for Mass.

This Baroque church (1564–1633) is also known as the church of the Casa Professa. The interior is an example of the skill of Sicilian craftsmen in the treatment of marble carving and inlay. The oldest Jesuit church in Sicily, it was restored after World War II.

Ruined cloister with the red domes of San Giovanni degli Eremiti behind

🏛 San Giovanni degli Eremiti

Via dei Benedettini. **Tel** 091 651 50 18. **Open** 9am–7pm Tue–Sun. 🎫

Reflecting Islamic architectural tradition with bulbous domes, corner arches, and filigreed windows, this deconsecrated Norman church (1132–48) was built in the grounds of a mosque. Beyond church and mosque, a ruined cloister from a 13th-century monastery encloses a pretty garden.

🏛 Palazzo dei Normanni

Piazza Indipendenza. **Tel** 091 626 28 33. **Open** 8:30am–5pm daily (to 12:30pm Sun & hols). Last adm: 45 mins before closing. 🎫 Cappella Palatina **Open** 8:30am–noon, 2:30–5pm Mon–Sat; 8:30am–2pm Sun. **Closed** for Mass; Easter, Apr 25, May 1, Dec 26. 🎫 🏛 Sun.

This site has been the focus of power since the days of Byzantine rule and is now home to Sicily's regional government. The nucleus of the present building was constructed by the Arabs, but after the Norman conquest of the city in 1072, it was enlarged for the Norman court. See the luxurious royal apartments, especially the Sala di Ruggero, and the splendid Cappella Palatina. Built by Roger II (1132–40), this dazzling chapel blends Byzantine, Islamic, and Norman styles. It is lavishly adorned with fine mosaics and marble inlaid with gold. Next to the palace is the eccentrically decorated Porta Nuova (1535).

Sumptuous interior of the Cappella Palatina, Palazzo dei Normanni

Duomo's exterior displaying a mixture of styles

Sights at a Glance

① San Giovanni degli Eremiti
② Palazzo dei Normanni
③ Gesù
④ Duomo
⑤ Santa Caterina
⑥ La Martorana
⑦ Vucciria
⑧ Oratorio del Rosario di San Domenico
⑨ San Domenico
⑩ Museo Archeologico Regionale
⑪ Oratorio di Santa Zita
⑫ Oratorio di San Lorenzo
⑬ Palazzo Abatellis and Galleria Regionale di Sicilia
⑭ La Magione
⑮ Villa Giulia

🏛 Santa Caterina
Piazza Bellini. **Tel** 091 616 24 88. **Open** 9:30am–1pm daily (summer: also 5–7pm Mon–Sat).

Although begun in 1580, most of the internal decoration of this unique church dates from the 17th and 18th centuries. A powerful example of the Palermitan Baroque, it boasts sculpture, marble inlay, and illusionistic ceiling frescoes (18th century) – by Filippo Randazzo in the nave and by Vito d'Anna in the dome.

The church is flanked by Piazza Pretorio, which is dominated by the huge Mannerist Fontana Pretoria (1544).

🏛 Duomo
Corso Vittorio Emanuele. **Tel** 091 33 43 73. **Open** 7am–7pm Mon–Sat, 9am–5:30pm Sun & hols. **Closed** during Mass. Treasury **Open** 9:30am–1:30pm, 2:30–5:30pm daily. cattedrale.palermo.it

Founded in 1184, the Duomo displays many architectural styles. The exterior shows the development of the Gothic style from the 13th–14th centuries. The south porch (1453) is a masterpiece of the Catalan style, and at the apse end, sturdy Norman work can be seen through an Islamic-inspired overlay. The dome is 18th century. Within the much-altered interior are the tombs of Sicily's kings. Squeezed into an enclosure by the south porch are the remains of Emperor Frederick II; his wife, Constance of Aragon; his mother, Constance, daughter of Roger II (also entombed here); and his father, Henry VI. The Treasury houses the 12th-century Imperial Diadem of Constance of Aragon, which was removed from her tomb in the 18th century.

Fontana Pretoria with Santa Caterina in the background

For keys to symbols *see back flap*

Exploring Palermo

East of the Quattro Canti, where Via Maqueda and Corso Vittorio Emanuele meet, the city is sprinkled with ornate palaces and more churches. Squeezed behind them are labyrinthine medieval quarters where ancient buildings with crumbling fabric still survive.

⬆ La Martorana

Piazza Bellini. **Tel** 091 616 16 92.
Open 8am–1pm, 3:30–5:30pm
Mon–Sat; 8:30am–1pm Sun & hols
(to 7pm in summer).

Also called Santa Maria dell' Ammiraglio, this church was built around 1140 by George of Antioch, Roger II's admiral. The design derives from Norman and Islamic traditions with mosaics possibly by Greek artisans. In the right aisle, King Roger receives the Imperial Diadem from Christ; in the left aisle, George of Antioch is portrayed.

A nearby convent, founded by Eloisa Martorana in 1193, was the site where the Sicilian Parliament met in 1295 and decided to hand the crown of Sicily to Frederick of Aragon. The church was presented to the convent in 1433.

Mosaic of Christ with Four Angels in the dome of La Martorana

🛒 Vucciria

Via Roma. **Open** daily.
Nowhere is Palermo's Arabic past more apparent than in this medieval casbah-style market that burrows through the ruinous Loggia district below Via Roma. Merchants, hawkers, shoppers, and pickpockets crowd an area once the haunt of artisans. The alleys all around are named after their professions, such as silversmiths, dyers, and keymakers. This busy market, the largest in Palermo, offers the usual market ware from daily objects to junk, as well as a wide selection of fresh fruit, vege-tables, fish, and meat.

Stuccoed interior of the Oratorio del Rosario di San Domenico

⬆ Oratorio del Rosario di San Domenico

Via dei Bambinai 2. **Open** 9am–1pm daily. 🎨 ♿
The interior of this tiny 16th-century chapel displays elegant Baroque decoration by the master of stucco, Giacomo Serpotta. Created around 1720–30, this was possibly his finest work. Serpotta's technical virtuosity, not to mention the sensory indulgence and whimsical fantasy in evidence here, is remarkable. The altar-piece is the famous *Madonna of the Rosary* (1624–8) by

Anthony Van Dyck, and there are wall paintings by Luca Giordano and Pietro Novelli.

⬆ San Domenico

Piazza San Domenico. **Tel** 091 32 95 88. **Open** 9–11:30am Tue–Sat (also 5–7pm Sat & Sun). Cloister **Open** call to check. Museo del Risorgimento **Tel** 091 58 27 74. **Open** 9am–1pm Mon, Wed, & Fri. **Closed** Aug.
🌐 storiapatria.it

Although the present building was begun in 1640, there has been a Dominican church on the site since the 14th century. Tommaso Maria Napoli, one of the masters of Sicilian Baroque, created the exuberant church façade (1726) and square in front (1724).

Within, the most interesting feature is Antonello Gagini's bas-relief of *Santa Caterina* (1528) in the third chapel on the left. Next to the church is a 14th-century cloister that gives access to the Museo del Risorgimento.

🏛 Museo Archeologico Regionale

Piazza Olivella 24. **Tel** 091 68 06 07. **Closed** for repairs. End date not known; call ahead before visiting. 🎨
Housed in a former monastery of the Filippini, Sicily's most important museum contains sculpture, architectural fragments and ceramics, bronzes, glassware, jewelry, weapons, and terracottas. The collection is taken from the island's Phoenician, Greek, and Roman sites of antiquity – Tindari, Termini, Imerese, Agrigento, Siracusa, Selinunte, and Mozia. The highlights are sculptures from the friezes of the ancient Greek temples at Selinunte.

Palermo's noisy, bustling Vucciria market east of Via Roma

For hotels and restaurants in this region see pp562–77 and pp580–605

⚐ Oratorio del Rosario di Santa Cita

Via Valverde 3. **Tel** 091 843 16 05 or 091 609 03 08 (for reservations).
Open 9am–1:30pm Mon–Sat.

This small chapel is dedicated to the Virgin of the Rosary after her miraculous intervention at the Battle of Lepanto *(see pp62–3)*. The stucco relief decoration is the work of Giacomo Serpotta (after 1688): the panel on the rear wall depicts the battle, and other reliefs show scenes from the New Testament. The neighboring 16th-century church of Santa Zita, from which the oratory takes its name, is filled with sculptures (1517–27) by Antonello Gagini.

Ornate interior of the Oratorio di Santa Cita

⚐ Oratorio di San Lorenzo

Via Immacolatella 5. **Tel** 091 611 81 68.
Open 10am–6pm daily.

Lining the walls of this tiny oratory are incredible stucco scenes from the lives of St. Francis and St. Lawrence, and allegorical figures and putti by Giacomo Serpotta (1699–1706). These remarkable works exhibit the virtuosity of their creator in the handling of his medium. Caravaggio's *Nativity with St. Francis and St. Lawrence* (1609) was stolen from above the altar in 1969. The oratory lies hidden next to the 13th-century church of San Francesco d'Assisi, which brims with great sculpture. The highlight of the church is the triumphal arch (1468) by Pietro da Bonitate and Francesco Laurana in the Cappella Mastrantonio.

The Palazzina Cinese (c.1799) set in the Parco della Favorita

▥ Palazzo Abatellis and Galleria Regionale di Sicilia

Via Alloro 4. **Tel** 091 623 00 11.
Open 9am–6pm Tue–Fri, 9am–1pm Sat & Sun.

Matteo Carnelivari built this palace combining Spanish late-Gothic and Italian Renaissance styles in the 15th century. It is home to the Galleria Regionale di Sicilia, which houses Antonello da Messina's *Vergine Annunziata* (1476) and Francesco Laurana's marble head of Eleanor of Aragon (15th century). Nearby, the 15th-century church of Santa Maria degli Angeli (or La Gancia) contains works by Antonello Gagini and Giacomo Serpotta.

Vergine Annunziata (1476) by da Messina in the Galleria Regionale

⚐ La Magione

Via Magione 44. **Tel** 091 617 05 96 or 339 377 41 37 (mobile). **Open** 8:45–11:45am, 3–6pm Mon–Sat; 8:45am–12:30pm Sun.
Ⓦ basilicalamagione.diocesipia.it

Restorations have revealed the ancient structure of this church founded in 1191 by Roger II's chancellor, Matteo d'Aiello. A highlight of Norman architecture, it has a simple nave flanked by fine Gothic columns.

◖ Villa Giulia

Via Abramo Lincoln. **Open** 9am–5pm daily. Orto Botanico **Tel** 091 740 40 28. **Open** Nov–Mar: 8am–5pm daily (to 2pm Sun); longer opening hours in summer. **Closed** public hols.

The villa's formal gardens were established in the 1700s. Once, with their statues and fountains, they evoked the antique world. Nowadays, their tropical flora and faded grandeur make them delightful for walks. There are splendid tropical plants in the adjacent Orto Botanico (botanical gardens), and plant specimens can be examined in Léon Dufourny's Neo-Classical Gymnasium (1789). Palermo's only central park, Villa Giulia has good children's facilities.

◖ Parco della Favorita

Entrance on Piazza Leoni & Piazza Generale Cascino. **Open** daily. Museo Etnografico Siciliano Pitré, Via Duca degli Abruzzi 1. **Tel** 091 740 48 90. **Open** 8:30am–7:30pm Sat–Thu. **Closed** public hols.

This park, laid out as a hunting ground in 1799 by the Bourbon Ferdinand IV, was surrounded by the nobles' summer villas. One of these, the Palazzina Cinese (c.1799), was built in a Chinese style for Ferdinand III and Maria Carolina, the sister of Marie Antoinette. The Museo Etnografico Siciliano Pitré, in the stables of the Palazzina Cinese, has a fine collection of Sicilian objects.

❷ Monreale

Magnificently adorned, and with a splendid view of the Conca d'Oro, the Duomo at Monreale is one of the great sights of Norman Sicily. Founded in 1172 by the Norman King William II, it flanks a monastery of the Benedictine Order. The interior of the cathedral glitters with mosaics carried out by Sicilian and Byzantine artists – the inspiration of a king who wanted to rival the power of the Archbishop of Palermo. Like Cefalù, and later Palermo, it was to serve as a royal sepulchre.

★ Christ Pantocrator
The cathedral's Latin-cross plan focuses on the imposing mosaic of the all-powerful Christ (12th–13th century).

Apse Exterior
With their rich multicolored ornamentation in tufa and marble, the three apses represent the apogee of Norman decoration.

KEY

① **Barisano da Trani's bronze door** (1179) on the north side is shielded by a portico designed by Gian Domenico and Fazio Gagini (1547–69).

② **Original Cosmati floor in choir**

③ **Nave and aisles separated by Roman columns**

④ **The royal tomb** of William II, in white marble, flanks the porphyry tomb of William I in the corner of the transept.

⑤ **Magnificent gilded wood ceiling**

⑥ **The south wall and cloisters** survive as elements from the Benedictine monastery.

⑦ **Small Oriental-inspired fountain**

⑧ **The 18th-century porch** is surrounded by two squat towers.

Entrance to Cappella del Crocifisso and Treasury

★ Mosaic Cycle
Completed in 1182, the rich mosaics show scenes from the Old Testament (nave), Teachings of Christ (aisles, choir, and transepts), and the Gospels (side apses). The story of Noah's Ark is depicted here.

★ **Cloisters**
A masterpiece of Norman artistic expression from the time of William II, the columns – plain, carved, or inlaid with richly lustered tiles – support elaborate capitals from which spring Saracenic-style arches.

VISITORS' CHECKLIST

Practical Information
Piazza Duomo.
[W] duomomonreale.it
Church Tel 091 640 44 13.
Open May–Sep: 9am–6:30pm daily; Oct–Apr: 8am–12:30pm, 3:30–6pm daily. 🔒 🚻
Cloister: **Tel** 091 640 44 03.
Open 9am–1pm Mon–Sat. 🚻
Treasury: **Open** same as the church. 🚻

Transportation
🚌 389, 809, 8/9, and many others going west.

Column Detail
Craftsmen from Campania, Puglia, Lombardy, and Sicily worked on the cloister columns. The detail here shows Adam and Eve.

Bronze Door Panel
Bonanno da Pisa's fine bronze door (1185), signed by him, depicts 42 scenes from the Bible set within elaborate borders. The lion and griffin are symbols of the Norman kingdom.

❸ Bagheria

Palermo. 🚹 50,000. **FS** 🚌 **ℹ** Corso
Umberto I (091 90 90 20). 🛍 Wed.
w comune.bagheria.pa.it

Today Bagheria is almost a
suburb of Palermo, though open
countryside with olive and
orange groves once separated
them. In the 17th century
Giuseppe Branciforte, Prince of
Butera, built a summer retreat
here, starting a fashion that
was quickly followed by other
Palermitan aristocrats. The town's
core is sprinkled with their
Baroque and Neo-Classical villas.

The **Villa Palagonia** was
designed in 1705 by the architect
Tommaso Maria Napoli for
Ferdinando Gravina, the
Prince of Palagonia. It has
remarkable architectural
qualities: a complex
outdoor staircase leads
to the first floor, and the
principal rooms, all with
unusual shapes, are
arranged around a
curved axis. A later
prince adorned the
perimeter wall with the
grotesque stone monsters
that amused the 18th-century
traveler Patrick Brydone, and

Stone figure on
Villa Palagonia

horrified Goethe, who also
traveled here and called this
the "Palagonian madhouse."
Across the piazza are **Villa
Valguarnera** (begun in 1713
by Napoli), set in its own park,
and **Villa Trabia** (mid-18th
century), but
neither is open to
the public. **Museo
Guttuso** (18th
century) houses a
modern art gallery.

🏛 Villa Palagonia
Piazza Garibaldi 3.
Tel 091 93 20 88.
Open daily (except
during functions). 🖼

🏛 Museo Guttuso
Via Rammacca 9. **Tel** 091 94 39 02.
Open daily. 🖼

Fishing and pleasure boats moored in the harbor of Trapani

❹ Trapani

🚹 70,000. **FS** 🚌 🚢 **ℹ** Piazza
Scarlatti 1 (0923 290 00). 🛍 daily.
w apt.trapani.it

Old Trapani occupies a narrow
peninsula. The best buildings
in this lively quarter are the
churches, such as the **Cathedral
of San Lorenzo** (1635) and the
Chiesa del Collegio dei Gesuiti
(c.1614–40). The façades of both,
and that of the **Palazzo d'Ali**
(17th century) on Via Garibaldi,
display magnificently the
ebullience of west Sicilian
Baroque architecture.

The 17th-century **Purgatorio**
on Via San Francesco d'Assisi
contains 18th-century *Misteri* –
realistic, life-size wooden statues
used annually in the Good
Friday procession. **Santa Maria
del Gesù** on Via Sant' Agostino
should be visited for the
Madonna degli Angeli by Andrea
della Robbia (1435–1525) and
for Antonello Gagini's canopy
(1521). In the Jewish quarter,
west of Via XXX Gennaio,
the **Palazzo della Giudecca**
(16th century) has a strangely
textured façade.

The **Museo Pepoli** has a
collection of local antiquities.
Of interest are the coral objects
and the Christmas figurines
(presepi), modern versions of
which are made here. Next to
the museum, the **Santuario di
Maria Santissima Annunziata**
contains the *Madonna di Trapani*,
a statue revered by fishermen
and sailors for its legendary
miraculous powers.

🏛 Museo Pepoli
Via Conte Agostino Pepoli. **Tel** 0923 55
32 69. **Open** 9am–1:30pm Mon–Sat,
9am–12:30pm Sun & hols (also
3–5:30pm Tue & Thu). 🖼

Outdoor staircase of the eccentric Villa Palagonia in Bagheria

❺ Erice

Trapani. 🚗 29,000. 🚌 ℹ️ Via Conte a Repoli 11 (0923 50 21 11). 🛒 Mon.

Poised on a crag overlooking Trapani, the medieval town of Erice was once the seat of the cult of the fertility goddess Venus Erycina. Her temple stood on the present site of the Norman castle (**Castello di Venere**), beyond the **Villa Balio** public gardens. On a clear day, you can see all the way to Tunisia from the castle. The ancient town of Eryx was renamed Gebel-Hamed by the Arabs, Monte San Giuliano by the Normans, and finally Erice in 1934 by Mussolini.

The **Duomo** (14th century) has a battlemented campanile and a 15th-century porch. Inside is a *Madonna and Child* (c.1469), attributed to either Francesco Laurana or Domenico Gagini. The deconsecrated 13th-century **San Giovanni Battista** on Viale Nunzio Nasi (now a hotel) contains Antonello Gagini's *St. John the Evangelist* (1531) and Antonino Gagini's *St. John the Baptist* (1539). **San Cataldo**, a plain 14th-century building on Via San Cataldo, houses a holy water stoup (c.1474) from Domenico Gagini's workshop. In the **Museo Cordici** are Antonello Gagini's *Annunciation* (1525), a variety of Classical remains and an old library.

🏛 **Museo Cordici**
Piazza Umberto I. **Open** 8:30am–1:30pm, 2:30–5:30pm Mon & Thu; 8am–1:30pm Tue, Wed & Fri.

A typical medieval street in the small hill town of Erice

Sicilian Islands

Surrounding Sicily are several island groups. The Isole Eolie (Aeolian Islands), to which Panarea, Lipari, Vulcano, and Stromboli belong, are a mass of volcanoes (most of them nearly extinct) poking out of the sea off the coast of Milazzo. The Isole Egadi (Egadi Islands), off the coast of Trapani, have a distinctly Arabic flavor. They include Favignana, Levanzo (which has Palaeolithic and Neolithic paintings and drawings), and Marettimo – the smallest and most unspoiled. Ustica, renowned for its marine life and popular among divers, lies north of Palermo. To the south are the remarkably tourist-free Isole Pelagie (Pelagic Islands) – Lampedusa and Linosa, which are North African in character. Remote Pantelleria lies closer to Tunisia than to Sicily.

The biggest and most popular of the Isole Eolie is Lipari, which has a pretty port and a good range of bars, restaurants, and hotels. Nearby sulfur-smelling Vulcano offers hot mud baths and black beaches.

Favignana, the largest and most populous of the Isole Egadi, is the scene of the traditional tuna slaughter – *la mattanza*. This takes place, as it has for centuries, in May. These fishermen are bringing in the nets following the slaughter.

Part of the Isole Pelagie, Lampedusa was once owned by the family of Giuseppe Tomasi di Lampedusa, author of *The Leopard*, Sicily's most famous novel. The island is nearer to Malta than Sicily and has limpid water and white beaches.

❻ Marsala

Trapani. 🗺 83,000. 🚇 🚌 🚢 ℹ️ Via
XI Maggio 100 (0923 71 40 97).
🏛 Tue. 🌐 consorziovinomarsala.it

The port of Marsala is the
home of a thick, strong,
sweet wine that has been in
production here since
the 18th century. In
1798 Admiral Nelson
ordered vast quantities
of it following the Battle
of the Nile. Its early
manufacture was
presided over by three
British families living in
Sicily. One of the old
warehouses where the
wine was produced is
now the **Museo
Archeologico di
Baglio Anselmi**,
housing important
Phoenician artifacts.

The ruins of **Lily-
baeum** are another
attraction. Founded in
397 BC, this outpost of the
Phoenician Empire was peopled
by the survivors of the massacre
at Mozia (ancient Motya) – the
island used by the Phoenicians
as a commercial center. Best of
all are the reconstructed
remains of a Punic ship thought
to have been active in the First
Punic War (263–241 BC). The
Museo di Mozia in the Whitaker
villa contains a remarkable early
5th-century BC statue of a
Greek youth.

The excavations here are
important; what we know of
the Phoenicians today comes
mostly from the Bible, and from
Mozia. The **Duomo**, begun in
the 17th century, was built on
the site of an earlier church;
both were dedicated to
Marsala's patron saint, Thomas
Becket of Canterbury. Its
interior is full of sculptural
works by members of the
Gagini family. The small
Museo degli Arazzi,
behind the Duomo,
contains several
magnificent 16th-century
Brussels tapestries.

Statue of a
Greek youth in
Museo di Mozia

🏛 **Museo Archeologico di
Baglio Anselmi**
Via Lungomare. **Tel** 0923 95 25
35. **Open** 9am–6pm daily. ♿

🏛 **Museo degli Arazzi**
Via Garaffa 57. **Tel** 0923 71 13
27. **Open** 9:30am–1pm daily
(and 4:30–6pm Tue–Sat). 📷

🏛 **Museo di Mozia**
Isola di Mozia. **Tel** 0923 71 25
98. **Open** 9am–1pm, 3–6pm
daily. 📷 ♿

❼ Segesta

Trapani. 🗺 7,500. 🚌 from Trapani &
Palermo. **Tel** 0924 95 58 41. **Open**
9:30am–6pm daily (to 4pm in winter).

According to legend, the ancient
town of Segesta – still largely
unexcavated – was founded by
Trojan followers of Aeneas. It
presents one of the most
spectacular sights on the island:
a massive unfinished **temple**
stranded on a remote hillside.
Its construction was started
between 426 and 416 BC, and it
was left incomplete following
the devastation of Selinunte by

the Carthaginians in 409 BC.
Archaeologists regard the temple
as a good example of "work in
progress." Nearby, close to the
summit of Monte Barbaro, the
ruins of an ancient theater (3rd
century BC) can be visited. Summer concerts are now held here.

❽ Selinunte

Trapani. **Tel** 0924 462 77. 🚇 Castelvetrano then bus. **Open** 9am–6pm
daily (to 4pm in winter). **Closed** Sun
pm. 📷

Founded in 651 BC, Selinunte
became one of the great cities
of Magna Graecia – the part of
southern Italy that was colonized
by ancient Greece – and its
toppled ruins are among Sicily's
most important historic sites. Its
ancient name, Selinus, derives
from the wild celery that still
grows here. The city was an
important port, and its wall
defenses can still be seen around
the Acropolis. The Carthaginians,
under Hannibal, completely
destroyed the city in 409 BC in
a battle famous for its epic and
spectacularly savage proportions.

While the city itself has virtually
disappeared, eight of its temples
are distinguishable, particularly
the so-called **Eastern Temples**
(E, F, and G). Of these, the
columns of huge Doric **Temple
E** (490–480 BC) have been
partially re-erected. **Temple F**
(c.560–540 BC) is in ruins.
Temple G (late 6th century BC),
which had 17 massive side
columns, was one of the greatest
Greek temples ever built.

Higher on the Acropolis lie the
remains of **Temples A, B, C, D,**
and **O**. Metope sculpture from
Temple C (early 6th century),
originally located on the frieze
between the triglyphs, can be
seen in the Museo Archeologico
Regionale in Palermo (see p532),
along with ceramics, jewelry, and
other artifacts excavated here.
A small **museum** on site houses
less important finds, as does
one in Castelvetrano, 8.5 miles
(14 km) north of Selinunte. The
ancient city is still being excavated; its **North Gate** entrance
is well preserved, and further
north there is also a **necropolis**.

The spectacularly situated, unfinished Doric temple at Segesta

❾ Cefalù

Palermo. 🚗 14,000. 🚆 🚌 ℹ️ Corso Ruggero 77 (0921 42 10 50). 🗓️ Sat. 🌐 **cefalu.it**

This pretty seaside town, with sandy beaches, restaurants, and hotels, is dominated by a huge rock known as **La Rocca** – once the site of a Temple of Diana – and by one of the finest Norman cathedrals in Sicily. Begun in 1131 by Roger II, the **Duomo** was intended as the main religious seat in Sicily. Though it failed to fulfill this function, the building's magnificence has never been eclipsed. Its splendid mosaics (1148), which feature an image of Christ Pantocrator in the apse, are remarkable and often celebrated as purely Byzantine works of art on Sicilian soil.

The **Museo Mandralisca** houses a fine *Portrait of a Man* (c.1465) by Antonello da Messina and a collection of coins, ceramics, vases, and minerals.

🏛️ Museo Mandralisca

Via Mandralisca. **Tel** 0921 42 15 47. **Open** 9am–1pm, 3–7pm daily (later in summer). 📷 🌐 **museomandralisca.it**

The lavish apse of Cefalù's Duomo

❿ Agrigento

🚗 59,000. 🚆 🚌 🚢 ℹ️ Via Empedocle 73 (0922 203 91); Piazzale Aldo Moro (0922 204 54). 🗓️ Fri. 🌐 **comune.agrigento.it**

Modern Agrigento occupies the site of Akragas, an important city of the ancient Greek world. Founded by Daedalus, according to legend, it was famed for the luxurious lifestyle of its

The twin-towered façade of the Norman Duomo in Cefalù

inhabitants, and was a great power and rival to Siracusa. In 406 BC it fell to the Carthaginians, who sacked and burned it.

The historic core of the city, with its medieval streets, focuses on the Via Atenea. **Santo Spirito** (13th century) houses stuccoes by Giacomo Serpotta (1695). **Santa Maria dei Greci** was built on the remains of a 5th-century BC temple – see the flattened columns in the nave. The **Duomo**, founded in the 14th century and altered in the 16th and 17th centuries, exhibits a unique mixture of Arab, Norman, and Catalan detailing.

Environs

The chief reason to visit Agrigento is to see the archaeological zone known as the Valley of the Temples *(see p540)*. The **Museo Regionale Archeologico** houses an interesting display of artifacts from the temples and the city, including a collection of vases, coins, and Greek and Roman sculpture.

🏛️ Museo Regionale Archeologico

Contrada San Nicola, Viale Panoramica. **Tel** 0922 40 15 65. **Open** 9am–7:30pm daily (to 1:30pm Mon, Sun). 📷 ♿

The Mafia

An international organization founded in Sicily, the Mafia developed as a result of the cruel State and severe poverty. By the late 19th century it had become a criminal organization thriving on property speculation and drug trafficking. Since the "singing" of Tommaso Buscetta and the capture of Toto Riina, the Mafia has been on the defensive against a State that has doubled its efforts against it. The "Boss of Bosses," Bernardo Provenzano, was arrested in 2006 after 43 years on the run. Violence is common in Sicily, but it is not directed at tourists.

Mafia assassination depicted in this scene from the film *The Godfather Part III* (1990)

Valley of the Temples

Straddling a low ridge to the south of Agrigento, the Valley of the Temples (Valle dei Templi) is one of the most impressive complexes of ancient Greek buildings outside Greece. Its Doric temples, dating from the 5th century BC, were destroyed in part by the Carthaginians in 406 BC, and in part by Christians, who believed the temples to be pagan, in the 6th century. Earthquakes wreaked further havoc. Nine of the original ten temples are still visible, and the whole area can be covered in a day. To avoid crowds, visit early in the morning (some temples open as early as 8:30am) or late afternoon.

Telamone from the Temple of Olympian Zeus

① Temple of Hephaistos
Apart from a couple of incomplete columns still standing, very little remains of this temple, built c.430 BC. It is also called the Temple of Vulcan.

② Sanctuary of the Chthonic Divinities
At this group of shrines, the forces of nature were worshipped.

(see p519)
Museo Regionale Archeologico
San Nicola

Via dei Templi
Via dei Templi
Via Sacra

Hellenistic and Roman Quarter

San Biagio

Rock Sanctuary of Demeter →

Strada Panoramica

Catacombs

P

S115

Temple of Asklepios

S115

④ Temple of Olympian Zeus
Begun c.480 BC, this was the biggest Doric temple ever built. Unfinished at the time of the Carthaginian attack, it is now a toppled ruin. Giant figures known as telamones were used in its construction.

⑤ Tomb of Theron
Here are the ruins of a Roman tomb (1st century AD).

⑥ Temple of Herakles
This is the oldest temple in the valley (late 6th century BC).

⑧ Temple of Juno
Built around 450 BC, this temple still has many intact columns.

③ Temple of Castor and Pollux
This is a controversial assemblage of pieces from other buildings, erected in the 19th century. Modern Agrigento (see p535) is in the background.

Key
— Suggested route
— Parking
Ancient walls

0 meters 500
0 yards 500

⑦ Temple of Concord
This beautifully preserved temple (c.430 BC) was converted into a Christian church in the 4th century AD, thus saved from destruction.

⓫ Piazza Armerina

Enna. 🏔 21,000. 🚌 ℹ Via Generale
Muscara (0935 68 02 01). 🛍 Thu.
🌐 piazzaarmerina.org

This active town is half medieval
and half Baroque. The 17th-
century **Duomo**, at its highest
point, is the most interesting of
the Baroque buildings.

In August, the lively *Palio dei
Normanni* festival attracts many
visitors, but the real draw are
the mosaics in the UNESCO-
listed **Villa Romana del Casale**,
3 miles (5 km) southwest of the
town. The mosaics were only
excavated in the 20th century.

It is thought that this huge,
once sumptuous villa with its
public halls, private quarters,
baths, and courtyards, belonged
to Maximianus Herculeus,
Diocletian's co-emperor, from
AD 286 to 305. His son and
successor, Maxentius, probably
continued its decoration, with
Constantine taking over on
Maxentius's death in 312.

Although little remains of the
building fabric, the floors have
some of the finest surviving
mosaics from Roman antiquity.
The hunting, mythological, and
domestic scenes, and exotic
landscapes, all exhibit realistic
attention to detail.

🏛 **Villa Romana del Casale**
Contrada Casale. **Tel** 0935 68 00 36.
Open 9am–4:30pm Fri–Sun. 🖼

Roman *Girls in Bikinis* mosaic from the Villa Romana del Casale

⓬ Enna

🏔 28,000. 🚊 🚌 ℹ Piazza
Colaianni 6 (0935 50 08 75). 🛍 Tue.
🌐 apt-enna.com

Impregnable on a crag above
a fertile landscape where
Persephone, mythological
daughter of Demeter, once
played, Sicily's highest town
(3,090 ft /942 m) has been
coveted by successive invaders
since its earliest days. The
venerated seat of the Cult of
Demeter (goddess of fertility)
was at Enna. Her temple stood
on the **Rocca Cerere**, not far from
the huge **Castello di Lombardia**
(13th century) built by Frederick II.

Most of Enna's sights are
clustered in the old town, among
the ancient streets that open out
of the Via Roma. The church of
San Francesco has a 16th-century
tower. **Piazza Crispi**, with its fine
views to nearby Calascibetta,
is dominated by a copy of
Bernini's *Rape of Persephone*. The
14th-century **Duomo**, altered in
later centuries, contains parts of
Demeter's temple.

The **Museo Alessi** houses
the Cathedral Treasury and an
interesting coin collection. The
Museo Varisano has exhibits
on the area's history, from
Neolithic to Roman. Away from
the center, the octagonal **Torre
di Federico II** (13th century) is a
former watchtower.

Environs
The ancient hill town of **Nicosia**,
northeast of Enna, was damaged
in the 1967 earthquake, but still
contains a smattering of
churches. San Nicola, built in the
14th century, has a magnificent,
carved entrance portal. Inside
there is a much venerated
wooden crucifix (17th century)
by Fra Umile di Petralia. Santa
Maria Maggiore houses a 16th-
century marble polyptych by
Antonello Gagini and a throne
reputedly used by Charles V in
1535. Farther east is **Troina**. It
was captured in 1062 by the
Normans, whose work survives
in the Chiesa Matrice. Southeast
of Enna, **Vizzini** commands fine
views of the countryside.

🏛 **Museo Alessi**
Via Roma 475. **Open** 8am–8pm daily.
🖼

🏛 **Museo Varisano**
Piazza Mazzini. **Tel** 0935 52 81 00.
Open 9am–6:30pm daily.

A view from the hills overlooking Vizzini, southeast of Enna

For hotels and restaurants in this region see pp562–77 and pp580–605

Taormina's magnificently situated Greek theater, with Mount Etna in the distance

⑬ Tindari

Messina. ℹ️ **Tel** 0941 24 11 36. 🚆 Patti or Oliveri, then bus. **Open** 9am–7pm daily (to 4pm in winter). ♿ 📷

Poised on the edge of a cliff overlooking the Golfo di Patti are the ruins of **Tyndaris**, one of the last Greek cities to have been founded in Sicily (395 BC). Apart from the city walls, the ruins are mostly Roman, including the **basilica** and **theater**. An **antiquarium** houses artifacts from the site. A combined ticket allows entry at the massive 2nd-century **Villa Romana** in Patti Marina.

Tindari is also known for its shrine to a Byzantine icon, the **Black Madonna** on Piazzale Belvedere.

⑭ Messina

🏔️ 250,000. 🚆 🚌 ⛴️ ℹ️ Piazza Cairoli 45 (090 293 52 92). 🏪 daily. 🌐 **azienturismomessina.it**

Messina has been the victim of earthquakes and World War II bombing. The **Museo Regionale** houses treasures that include works by Antonello da Messina and Caravaggio. **Santissima Annunziata dei Catalani** in Piazza Catalani displays the eclecticism of 12th-century

Norman architecture, with rich decoration. To visit the church, ask at the tourist office.

Outside, G.A. Montorsoli's **Fontana d'Orione** (1547) is the finest fountain of its kind from 16th-century Sicily. His **Fontana di Nettuno** (1557) celebrates Messina's foundation and position in the world as a principal commercial port.

🏛️ Museo Regionale

Via Libertà 465. **Tel** 090 36 12 92. **Open** 9am–1:30pm Thu–Tue (12:30pm Sun, hols; Tue, Thu, & Sat also pm). 📷 ♿

Antonello da Messina's *Madonna and Child* (1473), Museo Regionale

⑮ Taormina

Messina. 🏔️ 10,000. 🚆 🚌 ℹ️ Palazzo Corvaja, Piazza Santa Caterina (0942 232 43). 🏪 Wed.

Splendidly situated, Taormina is Sicily's best-known resort. It retains an air of exclusivity while being on the tourist trail, with sandy beaches and a wide range of restaurants and hotels.

The most illustrious relic of the past is the **theater**. Begun in the 3rd century BC by the Greeks, it was subsequently rebuilt by the Romans. Among other Classical remains are the ruins of the **odeon** (for musical performances) and the **naumachia** (an artificial lake for mock battles). On Piazza Vittorio Emanuele (site of the Roman Forum), **Palazzo Corvaia** (14th century) was built using stone from a temple that once stood here. The 13th-century **Duomo** (renovated in 1636) is a fortresslike building.

Environs

Taormina's main beach, **Mazzarò**, boasts clear waters and is easily reached from the town. South of Taormina at **Capo Schisò** are the ruins of ancient **Naxos**. To the west is **Gole dell'Alcantara**, a 66-ft (20-m) deep gorge of basalt rock, a river, and waterfalls.

⑯ Mount Etna

Catania. 🚉 Linguaglossa or Randazzo; Circumetnea railway from Catania to Riposto. 🚌 to Nicolosi. 🛈 Via G. Garibaldi 63, Nicolosi (095 91 15 05). To hire a guide: 095 791 47 55. 🌐 http://turismo.provincia.ct.it

Europe's highest (11,050 ft/ 3,370 m) and most active volcano, Mount Etna was thought by the Romans to have been the forge of Vulcan (god of fire). The climb to the summit should be made only with an experienced guide. The Circumetnea railroad runs around the base, offering a good alternative to hiking and good views.

⑰ Catania

🚹 315,000. ✈ 🚉 🚌 🛈 Via Cimarosa 10 (095 73 06 211). 🛒 Mon–Sat (general); Sun (antique & bric-a-brac). 🌐 apt.catania.it

Having been decimated by the earthquake of 1693, Catania was comprehensively rebuilt. While it is not immediately beautiful, it

The façade of Catania's Duomo

contains some of the most imaginative lava-built Baroque buildings in Sicily. **Piazza del Duomo**, featuring a lava elephant (Catania's symbol) carrying an Egyptian obelisk, offers a dramatic vista to Mount Etna. In 1736 the Norman **Duomo** was given a new façade by Vaccarini, who also worked on the **Municipio** (finished 1741), on the façade of **Sant'Agata** (1748), on the designs of **Collegio Cutelli**,

built around 1779, and on **Palazzo Valle** (c.1740–50).

Carrying on the Vaccarini tradition is Stefano Ittar's **San Placido** (around 1768). The frenzied stone carving on the **Palazzo Biscari** (early 18th century) is exceeded by Antonino Amato's unrestrained decoration of the vast Benedictine **convent** (1704) and the adjacent huge church of **San Niccolò** (1730).

On Via Vittorio Emanuele is the **Museo Belliniano**, birthplace of composer Vincenzo Bellini (1801–35). The lava ruins of the **Teatro Romano** (21 BC) are at Piazza Stesicono. **Verga's House**, home of the great Sicilian novelist Giovanni Verga (1840–1922), is on Via Sant' Anna. Via Crociferi is home to 18th-century churches **San Francesco Borgia**, **San Benedetto**, and **San Giuliano**, whose interior is Vaccarini's masterpiece (1760). Further along Via Crociferi, the church of **Santo Carcere** contains the prison of St. Agatha, who was martyred in AD 253.

Influences on Traditional Sicilian Cuisine

Sicily has one of Italy's most varied cuisines. The island's unique location – marooned between North Africa, Europe, and the eastern Mediterranean – and the invaders it attracted are responsible for this culinary diversity. The earliest Western cookbook, the now lost *Art of Cooking* (5th century BC), was written by Mithaecus, a Siracusan Greek. Sicily's fertility attracted Greek colonists, who exported oil, wheat, honey, cheese, fruit, and vegetables to their homeland. The Arabs introduced oranges, lemons, eggplant, and sugar cane. Their love of sweet confections inspired *granita*, a form of flavored ice, and *cassata*, an elaborate sponge cake with ricotta and candied

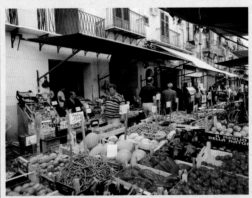
A colorful selection of vegetables at a Sicilian market stall

Marzipan fruits made from almond paste

fruit. The Sicilians love to claim an Arabic origin for their ice cream, but the Greeks and Romans had created an earlier version by chilling their wine with snow from Mount Etna. Traditionally, the peasants existed on a subsistence diet while the aristocracy enjoyed extravagant fare, and one

of the peculiarities of Sicilian food today is that it can be both frugal and handsomely ornate. All of the usual Italian dishes are available, but the more interesting meals are those that use local ingredients like swordfish, sardines, ricotta cheese, red chilies, eggplant, capers, olives, and almond paste to create unusual taste combinations.

Boats on the beach in the pretty seaside town of Cefalù ▶

Shorefront in Siracusa, one of the most beautiful cities of the ancient Greek world

⑱ Pantalica

Siracusa. 🚌 from Siracusa to Sortino then 3-mile (5-km) walk to entrance (partial access), or bus from Siracusa to Ferla then 6-mile (10-km) walk to entrance. Necropolis ℹ️ Pro Loco, Ferla. **Tel** 0931 79 06 81.

Remote in the desolate Monti Iblei and overlooking the River Anapo is the prehistoric **necropolis** of Pantalica – a pleasant place to walk and picnic. The dead of a large, unexcavated village (occupied from 13th–8th century BC) were buried here in cavelike tombs cut into the rock. More than 5,000 of these tombs were arranged in tiers with a single flat stone sealing each opening.

The inhabitants of Pantalica are thought to have come from coastal **Thapsos**, which was abandoned after raids by warlike tribes from mainland Italy. The site was re-inhabited in the Byzantine period when some tombs were made into cave dwellings and chapels.

Rock-cut tombs in the prehistoric necropolis of Pantalica

Artifacts from the necropolis are displayed in Siracusa's Museo Archeologico Regionale.

Interior of Duomo in Siracusa

⑲ Siracusa

🗺️ 125,000. **FS** 🚌 🚢 ℹ️ Via Maestranza (0931 46 42 55). 🛍️ Wed.

Siracusa (Syracuse) was the most important and powerful Greek city from the 5th to the 3rd centuries BC, and according to the Roman consul Cicero, the most beautiful. The peninsula **Ortigia** is the hub of the old city. On the mainland, **Achradina**, **Tyche**, and **Neapolis** have been occupied almost without a break since the expansion of the city in 480 BC. These were the years of Gelon, tyrant of Gela, when Siracusa was enriched with new temples, theaters, and dockyards. The city was a powerful force until 211 BC, when it fell to the Romans in a battle that also killed the

mathematician Archimedes, its most famous inhabitant.

The highlight of Ortigia is the extraordinary **Duomo**, begun in 1728 by architect Andrea Palma. Its Baroque façade masks the **Temple of Athena** (5th century BC), which has been absorbed into the Duomo. Facing the Ponte Nuovo are the ruins of Sicily's earliest Doric temple, the **Temple of Apollo**, which had monolithic columns.

Across from the Duomo is the **Palazzo Beneventano del Bosco** (1778–88), a bold example of Siracusan Baroque, as is **Santa Lucia alla Badia** (1695–1703). In the Municipio a small museum records the history of Ionic temples, and the coin collection of the Galleria Numismatica records Siracusa's past wealth. The delightful **Fonte Aretusa** is frequently referred to by Classical writers as the point where Aretusa emerged from the ground, having been changed into a spring by Artemis to help her escape her lover Alpheus.

At Ortigia's furthest point is the **Castello Maniace**, built by Frederick II around 1239. Here too is the **Gallerie Regionale di Palazzo Bellomo**, with sculpture and paintings including the *Burial of St. Lucy* (1608) by Caravaggio.

The painting comes from the church of **Santa Lucia** in the Achradina quarter. This area was flattened during World War II, but the church survived. It is mostly 17th century with a

Norman campanile, and occupies the site where St. Lucy, patron saint of Siracusa, was martyred in AD 304. Achradina is now the center of modern Siracusa.

To the north, in Tyche, is the **Museo Archeologico Regionale Paolo Orsi**, with its important collection of artifacts from the Palaeolithic to the Byzantine era, taken from southeastern sites in Sicily. Included are vases, coins, bronzes, sculpture, and fragments from Siracusan temples.

The Neapolis quarter and its **Parco Archeologico** feature the Teatro Romano, the Altar of Hieron II, and the spectacular Teatro Greco, carved into the hillside. Beyond the Nymphaeum is the 2nd-century AD Roman amphitheater and the stone quarries – the Latomia del Paradiso featuring the **Ear of Dionysius**. It is thought that 7,000 Athenians were incarcerated here and left to die after their calamitous defeat in 413 BC, in a battle described by Thucydides as "the greatest action in Hellenic history."

Environs
At **Epipolae**, 5 miles (8 km) north of Neapolis is the **Castle of Euryalus** – the most important ancient Greek fortification to have survived.

🏛 **Gallerie Regionale di Palazzo Bellomo**
Palazzo Bellomo, Via Capodieci 14. **Tel** 0931 695 11. **Open** 9am–6:30pm Tue–Sun (to 1pm public hols). 🎫 ♿

🏛 **Museo Archeologico Regionale Paolo Orsi**
Viale Teocrito 66. **Tel** 0931 46 40 22. **Open** 9am–6:30pm Tue–Sun (to 1pm Sun). Last adm: 1 hr before closing. 🎫 ♿

⑳ Noto
Siracusa. 🔼 24,000. 🚆 🚌 ℹ Piazza XVI Maggio (0931 83 67 44). 🗓 Mon & 1st & 3rd Tue of the month.
🌐 comune.noto.sr.it

Noto was built from scratch in the early 18th century to replace Noto Antica, which was devastated by an earthquake in 1693. The town was comprehensively designed in Baroque style, using

The façade of the Duomo in Noto rises above a huge staircase

the local white tufa, a limestone that has turned a honey-brown color from the sun. Noto is a UNESCO World Heritage site, but unfortunately much of its beauty is behind scaffolding due to ongoing restoration.

The twin-towered **Duomo** (completed 1770s) that dominates Noto is by architect Rosario Gagliardi, who also designed the eccentric tower façade of the seminary of **San Salvatore** (18th century) in Piazza Municipio, the convex façade of **San Domenico** (1730s) in Piazza XVI Maggio, and the oval interior of **Santa Chiara** (1730) on Corso Vittorio

Emanuele. The magnificent **Palazzo Trigona** (1781) stands on Via Cavour behind the Duomo. On Via Nicolaci, the **Palazzo Villadorata** (1730s) features a splendid façade adorned with elaborate stone carvings. At the north end of Via Nicolaci, the **Monastery of Montevergine** has a striking curved façade. In mid-May, Via Nicolaci is the site of the Infiorata flower festival. Gagliardi's church of the **Crocifisso** (1728) stands on the town's summit. It contains a sculpture of the Madonna by Francesco Laurana (1471). The **Municipio** (1740s), facing the Duomo, has a fine "billowing" ground floor design.

Environs
The earthquake of 1693 also devastated the towns of **Modica**, around 19 miles (30 km) to the west, and **Ragusa**, a short distance further. Like Noto, they were rebuilt in the region's rich Baroque style. Gagliardi worked on Modica's **San Giorgio** (early 18th century), on Ragusa's **San Giorgio** (begun around 1746, and one of his masterpieces), and on **San Giuseppe** (mid-18th century).

Boisterous carving on the façade of the Palazzo Villadorata in Noto

Exploring Sardinia

This island, called Sardegna in Italian, is characterized by an interior of dramatic, rolling uplands covered in *macchia* – grassland mingled with myrtle, wild thyme, prickly pears, and dwarf oaks – and a coastline of beguiling, translucent sea, isolated coves, long sandy beaches, and caves. The Gennargentu mountains, with the highest peak at 6,017 ft (1,834 m), shield a nearly impenetrable area of rural villages. In the northeast, mountains fall away dramatically to the Costa Smeralda, Sardinia's most exclusive coastal area. Farther south, the shoreline around the Golfo di Orosei is fairly unspoiled. Around Oristano in the west the land is flat, leading to the plain of Campidano where the island's corn, fruit, and vegetables grow.

A typical scene of clothes hanging out to dry in Alghero

Sights at a Glance

1. Costa Smeralda
2. Sassari
3. Alghero
4. Bosa
5. Nuoro
6. Cala Gonone
7. Nuoro Oristano
8. Sant'Antioco
9. Cagliari

Getting Around

Ferries from a wide range of ports on the Italian mainland dock at Cagliari, Olbia, and Porto Torres. International and domestic flights use the airports at Cagliari, Olbia, and Alghero. The island is neatly cut by the S131. It skirts the Gennargentu mountains, which are accessible only by tortuously winding passes. Branches of the S131 reach Olbia and Nuoro. Express bus services connect the major cities, while the smaller towns are linked by slow and infrequent public transport.

For additional map symbols *see back flap*

Isola Asinara
la Reale
Fornelli
Golfo dell' Asinara
Stintino
Porto Torres
Sorso
Palmadula
Osilo
SASSARI
Capo dell' Argentiera
Ploaghe
Olmedo
Ittiri
Ardara
Grotta di Nettuno
ALGHERO
Torralba
Monteleone Rocca Doria
Bonorva
Montresta
Capo Marargiu
BOSA
Bosa Marina
Macomer
MAR
Cuglieri
DI
Monte Ferru 1050m
Ghila
Capo Mannu
Riola Sardo
Fordongianu
Stagno di Cabras
Solaru
ORISTANO
Simax
SARDEGNA
Santa Giusta
Use
Arborea
Ales
Capo della Frasca
Terralba
Uras
Pardu Atzei
Sardar
Guspini
Capo Pecora
Villacidro
Monte Linas 1236m
Buggerru
Masua
Vallermosa
Iglesias
Siliqu
Gonnesa
Portoscuso
Narcao
Carbonia
Monte Caravius 1116m
Isola di San Pietro
Calasetta
Sant
SANT'ANTIOCO
Porto Botte
Isola di Sant'Antioco
Golfo di Palmas
Teulada
Capo Teulada

Waves lapping at the rocks on Isola di San Pietro, northwest of Sant'Antioco

Key

═══ Major road

──── Secondary road

──── Minor road

──── Scenic route

┄┄┄ Main railroad

──── Minor railroad

▲ Summit

0 kilometers   50

0 miles   25

Southernmost reach of the Gennargentu mountains

The extravagantly beautiful, macchia-scented Costa Smeralda

❶ Costa Smeralda

Sassari. **FS** 🚌 Olbia. 🚌 Porto Cervo.
i AAST La Maddalena, Cava Civetta
(0789 73 63 21); AAST Palau, Via
Nazionale 94 (0789 70 95 70).
w quicostasmeralda.it

Stretching from the Golfo di
Cugnana to the Golfo di
Arzachena, the Costa Smeralda
was developed by a consortium of magnates in the 1950s.
One of the world's most opulent
holiday resorts, it is kept
immaculate by strict controls.

In **Porto Cervo**, the main
town, boutiques jostle with
nightclubs, fine restaurants, and
luxury hotels. It caters to the
seriously rich – billionaires,
crowned heads, and pop stars.

Environs

Head north to rural **Baia
Sardinia** and **Cannigione**. From
Palau ferries leave for **La
Maddalena** and **Isola Caprera**,
the home of Garibaldi and the
Museo Nazionale Garibaldino.

🏛 **Museo Nazionale Garibaldino**
Frazione Caprera, La Maddalena.
Tel 0789 72 71 62. **Open**
9am–1:30pm, 2–7:15pm Tue–Sun.
Closed Jan 1, May 1, Dec 25. 🅿 ♿

❷ Cassari

🏘 130,000. ✈ **FS** 🚌 **i** Viale
Caprera 36 (079 27 99 54). 🛒 Mon.
w comune.sassari.it

Founded by Genoese and Pisan
merchants early in the 13th
century, Sassari is known for its
spectacular *Cavalcata Sarda*
festival on Ascension Day, and

for being the site of Sardinia's
first university. There is a church-
filled medieval quarter around
the **Duomo** (11th
century, with later,
mostly Baroque,
additions), and to
the north is the
Fonte Rosello, a
late-Renaissance
fountain. The **Museo
Archeologico
Nazionale "G.A.
Sanna"** is a good
starting point for an
investigation into
the region's
nuraghic history.

Environs

To the southeast
along the S131 is
the Pisan-Romanesque church
of **Santissima Trinità di
Saccargia** (1116), with the only
extant 13th-century fresco cycle
in Sardinia. Farther on is the
12th-century church of **San
Michele di
Salvenero**, and
at **Ardara** the
basalt-built
Romanesque
**Santa Maria del
Regno**, or "Black
Cathedral."

🏛 **Museo
Archeologico
Nazionale
"G.A. Sanna"**
Via Roma 64.
Tel 079 27 22 03.
Open 9am–7:30pm
Tue–Sun (to 7pm
Sun). 🅿 ♿

Façade of Santissima
Trinità di Saccargia

❸ Alghero

Sassari. 🏘 41,000. ✈ **FS** 🚌 🚢 **i**
Lungomare Dante 1 (079 97 59 96).
🛒 Wed. **w** comune.alghero.ss.it

Founded on a peninsula facing
the Bay of Alghero early in the
12th century, and taken from
the Genoese Dorias by the
Aragonese in 1353, Alghero
was peopled by settlers from
Barcelona and Valencia. Its
original occupants – Ligurians
and Sardinians – were expelled
with such thoroughness that
today the Catalan language
and culture is enjoying a revival
and the look of old Alghero is
consistently Spanish.

Filled with labyrinthine alleys
and cobbled streets, the lively
port of old Alghero is flanked
by battlemented walls and
defensive towers on all but the
landward section. Facing the
Giardino Pubblico is the massive
16th-century **Torre di Porta
Terra**, also known as the Jewish
Tower after its
builders. Around
the periphery of the
old town are more
towers, including
**Torre dell'Espero
Reial** and **Torre
San Giacomo** on
Lungomare
Colombo, and **Torre
della Maddalena** on
Piazza Porta Terra.

The 16th-century **Duomo** at
the bottom of Via Umberto is
predominantly Catalan-Gothic
with an Aragonese portal. Off
Via Carlo Alberto, **San
Francesco** (14th century) has a

A typical house in Alghero

The waterfront at Bosa

pretty cloister and octagonal campanile towering over Alghero, and Baroque **San Michele** has a bright tiled dome. In Via Principe Umberto is the **Casa Doria**, the house where the pre-Hispanic rulers of Alghero lived. It has a beautiful Renaissance portal and Gothic arched window.

Environs
Take a boat or car trip (the latter involves much climbing down) to the spectacular **Grotta di Nettuno**, a deep natural cave round the point of Capo Caccia, or the nearby **Grotta Verde**.

❹ Bosa

Nuoro. 🏛 8,500. 🚇 🚌 🚍 🛈 Pro Loco, Via Azuni 5 (0785 37 61 07). 🗓 Tue. 🆆 comune.bosa.nu.it

Bosa is a small, picturesque seaside town at the mouth of Sardinia's only navigable river, the Temo. The historic **Sa Costa** district struggles up the side of a low hill capped by the **Castello di Serravalle**, built in 1122 by the Malaspina family. The narrow passages and alleys here have changed little since the Middle Ages. By the Temo are **Sas Conzas** – the former dyers' houses and workshops.

Languishing on the riverside, the cosmopolitan **Sa Piatta** district houses the Aragonese-Gothic **Duomo** (15th century) and Romanesque **San Pietro Extramuros** (11th century), with a Gothic façade added by Cistercian monks in the 13th century.

Nuraghe in Sardinia

The dominant feature of Sardinia is the 7,000 or so *nuraghe* dotted around the island. Dating from 1800 to 300 BC, these strange, truncated cone structures were built without any bonding from huge basalt blocks taken from extinct volcanoes. To this day, little is known about the identity of the nuraghic people. They must have been well organized and have possessed remarkable engineering skills, judging by their buildings, but they appear to have left no written word. The mystery of these enigmatic people has intrigued Sardinians for years.

The individual nuraghe are fairly small. A few were fortresses, equipped with wells and other defensive features.

Su Nuraxi at Barumini *(above)*, Serra Orrios, near Dorgali, and Santu Antine at Torralba are among the most important *nuraghe* complexes. Houses, temples, tombs, and even a theater have been identified.

This bronze figure of a hero with four eyes and four arms is among the many objects and statues discovered on nuraghic sites and associated with the nuraghic people.

SARDINIA

Key
• Nuraghic sites

0 kilometers   100
0 miles   50

Nobel Prize–winning novelist Grazia Deledda from Nuoro

❺ Nuoro

�︎ 38,000. 🚇 🚌 ℹ️ Piazza d'Italia 19 (0784 300 83). 🛒 Fri & Sat. 🎉 Aug 29: Sagra del Redentore. 🌐 comune.nuoro.it

This town, in a spectacular setting beneath Monte Ortobene and the dramatic Supramonte, was the home of Grazia Deledda, who won the Nobel Prize for Literature in 1926 for her portrayal of the power and passions in the primitive communities around her. A comprehensive collection of ethnic items, such as traditional Sardinian costumes and jewelry, can be seen in the excellent **Museo Etnografico Sardo**. Attending the *Sagra del Redentore* festival is the best way to witness the region's dancing and dialects.

Environs
Nuoro is on the edge of the Barbagia region, which has isolated villages of shepherds who have never experienced the hand of any overlord, so impenetrable are the **Gennargentu** mountains. This region was known to the Romans as Barbaria, an area they were never able to subdue. Traces of the traditional lawlessness of the Barbagia can be seen in **Orgosolo**, with its wall murals calling for Sardinia's independence. Rival clans were locked in bloody vendetta for almost 50 years, and the deeds of native bandits form part of local folklore.

In **Mamoiada**'s *Feast of the Mamuthones*, men in sinister masks and traditional costume perform a ritual dance ending with a symbolic "killing" of a scapegoat. The fervor of the event is indicative of the fierce folkloric tradition and deep resistance to change.

🏛️ **Museo Etnografico Sardo**
Via Mereu 56. **Tel** 0784 25 70 35.
Open 10am–1pm, 3–7pm Tue–Sun.
📷 ♿ 🌐 isresardegna.it

❻ Cala Gonone

Nuoro. �︎ 800. 🚌 ℹ️ Pro Loco, via Lamormara 108, Dorgali (0784 962 43). 🛒 daily. 🚤 from Dorgali to grottoes (Apr–mid-Oct). **Tel** 0784 933 05.

East of Nuoro, between the sea and the mountains, is the hamlet of Cala Gonone – a bustling seaside resort and fishing port, with magnificent beaches. Along the unspoiled coast are the isolated coves of **Cala Luna**, linked with Cala Gonone by a well-marked two-hour trail, and Cala Sisine. The famous **Grotta del Bue Marino**, adorned with weird rock formations, can only be reached by boat.

Environs
To the south, the villages of **Urzulei**, **Baunei**, and **Santa Maria Navarrese**, along the spectacular SS125 road to Tortolì, feature breathtaking landscapes.

Ruins of Tharros near Oristano

❼ Oristano

Cagliari. 🚫 32,000. 🚇 🚌 ℹ️ EPT, Piazza Eleonora 1 (0783 79 13 06); Pro Loco, Via Vittorio Emanuele 8 (0783 706 21). 🛒 Tue & Fri.

The province of Oristano corresponds roughly with historical Arborea, over which Eleonora ruled (*see opposite*). She is commemorated by an 18th-century statue in **Piazza Eleonora**. On Corso Vittorio Emanuele is the 16th-century **Casa di Eleonora**, and nearby the **Antiquarium Arborense**, which has Neolithic, nuraghic, Punic, and Roman artifacts. The **Torre di San Cristoforo** (1291) in Piazza Roma once formed part of Oristano's fortifications. The **Duomo** (13th century) was later rebuilt in the Baroque style. More interesting are the churches of **Santa Chiara** (1343) on Via Garibaldi and 14th-century **San Martino** on Via Cagliari.

Environs
The 12th-century Pisan-Romanesque **Cathedral** at Santa Giusta has columns probably taken from Tharros, an 8th-century BC Punic

Entrance to the Grotta del Bue Marino, south of Cala Gonone

The tiny resort of Carloforte, the capital of Isola di San Pietro

settlement, 12 miles (20 km) west of Oristano on the Sinis peninsula.

🏛 Antiquarium Arborense
Palazzo Parpaglia. **Tel** 0783 79 12 62. **Open** 9am–2pm, 5–8pm Tue, Thu, Sun. ♿️✅

❽ Sant'Antioco
Cagliari. 🚉 🚌 ℹ️ Pro Loco, Piazza Repubblica 31a (0781 84 05 92).

The main town on this unspoiled island off Sardinia's southern coast is **Sant'Antioco**, once a Phoenician port and an important Roman base. Proof of almost continuous occupation is clear from the **catacombs**, a Phoenician burial place later used by Christians, under the 12th-century basilica of **Sant'Antioco Martire**. The **Museo Archeologico** contains Phoenician artifacts. The Punic **Tophet** (sanctuary of the goddess Tanit) and the **necropolis** are nearby. The small **Isola di San Pietro** can be reached by ferry from Calasetta.

🏛 Catacombs
Piazza Parrocchia. **Tel** 0781 830 44. **Open** 9am–noon, 3:30–6pm daily. ✅ only. ♿️✅

🏛 Museo Archeologico
Via Regina Margherita 113. **Tel** 0783 744 33. **Open** 9am–2pm, 3–8pm daily. **Closed** Dec 8, 25, & 26. ✅♿️ (& Tophet & necropolis). ✅

❾ Cagliari
🏠 165,000. ✈️ 🚉 🚌 ⛴ ℹ️ Piazza Matteotti 📞 (070 66 92 55). 🛒 daily; also Sun (flea) and 2nd Sun of month (antiques). 🌐 visit-cagliari.it

The capital of Sardinia, this site was occupied by the Phoenicians, Carthaginians, and Romans, and extensive ruins of the Phoenician city of Nora lie to the southwest of Cagliari. A 2nd-century **amphitheater** survives from the Roman era, cut from rock. Discover the town's earlier history in the **Cittadella dei Musei**, the former royal arsenal. It houses several museums, including the **Museo Archeologico Nazionale**. The nuraghic items are the most interesting in the collection, especially the bronze votive statuettes. Also in the Cittadella dei Musei is the **Pinacoteca**, an art gallery.

The 6th-century church of San Saturnino in Cagliari, built on a Greek-cross plan

The old core of Cagliari has a North African character. In the high **Castello** district, the Romans and, later, Pisans built defenses. The gracious **Bastione San Remy** on Piazza Costituzione offers magnificent views over the city and surrounding countryside. The **Duomo** is a 20th-century rehash of a Romanesque building. Flanking the entrance are two 12th-century pulpits originally destined for the cathedral in Pisa.

Nearby is the Pisan tower **Torre San Pancrazio** (14th century). From the partially ruined **Torre dell'Elefante** on Via dell'Università to the port lies the **Marina** quarter, which expanded from the old town in the 16th to 17th centuries. In Piazza San Cosimo, the 6th-century church of **San Saturnino** is a rare monument to Byzantine occupation.

🎭 Amphitheater
Viale Sant'Ignazio. **Tel** 070 677 64 70. **Open** 9am–5pm Tue–Sun (summer: 9am–1pm, 3:30–7:30pm). ♿️✅

🏛 Cittadella dei Musei
Piazza Arsenale. **Tel** 070 675 76 27. **Museo Archeologico Nazionale Open** 9am–8pm Tue–Sun. ♿️✅ **Pinacoteca Tel** 070 66 24 96. **Open** 9am–8pm Tue–Sun. **Closed** Jan 1, May 1, Dec 25. ♿️✅

Eleonora of Arborea
A champion against rule from abroad, Eleonora was governing *giudicessa* (judge) of Arborea, one of four administrative divisions of Sardinia, from 1383–1404. Her marriage to Brancaleone Doria consolidated Genoese interests in Sardinia. She rallied the island to keep out Spanish invaders who tried to claim land that had been given to the Aragonese King James II. Her greatest legacy was the completion of the codifying of laws begun by her father. Written in Sardinian, they called for community of property in marriage and the right of women to seek redress from rape.

WHERE TO STAY

People come from all over the world to visit Italy, and most Italians spend their vacations here as well, particularly in the mountains or by the sea. This means that there is a dazzling range of accommodation options, from splendid hotels in old palazzi and historic residences, to simple family-run *pensioni* and hostels. Most major cities also offer upscale guest houses. Those who want accommodations with cooking facilities are well served too, with everything from stately villas in Tuscany to purpose-built vacation flats in, or near, seaside resorts. Italian hotels can have a reputation for being expensive and short on services, but this is not always the case, and you can find excellent value in all price ranges. The hotels listed on pages 562–77 have been selected from every price category as among the best value in each area for style, comfort, or location.

The Gritti Palace, one of Venice's historic palazzi *(see p563)*

Ratings

Hotels in Italy are classified with a rating system of one to five stars. The grading depends on the facilities offered, and each region awards stars according to slightly different criteria.

Sometimes a hotel has a lower rating than it deserves. This may be because the local tourist office has not upgraded the rating or because the hotel itself has opted to stay in a lower category to avoid higher taxes.

Alberghi

Albergo is Italian for hotel, but the term tends to refer to establishments classified as three-star or above. Room sizes vary considerably: in city centers even expensive hotels can have small rooms, especially if the hotel is located in a historic building, whereas you get far more space for your money in rural areas. *Alberghi* will have private baths or showers in all rooms. Many high-end and boutique hotels also offer spa and fitness facilities.

Pensioni

Although the term *pensione* is no longer in official use, one- and two-star hotels still use the term to describe their status. On the whole you will find immaculate standards of cleanliness and friendly, helpful service with basic, although perfectly functional, rooms. Be aware that while your *pensioni* may be in an old building full of historic charm, this can also mean noisy, erratic plumbing and dark rooms. Many *pensioni*

Street sign showing the direction and location of hotels

do not have public rooms other than a sparsely furnished breakfast room. Most will offer at least some bedrooms with a private shower although rarely a bath. If you intend to be out late, check that you'll be able to get back into the *pensione*. Not all of them are staffed after midnight or 1am, but most will at least be able to provide a key to the main door.

A *locanda* was traditionally an inn, offering cheap food and a place to sleep for the traveler. The word is still in use, particularly in central and northern Italy, but is now synonymous with *pensione* and may be more of an affectation for the benefit of the tourist.

Chain Hotels

There are various Italian chain hotels, including **Atahotels** and **Una Hotels and Resorts**, as well as the usual big internationals. **NH Hoteles** hotels appeal to the business traveler, and there are one or two in most large cities; **Marriott**, **Hyatt**, and **Best Western** are international luxury chains, while **Italia Lodging** caters to the more modest budget. **Relais et Châteaux** run charming hotels in historic castles, villas, and monasteries, with facilities to match.

Meals and Facilities

There has been a general improvement in the facilities offered by Italian hotels, especially in the more modern four- and five-star hotels. However, in some older establishments there may not

Romantic Hotel Villa Pagoda in Nervi, Genoa *(see p568)*

always be air-conditioning or 24-hour room service, so it's best to check before you book.

Some hotels may insist on full board *(pensione completa)* or half board *(mezza pensione)* in peak season. Most hotel rates include breakfast, which in many establishments will consist of a large buffet, although smaller hotels and *pensioni* may offer a simple continental breakfast.

For a double room, state if you want twin beds *(letti singoli)* or a double bed *(matrimoniale)*. Bathrooms in most hotels will have showers rather than baths.

Most hotels offer Internet access, but it is not always free, and charges will vary. If a city center hotel does not have its own parking spaces, it may have an arrangement with a nearby garage. Check the availability and cost of parking with the hotel before making a reservation.

Children

Italians love children, and although most hotels may not offer special facilities for families, kids are always welcome.

Some of the cheaper hotels may not be able to provide cots. However, virtually all hotels will be happy to put a small bed into a double room for families traveling together. The price of this is usually an extra 30–40 percent of the double room rate per bed. Many large hotels also offer babysitting services.

Prices

As a rule hotels in Italy are not cheap, although prices vary considerably between regions. Hotels in major cities and resorts are likely to be more expensive. Booking online is one way to secure a better rate, as hotel websites may offer special deals. Or you can save money by booking your hotel and flight together on most travel websites.

Prices, which include tax and service and are quoted per room, start from around €60 for a double room without a bathroom, and can rise to at least €80 with a bath, even for a very basic hotel. A single room will cost about two thirds of a double. Outside the big cities, €100 should get you something comfortable and often picturesque, although not particularly luxurious. For €210 and upward you can expect a good range of facilities, a pleasant or central location, and often a hotel with local or historic charm. In Rome, all campsites, guest houses and hotels must add a city tax *(contributo di soggiorno)* to the bill. At present, these rates are fixed at €1 per day per person for campsites, €2 for establishments up to and including three-star hotels, and €3 for four- and five-star hotels.

In larger hotels there is often a considerable difference in quality and price between standard and more luxurious, deluxe rooms. If you would like a view or a terrace, this is also likely to be more expensive, though for those who prefer peaceful nights, it is generally best to avoid rooms facing the street in busy cities.

Also, beware of extra charges: the minibar can be very expensive as can the cost of parking, laundry, or making telephone calls directly from your hotel bedroom.

Reservations

Book as soon as possible, particularly if you have special requests such as a room with a view, off the street, or with a bath. August tends to be very busy at beach resorts, and February is peak season at mountain resorts. Peak times for cities and towns depend on their particular cultural calendars *(see pp70–73)*.

You will be asked for a deposit when you book; this can usually be paid for by credit card (even in hotels that do not accept credit cards for final payment); otherwise you can use PayPal for online transactions, or transfer the money via EFT from your bank account.

Under Italian law the hotel must issue you with a receipt *(ricevuta fiscale)* for final payment, which you must keep until you leave Italy.

The Italian State Tourist Office (**ENIT**) has accommodation lists for every region, although this might not be the most up-to-date resource. Rooms can also be booked via the **APT** (Azienda Provinciale per il Turismo).

A traditional Florentine hotel interior

The multilevel terrace of the Raphael in Rome *(see p574)*

Checking In and Out

Italian hotels are legally obliged to register you with the police, which is why you'll always be asked for your passport when checking in. This is a mere formality, and your passport should be returned to you within an hour or two.

Checking-out time is usually before noon, although some larger hotels may extend your checking-out time upon request, but only if your room is not already reserved for another guest. All rooms must be vacated on time, but most hotels will allow you to leave your luggage in a safe place to be collected later in the day.

Al Sole, Venice *(see p563)*

Self-Catering and Agriturismo

Across rural Italy, there are more than 2,000 farms, villas, and mountain chalets offering reasonably priced apartment- or hotel-style accommodations with cooking facilities as part of the **Agriturismo** scheme. Options range from beautifully kept villas or ancient castles with first-class facilities, to simple rooms in the family home on a working farm. Some places have excellent restaurants that serve farm and local produce, while others can arrange riding, fishing,

or other sporting activities *(see p610)*. Note that there may be a minimum stay requirement at some of these establishments, especially during peak season. The annual *Agriturist* publication can be found in the central tourist office in Rome, in regional offices, and in bookstores. Other self-catering options can be arranged through specialized agencies such as **Villas4you** and **Simply Travel** before you leave for Italy, but again, make sure you do this well in advance, as accommodations can be booked up months ahead.

There are also so-called *residenze*, found in the ENIT accommodation lists. These are halfway between hotels and apartments and normally offer cooking facilities and some sort of restaurant service.

For stays of several months or more, accommodation agencies for apartments in the city center, as well as the nearby countryside, can be found under *Immobiliari* in the *Pagine Gialle* (Yellow Pages).

Budget Accommodations

As well as the International Youth Hostels Association (**AIG** in Italy), tourist offices in the major cities have lists of hostels. Prices start at around €12 per person per night (€15 during peak season), and are much lower than even the cheapest *pensione*. Accom-

modation may be in single- or mixed-sex dormitories, though many hostels also have small private rooms. A room in a private house is another cheap option, often offering small but clean rooms. Guest house accommodations are available but are of variable quality.

The **Centro Turistico Studentesco** can help students find rooms in university accommodations across Italy. This is not limited to students, however, particularly in the summer when resident students are on vacation.

A peaceful alternative is to stay in a convent or monastery with guest accommodations. The rooms are clean, if a little spartan, and they are usually in a secluded area. Note that strict rules may be the price for a cheap room: most have early curfews and many will not admit members of the opposite sex even when with their spouses. There is no central agency dealing with these, but they are included in the ENIT accommodation lists for each region.

Mountain Refuges and Campsites

Basic accommodation in huts and refuges is available in mountainous areas where there are hiking trails. Most of these huts are owned and run by the **Club Alpino Italiano**, whose headquarters are in Milan.

Campsites abound in the mountains and around the

A boat carrying visitors' luggage to a hotel in Venice

coastal regions. Many of them offer basic accommodations in family-sized cabins *(bungalow)* as well as spaces for tents, RVs, and trailers, along with facilities such as water, electricity, and laundry. There is usually a restaurant, and, especially in campsites by the sea, there may also be sports facilities such as swimming pools, boat and water sports equipment rental, and tennis courts. The **Touring Club Italiano** publishes a good list of

A Park Spa Suite bedroom in the Park Hyatt Milano *(see p566)*

A high-altitude refuge in the Valsesia Alps

campsites with details of facilities for each one, as does **Federcampeggio**.

Disabled Travelers

In general, only newer hotels in Italy have special facilities for disabled travelers, although in many cases, older hotels will do all they can to accommodate people in wheelchairs by giving them downstairs rooms (when available) and help with elevators or stairs. It is best to contact the hotel of your choice directly before making a reservation, to check whether they are wheelchair accessible and what facilities they have *(for more information see pp616–17)*.

Recommended Hotels

The hotels listed in this guide-book have been chosen because they represent the best Italy has to offer in hospitality, service, value, or location. A huge variety of accommodation options is covered, from simple farmhouses and alpine chalets to family-run guest houses and luxury palaces.

Entries labeled DK Choice are outstanding in some way. They may be set in beautiful surroundings or in a historically important building, offer excellent service, have a romantic atmosphere, be particularly charming or environmentally friendly, or have a great spa. Whatever the reason it is a guarantee of a memorable stay.

DIRECTORY

Chain Hotels

Atahotels
Tel 066 964 69 64.
W atahotels.com

Best Western Hotels
Tel 800 820 080.
W bestwestern.it

Hyatt
Tel 800 872 021.
W hyatt.com

Marriott
Tel 800 876 022.
W marriott.com

NH Hoteles
Tel 848 390 227.
W nh-hotels.com

Relais & Châteaux
Tel 02 62 69 00 64.
W relaischateaux.com

Una Hotels and Resorts
Tel 800 60 61 62.
W unahotels.it

Reservations

ENIT
Via Marghera 2–6, 00185 Rome. **Tel** 06 497 11.
W enit.it

Italian State Tourist Board
1 Princes Street, London W1B 2AY. **Tel** 020 7408 1254. **W** italiantourist board.co.uk

Self-Catering and Agriturismo

Agriturismo
Corso Vittorio Emanuele II 101, 00186 Rome.

Tel 06 685 23 37.
W agriturist.it

Simply Travel
Tel 0871 231 40 50.
W simplytravel.co.uk

Villas4you
PO Box 1310, Maidstone ME14 9QH.
Tel 0800 096 3439.
W villas4you.co.uk

Budget Accommodations

AIG (Associazione Italiana Alberghi per la Gioventù)
Via Cavour 44, 00184 Rome. **Tel** 06 487 11 52.
W aighostels.com

Bed and Breakfast
W bed-and-breakfast.it

Centro Turistico Studentesco
Tel 06 462 04 31.
W cts.it

Italia Lodging
Tel 06 77 25 05 43.
W italialodging.com

Mountain Refuges and Campsites

Club Alpino Italiano
Via E. Petrella 19, Milan.
Tel 02 205 72 31. **W** cai.it

Federcampeggio
Via Vittorio Emanuele 11, 50041 Calenzano, Firenze.
Tel 055 88 23 91.
W federcampeggio.it

Touring Club Italiano
Corso Italia 10, 20122 Milano. **Tel** 02 852 61.
W touringclub.it

Where to Stay

Venice

CANNAREGIO: Al Saor €
B&B   **Map** 3 A4
Calle Zotti 3904/A, 30121
Tel *041 296 06 54*
W alsaor.com
Simple and elegant, this guesthouse offers cozy rooms and a friendly atmosphere.

CANNAREGIO: Hotel
Giorgione €€
Luxury   **Map** 3 B5
Calle dei Proverbi 4587, 30121
Tel *041 522 58 10*
W hotelgiorgione.com
Lovely old building, completely and charmingly refurbished.

CANNAREGIO: Palazzo
Abadessa €€
Historic   **Map** 3 A4
Calle Priuli 4011, 30131
Tel *041 24 137 84*
W abadessa.com
Charming 16th-century palace furnished with antiques and rich colors. Spacious rooms.

CANNAREGIO: Ca' Sagredo €€€
Historic   **Map** 3 A5
Campo Santa Sofia 4198, 30121
Tel *041 241 31 11*
W casagredohotel.com
Just across from Rialto market, this modernized 13th-century palazzo offers superb views.

CASTELLO: Locanda La Corte €€
Historic   **Map** 3 C5
Calle Bressana 6317, 30122
Tel *041 241 13 00*
W locandalacorte.it
Inviting rooms in a converted 16th-century palace with a charming courtyard.

CASTELLO: Metropole €€
Luxury   **Map** 8 D2
Riva degli Schiavoni 4149, 30122
Tel *041 520 50 44*
W hotelmetropole.com
The somewhat nondescript exterior belies the comforts within.

CASTELLO: Pensione Wildner €€
Pensione   **Map** 8 D2
Riva degli Schiavoni 4161, 30122
Tel *041 522 74 63*
W hotelwildner.com
Family-run establishment with wonderful views from the terrace.

CASTELLO: Londra Palace €€€
Boutique   **Map** 8 D2
Riva degli Schiavoni 4171, 30122
Tel *041 520 05 33*
W londrapalace.com

Excellent service and spacious, luxurious rooms. Splendid views of the lagoon and city.

DORSODURO: Instituto
Artigianelli €
Historic   **Map** 6 E4
Rio Terrà Foscarini 909/A, 30123
Tel *041 522 40 77*
W donorione-venezia.it
Religious institution offering simple, modern rooms with en suite bathrooms. Nice, quiet courtyard.

DORSODURO: Locanda
Ca' Zose €
B&B   **Map** 6 F4
Calle del Bastion 193/B, 30123
Tel *041 522 66 35*
W hotelcazose.com
Charming guesthouse run by two sisters with an eye for quality.

DORSODURO: Agli Alboretti €€
Pensione   **Map** 6 E4
Rio Terrà Foscarini 884, 30123
Tel *041 523 00 58*
W aglialboretti.com
Simple, comfortable rooms equipped with free minibar.

DORSODURO: Locanda
San Barnaba €€
Rooms with a view   **Map** 6 E4
Calle del Traghetto 2785–2786, 30123
Tel *041 241 12 33*
W locanda-sanbarnaba.com
The perfect place to return to after a hard day's sightseeing. Spacious foyer and spotless rooms, most overlooking the canal.

DORSODURO: Hotel
Pausania €€€
Historic   **Map** 6 D3
Fondamenta Gerardini 2824, 30123
Tel *041 522 20 83*
W hotelpausania.it

Elegant interiors and great views at the Cipriani hotel, Giudecca

Elegant light-filled rooms and a lovely veranda for breakfast.

GIUDECCA: Cipriani €€€
Luxury   **Map** 7 C5
Giudecca 10, 30133
Tel *041 520 77 44*
W hotelcipriani.com
Exquisite rooms in this Venice institution. There's a private launch to and from Piazza San Marco.

LIDO: Villa Mabapa €€
Rooms with a view
Riviera San Nicolò 16, 30126
Tel *041 526 05 90*
W villamabapa.com
Attractive period villas overlooking the Venice lagoon.

> ## DK Choice
>
> ### MAZZORBO: Venissa €€
> Pensione   **Map** 3 B4
> *Fondamenta Santa Caterina 3, 30170*
> **Tel** *041 527 22 81*
> W venissa.it
> A stylish option on a little known island for those who want a more exclusive Venetian experience. Rooms are modern and spacious. A plentiful breakfast is served in the restaurant, which is also open for lunch and dinner.

SAN MARCO: Bauer €€€
Luxury   **Map** 7 A3
Campo San Moisè 1459, 30124
Tel *041 520 70 22*
W bauerhotels.com
Beautifully decorated rooms and stunning views of the Grand Canal.

SAN MARCO: Europa &
Regina €€€
Luxury   **Map** 7 A3
Calle Larga XXII Marzo 2159, 30124
Tel *041 240 00 01*
W westineuropareginavenice.com
Panoramic terraces with magnificent views. Impeccable service.

SAN MARCO: Gritti Palace €€€
Luxury   **Map** 7 A3
Santa Maria del Giglio 2467, 30124
Tel *041 296 12 22*
W thegrittipalace.com
Iconic palazzo, dating back to 1475, with modern comforts.

SAN MARCO: Luna Hotel Baglioni
Luxury €€€
Map 7 B3
Calle Large dell'Ascension 1243, 30124
Tel *041 528 98 40*
w baglionihotels.com
Spacious rooms in a historic palazzo. Private jetty for guests.

SAN MARCO: Saturnia and International
Luxury €€€
Map 7 A3
Via XXII Marzo 2398, 30124
Tel *041 520 83 77*
w hotelsaturnia.it
Opulence wrapped in a simple setting. Antique furnishings and a pretty courtyard.

SAN MARCO: Splendid Venice
Luxury €€€
Map 7 B7
Mercerie 760, 30124
Tel *041 520 07 55*
w splendidvenice.starhotels.com
This hotel is comfortable and quiet, yet eclectic and vibrant. Well-stocked library and peaceful reading areas.

SAN POLO: Al Campaniel
B&B €
Map 6 E2
Calle del Campaniel 2889, 30125
Tel *041 275 07 49*
w alcampaniel.com
Clean and cozy guesthouse in a quiet street. The small apartment is great for families.

DK Choice

SANTA CROCE: Al Sole
Historic €€
Map 5 C1
Fondamenta Minotto 136, 30135
Tel *041 244 03 28*
w alsolehotels.com
Housed in Palazzo Marcello, a 15th-century palace with a beautiful façade and marble-floored reception area, this hotel offers well-appointed rooms. Enjoy the rich breakfast spread served in a patio garden.

SANTA CROCE: Hotel Falier
Charming €€
Map 5 C1
Salizzada San Pantalon 130, 30135
Tel *041 71 08 82*
w hotelfalier.com
This hotel is full of light, airy rooms and has a pretty wisteria-filled garden and helpful staff.

TORCELLO: Locanda Cipriani
Rooms with a view €€
Piazza Santa Fosca 29, 30012
Tel *041 73 01 50*
w locandacipriani.com
Comfortable old-world inn located far from the madding crowd. Famed for its discerning guests and quiet elegance.

Romantic natural setting of Hotel Cappella in Colfosco

The Veneto and Friuli

ASOLO: Albergo al Sole
Rooms with a view €€
Via Collegio 33, 31011
Tel *0423 95 13 32*
w albergoalsoleasolo.com
Pleasant, spacious rooms looking out over the town square.

ASOLO: Villa Cipriani
Historic €€
Via Canova 298, 31011
Tel *0423 52 34 11*
w villaciprianiasolo.com
Comfortable hotel in a 16th-century villa once home to poet Robert Browning.

CASTELROTTO: Cavallino d'Oro €
Spa hotel
Piazza Kraus 2, 39040
Tel *0471 70 63 37*
w cavallino.it
Charming hotel in a pretty setting with a cozy atmosphere.

CIVIDALE DEL FRIULI: La Cjase dai Toscans
B&B €
Corso Mazzini 15/1, 33043
Tel *349 076 52 88*
w lacjasedaitoscans.it
Friendly, well-positioned B&B with a terrace for summer breakfasts.

CIVIDALE DEL FRIULI: Locanda al Pomo d'Oro
Historic €
Piazzetta San Giovanni 20, 33043
Tel *0432 73 14 89*
w alpomodoro.it
Traditional family inn set in a quiet square in the historic center.

COLFOSCO: Hotel Cappella
Rooms with a view €€
Strada Pecei 17, 39033
Tel *0471 83 61 83*
w hotelcappella.com

A chalet in the Dolomites opened by the present owner's grandfather. Various styles of suite to choose from.

CONEGLIANO: Il Faè
Rooms with a view €
Via Faè 1, San Pietro di Feletto, 31020
Tel *0438 78 71 17*
w ilfae.com
Pleasant guesthouse surrounded by vineyards. Good views over the foothills of the Alps.

CORNO DI ROSAZZO: Villa Butussi
Rooms with a view €
Via San Martino 29, Visinale dello Judrio, 33040
Tel *0432 75 99 22*
w butussi.it
A 17th-century villa tastefully converted into a guesthouse that offers both rooms and apartments.

CORTINA D'AMPEZZO: Cristallo Hotel
Luxury €€€
Via R. Minardi 42, 32043
Tel *0436 88 11 11*
w cristallo.it
Beautifully presented rooms, some with balconies that have views of the Alps. Excellent facilities include a spa and a nine-hole golf course.

CORTINA D'AMPEZZO: Montana
Pensione €€€
Corso Italia 94, 32043
Tel *0436 86 04 98*
w cortina-hotel.com
Quiet hotel with simple, tasteful rooms and a hearty breakfast.

FOLLINA: Villa Abbazia
Historic €€
Via Martiri della Libertà 9, 31051
Tel *0438 97 12 77*
w hotelabbazia.it
Delightful 17th-century villa with spacious rooms decorated in English country-house style.

For more information on types of hotels *see p561*

GARDA: Locanda San Vigilio €€€
Rooms with a view
Località San Vigilio 17, 37016
Tel *045 725 66 88*
W locanda-sanvigilio.it
Exuding old-world charm, this
is one of the loveliest, most
exclusive hotels on Lake Garda.

**MALCESINE: Sailing Center
Hotel** €€
Rooms with a view
Via Gardesana 187, 37018
Tel *045 740 00 55*
W hotelsailing.com
Located on the shores of Lake
Garda, this hotel has comfortable
rooms and its own private beach.

PADUA: Belludi 37 €€
Boutique
Via L. Beato Belludi 37, 35124
Tel *049 66 56 33*
W belludi37.it
Steps from the Basilica del Santo,
this hotel is decorated with a
flair of contemporary design.

PADUA: Augustus Terme €€€
Spa Hotel
Viale Stazione 150, 35036
Tel *049 79 32 00*
W hotelaugustus.com
Comfortable hotel with opulent
rooms, thermal swimming pools,
and a reputable restaurant.

**PESCHIERA DEL GARDA:
Active Hotel Paradiso & Golf** €
Boutique
Via Coppo 2/b, 37014
Tel *045 640 58 11*
W golfhotelparadiso.it
A stylish hotel with pleasant, airy
rooms. Amenities include an
18-hole golf course.

POVOLETTO: La Faula €€
Agriturismo
Via Faula 5, 33040
Tel *334 399 67 34*
W faula.com
Lovingly restored farmhouse
surrounded by vineyards and
farmland. The rooms are spacious.

Comfortable furnishings at Hotel Laurin
in Bolzano

**TORRI DEL BENACO: Hotel
Gardesana** €
Historic
Piazza Calderini 5, 37010
Tel *045 722 54 11*
W gardesana.eu
A 15th-century former harbor-
master's house converted into
a friendly, comfortable hotel.

TREVISO: Locanda da Renzo €
B&B
Strada Terraglio 108, 31100
Tel *0422 40 20 68*
W locandadarenzo.it
A small family-run guesthouse
with a home-cooked evening
meal available on request.

TRIESTE: Le Corderie €€
Boutique
Via di Calvola 43, 34143
Tel *040 322 92 77*
W lecorderiehotel.it
You're assured of a warm welcome
at this comfortable, modern hotel.
Great breakfast spread.

**UDINE: Hotel Clocchiatti &
Next** €€
Boutique
Via Cividale 29, 33100
Tel *0432 50 50 47*
W hotelclocchiatti.it
Choose between rooms with
traditional period decor or
modern fittings.

DK Choice

**VALDOBBIADENE: Villa
Barberina** €€
Historic
Via Roma 2, 31049
Tel *0423 97 24 79*
W villabarberina.it
In past centuries, wealthy
Venetians would live part of the
year in their country estates. This
hotel gives guests an idea of the
opulence of such residences.
This handsome 18th-century
villa has elegantly decorated
rooms, magnificent grounds,
and a well-stocked library.

VERONA: Giulietta e Romeo €€
Charming
Vicolo Tre Marchetti 3, 37121
Tel *045 800 35 54*
W giuliettaeromeo.com
The rooms are comfortable and
bright. The breakfast is hearty.

VERONA: Il Torcolo €€
Charming
Vicolo Listone 3, 37121
Tel *045 800 75 12*
W hoteltorcolo.it
Small, family-run hotel with
simple rooms and a pleasant
terrace where breakfast is served.

**VICENZA: Glam Boutique
Hotel** €€€
Boutique
Via A. Giuriolo 10, 36100
Tel *0444 32 64 58*
W gboutiquehotel.com
Stylish hotel with a perfect blend
of traditional and modern decor.

Trentino–Alto Adige

BOLZANO: Hotel Laurin €€
Historic
Via Laurin 4, 39100
Tel *0471 31 10 00*
W laurin.it
Marvel at the original Art Nouveau
features in this charming hotel.

BOLZANO: Luna-Mondschein €€
Spa hotel
Via Piave 15, 39100
Tel *0471 97 56 42*
W hotel-luna.it
This stylish hotel in the city
center has fabulous grounds.

BRESSANONE: Hotel Dominik €
Rooms with a view
Via Terzo di Sotto 13, 39042
Tel *0472 83 01 44*
W hoteldominik.com
Furnished with antiques, most
rooms boast views of the river.

**FIE ALLO SCILIAR: Edelansitz
Zimmerlehen** €
Agriturismo
Via Kühbach 15, Obervöls, 39050
Tel *0471 72 50 53*
W zimmerlehen.it
A 13th-century manor farm with
four towerlike buildings converted
into simple apartments. Enjoy a
breakfast of farm produce.

**MERANO: Hotel Castel
Fragsburg** €€
Rooms with a view
Via Fragsburg 3, 39012
Tel *0473 24 40 71*
W fragsburg.com
This hotel boasts fine views of the
mountains and the town below.

DK Choice

MERANO: Ottmanngut €€
Boutique
Via Verdi 18, 39012
Tel *0473 44 96 56*
W ottmanngut.it
Surrounded by lush greenery,
this family-run guesthouse is
within walking distance of the
spa town. The suites are
elegantly decorated with
period furnishings and modern
conveniences. There is also a
lovely garden to relax in.

**ORTISEI: Adler Dolomiti Spa
& Sport Resort** €€€
Spa hotel
Via Rezia 7, 39046
Tel *0471 77 50 01*
W adler-dolomiti.com
A good choice for all seasons.
Excellent service and facilities,
including vast gardens.

**REDAGNO: Berghotel
Zirmerhof** €€
Agriturismo
Oberradein 59, 39040
Tel *0471 88 72 15*
W zirmerhof.com
Simple accommodations in a
beautiful mountain setting.

TRENTO: Accademia €€
Historic
Vicolo Colico 4-6, 38122
Tel *0461 23 36 00*
W accademiahotel.it
Restored medieval building with
a pleasant courtyard.

Lombardy

APRICA: Relais Volla Brioschi €€
Boutique
Via Valeriana 187, 25040
Tel *0342 74 56 81*
W relaisvillabrioschi.com
A luxury Art Nouveau–style
country house with a garden,
parking, and its own restaurant.

BELLAGIO: Hotel Florence €€
Spa hotel
Piazza Mazzini 46, 22021
Tel *031 95 03 42*
W hotelflorencebellagio.it
This lakeside hotel offers stylish
decor, canopy beds, claw-foot
tubs, and a gourmet restaurant.

BELLAGIO: Hotel Suisse €€
Historic
Piazza Mazzini 8/10, 22021
Tel *031 95 17 55*
W hotelsuissebellagio.com
This lakeside hotel has an
excellent restaurant.

**BELLAGIO: Grand Hotel
Villa Serbelloni** €€€
Luxury
Via Roma 1, 22021
Tel *031 95 02 16*
W villaserbelloni.com
The hotel boasts frescoed ceilings
and views of Lake Como.

BERGAMO: Hotel Gombit €€€
Design
Via Mario Lupo 6, 24129
Tel *035 24 70 09*
W gombithotel.it
A concept hotel with distinctive
architecture and interior design.

The stately Grand Hotel Villa Serbelloni in Bellagio

BORMIO: Hotel Cristallo €€
Spa hotel
Via Milano 44, 23032
Tel *0342 90 27 00*
W cristallohotelresidence.it
A short stroll from ski lifts and
thermal baths, this hotel offers
a large garden, a ski room, and
a games room.

BRATTO: Hotel Milano €€
Spa hotel
Via Silvio Pellico 3, 24020
Tel *0346 31 211*
W hotelmilano.com
Large Alpine resort hotel and spa.
Plenty of comfort and style.

BRESCIA: Park Hotel Cà Noa €
Rooms with a view
Via Triumplina 66, 25123
Tel *030 39 87 62*
W hotelcanoa.it
Situated in a quiet park, this hotel
has an outdoor pool.

BRESCIA: AC Hotel Brescia €€
Design
Via Giulio Quinto Stefana 3, 25126
Tel *030 24 05 511*
W hotelacbrescia.com
This minimalist design hotel with
modern facilities has a fitness
center and a gourmet restaurant.

CERNOBBIO: Villa d'Este €€€
Luxury
Via Regina 40, 22012
Tel *031 34 81*
W villadeste.it
An elegant and sumptuous
hotel set in 25 acres (10 ha)
of lush parkland.

**CERVESINA: Hotel Castello
di San Gaudenzio** €€
Historic
Via Mulino 1, 27050
Tel *0383 33 31*
W castellosangaudenzio.com
A 15th-century castle boasting
romantic rooms, a gym, and a
pool, plus a top-class restaurant.

COLOGNE: Cappuccini €€
Historic
Via Cappuccini 54, 25033
Tel *030 715 72 54*
W cappuccini.it
This former monastery has a
wellness center, an outdoor pool,
and a restaurant.

COMO: Hotel Firenze €
Rooms with a view
Piazza Volta 16, 22100
Tel *031 30 03 33*
W albergofirenze.it
A renovated Neo-Classical hotel
situated in a pedestrianized
square in the town center.

COMO: In Riva al Lago €
B&B
Via Crespi 4, 22100
Tel *031 30 23 33*
W inrivaallago.com
Basic, spotless hotel that also
offers self-contained apartments.

**CREMONA: Dellearti Design
Hotel** €€
Boutique
Via Bonomelli 8, 26100
Tel *0372 231 31*
W dellearti.com
Accommodations with artsy
touches. Close to the cathedral
and the medieval bell tower.

**DESENZANO DEL GARDA:
Park Hotel** €€
Luxury
Lungolago Cesare Battisti 19, 25015
Tel *030 914 34 95*
W parkhotelonline.it
Elegant hotel with well-furnished
rooms, some with lake views.

**GARDONE RIVIERA:
Villa del Sogno** €€€
Historic
Via Zanardelli 107, 25083
Tel *0365 29 01 81*
W villadelsogno.it
A Neo-Classical villa with tennis
courts and an outdoor pool.

For more information on types of hotels *see p561*

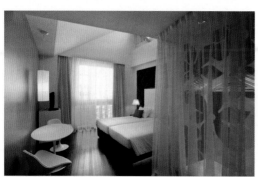

Stylish minimalist decor at Nhow Milano in Milan

GARDONE RIVIERA: Villa Fiordaliso €€€
Luxury
Corso Zanardelli 132, 25083
Tel *0365 201 58*
W *villafiordaliso.it*
Beautiful three-story villa overlooking Lake Garda. Furnished with eclectic decor with a floral theme.

GARGNANO: Villa Sostaga €€€
Boutique
Via Sostaga 19, 25084
Tel *0365 79 12 18*
W *villasostaga.it*
This family-run hotel offers large rooms with modern facilities and an Art Nouveau dining room.

ISEO: Iseolago €€
Spa hotel
Via Colombera 2, 25049
Tel *030 98 891*
W *iseolagohotel.it*
Extensive gardens with swimming pools, a tennis court, and a children's playground.

DK Choice
LIMONE SUL GARDA: Hotel Capo Reamol €
Budget
Via IV Novembre 92, 25010
Tel *0365 95 40 40*
W *hotelcaporeamol.it*
This hotel's idyllic location offers breathtaking views of Lake Garda. Rooms are compact but clean and the staff are friendly. A fitness room and spa services are available to guests, along with a private beach and a swimming pool. Excellent value for money.

LIVIGNO: Hotel Capriolo €
Pensione
Via Borch 96, 23030
Tel *0342 99 67 23*
W *capriololivigno.com*
Family-run hotel located close to ski lifts and hiking paths. Offers traditional *Valtellina* cuisine.

MANTUA: Casa Poli €€
Boutique
Corso Giuseppe Garibaldi 32, 46100
Tel *0376 28 81 70*
W *hotelcasapoli.it*
Near the harbor, this hotel has cozy rooms and minimalist decor.

MANTUA: Hotel La Favorita €€
Business
Via S. Cognetti De Martiis 1, 46100
Tel *0376 25 47 11*
W *hotellafavorita.it*
A modern and elegant hotel with an excellent restaurant.

DK Choice
MILAN: Antica Locanda Leonardo €€
Boutique
Corso Magenta 78, 20123
Tel *02 48 01 41 97*
W *anticalocandaleonardo.com*
Peacefully located in an elegant 19th-century palazzo, this family-run hotel has well-decorated rooms overlooking a charming and picturesque inner garden. The staff are helpful and friendly.

MILAN: Antica Locanda Solferino €€
Boutique
Via Castelfidardo 2, 20121
Tel *02 65 70 12 9*
W *anticalocandasolferino.it*
A welcoming guesthouse with eclectic old-world charm.

MILAN: Ata Hotel Executive €€
Business
Viale Sturzo 45, 20100
Tel *02 62 941*
W *atahotels.it/executive*
Rooms are spacious, and facilities include a gym and sun terrace.

MILAN: Nhow Milano €€
Design
Via Tortona 35, 20144
Tel *02 48 98 861*

W *nh-hotels.it*
This hotel boasts an interesting collection of contemporary art.

MILAN: Una Hotel Century €€
Business
Via Fabio Filzi 25/B, 20100
Tel *02 67 50 41*
W *unahotels.it*
Modern facilities are available in this contemporary hotel.

MILAN: Hotel Manzoni €€€
Luxury
Via Santo Spirito 20, 20121
Tel *02 76 00 57 00*
W *hotelmanzoni.com*
Beautiful hotel set in a quiet, yet central location.

MILAN: Park Hyatt Milano €€€
Luxury
Via Tommaso Grossi 1, 20121
Tel *02 88 21 12 34*
W *milan.park.hyatt.com*
Housed in a former bank, this elegant hotel has a spa and gym.

PAVIA: Hotel Italia €
Pensione
Corso Partigiani 48, 27012
Tel *0382 92 56 56*
W *italiacertosa.pavia.it*
Family-run hotel in an 18th-century farmhouse. Rooms are simply but tastefully decorated with antique pieces.

RANCO: Il Sole di Ranco €€
Rooms with a view
Piazza Venezia 5, 21020
Tel *0331 97 65 07*
W *ilsolediranco.it*
Overlooking Lake Maggiore, this hotel boasts a private garden and an infinity pool.

RIVA DI SOLTO: Albergo Ristorante Miranda €
Pensione
Via Cornello 8, 24060
Tel *035 98 60 21*
W *albergomiranda.it*
This family-run guesthouse has views over Lake Iseo and comfortable rooms with balconies.

RODIGO: Hotel Villa dei Tigli €€
Historic
Via Cantarana 20/I, 46040
Tel *0376 65 06 91*
W *hotelvilladeitigli.it*
A 20th-century former aristocratic villa with an outdoor pool and a high-class terrace restaurant.

SALÒ: Romantik Hotel Laurin €€
Boutique
Viale Landi 9, 25087
Tel *0365 22 022*
W *laurinhotelsalo.com*
A romantic lakeside villa with a restaurant and an outdoor pool.

SIRMIONE: Hotel Catullo €€
Historic
Piazza Flaminia 7, 25019
Tel *030 990 58 11*
w hotelcatullo.it
This hotel offers rooms with
balconies and a rooftop terrace.

TREMEZZO: Hotel la Darsena €€
Rooms with a view
Via Regina 3, 22019
Tel *0344 431 66*
w hotelladarsena.it
A lakeside hotel-cum-restaurant
in a great location for visiting
nearby villas and other sights.

**TREMEZZO: Grand Hotel
Tremezzo** €€€
Historic
Via Regina 8, 22019
Tel *0344 424 91*
w grandhoteltremezzo.com
A prestigious lakeside hotel, in
Art Nouveau style; great facilities.

VARENNA: Hotel Du Lac €€
Rooms with a view
Via del Prestino 11, 23829
Tel *0341 83 02 38*
w albergodulac.com
A peaceful hotel at the water's
edge with enchanting views.

Valle d'Aosta and Piedmont

ACQUI TERME: Hotel Rondò €
Spa hotel
Viale Acquedotto Romano 44, 15011
Tel *0144 32 28 89*
w albergorondo.it
Rooms are bright and basic, and
the staff friendly and helpful.

**ACQUI TERME: Hotel Talice
Radicati** €€
Historic
Piazza Conciliazione 12, 15011
Tel *0144 32 86 11*
w taliceradicati.com
The rooms in this 15th-century
palazzo are elegant and refined.

DK Choice

**ALBA: Villa La Meridiana
Cascina Reinè** €
Agriturismo
Località Altavilla 9, 12051
Tel *0173 44 01 12*
w villalameridianaalba.it
This 18th-century villa benefits
from enchanting views over the
surrounding vineyards. Rooms
are comfortable and furnished
with the family's antique collection, and there are three cozy
apartments with small kitchens.

Guests can participate in
harvesting the crop from the
estate's vineyards and hunt for
truffles in the woods.

**ALESSANDRIA: Hotel Alli
Due Buoi Rossi** €€
Historic
Via Cavour 32, 15121
Tel *0131 51 71 71*
w hotelalliduebuoirossi.com
A welcoming and friendly hotel
with a renowned *trattoria*.

AOSTA: Hotel Village Aosta €€
Resort
Località Torrent de Maillod 1, 11020
Tel *0165 77 49 11*
w hotelvillageaosta.it
This small but charming hotel
offers both rooms and chalets.

ARONA: Hotel Giardino €
Pensione
Corso Repubblica 1, 28041
Tel *0322 459 94*
w giardinoarona.com
A comfortable hotel with splendid
views across Lake Maggiore from
the large terrace and grounds.

**BARDONECCHIA: Hotel
Jafferau** €€
Resort
Località Fregiusia, 10052
Tel *0122 998 99*
w hoteljafferau.it
Well-equipped hotel with a pool,
a sauna, and hydromassage.

DK Choice

BAVENO: Hotel Splendid €€
Resort
Via Sempione 12, 28831
Tel *0323 92 41 27*
w zaccherahotels.com
This elegant hotel has its own
private beach (which has sun
beds and a private jetty), and an
outdoor pool. The rooms are

Stone steps leading to the charming Villa
La Meridiana Cascina Reinè in Alba

comfortable and well
appointed – most have
balconies with lakeside views.
Helpful and attentive staff
provide excellent service.

**CANNOBIO: Residenza
Patrizia** €
Pensione
Viale Vittorio Veneto 37, 28822
Tel *0323 73 97 13*
w residenzapatrizia.com
Inviting rooms and self-contained
apartments as well, plus amenities
such as a sauna and a pool.

**ORTO SAN GIULIO: Hotel
San Rocco** €€
Historic
Via Gippini 11, 28016
Tel *0322 91 19 77*
w hotelsanrocco.it
Unwind at the lakeside pool or
enjoy the excellent restaurant,
and views of San Giulio Island.

STRESA: Hotel La Palma €€
Resort
Lungolago Umberto I 33, 28838
Tel *0323 324 01*
w hlapalma.it
This hotel offers a private beach,
an outdoor pool, spa facilities,
and a terrace bar. There is also
a well-regarded restaurant.

TORTONA: Villa Giulia €
Boutique
Corso Alessandria 7/A, 15057
Tel *0131 86 23 96*
w villagiulia-hotel.com
Former private villa, with elegant
decor. Homey atmosphere and
an ample breakfast.

TURIN: Albergo Serenella €
Pensione
Via Tarino 4, 10124
Tel *011 83 70 31*
w albergoserenella.com
This family-run establishment has
clean and basic rooms at unbeat-
able prices for the city center.

**TURIN: Hotel Conte
Biancamano** €
Pensione
Corso Vittorio Emanuele 73, 10128
Tel *011 562 32 81*
w hotelcontebiancamano.it
An intimate hotel with elegant
decor located on the third floor
of a 19th-century palazzo.

TURIN: Grand Hotel Sitea €€
Luxury
Via Carlo Alberto 35, 10123
Tel *011 517 01 71*
w grandhotelsitea.net
Set in a Neo-Classical palazzo,
this place offers elegant suites
and a top-class restaurant.

For more information on types of hotels *see p561*

TURIN: NH Lingotto Tech €€
Design
Via Nizza 230, 10126
Tel *011 664 20 00*
W nh-hotels.com
A contemporary hotel located in the Lingotto Building, once a huge Fiat factory.

TURIN: Turin Golden Palace €€€
Luxury
Via dell'Arcivescovado 18, 10121
Tel *011 551 21 11*
W goldenpalace.it
This hotel, set in a 19th-century palazzo, offers a spa with a pool, sauna, and fitness center.

VARALLO SESIA: Albergo Sacro Monte €
Pensione
Località Sacro Monte 14, 13019
Tel *0163 542 54*
W sacromontealbergo.it
A comfortable hotel with simple rooms and a small private garden.

Liguria

DK Choice

CAMOGLI: Locanda I Tre Merli €€
Rooms with a view
Via Scalo 5, 6032
Tel *0185 77 67 52*
W locandaitremerli.com
Located right on the enchanting fishing port of Camogli, this cozy hotel offers wonderful views and personalized service. Room amenities include basic cooking facilities. A small spa area offers a Jacuzzi and a steam bath. Ferries to Portofino and the Cinque Terre are nearby. Parking is available upon request.

CAMOGLI: Villa Rosmarino €€
Rooms with a view
Via Figari 38, 16032
Tel *0185 77 15 80*
W villarosmarino.com
At the foot of Monte di Portofino, this villa has an outdoor pool.

CAMOGLI: Cenobio dei Dogi €€€
Luxury
Via Nicolò Cuneo 34, 16032
Tel *0185 72 41*
W cenobio.it
Built for the Doges of Genoa, this 17th-century villa houses a vast hotel with a private beach.

FINALE LIGURE: Punta Est €€€
Luxury
Via Aurelia 1, 17024
Tel *019 60 06 11*
W puntaest.com

An 18th-century villa with superb views over the Ligurian bay.

GARLENDA: La Meridiana €€
Resort
Via ai Castelli, 17033
Tel *0182 58 02 71*
W lameridianaresort.com
This relaxing country house–style hotel is perfect for walking vacations and outdoor activities.

GENOA: Hotel Villa Pagoda €€
Rooms with a view
Via Capolungo 15, 16167
Tel *010 372 61 61*
W villapagoda.it
This luxurious 19th-century villa is only steps from the coast.

ISOLA PALMARIA: Locanda Lorena €€
Rooms with a view
Via Cavour 4, 19025
Tel *0187 79 23 70*
W locandalorena.com
A small beach hotel accessible by stylish Venetian motorboats.

LEVANTO: Hotel Stella Maris €€
Boutique
Via Marconi 4, 19015
Tel *0187 80 82 58*
W hotelstellamaris.it
Close to the beach, this place is exquisitely decorated.

MANAROLA: Ca' d'Andrean €
Pensione
Via Discovolo 101, 19017
Tel *0187 92 00 40*
W cadandrean.it
This family-run guesthouse serves breakfast alfresco in summer.

MONTEROSSO: Hotel Marina €
Pensione
Via Buranco 40, 19016
Tel *0187 81 76 13*

Charming views from the vibrant Locanda I Tre Merli, Camogli

W hotelmarina5terre.com
Cooking lessons are available on request from this quiet hotel.

NERVI: Villa Pagoda €€
Boutique
Via Capolungo 15, 16167
Tel *010 32 32 00*
W villapagoda.it
An elegant, romantic hotel with Oriental touches. Opulent interiors and an excellent restaurant.

OSPEDALETTI: Hotel Firenze €
Rooms with a view
Corso Regina Margherita 97, 18014
Tel *0184 68 92 21*
W firenze.azurline.com
A small hillside hotel with basic but cheerful rooms, most of which have balconies.

PORTO VENERE: Hotel della Baia €
Rooms with a view
Via Lungomare 111, 19025
Tel *0187 79 07 97*
W baiahotel.com
All rooms have balconies and views over the bay. There's an outdoor pool and a restaurant.

PORTOFINO: Splendido €€€
Luxury
Salita Baratta 16, 16034
Tel *0185 26 78 01*
W hotelsplendido.com
Housed in a former monastery, this hotel has elegantly furnished rooms, many with private terraces.

RAPALLO: Hotel Stella €
Rooms with a view
Via Aurelia Ponente 6, 16035
Tel *0185 503 67*
W hotelstella-riviera.com
This small hotel lies in the center of Rapallo, close to the beach and seafront promenade.

RAPALLO: Hotel Italia e Lido €€
Rooms with a view
Lungomare Castello 1, 16035
Tel *0185 504 94*
W italiaelido.com
Overlooking the Gulf of Tigullio, this hotel has bright, airy rooms.

SANREMO: Hotel Nazionale €€
Rooms with a view
Corso Matteotti 3, 18038
Tel *0184 57 75 77*
W hotelnazionalesanremo.com
A high level of service and classically furnished rooms.

SANREMO: Royal Hotel €€€
Luxury
Corso Imperatrice 80, 18038
Tel *0184 53 91*
W royalhotelsanremo.com
Located on the seafront, this place is renowned for its restaurants.

SESTRI LEVANTE: Hotel Helvetia €€
Boutique
Via Cappuccini 43, 16039
Tel *0185 411 75*
W hotelhelvetia.it/
This hotel boasts its own private beach, garden, and solarium.

VENTIMIGLIA: La Riserva di Castel d'Appio €€
Rooms with a view
Via Peidaigo 71, 18039
Tel *0184 22 95 33*
W lariserva.it
Enjoy panoramic views over the Italian Riviera and the Côte d'Azur at this hotel. Excellent service.

Emilia-Romagna

BOLOGNA: Delle Drapperie €
Pensione
Via Drapperie 5, 40124
Tel *051 223 955*
W albergodrapperie.com
Decoratively painted ceilings and luxurious bathrooms characterize this well-priced option.

BOLOGNA: Il Guercino €
Boutique
Via Luigi Serra 7, 40129
Tel *051 369 893*
W guercino.it
An Indian flavor prevails at this charming hotel, which has two solariums and a relaxation area.

BOLOGNA: Indipendenza Suite €
Pensione
Via dell'Indipendenza 30, 40121
Tel *331 4575 920*
W indipendenza-suite.it
Four independent apartments decorated in simple, classic style.

BOLOGNA: Panorama Hotel €
Budget
Via Giovanni Livraghi 1, 40121
Tel *051 221 802*
W hotelpanoramabologna.it
A clean and central option; some rooms have a private bath.

BOLOGNA: Commercianti €€
Historic
Via De' Pignattari 11, 40124
Tel *051 745 75 11*
W bolognarthotels.it
A 13th-century building bursting with romantic details.

BOLOGNA: Corona d'Oro €€
Romantic
Via Guglielmo Oberdan 12, 40126
Tel *051 7457 611*
W hco.it
Historic hotel with an eclectic style: from medieval to Art Deco.

Outdoor swimming pool at La Riserva di Castel d'Appio in Ventimiglia

BOLOGNA: Il Convento dei Fiori di Seta €€
Historic
Via Orfeo 34, 40124
Tel *051 272 039*
W ilconventodeifioridiseta.com
Ten well-appointed rooms in this converted medieval convent.

BOLOGNA: Roma €€
Pensione
Via Massimo D'Azeglio 9, 40123
Tel *051 231 330*
W hotelroma.biz
Quaint rooms, ask for one of the few with balconies.

DK Choice

BOLOGNA: Grand Hotel Majestic €€€
Luxury
Via Indipendenza 8, 40121
Tel *051 225 445*
W grandhotelmajestic.
duetorrihotels.com
This legendary hotel expertly combines opulent old-world elegance with modern comfort and hospitality. Each room is individually decorated with lush fabrics and antique furniture. Breakfast is served on the romantic rooftop terrace with sweeping views of the city. The dining room boasts beautiful frescoes.

BOLOGNA: Royal Hotel Carlton €€€
Luxury
Via Montebello 8, 40121
Tel *051 249 361*
W monrifhotels.it/RoyalCarltonHotel
Elegant, grand hotel with a fully-equipped wellness center.

FERRARA: Principessa Leonora €€
Boutique
Via Mascheraio 39, 44121
Tel *0532 20 60 20*
W principessaleonora.it

A 16th-century residence exquisitely decorated with antique French tapestries and traditional furniture.

FERRARA: Duchessa Isabella €€€
Historic
Via Palestro 70, 44121
Tel *0532 20 21 21*
W duchessaisabella.it
Minute attention to detail in both decor and service. Rooms are sumptuously furnished.

MODENA: Daunia €
Pensione
Via del Pozzo 158, 41125
Tel *059 37 11 82*
W hoteldaunia.it
A simple, modern building with restaurant. Breakfast is served in the garden, weather permitting.

MODENA: Canalgrande €€€
Historic
Corso Canal Grande 6, 41100
Tel *059 21 71 60*
W canalgrandehotel.it
Housed in a former convent and with fresh, Neo-Classical decor.

PARMA: Button €
Budget
Borgo della Salina 7, 43121
Tel *0521 20 80 39*
W hotelbutton.it
Courteous service makes up for the basic accommodations.

PARMA: Stendhal €€
Romantic
Via Giambattista Bodoni 3, 43121
Tel *0521 20 80 57*
W hotelstendhal.it
Eclectically decorated rooms in a centrally located old palazzo.

PIACENZA: San Francesco €
Pensione
Galleria San Francesco 2, 29121
Tel *0523 32 66 88*
Excellent location and prices for spotlessly clean accommodations.

For more information on types of hotels *see p561*

PIACENZA GENEPRETO:
La Pobiella €€
Agriturismo
Località Pobiella 16, 29010
Tel *347 22 12 91*
This rustic stone villa is ideal for
a relaxed hillside vacation.

RAVENNA: Sant'Andrea €
Boutique
Via Carlo Cattaneo 33, 48121
Tel *0544 21 55 64*
W santandreahotel.com
A converted convent with a
tranquil cloister-garden.

RAVENNA: Cappello €€
Romantic
Via IV Novembre 41, 48121
Tel *0544 21 98 13*
W albergocappello.it
The rooms in this exquisite hotel
have coffered ceilings.

RIMINI: Acasamia €
Budget
Viale Renato Parisano 34, 47921
Tel *0541 39 13 70*
W hotelacasamia.com
Colorful rooms, and located
a short stroll from the beach.

RIMINI: Grand Hotel Rimini €€€
Luxury
Parco Federico Fellini 1, 47900
Tel *0541 560 00*
W grandhotelrimini.com
Deluxe seaside establishment
made famous by Federico Fellini.

Florence

Antica Dimora Firenze €
B&B **Map** 2 D3/4
Via San Gallo 72/r, 50129
Tel *055 462 72 96*
W anticadimorafirenze.it

Pleasantly bright, large rooms at the Relais
Uffizi in Florence

Canopy beds and antique
furniture set this B&B apart.

Palazzo Guadagni €
Historic **Map** 5 B5
Piazza di Santo Spirito 9, 50125
Tel *055 265 83 76*
W palazzoguadagni.com
Fantastic service, a great location,
and reasonable prices.

Relais Il Campanile €
B&B **Map** 6 E1
Via Ricasoli 10, 50125
Tel *055 21 16 88*
W relaiscampanile.it
Quaint rooms with wrought iron
accents in a 17th-century palazzo.

Residenza Johanna €
Pensione **Map** 2 D3
Via Bonifacio Lupo 14, 50129
Tel *055 48 18 96*
W johanna.it
This tiny and charming hotel is
fantastic value. Free parking.

Brunelleschi €€
Historic **Map** 6 D2
Piazza Sant'Elisabetta 3, 50122
Tel *055 27 37 52*
W hotelbrunelleschi.it
Located in a Byzantine tower, this
place offers classy, opulent rooms.

David €€
Pensione **Map** 4 E3
Viale Michelangiolo 1, 50125
Tel *055 681 16 95*
W davidhotel.com
Some rooms have balconies that
look out over leafy Oltrarno in
this family-owned guesthouse.

Grifone €€
Business
Via Gaetano Pilati 20, 50136
Tel *055 67 74 74*
W hotelgrifonefirenze.com
Comfortable and spacious rooms,
some with a kitchenette.

Hotel Home €€
Boutique **Map** 4 F2
Piazza Piave 3, 50122
Tel *055 24 36 68*
W hhflorence.it
All white and extremely elegant
decor in this stylish hotel.

DK Choice

Relais Uffizi €€
Romantic **Map** 6 D4
Chiasso del Buco 16, 50122
Tel *055 267 62 46*
W relaisuffizi.it
Located behind the Piazza della
Sugnoria, this affordable hotel
offers fantastic quality for the
price. All rooms are large and
charmingly decorated, and

several have canopy beds. The
quaint, spacious bathrooms are
spotlessly clean and may have
bathtubs. The breakfast room
looks out onto the Piazza.

Four Seasons Hotel Firenze €€€
Luxury **Map** 2 E4
Borgo Pinti 99, 50121
Tel *055 262 61*
W fourseasons.com/florence
The epitome of elegance, with
silk wall hangings, frescoes, and
bas-reliefs. Impeccable service.

Grand Hotel Minerva €€€
Historic **Map** 5 B2
*Piazza di Santa Maria Novella 16,
50123*
Tel *055 272 30*
W grandhotelminerva.com
A panoramic terrace with a pool
gives a modern touch to one
of the city's oldest hotels.

The Westin Excelsior €€€
Luxury **Map** 5 A2
Piazza d'Ognissanti 3, 50123
Tel *055 271 51*
W westinflorence.com
Opulent rooms, some with
balconies that have views of
the Arno. The roof terrace is
exquisitely presented.

Tuscany

DK Choice

AREZZO: Badia di Pomaio €€
Boutique
Loc. Pomaio 4, 52100
Tel *0575 37 14 07*
W badiadipomaio.it
This superbly converted
17th-century abbey is situated
in a picturesque spot amidst
lush gardens with a swimming
pool and panoramic views
of the medieval town below.
Comfortable and quiet rooms
with elegant furnishings. The
staff are warm and hospitable.

AREZZO: Graziella Patio Hotel €€
Boutique
Via Cavour 23, 52100
Tel *0575 40 19 62*
W hotelpatio.it
Charming hotel with rooms in
African and Far Eastern styles.

CORTONA: Italia €
Budget
Via Ghibellina 5/7, 52044
Tel *0575 63 02 54*
W hotelitaliacortona.com
Excellent value at this lovely
central spot full of character.

CORTONA: San Michele €€
Historic
Via Guelfa 15, 52044
Tel *0575 60 43 48*
w hotelsanmichele.net
Modern comfort in Renaissance
setting. Very classy decor.

DK Choice

**ELBA MARCIANA: Cernia
Isola Botanica** €€
Rooms with a view
Via San Gaetano 23, 57030
Tel *0565 90 82 10*
w hotelcernia.it
A lush, flower-filled park and
botanical garden surround this
charming hotel. Rooms are
spacious and minimalist, with
interesting design elements.
There is a freshwater swimming
pool and wellness center.
Situated a short walk from
Capo Sant'Andra, the location
is hard to beat.

ELBA SPARTAIA: Desiree €€
Rooms with a view
Spartaia, Procchio, 57030
Tel *0565 90 73 11*
w htdesiree.it
Clean rooms and private beach
access at this comfortable hotel.

LUCCA: Piccolo Hotel Puccini €
Pensione
Via di Poggio 9, 55100
Tel *0583 554 21*
w hotelpuccini.com
The prices may be low but you get
warm service and charming rooms.

**LUCCA: Alla Corte degli
Angeli** €€
Boutique
Via degli Angeli 23, 55100
Tel *0583 46 92 04*
w allacortedegliangeli.it
A jewel of a hotel with distinc-
tively personalized rooms.

MONTEPULCIANO: San Biagio €
Budget
Via San Bartolomeo 2, 53045
Tel *0578 71 72 33*
w albergosanbiagio.it
Located just outside of the town
with glorious views, this hotel has
comfortable and clean rooms,
and a heated swimming pool.

**MONTERIGGIONI: Borgo
Gallinaio** €€
Agriturismo
Strada del Gallinaio 5, 53035
Tel *0577 30 47 51*
w gallinaio.it
This converted 15th-century
stone-built farmhouse is
surrounded by cypress and olive
trees. There is an outdoor pool.

Dining area with medieval details in the
Antica Residenza Cicogna, Siena

PISA: Guerrazzi €
B&B
Via Francesco da Buti 4, 56125
Tel *3389 32 81 69*
w bbguerrazzi.hostel.com
Simple but quaint, with
comfortable and clean rooms.

PISA: Royal Victoria Hotel €€
Historic
Lungarno Antonio Pacinotti 12, 56126
Tel *050 94 01 11*
w royalvictoria.it
Housed in a 10th-century tower,
Pisa's very first hotel has stately
decor and spacious rooms.

PISA: Relais dell'Orologio €€€
Historic
Via della Faggiola 12, 56126
Tel *050 83 03 61*
w hotelrelaisorologio.com
Built into a 14th-century tower,
this hotel has elegant rooms and
a delightful reading room. Enjoy
breakfast on the veranda.

**SAN GIMIGNANO:
Bel Soggiorno** €
Budget
Via San Giovanni 91, 53037
Tel *0577 94 03 75*
w hotelbelsoggiorno.it
Comfortable and well-priced
hotel run by the same family
since 1886. Excellent restaurant.

**SAN GIMIGNANO:
Leon Bianco** €€
Rooms with a view
Piazza Cisterna 13, 53037
Tel *0577 94 12 94*
w leonbianco.com
Elegant rooms with spectacular
views of the hillside piazza.

**SIENA: Antica Residenza
Cicogna** €
Pensione
Via Termini 67, 53100
Tel *0577 28 56 13*
w anticaresidenzacicogna.it

Romantic location set in a
medieval building full of
charming details.

SIENA: Palazzo Ravizza €€
Romantic
Piano dei Mantellini 34, 53100
Tel *0577 28 04 62*
w palazzoravizza.it
Lovely rooms with original period
furniture. Some rooms overlook
a picturesque garden.

**SIENA: Grand Hotel
Continental** €€€
Luxury
Via Banchi di Sopra 85, 53100
Tel *0577 560 11*
w grandhotelcontinentalsiena.com
The most prestigious address in
Siena. This 17th-century building
has impressive frescoes and
luxurious rooms.

VIAREGGIO: London €€
Rooms with a view
Viale Daniele Manin 16, 55049
Tel *0584 498 41*
w hotellondon.it
Simple, comfortable rooms and
an elegant lobby. Located a short
walk from the sea.

VOLTERRA: Villa Rioddi €
Historic
*Strada Provinciale del Monte
Volterrano 71, 56048*
Tel *0588 880 53*
w hotelvillarioddi.it
Experience ultimate relaxation in
this medieval 15th-century villa.

VOLTERRA: Marcampo €€
Agriturismo
*Località San Cipriano, Podere
Marcampo 30, 56048*
Tel *0588 853 93*
w agriturismo-marcampo.com
There are just six rooms in this
tranquil slice of Tuscan paradise.
Enjoy the pool with views of the
surrounding vineyards.

Umbria

ASSISI: Sole €
Budget
Corso Giuseppe Mazzini 35, 06081
Tel *075 81 23 73*
w assisihotelsole.com
Basic but spacious rooms in a
15th-century medieval building.

ASSISI: Subasio €€
Romantic
Via Elia Frate 2c, 06081
Tel *075 81 22 06*
w hotelsubasio.com
Located beside the famous
basilica: atmospheric and spacious
rooms, some with a terrace.

For more information on types of hotels *see p561*

GUBBIO: Le Cinciallegre €
Agriturismo
Fraz. Pisciano, 06024
Tel *075 925 59 57*
🆆 lecinciallegre.it
This is a jewel hidden in the
countryside. Small but cozy rooms.

GUBBIO: Relais Ducale €€
Romantic
Via Galeotti 19, 06024
Tel *075 922 01 57*
🆆 mencarelligroup.com
Beautiful rooms in a converted
manor house. Panoramic views.

**NORCIA: Casale nel Parco dei
Monti Sibillini** €
Agriturismo
Vocabolo Fontevena 8, 06046
Tel *0743 81 64 81*
🆆 casalenelparco.com
Canopy beds and wood-beamed
ceilings; some rooms also have
kitchenettes. Great service.

ORVIETO: Filippeschi €
Budget
Via Filippeschi 19, 05018
Tel *0763 34 32 75*
🆆 albergofilippeschi.it
Basic but comfortable rooms in
the historic center. Spacious lobby.

ORVIETO: La Badia €€
Historic
Località la Badia 8, 05018
Tel *0763 30 19 59*
🆆 labadiahotel.it
Breathtaking hotel built into the
ruins of an 8th-century monastery.

ORVIETO: Locanda Pallazone €€
Agriturismo
Località Rocca Ripesena 66, 05018
Tel *0763 39 36 14*
🆆 locandapalazzone.it
Elegant accommodations in
a former cardinal's residence;
surrounded by vineyards.

PERUGIA: Fortuna €
Historic
Via Luigi Bonazzi 19, 06121
Tel *075 572 28 45*
🆆 hotelfortunaperugia.com
Restoration work revealed over-
300-year-old frescoes at this hotel.

**PERUGIA: Castello di
Monterone** €€
Historic
Strada Monteville 3, 06126
Tel *075 572 42 14*
🆆 castellomonterone.com
Luxurious rooms and two stellar
restaurants are available here.

PERUGIA: La Rosetta €€
Boutique
Piazza Italia 19, 06121
Tel *075 572 08 41*
🆆 larosetta.eu

Fantastic rooms, decorated either
in 1920s or Baroque style.

PERUGIA: Brufani Palace €€€
Luxury
Piazza Italia 12, 06121
Tel *075 573 25 41*
🆆 brufanipalace.com
Sumptuous accommodations
plus a roof garden with views of
the town and countryside.

SPOLETO: Hotel Aurora €
Budget
Via dell'Apollinare 3, 06049
Tel *0743 22 03 15*
🆆 hotelauroraspoleto.it
Great value at this central but
quiet family-run hotel.

SPOLETO: San Luca €€
Boutique
Via Interna delle Mura 21, 06049
Tel *0743 22 33 99*
🆆 hotelsanluca.com
Sophisticated elegance in one of
the loveliest palaces in Spoleto.

**TODI CANONICA: Tenuta
di Canonica** €€
Agriturismo
Vocabolo Casalzetta 75, 06059
Tel *075 894 75 45*
🆆 tenutadicanonica.com
Sublime country residence on
the site of a 9th-century farm.
Superb location.

Le Marche

ANCONA: Grand Hotel Palace €€
Historic
Lungomare Luigi Vanvitelli 24, 60121
Tel *071 20 18 13*
🆆 hotelancona.it
Old-world elegance at this grand
17th-century portside palazzo.

Luxuriously decorated room in the Locanda
Pallazone in Orvieto

ANCONA: NH Ancona €€
Rooms with a view
Via XXIX Settembre 14, 60122
Tel *071 20 11 71*
🆆 nh-hotels.it
Stylish, contemporary hilltop
hotel with simple rooms.

ASCOLI PICENO: Pennile €
Budget
Via Gaetano Spalvieri 1, 63100
Tel *0736 416 45*
🆆 hotelpennile.it
Reasonable prices for simple and
well-kept rooms.

DK Choice

**ASCOLI PICENO:
Villa Cicchi** €€
Agriturismo
Via Salaria Superiore 137, 63100
Tel *0736 25 22 72*
🆆 villacicchi.it
An exquisite, meticulously
presented villa is at the heart of
this agriturismo that combines
luxury accommodations with
rustic hospitality. There are
magnificent grounds, a large
pool, period furniture, and
frescoed ceilings. Available
activities include trekking, wine
tasting, cooking and photography courses, and yoga.

PESARO: Bellevue €
Resort
Viale Trieste 88, 61121
Tel *0721 690 18*
🆆 bellevuehotel.net
Great value for this simple but
accommodating beach resort.

DK Choice

**PESARO: Alexander
Museum Palace Hotel** €€
Historic
Viale Trieste 20, 61121
Tel *0721 344 41*
🆆 alexandermuseum.it
As the name implies, this
unique accommodation is part
museum, part hotel. Both
established and emerging Italian
artists have collaborated to
transform this elegant hotel
into a literal work of art. Each
room is different, and every
single design element from
the colors to the chairs and
floors is one of a kind. The sea
views are a bonus.

SAN MARINO: Villa Giardi €
B&B
Via Palamede Ferri 22, 47890
Tel *0549 99 10 74*
Warm atmosphere and a handful
of simple rooms.

Key to prices *see p562*

SAN MARINO: Cesare €€
Boutique
Salita alla Rocca 7, 47890
Tel *0549 99 23 55*
W hotelcesare.com
This hotel blends convenience
with refined elegance. Rooms
are clean and bright. The staff are
very attentive.

URBINO: Cà Andreana €
Agriturismo
Via Gadana 119, 61029
Tel *0722 32 78 45*
W caandreana.it
This farm stay is located in a
magnificent country setting
with stunning views. Rooms
are quaint and well-presented.

URBINO: Raffaello €
Rooms with a view
Via Santa Margherita 38, 61029
Tel *0722 47 84*
W albergoraffaello.com
Situated near the famous artist's
childhood home. Rooms are
simple but inviting.

Glass walls of the Alexander Museum Palace Hotel in Pesaro

Rome

The Ancient Center

Nicolas Inn €
B&B **Map** 3 B5
Via Cavour 295, 00184
Tel *06 97 61 84 83*
W nicolasinn.com
Basic service, but the rooms are
pleasant and cozy, and all have
en suite bathrooms. The hosts
are warm and friendly.

Hotel Forum €€
Rooms with a view **Map** 3 B5
Via Tor de' Conti 25, 00184
Tel *06 679 24 46*
W hotelforum.com
Enjoy magnificent views of
ancient Rome from a charming
terrace. Graceful interiors and
plenty of old-world charm.

Fortyseven €€€
Rooms with a view **Map** 6 E1
Via Luigi Petroselli 47, 00186
Tel *06 69 20 01 08*
W fortysevenhotel.com
Stellar views of the ancient city
from this retro-styled hotel.
Elegant rooms, including two
suites, both with private terraces.

Palazzo Manfredi €€€
Rooms with a view **Map** 7 A1
Via Labicana 125, 00184
Tel *06 77 59 13 80*
W hotelgladiatori.it
The Colosseum seems close
enough to touch at this hotel.
Elegantly decorated rooms and
excellent service.

Around Piazza Navona

Albergo Santa Chiara €€
Boutique **Map** 10 D3
Via di Santa Chiara 21, 00186
Tel *06 687 29 79*
W albergosantachiara.com
The lobby is the most impressive
part of this hotel, the rooms are
pleasant but don't compare.
Enjoy a drink in the alfresco bar.

Casa di Santa Brigida €
Religious institution **Map** 9 B4
Via Monserato 54, 00186
Tel *06 68 89 25 96*
W brigidine.org
Not the cheapest convent in town,
but the location is worth the
price. Clean and spacious rooms.

Sole al Biscione €
Historic **Map** 9 C4
Via del Biscione 76, 00186
Tel *06 68 80 68 73*
W solealbiscione.it
This basic but charming hotel
claims to be the oldest in Rome.

Campo de'Fiori Hotel €€
Rooms with a view **Map** 9 C4
Via del Biscione 6, 00186
Tel *06 68 80 68 65*
W hotelcampodefiori.com
Romantically decorated rooms
with refined furnishings, and
views of rooftops and domes.

Due Torri €€
Historic **Map** 9 C1
Vicolo del Leonetto 23, 00186
Tel *06 68 80 69 56*
W hotelduetorriroma.com
Small but lovely rooms in a
converted Renaissance palace.

Locanda Cairoli €€
Boutique **Map** 10 D4
Piazza Benedetto Cairoli 2, 00186
Tel *06 68 80 92 78*
W locandacairoli.it
Centrally located hotel with
comfortable rooms. Spacious
family-style breakfast room.

Portoghesi €€
Charming **Map** 10 D2
Via dei Portoghesi 1, 00186
Tel *06 686 42 31*
W hotelportoghesiroma.it
Nestled in a quiet cobbled
alley, this hotel has a charming
breakfast terrace.

Teatro di Pompeo €€
Historic **Map** 9 C4
Largo del Pallaro 8, 00186
Tel *06 68 30 01 70*
W hotelteatrodipompeo.it
Built on the ruins of Pompey's
ancient theater, this hotel has
simple rooms and friendly staff.

Teatropace33 €€
Rooms with a view **Map** 9 C3
Via del Teatro Pace 33, 00186
Tel *06 687 90 75*
W hotelteatropace.com
Excellent price-quality ratio
at this charming Baroque-style
hotel with elegant decor.

Albergo del Sole al Pantheon €€€
Rooms with a view **Map** 9 C4
Piazza della Rotonda 63, 00186
Tel *06 678 04 41*
W solealpantheonrome.com
Unparalleled views of the
bustling Piazza Navona, if you
don't mind the noise.

Grand Hotel de La Minerve €€€
Luxury **Map** 10 D3
Piazza della Minerva 69, 00186
Tel *06 69 52 01*
W grandhoteldelaminerve.com
Excellent views from nearly every
room. The decor is luxurious and
the service is excellent.

Raphael €€€
Romantic **Map** 9 C2
Largo Febo 2, 00186
Tel *06 68 28 31*
W raphaelhotel.com
World-class service, gorgeous
decor, and a terrace with views.

For more information on types of hotels *see p561*

Charming outdoor garden area at Beehive, Northeast Rome

St. George Hotel €€€
Luxury Map 9 A3
Via Giulia 62, 00186
Tel *06 68 66 11*
W stgeorgehotel.it
This elegant five-star hotel offers
rooms with contemporary design.

Northeast Rome

DK Choice

Beehive €
Budget Map 4 E3
Via Marghera 8, 00185
Tel *06 44 70 45 53*
W the-beehive.com
A gem of a hotel with both
private rooms and small dormitories available. The rooms are
basic, clean, and comfortable;
some with en suite bathrooms.
Enjoy the extras, such as yoga
lessons, massage, and a café
serving freshly baked bread
and organic coffee. .

Blue Hostel €
Budget Map 4 D4
Via Carlo Alberto 13, 00185
Tel *34 09 25 85 03*
W bluehostel.it
A charming hotel with clean and
spacious rooms.

DK Choice

Casa Howard €
B&B Map 3 A3
*Via di Capo le Case 18, 00187 &
Via Sistina 149, 00187*
Tel *06 69 92 45 55*
W casahoward.com
This funky B&B, inspired by E. M.
Forster's novel *Howard's End*,
comprises 10 uniquely decorated
rooms in two adjacent locations.
What it lacks in round-the-clock
service (there is no reception;
each guest is provided with a
set of keys), it makes up for in
style, character, and location.

Hostel des Artistes €
Budget Map 4 E2
Via Villafranca 20, 00185
Tel *06 445 43 65*
W hostelrome.com
Friendly and clean, with private
rooms and dorm accommodations.

Daphne Inn €€
B&B Map 3 B2
Via di San Basilio 55, 00187
Tel *06 87 45 00 86*
W daphne-rome.com
Top-notch B&B with personal
service and a modern look.

Deko Rome €€
Pensione Map 3 C1
Via Toscana 1, 00187
Tel *06 42 02 00 32*
W dekorome.com
Small rooms in minimalist style;
surprisingly luxurious bathrooms.

Hotel Suisse €€
Pensione Map 3 A2
Via Gregoriana 54, 00187
Tel *06 678 36 49*
W hotelsuisserome.com
Great value at this elegantly
appointed hotel.

Residenza Cellini €€
Pensione Map 3 C3
Via Modena 5, 00184
Tel *06 47 82 52 04*
W residenzacellini.it
Large, simply furnished rooms;
some bathrooms have Jacuzzi tubs.

Aldrovandi Palace €€€
Luxury
Via Ulisse Aldrovandi 15, 00197
Tel *06 322 39 93*
W aldrovandi.com
A spectacular five-star hotel with
airy rooms and views of the park.

Aleph €€€
Luxury Map 3 B2
Via di San Basilio 15, 00185
Tel *06 42 29 01*
W aleph-roma.boscolohotels.com
Experience modern opulence at
this relaxing, luxurious spa.

Babuino181 €€€
Boutique Map 2 F1
Via del Babuino 181, 00187
Tel *06 32 29 52 95*
W romeluxurysuites.com
Splendid modern hotel with
luxurious details. Set in a
Renaissance palace with a leafy
roof terrace.

Eden €€€
Luxury Map 3 B2
Via Ludovisi 49, 00187
Tel *06 47 81 21*
W edenroma.com
A grand hotel with elegantly
furnished rooms and a rooftop
dining area. Service is exceptional.

es Hotel €€€
Rooms with a view Map 4 E4
Via Filippo Turati 171, 00185
Tel *06 44 48 41*
W radissonblu.com/eshotel-rome
Splendid five-star hotel with
sleek modern design and all
white rooms.

Excelsior €€€
Romantic Map 3 B2
Via Veneto 125, 00187
Tel *06 470 81*
W westin.com/excelsiorrome
This favorite with honeymooners
is the perfect place to enact
la dolce vita.

Exedra €€€
Luxury Map 3 C3
Piazza della Repubblica 47, 00185
Tel *06 48 93 80 12*
W exedra-roma.boscolohotels.com
Lavish five-star hotel with plush
rooms, a rooftop pool, and an
award-winning spa.

DK Choice

Hassler €€€
Luxury Map 3 A2
Piazza Trinità dei Monti 6, 00187
Tel *06 69 93 47 26*
W hotelhasslerroma.com
The discreet service, plush
furnishings, and stunning
bedrooms make this a firm
favorite with celebrities. Guests
can also take advantage of the
Michelin-stared Imàgora
restaurant or enjoy a signature
Venschuas cocktail in the
Hassler Bar.

Hotel d'Inghilterra €€€
Romantic Map 3 A2
Via Bocca di Leone 14, 00187
Tel *06 69 98 11*
W hoteldinghilterrarome.com
Spacious accommodations in
an enviable location near the
Spanish Steps. All the rooms and
suites are individually styled.

Locarno €€€
Historic Map 2 F1
Via della Penna 22, 00186
Tel *06 361 08 41*
W hotellocarno.com
A masterpiece of Art Deco and
the location for many classic films.

Piranesi €€€
Boutique Map 2 F1
Via del Babuino 196, 00187
Tel *06 32 80 41*
W hotelpiranesi.com
Quiet elegance in an ideal
location. There's a roof garden,
sauna, and a solarium. It also has
a small gym.

Portrait Suites €€€
Boutique Map 3 A2
Via Bocca di Leone 23, 00187
Tel *06 69 38 07 42*
W lungarnocollection.com
Accommodations with style; this
hotel is owned by famed shoe
designer Salvatore Ferragamo's
family, and it shows.

The Vatican and Trastevere

Arco del Lauro €
B&B Map 6 D1
Via dell'Arco de' Tolomei 27, 00153
Tel *06 97 84 03 50*
W arcodellauro.it
Tiny hotel in a picturesque
medieval location with simple
but lovely rooms.

**Casa Internazionale delle
Donne** €
Budget Map 2 D5
*Vicolo di San Francesco di Sales 47,
00165*
Tel *06 68 89 24 65*
W casainternazionaledelledonne.org
Basic accommodations in a quiet
but central area; women only.

Centro Diffusione Spiritualità €
Religious institution Map 2 D5
Via dei Riari 44, 00153
Tel *06 68 80 61 22*
Budget accommodations
including breakfast and dinner.
There is an 11pm curfew.

Domus Tiberina €
Budget Map 6 D1
Via in Piscinula 37, 00153
Tel *06 581 36 48*
W hoteldomustiberina.it
This tiny, quaint hotel is just steps
from the Tiber. Offers simple
rooms and continental breakfast.

Hotel Ottaviano €
Budget Map 1 C2
Via Ottaviano 6, 00192
Tel *06 39 73 81 38*
W pensioneottaviano.com

Two steps from the Vatican
Museums, this hotel is a back-
packer's paradise. Great views of
St. Peter's square.

Hotel Trastevere €
Budget Map 5 C1
Via Luciano Manara 24, 00153
Tel *06 581 47 13*
W hoteltrastevere.net
Simple, clean, and large rooms at
this hotel, which offers good value
for money. Good breakfast spread.

Relais Casa della Fornarina €
Historic Map 2 D5
Via di Porta Settimiana 7, 00153
Tel *06 64 56 22 68*
W casadellafornarina.com
Guesthouse where Raphael's muse
once lived. Spacious rooms and
good service.

Bramante €€
Historic Map 1 C3
Vicolo delle Palline 24, 00193
Tel *06 68 80 64 26*
W hotelbramante.com
In the shadow of St. Peter's, this
family-run accommodation has
quiet and tasteful rooms.

DK Choice

Donna Camilla Savelli €€
Romantic Map 5 B1
Via Garibaldi 27, 00153
Tel *06 58 88 61*
W hoteldonnacamillasavelli.com
Designed by Baroque genius
Borromini, this meticulously
restored monastery still belongs
to the nuns of the original
order, but is now a four-star
hotel. All rooms are decorated
with period furniture, and some
have Jacuzzi tubs. The cloister is
an oasis in the heart of the
bustling city; breakfast is served
here in good weather.

Chic and comfortable sitting area at Portrait
Suites, Northeast Rome

Sant'Anna €€
Boutique Map 1 C3
Borgo Pio 134, 00193
Tel *06 68 80 16 02*
W santannahotel.net
Modern convenience with an
old-world feel. Rooms are spacious,
and there is an exquisite courtyard.

Aventine and Lateran

Domus Aventina €
Budget Map 5 E2
Via di Santa Prisca 11b, 00153
Tel *06 574 61 35*
W hoteldomusaventina.com
Simple but elegant rooms
opening onto a lush courtyard.

Sant'Anselmo €€
Romantic Map 6 E3
Via Santa Melania 19, 00153
Tel *06 57 00 57*
W aventinohotels.com
Four-poster beds and claw-foot
tubs are available at this simple
and graceful hotel. Free parking.

Villa San Pio €€
Romantic Map 6 E3
Via Santa Melania 19, 00153
Tel *06 57 00 57*
W aventinohotels.com
Quiet and secluded, but located
conveniently in the city center.

Lazio

Casale Poggio Nebbia €
Agriturismo
*S.S. Aurelia km 84, 100, Loc.
Farnesiana, 01016*
Tel *0766 84 12 68*
W poggionebbia.it
Relaxing farm stay nestled in
a valley. Ideal for families.

Hotel all'Olivo €
Budget
Via Palmiro Togliatti 15, 01016
Tel *0766 85 73 18*
W allolivo.it
Old-fashioned hotel in the
countryside with an excellent
traditional restaurant.

Hotel Viterbo Best Western €
Budget
Via San Camillo de Lellis 6, 01100
Tel *0761 27 01 00*
W hotelviterbo.com
Comfortable hotel with good
service and an abundant breakfast.

Palazzo Maggiore €
B&B
Via Domenico Giuliani 89, 00019
Tel *393 104 49 37*
W palazzomaggiore.com
This sweet hotel provides the
perfect base to explore Tivoli.

For more information on types of hotels *see p561*

Poggio Regillo €
Agriturismo
Via Pietra Porzia 30, 00044
Tel *06 941 78 00*
w poggioregillo.it
An environmentally friendly hotel
that offers excellent value for
money. The breakfast room has
splendid views of the countryside. Pets welcome.

Grotta di Tiberio €€
Rooms with a view
Via Flacca km 15, 700, 04029
Tel *0771 54 81 37*
w hotelgrottaditiberio.it
Charming beachside hotel with a
large pool. Rooms are spacious,
and most have balconies.

L'Isola di Rosa €€
Spa hotel
Via del Grano 20, 00052
Tel *06 99552819*
w isoladirosa.com
Old manor house on a sprawling
property with a modern spa.
Romantic ambience and well-
appointed rooms.

Niccolò V €€
Spa hotel
Strada Bagni 12, 01100
Tel *0761 35 05 55*
w termedeipapi.it
Historic thermal baths and
wellness center in an elegant
four-star hotel.

Villa Clementina Spa & Resort €€
Spa hotel
Traversa Quarto del Lago 12, 00062
Tel *06 998 62 68*
w hotelvillaclementina.it
Beautifully frescoed rooms in lush
surroundings with a large and
inviting pool.

Grand Hotel Duca d'Este €€€
Business
Via Tiburtina Valeria 330, 00019
Tel *0774 38 83*
w ducadeste.com
Large, comfortable hotel with
fully equipped wellness center.

Naples and Campania

AMALFI COAST: Hotel Desirée €
Rooms with a view
Via Capo 31, 80067
Tel *081 878 15 63*
w desireehotelsorrento.com
This simple, cliff-side hotel offers
excellent value. There's an eleva-
tor to a small private beach.

**AMALFI COAST: Antica
Repubblica** €€
Boutique
Vico dei Pastai 2, 84011
Tel *089 873 63 10*
w anticarepubblica.it
A charming hotel with elegantly
furnished rooms and a terrace.

AMALFI COAST: Miramare €€
Rooms with a view
Via Trara Genoino, 84017
Tel *089 87 50 02*
w miramarepositano.it
Rooms are brightly decorated
and have views looking out over
Positano and the ocean beyond.

**AMALFI COAST: Bellevue
Syrene** €€€
Luxury
Piazza della Vittoria 5, 80067
Tel *081 807 38 99*
w bellevue.it
A dreamy 18th-century villa with
a flowering terrace and private
beach access.

AMALFI COAST: La Sirenuse €€€
Luxury
Via Cristoforo Colombo 30, 84017
Tel *089 87 50 66*
w sirenuse.it
World-class hotel with spectacular
views of Sorrento and the coast.

CAPRI: Bellavista €€
Boutique
Via Giuseppe Orlandi 10, 80071
Tel *081 837 14 63*
w bellavistacapri.com

Enjoy the spectacular views from
this sweet 1960s-style hotel.

**CAPRI: Grand Hotel
Quisisana** €€€
Luxury
Via Camerelle 2, 80073
Tel *081 837 07 88*
w quisisana.com
Deluxe accommodations in an
extraordinary setting.

CASERTA: Amadeus €
Boutique
Via Giuseppe Verdi 72/76, 81100
Tel *0823 35 26 63*
w hotelamadeuscaserta.it
A centrally located, comfortable
hotel with spacious rooms.

DK Choice

**ISCHIA AND PROCIDA:
Miramare** €€
Spa hotel
*Via Maddalena Comandante 29,
Sant'Angelo, 80070*
Tel *081 99 92 19*
w hotelmiramare.it
This gorgeous old-world hotel
is perched on the rocks right
over the Tyrrhenian Sea. The
lovely rooms, most with canopy
beds and balconies, all face the
sea. A short walk leads to the spa
complex with thermal pools and
a private beach. The ample
breakfast is served on a flowering
terrace with spectacular views.

NAPLES: L'Alloggio dei Vassalli €
B&B
Via Donnalbina 56, 80134
Tel *081 551 51 18*
w alloggiodeivassalli.it
Lovely rooms, a wellness center,
and cordial service.

NAPLES: Decumani €€
Historic
Piazzetta Giustino Fortunato 8, 80100
Tel *081 420 13 79*
w palazzodecumani.com
Tasteful furnishings and elegant
bathrooms in a Baroque palace.

**NAPLES: Grand Hotel
Vesuvio** €€€
Rooms with a view
Via Partenope 45, 80121
Tel *081 764 00 44*
w vesuvio.it
Sumptuous lodgings with views
of the gulf and Castel dell'Ovo.

SALERNO: Lloyd's Baia €€
Rooms with a view
Via Enrico de Marinis 2, 84013
Tel *089 763 31 11*
w lloydsbaiahotel.it
Lovely hotel hanging over a cliff
and offering remarkable views.

Outdoor pool beside the beach at Grotta di Tiberio hotel in Lazio

Key to prices *see p562*

Abruzzo, Molise, and Puglia

DK Choice

ALBEROBELLO: B&B Fascino Antico €
Historic
Strada Statale 172, 74015
Tel *080 432 50 89*
W fascinoantico.eu
At this charming B&B, you can lodge in one of the five 19th-century huts without losing the comforts of a modern vacation. Surrounded by centuries-old olive trees, the apartments face a large courtyard, and there is an outdoor pool.

BARI: Boston €
Business
Via Niccolò Piccinni 155, 70122
Tel *080 521 66 33*
W bostonbari.it
Functional and comfortable rooms in a convenient location.

ISOLE TREMITI: Baely Resort €€
Resort
Via Matteotti, 71040
Tel *0882 46 37 67*
W baely.it
Intimate hotel with comfortable, distinctively decorated rooms.

L'AQUILA: Magione Papale €€
Boutique
Via Porta Napoli 67, 67100
Tel *0862 41 49 83*
W magionepapale.it
Set in a restored mill, this quaint country inn has plenty of character.

Basilicata and Calabria

MARATEA: La Locanda delle Donne Monache €€
Romantic
Via Carlo Mazzei 4, 85046
Tel *0973 87 61 39*
W locandamonache.com
Spacious, bright rooms at this lovely former convent.

DK Choice

MATERA: Sassi Hotel €
Historic
Via San Giovanni Vecchio 89, 75100
Tel *0835 33 10 09*
W hotelsassi.it
Matera's famous rock dwellings make an evocative setting for this one-of-a-kind hotel. Each

Ultramodern lounge area in Riva del Sole in Cefalù

room is carved into the mountain, with distinctive vaulted stone ceilings and panoramic views of the medieval town below. Furnishings are simple and classic, letting the natural elements of the 18th-century building shine.

MELFI: Relais la Fattoria €
Agriturismo
Località la Cavallerizza, 85025
Tel *0972 247 76*
W relaislafattoria.it
A country inn set amid olive trees and vineyards. Charming rooms.

TROPEA: Cala di Volpe €€
Resort
Località Torre Marino, 89865
Tel *0963 66 92 22*
W caladivolpe.it
A beautiful seaside resort surrounded by a lush tropical garden. A short walk to the beach.

Sicily

AGRIGENTO: Camere a Sud €
B&B
Via Ficani, 92100
Tel *349 638 44 24*
W camereasud.it
Warm, simple rooms in this sunny B&B. Friendly, helpful owners.

CEFALÙ: Riva del Sole €€
Rooms with a view
Lungomare Giardina 25, 90015
Tel *0921 42 12 30*
W rivadelsole.it
A modern hotel ideally located between the sea and city center.

ERICE: Elimo €€
Rooms with a view
Via Vittorio Emanuele 73, 91016
Tel *0923 86 93 77*
W hotelelimo.it
Small but lovely rooms with panoramic views of the countryside.

PALERMO: Principe di Villafranca €€€
Luxury
Via Giuseppina Turrisi Colonna 4, 90141
Tel *091 611 85 23*
W principedivillafranca.it
Elegant hotel full of intricate details and antique art and furnishings.

Sardinia

ALGHERO: Villa Las Tronas €€€
Spa hotel
Lungomare Valencia 1, 07041
Tel *079 98 18 18*
W hotelvillalastronas.it
Scenic views at this elegant hotel, with indoor and outdoor pools.

CAGLIARI: T Hotel €€
Design
Via dei Giudicati 66, 09131
Tel *070 474 00*
W thotel.it
Modern design hotel with large rooms and a fitness center.

COSTA SMERALDA: Nibaru €€
Resort
Località Cala di Volpe
Tel *0789 960 38*
W hotelnibaru.it
A tranquil oasis a short walk from the sea. Comfortable and clean rooms, and a lovely pool.

COSTA SMERALDA: Pitrizza €€€
Luxury
Via Nazionale 35, 07020
Tel *0789 93 01 11*
W pitrizzahotel.com
A grand hotel with fabulous amenities and breathtaking views.

SASSARI: Grazie Deledda €
Business
Viale Dante 47, 07100
Tel *079 27 12 35*
W hotelgraziadeledda.it
Remarkable low prices for this large and comfortable hotel.

For more information on types of hotels *see p561*

WHERE TO EAT AND DRINK

Food is a serious subject in Italy. The Italians are justly proud of their fine cuisine and wines and many sociable hours are spent around the table. One of the great pleasures of travelling in Italy is sampling regional variations in pasta, breads, and cheeses. You don't have to head to the most expensive places for good food; a simple *trattoria*, which serves the local clientele, will often produce a better meal than the nearby international restaurant. However, whether it is a crowded *osteria*, a local *pizzeria*, or a terrace with sea views, this introduction gives plenty of practical tips on types of restaurants, ordering, and service to help you enjoy eating out in Italy.

Places to Eat

Traditionally a *trattoria* and an *osteria* are cheaper and more casual alternatives to the smarter *ristorante*.

A *pizzeria* is usually a cheap place to eat (as little as €18 with beer) and many serve pasta, meat, and fish dishes as well as pizzas. *Pizzerie* are often open in the evening only, especially those with wood-fired ovens *(forno a legna)*.

A *birreria* is another cheap option, serving pasta and snacks such as sausages and hamburgers. An *enoteca*, or *vineria*, will offer a selection of wines to try, along with a range of light dishes. Prices vary and tend to be relatively expensive for the quantities served.

At lunch time and in the early evening, *rosticcerie* sell roast chicken, slices of pizza *(pizza al taglio)*, and other snacks to take out. *Pizza al taglio* can also be bought straight from the baker. Many bars offer filled rolls *(panini)* and sandwiches *(tramezzini)*, and some also

A restaurant in Chioggia offering a cozy environment in a vaulted room

serve simple hot dishes from the *tavola calda* counter for around €8.

Stop at a *gelateria* for ice cream, with a sometimes bewildering choice of different flavours, or a *pasticceria* for one of a dazzling variety of sweet and savory pastries, cakes, and biscuits.

Opening Times

Lunch is generally served between 12:30pm and 2:30pm and, particularly in the south, all other activity stops between these hours. Dinner is at about 7:30pm and goes on until 11pm or later (in the south eating hours tend to be later). It is not unusual to see tables still full from lunch at 4pm or diners sipping *digestivi* well after midnight.

Reservations

Good restaurants in Italy are likely to be popular, so reserve a table in advance if you can *(prenotazione)*. Otherwise, get there early to avoid having to wait in line. Many restaurants close one day a week and for a few weeks in either winter or the summer vacation season; this information will be included in the list of restaurants on the pages that follow, but phone first if in doubt.

The Menu

Italian meals consist of three or four courses, and restaurants generally expect patrons to order at least two, though you should not feel obliged to do so. The *antipasto* (starter), is followed by the *primo*, of pasta, rice, or soup. The *secondo* is the main meat or fish course, for which you will need to order vegetables *(contorni)* separately. Fruit *(frutta)*, cheese *(formaggi)*, or dessert *(dolce)* follow, with coffee and the preferred *digestivo* of the region to finish the meal.

Menus usually change with the season to make use of the freshest local produce, and the day's specials may be recited to you by the waiter rather than written down. Persevere, if you don't immediately understand, using the menu information at the beginning of each section. Try to avoid restaurants that do not state prices on their menus.

Villa Crespi in Piedmont, inspired by the *Arabian Nights (see p588)*

Vegetarians

Italian restaurants offer plenty of choices for vegetarians as the menu will always feature a selection of seasonal vegetables and pulses. Many pasta and *antipasto* dishes use no meat at all and for a main course you can ask for an omelette *(frittata)* with a side dish of vegetables from the *contorni*. Most menus are adaptable because dishes are prepared to order – tell your waiter that you are *vegetariano* (female – *vegetariana*) and they will advise you accordingly.

Wine and Drinks

Many regions have their own *aperitivo* served before the meal and a *digestivo* for afterwards. Universal alternatives are *prosecco* (dry, fizzy white wine) or an *analcolico* (nonalcoholic) aperitif, and *grappa* as a digestive. House wine (red or white) will be a simple local wine served by the liter or by the glass and will generally be perfectly palatable. In addition, all but the cheapest eateries have a range of other local and regional wines specially selected to accompany the food on the menu, with smarter establishments also offering foreign vintages.

Tap water *(acqua del rubinetto)* is always drinkable and often very good, but Italy has a large range of mineral waters. Fizzy ones *(frizzante)* may contain carbon dioxide, while *naturale* can mean still or naturally sparkling. If you particularly want a still water, ask for *non gassata*. Espresso bars usually charge more for table service.

Paying

Tax and service are usually included in the menu prices, but it is normal to leave a tip of around 10 percent. Note that many restaurants include a cover charge *(coperto)*, on the bill *(il conto)*, which covers bread (whether you eat it or not) and is charged per person.

Credit cards are not always accepted in Italy, particularly in smaller towns, so it is wise to check before you order.

Diners enjoying a meal *al fresco* in Chianti, Tuscany

Dress

Italians generally tend to look stylish but don't necessarily expect visitors to do the same. However, very scruffy or dirty clothes are unlikely to get you good, efficient, or particularly friendly service.

Children

Children are welcome in all but the smartest establishments and restaurants are likely to be filled with extensive Italian families for Sunday lunch. Facilities such as high chairs or special menus are rare, but most places will provide a small or half portion *(mezza porzione)*.

Smoking

Smoking is still popular in Italy. However, smoking laws now mean that all restaurants in the country are nonsmoking establishments. Unless a smokers' room is provided, you should step outside if you want to light up.

Outdoor tables at the seafood restaurant Il Riccio on Capri *(see p600)*

Wheelchair Access

Few restaurants have special facilities for people in wheelchairs, but if you book in advance, the establishment can reserve a suitable table and be ready to help if necessary when you arrive.

The charming interior of U'Giancu in Rapallo, Liguria *(see p590)*

Recommended Restaurants

The restaurants listed in this guidebook cover a wide range of eateries, from the simple *pizzeria* and *tavola calda* (cafeteria) to family-run *trattoria* and elegant *ristorante*. Each restaurant has a cuisine type listed beneath the name of the establishment. Most of these descriptions are self explanatory but the *Places to Eat* section will provide more information on what you can expect from the menu.

The DK Choice label means the restaurant has outstanding qualities and is highly recommended. It may serve delicious local dishes, offer excellent value for money, be in a beautiful location, have a romantic atmosphere, or be particularly charming. Whatever the reason it is a guarantee of a great meal.

Where to Eat and Drink

Venice

BURANO: Da Romano   €€
Seafood
Via Piazza Galuppi 221, 30012
Tel *041 73 00 30* **Closed** *Sun dinner; mid-Dec–Jan: Tue*
A wide range of fish dishes served in the traditional Venetian fashion. Advance reservations advised.

DK Choice

BURANO-MAZZORBO:
Venissa   €€€
Modern Italian
Fondamenta Santa Caterina 3, 30170
Tel *041 527 22 81* **Closed** *Mon; Nov: Mon, Tue, Wed; Dec–Mar*
Dine at the elegant Venissa restaurant for an extraspecial gastronomic experience. The menu features a wide selection of seafood, meat, and vegetarian options using fresh, seasonal ingredients grown in the restaurant's own garden. The menu changes daily.

DK Choice

CAMPALTO-MESTRE:
Ristorante al Passo   €€€
Seafood
Via Passo Campalto 118, 30173
Tel *041 90 04 70* **Closed** *Mon, Tue; 3 wks Aug, Dec 27–Jan 6*
Family-run for several generations, this noteworthy restaurant has an exclusive focus on fish. On the pricy side, but worth it.

CANNAREGIO: Osteria al Timon €
Regional Italian   **Map** 2 E3
Fondamenta Ormesini 2754, 30121
Tel *041 524 60 66* **Closed** *Wed; 2 wks Oct*
Fantastic range of *cicchetti* (finger food) to accompany a glass of wine, but also good meat dishes.

CANNAREGIO:
Trattoria da Gigio   €
Regional Italian   **Map** 2 D3
Rio Terrà San Leonardo 1593, 30121
Tel *041 71 75 74* **Closed** *Sun*
Seafood is a popular option at this restaurant, as are the generous hors d'oeuvres.

CANNAREGIO:
Osteria l'Orto dei Mori   €€
Regional Italian   **Map** 2 F3
Campo dei Mori 3386, 30121
Tel *041 524 36 77*   **Closed** *Tue*

This off-the-beaten-track *osteria* has a refined take on local cuisine. Elegant Modernist interiors.

CANNAREGIO: Vini da Gigio €€
Regional Italian   **Map** 3 A4
Fondamenta San Felice 3628A, 30121
Tel *041 528 51 40* **Closed** *Mon, Tue; mid-Jan–1st wk Feb, 2 wks Aug*
The menu largely depends on what Rialto market has to offer that morning. Reservations advised.

CANNAREGIO:
Fiaschetteria Toscana   €€€
Seafood   **Map** 3 B5
Salizzada San Giovanni Grisostomo 5719, 30131
Tel *041 528 52 81* **Closed** *Tue, Wed lunch; end Jul–mid-Aug, 1 wk Dec*
Try the delectable warm octopus salad and the turbot in caper sauce. Book ahead.

CASTELLO:
Enoteca La Mascareta   €
Enoteca   **Map** 7 C1
Calle Santa Maria Formosa 5183, 30122
Tel *041 523 07 44*   **Closed** *lunch*
Wine expert Mauro Lorenzon provides some delicious food to accompany the excellent drinks.

CASTELLO:
Ristorante Giorgione   €€
Regional Italian   **Map** 8 F3
Via Garibaldi 1533, 30122
Tel *041 522 87 27*   **Closed** *Wed; 2 wks Nov*
Great neighborhood *trattoria* serving flavorsome fish dishes, including lasagna and risotto.

CASTELLO: Ristorante Wildner €€
Regional Italian   **Map** 8 D2
Riva degli Schiavoni 4161, 30122
Tel *041 522 74 63*   **Closed** *Tue; 3 wks Jan*
Fresh fish, locally grown organic vegetables, and an interesting wine list at this restaurant.

CASTELLO: Al Covo   €€€
Seafood   **Map** 8 E2
Campiello della Pescaria 3968, 30122
Tel *041 522 38 12* **Closed** *Wed, Thu; 2 wks Jan, 1 wk Aug*
Tucked away behind the Arsenale boat strip, Al Cova has interesting tasting menus.

CASTELLO: Da Remigio   €€€
Seafood   **Map** 8 D2
Salizzada dei Greci 3416, 30122
Tel *041 523 00 89* **Closed** *Mon dinner, Tue; 2 wks Jul–Aug, 3 wks Dec–Jan*
Book early as space is limited. Specials include the fish and shellfish risotto.

Price Guide
Prices are based on a three-course meal per person, with a half-bottle of house wine, including tax and service.

€   up to €40
€€   €40 to 75
€€€   over €75

CASTELLO:
Osteria di Santa Maria   €€€
Regional Italian   **Map** 3 B5
Campo Santa Marina 5911, 30122
Tel *041 528 52 39* **Closed** *Sun, Mon lunch; 2 wks Jan, 2 wks Aug*
A restaurant with a reputation for its creative take on local cuisine.

DORSODURO: La Rivista   €
Vegetarian   **Map** 6 E4
Rio Terà Foscarini 979/A, 30123
Tel *041 240 14 25*   **Closed** *Mon; 2 wks Jan*
A welcoming restaurant offering salads and cold platters for lunch.

DORSODURO: Ai Gondolieri €€€
Regional Italian   **Map** 6 F4
San Vio 366, 30123
Tel *041 528 63 96*   **Closed** *Tue; 1 wk Aug: lunch; Dec 25.*
Here, regional meat and vegetable dishes are served with flair.

GIUDECCA: Cipriani   €€€
Fine Dining
Giudecca 10, 30133
Tel *041 520 77 44* **Closed** *Nov–Mar*
Guests are ferried from the San Marco waterfront to these exclusive island hotel restaurants.

MIRANO:
Trattoria la Ragnatela   €€
Regional Italian
Via Caltana 79, 33035
Tel *041 43 60 50*
Local herbs and spices are used at this cooperative *trattoria*.

Spectacular setting of one of the waterfront restaurants at Cipriani, Giudecca

SAN MARCO: Acqua Pazza €€
Seafood   Map 7 A2
Campo Sant'Angelo 3808, 30124
Tel *041 277 06 88*   **Closed** *Sun;*
Jan–Feb
This is where the Amalfi Coast
meets Venice. A different take on
fish, with wines to match.

SAN MARCO: Gran Caffè e
Ristorante Quadri €€€
Fine Dining   Map 7 B2
Piazza San Marco 121, 30124
Tel *041 522 21 05*   **Closed** *Mon*
Fantastic historic site now in the
capable, creative hands of star
chef Massimiliano Alajmo.

SAN MARCO:
Trattoria Do Forni €€€
Fine Dining   Map 7 B2
Calle dei Specchieri 468/457, 30122
Tel *041 523 21 48*
Two dining areas with different
decors serve careful interpreta-
tions of classic Venetian cuisine.

SAN POLO: Muro €
Pizzeria   Map 6 E1
Rio Terà dei Frari 2604, 30125
Tel *041 524 53 10*   **Closed** *Thu*
A branch of the Muro pizza
restaurants, popular with young
locals. Mega salads also available.

SAN POLO: Osteria da Fiore €€€
Fine Dining   Map 6 D1
Calle del Scaleter 2202, 30125
Tel *041 72 13 08*   **Closed** *Sun, Mon;*
Jan 8–22, 3 wks Aug
Many deem this the city's best
restaurant. Seasonal produce is
the rule. Leave room for dessert.

SANTA CROCE:
Antiche Carampane €
Seafood   Map 2 F5
Rio Terà Carampane 1911, 30125
Tel *041 524 01 65*   **Closed** *Sun, Mon;*
10 days Jan, 3 wks Aug
Seek out this local favorite, for
great fish and pasta dishes. Don't
miss the seafood stir-fry.

SANTA CROCE:
Enoteca al Prosecco €
Enoteca   Map 2 E3
Campo San Giacomo dell'Orio
1503, 30135
Tel *041 524 02 22*   **Closed** *Sun;*
Jan, Aug
Enjoy light meals indoors or
outside in the square, with a
glass of excellent wine.

SANTA CROCE: Il Rèfolo €
Pizzeria   Map 2 E5
Campo del Piovan 1459, 30135
Tel *041 524 00 16*   **Closed** *Mon,*
Tue lunch; Jan
Set in a picturesque square, this
modern establishment serves
innovative gourmet pizzas.

Tasteful interiors and charming garden at Villa Cipriani, Asolo

SANTA CROCE:
Osteria La Zucca €
Regional Italian   Map 2 E5
Ponte del Megio 1762, 30135
Tel *041 524 15 70*   **Closed** *Sun*
Pretty canalside restaurant popular
with Venetians as well as visitors.

TORCELLO: Locanda Cipriani €€€
Fine Dining
Piazza Santa Fosca 29, 30012
Tel *041 73 01 50* **Closed** *Tue; Jan–Feb*
Charming and exclusive island
restaurant with a shady courtyard
and its own vegetable garden.

The Veneto
and Friuli

ARCO: Alla Lega €
Regional Italian
Via Vergolano 8, 38062
Tel *046 451 62 05*   **Closed** *end Jan–*
mid-Mar; Nov–Jan: Wed
Lively restaurant serving traditional
regional fare. Housed in a rustic
18th-century building with a
lovely courtyard.

ASOLO: Locanda Baggio €€
Regional Italian
Via Bassane 1, Località Casonetto,
31011
Tel *0423 52 96 48*   **Closed** *Mon,*
Tue lunch
Changing seasonal menu with
innovative interpretations of
traditional fare.

ASOLO: Villa Cipriani €€€
Fine Dining
Via Canova 298, 31011
Tel *0423 52 34 11*
Creative cuisine overlooking a
glorious garden, with breath-
taking views of the hills below.

BASANO DEL GRAPPA:
Osteria Trinità €
Regional Italian
Contrà San Giorgio 17, 36061
Tel *042 450 37 00*   **Closed** *Wed,*
Sat lunch

Traditional eatery serving Venetian
classics such as *pasta e fagioli*
(bean and pasta soup) and
baccalà (cod) in various forms.

BASSANO DEL GRAPPA:
Pulierin Enotavola €€
Enoteca
Strada Soarda 26, San Michele,
36061
Tel *042 450 55 62*   **Closed** *Sat*
lunch, Sun
A wine-tasting facility in a lovely
rural setting serving food based
on local products.

BELLUNO:
Ristorante Terracotta €€
Regional Italian
Via Garibaldi 61, 32100
Tel *043 729 16 92*   **Closed** *Tue, Wed*
lunch; Aug
Friendly family-run restaurant
specializing in regional seasonal
dishes. Delicious selection of
desserts and extensive wine list.

CASTELFRANCO: Barbesin €€
Regional Italian
Via Circonvallazione Est 41, 31033
Tel *042 349 04 46*   **Closed** *Wed*
dinner, Thu; 2 wks Jan, 3 wks Aug
Dishes based on local radicchio
predominate, but there are also
mixed grills and salted cod in the
Vicenza tradition.

CHIOGGIA: La Taverna €€
Seafood
Via Felice Cavallotti 348, 30015
Tel *041 40 18 06*   **Closed** *Wed; mid-*
Jan–mid-Feb
Classic seafood dishes in an
elegant setting. The outdoor
tables look over the main square.

CHIOGGIA: Osteria Penzo €€
Seafood
Calle Larga Bersaglio 525, 30015
Tel *041 400992* **Closed** *Mon dinner,*
Tue; 2 wks Nov
Just the place for traditional fare
such as squid with peas or
gnocchi with onions, mussels,
and radicchio.

For more information on types of restaurants *see p579*

CIVIDALE DEL FRIULI:
Alla Speranza   €
Regional Italian
Via Foro Giulio Cesare 15, 33043
Tel *043 273 11 31*   **Closed** *Tue; late Jan, late Sep*
Cozy wood-paneled interior for winter meals and a shady courtyard for summer lunches.

CONEGLIANO: Al Salisa   €€
Regional Italian
Via XX Settembre 4, 31015
Tel *0438 242 88*   **Closed** *Tue dinner, Wed; last 2 wks Jun*
An elegant restaurant housed in a medieval building. Serving fresh fish, game, and even sushi.

CORMONS: Ristorante al Cacciatore – La Subida   €€€
Regional Italian
Via Subida 52, 34071
Tel *048 16 05 31*   **Closed** *lunch: Mon, Thu, Fri; Tue, Wed; 2 wks Feb, 1 wk Mar*
Inventive Friulian and Slovenian menu that changes with the seasons. Beautiful country setting.

CORTINA D'AMPEZZO:
Baita Fraina   €€
Regional Italian
Località Fraina 1, 32043
Tel *0436 36 34*   **Closed** *off-season: Mon; after Easter–Jun, Oct–Nov*
Attractive wood-paneled B&B with an on-site restaurant, panoramic terrace, and spacious play area for kids.

CORTINA D'AMPEZZO:
Ristorante El Zoco   €€
Regional Italian
Cademai 18, 32043
Tel *043 686 00 41*   **Closed** *Mon; May, Nov*
Small but cozy restaurant on the outskirts of trendy Cortina. Good grilled meats and fresh vegetables.

FUMANE: Ristorante Scamperle alla Rosa   €€
Regional Italian
Via Incisa 8, 37022
Tel *045 770 10 06*   **Closed** *off-season: Mon, Sat lunch; 1st wk Jul, 2nd wk Jan*

One of the oldest restaurants in the Valpolicella. All pasta, bread, and pastries are made on-site.

GARDA:
Locanda San Vigilio   €€€
Traditional Italian
Vicolo San Vigilio, 37016
Tel *045 725 66 88*   **Closed** *mid-Nov–end Mar*
Five centuries of experience in delighting guests with excellent food, wine, and gorgeous views.

GRADO: Trattoria de Toni   €€
Seafood
Piazza Duca d'Aosta 37, 34073
Tel *043 18 01 04*   **Closed** *Wed; Dec–Feb*
The house specialty here is *boreto alla gradese*, a delicious fish stew cooked in vinegar.

GRANCONA: Isetta   €€
Regional Italian
Via Pederiva 96, 36040
Tel *044 488 99 92*   **Closed** *Tue dinner, Wed; 1 wk Jan, 2 wks Jul*
Pretty restaurant in a hilly area outside Vicenza. Regional food, with emphasis on grilled meats.

LONIGO: La Peca   €€€
Fine Dining
Via Giovanelli 2, 36045
Tel *044 483 02 14*   **Closed** *Sun, Mon; 1 wk mid-Aug*
Traditional ingredients revisited with inventive flair. Similar mixture of classic and creative in the decor.

MESTRE: La Vivanderia   €
Regional Italian
Via Pasqualigo 59/H, 30175
Tel *041 61 07 42*   **Closed** *Sat lunch; Jun–Aug: Sun; Sep–May: Thu*
Dishes based on seasonal ingredients are the focus at this *osteria*. Limited but excellent wine selection.

MIANE: Da Gigetto   €€
Regional Italian
Via De Gasperi 5, 31050
Tel *043 896 00 20*   **Closed** *Mon dinner, Tue; 2 wks Jan, 3 wks Aug*

An elegant take on traditional dishes made with seasonal ingredients, including pumpkin and mushrooms in fall.

MONTECCHIA DI CROSARA:
Alpone   €€
Regional Italian
Via Pergola 17
Tel *045 617 53 87* **Closed** *Sun dinner, Tue; 2 wks Jan, 2 wks Aug*
A refined country restaurant with a seasonal tasting menu. Local cheeses and chutneys served.

NOVENTA PADOVANA:
Boccadoro   €€
Regional Italian
Via della Resistenza 49, 35027
Tel *049 62 50 29*   **Closed** *Wed; 3 wks Aug, Dec 27–Jan 6*
Quietly elegant family-run restaurant offering well-balanced fish and meat dishes.

PADUA: Da Giovanni   €
Regional Italian
Via Pietro Maroncelli 22, 35129
Tel *049 77 26 20*   **Closed** *Sat lunch, Sun; Aug, 10 days Dec*
Time-honored *trattoria* offering classics such as homemade pasta, risotto, and meat stews.

PADUA: Trattoria San Pietro   €
Regional Italian
Via San Pietro 95, 35139
Tel *049 876 03 30*   **Closed** *Sun*
The perfect place for regional dishes cooked with fresh local ingredients. Informal atmosphere.

RUBANO: Le Calandre   €€€
Fine Dining
Via Liguria 1, 35030
Tel *049 630303*   **Closed** *Sun, Mon; 2 wks Jan, 2 wks Aug*
The cuisine at this three-Michelin-starred restaurant will enchant the senses.

> ## DK Choice
>
> **SAN GIORGIO DI VALPOLICELLA: Trattoria Dalla Rosa Alda**   €€
> Regional Italian
> *Strada Garibaldi 4, 37015*
> **Tel** *045 770 10 18*   **Closed** *Sun dinner, Mon; Jan–Feb*
> Nestled in a charming village surrounded by vineyards, this family-run *trattoria* has been serving excellent traditional fare for several generations. The ingredients are carefully sourced from local producers. The cellars are full of carefully chosen wines, from the Valpolicella region, to accompany your meal. Guests can eat alfresco on a beautiful terrace, weather permitting.

Guests relaxing under the shade of umbrellas at Locanda San Vigilio in Garda

SANTA MARIA DI SALA:
Trattoria Barison €
Regional Italian
Via della Pieve 113, Borgoricco,
35010
Tel *049 579 80 63* **Closed** *Mon*
dinner, Tue; 2 wks Jan, 3 wks Aug
Serves not only the traditional
baccalà, but also grilled meats,
cooked vegetables, and wild salads.

SOLIGHETTO:
Locanda da Lino €€
Regional Italian
Via Roma 19, 31050
Tel *043 88 21 50* **Closed** *Mon;*
last 2 wks Jul
This restaurant is part of an inn
overlooking the Prosecco
hillsides. Offers homemade pasta
and good grilled meats.

TREVISO:
Antico Ristorante Beccherie €€
Regional Italian
Piazza Ancilotto 11, 31100
Tel *042 254 08 71* **Closed** *Sun dinner,*
Mon; last 2 wks Jul
The name is derived from a word
in the local dialect that means
"butcher's," so not surprisingly,
meat is the specialty here.

TRIESTE: Antica Ghiacceretta €€
Regional Italian
Via dei Fornellli 2, 34121
Tel *040 322 03 07* **Closed** *Sun;*
1 wk Feb, 1 wk Aug
Enjoy fish dishes revisited with
an inventive, light touch in a
modern setting. Wines to match.

UDINE: Da Raffaele €
Pizzeria
Via Leonardo da Vinci 56, 33100
Tel *043 229 58 31* **Closed** *Sun lunch,*
Wed; 3 wks Jul–Aug
More than just a classic pizzeria,
this place boasts a traditional
wood-fired oven and beer on tap.

DK Choice

UDINE: Agli Amici €€€
Fine Dining
Via Liguria 252, 33100
Tel *043 256 54 11* **Closed** *Mon;*
winter: Sun dinner, Tue lunch;
2 wks end Jan–early Feb
Agli Amici whips up a cuisine
that draws on local influences,
traditions, and ingredients and
is served with elegance. Sample
one of the tasting menus for a
chance to taste a few dishes.

VALEGGIO SUL MINCIO:
Antica Locanda Mincio €
Traditional Italian
Via Michelangelo Buonarroti 12, 37067
Tel *045 795 00 59* **Closed** *Wed, Thu;*
2 wks Feb, 2 wks Nov

Frescoed walls, open fireplaces,
and an outdoor terrace. Specials
include trout from Lake Garda.

VERONA: Al Bersagliere €€
Regional Italian
Via Dietro Pallone 1, 37121
Tel *045 820 48 24* **Closed** *Sun, Mon*
This pleasantly informal, yet chic
restaurant offers great risotto
with Amarone and pasta dishes
such as *bigoli* with duck sauce.

VERONA: Arche €€
Regional Italian
Via Arche Scaligere 6, 37121
Tel *045 800 74 15* **Closed** *Sun, Mon*
lunch; 2 wks Jan
Established in 1879, this seafood
restaurant serves unmatched
marinated rock lobster.

VERONA: Il Desco €€€
Fine Dining
Via Dietro San Sebastiano 5–7, 37121
Tel *045 59 53 58* **Closed** *Sun; 2 wks*
Jun & Dec; Jul–Aug & Dec: Mon lunch
This elegant Michelin-starred
restaurant offers a creative take
on traditional dishes.

VICENZA:
Antica Casa della Malvasia €
Regional Italian
Contrà delle Morette 5, 36100
Tel *044 454 37 04* **Closed** *Mon;*
2 wks Jul
Osteria serving pumpkin pancakes,
local cheeses, and cold cuts, and
pork fillet with truffles.

VICENZA: Locanda Veneta €
Regional Italian
Via Battaglione Valtellina 138, 36100
Tel *044 456 80 07* **Closed** *Mon*
A wide range of fish and meat
dishes is served at this family
restaurant with a kids' play area.

Trentino–Alto Adige

DK Choice

BOLZANO: Cavallino Bianco €
Regional Italian
Via dei Bottai 6, 39100
Tel *0471 97 32 67* **Closed** *Sat*
dinner, Sun
Also known by its German
name, Weisses Rössl, this busy
family restaurant serves
traditional South Tyrol fare.
A large buffet breakfast is
followed by good lunch options
and a waiter-service dinner at
this hotel restaurant. The
gastronomic theme evenings
are popular with the locals.
Good value and speedy service.

Wood-beamed ceilings and soft lighting
at the informal Al Bersagliere, Verona

BOLZANO: Forst €
Birreria
Goethestrasse 6, 39042
Tel *0471 97 72 43* **Closed** *Sun*
Popular restaurant serving not
only the hallmark beer, but also
good wines and excellent food.

BOLZANO: Hopfen & Co €
Birreria
Obstplatz 17, 39100
Tel *0471 30 07 88* **Closed** *Dec 24*
A sought-after brewery serving
cold cuts, sausages, and desserts.

BRESSANONE: Fink €
Regional Italian
Via Portici Minori 4, 39042
Tel *0472 83 48 83* **Closed** *Wed;*
3 wks May; Oct–Jun: Tue dinner
Dining areas comprise elegant
seating upstairs, and more casual
rooms on the ground floor. Classic
local cuisine revisited with flair.

BRUNICO: Oberraut €
Regional Italian
Via Ameto 1, Località Amaten, 39031
Tel *0474 55 99 77* **Closed** *Thu;*
2 wks Jan
Nestled in the countryside, this
Tyrolean-style guesthouse special-
izes in game and seasonal dishes.

CALDARO: Castel Ringberg €€
Regional Italian
San Giuseppe al Lago 1, 39052
Tel *0471 96 00 10* **Closed** *Tue;*
Jan–mid-Mar
Housed in a 17th-century castle
set among vineyards. Fine fare
and a seasonally changing menu.

CERMES: Restaurant Miil €€
Fine Dining
Gampenstrasse 1, 39010
Tel *0473 56 37 33* **Closed** *Sun, Mon;*
2 wks Jan
Head to the Kränzelhof wine estate
for a modern take on classic fare.

For more information on types of restaurants *see p579*

GUDON: Unterwirt €€€
Regional Italian
Chiusa (Klausen), 39043
Tel *0472 84 40 00* **Closed** *Sun, Mon; 2 wks mid-Jun*
Chef Thomas Haselwanter's homemade breads are a tasty introduction to the seasonal menu.

LEVICO TERME: Boivin €€
Regional Italian
Via Garibaldi 9, 38056
Tel *0461 70 16 70* **Closed** *lunch (except Sun, Jul, Aug), Mon; 2 wks Jan*
Cozy *trattoria* serving classic dishes such as potato dumplings stuffed with cheese and walnuts.

ROVERETO: Novecento €
Regional Italian
Corso Rosmini 82d, 38068
Tel *0464 43 54 54* **Closed** *Sun*
Run by the Zani family, this restaurant is renowned for its homemade pasta.

TRENTO: Happy Hour €€
Seafood
Via Perini 57, 38122
Tel *0461 39 23 94* **Closed** *Sun dinner, Mon*
Pleasantly informal, with a menu that changes daily, according to the top picks from the fish market.

TRENTO:
Osteria Alle Due Spade €€
Regional Italian
Via Don Rizzi 11, 38100
Tel *0461 23 43 43* **Closed** *Sun, Mon lunch; last 2 wks Jun*
Welcoming cellar restaurant serving traditional fare including game and freshwater fish.

VAL SENALES:
Zur Goldenen Rose €€
Regional Italian
Kartaus 29, 39020
Tel *0473 67 91 30* **Closed** *Apr 20–May 25; Nov 10–Dec 5*
Explore the surrounding countryside and then unwind at this excellent hotel restaurant.

Lombardy

BELLAGIO:
Albergo Ristorante Silvio €
Regional Italian
Via Carcano 12, 22021
Tel *031 95 03 22* **Closed** *Nov–mid-Mar*
Enjoy freshwater fish on a vine-clad terrace. Offers fishing trips.

BELLAGIO: Barchetta €€
Regional Italian
Salita Mella 13, 22021
Tel *031 95 13 89* **Closed** *Tue; Nov–Easter*

A creative Mediterranean menu, including fresh fish and homemade desserts.

BERGAMO:
Colleoni dell'Angelo €€
Modern Italian
Piazza Vecchia 7, 24129
Tel *035 23 25 96* **Closed** *Mon*
Offers excellent service and imaginative cuisine.

BERGAMO: Vineria Cozzi €€
Enoteca
Via Colleoni 22, 24129
Tel *035 23 88 36* **Closed** *1 wk end Jan, 1 wk Jun*
A century-old Bergamo favorite serving local dishes.

BERGAMO: Roof Garden €€€
Mediterranean
Piazzale della Repubblica 6, 24122
Tel *035 36 61 59* **Closed** *Sat lunch, Sun*
This eight-floor restaurant offers a fusion of world flavors and Mediterranean dishes.

BORMIO: Al Filò €
Regional Italian
Via Dante 6, 23032
Tel *0342 90 17 32* **Closed** *Mon & Tue lunch; 3 wks Jun, 3 wks Nov*
Dishes based on game, cured meats, and mushrooms are served in a converted barn.

BRESCIA: Osteria Delle Streghe €
International
Via Sorbana 72, 25100
Tel *030 32 12 15* **Closed** *Sat lunch, Sun; 2 wks Aug, 2 wks Dec*
Serves grilled meats and local products. Reservations required.

BRESCIA: Trattoria Mezzeria €
Regional Italian
Via Trieste 66, 25121
Tel *030 40 306* **Closed** *Sun, Aug*

The welcoming entrance to Barchetta, in Bellagio, which specializes in local cuisine

Try the homemade *gnocchi di zucca* (pumpkin dumplings) in this busy little *trattoria*.

CANTÙ: Le Querce €
Modern Italian
Via Marche 27, 22063
Tel *031 73 13 36* **Closed** *Mon, Tue; 3 wks Aug; Dec 27–Jan 6*
Set amid oak and rhododendron, Le Querce serves local dishes and offers a rich selection of wines.

CASTELVECCANA:
Sant'Antonio €
Traditional Italian
Località Sant'Antonio, 21010
Tel *334 276 65 85* **Closed** *Sep–May (except weekends & public hols)*
Trattoria set in an old farmhouse overlooking Lake Maggiore. Try the local cheeses and cured meats.

COMO: Al Giardino €
Regional Italian
Via Monte Grappa 52, 22100
Tel *031 26 50 16* **Closed** *Sun dinner, Mon; 2 wks Aug*
Child-friendly restaurant serving local and regional specialties.

DK Choice

COMO: L'Angolo del Silenzio €
Regional Italian
Viale Lecco 25, 22100
Tel *031 377 21 57* **Closed** *Mon & Tue lunch, 2 wks Aug*
This reasonably priced *osteria*, just a few steps from the cathedral and lake, offers homemade pasta, meat, game, and fish dishes in a friendly atmosphere. Try the wild boar with red currant sauce and Roquefort. An inexpensive one-dish lunch is available on weekdays, and gluten-free dishes are available upon request. Book ahead.

COMO: Sant'Anna 1907 €
Regional Italian
Via Turati 3, 22100
Tel *031 50 52 66* **Closed** *Sat lunch, Sun*
Creative local cuisine, including seafood and vegetarian options.

CREMONA: Il Violino €€
Traditional Italian
Via Sicardo 3, 26100
Tel *0372 46 10 10* **Closed** *Tue*
Traditional local cuisine is served in this elegant restaurant.

GARGNANO DEL GARDA:
La Tortuga €€
Modern Italian
Via XXIV Maggio 5, 25084
Tel *0365 712 51* **Closed** *Tue; Mar–Oct: lunch*
Light, imaginative cuisine in this renowned lakeside restaurant.

ISEO: Trattoria Al Castello   €€
Modern Italian
Via Mirolte 53, 25049
Tel *030 98 12 85*   **Closed** *Mon–Fri lunch, Wed; 2 wks Jan; 10 days Nov*
Classic and creative dishes in a restored 17th-century wine cellar in the historic center of Iseo.

LAKE COMO:
Locanda dell'Isola Comacina   €€
Seafood
Isola Comacina, 22010
Tel *034 455 083*   **Closed** *Tue; Nov–Mar*
A unique experience on this wonderful island, deserted except for this spot serving fresh fish.

LECCO: Osteria del Filet   €
Regional Italian
Corso Matteotti 71, 23900
Tel *0341 28 30 17*   **Closed** *Jun–Sep: Sun; Oct–May: Thu*
Offers grilled meat, fish, and local salami. A fixed-price two-course lunch is offered on weekdays.

LECCO:
Antica Osteria Casa di Lucia   €€
Fine Dining
Via Lucia 27, Località Acquate, 23900
Tel *0341 49 45 94*   **Closed** *Sat lunch, Sun; 2 wks Aug*
A superb gourmet restaurant set in a 17th-century house.

LEGNANO: Al Vintun Osteria   €
Modern Italian
Via Bramante 95, 20025
Tel *0331 44 10 76*   **Closed** *lunch, Mon*
Serves Italian fish and meat dishes. A fixed-price menu is offered every Thursday evening.

MANERBA DEL GARDA:
Capriccio   €€€
Regional Italian
Piazza San Bernardo 6, Località Montinelle, 25080
Tel *0365 55 11 24*   **Closed** *Tue; Jan–Feb*
Refined dining in an elegant setting with a breathtaking view of Lake Garda from all tables.

MANTUA:
Antica Osteria Ai Ranari   €
Regional Italian
Via Trieste 11, 46100
Tel *0376 32 84 31*   **Closed** *Mon*
Traditional Mantuan dishes, including the famous *tortelli di zucca* (pumpkin-filled pasta).

MANTUA: L'Ochina Bianca   €
Regional Italian
Via Finzi 2, 46100
Tel *0376 32 37 00*   **Closed** *Mon–Thu lunch; Jul–Aug: Fri–Sun lunch*
Regional dishes with a modern touch; try the local *torta sbrisolona*, a classic Mantuan sweet cake.

Casual dining at Pasta Madre, near Porta Romana, Milan

MANTUA: Il Cigno Trattoria dei Martini   €€
Modern Italian
Piazza Carlo D'Arco 1, 46100
Tel *0376 32 71 01*   **Closed** *Mon, Tue; Aug*
Fine fare complemented by an impeccable wine list.

MILAN: Be Bop Ristorante   €
Pizzeria
Viale Col di Lana 4, 20136
Tel *02 83 76 972*   **Closed** *Aug*
This restaurant offers gluten-free and vegetarian pizzas.

MILAN: Bianco Latte   €
Mediterranean
Via Turati 30, 20121
Tel *02 60 08 61 77*   **Closed** *Mon dinner; 2 wks Aug*
Stop here for a hearty brunch or light dinner. Great bread selection and excellent coffee.

MILAN: Erba Brusca   €
Mediterranean
Alzaia Naviglio Pavese 286, 20144
Tel *02 87 38 07 11*   **Closed** *Mon, Tue*
This small restaurant has its own kitchen garden, where the creative cuisine can be enjoyed alfresco.

MILAN: Omelette e Baguette   €
Bistro
Via Pollaiuolo 9, 20159
Tel *02 688 46 87*   **Closed** *Mon; Aug*
Burgers, sandwiches, quiches, and salads to eat in or take out.

MILAN: Osteria Brunello   €
Regional Italian
Corso Garibaldi 117, 20121
Tel *02 659 29 73*   **Closed** *lunch; 2 wks Aug*
Dishes based on Tuscan traditions; try the *pappardelle* (broad, flat pasta) with wild boar.

MILAN: Pasta Madre   €
Modern Italian
Via Bernardino Corio 8, 20135
Tel *02 55 19 00 20*   **Closed** *Sun; Aug*

Contemporary decor with an relaxed atmosphere and creative Italian cuisine. Gluten-free desserts available.

MILAN: Premiata Pizzeria   €
Pizzeria
Via Alzaia Naviglio Grande 2, 20144
Tel *02 89 40 06 48*
A great pizzeria with delicious toppings like salami, *gorgonzola* (blue cheese), and truffle oil. Casual dining on shared tables.

MILAN: Trattoria Aurora   €
Traditional Italian
Via Savona 23, 20144
Tel *02 89 40 49 78*   **Closed** *Mon*
This upscale brasserie near the Navigli district offers hearty Piedmontese food. Finish your meal with a slice of *tiramisù*.

MILAN: U Barba   €
Regional Italian
Via Decembrio 33, 20137
Tel *02 45 48 70 32*   **Closed** *Mon, Tue–Fri lunch*
Friendly traditional Genoese *osteria* with a bocce ball court. Great fish and game dishes. Try the freshly made gnocchi.

MILAN:
Alla Cucina delle Langhe   €€
Traditional Italian
Corso Como 6, 20144
Tel *02 65 54 279*   **Closed** *Sun; last 3 wks Aug*
Delectable interpretations of classic Piedmontese fare, just a few steps from designer store 10 Corso Como.

MILAN: Da Giacomo   €€
Regional Italian
Via Sottocorno 6, corner of Via B. Cellini, 20129
Tel *02 76 02 33 13*   **Closed** *2 wks Aug, 2 wks Dec*
An insider Milanese address offering simply cooked fish and seafood in a friendly atmosphere.

For more information on types of restaurants *see p579*

Exquisite grounds of the lovely Locanda del Pilone di Alba, Alba

MILAN: Giglio Rosso €€
Fine Dining
Piazza Luigi di Savoia 2, 20124
Tel *02 669 41 74* **Closed** *Sat & Sun lunch; Aug, Dec 23–Jan 6*
This elegant restaurant offers innovative Tuscan dishes, staples such as variations of risotto, gnocchi, and ravioli.

DK Choice

MILAN:
Nobile Bistrò de Milan €€
Regional Italian
Corso Venezia 45, 20121
Tel *02 49 52 65 92* **Closed** *2 wks Aug*
This reasonably priced restaurant is a short walk from the Monte-napoleone shopping area. Well-known Milanese chef Claudio Sadler offers traditional regional meat and fish dishes with a modern twist. Continental breakfast, lunch, afternoon tea, *aperitivo*, and dinner are all served in an informal atmosphere, with tables both indoors and in a private courtyard.

MILAN: Victoria €€
Pizzeria
Via Clerici 1, 20121
Tel *02 869 07 92*
A few steps behind La Scala, Victoria offers traditional fare and pizza in an Art Nouveau setting.

MILAN:
Il Ristorante Bulgari Hotel €€€
Fine Dining
Via Privata Fratelli Gabba 7/B, 20122
Tel *02 80 50 52 33*
A luxury dining experience a few steps from Via Montenapoleone.

MONTE ISOLA: La Foresta €€
Regional Italian
Via Peschiera 174, Maraglio, 25050
Tel *030 988 62 10* **Closed** *Wed; 10 days Dec*

Family-run lakeside restaurant serving fresh Lake Iseo fish; sun-dried salted fish is a specialty.

PAVIA: Le Tre Torri €
Pizzeria
Via Lazzaro Spallanzani 6, 27100
Tel *0382 30 28 20* **Closed** *Sun, Mon, Sat lunch; Aug*
This restaurant offers a varied selection of pizza and pasta dishes.

PAVIA: La Locanda
Vecchia Pavia "al Mulino" €€
Regional Italian
Via al Monumento 5, Località Certosa, 27012
Tel *0382 92 58 94* **Closed** *Mon; Apr–Oct: Tue lunch; Nov–Mar: Sun dinner*
Located on the grounds of the Certosa di Pavia, this restaurant offers local specialties.

SALÒ: Osteria dell'Orologio €
Traditional Italian
Via Butturini 26, 25087
Tel *0365 29 01 58* **Closed** *Wed; 1 wk end Jan, 1 wk end Nov*
This bistro offers great-value, traditional, local cuisine and a reasonably priced wine list.

SALÒ:
Antica Trattoria alle Rose €€
Regional Italian
Via Gasparo da Salò 33, 25087
Tel *0365 432 20* **Closed** *Wed; Nov*
A traditional *trattoria* offering lake fish, local dishes, and home-made pasta. There is a delicious selection of desserts.

SALÒ: La Campagnola €€
Modern Italian
Via Brunati 11, 25087
Tel *0365 22 153* **Closed** *Mon, Tue lunch*
One of the oldest establishments around Lake Garda, La Campagnola has a extensive selection of dishes, with a separate steak menu and an extensive wine list. Book ahead.

Valle D'Aosta and Piedmont

ACQUI TERME: La Schiavia €
Regional Italian
Vicolo della Schiavia, Acqui Terme, 15011
Tel *0144 559 39* **Closed** *Sun; 3 wks Aug*
Piedmontese and Ligurian cuisine in a renovated ancient palace. Extensive wine list. Reservations required.

ALBA:
Ristorante Madonna di Como €
Regional Italian
Frazione Madonna di Como 31, 12051
Tel *017 336 33 21* **Closed** *Tue*
Set in the hills above Alba and with panoramic views, this restaurant offers regional dishes.

DK Choice

ALBA:
Locanda del Pilone di Alba €€
Regional Italian
Strada della Cicchetta Frazione Madonna di Como 34, 12051
Tel *0173 36 66 16* **Closed** *Tue; Jan–Feb*
Set in a stunning location, this converted *cascina* (barn) has views over the Alps. The menu features classic Piedmontese cuisine with touches of Neapolitan cooking. Each dish is served with a carefully selected wine. The wide range of desserts are delicious. Cooking classes and wine tasting also provided.

ALBA: Piazza Duomo €€€
Regional Italian
Piazza Risorgimento 4, 12050
Tel *0173 36 61 67* **Closed** *Sun dinner, Mon; 2 wks Aug, 3 wks Dec–Jan*
Gourmet fare and impeccable service on offer near the main square of Alba.

ALESSANDRIA: Il Grappolo €€
Regional Italian
Via Casale 28, 15121
Tel *0131 25 32 17* **Closed** *Mon dinner, Tue*
Located in a 17th-century palace. Offers Piedmontese food with a modern twist; good wine list.

AOSTA: Au Bourg €
Regional Italian
Fraz Bourg 71, Montjovet, 11020
Tel *340 009 47 88* **Closed** *Wed*
Situated in the old center of Aosta, Au Bourg is notable for traditional cheese-based dishes – *fonduta* (fondue) and raclette.

AOSTA: Grotta Azzurra €
Pizzeria
Via Croce di Citta' 97, 11100
Tel *0165 26 24 74* **Closed** *Wed; Jul*
Reasonably priced pizzeria in the town center. Varied menu features a delicious fish soup.

**AOSTA:
Trattoria degli Artisti** €€
Regional Italian
Via Maillet 5–7, 11100
Tel *0165 40 96 04* **Closed** *Sun, Mon; 15 days Jan, 15 days Nov*
On a cobbled street in the town center, this *trattoria* offers a regional menu and great home-made cakes and desserts.

ARONA: Il Calicanto €€
Mediterranean
Piazza Nazario Sauro 6, 28041
Tel *0322 24 33 50* **Closed** *Mon*
A well-chosen wine list accompanies fish and meat dishes of high quality.

DK Choice

**ARONA:
La Taverna del Pittore** €€
Fine Dining
Piazza del Popolo 39, 28041
Tel *0322 24 33 66* **Closed** *Mon*
With a veranda offering stunning views of the Rocca di Angera, this restaurant whips up creative Italian cuisine using seafood, fish, and meat. Dishes include ravioli with truffles, tagliolini with lobster sauce, and grilled beef fillet with porcini mushrooms. The menu is presented on an artist's palette, owing to the restaurant's past as a meeting place for painters.

ASTI: L'Angolo del Beato €
Regional Italian
Vicolo Cavalleri 2, 14100
Tel *0141 53 16 68* **Closed** *Sun*
Family-run spot in a medieval setting offering Piedmontese dishes; try the varied antipasti.

ASTI: Gener Neuv €€
Traditional Italian
Lungo Tanaro dei Pescatori 4, 14100
Tel *0141 55 72 70* **Closed** *Sun, Mon dinner*
Family-run restaurant near the river with excellent local cuisine; reservations required.

ASTI: Osteria da Marisa al Castello €€
Regional Italian
Piazza Castello 1, 14100
Tel *0141 20 41 15* **Closed** *Mon, Tue*
Set in an 18th-century castle overlooking the Monferrato hills. Excellent Piedmontese cuisine.

BRA: Battaglino €
Regional Italian
Piazza Roma 18, 12042
Tel *0172 41 25 09* **Closed** *Sun dinner, Mon; 2 wks Jan, 3 wks Aug*
Traditional Piedmontese meat dishes offered in this convivial restaurant in the heart of Bra.

BRA: Guido Ristorante €€
Regional Italian
Via Fossano 19, 12042
Tel *0172 45 84 22* **Closed** *Mon, Tue-Fri: lunch; 2 wks Jan, 1st wk Aug*
Located inside the castle of Pollenzo. Refined regional meat and fish dishes à la carte, or a high-price tasting menu.

**BREUIL-CERVINIA:
Al Solito Posto** €
Regional Italian
Via Meynet 10 11021
Tel *0166 94 91 26*
Charming, rustic restaurant with a good fixed-price menu.

**BREUIL-CERVINIA:
Les Neiges d'Antan** €€
French
Cretes Perreres
Tel *0166 94 87 75* **Closed** *May-mid-Jun, mid-Sep-end Oct*
This restaurant-cum-hotel serves refined rustic and rich mountain fare accompanied by great wines.

CANNOBIO: Del Lago €
Traditional Italian
Via Nazionale 2, Località Carmine Inferiore, 28822
Tel *0323 705 95* **Closed** *Tue, Wed lunch; Nov*
Simple yet imaginative dishes and views of Lake Maggiore.

CANNOBIO: Osteria Vino Divino €
Modern Italian
Strada Valle Cannobina 1, 28822
Tel *0323 719 19* **Closed** *Wed; Jan-Feb*

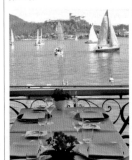

Traditional dishes reinvented with a twist in a converted 19th-century stable block. Good wine.

CANNOBIO: Lo Scalo €€
Seafood
Piazza Vittorio Emanuele 32, 28822
Tel *0323 714 80* **Closed** *Apr & Oct: Wed; Nov-Easter*
Daily catch of lake fish baked in foil, plus an array of shellfish and local produce.

**CASALE MONFERRATO:
La Torre** €€
Modern Italian
Via Candiani d'Olivola 36,15033
Tel *0142 702 95* **Closed** *Tue, Wed lunch; 3 wks Aug*
La Torre offers creative regional cuisine and has a good wine list.

**CHIUSA SAN MICHELE:
Ristorante della Sacra** €
Mediterranean
Piazzale della Sacra di San Michele, 10057
Tel *011 93 98 43* **Closed** *Apr-mid-Oct: Mon; mid-Oct-end Mar: Mon, Tue, Wed*
Good-quality café, hotel, and restaurant next to the famous Sacra San Michele monastery.

COGNE: Lou Rossignon €
Traditional Italian
Rue Mines de Cogne 22, 11012
Tel *0165 740 34* **Closed** *Mon dinner, Tue (except Aug, Dec-Feb); May, Nov*
Traditional Alpine and local fare in a cozy mountain taverna.

COSSANO BELBO: Trattoria della Posta da Camulin €
Regional Italian
Corsi Fratelli Negro 3, 12054
Tel *0141 881 26* **Closed** *Sun dinner, Mon; mid-Jul-mid-Aug*
Friendly, century-old *trattoria* serving regional dishes and homemade pasta.

**COSTIGLIOLE D'ASTI:
Caffè Roma** €
Traditional Italian
Piazza Umberto I 14, 14037
Tel *0141 96 65 44* **Closed** *Mon; 1 wk end Feb, 1 wk Jun*
A wine bar at the foot of the castle with light dishes in a cozy atmosphere.

**COSTIGLIOLE D'ASTI:
Cascina Collavini** €
Traditional Italian
Strada Traniera 24, 14037
Tel *0141 96 64 40* **Closed** *Tue dinner, Wed; 2 wks Jan, 2 wks Aug*
Simple, elegant restaurant located in an old farmhouse. The menu features traditional regional fare. Wines come from the local vineyard.

Stunning views of the Rocca di Angera from La Taverna del Pittore, Arona

For more information on types of restaurants *see p579*

COURMAYEUR: Du Tunnel   €
Pizzeria
Via Circonvallazione 80, 11013
Tel *0165 84 17 05*   **Closed** *winter: Wed lunch*
A simple snack bar–pizzeria offering wood-fired pizzas and a convivial atmosphere.

**COURMAYEUR:
Cadran Solaire**   €€
Traditional Italian
Via Roma 122,11013
Tel *0166 84 46 09*   **Closed** *Tue; May, 2 wks Nov*
Local dishes including *risotto alla Valdostana* (made with Fontina cheese) served in a cozy setting.

**CUNEO:
Osteria della Chiocciola**   €
Regional Italian
Via Fossano 1, 12100
Tel *0171 662 77*   **Closed** *Sun*
Top-quality regional cuisine. Homemade classics such as gnocchi, ravioli, and risotto are served with excellent wine.

**CUNEO:
La Ciau del Tornavento**   €€
Regional/Modern Italian
Piazza Baracco 7, 12050
Tel *0173 63 83 33*   **Closed** *Wed, Thu lunch; Feb*
Regional slow-cooked food and creative dishes, with a good selection of local cheeses.

DOMODOSSOLA: Antica Ristorante Piemonte da Sciolla   €
Regional Italian
Piazza della Convenzione 4, 28845
Tel *0324 24 26 33* **Closed** *Sun dinner, Wed; 10 days Jan, 1 wk Aug, 1 wk Sep*
Known for its local mountain fare of hearty meat and game dishes.

IVREA: Trattoria Boccon Divino €
Regional Italian
Via Aosta 47,10015
Tel *0125 489 98*   **Closed** *Thu*
A small *trattoria* in the historic center of Ivrea serving traditional regional cuisine.

NOVARA: I Due Ladroni   €
Traditional Italian
Corso Cavallotti 15, 28100
Tel *0321 62 45 81*   **Closed** *Sun*
Classic cuisine in a 16th-century palazzo in the heart of town. Excellent food with great flavors.

**NOVARA:
Osteria Del Laghetto**   €€
Regional Italian
Via Case Sparse 11, 28100
Tel *0321 47 29 62*   **Closed** *Sun; 10 days Aug, Dec 24–Jan 7*
Truffles, mushrooms, and fish are offered at this restaurant set in its own grounds. Book ahead.

Rustic and charming entrance of the popular Al Sorriso, Soriso

**ORTA SAN GIULIO:
Ristoro Olina**   €
Traditional Italian
Via Olina 40, 28016
Tel *0322 90 56 56*   **Closed** *Wed; mid-Nov–mid-Dec*
Serves homemade pasta. Local mushrooms and truffles feature on the menu, as do fish dishes.

**ORTA SAN GIULIO:
Villa Crespi**   €€€
Modern Italian
Via Fava 18, 28016
Tel *0322 91 19 02*   **Closed** *Mar–Dec: Mon, Tue (except Apr–Oct: Tue dinner)*
Set in a 19th-century folly, this restaurant offers high-level gastronomy and a vast wine list.

RIVOLI: Combal.Zero   €€€
Modern Italian
Il Castello, Piazza Mafalda di Savoia 62, 10098
Tel *010 956 52 25*   **Closed** *Sun, Mon, Sat lunch; Aug*
Located in the grounds of the Castello di Rivoli, this restaurant offers a creative Italian menu.

DK Choice

SAINT VINCENT: Le Grenier €€
Modern Italian
Piazza Monte Zerbion 1, 11010
Tel *0166 51 01 38*   **Closed** *Mon–Fri lunch, Wed; Jul*
Housed in an old barn, where soft lighting and a copper fireplace create a warm ambience. Try the *carpaccio di filetto* (thin slices of raw beef) with curry sauce, the venison, or the *ravioli di carciofi e robiola con gamberi rossi* (pasta filled with artichokes, robiola cheese, and shrimp). Ample choice of Italian and French wines and a good cheese selection.

**SESTRIERE:
La Vineria del Colle**   €€
Enoteca
Via Assietta 1, 10058
Tel *0122 764 76*   **Closed** *Mon; May, Oct*
Housed in an old wine cellar next to the ski slopes, this *enoteca* combines traditional flavors with contemporary tastes.

SORISO: Al Sorriso   €€€
Regional Italian
Via Roma 18, 28016
Tel *0322 98 32 28*   **Closed** *Mon, Tue; 1 wk Jan, 10 days Aug*
Renowned for its good, creative cuisine with a range of seasonal specialties. Book ahead.

STRESA: Il Vicoletto   €€
Modern Italian
Vicolo del Poncivo 3, 28838
Tel *0323 93 21 02*   **Closed** *Nov–Mar: Thu*
Piedmontese cuisine, including classic dishes with a touch of creativity. Good wine cellar.

STRESA: Piemontese   €€
Regional Italian
Via Mazzini 25, 28838
Tel *0323 30 235*   **Closed** *Mon; Dec–Jan*
Intimate family-run restaurant with interesting versions of local fare. There is also a pretty asfresco terrace for summer dining.

TORTONA: Aurora Girarrosto   €
Regional Italian
Strada Statale per Genova 13, 15057
Tel *0131 86 30 33*   **Closed** *2 wks Aug*
The specialty here is barbecued meats, with all produce coming from local organic farmers.

TURIN: Birilli   €€
Modern Italian
Strada Val San Martino 6, 10131
Tel *011 819 05 67* **Closed** *1st wk Jan; Oct–May: Sun*
Hearty home cooking offering a good variety of pasta, grilled fish, and meat dishes.

TURIN: Dai Saletta   €€
Regional Italian
Via Belfiore 37, 10126
Tel *011 668 78 67*   **Closed** *Sun; 1st week Jan, Aug*
Typical *trattoria* ambience. Has a classic Piedmontese menu and a good wine list. Good selection of homemade desserts.

TURIN: La Porta Rossa   €€
Seafood
Via Passalacqua 3/B, 10122
Tel *011 53 08 16*   **Closed** *Sat lunch, Sun; Aug 7, Dec 25–Jan 6*
Serving fresh fish accompanied by fine wines.

TURIN: Neuv Caval' Brons €€€
Fine Dining
Piazza San Carlo 155, 10123
Tel *011 53 90 30*
Set in a beautiful square, this
restaurant offers Piedmontese
dishes with an international twist.

VENARIA REALE:
Il Convito della Venaria €
Regional Italian
Via Andrea Mensa 37G, 10078
Tel *011 459 83 92* **Closed** *Sun
dinner, Mon*
A menu of meat and fish dishes,
pizza cooked in a wood-fired
oven, and homemade desserts.

VERBANIA PALLANZA:
Osteria del Castello €
Enoteca
Piazza Castello 9, 28921
Tel *0323 51 65 79* **Closed** *Sun;
1 wk Dec*
A local favorite serving pasta and
Piedmontese beef. Good wine list.

VERBANIA PALLANZA:
Osteria dell 'Angolo €
Regional Italian
Piazza Garibaldi 35, 28048
Tel *0323 55 63 62* **Closed** *Mon; Nov*
Typical regional taverna offering
fish dishes and Piedmontese and
Lombardy cuisine. Book ahead.

VERBANIA PALLANZA:
Milano €€
Regional Italian
Corso Zanitello 2, 28922
Tel *0323 55 68 16* **Closed** *Tue;
Nov–Easter*
Choose from a selection of fish
served with organic vegetables.

VERCELLI: Acqua Pazza €
Pizzeria
Corso Gastaldi 25, 13100
Tel *0161 21 74 20* **Closed** *Wed*
In addition to a range of pizzas,
this centrally located restaurant
also offers Vercellese dishes.

VERCELLI: Il Giardinetto €
Regional Italian
Via Sereno 3, 13100
Tel *0161 25 72 30* **Closed** *Mon;
1 wk Jan, 3 wks Aug*
Housed in a 19th-century villa,
this restaurant serves delicious
fare using Piedmontese delicacies.

VERCELLI: Il Paiolo €
Regional Italian
Viale Garibaldi 72, 13100
Tel *0161 25 05 77* **Closed** *Thu;
mid-Jul–mid-Aug*
A *trattoria* set in the rice-growing
country. Serves excellent risotto.

Liguria

DK Choice

CAMOGLI:
La Cucina di Nonna Nina €€
Regional Italian
Via Molfino 126, 16032
Tel *0185 77 38 35* **Closed** *Wed;
10 days Jan, Nov*
This restaurant is nestled on a
picturesque hill and encircled
by citrus and olive trees. The
chef produces excellent dishes,
using top-quality local products
including olive oil from the
Ligurian coast, fish bought from
local fishermen, and organic
vegetables grown in its own
garden. The focaccia, among
other breads, cakes, and Ligurian
pasta, are all homemade on the
day of serving.

CAMOGLI: Rosa €€
Seafood
Via Jacopo Ruffini 13, 16032
Tel *0185 77 34 11* **Closed** *Tue, Wed
lunch; Jun–Aug: Tue lunch*
Try the seafood and pasta in this
Art Nouveau–style restaurant.

CERVO: San Giorgio €€
Seafood
Via Volta 19, 18010
Tel *0183 40 01 75* **Closed** *Sep–Jun:
Tue lunch; Oct–Easter: Mon dinner*
Popular, charming restaurant
offering simple dishes. Book ahead.

GENOA: Da Genio €
Regional Italian
Salita San Leonardo 61r, 16128
Tel *010 58 84 63* **Closed** *Sun; Aug*
Sample the classic *trenette al
pesto* (local pasta with pesto
sauce) and fish dishes.

GENOA: Da O' Colla €
Regional Italian
Via alla Chiesa di Murta 10, 16162
Tel *010 740 85 79* **Closed** *Mon,
Sun dinner*
Excellent home-cooked Ligurian
cuisine. Located away from the
city center, but worth the taxi fare.

GENOA: Cantine Squarciafico €€
Regional Italian
Piazza Invrea 3r, 16123
Tel *010 24 70 82 3* **Closed** *1 wk Jan,
2 wks Aug*
Ligurian wine bar offering local
specialties including *stracci*
(a type of lasagna).

LEVANTO: Cavour €€
Regional Italian
Piazza Cavour 1, 19015
Tel *0187 80 77 86* **Closed** *Mon;
Dec–Jan*
Traditional *trattoria* specializing
in local seafood dishes.

MANAROLA: La Scogliera €€
Regional Italian
Via Birolli 103, 19017
Tel *0187 92 07 47* **Closed** *Thu*
A pretty, family-run restaurant
renowned for seafood specialties.

NERVI: Astor €
Regional Italian
Viale delle Palme 16, 16167
Tel *010 32 90 11*
Steps away from the seashore,
Astor offers local cuisine in a
simple and elegant setting.

PORTOFINO: Da U Batti €€
Seafood
Vico Nuovo 18, 16034
Tel *0185 26 93 79* **Closed** *Mon;
Nov–mid-Jan*
A chic, intimate restaurant, in
Liguria's most elegant town,
offers exceptional fish cuisine.

PORTOVENERE: Da Iseo €€
Regional Italian
Calata Doria 9, 19025
Tel *0187 79 06 10* **Closed** *Wed;
20 days Nov*
This *trattoria* on the waterfront
serves typical fish dishes.

Spacious terrace with spectacular views, perfect for alfresco dining at Rosa in Camogli

For more information on types of restaurants *see p579*

PORTOVENERE: Le Bocche €€
Regional Italian
Calata Doria 102, 19025
Tel *0187 79 06 22* **Closed** *Jan;
Sep–Apr: Tue*
Delicate Ligurian fish dishes served
alfresco overlooking Portovenere.

RAPALLO: U'Giancu €
Regional Italian
Via San Massimo 78, 16035
Tel *0185 26 05 05* **Closed** *lunch, Thu;
last 2 wks Dec*
Classic Ligurian specialties
complemented by vegetables
from the restaurant's garden.

**RAPALLO:
Hostaria Vecchia Rapallo** €€
Seafood
Via Cairoli 10, 16035
Tel *0185 500 53* **Closed** *Mon;
Dec–1st wk Feb*
This elegant restaurant offers
creative seafood dishes and
a good selection of wine.

RAPALLO: La Nave €€
Seafood
Via Pomaro 15, 16035
Tel *0185 66 95 02* **Closed** *Wed*
Excellent location on the beach.
Sample the *frittura di pesce* (fried
fish) and homemade pesto.

DK Choice

**SANREMO:
Da Paolo e Barbara** €€
Seafood
Via Roma 47, 18038
Tel *0184 53 16 53* **Closed** *Mon–Fri
lunch, Wed, Thu; 1 wk Jan,
2 wks mid-Jun, Dec 17–28*
This small family-run restaurant
serves local fresh fish, meat
sourced from the nearby Langhe
region, vegetables from its own
farm, and homemade focaccia.
Try the pasta with *gambero rosso
di Sanremo* (local red prawn) or
trofie al Marò (pasta with bean
and mint sauce). A special
"Saturday shopping" menu is
offered to shoppers.

SANREMO: Da Vittorio €€
Seafood
Piazza Bresca 16, 18038
Tel *0184 50 19 24* **Closed** *2 wks Nov*
A traditional favorite close to the
shore. Daily caught fish and
seafood are the main draw.

**SANTA MARGHERITA:
Cinzia e Mario** €
Seafood
Via Palestro 6, 16038
Tel *0185 28 75 05* **Closed** *Thu*
Good choice of four different
tasting menus, together with à la
carte dishes and a range of pizzas.

**SANTA MARGHERITA:
L'Insolita Zuppa** €
Traditional Italian
Via Romana 7, 16038
Tel *0185 28 95 94* **Closed** *lunch,
Wed; 2 wks Feb, Nov*
A cozy place offering traditional
meat and fish dishes.

**SESTRI LEVANTE:
Ristorante Olimpo** €€
Mediterranean
Via Della Chiusa 28, 16039
Tel *0185 426 61* **Closed** *Jan 7–
Mar 22, Nov 4–Dec 26*
Overlooking the Baia del Silenzio,
this restaurant serves fine cuisine
with an emphasis on fish.

VERNAZZA: Gambero Rosso €€
Seafood
Piazza Marconi 7, 19018
Tel *0187 81 22 65* **Closed** *Thu;
mid-Jan–Feb*
Inventive modern interpretations
of Ligurian seafood dishes.

Emilia-Romagna

**BOLOGNA:
Antica Trattoria della Gigina** €
Regional Italian
Via Stendhal 1, 40128
Tel *051 32 23 00*
Delivers a modern take on
regional cuisine without
compromising the flavors.

BOLOGNA: Battibecco €
Regional Italian
Via Battibecco 4, 40123
Tel *051 22 32 98*
Classic Bolognese cuisine and
seafood dishes in this centrally
located, elegant restaurant.

BOLOGNA: Pepperoni €
Pizzeria
Via di Barbiano 7, 40136
Tel *051 33 36 58*
Minimalist decor in this trendy
spot serving high-quality pizzas.

BOLOGNA: Pino €
Pizzeria
Via Goito 2, 40126
Tel *051 22 72 91* **Closed** *Mon*
Boisterous spot in the heart of
town offering first-rate pizzas
topped with quality ingredients.

BOLOGNA: Posta €
Regional Italian
Via della Grada 21, 41022
Tel *051 649 21 06* **Closed** *Mon;
last 2 wks Aug*
Enjoy Tuscan cuisine at this rustic
spot with wood-beamed ceilings
and terracotta-tiled floors.

BOLOGNA: Cesarina €€
Regional Italian
Via Santo Stefano 19, 40125
Tel *051 23 20 37* **Closed** *Mon, Tue*
This over 100-year-old restaurant,
situated beside an exquisite
church, offers regional dishes
with many seafood options.

BOLOGNA: Il Cantuccio €€
Seafood
Via Volturno 4, 40121
Tel *051 23 34 24* **Closed** *Mon, Tue &
Sat dinner, Sun lunch; Aug*
Fresh Mediterranean cuisine in
an intimate setting. Family-run,
with courteous service.

BOLOGNA: Marco Fadiga €€
Bistro
Via Rialto 23/C, 40124
Tel *051 22 01 18* **Closed** *Mon, Sun;
1 wk Aug*
Part bistro, part *osteria* offering
local cuisine with a creative
spin; classic French dishes are
available too.

BOLOGNA: Pappagallo €€
Fine Dining
Piazza della Mercanzia 3, 40125
Tel *051 23 28 07*
Excellent traditional cuisine
is served here, under dramatically
high ceilings. The desserts are
delicious and the cellar is well
stocked.

Elegant seating at Sanremo's noted Da Paolo e Barbara restaurant

BOLOGNA: Bitone €€€
Fine Dining
Via Emilia Levante 111, 40134
Tel *051 54 61 10* **Closed** *Mon, Tue; Aug*
Just outside the city center, this find is more than worth the trek. Fantastic Bolognese dishes and attentive service.

BOLOGNA: I Portici €€€
Fine Dining
Via dell'Indipendenza 69, 40121
Tel *051 421 85* **Closed** *Mon, Sun*
The Michelin-starred chef here creates traditional Bolognese and modern Italian cuisine. Romantic setting in a former theater.

**CASTELL'ARQUATO:
Da Faccini** €€
Regional Italian
Località S. Antonio, 29014
Tel *0523 89 63 40* **Closed** *Wed; Jun, Jul*
In-season local ingredients decide the daily changing menu at this warm, family-run eatery.

FAENZA: La Pavona €
Regional Italian
Via Santa Lucia 45, 48018
Tel *0546 310 75* **Closed** *Tue, Sat lunch; 3 wks Jul*
Just outside the historic center, this rustic and cozy spot serves the favorites of Emilian cooking.

FERRARA: Ca d'Frara €
Regional Italian
Via del Gambero 4, 44121
Tel *0532 20 50 57* **Closed** *Tue, Wed*
A slightly sterile atmosphere does not detract from the quality of the Emilian cuisine; low prices.

**FERRARA:
Big Night-da Giovanni** €€
Regional Italian
Largo Castello 38, 44121
Tel *0532 24 23 67* **Closed** *winter*
Large windows afford castle views at this restaurant serving traditional dishes from land and sea.

**FIDENZA FORNIO:
Osteria di Fornio** €
Regional Italian
Via Fornio 78, 43036
Tel *0524 601 18* **Closed** *Mon dinner, Tue*
Tucked away in the countryside, this restaurant has a changing menu of regional delicacies.

**MODENA:
Al Boschetto da Loris** €
Regional Italian
Via Due Canali Nord 218, 41122
Tel *059 25 17 59*
Housed in a 16th-century hunting lodge, this place serves home-cooked style meals.

DK Choice

**MODENA: Osteria
Francescana** €€€
Fine Dining
Via Stella 22, 41121
Tel *059 21 01 18* **Closed** *Jan– Aug; Sat lunch, Sun*
This two-Michelin-starred restaurant is avant-garde and experimental. The regional specialty – Parmigiano Reggiano – is available in five different stages of aging, and the most notable dishes include ravioli with veal offal, chlorophyll, and black truffles. Sample the marinated suckling pig with cream of fennel, and the famous Modena balsamic vinegar.

PARMA: I Tri Siochètt €
Regional Italian
Strada Farnese-Vigheffio 74/A, 43125
Tel *0521 96 88 70*
Named for the three "mad" siblings who opened this *trattoria* years ago. Hearty local cuisine.

PARMA: Parizzi €€
Fine Dining
Strada della Repubblica 71, 43100
Tel *0521 28 59 52* **Closed** *Mon; last 3 wks Aug*
Modern decor with spotlights and gold floors and a menu of contemporary and classic dishes.

PARMA: Le Viole €
Modern Italian
Strada Nuova di Castelnuovo, 60
Tel *0521 60 10 00* **Closed** *Jan 15; Jul & Aug: Mon, Sun (Aug 15–30); Dec–Feb: Wed, Thu (Feb 10)*
Seasonal produce inspires gastronomic inventions by the two sisters who run this friendly spot.

PIACENZA: Vecchia Piacenza €€
Modern Italian
Via Taverna/C.ne S. Bernardo 1, 29100
Tel *0523 30 54 62* **Closed** *Sun*
A husband and wife team combine innovative cuisine with original interior artwork.

**PIACENZA:
Antica Osteria del Teatro** €€€
Fine Dining
Via Giuseppe Verdi 16, 29121
Tel *0523 32 37 77*
Housed in a beautifully restored 15th-century palazzo. Frenchinspired choices include *foie gras* marinated in port and Armagnac.

**RAVENNA:
Antica Trattoria al Gallo 1909** €
Regional Italian
Via Maggiore 87, 48123
Tel *0544 21 37 75* **Closed** *Sun dinner, Mon, Tue*

Sophisticated at the Michelin-starred Osteria Francescana, Modena

The rustic exterior of this historic *trattoria* hides an Art Deco interior. Ample Emilian specialties.

RAVENNA: Ca de Ven €
Regional Italian
Via Corrado Ricci 24, 48121
Tel *0544 301 63* **Closed** *Mon*
Authentic eatery popular with locals. Shared tables available for a more casual dining experience.

RAVENNA: Bella Venezia €€
Regional Italian
Via 4 Novembre 16, 48121
Tel *0544 21 27 46* **Closed** *Sun; 3 wks Jan, 1 wk Jul*
Excellent pasta and fresh fish in a romantic, intimate setting. Great service and a central location.

RIMINI: Osteria de Borg €
Regional Italian
Via Forzieri 12, 47921
Tel *0541 225 30*
A rustic setting in which to sample meat specialties, local cheeses, and cured meats.

RIMINI: Dallo Zio €€
Seafood
Via Santa Chiara 16, 47921
Tel *0541 78 67 47*
The cuisine at this fresh, modern spot is inspired from the classic flavors of the Adriatic.

RIMINI: Europa €€
Seafood
Via Roma 51, 47922
Tel *0541 287 61*
Traditional yet inventive restaurant serving fresh fish and meat dishes.

RIMINI: Guido €€
Seafood
Lungomare Guido Spadazzi 12, 47924
Tel *0541 37 46 12* **Closed** *Mon; 1 wk Dec*
Cuttlefish, oysters, and calamari are just a few of the specialties served at this spot on the beach.

Florence

Bar 53 Bottega €
Enoteca   Map 2 D3
Via di Santa Caterina d'Alesssandria 3, 50129
Tel *055 463 38 95*   **Closed** *Sat*
There's a chilled vibe at this wine bar that's also a popular spot for breakfast and lunch. Free Wi-Fi.

Il Pizzaiuolo €
Pizzeria   Map 4 E1
Via de' Macci 113, 50122
Tel *055 24 11 71*   **Closed** *Sun; 3 wks Aug, 1 wk Dec*
Treat yourself to a thick-crusted Neapolitan-style pizza.

Il Vegetariano €
Vegetarian   Map 2 D3
Via delle Ruote 30, 50129
Tel *055 47 50 30*   **Closed** *Mon; last 2 wks Aug*
There is excellent value is to be had at this long-established restaurant. Service is meager, portions are not.

La Bussola €
Pizzeria   Map 5 C3
Via Porta Rossa, 58 50123
Tel *055 293376*
Charming, low-key pizzeria with a wood-burning oven. The service is excellent, and the wine list surprisingly ample.

Ruth's €
Kosher/Vegetarian   Map 2 E5
Via Luigi Carlo Farini 2, 50121
Tel *055 248 08 88*   **Closed** *Fri, Sat, Jewish festivities*
Located beside the synagogue, this kosher restaurant serves Jewish-inspired recipes; many vegetarian and seafood options.

Tarocchi €
Pizzeria   Map 6 E5
Via dei Renai 12, 50125
Tel *055 234 39 12*   **Closed** *Mon*
Great prices at this off-the-beaten-path pizzeria. Pasta dishes are available, too.

Trattoria Zàzà €
Regional Italian   Map 1 C4
Piazza del Mercato Centrale 26, 50123
Tel *055 21 54 11*
Traditional Florentine favorites from land and sea, as well as, vegetarian and gluten-free fare.

Da Kou €€
Japanese   Map 5 C1
Via del Melarancio 19/r, 50123
Tel *055 28 29 22*
Fresh and authentic sushi prepared with skill; portions are generous. The decor is modern and informal.

DK Choice

Alle Murate €€
Regional Italian   Map 6 E2
Via del Proconsolo 16/r, 50122
Tel *055 24 06 18*   **Closed** *Sun lunch, Mon*
This unique restaurant offers a one-of-a-kind opportunity to combine Florentine art and food. Housed in a 14th-century palace, it boasts original frescoes on the walls and vaulted ceilings, hidden for centuries and uncovered in a painstaking restoration process. The excellent, understated local cuisine is a perfect companion to the stunning early-Renaissance art.

Dei Frescobaldi €€
Enoteca   Map 6 D3
Via dei Magazzini 2, 50122
Tel *055 28 47 24*   **Closed** *Sun, Mon lunch; 1 wk Jan, 3 wks Aug*
Sample top fine wines and meticulously matched dishes in a setting of frescoed walls and exposed stonework.

Ora d'Aria €€
Modern Italian   Map 6 D4
Via dei Georgofili 11/r, 50100
Tel *055 200 16 99*   **Closed** *Sun, Mon lunch; 2 wks Jan, 2 wks Aug*
Tucked away in an alley, this place is well worth the hunt for its authentic specialty dishes.

Osteria Santo Spirito €€
Regional Italian   Map 5 A5
Piazza Santo Spirito 16, 50125
Tel *055 238 23 83*   **Closed** *Mon, public hols*
Tuscan specialties with a twist at this cozy eatery.

Pane e Vino €€
Modern Italian   Map 3 A1
Piazza di Cestello 37/r, 50124
Tel *055 247 69 56*
Cozy and familial restaurant offering traditional Florentine dishes and more modern ones.

Bistrò Del Mare €€€
Fine Dining   Map 5 C3
Lungarno Corsini 4/r, 50123
Tel *055 239 92 24*   **Closed** *Mon; 1 wk Aug*
Steps away from Ponte Vecchio, this refined restaurant serves dishes inspired by old Tuscan recipes but brought up to date.

Cibrèo €€€
Modern Italian   Map 4 E1
Via Andrea del Verrocchio 8/r, 50122
Tel *055 234 11 00*   **Closed** *Mon; 3 wks Aug*
This trendy place delights diners with its take on local cuisine.

Interiors of Pane e Vino, popular for traditional Florentine dishes, Florence

DK Choice

Enoteca Pinchiorri €€€
Fine Dining   Map 4 E1
Via Ghibellina 87, 50122
Tel *055 24 27 57*   **Closed** *Sun, Mon; Aug, public hols*
This triple Michelin-starred restaurant is considered by some to be the finest in Italy. Its modern, understated interior and soft lighting provide the ideal setting to indulge in any of the exquisite gastronomic creations. Specials include the ravioli with *taggiasche* olives and burrata cheese, and the roast pigeon with honey, spices, and breaded eggplant. The wine cellar is legendary. A private dining room is available.

Tuscany

AREZZO:
La Lancia d'Oro €€
Regional Italian
Piazza Grande 18, 52100
Tel *0575 210 33*   **Closed** *Mon; 2 wks Feb, 2 wks Nov*
Hearty Tuscan meals served in a stunning setting with outdoor seating under *Vasari's Loggias* (Vasari's Corridor).

AREZZO:
Le Chiavi d'Oro €€
Modern Italian
Piazza San Francesco 7, 52100
Tel *0575 403 313*   **Closed** *Mon; 1 wk Feb, 1 wk Aug*
This stylish Danish-designed restaurant is elegantly decorated with 1960s swivel stools and blond wood floors. The kitchen specializes in contemporary, regionally inspired cuisine.

Key to prices *see p580*

ARTIMINO: Da Delfina €€
Regional Italian
Via della Chiesa 1, 59015
Tel *055 871 80 74* **Closed** *Mon, Tue;
1 wk Jan, 1 wk Feb*
The chef's creations are inspired
by his mother's cooking. Hidden
away in a delightful walled town.

**CORTONA:
Hostaria la Bucaccia** €
Regional Italian
Via Ghibellina 17, 52044
Tel *0575 606 039* **Closed** *Jan 15–30;
Dec–Feb: Mon*
This restaurant has original
features, built over a Roman road.
Home cooking is served.

CORTONA: Il Falconiere €€€
Fine Dining
Località San Martino 370, 52044
Tel *0575 612 679* **Closed** *Jan 7–30*
Nestled among olive and cypress
trees, this restaurant is out of a
fantasy. Great place to sample
exalted Tuscan cuisine.

ELBA: La Lucciola €€
Seafood
Lungomare Pino Nomellini 64, 57034
Tel *0565 976 395* **Closed** *Nov–Apr*
The catch of the day is served
directly on the beach at this
romantic and intimate spot.

ELBA: Publius €
Regional Italian
Piazza del Castagneto 11, 57030
Tel *0565 992 08* **Closed** *Mon;
Nov–Mar*
A wide variety of dishes and an
impressive wine cellar at this
charming restaurant boasting
fantastic sea views.

ELBA: Stella Marina €€
Seafood
Via Vittorio Emanuele II 1, 57037
Tel *0565 915 983* **Closed** *Mon*
Fish doesn't get much fresher
than at this tiny restaurant on
the edge of the port; excellent
wine list.

LUCCA: Da Giulio in Pelleria €
Regional Italian
Via delle Conce 47, 55100
Tel *0583 559 48* **Closed** *Sun;
3 wks Jan*
Prices are reasonable at this
popular *trattoria* serving Tuscan
fare such as polenta and *zuppa di
farro* (bean and spelt soup).

LUCCA: La Tana dell'Orco €
Pizzeria
Viale Regina Margherita 225, 55100
Tel *0583 558 81* **Closed** *Tue*
The concept is simple at this
pizzeria just outside the city walls
– minimal service and low prices.

LUCCA: Buca di Sant'Antonio €€
Regional Italian
Via della Cervia 3, 55100
Tel *0583 558 81* **Closed** *Sun dinner,
Mon; 1 wk Jan, 1 wk Jun*
Ancient local recipes are lovingly
prepared at this historic eatery
in a medieval stable.

**MONTALCINO:
Il Boccon Divino** €€
Regional Italian
*Strada Provinciale Traversa dei
Monti 201, 53024*
Tel *0577 848 233* **Closed** *Tue*
Favorites from Tuscany and
beyond with sweeping views of
the countryside. Fantastic wines.

**MONTE ARGENTARIO:
Osteria dei Nobili Santi** €€
Seafood
Le Piane, 58019
Tel *0564 833 015* **Closed** *Mon*
Good prices at this intimate
restaurant serving plenty of
delectable fish dishes.

**MONTEPULCIANO:
Osteria Acquacheta** €
Regional Italian
Via del Teatro 22, 53045
Tel *0578 717 086*
This tiny, popular restaurant is
always packed. The Tuscan meat
dishes are a specialty.

MONTEPULCIANO: La Grotta €€
Regional Italian
Via di San Biagio 15, 53045
Tel *0578 757 479* **Closed** *Wed;
Jan, Feb*
A restaurant set in a 16th-century
building. The menu features
expertly revisited Tuscan classics.

MONTERIGGIONI: Il Pozzo €€
Regional Italian
Piazza Roma 20, 53035
Tel *0577 304 127* **Closed** *Sun
dinner, Mon; 2 wks Jan, 2 wks Feb*
Well located in the center of the
walled town, this rustic *osteria*
serves traditional fare.

PIENZA: Latte di Luna €
Regional Italian
Via San Carlo 2, 53026
Tel *0578 748 606*
Classic Tuscan dishes at this
quaint, family-friendly eatery.
Dont forget to try the locally
produced Pecorino cheese.

PISA: La Taverna di Emma €
Modern Italian
Carlo Salomone Cammeo 50, 56122
Tel *050 555 003* **Closed** *Sun;
1 wk Feb, last wk Aug*
Simple local eatery with a
talented chef who whips up
imaginative yet tradition-inspired
recipes. Gorgeous desserts.

PISA: Osteria del Porton Rosso €
Regional Italian
Via Porton Rosso 11, 56126
Tel *050 580 566* **Closed** *Mon*
The menu of classic Tuscan meat
and seafood are scrawled on a
blackboard at this eatery hidden
in the backstreets.

PISA: V. Beni €€
Seafood
Piazza Chiara Gambacorti 22, 56125
Tel *050 250 67* **Closed** *Sun;
2 wks Aug*
Slightly off the tourist track, this
favorite with the locals is housed
in a rustic 600-year-old building.

PISA: A Casa Mia €
Regional Italian
Via Provinciale Calcesana 10, 56010
Tel *050 879 265* **Closed** *Sun;
1 wk Jan, Aug*
Traditional recipes are served
with familial warmth in the
one-time home of the owners.

PISTOIA: La Bottegaia €
Enoteca
Via Del Lastrone 17, 51100
Tel *0573 365 602* **Closed** *Mon;
2 wks Aug*
Cheeses, cured meats, tempting
desserts, and, of course, plenty of
fantastic bottles at this friendly,
unpretentious wine bar.

The well-stocked wine cellar at Da Delfina in Artimino

For more information on types of restaurants *see p579*

The traditionally decorated dining area of Osterie le Logge in Siena

PRATO: Osteria Cibbè €
Regional Italian
Piazza Mercatale 49, 59100
Tel *0574 607 509* **Closed** *Sun; 3 wks Aug*
Try the traditional Tuscan recipes and comforting homemade desserts at this charming eatery.

SAN GIMIGNANO: Antica Macelleria €
Regional Italian
Via Dei Marsili 1/3, 53037
Tel *0577 942 228*
Pick your meat from the old-style butcher's counter and the chef will prepare it to your liking.

SAN GIMIGNANO: Dorandò €€
Regional Italian
Vicolo dell'Oro 2, 53037
Tel *0577 941 862* **Closed** *Dec–Feb*
Enjoy the Slow Food dining experience at Dorandò.

SAN SEPOLCRO: Ristorante da Ventura €
Regional Italian
Via Aggiunti Niccolò 30, 52037
Tel *0575 742 560* **Closed** *Sun dinner, Mon; 2 wks Aug*
Enjoy homemade delights at this family-run eatery. Try the slow-cooked veal, or truffle-filled ravioli.

DK Choice

SIENA: 53 Cento €
Enoteca
Viale Pietro Toselli 19, 53100
Tel *0577 050 169* **Closed** *Sun; 2 wks Aug*
This eclectic wine bar is open from breakfast to the early hours. The well-stocked cellar and the capable staff are happy to make suggestions. The cuisine is pan-Mediterranean with imaginative takes on Italian staples, including many vegetarian options. There is also an oyster bar.

SIENA: Enoteca i Terzi €
Enoteca
Via dei Termini 7, 53100
Tel *0577 443 29* **Closed** *Sun*
Airy, spacious wine bar with copious varieties of cheeses and smoked and cured meats.

SIENA: Grotta Santa Caterina da Bagoga €
Regional Italian
Via della Galluzza 26, 53100
Tel *0577 282 208* **Closed** *Sun dinner, Mon; 2 wks Jan, 1 wk Jul*
Tucked in a narrow backstreet, this authentic restaurant offers good food and great service.

SIENA: La Taverna di San Giuseppe €
Regional Italian
Via Giovanni Duprè 132, 53100
Tel *0577 422 86* **Closed** *Sun; 2 wks Jul, 2 wks Dec*
Rustic eatery with local flavors. Check out the wine cellar, carved from an ancient Etruscan dwelling.

SIENA: Trattoria Papei €
Regional Italian
Piazza del Mercato 6, 53100
Tel *0577 280 894*
This informal spot is run by an entire family, with mama preparing Tuscan specialties.

SIENA: Osteria le Logge €€
Modern Italian
Via del Porrione 33, 53100
Tel *0577 480 13* **Closed** *Sun; 1 wk Jan*
This lovely restaurant with traditional furnishings presents a novel interpretation of classic cuisine and has a fine wine list.

SIENA: Il Canto €€€
Modern Italian
Strada di Certosa 82, 53100
Tel *0577 288 180* **Closed** *Nov–Feb*
Siena's most experimental and creative restaurant offers a gastronomic adventure.

VIAREGGIO: Cabreo €€
Seafood
Via Firenze 14, 55049
Tel *0584 546 43* **Closed** *Sun; Nov*
Whatever is caught on any given day ends up on the plate at this authentic fish eatery. Meat dishes are available.

VIAREGGIO: Piccolo Principe €€€
Fine Dining
Piazza Giacomo Puccini 1, 55049
Tel *0584 401 86 22* **Closed** *Nov–May*
Creative and sophisticated cuisine served in a rooftop garden with magnificent sea views. Its Michelin star is well earned.

VOLTERRA: Enoteca del Duca €
Enoteca
Via di Castello 2, 56048
Tel *0588 815 10* **Closed** *Tue; Jan, Feb*
Cozy wine bar serving rustic snacks. There's also an elegant restaurant for full meals in the typical Tuscan tradition.

VOLTERRA: Il Sacco Fiorentino €
Regional Italian
Via Turazza 13, 56048
Tel *0588 885 37* **Closed** *Wed; 1 wk Jan*
An intriguing tasting menu, as well as numerous à la carte options, offering traditional Tuscan with international touches.

Umbria

ASSISI: I Monaci €
Pizzeria
Via Scalette 10, 06081
Tel *075 81 25 12*
A warm and rustic pizzeria in the heart of the medieval center.

ASSISI: La Fortezza €
Regional Italian
Vicolo della Fortezza 2b, 06081
Tel *075 81 29 93* **Closed** *Thu; Jul*
Mostly traditional cuisine, with some creative touches. Friendly but professional service and good price-quality ratio.

GUBBIO: Grotta dell'Angelo €€
Enoteca
Via Gioia 47, 06024
Tel *075 9271 747* **Closed** *Tue; Jan 7, Feb 7*
This rustic wine bar is carved into a 13th-century cave. Enjoy dining in the garden in summer.

GUBBIO: Taverna del Lupo €€
Regional Italian
Via Ansidei 6, 06024
Tel *075 92743 68*
Succulent local cuisine at this centrally located spot run by a husband and wife team.

MONTEFALCO: Coccorone €
Regional Italian
Largo Tempestivi 11, 06036
Tel *074 2379 535* **Closed** *Wed*
Traditional seasonal ingredients, including truffles and porcini mushrooms, make for a fresh and authentic dining experience.

NORCIA: Beccofino €
Regional Italian
Piazza San Benedetto 12, 06046
Tel *0743 81 60 86* **Closed** *Wed; Dec 25*
Traditional Umbrian cuisine served in a simple setting. Ample wine cellar with over 250 labels.

NORCIA:
Taverna de' Massari €€
Regional Italian
Via Roma 13, 06046
Tel *0743 81 62 18* **Closed** *Tue; 2 wks Jan, 1 wk Jul*
Intimate spot offering the time-honored cured meats and dishes that make this tiny town famous.

ORVIETO: Del Moro-Aronne €
Regional Italian
Via San Leonardo 7, 05018
Tel *0763 34 27 63*
Simple, home-style cooking is served up enthusiastically at this restaurant with low prices.

ORVIETO: La Volpe e l'Uva €
Regional Italian
Via Ripa Corsica 2, 05018
Tel *0763 34 16 12*
A wide variety of tempting options – even for vegetarians – at this bustling restaurant in town.

ORVIETO: Duca di Orvieto €€
Regional Italian
Via della Pace 5, 05018
Tel *0763 34 46 63*
A family-run restaurant using centuries-old local recipes. Patient servers will explain the day's specials in detail.

Traditional rustic charm at the cozy Duca di Orvieto, Orvieto

ORVIETO: I Sette Consoli €€
Modern Italian
Piazza Sant'Angelo 1A, 05018
Tel *0763 343 911* **Closed** *Sun dinner, Wed*
Original and imaginative cuisine in a rustic yet dignified setting. Dine in the garden in summer, weather permitting.

PASSIGNANO SUL TRASIMENO:
Cacciatori da Luciano €€€
Seafood
Lungolago Aganor Pompilj 3, 06061
Tel *075 827 210* **Closed** *Wed; Jan 6–30*
Fresh fish from the adjacent lake and delicacies from the sea are cooked using authentic recipes. Extensive wine list.

PERUGIA: Il Falchetto €
Modern Italian
Via Bartolo 20, 06123
Tel *075 5731 775* **Closed** *Mon*
Gorgeous little restaurant inside a medieval building, with seating on the piazza in summer. Classic Umbrian dishes fill the menu.

PERUGIA: La Botte €
Pizzeria
Via Volte della Pace 31, 06122
Tel *075 5722 679* **Closed** *Sun*
Simple, no-frills pizzeria serving time-honored family recipes.

PERUGIA:
Antica Trattoria San Lorenzo €€
Modern Italian
Piazza Danti 19/a, 06122
Tel *075 5721 956*
Creative Umbrian-inspired cuisine at a cozy spot just behind the Duomo.

PERUGIA: Il Gradale €€
Modern Italian
Strada Montevile, 06126
Tel *075 5717 402*
A branch of Castello di Monterone's restaurants delights diners with a choice of light and sophisticated dishes.

PERUGIA: Il Postale €€€
Fine Dining
Strada Montevile 3, 06126
Tel *075 5724 214* **Closed** *Sun dinner, Mon, Tue; Jan 15–Feb 15*
Set within a wonderful castle location, this award-winning restaurant serves meals rich with local ingredients.

SPOLETO: Il Tempio del Gusto €
Modern Italian
Via Arco di Druso 11, 06049
Tel *0743 471 21* **Closed** *Thu*
Stone floors and small tables create an intimate atmosphere in this restaurant serving creative and top-notch cuisine.

DK Choice

SPOLETO: Il Tartufo €
Regional Italian
Piazza Giuseppe Garibaldi 24, 06049
Tel *0743 40 236* **Closed** *Mon*
The decor may be simple and old-fashioned, but the local truffles that this restaurant is proudly named for make it worth a special trip. The owners, members of the family who opened the restaurant in 1927, are dedicated to creating dishes based on traditional local recipes. Look out for the ancient Roman paving tiles in one of the dining rooms. In good weather, it's possible to eat outside on the bustling piazza.

TODI:
Antica Hostaria della Valle €
Modern Italian
Via Augusto Ciuffelli 19, 06059
Tel *075 894 48 48* **Closed** *Thu*
Imaginative gastronomic delights at this cozy and welcoming *osteria*. The homemade pasta is the star of the show.

TODI: Umbria €€
Regional Italian
Via San Bonaventura 13, 06059
Tel *075 894 27 37* **Closed** *Tue*
Traditional cuisine is carefully prepared at this legendary restaurant. There is a picturesque dining terrace with views over a lush valley.

Le Marche

ANCONA: Boccon Divino €
Regional Italian
Via Giacomo Matteotti 13, 60121
Tel *071 572 69* **Closed** *Sun; Aug*
Classic Marchegiana cuisine is served up here by a young but capable staff.

ANCONA: La Moretta €
Regional Italian
Piazza Plebiscito 52, 60121
Tel *071 20 23 17* **Closed** *Sun; Jan 1–6*
This traditional restaurant has been in the same family for over 100 years. Sample the excellent *stoccafisso* (dried cod) in broth.

ANCONA: Sale Grosso €€
Modern Italian
Via Guglielmo Marconi 3, 60125
Tel *071 207 52 79*
Imaginative reinvention of Italian cuisine using local ingredients from land and sea. The decor is fresh and minimalist.

ASCOLI PICENO: Gallo d'Oro €
Regional Italian
Corso Vittorio Emanuele 54, 63100
Tel *0736 25 35 20* **Closed** *Sun dinner, Mon*
Despite the sophisticated interior, prices are reasonable at this spot serving regional fare.

ASCOLI PICENO: Del Corso €€
Seafood
Corso Giuseppe Mazzini 277, 63100
Tel *0736 25 67 60* **Closed** *Sun dinner, Mon; 3 wks Jan, Dec 2*
Tiny stone-walled restaurant located in a historic palazzo. Most dishes on the changing menu are fish-based.

LORETO: Andreina €
Regional Italian
Via Buffolareccia 14, 60025
Tel *071 97 01 24* **Closed** *Tue, Wed; Jun*
Rustic with a few modern touches. Tuscan specialties reign, with tempting options from the grill.

LORETO: Vecchia Fattoria €
Regional Italian
Via Manzoni 19, 60025
Tel *071 97 89 76*
This converted farmhouse offers classic regional dishes in a welcoming family atmosphere.

PESARO: Da Gennaro €
Seafood
Via Santa Marina Alta 30/1, 61100
Tel *0721 273 21* **Closed** *Sun dinner, Mon; Sep 1–20*
Perched in the mountains 4 miles (7 km) west of the sea, this is one of the most authentic eateries in town.

PESARO: Il Commodoro €€
Enoteca
Viale Trieste 269, 61121
Tel *0721 326 80* **Closed** *Mon*
This inviting modern spot serves up fresh fish and much more. Cozy wine bar attached.

PESARO: Da Alceo €€€
Seafood
Strada Panoramica Ardizio 101, 61100
Tel *0721 513 60*
A panoramic seaside terrace provides an exquisite setting in which to sample some of the best seafood in the area.

SAN MARINO:
Righi la Taverna €€€
Fine Dining
Piazzale della Libertà 10, 47825
Tel *0549 99 11 96* **Closed** *Sun dinner, Mon; Jan, Feb*
The most famous restaurant in this republic serves a mix of age-old and modern Italian cuisine.

URBANIA: Big Ben €
Regional Italian
Corso V. Emanuele 61, 61049
Tel *0722 31 97 95*
Marchegiana specialties such as truffles, snails, and wild fennel are offered at this restaurant.

URBINO: Guanábana €
Modern Italian
Via Giuseppe Mazzini 65, 61029
Tel *366 726 55 51*
This quirky little restaurant offers an interesting fusion of local and Venezuelan cuisines. The flavors are surprisingly complementary.

URBINO: Taverna degli Artisti €
Regional Italian
Via Donato Bramante 52, 61029
Tel *0722 26 76*
Opulent frescoed ceilings make a dramatic contrast to the simple home-style cooking.

URBINO:
Antica Osteria da la Stella €€
Regional Italian
Via Santa Margherita 1, 61029
Tel *0722 320228*
This historic restaurant counts famous painters Raphael and Piero della Francesca among its one-time clientele. Elegant interior with a cozy fireplace.

Rome

The Ancient Center

Enoteca Provincia Romana €€
Enoteca **Map** 3 A4
Largo di Foro Traiano 82-84, 00187
Tel *06 69 94 02 73* **Closed** *Sun & Mon lunch*
Both the wine list and the menu ingredients are refreshingly local at this *enoteca*. Good snack food to accompany a long wine list.

Aroma €€€
Fine Dining **Map** 7 1A
Via Labicana 125, 00184
Tel *06 77 59 13 80*
A sleek interior and unequaled views of the Colosseum. Seasonal menu of regional favorites.

Around Piazza Navona

Acchiappafantasmi €
Pizzeria **Map** 9 B3
Via dei Cappellari 66, 00186
Tel *06 687 34 62* **Closed** *Mon*
It's name means "Ghostbusters," and the ghost-shaped pizzas are as tasty as they are amusing.

Baffetto €
Pizzeria **Map** 9 B3
Via del Governo Vecchio 114, 00186
Tel *06 686 16 17*

The crunchy Roman-style pizza is considered by many to be the best in Rome, but be prepared for a long wait.

Nonna Betta €
Regional Italian **Map** 10 D5
Via del Portico d'Ottavia 16, 00186
Tel *349 667 16 20* **Closed** *Tue*
An authentic Jewish eatery. Don't expect an English translation on the handwritten menu, but the food is glorious.

Old Bear €
Regional Italian **Map** 9 C2
Via dei Gigli d'Oro 3, 00186
Tel *06 68 21 00 09* **Closed** *Apr; Nov: Mon, Tue*
Dark wood beams and low ceilings create a warm and inviting ambience. Don't miss the Tuscan soup with truffle oil.

Open Baladin €
Birreria **Map** 10 D5
Via degli Specchi 6, 00186
Tel *06 683 89 89* **Closed** *2 wks Aug, Dec 24, 25, & 31*
Over 120 labels of craft beers served here, as well as original, all-natural sodas. Staple snack food is served.

Angolo Divino €€
Enoteca **Map** 9 C4
Via dei Balestrari 12, 00186
Tel *06 686 44 13* **Closed** *Mon & Tue lunch; Aug 10–20*
Intimate and romantic spot. The warm chocolate cake is almost as divine as the wine list.

Capricci Siciliani €€
Regional Italian **Map** 9 B2
Via di Panico 83, 00186
Tel *06 45 43 38 23* **Closed** *Aug*
Elegant Sicilian dining in the heart of the historic center; specialties include swordfish medallions and anchovy rolls.

Diners at the well-known Jewish-Roman eatery Nonna Betta

Cul de Sac €€
Enoteca **Map** 9 C3
Piazza di Pasquino 73, 00186
Tel *06 68 80 10 94* **Closed** *Dec 24, 25, & 31*
This narrow wine bar boasts hundreds of labels as well as a wide variety of tasty eats.

Da Giggetto €€
Regional Italian **Map** 10 E5
Via del Portico d'Ottavia 21/22, 00186
Tel *06 686 11 05* **Closed** *Mon; last 2 wks Aug, Dec 24 & 31*
Dine in the shadow of ancient ruins at this famous Jewish-Roman eatery. Don't miss the deep-fried artichokes.

Il Bacaro €€
Modern Italian **Map** 10 D2
Via degli Spagnoli 27, 00186
Tel *06 687 25 54*
Romantic with specialties such as *trofie* with asparagus and beef *carpaccio* with endive and truffles.

Roscioli €€
Enoteca **Map** 9 C4
Via dei Giubbonari 21, 00186
Tel *06 687 52 87*
Part wine bar, part *salumeria*, with drool-worthy meats and cheeses and a dizzying selection of labels.

Terra di Siena €€
Regional Italian **Map** 9 C3
Piazza di Pasquino 77, 00186
Tel *06 68 30 77 04*
Hearty Tuscan dishes such as Florentine steak and *ribollita* soup; seating in a cheerful dining room or on the buzzing piazza.

Al Bric €€€
Enoteca **Map** 9 C4
Via del Pellegrino 51, 00186
Tel *06 687 95 33* **Closed** *Mon; 2 wks Aug*
The impeccable wine list at Al Bric is matched with tempting creations from the kitchen. The setting is cozy.

Camponeschi €€€
Fine Dining **Map** 9 C4
Piazza Farnese, 50/50a, 00186
Tel *06 687 49 27*
World-class dining in the heart of town. Try tagliolini with lobster and black truffles; wild game is the house specialty.

Hostaria dell'Orso €€€
Fine Dining **Map** 9 C2
Via dei Soldati 25c, 00186
Tel *06 68 30 11 92* **Closed** *Sun & Mon lunch; Aug*
This legendary restaurant and nightclub has been welcoming guests since the start of the 16th century.

Bright and inviting interior of Al Bric, around Piazza Navona

Il Pagliaccio €€€
Fine Dining **Map** 9 B2
Via dei Banchi Vecchi 129, 00186
Tel *06 68 80 95 95* **Closed** *Sun, Mon & Tue lunch; Aug*
Surprising blend of pan-Asian and Mediterranean fare offered here. Try one of the tasting menus, some of which have up to 12 courses.

Northeast Rome

Ai Tre Scalini €
Enoteca **Map** 3 C4
Via Panisperna 251, 00184
Tel *06 48 90 74 95*
One of the hippest wine bars in town, with excellent wines, beers, and savory delicacies.

Antica Birreria Peroni €
Birreria **Map** 10 F3
Via di San Marcello 19, 00187
Tel *06 679 53 10* **Closed** *Sun; Aug 2 & 5; Dec 24, 25, & 31*
Casual spot that's been serving beer for over 100 years. All-Italian grilled beef and pork.

Cavour 313 €
Enoteca **Map** 3 C5
Via Cavour 313, 00184
Tel *06 678 54 96* **Closed** *Aug*
Highly trained staff help guests select a memorable vintage in this wood-lined wine bar.

La Carbonara €
Regional Italian **Map** 3 C4
Via Panisperna 214, 00184
Tel *06 482 51 76* **Closed** *Sun; Aug*
This *osteria* serves hearty local fare and of couse Carbonara.

San Marco €
Pizzeria **Map** 3 C1
Via Sardegna 38, 00187
Tel *06 42 01 26 20* **Closed** *1 wk Aug, Dec 24*
A wine bar and grill noted for its pizzas and warm service. Blackboard-covered walls list the day's specials.

Trattoria Monti €
Regional Italian **Map** 4 D4
Via di San Vito 13, 00185
Tel *06 446 65 73* **Closed** *Sun dinner, Mon; Aug, Dec 24–Jan 3*
The day's specials, featuring local seasonal ingredients, are explained by the brothers who own this heavenly spot. Good range of beverages.

Trimani il Wine Bar €
Enoteca **Map** 4 D2
Via Cernaia 37b, 00185
Tel *06 446 96 30* **Closed** *Sun; Jan 1, 2 wks Aug, Dec 25 & 26*
Modern wine bar with labels that pair perfectly with cold and hot dishes, as well as Italian cheeses.

Urbana 47 €
Modern Italian **Map** 3 C4
Via Urbana 47, 00184
Tel *06 47 88 40 06* **Closed** *2 wks Aug*
Funky and eclectic place offering creative and delicious dining. Great range of desserts and exceptional value.

'Gusto €€
Pizzeria **Map** 2 E2
Piazza Augusto Imperatore 9, 00186
Tel *06 322 62 73* **Closed** *Jan 1, Dec 24*
Factory-like setting with exposed brick and iron. The Neapolitan-style pizzas are thick-crusted.

Ambasciata d'Abruzzo €€
Regional Italian
Via Pietro Tacchini, 26
Tel *06 807 82 56* **Closed** *Aug 2–4*
Traditional Abruzzese dishes such as *maccheroni* with lamb *ragu* mingle with Roman favorites in a convivial setting.

Cuoco e Camicia €€
Modern Italian **Map** 3 C5
Via Monte Polacco 2/4, 00184
Tel *06 88 92 29 87* **Closed** *Sun, Sat lunch; 2 wks Aug, Dec 24 & 25*
Cheerful eatery that prides itself on using only the freshest local ingredients. Good tasting menu.

For more information on types of restaurants *see p579*

Hamasei €€
Japanese Map 10 F1
Via della Mercede 35/36, 00187
Tel *06 679 21 34* **Closed** *Mon; Aug*
Inventive sushi and sashimi
dishes are served in a minimalist
setting, with low tables for
authentic Nipponese dining.

Hang Zhou €€
Chinese Map 9 E5
Via Principe Eugenio 82, 00184
Tel *06 487 27 32* **Closed** *Aug*
Unanimously touted the best
Chinese food in town. The all-
you-can eat buffet is a steal; other
meals are higher than average.

La Campana €€
Regional Italian Map 10 D1
Vicolo della Campana 18, 00186
Tel *06 687 52 73* **Closed** *Mon; Aug*
Packed any night of the week,
this is the oldest restaurant in
Rome, dating back to 1518.
Traditional favorites are served.

Doozo €€€
Japanese Map 3 C4
Via Palermo 51, 00184
Tel *06 481 56 55* **Closed** *Sun lunch,
Mon; 1 wk Aug, Dec 22–Jan 15*
Excellent sushi, and origami
courses, at this restaurant and
Japanese cultural center.

Imàgo €€€
Fine Dining Map 3 A2
Piazza Trinità dei Monti 6, 00187
Tel *06 69 93 47 26*
Creative Italian cuisine and
exceptional views from the top
of the Spanish Steps. The desserts
are divine and the wine list is
expertly chosen.

L'Olimpo €€€
Fine Dining Map 3 B2
Piazza Barberini 23, 00187
Tel *06 48 83 051*
Dine with sweeping views of the
entire city. Considerable savings
at lunchtime; a more expensive
menu in the evenings.

Oliver Glowig €€€
Fine Dining
Via Ulisse Aldrovandi, 15 00197
Tel *06 321 61 26*
Try Mediterranean delicacies such
as scampi with artichoke heart and
burrata cheese at this exquisite
poolside restaurant.

Osteria Margutta €€€
Modern Italian Map 3 A2
Via Margutta 82b, 00187
Tel *06 323 10 25* **Closed** *Sun dinner,
Mon lunch; 1 wk Aug*
Historic restaurant located on a
vine-covered street. This tradi-
tional restaurant serves classic
Roman fare with a modern twist.

Sleek interiors at the Japanese restaurant Doozo, Northeast Rome

The Vatican and Trastevere

Akropolis €
Greek Map 5 C2
*Via di San Francesco a Ripa 103,
00153*
Tel *06 58 33 26 00*
Tempting appetizers include
stuffed vine leaves and
spanakopita. Fantastic gyros.

Arian €
Persian Map 2 D2
Via Tacito 54a, 00193
Tel *06 45 44 11 22* **Closed** *Sun &
Mon lunch; 1 wk Aug*
Iranian cuisine in a vibrant
atmosphere. Live belly dancing
on Friday and Saturday nights.

Arlù €
Regional Italian Map 1 C3
Borgo Pio 135, 00193
Tel *06 686 89 36* **Closed** *Sun; Jan 1,
2 wks Aug, Dec 25 & 26*
The most authentic restaurant in
the area. A husband and wife
team serve up delectable cuisine.
Great choice of beverages.

Da Lucia €
Regional Italian Map 5 B1
Vicolo del Mattonato 2b, 00153
Tel *06 580 36 01* **Closed** *Mon; 2 wks
Aug; Dec 24, 25, & 31*
Simple pasta dishes as well as
more hearty meals and delicious
homemade desserts are served
on a beautifully lit street.

Dar Poeta €
Pizzeria Map 2 E5
Vicolo del Bologna 45, 00153
Tel *06 588 05 16* **Closed** *Dec 24 & 31*
Perfect balance between thick-
and thin-crusted pizza; the buffalo
mozzarella topping is unmatched.

In Vino Veritas €
Enoteca Map 2 D5
Via Garibaldi 2a, 00153
Tel *347 194 75 80*

Cozy and informal wine bar with
over 200 varieties of wine. Food
is simple and made for sharing.

Ivo a Trastevere €
Pizzeria Map 5 C1
*Via di San Francesco a Ripa 158,
00153*
Tel *06 581 70 82*
Snacks and thin-crusted pizza have
this eatery bustling with locals.

Pizzeria ai Marmi €
Pizzeria Map 5 C1
Viale di Trastevere 53, 00153
Tel *06 580 09 19* **Closed** *Wed;
Aug 10 & 28*
Nicknamed "the morgue" for its
long marble-top tables. Try the
suppli al telefono (fried rice balls).

Rajdhani €
Indian Map 6 D1
Via di Santa Cecilia 8, 00153
Tel *06 581 85 08* **Closed** *Mon*
Tandoori chicken and creamy *tikka
masala* (spicy roasted meat) are
the specialties at this friendly spot.

Bir and Fud €€
Birreria Map 2 E5
Via Benedetta 23, 00153
Tel *06 589 40 16* **Closed** *Dec 25 & 31*
Boutique beers and microbrews
accompany crusty pizzas and
gourmet chips.

BRASSERIE 4:20 €€
Birreria Map 5 C3
Via Portuense 82, 00153
Tel *06 58 31 07 37*
Craft beers from around the
world are meticulously paired
with a wide selection of dishes.

Da Gildo €€
Regional Italian Map 2 D5
Via della Scala 31/A, 00153
Tel *06 580 07 33* **Closed** *Thu*
Quirky decoration and a cozy
outdoor seating area. Try the
divine *gnocchi alla romana* (baked
gnocchi with cheese on top).

DK Choice

Isole di Sicilia €€
Regional Italian **Map** 5 B1
Via Garibaldi 68, 00153
Tel *06 58 33 42 12* **Closed** *Wed*
This cheerful restaurant dishes
up some of the best Sicilian
food in town. The elaborate
dishes are inspired by the native
cuisine of the tiny islands
around Sicily. A vast antipasto
spread kicks off a memorable
meal. In good weather, dine on
the tree-lined street.

Antica Pesa €€€
Fine Dining **Map** 5 B1
Via Garibaldi 18, 00153
Tel *06 580 92 36* **Closed** *Sun; Jan 1,
Dec 26*
Eat exquisite cuisine in a beautifully
decorated restaurant with murals
covering the walls. Dine alfresco
in warm weather.

Antico Arco €€€
Fine Dining **Map** 5 A1
Piazzale Aurelio 7, 00152
Tel *06 581 52 74* **Closed** *Jan 1*
Truffles, wild strawberries, and
other such delights are available.
The vast wine list is as tantalizing.

Settembrini €€€
Modern Italian
Via Luigi Settembrini 25, 00195
Tel *06 323 26 17* **Closed** *Sun, Sat
lunch; 2 wks Aug*
Renowned chef Gigi Nastri serves
creative Italian cuisine that is as
beautiful as it is tasty; delectable
seafood.

Spirito Divino €€€
Modern Italian **Map** 6 D1
Via dei Genovesi 31, 00153
Tel *06 589 66 89* **Closed** *Sun*
Fine dishes served in a converted
medieval synagogue; take a peek
in the 2,000-year-old wine cellar.

Taverna Trilussa €€€
Regional Italian **Map** 2 E5
Via del Politeama 23, 00153
Tel *06 581 89 18* **Closed** *lunch, Sun;
3 days mid-Aug; Dec 24, 25, & 31*
A bustling yet elegant spot.
Some pasta dishes are served in
the pan they were cooked in.

Aventine and Lateran

Angelina a Testaccio €
Regional Italian **Map** 6 D3
Via Galvani 24, 00153
Tel *06 57 28 38 40*
The gem of Testaccio, this shabby
chic bistro offers a tempting
Sunday brunch. The desserts are
scrumptious and there is a good
choice of beverages.

Oasi della Birra €
Birreria **Map** 6 D3
Piazza Testaccio 39, 00153
Tel *06 574 61 22* **Closed** *1 wk Aug,
Dec 24 & 25*
This oasis of beer starts serving
in the early afternoon and no
one leaves thirsty.

Checchino dal 1887 €€
Regional Italian **Map** 6 D4
Via di Monte Testaccio 30, 00153
Tel *06 574 38 16* **Closed** *Sun,
Mon; Aug*
Lovingly prepared hearty Roman
dishes make this restaurant a
favorite with discerning diners.

Further Afield

La Gatta Mangiona €€
Pizzeria
*Via Federico Ozanam 30, Monteverde
Nuovo, 00152*
Tel *06 534 67 02* **Closed** *Mon;
Aug 10–25, Dec 24–26 & 31*
Creative toppings and daily specials
make this spot popular with locals
and in-the-know visitors.

DK Choice

Momò Republic €€
Pizzeria
*Piazza Forlanini 10, Monteverde
Nuovo, 00151*
Tel *06 537 30 87*
A 19th-century mansion in a
garden is the setting for this
trendy pizzeria. Huge
chandeliers and parquet floors
add to the ambience. In
summer, start with *aperitivo* on
the lawn. Pasta, meat, and fish
are also available.

Osteria Flaminio €€
Modern Italian
Via Flaminia 297, 00196
Tel *06 323 69 00* **Closed** *lunch*
Trek north of the center to try the
innovative and original Italian
cuisine available here.

Bastianelli al Molo €€€
Fine Dining
Via Torre Clementina 312, 00054
Tel *06 650 53 58*
A terrace overlooking the
Tyrrhenian Sea is the setting for a
meal of ultra-fresh seafood.

DK Choice

La Pergola €€€
Fine Dining
Via Alberto Cadlolo 101, 00136
Tel *06 350 91* **Closed** *Sun, Mon*
Rome's finest restaurant, La
Pergola is also the only one to
earn the coveted three Michelin
stars. Chef Heinz Beck dazzles
with exquisite Mediterranean
creations. Perched atop Monte
Mario hill, it offers great views of
St. Peter's Basilica. The award-
winning wine cellar boasts
more than 53,000 bottles, the
oldest dating from 1888.

Lazio

BRACCIANO: Cibus €
Modern Italian
Piazza Roma 8, 00062
Tel *339 848 58 34*
Imaginative take on traditional
recipes, in a welcoming setting.

**BRACCIANO:
Quattro Castagni** €€
Regional Italian
Via Olmata Tre Cancelli, 7
Tel *06 99 80 31 30*
Traditional cuisine, specializing
in wild game, served in a rustic
setting with exposed stonework.

**CASTELLI ROMANI FRASCATI:
Pezzafina** €€
Modern Italian
Vicolo Manara 2, 00044
Tel *06 60 65 17 80* **Closed** *lunch, Sun*
Cheerful restaurant with a menu
featuring daring ingredient
combinations, while maintaining
traditional flavors.

CERVETERI: Trattoria Zi Maria €
Regional Italian
Via Sasso Manziana 2, 00050
Tel *06 99 07 90 29* **Closed** *Tue*
Typical regional cuisine at good
prices. Hearty specialties include
venison with wild berries and
pork with pear and stilton.

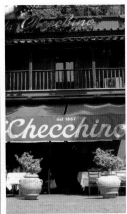

Exterior of the friendly Checchino dal 1887,
known for its filling Roman dishes

For more information on types of restaurants *see p579*

CERVETERI:
Il Cavallino Bianco   €€
Regional Italian
Via Bastioni 46, 00052
Tel 345 42 91 637
Classic Roman cuisine served
with warmth. "Quick lunch"
options are popular, as is the
well-stocked cellar.

GAETA: Narì   €€
Seafood
Via Duomo 15, 04024
Tel 0771 46 30 94   **Closed** Mon
Excellent fish and pasta dishes in
the medieval center of Gaeta.

OSTIA: La Bussola   €€
Seafood
Lungomare A. Vespucci 72, 00122
Tel 06 56 47 08 67   **Closed** Mon
Inspired by the recipes of the
owners' great aunt. Try the gnocchi
with octopus and the fish stew.

SERMONETA: Il Giardino del
Simposio   €
Modern Italian
Corso Garibaldi 33, 04010
Tel 339 284 69 05   **Closed** Mon;
Jan–Feb: Sat & Sun
Innovative dishes such as pasta
with fresh ricotta and wild fennel.

SPERLONGA: Gli Archi   €€
Traditional Italian
Via Ottaviano 17, 04029
Tel 0771 54 83 00   **Closed** Wed; Jan
Simple traditional cuisine in the
heart of this seaside village.
Outdoor seating in warm weather.

TARQUINIA: La Cantinetta   €
Regional Italian
Via XX Settembre 27, 01016
Tel 0766 85 68 10   **Closed** Tue;
summer
Simple spot offering staples from
land and sea. Try the spaghetti
with octopus and clams.

TIVOLI: Avec 55   €€
Modern Italian
Via Domenico Giuliani 55, 00019
Tel 0774 31 72 43   **Closed** Mon

Gastronomic feats paired with
excellent wine. Divine desserts.

TIVOLI: La Sibilla   €€
Regional Italian
Via della Sibilla 42, 00019
Tel 0774 33 52 81   **Closed** Apr, Oct,
Dec–Feb: Mon
Fine views of the Roman ruins
provide a great setting to indulge
in high-quality regional cuisine.

DK Choice

VITERBO: Il Labirinto   €
Pizzeria
Via di San Lorenzo 46, 00100
Tel 0761 30 70 26   **Closed** Mon
This charming restaurant
prepares a variety of bruschetta,
pizza, pasta, and main courses in
traditional style. The outdoor
seating area is next to a quaint
fountain and a medieval church.
Service is friendly and prices low.

VITERBO: Enoteca La Torre   €€€
Fine Dining
Via della Torre 5, 01100
Tel 0761 22 64 67   **Closed** Tue, Wed;
3 wks Aug
The chef and sommelier create
an unforgettable dining
experience at this vibrant spot.

VITERBO: Villa San Michele   €€€
Fine Dining
Via Pian di Quercia, 01030
Tel 338 501 03 87   **Closed** Mon, Tue
Icelandic *baccalà* (salt cod) in
coconut milk, cinnamon, and
orange zest is a menu highlight.

Naples and Campania

AMALFI:
Da Ciccio Cielo Mare Terra   €€
Regional Italian
Via Giovanni Augustariccio 21, 84011
Tel 089 83 12 65   **Closed** Tue; Jan, Nov

Great views of the coastline are
matched by the delicious food.

AMALFI: La Caravella   €€€
Fine Dining
Via Matteo Camera 12, 84011
Tel 089 87 10 29**Closed** Tue; Jan, Nov
The award-winning chef here
uses local flavors to exalt the
regional cuisine.

BENEVENTO: Pascalucci   €
Regional Italian
Via Appia 1, 82010
Tel 0824 77 84 00   **Closed** winter
Simple recipes prepared with
fresh local ingredients.

CAPRI: Da Gelsomina   €€
Regional Italian
Via Migliara 72, 80071
Tel 081 837 14 99   **Closed** Tue;
Jan–Feb
Much of the produce is grown
on-site at this delightful restaurant.

CAPRI: Da Paolino   €€
Regional Italian
Via Palazzo a Mare 11, 80073
Tel 081 837 61 02   **Closed** Oct–Apr
Rustic country restaurant with
rich regional cuisine.

CAPRI: L'Olivo   €€
Fine Dining
Via Capodimonte 14, 80071
Tel 081 978 01 11   **Closed** mid-Oct–
mid-Apr
Uses saffron, bergamot, fava
beans, and asparagus to make
gorgeous flavor combinations.

CAPRI: Il Riccio   €€€
Seafood
Via Grotta Azzurra 11, 80071
Tel 081 837 13 80   **Closed** Nov–Mar
Pleasant atmosphere in which to
enjoy exceptional seafood dishes.

CASERTA: Antica Locanda   €
Regional Italian
Piazza della Seta 7, 81100
Tel 0823 30 54 44 **Closed** Sun dinner,
Mon; Aug, Dec 24 & 31
Simple, characterful *osteria* with
rustic details. Southern Italian
cooking and excellent risotto.

CASERTA: Leucio   €
Seafood
Via Giardini Reali 86, 81100
Tel 0823 30 12 41 **Closed** Sun dinner,
Mon; 1 wk Aug
Exceptional prices at this simple
fish restaurant run by a father
and son. Also serves great pasta.

CASERTA: Le Colonne   €€
Fine Dining
Viale Giulio Douhet 7, 81100
Tel 0823 46 74 94   **Closed** Tue
Indulge in superbly reinterpreted
local cuisine in a luxurious setting.

Romantic dining amid lemon trees at Da Paolino, Capri

Sunny patio of the Neapolitan gem, Il Comandante, Naples

ISCHIA AND PROCIDA: La Stadera €
Enoteca
Via C. Maddalena 15, Sant'Angelo, 80070
Tel *081 99 98 93*
Narrow alleys lead to this *enoteca* where the owners delight with unusual wines and liqueurs. The food here is also delicious.

ISCHIA AND PROCIDA: La Tinaia €
Pizzeria
Via Matteo Verde 39, Forio, 80075
Tel *081 99 84 48*   **Closed** *Dec 24*
Fantastic thick-crusted pizza, as well as pasta and seafood. Basic but friendly service.

ISCHIA AND PROCIDA: Lo Scoglio €
Seafood
Via Cava Ruffano 58, Sant'Angelo, 80077
Tel *081 999529*
Stunningly located on a rock jutting over the sea, this simple restaurant serves quality fish. There is also a good selection of wine.

ISCHIA AND PROCIDA: Alberto €€
Modern Italian
Via Cristoforo Colombo 8, Ischia, 80077
Tel *081 98 12 59*   **Closed** *Nov–Mar*
Sample traditional Italian seafood specialties with creative reinterpretation at this lovely beachfront restaurant.

ISCHIA AND PROCIDA: Gorgonia €€
Seafood
Via Marina di Corricella 50, Procida, 80079
Tel *081 810 10 60*
Set high above a picturesque bay, Gorgonia serves the catch of the day.

ISCHIA AND PROCIDA: Il Mosaico €€€
Fine Dining
Piazza Bagni, Casamicciola Terme, 80074
Tel *081 99 47 22*   **Closed** *Tue; mid-Oct–Mar*
Rich Neapolitan cuisine inspires this multitalented chef's innovative and exquisite menu. The wine list is excellent and the desserts are divine.

DK Choice

ISCHIA AND PROCIDA: Umberto a Mare €€€
Fine Dining
Via del Soccorso 2, Forio, 80075
Tel *081 99 71 71* **Closed** *Nov–Mar*
Time seems to stand still as you take a seat on the tiny terrace that juts out over the sea in the shadow of the evocative Santa Maria del Sorrorso church. The tasting menus feature the gastronomic delights of the Mediterranean. The wine selection is outstanding, and the staff attend to every need.

DK Choice

NAPLES: Da Michele €
Pizzeria
Via Cesare Sersale 1, 80139
Tel *081 553 92 04*   **Closed** *Sun*
A trip to Naples wouldn't be complete without tasting a Margherita at this institution, probably the most famous pizzeria in the world. Only Margherita and Marinara pizzas are served here.

NAPLES: Di Matteo €
Pizzeria
Via dei Tribunali 94, 80138
Tel *081 455 262*   **Closed** *Sun*
A Naples institution serving classic chewy pizza and tasty *fritti* (fried food). Popular with locals and celebrities.

NAPLES: La Notizia €
Pizzeria
Via Michelangelo da Caravaggio 53, 80126
Tel *081 714 21 55*   **Closed** *Mon; Aug, Dec 25*
Tiny pizzas with intense flavors at this popular spot, considered one of the world's best pizzerias.

NAPLES: La Piazzetta €
Regional Italian
Via Nazario Sauro 21, 80132
Tel *081 764 61 95*   **Closed** *Mon*
Traditional local fare and pizzeria at this quaint restaurant designed to look like a small-town piazza.

NAPLES: Sorbillo €
Pizzeria
Via dei Tribunali 38, 80138
Tel *081 033 10 09*   **Closed** *Sun; 1 wk Feb*
A comfortable setting, good pizza, and attentive service for a great price.

NAPLES: Kukai Nibu €€
Japanese
Via Carlo de Cesare 52, 80132
Tel *081 42 58 88*
Generous portions of sushi and sashimi; a glass kitchen allows diners a great view of the action.

NAPLES: La Cantinella €€
Fine Dining
Via Cuma 42, 80132
Tel *081 764 86 84*   **Closed** *Sun*
A bamboo forest is re-created in this award-winning restaurant with an imaginative chef.

NAPLES: La Scialuppa €€
Seafood
Piazzetta Marinari 4, 80132
Tel *081 764 53 33*   **Closed** *Mon; Jan*
Right on the gulf, this traditional restaurant serves fresh fish, as well as pasta and pizza.

NAPLES: Palazzo Petrucci €€
Modern Italian
Piazza San Domenico Maggiore 4, 80134
Tel *081 552 40 68* **Closed** *Sun dinner, Mon lunch; Aug 2–4, Dec 25*
This Michelin-starred restaurant in an ancient setting serves modern fare made with local ingredients.

NAPLES: Il Comandante €€€
Fine Dining
Via Cristoforo Colombo, 80133
Tel *081 01 75*   **Closed** *Tue*
The chef creates exquisite dishes from a few basic ingredients.

POSITANO: Chez Black €€
Seafood
Via del Brigantino, 84017
Tel *089 87 57 96*   **Closed** *mid-Jan–mid-Feb*
Idyllic beachfront location. Serves traditional fish recipes.

POSITANO: Le Terrazze €€
Regional
Via Grotte Dell'Incanto 51, 84017
Tel *089 87 58 74*   **Closed** *Oct–Apr*
Wine bar with panoramic sea views. The wine cellar is carved right into the hillside rock.

POSITANO: Zass €€€
Fine Dining
Via Laurito 2, 84017
Tel *089 87 54 55*
Mouthwateringly delicious elevation of regional cuisine. Desserts to die for.

For more information on types of restaurants *see p579*

SALERNO: Addor I Pizza €
Pizzeria
Piazza San Francesco d'Assisi, 84122
Tel *089 24 18 76* **Closed** *Mon, Sun*
Courteous service in this tiny
pizzeria that also serves pasta.

SALERNO: Il Timone €€
Seafood
Via Generale Allende 29/35, 84122
Tel *089 33 51 11* **Closed** *Mon;*
Aug 15–31
Friendly, bright fish restaurant
with fast, courteous service.

**SALERNO: Osteria Dedicato
a mio Padre** €€
Seafood
Vicolo Giudaica 8, 84100
Tel *089 23 15 55* **Closed** *Sun*
Numerous varieties of fresh fish,
served up in a cozy setting in the
heart of the historic center.

SORRENTO: La Basilica €
Regional Italian
Via Sant'Antonino 28, 80067
Tel *081 877 47 90* **Closed** *Mon*
It's possible to dine until 1am at
this restaurant. Fish, meat and
vegeatrian options in classic
regional style.

SORRENTO: Zi'ntonio €
Regional Italian
Via Luigi De Maio 11, 80067
Tel *081 878 16 23*
Local favorites served in a room
with exposed tufa blocks and
wood-beamed ceilings.

SORRENTO: Il Buco €€
Modern Italian
Il Rampa Marina Piccola 5, 80067
Tel *081 878 23 54* **Closed** *Wed; Jan*
Elegant yet informal restaurant
housed in the cellar of an ancient
monastery. A perfect blend of
tradition and more daring cuisine.

Abruzzo, Molise, and
Puglia

ALBEROBELLO: Trullo d'Oro €
Regional Italian
Via Felice Cavallotti 27, 70011
Tel *080 432 18 20* **Closed** *Mon*
Local cuisine in the characterful
setting of an authentic *trullo*.
Great antipasto spread.

**ALBEROBELLO: Il Poeta
Contadino** €€
Fine Dining
Via Indipendenza 21, 70011
Tel *080 432 19 17* **Closed** *Mon;*
Jan (except for group reservations)
Awarded a Michelin star for its
delectable regional cuisine and
a stunning location. The desserts
are heavenly.

Homey setting for regional cuisine at Il Cortiletto, Lucera

**BARI:
Osteria delle Travi "Il Buco"** €
Regional Italian
Largo Ignazio Chiurlia 12, 70122
Tel *339 157 88 48* **Closed** *Sun*
dinner, Mon
Authentic home-style cooking in
the old Pugliese style *osteria*.

BARI: Bacco €€
Modern Italian
Corso Vittorio Emanuele II 126, 70122
Tel *080 527 58 71* **Closed** *Sun*
dinner, Mon; Aug
Both meat and fish are on the
menu at this award-winning
restaurant. Ample wine list.

**GARGANO PENINSULA:
Medioevo** €
Regional Italian
Via Castello 21, 71037
Tel *0884 56 53 56* **Closed** *Nov: dinner;*
Dec–Feb: Mon
This simple *osteria* uses the best
seasonal produce available. Meat
and soup specialties.

**GARGANO PENINSULA:
Porta di Basso** €€
Seafood
Via Cristoforo Colombo 38, 71010
Tel *0884 91 53 64* **Closed** *Thu*
Creative reinterpretations of
Pugliese fish recipes. Located
on a cliff above the sea.

**GARGANO PENINSULA:
Al Dragone** €€
Regional Italian
Via Duomo 8, 71019
Tel *0884 70 12 12* **Closed** *Apr–Nov:*
Tue; Dec–Mar
Dining in this restaurant built into
a natural cave is an experience in
itself. Delicious regional dishes
and a good wine list.

ISOLE TREMITI: La Nassa €
Seafood
Via Aldo Moro 24, 71040
Tel *0882 46 33 45* **Closed** *Easter;*
Apr–Oct
Nestled in a lush garden, this
restaurant offers fresh fish served in
the simple but rich local tradition.

L'AQUILA: Le Rocce dell'Aquila €
Regional Italian
Viale della Croce Rossa 40, 67100
Tel *0862 41 90 12*
Creativity meets local produce at
this small restaurant.

L'AQUILA: Elodia €€
Fine Dining
Via Valle Perchiana 22, 67100
Tel *0862 60 68 30* **Closed** *Mon, Tue*
Gourmet interpretations of great
local recipes; delicious desserts.

LECCE: Osteria degli Spiriti €
Regional Italian
Via Cesare Battisti 4, 73100
Tel *0832 24 62 74*
Local cuisine served in a high-
ceilinged *trattoria* that was once
a warehouse.

LUCERA: Il Cortiletto €
Regional Italian
Via Famiglia de Nicastri 26, 71036
Tel *0881 54 25 54* **Closed** *Sun dinner*
The short weekly menu is
described by the staff. Regional
favorites with original touches.

DK Choice

LUCERA: Osteria Utz €
Modern Italian
Corso Garibaldi 103, 71036
Tel *0881 61 82 34* **Closed** *Sun*
This warm, cozy restaurant
selects only the freshest local
ingredients – from cured meats
and cheeses to native herbs –
and uses them to craft innovative dishes inspired by the area's
cuisine. The atmosphere is
informal but romantic. The
specialty is numerous varieties
of fresh homemade bread.

**OSTUNI: Osteria Piazzetta
Cattedrale** €
Modern Italian
Largo Arcidiacono T. Trinchera 7,
72017
Tel *0831 33 50 26* **Closed** *Tue*
This elegant restaurant serves local
cuisine with a modern touch.

OSTUNI:
Osteria del Tempo Perso €€
Modern Italian
Via Gaetano Tanzarella Vitale 47, 72017
Tel *0831 30 48 19* **Closed** *Mon; Jan 15–20*
Set in an antique mill, the dishes are reinventions of classic recipes.

OSTUNI: Porta Nova €€
Seafood
Via Gaspare Petrarolo 28, 72017
Tel *0831 33 89 83*
This fish restaurant boasts fine food and views of the surrounding area from its large terrace.

OTRANTO: Peccato di Vino €€
Modern Italian
Via Rondachi 7, 73028
Tel *0836 80 14 88* **Closed** *Tue*
One of the finest restaurants in town, serving creative Pugliese cuisine in a jovial atmosphere.

SULMONA: Rigoletto €
Regional Italian
Via Stazione Introdacqua 46, 67039
Tel *086 45 55 29*
Homemade dishes with local ingredients such as rabbit, truffles, and scamorza cheese.

TARANTO: Al Canale €€
Seafood
Scesa Vasto, 74100
Tel *099 476 42 01* **Closed** *Sun dinner; Nov 1–15*
Seafood specialties are prepared at this luminous restaurant.

TARANTO:
Trattoria al Gatto Rosso €€
Regional Italian
Via Cavour 2, 74123
Tel *099 452 98 75* **Closed** *Sun lunch, Mon*
Innovative contemporary cuisine based on local recipes.

TRANI: Torrente Antico €€€
Fine Dining
Via Edoardo Fusco 3, 70059
Tel *0883 48 79 11* **Closed** *Mon*
Light and modern versions of Puglia's traditional recipes at the finest restaurant in the area.

Basilicata and Calabria

MARATEA:
Il Giardino di Epicuro €
Regional Italian
Contrada Massa Piano, 85046
Tel *0973 87 01 30* **Closed** *Jan, Feb, Nov*
The owner's mother creates heavenly traditional meals.

MARATEA: Zà Mariuccia €€
Seafood
Via Grotte 2, 85040
Tel *0973 87 61 63* **Closed** *Mon; mid-Oct–Mar*
Call ahead to secure one of the few terrace tables with splendid sea views. Top-notch local seafood with an excellent wine list.

MARATEA: Taverna Rovita €€€
Regional Italian
Via Rovita 12, 85046
Tel *0973 87 65 88*
Serves tempting meat and fish dishes and homemade pasta with seasonal ingredients.

MATERA: Alle Fornaci €
Seafood
Piazza Cesare Firrao 5/7, 75100
Tel *0835 33 50 37* **Closed** *Mon*
Fresh fish from the Ionian and Tyrrhenian seas is brought in daily for the no-fuss dishes.

MATERA: Don Matteo €€
Modern Italian
Via San Potito 12, 75100
Tel *0835 34 41 45* **Closed** *lunch*
Dine inside a *sassi* (characteristic stone dwelling). A modern take on traditional local recipes.

DK Choice

MELFI: La Villa €
Regional Italian
Contrada Cavallerizza, 85025
Tel *0972 23 60 08* **Closed** *Sun dinner, Fri; 2 wks mid-Jul*
Set in the heart of the countryside, this rustic restaurant mills its own flour and grows its own grapes. Every ingredient used is local, and the traditional recipes are executed with attention to detail. The family who run the estate treat guests like family members.

The warmly lit entrance to seafood restaurant Porta Nova in Ostuni

MELFI: Novecento €
Regional Italian
Contrada Incoronata, 85025
Tel *0972 23 74 70*
Authentic local cuisine served in a welcoming restaurant. Worth the trek outside town.

MELFI: La Grotta Azzurra €€
Regional Italian
Via Carmine 13, 85025
Tel *0972 23 81 34*
Bring a big appetite to this excellent restaurant with hearty Lucano specialties. Heavenly desserts and a good wine list.

REGGIO DI CALABRIA:
Il Fiore del Cappero €
Seafood
Via Zaleuco 7, 89125
Tel *0965 209 55* **Closed** *Sun, 1st wk Jan*
Sicilian cuisine, based mostly on fish, in this welcoming restaurant with ample Calabrian wines.

REGGIO DI CALABRIA:
Bistrot 15 €€
Bistro
Via Nazionale Pellaro 15, 89134
Tel *0965 35 03 41* **Closed** *May–Sep; Dec–Feb: Mon*
Innovative and artistic seafood served in a modern setting. Worth the small journey out of the center.

ROSSANO: Bella Napoli €
Pizzeria
Via Capri 5, 87067
Tel *0983 51 01 53*
Authentic Neapolitan-style pizzas are served in generous portions. Pasta and meat dishes also on the menu.

ROSSANO: Paridò €
Modern Italian
Via dei Normanni, 87067
Tel *0983 29 07 31*
Regional staple ingredients such as cuttlefish, swordfish, citrus fruits, and eggplant are reinterpreted in modern Mediterranean style.

TROPEA: Al Pinturicchio €
Pizzeria
Via Dardano, 89861
Tel *0963 60 34 52*
Come early to this popular pizzeria with tables that spill out onto the narrow street.

TROPEA: La Lamia €
Modern Italian
Largo Vulcano, 89861
Tel *0963 612 74*
Both meat and fish dishes feature heavily on the menu at this characteristic and popular neighborhood *osteria*.

For more information on types of restaurants *see p579*

TROPEA: Pimm's €€
Seafood
Largo Migliarese 10, 89861
Tel *0963 66 61 05*   **Closed** *Mon*
Elegant and quiet restaurant in
the heart of town.

**VENOSA: Locanda Accademia
dei Piacevoli** €€
Modern Italian
Via Discesa Capovalle 1, 85029
Tel *0972 360 82*   **Closed** *Mon;
first 2 wks Nov*
Small gourmet restaurant built
into a tiny stone house.

Sicily

**AGRIGENTO:
Trattoria dei Templi** €
Seafood
*Via Panoramica Valle dei Templi 15,
92100*
Tel *0922 40 31 10*
This inviting restaurant overlook-
ing the temples offers expertly
prepared seafood specialties.

AGRIGENTO: Kokalos €€
Regional Italian
Via Cavaleri Magazzeni 3
Tel *0922 60 64 27*
Traditional Sicilian cuisine using
local ingredients such as oranges,
almonds, and sun-dried
tomatoes.

CATANIA: La Siciliana €
Regional Italian
Viale Marco Polo 52, 95126
Tel *095 37 64 00*   **Closed** *Sun dinner*
Classic Sicilian recipes, including
dishes specific to the town. One
of Catania's best restaurants.

CATANIA: Il Cuciniere €€
Modern Italian
Via Finocchiaro Aprile 110, 95129
Tel *095 747 07 02*   **Closed** *Sun*

Erice's Monte San Giuliano restaurant,
serving local dishes

The chef uses traditional Sicilian
ingredients in unique ways, such
as fish with Modica chocolate.

CEFALÙ: La Brace €
Bistro
Via 25 Novembre 10, 90015
Tel *0921 42 35 70*   **Closed** *Mon, Tue;
Dec 15–Jan 15*
Hints of the Orient mingle with
local flavors at this bistro hidden
away in the historic center.

ENNA: Ariston €
Regional Italian
Piazza Napoleone Colajanni 6, 94100
Tel *0935 260 38*
Fresh local ingredients from land
and sea served with enthusiasm
at this friendly spot.

ERICE: Monte San Giuliano €
Regional Italian
Vicolo San Rocco 7, 91016
Tel *0923 86 95 95*   **Closed** *Mon;
Nov 15*
The remarkable terrace garden
here is an ideal setting to enjoy
some authentic local cuisine.

ERICE: Osteria di Venere €€
Regional Italian
Via Roma 6, 91016
Tel *0923 86 93 62*
Sample diverse Mediterranean
cuisine including homemade
pasta and grilled catch of the day.

MARSALA: Garibaldi €
Regional Italian
Piazza dell'Addolorata 1, 91025
Tel *0923 95 30 06*   **Closed** *Sat lunch,
Sun dinner*
Dizzying selection of regional
favorites, as well as fish cooked
any way you please.

MESSINA: La Durlindana €
Regional Italian
Via Nicola Fabrizi 143, 98123
Tel *090 641 31 56*
This modern restaurant with an
open kitchen offers regional
dishes and wines

MESSINA: Piero €€
Regional Italian
Via Ghibellina 119, 98123
Tel *090 640 93 54*   **Closed** *Aug*
This restaurant has been serving
large plates of fish, big salads,
and hearty meat dishes since its
opening in 1962.

**MONREALE:
Taverna del Pavone** €
Regional Italian
Vicolo Pensato 18, 90046
Tel *091 640 62 09*   **Closed** *Mon;
2 wks Jan, 2 wks Jul*
Sample authentic, no-frills Sicilian
specialties served in a cozy and
friendly setting.

**PALERMO:
Antico Caffè Spinnato** €
Enoteca
Via Principe di Belmonte 111, 90139
Tel *091 749 51 04*   **Closed** *Christmas*
Come for the wines, liqueurs, and
espresso, but stay for the *cassata*
(traditional Sicilian dessert),
cannoli (fried pastry with a
creamy filling), and gelato.

PALERMO: Santandrea €
Regional Italian
Piazza Sant'Andrea 4, 90133
Tel *091 33 49 99*
In a tranquil oasis of exposed
wood and stone, this eatery
dishes up time-honored
regional fare.

PALERMO: Bye Bye Blues €€
Fine Dining
Via del Garofalo 23, 90149
Tel *091 684 14 15*   **Closed** *Mon;
2 wks Jan*
Fantastic prices for a Michelin-
starred restaurant. Diners can
watch their dishes being
prepared at this restaurant.

PALERMO: Lo Scudiero €€
Seafood
Via Filippo Turati 7, 90139
Tel *091 58 16 28*   **Closed** *Sun;
2 wks Aug*
The impeccable and attentive
service is almost as refreshing as
the delectable fish.

PALERMO: Sapori Perduti €€
Modern Italian
Via Principe di Belmonte 32, 90139
Tel *091 32 73 87*   **Closed** *Mon; Aug*
Modern design goes hand-in-
hand with expertly prepared
modern Italian cuisine.

SIRACUSA: Enoteca Solaria €
Enoteca
Via Roma 86, 96100
Tel *0931 46 30 07*
The oldest wine bar in the city,
with labels from Italy and France.

SIRACUSA: Oinos €€
Modern Italian
Via della Giudecca 69/75, 96100
Tel *0931 46 49 00*
Intimate and informal setting
for a variety of modern dishes
based on recipes from across
Italy. There is also a good range
of beverages to accompany meals.

SIRACUSA: Porta Marina €€
Regional Italian
Via dei Candelai 35, 96100
Tel *0931 225 53*   **Closed** *Mon;
2 wks Feb*
A lovely restaurant set in a
crumbling early Renaissance
palazzo. It offers good value for
the quality of food it serves.

DK Choice

TAORMINA: Al Duomo €€
Seafood
Vico Ebrei (Piazza Duomo), 98039
Tel *0942 62 56 56* **Closed** *Mon*
The picturesque location for
this restaurant is on a terrace in
Taormina's most beautiful
piazza, with the backdrop of
a 12th-century cathedral.
Classic and modern fish dishes
are whipped up by the chefs
with enthusiasm. The kitchen
is open well past midnight.

TAORMINA: Principe Cerami €€€
Fine Dining
Piazza San Domenico 5, 98039
Tel *0942 61 31 11* **Closed** *lunch, Mon*
Heavenly terrace overlooking
crystal waters offering uber-
refined Sicilian fare. Book early.

TRAPANI: Taverna Paradiso €€
Seafood
Lungomare Dante Alighieri 22, 91100
Tel *0923 223 03*
Ask the friendly staff for their
recommendations at this lovely
eatery with super-fresh fish.

Sardinia

ALGHERO: Al Tuguri €€
Seafood
Via Maiorca 113, 07041
Tel *079 97 67 72* **Closed** *Sun;*
mid-Dec–Mar
Just a few tables are available in
this cozy seafood restaurant.

ALGHERO: Andreini €€€
Modern Italian
Via Ardoino 45, 07041
Tel *079 98 20 98* **Closed** *Dec–Apr*
A romantic, family-run place
offering Mediterranean cuisine.

BOSA:
Mannu da Giancarlo e Rita €€
Seafood
Viale Alghero 14, 08013
Tel *0785 37 53 07* **Closed** *winter*
A modern restaurant where
lobster dominates the menu.

CAGLIARI: La Stella
Marina di Montecristo €
Seafood
Via Sardegna 140, 09124
Tel *347 578 89 64* **Closed** *Sun*
This is a simple *osteria* with cordial
service. Wild game on Thursdays.

CAGLIARI: Dal Corsaro €€
Modern Italian
Viale Regina Margherita 28, 09124
Tel *070 66 43 18* **Closed** *Sun;*
3 wks Jan

Buzzing atmosphere at Hivaoa, Costa Smeralda

Sardinian classics are re-created
with a contemporary twist.

CALA GONONE: Il Pescatore €€
Seafood
Lungomare Acqua Dolce 1, 08022
Tel *0784 931 74*
A seaside spot serving classic
Sardinian fish dishes.

COSTA SMERALDA:
Corbezzolo €€
Seafood
Piazzetta della Fontana, Baia
Sardinia, 07021
Tel *0789 998 93* **Closed** *Dec–May*
Tasty classic seafood dishes
served on a sea-view terrace.

COSTA SMERALDA: Hivaoa €€
Pizzeria
Via della Marina, Porto Cervo, 07021
Tel *0789 914 51*
Dine on a breezy terrace. Pizza,
pasta, and excellent seafood.

COSTA SMERALDA:
Spinnaker €€€
Seafood
Res. Alba Ruja, Porto Cervo, 07020
Tel *0789 912 26* **Closed** *winter*
One of the Emerald Coast's best-
known restaurants. Excellent fish.

DK Choice

COSTA SMERALDA:
Pedristellas €€
Regional Italian
Via Monte Ladu, Porto Rotondo,
07026
Tel *377 236 92 01* **Closed** *winter*
Literally "rocks and stars" in the
Sardinian dialect, this restaurant
is set in a rock garden dotted
with centuries-old pine trees.
The tables, lighting, and
meandering paths complement
the natural setting. It offers an
abundant menu of seafood and
meat in the Sardinian tradition.

COSTA SMERALDA:
Stella di Gallura €€
Regional Italian
Loc. Monte Ladu, Porto Rotondo,
07026
Tel *0789 344 02* **Closed** *winter*
Dine by the poolside and sample
typical Sardinian dishes from
both land and sea.

COSTA SMERALDA:
Da Giovannino €€€
Fine Dining
Piazza Quadra 10, Porto Rotondo,
07026
Tel *0789 352 80* **Closed** *winter*
High-profile restaurant with a
pretty garden. Excellent
Mediterranean cuisine.

NUORO: Il Rifugio €€
Regional Italian
Via Antonio Mereu 28, 08100
Tel *0784 23 23 55* **Closed** *winter*
An ample variety of classic
Sardinian dishes. Excellent pizza.

ORISTANO: Craf da Banana €€
Regional Italian
Via De Castro S. A. 34, 09170
Tel *0783 42 01 82* **Closed** *winter*
Wild game is the house specialty.
Try the mixed grill for a range.

SANT'ANTIOCO:
Moderno-da Achille €€
Regional Italian
Via Nazionale 82, 09017
Tel *0781 831 05* **Closed** *winter*
Tasty Sardinian fare expertly
prepared by a talented chef who
makes each dish his own, served
in an elegant setting.

SASSARI: Liberty €€
Seafood
Piazza Nazario Sauro, 07100
Tel *079 23 63 61* **Closed** *winter*
The look is distinctly Art Deco at
this sophisticated spot serving
super-fresh fish. Long list of
Sardinian wines.

For more information on types of restaurants *see p579*

SHOPPING IN ITALY

Italy is known for its quality designer goods, ranging from chic clothing and sleek cars to stylish household items. There is a strong tradition of craftsmanship, often from family-run businesses, and there are numerous markets selling regional specialties. Apart from the town markets, it is not a country for bargains, but the joys of window shopping will offer plenty of compensation. If you come from outside the European Union, you may be able to claim back the 10 percent IVA tax (VAT). Make sure you leave time at your departure airport to fulfil all administrative requirements.

Fresh vegetables on display at a Venetian market stall

Opening hours

Open hours for shops are usually 9:30am–1pm and around 3:30–8pm, Tuesday to Saturday and Monday afternoons. However, shopkeepers are increasingly using more flexible hours. There are few department stores, but most large towns will have a Standa, Upim, Coin, or Rinascente. These stores are often open nonstop (orario continuato) from 9am–8pm, Monday to Saturday. Music stores and book-stores sometimes stay open after 8pm and on Sundays.

Food shops

Even though there are super-markets throughout Italy, the specialist shops, although more expensive, are still the most interesting way to shop. A forno has the best bread and a macellaio has the finest meat (go to a norcineria for pork products). Vegetables are freshest from market stalls or the fruttivendolo. You can buy cakes at the pasticceria, milk at the latteria, and pasta, ham, cheese, and general foods at the often impressively stocked alimentari. Here you can also buy wine, but for a wider choice, head for the enoteca, vineria, or vinaio, where you can sometimes taste the wine before purchasing.

Markets

All towns have regional weekly markets. Large towns will have several small daily markets followed by a weekly flea market, usually on Sunday. In this guide the main market days are listed under each town. Traders set up at 5am and start to clear away at about 1:30pm. Food is sold by the etto (100 grams, or 3.5 oz) and the chilo (kilo, or 2.2 pounds) (see p665), or in numbers (two onions, etc.). Food stalls selling seasonal products generally have fresher and cheaper produce than the shops. Bargaining is not usual when buying food, but it is worth asking for a discount (sconto) for clothes.

Seasonal produce

To make the most of Italian food, try to buy and eat what is in season. Grapes and mushrooms are best in autumn, whereas spring is the season for asparagus and strawberries. In winter, vegetables such as Roman artichokes, cauliflower, and broccoli are at their best, as are lemons from Amalfi and Sicilian blood oranges. Summer is the time for plums, pears, and cherries, as well as zucchini, eggplant, tomatoes, and melons.

Clothes and designer shops

Italy is renowned worldwide for its fashion industry. Milan is the fashion capital and Via Monte Napoleone, in the city center, is lined with designer boutiques. All large towns will have a selection of designer shops, usually situated near each other. Less expensive clothes are

Souvenir shop in Ostuni, near Brindisi, Puglia

available in markets and many department stores, where the styles tend to be more conventional. Italy is also famous for leather shoes and bags, the prices of which tend to be reasonable.

Sales (*saldi*) are held in summer and winter. Second-hand shops can be expensive, but the quality and condition of the clothes are usually very good. Larger markets have stalls piled high with used clothes. Rummage through and you will often find bargains.

An elegant designer clothes boutique in Treviso

Colorful shop display of leather handbags in Florence

Jewelry and antique shops

Glitzy gold jewelry is very popular in Italy and every *gioielleria* (jewelry shop) will have a wide selection. For more unusual items, try the *bigiotteria* or artisan shops (*oreficeria*). Antique stores like *Antichità* and *Antiquariato* sell furniture and ornaments of varying quality and prices. You will rarely find bargains in Italy, except perhaps at the *Fiere dell'Antiquariato* (antique fairs), held throughout the year all over the country.

Interior design and household wares

Interior design is another Italian sector where top names demand extravagant prices, with many shops concentrating on modern, high-tech styles. There are household stores in cities and towns throughout the country. Italian kitchenware is particularly striking, with its stainless steel and copper pots, pans, and utensils. For the lowest prices, avoid the tourist shops and, if possible, buy directly from the manufacturer. Less expensive items include the characteristic brown espresso and cappuccino cups sold in all markets.

Regional specialties

Many of Italy's regional specialties are world famous: Parma ham, Chianti wine, olive oil, and *grappa*. Regional sweets, including the Sienese *panforte* and Sicilian marzipan, are also well-known, as are cheeses such as Gorgonzola from Lombardy and Parmesan from Emilia-Romagna. Traditional crafts are still practiced in Italy and range from delicate lacework and glassware in the Veneto to leatherwork, jewelry, and marbled paper in Florence. Italian ceramics include elaborate Tuscan pottery, hand-painted dishes around Amalfi and De Simone's stylized designer plates from Sicily.

Display of decorative glazed pottery from Tuscany

Size Chart

For Australian sizes follow the British and American conversions.

Women's dresses, coats, and skirts

Italian	38	40	42	44	46	48	50
British	8	10	12	14	16	18	20
American	6	8	10	12	14	16	18

Women's shoes

Italian	36	37	38	39	40	41
British	3	4	5	6	7	8
American	5	6	7	8	9	10

Men's suits

Italian	44	46	48	50	52	54	56	58 (size)
British	34	36	38	40	42	44	46	48 (inches)
American	34	36	38	40	42	44	46	48 (inches)

Men's shirts (collar size)

Italian	36	38	39	41	42	43	44	45 (cm)
British	14	15	15$\frac{1}{2}$	16	16$\frac{1}{2}$	17	17$\frac{1}{2}$	18 (inches)
American	14	15	15$\frac{1}{2}$	16	16$\frac{1}{2}$	17	17$\frac{1}{2}$	18 (inches)

Men's shoes

Italian	39	40	41	42	43	44	45	46
British	6	7	7$\frac{1}{2}$	8	9	10	11	12
American	7	7$\frac{1}{2}$	8	8$\frac{1}{2}$	9$\frac{1}{2}$	10$\frac{1}{2}$	11	11$\frac{1}{2}$

ENTERTAINMENT IN ITALY

Italians exude strong national pride and passion about every aspect of their cultural heritage. One of Europe's key centers of culture since Roman times, Italy was the cradle of the Renaissance, and it is known today as the home of opera and a mixed bag of regional styles of folk music. The country holds one of the most acclaimed international film festivals and every town boasts a *teatro*, an elaborate classical venue with mixed programs incorporating every aspect of classic and traditional culture. Add to this the many street festivals and fairs, often in celebration of food, wine, and *la dolce vita*, and you will never have a dull moment.

Practical Information

Most venues have booking facilities online or a reservations line to call. However, major events and most opera performances tend to sell out well in advance, so it is wise to reserve tickets through ticket companies such as **Liaisons Abroad** that may still have availability when the venue itself has sold out.

If you wish to find out what's happening in Italy during your stay, check the Italian tourism website (www.italiantourism. com) or pick up a copy of *Dove*, a monthly publication about culture, travel, and gastronomy that also highlights the month's events in Rome and Milan.

Il Corriere della Sera, Italy's oldest daily, contains sections on events and culture; its ViviMilano website (www. corriere.it/vivimilano) is a mine of information on events taking place in the fashion capital. Another website (www.romaturismo.it) offers excellent service for Rome.

Tourist information offices *(see p617)* will also provide information on programs, events, and venues, as will the **Italian State Tourist Board**. Few Italian venues provide easy access for people with restricted mobility. The situation improves a little in the summer, when many events are held outside.

Opera and Classical Music

Italy has some of the world's most beautiful and historic opera houses. Venice's **La Fenice**, destroyed by fire in 1996, has been restored to its former splendor, and **Teatro alla Scala** *(see p197)* in Milan also underwent a major renovation. In addition to the original building, there is also an extra theater, **Teatro degli Arcimboldi**, allowing the Scala to host more performances.

Verona hosts a summer season of opera and classical music in the outdoor **Arena di Verona** *(see p151)*, while Rome's venues include the open-air **Baths of Caracalla** *(see p441)*, the breathtaking Renzo Piano–designed auditorium **Parco della Musica**, and the **Teatro dell'Opera**.

In May and June, Florence's **Maggio Musicale** *(see p70)* is packed with opera, ballet, and classical performances.

Poster advertising the Venice Film Festival

Rock, Jazz, and Contemporary Music

Large concerts tend to be held in classic theaters or in sports stadiums. The **Arena di Verona** hosts big names in summer, as does the **Stadio Olimpico** in Rome. In Milan, the **Forum di Assago** sports stadium is a popular venue. Tickets for concerts are sometimes sold in record stores.

World-class jazz performers gather annually in Perugia for the **Umbria Jazz** festival in July. The website provides booking details and information.

Theater and Ballet

Italy has the highest concentration of traditional theaters in Europe, offering a mixture of theater, ballet, and classical music all under one roof. All theaters also hold ballet performances, mainly by international touring troupes. The **Scala**'s ballet company has gained international renown. Both tradition and innovation can be seen at the international festival of ballet that takes place at Genoa's **Teatro Carlo Felice** in July.

The opera festival in Verona attracts huge crowds to the Roman arena

Cinema

One of the highlights of the cinema year is the **Venice Film Festival** *(see p71)*, which takes place from August to September. The Rome International Festival of Cinema *(see p72)* also draws major film stars. A smaller International Film Festival *(see p71)* is held in Taormina, Sicily, while Florence has the Festa dei Popoli *(see p72)* in winter.

A thrilling moment in the Sienese Palio race held in Piazza del Campo

Regional Dance, Music, and Festivals

Seasonal festivals are either religious, relating to patron saints, or food-oriented. The best known is *Carnevale* (literally "farewell to meat") *(see p73)*, which celebrates the end of winter and introduces Lent. Venice holds the most opulent and the oldest masquerade party, while Viareggio, in Tuscany, is famous for its lively themed floats.

Another festival highlight is the *Sienese Palio (see pp71 and 345)*, a bareback horse race that takes place twice a year in one of Italy's most beautiful squares. For further details on festivals throughout Italy, see pp70–73.

An elaborate Carnival mask

Every region in Italy has its own ancient music and dance, but the best known is the *tarantella*, a lively dance and rhythmic song from Puglia *(see p515)*. Legends trace the origins of the name to the tarantula spider, since victims of a tarantula bite would perform a frenzied dance in order to sweat out the poison.

Culture

Spectating, whether at sporting events, rural festivals, or even grand events, is what entertainment is all about. And part of this, of course, involves that very Italian pastime – seeing and being seen. You can witness this in daily life in the café culture – visit any of the large cities' popular squares, such as Piazza di Spagna or Piazza Navona in Rome, Piazza del Duomo in Milan, or Piazza San Marco in Venice, and you will see people of all ages parading around in their best clothes. This is referred to as *la passeggiata*, a walk around that becomes a ritual at weekends, along the seafront and lakeside promenades in summer and in city and town centers.

Another aspect of daily life is *l'aperitivo*. This ritual of joining friends for an early evening drink after work or before going on to dinner or to a nightclub is back in fashion. Bars provide abundant finger-food buffets to accompany the drinks, which are generally priced higher than at other times of day. This trend has spawned new lounge clubs in the major cities.

DIRECTORY

Practical Information

Italian State Tourist Board
1 Princes Street, London W1B 2AY.
Tel 020 7408 1254.
w italiantouristboard.co.uk

Liaisons Abroad
Tel 020 7808 7330.
w liaisonsabroad.com

Opera and Classical Music

Arena di Verona
Piazza Brà, Verona.
Tel 045 800 51 51.
w arena.it

Baths of Caracalla
Via delle Terme di Caracalla 52, Rome.
Map 7 A3.

La Fenice
Campo San Fantin, Venice.
Map 7 A2. **Tel** 041 24 24.
w teatrolafenice.it

Maggio Musicale
Florence.
w maggiofiorentino.it

Parco della Musica
Viale de Coubertin 30, Rome. **Tel** 06 80 24 12 81.
w auditorium.com

Teatro alla Scala
Piazza della Scala, Milan.
Tel 02 72 00 37 44.
w teatroallascala.org

Teatro degli Arcimboldi
Viale dell'Innovazione 20, Milan.
Tel 02 641 142 212.
w teatroarcimboldi.it

Teatro dell'Opera
Piazza B. Gigli 7, Rome.
Map 3 C3.
Tel 06 48 16 02 55.
w operaroma.it

Rock, Jazz, and Contemporary Music

Forum di Assago
Via G. Di Vittorio 6, Assago, Milan.
Tel 199 128 800.
w forumnet.it

Stadio Olimpico
Viale dei Gladiatori, Rome.

Umbria Jazz
Tel 075 573 24 32.
w umbriajazz.com

Theater and Ballet

Teatro Carlo Felice
Passo E. Montale 4, Genova.
Tel 010 58 93 29.
w carlofelice.it

Cinema

Venice Film Festival
Tel 041 521 87 11.
w labiennale.org

Specialist Vacations and Outdoor Activities

Italy offers an amazing variety of cultural, sporting, and leisure activities. However, many schools and groups require annual membership and short-term activities are often expensive and difficult to find. Information on current recreation and sporting events in a specific region is available from the tourist office listed for each town in this guide. For details on annual festivals, see *Italy Through the Year* on pages 70–73. The following suggestions include some of the most popular as well as some more unusual pursuits.

The **Federazione Arrampicata Sportiva Italiana** has a list of mountain-climbing schools that arrange climbs for all levels.

Ski lift near the desolate Falzarego Pass, in the heart of the Dolomites

Cycling on the tree-lined flatlands of the Po Delta

maps are the most detailed but unfortunately are only available from specialized map stores.

Cycling is popular despite Italy's mountainous landscape. Travel bookstores stock publications with suggested routes, such as the Po Delta, which has miles of scenic flatlands.

Many riding schools organize trips and outings, which are also advertised in the local press. For general information, contact the **Federazione Italiana Sport Equestri**.

Walking, Cycling, and Horseback Riding

Some Italian branches of the **World Wide Fund for Nature (WWF)** organize walks and treks. **Club Alpino Italiano (CAI)** runs trekking and climbing excursions, and the **Italian Birds Protection League (LIPU)** arranges nature walks and bird-watching trips. The military *IGM*

Mountain Sports

The most well-equipped and famous ski resorts are in the Dolomites, in the Italian Alps and around Turin, the city chosen to host the 2006 Winter Olympics. There are also smaller and less expensive resorts in the Apennines and in Sicily. Package ski vacations, arranged from outside Italy, offer the best deals.

Archaeological Digs

The British monthly magazine *Archaeology Abroad*, available in the UK, gives a comprehensive list of archaeology groups and digs worldwide. In Italy, the **Gruppo Archeologico Romano** runs two-week digs in various regions. There are summer and winter digs for both adults and children. The group has contacts with local archaeological organizations as well.

Italian Language and Culture

For a wide selection of material on courses and schools in Italy, contact the Italian consulate in your home country. The **Società Dante Alighieri** provides courses in the Italian language, history of art, literature, and culture. There are both full- and part-time courses available, for every level. Language schools abound in Italy's main cities and are advertised in the Yellow Pages *(Pagine Gialle)* or foreign language bookstores and newspapers. For young students, **Intercultura** will organize weekly, monthly, and yearlong exchanges including language courses, homestays with Italian families, and enrollment in Italian schools. Cooking courses run

Group hiking tour in the Dolomites of Trentino–Alto Adige *(see p82)*

A lesson in Italian cooking in Sicily

by English-speaking experts in Italian cooking have become very popular. **Tasting Places**, for example, does wine tours and weeklong courses in Italian cuisine, and provides beautiful accommodations. The course locations include the Veneto, Sicily, Tuscany, and Umbria. Wine tasting tours are organized by local tourist boards. The Università per Stranieri in Perugia runs courses in Italian, art history, and literature (www. unistrapg.it).

Water Sports

Most lakes and many seaside resorts rent out sailing boats, canoes, and windsurfing equipment. Lessons and courses are organized by clubs, which usually require membership. For a list of authorized associations contact the **Federazione Italiana Canoa Kayak** and the **Federazione Italiana Vela**. Weekend and weekly sailing vacations and courses are featured in the magazine *Avventure nel Mondo* and most travel agents have a selection of sailing vacations.

Swimming pools are expensive in Italy and many do not accept people on a daily basis. You often have to pay a membership fee and a monthly tariff. Some of the luxurious hotels open their pools to the public in summer, but at pricy rates. Water parks are popular and provide pools, slides, wave machines, and games. Before diving into any lakes or rivers (and even the sea near main towns) it is best to check that the water is not polluted. The **Federazione Italiana di Attività**

Subacquee runs underwater diving courses, and can give information on all local centers.

Air Sports

There are schools nationwide that offer hang-gliding and flying courses, but the minimum duration of each course is one month. For information and a list of schools contact the **AeroClub Italia**. You must be licensed before you can fly and all crafts must be registered with AeroClub.

Other Sports

Golf is a popular sport in Italy and there are plenty of courses to choose from. Home membership and handicap are often required for daily access to a club. Italian tennis clubs usually operate on a membership basis, unless you are invited as a member's guest. The national **Federazione Italiana di Tennis** has a list of all the tennis clubs in Italy. The opportunity to watch a professional soccer game should not be missed. Seats can be scarce, so book tickets in advance from the stadium. Most Serie A matches are played on Sundays, with international games taking place on Tuesdays and Wednesdays.

Playing golf

Sailing in Italy, a popular leisure activity and competitive sport

DIRECTORY

AeroClub Italia
Via Cesare Beccaria 35a, 00196 Rome. **Tel** 06 36 08 46 00.
🌐 **aeci.it**

Club Alpino Italiano
Via E. Petrella 19, Milan.
Tel 02 205 72 31. 🌐 **cai.it**

Federazione Arrampicata Sportiva Italiana
Via del Terrapieno 27, 40127 Bologna. **Tel** 051 601 48 90.
🌐 **federclimb.it**

Federazione Italiana Attività Subacquee
Via A. Doria 8, Milan.
Tel 02 670 50 05. 🌐 **fias.it**

Federazione Italiana Canoa Kayak
Viale Tiziano 70, 00196 Rome.
Tel 06 36 85 81 88.
🌐 **federcanoa.it**

Federazione Italiana Sport Equestri
Viale Tiziano 74, 00196 Rome.
Tel 06 836 68 41. 🌐 **fise.it**

Federazione Italiana di Tennis
Stadio Olimpico, Rome.
Tel 06 36 85 82 18.
🌐 **federtennis.it**

Federazione Italiana Vela
Piazza Borgo Pila 40, Genova.
Tel 010 54 45 41. 🌐 **federvela.it**

Gruppo Archeologico Romano
Via Baldi degli Ubaldi 168, 00167 Rome. **Tel** 06 638 52 56.
🌐 **gruppoarcheologico.it**

Intercultura
Via Venezia 25, 00184 Rome.
Tel 06 48 88 24 01.
🌐 **intercultura.it**

Italian Birds Protection League (LIPU)
Via Trento 49, 43100 Parma.
Tel 0521 27 30 43. 🌐 **lipu.it**

Società Dante Alighieri
Via Gino Capponi 4, 50121 Florence. **Tel** 055 247 89 81.
🌐 **dantealighieri.it**

Tasting Places Cooking and Wine Tours
P.O. Box 38174, London W10 5ZP.
Tel 020 8964 5333.
📺 **tastingplaces.com**

World Wide Fund for Nature
Via Po 25c, 00198 Rome.
Tel 06 84 49 71. 🌐 **wwf.it**

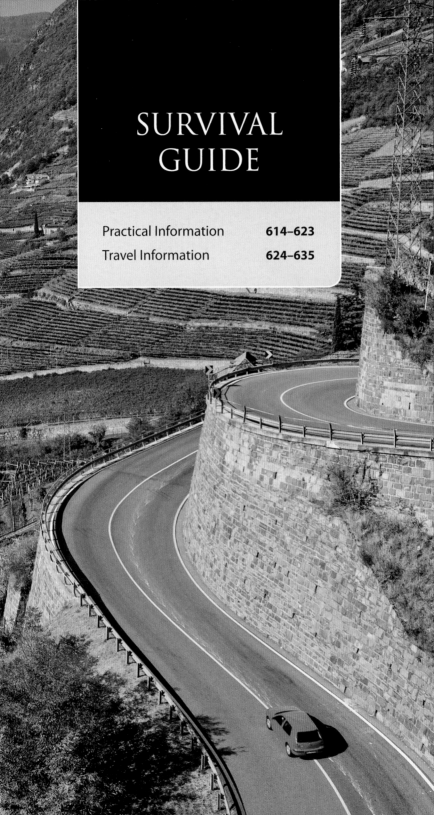

SURVIVAL GUIDE

Practical Information   614–623

Travel Information   624–635

PRACTICAL INFORMATION

Ask any Italian and they will almost certainly tell you that Italy is the most beautiful country in the world. They may not be far wrong. However, the charm and allure of Italy may help to veil some of her numerous practical problems. Getting information is rarely straightforward; public offices and banks are nearly always crippled by long lines and bureaucracy; and the postal service is renowned for its inefficiency. This section, together with some forward planning and a little patience, should help you cope with some of Italy's idiosyncrasies.

Tourists crossing the Ponte della Paglia in Venice *(see p113)*

When to Visit

The northern part of Italy is generally more temperate than the south, which has a Mediterranean climate. From June to September the weather is hot throughout the country and, in peak summer, also humid. Seaside resorts tend to get very busy. Spring and autumn are ideal for visiting cities as temperatures are milder, making sightseeing much more comfortable, although you should be prepared for the unexpected downpour.

Italy's towns and historic sites are extremely popular attractions and it is worth considering this when planning your trip. Most sights are open all year, except on some public holidays *(see p73)*, and most close one day a week. Rome, Florence, and Venice are all crowded from spring to October and it is a good idea to reserve a hotel room well in advance. In August the cities are generally slightly less busy, abandoned by their inhabitants for summer vacations.

In February, Venice triples its population during Carnevale *(see p73)*, and at Easter, Rome is overrun by pilgrims and tourists. Winter can be bitterly cold, especially in the north, and December to March is the time of year for skiing in the high-altitude resorts of the Italian Alps. *The Climate of Italy* on pages 76–7 takes a detailed look at the country's regional weather.

Visas and Permesso di Soggiorno

European Union nationals and citizens of the United States, Canada, Australia, and New Zealand do not need visas for stays of up to three months. Most European Union (EU) visitors need only a valid identity document with photograph, but visitors from the UK, Ireland, Denmark and Sweden, must have a passport.

All visitors should check requirements with the Italian embassy before traveling and officially declare themselves to the Italian police within eight days of arrival. If you are staying in a hotel or campsite, this will be done for you by the staff, otherwise contact the local *Questura* (police station).

Anyone wishing to stay in Italy for more than three months will have to obtain a *permesso di soggiorno* (permit to stay or residence permit). Non-EU citizens must apply for one within eight days of arrival. You can apply for a residence permit at any main police station, *Questura di Provincia*. In some cases you can obtain a packet containing the necessary application form from main post offices. You must apply for the correct permit, either a permit to work *(lavoro)* or a permit to study *(studio)*. The necessary documentation is listed on the *Questura* website *(see p617)*.

To apply for a study permit, it is necessary to get a letter from the relevant school or university at which you intend to study, giving details of your course of study. This then has to be sent to the Italian consulate in your own country of origin to obtain an official cover letter, or declaration.

You will also need some form of guarantee that your medical bills will be paid if you become ill or have an accident where you require medical treatment. A comprehensive insurance policy for the length of your stay *(see p619)* will usually be sufficient.

Rome's renowned Tazza d'Oro café, an ideal rest stop after sightseeing

◄ The wonderful view from the A22 road that carves through the mountains and vineyards that surround Bolzano

Customs

On June 30, 1999, the intra-EU Duty and Tax Free Allowances, better known as Duty-free and mainly affecting such high-tax items as alcohol, perfumes, and tobacco, were abolished. However, for EU residents the amount of these goods that can be imported for personal use has increased.

Consulates can generally provide up-to-date information on particular customs regulations. To find out what you can take back from Italy to non-EU countries, contact that particular country's customs department, which will be able to advise you.

Tax Exemption

Value Added Tax (IVA in Italy) ranges from about 20 percent, with a reduced rate of 4–10 percent on some items. Non-European Union citizens making purchases in Italy can claim an IVA rebate, provided that total purchases in the one shop are over €155. It is a long process, and it is easier to get a refund if you shop where you see the "Euro Free Tax" sign, rather than from a market stall. In this instance, show your passport to the shop assistant, complete a form, and the IVA will be deducted from your bill. Alternatively, present a customs officer with your purchases and their receipts on your departure from Italy. He or she will stamp the receipts, which you then send to the vendor. A refund should eventually be sent to you.

Tourist Information

The national tourist board, **ENIT**, has a good website as well as branches in capital cities worldwide, and offers general information on Italy. For specific requests, contact the local tourist office. The addresses and telephone numbers are listed under each town or city, directly under the title, and they are plotted on the town and city

Sign for tourist information

maps. An EPT *(Ente Provinciale di Turismo)* has information on its town and surrounding province, whereas an APT *(Azienda di Promozione Turistica)* deals exclusively with individual towns. Both offices help with practical information such as hotel reservations and tours. They also provide free maps and guidebooks in various languages. The EPT and APT can refer you to local tour guides and offer advice on trips and excursions.

Small towns will have a *Pro Loco*, a tourist office run by the local administration, which is sometimes open only during the tourist season. It is usually located in the town hall.

Tours

Many tour companies organize bus tours, with English-speaking guides, that include all the main tourist attractions in Italy. Companies such as the UK-based **Leger Holidays** offer bus tours that go all over the country. If you are looking for something a little more personal and off the beaten track, check the local pages of national newspapers for tour groups or organizations. Local tourist boards will also be able to advise you. Always employ official guides and be sure to establish the fee in advance. For information on theme vacations, including sporting and cultural activities, turn to pages 610–11.

A guided group tour through the streets of Florence

Daytime sightseeing on a tranquil canal in Venice

Sightseeing Opening Hours

Italian museums are gradually conforming to regulations, particularly in the northern and central regions of the country, opening from 9am–7pm daily, except for Mondays. In winter, however, many museums revert to slightly earlier closing times, particularly on Sundays, but it is best to check.

Privately run and smaller museums set their own opening times, so it is a good idea to phone in advance to avoid disappointment. Archaeological sites are generally open from 9am to one hour before sunset, Tuesday to Sunday. Churches are usually open from about 7am–12:30pm and 4–7pm. However, they often prefer not to let tourists in during services, so Sunday is not the best day to visit.

Admission Charges

Sightseeing fees range from €2 to €10. Churches are usually free, but some expect a donation, and you will need coins to illuminate some works of art. Discounts for students are not always offered but many state-run museums and archaeological sites allow free entry for EU residents under 18 and over 60 years of age. Large groups are often entitled to a discount as well. If discounts are available, you will need to show a valid form of identification.

Etiquette and Tipping

People in Italy are friendly toward foreign visitors. On entering a shop or bar it is customary to greet people with a general *buon giorno* (good morning) or *buona sera* (good evening), and the same applies when leaving. They will also try to be helpful when asked directions in the street. If your Italian is slight, simply saying *scusi*, followed by the name of the place you wish to go to, will often suffice. *Grazie* (thank you) is replied to with *prego* (you're welcome).

Tipping in restaurants is expected when the 10–15 percent service is not included. However, as much as 10 percent would be considered generous, and a tip is often not expected at all in more basic restaurants. Taxi drivers and hotel porters expect a few euros if they have been helpful. You could simply round the bill up to the nearest €2.

Italians are very dress-conscious and unusual clothes do get noticed. Be aware that in places of worship you should cover your torso and upper arms; shorts and skirts must reach below the knee.

Smoking is forbidden in all buildings open to the public (including offices, shops, bars, and restaurants). However, it is tolerated in outdoor public places, whereas drunkenness is definitely frowned upon.

A student relaxing in the sun in Gaiole in Chianti

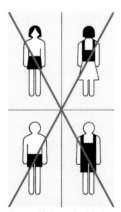

Unacceptable dress in church: both sexes are required to cover torsos and upper arms

Religious Services

Around 35 percent of the population is practicing Catholic. Sunday mass is celebrated throughout the country, while in the principal churches, services are also held during the week. In major cities some churches, such as the church of Santa Susanna (Via XX Settembre 14) in Rome, offer services and confession in English. For some visitors, a trip to Rome will include an audience with the pope *(see p423)*.

With increasing numbers of foreigners making their home in Italy, all the main religious beliefs are also represented. For details contact the main centers in Rome.

Student Information

The national student travel organization, **CTS** (Centro Turistico Studentesco), has branches throughout Italy and Europe. They issue the International Student Identity Card (ISIC) and the Youth International Educational Exchange Card (YIEE). Both can be used, along with a passport, for discounts at museums and other tourist attractions. The ISIC card also gives holders access to a free 24-hour telephone helpline in cases of emergency. As well as issuing youth cards, CTS offers cut-rate car rental and will organize vacations and courses. For details about youth hostels,

ISIC card

contact the **Associazione Italiana Alberghi per la Gioventù** (the Italian YHA), providing that you are a current member.

Traveling with Children

On the whole, Italians love children, to an extent that sometimes seems over-indulgent. Most trattorias and pizzerias welcome them and there are no rules excluding children from bars; however, high chairs are unusual. Hotels also welcome children, but smaller establishments may have limited facilities. Some of the more upscale hotels will arrange a babysitting service. Very few museums, on the other hand, provide special child-oriented activities. It is common to see children playing outside fairly late at night, especially in summer. Most towns have city parks with playgrounds, and many have summer amusement parks. Regular stops for *gelato* are guaranteed to go down well with youngsters. For young swimmers, the calm Mediterranean is ideal, though care should always be taken.

Disabled Travelers

Awareness of the needs of the disabled is improving in Italy, especially in major cities, with ramps being added to museums and some churches. Trains and buses are also becoming more disabled-friendly. In Milan **AIAS**

(Associazione Italiana Assistenza Spastici) and in Rome **CO.IN. Sociale** and **Roma per Tutti** provide information and general assistance. Train travelers with **Trenitalia** on both international and domestic routes receive help with reservations and assistance at stations.

Public Conveniences

Gabinetto means public restroom, though signs often say WC. Tourist cities have well-marked public conveniences that charge around €1. Some have cleaning staff on hand and a tip may be left. Italian cafés usually have a restroom for their customers, but it is worth checking first. Old-style "crouch" toilets are still common.

Electrical Adapters

The voltage in Italy is 220 volts, with two-pin round-pronged plugs, so it is a good idea to bring a universal adapter with you or buy one in the country. Most hotels with three or more stars have hair-dryer points in all bedrooms, but check the voltage first, to be safe.

Italian Time

Italy is one hour ahead of Greenwich Mean Time (GMT). The clocks are put forward one hour in March and back in October. For example: London is 1 hour behind Italy; Sydney is 9 hours ahead; while Ottawa is 6 hours behind.

Responsible Travel

Local attitudes toward environmental issues are developing rather slowly in Italy, despite the efforts of many concerned groups such as the Verdi political party. However, there are opportunities for low-impact travel and alternative green options available.

Staying at family run guest-houses instead of international hotel chains helps support local economies. National and regional parks award eco labels to hotels and guesthouses that adhere to EU rules governing sustainable tourism, which cover issues such as energy and water saving, waste disposal, and use of local products. The **National Association for Agritourism and Agriturismo** *(see p560)*

offers countrywide farm stays. These are a great way of enjoying the countryside and experiencing local traditions, as well as helping supplement the income of small farm owners. Facilities vary and some farms offer visitors the opportunity to help out.

Farmers' markets and growers who sell their produce direct to the public are now more common, guaranteeing fresh, seasonal produce. Look for the label *biologico* when searching for organic produce.

Conversion Chart

Imperial to Metric
1 inch = 2.54 centimeters
1 foot = 30 centimeters
1 mile = 1.6 kilometers
1 ounce = 28 grams
1 pound = 454 grams
1 pint = 0.57 liter
1 gallon = 4.6 liters

Metric to Imperial
1 centimeter = 0.4 inch
1 meter = 3 feet 3 inches
1 kilometer = 0.6 mile
1 gram = 0.04 ounce
1 kilogram = 2.2 pounds
1 liter = 1.8 pints

DIRECTORY

Questura and Permits

w poliziadistato.it

w portaleimmigrazione.it

w esteri.it/visti

Italian Customs and Tax

w agenziadogane.it

Tourist Information and Tours

APT Florence
Via Cavour 1r. **Map** 2 D4.
Tel 055 29 08 32.
w firenzeturismo.it

APT Siena
Piazza del Campo 56.
Tel 0577 28 05 51.
w terresiena.it

APT Venice
Piazza San Marco 71f.
Map 7 B2.
Tel 041 529 87 11.
w turismovenezia.it

ENIT
w italia.it

IAT Milan
Piazza Castello 1.
Tel 02 77 40 43 43.
w visitamilano.it

Leger Holidays
Tel 0844 504 62 51.
w leger.co.uk

Rome Tourist Office
Termini Station, Platform
24. **Map** 4 D3. **Tel** 06 06
08. w 060608.it

Religious Organizations

Catholic
Ufficio Informazioni
Vaticano, Piazza San

Pietro, Vaticano, Rome.
Map 1 B3.
Tel 06 69 88 16 62.

Jewish
Unione delle Comunità
Ebraiche Italiane,
Lungotevere Sanzio 9,
Rome. **Map** 6 D1.
Tel 06 45 54 22 00.
w ucei.it

Muslim
Centro Islamico Culturale
d'Italia, Viale della
Moschea 85, Rome.
Tel 06 808 22 58.

Student Information

**Associazione Italiana
Alberghi per la
Gioventù**
Via Cavour 44 (3rd floor),
Rome. **Map** 3 C5.
Tel 06 487 11 52.
w aighostels.com

CTS
Via Solferino 6A, Rome.
Map 4 D3.
Tel 06 462 04 31.
w cts.it

Disabled Tours

AIAS
Via P. Mantegazza 10,
Milan. **Tel** 02 330 20 21.
w aiasmilano.it

CO.IN.Sociale
Via E. Giglioli 54A, Rome.
w coinsociale.it

Roma per Tutti
Tel 06 57 17 70 94.
w romapertutti.it

Responsible Travel

**National Association
for Agritourism**
w agriturist.it

Personal Security and Health

Although Italy is generally a safe place for visitors, it is wise to keep a watchful eye on your personal belongings, especially in the larger towns and cities. There is a conspicuous police presence throughout the country, and in the event of an emergency or crime, any of the police officers described in this section will be able to assist you and tell you where to go to report an incident. If you fall ill, pharmacies are a good first stop where medically trained staff can give advice or tell you where to find further help. In an emergency, the Emergency Department (*Pronto Soccorso*) of any hospital will treat you and it is likely that you will encounter English-speaking staff, especially in large towns.

Commissariato di Polizia – a police station

Police car

Green Cross ambulance in Venice

Roman fire engine

Personal Property

Petty theft such as pickpocketing, bag snatching, and car theft is common in Italian cities. In the event of a theft you must report it within 24 hours to the nearest *questura* or *commissariato di polizia* (police station). If possible, show them some ID.

Avoid leaving anything visible in an unattended car, including a car radio. If you have to leave luggage in a car, find a hotel that has private parking. When making a purchase, always check your change, and do not keep wallets in back pockets, especially on buses or in other crowded places. "Fanny packs" and money belts are a favorite target for pickpockets, so try to keep them hidden. When

walking, hold bags and cameras in front of you and on the inside of the sidewalk so as not to tempt motorized snatchers, and do not show expensive cameras and video equipment in areas off tourist routes.

If attacked, never attempt to hang on to your things, as you could be seriously injured and dragged along the street.

Avoid carrying large sums of money – take out only what you need for the day. It is recommended to get comprehensive travel insurance that covers theft of personal possessions in addition to covering cancellation/delay of flights; loss/damage of luggage, money, and other valuables; and personal liability and accidents. It should include coverage for legal assistance and advice.

If you do need to make an insurance claim for stolen or lost property, you must get a copy of the report (*denuncia*) from the police station when you report the incident. In case of lost passports, go to your embassy or consulate; for lost credit cards or travelers' checks, contact the issuing company's nearest office.

If you do not have insurance coverage, contact your embassy as soon as possible after an incident, such as an accident,

occurs. The embassy can offer advice and should provide you with a list of English- and Italian-speaking lawyers who are knowledgeable about both the Italian and other legal systems.

Personal Security

Although petty crime in cities is frequent, violent crime in Italy is rare. However, it is common for people to raise their voices aggressively during an argument. Usually, remaining calm and being polite will help to defuse the situation.

Always be wary of unofficial tour guides, taxi drivers, or strangers who wish to assist you or advise you on accommodations, restaurants, or shops, as they may expect something in return. Decline their offers politely but firmly.

A team of *carabinieri* in traffic police uniform

Women Travelers

Women traveling on their own in Italy are likely to meet with a lot of attention. This is often more of an irritation than a danger, but it is best to keep away from lonely, unlit streets and areas near train stations at night, and to carry an alarm or whistle and be equipped with the telephone numbers of your hotel and a local taxi service. Walking quickly and purposefully is a good way to avoid any unwanted attention. The staff at hotels and restaurants generally treat their single female guests and customers with extra care and attention.

The Police

There are several different police forces in Italy and each one fulfills a particular role. The state police, *la polizia*, wear blue uniforms and drive blue cars. They deal with most crimes.

The *carabinieri* are militarily trained and wear dark blue and black uniforms with red striped trousers. These officers deal with a variety of offenses from organized crime to speeding and can also conduct random security checks.

The *guardia di finanza* are the financial police force (the fraud squad), and wear gray uniforms with yellow striped trousers. The *vigili urbani*, or the municipal traffic police, wear blue and white uniforms in winter

Municipal policeman

and white during the summer.

Even though they are not official police officers, the *vigili urbani* can issue heavy fines for traffic and parking offenses. They can usually be spotted patrolling the streets, enforcing laws, or directing traffic. Officers from any of the forces will be able to help in an emergency.

Outside a Florentine pharmacy with a green cross sign

Medical Treatment

Emergency medical care in Italy is free for all EU and Australian citizens, thanks to reciprocal agreements. The EHIC European Health Insurance Card, which is available from the UK Department of Health offices and website, or from a main post office, covers emergencies only; private medical insurance is needed for all other types of treatment. The card comes with a booklet that contains general health advice and information about how to claim free medical treatment when traveling abroad. You may find you have to pay and reclaim the money later. Australians need to apply to Medicare.

Non-EU citizens should try to arrive in Italy with comprehensive private medical insurance to cover all eventualities. If you do need emergency treatment, go to the *Pronto Soccorso* (Emergency Department) of the nearest hospital. If necessary, you will be referred to the appropriate specialist or department within the same structure.

As an alternative, ask your hotel to call the night doctor – *guardia medica* – who can be consulted on the phone.

No inoculations are needed for Italy, but mosquito repellent is recommended in summer. Repellent creams and sprays are found in pharmacies, as are electric insect repellers, which burn pellets to deter the bugs.

Pharmacies

Various medical products, including homeopathic medicines, are available in any pharmacy (*farmacia*), but a prescription is often required. Qualified staff will offer advice for minor ailments and common illnesses and provide appropriate medicines. Thanks to a night duty roster (*servizio notturno*), there is always a pharmacy open in all cities and most towns. Those that are open at night are listed in the local pages of daily newspapers and on all pharmacy doors.

Pharmacies also sell toiletries and beauty items. Common nonprescription pharmaceutical products such as aspirin are also sold at lower prices in many large supermarkets.

Banking and Local Currency

Virtually all Italian hotels, many shops, large restaurants, and gas stations accept major credit cards. Only in the more off-the-beaten-track locations will you have difficulties without euros, and some establishments will offer a discount for payments made in cash, especially in the off-season. When you pay with a credit card, you might be asked to show identification, such as your passport. Foreign currency can be changed in banks, although these are often crowded and service tends to be slow. All banks will cash travelers' checks, and cash machines *(bancomat)* will accept cards with a PIN. Most machines also accept MasterCard, VISA, and American Express cards. Although banks often have the best exchange rates, bureaux de change and foreign exchange machines can be more convenient.

Bureaux de change, however, are often open all day, and in some places they also stay open until late at night.

Using banks

For security purposes, most banks have electronic double doors with metal detectors, allowing one person in at a time. Metal objects and bags should first be deposited in lockers situated in the foyer. Press the button to open the outer door, then wait for it to close behind you. The inner door then opens automatically. Do not be alarmed by the heavily armed guards who patrol most banks in Italy.

Changing money at a bank can be a frustrating process involving endless form-filling and standing in line. First you have to go to the window that displays the *cambio* sign and then to the *cassa* to obtain your money. If in doubt, ask someone in order to avoid waiting in the wrong line.

If you need to have money sent to you in Italy, banks at home can transfer money to an Italian bank, but it can take up to a week. American Express, Thomas Cook, and Western Union all provide swifter money transfer services, with a charge to the sender.

ATM, which also accepts VISA and MasterCard (Access)

Changing money

Banking hours are somewhat restrictive and can also be slightly erratic, so it is safest to acquire a small amount of local currency before you arrive in Italy. Exchange rates will vary from place to place.

Travelers' checks are still a safe way to carry money, though commission charges can be hefty. Choose a well-known name such as Thomas Cook or American Express. Once you arrive, the most convenient way to change money is to use the electronic exchange machines, which are located at all major airports, train stations, and some banks. The machines have multilingual instructions and the exchange rate is clearly displayed on the screen. Simply feed in bills of the same foreign currency and you will receive euros in return.

Bureaux de change can be found in all main towns. Although they are easier to

use, they usually have worse exchange rates and charge more commission than banks.

Regional differences in cost of living

The north is generally more expensive than the south, but there are many exceptions. Restaurants and hotels off the beaten track are usually better value, and buying locally made produce is cost effective if you avoid obvious tourist traps.

Banking hours

Banks are usually open between 8:30am and 1:30pm, Monday to Friday. Most also open for an hour in the afternoon, from about 2:15pm to 3pm or 2:30pm until 3:30pm, depending on the bank. All banks close on weekends and for public holidays, and they also close early the day before a major holiday.

Metal-detecting security doors found at most banks

Cash machines

Withdrawing cash from an ATM (automatic teller machine) with a credit card is a straightforward process. Choose your language on the screen and follow the instructions. You will need to type in your PIN, so have it handy. Should your card be swallowed up by a cash machine for some reason (for example if you typed an incorrect number), it may be sent back to the issuing bank. However, if the bank is open do ask inside. Costs for cash withdrawals are set by your bank so check before you travel. It may be a good idea to take out a largish amount of money in one go, but bear in mind that ATMs may run out of bills on weekends.

The euro

The euro (€) is the common currency of the European Union. It came into general circulation on January 1, 2002, initially for twelve participating countries. Italy was one of those twelve countries, and the lire was phased out by March 2002.

EU members using the Euro as sole official currency are known as the Eurozone. Several EU members have opted out of joining this common currency. Euro bills are identical throughout the Euro-zone countries, each one including designs of fictional architectural structures. The coins, however, have one side identical (the value side) and one side with an image unique to each country. Bills and coins are exchangeable in each participating country.

Euro Bills

The EU prints euro bills in seven denominations. The €5 bill (gray in color) is the smallest, followed by the €10 bill (pink), €20 bill (blue), €50 bill (orange), €100 bill (green), €200 bill (yellow), and €500 bill (purple). All euro bills show the 12 stars of the European Union.

€5 bill

€10 bill

€20 bill

€50 bill

€100 bill

€200 bill

€500 bill

€2 coin

€1 coin

50 cents

20 cents

10 cents

Euro Coins

The euro has eight coin denominations: €1 and €2; 50 cents, 20 cents, 10 cents, 5 cents, 2 cents, and 1 cent. The €2 and €1 coins are both silver and gold in color. The 50-, 20-, and 10-cent coins are gold. The 5-, 2-, and 1-cent coins are bronze.

5 cents

2 cents

1 cent

Communications and Media

Although the Italian postal service is known for being very slow, Italy's other forms of communication, at least in the cities, are more efficient. Fax machines, courier services, and telephones are all widespread, and Internet access is available throughout Italy. Foreign-language newspapers and magazines are on sale in all cities and most large towns. Both state-run and privately owned television stations exist, but only satellite television and radio stations broadcast foreign-language programs.

Telephone company logo

Public telephones

The Italian national telephone company is Telecom Italia. Coin-operated telephones have been phased out and replaced by card-operated machines. Most public telephones have instructions in five languages (Italian, English, French, Spanish, and German). To select a language, push the top right-hand button. To use a public telephone you will need a Telecom Italia phone card. Phone cards (*carta* or *scheda telefonica*) can be purchased from bars, newspaper kiosks, post offices, and *tabacchi* displaying the black-and-white T sign.

International phone cards, on sale at *tabacchi* and newsstands, are still a very cheap way to call abroad. Some cards offer as many as 3 hours of calls for about €10, depending on the country being called. Dial the toll-free number on the card and then enter the secret code found by scratching off the silver strip on the back of the card. You will be told the amount of credit available and

Telephone sign

then asked to dial the number you wish to call. Rates are slightly higher when calling from a mobile or public phone. Check with your hotel before using a card from your room as extra charges may be applied.

Email and Internet

Internet and email services are widely available throughout Italy, particularly in urban areas, so it should not be difficult to access email accounts or connect to the web. Telecom Italia, the Italian national phone company, has set up Internet service in the country's major train stations and public phone centers. Internet time can be purchased using a regular phone card.

Some major chains of Internet providers sell magnetic cards with credit that can be used in any of their stores throughout Italy. **Internet Train**, with branches in over 40 towns, is the most visible. Visit its website for a full list of stores. In addition, small Internet shops are very common. These are usually

clustered around train stations, cheap hotels, and university areas and can range from the back room of a café or bar to the corner of a launderette. Users can buy computer time in blocks as short as 15 minutes. There are usually student discounts available, and cost per minute decreases as the amount of time purchased increases.

Many hotels have Wi-Fi so travelers with their own laptop can have easy access. You'll probably need a plug adapter too. Remember that with **Skype** or **Voip Stunt** installed it's possible to make phone calls over the Internet with the help of a small microphone. Calls are free between Skype users.

Mobile phones

There are four main GSM frequencies (Global System for Mobile Communications) in use around the world, so to guarantee that your phone will work, make sure you have a quad-band phone. Tri-band phones from outside the United States are also usually compatible, but because the United States uses two frequency bands itself, a U.S. tri-band phone may only have limited global coverage. Contact your service provider for clarification.

To use your mobile phone abroad you may need to get "permission" from your network operator, as often they need to enable "roaming" for your phone. At the moment, you are charged for the calls you receive as well as the calls you make, and you have to pay a substantial premium for the international leg of the call.

Another option is to purchase a local SIM card – the electronic chip that links your phone to a particular network – that can

Using a public Telecom Italia telephone

be topped up with credit and uses the local mobile phone networks. You can only do this if your handset is "unlocked" – some operators lock their phones to specific networks.

It is worth checking your insurance policy in case your phone gets stolen. You should also keep your network operator's helpline number handy for emergencies.

TV and radio

Television channels in Italy include the state-owned RAI (Uno, Due, and Tre) and Mediaset (Retequattro, Canale Cinque, and Italia Uno). There are also many local channels. Most foreign programs are dubbed into Italian, although satellite channels, such as BBC World News, Sky, and CNN, show news and sports programs in English. There are three national radio stations and hundreds of local stations.

A selection of newspapers available at a newsstand

Newspapers

There are several national daily newspapers, including *La Stampa*, *Il Corriere della Sera*, and *La Repubblica*. Papers with the most detailed news of Italy's major cities include *Il Mattino* for Naples, *Il Messaggero* for Rome, *La Nazione* for Florence, and *Il Giornale* for Milan.

All newspapers will have local pages and listings for movies, theaters, main concerts, and other cultural events. In Rome and Milan, *La Repubblica* also publishes regular "what's happening and where to go" supplements called *TrovaRoma* and *ViviMilano* respectively.

Florence's *Firenze Spettacolo* and Rome's *Roma c'è* are weekly magazines with entertainment listings. The latter also has a useful restaurant section and a summary of listings in English at the back.

British and American papers, such as the *International Herald Tribune*, *The Guardian*, and *USA Today*, are readily available and tend to arrive in the main cities at around midday on the day of publication.

Post office

Local post offices open from 8:25am–1:50pm weekdays, and from 8:25am–noon on Saturday. Main city post offices are open from 8:25am–7pm nonstop. Many tobacconists also sell stamps.

The Vatican City and the state of San Marino have their own postal systems and stamps. Bear in mind that letters bearing San Marino or Vatican stamps can only be posted in San Marino and Vatican mailboxes.

The red mailboxes (blue in the Vatican) usually have two slots labeled *per la città* (for the city only) and *tutte le altre destinazioni* (for all other destinations).

The Italian postal service is notorious for its unreliability, and letters can take between four days and two weeks to arrive.

For faster service it is best to send letters by express mail (*posta prioritaria*). A more reliable option is recorded delivery (*raccomandata*). Anything of value should be sent by insured mail (*assicurata*).

For urgent communications, try state couriers *Postacelere* and *Paccocelere*, which are based at all main post offices. They guarantee delivery within 24–72 hours and are far cheaper than private couriers.

City letters   Other destinations

Italian mailbox

DIRECTORY

Remember to always use the full area code (including the first zero), even when making a call within a city.

Useful Numbers

Directory Enquiries
Tel 1254 (Option 1).

Multilingual Directory Enquiries
Tel 1254 (Option 2).

Operator Services
Tel 170 (also for collect and calling card calls).

American Operators
Tel 800 17 24 44 (AT&T).
Tel 800 17 24 01 (Verizon).
Tel 800 17 24 05 (Sprint).

Australian Operators
Tel 800 17 26 10 (Telstra).
Tel 800 17 26 11 (Optus).

Country Codes

To call Italy from these countries, dial the code and then the full area code (including the 0) and the number.

Tel 00 39 – UK
Tel 0 1139 – U.S. & Canada
Tel 00 39 – Ireland
Tel 00 1139 – Australia

Email and Internet

Internet Train
W internettrain.it

Skype
W skype.com

Voip Stunt
W voipstunt.com

Mail and Couriers

Italian Post Office
W poste.it

Private Couriers

DHL
Tel 199 199 345.
W dhl.it

FedEx
Tel 199 151 119.
W fedex.com

UPS
Tel 02 30 30 30 39.
W ups.com

TRAVEL INFORMATION

Italy has transportation systems of varying efficiency, from the modern road, bus, and railroad networks of the north to the slower systems of the south. Numerous airlines operate flights to several of the country's major airports, while within Italy itself the national carrier Alitalia, and several smaller companies, provide an extensive network of internal flights. Connections by road to the rest of Europe are good, though Alpine roads can be adversely affected by the weather in winter. Highways and other roads within the country are generally good, but can be busy on weekends and during peak periods. Italy also has an efficient system of ferries connecting Sicily, Sardinia, and many of the smaller off-shore islands. Many of these are car ferries, and are busy in summer.

Green Travel

Traveling in Italy without using high-impact flights or long car drives is straight-forward, thanks to an excellent public transportation network. Train and bus systems both offer regular and reliable services and are reasonably priced. Connections with major European cities are good and travelers can often choose between day services on the Eurocity trains and overnight services on the EuroNight trains. There are also high-speed trains, known as the *Alta Velocita* (*see pp628–9*).

Where only a few people use a particular route (such as to outlying hamlets in the Alps and Apennines), some authorities have set up a *servizio a chiamata* (demand-responsive service), whereby passengers phone a toll-free number to reserve a vehicle. This results in cost savings for the council and a reduction in carbon emissions, plus passengers get a personalized taxi for the price of a single bus ticket. Within cities, less polluting vehicles such as battery- or methane-powered buses and *vaporetti* have been introduced.

Bicycle routes and rentals are increasing in number, and many cities such as Milan and Rome have plenty of rental shops and marked safe bicycle lanes. The Trentino–Alto Adige regions are especially well organized with long-distance cycle routes. For a small charge bicycles can be transported on many regional and international trains.

Arriving by Air

Rome's Leonardo da Vinci (Fiumicino) and Milan's Malpensa are the key airports for long-distance flights into Italy. Milan's Linate airport handles some European flights, and most European airlines also fly to Venice, Turin, Naples, and Pisa (for Florence). Many airlines are now flying regularly to smaller cities such as Florence, Genoa, Bologna, Verona, and Bergamo, while charter flights serve summer destinations such as Catania, Olbia, and Rimini in peak season.

Part of the extension to Fiumicino airport, Rome

Long-Distance Flights

If you are flying from the United States, **Delta** and **United Airlines** operate regular direct scheduled flights to Rome and Milan, with service from New York, Philadelphia, Los Angeles, Boston, and Chicago. **Air Canada** flies from Montreal and Toronto, and **Qantas** flies from Sydney and Melbourne.

Regular service between Rome and Milan and New York, Boston, Chicago, Miami, and Toronto is also offered by the Italian state airline, **Alitalia**.

It may, however, be more convenient and cheaper for long-distance passengers to take a budget flight to London, Frankfurt, Paris, Athens, or Amsterdam and then continue to Italy from there.

European Low-Cost Flights

It has never been so easy to get to Italy by air. **British Airways** and **Alitalia** and its partners fly to major destinations in Italy from large European cities. However, low-cost, "no-frills" airlines offer many more destinations.

Ryanair flies to more than 20 airports (including Genoa, Rome-Ciampino, Turin, and Venice-Treviso) from Stansted; while **easyJet**, from Gatwick or Stansted, serves Rome-Ciampino, Milan, Venice, Pisa, Palermo, and Naples, and also Rome, Olbia, and Pisa from Bristol. **Meridiana** flies to Florence and Olbia from Gatwick and, like **Blu-Express**, also offers a number of domestic flights.

The entrance hall at Pisa airport

Tickets and Fares

Fares vary enormously according to season and supply and demand. You can usually get the best deals by booking online well in advance.

Consult a good travel agent or check availability on the Internet. If you are based in the UK, it may be worthwhile to scour the small ads of newspapers for charter and discounted scheduled flights on major routes. Most charters leave from Gatwick or Luton, and may land at a city's second (and often less convenient) airport. Fares tend to vary greatly during the year, but the most expensive periods are during the summer months and over the Christmas and Easter holidays. Where possible, ask for available student discounts.

Package Vacations

Package vacations to Italy are usually cheaper than traveling independently, unless you are traveling on a tight budget and are prepared to make use of youth hostels and campsites. Rome, Florence, and Venice are often offered as separate or linked package deals, and many operators have packages to the Tuscan and Umbrian countryside, Sicily, the Italian Lakes, the Italian Riviera, Naples, and the Amalfi coast. In winter, ski packages are available to many Alpine resorts. Themed vacation packages, such as cooking, walking, and art tours, are also common.

In cities, different tour operators may use different hotels, so it is worth researching the most pleasant (and centrally located) accommodation options. Many operators include transfers from the airport to your hotel. Some include tour guides.

DIRECTORY

Green Travel

Cycling in Trentino
W visittrentino.it

Airlines

Air Canada
W aircanada.com

Alitalia
Tel 89 20 10. W alitalia.com

Blu-Express
W blu-express.com

British Airways
Tel 02 69 63 36 02.
W britishairways.com

Delta
W delta.com

easyJet
W easyjet.com

Meridiana
W meridiana.it

Qantas
W qantas.com

Ryanair
W ryanair.com

United Airlines
W united.com

Airport	Information	Distance to city center	Taxi fare to city center	Public transportation to city center
Rome (Fiumicino)	06 659 51 W adr.it	22 miles (35 km)	€40	FS 30 mins
Rome (Ciampino)	06 659 51 W adr.it	9 miles (15 km)	€30	M 45 mins
Milan (Linate)	02 23 23 23 W seamilano.eu	5 miles (8 km)	€20	15 mins
Milan (Malpensa)	02 23 23 23 W seamilano.eu	31 miles (50 km)	€90	FS M 60 mins
Pisa (Galileo Galilei)	050 84 91 11 W pisa-airport.com	1 mile (2 km)	€10	FS to Pisa: 10 mins FS to Florence: 80 mins
Venice (Marco Polo)	041 260 92 60 W veniceairport.it	8 miles (13 km)	€35 (€100 water taxi)	60 mins 20 mins
Venice (Treviso)	0422 31 51 11 W trevisoairport.it	15 miles (25 km)	€70 to Venice	to Treviso: 20 mins to Venice: 70 mins
Verona	045 809 56 66 W aeroportoverona.it	7 miles (12 km)	€25	15 mins
Bergamo	035 32 63 23 W orioaeroporto.it	3 miles (5 km)	€18	25 mins
Turin	011 567 63 61 W turin-airport.com	9 miles (15 km)	€30	20 mins
Naples	081 789 61 11 W portal.gesac.it	4 miles (7 km)	€20	30 mins
Palermo	091 702 02 73 W gesap.it	21 miles (35 km)	€40–€45	50 mins 1 hr

Arriving by Sea, Rail, and Road

Italy is served by an extensive network of roads, railroads, and international ferry lines. Road and railroad links cross into the country from France, Switzerland, Austria, and Slovenia, and there are through train services from as far afield as Budapest, London, and Barcelona. Road connections into the country are generally of highway standard, though delays can occur at some of the many Alpine passes and tunnels during bad weather or peak summer vacation periods.

Do-it-yourself help kiosks with train information on screens

Ticket windows at Florence's Santa Maria Novella station

Arriving by Car

Most roads into Italy from the rest of Europe involve Alpine crossings by tunnel or mountain passes. The notable exceptions are the approach from Slovenia in the northeast (on the A4 highway) and the route along the French Riviera that enters Italy as the A10 highway at Ventimiglia.

The most popular route from Geneva and southeast France is via the Mont Blanc tunnel and A5 highway, entering Italy close to Aosta and Turin. Another busy approach (from Switzerland) uses the St. Bernard Pass and tunnel.

Further east, the main route from Austria and southern Germany crosses the Brenner Pass and goes down to Verona on the A22 highway via Trento and the Adige valley. Weather conditions rarely close the passes, but snow and fog can make progress slow on the winding roads through the mountains. Most highways are toll roads; you pay as you exit the highway.

Arriving by Train

After air travel, arriving by train is the least painful way to reach Italy. Countless through services (including many sleepers) link Italian towns and cities with places as far afield as Brussels, Budapest, and Barcelona. Connections from Paris (and London, via Eurostar) run to Turin, Milan, Venice, Bologna, Florence, or along Italy's west coast, via Genoa and Pisa, to Rome and Naples. Train services also operate from German, Swiss, and other northern European cities to

Platform sign

Exit sign

The sleeping car on an international Eurocity train

Milan, Turin, Venice, and Verona. There are also direct services from Vienna, Spain, and the south of France. Motorail connections exist from several centers in northern Europe and the Channel ports.

The popularity of low-cost airlines has forced international train travel to be a little more competitive – if booked online. Special discount fares, however, are often available for senior travelers and for travelers under 26.

Trains can be extremely busy during peak periods, particularly on Friday and Sunday evenings, and during the Christmas and Easter holiday periods. July and August can also be frantically busy, especially on routes from Germany and ports connecting with Greek ferries in the south. Reservations are recommended on most routes.

Arriving by Boat

Most people arriving in Italy by boat do so from Greece, using services from Corfu and Patras to Brindisi and other southeastern ports. Boats are crowded in summer, as are connecting train services from Brindisi to the rest of Italy.

Other international connections include ferries from Malta and North African ports to Palermo, Naples, and various southern Italian ports. Boats also run from towns in the south of France to Genoa, Livorno, and ports on the Italian Riviera, and from the Croatian coast across the Adriatic to Venice.

Arriving by Bus

Bus travel to Italy is relatively cheap, but long travel times make it one of the least comfortable ways to travel. The travel time from London to Milan is about 24 hours, and it is about 33 hours from London to Rome. A night on the road is thus unavoidable. **Eurolines** runs buses from London's Victoria Coach Station to most of Italy's major cities as far as Rome and Naples (a change at Milan or Paris is often necessary). Buses travel via Dover, Calais, Paris, and Dijon and it is useful to have some euros with you for stops en route. Travel around Italy by long-distance bus is feasible with SITA.

SITA bus arriving at the station in Florence

Traveling Around by Ferry

Italy's large number of off-shore islands mean that it has a large and well-developed network of ferries, as well as services to the rest of Europe and North Africa.

One of the Moby Lines car ferries that sail the Mediterranean

Ferries

Car ferries are a convenient link with the beautiful islands scattered off the Italian mainland. Boats for Sardinia leave from Civitavecchia (north of Rome), Livorno, and Genoa, and depart for Sicily from Naples and Reggio di Calabria. Ferries run from the major Sicilian ports to the Egadi and the Aeolian archipelagoes, as well as to countless other small islands around Sicily (although be aware that ferries to the smaller islands do not always carry cars).

Boats also ply between Elba and Piombino, as well as the smaller islands of the Tuscan archipelago such as Capraia. Ferries run from ports close to Rome to Ponza and its surrounding islands, and from Naples to Capri and Ischia. On the east coast the Tremiti islands are linked to ports on the Gargano peninsula.

Hydrofoils are increasingly complementing conventional ferries, particularly on busy routes to Capri and Ischia. Hydrofoils, and ferries, also run on some of Italy's lakes, such as Como and Garda.

Lines for ferries are common in summer, so make reservations well in advance if you wish to travel in July or August, especially if taking a vehicle. Ferry services are more frequent and reliable in summer than in winter.

Reservations can be made online, through travel agents, or at a ferry line's agents in your own country. Ticket prices can vary according to the time of year but are generally reasonable. To check schedules and fares, visit the relevant website.

DIRECTORY

Arriving by Train

Ferrovie dello Stato
Tel 89 20 21 (in Italy).
W trenitalia.com

Arriving by Bus

Eurolines
Tel 0861 199 19 00.
W eurolines.co.uk

SITA
W sitabus.it

Ferries

Corsica Sardinia Ferries
Tel 199 400 500.
W corsicaferries.com
Civitavecchia/Livorno –
Golfo Aranci

Grandi Navi Veloci
Tel 010 209 45 91.
W gnv.it Genoa/
Civitavecchia – Palermo
Genoa – Porto Torres/
Olbia

Moby Lines
Tel 199 303 040;
02 76 02 81 32.
W moby.com
Piombino – Elba
Genoa/Livorno – Olbia

SNAV
Tel 081 428 55 55.
W snav.it
Ancona – Split
Naples/Sorrento –
Capri/Ischia
Naples – Aeolian Islands

Tirrenia
Tel 892 123; 02 26 30 28
03. W tirrenia.it
Bari – Durazzo
Genoa – Porto Torres
Civitavecchia – Olbia
Naples – Palermo/Cagliari
Cagliari – Palermo

Venezia Lines
Tel 041 882 11 01.
W venezialines.com
Venice – Rabac
Venice – Porec/Rovinj/Pula
Bari – Durazzo

Traveling Around by Train

Train travel is one of the best ways to explore Italy. Tickets are inexpensive, services frequent, and rolling stock some of the most modern in Europe. Routes can be busy, but the days of rampant overcrowding are mostly over. Lines often run through lovely countryside, from mountain lakes to rolling plateaus, and railroad lines provide more convenient links between cities than roads or air travel. Only in the south, or deeply rural areas, are train services slow and infrequent.

A Eurostar – one of Italy's fastest trains

The Network

The bulk of Italy's railroad network is an integrated state-run system operated by **Trenitalia** of the Ferrovie dello Stato (FS), which has introduced superfast services reducing travel times between major cities. In this, it competes with the **NTV** consortium. Smaller privately run lines also fill crucial gaps left by the FS, but through-tickets are generally available where travel involves both networks. State and private lines often share the same main station (*stazione*), and also charge similar fares.

Trains

Trenitalia and NTV take advantage of the *Alta Velocità* (AV) network between major cities in the north as well as southward as far as Naples. These, the fast Eurostar (ES) and a handful of other special high-speed trains always require advance seat reservations. Intercity (IC) trains and Eurocity (EC) trains stop only at major stations and require the payment of a supplement (*un supplemento*) on top of the standard ticket (supplements can be bought on the train, but are more expensive). *Regionali*

and *Interregionali* trains make more stops and require no supplement.

AV, ES, EC, and Intercity trains are usually all air-conditioned. Railroad cars on branch lines can still be ancient.

Facilities for the disabled, including assistance at stations, exist on all fast trains and international services. For assistance ask at the special *Sale Blu* (Blue Halls) in mainline train stations.

Tickets and Fares

Tickets (*biglietti*) are available as single (*andata*) or return (*andata e ritorno*) in first (*prima*) or second class (*seconda classe*). They can be bought at some travel agents or at any station ticket office (*biglietteria*).

Major stations have automatic ticket machines and you can also buy tickets for journeys of up to 155 miles (250 km) from newsstands or station tobacconists (such a ticket is called *biglietto a fascia chilometrica*). Be sure to validate all tickets on both outbound and return journeys, or you will be fined. A ticket's validity usually starts on the day of purchase, so be sure to specify the day of travel when buying

tickets. Fares are calculated on a kilometric basis and are among the cheapest in western Europe. Many discounted fares are offered, including special family tickets. Some online ticket purchases also carry discounts.

Refunds involve a complicated process – inquire at the *Assistenza* counter at major stations. It is important, therefore, to buy the correct ticket before traveling.

Passes

The most useful pass for visitors is the **Interrail Pass**, which gives unlimited travel for consecutive or nonconsecutive days over varying periods, with special rates for travelers under 26. It can be purchased online or at most mainline stations and at various agencies outside Italy. An Interrail One Country Pass allows travel on any 5 or 10 days within a specific period.

Timetables

If you plan to use trains often, it is a good idea to pick up an official Trenitalia timetable (*un orario*) at a train station or newsstand. It is updated yearly. Alternatively, find the online time-table at www.trenitalia.com.

Validity and Reservations

Single or return tickets are valid for up to two months from the date of purchase. If a seat reservation is made with the ticket, however, the date you wish to travel will be stamped automatically on the ticket. Reservations are automatic on AV and Eurostar services, and they are a good idea on all trains on and around public holidays. Reservations can be made at most main stations or online.

The concourse at Stazione Termini, Rome

Discounts

The Smart Price deal offers discounts on international trains between Italy and various European countries. Prices range from €19 to €70 one way, with extra fees for pull-down bunks (couchettes) and sleeping cars. You can buy tickets at mainline stations or on the Trenitalia website; only a fixed number are available so reserve in advance.

Baggage Storage

Main city stations usually have bag-check facilities. Most are staffed (but the smaller stations have self-service lockers), and you may need to present identification when depositing or collecting bags. Fees are calculated per bag and by the number of hours bags are left.

Scenic Railroad Routes

Italy's varied geography makes for some memorable train trips across the length and breadth of the country. The glacially shaped Adige valley between Bolzano and Verona in the north is thick with apple orchards and surrounded by soaring alpine peaks, with the pretty Trento-Male line branching off it. The Tuscan countryside south of Florence boasts views of hill towns and rolling wheat fields, while close by in Lazio the Roma Nord-Viterbo line winds its way through beautiful rural scenery.

Farther south, trains cross the Straits of Messina to Sicily on a special ferry, while a narrow-gauge line circles Mount Etna. For steam train enthusiasts there are trips run by the FTI (Ferrovie Turistiche Italiane) groups in the north through alpine foothills and past picturesque lakes, as well as in the countryside outside Siena.

Machines for Trenitalia Train Tickets

These machines are easy to use, and most have instructions on screen in a choice of six languages. They accept coins, bills, and credit cards.

1 Touch screen: choose destination, train, and ticket type, make seat reservations, and choose payment method.

2 Insert coins here.

3 Insert bills here.

4 Pay with credit card: touchpad with slot for card below.

5 Receive train tickets, seat reservations, and change here.

Italy's Principal FS Network

The Italian state railroad network operates various types of service. Check what is available before buying your ticket.

Key

● Main stations

○ Other stations

— Principal route

-- Route over water

DIRECTORY

Railroad information

Erail Travel Ltd
Tel 020 7619 1083 (UK).
🅦 erail.co.uk

FTI (Ferrovie Turistiche Italiane)
🅦 ferrovieturistiche.it

Interrail Pass
🅦 interrailnet.com

NTV
🅦 ntvspa.it

Trenitalia
Information for travel all over Italy. **Tel** 89 20 21.
🅦 trenitalia.com

Traveling Around by Car

A road trip is a practical way of exploring the country, though you should take into account high gas prices, difficulties parking, driving restrictions in cities, and the Italians' occasionally erratic approach to driving. A car is invaluable in the countryside and for extensive touring, but less useful in major towns and cities, due to congestion and the fact that most city centers are off-limits to nonresidents' cars.

One-way street

Blue signs showing main roads and green signs showing highways

Automatic tollbooths on the highway outside Florence

What to Take

Drivers from outside Italy who bring their own foreign-registered cars into the country must carry a Green Card (for insurance purposes), all the vehicle's registration documents, and a full, valid driver's license (*patente* in Italian). Any EU nationals who do not have the standard EU "pink" license and are planning to stay for more than six months will need an Italian translation of their license, obtainable from most automobile organizations or from the Italian state tourist office in your home country. A red warning triangle and fluorescent vests must also be carried at all times, for use in the event of a breakdown or emergency.

Gas

Gas (*benzina*) in Italy is some of the most expensive in Europe (diesel, or *gasolio*, is a little cheaper). Although many gas stations are now self-service, it is still common to be served by an attendant. Most gas stations follow normal business hours, so make sure you have a full tank before lunchtime or public holidays. On highways

gas stations tend to be open 24 hours a day. Credit cards are usually accepted.

Roads

Italy has a good network of highways, though many have a total of only four lanes, often leading to congestion. Busy routes include the A1 from Bologna to Florence and between Bologna, Parma, and Milan. Tolls must be paid on most highways (*autostrade*), again leading to congestion

Rules and Regulations

Drive on the right and yield to traffic from the right. Seat belts are required for all passengers. Heavy fines are levied for using a mobile phone while driving. Headlights must be turned on even during the day on highways and outside built-up areas. The speed limit in urban areas is 30 mph (50 km/h); outside urban areas it is 70 mph (110 km/h) on divided highways and 55 mph (90 km/h) on other secondary roads. On highways the limit is 80 mph (130 km/h) for vehicles over 1100cc, 70 mph (110 km/h) for those under 1100cc.

at tollbooths (*Alt Stazione*) during busy periods. Payment is made at the end of the journey in cash, credit card, or prepaid magnetic VIA cards, available from tobacconists and the **ACI**. There is a congestion charge in Milan (7:30am–7:30pm Mon–Fri); call 800 437 437 or visit www.comunemilano.it/ecopass before entering the city.

Secondary roads are known as *Nazionali* (N) or as *Strade Statali* (SS), and vary enormously in quality. Mountain roads are usually good, but distances can be deceptive. In winter, snow chains are obligatory on many higher routes. Some back roads (known as *strade bianche*, or "white roads") have only a gravel surface. These are slow, but usually passable for cars.

No stopping

End of speed restriction

Pedestrianized street – no traffic

Yield to oncoming traffic

continua

No parking

Danger (often with description)

Logo for international car rental company

Car Rental

Car rentals *(autonoleggio)* in Italy are expensive, and should be organized beforehand through package airfare-plus-rental deals or advance reservations with rental agencies that have branches in Italy. For on-the-ground rentals, Italian firms may be cheaper than big international names. Agencies are listed in the Yellow Pages *(Pagine Gialle)* under Autonoleggio. Most airports have car rental offices on site.

To rent a car in Italy you must generally be over 21 (sometimes older) and have held a valid driver's license for at least a year. Visitors from outside the EU must have an international license, though in practice not all rental agencies insist on this. Check the fine print of the agreement for insurance coverage.

Accidents and Breakdowns

If you have an accident or a breakdown, switch on your hazard warning lights and place a warning triangle 164 ft (50 m) behind your car. Then (for breakdowns) call the **ACI** emergency number (803 116) or emergency services (112 or 113). The ACI will tow any foreign-registered car free to the nearest ACI-affiliated garage. They also do free repairs for members of affiliated automobile associations, such as the AA and RAC in Britain.

If you have an accident, stay calm, and do not admit liability or make any statements that might incriminate you later. Simply exchange car and insurance details, names, and addresses.

Parking

Parking in most Italian cities and large towns is a problem. Many historic centers have restricted daytime access and baffling one-way systems. Other areas may be reserved for residents' parking (marked *riservato ai residenti*). Most towns have metered parking areas that charge an hourly fee paid with coins, cards, or coupons bought from *tabacchi*. Cars can be towed away or have their wheels clamped, especially in areas marked *zona rimozione*, particularly on street-cleaning days. Call the Municipal Police *(Vigili)* to retrieve your car.

Official parking area patrolled by attendant

Safety

Car theft is rife in Italy. Never leave anything in your car, and (if possible) always remove radio-CD players and GPS devices.

Leave your car in a guarded parking lot whenever you can. Be especially careful driving at night, when Italian driving is more cavalier than usual, and when many traffic lights switch to flashing amber. Hitchhiking *(autostop)* is not a good idea (and is not common), certainly never for women on their own.

DIRECTORY

Car Rental

Avis
Tel 06 452 10 83 91.
w avisautonoleggio.it

Europcar
Tel 199 307 030.
w europcar.it

Hertz
Tel 06 65 01 15 53 (Rome airport).
w hertz.it

Maggiore
Tel 199 151 120.
w maggiore.it

Sixt
Tel 06 65 21 11 (Rome).
w sixt.it

Emergencies

ACI emergency
Tel 803 116. w aci.it

Police
Tel 112 or 113.

Ambulance
Tel 118.

Distance Chart

	10 Distance in kilometers
	10 Distance in miles

Rome											
286	Ancona										
178											
748	**617**	Aosta									
465	383										
383	**219**	**401**	Bologna								
238	136	249									
645	**494**	**449**	**280**	Bolzano							
401	307	279	174								
278	**262**	**470**	**106**	**367**	Florence						
173	163	292	66	228							
510	**506**	**245**	**291**	**422**	**225**	Genoa					
317	315	152	181	262	140						
601	**614**	**1220**	**822**	**1097**	**871**	**1103**	Lecce				
373	382	758	511	682	541	685					
575	**426**	**181**	**210**	**295**	**299**	**145**	**1029**	Milan			
357	265	113	130	183	186	90	639				
219	**409**	**959**	**594**	**856**	**489**	**714**	**393**	**786**	Naples		
136	254	596	369	532	304	444	244	488			
673	**547**	**110**	**332**	**410**	**395**	**170**	**1150**	**138**	**884**	Turin	
418	340	68	206	255	245	106	715	86	549		
530	**364**	**442**	**154**	**214**	**255**	**397**	**967**	**273**	**741**	**402**	Venice
329	226	275	96	133	158	247	601	170	460	250	

Traveling within Cities

The best ways of getting around Italian cities differ from place to place. In Rome buses are most useful, in Milan the metro is more efficient, and in Venice you will need to take a boat to get about. Streetcars still run in some cities, such as Milan and Rome. Cars are a liability almost everywhere, unlike walking, which in many cases is the easiest way to negotiate the tight historic cores of Italian towns and cities. Florence has a large limited-traffic zone, and most towns now have a pedestrian area in the center.

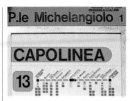
Bus stop displaying the route

A Roman bus in the red and gray livery of ATAC

One of the distinctive orange city buses, central Verona

Buses and Streetcars

Virtually every Italian city and large town has a bus system. Most are cheap, comprehensive, and as efficient as traffic and narrow streets will allow, and systems vary only slightly from city to city. Bus stops are known as *fermate*, and increasingly (notably in Rome) list full details of the routes they serve. Buses (*autobus*) usually run from about 6am to midnight, and there are night buses (*servizio notturno*) in larger cities. If you arrive in a town by train, stations are invariably linked to the center by shuttle buses from the front of the station (tickets are usually available from the station bar or tobacconist).

Tickets

Tickets (*biglietti*) must be bought before boarding the bus, and can be found at kiosks belonging to the bus company (ATAF in Florence, ATAC in Rome), bars, newsstands, or tobacconists displaying the bus company's sticker. A few cities also have on-street vending machines around main transportation hubs. It is worth buying more than one ticket at a time, as outlets often close in the afternoon or early evening. Discounted tickets (*un blocchetto*), or day- or weeklong visitors' tickets and passes (*una tessera* or *tesserino*) are also available. In some cities tickets are valid for any number of trips within a given time. The ATAC website has more details on buses in Rome.

ATAC
w atac.roma.it

Using Buses and Streetcars

Board buses via the front and rear doors, and exit via the central doors. Buses usually have a driver and no conductor (night buses may have a conductor from whom tickets can be bought).

Tickets must be validated by punching them in machines at the front or rear of the bus. There are large on-the-spot fines if you are caught without a properly validated ticket. The front, low seats on buses are for people with children, the elderly, and the disabled.

Most larger cities have transportation information offices at the main train station or piazza that provide free maps, timetables, and tickets.

The majority of city buses are painted bright orange and display the final destination (*capolinea*) on the front.

Metropolitana

Underground systems, known as *metropolitana* (*la metro* for short), are found in Rome and Milan. Rome's network amounts to just two lines, A and B, which converge at Stazione Termini, the city's central train station. Several stations are useful for key sights, and at peak times the lines provide the best way of crossing the city quickly. Stations are fairly dingy – though rarely dangerous – and train cars can be stiflingly hot in summer. In Milan the network is more extensive, with three principal lines – MM1 (the red line), MM2 (green), and MM3 (yellow) – that meet at the hub stations of Stazione Centrale, Duomo, Cadorna, and Loreto. These

Metro sign

Termini metro station, Rome

An official taxi waiting at a pedestrian crossing

three lines give easy access to the majority of the city's main sights.

Metro tickets in both cities are available from the same sources as bus and streetcar tickets, and from machines and ticket offices in underground stations. Tickets in Rome are valid for 75 minutes for one metro journey only, but can be used on any number of bus and streetcar trips. One-day, three-day, and seven-day tickets are also available and offer unlimited metro, bus, and streetcar travel. In Milan, by contrast, ordinary metro tickets are valid for 90 minutes for one metro journey and can also be used on the buses and streetcars.

Stay on the sidewalk at all costs

Marginally less dangerous to cross

Walking

Walking can be a wonderful way to explore Italy's historic towns and cities, most of whose historic centers are smaller than you might expect. Traffic can be a curse, however, especially in narrow streets (Rome is worst in this respect), but many cities are introducing pedestrianized areas or cutting down on car access around key tourist sights. On certain Sundays (*Domenica a Piedi*), entire town centers may be designated traffic-free zones.

Italian towns have plenty of shady squares and cafés to escape the heat of the summer sun, and churches and cathedrals also provide cool retreats from the rigors of sightseeing. Most sights are well marked

(churches, museums, and other places of interest are often indicated by yellow signs). Always carry your valuables well out of sight. The best times to walk are in the cool of the morning, or in the early evening, when you can join in the pre-dinner stroll known as the *passeggiata*.

Taxis

Only accept rides in official taxis. Most drivers are honest but there are many supplements that can be legitimately levied. Generally an extra charge is made for each piece of luggage placed in the

trunk, for rides between 10pm and 7am, on Sundays and public holidays, and for travel to and from airports.

In theory, taxis cannot be hailed. Take one at an official taxi stand (usually found at the train station or main piazza, or close to key tourist sights) or reserve one by phone. When you order a taxi by phone, take the driver's code name, e.g., Napoli 18. If you call a cab, the meter will start at the time of your call.

Bicycle Rental

Many towns and cities, especially those popular with visitors, have stands and shops offering bikes and scooters for rent. You can usually rent hourly or by the day, and you may have to leave your passport with the shop as a deposit. Be very careful, however, if riding a bike in the busy traffic of the larger towns and cities.

BikeMi in Milan provides access to bikes at various places in the city. The initial fee is €2.50 a day (€6 a week), which covers the first 30 minutes' rental. Rates are then €0.50 for 30 minutes, rising to €2 per hour after the first two hours. You can register by phone (800 80 81 81) or via the website (www.bikemi.it).

Intercity Transportation: Buses

Long-haul buses (*pullman* or *corriere*) between towns operate in a similar way to local buses, though you can usually buy tickets on board, and services are often run by different companies in different-colored buses (blue is the most common color for *pullman*, orange for city buses). Buses in some areas

Rome to Gubbio bus

may be run by several companies (notably around Florence and in Tuscany), and not all operate from the same terminals. Intercity bus routes often depart from outside train stations, or from a town's main piazza. If in doubt, ask at a local tourist office. Reduced schedules may be offered on weekends, when offices are closed.

Rome
COTRAL
Tel 800 174 471
or 06 72 05 72 05.
W **cotralspa.it**

Appian
Tel 06 48 78 66 01.
W **appianline.it**

Tuscany
Lazzi **Tel** 0573 193 79
00. W **lazzi.it**
Sita **Tel** 800 37 37 60.
W **sitabus.it**
Tra-In **Tel** 0577 20 41
11. W **trainspa.it**

National & International
Eurolines
Tel 0861 199 19 00.
W **eurolines.it**

Traveling Around Venice

For visitors to Venice, the *vaporetti* or waterbuses *(see pp140–41)* provide an entertaining form of public transportation, although most journeys within the city can usually be covered more quickly on foot. The main route through the city for the *vaporetti* is the Grand Canal. Waterbuses also supply a useful service connecting outlying points on the periphery of Venice, and linking the city to the islands in the lagoon. The most important service from a visitor's point of view is the No. 1. This operates from one end of the Grand Canal to the other and travels slowly enough for you to admire the parade of palaces at the waterside *(see pp92–95)*.

Vaporetto stop at the Giardini Pubblici, Venice

A *vaporetto* or waterbus

The smaller, sleeker *motoscafo*

The Boats

The original *vaporetti* were steam-powered (*vaporetto* means little steamer); today they are mostly diesel-run motorboats, with a handful of electric, battery-powered prototypes. Although all the boats tend to be called *vaporetti*, the word only really applies to the large, wide boats used on slow routes, such as No. 1. These boats provide the best views. *Motoscafi* are the slimmer, smaller boats that look old but go at a fair pace, while *motonavi* are two-tier boats that run to the islands. To visit the islands of Murano, Burano, or Torcello, take the LN Line, which departs from San Zaccaria and Fondamente Nuove.

Types of Ticket

If booths at landing stages are closed, single tickets can be purchased on board at no extra charge – the tickets are valid for 1 hour from purchase. A good way to save money, however, is by buying a travel card, available for 12, 24, 36, 48, or 72 hours. Such a card entitles the holder to unlimited travel on most lines. Discounts on advance tickets are also available, especially if you reserve seven days in advance. A single- or round-trip supplement to/from Marco Polo airport can also be added to the price of the card (see www.veniceconnected.com).

If you are staying more than a few days, it is worth buying a weekly season ticket (*abbonamento*), available from ticket offices, though non-residents are charged €50 for the privilege. Holders of Rolling Venice cards (with information packs and discounts for 14–29-year-olds) can buy a three-day youth pass. Tickets include transporting one piece of luggage: be prepared to buy another ticket for extra items.

Hours of Service

The main routes run every 10 to 20 minutes until the early evening. Services are less frequent after midnight, but run all night. From June to September the services are more frequent and certain routes are extended. Timetables are available at main landing stages. Be warned: from May to September the main routes and island boats are very crowded.

Vaporetto Information

ACTV (Hello Venezia Office) Piazzale Roma, Venice. **Map** 5 B1. **Tel** 041 2424. W actv.it

Traghetti

Traghetti are gondola ferries that cross the Grand Canal at seven different points, providing a useful service for pedestrians. Few tourists make use of this cheap (about 50 euro cents per trip) and constant service. Points where *traghetti* cross the Grand Canal are marked on the Street Finder maps *(see pp130–39)*. A gondola on yellow street signs points to *traghetti* stops.

A two-tier *motonave* boat

Gondolas

Gondolas are a luxury form of transportation used only by visitors and Venetians at weddings. Before boarding, check the official tariffs and agree on a price with the gondolier. Official costs are around €80 for 40 minutes, increasing to €100 after 7pm. During the off-season, you may be able to negotiate a lower fee, and a journey shorter than the usual 40 minutes.

Water Taxis

For those with little time and sufficient funds, the fastest and most practical means of getting from A to B in Venice is by water taxi. The craft are sleek, white or polished wood motorboats, and all are equipped with a cabin.

They zip efficiently to and from the airport in only 20 minutes. There are 16 water taxi ranks, including one at the airport and one at the Lido.

A water taxi

Beware of extra charges for transporting luggage, waiting, night service, and for calling a taxi. When the *vaporetti* go on strike, taxis are scarce.

Water Taxi Stands

Radio Taxi (all of Venice)
Tel 041 522 23 03.

Piazzale Roma
Map 5 B1. **Tel** 041 71 69 22.

Crossing the Grand Canal by *traghetto*

The Main Routes

① This is the slow boat down the Grand Canal, stopping at every landing stage. The route starts at Piazzale Roma, travels the length of the Grand Canal, then from San Marco it heads east to the Lido.

② The No. 2 is the faster route down the Grand Canal. With an extension to the Lido during the summer months, the route serves San Zaccaria, continuing westward along the Giudecca Canal to Tronchetto and Piazzale Roma, then down the Grand Canal back to San Zaccaria.

④ ④2 ⑤1 ⑤2 ⑥ These lines all sail around the central islands. The circular *Giracittà* routes 4.1–4.2 provide a scenic tour of Venice and Murano, while lines 5.1–5.2 and 6 also extend to the Lido.

⑫ ⑭ The 12 departs from the Fondamente Nuove and runs to the main islands in the northern lagoon – Murano, Mazzorbo, and Burano (with a connection to Torcello) – then calls at Punta Sabbioni. The 14 takes you to the Lido, before concluding at San Zaccaria.

Using the Vaporetti

1 Tickets are available at most landing stages, some bars, and at shops and tobacconists displaying the ACTV sign. It is also possible to buy tickets on board. The price of a ticket remains the same whether you are going one stop or traveling the whole line.

2 Signs on the landing stage tell you the direction of the boats stopping there.

3 Imob electronic chip tickets are in use and should be validated before each journey at the electronic machines on the landing stages. Inspectors rarely board the boats, and this makes it surprisingly easy to hop on and off the boats without a validated ticket. However, there are steep fines for any passengers caught without tickets.

4 An indicator board at the front of each boat gives the line number and main stops. (Ignore the black numbers on the boat's side.)

5 Each landing stage has its name clearly marked on a board. Most stops have two landing stages and it is quite easy, particularly if it is crowded and you can't see which way the boat is facing, to board a boat traveling in the wrong direction. It is helpful to watch which direction the boat is approaching from; if in doubt, check with the boatman.

General Index

Page numbers in **bold** type refer to main entries

A

Abbadia dell'Isola 338
Abbadia di San Salvatore
  festivals 73
Abbazia di Monte Maria 174
Abbazia di Novacella 175
Abbazia di Praglia 163
Abbazia di San Fruttuoso 244
Abbazia di Santo Stefano (Bologna) 268–9
  Street-by-Street map 267
Abruzzo, Molise, and Puglia 505–17
  climate 77
  Exploring Abruzzo, Molise, and Puglia 506–7
  hotels 577
  Parco Nazionale d'Abruzzo, Lazio e Molise 510–11
  regional food 480–81
  restaurants 602–3
Acaia family 223
Accademia (Venice) 94, **110–11**
Accademia, Galleria dell' (Florence) 13, 278, **279**
Accademia Filarmonica Romana (Rome) 449, 450
Accessory shops
  Florence 309, 310
  Milan 200, 201
  Venice 128, 129
Accidents, cars 631
Achradina 546–7
ACTV 634
Adelaide, Countess 222
Admission charges 615
Adoration of the Magi (Gentile da Fabriano) 31
Adoration of the Magi (Pinturicchio) 427
Adriatic Sea 89
Aeneas 54
Aeolian Islands 537
AeroClub Italia 611
Aeschylus 484
Agatha, St. 543
Agnelli family 224
Agnes, St. 403, 445
Agostino di Duccio 270, 356, 357
Agrigento 478, 527, **539**
  festivals 73
Agrippa 415, 444
Agriturismo **560**, 561
Agropoli 502
AIAS 617
Aiello, Matteo d' 533
AIG (Associazione Italiana per la Gioventù) 561
Air Canada 625
Air sports 611
Air travel 624–5
Airports 624–5
Aistulf, King of the Lombards 55
Al Pellegrino Cattolico (Rome) 447, 448

Alaric the Visigoth 54
Alatri 474
Alba 215
  festivals 72
Alban hills 471
Albenga 239
Alberello 506
Alberghi 558
Alberobello 515
Alberti, Leon Battista
  Basilica di Sant'Andrea (Mantua) 211
  d'Este statues 265
  On Painting 60
  Palazzo Rucellai (Florence) 301
  Santa Maria Novella (Florence) 35, 257, 300
  Santo Stefano Rotondo (Rome) 438
  Tempio Malatestiano (Rimini) 270
Alberto Valese-Ebru (Venice) 129
Alemagna, Emilio 199
Alemanno 377
Alessi 25, 42
Alessi (Florence) 310
Alessi, Galeazzo 245
Alexander VI, Pope 405, 431
  Borgia Apartment, Vatican Museums (Rome) 424, 427
Alexander VII, Pope 404
  monument to 422
Alexanderplatz (Rome) 449, 450
Alfieri, Vittorio
  statue of 232
Alfonso of Aragon 60, 496
Alghero 549, 550, **552–3**
Aliani (Casa del Parmigiano, Venice) 128, 129
Alinari brothers 301
Alitalia 625
Allegory of Good Government (Lorenzetti) 344
Alpe Cermis 177
Alpe di Siusi 176
Alpe Tognola 177
Alpheus (Rome) 450
Alpi Apuane 322
Alps 215
  Monte Bianco 218
  Monte Cervino (Matterhorn) 218
  road tunnels 626
Alta Val Susa 222
Altemps, Cardinal Marco Sittico 404
Alto Adige *see* Trentino–Alto Adige
Alunno, Niccolò 365
Amadeo, Giovanni Antonio 207, 208
Amalfi 501
  festivals 71
Amalfi Coast (Costiera Amalfitana) 15, 478, 487, 489, **501**
Amati, Andrea 210
Amati, Niccolò 210
Amato, Antonio 543
Amatrice, Cola dell' 377, 508
Ambrogio da Predis 199
Ambrose, St. 168, 204
Amedeo D (Milan) 200, 201

Amedeo di Castellamonte 228
Amici della Musica (Florence) 72
Amiternum 508
Ammannati, Bartolomeo
  Fontana di Nettuno (Florence) 294
  Ponte Santa Trinita (Florence) 296
  San Lorenzo (Florence) 298
  tomb of Marco Benavides 162
  Villa Giulia (Rome) 444
Ampezzo 166
Anacapri 502
Anagni 474
Ancona 369, **376–7**
Andrea del Castagno 123, 278, 332
Andrea da Firenze 490
Andrea del Sarto 281
  The Birth of the Virgin 281
Anfiteatro Romano (Lucca) 326
Angel Delivering St. Peter from Prison (Raphael) 32
Angelico, Fra 357, 363
  The Annunciation 31, 278, 336
  Christ 329
  Convento di San Marco frescoes (Florence) 280
  The Crucifixion 333
  Deposition 280
  Madonna with Angels and Saints 333
  tomb of 408
  Vatican frescoes 427
  Virgin Enthroned with the Child and Saints 36
Angels in Armor (Guariento) 162
Anguillara, Rodolfo 433
Anguillara (Lazio) 470
Annigoni, Pietro 299
Annunciation (Fra Angelico) 31, 278, 336
Annunciation (Ghirlandaio) 348
Annunciation (Leonardo da Vinci) 293
Annunciation (Martini) 290
Annunciation (Pinturicchio) 366
Annunciation (Pontormo) 308
Antelami, Benedetto 232, 262, 263
Anthony of Padua, St.
  tomb of 162
Antica Caciara Trasteverina (Rome) 447, 448
Antigorio valley 230
Antinori family 301
Antiquarium Forense (Rome) 395
Antique shops 607
  Florence 309, 310
Antonelli, Alessandro
  Duomo (Novara) 231
  Mole Antonelliana (Turin) 189, 228
Antonello da Messina 542
  Portrait of a Man 539
  Portrait of an Unknown Man 225
  Vergine Annunziata 533
Antoniazzo Romano 408, 470
Antony, Mark 51, 149
Aosta 219
  festivals 73

Aosta, Dukes of 219
Apennines 505
Apollo and Daphne (Bernini) 443
Apollodorus of Damascus 392
Aprosio & Co. (Florence) 310
APT Florence 617
APT Rome 617
APT Siena 617
APT Venice 617
Apuleius 211
Aqua Appia 50
Aquariums
　Acquario Marino (Trieste) 169
　Genoa 241
Aqueducts, Roman 50
Aquileia 81, **168**
Aquinas, St. Thomas 36, 493
Ara Pacis (Rome) 52, **414**
Aracoeli Steps (Rome) 388
Arch of Constantine (Rome) 34, 384,
　393
Arch of Janus (Rome) 437
Arch of Septimius Severus (Rome)
　394, 396
Arch of Titus (Rome) 395
Archaeological digs 610
Archimedes 45, 50, 485, 546
Architecture 34–5
　Central Italy 256–7
　Etruscan 34
　Northwest Italy 178–9, **188–9**
　Romanesque churches in Umbria
　　364–5
　Rome and Lazio 384–5
　Southern Italy 482–3
　trulli houses 505, 506
　Venice and the Veneto 84–5
Archytas 485
Ardara 552
Area Sacra di Largo Argentina
　(Rome) 407
Arena (Verona) 146, 147, 609
Aretino, Spinello 59, 117, 308
Arezzo 333–5
　festivals 72
　San Francesco 334–5
Ariosto, Ludovico 259, 265
Aristoxenes 485
Armani, Giorgio 25, 28, 43
Armani (Florence) 322
Armani (Venice) 128, 129
Arno, river 69, 275, 319
Arnolfo di Cambio
　Duomo pulpit (Siena) 346
　Museo dell'Opera del Duomo
　　(Florence) 283
　St. Peter 423
　San Paolo fuori le Mura (Rome)
　　446
　Santa Cecilia in Trastevere altar
　　canopy (Rome) 433
Arona 195
Arpino 474
Arpino, Cavalier d' 508
*Arrival of Cardinal Francesco
　Gonzaga* (Mantegna) 31

Arsenale (Venice) 124
Art
　fresco technique **31**
　High Renaissance art **32–3**
　medieval and early Renaissance
　　30–31
　saints and symbols 36–7
　shopping in Florence 309, 310
　symbolism in early Christian art
　　168–9
　see also Architecture
Art galleries *see*
　Museums and galleries
Arte di Calimala 308
Artemide 43
Artemide (Milan) 200, 201
Artimino 332
Ascoli Piceno 369, 370, **377**
Asolo 153
Aspertini 325
Aspromonte mountains 519
Aspurucci, Antonis 442
Assisi 353, **358–9**
　architecture 365
　Basilica di San Francesco 358–9
　earthquake 69
　festivals 72
Associazione Italiana Alberghi per
　la Gioventù 617
Assumption of the Virgin (Correggio)
　33, 263
Assumption of the Virgin (Titian)
　102, 149
Asti 232–3
　festivals 72
Athletics 75
Atrani 501
Atri 508
Atti, Isotta degli 270
Attila the Hun 127
Attombri (Venice) 128, 129
Aue, Hartmann von 175
Augustine, St. 207
Augustinian order 305
Augustus, Emperor 52, 53
　Aosta 219
　Aquileia 168
　Ara Pacis (Rome) 414
　Forum of Augustus (Rome) 393
　Mausoleum of Augustus (Rome)
　　414
　Museo Archeologico (Verona) 149
　Palatine (Rome) 398, 399
　Piazza di Montecitorio (Rome) 409
　Ravenna 272
　statues of 224, 416, 426
　Susa 222
　Via Appia Antica (Rome) 445
Aula Magna dell'Università La
　Sapienza (Rome) 449, 450
Aurelian, Emperor 421
Aurelian Wall 54, 441
Automobile racing 74, 75
Aventine and Lateran (Rome)
　435–41
　hotels 575–6

Aventine and Lateran (Rome) (cont.)
　restaurants 599
Avenzo, Jacopo 163
Avigliana 223
Avis 631
Ayas valley 218
Azzurro Scipioni (Rome)
　449, 450

B

B&B (Milan) 200, 201
Babington's Tea Rooms (Rome) 412
Bacanal del Gnoco (Verona) 73
Bacchus (Caravaggio) 290
Bacchus (Michelangelo) 287
Baccio d'Agnolo 285
Baceno 230
Il Baciccia 407
Baciocchi, Elisa 324
Bacon, Francis 109, 424
Badia Fiorentina (Florence)
　Street-by-Street map 283
Badia a Passignano 255
Badoglio, Pietro 68
Baggage storage 629
Bagheria 536
Bagni di Lucca 323
Baia Sardinia 552
Baldini, Stefano 75
Ballet **608**, 609
　Rome 449, 450
Balzi Rossi 238
Bandinelli, Baccio 285
Bank notes 621
Banks 620
Banner (Milan) 200, 201
Baptism of St. John the Baptist
　(Andrea Pisano) 30
Baptistry (Florence) 13, 282, **284–6**
　Street-by-Street map 282
Baptistry (Pisa) 328
Barbarigo, Antonio 163
Barbera d'Alba wine 186
Barberini (Rome) 449, 450
Barberino Designer Outlet
　(Florence) 309, 310
Barcelona, Treaty of (1529) 62
Bardolino 152
Bardonecchia 222
Barga 322
Bargello (Florence) 13, **287**
　Street-by-Street map 283
Bari 505, **514**
　architecture 483
　festivals 70
Barisano da Trani
　Duomo (Monreale) 534
　Duomo (Ravello) 501
　Duomo (Trani) 513
Barocci, Federico 375, 443
Barolo 215
Barolo wine 186, 187
Baroque era 62
　architecture 35, 84, 188, 384, 482
　music 40–41
Barovier, Angelo 125

Barrea, Lake 511
Bartolini, Lorenzo 279
Bartolo di Fredi
  Christ 349
  The Creation 348
Bartolomeo, Fra 279
  *God the Father with Saints
  Catherine and Mary Magdalene*
  327
  Madonna della Misericordia 327
Barumini 478, 549, 553
Barzaghi, Francesco 199
Basilian monks 519
Basilica Aemilia (Rome) 396
Basilica of Constantine and
  Maxentius (Rome) 395, 396
Basilica Julia (Rome) 394
Basilica Paleocristiana (Trieste) 169
Basilica di Sant'Antonio (Padua) 162
Basilica di San Francesco (Assisi)
  251, 353, **358–9**
Basilica di San Marco (Venice) 13,
  34, 81, 84, **114–17**
  Baptistry and chapels 117
  the building of St. Mark's 115
  floorplan 116–17
  mosaics 114–17
  Museo Marciano 117
  Pala d'Oro 117
  Street-by-Street map 113
Basilica di San Nicola (Bari) 483
Basilica di Superga 229
Basilicata and Calabria 519–25
  climate 77
  Exploring Basilicata and Calabria
  520–21
  hotels 577
  regional food 481
  restaurants 603
Bassano 199
Bassano del Grappa 143, **153**
Bata (Florence) 310
Baths of Caracalla (Rome) 53, **441**,
  609
Battle of San Romano (Uccello) 31, 292
Baunei 554
Becket, St. Thomas à 327, 538
La Befana 73
Belisarius 54
Bellagio 14, 194
Bellini, Giovanni 102, 202, 205, 227,
  265, 293
  Baptism of Christ 156
  Coronation of the Virgin 372
  Madonna and Child 103
  *Madonna and Child between St.
  John the Baptist and a Saint* 110,
  111
  *Madonna and Child with Four
  Saints* 32, 37
  Madonna and Child with Saints 123
  Madonna of the Beautiful Eyes 98
  Madonna with Child 98
  Pietà 112, 427
  Polyptych 122
  *St. Jerome with Saints Christopher
  and Augustine* 99
  San Giobbe Altarpiece 32
Bellini, Vincenzo 41

Bellini, Vincenzo (cont.)
  Museo Belliniano (Catania) 543
Belluno 165
Beltrami (Florence) 310
Bembo, Cardinal Pietro 153
Benavides, Marco
  tomb of 162
Benedetto da Maiano
  Annunciation 493
  Palazzo Strozzi (Florence) 297
  Sant'Agostino altar (San
  Gimignano) 349
  Strozzi Tomb 301
Benedict, St. 366–7, 473
Benedict XI, Pope
  tomb of 357
Benedict XVI, Pope 69
Benedictines
  Abbazia di Praglia 163
  Monreale 534
  Montecassino 473
  San Gregorio Armeno (Naples)
  492
  Subiaco 473
Benetton (Venice) 128, 129
Beneventano, Oderisio da 513
Benevento 487, **500–501**
Benigni, Roberto 69
Bentivoglio, Annibale 267
Bentivoglio, Anton Galeazzo 267
Bentivoglio family 259
Bergamo 188, 191, 192, **205**
Bergognone 199, 207
  Certosa di Pavia 208, 209
  Susa polyptych 222
Berio, Luciano 41
Berlinghieri, Bonaventura
  St. Francis Altarpiece 30
Berlioz, Hector 413
Berlusconi, Silvio 69
Bernard of Aosta, St. 218
Bernard of Clairvaux, St. 473
Bernardino of Siena, St. 210, 356
  tomb of 508
Bernini, Gian Lorenzo 35, 264, 385,
  408
  Apollo and Daphne 443
  Chigi chapel, Santa Maria del
  Popolo (Rome) 414
  David 443
  Ecstasy of Beata Ludovica Albertoni
  433
  The Ecstasy of St. Teresa 63, 416
  Fontana dei Quattro Fiumi 380, 403
  Fontana del Tritone (Rome) 27
  Medusa 391
  model for a fountain 93
  Palazzo Barberini (Rome) 415
  Palazzo di Montecitorio (Rome)
  409
  Piazza San Pietro (Rome) 420
  The Rape of Proserpina 443, 541
  St. Peter's (Rome) 422
  Sant'Andrea delle Fratte angels
  (Rome) 413
  Sant'Andrea al Quirinale (Rome)
  415
  Santa Maria sopra Minerva (Rome)
  406

Bernini, Pietro 413, 442
Berruguete, Pedro
  Duke Federico 375
Berry, Duc de 225
Bertini, Giovanni 493
Bertini, Pacio 493
Bessarion, Cardinal 61
Best Western Hotels 561
Bevagna 366
  architecture 365
Bialetti 42
Bianco, Bartolomeo 242
Bicycling *see* Cycling
Bicheri, Cardinal Guala 232
Biennale (Venice) 71
Big Mama (Rome) 449, 450
BikeMi (Milan) 633
Birds
  Lago Massaciuccoli 323
  Valli di Comacchio 271
  see also Wildlife
Birreria 578
The Birth of Venus (Botticelli) 32, 291,
  293
The Birth of the Virgin (Andrea del
  Sarto) 281
Il Bisonte (Florence) 310
Bizzaccheri, Carlo 436
Black Death 59, 319
"Blockhead" Captive (Michelangelo)
  33
Blu-Express 625
Boats
  ferries 626, **627**
  gondolas of Venice 92, 112
  Museo Storico Navale (Venice)
  124
  sailing 611
  traveling to Italy 626
  Venetian vaporetto routes 140–41
  in Venice 634–5
Boboli Gardens (Florence) 13, 257, **307**
Boccaccino 210
Boccaccio, Giovanni 38, 40, 58, 345,
  492
Boccanegra, Simon 59
Boccioni, Umberto
  Unique Forms of Continuity in Space
  68
Bodoni, Giambattista 43
Boëthius
  tomb of 207
Boldi 243
Bologna 259, **266–9**
  A Gourmet Tour of Central Italy 16
  Roman remains 51
  San Petronio 268–9
  Street-by-Street map 266–7
Bologna University 56
Bolsena 469
Bolzano (Bozen) 176
  festivals 72
Bomarzo 469
Bon, Bartolomeo
  San Rocco (Venice) 105
  Santi Giovanni e Paolo (Venice)
  122
  Santa Maria Gloriosa dei Frari rood
  screen (Venice) 102

Bon, Bartolomeo (cont.)
Santo Stefano (Venice) 121
Scuola Grande di San Rocco
(Venice) 104
Bon family 107
Bonanno da Pisa 535
Bonaparte, Joseph, King of Naples
65
Boniface VIII, Pope 58, 474
Boniface VIII fresco (Giotto) 440
Bonitate, Pietro da 533
Bookstores
Florence 309, 310
Milan 200, 201
Rome 447, 448
Venice 129
Bordone, Paris
Fisherman Delivering the Ring 33
Borghese, Prince Camillo 443
Borghese, Pauline 65, 443
Borghese, Cardinal Scipione 442,
443
Borgia, Lucrezia 265
Borgo San Martino
festivals 71
Borgomaggiore 372
Bormio 206
Borromean islands 195
Borromeo, Cardinal Carlo 62, 230
statue of 195
Borromeo, Cardinal Federico 199
Borromini, Francesco
Collegio di Propaganda Fide
(Rome) 412
Palazzo Barberini (Rome) 415
Palazzo Spada (Rome) 405
San Carlo alle Quattro Fontane
(Rome) 415
Sant'Agnese in Agone (Rome) 403
Sant'Ivo alla Sapienza (Rome) 403,
404
Torre dell'Orologio (Rome) 402
Borsalino (Milan) 200, 201
Bosa 553
Bosco della Mesola 271
Bossea Caves 233
Botanical Gardens (Rome) 432
La Bottega dei Cristalli (Florence)
310
Bottega dell'Olio (Florence) 310
Botticelli, Sandro 196, 205, 275, 281,
375
The Birth of Venus 32, 291, 293
*Madonna and Child with John the
Baptist* 262
Madonna del Mare 279
Madonna of the Canopy 199
Primavera 292, 293
Sistine Chapel (Rome) 430
tomb of 301
Bourbon dynasty 66
Bozen *see* Bolzano
Bracciano 470
Bracciano, Lake 470
Bramante, Donato di Angelo 363,
431
Basilica (Loreto) 377
Castello Sforzesco (Milan) 196
Duomo (Pavia) 207

Bramante, Donato di Angelo (cont.)
Palazzo Corsini (Rome) 432
San Satiro (Milan) 199
Santa Maria della Consolazione
(Todi) 256
Santa Maria delle Grazie (Milan)
204
Santa Maria della Pace (Rome)
402, **404**
Santa Maria del Popolo (Rome)
414
Tempietto (Rome) 35, **433**
Brancacci, Felice 302
Brancaccio, Cardinal Rinaldo
tomb of 492
Brancaleone (Rome) 450
Branciforte, Giuseppe, Prince of 536
Brancusi, Constantin
Maiastra 109
Braque, Georges 109
Breakdowns, cars 631
Breakfast 559
Brenner Pass 143
Brenta, river 153
Brenta Canal 164
Brescia 207
Bressanone (Brixen) 172, **175**
Breuil-Cervinia 218
Bridge of Sighs (Venice)
Street-by-Street map 113
Briosco, Andrea "Il Riccio" 98
British Airways 625
British School at Rome 442
Brixen *see* Bressanone
Bronzino, Agnolo 279
Cappella di Eleonora (Florence) 295
Cosimo I 293
Eleonora di Toledo 293
The Martyrdom of St. Lawrence 298
Portrait of Lucrezia Panciatichi 33
Ritratto di Gentiluomo 227
Browning, Pen 94, 107
Browning, Robert 94, 107, 153
Brueghel, Pieter 205
Brunelleschi, Filippo
Baptistry doors (Florence) 286
Duomo (Florence) 35, 60, 257, 275,
283, **285**
Duomo (Pistoia) 331
Palazzo Pitti (Florence) 306
Pazzi Chapel, Santa Croce
(Florence) 288
Piazza della Santissima Annunziata
(Florence) 281
portrait of 60
The Sacrifice of Isaac 287
San Lorenzo (Florence) 298, 299
Santa Croce (Florence) 256
Santo Spirito (Florence) 304, **305**
Spedale degli Innocenti (Florence)
61, 279, **281**
Brunello di Montalcino wine 254,
255
Bruni, Leonardo
tomb of 288
Brunico (Bruneck) 175
Bruno, Giordano 62, 405
Brusazorzi, Domenico 156
Brustolon, Andrea 107, 165

Brutus 393, 407
Brydone, Patrick 536
Budget accommodations 560
Bulgari (Florence) 310
Bulgari (Milan) 200, 201
Bulgari (Venice) 128, 129
Buontalenti, Bernardo
Forte di Belvedere (Florence) 307
Piazza de' Frescobaldi fountain
(Florence) 305
San Lorenzo (Florence) 298
Tribune 293
Uffizi (Florence) 290
Villa di Artimino (Artimino) 332
Burano 13, 89, **125**
Bureaux de change 620
Buscetta, Tommaso 539
Buscheto 328
Buses 632
Bus tours 615
Bus travel 627, 633
Rome bus routes 462–3
Bussana Vecchia 238–9
Byron, Lord 64, 412
Palazzo Mocenigo (Venice) 94
Byzantine Empire 259
architecture 34, 84, 482
Ravenna 272

C

Ca' Foscari (Venice)
Street-by-Street map 107
Ca' Macana (Venice) 128, 129
Ca' d'Oro (Venice) 85, 93, **98–9**
Ca' Pesaro (Venice) 85, 93
Ca' Rezzonico (Venice) 94, **107**
Street-by-Street map 107
Caccini, Giovanni 305
Caecus, Appius Claudius 445
Caesar, Julius **50**, 51
assassination 393, 407
Basilica Julia (Rome) 394
Forum of Caesar (Rome) 393
Gallic Wars 39
Caetani family 474
Caffè Florian (Venice) 13
Caffè Greco (Rome) 412
Caffè Pedrocchi (Padua) 159
Cagliari 549, **555**
ferries 627
festivals 70
Caius Cestius, Pyramid of (Rome)
441
Cala Gonone 554
Cala Luna 554
Cala Sisine 554
Calabria *see* Basilicata and Calabria
Calcio Fiorentino 74
Calcio Storico (Florence) 71
Caligula, Emperor 52
The Calling of St. Matthew
(Caravaggio) 404
Callisto, Patriarch 167
Callixtus I, Pope 432
Cambiaso, Luca 242
Camogli 244
Camorra 487
Camosciara 511
Campanella, Tommaso 524

Campania *see* Naples and Campania
Campanile (Venice) 121
  Street-by-Street map 113
Campi family 210
Campo de' Fiori (Rome) **405**, 448
Campo Formio, Treaty of (1797) 65
Camposanto (Pisa) 328
Campsites 561
Canaletto 107, 111, 202, 205, 227
Canals
  Brenta Canal 164
  Torcello 127
  Venice 92–5
Canazei 176–7
Cannae, Battle of (216 BC) 50
Cannigione 552
Cannobio 195
Canova, Antonio 227
  Cupid and Psyche 195
  Museo Correr (Venice) 121
  statue of Napoleon 202
  tomb of 103
  Venus 65
  Venus Italica 306
  Venus Victrix 443
Capitoline Hill (Rome)
  Street-by-Street map 388–9
Capitoline Museums (Rome) 12,
  381, **390–91**
  Street-by-Street map 388
Capo Schisò 542
Capodanno 73
Caporetto, Battle of (1917) 68
Cappella Brancacci (Florence) 13,
  302–3
Cappelle Medicee (Florence) 299
Cappella Palatina 482
Cappella Sansevero (Naples) 491
Cappella degli Scrovegni (Padua)
  160–61
Cappella del Tau (Pistoia) 331
Cappellini, Giulio 42
Cappello, Bianca 304
Capponi family 308
Caprarola 465, 469
Capri 15, 487, **502–3**
Caracalla, Baths of (Rome) *see*
  Baths of Caracalla
Caravaggio 202, 243, 408, 415, 542
  Bacchus 290, 293
  Burial of St. Lucy 546
  The Calling of St. Matthew 404
  Campo de' Fiorio (Rome) 405
  Conversion of St. Paul 414
  Crucifixion of St. Peter 414
  Deposition 427
  Fruit Basket 199
  Martyrdom of St. Matthew 404
  Medusa 293
  *Nativity with St. Francis and
  St. Lawrence* 491
  Sacrifice of Isaac 293
  St. John the Baptist 391, 432
  St. Matthew and the Angel 404
  San Luigi dei Francesci paintings
  (Rome) 403
  Seven Acts of Mercy 491
  The Sleeping Cupid 306
Carbonari 66

Carignano family 227
Carloforte 549
Carlone 242
Carnelivari, Matteo 533
Carnevale (Carnival)
  Marmoiada 73
  Venice 64, 73
  Viareggio 73
Carnic Alps 166
Caroline of Brunswick, Queen of
  England 194
Carpaccio, Vittore 293
  Annunciation 98
  Death of the Virgin 98
  Healing of the Madman 111
  *Portrait of a Young Man in a Red
  Hat* 121
  St. Augustine 61
  St. George Slaying the Dragon
  124
  *St. Jerome Leading the Tamed Lion
  to the Monastery* 124
  Scenes from the Legend of St. Ursula
  111
  Scuola di San Giorgio degli
  Schiavoni (Venice) 124
  Two Venetian Ladies 121
Carpano, Antonio Benedetto 227
Carrà, Carlo 198, 424
  Mother and Son 203
Carracci, Annibale 405
Carracci family 264, 269
Carrara 322
Carreras, José 41
Carretto, Ilaria del
  tomb of 326
Cars 626, **630–31**
  accidents 631
  breakdowns 631
  driving to Italy 626
  ferries 627
  rental of 631
  Museo dell'Automobile (Turin) 229
  parking 631
  gas 630
  roads 630
  rules and regulations 630
  safety 631
  see also Tours by car
Carso 167
Carthage 50, 538, 539, 540
Carthusians 208
Cartier (Venice) 128, 129
Casa del Cinema (Rome) 449, 450
Casa dei Crescenzi (Rome) 436
Casa del Jazz (Rome) 449, 450
Casa dei Latticini Micocci (Rome)
  447, 448
Casa Natale di Puccini (Lucca) 325
  Street-by-Street map 324
Casa Pigafetta (Vicenza)
  Street-by-Street map 155
Casa dei Tessuti (Florence) 309, 310
Casamari 473
Casanova 120
Cascate delle Marmore 367
Caserta 500
  architecture 482
Caserta Vecchia 500

Cash machines 620
Casole d'Elsa 319
Cassina (Milan) 200, 201
Cassini, Gian Domenico 44, 268
Cassius 393, 407
Cassone Adimari (Lo Scheggia) 279
Castel Gandolfo 471
Castelfranco Veneto 153
Castell'Arquato 262
Castelli Romani 471
  festivals 72
Castello di Avio 179
Castelluccio 353, 355, 366
Castelnuovo di Garfagnana 322
Castiglione, Achille 42
Castiglione, Giovanni Benedetto
  242
Castiglione del Lago 357
Castles and fortresses
  Bari 514
  Castel Beseno 179
  Castel Capuano (Naples) 490
  Castel Coira 174
  Castel del Monte 513
  Castel Nuovo (Naples) 496
  Castel dell'Ovo (Naples) 497
  Castel Sant'Angelo (Rome) 421
  Castel Sant'Elmo (Naples) 496
  Castel Tirolo 173, 174
  Castel Trauttmansdorff 174
  Castello di Aymavilles 220
  Castello del Buonconsiglio
  (Trento) 178
  Castello di Casotto 233
  Castello Estense (Ferrara) 265
  Castello di Fénis 188, 218, 219
  Castello di Graines 218
  Castello dell'Imperatore (Prato) 57,
  332
  Castello di Issogne 218, 219
  Castello di Lerici 245
  Castello di Lombardia (Enna) 541
  Castello di Miramare (Grignano) 169
  Castello di Montmayer 218
  Castello Principesco (Merano) 174
  Castello di Rodengo 175
  Castello di San Giusto (Trieste) 169
  Castello di Sarre 218
  Castello Sforzesco (Milan) 188, 196
  Castello di Ussel 218
  Castello di Velturno 175
  Castello di Venere (Erice) 537
  Castello di Verrès 218
  Castelvecchio (Verona) 146–7
  Châtelard 215, 218
  Dolceacqua 238
  Euryalus 547
  Fortezza Medicea (Arezzo) 333
  Fortezza Medicea (Siena) 347
  Lagopesole 522
  Lecce 517
  Lucera 512
  medieval castles and forts in the
  Valle d'Aosta **218**
  Melfi 522
  Otranto 517
  St. Pierre 217
  San Leo 372
  Taranto 515

Castles and fortresses (cont.)
Trani 513
Venosa 522
Catacombs (Rome) 446
Catacombs of San Gennaro (Naples) 497
Catanei, Vannozza 405
Catania 527, **543**
Cathedrals see Duomos
Catherine of Alexandria, St. 37
Catherine of Austria
tomb of 492
Catherine of Siena, St. 344, 345
tomb of 408
Catholic Church 29, 47, 617
Council of Trent 178
Counter-Reformation 62–3
religious services 616
saints and symbols in Italian art 36–7
Vatican 420–21
Catullus 399
Cavalese 177
Cavallini, Pietro 357, 433, 446
Last Judgment 30
Life of the Virgin 380
Caves
Balzi Rossi 238
Bossea Caves 233
Grotta Azzurra (Capri) 502
Grotta del Bue Marino 554
Grotte di Castellana 515
Grotta del Gigante 169
Grotte di Frasassi 376
Grotta di Nettuno 553
Grotte di Toirano 239
Grotta Verde 553
Matera 522–3
Cavour, Count Camillo di 66, **67**, 227
Cecilia, St. 433
Cefalù 482, 527, **539**
Celestine V, Pope 508
Cellini, Benvenuto 287, 289, 405
Perseus 295
Cell phones 622–3
Cembra 177
Cenacolo di Santo Spirito (Florence) 304
Central Italy 249–377
architecture 256–7
A Gourmet Tour of Central Italy 16
map 250–51
regional food 252–3
wines 254–5
Centro Turistico Studentesco 561
Ceramics
Faenza 270
Ruvo di Puglia 514
Ceresole Reale 222
Cernobbio 194
Certosa di Pavia 183, 191, **208–9**
Certosa di San Giacomo (Capri) 503
Cerveteri 17, 380, **470**
Cervo 236, **239**
Cesena, Biagio da 430
Cesenatico 261, 270
Cézanne, Paul 198
Chagall, Marc 109, 270
Chain hotels 558–9
Challant family 219

Charlemagne, Emperor 47, 55
coronation 55, 207
Santi Apostoli (Florence) 296
Charles II, King of Naples 512
Charles III, King of Naples 64
Charles III, King of Spain 482, 497, 500
Charles V, Emperor 61, 62, 228
Lecce 517
Nicosia throne 541
Piazza del Campidoglio (Rome) 389
Charles VIII, King of France 61
Charles of Anjou 57, 496
Charles of Calabria 493
Châtelard 215, 218
Cheese, Parmesan 263
Cherubini, Luigi 278
Chess 72
Chiaiolella 503
Chianti
festivals 72
wine 254, 255
Chiaramonti Museum (Rome) 426
Chiesa degli Eremitani (Padua) 162
Chiesa Nuova (Rome) 404
Street-by-Street map 402
Chiesa del Rosario (Lecce) 483
Street-by-Street map 516
Chigi, Agostino 414, 432
Children 616
in hotels 559
in restaurants 579
Chini, Galileo 323
Chioggia 59
Chirico, Giorgio de 109, 198
Mysterious Baths 199
Chiusi 17, **336**
Christ (Bartolo di Fredi) 349
Christ Delivering the Keys of the Kingdom to St. Peter (Perugino) 32
Christian Democrats 28, 68
Christianity
Constantine's conversion 54, 168, 205, 438
Counter-Reformation 62–3
Edict of Milan 205
saints and symbols in Italian art 36–7
symbolism in early Christian art 168–9
Turin Shroud 225
Christina, Queen of Sweden 432, 444
Christmas 73
Christopher, St. 98
Church of Gesù (Genoa)
Street-by-Street map 241
Churches
admission charges 615
dress code 616

opening hours 615
religious services 616
Romanesque churches in Umbria 364–5
see also Duomo and individual saint's names, towns, and cities

Ciampino Airport (Rome) 624–5
Cicero 39, 399, 502
birthplace 474
Senate 51
Cignani, Carlo
Flora 264
Cilento 487, 502
Cima da Conegliano 98, 124, 165
Cima della Rosetta 177
Cimabue
Christ in Majesty 328
Crucifixion 288
Madonna Enthroned with Angels and Prophets 30
Maestà 292
St. Francis 358
Cinecittà 28
Cinema see Movies
Cino da Pistoia
tomb of 331
Cinque Terre 13, 14, 237, **245**
Cinque Torri (Dolomites) 86
Cipollini, Mario 74
Cipriani, Giuseppe 95, 112
Cislano 206–7
Cistercian Order 339, 473
Cisternino (Rome) 447, 448
Città Vecchia 515
Cittadella dei Musei (Cagliari) 555
Cividale del Friuli 145, **167**
Civitali, Matteo 326, 327
Civitavecchia
ferries 627
Clare, St.
tomb of 359
Claude Lorrain 227, 408, 442
Claudius, Emperor 52
Clement, St. 439
Clement V, Pope 58
Clement VII, Pope 62, 363
tomb of 408
Clement X, Pope 413
Clement XII, Pope 392, 440
Cleopatra 51, 149
Climate **76–7**, 614
Clothes 28
in churches 616
Florence 309, 310
Milan 200, 201
in restaurants 579
shops 606–7
size chart 607
Venice 128, 129
Club Alpino Italiano 561, 611
Coccinelle (Florence) 310
Coccinelle (Milan) 200, 201
Cocullo 509
festivals 70
Coducci, Mauro 99, 121, 123
Cogne 221
Coin (Florence) 310
Coin (Milan) 200, 201
Coins 621
CO.IN.Sociale 617
Colle del Gran San Bernardo 218
Collegiata (San Gimignano) 349
Street-by-Street map 348
Collegio di Propaganda Fide (Rome) 412

Colleoni, Bartolomeo
monument to 32
statue of 123
tomb of 205
Collodi, Carlo 38
Colonna, Vesapasiano Gonzaga
210
Colonna dell'Immacolata (Rome)
412
Colonna di Sant'Oronzo (Lecce)
Street-by-Street map 517
Colonnata 322
Colosseum (Rome) 12, 52, 65, 381,
387, **397**
Columbus, Christopher 44, 264, 301
in Genoa 235, 241, **242**
portrait of 243
Comacchio 271
Coming Out (Rome) 450
Communications 622–3
Como 194, 195
Como, Lake see Lago di Como
Condottieri (mercenaries) 58
Conegliano 165
Conero Peninsula 371, **377**
Constance of Aragon
tomb of 531
Constantia 445
Constantine I, Emperor 115
Arch of Constantine (Rome) 393
Basilica of Constantine and
Maxentius (Rome) 396
Battle of the Milvian Bridge 54,
393, 396, 431
conversion to Christianity 54, 168,
205, 438
Edict of Milan 205
Iron Crown 205
Legend of the True Cross 334–5
St. Peter's (Rome) 422
San Giovanni in Laterano (Rome)
440
statue of 204, 391
Villa Romana del Casale (Piazza
Armerina) 541
Consulates 619
Contarini, Marino 98
Contrà Porti (Vicenza) 155
Convento di San Marco (Florence)
278, **280**
Conversion chart 617
Cooking courses 611
Coppo di Marcovaldo
Madonna and Child 30
Cordonata (Rome) 388
Corelli, Arcangelo 41
The Coretti (Giotto) 160
Cornaro, Queen Caterina 153
Cornaro family 416
Corneliani (Milan) 200, 201
Corniglia 245
Coronation of the Virgin (Bellini) 372
Coronation of the Virgin (Veneziano)
110, 111
Corradini, Antonio 491
Correggio, Antonio da 293
Assumption of the Virgin 33, 263
Danäe 443
Palazzo Pilotta frescoes (Parma) 263

Correggio, Antonio da (cont.)
Vision of St. John at Patmos 263
Correr, Teodoro 121
Corsa del Palio (Siena) 71
Corsini family 432
Cortenuova, Battle of (1237) 57
Cortile della Pigna (Rome) 421
Cortina d'Ampezzo 145, **165**
Cortona 320, **336**
Cosmas, St. 36
Cosmati 417, 438, 439
Cossa, Francesco del 269
Cost of living, regional differences
620
Costa, Lorenzo
Apocalypse 267
Madonna Enthroned 267
The Martyrdom of St. Sebastian 266
Triumph of Death 267
Costa Smeralda 549, **552**
Costiera Amalfitana see Amalfi Coast
Costume shops
Venice 128, 129
Council of Ten (Venice) 120
Counter-Reformation 62–3
Courmayeur 215, 218
Couture, Thomas
Romans of the Decadence 399
Craxi, Bettino 69
The Creation (Bartolo di Fredi) 348
Credit cards 620
in restaurants 579
Cremona 191, **210**
Cremona school 210
Crete Senesi 338
Crime 618
Cristo degli Abissi 244
Crivelli, Carlo 205, 377
Madonna della Candeletta 203
Crivelli, Taddeo 264
Croce, Baldassare 468
Crocifissi, Simone dei 269
Crodo 230
Cronaca (Simone del Pollaiuolo)
297, 305
Crotone 484, 485, 519, 521
Crucifixion (Tintoretto) 100, 104
Crusades 56, 57, 89, 235
Cryptoporticus (Rome) 399
CTS 617
Cucina Romana 382–3
Cultural breaks 610
Culture 609
Cumae 49
Cuneo 233
Cupid and Psyche (Canova) 195
Curia (Rome) 394, 396
Currency 620–21
Customs and excise 615
Cycling
bicycle rental 633
races 74
vacations 610

D

Daddi, Bernardo 287
Daedalus 539
D'Alema, Massimo 28
Dalí, Salvador 109

Damian, St. 36
Damned Consigned to Hell
(Signorelli) 32
Danaë and the Shower of Gold
(Titian) 497
Dance
ballet **608**, 609
regional dance, music, and
festivals 609
Rome 449, 450
tarantella 515
Dance of the Devils (Prizzi) 70
Dandolo, Andrea, Doge of Venice
tomb of 117
Dandolo, Enrico, Doge of Venice 56
Daniela Porto (Venice) 129
D'Annunzio, Gabriele
Il Vittoriale (Gardone) 152
Dante Alighieri 38, 57, 58, 259, 275
birthplace 282, 283
Divine Comedy 58, 146, 199, 264,
285, 300
Duomo (Florence) 284
Inferno 58, 160, 179, 268, 338, 430,
523
Paradiso 377
Purgatorio 372
Ruina Dantesca 179
statue of 148
tomb of 273
Dante Explaining the Divine Comedy
(Michelino) 285
Danti, Ignazio 424
D'Ascanio, Corradino 43
David (Donatello) 31, 287
David (Michelangelo) 32, 279, 294,
322
David (Verrocchio) 31
David and Goliath (Titian) 33
De Sica, Vittorio 28, 69
Dead Christ (Mantegna) 32, 202
Dead Christ (Sammartino) 491
Death of the Saint (Martini) 359
Debussy, Claude Achille 413
Deledda, Grazia 554
Delitio, Andrea 508
La Deliziosa (Rome) 447, 448
della Rovere family 414
Delta 625
Demeter 485, 541
Deposition (Fra Angelico) 280
Deposition (Lorenzetti) 358
Design 42–3
shopping in Milan 200, 201
Designer shops 606–7
D'Este, Alfonso I 265
D'Este, Beatrice
tomb of 208
D'Este, Ercole I 265
D'Este, Ferrante 265
D'Este, Giulio 265
D'Este, Cardinal Ippolito 472
D'Este, Leonello 205
D'Este, Nicolò II 265
D'Este, Nicolò III 265
D'Este, Parisina 265
D'Este family 259, 264, **265**
Dialectic (Veronese) 120
Dialing codes 623

Diano Marina
  festivals 71
Dickens, Charles 413
Diffusione Tessile (Milan) 200, 201
Diocletian, Emperor 54, 115, 372
Dionysius I of Siracusa 538
Dionysius II of Siracusa 485
Disabled travelers 616
  in hotels 561
  in restaurants 579
Discount dell'Alta Moda (Rome) 447, 448
Discounts
  student 616
  train tickets 626, 629
Distance chart 631
DMagazine (Milan) 200, 201
Doge's Palace (Venice) see Palazzo Ducale
Dolce & Gabbana (Florence) 310
Dolce & Gabbana (Milan) 200, 201
Dolceacqua 238
  festivals 73
Dolceforte (Florence) 310
Dolcetto wine 186
Dolomites 80, **86–7**, 171, 173
  Canazei 176–7
  Cortina d'Ampezzo 165
  Parco Nazionale dello Stelvio 193, **206**
  San Martino di Castrozza 177
Dolomiti Ski Jazz Festival (Trentino–Alto Adige) 70
Domenichino 471, 491
Domingo, Placido 41
Dominic, St. 36
  tomb of 266, 269
Dominican Order 57, 280
  Santi Giovanni e Paolo (Venice) 122
  Santa Maria sopra Minerva (Rome) 408
  Santa Maria Novella (Florence) 300–301
  Santa Sabina (Rome) 441
Domitian, Emperor 426
  Arch of Titus (Rome) 395
  Forum of Caesar (Rome) 393
  Palatine (Rome) 398, 399
  Piazza Navona (Rome) 403
  statue of 28
Domodossola 230
Domus Flavia (Rome) 398
Donà, Leonardo, Doge of Venice 121
Donatello 102, 123, 275, 286
  Annunciation 288
  Baptismal font 346
  Baptistry (Siena) 342
  choir loft 283
  David 31, 287
  Duomo (Siena) 346
  Gattamelata 159, **162**
  Judith and Holofernes 295
  La Maddalena 283
  Madonna and Child 347
  Marzocco 294
  Orsanmichele (Florence) 287

Donatello (cont.)
  Pulpit of the Holy Girdle (Prato) 332
  St. George 282, 287
  St. John 283
  San Lorenzo (Florence) 298, 299
  San Rossore 329
  tomb of Cardinal Rinaldo Brancaccio 492
Donizetti, Gaetano 41, 67, 191
  tomb of 205
Donnino, San 262
Doria, Andrea 235
Doria, Brancaleone 555
Doria family 238, 240, 552
Dorsoduro (Venice)
  Street-by-Street map 106–7
Double Portrait (Tullio Lombardo) 98
Dramatists 38–9
The Dream of Constantine (Piero della Francesca) 31
The Dream of Pope Innocent III (Giotto) 57
Drogheria Mascari (Venice) 128, 129
Drovetti, Bernardo 226
Drugs, pharmacies 619
Drunkenness 616
Ducci (Florence) 310
Duccio di Buoninsegna 58
  Madonna dei Francescani 345
  Maestà 292, 339, 342, 347
  Rucellai Madonna 30
Duchamp, Marcel 109
Dufourny, Léon 533
The Duke and Duchess of Urbino (Piero della Francesca) 291, 292
Duke Federico (Berruguete) 375
Duomos (cathedrals)
  Agrigento 539
  Albenga 239
  Alghero 552
  Amalfi 501
  Anagni 474
  Aosta 219
  Arezzo 333
  Ascoli Piceno 377
  Assisi 359, 365
  Asti 233
  Atri 508
  Belluno 165
  Benevento 500
  Bolzano 176
  Bosa 553
  Brescia 207
  Bressanone 175
  Cagliari 555
  Carrara 322
  Castelfranco Veneto 153
  Catania 543
  Cefalù 539
  Chiusi 336
  Cividale del Friuli 167
  Como 195
  Conegliano 165
  Cremona 210
  Enna 541
  Erice 537
  Fidenza 262
  Fiesole 333

Duomos (cathedrals) (cont.)
  Florence 12–13, 35, 250, 257, 275, 282, **284–6**
  Gaeta 475
  Genoa 240, **241**
  Gerace 525
  Grado 168
  Gubbio 356
  Lanciano 511
  L'Aquila 508
  Lecce 516
  Lucera 512
  Mantua 211
  Marsala 538
  Massa Marittima 339
  Matera 523
  Melfi 522
  Milan 183, 197
  Modena 264
  Monreale 34, 478, 482, 527, **534–5**
  Montepulciano 337
  Monza 188, **205**
  Naples 491
  Norcia 367
  Noto 547
  Novara 231
  Oristano 554
  Ortigia 546
  Orvieto 34, **362–3**
  Otranto 517
  Padua 158, 159
  Palermo 531
  Parma 263
  Pavia 207
  Perugia 356
  Piacenza 262
  Piazza Armerina 541
  Pienza 256
  Pinerolo 223
  Pisa 250, 319, 328
  Pistoia 331
  Pitigliano 351
  Pordenone 166
  Prato 332
  Ravello 501
  Ruvo di Puglia 483
  Salerno 502
  San Leo 372
  San Miniato 332
  Sassari 552
  Sermoneta 474
  Siena 35, 342, **342–7**
  Siracusa 483
  Spoleto 364
  Stilo 524
  Susa 222
  Syracuse 35
  Taormina 542
  Taranto 515
  Terracina 475
  Todi **363**, 365
  Trani 513
  Trento 178
  Treviso 164
  Trieste 169
  Troia 483, **512–13**
  Turin 224–5
  Udine 166

Duomos (cathedrals) (cont.)
Urbino 375
Venosa 522
Vercelli 232
Verona 149
Vicenza 154
Viterbo 468
Volterra 338
Dürer, Albrecht 205, 243, 405
Dying Slave (Michelangelo) 32

E

Email 622
Easter 70
EasyJet 625
Ecce Homo with Angel (Moretto) 33
Eco, Umberto 38
Ecstasy of Beata Ludovica Albertoni (Bernini) 433
Ecstasy of St. Cecilia (Raphael) 269
Ecstasy of St. Teresa (Bernini) 63, 416
Edison (Florence) 310
Egadi Islands 537
Egesta 484
Elba 350
ferries 627
Elea 502
Eleanor of Aragon 533
Electrical adapters 617
Eleonora of Arborea 555
statue of 554
Eleonora of Portugal 346
Eleonora of Toledo 300
Eliseo (Rome) 450
Emanuele Filiberto, Duke of Savoy 215, 224
statue of 227
Embassies 619
Emilia-Romagna 259–73
climate 76
Exploring Emilia-Romagna 260–61
hotels 569–70
regional food 252
restaurants 590–92
ENIT (Ente Nazionale Italiano per il Turismo) 561
ENIT UK 617
Enna 541
Enotecas 578
Entertainment 60–61, **608–9**
Rome 449–50
Enthroned Christ with Madonna and Saints (Orcagna) 31
Epicentro (Venice) 128, 129
Epipolae 547
Epomeo, Monte 503
Equestrian Monument of Bartolomeo Colleoni (Verrocchio) 32
Equilibrio Festival (Rome) 449
Erasmus 432
Erice 537
Ermenegildo Zegna (Milan) 200, 201
Ernst, Max 109, 424
Estate Romana (Rome) 71
Este, d' *see* D'Este
Etiquette 616
Etna, Mount 63, 479, 484, **543**
Etruscans and Etruria 48–9, 259

Etruscans and Etruria (cont.)
architecture **34**, 384
Campania 487
Cerveteri 470
Chiusi 336
Cortona 336
Lazio 465
Maremma 350
Museo Archeologico e Necropoli (Tarquinia) 470
Museo Civico (Gubbio) 356
Museo Etrusco (Pitigliano) 351
Museo Nazionale Etrusco (Rome) 17, 444
Necropoli Etrusca – Crocefisso del Tufo (Orvieto) 363
Tarquinia 470
A Tour of Etruscan Italy 17
Vatican Museums (Rome) 424, 425, 426
Viterbo 468
Volterra 338
Eudoxia, Empress 416
Euganean Hills 163
EUR (Rome) 442, **446**
Eurolines 627, 633
Europcar 631
European Economic Community 69
European Health Insurance Card 619
Euros 621
Eusebio, Sant', Bishop of Vercelli 230
Eusebio di San Giorgio 357
Evelyn, John 149
Explorers 44–5
Expulsion of the Merchants (Giotto) 160

F

Fabriano (Milan) 200, 201
Fabric shops
Venice 128, 129
Faenza 270
Fair of St. Orsa (Aosta) 73
Falcone, Judge Giovanni 69
Fall in Italy 72
The Fall (Niccolò di Tommaso) 331
Fallopio, Gabriele 163
Fancelli, Luca 490
Fano 371, 373
Fantiscritti 322
Fanzago, Cosimo 493, 496
Farnese, Alessandro
statue of 262
Farnese, Ranuccio
statue of 262
Farnese family 259
Museo di Capodimonte (Naples) 497
Palazzo Farnese (Caprarola) 469
Palazzo Farnese (Rome) 441
Palazzo Pilotta (Parma) 263
Villa Farnesina (Rome) 432
Fascism 47, 68
Fashion shops
Milan 200, 201
Rome 447, 448
Fattori, Giovanni 243
The Palmieri Rotonda 307
Favignana 537

Feast in the House of Levi (Veronese) 110, 111
Federazione Arrampicata Sportiva Italiana 611
Federazione Italiana Attività Subacquee 611
Federazione Italiana Canoa Kayak 611
Federazione Italiana Sport Equestri 611
Federazione Italiana di Tennis 611
Federazione Italiana Vela 611
Federcampeggio 561
Federico Buccellati (Milan) 200, 201
Fellini, Federico 28, 69, 270
Feltre
festivals 71
Feltrinelli International (Florence) 310
Feltrinelli International (Rome) 447, 448
Fendi (Rome) 447, 448
La Fenice (Venice) 69, 609
Fénis 218, 219
Ferdinand I, King of Aragon 496
Ferdinand II, Grand Duke of Tuscany 66, 289
Ferdinand IV, King of Naples 494, 500, 533
Ferdinando I, Grand Duke of Tuscany 289, 332
statue of 278, 281
Fermi, Enrico 45
Ferragamo 25
Ferragamo (Florence) 310
Ferrara 259, **265**
Ferrarese School 264, 268, 269
Ferrari 42, 264
Ferrari, Defendente 223, 226
Ferrari, Enzo 264
Ferrari, Gaudenzio
St. Peter and a Donor 226
San Cristoforo frescoes (Vercelli) 232
San Gaudenzio altarpiece (Novara) 231
Santa Maria delle Grazie frescoes (Varallo) 230
Virgin and Child Enthroned 231
Ferrata, Ercole 402
Ferraù da Faenza 363
Ferrer, St. Vincent 122
Ferrero 215
Ferri, Ciro 306
Ferries 626, **627**
Festa degli Aquiloni (San Miniato) 70
Festa dei Candelieri (Sassari) 71
Festa dei Ceri (Gubbio) 70
Festa d'o' Cippo di Sant'Antonio (Naples) 73
Festival dei Due Mondi (Spoleto) 71
Festa della Fragola (Borgo San Martino) 71
Festa della Madonna della Bruna (Matera) 71
Festa della Madonna di Loreto (Loreto) 73

Festa della Madonna che Scappa in
  Piazza (Sulmona) 70
Festa dei Noiantri (Rome) 71
Festa del Mare (Diano Marina) 71
Festa dei Popoli (Florence) 72
Festa della Salute (Venice) 72
Festa di San Domenico Abate
  (Cocullo) 70
Festa di San Francesco (Assisi) 72
Festa di San Giovanni (Turin) 71
Festa di San Marco (Venice) 70
Festa di San Nicola (Bari) 70
Festa di San Sebastiano
  (Dolceacqua) 73
Festa di Sant'Ambrogio (Milan) 73
Festa di Sant'Andrea (Amalfi) 71
Festa di Sant'Efisio (Cagliari) 70
Festa di Santa Lucia (Sassari) 72
Festa della Santa Maria del Carmine
  (Naples) 71
Festa dello Speck (Bolzano) 70
Festa dell'Uva (Bolzano) 72
Festivals 70–73
  regional dance, music, and
    festivals 609
Fiaccole di Natale (Abbadia di San
  Salvatore) 73
Fiamma (Rome) 449, 450
FIAT 25, 43, 215, 224, 228
  Lingotto building (Turin) 189
  Museo dell'Automobile (Turin) 229
  "Topolino" car 68
Fidenza 262
Fiera del Tartufo (Alba) 72
Fiesole 332–3
Filangieri, Prince Gaetano 492
Filarete 196, 423
Filipucci, Memmo di
  Wedding Scene 349
Finding the Body of St. Mark
  (Tintoretto) 33
Fire service 619
Fisherman Delivering the Ring
  (Bordone) 33
Fisichella, Giancarlo 75
Fiumicino Airport (Rome)
  624–5
The Flagellation (Piero della
  Francesca) 374
The Flight into Egypt (Tintoretto) 104
Flora (Cignani) 264
Florence **275–317**, 319
  architecture 256–7
  Cappella Brancacci 302–3
  Discovering Italy 12–13
  Duomo and Baptistry 35, 250, 257,
    275, 282, **284–6**
  festivals 70, 71, 72, 73
  floods 69
  hotels 570–71
  map 20, 276–7
  Palazzo Pitti 305, **306–7**
  Piazza della Signoria 294–5
  restaurants 592
  San Lorenzo 298–9
  Santa Croce 256, **288–9**
  Santa Maria Novella 35, 257,
    300–301
  shopping 309–10

Florence (cont.)
  Street-by-Street maps
    around the Duomo 282–3
    around San Marco 278–9
    Oltrarno 304–5
    Piazza della Repubblica 296–7
  Street Finder 311–17
  A Tour of Etruscan Italy 17
  Uffizi 250, **290–93**
Florentine School 292
Flos (Milan) 200, 201
Fo, Dario 38, 69
Focacci (Rome) 447, 448
Fondaco dei Turchi (Venice) 92
Fondamenta Gherardini (Venice)
  Street-by-Street map 106
Fondazione Cini (Venice) 125
Fontana, Carlo 409, 469
Fontana, Domenico 417, 497
  tomb of 493
Fontana di Nettuno (Bologna)
  Street-by-Street map 266
Fontana di Trevi (Rome) 12, 384
Fontana dei Tritoni (Rome) 27, 436
  Street-by-Street map 436
Food and drink
  Central Italy 252–3
  cooking courses 611
  Florence 309, 310
  Milan 200, 201
  Northeast Italy 82–3
  Northwest Italy 184–5
  Parmesan cheese and Parma ham
    263
  Rome 447, 448
  Rome and Lazio 382–3
  shops 606, 607
  Southern Italy 480–81
  traditional Sicilian cuisine 543
  Venice 128, 129
  see also Restaurants; Wine
Football see Soccer
Forest Umbra 512
Formazza valley 230
La Fornarina 415
Fortresses see Castles and fortresses
Forum (Rome) 53, **394–6**
Forum di Assago (Milan) 609
Forum of Augustus (Rome) 393
Forum Boarium (Rome) 437
  Street-by-Street map 436
Forum of Caesar (Rome) 393
"Forza Italia" 69
Foscari, Francesco, Doge of
  Venice
  Ca' Foscari (Venice) 107
  monument to 102
Four Crowned Martyrs (Nanni di
  Banco) 31
Francesco I, Grand Duke of Tuscany
  290, 304
Franchetti, Baron Giorgio 98
Francia, Francesco 267
Francis I, King of France 61
Francis of Assisi, St. 57, 162, 353
  Basilica di San Francesco (Assisi)
    358–9
  San Francesco d'Assisi (Matera) 523
  San Francesco a Ripa (Rome) 433

Francis of Assisi, St. (cont.)
  writings 39
Franciscan Order 57
Franks 55
Frari (Venice) see Santa Maria
  Gloriosa dei Frari
Frascati 471
Fratelli Fabbi (Rome) 447, 448
Frederick II, Emperor 57
  Bari 514
  Castel Capuano (Naples) 490
  Castel del Monte 513
  Castello dell'Imperatore (Prato)
    332
  Castello di Lombardia (Enna) 541
  Castello Maniace (Siracusa) 546
  Constitutiones Augustales 522
  Lagopesole 522
  L'Aquila 508
  Lucera 512
  Puglia 505
  Rocca (San Miniato) 332
  tomb of 531
  Trani 513
  Troia 512
Frederick III, Emperor 346
Frederick of Aragon 515, 532
Frederick Barbarossa, Emperor 57
  coronation 207
  Lagopesole 522
  and the Lombard League 191
Fresco of Malatesta and St. Sigismund
  (Piero della Francesca) 270
Fresco technique 31
Frieze of Papier Mâché (Florence) 304
Friso, Alvise dal 108
Friuli see Veneto and Friuli
Fruit Basket (Caravaggio) 199
Fuga, Ferdinando
  Gesù Nuovo (Naples) 493
  Palazzo Corsini (Rome) 432
  Santa Maria Maggiore (Rome) 417
  Teatro di Corte (Naples) 497
Fumiani, Gian Antonio 105
Funeral of San Bernardino
  (Pinturicchio) 389
Furla (Florence) 310
Furla (Milan) 200, 201

G

Gaddi, Agnolo 332
Gaddi, Taddeo 288, 289
Gaeta 475
Gagini, Antonello 541
  Oratorio di Santa Zita sculptures
    (Palermo) 533
  St. John the Evangelist 537
  Santa Caterina 532
  Santa Maria del Gesù canopy
    (Trapani) 536
Gagini, Antonino 537
Gagini, Domenico 537
Gagini, Fazio 534
Gagini, Gian Domenico 534
Gagini family 533, 538
Gagliardi, Rosario 483, 547
Galatina 515, **517**
Galgano, San 339
Galileo Galilei 44, 45, 62, 319

Galileo Galilei (cont.)
Campanile (Venice) 121
Leaning Tower of Pisa 330
Museo di Storia della Scienza
(Florence) 289
Palazzo del Bo (Padua) 163
portrait of 330
tomb of 288
trial 63, 408
Galileo Galilei Airport (Pisa)
624–5
Galleria dell'Accademia (Florence)
13, **279**
Street-by-Street map 278
Galleria Nazionale d'Arte Antica
(Rome) 432
Galleria Regionale di Sicilia
(Palermo) 533
Galleria Tornabuoni (Florence) 309,
310
Galleria Umberto I (Naples) 497
Galleria Vittorio Emanuele II (Milan)
35, 189, **198**
Galleries see
Museums and galleries
Gallery of Views of Ancient Rome
(Pannini) 64
Gallo, Francesco 233
Galuppi, Baldassare 125
Gambara, Cardinal 469
Gambello, Antonio 123, 124
Gandolfino d'Asti 232
Garda, Lake 152
Gardens see Parks and gardens
Gardone 152
Garessio 233
Garfagnana 322
Gargano Peninsula 506, **512**
Garibaldi, Anita 243
Garibaldi, Giuseppe 47, 235
Mille 243
monument to 372
Museo Nazionale Gariboldino
(Isola Caprera) 552
Museo Nazionale del
Risorgimento (Turin) 227
Risorgimento 66–7
Garlando (Milan) 200, 201
Gas 630
Gates of Paradise (Ghiberti) 31, 286
Gattamelata 159, 162
Gattapone 356, 364, 365
Gatti 210
Gauguin, Paul 198
Gauls 49, 50
Gelaterias 578
Gelon 546
Geminiano, San
tomb of 264
Gennargentu mountains 549, 551,
554
Gennaro, San 491, 497
Genoa 143, 235, 236, **240–43**
architecture 189
ferries 627
Street-by-Street map 240–41
Gentile da Fabriano
Adoration of the Magi 31, 292
Madonna of Humility 329

Gentileschi, Artemisia 405, 415
Judith 306
Genzano
festivals 71
George of Antioch 532
Gerace 525
Gerolamo Romanino 178
Gesù (Palermo) 530
Gesù (Rome) 35, 385, **407**
Street-by-Street map 407
Gesù Nuovo (Naples) 493
Gesualdo, Carlo 40
Ghetto (Rome) 405
Ghibellines 57, 58
Ghiberti, Lorenzo
Baptismal font 346
Baptistry (Siena) 342
Baptistry doors (Florence) 31, 284,
286
Gates of Paradise 31, 286
Orsanmichele (Florence) 287
The Sacrifice of Isaac 287
stained glass 285
Ghigodonna (Milan) 200, 201
Ghirlandaio, Domenico 281, 295,
305, 349
The Annunciation 348
Christ in Majesty 338
Last Supper 280, 301
Life of St. John 301
The Madonna and Saints 326
Madonna della Misericordia 301
portrait of Christopher Columbus
243
Santa Trinita frescoes (Florence)
296
Sistine Chapel (Rome) 430
Ghirlandaio, Ridolfo del 279
Giambelli, Pietro 281
Giambologna 262
Fontana di Nettuno (Bologna) 266
Mercury 283, 287
Oceanus Fountain 307
The Rape of the Sabine Women 295
statue of Ferdinando I 278, 281
Giambono, Michele 111, 373
Gianfranco Ferrè (Milan) 200, 201
Giannicola di Paolo 356, 363
Giardino del Lago (Rome) 442
Gift shops
Florence 309, 310
Milan 200, 201
Rome 447, 448
Venice 129
Gioco del Ponte (Pisa) 71
Giordano, Luca 491, 492, 532
Giorgio Armani (Milan) 200, 201
Giorgione 105
birthplace 153
Madonna and Child with Saints
Liberal and Francis 153
Sleeping Venus 291
The Tempest 110, 153
The Three Ages of Man 306
Giostra del Saracino (Arezzo) 72
Giotto 58, 159, **161**, 162
Basilica di San Francesco frescoes
(Assisi) 69, 251, 353
Boniface VIII fresco 440

Giorgione (cont.)
Campanile (Florence) 284
Cappella Bardi frescoes (Florence)
288, 289
Cappella degli Scrovegni frescoes
(Padua) 81, 160
The Coretti 160
The Dream of Pope Innocent III 57
Expulsion of the Merchants 160
Injustice 161
Lament over the Dead Christ 161
The Last Judgment 161
Life of St. Francis 358, 359, 365
Mary Is Presented at the Temple 161
The Meeting at the Golden Gate 30
mosaic 423
Ognissanti Madonna 290, 292
St. Francis Appearing to the Friars at
Arles 360–61
Stefaneschi Triptych 427
Giovanna I, Queen of Naples 59
Giovanna Zanella (Venice) 128, 129
Giovanni d'Alemagna 123
Giovanni di Bartolo 147
Giovanni Galli Marroni e Canditi
(Milan) 200, 201
Giovanni de' Santi 98
Giovanni di Simone 328
Giovanni da Verona 493
Giovine Italia (Young Italy) 66
Giugiaro, Giorgio 42
Giuliano da Maiano 490
Giulio Romano 33, 211
Glassware
Museo Vetrario (Murano) 125
shops in Venice 128, 129
Glorenza 174
Glykon of Athens 495
Goa (Rome) 450
Goethe, Johann Wolfgang von 64,
412, 536
Goldoni, Carlo 39, 64
Gole dell'Alcantara 542
Gondolas 92, 112, 635
Gonzaga, Federico II 211
Gonzaga, Lodovico 211
Gonzaga family 211
Good Government Enthroned
(Lorenzetti) 30
Gorizia 167
Gothic architecture 34
Venice 84
Goths 54
Gozzoli, Benozzo 329, 349, 363
Life of St. Augustine 349
Life of St. Francis 365
The Procession of the Magi 60–61
Sermoneta 474
Grado 168
Gran Paradiso, Parco Nazionale del
182, 215, **220–21**
Gran Sasso 507, 508
Grancaffè Quadri (Venice) 13
Grand Canal (Venice) 13, **92–5**
Grand Tours 64–5
Grapes
Central Italy 255
Northwest Italy 187
Graves, Michael 42

Gravina, Ferdinando, Prince of Palagonia 536
Greco, Emilio 159
  Museo d'Arte Moderna "Emilio Greco" (Orvieto) 362
Greek Drama in Theater (Syracuse) 70
Greeks, Ancient 48, 369
  Agrigento 539
  Ancona 376
  Basilicata and Calabria 519
  Campania 487
  Elea 502
  Lecce 516
  Locri Epizephiri 519, 525
  Museo Nazionale della Magna Grecia (Reggio di Calabria) 525
  Paestum 502–3
  Selinunte 538
  Sicily 527
  Siracusa 546
  in Southern Italy 484–5
  Tindarys 542
  Valley of the Temples (Agrigento) 539, **540**
Green travel 624
Greenaway, Peter 228
Gregorian Profane Museum (Rome) 426
Gregory VII, Pope 56
Gregory IX, Pope 57
Gregory XI, Pope 59, 344
Gregory XIII, Pope 404
Gregory XV, Pope 409
Gregory the Great, Pope 55, 421
Gressoney valley 218
Gritti family 95
Grom (Florence) 309
Grotta Azzurra (Capri) 502
Grotta del Bue Marino 554
Grotta di Nettuno 553
Grotta Verde 553
Grottaferrata 471
Grotte di Castellana 515
Grotte di Frasassi 376
Grotte di Toirano 239
Gruppo Archeologico Romano 611
Guardi, Francesco 107, 205
Guariento
  Angels in Armor 162
Guarini, Guarino 62
  Cappella della Sacra Sindone (Turin) 225
  Palazzo dell'Accademia delle Scienze (Turin) 226
  Palazzo Carignano (Turin) 188, 227
  San Lorenzo (Turin) 189, 228
Gubbio 353, 355, **356**
  festivals 70
  A Tour of Etruscan Italy 17
Gucci 43
Gucci (Florence) 310
Gucci (Milan) 200, 201
Gucci (Venice) 128, 129
Guelphs 57, 58, 297
Guercino 269, 373, 405, 408
  Assumption 327
  Duomo (Piacenza) 262
  St. Lucy 327

Guggenheim Collection (Venice) *see* Peggy Guggenheim Collection
Guglielmo da Pisa 331
Guicciardini, Francesco 305
Guidetto da Como 326
Guido d'Arezzo 40
Guido da Como 328
Guidoriccio da Fogliano 58
Guillaume le Moine 496
Guinigi, Paolo 326, 327
Guiscard, Robert 56, 522
'Gusto (Rome) 450

H

Habsburg dynasty 171
Hadrian, Emperor 52, 53
  Castel Sant'Angelo (Rome) 421
  Hadrian's Villa (Tivoli) 53, 392, 472
  Pantheon (Rome) 406, **408**
  Plutei of Trajan 396
  Temple of Venus and Rome (Rome) 395
Hadrian's Villa (Tivoli) 12
Ham, Parma 263
Hanbury, Sir Thomas 238
Handing over the Keys of St. Peter (Perugino) 60
Hannibal 522, 538
  Battle of Lake Trasimeno 357
  crosses Alps 50
Hannibalianus 445
Harry's Bar (Venice) 95
  Street-by-Street map 112
Hauteville, Roger de 56
Hawkwood, Sir John 339
Hayez, Francesco
  The Kiss 202
Healing of the Madman (Carpaccio) 111
Health care 619
Helena (daughter of Emperor Constantine) 445
Helena, St. 334
Heliodorus, St. 126
Hemingway, Ernest 112
Henry IV, Emperor 56
Henry VI, Emperor
  tomb of 531
Henry VII, Emperor 242
Herculaneum 52, 484, 487, 499
  Museo Archeologico Nazionale (Naples) 494
Hernici 474
Herod the Great, King of Judea 168
Hertz 631
High Tech (Milan) 200, 201
Highways 626, 630
History 47–69
Hitching 631
Hogan (Milan) 200, 201
Holbein, Hans 205
Holidays, public 73
The Holy Family (Michelangelo) 291, 293
Holy Roman Empire 55, 191, 369
Holy Shroud (Turin) 225
Homer 475, 485

Horace 38, 502, 522
Horseback riding 610
Hotels 558–77
  Abruzzo, Molise, and Puglia 577
  Agriturismo 560
  alberghi 558
  Basilicata and Calabria 577
  budget accommodations **560**, 561
  chain hotels **558–9**, 561
  checking in and out 560
  children in 559
  disabled travelers 561
  Emilia-Romagna 569–70
  Florence 570–71
  Lazio 576
  Liguria 568–9
  Lombardy 565–7
  Le Marche 572–3
  meals and facilities 559
  Naples and Campania 576
  pensioni 558
  prices 559
  ratings 558
  reservations 559
  Rome 573–6
  Sardinia 577
  Sicily 577
  Trentino–Alto Adige 564–5
  Tuscany 571–2
  Umbria 572
  Valle D'Aosta and Piedmont 567–8
  Veneto and Friuli 563–4
  Venice 562–3
House of Augustus (Rome) 398
House of Livia (Rome) 398
House of the Vestal Virgins (Rome) 394, 396
House of the Vettii (Pompeii) 52–3
Household wares shops 607
Hugo Boss (Milan) 200, 201
Human chess game (Marostica) 72
Hunt, Leigh 245

I

IAT Milan 617
Imperia 432
Incisioni Rupestri, Parco Nazionale delle 206
Infiorata (Genzano) 71
Injustice (Giotto) 161
Innocent III, Pope 57
Innocent VIII, Pope 424
Innocent X, Pope 403, 404, 408
Inoculations 619
Inquisition 62, 63
Insect repellent 619
Insurance
  cars 630
  travel 618
Intercultura 611
Interior design shops 607
  Venice 128, 129
International Festival of Cinema (Rome) 72, 609
International Film Festival (Taormina) 71
Internet 622
Interrail One Country Pass 628

Interrail Pass 628
Intimissimi (Florence) 310
Inventors 44–5
Iron Age 48
Ischia 487, **503**
Ischia Ponte 503
Ischia Porto 503
Iseo, Lago d' 206–7
Islam 617
L'Isola – Carlo Moretti (Venice) 128, 129
Isola Bella 183, 192, 195
Isola Caprera 552
Isola Maggiore 357
Isola San Giulio 231
Isola di San Pietro 549, 551, 555
Isole Egadi 537
Isole Eolie 537
Isole Pelagie 537
Isole Tremiti 511
Issime 218
Issogne 218, 219
Italia Lodging 558
Italian Birds Protection League (LIPU) 611
Italian Grand Prix 75
Italian State Railway Information Office 629
Italian State Tourist Board 561, 609
Ittar, Stefano 543
Ivrea 215

J

Jacob of Ulm 268
Jacopone da Todi
tomb of 363
James II, King of Aragon 555
James, Henry 94, 105, 109
Jazz 608, **609**
festivals 71
Rome 449, 450
Jerome, St. 37, 168
Jesi 376
Jesuits 62, 65
Collegio di Propaganda Fide (Rome) 412
Gesù (Rome) 35, **407**
Sant'Andrea al Quirinale (Rome) 415
Sant'Ignazio di Loyola (Rome) 409
Jewelry shops 607
Florence 309, 310
Venice 128, 129
Jews
Ghetto (Rome) 405
Pitigliano 350–51
religious services 616
John, St. 36
John the Baptist, St. 205, 241
John of Durazzo
tomb of 493
John Paul II, Pope 69
Joseph II, Emperor 65
Judith (Gentileschi) 306
Julia 509, 511
Julius II, Pope 61
Piazza di Montecitorio (Rome) 409
Raphael Rooms (Rome) 431

Julius II, Pope (cont.)
Santa Maria del Popolo (Rome) 414
Sistine Chapel 428
statue of 356
tomb of 279, 416
Vatican Museums (Rome) 424
Julius III, Pope 444
Justinian, Emperor 54–5
Juvarra, Filippo
Armeria Reale (Turin) 228
Basilica di Superga 229
Chiesa Vecchia (Santuario d'Oropa) 230
Duomo (Como) 195
Duomo (Turin) 225
Palazzo Madama (Turin) 225
Palazzo Reale (Turin) 228
Santa Cristina (Turin) 227
Stupinigi 229
Juvenal 39

K

Kandinsky, Wassily 109, 198
Keats, John 64
grave of 441
Keats-Shelley Memorial House (Rome) 412
Kisling, Moïse 203
The Kiss (Hayez) 202
Klee, Paul 109, 198
Knights of St. John of Jerusalem 232
Knights Templar 513
Kublai Khan 45, 56
Kubrick, Stanley 129

L

La Scala (Milan) 65
Lace, Burano 125
Ladislas, King of Naples
tomb of 490
Lago di Como 14, 191, **194–5**
map 194
Lago di Garda 152
Lago d'Iseo 206–7
Lago Maggiore 183, 191, 192, **195**
Lago di Misurina 87
Lago d'Orta 231
Lago di Sauris 166
Lago di Scanno 509
Lago di Vico 469
Lagopesole 522
Lament over the Dead Christ (Giotto) 161
Lamezia Terme 521
Lampedusa 537
Lampedusa, Giuseppe Tomasi di 537
Lanci, Baldassare 347
Lanciano 511
Landini, Francesco 40
Lanfranco 264, 491, 493
Language courses 610
L'Aquila 508
Lascaris, Giorgio 99
Last Judgment (Cavallini) 30
Last Judgment (Giotto) 161
Last Judgment (Michelangelo) 33, 62, 430
Last Judgment (Signorelli) 363

Last Supper (Ghirlandaio) 301
Last Supper (Leonardo da Vinci) 32, 191, 204, 293
Latin people 465
Laura Biagiotti (Rome) 447, 448
Laurana, Luciano 374
Laurana, Francesco
head of Eleanor of Aragon 533
Madonna 496, 547
Madonna and Child 537
Oratorio di San Lorenzo (Palermo) 533
Lawrence, St. 36
Lawrence, D.H. 244, 245, 549
Lazio 465–75
Exploring Lazio 466–7
hotels 576
monasteries 473
restaurants 599–600
Le Corte, Giusto 109
Leaning Tower of Pisa 250, 319, 328, **330**
Lear, Edward 238, 519
Leather shops
Florence 309, 310
Lecce 479, 505, 507
architecture 483
Street-by-Street map 516–17
Lecco 194, 195
Left luggage 629
Lega Nord 191
Legal assistance 618
Léger, Fernand 109
Leger Holidays 615, 617
Legros, Pierre
Triumph of Faith over Idolatry 407
Lenzi, Lorenzo 300
Leo, St. 372
Leo III, Pope 431
Leo IV, Pope 55, 431
Leo X, Pope 61, 431, 438
tomb of 408
Leo XIII, Pope 405
Leon d'Oro (Venice) 128, 129
Leonardo da Vinci 60, 431
Adoration of the Magi 293
The Annunciation 293
Atlantic Codex 199
birthplace 331
Duomo (Pavia) 207
inventions 44
Last Supper 32, 191, 204, 293
Mona Lisa 32
Museo Leonardiano (Vinci) 331
Portrait of a Musician 199
St. Jerome 425, 427
self-portrait 228
Uomo Vitruviano 32
Virgin of the Rocks 32
Leone, Sergio 69
Leonello d'Este (Pisanello) 205
Leopardi, Alessandro 32, 123
Leopold, Grand Duke of Tuscany 65
Lepanto, Battle of (1571) 62, 63, 168
Lerici 245
Lesina 512
Levanzo 537

Levi, Carlo 523
Levi, Primo 38
Levico Terme 179
Liaisons Abroad 609
Libreria Belardetti (Rome) 447, 448
Libreria Marco Polo (Venice) 129
Life of St. Francis (Giotto) 358, 359, 365
Life of St. Francis (Gozzoli) 365
Life of St. John (Ghirlandaio) 301
Life of St. Peter (Masaccio) 302–3
Life of the Virgin (Cavallini) 380
Ligorio, Pirro 472
Liguria 235–47
   climate 76
   Exploring Liguria 236–7
   hotels 568–9
   regional food 185
   restaurants 589–90
Lillaz 221
Lilybaeum 538
Linate Airport (Milan) 624–5
Linosa 537
Lipari 537
Lippi, Filippino 279, 349
   Capella di Filippo Strozzi frescoes (Florence) 301
   Life of St. Peter 302, 303
   Madonna and Child 305
   Madonna with Saints 243
   Saints Helena, Jerome, Sebastian and Roch 325
   Santa Maria sopra Minerva frescoes (Rome) 406, 408
   The Virgin Appearing to St. Bernard 283
Lippi, Fra Filippo 415
   Crucifixion 332
   Life of John the Baptist 332
   Life of the Virgin 364
   Madonna and Child 306
   Madonna and Child with Angels 31, 292–3
   Madonna del Ceppo 332
Liszt, Franz 412
Literature 38–9
Little St. Bernard Pass 218
Livia 398, 416, 426
Livorno 319
   ferries 627
Livy 39
Locanda Atlantide (Roma) 450
Locorotondo 515
Locri Epizephiri 485, 519, 525
Lodi 207
Loggia del Bigallo (Florence)
   Street-by-Street map 282
Loggia del Capitaniato (Vicenza) 155
   Street-by-Street map 154
Loggia della Gran Guardia (Padua)
   Street-by-Street map 158
Loggia della Mercanzia (Siena) 343
Lombard League 57, 191
Lombardi family 122
Lombardo, Pietro
   Santa Maria Gloriosa dei Frari rood screen (Venice) 102
   Santa Maria dei Miracoli (Venice) 99

Lombardo, Pietro (cont.)
   tomb of Andrea Vendramin 123
   tomb of Nicolò Marcello 122
Lombardo, Tullio 98, 99
   Double Portrait 98
Lombards 54, 55, 353, 364
Lombardy 191–213
   climate 76
   Exploring Lombardy 192–3
   hotels 565–7
   regional food 184
   restaurants 584–6
Longhena, Baldassare
   Ca' Rezzonico (Venice) 107
   Santi Giovanni e Paolo (Venice) 123
   Santa Maria della Salute (Venice) 109
Longhi, Martino the Elder 404
Longhi, Pietro 107, 111
Loren, Sophia 27
Lorenzetti, Ambrogio 292
   Allegory of Bad Government 344
   Allegory of Good Government 30, 344
   map of the world 344
   San Galgano frescoes 339
Lorenzetti, Pietro 292
   Crucifixion 336
   The Deposition 358
   Two Views 345
Lorenzo da Viterbo 468
Loreto 377
   festivals 73
Loreto Aprutino 508
Lorraine, Dukes of 307
Losey, Joseph 157
Lotto, Lorenzo 147, 164, 207, 376, 377
Louis IX, King of France 156
Louis XIV, King of France 413
Louis Vuitton (Florence) 310
Loyola, St. Ignatius 63, 407, 409
Lucca 319, **324–7**
   Discovering Italy 13, 14
   festivals 70
   Street-by-Street map 324–5
Lucera 512
Lucy, St. 37, 92, 547
Ludovico il Moro
   tomb of 208
Luke, St. 36, 37, 230
Lumiei, river 166
Luther, Martin 268
Lutyens, Edwin 442
Lysippus 495

M

Macchiaioli 307
Macedonian Wars 51
Machiavelli, Niccolò 275, 372
   portrait of 61
   The Prince 61
   tomb of 288
La Maddalena (Costa Smeralda) 552
La Maddalena (Rome) 409
Maderno, Carlo 415, 423
Maderno, Stefano 433
Madonna and Angels (Parmigianino) 33
Madonna di Campiglio 173, **178**
   festivals 70

Madonna della Candeletta (Crivelli) 203
Madonna di Ca' Pesaro (Titian) 102
Madonna del Ceppo (Lippi) 332
Madonna of the Chair (Raphael) 306
Madonna and Child (Bellini) 103
Madonna and Child (Coppo di Marcovaldo) 30
Madonna and Child between St. John the Baptist and a Saint (Bellini) 110, 111
Madonna and Child with Angels (Lippi) 31, 292–3
Madonna and Child with Four Saints (Bellini) 32, 37
Madonna Enthroned with Angels and Prophets (Cimabue) 30
Madonna of the Goldfinch (Raphael) 32, 293
Madonna of the Long Neck (Parmigianino) 293
Madonna della Misericordia (Ghirlandaio) 301
Madonna di Nicopeia (icon) 116, 117
Madonna dell'Orto (Venice) 98
Madonna of the Pesaro Family (Titian) 32
Maestà (Duccio) 339, 342
Mafia 69, 487, 519, **539**
Magellan, Ferdinand 155
Magenta, Battle of (1859) 67
Maggio Musicale (Florence) 70, 609
Maggiore (Rome) 631
Maggiore, Lake *see* Lago Maggiore
La Magione (Palermo) 533
Magna Graecia 369, 484, 519, 538
Magritte, René 109
Maiastra (Brancusi) 109
Maiella National Park 509
Mail services 623
Maitani, Lorenzo 362, 363
Malaspina family 553
Malatesta, Sigismondo 270
Malatesta family 259, 373
Malevich, Kasimir 109
The Mall (Florence) 310
Malles Venosta (Mals im Vinschgau) 174
Malpensa Airport (Milan) 624–5
Mamertine Prison (Rome) 393
Mamoiada 554
"Man in the Iron Mask" 223
Manarola 245
Mandragora (Florence) 310
Manfredonia 512
Manin, Daniel 66
Manin, Ludovico, Doge of Venice 167
Mannerism 293
Mantegna, Andrea 196, 205, 227, 265, 293
   Arrival of Cardinal Francesco Gonzaga 31
   Dead Christ 32, 202
   The Martyrdom of St. Christopher 162
   The Martyrdom of St. James 162
   Palazzo Ducale frescoes (Mantua) 211
   St. Sebastian 98

Mantegna, Andrea (cont.)
Virgin and Child with Saints 150
Mantua 191, **211**
Manzoni, Alessandro 194, 195
Maps
Abruzzo, Molise, and Puglia 506–7
ancient 47
Basilicata and Calabria 520–21
Bologna 266–7
Capri 502–3
Central Italy 250–51
Emilia-Romagna 260–61
Florence 276–7
Florence: Around Piazza della
Repubblica 296–7
Florence: Duomo 282–3
Florence: Oltrarno 304–5
Florence: San Marco 278–9
Florence and Environs 20
Florence Street Finder 311–17
Genoa 240–41
The Greeks in Southern Italy 484–5
Italy 18–19
Italy in 650 BC 48
Italy in AD 600 54
Italy in 1350 58
Italy in 1492 60
Italy in 1550 62
Italy in 1861 66
Lago di Garda 152
Lake Como 194
Lazio 466–7
Lecce 516–17
Liguria 236–7
Lombardy 192–3
Lucca 324–5
Le Marche 370–71
Maremma 350–51
Mediterranean in 1250 56
Milan 196–7
Naples 490–91
Naples and Campania 488–9
Northeast Italy 80–81
Northern Italy 20–21
Northwest Italy 182–3
Nuraghe in Sardinia 553
Padua 158–9
Palermo 530–31
Parco Nazionale d'Abruzzo, Lazio,
e Molise 510–11
Parco Nazionale del Gran Paradiso
220–21
Pompeii 499
Ravenna 272–3
Roman Empire 50–51, 52
Rome: Ancient Center 387
Rome: Around the Pantheon 406–7
Rome: Around Piazza Navona 401,
402–3
Rome: Aventine and Lateran 435
Rome: Capitoline Hill 388–9
Rome: Further Afield 442
Rome: Northeast Rome 411
Rome: Piazza della Bocca della
Verità 436–7
Rome: Piazza di Spagna 412–13
Rome: Vatican and Trastevere 419
Rome and Environs 23
Rome and Lazio 380–81

Maps (cont.)
Rome Street Finder 451–61
San Gimignano 348–9
Sardinia 22, 550–51
scientists, inventors, and explorers
44–5
Sicilian islands 537
Sicily 22, 528–9
Siena 342–3
Southern Italy 22–3, 478–9
Strada delle Dolomiti 86
train routes 629
Trentino–Alto Adige 172–3
Turin 224
Tuscany 320–21
Umbria 354–5
Valle d'Aosta and Piedmont 216–17
Valley of the Temples (Agrigento)
540
Veneto and Friuli 144–5
Venice 21, 81, 90–91
Venice: Dorsoduro 106–7
Venice: Grand Canal 92–5
Venice: Piazza San Marco 112–13
Venice: San Polo 100–101
Venice: vaporetto routes 140–41
Venice Street Finder 130–39
Verona 146–7
Vicenza 154–5
wines of Central Italy 254–5
writers, poets, and dramatists
38–9
Maratea 521, **523**
Marcellinus 445
Marcello, Nicolò, Doge of Venice
tomb of 122
Marcellus
tomb of 522
Le Marche 369–77
climate 77
Exploring Le Marche 370–71
hotels 572–3
regional food 253
restaurants 595–6
Marchiol (Venice) 128, 129
Marco da Firenze 490
Marco Polo Airport (Venice) 624–5
Marconi, Guglielmo 44
Marcus Aurelius, Emperor 52, 53
Column of Marcus Aurelius
(Rome) 409
statue of 388
Mare di Carta (Venice) 129
Maremma 16, **350–51**
Marettimo 537
Margaret of Brabant
tomb of 240, 242
Maria d'Aragona 493
Maria Carolina, Queen 533
Marie Louise of Lucca 326
Marina Grande (Capri) 503
Marina di Pisa 26
Marina e Susanna Sent (Venice) 128,
129
Marinetti, Filippo 68
Marini, Marino 109, 331
Marinus, St. 372
Mark the Evangelist, St. 36, 37
Basilica di San Marco (Venice) 115

Markets 606
Florence 309, 310
Mercato Centrale (Florence) 299
Rome 448
Venice 128, 129
Vucciria (Palermo) 532
see also Shopping
Marmoiada
festivals 73
Marmolada (Dolomites) 86
Marocchetti, Carlo 227
Marostica
festivals 72
Marriage of Alexander and Roxana
(Sodoma) 32
Marriage of the Virgin (Raphael) 203
Marsala 538
Martin IV, Pope
tomb of 356
Martin V, Pope 60
Martina Franca 515
Martini, Francesco di Giorgio 372
Martini, Francesco di Giovanni 356
Martini, Simone 58
Annunciation 290, 292
*The Blessed Agostino Novello and
Four of His Miracles* 345
Death of the Saint 358, 359
Guidoriccio da Fogliano 344
The Madonna and Saints 329
Maestà 344
The Virgin and Child 329
Vision of St. Martin 30
Martorana, Eloisa 532
La Martorana (Palermo) 532
The Martyrdom of St. Lawrence
(Bronzino) 298
The Martyrdom of St. Sebastian
(Costa) 266
Mary, Virgin 377
Mary Is Presented at the Temple
(Giotto) 161
Mary of Valois
tomb of 493
Masaccio
Life of St. Peter (Cappella Brancacci)
302–3
St. Paul 329
The Tribute Money 31
Trinity 300
Masaniello, Revolt of (1647) 63
Maserati 264
Mask shops, Venice 128, 129
Maso di Bartolomeo 374
Masolino da Panicale
Life of St. Peter 302–3
Madonna and Child 363
San Clemente frescoes (Rome)
439
The Mass of Bolsena (Raphael) 431
Massa Marittima 339
Massaciuccoli, Lago 323
Massari, Giorgio 94, 107
Matas, Niccolò 288
Matera 519, **522–3**
festivals 71
Matilda, Countess of Tuscany 56,
264
Matisse, Henri 270

Matteo da Gualdo 359
Matterhorn (Monte Cervino) 218
Matthew, St. 36, 37
  tomb of 502
Mausoleum of Augustus (Rome) 414
Maxentius, Emperor
  Basilica of Constantine and Maxentius (Rome) 396
  Battle of the Milvian Bridge 54, 393, 396, 431
  Villa Romana del Casale (Piazza Armerina) 541
Maximian, Emperor 115
Maximianus Herculeus 541
Maximilian, Archduke 169
Maximinian, Archbishop of Ravenna 55
MaxMara (Venice) 128, 129
Mazzarò 542, 543
Mazzini, Giuseppe 66, 227, 235
  grave of 243
Mazzoni, Guido
  Pietà 493
Medical treatment 619
Medici, Alessandro de' 62
Medici, Anna Maria Lodovica 292
Medici, Cosimo de' (il Vecchio) 60, 293
  Convento di San Marco (Florence) 280
  tomb of 299
Medici, Cosimo I de'
  Cappelle Medicee (Florence) 299
  Fortezza Medicea (Siena) 347
  Palazzo Vecchio (Florence) 295
  statue of 329
  Uffizi (Florence) 290
Medici, Cosimo III de' 293
Medici, Cardinal Ferdinando de' 413
Medici, Giuliano 299
Medici, Lorenzo the Magnificent 60, 61
  Museo degli Argenti (Florence) 307
  Poggio a Caiano 332
  tomb of 299
Medici, Princess Maria Maddalena de' 281
Medici, Piero de' 60
Medici family 60, 319
  Boboli Gardens (Florence) 307
  Cappelle Medicee (Florence) 299
  coat of arms 64
  Corridoio Vasariano (Florence) 289
  Florence 275
  Fortezza Medicea (Arezzo) 333
  Palazzo Madama (Rome) 403
  Palazzo Pitti (Florence) 250, 306, 307
  Pazzi conspiracy 405
  Piazza della Signoria (Florence) 294
  San Lorenzo (Florence) 298
  tombs 298, 299
Medici Venus 293, 306
Medieval Italy 58–9
  art 30–31
Medieval Palio (Feltre) 71
Medusa (Bernini) 391

The Meeting at the Golden Gate (Giotto) 30
Meier, Richard 414
Melanzio, Francesco 365
Melfi 522
Melozzo da Forlì 47
Memling, Hans 156
Memmi, Lippo 290
  Life of Christ 349
  Madonna dei Raccomandati 362
  Maestà 348, 349
Memmo di Filipucci 349
Menabuoi, Giusto de' 158, 159
Menaggio 194
Mengoni, Giuseppe
  Galleria Vittorio Emanuele II (Milan) 35, 189, **198**
  Mercato Centrale (Florence) 299
Menus 578–9
Merano (Meran) 174
Mercato della Befana (Rome) 73
Mercato Centrale (Florence) **299**, 310
Mercato Nuovo (Florence) 297
Mercato di Sant'Ambrogio (Florence) 310
Mercato delle Stampe (Rome) 448
Mercury (Giambologna) 283
Messina 542
  history 55, 63
  Revolt of (1848) 66
Messina (artist) 243
Messina, Straits of 485
Metaponition 485
Metaponto 519, **523**
Metropolitana (underground railroads) 632–3
Il Mezzogiorno 25
Michelangelo 60, 61, 269, 275, 286, 302, 426, 431
  Bacchus 287
  "Blockhead" Captive 33
  Brutus 287
  Capitol (Rome) 388
  Cappelle Medicee (Florence) 299
  Carrara house 322
  David 32, 279, 294, 322
  Duomo (Padua) 159
  Duomo (Siena) 346
  Dying Slave 32, 416
  The Holy Family 291, 293
  Last Judgment 33, 62, 363, 416, 430
  Madonna and Child 287, 299
  Moses 416
  Palazzo Corsini (Rome) 432
  Palazzo Farnese (Rome) 405
  Palazzo Nuovo (Rome) 392
  Piazza del Campidoglio (Rome) 389
  Piazzale Michelangelo (Florence) 308
  Pietà 283, 423
  Quattro Prigioni 279
  Risen Christ 408
  Rondanini Pietà 196
  St. Peter's (Rome) 380, 396, 422
  San Lorenzo (Florence) 298, 299
  Santa Maria sopra Minerva (Rome) 406
  Sistine Chapel 32, 61, 420, **428–30**

Michelangelo (cont.)
  The Tomb of the Duke of Nemours 299
  tomb of 288
  tomb of Julius II 416
  Venus and Cupid 279
  Victory 294, 295
  Villa Giulia (Rome) 444
Michelino
  Dante Explaining the Divine Comedy 285
Michelozzo
  Cappella del Crocifisso (Florence) 308
  Convento di San Marco (Florence) 280
  Ospedale del Ceppo (Pistoia) 331
  Pulpit of the Holy Girdle (Prato) 332
  Santissima Annunziata (Florence) 281
  tomb of Cardinal Rinaldo Brancaccio 492
Middle Ages 58–9
Miel 228
Miglionico 521
Milan 26, 69, 191, **196–205**
  airports 624–5
  architecture 35, 189
  congestion charge 630
  Discovering Italy 14
  festivals 73
  map 196–7
  Pinacoteca di Brera 191, **202–3**
  shopping 200–201
Milan, Edict of (AD 313) 54, 205
Milazzo 537
Milvian Bridge, Battle of (312 AD) 54, 393, 396, 431
Miniato, San 308
Minori 501
Miracle of San Gennaro (Naples) 72, 73
Miretto, Nicola 159
Miró, Joan 109
Missoni (Venice) 128, 129
Misurina, Lago di 87
Mithras, cult of 439
Mobile phones 622–3
Mocenigo, Pietro, Doge of Venice
  tomb of 122
Mochi, Francesco 262
The Mocking of Christ (Fra Angelico) 280
Modena 16, 259, **264**
Modern Italy 68–9
Modica 527, 547
Modigliani, Amedeo 198, 227
  Portrait of Moisè Kisling 203
Mole Antonelliana (Turin) 35, 189, 228
Molise *see* Abruzzo, Molise, and Puglia
Momo, Giuseppe 421
Mona Lisa (Leonardo da Vinci) 32
Monasteries of Lazio 473
Mondrian, Piet 109, 198
Money 620–21

Monreale 478, 482, 527, **534–5**
  architecture 34
Mont Blanc (Monte Bianco) 218
Montagna, Bartolomeo 156, 157, 165
Montalcino 337
  festivals 72
Montaperti, Battle of (1260) 319
Monte Argentario 351
Monte Berico (Vicenza) 157
Monte Bianco (Mont Blanc) 218
Monte Bondone 179
Monte Cervino (Matterhorn) 218
Monte Rosa 218
Monte Spinale 171
Monte Vettore 366
Montecassino 465, **473**
Montecatini Terme 323
Montefalco 353, **365**
Montefeltro, Dukes of 356, 373
Montefeltro, Federico da, Duke of
  Urbino 60, 369
  Fano 373
  Palazzo Ducale (Urbino) 374–5
  portrait of 291, 292
Montefiascone 469
Montepulciano 337
Monteriggioni 338
Monterosso al Mare 245
Monteverdi, Claudio 40–41, 63, 191,
  210
Monti Sibillini **366**, 369
Montmayer 218
Montorsoli, GA 542
Monza 205
  architecture 188
Moore, Henry 322
Morandi, Giorgio
  Still Life 198
Moravia, Alberto 39
Morazzone, Pier Francesco 231
Morelli, Cosimo 402
Morello 228
Moretto
  Ecce Homo with Angel 33
Moriondo e Gariglio (Rome) 447,
  448
Moro, Aldo 69
La Mortella (Forie) 503
Mosaico di Pitti (Florence) 310
Mosaics
  Basilica di San Marco (Venice)
  114–17
  Monreale 534
  Ravenna 272–3
  Santa Maria Maggiore (Rome) 417
Mosca, Ferdinando 508
Moscato d'Asti wine 187
*Moses Defends the Daughters of
  Jethro* (Rosso Fiorentino) 33
Mosquito repellent 619
Mostra Mercato Internazionale
  dell'Artigianato (Florence) 70
Mother and Son (Carrà) 203
Motorcycle racing 74
Mount Etna 63, 479, 484, **543**
Mountain refuges 561
Mountain sports 610
Movies 28, **609**
  festivals 71

Movies (cont.)
  Italian cinema since World War II
  69
  Rome 449, 450
Mozart, Leopold 211
Mullooly, Father 439
Multscher, Hans
  Museo Multscher (Vipiteno) 174
Murano 13, **125**
Murat, Joachim, King of Naples 65
Murge dei Trulli 515
Murillo, Bartolomé Esteban 432
Museums and galleries (general)
  admission charges 615
  opening hours 615
Museums and galleries
  Accademia (Florence) 13
  Accademia (Venice) 94, **110–11**
  Antiquarium Arborense (Oristano)
  554, 555
  Armeria Reale (Turin) 228
  Bargello (Florence) 283, **287**
  Borgo Medioevale (Turin) 227
  Ca' Rezzonico (Venice) 107
  Capitoline Museums (Rome) 12,
  381, 388, **390–91**
  Casa di Petrarca (Padua) 163
  Casa di Puccini (Lucca) 325
  Casa Rossini (Pèsaro) 372–3
  Castelvecchio (Verona) 146–7
  Centro per l'Arte Contemporaneo
  Pecci (Prato) 332
  Centro Camuno in Studi Preistorici
  206
  Cinema Museum (Turin) 228
  Cittadella dei Musei (Cagliari) 555
  Civico Museo Archeologico
  (Milan) 193
  Etruscan Museum of the
  Vatican (Rome) 17
  Fondazione Cini (Venice) 125
  Galleria d'Arte Moderna (
  Florence) 306, 307
  Galleria d'Arte Moderna (Nervi)
  243
  Galleria dell'Accademia (Florence)
  13, 278, **279**
  Galleria dell'Accademia Carrara
  (Bergamo) 205
  Galleria del Costume (Florence)
  307
  Galleria Estense (Modena) 264
  Galleria Ferrari (Modena) 264
  Galleria Nazionale d'Arte Antica
  (Rome) 432
  Galleria Nazionale d'Arte Moderna
  (Rome) 443
  Galleria Nazionale dell'Umbria
  (Perugia) 357
  Galleria Palatina (Florence) 306
  Galleria Regionale di Sicilia
  (Palermo) 533
  Galleria Sabauda (Turin) 226–7
  Galleria Umberto I (Naples) 497
  Keats-Shelley Memorial House
  (Rome) 412
  MADRE (Naples) 490
  MAUTO – Museo dell'Automobile
  di Torino (Turin) 228

Museums and galleries (cont.)
  MAXXI (Rome) 445
  Museo dell'Accademia Etrusca
  (Cortona) 336
  Museo Alessi (Enna) 541
  Museo degli Alpini (Bassano del
  Grappa) 153
  Museo degli Arazzi (Marsala)
  538
  Museo Archeologico (Ascoli
  Piceno) 377
  Museo Archeologico (Bolzano)
  176
  Museo Archeologico (Florence)
  17, 279, **281**
  Museo Archeologico
  (Sant'Antioco) 555
  Museo Archeologico (Terracina)
  475
  Museo Archeologico (Verona)
  149
  Museo Archeologico dell'Antica
  Capua (Capua) 500
  Museo Archeologico di Baglio
  Anselmi (Marsala) 538
  Museo Archeologico e Museo
  d'Arte Sacra (Massa Marittima)
  339
  Museo Archeologico Etrusco
  (Artimino) 332
  Museo Archeologico Faina
  (Orvieto) 362
  Museo Archeologico Nazionale
  (Aquileia) 168
  Museo Archeologico Nazionale
  (Cagliari) 555
  Museo Archeologico Nazionale
  (Cividale del Friuli) 167
  Museo Archeologico Nazionale
  (Ferrara) 265
  Museo Archeologico Nazionale
  (Naples) 479, **494–5**
  Museo Archeologico Nazionale
  (Sperlonga) 475
  Museo Archeologico Nazionale
  (Taranto) 515
  Museo Archeologico Nazionale
  (Venosa) 522
  Museo Archeologico Nazionale
  "G.A. Sanna" (Sassari) 552
  Museo Archeologico Nazionale
  Jatta (Ruvo di Puglia) 514
  Museo Archeologico Nazionale
  delle Marche (Ancona) 376, 377
  Museo Archeologico Nazionale
  dell'Umbria (Perugia) 357
  Museo Archeologico e Necropoli
  (Tarquinia) 470
  Museo Archeologico Oliveriano
  (Pèsaro) 372, 373
  Museo Archeologico Regionale
  (Palermo) 532
  Museo Archeologico Regionale
  Paolo Orsi (Siracusa) 547
  Museo di Architettura e Scultura
  Ligure (Genoa) 242
  Museo degli Argenti (Florence)
  306, 307
  Museo d'Arte (Pordenone) 166

Museums and galleries (cont.)
Museo d'Arte e di Ammobiliamento (Stupinigi) 229
Museo di Arte Contemporanea di Trento e Rovereto (MART, Rovereto) 179
Museo d'Arte Medioevale e Moderna (Arezzo) 333
Museo d'Arte Moderna "Emilio Greco" (Orvieto) 362
Museo delle Arti Popolari (Tolmezzo) 166
Museo Belliniano (Catania) 543
Museo della Canonica del Duomo (Novara) 231
Museo di Capodimonte (Naples) 497
Musei del Castello (Milan) 196
Museo della Cattedrale (Chiusi) 336
Museo della Cattedrale (Ferrara) 265
Museo delle Cere Anatomiche (Bologna) 269
Musei Civici (Pèsaro) 372, 373
Musei Civici e Galleria di Storia e Arte Antica (Udine) 166, 167
Museo Civico (Belluno) 165
Museo Civico (Cremona) 210
Museo Civico (Fano) 373
Museo Civico (Gubbio) 356
Museo Civico (Naples) 496
Museo Civico (Orvieto) 362
Museo Civico (Pavia) 207
Museo Civico (Piacenza) 262
Museo Civico (Prato) 332
Museo Civico (Rovereto) 179
Museo Civico (San Gimignano) 349
Museo Civico (Sansepolcro) 336
Museo Civico (Siena) 344
Museo Civico (Sulmona) 509
Museo Civico (Treviso) 164
Museo Civico (Vicenza) 156
Museo Civico d'Arte Antica (Turin) 225
Museo Civico Borgogna (Vercelli) 232
Museo Civico Eremitani (Padua) 162
Museo Civico Fiorelli (Lucera) 512
Museo Civico del Marmo (Carrara) 322
Museo Civico di San Francesco (Montefalco) 365
Museo Cordici (Erice) 537
Museo Correr (Venice) 112, **121**
Museo Cristiano (Cividale del Friuli) 167
Museo Diego di Aragona Pignatelli Cortes (Naples) 496
Museo Diocesano (Arezzo) 333
Museo Diocesano (Bressanone) 175
Museo Diocesano (Cortona) 336
Museo Diocesano (Rossano) 524
Museo Diocesano (Salerno) 502
Museo Diocesano (San Miniato) 332
Museo Diocesano (Urbino) 375
Museo Diocesano Tridentino (Trento) 178

Museums and galleries (cont.)
Museo del Duomo (Milan) 198
Museo Egizio (Turin) 226
Museo dell'Estuario (Torcello) 127
Museo Etnografico (San Pellegrino in Alpe) 322
Museo Etnografico Sardo (Nuoro) 554
Museo Etnografico Siciliano Pitré (Palermo) 533
Museo Etnografico di Teodone (Brunico) 175
Museo Etnografico della Val Varatella (Grotte di Toirano) 239
Museo Etrusco (Pitigliano) 351
Museo Etrusco-Romano (Todi) 363
Museo Faesulanum (Fiesole) 333
Museo Filangieri (Naples) 492
Museo Galileo (Florence) 289
Museo e Galleria Borghese (Rome) 443
Museo di Geologia e Etnografia (Predazzo) 177
Museo Guarnacci (Volterra) 338, 339
Museo Guttuso (Bagheria) 536
Museo Internazionale delle Ceramiche (Faenza) 270
Museo Ladino (Vigo di Fassa) 177
Museo Leonardiano (Vinci) 331
Museo Mandralisca (Cefalù) 539
Museo Marciano (Venice) 117
Museo del Merletto (Burano) 125
Museo della Miniera (Massa Marittima) 339
Museo di Mozia (Marsala) 538
Museo Multscher (Vipiteno) 174
Museo Navale Romano (Albenga) 239
Museo Nazionale (Locri Epizephiri) 525
Museo Nazionale (Ravenna) 271
Museo Nazionale d'Abruzzo (L'Aquila) 508
Museo Nazionale Alinari della Fotografia (Florence) 277, **301**
Museo Nazionale Archeologico (Palestrina) 472
Museo Nazionale dei Balzi Rossi (Balzi Rossi) 238
Museo Nazionale della Ceramica Duca di Martina (Naples) 497
Museo Nazionale Cerite (Cerveteri) 470
Museo Nazionale Etrusco (Chiusi) 336
Museo Nazionale Etrusco (Rome) 17, 444
Museo Nazionale Garibaldino (Isola Caprera) 552
Museo Nazionale della Magna Grecia (Reggio di Calabria) 525
Museo Nazionale del Melfese (Melfi) 522
Museo Nazionale di Metaponto (Metaponto) 523
Museo Nazionale Ridola (Matera) 523

Museums and galleries (cont.)
Museo Nazionale del Risorgimento (Turin) 227
Museo Nazionale Romano (Rome) 416
Museo Nazionale di San Marino (Naples) 496
Museo Nazionale di San Matteo (Pisa) 329
Museo Nazionale della Siritide (Policoro) 523
Museo Nazionale di Villa Guinigi (Lucca) 327
Museo dell'Opera del Duomo (Florence) 283
Museo dell'Opera del Duomo (Lucca) 324, 326–7
Museo dell'Opera del Duomo (Orvieto) 362
Museo dell'Opera del Duomo (Pisa) 329
Museo dell'Opera del Duomo (Siena) 342, **347**
Museo Paleocristiano (Aquileia) 168
Museo Pepoli (Trapani) 536
Museo-Pinacoteca (Loreto) 377
Museo Poldi-Pezzoli (Milan) 196
Museo dei Presepi (Bressanone) 175
Museo Provinciale (Gorizia) 167
Museo Provinciale (Salerno) 502
Museo Provinciale (Trento) 178
Museo Regionale (Messina) 542
Museo Regionale Archeologico (Agrigento) 539
Museo del Risorgimento (Venice) 121
Museo San Gimignano 1300 (San Gimignano) 349
Museo di San Marco (Florence) 280
Museo del Sannio (Benevento) 500, 501
Museo di Santa Giulia (Brescia) 207
Museo di Storia ed Arte ed Orto Lapidario (Trieste) 169
Museo Storico Italiano della Guerra (Rovereto) 179
Museo Storico Navale (Venice) 124
Museo Stradivariano (Cremona) 210
Museo Teatrale (Milan) 197
Museo del Tesoro (Aosta) 219
Museo e Tesoro del Duomo (Milan) 205
Museo del Tesoro di San Gennaro (Naples) 491
Museo del Tesoro di San Lorenzo (Genoa) 241
Museo del Tessile e del Costume (Spoleto) 365
Museo del Tessuto (Prato) 332
Museo della Tortura (Matera) 523
Museo della Val Gardena (Ortisei) 176
Museo Varisano (Enna) 541
Museo Vetrario (Murano) 125

Museums and galleries (cont.)
Museo Villa Puccini (Torre del Lago Puccini) 323
Museo Zuccarelli (Pitigliano) 351
Palazzo Bianco (Genoa) 242–3
Palazzo Davanzati (Florence) 296, **297**
Palazzo dei Diamanti (Ferrara) 265
Palazzo Pitti (Florence) 305, **306–7**
Palazzo della Ragione (Milan) 205
Palazzo Reale (Milan) 196, **198**
Palazzo Sturm (Bassano del Grappa) 153
Peggy Guggenheim Collection (Venice) 13, 95, **108–9**
Pinacoteca (Cagliari) 555
Pinacoteca (Rome) 425, 426
Pinacoteca Ambrosiana (Milan) 199
Pinacoteca Civica (Ascoli Piceno) 377
Pinacoteca Civica Tosio Martinengo (Brescia) 207
Pinacoteca Comunale (Assisi) 359
Pinacoteca Comunale (Todi) 363
Pinacoteca Comunale F Podesti e Galleria d'Arte Moderna (Ancona) 376, 377
Pinacoteca di Brera (Milan) 191, **202–3**
Pinacoteca Giovanni e Marella Agnelli (Turin) 227
Pinacoteca Malatestiana (Fano) 373
Pinacoteca e Musei Civici (Jesi) 376
Pinacoteca e Museo Civico (Volterra) 338, 339
Pinacoteca Nazionale (Bologna) 269
Pinacoteca Nazionale (Siena) 345
Pio-Christian Museum (Rome) 425
Pio-Clementine Museum (Rome) 425, 426
Uffizi (Florence) 13, 250, **290–93**
Vatican Museums (Rome) 12, 421, **424–7**
Villa Belgiojoso Bonaparte (Milan) 198
Villa Doria (Pegli) 243
Villa Grimaldi (Nervi) 243
Music 40–41
Antonio Stradivari and his violins 210
classical music and dance 449, 450
festivals 70–72
opera and classical music 27, **608**, 609
regional dance, music, and festivals 609
rock, jazz, and contemporary music 449, 450, **608**, 609
Muslims 617
Mussolini, Benito 68
Erice 537
EUR (Rome) 442
Palazzo Venezia (Rome) 388
Pontine marshes 465

Mussolini, Benito (cont.)
Republic of Salò 152
La Muta (Raphael) 375
Muti, Riccardo 41
Muttoni, Antonio 157
Mythology, Greek 485

N

Nanni di Banco
Four Crowned Martyrs 31
Naples 26, 487, 488, **490–97**
architecture 482
Discovering Italy 15
ferries 627
festivals 71, 72, 73
history 56, 60, 63, 64
map 490–91
Museo Archeologico Nazionale 494–5
Naples and Campania 487–503
climate 77
Exploring Naples and Campania 488–9
hotels 576
regional food 480
restaurants 600–601
Napoleon I, Emperor 44
Accademia (Venice) 110
conquest of Italy 47, 64, 65, 89
exile in Elba 350
and Farnese Hercules 495
and Pala d'Oro (Venice) 117
Piazza San Marco (Venice) 112
statue of 202
and the *Venus Italica* 306
Napoleon III, Emperor 67
monument to 199
Napoli, Tommaso Maria 532, 536
Nardi (Venice) 128, 129
Nardo di Cione 300
Natale Oggi (Rome) 448
National parks
Abruzzo, Lazio, e Molise 478, **510–11**
Delta del Po 271
Gran Paradiso 182, 215, **220–21**
Incisioni Rupestri 206
Maiella 509
Maremma 350
Monti Sibillini **366**, 369
Stelvio 193, **206**
Natisone, river 167
Natissa, river 168
'Ndrangheta 519
Neapolis 546
Necropoli Etrusca – Crocefisso del Tufo (Orvieto) 363
Nelli, Ottaviano 356
Nelson, Admiral 538
Nemi 471
Nemi, Lake 471
Nemours, Duke of
tomb of 299
Neri, San Filippo 402, 404
Nero, Emperor 52, 397, 517
Nervi 243
Nervi, Pier Luigi 35, 189
Nervia, river 238
New World (Tiepolo) 107

Newspapers 623
NH Hoteles 561
Niccolò di Tommaso
The Fall 331
Nicholas, St. 514
Nicholas II, Pope 522
Nicholas V, Pope 427
Nicholas the Pilgrim, St. 513
Nicolò di Angelo 446
Nicola di Bari 269
Nicolò di Pietro 99
Nicosia 541
Nigetti, Matteo 298
Nightlife
Rome 450
Ninfa 474
Noah and the Flood (mosaic) 117
Noasca 222
Nobel, Alfred 238
Norchia 470
Norcia 16, 353, **366–7**
Normans 56
architecture 482
Melfi 522
Palazzo Reale (Palermo) 530
Sicily 527
Northeast Italy 79–179
Discovering Italy 14
map 80–81
regional food 82–3
Northern League 26
Northwest Italy 181–247
architecture 178–9
Discovering Italy 14
map 182–3
regional food 184–5
wines 186–7
Noto 15, 527, **547**
La Notte Bianca (Rome) 72
Novara 231
Novelli, Pietro 532
Numa Pompilius, King 48
Numana 377
Nuoro 549, **554**
Nuovo Mercato Esquilino (Rome) 448
Nuovo Olimpia (Rome) 449, 450
Nuraghe **58**, 549

O

Oceanus Fountain (Giambologna) 307
Ognissanti (Florence) 301
Ognissanti Madonna (Giotto) 290
Olbia 549
Olivetti 25, 42, 43, 215
Oltrarno (Florence)
Street-by-Street map 304–5
Olympic Games (1960) 69
Ombrone estuary 350
Opening hours
banks 620
churches 615
museums 615
restaurants 578
shops 606
Opera 27, **41**, 608, 609
Opera Festival (Verona) 71

Ora
 festivals 70
Oratorio dei Filippini (Rome) 402
Oratorio del Rosario di Santa Cita
 (Palermo) 533
Oratorio del Rosario di San
 Domenico (Palermo) 532
Oratorio di San Giorgio (Padua) 163
Oratorio di San Lorenzo (Palermo)
 533
Oratorio di Santa Zita (Palermo) 482
Orbetello 351
Orbis (Rome) 449, 450
Orcagna, Andrea
 Cappella Strozzi frescoes
  (Florence) 300
 Cenacolo di Santo Spirito fresco
  (Florence) 304
 *Enthroned Christ with Madonna
  and Saints* 31
 Loggia dei Lanzi (Florence) 295
 Orsanmichele (Florence) 287
Orgosolo 554
Oristano 549, **554–5**
 festivals 70
Ormea 233
Oronzo, St. 517
Orsanmichele (Florence) 287
 Street-by-Street map 282
Orseolo, Pietro, Doge of Venice 56,
 112
Orsini, Duke Vicino 469
Orsini family 517
Orso, St.
 tomb of 219
Orta, Lake (Lago d'Orta) 231
Orta San Giulio 231
Ortigia 546
Ortisei (Sankt Ulrich) 176
Orvieto 353, **362–3**
 architecture 364
 Duomo 34, **362–3**
 A Gourmet Tour of Central Italy
  16
 A Tour of Etruscan Italy 17
Orvieto Classico wine 255
Ospedale del Ceppo (Pistoia) 331
Ossola valley 230
Osterias 578
Ostia Antica 471
Ostrogoths 54
Otranto 517
Ötzi 176
Outdoor activities 610–11
Outdoor entertainment in Rome
 449, 450
Ovid 38, 39, 405, **509**, 511
 birthplace 508
Oviesse (Milan) 200, 201

P

Padua 81, 143, **158–63**
 Cappella degli Scrovegni 160–61
 Discovering Italy 14
 Street-by-Street map 158–9
Padua University 45
 Street-by-Street map 159
Paestum 49, 484, 487, **502–3**
Pal Zileri (Milan) 200, 201

Palaces
 Ca' Foscari (Venice) 107
 Ca' d'Oro (Venice) 85, 93, **98–9**
 Ca' Pesaro (Venice) 85, 93
 Ca' Rezzonico (Venice) 107
 Palace of Septimius Severus
  (Rome) 399
 Palazzo Abatellis (Palermo) 533
 Palazzo Altemps (Rome) 404
 Palazzo Altieri (Rome) 407
 Palazzo Antinori (Florence) 301
 Palazzo Barbaro (Venice) 94
 Palazzo Barberini (Rome) 415
 Palazzo Barzizza (Venice) 95
 Palazzo di Bianca Cappello
  (Florence) 304
 Palazzo Bianco (Genoa) 242–3
 Palazzo del Bo (Padua) 163
 Palazzo Borromeo (Isola Bella) 195
 Palazzo Braschi (Rome) 402
 Palazzo della Cancelleria (Rome)
  404–5
 Palazzo Capello Malipiero (Venice)
  94
 Palazzo del Capitanio (Padua) 158
 Palazzo del Capitano (Verona) 148
 Palazzo Carignano (Turin) 188, 227
 Palazzo Chiericati 84
 Palazzo del Comune (Ferrara) 265
 Palazzo del Comune (Piacenza)
  262
 Palazzo dei Conservatori (Rome)
  391
 Palazzo dei Consoli (Gubbio) 356
 Palazzo Corsini (Rome) 432
 Palazzo Dario (Venice) 95
 Palazzo Davanzati (Florence) 296,
  297
 Palazzo Doria Pamphilj (Rome)
  406, **408**
 Palazzo Ducale (Genoa) 240
 Palazzo Ducale (Gubbio) 356
 Palazzo Ducale (Mantua) 211
 Palazzo Ducale (Urbino) 251, 256,
  374–5
 Palazzo Ducale (Venice) 13, 113,
  118–20
 Palazzo Farnese (Caprarola) 384,
  469
 Palazzo Farnese (Rome) **405**, 441
 Palazzo Garzoni (Venice) 94
 Palazzo Giustinian (Venice) 107
 Palazzo del Governatore (Parma)
  25
 Palazzo Grassi (Venice) 94
 Palazzo Gritti-Pisani (Venice) 95
 Palazzo Guadagni (Florence) 304
 Palazzo Guicciardini (Florence) 305
 Palazzo Labia (Venice) 92
 Palazzo Madama (Rome) 403
 Palazzo Madama (Turin) 225
 Palazzo Maffei (Verona) 148
 Palazzo Michiel dalle Colonne
  (Venice) 93
 Palazzo Mocenigo (Venice) 94
 Palazzo dei Musei (Modena) 264
 Il Palazzo Nonfinito (Venice) 109
 Palazzo dei Normanni (Palermo)
  527, 530

Palaces (cont.)
 Palazzo Nuovo (Rome) 389, **390**
 Palazzo Pandolfini (Florence) 278
 Palazzo di Parte Guelfa (Florence)
  297
 Palazzo Pfanner (Lucca) 327
 Palazzo Piccolomini (Siena) 345
 Palazzo Pilotta (Parma) 263
 Palazzo Pitti (Florence) 13, 250,
  305, **306–7**
 Palazzo del Popolo (San
  Gimignano) 348
 Palazzo dei Priori (Perugia) 357
 Palazzo Pubblico (Siena) 343, 344
 Palazzo della Ragione (Padua) 159
 Palazzo della Ragione (Verona)
  148
 Palazzo Reale (Caserta) 482
 Palazzo Reale (Genoa) 242
 Palazzo Reale (Naples) 497
 Palazzo Reale (Turin) 228
 Palazzo dei Rettori (Belluno) 165
 Palazzo Rosso (Genoa) 243
 Palazzo Rucellai (Florence) 301
 Palazzo Sagredo (Venice) 93
 Palazzo Schifanoia (Ferrara) 265
 Palazzo Senatorio (Rome) 389
 Palazzo Spada (Rome) 405
 Palazzo Strozzi (Florence) 256, 296,
  297
 Palazzo Tè (Mantua) 211
 Palazzo Valmarana Braga (Vicenza)
  154
 Palazzo Vecchio (Florence) 13, **295**
 Palazzo Vendramin Calergi
  (Venice) 93
 Palazzo Venezia (Rome) 388
 Palazzo Vescovile (Lecce) 516
 Palazzo Zenobio (Venice) 106
 see also Villas
Palalottomatica (Rome) 449, 450
Palatine (Rome) 398–9
Palau 552
Palazzina di Caccia di Stupinigi 229
Palermo 527, 529, **530–33**
 Discovering Italy 15
 ferries 627
 map 530–31
Palestrina 467, **472**
Palestrina, Giovanni Pierluigi da
 40, 62
Palio (Asti) 72
Palio (Siena) 345
Palladio, Andrea 35, 80, 143
 Accademia (Venice) 110
 Arco Bollani (Udine) 166
 Loggia del Capitaniato (Vicenza)
  155
 memorial 154
 Palazzo Chiericati (Vicenza) 84,
  156
 Palazzo Ducale (Venice) 120
 Palazzo Valmarana Braga (Vicenza)
  154
 Piazza della Loggia (Brescia) 207
 Piazza dei Signori (Vicenza) 155
 Ponte degli Alpini (Bassano del
  Grappa) 143, **153**
 portrait of 62, 84

Palladio, Andrea (cont.)
  Il Redentore (Venice) 125
  La Rotonda (Vicenza) 157
  San Giorgio Maggiore (Venice) 125
  Santa Maria Gloriosa dei Frari (Venice) 103
  Teatro Olimpico (Vicenza) 156
  Vicenza 154, 155
  Villa Barbaro (Masèr) 84, 153
  Villa Emo (Fanzolo) 153
  Villa Foscari (Malcontenta) 164
Pallavicini, Cardinal 433
Palma, Andrea 483, 546
Palma il Giovane 101, 123
Palma il Vecchio
  St. Barbara 123
Palmanova 168
The Palmieri Rotonda (Fattori) 307
Pamphilj family 408
Panarea 537
Panciatichi, Lucrezia 33
Pannini, Giovanni
  Gallery of Views of Ancient Rome 64
Pantalica 546
Pantelleria 537
Pantheon (Rome) 12, 53, 381, 385, **408**
  Street-by-Street map 406–7
Paolo Olbi (Venice) 129
Papal Address (Rome) 70
Papal States 259, 353, 465
Paperback Exchange (Florence) 310
Papier Mâché (Venice) 128, 129
Il Papiro (Florence) 310
Il Papiro (Rome) 447, 448
Paradise (Tintoretto) 118, 120
Parco delle Cascine (Florence) 310
Parco Delta del Po 271
Parco della Musica (Rome) 449, 450, 609
Parco Nazionale d'Abruzzo, Lazio, e Molise 478, **510–11**
Parco Nazionale del Gran Paradiso 182, 215, **220–21**
Parco Nazionale delle Incisioni Rupestri 206
Parco Nazionale dello Stelvio 193, **206**
Parco dell'Orecchiella 322
Parenti (Florence) 310
Parigi, Giulio 281
Parking 631
Parks and gardens
  Boboli Gardens (Florence) 13, **307**
  Botanical Gardens (Rome) 432
  Giardino Botanico Alpino Retia (Bormio) 206
  Giardino Giusti (Verona) 149
  Giardino del Lago (Rome) 442
  La Mortella (Forie) 503
  Ninfa 474
  Orto Botanico (Padua) 163
  Orto Botanico (Palermo) 533
  Orto Botanico (Turin) 227
  Orto Botanico Pania di Corfino 322
  Palazzo Pfanner (Lucca) 327
  Paradisia Alpine Garden 221
  Parco della Favorita (Palermo) 533

Parks and gardens (cont.)
  Parco Municipale (Nervi) 243
  Parco Savelli (Rome) 435
  Parco Sempione (Milan) 199
  Parco del Valentino (Turin) 227
  Vatican Gardens (Rome) 421
  Villa Barbarigo 163
  Villa Borghese (Rome) 17, 442
  Villa d'Este (Tivoli) 472
  Villa Giulia (Palermo) 533
  Villa Hanbury 238
  Villa Lante (Viterbo) 469
Parma 16, 25, 259, **263**
Parma ham 263
Parmesan cheese 263
Parmigianino 263
  Madonna and Angels 33
  Madonna of the Long Neck 293
Parodi 242
Paschal I, Pope 433, 438
Paschal II, Pope 416
Pasolini, Pier Paolo 28, 69
Pasquino (Rome)
  Street-by-Street map 402
Passes, trains 628
Passignano sul Trasimeno 357
Passirio, river 174
Passo del Gavia 193
Passports 560, 614
Pasticcerias 578
Patrizia Reppe (Florence) 304
Paul, St. 52, 517
  Catacombs (Rome) 446
  Mamertine Prison (Rome) 393
  San Paolo fuori le Mura (Rome) 446
  Via Appia Antica (Rome) 445
Paul III, Pope 389, 405, 430
Paul IV, Pope 405
Paul V, Pope 417, 442
Pavia 54, **207–9**
  Certosa di Pavia 183, 191, **208–9**
Pavia, Battle of (1525) 61
PayPal 559
Pazzi Chapel *see* Santa Croce (Florence)
Peck (Milan) 200, 201
Peggy Guggenheim Collection (Venice) 13, 95, **108–9**
Pegli 243
Pegna (Florence) 310
Pelagic Islands 537
Penne 508
Pensioni 558
Pentedattilo 519
Pepin, King of the Franks 55
  tomb of 150
Peppe Peluso (Florence) 310
La Perla (Florence) 310
Perle e Dintorni (Venice) 128, 129
Permesso di soggiorno 614
Persephone 485, 541
Perseus (Cellini) 295
Personal security 618–19
Perugia 16, 353, **356–7**
  festivals 71

Perugia (cont.)
  town square 58–9
Perugino, Pietro 205, 293, 365, 431
  Certosa di Pavia altarpiece 209
  Christ Delivering the Keys of the Kingdom to St. Peter 32
  Collegio del Cambio frescoes (Perugia) 357
  Handing over the Keys of St. Peter 60
  Madonna in Glory 269
  Perugia 356
  Sistine Chapel (Rome) 430
Peruzzi, Baldassare 432
Pesarina Valley 166
Pèsaro 372–3
  festivals 71
Pescasseroli 510
Peschici 512
Peschiera 152
Peter, St. 37, 52
  Catacombs (Rome) 446
  Mamertine Prison (Rome) 393
  St. Peter's (Rome) 422–3
  San Pietro in Vincoli (Rome) 416
  Tempietto (Rome) 433
  Vatican 419
  Via Appia Antica (Rome) 445
Peter of Aragon 58
Peter of Illyria 441
Peter Martyr, St. 36
Petralia, Fra Umile di 541
Petrarch 38, 40, 265, 275
  Casa di Petrarca (Padua) 163
  portraits of 39, 58, 158
  San Lorenzo Maggiore (Naples) 492
Petronius, St.
  tomb of 269
Pharmacies 619
Phidias 525
Phoenicians 538, 555
Piacenza 259, 260, **262**
Piaggio 43
Pianegonda (Milan) 200, 201
Piano, Renzo 189
Piano Grande 366
Pianta, Francesco 104
Pianura Padana 259
Piazza Armerina 15, **541**
Piazza della Bocca della Verità (Rome)
  Street-by-Street map 436–7
Piazza del Campidoglio (Rome) 389
  Street-by-Street map 388–9
Piazza del Campo (Siena) 343
Piazza dei Cavalieri (Pisa) 329
Piazza Cavour (Bologna)
  Street-by-Street map 266
Piazza della Cisterna (San Gimignano)
  Street-by-Street map 349
Piazza Colonna (Rome) 409
Piazza delle Erbe (Padua)
  Street-by-Street map 159
Piazza Erbe (Verona) 148
Piazza della Minerva (Rome) 406
Piazza di Montecitorio (Rome) 409
Piazza Napoleone (Lucca)
  Street-by-Street map 324

Piazza Navona (Rome) 12, 380, **401–9**
　area map 401
　Street-by-Street map 402–3
Piazza della Repubblica (Florence)
　Street-by-Street map 296–7
Piazza San Marco (Venice) 13
　Street-by-Street map 112–13
Piazza San Matteo (Genoa)
　Street-by-Street map 240
Piazza San Pietro (Rome) 420, 423
Piazza dei Signori (Verona) 148
Piazza dei Signori (Vicenza) 155
　Street-by-Street map 155
Piazza della Signoria (Florence) 13, **294–5**
Piazza di Spagna (Rome) 12, **413**
　Street-by-Street map 412–13
Piazzale Michelangelo (Florence) 308
Piazzetta, Giovanni Battista 110
Picasso, Pablo
　ceramics 270
　The Poet 109
Piccolomini family 345
Pickpockets 618
Pie' di Marmo (Rome) 407
Piedmont *see* Valle d'Aosta and Piedmont
Pienza 337
　architecture 256
Piero della Francesca 196, 202, 319, 357
　birthplace 336
　The Dream of Constantine 31
　The Duke and Duchess of Urbino 291, 292
　The Flagellation 374
　Fresco of Malatesta and St. Sigismund 270
　Legend of the True Cross 334–5
　Madonna della Misericordia 336
　Madonna del Parto 336
　Mary Magdalene 333
　The Resurrection 31, 336
Piero di Cosimo 281
Pierozzi, Antonino 280
Pietà (Bellini) 112, 427
Pietà (Mazzoni) 493
Pietà (Michelangelo) 423
Pietro da Cortona
　Annunciation 336
　Chiesa Nuova (Rome) 404
　Palazzo Barberini (Rome) 415
　Palazzo Pitti (Florence) 306
　The Rape of the Sabine Women 391
　Santa Maria della Pace (Rome) 402, **404**
Pietro da Domenico
　Adoration of the Shepherds 345
Pietro Leopoldo, Grand Duke of Tuscany 287
Pigafetta, Antonio 155
Pila, Jacopo della 493
Pilet, Christophe 42
Pinacoteca (Rome) 425, 426, 427
Pinacoteca di Brera (Milan) 191, **202–3**

Pinerolo 223
Pininfarina 42
Pinturicchio 349
　Adoration of the Magi 427
　Annunciation 366
　Duomo frescoes (Siena) 346
　Funeral of San Bernardino 389
　Madonna and Child 364
　Santa Maria del Popolo frescoes (Rome) 414
Pinzolo 178
Pio, Padre
　tomb of 512
Pio-Christian Museum (Rome) 425, 427
Pio-Clementine Museum (Rome) 425, 426
Pio Monte della Misericordia (Naples) 491
Piola, Domenico 242, 243
Piombino
　ferries 627
Piramidi di Segonzano 177
Pirandello, Luigi 39
Piranesi, Giovanni Battista
　View of the Roman Forum 65
Pirelli 25
Pirelli building (Milan) 35
Pisa 13, 319, **328–30**
　airport 624–5
　Discovering Italy 14
　festivals 71
　A Gourmet Tour of Central Italy 16
　Leaning Tower 250, 319, 328, **330**
Pisanello 98, 147, 148, 211
　Leonello d'Este 205
Pisano, Andrea 362
　Baptism of St. John the Baptist 30
　Baptistry doors (Florence) 284
　Campanile reliefs (Florence) 284
　Madonna del Latte 329
Pisano, Bonanno 328
Pisano, Giovanni 347
　Baptistry (Pisa) 30, 328
　Duomo pulpit (Siena) 346
　Fontana Maggiore (Perugia) 356
　Pisa Duomo pulpit 328
　San Giovanni Fuorcivitas (Pistoia) 331
　tomb of Margaret of Brabant 240
　Virgin and Child 329
Pisano, Nicola 329
　Baptistry (Pisa) 30, 328
　Duomo pulpit (Siena) 346
　Fontana Maggiore (Perugia) 58, 356
　San Martino (Lucca) 326
　tomb of St. Dominic 269
Piscopia, Elena 159
Pistoia 331
Pitigliano 350–51
Pitti, Luca 250, 306
Pitti Immagine Uomo (Florence) 73
Pius II, Pope
　Duomo (Pienza) 256
　Duomo (Siena) 346
　Logge del Papa (Siena) 343
　Pienza 337
　Tempio Malatestiano (Rimini) 270

Pius V, Pope 427
Pius VII, Pope 65
Pius IX, Pope 67, 412
Pizzerias 578
Pizzo 520, 524
Plato 61, 485
Plautus 39
Pliny the Elder 39, 45, 499
　statue of 148
Pliny the Younger 499
Po, river 191, 259
Po Delta 16, 260, **270–71**
Poccetti, Bernardino 280
Poets 38–9
Poggi, Giuseppe 308
Poggio a Caiano 257, 332
Poldi-Pezzoli, Giacomo 196
Police 619
Policoro 523
Politics 28
Pollaiolo, Antonio 287
　Portrait of a Young Woman 196
　Tobias and the Archangel Raphael 226–7
Pollaiolo, Piero
　Coronation of the Virgin 349
　Tobias and the Archangel Raphael 226–7
Pollock, Jackson 109
Polo, Maffeo 57
Polo, Marco 44, 45, 56–7, 58
Polo, Nicolò 56, 57
Polyclitus 426, 525
Polyptych (Bellini) 122
Pomarancio, Niccolò 438
Pomellato (Florence) 310
Pompeii 51, 479, 487, **498–9**
　Discovering Italy 15
　excavations 64
　House of the Vettii 52–3
　Museo Archeologico Nazionale (Naples) 494, 495
Pompey 50, 51
Ponte dei Pugni (Venice)
　Street-by-Street map 107
Ponte Rotto (Rome) 436
Ponte Santa Trinita (Florence)
　Street-by-Street map 296
Ponte Scaligero (Verona) 147
Ponte delle Torri (Spoleto) 364–5
Ponte Vecchio (Florence) 13, 275, 276, **289**, 308
Ponti, Gio 35, 189, 199
Pontine marshes 465
Pontormo, Jacopo
　The Annunciation 308
　Charity 293
　Cosimo il Vecchio 293
　The Deposition 308
　Santissima Annunziata frescoes (Florence) 281
　Venus and Cupid 279
　The Visitation 332
Ponzio, Flaminio 417, 443
Poor Clares 359
Pope Innocent X (Velázquez) 408
Pope Julius II (Raphael) 61
Pordenone 166

Il Pordenone 99, 100, 164, 166
Porta Capuana (Naples) 490
Porta Portese (Rome) 448
Porta Rudiae (Lecce)
    Street-by-Street map 516
Porta Soprana (Genoa)
    Street-by-Street map 241
Porto, Luigi da 149
    tomb of 156
Porto Cervo 552
Porto Ercole 351
Porto Santo Stefano 351
Portofino 183, 235, 244
Portofino Peninsula 244
Portonovo 371, 377
Portovenere 245
Portrait of Alfonso I d'Este (Titian)
    265
Portrait of Lucrezia Panciatichi
    (Bronzino) 33
Portrait of Moisè Kisling (Modigliani)
    203
*Portrait of Pope Paul III Farnese with
    His Nephews* (Titian) 33
Portrait of a Young Man in a Red Hat
    (Carpaccio) 121
Portrait of a Young Woman
    (Pollaiuolo) 196
Positano 15, 501
Post offices 623
Pound, Ezra 244
Poussin, Nicolas 442
Pozzo, Andrea 63, 406, 409
Pozzo di San Patrizio (Orvieto) 363
Pozzuoli 487
Prada 25, 43
Prada (Florence) 310
Prada (Milan) 200, 201
Prada (Rome) 447, 448
Prada, Miuccia 43
Praiano 501
Prato 57, **332**
Praxiteles 443
Predazzo 177
Prehistoric sites 171
    Balzi Rossi 238
    Grotte di Toirano 239
    Pantalica 546
    Sardinian *nuraghe* 549, **553**
    Val Camonica 206
Preti, Mattia 491, 492
Primavera (Botticelli) 292, 293
Private couriers 623
Prizzi
    festivals 70
Procacci (Florence) 310
Procession of the Grieving
    Madonna (Procida) 70
Procession of the Macchina di Santa
    Rosa (Viterbo) 72
The Procession of the Magi (Gozzoli)
    60–61
Procida 487, **503**
    festivals 70
Promod (Venice) 128, 129
Protestant Cemetery (Rome) 441
Provenzano, Bernardo 539
Public restrooms 617
Public holidays 73

Puccini, Giacomo 41
    Casa di Puccini (Lucca) 324, 325
    Museo Villa Puccini (Torre del
        Lago Puccini) 323
    Torre del Lago Puccini 323
    Tosca 402
Puglia *see* Abruzzo, Molise, and
    Puglia
Punic Wars 50, 51
Punta Colomion 222
Punta della Dogana (Venice) 95, **109**
Pyramid of Caius Cestius (Rome)
    441
Pyrrhus, King 50
Pythagoras 485, 523

Q

Qantas 625
Quartieri Spagnoli (Naples) 487, 496
Quercia, Jacopo della 286, 327, 347
    Baptismal font 346
    Baptistry (Siena) 342
    Fonte Gaia 343, 345
    Madonna of the Pomegranate 265
    San Frediano altarpiece (Lucca)
        325
    tomb of Anton Galeazzo
        Bentivoglio 267
    tomb of Ilaria del Carretto 326
Quercioli (Florence) 309

R

Radio 623
Raffaello da Brescia 269
Ragusa 527, 547
Railroads *see* Trains
Raimondo, Prince 491
Rainfall 76–7
Rainulf 56
Ramparts (Lucca) 327
Randazzo, Filippo 531
Rapallo 244
The Rape of Proserpina (Bernini) 443,
    541
The Rape of the Sabine Women
    (Giambologna) 295
The Rape of the Sabine Women
    (Pietro da Cortona) 391
Raphael 60, 61, 202, 205, 207, 357
    *Angel Delivering St. Peter from
        Prison* 32
    Casa Natale di Raffaello (Urbino) 375
    Chigi chapel, Santa Maria del
        Popolo (Rome) 414
    Deposition 443
    Donna Velata 306
    Ecstasy of St. Cecilia 269
    La Fornarina 415
    Madonna of the Chair 306
    Madonna of Foligno 427
    Madonna of the Goldfinch 32, 293
    Marriage of the Virgin 203
    The Mass of Bolsena 431
    monument to 444
    La Muta 375
    Palazzo Pandolfini (Florence) 278
    Pope Julius II 61
    Raphael Rooms (Vatican Museums,
        Rome) 12, 420, 424, **431**

Raphael (cont.)
    Santa Maria della Pace (Rome)
        402, **404**
    The School of Athens 32, 199, 420,
        431
    Three Graces 432
    Transfiguration 427
    Villa Farnesina frescoes (Rome)
        432
Rassegna del Chianti Classico
    (Chianti) 72
Ratchis, King 167
Ravello 15, 489, 501
Ravenna 259, **271–3**
    history 54
    mosaics 272–3
Red Brigades 69
Regata Storica (Venice) 72
Reggio di Calabria 525
Relaix & Châteaux 561
Religious services 616
    see also Catholic Church;
        Christianity
Rembrandt 227, 293
Remus *see* Romulus and Remus
Renaissance 60–61
    architecture 35, 384
    early Renaissance art 30–31
    High Renaissance art 32–3
    music 40
    scientists 44–5
René Caovilla (Milan) 200, 201
Reni, Guido 264, 269, 293, 329, 373,
    377
    Salome 432
Rentals
    bicycles 633
    cars 631
Reservations
    hotels 559
    restaurants 578–9
    trains 629
Respighi, Ottorino 41,
    443
Responsible travel
    617
Restaurants 578–605
    Abruzzo, Molise, and Puglia 602–3
    Basilicata and Calabria 603
    children in 579
    dress code 579
    eating hours 578
    Emilia-Romagna 590–92
    Florence 592
    in hotels 559
    Lazio 599–600
    Liguria 589–90
    Lombardy 584–6
    Le Marche 595–6
    menus 578–9
    Naples and Campania 600–601
    paying 579
    reservations 578
    Rome 596–9
    Sardinia 604–5
    Sicily 603–4
    smoking 579
    tipping 615
    Trentino–Alto Adige 583–4

Restaurants (cont.)
Tuscany 592–4
types of 578
Umbria 594–5
Valle D'Aosta and Piedmont 586–9
vegetarian food 579
Veneto and Friuli 581–3
Venice 580–81
wheelchair access 579
wine and drinks 579
see also Food and drink
The Resurrection (Piero della Francesca) 31, 336
Rezzonico family 107
Rialto (Venice) 13, **101**
Street-by-Street map 101
Rialto Bridge (Venice) 93
Rialto Markets (Venice)
Street-by-Street map 100
Riario, Cardinal Domenico 432
Riario, Girolamo 404
Riario, Raffaele 405
Ribera, José 492, 493
Ricci, Marco 111
Ricci, Sebastiano 165
Il Riccio 162
Ricordi Music Store (Rome) 449, 450
Rienzo, Cola di 59
Riina, Toto 539
Rimini 259, **270**
Rinaldo, Muccio and Francesco di 344
La Rinascente (Florence) 310
La Rinascente (Milan) 200, 201
Rio di Pusteria 175
Riomaggiore 237, 245
Risorgimento **66–7**, 215
Museo del Risorgimento (Venice) 121
Museo Nazionale del Risorgimento (Turin) 227
Ristorantes 578
Riva del Garda 152
Riva del Vin (Venice) 95
Rivello 520, 523
Riviera Levante 235
Rizzo, Antonio 118, 120, 164
Rizzo (Venice) 128, 129
Roads 630
Roman 51
Robbia, Andrea della 508
Madonna degli Angeli 536
Spedale degli Innocenti roundels (Florence) 279, **281**
Robbia, Giovanni della 331
Robbia, Luca della
choir loft 283
Pazzi Chapel roundels (Florence) 288
Santa Croce (Florence) 256
San Miniato al Monte roundels (Florence) 308
Robert the Wise of Anjou 58, 492, 493
Roberti, Ercole de' 269
Roberto Cavalli (Venice) 128, 129
Rocco, San (St. Roch) 104
Rock music 608, **609**
Rome 449, 450

Rodi Garganico 512
Rodriguez, Cardinal tomb of 417
Roger, King of Naples 501
Roger II, King of Sicily 56
Bari castle 514
Cefalù cathedral 482, 539
La Martorana (Palermo) 532
Palazzo Reale (Palermo) 530
tomb of 531
Roma per Tutti 617
Romagna see Emilia-Romagna
Roman Empire 47
architecture 34, **384–5**
Battle of Lake Trasimeno 357
classical Roman writers 39
from Republic to Empire 50–51
Golden Age 52–3
roads 51
splitting of the Empire 54–5
Veneto and Friuli 143
Roman Forum (Rome) 12
Roman remains
Amiternum 508
Aosta 219
Aquileia 168
Benevento 500
Bologna 51
Campania 487
Elea 502
Fano 373
Lecce 517
Lucca 326
Lucera 512
Milan 204
Ostia Antica 471
Pompeii 51, **498–9**
Rome, Ancient Center 387–99
Santa Maria Capua Vetere 500
Sardinia 51
Siracusa 546, 547
Susa 222
Temples of the Forum Boarium (Rome) 437
Terracina 475
Tindari 542
Venosa 522
Verona 53, 147, 149
Zuglio 166
Romanelli (Florence) 310
Romanesque architecture 34
Northwest Italy 188
Southern Italy 482
Umbrian churches 364–5
Romans of the Decadence (Couture) 399
Rome 379–463
airports 624–5
Ancient Center 387–99
Arch of Constantine 34
Aventine and Lateran 435–41
bus routes 462–3
Capitoline Museums 381, 388, **390–91**
Colosseum 52, 65, 381, 387, **397**
Discovering Italy 12
entertainment 449–50
festivals 70, 71, 72, 73
Further Afield 442–6

Rome (cont.)
Gesù 35
Golden Age 52–3
hotels 573–6
intercity buses 633
Jubilee 69
map 23
Northeast Rome 411–17
Palatine 398–9
Piazza Navona 401–9
Raphael Rooms 431
Roman Forum 394–6
sack of (1527) 61, 62
St. Peter's 380, 419, 420, **422–3**
San Clemente 439
San Giovanni in Laterano 440
Santa Maria Maggiore 381, **417**
shopping 447–8
Sistine Chapel 32, **428–30**
Street-by-Street maps
Around the Pantheon 406–7
Around Piazza Navona 402–3
The Capitoline Hill 388–9
Piazza della Bocca della Verità 436–7
Piazza di Spagna 412–13
Street Finder 451–61
A Tour of Etruscan Italy 17
Vatican and Trastevere 419–33
Rome, Treaty of (1957) 69
Rome and Lazio 379–475
architecture 384–5
climate 77
map 380–81
regional food 382–3
Romeo and Juliet **149**, 156, 211
Romulus and Remus 48, 395, 398, 399, 465
Rondanini Pietà (Michelangelo) 196
Rosolino, Massimiliano 75
Rossano 524
Rosselli, Cosimo 305
Rossellini, Roberto 69
Rossellino, Antonio 493
Rossellino, Bernardo
The Annunciation 333
Duomo (Pienza) 256
Madonna 333
Palazzo Piccolomini (Siena) 345
Pienza 337
tomb of Leonardo Bruni 288
Rossini, Gioacchino 40, 41, 67
birthplace 372
Casa Rossini (Pèsaro) 372–3
Rossini Festival (Pèsaro) 71
Rosso Fiorentino 329
The Deposition 336, 338
Moses Defends the Daughters of Jethro 33
Santissima Annunziata frescoes (Florence) 281
Rosticcerie 578
Rothko, Mark 109
La Rotonda (Vicenza) 157
Rovereto 179
Rubelli (Venice) 128, 129
Rubens, Peter Paul 202, 211, 243, 293, 432

Rubens, Peter Paul (cont.)
Chiesa Nuova paintings (Rome) 404
Rucellai, Giovanni 301
Rucellai Madonna (Duccio di Buoninsegna) 30
Ruffo, Niccolò
tomb of 525
Rugby 74
Ruggieri, Ferdinando 308
Ruina Dantesca 179
Rules of the road 630
Ruskin, Effie 98
Russi, Franco 264
Ruvo di Puglia 483, **514**
Ryanair 625

S

Sa Sartiglia (Oristano) 70
Sabbioneta 210
Sabines 465
Sacra di San Michele 223
Sacred and Profane Love (Titian) 443
The Sacrifice of Isaac (Brunelleschi) 287
Safety, cars 631
Sagra delle Mandorle in Fiore (Agrigento) 73
Sagra Musicale Lucchese (Lucca) 70
Sagra del Tordo (Montalcino) 72
Sailing 611
St. Augustine (Carpaccio) 61
St. Barbara (Palma il Vecchio) 123
St. Bernard Pass 218
St. Francis (Cimabue) 358
St. Francis Altarpiece (Berlinghieri) 30
St. George (Donatello) 282
St. George Slaying the Dragon (Carpaccio) 124
St. Jerome (Leonardo da Vinci) 425, 427
St. Jerome with Saints Christopher and Augustine (Bellini) 99
St. John the Baptist (Caravaggio) 391
St. Mark's (Venice) *see* Basilica di San Marco
St. Peter and a Donor (Ferrari) 226
St. Peter's (Rome) 12, 380, 419, 420, **422–3**
history 54, 63
Saints and symbols in Italian art 36–7
Salerno 56, **502**
Salimbeni, Giacomo 375
Salimbeni, Lorenzo 375
Sallust 508
Salò, Republic of 152
Salomé (Titian) 406
Salvagente (Milan) 200, 201
Salvi, Nicola 414
Sammartino, Giuseppe
The Dead Christ 491
San Barnaba (Venice)
Street-by-Street map 107
San Benedetto (Subiaco) 473
San Carlo alle Quattro Fontane (Rome) 415
San Cassiano (Venice)
Street-by-Street map 100

San Clemente (Rome) 12, **439**
San Domenico (Bologna) 269
San Domenico (Palermo) 532
San Domenico (Siena) 345
San Domenico Maggiore (Naples) 493
San Domino 511
San Fermo Maggiore (Verona) 147
San Francesco (Arezzo) 334–5
San Francesco a Ripa (Rome) 433
San Frediano (Lucca) 325
San Galgano 339
San Giacomo Maggiore (Bologna) 267
Street-by-Street map 267
San Giacomo dell'Orio (Venice) 101
San Giacomo di Rialto (Venice)
Street-by-Street map 101
San Gimignano 27, **348–9**
Discovering Italy 14
Street-by-Street map 348–9
A Tour of Etruscan Italy 17
San Giobbe Altarpiece (Bellini) 32
San Giorgio Albanese 519
San Giorgio in Braida (Verona) 149
San Giorgio Maggiore (Venice) 85, **124–5**
San Giorgio in Ragusa 483
San Giorgio in Velabro (Rome) 437
San Giovanni in Bragora (Venice) 124
San Giovanni Decollato (Rome) 436
San Giovanni Elemosinario (Venice)
Street-by-Street map 100
San Giovanni degli Eremiti (Palermo) 530
San Giovanni Fuorcivitas (Pistoia) 331
San Giovanni Grisostomo (Venice) 99
San Giovanni in Laterano (Rome) 381, **440**
San Giovanni Rotondo 512
San Gregorio Armeno (Naples) 492
San Leo 369, **372**
San Leucio 500
San Lorenzo (Duomo, Genoa) 241
Street-by-Street map 240
San Lorenzo (Florence) 298–9
San Lorenzo (Verona) 147
San Lorenzo (Vicenza) 157
San Lorenzo Maggiore (Milan) 204
San Lorenzo Maggiore (Naples) 492
San Luigi dei Francesi (Rome) 404
Street-by-Street map 403
San Marco (Rome) 388
San Marco (Venice) 56
San Marco area (Florence)
Street-by-Street map 278–9
San Marco in Lamis 512
San Marino 369, **372**
San Marino Grand Prix 74
San Martino (Lucca) 326
Street-by-Street map 325
San Martino di Castrozza 177
San Michele (Carmignano) 332
San Michele in Foro (Lucca) 325
Street-by-Street map 324
San Miniato 332
festivals 70

San Miniato al Monte (Florence) 308
San Nicolò dei Mendicoli (Venice) 108
San Pantalon (Venice) 105
San Paolo fuori le Mura (Rome) 446
San Pellegrino in Alpe 322
San Petronio (Bologna) 268–9
Street-by-Street map 266
San Pietro in Montorio (Rome) 433
San Pietro in Valle 367
San Pietro in Vincoli (Rome) 416
San Polo (Venice) 101
Street-by-Street map 100–101
San Rabano 351
San Rocco (Venice) 105
San Satiro (Milan) 199
San Sebastiano (Venice) 108
San Severo 512
San Teodoro (Rome) 437
San Vitale (Ravenna) 54–5, 251
San Zaccaria (Venice) 123
San Zanipolo (Venice) *see* Santi Giovanni e Paolo
San Zeno Maggiore (Verona) 150–51
Sanctis, Francesco de 413
Sangallo, Antonio da 469
Fortezza Medicea (Arezzo) 333
Palazzo Farnese (Rome) 405
Pozzo di San Patrizio (Orvieto) 363
Sangallo, Francesco da 285, 287
Sangallo, Giuliano da
Basilica (Loreto) 377
Palazzo Strozzi (Florence) 297
Poggio a Caiano 257, 332
Santo Spirito (Florence) 305
Sangro di Sansevero, Princes di 491
Sankt Ulrich *see* Ortisei
Sanmicheli, Michele 149
Sanremo 182, 235, 237, **238**
Sanremo Car Rally 75
Sansepolcro 336
Sansovino, Andrea
Basilica (Loreto) 377
Santa Maria in Domnica (Rome) 438
Sansovino, Jacopo
Madonna and Child 98
Palazzo Ducale (Venice) 118, 120
tomb of 117
Zecca (Venice) 113
Sant'Agnese in Agone (Rome) 401
Street-by-Street map 403
Sant'Agnese fuori le Mura (Rome) 445
Sant'Agostino (Genoa) 242
Street-by-Street map 240
Sant'Agostino (San Gimignano) 349
Sant'Ambrogio (Milan) 204
Sant'Anastasia (Verona) 148
Sant'Andrea (Genoa)
Street-by-Street map 241
Sant'Andrea delle Fratte (Rome) 413
Sant'Andrea al Quirinale (Rome) 385, **415**
Sant'Andrea della Valle (Rome) 402
Sant'Angelo 503
Sant'Angelo, Monte 512
Sant'Angelo a Nilo (Naples) 492
Sant'Anna e San Bartolomeo dei Lombardi (Naples) 493

Sant'Antioco 555
Sant'Aponal (Venice)
  Street-by-Street map 100
Santi Apostoli (Florence) 296
Santa Caterina (Palermo) 531
Santa Cecilia in Trastevere (Rome) 433
Santa Chiara (Naples) 493
Santa Corona (Vicenza) 156
Santa Costanza (Rome) 55, **445**
Santa Croce (Florence) 13, 256, **288–9**
Santa Croce (Lecce)
  Street-by-Street map 517
Santa Felicita (Florence) 308
Santa Francesca Romana (Rome) 395
Santi Giovanni e Paolo (Venice) 122–3
Sant'Ignazio di Loyola (Rome) 409
  Street-by-Street map 406
Sant'Ivo alla Sapienza (Rome) 385, **404**
  Street-by-Street map 403
Santa Maria in Aracoeli (Rome) 389
  Street-by-Street map 389
Santa Maria dell'Assunta (Torcello) 126–7
Santa Maria Capua Vetere 487, **500**
Santa Maria del Carmine (Florence)
  Cappella Brancacci 302–3
Santa Maria dei Carmini (Venice)
  Street-by-Street map 106
Santa Maria della Concezione (Rome) 415
Santa Maria della Consolazione (Rome) 437
Santa Maria della Consolazione (Todi) 256
Santa Maria in Cosmedin (Rome) 438
  Street-by-Street map 436
Santa Maria in Domnica (Rome) 438
Santa Maria Forisportam (Lucca) 327
Santa Maria Formosa (Venice) 123
Santa Maria Gloriosa dei Frari (Venice) 13, **102–3**
Santa Maria delle Grazie (Milan) 204
Santa Maria Maggiore (Rome) 381, **417**
Santa Maria sopra Minerva (Rome) 408
  Street-by-Street map 406
Santa Maria dei Miracoli (Venice) 99
Santa Maria Navarrese 554
Santa Maria Novella (Florence) 13, 35, 257, **300–301**
Santa Maria della Pace (Rome) 404
  Street-by-Street map 402
Santa Maria del Patirion 524
Santa Maria del Popolo (Rome) 414
Santa Maria della Salute (Venice) 89, 90, 95, **109**
Santa Maria della Spina (Pisa) 329
Santa Maria in Trastevere (Rome) 380, **432–3**
Santa Maria della Vittoria (Rome) 416
Sant'Omobono (Rome) 436
Sant'Orso (Aosta) 219

Santi Pietro e Paolo 527
Santa Prassede (Rome) 416
Santi Quattro Coronati (Rome) 438
Santa Sabina (Rome) 441
Santa Scolastica (Subiaco) 473
Santo Spirito (Florence) 305
  Street-by-Street map 304
Santo Stefano (Venice) 121
Santo Stefano Rotondo (Rome) 438
Santa Trinita (Florence)
  Street-by-Street map 296
Santissima Annunziata (Florence) 281
  Street-by-Street map 278
Santuario e Casa di Santa Caterina (Siena) 344
Santuario d'Oropa 230
Saracens 55, 56, 235, 487
Sardinia 478, **549–55**
  climate 76
  Exploring Sardinia 550–51
  ferries 627
  hotels 577
  map 22
  Nuraghe 553
  regional food 481
  restaurants 604–5
  Roman remains 51
Sarre 218
Sassari 549, **552**
  festivals 71, 72
Sassi 522–3
Sasso Lungo (Dolomites) 86
Sauris, Lago di 166
Sauze d'Oulx 222
Savonarola, Girolamo
  Convento di San Marco (Florence) 280
  execution 60, 61, 280
  portrait of 294
Savoy 215
Savoy, House of 64, 67
  Armeria Reale (Turin) 228
  Castello di Casotto 233
  Palazzo Reale (Genoa) 242
  Palazzo Reale (Turin) 228
  Parco Nazionale del Gran Paradiso 220
  Pinerolo 223
  tombs of 229
  Turin Shroud 225
Sawaya, William 42
Sawaya & Moroni 42
Sbigoli Terracotte (Florence) 310
Scaligeri, Cangrande I 146
  tomb of 146, 148
Scaligeri, Cangrande II 146, 147
Scaligeri, Cansignorio
  tomb of 148
Scaligeri, Mastino II
  tomb of 148
Scaligeri family 146
  tombs of 148
Scamozzi, Vincenzo 156, 210
Scanno 505, **509**
Scarlatti, Alessandro 41
Scarpagnino 104
Scenic railroad routes 629
Lo Scheggia
  Cassone Adimari 279

The School of Athens (Raphael) 32, 199, 420, 431
Scientists 44–5
Scilla 524
Scoppio del Carro (Florence) 70
Scriptorium (Florence) 309, 310
Scrovegni, Enrico 160, 161
Scuola del Cuoio (Florence) 310
Scuola Grande dei Carmini (Venice)
  Street-by-Street map 106
Scuola Grande di San Rocco (Venice) 104–5
Scuola di San Giorgio degli Schiavoni (Venice) 124
Scuola del Santo (Padua) 163
Seasonal produce shops 606
Sebastiano del Piombo 99, 432
Security 618–19
Segesta 528, **538**
Self-catering **560**, 561
Selinunte 538
Sella Chianzutan 166
Seneca 39, 494
Sentino, river 376
Septimius Severus, Emperor 53
  Arch of Septimius Severus (Rome) 394, 396
  Baths of Caracalla (Rome) 441
  Palatine (Rome) 398, 399
Seravezza 322
Sermoneta 474
Serpotta, Giacomo 62–3
  Oratorio del Rosario di San Domenico (Palermo) 532
  Oratorio del Rosario di Santa Cita (Palermo) 533
  Oratorio di San Lorenzo (Palermo) 533
  Oratorio di Santa Zita (Palermo) 482
  Santo Spirito (Agrigento) 539
Servite order 281
Sesia valley 230
Sestriere 222
Settimane Musicali di Stresa (Stresa) 71
Seyter 228
Sforza, Battista 291
Sforza, Francesco 196, 210
Sforza, Galeazzo Maria 60, 198
Sforza family 191
Shakespeare, William 41, 156
  Romeo and Juliet **149**, 156, 211
Shakespeare Festival (Verona) 71
Shelley, Percy Bysshe 64, 245
  grave of 441
  Keats-Shelley Memorial House (Rome) 412
Shoe stores
  Florence 309, 310
Shopping 606–7
  Florence 309–10
  Milan 200–201
  Rome 447–8
  Venice 128–9
  see also Markets
Sicilian Vespers (1282) 58
Sicily 478, **527–47**
  architecture 482

Sicily (cont.)
climate 77
Discovering Italy 15
earthquakes 63, 68
Exploring Sicily 528–9
history 51, 55, 67
hotels 577
islands 537
map 22
regional food 481
restaurants 603–4
traditional cuisine 543
Siena 251, 319, **342–7**
Discovering Italy 14
Duomo 35, **346–7**
festivals 71
A Gourmet Tour of Central Italy 16
history 58
Palio 345
Street-by-Street map 342–3
Sienese School 337, 344, 345, 347
Sigismund, Archduke 174
Signor Blum (Venice) 129
Signorelli, Luca 377
Annunciation 338
Crucifixion 336
Damned Consigned to Hell 32
Deposition 336
Flagellation 98
Last Judgment 363
Sistine Chapel (Rome) 430
tomb of 336
Virgin and Child with Saints 338
Signum (Florence) 310
Sila mountains 519
Sile, river 164
Simius, Bay of 549
Simply Travel 560
Siponto 512
Siracusa 527, 528, **546–7**
architecture 35, 483
festivals 70
history 55
Sirmione 152
Sirmione Peninsula 152
Sirolo 377
Sistine Chapel (Rome) 12, 32, 61, **428–30**
ceiling 420, **428–9**
walls 420, **430**
Sixt (Rome) 631
Sixtus I, Pope 405
Sixtus IV, Pope 47, 404
Capitoline Museums (Rome) 392
Santa Maria della Pace (Rome) 404
Santa Maria del Popolo (Rome) 414
Sistine Chapel (Rome) 61
Vatican Museums (Rome) 424
Sixtus V, Pope
tomb of 417
Skiing 75
Cortina d'Ampezzo 165
Skira (Milan) 200, 201
Smoking 616
in restaurants 579
Snack bars 578
Soccer 28–9, 74, 75

Società Dante Alighieri 611
Sodoma 345
Marriage of Alexander and Roxana 32
Solari, Cristoforo
tomb of Ludovico il Moro and Beatrice d'Este 208
Solferino, Battle of (1859) 67
Solimena 493
Sophocles 156
Sorrento 15, 501
Sorri, Pietro 344
Sottsass, Ettore 42, 43
Southern Italy 477–555
architecture 482–3
Discovering Italy 15
Greeks in 484–5
map 478–9
regional food 480–81
Sovana 49, **350**
Spada, Cardinal Bernardino 405
Lo Spagna 365
Spanish Steps (Rome) 12, 411, **413**
Street-by-Street map 412
Spartacus 51, 500
Spartans 515
Spas
Bagni di Lucca 323
Levico Terme 179
Merano 174
Montecatini Terme 323
Spazio 900 (Milan) 200, 201
Spedale degli Innocenti (Florence) 61, **281**
Street-by-Street map 279
Spello 366
Sperlonga 467, **475**
Spoleto 353, **364–5**
architecture 364
festivals 71
Spoleto, Vale of 353
Sports 610–11
sporting year 74–5
Spring in Italy 70
Stabiae 499
Stadio Olimpico (Rome) 449, 450, 609
Staglieno Cemetery (Genoa) 243
Starwood Westin 561
Statue of Colleoni (Venice) 123
Stefaneschi Triptych (Giotto) 427
Stelvio, Parco Nazionale dello 193, **206**
Sterzing *see* Vipiteno
Still Life (Morandi) 198
Stilo 55, 519, **524**
Strada delle Dolomiti 86
Strada Panoramica dei Sassi 522–3
Stradivari (Stradivarius), Antonio 191, **210**
Streetcars 632
Street names
Venice 130
Stresa 195
festivals 71
Stromboli 537
Strozzi, Bernardo 111, 242
Strozzi, Filippo 297
Student information 616

Study permits 614
Su Nuraxi (Barumini) 478, 550, 553
Su e zo per i ponti (Venice) 70
Subiaco 465, **473**
Suetonius 39
Sulla 445, 472
Sulmona 508–9
festivals 70
Summer in Italy 71
Sunshine 76–7
Super-Tuscan wines 254
Susa 222
Sustermans, Justus 307
Sutri 17, 470
Swanson, Gloria 229
Swimming championships 75
Sybarites 485
Sylvester, Pope 54
Symbolism
early Christian art 168–9
saints and symbols in Italian art 36–7
Syracuse *see* Siracusa

T

Tacca, Pietro 281
Tacitus 39, 499
Taddeo di Bartolo 349
Abbadia dell'Isola frescoes 338
Assumption 337
Life of the Virgin 344
Tadoline 195
Taglioni, Maria 98
Tamagni, Vincenzo 338
Tanzio da Varallo 230, 231
Taormina 527, **542**
festivals 71
Tarantella 515
Taranto 505, **515**
Taras 485
Tarpeian Rock (Rome) 389
Tarquinia 17, 48, **470**
Tarquinii 50
Tarquinio the Older 48
Tarquinius Superbus, King 49
Tasso, Torquato 265
Tassoni 264
Tasting Places Cooking and Wine Tours 611
Tavarone 242
Tax exemption 615
Taxis 633
tipping 616
Tchaikovsky, Peter Ilyich 238
Teatro degli Arcimboldi (Milan) 609
Teatro Argentino (Rome) 450
Teatro Carlo Felice (Genoa) 609
Teatro India (Rome) 450
Teatro Olimpico (Vicenza) 156–7
Teatro dell'Opera (Rome) 449, 450, 609
Teatro Quirino (Rome) 450
Teatro Romano (Verona) 149
Teatro San Carlo (Naples) 497
Teatro alla Scala (Milan) 197, 609
Telephones **622**, 623
Television 623
Temperatures 76–7

The Tempest (Giorgione) 110, 153
Tempesta, Antonio 438
Tempietto (Rome) 35, **433**
Temple of Antoninus and Faustina (Rome) 394
Temple of Castor and Pollux (Rome) 394, 396
Temple of Concord (Agrigento) 527
Temple of Hadrian (Rome) 406
Temple of Jupiter (Rome) 389
Temple of Romulus (Rome) 395
Temple of Saturn (Rome) 396
Temple of Venus and Rome (Rome) 395
Temple of Vesta (Rome) 396
Temples of the Forum Boarium (Rome) 437
Street-by-Street map 436
The Temptation of Christ (Tintoretto) 104, 105
10 Corso Como (Milan) 200, 201
Terracina 475
Tesero 177
Testa Grigia 218
Thapsos 546
Tharros 51
Theater 608, **609**
Rome 449–50
Theft 618, 631
Theme vacations 610–11,625
Theodolinda, Queen 54, 205
Theodoric the Ostrogoth 54
Théudon 407
Thomas the Apostle, St. 332
The Three Ages of Man (Giorgione) 306
Three Graces (Raphael) 432
Thucydides 547
Tibaldi, Pellegrino 421
Tiber Island (Rome) 405
Tiberio d'Assisi 365
Tiberius, Emperor 52, 475, 503
Tickets
    air travel 625
    buses 631
    entertainment in Rome 449, 450
    trains 628, 629
    vaporetti in Venice 634, 635
Tiepolo, Giambattista 111, 205
    New World 107
    Nuptial Allegory 107
    Palazzo Labia (Venice) 92
    Scuola Grande dei Carmini (Venice) 106
    Udine 166
    Villa Nazionale (Strà) 164
    Villa Valmarana ai Nani (Vicenza) 157
Tiepolo, Giandomenico 101, 107, 157
Time zone 617
Timetables, trains 628
Tindari 542
Tino da Camaino 328, 493
Tintoretto, Domenico 125
    Paradise 118, 120
Tintoretto, Jacopo 109, 115, 117, 202, 264, 326, 391
    The Adoration of the Golden Calf 98

Tintoretto, Jacopo (cont.)
    The Adoration of the Shepherds 104
    Annunciation 104
    The Ascent to Calvary 105
    Assumption 104
    Baptism of Christ 149
    Christ before Pilate 105
    Christ Carrying the Cross 104–5
    The Crowning with Thorns 105
    Crucifixion 100, 104
    The Deposition 125
    The Fall of Manna in the Desert 104
    Finding the Body of St. Mark 33
    The Flight into Egypt 104
    Gathering of the Manna 125
    Last Judgment 98
    Last Supper 101, 125
    The Miracle of the Bronze Serpent 104
    The Miracle of St. Mark Freeing a Slave 111
    Moses Strikes Water from the Rock 104
    Palazzo Ducale (Venice) 120
    Paradise 118, 120
    St. Mary of Egypt 104
    St. Mary Magdalene 104
    San Rocco (Venice) 105
    San Rocco in Glory 105
    Scuola Grande di San Rocco (Venice) 104
    The Temptation of Christ 104, 105
    tomb of 98
Tipping 615
    in restaurants 579
Titian 61, 103, 427
    Annunciation 105, 164
    Assumption of the Virgin 102, 149
    Basilica di San Marco paintings (Venice) 115
    Brescia altarpiece 207
    Ca' d'Oro paintings (Venice) 99
    Cain and Abel 109
    Crucifixion 105
    David and Goliath 33, 109
    Lavinia Vecellio 497
    Madonna di Ca' Pesaro 32, 102
    Palazzo dei Conservatori paintings (Rome) 391
    Palazzo Doria Pamphilj (Rome) 408
    Portrait of Alfonso I d'Este 265
    Portrait of a Gentleman 306
    Portrait of Pope Paul III Farnese with His Nephews 33
    Sacred and Profane Love 443
    The Sacrifice of Abraham and Isaac 109
    St. Mark Enthroned with Saints Cosmas, Damian, Roch, and Sebastian 109
    Salomé 406
    Scuola del Santo paintings (Padua) 163
    The Venus of Urbino 33, 291, 293
    The Wedding at Cana 109
Titus 395
Tivoli 12, **472**
Tobias and the Archangel Raphael (Pollaiuolo) 226–7

Todi 17, 353, **363**
    architecture 256, 365
Tod's (Milan) 200, 201
Tolfa hills 466
Tolmezzo 166
Tomba, Alberto 75
Torcello 13, **126–7**
Il Torchio (Florence) 310
Torgiano 353
Torquemada, Cardinal Juan de 408
Torre del Lago Puccini 323
Torre dei Lamberti (Verona) 148
Torre del Merlo, Giovanni 239
Torre dell'Orologio (Rome) 402
Torre dell'Orologio (Venice) 121
    Street-by-Street map 112
Torre Velasca (Milan) 35
Torri degli Asinelli e Garisenda (Bologna) 268
    Street-by-Street map 267
Torri del Vaiolet (Dolomites) 87
Torrini (Florence) 310
Torriti, Jacopo 417
Toscanini, Arturo 195
Touring Club Italiano 561
Tourist offices **615**, 617
Tours 615
Town squares 58–9
Traghetti, Venice 634
Tragicomica (Venice) 128, 129
Traini, Francesco
    Scenes from the Life of St. Dominic 329
    Triumph of Death 31
Trains 626, **628–9**
Trajan, Emperor 52, 53
    Arch of Trajan (Benevento) 500
    Forum of Caesar (Rome) 393
    Plutei of Trajan 396
    Trajan's Column (Rome) 52, 392
    Trajan's Forum and Markets (Rome) 392
Trani 513
Trapani 536
Trasimeno, Lake 357
    Battle of (217 BC) 357
Trastevere (Rome) *see* Vatican and Trastevere
Trattorias 578
Travel 624–35
    Abruzzo, Molise, and Puglia 506
    air 624–5
    Basilicata and Calabria 521
    bicycles 624, 633
    buses 627, 632–3
    cars 626, **630–31**
    in cities 632–3
    Emilia-Romagna 261
    ferries 626, **627**
    Lazio 467
    Liguria 237
    Lombardy 193
    Le Marche 371
    metropolitana (underground railroads) 632–3
    Naples and Campania 489
    Sardinia 551
    Sicily 528

Travel (cont.)
streetcars 632
taxis 633
trains 626, **628–9**
Trentino–Alto Adige 173
Tuscany 321
Umbria 354
Valle d'Aosta and Piedmont 217
Veneto and Friuli 145
Venice 91, **634–5**
Travelers' checks 620
Tre Cime di Lavaredo (Dolomites) 87
Le Tre Ghinee (Rome) 447, 448
Tremiti Islands 511
Trenitalia 627
Trent, Council of (1545–63) 62, 178, 268
Trentino–Alto Adige 80, **171–9**
climate 76
Exploring Trentino–Alto Adige 172–3
hotels 564–5
regional food 83
restaurants 583–4
Trento 178–9
Trevi 365
Trevi Fountain (Rome) 12, **414–15**
Treviso 143, **164**
airport 624–5
The Tribute Money (Masaccio) 31
Triennale (Milan) 200, 201
Trieste 169
Trinità dei Monti (Rome) 412
Trinity (Masaccio) 300
Triumph of Death (Costa) 267
Triumph of Death (Traini) 31
Triumph of Faith over Idolatry (Legros) 407
Triumph of Mordecai (Veronese) 33
Trivia 415
Troia 512–13
architecture 483
Troina 541
Trois (Venice) 128, 129
Trojans 538
Tropea 524
Troubetzkoy, Prince 98
Trulli houses 505, 506
Murge dei Trulli 515
TSL Tessile San Leonardo (Venice) 128, 129
Tura, Cosmè 265
Turin 182, 215, 217, **224–9**
architecture 35, 189
festivals 71
map 224
Turin Shroud see Holy Shroud
Tuscania 468
Tuscany 319–51
climate 76
Discovering Italy 14
Exploring Tuscany 320–21
hotels 571–2
intercity buses 633
regional food 253
restaurants 592–4
Twain, Mark 293
Tyche 546, 547
Tyrol, Counts of 171

U

Uccellina Hills 351
Uccello, Paolo
The Battle of San Romano 31, 292
Santa Maria Novella frescoes (Florence) 300
Udine 81, **166–7**
Ufficio Monumenti Antichi e Scavi 616
Uffizi (Florence) 13, 250, **290–93**
early Renaissance 292–3
floorplan 290–91
Gothic art 292
high Renaissance and Mannerism 293
later paintings 293
Ugo Poggi (Florence) 310
Ugolini (Florence) 310
Ugolino di Prete Ilario 362
Umberto I, King 67, 68
Umbria 353–67
climate 77
Exploring Umbria 354–5
hotels 572
regional food 253
restaurants 594–5
Romanesque churches 364–5
Umbria Jazz (Perugia) 71, 609
Underground railroads 632–3
UNESCO 206
UNESCO World Heritage Sites 515, 523, 547
Ungarelli, Father 425
Unique Forms of Continuity in Space (Boccioni) 68
Uomo Vitruviano (Leonardo da Vinci) 32
Urban III, Pope 339
Urban IV, Pope 57
tomb of 356
Urban VIII, Pope 443
coat of arms 419
Palazzo Barberini (Rome) 415
St. Peter's (Rome) 422
Sant'Ivo alla Sapienza (Rome) 404
Urbania 373
Urbania 369, **373**
Urbino 369, **374–5**
Palazzo Ducale 251, 256, **374–5**
Urbino, Duke of
tomb of 299
Urzulei 554
Ussel 218
Ustica 537
Utens, Giusto 305
Utrecht, Treaty of (1713) 64

V

Vacations, theme 610–11, 625
Vaccarini 543
Vaccaro 493
Vaga, Perin del 421
Val Camonica 206
Val Genova 178
Val di Racines 174
Val di Rhêmes-Notre-Dame 220
Val Sugana 179
Valentino (Florence) 310
Valentino (Rome) 447, 448
Valerian, Emperor 115

Valeriano 493
Valle d'Aosta and Piedmont 215–33
climate 76
Exploring Valle d'Aosta and Piedmont 216–17
history 47
hotels 567–8
regional food 184–5
restaurants 586–9
Valle dei Nuraghe 549
Valley of the Temples (Agrigento) 478, 527, 539, **540**
Valli di Comacchio 271
Valnerina 367
Valnontey 221
Value Added Tax (IVA) 615
Van Dyck, Anthony 99, 202, 227, 242, 243, 293, 391, 432
Madonna of the Rosary 532
Van Egmont, J. 432
Van Eyck, Jan 227
Vanni, Andrea 345
Vanni, Francesco 344
Vanvitelli, Luigi 349, 482, 500
Vaporetti (waterbuses) 634, 635
route map 140–41
Varallo 230
Varano 512
Varenna 194
Vasari, Giorgio 287
Casa di Vasari (Arezzo) 333
Corridoio Vasariano (Florence) 289
Last Judgment 285
Palazzo dei Cavalieri (Pisa) 329
Palazzo Vecchio (Florence) 294, **295**
Piazza Grande (Arezzo) 333
Sant'Anna e San Bartolomeo dei Lombardi frescoes (Naples) 493
Santa Felicita (Florence) 308
tomb of Michelangelo 288
Uffizi (Florence) 290, 291
Villa Giulia (Rome) 444
Vassalletto, Pietro 446
Vassalletto family 440
Vatican and Trastevere (Rome) 419–33
Raphael Rooms 431
Sistine Chapel 428–30
tour of the Vatican 420–21
Vatican Gardens (Rome) 421
Vatican Museums (Rome) 12, 421, **424–7**
early Christian and medieval art 427
Egyptian and Assyrian art 425, 426
15th- to 19th-century art 427
floorplan 424–5
Greek, Etruscan, and Roman art 17, 424, 426
Vatican Radio 420
Vegetarian food 579
Veii 49
Velázquez, Diego Rodriguez de Silva y 205, 264
Pope Innocent X 408
Venaria Reale 230

Vendramin, Andrea, Doge of Venice
  tomb of 123
Veneto and Friuli 143–71
  architecture 84–5
  climate 77
  Discovering Italy 14
  Exploring the Veneto and Friuli
    144–5
  hotels 563–4
  regional food 82, 83
  restaurants 581–3
Venezia see Venice
Veneziano, Paolo 152
  Coronation of the Virgin 110, 111
Venice 89–141
  Accademia 94, 110–11
  airports 624–5
  architecture 84–5
  Basilica di San Marco 34, 114–15
  Carnival 64, 73
  Discovering Italy 13
  Exploring Venice 90–91
  festivals 70, 71, 72
  gondolas 92, 112
  Grand Canal 92–5
  hotels 562–3
  map 21, 81
  Palazzo Ducale 118–20
  restaurants 580–81
  rise of 56–7
  San Marco 56
  Santi Giovanni e Paolo 122–3
  Santa Maria Gloriosa dei Frari
    102–3
  Scuola Grande di San Rocco
    104–5
  shopping 128–9
  Street-by-Street maps
    Dorsoduro 106–7
    Piazza San Marco 112–13
    San Polo 100–101
  Street Finder 130–39
  street names 130
  Torcello 126–7
  travel 634–5
  vaporetto routes 140–41
Venice Film Festival 71, 609
Venice Pavilion Bookshop (Venice)
  129
Venice in Peril fund 98, 108
Venier, Sebastiano, Doge of Venice
  monument to 122
Venini (Venice) 128, 129
Venosa 522
Venus (Canova) 65
The Venus of Urbino (Titian) 33, 291
Vercelli 182, 216, 232
Vercelli school 32, 231
Verdi, Giuseppe 41, 67, 211
Verdicchio wine 255, 376
Verga, Giovanni
  Verga's House (Catania) 543
Vergine Annunziata (Antonello da
  Messina) 533
Vernaccia di San Gimignano wine
  254
Vernazza 245
Verona 80, 143, 144, 146–51
  Discovering Italy 13, 14

Verona (cont.)
  festivals 71, 73
  map 146–7
  Roman remains 53
  Romeo and Juliet 149
  San Zeno Maggiore 150–51
Veronese, Paolo 117, 202, 227, 243,
  264, 391
  Adoration of the Magi 156
  Age and Youth 120
  Coronation of the Virgin 108
  Deposition 147
  Dialectic 120
  Feast in the House of Levi 110, 111
  Four Evangelists 108
  Juno Offering the Ducal Crown to
    Venice 120
  Martyrdom of St. George 149
  Rape of Europa 120
  St. Helen 427
  San Giacomo dell'Orio (Venice) 101
  San Sebastiano paintings (Venice)
    108
  The Supper of St. Gregory the Great
    157
  tomb of 108
  Triumph of Mordecai 33
  Villa Barbaro (Masèr) 153
Verrès 218
Verrocchio, Andrea del
  bust of Christ 332
  David 31
  Equestrian Monument of
    Bartolomeo Colleoni 32
  Orsanmichele (Florence) 287
  Putto fountain 295
  statue of Colleoni 123
Versace (Florence) 310
Vespasian, Emperor 426
  Arch of Titus (Rome) 395
  Colosseum (Rome) 381, 397
Vespucci, Amerigo 44, 301
Vespucci family 301
Vestal Virgins 394, 395, 396
Vesuvius, Mount 484, 487, 498,
  499
Vezzano 179
Via Aemilia 259, 262
Via Appia Antica (Rome) 50, 51, 445
Via Fillungo (Lucca) 325
Via Lattea 222
Viareggio 323
  festivals 73
Vicenza 80, 143, 154–7
  Discovering Italy 14
  Street-by-Street map 154–5
Victor Emmanuel Monument
  (Rome) 67
  Street-by-Street map 388
Vienna, Congress of (1815) 65
Vienna, Peace of (1735) 64
Vieste 506, 512
View of the Roman Forum (Piranesi) 65
Vignola, Giacomo Barozzi da
  Castellina (Norcia) 367
  Gesù (Rome) 35
  Palazzo Farnese (Caprarola) 469
  Villa Giulia (Rome) 444
  Villa Lante (Viterbo) 465, 468, 469

Vigo di Fassa 177
Viligiardi, Arturo 336
Villaggio Globale (Rome) 449, 450
Villanovan period 48
Villas
  Barchessa Valmarana (Mira) 164
  Hadrian's Villa (Tivoli) 472
  Poggio a Caiano 257, 332
  La Rotonda (Vicenza) 157
  Villa Aldobrandini (Frascati) 471
  Villa di Artimino (Artimino) 332
  Villa Barbarigo 163
  Villa Barbaro (Masèr) 84, 153
  Villa Borghese (Rome) 12, 17, 442–3
  Villa Carlotta (Como) 194, 195
  Villa Doria (Pegli) 243
  Villa Durazzo-Pallavicini (Pegli) 243
  Villa Emo (Fanzolo) 153
  Villa d'Este (Tivoli) 472
  Villa Farnesina (Rome) 432
  Villa Floridiana (Naples) 497
  Villa Foscari (Malcontenta) 164
  Villa Giulia (Palermo) 533
  Villa Giulia (Rome) 17, 444
  Villa Gregoriana (Tivoli) 472
  Villa Grimaldi (Nervi) 243
  Villa Hanbury 238
  Villa Jovis (Capri) 503
  Villa Lante (Viterbo) 465, 468, 469
  Villa Luxoro (Nervi) 243
  Villa Manin (Codroipo) 167
  Villa Manzoni (Lecco) 195
  Villa Medici (Rome) 413
  Villa Nazionale (Strà) 164
  Villa Opicina (Trieste) 169
  Villa Palagonia (Bagheria) 482, 536
  Villa Romana (Tindari) 542
  Villa Romana del Casale (Piazza
    Armerina) 541
  Villa Taranto (Verbania) 195
  Villa Trabia (Bagheria) 536
  Villa Valguarnera (Bagheria) 536
  Villa Valmarana ai Nani (Vicenza) 157
  see also Palaces
Villas4you 560, 561
Vincenzo di Michele 327
Vinci 331
Vinerias 578
Vino Nobile di Montepulciano 254, 255
Violins 210
Vipiteno (Sterzing) 174
Virgil 38, 39, 191, 431, 465, 475
  birthplace 211
  statue of 211
The Virgin and Child (Martini) 329
Virgin and Child with Saints
  (Mantegna) 150
The Virgin Appearing to St. Bernard
  (Lippi) 283
Virgin Enthroned with the Child and
  Saints (Angelico) 36
Virgin of the Rocks (Leonardo da
  Vinci) 32
Visas 614
Visconti, Bianca 210
Visconti, Prince Gian Galeazzo 59,
  197, 198, 208
  tomb of 208
Visconti, Luchino 28, 69

Visconti family 191
  Milan 196, 197
  Verona 146
Vision of St. Martin (Martini) 30
Vitale di Bologna 269
Viterbo 17, **468–9**
  festivals 72
Vitruvius
  statue of 148
Vittoria, Alessandro 98, 120, 123
Vittorio Amedeo II, Duke of Savoy 229
Vittorio Emanuele II, King
  birthplace 227
  Risorgimento 66
  Sarre 218
  unification of Italy 344
  Victor Emmanuel Monument
    (Rome) 388
Vivaldi, Antonio 40, 41, 63, 64
Vivarini, Alvise 98
Vivarini, Antonio 123
Vivarini, Bartolomeo 123, 124
Vizzini 541
Voiello 42
Volpetti (Rome) 447, 448
Volta, Alessandro 44
Volterra 17, **338–9**
  history 59
Vucciria (Palermo) 532
Vulcano 537

W

Wagner, Richard
  Caffè Greco (Rome) 412
  Palazzo Giustinian (Venice) 107
  Palazzo Vendramin Calergi
    (Venice) 93
  Parsifal 501

Walking
  in cities 633
  vacations 610
Walser people 218
Walther von der Vogelweide
  statue of 176
Water, drinking 579
Water polo 74
Water sports 611
Water taxis 635
Waterbuses 634, 635
Waterfalls
  Cascata di Lillaz 221
  Cascate delle Marmore 367
  Cascate di Nardis 178
  Domodossola 230
  Gole dell'Alcantara 542
  Goletta 220
  Noasca 222
Weather **76–7**, 614
Wedding Scene (Filipucci) 349
Wheelchair access *see* Disabled
  travelers
Wildlife
  Bosco della Mesola 271
  Dolomites 87
  Maremma 351
  Parco Nazionale d'Abruzzo, Lazio,
    e Molise 510–11
  Parco Nazionale del Gran Paradiso
    220
  see also Aquariums; Birds; Zoo
Wiligelmus 264, 265
William I, King 490
  tomb of 534
William II, King 482, 534
  tomb of 534
William the Bad 522

Wine
  Central Italy 254–5
  festivals 72
  Northwest Italy 186–7
  in restaurants 579
Winter in Italy 73
Women travelers 619
Work permits 614
World music, Rome 449, 450
World War II 68
World Wide Fund for Nature 611
Writers 38–9

Y

Yeats, WB 245

Z

Zanotta 42
Zanussi 25
Zecca (Venice) 521
  Street-by-Street map 113
Zelotti 153, 163, 164
Zen, Cardinal 117
Zeno, San 150, 151
Zevio, Altichiero da 162, 163
Zevio, Stefano da 147
Lo Zingarello (Giuseppe Zimbalo)
  483, 516
Zoo
  Villa Borghese (Rome) 442
Zuccarelli, Francesco 111
  Museo Zuccarelli (Pitigliano) 351
Zuccari brothers 285, 469
Zuglio 166

Acknowledgments

Dorling Kindersley would like to thank the following people whose contributions and assistance have made the preparation of this book possible.

Contributors
Paul Duncan is an expert on art and architectural history and has published a guide to Sicily as well as one on Italy's hill-towns.

Tim Jepson, formerly Rome correspondent for the *Sunday Telegraph*, has written guides to Tuscany, Umbria, Rome and Venice, a complete guide to Italy, *Italy by Train* and *Wild Italy*, a guide to Italy's nature reserves.

Andrew Gumbel, former Reuters correspondent in Rome, has written a number of guide books and is the correspondent for the *Independent* in Rome.

Christopher Catling has written guides to Florence and Tuscany, the Veneto and the Italian Lakes and is particularly interested in archaeology.

Sam Cole works for Reuters in Rome, where he has lived for some years, and contributes regularly to guidebooks on Rome and the Lazio region.

Additional Contributors
Dominic Robertson, Mick Hamer, Richard Langham Smith, Gillian Price.

Additional Photography
Francesco Allegretto, Giuseppe Carfagna & Associati, Peter Chadwick, Andy Crawford, Philip Dowell, Mike Dunning, Philip Enticknap, Steve Gorton, Dave King, Rough Guides/James McConnachie, Neil Mersh, Anna Mockford, Roger Moss, Poppy, Rough Guides/Martin Richardson; Kim Sayer, Helena Smith, James Stevenson, Clive Streeter, Jo-Ann Titmarsh, David Ward, Matthew Ward, Christine Webb.

Additional Illustrations
Andrea Corbella, Richard Draper, Kevin Jones Associates, Chris Orr and Associates, Robbie Polley, Simon Roulstone, Martin Woodward.

Cartographic Research
Jane Hugill, Samantha James, Jennifer Skelley.

Design and Editorial Assistance
Tora Agarwala, Beverley Ager, Gillian Allan, Gaye Allen, Douglas Amrine, Emily Anderson, Peter Bently, Marta Bescos Sanchez, Sonal Bhatt, Uma Bhattacharya, Tessa Bindloss, Hilary Bird, Sally-Ann Bloomfield, Samantha Borland, Isabel Boucher, Hugo Bowles, Reid Bramblett, Caroline Brooke, Nick Bruno, Paola Cacucciola, Stefano Cavedoni, Margaret Chang, Susi Cheshire, Elspeth Collier, Sherry Collins, Lucinda Cooke, Cooling Brown, Imogen Corke, Michelle Crane, Gary Cross, Felicity Crowe, Cristina Dainotto, Peter Douglas, Mandy Dredge, Stephanie Driver, Julia Dunn, Michael Ellis, Adele Evans, Mariana Evmolpidou, Danny Farnham, Emer FitzGerald, Karen Fitzpatrick, Sarah Fraser, Kyra Freestar, Anna Freiberger, Camilla Gersh, Jackie Gordon, Angela-Marie Graham, Caroline Greene, Vanessa Hamilton, Amy Harrison, Sally-Ann Hibbard, Elinor Hodgson, Tim Hollis, Paul Jackson, Gail Jones, Roberta Kedzierski, Amy Knauff, Steve Knowlden, Shikha Kulkarni, Suresh Kumar, Jude Ledger, Leonie Loudon, Siri Lowe, Carly Madden, Hayley Maher, Nicola Malone, Sarah Martin, Georgina Matthews, Alison McGill, Ferdie McDonald, Sam Merrell, Ian Midson, Rebecca Milner, Adam Moore, Cherrye Moore, John Murphy, Cristina Murroni, Jennifer Mussett, Catherine Palmi, Tiffany Parks, Helen Partington, Alok Pathak, Julia Paynton, Susie Peachey, Alice Peebles, Tamsin Pender, Marianne Petrou, Gillian Price, David Pugh, Alessandra Pugliese, Rada Radojicic, Jake Reimann, Catherine Richards, David Roberts, Evelyn Robertson, Ellen Root, Carolyn Ryden, Simon Ryder, Giuseppina Russo, Collette Sadler, Sands Publishing Solutions, Baishakhee Sengupta, Marcella Simoni, Kunal Singh, Kate Singleton, Ellie Smith, Susana Smith, Alison Stace, Solveig Steinhardt, Donald Strachan, Hugh Thompson, Jo-Ann Titmarsh, Conrad Van Dyk, Elaine Verweymeren, Ingrid Vienings, Karen Villabona, Stewart J Wild, Rebecca Winke, Debra Wolter, Veronica Wood.

Dorling Kindersley would also like to thank the following for their assistance: Azienda Autonoma di Soggiorno Cura e Turismo, Napoli; Azienda Promozione Turistica del Trentino, Trento; Osservatorio Geofisico dell'Università di Modena; Bell'Italia; Enotria Winecellars.

Photography Permission
Dorling Kindersley would like to thank the following for their assistance and kind permission to photograph at their establishments: Assessorato Beni Culturali Comune di Padova. Le Soprinten-denze Archeologiche di Agrigento, di Enna, di Etruria Meridionale, per il Lazio, di Napoli, di Pompei, di Reggio Calabria e di Roma. Le Soprintendenze per i Beni Ambientali e Architettonici di Bolzano, di Napoli, di Potenza, della Provincia di Firenze e Pistoia, di Ravenna, di Roma, di Siena e di Urbino. Le Soprintendenze per i Beni Ambientali, Architettonici, Artistici e Storici di Caserta, di Cosenza, di Palermo, di Pisa, di Salerno e di Venezia. Le Soprintendenze per i Beni Artistici e Storici della Provincia di Firenze e Pistoia, di Milano e di Roma. Also all the other churches, museums, hotels, shops, restaurants, galleries and sights too numerous to thank individually.

Picture Credits
a-above; b-below; c-centre; f-far; l-left; r-right; t-top.

Works of art have been reproduced with the permission of the following copyright holders: © ADAGP, Paris and DACS, London 2006 *Bird in Space* by Constantin Brancusi 109cl; © DACS, 2006 *Mother and Son* by Carlo Carrà 203tl.

Dorling Kindersley would like to thank the following for their assistance: **Eric Crighton:** 87cra, **FIAT:** 224c, **Gucci Ltd:** 43cr, **Prada, Milan:** 43c, **National Archaeological Museum, Naples:** 499br, **National Maritime Museum:** 44cla, **Royal Botanic Gardens, Kew:** 87ca, **Science Museum, Telecom Italia:** 622tr.

The publisher would like to thank the following individuals, companies and picture libraries for permission to reproduce their photographs: **Accademia Italiana:** Sue Bond 499c; **Actv S.p.A:** 634br, 635crb; **AFE, Rome:** 42cb, 43tl; Giuseppe Carfagna 198br, 206br, 222tl, 222br, 225bl, 226cla, 229tl, 239tr, Claudio Cerquetti 72tc, 73bl, 73tr; Enrico Martino 62clb, 70tr; Roberto Merlo 240bl, 243tl, 243br; Piero Servo 271t, 273bl, Gustavo Tomsich 231tl; **APT Turin:** 228bl, 228tr; **Archivio APT Monregalese:** 233tr; **Action Plus:** Mike Hewitt 74cla; Glyn Kirk 75tr; **Alamy Images:** Peter Adams Photography 16bl; Arco Images GmbH 17cr; Krys Bailey 618cl, Adriano Bacchella 185tl, Bluered 329tl; Enrico Caracciolo 253c; Caro 582bl; Cristina Fumi 28br; funkyfood London - Paul Williams 96-7; gkphotography 83cl; INTERFOTO 225cr; Jon Arnold Images Ltd. 8-9, 434; Norma Joseph 352, 368; Jtb Media Creation, inc. 13br; Theodore Liasi 618cla, LOOK Die Bildagentur der Fotografen GmbH 142; David Lyons 13tl, 24, 212-3; Marka 17tr; Steven May 634cla; David Noton Photography 258, 318; Chuck Pefley 26tr; Prisma Bildagentur AG 410; Robert Harding Picture Library Ltd. 173cr; Robert Harding World Imagery 170; tbkmedia.de 603bc; Travel Pictures 15tr; vario images GmbH & Co.KG/ Ulrich Baumgarten 620cl, 622bl; Steve Vidler 398cla; Woodstock 548; **Alexander Museum Palace Hotel:** 573 tr; **Allsport:** Mark Thompson: 75ca; **Ancient Art and Architecture:** 485br; **Antica Residenza Cicogna:** 571tc; Archiv für Kunst und Geschichte, London: 32bl, 38b, *Rossini* (1820), Camuccini, Museo Teatrale alla Scala, Milan 40br, 41bl, 45br, *Pope Sixtus IV Naming Platina Prefect of the Library,* Melozzo da Forlì (1477), Pinacoteca Vaticana, Rome 48cla, *Statue of Augustus from Prima Porta* (1st century AD) 53tl, *The Gift of Constantine* (1246), Oratorio di San Silvestro, Rome 54cl, *Frederick I Barbarossa as a Crusader* (1188), Biblioteca Apostolica Vaticana, Rome 57bl, *Giving the Keys to St Peter,* Perugino (1482), Sistine Chapel, Vatican, Rome 60cla, 60bl, *Machiavelli,* Santi di Tito, Palazzo Vecchio, Florence 61br, Andrea Palladio, Meyer 62cb, *Goethe in the Campagna,* Tischbein (1787), Stadelsches Kunstinstitut, Frankfurt 64cl, *Venetian Carnival in the Eighteenth Century,* Anon (19th century) 64clb, *Bonaparte Crossing the Alps,* David, Schloss Charlottenburg, Berlin 65cr, 65bl, 110tr, 110bl, 203bc, 470bl, *Archimedes,* Museo Capitolino, Rome 485bl, 509tc, 513cl; Stefan Diller *St Francis Appearing to the Brothers at Arles* (1295–1300), San Francesco, Assisi 57tl; Erich Lessing Margrave *Gualtieri of Saluzzo Chooses the Poor Farmer's Daughter, Griseldis, for his Wife, di Stefano,* Galleria dell'Accademia Carrara, Bergamo 38crb, *The Vision of St Augustine* (1502), Carpaccio, Chiesa di San Giorgio degli Schiavoni, Venice 61cr, 226bl, 272b, 495cr; **Archivio IGDA, Milan:** 208cl, 208br, 209bc, 525br; **Emporio Armani:** 43tc; **Artemide, GB Ltd:** 43clb.

Badio & Coltibuono: 579; **Beehive, Rome:** 574; **Al Bersagliere:** 583tr; **Mario Bettella:** 539clb, 546c; **La Biennale di Venezia:** 608cra; **Frank Blackburn:** 271c; **Osvaldo Böhm, Venice:** 93tc, 98c, 115tc; **Bridgeman Art Library, London/ New York:** 50c, Ambrosiana, Milan 199tl; Bargello, Florence 283bc, 287c; **Bibliothèque Nationale, Paris:** *Marco Polo with Elephants and Camels Arriving at Hormuz, Gulf of Persia, from India,* Livre des Merveilles Fr 2810 f.18v 45tr; British

Museum, London *Etruscan Vase Showing Boxers Fighting* 49tl, *Flask Decorated with Christian Symbols* 54tl, *Greek Attic Red-Figure Vase depicting Odysseus with the Sirens,* Stamnos 485cb; Galleria dell'Accademia Carrara, Bergamo 205tc; Galleria Borghese, Rome 443cl; Galleria degli Uffizi, Florence 30tc, 30tr, 33tl, 33cb, *Self-Portrait,* Raphael Sanzio of Urbino 61bl, 291br, 293bc; K & B News Photo, Florence 280tl; Santa Maria Novella, Florence 301bl; Museo Civico, Prato 332bl; Ravenna 272tr; Louvre, Paris *Statuette of Herakles Brandishing his Club,* Classical Greek, Argive period 484tc; Mausoleo di Galla Placidia, Ravenna 272tr; Museo di San Marco, Florence 301bl; Musée d'Orsay, Paris - Giraudon *Les Romains de la Decadence,* Thomas Couture 399tr; Museo delle Sinopie, Camposanto, Pisa 31clb; Palazzo dei Normanni, Palermo *Scene with Centaurs from the Room of King Ruggero* 527b; Pinacoteca di Brera, Milan 202cla, 202bl, 203ca, Private Collection *Theodoric I* (455–526 AD) *Ostrogothic King of Italy* 54br; San Francesco, Arezzo 31tr; San Francesco, Assisi 359cb; San Sebastiano, Venice 33crb; San Zaccaria, Venice 37c, 37tr, 103cr; Santa Croce, Florence 288bl, 289cl; Santa Maria Gloriosa dei Frari, Venice 32tr; Santa Maria Novella, Florence 31cla; Scrovegni (Arena) Chapel, Padua 31tr; Scuola di San Giorgio degli Schiavoni, Venice 124b; Staatliche Museen, Berlin *Septimius Severus and Family* 53b; Vatican Museums and Galleries, Rome 425bl; Walker Art Gallery, Liverpool *Aeschylus and Hygieia* 484bc; **Al Bric, Rome:** 597tr; **British Museum, London:** 50cl; **Brufani Palace:** 572bc.

Capitoline Museum, Rome: 391cr; **Hotel Cappella Romantik:** 563tr; **Demetrio Carrasco:** 106br, 634tr; **Cephas Picture Library** Mick Rock: 28tl, 186tr, 187bl, 187tr, 255tl, 255tr; **JL Charmet, Paris:** 357br; **Ciga Hotels:** 95cl; **Foto Elio e Stefano Ciol:** 81cra, 168bc, 168br, 169bl, 169bc, 169br; **Hotel Cipriani, Guidecca:** 562bc; Fortuny Restaurant 580br; **Villa Cipriani:** 581tr; **Stephani Colasanti:** 80bl; **Il Comandante:** 601tr; **Comune di Asti:** 72cl; **Consorzio Motoscafi Venezia:** 634clb; **Corbis:** Assignments Photographers/Bryn Colton 184cla; Dave Bartruff 480cla; Owen Franken 252cla, 253tl, 481c; Michelle Garrett 481tl; In Pictures/Michael Aitchison 16tr; John Heseltine 382cla; Robert Harding World Imagery/ Jeremy Bright 112cla; Robert Holmes 83tl; Hemis/ Stefano Torrione 556-7; Frank Krahmer 2-3; Jose Fuste Raga 180-1; Reuters/Tony Gentile 383tl; Sylvain Sonnet 378-9, 400; Hubert Stadler 543crb; **Joe Cornish:** 86tr, 164tl, 337br, 465b, 541bl; **Il Cortiletto:** 602tr; **Giancarlo Costa:** 39cr, 39cra, 39tl, 79c.

Il Dagherrotipo: 549b, 628bl; Archivio Arte 211tl; Archivio Storico 39br, 210br, 265bc; Alberto Berni 229cl; Riccardo Catani 505b; Marco Cerruti 182cla, 217crb, 219br, 220cl; Antonio Cittadini 193tr, 196bl, 206tl; Gianni Dolfini 554bl; Riccardo d'Errico 74tr, 251tl, 272cl; Maurizio Fraschetti 500br; Diane Haines 177br, 611bc; Maurizio Leoni 71c; Marco Melodia 510clb, 510br, 511cb, 551tr, 610cl; Stefano Occhibelli 73c, 405bl; 256t, 517tr; Donato Fierro Perez 537cb; Marco Ravasini 174tl, 553cr; Giovanni Rinaldi 29t, 70bl, 71tl, 183bl, 235b, 402c, 371tr, 377tl, 470cr, 503tc, 511c, 537cr, 555tl, 555crb; Lorenzo Scaramella 472cr; Stefania Servili 176tl; **Da Delfina:** 593bl; **CM Dixon:** 425cb; **Chris Donaghue** The Oxford Photo Library: 121cla; **Doozo, Rome:** 598tr;

Dreamstime: Abey79 12br; Ange84 476-7; Cipriansalceanu 12tl; Gmv 214; Mcristale 157tr; Mirohasch 11br; Rundywong 234; Sborisov 386; **Duca di Orvieto:** 596bc.

Electa: 160c, 161c, 161tc; **Empics:** 74clb; **ET Archive:** 40bc, 49c, 53cr, 56–7c, 61tl, 63tl, 67bc, 416tr, 485cra, 535br; **Mary Evans Picture Library:** 38bl, 45ca, 66b, 66crb, 67cr, 68cb, 84tr, 324cla, 330tc, 395ca, 397bl, 413br, 446clb, 515cr, 515br, 554tl.

Ferrari: 42b; **Archivio Storico Fiat,** Turin: 68tr; **Fiat Press Office:** 224ca; **APT Folignate e Nocera Umbra:** 365tr; by kind permission of **Fondazione Arena di Verona:** Gianfranco Fainello 608bl; **Werner Forman Archive:** 49br, 55tr, 439br; **Fotolia:** LianeM 14tr; **Consorzio Frasassi:** 376br.

Studio Gavirati, Gubbio: 356c; **APT Genova:** Roberto Merlo 242bl; **Getty Images:** Peter Adams 504, 544-5; AFP/ Valery Hache 75bl; Daryl Benson 91tr; Mel Curtis 464; Garrett Ellwood 74ca; Robert Everts 190; Julian Finney 74bc; Godong 46; Robert Harding 10cla; The Image Bank/ Andrea Pistolesi 82cla; Image Source 340-1; Jean-Pierre Lescourret 14bl; Adam Jones 248-9; Michal Krakowiak 486; David Lyons 526; Maremagnum 623cl; Clive Mason 75cb; Sergio Pitamitz 78-9; Roy Rainford 15cb; Stefano Scata 518; SOPA RF/SOPA/Franco Cogoli 88; Stone/Simone Huber 609tr; Steve Sucsy 246-7; Guy Vanderelst 418; **Giraudon, Paris:** *Aphrodite Persuading Helen to Follow Paris to Troy,* Museo Nazionale di Villa Giulia, Rome 49clb, *Pharmacy,* Museo della Civiltà Romana 52cb, *Grandes Chroniques de France; Coronation of Charlemagne in St Peter's by Leon III,* Musée Goya, Castres 55tl, *Taking of Constantinople,* Basilica of St John the Evangelist, Ravenna 57cr, *Dante's Hell with Commentary of Guiniforte delli Bargigi* (Ms2017 fol 245), Bibliothèque Nationale, Paris 58crb, *Portrait of St Ignatius of Loyola,* Rubens, Musée Brukenthal, Sibiu 63ca, *Charles III's Fleet at Naples 6th October 1759,* Joli de Dipi, Museo del Prado, Madrid 64tr, *Inauguration of the Naples-Portici Railway,* Fergola (1839), Museo Nazionale di San Martino, Naples 66clb, *Piedmontese and French at the Battle of San Martino in 1859* Anon, Museo Centrale del Risorgimento, Rome 67tl, 110crb, 111tl, 203cr; **Alinari-Giraudon:** *St Mark Appearing to the Venetians Looking for His Body,* Tintoretto (1568), Brera Art Gallery, Milan 33tr, *Shrine,* House of the Vettii, Pompeii 53cb, *St Gregory in his Study* (Inv 285), Pinacoteca Nazionale, Bologna 55bl, *Portrait of Victor Emmanuel II,* Dugoni (1866), Galleria d'Arte Moderna, Palazzo Pitti, Florence 111br, 203tl, *Louis II of Gonzaga and his Court,* Andrea Mantegna (1466–74), Museo di Palazzo Ducale, Mantova 291tl-tc, *History of Pope Alexander III:* Building of the City of Alexandria, Aretino Spinello (1407), Palazzo Pubblico, Siena 59cr; **Alinari-Seat-Giraudon:** 231c; **Flammarion-Giraudon:** *Poem by Donizo in Honour of Queen Matilda,* Biblioteca Apostolica, Vatican 56ca; **Lauros-Giraudon:** *Portrait of Francis Petrarch* 58bc, *Liber notabilium Philippi Septimi, francorum regis a libris Galieni extractus* (Ms 334 569 fig17), Guy of Pavia (1345), Musée Condé, Chantilly 59bl, *Gallery of Views of Ancient Rome,* Pannini (1758), Musée du Louvre, Paris 64–5c, *Four Angels and Symbols of the Evangelists,* 36tr, 37t; **Orsi-Battaglini-Giraudon:**

Madonna of the Shadow, Museum of San Marco, Florence 36c, *Supplice de Savonarola* Anon 60clb; **Grand Hotel Villa Serbelloni:** 565tr; **The Ronald Grant Archive:** 69bc; Paramount *The God-father Part III* (1990) 539br; Riama *La Dolce Vita* (1960) 68cra; TCF *Boccaccio '70 The Name of the Rose* (1986) 38cla; **Grotta di Tiberio:** 576bl; **Palazzo Venier dei Leoni, Peggy Guggenheim Collection,** Venice: 95cla.

Photo Halupka: 124tr; **Robert Harding Picture Library:** 41br, 195br, 394cl, 423br, 610bl; Dumrath 273crb; Gavin Hellier 12crb; 610tr; Roy Rainford 503cr; **John Heseltine:** 471tr; **Hivaoa:** 605tr; **Michael Holford:** 51ca; **Hotel Raphaël - Relais & Châteaux:** 560tl; **Hotel Villa Pagoda:** 559tl; **HSL:** 631tl; **The Hulton Deutsch Collection:** 68br, 93cla, 94cla, 94br, 161br; Keystone 68ca.

Icona Roma: 4cla; **The Image Bank,** London: 51cb, 338br; Marcella Pedone 191b; Andrea Pistolesi 259b; **The Image Bank,** Milan: 199br; **Impact:** 319b; **Index,** Florence: 286c, 331tr, 331cr; **Istituto e Museo di Storia della Scienza di Firenze:** Franca Principe 44br, 289c.

Tim Jepson: 355tr.

Frank Lane Picture Agency: 220tr, 221tl, 221ca, 221cr; M Melodia/Panda 510cla; **La Riserva di Castel D'appio:** 569tr; **Hotel Laurin,** Bolzano: 564bl; **Locanda del Pilone di Alba:** 586tl; **Locanda I Tre Merli:** 568bc.

Magnum, London: Abbas 68crb; **The Mansell Collection:** 56clb; **Marconi Ltd:** 44cl; **Marka:** L Barbazza 101tr; E Cerretelli 125br; M Motta 619tc; **Masterstudio,** Pescara: 508cr; su concessione del **MAXXI:** Roberto Galasso 445tl; **Ministero per i Beni Culturali e Ambientali:** *The Last Supper,* da Vinci, Leonardo 204b; **Mirror Syndication International:** 44c; **Moby Lines:** 627cl; **Foto Modena:** 270tl, 375c; **Monte san Giuliano:** 604bl; **Tony Mott:** 474t; **Museo Diocesano di Rossano:** 524tl.

NHPA: Laurie Campbell 87crb; Gerard Lacz 87br; Silvestris Fotoservice 87cr; **Grazia Neri:** Marco Bruzzo 72br; Cameraphoto 112bl; Marcello Mencarini 92br; **Newimage s.r.l:** Rolando Fabriani 606cla; **Nhow Milano:** 566tl; **Nippon Television Network:** 428–9 all pics, 430bl; **Peter Noble:** 322tr, 345br, 618br; **Nonna Betta:** 596br.

L'Occhio di Cristallo/Studio Fotografico di Giorgio Olivero: 233bl; **APT Orvieto:** Massimo Roncella 362tr; **Osteria Francescana:** 591tr; **Osteria Le Logge:** 594tl; **Oxford Scientific Films:** Stan Osolinski 351cr.

Padova - Musei Civici - Cappella Scrovegni: 81cr, 160 all pics, 161cra, 161crb, 161bl; **Padova - Musei Civici Agli Eremitani:** 162tr, 162c; **Palazzo Grassi S.p.A:** Thomas Mayer 109br; **Pane e Vino:** 592tc; **Pasta Madre:** 585tr; **Da Paolo e Barbara:** Toni Meneguzzo 590br; **Da Paolino:** 600bl; **Luciano Pedicini - Archivio dell'Arte:** 366bl, 408tr, 479tc, 494tr, 494cl, 494clb, 495tl, 495ca, 495br, 497tr, 534b; **APT Pesaro - Le Marche:** 372br; **Pictures Colour Library:** 550clb, 552tl; **Andrea Pistolesi:** 25; **PNALM Archive:** in association with www.abruzzonatura.com 510bc;

Polis Photo Library; Popperfoto: 68tl, 69tl, 69clb; Portrait Suites, Rome: 575bc.

Sarah Quill, Venice: 94t, 98bc, 104tl.

Relais Uffizi, Florence: 570bl; Retrograph Archive: 41c; Rex Features: 41tl; Steve Wood 43tr; Reuters: Toru Hanai 74crb; Ferran Paredes 75tl; Il Riccio Restaurant: 579bc; Hotel Riva Del Sole: 577tr; Ristorante Rosa: 589bl.

Sauraya & Moroni Milton: 42cr; Scala Group S.p.A: 30bl, 31br, 32br, 33ca, 33bl, 92cla, 56bl, 402cla, Portrait of Claudio Monteverdi, Domenico Feti, Accademia, Venice 40bl, Portolan of Italy (16th century), Loggia dei Lanzi, Firenze 295bl, Museo Correr, Venice 47b, Etruscan Bronze Liver, Museo Civico, Piacenza 48clb, Earrings, Museo Etrusco Guarnacci, Volterra 48br, 48r–9c, Crater from Pescia Romana, Museo Archeologico, Grosseto 49bc, Terracotta Vase in the Shape of an Elephant, Museo Nazionale, Naples 50cr, Cicero denounces Catiline, Palazzo Madama, Rome 51tl, 51bl, Circus Scene Mosaic - Gladiator Fight, Galleria Borghese, Rome 52ca, 52br, Theodolinda Melts the Gold for the New Church (15th century), Famiglia Zavattari, Duomo, Monza 54clb, 54–5, 55br, Tomb Relief depicting a School, Matteo Gandoni, Museo Civico, Bologna 56bc, Detail from an Ambo of Frederick II (13th century), Cattedrale, Bitonto 57cb, Guidoriccio da Fogliano at the Siege of Note Massi, Simone Martini, Palazzo Pubblico, Siena 58clb, 59tl, Return of Gregory XI from Avignon Giorgio Vasari, Sala Regia, Vatican 59crb, 60br, 60r–61c, 61crb, Clement VII in Conversation with Charles V, Giorgio Vasari, Palazzo Vecchio, Florence 62cla, Portrait of Pierluigi da Palestrina, Istituto dei Padri dell'Oratorio, Rome 62br, Revolt at Masaniello, Domenico Gargiulo, Museo di San Martino, Naples 63crb, 64br, 65tl, 65crb, 66cla, 66–7c, 67crb, 99cla, 104c, 122br, 150cla, 226tr, 230br, 264tl, 267tl, 269tr, 273tl, 278cla, 278bl, 279tr, 280c, 280bl, 281tl, 281b, 284cl, 286tc, 287tr, 287br, 290cl, 290cb, 290br, 291ca, 291cb, 292tr, 292b, 293tr, 293cl, 295bl, 296cl, 296bc, 297tr, 297clb, 298tr, 298cl, 299tc, 300cl, 302–3 all, 305clb, 306tr, 306cla, 306c, 307tl, 307cl, 307bl, 329c, 329br, 334–5 all, 336tl, 336br, 342bl, 344tl, 345cl, 348cla, 349br, 358clb, 358br, 359bl, 362bl, 363cl, 374tr, 375tl, 375bc, 381br, 388cl, 404bl, 406tr, 408cl, 415c, 420cla, 421bl, 421tl, 423tl, 424tr, 424c, 425cr, 427tr, 427clb, 427br, 431cla, 431br, 494bc, 515clb, 517tl, 533b, 534tr, 540tc, 541tr, 542bc, 553bc; Science Photo Library: Argonne National Laboratory 45cr; John Ferro Sims: 369b, 546bl; Agenzia Sintesi, Rome: Antonella

Girolamo 618clb; Al Sorriso: 588tc; Mario Soster di Alagna: 561cl; Frank Spooner Pictures: Diffidenti 552br; Gamma 69tr; Sporting Pictures: 75cra; STA Travel Group: 616crb; Tony Stone Images: 87cla; Stephen Studd 35tr, 189cr; Agenzia Fotografica Stradella, Milan: Bersanetti 195tl; Francesco Gavazzini 221br; F Giaccone 530cla; Mozzati 263bc, 374bc; Massimo Pacifico 511tl; Ettore Re 503crb; Ghigo Roli 503bl; Giulio Vegi 537ca; Amedeo Vergani 218br, 238tl, 261tr; SuperStock: age fotostock 383c; Sygma: 71tr.

Tasting Italy: Martin Brigdale 611tl; Tate Gallery Publications: 68bl; Taverna del Pittore: 587bc; Tipsimages: Mario Verin 612-3; Touring Club of Italy: 208cb, Cresci 538ca; Archivio Città di Torino Settore Turismo: 225tl; Davide Bogliacino 217tr; Travel Library: 279cb; Fototeca APT del Trentino: Foto di Banal 178tl; Foto di Faganello 177tr, 179cr.

U'Giancu Restaurant: 579cr.

Vela SpA: 635cr, 635br; Villa Crespi: 578bl; Villa Meridiana Cascina Reine: 567.

Edizione White Star: Giulio Veggi 79; Peter Wilson: 5t..

Front Endpaper
Alamy Images: David Noton Photography Rftl, Lcra, Norma Joseph Rcla, Rcra, LOOK Die Bildagentur der Fotografen GmbH Rtr, Robert Harding World Imagery Rtl, Woodstock Lfclb; Corbis: SOPA RF/SOPA/Franco Cogoli Rftr, Sylvain Sonnet Lfbr; Dreamstime: Gmv Ltc, Rudywong Lca; Getty Images: Peter Adams Rfcra, Mel Curtis Lbr, Robert Everts Lcla, Michal Krakowiak Lfcrb, David Lyons Rfbr, Stefano Scata Rfcrb.

Back Endpaper: Alamy Images: Jon Arnold Images Ltd Rcrb, Prisma Bildagentur AG Rtr; Corbis: Sylvain Sonnet Lca; Dreamstime.com: Rbl; Getty Images: Guy Vanderelst Ltl.

Front jacket and spine: Corbis: Atlantide Phototravel; Spine: Corbis: Atlantide Phototravel t.

Map Cover
Corbis: Atlantide Phototravel.

All other images © Dorling Kindersley. For further information: www.dkimages.com

---

Special Editions of DK Travel Guides

DK Travel Guides can be purchased in bulk quantities at discounted prices for use in promotions or as premiums. We are also able to offer special editions and personalized jackets, corporate imprints, and excerpts from all of our books, tailored specifically to meet your own needs.

To find out more, please contact:
in the United States SpecialSales@dk.com
in the UK travelspecialsales@uk.dk.com
in Canada DK Special Sales at general@tourmaline.ca
in Australia business.development@pearson.com.au